Handbook of Research on Digital Media and Advertising:
User Generated Content Consumption

Matthew S. Eastin
The University of Texas at Austin, USA

Terry Daugherty
The University of Akron, USA

Neal M. Burns
The University of Texas at Austin, USA

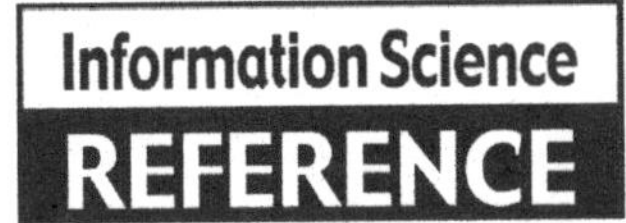

INFORMATION SCIENCE REFERENCE
Hershey · New York

Director of Editorial Content:	Kristin Klinger
Director of Book Publications:	Julia Mosemann
Acquisitions Editor:	Lindsay Johnston
Development Editor:	Christine Buffton
Publishing Assistant:	Tom Foley
Typesetter:	Deanna Jo Zombro
Production Editor:	Jamie Snavely
Cover Design:	Lisa Tosheff
Printed at:	Lightning Source

Published in the United States of America by
Information Science Reference (an imprint of IGI Global)
701 E. Chocolate Avenue
Hershey PA 17033
Tel: 717-533-8845
Fax: 717-533-8661
E-mail: cust@igi-global.com
Web site: http://www.igi-global.com

Library of Congress Cataloging-in-Publication Data

Handbook of research on digital media and advertising : user generated content consumption / Matthew S. Eastin, Terry Daugherty and Neal M. Burns, editors.

p. cm.

Includes bibliographical references and index.

Summary: "This book bridges the gap between professional and academic perceptions of advertising in new media environments, defining the evolution of consumerism within the context of media change and establishing the practical issues related to consumer power shifts from supplier to user"--Provided by publisher.

ISBN 978-1-60566-792-8 (hbk.) -- ISBN 978-1-60566-793-5 (ebook) 1. Advertising--Social aspects. 2. Internet marketing--Social aspects. 3. Consumer behavior. 4. Digital media--Social aspects.
I. Eastin, Matthew S. II. Daugherty, Terry, 1971- III. Burns, Neal M., 1933-
HF5821.H318 2010
659.14'4--dc22

2009053448

British Cataloguing in Publication Data
A Cataloguing in Publication record for this book is available from the British Library.

List of Reviewers

JoAnn Atkin, *Western Michigan University, USA*
Sam Bradley, *Texas Tech University, USA*
Yunjae Cheong, *University of Alabama, USA*
Marina Choi, *University of Texas, USA*
Steve Edwards, *Southern Methodist University, USA*
Lisa Fall, *University of Tennessee, USA*
David Fortin, *University of Canterbury, New Zealand*
Jennifer Gregg, *University of Louisville, USA*
Natalie Guinsler, *Ohio State University, USA*
Mi-Ra Lee, *Michigan State University, USA*
Dana Mastro, *University of Arizona, USA*
Ajay Madhok, *AmSoft Systems, USA*
Sally McMillan, *University of Tennessee, USA*
Greg Nuyens, *Teleplace.com, USA*
Elizabeth Quilliam, *Michigan State University, USA*
Martha G. Russell, *Stanford University, USA*
Kim Sheehan, *University of Oregon, USA*
Bob Weinschenk, *Smarty Pig, Inc, USA*

List of Contributors

Table of Contents

Section 4
Advertising Tactics in Gaming, Sports and Politics

Detailed Table of Contents

Preface xxv

Section 1
Digital: Shaping A Perspective

Chapter 1
An Overview of Digital Media and Advertising 1
Irene J. Dickey, University of Dayton, USA
William F. Lewis, University of Dayton, USA

In an astonishingly short period of time, the Internet and mobile commerce have profoundly shaped the way consumers live their lives as well as the way organizations do business with them—and with each other. With these electronic technologies and tools, businesses have remarkable new opportunities to connect with their customers and to build their brands as never before. Consequently, this chapter provides a broad overview of digital media and its effects on marketing and advertising. In doing so, we identify and define the most important digital media and advertising tactics as well as explain how they can be introduced into traditional marketing and advertising programs. The innovations presented here will help the reader understand how digital technology can improve marketing and advertising strategy formulation and execution. With so many online changes and innovations happening daily, this is a challenging—and exciting—time to practice marketing and advertising. As such, it is imperative that organizations have a presence in the Internet spaces that their customers and potential customers are exploring on a daily basis. In essence, organizations need to provide online listening posts for customers so that they can communicate what they think, as well as what they want or don't want.

Chapter 2
Media Evolution and the Advent of Web 2.0 32
Laura F. Bright, Texas Christian University, USA

In today's marketplace, new technology innovations and the changing media environment offer endless opportunities to consumers: seemingly infinite amounts of information via the internet, a plethora of broadcast stations and channels, and higher functionality and control through such technologies as online content aggregators and digital video recorders. These technological changes have redefined the media landscape and thus the role of advertising in new media consumption. As interactive media mar-

kets become increasingly segmented, it is vital for advertisers to examine effective techniques for communicating with consumers via such customized and controlled channels. This chapter will examine how media has evolved over the last several decades and the impact Web 2.0 technologies are making within the interactive advertising space.

Geraldine Ryan, University College Cork, Ireland
Edward Shinnick, University College Cork, Ireland

Changes in technology bring new challenges and opportunities for every industry, and the media industry is no different. Today people use mass media, and in particular the Internet, to participate in discussions and debate, to advertise and sell their products, to collect and store knowledge and to interact with the global community on the information super-highway. Given both the fast pace of innovation in the media industry and consumer demands for ever greater media content regulatory authorities are faced with challenging times. In this chapter, the authors examine how vertical mergers, vertical restraints, regulations, and competition policy are impacting on the European and American media industries. The authors examine how the internationalisation of the industry, increased merger activity, and the move towards cross media ownership, are impacting on market concentration and diversity. The authors conclude that a balance must be struck between encouraging greater capital flows into the industry to help develop innovation, and the need to protect the public's long term interest through ensuring competitive markets.

Paul R. Messinger, University of Alberta, Canada
Xin Ge, University of Northern British Columbia, Canada

This chapter describes how virtual worlds can be used for advertising and other communications to consumers. To help conceptualize how virtual worlds enable enhanced forms of communications to consumers, the authors introduce a conceptual framework which we call a *hierarchy of engagement* in advertising communications. They argue that virtual worlds facilitate deeper levels of engagement in this hierarchy. The authors then describe, from a practical standpoint, how to manage the traditional elements of advertising campaigns — message, media, timing, intensity, and budget — in the context of virtual worlds to help achieve deeper levels of engagement, which we argue lead to greater brand recall and loyalty. To put these points in context, they begin with a short history of gaming and social computing. To assist with selection of virtual worlds in which to conduct communication campaigns, the authors present a typology of virtual worlds and provide a description of some extant virtual worlds using this typology. The chapter concludes with a description of needed future work to harness virtual worlds for customer engagement.

With a focus on the factors that determine the effectiveness of product placements, we compare the use of product placements in traditional and digital media. Despite the enthusiastic use of product placements in both forms of media, research has not provided conclusive results as to the effectiveness of this form of marketing. After reviewing the factors that alter product placement outcomes, we present a conceptual model designed to highlight the processes that we perceive as altering the consequences of product placements. We presume that whether or not a product placement results in positive consequences for an embedded brand depends on a combination of influences that stem primarily from the degree of a consumer's immersion within the media experience. The highly stimulating and self-directed nature of digital media is predicted to produce profitable consequences for embedded brands, making it a prosperous venue for marketers to utilize to feature their brands.

This chapter stems from recent discussions with academic, advertising and network researchers. In this review, four types of issues relevant to new agendas for advertising research are highlighted: the legacy of metrics based on the interrupted narrative model of advertising and assumed attention; real advertising campaigns as a source of innovations in developing new metrics for earned engagement; the interdisciplinary theoretical foundations for studying engagement and persuasion in advertising; and the need for advertisers, media developers and academicians to collaborate and expedite the creation of metrics to rationalize the monetization of new media used for advertising. Measuring engagement and persuasion in the current media ecology requires metrics that consider simultaneous media exposure and continuous partial attention in the context of a participatory culture and multifaceted objectives for advertising campaigns.

Consumers today have more control over media consumption than ever before, with interactive media helping to transform the industry away from a traditional publisher-centric focus towards a new dynamic user-centric model. Examples of prominent Web 2.0 media environments that support the creation, distribution and consumption of user-generated content (UGC) include YouTube, MySpace, Facebook, Wikipedia, StupidVideos, Flickr, Blogger, and personal Web pages, among others. In addition, recent media research involving Social Cognitive Theory has emerged to offer explanatory power for Internet use and could provide a better understanding of the UGC phenomenon. Therefore, a theoretical model grounded in Social Cognitive Theory was tested examining the relationships between media experience, desirability of control, attitude and the consumption of UGC. A survey was administered to an opt-in online panel (N=325) recruited for Web-based research with the findings confirming the hypothesized model.

Avatars and anthropomorphic characters by marketers are becoming more commonplace on commercial web sites. Moreover, a trend among marketers is to use ethnically ambiguous models in advertising to appeal to specific consumer segments. This study helps our understanding of not only how best to segment and appeal to racially diverse consumers but how people interact with virtual human agents in relationship to the literature on audience response to real humans. It was predicted that Blacks would respond more positively to a Black agent, than they would to either a White agent or an ethnically ambiguous agent. It was also expected that Whites would show no difference in their response based on the race of the computer agent. The findings demonstrate that Blacks had more positive attitudes toward a computer agent, had more positive attitudes toward a web site and recalled more product information from a site when the site featured a Black agent vis-à-vis a White agent. Whites showed no significant response difference concerning the agent, the brand or the site based on the racial composition of the computer agents. Interestingly, the ethnically ambiguous character was overall just as effective in persuading both White and Black browsers as were the same-race agents.

Around the world today we have convenient, fingertip access to continual, informational content. At first the free flow of information seems convenient, empowering, and endlessly beneficial for those world citizens with access to it. This chapter takes a closer look at this relationship in terms of today's consumer and the mediated information they are exposed to and asks the question of whether or not this is necessarily a good thing. The chapter looks at the historical relationship of power and information for guidance in this examination while considering active and inactive audience, corporate and independent media texts, and the possible relationships between Victor Frankl's 'existential void' and mediated messages today.

Consumer reviews on retail websites are now established as a common type of user-generated marketing communication online. To provide a comprehensive and well-defined framework for researchers and marketers who are interested in its implementation and evaluation, a synthetic review of existing studies on the consumer reviews are conducted here. More specifically, the prevalence and popularity of consumer reviews of retail websites, the motivations behind the review activities, and the effects are examined in detail. Three important message characteristics of the reviews - volume, valence, and value - are also identified and discussed. After this assessment of the current status is completed, the focus is shifted to a more existential question about the consumer reviews: Whether the reviews posted by consumers are essentially "commons," an entity created by members of a wide open community and amendable to exploitation by consumers and marketers alike, or "intellectual properties" of the online retailers who collect and manage them. Subsequently, a view that regards the consumer reviews as social capital is presented, followed by a discussion concerning moderation and reputation systems as quality control mechanisms.

With the Internet, even ordinary Web users can conveniently create and disseminate media content. The notion of User-Generated Content (UGC) or Consumer-Generated Content (CGC) captures the user-as-producer feature, and refers to content that is not generated or published by professionals on the Internet, unlike traditional media. An important type of online advertising that makes use of CGC is eWOM advertising. Defined in terms of situations where consumers refer products or services to other consumers on the Internet, eWOM is closely related to CGC and can be applied to many online forums for UGC and CGC. With this in mind, this chapter seeks to define and categorize eWOM based on different online platforms of CGC, review existing research in eWOM, and, finally, extend the use of eWOM to health promotion by examining characteristics of eWOM in an online breast cancer bulletin board.

In this chapter, the authors explore the unique social dimension of shopping in virtual worlds, namely *Second Life*, by examining the role of avatar-based interactions in determining consumer shopping experience. To this end, an overview of *Second Life,* and other similar virtual worlds, is provided. This chapter then introduces the concept of social presence and offers a conceptual discussion of how avatar-based shopping in virtual environments is distinctive from shopping in other Web environments. Next, the authors present the preliminary findings of our ongoing research study investigating how consumers' interactions with salespersons and peer consumers via avatars influence their shopping experience in *Second Life*. This chapter concludes with a future prospect of virtual worlds and directions for future research.

Blogs are the newest and potentially most attractive online media available to marketers. This chapter discusses the unique nature of blogs and the growing power of consumer generated content. This raises a number of questions as well as new opportunities. As the authors point out that existing literature on blog marketing only discusses the possible advantages of using blogs as a marketing tool and the addition of blogs into the marketing mix. However, the problem is that these studies totally ignored consumers' perception towards blogs that carry advertisements. The rise of advertising companies that have stepped in to fill the gap between companies and bloggers, are discussed. Some examples of successful blog advertising campaigns are also provided. This chapter also presents a conceptual model that examines the salient factors that are likely to influence consumer attitude towards blogs and towards advertising in blogs, and more specifically on sponsored posts on blogs. It is hoped that this chapter would encourage other researchers to take a look at this unique media which in turn will help shed new light on how blogs are enabling a new model of consumer collaboration and consumer generated advertising.

Social networking sites (SNSs) are being increasingly used by businesses to add value to companies as well as consumers. Yet, very little is known as to why individuals adopt and use SNS. The current chapter reviews literature on uses and gratification and technology acceptance model (TAM) to propose a framework for SNS adoption. Six main motivational factors are identified from literature and are expected to influence SNS adoption: need to belong, entertainment, communication, information, commercial value, and self-expression. Further, two main barriers to SNS adoption, technology and privacy, are expected to hinder adoption. The proposed theoretical framework is a first step toward understanding SNS adoption and both managerial and theoretical implications are drawn.

This chapter explores the profound impact of the digital revolution on the advertising business. Specifically, it looks at how advertisers and their agencies are changing the ways they plan media, create advertising ideas, and integrate their campaigns using digital and traditional media. Three key themes are explored: 1) the critical importance of *context*, which challenges advertisers to fundamentally reevaluate the relationship between media placement and messaging; 2) the challenge of *fragmentation* to goals of integration: in the digital scenario, the ability to manage complexity has become a key competitive advantage; 3) the need for a new process to ensure the creative development process is in tune with context and focused on simplicity: this process is called the *contextual creative brief.* A number of case studies are provided of advertising campaigns that have pioneered in these areas. They are: Mitsubishi's "Which Car?" campaign, Lexus' "Mosaic" campaign, Toyota's "Best in Jest" and "Sketchies" campaigns, Ambien CR's "Points of Stress" campaign, and the Simpsons Movie launch campaign.

Section 3
Digital Engagement and New Metrics

Chapter 16
Point of Involvement, Purchase and Consumption: The Delivery of Audience Engagement 300
Neal M. Burns, The University of Texas at Austin, USA

Advertising effectiveness and its measurement has characteristically been a subject of concern and debate and with the availability and access of the Internet and digital technology the issue is still elusive and complex. This chapter provides a review of the measures that were frequently used to determine the audience that was impacted with traditional media resources as well as those media and message processes generally called new or "alternative" - in that they are different than the traditional electronic, print and out-of home that have been used by advertisers and their agencies for more than 100 years. The chapter reviews and discusses which measures are simply cost indices and which are measures of effectiveness. The emphasis reflects the interests of both those working in the field as practitioners as well as those involved in its research and instruction. In a profession in which decisions in the past were built upon cost per thousand (CPT or CPM), cost per point (CPP) and the challenges of ROI and share fight, the metrics for new media must be precisely defined, valid and reliable. Assessing advertising effectiveness is – as has been said – challenging. The need to inform, persuade and sell in a global marketplace with a technological base that incorporates all we have used in the past plus the networks and mobile delivery now available have already served to make this aspect of communication a compelling set of opportunities. Digital media and delivery are revolutionary and their impact will be profound. Ideally, the problems to be solved will bring those doing the research and those in practice closer than they have been in the past. The metrics to be developed and the narratives that will follow will reflect the ways in which we relate to products and services and to each other in the 21st Century.

Chapter 17
Digital Metrics: Getting to the Other 50 Percent 314
Michelle R. Nelson, University of Illinois at Urbana-Champaign, USA
Helen Katz, Starcom Mediavest Group, USA

This chapter, authored by an industry professional and an academic, reviews measures of advertising effectiveness in research and practice from the pre-digital to the digital era. A focus on efficacy and ethics in terms of measurement and consumer privacy issues associated with collecting, monitoring and learning from digital metrics is discussed. Research questions related to persuasion knowledge and digital privacy are posed.

Chapter 18
Virtual Identities from Virtual Environments 335
Melvin Prince, Southern Connecticut State University, USA

The creation of identities in immersive online digital environments has become commonplace in consumer behavior. Consumers frequently enter into socially networked, computer mediated environments (CME's) as *avatars*. A user can design his or her avatar by choosing typologies of facial features, body types and clothing styles. The chapter concerns Avatar analysis as a system for generating and analyzing consumer information of practical value to marketers. Avatar analysis enhances understanding of brand perceptions and meanings, discovers new ways of positioning and differentiating brands, and provides insights for improving the effectiveness of brand communications. Using websites such as Second Life to draw avatars, consumer identity projections are elicited based on consumers' perceptions and interpretations of their own digital figure drawings i.e., virtual social identities of consumers and brands. These identity projections disclose their real and ideal selves, brand-as-a-person, and imagery of a typical brand user.

Chapter 19
The "Digitalisation" of Youth: How Do They Manage and Integrate Digital Technologies? 345
Pedro Quelhas Brito, Universidade do Porto, Portugal

The digitalization of youth signifies their complete immersion, active participation and involvement in the production, consumption and sharing of digital content using various interconnected/interfaced digital devices in their social network interactions. A prerequisite to successful commercial communication with young people is having a good understanding of new media, along with their social and psychological framework. The behaviour, motivation and emotions of youth in general and in relation to digital technologies, especially the meaning attached to mobile phones, the Internet (mainly social network sites) and games (computer-based and portable) should also be addressed if advertisers aim to reach this target group.

Chapter 20
Consumption and Marketing in a 3D Virtual Space: The Second Life Experience............................ 374
Gulnur Tumbat, San Francisco State University, USA
Lisa Bennett, San Francisco State University, USA

Second Life (SL) established itself in 2003 as a virtual world where people can create an alternate life as an avatar. It provides a fertile ground for real-world businesses to market their products to a tech-savvy and brand-conscious group of potential consumers. The aim of this exploratory chapter is to gain an understanding about the SL experience for these consumers and provide examples of some of the

marketing practices. The authors conclude that while SL does provide an alternative for businesses for building, maintaining, and extending their real world brand presence, it remains *primarily* as a 3-dimension virtual social space for people to connect and communicate with the like-minded others.

Solving the problem of how to provide effective health education on diseases subject to social taboos is an immediate need. The social stigma of HIV/AIDS is particularly prominent in the developing world, where 95 percent of all HIV-infected persons live. Millions of people risk death from HIV/AIDS while cultures and laws resist change. New approaches must be created to provide education despite whatever social, structural, cultural, and legal barriers exist. Fortunately, the emergence of new media and information and communication technologies (ICT) has provided new ways to help bypass social taboos and provide effective education. This chapter discusses these challenges and presents criteria for evaluating the efficacy of educational campaigns aimed at promoting awareness relating to taboo topics using a specially designed HIV/AIDS curriculum—*Interactive Teaching AIDS*—as an exemplar. It incorporates key pedagogical and communication theories and approaches in order to maximize its efficacy. To provide psychological comfort and promote coherent understanding, this ICT-based application couples the presentation of biological aspects of transmission with culturally-familiar euphemisms and metaphors to communicate ideas about prevention measures. Created using a rigorous, iterative, and research-based process, the 20-minute application provides detailed yet accessible culturally-appropriate explanations of all key aspects of HIV/AIDS prevention. For people living in areas that cannot easily access explicit HIV/AIDS materials due to social, cultural or other constraints, the positive results of the authors' study suggest that it is possible to design curricula that are socially-acceptable and accurate, that promote significant gains in learning, retention, and changes in attitudes. Furthermore, these materials can encourage learners to proactively seek more information regarding the taboo topic and share prevention information with others. Educators who are reticent to teach about such subjects due to embarrassment or lack of health expertise can utilize similar approaches to educate students.

The diffusion of digital media technologies since the 1990s has opened many new channels through which advertisers may reach consumers. This chapter examines the manifestations and effects of advertising in video games. Although early video games rarely and purposefully included advertising, its presence in many contemporary game genres (particularly sports and racing titles) is impossible to ignore. In-game advertising has become a more than $60 million dollar industry (Gaudiosi, 2006) and is expected to grow to almost $2 billion by 2010 (Shields, 2006). The present chapter covers the history and types of advertising in video games before shifting to a discussion of research on its effectiveness. The chapter concludes by highlighting the potential of advertising in games, from both applied and research perspectives.

Online gaming has become a major part of our culture. In order to understand this new media in our society we must examine the motivations for playing these types of games and how that impacts individuals processing of information. This book chapter sets out to examine those motivations and how motivational processing influences in-game content during game play. More importantly how individuals recognize, process, and evaluate information relative to their motivations for playing an online game. Furthermore, this chapter not only explores the product-related segmentation variables, but also demographic segmentation variables. Thus, taken together variables such as motivations, demographics, and game features allows us to paint a clearer picture of the: who, how, and why of online gaming.

It is argued here that the potential connections video game advertisers can build with consumers makes this new medium a strong force in the digital media world. A meaning-based model is introduced to explain the fluctuation of meaning over time, which is caused by the individual and social interpretation and integration of signs and symbols. The history of video games will be comprehensively interpreted through this model to explain the active identification going on between consumers and video games.

Advertising and sponsorship in the area of sports continue to be a prominent way for companies to receive brand exposure to a desired target audience and obtain a brand association with a popular entity. The fundamental advantages of advertising and sponsorship in sports now combine with digital media to provide more extensive and unique opportunities for companies to promote their brands and potentially better connect with their customers. It is clear that digital media do not replace more traditional forms of sports advertising and sponsorship, but rather represent additional vehicles for promotional communication. This chapter begins by providing an explanation of the goals and advantageous characteristics of a sports sponsorship for a company. This review is necessary because developing an agreement with the sports property is required for sponsors to obtain rights to content (footage of that sport), and logos they could use on their product packaging or in their advertisements to better communicate a brand association. The chapter then offers four examples of companies using digital media to execute their sponsorships with sports properties: Sprite and the NBA, Sprint and the NFL, AT&T and the Masters Golf Tournament, and Wise Snack Foods and the Boston Red Sox and New York Mets. A fifth example looks at how sponsors are using another prominent media destination for the sports audience, ESPN. The chapter reveals the endless possibilities of what a sponsorship using digital media can include in the area of sports.

With the billions of dollars at stake in sport enterprises, it is not surprising that advertising permeates every facet of athletic competition as companies attempt to increase awareness of their products to the millions of sports fans around the world who continue to make it a multi-billion dollar industry. Today in sports, it seems that everything can be purchased, even "virtual space." For advertisers, however, the proliferation of exposure is not indicative of over-saturation, but rather presents a need for innovative ways to reach their target audiences. Like athletes who use intensive workouts and nutritional supplements, advertisers are looking for performance-enhancing broadcast options. Virtual advertising is a relatively new, performance-enhancing technique that can improve a company's competitive edge. Following an examination of mere exposure theory, this chapter will turn to a discussion of the benefits and opportunities of virtual advertising in sports events, and finally will explore the potential controversies and drawbacks surrounding virtual advertising technology.

A *virtual world* is an online representation of real world people, products, and brands in a computer-mediated environment (CME). Within the next few years CMEs are likely to emerge as the dominant internet interface. In addition to corporate websites, companies will operate virtual stores where customers can browse and interact with assistants. However, due to the newness of the medium advertisers still struggle to figure out the best way to talk to consumers in these environments – or to decide if they should enter them at all. In this chapter, the authors look at the role of avatars (digital spokes characters) as sources of in-world marketing communications. The authors discuss conceptual issues such as how an avatar's appearance and the ability of the visitor to customize this appearance may influence consumer attitudes and behavior and how conversations with other avatars can serve as a potentially valuable starting point for buzz-building and word of-mouth marketing campaigns. They conclude with some specific suggestions based upon "lessons learned" regarding issues advertisers need to consider when choosing a spokesavatar to communicate with residents of virtual worlds.

Chapter 28
Sounds of Web Advertising..535
Iben B. Jessen, Aalborg University, Denmark
Nicolai J. Graakjaer, Aalborg University, Denmark

Sound seems to be a neglected issue in the study of web ads. Web advertising is predominantly regarded as visual phenomena – commercial messages, as for instance banner ads, that we watch, read, and eventually click on – but only rarely as something we listen to. The present chapter presents an overview of the auditory dimensions in web advertising: What kinds of sounds do we hear in web ads? What are the conditions and functions of sound in web ads? Moreover, the chapter proposes a theoretical framework in order to analyse the communicative functions of sound in web advertising. The main argument is that an understanding of the auditory dimensions in web advertising must include a reflection on the hypertextual settings of the web ad as well as a perspective of how users engage with web content.

Chapter 29
Alternative Online Videos in the 2008 U.S. Presidential Election: Multiple Mix of Media Attributes Approach to Grassroots Mobilization 552
Gooyong Kim, University of California – Los Angeles, USA

This chapter examines a new form of popular political mobilization – online videos. Revising a "mix of attributes approach" to media effects (Eveland, 2003), grassroots participation is included as the Internet's new attribute, which renders a more sociopolitical impact of the medium. Furthermore, to examine its sociopolitical impact, the author suggests a "multiple" mix of attributes approach, which considers extrinsic attributes of audiences' media consumption contexts as well as intrinsic attributes of media configurations. In this regard, the author examines the grassroots participation attribute by interrogating how ordinary people participate in an online public sphere (www.dipdive.com) where they shared and reinforced their support for Obama by producing alternative videos. When it comes to the importance of individuals' critical appropriation of the Internet for political participation, through alternative video production, the potential of transformative human agency by shaping personal narratives toward a better future is realized. In online videos for the Obama campaign, identity politics and the democratization of campaign leadership as extrinsic attributes are enhancing the Internet's network politics for political mobilization. Nevertheless, there is ambivalence of online video's practical impact on society depending on each user's specific motivations and objectives of using it as seen in many cases of destructive, anti-social deployment of the Internet throughout the globe. Therefore, as an educational initiative to implement the multiple mixes of media attributes approach, this chapter concludes by proclaiming that it is a crucial issue for critical pedagogy practitioners to envisage Feenberg's (2002) "radical philosophy of technology" which demands individuals' active intervention in shaping technologies' social applications, as well as its redesign for a more egalitarian purposes. With critical media pedagogy as a premise of the strategic deployment of new media technologies for social change, common people can become leaders of democratic, grassroots political mobilization as well as active, popular pedagogues by producing alternative online videos.

The Internet has captured the attention of the media, the government and much of the public. It has changed the way Americans receive information and communicate. With a number of political candidates creating MySpace profiles, YouTube videos and Second Life avatars it appears that the Internet and web 2.0 technologies have been leveraged for political advertising and campaigning. In the early literature the Internet and its role in politics had been purely speculative, with research only making vague guesses as to where the Internet would lead politicians in their political ambitions. The following chapter first outlines a historical perspective of political advertising, then examines contemporary forms and avenues of political advertising.

The gold standard for customer service is catering to each individual's unique needs. This means providing them undivided attention and helping them find what they want as well as what they will like, based on their prior history. An illustrative metaphor of the ideal interpersonal relationship between retailers and consumers is the "sincere handshake," welcoming a familiar face to a familiar place and saying goodbye until next time, best symbolizes an ideal interpersonal relationship between retailers and consumers. In this chapter the authors offer a four-step cycle of this personalization process, which abstracts the key elements of this handshake in order to make it possible in mass digital consumerism. This model offers an ideal framework for drawing out the key lessons learned from the two previous stages of media evolution, *Micro* and *Mass*, as well as from social science and Human Computer Interaction (HCI) to inform the design and further the understanding of the rich capabilities of the current age of Digital Consumerism.

If reality television is any indication, people have an interest in being known. For some, creating and possibly starring in some form of user-generated content can be a route to being a reality star. The Internet provides a way for consumers to share their documentaries, antics, music videos, and even commercials with other users. Several marketers have capitalized on this trend by combining the desire of users to create their own content with the time-honored concept of a sweepstakes. The purpose of this chapter is to present a model of consumer engagement that encompasses user-generated advertising content. The model will then be placed into context by discussing specific examples from 15 user-generated advertising contests and making theoretical connections for each of the key contest elements.

Preface

When first thinking of putting together a compilation of writings on a particular topic, those that have such a notion believe they will give meaning to a paradigm, influence a research area, or at a minimum shed light exploring a critical phenomenon. Ultimately, the editors and authors hope that the exchange for the reader - in return for thoughtful consideration of and time invested with the material put before them - will be a level of understanding and newly acquired insight. Such was the thinking of the editors of this volume even though we knew that time would not be friendly to our efforts. The combination of advertising practice, available technology and media use has produced shifts in commercial and social communication that have become culturally defining. This volume provides both the baseline for such changes and the predictors of what comes next. In many ways the speed and the changes that have occurred during the compilation, editing and publication of this volume reflect Moore's Law and perhaps even surpassing the exponential levels of change implicit in his prophecy.

Throughout the book, authors integrate their beliefs and research findings by examining some of the most critical areas of interest within digital media. For example, the relationship between metrics and advertising theory, as well as conventional measurements of effectiveness, are presented early and remain an important element throughout the text. Further, chapters dealing with gaming and virtual realities stimulate provocative examination of consumer engagement and its relationship with individual characteristics. Likewise, the transformation of consumer preference from professionally created content and delivery to the consumption of user-generated content is fully explored. Certainly the prevalence of research illustrating how consumers respond to convenience, choice and control throughout several chapters reflects how significantly the mass media have transformed in recent years. Finally, social networks and the digital manifestations of word-of-mouth via blogs and wikis represent excellent examples of the strength of web-related efforts for stimulating consumer behavior. These digital experiences do not occur for consumers simply from being talked to by advertisers; rather they reflect a far more active – at times aggressive – level of communication.

The editors believe this book represents a wonderful cross-section of current research and understanding of digital media through contemporary communication. The metrics and theory throughout are well presented and reflect the multidisciplinary nature of digital media by connecting such industries as business, sports, politics, gaming and economics. Advertising within the realm of digital media goes well beyond simply identifying how much or how often a commercial message is delivered, but instead seeks to embrace consumer awareness, behavior and commercial impact that is unarguably attributed to mediated communication.

The time between submission of an edited manuscript and publication have seen – as mentioned earlier – new and significant additions to the complexity of digital media and advertising. Nevertheless, the material assembled here remains seminal in almost all respects and ahead of development in many others. The predictions for what is to come next in this age of digital media are clearly articulated in virtually every chapter and the breadth represented is unequalled. We hope you enjoy the read.

Matthew S. Eastin
The University of Texas at Austin, USA

Terry Daugherty
The University of Akron, USA

Neal M. Burns
The University of Texas at Austin, USA

Section 1
Digital:
Shaping A Perspective

Chapter 1
An Overview of Digital Media and Advertising

Irene J. Dickey
University of Dayton, USA

William F. Lewis
University of Dayton, USA

ABSTRACT

In an astonishingly short period of time, the Internet and mobile commerce have profoundly shaped the way consumers live their lives as well as the way organizations do business with them—and with each other. With these electronic technologies and tools, businesses have remarkable new opportunities to connect with their customers and to build their brands as never before. Consequently, this chapter provides a broad overview of digital media and its effects on marketing and advertising. In doing so, we identify and define the most important digital media and advertising tactics as well as explain how they can be introduced into traditional marketing and advertising programs. The innovations presented here will help the reader understand how digital technology can improve marketing and advertising strategy formulation and execution. With so many online changes and innovations happening daily, this is a challenging—and exciting—time to practice marketing and advertising. As such, it is imperative that organizations have a presence in the Internet spaces that their customers and potential customers are exploring on a daily basis. In essence, organizations need to provide online listening posts for customers so that they can communicate what they think, as well as what they want or don't want.

INTRODUCTION

It is well-documented that consumers are increasingly using the Internet and mobile commerce for shopping, for entertainment, and for accessing and sharing information. Brands that connect with consumers in these spaces—and listen to them—will have a greater chance of success. The utilization of these electronic platforms is no longer a matter of being innovative--it has become a necessity. To understand how things reached this point, we will briefly review the history of Internet marketing. Next, we will outline key marketing tactics for facilitating ecommerce (e-commerce,

DOI: 10.4018/978-1-60566-792-8.ch001

eCommerce) with the organization's website as well as for those outside of the organization's website. This will include a strategic approach for understanding customer needs and wants within the context of the marketing environment in an easy-to-understand framework. In addition, recommendations are provided for the effective implementation of ecommerce strategies that will build the brand and build relationships with customers using digital advertising and media. We will conclude with recommendations and applications for future research.

BACKGROUND

History of the Internet and the World Wide Web

The evolution of the Internet provides a relevant and substantive narrative and starting point for this chapter. While the World Wide Web was created in 1991, its origin dates back to 1957 when the Soviet Union launched the Sputnik I satellite. With Sputnik, the "space race" between the U.S.A. and the U.S.S.R. began. During this period, President Eisenhower created the Defense Advanced Research Projects Agency (DARPA) to fund scientific research among the Department of Defense, universities, and research organizations across the United States. What emerged from this effort was an attack-proof electronic infrastructure for the sharing of research results by multiple users, on their own computers, at the same time. The linking of computers allowed scientific communities to interconnect and exchange ideas as well as cooperate on scientific projects.

This new computer network enabled instant, electronic human communication in a time and distance environment that was completely unprecedented in our history. That said, the number of users was limited until the mid 1980's—when TCP/IP (Transmission Control Protocol/Internet Protocol), a standard language of Internet computing was invented and published. Initially developed by English researcher Tim Berners-Lee, the program was expanded to find and retrieve information for the European Particle Physics Laboratory (CERN) in Switzerland. Hypertext was then developed to allow a linked retrieval system that came to be known as the World Wide Web (WWW).

In June, 1993 CERN released this innovation—an interconnected network called the Internet—to the rest of the world. Described as being global and user-friendly, this standardized computer language opened the door to businesses and individuals to connect online. Soon, commercial traffic came rushing in. But in the beginning the Internet was difficult to navigate since search engines and directories did not exist. Moreover, many consumers felt it was too boring or of little use. In short, Internet adoption by consumers emerged slowly until a tipping point occurred in the early 1990s. After that, the rate of adoption skyrocketed past any previous media innovation. Reaching that tipping point, however, required several additional improvements and developments. For instance, in 1993 Mosaic (the forerunner of Netscape) allowed for the transmission of graphic files—something of broader interest. As a consequence, by 1995-1996, there emerged a significant public consciousness of this electronic tool and its potential. Nevertheless, few people fully anticipated the applications that would continue to emerge, much less the rapidly growing pace of change and development that was to come on the Web.

The next significant development occurred in 1996 when Yahoo! pioneered directory and search capabilities that allowed users to move around the Web. Not only could Web surfers find things more easily, as new and easier to use technologies were developed for the Internet, but they also found it more convenient to access information, initiate communications, discover entertainment, and more. Subsequently, the Internet diffused into the global society in a big way. This diffusion provided businesses with an understanding of many unique aspects of the Internet and of users' behaviors. During this period, various marketing, advertising, and promotion theories related to online marketing strategies and tactics were developed to increase the odds of success, and reduce the risk of failure. Consequently, 1996 was an important turning point, marking the transition from the first generation of digital marketing to the second generation. It was also a time in which valuable lessons were learned.

One of the important lessons learned from the decade of the 1990s was that a focus on digital technology alone, without an appropriate focus on consumer behavior, resulted in overestimating the willingness of consumers to change behaviors from physical shopping space to virtual shopping space. In addition, many Internet marketers abandoned old and proven business models and strategies for new, unproven ones resulting in many Internet business failures. The dramatic result was when the "dot-com era" ended abruptly and traumatically when many dot-com companies went bust in 2001. Much has been learned since that time. Practitioners and academics have aggressively researched and reported what works and what does not work, and have developed "best practices" that are increasing the probability of digital success. And what is Tim Berners-Lee doing these days? In January of 2009, he assisted in the re-launch of the British monarchy's website, royal.gov.uk, making it easier to navigate. The site now features new technology, including audio and video footage as well as interactive maps.

History of Internet Marketing

The enthusiastic, yet cautious adoption of the Internet by consumers and businesses led to changes in long-accepted marketing and advertising practices. At first, these new changes were largely trials, tests, and experiments. Questions emerged as quickly as technological changes occurred. Imagine the thoughts of marketers: "What is a web page?" "Can I advertise on the World Wide Web; and if I do, how do I do it?" The Internet clearly generated a need for new marketing "vocabulary" (Kalyanam and McIntyre (2002)—much of which we use in this chapter.

The accelerating growth of the Internet and its rapid adoption by consumers can be largely attributed to the positive impact this medium has had on their lives. This goes far beyond simply purchasing items online. Consumers began to use "...electronic networks to become and stay informed, perform services for themselves (such as banking, redeeming air miles, and trading stocks), interact with private and public institutions, and entertain themselves." (Watson, et al. 2002) The general public and consumers have continued to use every conceivable technological device to surf the Web and continue to adopt new technology at a rapid pace. Businesses, early on, responded to this rapid growth, and marketers, especially now, must explore, understand, and positively influence customers with digital media and advertising. Doing so has the potential to make positive changes that will deliver "value" to customers. The Internet is "...an enabler and driver of competitive marketing strategy" as well as an enabler of digital media and advertising. (Varadarajan (2002) As such, the Internet has the potential to gainfully leverage and enhance the effectiveness of a business's competitive marketing strategy. Given the enormous—and expanding—impact of the Internet it is beneficial for marketers to understand the evolution of digital media and advertising.

Early on, the attractiveness of the Internet as a commercial medium was due to its ability to facilitate the global sharing of information and its potential to provide an efficient channel for advertising, marketing and the selling of goods. (Hoffman, Novak and Chatterjee 1995) During the early development of the Internet, businesses used it to engage in electronic transactions as sellers or as buyers in the business-to-business market. (Bradlow and Schmittlein 2000) In addition, they also used the Internet to disseminate and gather information about customers, both in Internet advertising (acquiring new customers) and after sales support. (Bakos 1997, Hoffman and Novak 1996) As a result, the Internet has emerged as a rich source of managerial information that helps firms manage their brands and conduct marketing research. (Vikas, Manz and Glick 1998, Haubl and Trifts 2000)

As the Internet matured, marketers began to focus on the overall marketing value of an online presence. Marketing research is growing on the Internet, with firms collecting customer information using techniques such as search log analysis and click stream analysis. Both types of data provide precise records of an individual's movement on the Internet and can provide insights into a customer's behavior, types of demand, and their brand perceptions. (Burton and Walther 2001, Maxwell 2001) The ability to track advertising effectiveness and target specific online markets and individuals with web analytics and specific metrics are what truly propelled interest in digital media and advertising.

Web analytics allow firms to study and shape customers' online behavior. Specifically, off-site web analytics measure and analyze web behavior irrespective of whether the organization owns or maintains a website. It measures what is happening on the Internet as a whole. On-site web analytics measures a visitor's journey on the organization's website. The measurement includes its drivers and conversions; for example, which landing pages encourage consumers to make a purchase. A digital trail is left behind every campaign and every marketing and advertising program. The Internet can potentially be a marketing manager's dream (or nightmare if not managed properly). The ability to develop marketing programs based on research metrics, and then evaluate their subsequent effectiveness, has become a key strength of digital media and advertising.

Of course, along the way, many Internet strategies and tactics failed. One dramatic example is Webvan, which filed for bankruptcy in 2001. In spite of raising $375 million in its initial public offering, their grocery delivery business model never attained profitability. (Farmer and Sandoval 2009) Webvan's Internet business model depended on consumers ordering their groceries online; and then Webvan would deliver them to the customer's address. In spite of this dramatic Internet business failure, a variety of new digital marketing strategies and tactics have emerged and endured, becoming common marketing practices because they work well if implemented properly. For instance, search engine optimization (SEO) appears to be growing in acceptance and usage for many organizations. Therefore, if a business, or other type of organization, has a website it must engage in SEO or be left behind. Web search engines are commonly used to help locate information of all kinds and navigate the millions of pages on the World Wide Web. (Krishnamurthey, 2003) Brand managers today must recognize the way consumers use keywords on search engines to find suitable brands. To capitalize on the opportunity presented by search engines, managers want their brands listed at the top of appropriate web pages. That said, Owen (2000) found that brand managers initially gave insufficient thought to search engine tactics; especially in their infancy. With greater experience, however, the use of search engines has become more accepted by consumers and businesses. Likewise, Search Engine Marketing (SEM)—the tactic of paying for the placement of an ad on a searcher's click through—has become more popular. Each of these will be discussed in more detail later in the chapter.

Advertising on the Internet has generated many questions and much research. For instance, what are the different types of internet advertising? What is the influence of various types of ads on visitors and viewers? Which organizations and industries are engaging in Internet advertising? How much is being spent on Internet advertising, and by whom? We know that Internet technology makes it possible to target specific customers with relevant messages. Banner ads, button ads, tower ads, intromercials, sponsorships, as well as co-branded and co-marketed ads, are all attempting to integrate companies' brands and products with the editorial content on targeted websites.

However, the future of online advertising is expected to become more intrusive and "louder" in order to capture the desired attention of consumers. Krishnamurthy (2003) estimates that as the level of clutter on the Internet rises, creative approaches to grab consumers' attention will become the norm. For instance, Luk, Chan, and Li (2002) investigated the characteristics of manufacturers' online advertising, analyzing 472 product advertisements found on the websites of automobile manufacturers. In addition, they examined the possible impact of the content and enhancement devices of Internet advertising on the attractiveness and effectiveness of online advertisements. While they found Internet advertising facilitates selling activities, its impact was not as strong as expected. They also reported that various technologies are also making it possible to use creative, but less graphically intensive messages to achieve greater engagement of the customer with the message. Put simply, Internet advertising strategies are continuing to evolve.

Various forms of Internet advertising have come and gone. The bottom line is that firms with business models that focus on advertising revenue must find a way to deliver relevant and targeted ads to potential customers on their websites and in other digital media. The keys to success will be the specific relevance of the message, the resonance of the message, and the effectiveness of the delivery of the message or program in the time and space where the potential customers want to receive it, not where marketers want to shout it out.

Fundamental Differences between Digital and Traditional Advertising and Marketing Communication

The Internet is certainly the most recent significant development in the long history of steadily advancing communication media—techniques that began with the stone tablet and have culminated in various forms of electronic media. Internet marketing is a subset of e-commerce that focuses on the utilization of the Internet in the marketing component of business and other organizations. In recent years, the Internet has developed many unique properties that can help organizations perform marketing functions more effectively and efficiently, with greater value to customers. (Bierma 2002) Many firms have discovered that the Internet is an effective tool for differentiating their products (Trudell and Kolkin 1999), and building long-term relationships with current and potential customers. (Kalakota and Robinson (2000) Additional research indicates that the Internet can be used for positioning an organization in the e-environment (Cho, Yong-Sauk and Jae-Chase 2002), tapping into global markets more easily (Donada 2002), and fundamentally altering the way many companies do business (Krishnamurthy 2003).

When the Internet revolution began there were many unknowns. But it was clear then, and is still clear today, that the Internet did not, and should not, change everything in marketing. In other words, traditional marketing themes and tactics remain essential. The Internet does, however, provide new and powerful applications for traditional marketing strategies and tactics. Today, it is hard to imagine an effective marketing plan that does not incorporate the Internet and consider mobile marketing. At the macro level, an important dimension of Internet marketing is the opportunity for organizations and entrepreneurs to construct new business models and/or to change their existing business models. A business model (also called business design) is the primary mechanism by which a business intends to generate revenue and profits, and it is important to include how the Internet will help serve customers better.

Integrating the Internet into traditional marketing plans and strategies will help the organization discover its customers, as well as define and differentiate its product offerings. These plans and strategies need to be based on consumer demand in such a way as to create utility for its customers, acquire and keep customers, go to the market (promotion and distribution strategy), define the tactics and tasks that need to be performed, profitably administer its resources, and increase sales and profits. Some of the most well-known new business models include eBay, Priceline, Amazon, CarDirect, Google, and Weather.com. Practitioners should consider these and other new, innovative organizations and their business models to encourage wise decision making about how they might modify their own business model to deliver greater value to customers, and increased sales and profits for their organizations.

To be fully effective, any new advertising medium requires that advertisers do extensive marketing research to understand the medium and the process by which consumers adopt or reject it. It is necessary to develop a framework for defining the value that a medium can provide and the value received and perceived from the point of view of the target audience. The key question is—does the new medium provide the value and benefits sought by the target audience? If not, the new medium will be less effective, or even fail to become profitable. For example, one discovery early on was that advertising tactics and programs that worked offline did not always work online. For advertisers, the Web was the first interactive medium. Interactivity offers major challenges and opportunities for advertisers. Marketers needed to understand how the capability of interactivity could be used to develop on-going relationships with customers.

Traditional mass media is also a one-to-many distribution process (broad casting) where the same message is directed at everyone. The Internet offers the capability of one-to-one marketing (narrow casting), and targeted marketing. The potential for personalization of advertising messages and promotional offers evolved as the technology and software advanced. The challenge at the time was that sophisticated software was required as well as the educational and intellectual capital to develop, program, and implement such programs. In a short period of time, software was developed that made the Internet more readily accessible to nonprogrammers and more cost efficient. Such advances in software meant that businesses could shift from mass advertising to more personalized, or targeted marketing.

Another aspect that differentiates the Internet is that it is both a push and a pull promotion medium. Consequently, marketing and advertising programs need to be developed to consider and maximize both. When consumers type in the name of a Web address to obtain information they are pulling content back to their computer or other device, such as a cell phone or personal digital assistant (PDA). It can also be a push promotion medium where consumers are served ads or e-mails directly to their computers or other devices. Some advertising is both push and pull. This can happen when a consumer observes an ad online and then clicks through to connect with the desired content. Much has been learned over time, just as advertisers learned how to most effectively use radio and television when they became media options. The fact is that marketers need to continue to research and understand consumers and their media consumption habits as well as their attitudes and behaviors. So armed, marketers will be better able to incorporate digital media and advertising into their marketing programs in ways that accurately reflect the lifestyles and media habits of their target audiences. The real beauty of today's Internet environment is that extensive databases are readily available to assist marketers in these efforts. Web analytics should be at the core of the development, implementation, and evaluation of all digital media marketing programs. More about web analytics later in the chapter.

COMMERCE

Today, Internet marketing largely focuses on how the Internet has become a new channel for communication with customers and for the distribution of products. (Lal and Sarvary 1999; Bakos and Brynjolfsson 1999; Markilli 2004; Kalaignanam, Kushwaha and Varadarajan 2008) Online retailers are known as e-tailers, and online retailing is known as e-tail. Markillie (2004) explains how e-business is merging with traditional forms of retailing, and according to the Department of Commerce, online retail sales in the U.S. in 2007 rose by 26 percent, to $55 billion over 2006. However, this amounts to only 1.6 percent of total retail sales. The vast majority of consumers still buy most products in the traditional bricks-and-mortar world. These figures and other measures of better-than-expected growth appear to be signs of continued resilience and health of online retail sales. This might be fueled by the fact that online retailing has the potential to generate a greater profit than off-line retailing. For example, The Associated Press (2004) reported that traditional bricks-and-mortar stores generate a 3-10 percent operating profit margin whereas online retailers generate approximately 21 percent. Other research has found that the Internet offers a wide range of opportunities for firms to achieve marketing efficiency gains by lowering costs. For example, efficiency gains are possible even for Internet grocers, if an appropriate business model and be developed. (McTaggart 2004, Anckar 2002).

A survey of eCommerce in the *Economist* (2004) reported that both businesses and consumers are changing their behavior in significant ways. Not only are consumers spending more, but a broader range of consumers are spending online in a wider variety of ways. This study found that, each year, consumers are spending greater amounts on the Internet. For example, in November and December 2003, Americans spent $18.5 billion online (excluding travel)—35 percent more than they spent in the same two months of 2002. This overall growth has been driven by the rising number of high-speed broadband links which now connect over 50 million American homes to the Web. Spending patterns on the Internet are also getting closer to those in bricks-and-mortar outlets. For example, the survey also reports that 71% of females purchase online, and that growth was six times faster than spending for men. Older people are also shopping more online.

Much of the online shopping is heavily concentrated on a few sites. In January 2004, 83.5 million Americans, or just over half of the country's Internet users, visited either eBay or Amazon, making these sites among the most frequently visited retail outlets in the country; both online and offline. Half of the 60 million consumers in Europe who have an Internet connection bought products offline after having investigated prices and details, such as styles, availability, and colors, online. It is interesting to note that more and more consumers, who purchased products in brick-and-mortar stores, or by telephone from catalogues, are first checking out the merchandise online for styles, sizes, colors, availability, and price (Forester Research 2009).

Even in those years when retail industry sales are expected to be sluggish, American consumers will likely keep turning to the Internet for many of their shopping needs. In their 11th annual Shop.org study, Forrester Research (Mulpuru 2008) found that of the 125 retailers in their study, online retail sales was expected to rise 17 percent ($204 billion) in 2008. Apparel ($26.6 billion), computers ($23.9 billion), and autos ($19.3 billion) will be the three largest sales categories. This has enormous implications for businesses because websites are increasingly becoming the gateway to a firm's goods and services—even if the firm does not sell online. Therefore, even if a company does not sell directly online, they need to have a presence on the Web in order to gain sales leads or provide information needed by customers and potential customers.

FACILITATION OF ECOMMERCE IN A DIGITAL ENVIRONMENT

Websites and Branding

Branding should be at the core of website design and all digital advertising and media programs. The design should identify the seller and differentiate that seller's products from all others. The brand is the sellers' promise to deliver a specific set of features, benefits, and services consistently and reliably to the target market. (Kaferer, 1992 and Aaker, 1997) A brand needs to build trust in order to achieve brand equity in the minds of consumers. Consumer research has shown that powerful brands also create meaningful images in the minds of customers that help them differentiate among competing brands. (Shocker, Srivastava, and Ruekert, 1994 and Keller, 1993) For the seller, a strong branding strategy can build strong brand equity in the minds of consumers, which is the added value a brand name gives to a product beyond the functional benefits provided. (Aaker, 1996)

Marketers invest in branding because brand image and brand reputation enhance differentiation and can lead to stronger brand equity. (deChernatony and McEnally, 1999) Brandt and Johnson define brand equity as "the tangible product plus the intangible values and expectations attached to the product by the consumer or prospect." (Brandt and Johnson, 1997) Gardner & Levy (1955) proposed that a brand name is more than the label employed to differentiate among the manufacturers of competing products. It is a complex symbol that represents a variety of ideas and attributes. It tells the consumers many things, not only by the way it sounds, but, more importantly, via the body of associations (classical conditioning) it has built up and acquired as a public object over time. The net result is a public brand image, a character or personality that may be more important for the overall status (and sales) of the brand than many technical facts about the product.

Moore (2003) states that one of the beneficial characteristics of effective branding are the strong associations embedded in consumers' thought processes (classical conditioning). The goal of any branding project is to establish a strong and stable set of associations in the minds and long-term memories of consumers. Strategists work to help client companies achieve consistency across all "touch-points," so that the consumers' in-store experience, or the experience of the catalogue, the website, the call center, or any face-to-face dealings with any representatives of the company, are all consistent, and all of the company's communication mediums mutually reinforce the brand's values and image. Moore found that redundancy, in this case, is a virtue, and that it is essential that associations be multiplied and reinforced across all media and channels (print, online, in-store, and broadcast). The sheer quantity of associations is also important, since, to this way of thinking, the greater the number of associations in the consumers' mind, the stronger the recall (long-term memory).

So where and how does the Internet fit into branding strategy? Rubenstein and Griffith (2001) propose that, on the Internet the brand itself must be at the heart of the business strategy. The emphasis shifts from brand to "branded experience," and becomes an issue for the entire company. They argue that while the key principles of how to develop a brand remain the same, the need for speed and other experiential variables means that it must be managed differently. Many studies emphasize the differences found when consumers use digital as opposed to traditional media. deChernatony's (2001) research suggests that brand strategists need a new mental model to develop integrated brands in a digital age—brands that go beyond the classical models in recognizing the new roles consumers are taking. The need for this new mental model emerged as deChernatony considered, and then challenged, some of the assumptions that led some managers to migrate their brands onto the Internet. One significant aspect of online branding is that a looser degree of control is more appropriate because of the involvement and number of interactions within a brand's Internet communities. Both studies focused heavily on such differences and identified specific behaviors that are unique to online media, recommending changes to accommodate these differences.

For instance, deChernatony discovered that businesses need to switch from the classical model of talking to customers directly to interactively communicating with them using systems that enable organizations to respond rapidly to inquiries. Other research also suggests that an organization's website represents an opportunity to communicate the brand and the brand message, as well as differentiate a brand from competitive brands. It is obvious that further research is needed in order to capitalize on these potential opportunities. To date, a significant amount of Internet research has focused on website design, revealing many current and potential problems. For instance, Hauseman and Siekpe (2008) found that firms are increasingly relying on e-commerce solutions to reach their profit objectives; yet many websites fail to help companies reach these objectives. Their study finds that the "...use of human factors is stronger in evaluations of usefulness and entertainment of a site, which are more influential antecedents of attitudes towards a site and flow that, in turn, impact purchase and return intentions." This finding seems suggests that there should be increased emphasis on these human factors rather than technology elements in the development, testing, and ultimate design of a website. Human factors engineering is the science of understanding the properties of human capabilities (human factors science), and the development of systems and services that humans are capable of using effectively. Human factors engineering has also been called ergonomics. (Human Factors Engineering 2009)

WEBSITE CONTENT

8 Cs and a U

The traditional marketing mix or four Ps (product, price, place, and promotion) are well-accepted in marketing. In virtual space, there appears to have emerged some additional principles, particularly in the design of websites and website strategy. Before these principles are explored, it is vital that practitioners have a clear understanding of the purpose of their website. It might be to sell (Amazon), or to provide information (ESPN.com), or to build a brand and relationships with customers (Kraftfoods.com), or to collect data about visitors in order to deliver relevant and timely information and special offers to them (forresterresearch.com). This is what all organizations need to be doing. It requires an opt-in strategy. Once the organizations objective(s) are defined, the following table displays some of the basic principles that are essential for building a framework for an effective and efficient website strategy. (Krishnamurthy 2003) In essence, instead of the four Ps in physical space, the virtual space (the website) should contain the 8 Cs and a U (see Table 1). The first 7 Cs listed in the table were proposed by Krishnamurthy (2003).

Practitioners and consumers place a high value on convenience, which is the 8th "C." The term "usability" (U) was high on the list of practitioners, as well. To practitioners, this has more to do with Web design factors such as website navigation. As we progress through this chapter, many of these terms will emerge again, and take on a dual role. Not only should they be part of the website design, but marketers can also use them for branding and advertising purposes. For example content, connectivity, and community can be achieved by providing a consumer-generated media or social networking space on a website. Many organizations do this very successfully. Kraftfoods.com encourages readers to share thoughts about their huge recipe library, rate recipes, and share their

Table 1. The 8 Cs and a U of website design

8 Cs and U	Description or Common Meaning
Commerce	Encourage exchanges (goods, services, two-way information, etc.
Content	Give visitors what they want; do not lock up archives or all desired information
Communication	Talk with visitors and let them communicate with each other
Connectivity	Talk with visitors and let them communicate with each other
Community	Develop a community for viral marketing
Computing	Enable visitors to calculate (banking, stock prices, sports scores, track weight loss, etc.)
Cost Savings	Help visitors save money, time, and effort
Convenience	Make it easy for customers to find you and to do business with you
Usability	Make the website easy to navigate, fast, searchable, and visually appealing (human factors science)

own recipes with other readers. This network builds the Kraft brand as well as building stronger, on-going relationships with customers. An integrated marketing campaign is at the core of Kraft's digital marketing strategy which is supplemented with direct, permission-based e-mail campaigns, and a high quality magazine sent out to consumers who opted-into the program.

The 8 Cs and a U will be a running theme throughout this chapter. Moreover, the concepts of branding and integration of all forms of communication efforts through all forms of media should be considered as well. This is typically referred to as Integrated Marketing Communications (IMC). The purpose IMC is to ensure that all forms of communication display a uniform, recognizable brand image, and communicate the same basic message(s).

Website Personalization

It is becoming more and more common for people to customize their choice of product features from a menu the manufacturer displays on its website. An extension of this customization is to further personalize the customer's experience by allowing them to become a co-creator of the product experience. For example, Converse allows you to design your own tennis shoe online at their website. (Converse 2009) The customer can collaborate with the brand to get exactly what he or she wants, when he or she wants it. Content is tailored to the customer, and cost and time savings may be achieved. From the brand's point of view, personalization makes the customer part of its distinctive competency. And while customization does a good job of building brand loyalty, personalization does an even better job because it helps the customer to think, "Hey, I designed it, so it's mine." (Travis, 2001).

Personalization is targeting taken to the extreme because it envisions creating a unique marketing mix for each individual. For consumers, personalization reduces the transactional burden because they invest time and energy educating the supplier about their specific needs. What that means for the company is that this investment is significant enough that consumers will be unlikely to want to repeat the process elsewhere since the cost of switching would be so high. Switching costs include the time, effort, and money a consumer would have to expend to switch from one brand to another.

Consumers may also find it convenient to use personalization to track new products consistent with their tastes. This is a strategy used effectively by Amazon.com whereby a customer orders a book and periodically receives an e-mail or pop-up technology alert about new books by the same author, or similar types of books by different authors. On the other hand, there appears to be a need to ensure that the brand remains strong while implementing personalization strategies. If the site redesigns itself for each user, it may become hard to define what the site stands for in the first place. One viable approach would be to maximize the individual experience while creating a broader theme that defines and informs the customer what the brand is all about. (Krishnamurthy, 2003) It is clear that there are compelling reasons for organizations to offer personalization capabilities on their website. However, it can be very challenging to attract and retain the customers over the Internet due to low barriers to entry, and severe competition. Changchien et al. (2003) define personalization as a special form of product differentiation. When applied in market fragmentation segmentation (individualized segmentation), personalization can transform a standard good or service into a specialized solution for a specific individual. There are significant marketing opportunities to explore this topic across industries and customer segments to better understand how best to develop and offer personalization capabilities.

RSS Feeds: Website Content and Digital Advertising Capabilities

Most consumers are not aware of really simple syndication (RSS) feeds. (Beal, 2004) Yet, RSS feeds are an emerging theme in marketing, most commonly used by trade journals and the popular press, but now they are being embraced as valuable website content, and even a form of advertising for marketers. Netscape initially developed RSS feeds as a way of creating portals for online news organizations to allow users to download a program designed to accept information from websites that provide an RSS feed. That feed then pops up as a headline, or short summary, and a link to the webpage where the content is located. One of the unique capabilities of these feeds is where they can be displayed. They are most commonly found in a web browser and in small boxes that appear in the corner of a desktop (similar to some e-mail programs).

RSS is a method of extruding information from a website and making it available as a feed that can be viewed in an RSS reader, also known as a news, information, or entertainment aggregator. Some aggregators deliver feeds to a user's e-mail inbox, while others are stand-alone programs that run on a users' computer or are customizable web pages. (Palser, 2005) Clicking a headline in an RSS feed is equivalent to typing the URL into a web browser. Beal (2004) suggests that RSS feeds can potentially help a company's marketing program. In cases where an organization has a large number of products or product categories, generating a continual stream of changes that need to be communicated to customers, RSS feeds can efficiently and effectively provide information about product changes, new products, pricing changes, and other important topics.

Palser notes the emerging practice of placing text ads between headlines in the feeds themselves, and suggests that the biggest implication might be the link to promotion and branding. In a time when brand loyalty is waning in most consumer product categories, loyalty might be encouraged in an environment "...where people can compare coverage from competing newsrooms side by side, the very best way to cultivate affinity will be with timely, reliable, complete information." (Palser, 2005) Initially, the most common marketing applications of RSS feeds alerted customers to new products or to account information. Because RSS feeds are not e-mail, they do not run into content filters and are therefore, not considered spam. In fact, an RSS feed is considered to be a fine example of "pull" promotion, rather than "push" promotion that is commonly used to communicate with customers. Beal (2004) explains that it is users, not marketers, who determine what type of feed they receive; and whether they want to follow the feed to the site, or to simply ignore it.

RSS feeds have the added advantage of not having the same security risks as e-mail—because they are links, they are not subject to customers' fears of downloading unwanted files, viruses, or other unwanted attachments. Baker and Green (2005) report RSS as an innovation that has sent blogs catapulting into the mainstream on the Internet. Currently a user can subscribe to certain weblogs, or to key words, and then have all the relevant items land at a single destination. These personalized web pages bring together the music and video the user signs up for, as well as the news. These personalized web pages are also aggregators, and Yahoo!, MSN, and Google are working with them. Baker and Green (2005) reveal how "insidious" this really is. "If you set up your own aggregator page, such as my.yahoo.com, and subscribe to feeds, you soon discover that blog and mainstream postings mingle side by side. Feeds zip through the walls between blogs and the rest of the information world." (Green, 2005) People subscribe to RSS feeds only when they are interested in the content. For a marketer, this should mean that conversion rates into leads or sales should be higher because users are seeing what they want to see. Hrastnik (2005) claims that it is relatively easy and inexpensive for an organization to create, maintain, and support its own RSS feeds. For the user it does not require much of an orientation, and most of the time it is free. Many electronic devices are capable of receiving RSS feeds including iPods, PlayStation game consoles, and PDAs. Sony, Dell, and Yahoo! are among the many organizations embracing RSS feeds to communicate with consumers; including advertising to them. In fact, Apple's iTunes Music Store invites consumers to find their favorite podcasts from ABC News, CNN, ESPN, CNBC, etc. Subscriptions are free, and with the click of a button subscribers can get the most recent episodes, and all future episodes automatically delivered to an iTunes podcast playlist.

Websites and Podcasts: Content and Digital Advertising Capabilities

Podcasts are another innovation that is related to weblogs and RSS feeds. Podcasting is primarily associated with the iPod, but its real association is with RSS file casting. Once you know how RSS feeds work, the concept of podcasting is relatively easy. RSS feeds are the downloadable content that originated with news programs. However, these programs have merged into many different types of content from sports programs to music, and ever more frequently, into original programs. Podcasting allows individuals and businesses to create and distribute original audio and video programs via the Internet. Often formatted like a radio show, a podcast is a multimedia file downloaded by its audience. More than 25 million fans will "tune in" to podcasts in 2008. (PR NewWire 2006) This figure is expected to rise to 50 million by 2010. Podcasts have become popular largely because of their distinctive content, finding niche audiences, and giving voices to people outside the mainstream media.

West (2005) explains that the "podcast phenomenon" is largely fueled by the under 24-year-old age group. He reports that over one in four 8 to 18-year-olds use audio media while using other media such as personal computers, or even watching television. These young consumers are listening to audio while they do homework, shop, drive, and, especially when they are alone. West suggests that podcasts can be used for both internal and external communications, including marketing and branding. We are beginning to see corporations post and deliver their executive speeches and current news (publicity) as a podcast. Some college professors are now delivering their lectures via podcasts. Television stations are beginning to podcast their news programs, offering time and place convenience. The radio industry is profoundly changing their offerings to include podcasts. West (2005) reports that any radio station without a podcast/Internet strategy "...will run the risk of audience loss, and consequently advertising that is increasingly part of podcasts."

A major strength of podcasting is that it provides access to existing content, such as Web mail, anywhere, anytime, and with the computer phones, any place. This, of course, makes life easier by allowing consumers to access content anytime they want, such as during their commute to work, at lunch, or any time convenient to them. Podcasts are portable programs that can be heard on-demand using computers, portable media players, or other devices. Similar to a weblog, subscribers can receive podcasts automatically through RSS feeds. (PR NewWire 2006) Podcasts allow consumers and organizations to engage in social media, and create a conversation. The conversation is not a one-way conversation (narrowcasting) with the marketer sending a message to the customer, but rather a two-way conversation (dyadic) between marketer and customer. A good example of this is the CarTV podcast, a weekly video that covers the automobile industry and evaluates car models from different makers. The CarTV podcast can be downloaded to an iPod or other portable video player, and is popular with consumers with a strong interest in cars. Currently, there are podcasts available for almost any topic of interest. Audi is known for its use of non-traditional media to connect with its customers and to communicate its messages. Each year, Audi teams up with top music acts to back the launch of its latest TT model sports car through a digitally-led campaign. What Audi is trying to do is to sign up with established, well-known bands that create original content that will be available as podcasts on their website. This campaign is an example of how a growing number of marketers are focusing more on digital work, and less on conventional advertising. (Charles 2006) Music has long been used as a marketing tactic to connect with customers. Podcasts are another vehicle to deliver the same basic kind of connection. Deliso (2006) reports that only 8 percent of American adults listen to podcasts, however, he believes that marketers' embrace of this technology is not premature. There is some question as to just how fast podcasting is proliferating, but marketers seeking a low cost technology to reach audiences should consider podcasting.

There are, of course additional opportunities and tactics to exploit the rich capabilities of a website to meet organizational marketing and advertising goals. Marketing and advertising objectives are more likely to be met when the Internet focus is on online branding. This focus can be achieved by implementing various online marketing tactics such as using the 8 Cs and a U in website design, as well as utilizing media content broadcasting such as RSS Feeds and podcasts that can reach customers and potential customers on the Web. Connecting with customers can be as simple as providing clear contact information via e-mail, phone, chat, or even weblogs. Weblogs will be discussed later in this chapter.

DRIVING TRAFFIC TO A WEBSITE

Much of the chapter thus far has been devoted to websites and website content. We now shift to consideration of driving traffic to a website. Just as bricks and mortar retailers want to drive traffic to their stores, online marketers should strive to drive traffic to their websites. A major objective of a website is to generate "traffic" (visitations to the website). Generating more traffic will provide the organization with more connections with its customers and potential customers, potentially resulting in higher advertising rates (if profits are based on advertising), and potentially a greater return-on-investment (ROI). Traffic can and should be driven by offline and online tactics in an integrated manner. In cyberspace, hurling (distributing) your URL is a must. Practitioners must place their website address, or URL, on every communication piece they distribute. Other tactics include viral marketing, affiliate marketing, sales promotions and incentives, e-mail and search engine programs, including search engine marketing (SEM), and search engine optimization (SEO), directory listings, and more. Digital advertising clearly has the capacity to drive traffic to an organization's website as well. This will be discussed later in this chapter.

DIGITAL ADVERTISING

Digital advertising is simply an extension of the traditional media broadcast model (i.e., similar to advertising on television and radio). The website digital advertiser broadcasts content (typically for free, but not always) that contains various kinds of useful customer information. These broadcasts may also include such services as e-mail, chat rooms, and weblog services. Mixed in with this content and services are advertising messages, such as banner ads. For some advertisers banner ads are their sole sources of revenue.

These generally work best when the volume of viewer traffic is large or highly specialized. High volume sites such as Yahoo! and Google attract a large number of viewers and are desirable for their ability to reach large numbers of people. The Super Bowl is a good example of a program with high reach in traditional media--and therefore commands very high advertising rates. ESPN.com is desirable to advertisers because of its reach, as well as some strong sports-oriented specialization. The primary audience is comprised of males (sports enthusiasts) who are intensely interested in sports. Male sports enthusiasts often respond in similar ways to advertising messages targeted towards them. Enthusiasts tend to be the most frequent viewers of specialized websites as well as the most frequent purchasers of specific products. They are also the most brand loyal. There are many highly specialized sites focusing on everything from fly fishing to fashion. Advertising on these sites is desirable because of their enthusiast targeting capabilities.

Media kits for any site that sells advertising will provide traffic and visitor metrics. A media kit, or press kit, is a package of news and background information about a medium that is provided to potential advertisers. For example, among other things, information might be provided on the number of readers, viewers, visitors, demographics, advertising options and rates, and contact information. It assists the advertiser in understanding and comparing one medium relative to others. For example, CyberAtlas (http://www.cyberatlas.com) collects a vast array of Internet statistics and metrics that could be of interest to Internet marketers, advertisers, and others doing business on the Internet. Media Metrics (http://www.mediametrics.com.au/) provides a patented on-site web analytics methodology to measure a consumer's online behavior including click by click, page by page, minute by minute user activity, both online and off line. ACNielsen/NetRatings (http://www.nielsen-netratings.com) can provide data on Internet growth and consumer user patterns of Internet usage by using an off-site web analytics methodology. eMarketer (http://www.emarketer.com) proclaims to be the leading provider of eBusiness statistics and Internet statistics in the world. Burke, Inc. (http://www.burke.com) can provide custom, full-service Internet metric marketing research, market analysis, and consulting for both consumer and business-to-business goods and services organizations.

Marketers should understand both the opportunities and the threats associated with digital media and advertising. For example, Menon and Soman (2003) argue that the challenges of generating interest and educating consumers about your brand are especially relevant in digital advertising. Unlike advertising messages in traditional media, most digital advertising is in a form a banner or tower ad that generates sufficient interest and motivation on the part of the consumer to interact with the message. In addition, customers are often required to actively access information rather than be passive recipients of the advertising message.

Marketers must work to ensure that they are generating sufficient attention and motivation for viewers to click-through and view the full content of the advertisement. Unfortunately, many of the tactics that work well in traditional media may not work as well in digital spaces. For instance, television commercials do not always work well in a digital medium. Since the customer has a choice on a website he or she will most likely click away from a "lengthy" television style advertisement; unless they are very short in duration. Marketers should strive to develop messages that fit the medium and its users. Another consideration is ad placement. Chatterjee, et al. (2003) find that while repeated exposures to the same banner ad is negatively related to click-through rate, consumers are equally likely to click on banner ads that are placed early (primacy) in navigation, or later (recency) in navigation on a website. Moreover, clutter is a major weakness for digital ads. The greater the clutter in the ad the more likely it is to be ignored by customers. Using metrics that discover the most likely target market can help to deliver relevant messages to targeted prospects, increasing the success of digital advertising campaigns. They key word is *relevant*. Most consumers want relevancy in the ads they read or listen to on the Internet.

Although there are many forms of digital media and advertising, Table 2 presents some of the most common types in use today. There are two forms of digital advertising that are currently not considered to be common forms of digital advertising but appear to be gaining a large amount of interest with marketers. Both video and mobile advertising are on the rise and are generating attention. Consumers are beginning to see campaigns which include video and mobile messages. Both of these areas of digital advertising may grow in the future and become significant in some online marketing programs. (Business Week, 2009)

Video ads formats are not much different from ads that consumers might see on television, while others encourage and enable the interactivity of the Internet to engage viewers. (MacMillan 2009) The Interactive Advertising Bureau collaborated with more than 140 different online publishers, including Microsoft, Google, and Yahoo!, to create a set of guidelines for the five most common formats, some of which are not much different from television ads. Others are more sophisticated and use the interactivity of the Internet to engage viewers. The first is the "pre-roll" - a 15- or 30-second ad that viewers watch before a show or video clip ("pre-roll"), at some

Table 2. Most common forms of digital advertising

Form of Digital Advertising	Description or Common Meaning
A business's website	This is the most common form of advertising on the Internet. Ragu Spaghetti Sauce was one of the first. Remember to consider the 8 Cs and the U.
Banner	A banner is a rectangular graphic placed as an advertisement on web pages. They often employ graphics, or rotate to capture the user's attention. The user can even click-thru the web page.
Button	A button is similar to a banner, but square.
Tower	A tower is vertical display; usually down the right site side.
Intromercials	An intromercial is an animated, full-screen ad placed at the entry point of a website before the user reaches the intended content.
Search Engine Marketing (SEM)	SEM includes various forms of Internet marketing displays that seek to promote websites by increasing their visibility and/or ranking in search engine results pages.
Classified Ads	Classified ads are well-suited for the interactive environment. Users can enter requests, and the computer will search for the appropriate listings.
Weblog or Chat Room Ads	Yahoo! and HotWired are examples of sites that sell advertising in chat rooms.
Contest Sponsorship	Many sites offer contests which can be sponsored by an advertiser.

point during the video ("mid-roll"), or afterward ("post-roll"). The second is the "interactive." The Interactive is a pre-roll, mid-roll, or post-roll that offers viewers some form of interaction, such as entering a Zip Code or stock ticker, or playing a short game. The ad may last longer than 15 or 30 seconds if a viewer engages with it. The third form is the "overlay," a text or graphic that appears on the bottom or top portion of the video for a brief period while content is in progress. What generally occurs is that viewers can click on the ad to expand it or go to an advertiser's Web site. The fourth form is the "invitation," which is similar to an overlay, but the message briefly appears next to the actual video player rather than on top of it. Lastly, the "companion" is a static banner that appears alongside a video player, typically in conjunction with another ad from the same sponsor, like a pre-roll or overlay. (MacMillan 2009) As these and other forms of digital advertising methods develop, marketers will begin to and continue to explore video ads and their potential for engagement and ROI.

More than 80 percent of consumers now own cell phones—a potential advertising medium. Fast-food chains, car makers and TV reality shows have run contests and other promotions in which consumers participate by sending text messages to their Web addresses. Wireless carriers have begun allowing organizations to run banners ads in a mini version of what they might see on the Internet. Google Inc. and Yahoo! have distributed search ads to cell phones; and this appears to be just the beginning. Jesdanun (2009) reported that organizations will be able to use image-recognition software to determine what offers, video clips, or other content are delivered to cell phone users.

For example, Snap Tell Inc., an online wine retailer, offered discounts to anyone who sent a photo of its newspaper ad snapped with a camera phone. Soon it will be possible for cell phone users to snap a picture of a movie poster, billboard, or some other brand message and receive movie reviews, and/or receive discounts for tickets, goods, or services. The Mobile Advertising Report (2008) found that in the first quarter of 2008 there were more than 255 million mobile phone users in the U.S.; up from 251 million in the fourth quarter of 2007. A dramatic finding of the research was the significant rise in the number of consumers who were able to recall the brand they had seen advertised on their cell phones. Forty-one percent of those who remembered mobile advertising could remember at least one brand, which is up from 34 percent just three months before. This represents a 7 percentage point increase. Men are 10 percent more likely than women to recall a brand they have seen advertised on their cell phone, while those aged 25 to 34 were the highest-performing age group in terms of brand recall. There is certainly much to learn about this new medium, and form of advertising; and both researchers and marketers need to explore it.

Viral Marketing

Viral marketing is a term applied to a family of analogous marketing tactics, some of them quite old, though the term itself dates from the height of the Internet bubble economy. (Moore, 2003) According to one of the venture capitalists who launched it, viral marketing amounts to little more than "network-enhanced word-of-mouth." Word-of-mouth has consistently been one of the oldest, most credible, and most effective branding and advertising strategies. Viral marketing proposes that messages can be rapidly disseminated from consumer to consumer, leading to large-scale market acceptance because of the credibility of the source of the information—friends, family, relatives, co-workers, etc. (Krishnamurthy, 2003) The beauty of viral marketing on the Internet is that it can turn every user into "an involuntary salesperson." In viral marketing, the brand seems to underwrite (or sponsor) acts of communication, transforming users of the service—authors of e-mail messages sent over the network—into de facto product endorsers.

Viral marketing is more powerful than third-party advertising because it conveys an implied endorsement from a friend, relative, or co-worker. Close acquaintances have more credibility than an advertiser. Tactics that involve people in playful ways, which are passed on and disseminated organically, are far more likely to be successful. (Moore, 2003) Brands that are perceived to enhance personal relationships, and are worth sharing with friends, are the ones that will prosper. (Hodder, 2002) In addition, contacting individuals using the Web is much faster and less expensive than any other medium. The critical mass effect also plays an important role in viral marketing. As more customers spread information or sign up for a product, each one can contact many more. Soon the total number contacted rises exponentially; which illustrates Metcalfe's Law (Metcalfe's Law 2008) that the community value of a network grows as the square of the number of its users increase.

Affiliate Marketing

Affiliate marketing is a marketing practice in which a business rewards one or more affiliates for each visitor or customer brought in by the affiliate's marketing efforts. It is using the connectivity function of one website to drive traffic to another. Amazon.com and Barnesandnoble.com are affiliates for many other websites. A visitor to an Amazon.com affiliate might see an ad on that site for a book that Amazon sells. If a visitor clicks through and purchases something at the Amazon.com site, Amazon.com will pay their affiliate a fee. Therefore, the affiliates provide purchase-point click-through to the merchant (Amazon.com). It is a pay-for-performance business model. If an affiliate does not generate sales, no cost is incurred by the sponsor. This type of marketing may have another advantage. The algorithms search engines use for serving up listings usually consider the popularity of a website including what other sites that website is linked to. Search engines will reward those websites that have more links, and those that display more popular links with a higher natural, or organic, and perhaps less expensive paid listing.

Email

Commercial e-mail is an electronic message that can be promotional in nature, usually containing an incentive. It is a form of direct marketing, and is interactive. For marketers, e-mail introduces five capabilities, including the ability to initiate two-way communication, the ability to communicate quickly, the ability to provide almost instant feedback, and the ability to achieve worldwide reach, and it is relatively low-cost. On the negative side, consumers and businesses receiving unsolicited e-mail messages often perceive them to be spam, or junk, and may choose to "block" them.

Permission Marketing

Digital marketing works best when it is permission-based; that is, when a consumer gives a business the "permission" to send and receive relevant messages. Permission marketing is about each customer shaping the targeting behavior of marketers and receiving only the marketing messages desired. It is a scenario where consumers empower a marketer to send them messages in certain interest categories. Marketers then match anticipated, personal, and relevant messages with the interests of consumers who have opted-in. The use of e-mail to solicit permission to market to individuals is common and often successful.

Marketers can make good use of data mining techniques (discussed below) when seeking permission to send customized messages and offers to potential and existing customers. E-mail is relatively easy to use and e-mail lists are readily available. Marketers should work to ensure the delivery of legitimate e-mail communications and build an ongoing, mutually beneficial dialogue with customers and potential customers. Some suggestions for maximizing the effectiveness of e-mail communications include informing customers about the nature of e-mails they will receive and the frequency of those communications, should they give permission. The more specific the information is about the type of offer or product the better. Marketers should create and make readily available a clear privacy policy statement that is easily accessible to recipients—one that explains what data is collected and how it will and will not be used or shared.

Communications should be relevant to the recipient, should not contain objectionable content, and should only contain the type of content the customer originally agreed to. The content should clearly describe the offer and its benefits. Tips, special offers, and information based on each recipient's own behavior, interests, and needs often generate the best response rates and the fewest complaints. It is very important that the subject line accurately reflect the message, purpose, and content. In addition, a marketer's brand should be featured prominently in the "From" and/or the "Subject" lines. Although creative elements such as images often make a message more interesting, marketers should pretest them with anti-spam software to avoid words, phrases, coding, punctuation, and design common to spam. (Direct Marketing Association 2005) These recommendations are among the many that should help to improve the likelihood of permission-based e-mail being delivered to the inbox and read by the intended recipient.

Sales Promotions and Incentives

Consumers are accustomed to incentive tactics in the bricks and mortar environment; yet they often perceive few benefits from similar tactics on the Internet. (deChernatony, 2001) However, it is the marketer's task to develop and implement incentives to drive traffic to his or her website, and then employ additional incentives to convert potential customers into customers. Such tactics might included sales promotions designed to move the target market quickly towards a purchase, such as the use of a promotion code published in a magazine. Permission e-mail marketing directs marketing messages and incentives towards potential customers that are interested enough to allow their names to be included on a commercial e-mail distribution list. Further, with personalization, more customer data can be mined to target the right customer with the right messages.

Data Mining and the Marketing Decision Support System (MDSS)

Data mining, also called machine learning, or knowledge discovery, is a class of machine-driven methods that look for hidden patterns and relationships in databases and data warehouses. (Siegal 2004) It works by analyzing huge amounts of raw data to discover managerially useful summary information within the data that are not typically be revealed in the raw data. Siegal (2004) reports that data mining can substantiate what would otherwise be educated guesses about marketing relationships. This can be accomplished by using automated discovery whereby the marketer can search for hidden relationships among a multitude of variables. Siegel further claims that data mining is both a descriptive and predictive tool—one where the process creates its own theory about why a relationship exists. It requires drilling down through multiple layers of data such as customer transaction data to create profiles of customer purchase behaviors. The process of data mining creates models for segmenting customers and forecasting behaviors, such as future purchases (loyalty) or attrition (brand switching).

Data mining is relatively new addition to the traditional marketing decision support system (MDSS). A marketing decision support system is "…a coordinated collection of data systems, tools, and techniques with supporting software and hardware by which an organization gathers and interprets relevant information from business and the environment and turns it into a basis for marketing action." (Little 1979) The main reason data mining is important to marketers is that this information can be used to assist in developing marketing programs to include market segmentation, targeted marketing, personalization/customization, relationship marketing, direct marketing, cross selling and discovering customer lifetime value. Marketing research also does this, but in a different way. According to Yang (2005):

Data mining research incorporates methodologies from various research disciplines such as statistics, machine learning, database technology, optimization and pattern recognition, and hence has a richer pool of knowledge and model representation. It focuses more on the effectiveness of problem solving, and pays greater attention to the actual performance on data. In contrast, marketing research advocates more theory-based analysis and its theories are often built upon statistics, economics, econometrics and other social sciences.

An MDSS system has three basic components. The first is the data system which is composed of methods and processes for gathering useful internal and external information. The second component is the model system which provides routines, procedures, and techniques for manipulating information. And, the third component is the dialogue system (language) that allows the marketing manager to manipulate the data to solve ill-structured decision problems. There is evidence that these two basic forms of marketing research can work well together in a MDSS system. For example, as consumers continue to shift their purchasing toward shopping in multiple channels, the value of capturing information at various touch points has become increasingly important. This growing need for data mining is also occurring in the B2B marketplace as these markets become more complex, and the need for better targeting grows. One of the strongest applications of data mining results is the ability to deliver relevant offers to targeted consumers.

Coupons are one of the most visible forms of sales promotion. Many retailers participate in online coupon programs. Additionally, contests are popular online—such as those offered by General Mills, and NASCAR. To be sure, one of the most important tasks of the marketer is to employ data mining techniques to develop relevant messages and offers to targeted consumers. For example, data mining can be used to reduce shipping costs to specific geographic areas. It can also be used to discover specific market segments that are price sensitive, or responsive to incentives.

Cross-selling and up-selling are tactics that can be used on commerce sites. Other incentives might come in the form of cause-related marketing such as green marketing. Research by Changchien et al. (2003) evaluated a sales promotion application for distributing and redeeming coupons while shopping on the Internet. They found that during the online shopping experience, various sales promotions and coupons were offered. Various methods were also used to target coupons to select potential buyers. One threat that emerged, and which should be considered, is that security mechanisms are needed to prevent alterations, duplication, and trading of coupons by customers; as well as the fraudulent use of manufacturer's coupons by retailers. The impact of coupon trading and duplication Marketers, facilitated by the Internet can have an adverse effect on sales promotion campaigns. should consider that well-developed and targeted campaigns can be quite successful, but care should be taken in minimizing the potential for fraud.

Search Engine Programs

More and more marketing managers are adopting new ways of thinking about branding on the Internet; including the ability to recognize the way consumers use keywords in search engines to find suitable brands. To capitalize on the opportunity presented by search engines, some marketing mangers strive to get their brands posted at the top of the list on the website. (Owen 2000). The term "search engine" is commonly used for any type of website search—one that obscures valuable information about other types of search tools and other types of search sites. There are three types of Internet search tools including lists, directories, and search engines. A given search site may contain one or more of these search tools for the visitor to use.

Lists are the earliest and most popular form of organizing information about websites. They are literally a list of websites (or far less frequently of web pages) that may be organized by some scheme, such as letters of the alphabet, or subject area. These lists typically have only one or two levels of organization. The visitor uses a list by simply reading down the list until they (hopefully) find a website that is relevant to their interests. An online example of such a list is yellowpages.com.

Directories were the next development in search tools. Yahoo! is the earliest and best-known example. Two other examples are Open Directory and Looksmart. A directory is a logical extension of a list having multiple categories and subcategories; in some cases 10 to 20 levels deep. They list websites (not web pages). The visitor uses the directory by "drilling down" (clicking) through the subcategories until they find the appropriate subcategory they are looking for. Then they peruse the list of websites therein. A key feature, and as it has turned out, a key reason for the failure of directories, is that they have a human being review each website before listing the website in their directory. (Sonnenreicht 1997)

Search engines, and their cousins, meta-search engines, have proven to be the most popular search tools on the Web. A search engine consists of three elements. The first element is a database of web pages (not websites), the second element is a user interface, and the third element is an algorithm that determines the relevancy of web pages in the database for any given search term. Upon locating a new website or web page, the search engine searches the site by using a "robot," or "spider." A robot is a type of automated software, often referred to as spider. The robot collects the web page and places it in the search engine database. When a visitor requests a search for a specified word, phrase, or term, the search engine uses a proprietary, secret, multi-variable, non-linear algorithm to evaluate all the web pages in its index that contain the search term. The web pages are then presented to the visitor, ordered from highest to lowest in terms of relevancy by means of a relevancy score. Compared to lists and directories, search engines are more convenient to use, are more inclusive of the World Wide Web, and typically have more relevant results. (Brynn, 1999)

Meta-search engines function by first accepting the visitor's search term(s); it then searches other search engines, and finally presents the results. Meta-search engines do not contain their own database. The simplest of these meta-search engines presents the results from the search engines they contacted on the visitors behalf, in a list, engine by engine (see www.dogpile.com). A more sophisticated meta-search engine applies its own algorithm to the results it obtains from the search engines it contacts to provide another level of interpretation of relevancy. One example is www.ixquick.com.

Search sites are websites where the searcher may conduct searches for websites or web pages relevant to a given search term. Most search sites include both a search engine and a directory. The directory is typically a feed from Open Directory or Looksmart, rather than a directory unique to the search site. Also, the database of web pages is typically an amalgamation of the search site's own database supplemented by databases from other search sites. Search sites have struggled to develop sustainable revenues. Most are operating in the red, using additional investment or debt capital to sustain operations. A key element in the future survivability of individual search sites is the ability to develop a business model that generates adequate revenues. Revenue generation continues to be a major hurdle for search sites. However, four revenue sources have become prominent. One of these revenue sources is advertising. Search sites sell ad space typically in three areas. These areas include banner ads at the top of the web page, skyscraper ads on the right side of the page, and "sponsored listings" typically displayed as the first pages above the non-advertised pages.

Another source of revenue is paid inclusion. Search sites quickly realized that website owners often wanted their websites included as soon as possible on any newly launched website. This is because traffic is the key to the success of most websites; and placement in search engines generates traffic. In the past, most search sites were not indexing new pages or re-indexing existing pages in a timely manner. It was typical for months to go by before a robot would visit or revisit a website. In order to counter this slow indexing of websites, some search sites began offering a "premium" service. By paying a negotiated fee per page, a website owner could have their pages indexed within two to three days and then re-indexed every two to three days thereafter.

A third source of revenue is "pay for placement;" also known as "pay per click" or "PPC". This is a form of advertising in which a search engine allows website owners to "bid" for top placements in the engine on a keyword by keyword basis. The bid is what the website advertiser is willing to pay that search engine owner per visitor. Overture (formerly GoTo, now owned by Yahoo!) was the initial search engine to promulgate this model. It and has been extremely successful, both in obtaining market visibility, and in revenue generation (and suspected profitability). Based on traffic and revenues they remain the major "pay for placement" search engine. There are about 5 to 10 minor such search engines, and between 100 and 200 micro search engines.

A fourth source of revenue is the sharing of sponsored listings. Yahoo! is perhaps the greatest proponent of this approach—they provide their top three listings (based on bids) to another search site. Both Yahoo! and the other search site benefit from this arrangement. Yahoo! benefits because it gets more exposure for its listings, thereby generating more income, and it shares the income with the other search sites. There is continued growth in the number of listings being shared among search sites as they mimic Yahoo! Currently, Google, Yahoo! and MSN provide the great majority of searches. Because of this sharing among websites, marketers can have confidence in the extensive reach of their search engine marketing strategy when advertising on just these three search engines. The opportunities to advertise are becoming broader and more complex as these sites work to provide relevant listings to Internet searchers. The search engines are trying to accommodate the needs of advertisers while earning greater revenues and profits for their organizations.

A final observation about search engines is their ability to generate traffic. Website owners realize that high placements in search engines (and sometimes directories) can result in significant traffic to their websites. Currently, there are three ways to obtain visibility, and hence, traffic from search sites. One is through optimization. Optimization is the practice of creating web pages that will produce high relevancy scores in a search engine's algorithm. Since early algorithms employed by search engines were often simplistic, it was possible to significantly influence relevancy scores (and hence placements) by manipulating text on pages. But the era of simplistic and easy means to obtain high relevancy scores is past. (Farrelly, 1999 and Google 2002) Search engines now employ highly sophisticated, secret algorithms. Consequently, the practitioner of "optimization" must keep abreast of the state of the art in search engine algorithms. This is not easy to do. It is possible to influence relevancy scores by creating "optimized" pages, but it is no longer possible to manipulate search engines. A second means to generate traffic in search sites is through the "pay for placement" model as exemplified by Overture. A web page can be listed at the top of a search engine results page even though it is identified as a "sponsored link." That way it will obtain high visibility and receive traffic. A third means to generate traffic is through advertising such as banner ads, and skyscraper ads. Website marketers typically employ variations of all three techniques to obtain traffic.

Consumer-Generated Media

Smith (2006) suggests that the Internet is still evolving with the latest "killer application" being social engagement. Social engagement is a key characteristic of consumer-generated media (CGM). Perhaps the simplest way to describe CGM is to provide some well-known examples. Facebook, MySpace, YouTube, Craigslist, Angie's List, and PhotoBucket are among the most used websites by consumers. Examples of CGM include blog entries, consumer e-mail feedback, message board posts, forum comments, personal websites, and personal e-mail. Recently, Hart and Blackshaw (2006) included wikis, raves, profiles, networks, and mailing lists as other examples of CGM. CGM is not precisely defined, and generally refers to "…just about any website powered by the user on a constant and mandatory basis." (Levy and Stone 2006) The popular media refers to GCM as Web 2.0. Unlike paid media, CGM is created and driven by consumers. It is advancing as a major consumer resource for socializing and connecting with others, as well as obtaining various types of desired information. The central idea is "harnessing collective intelligence." (Surowiecki 2005, as cited in Levy and Stone 2006)

For instance, a good early example of a CGM website is Craigslist, an online community bulletin board where millions of consumer go to peruse classified-ad listings to find jobs, apartments, concert tickets, and more. In doing so, they connect with millions of people who provide postings in a self-service, community-moderated market space. Managed by a small staff of 19, Craigslist is the seventh largest website in the world. (Levy and Stone 2006) A similar kind of list is Angie's List that is a review, or rating site that gathers consumer ratings of various types of businesses and services, such as plumbers, painters, accountants, doctors, lawyers, dry cleaners, and so on. Table 3 describes the most common forms or types of CGM.

Consumer use of CGM is growing at an increasing rate. In 2006, MySpace.com was visited by 65 million consumers. In addition to final consumers, there is a growing list of marketers wishing to connect with them. (Levy and Stone 2006) Facebook has almost 200 million members. (Facebook 2009) Early in 2009, Facebook was growing by over 700,000 users a day. This growth translates into more 5 million new users a week world-wide and more than one million per week in the United States. This unprecedented growth

Table 3. Most common forms or types of CGM

Form or Type of GCM	Description, or Common Meaning
Blog	Website where entries are written in chronological order and displayed in reverse chronological order.
Message Boards/ Forum	Web application for holding discussions and posting user-generated content.
Review/Rating Site	Website where product and/or company reviews are posted by experienced consumers.
Direct Company Feedback	Media vehicle allowing consumers to provide direct feedback to companies.
Third-Party Web Site	Website, such as Complaints.com and My3cents.com, where smaller, yet active groups of consumers generate comments.
Moblog	Mobile-enabled blogs that let users post photos from anywhere.
Vlogs/Video blog	A blog that comprises video.
Podcast	A digital media file, or a series of such files, that is distributed over the Internet using syndication feeds for playback on portable media devices.

is now attracting over 10 percent of the global Internet population to its site. Facebook employs most of the 8 Cs and the U as it continues to differentiate itself through content, community, connectivity such as easy photo-sharing (it has more than a billion photos shared per month) and clear and aggressive privacy controls so people can make sure those who are most special in their lives can see certain information others cannot.

Each day around 35,000 videos are added to YouTube with about 30,000 daily visitors to the site, viewing millions of videos. (Levy and Stone 2006) Flickr—a 2.5 million member community of people with a passion for sharing photos—is another popular CGM site recently purchased by Yahoo! Google Video is another CGM site that lets users upload videos and even sell them. In all of this communication and engagement, what may interest marketers most is that consumers communicate frequently about products and brands.

Indeed, Klaassen (2007) reports that marketers are already starting to recognize the frequency with which people report their affinities for brands on CGM sites such as social nets, blogs, and personal web pages. Marketers also understand that consumer reviews and trusted recommendations (a level of credibility not enjoyed by advertisers) are increasingly important marketing factors. For example, Facebook has developed applications devoted to displaying visitors' favorite brands, purchases, and tastes. CGM communities provide value to consumers akin to the value of word-of-mouth, and their reach is limited only by the size of the online network. (Hart and Blackshaw 2006) Organizations such as Nike, Sears, and the Coca-Cola Company have pushed their advertising agencies to come up with CGM tactics. Nike built a social network for running geeks. The main point was to get feedback and learn what worked and what did not work. (Helm and Kiley 2009) Experimentation with social networking should continue because companies need to determine how to connect with consumers in the digital age.

Lenhart (2007) discovered that teenagers are one of the most influential consumer segments propelling CGM. MySpace grew to 50 million members in a little over two years. Websites such as MySpace, Facebook, and PhotoBucket have between 50 percent and 90 percent more visitors aged 12 to 24 than the Web as a whole. (Morrissey, 2006) Content creation is a common behavior on CGM sites and this behavior by teenagers continues to grow; with 64 percent of online teens ages 12 to 17 engaging in at least one type of content creation. Girls continue to dominate most elements of content creation with approximately 35 percent of all online teen girls blogging, compared with 20 percent of online boys. Lenhart (2007) also found that 54 percent of wired girls post photos online compared with 40 percent of online boys. Boys dominate the posting of video content online however, and are nearly twice as likely as online girls (19 percent vs. 10 percent) to have posted a video online. Lenhart also found that content creation is more than just about sharing creative output—it is also about participating in conversations based on that content. Almost half (47 percent) of online teens have posted photos in places where others can see them; and 89 percent of those teens say that people comment on the images at least some of the time. Parents of teenagers are more likely to be online (87 percent) than parents who do not have teenagers in the home (17 percent). The most common online behavior for the parents of teens is to check up on, and regulate their teens' media usage; including the Internet, but also television and video games. (Macgill 2008)

In order to use CGM as an effective marketing tool, marketers will need to analyze its costs and benefits. While the popularity of using CGM to spread information is growing rapidly, risks exist. On the one hand, marketers might successfully influence the consumer content and postings, and also gain a better understanding of consumers' attitudes toward their products, services, brands, and even their competition. On the other hand, CGM tactics can be time-consuming, require regular management, and can produce candid, sometimes negative, remarks about an organization or its products. It is this lack of control that may be the biggest fear of marketers when considering the risks of using and participating in CGM. While it is clear that CGM can be used to send and receive information, there is little substantiated research providing evidence as to their effective use in generating sales and profits. In the absence of valid and reliable studies, marketers must rely on case studies and specific examples from industry to gauge their potential success. Future research needs to consider these and other strategic and tactical variables so that marketers can develop a stronger understanding of CGM and their potential role in marketing programs.

Weblogs (blogs), are a type of CGM which has received significant attention in both in the academic literature and even more so in the trade literature. *Business Week* (2006) suggests that it is difficult to imagine a world without Weblogs. In the early stages of Weblogs, Winer (1999) reported that Weblogs were "...often-updated sites that pointed the reader to on-site articles and to articles elsewhere on the Web with comments on those articles. A Weblog is kind of a continual tour, with a human guide whom you get to know." Kahney (2000) proposes that the best Weblogs provide a diverse mix of resources including news stories, connections with other similar topic sites, essays, and opinions. Weblogs about cars, food, health, love, news and more have emerged online.

In a special report, *The Washington Times* reported that many companies have incorporated Weblogs and Weblog discussions (blogging) into their customer relationship programs. (Baker, 2006) Microsoft Corp., Dell Inc., and Sun Microsystems have given their employees permission to start Weblogs and are generally given free rein to discuss their business, as long as they do not give away trade secrets. Nike hired an agency that publishes several popular Weblogs to create a Weblog for a new campaign entitled "Art of Speed." The Weblog promotes a Nike-sponsored series of short films. On the other side of the business scenario, there is evidence that blogging might be appealing to customers who have become weary of traditional marketing methods. (Baker, 2006)

Blogging provides marketers with an opportunity to no longer have to rely on the printed press alone to publicize new goods and services. There are many other uses of Weblogs, as well. Some, like Nike's "Art of Speed" Weblog, have great attention-getting and entertainment value. Others, such as Microsoft's employee Weblogs, provide good information as well as good customer service to customers. The themes, or tactics, of Weblogs should be considered from the prospective of both the seller and the buyer. For example, Weblogs that are simple and useful might result in a potential shift in the way people get their news and how they learn about new goods and services. CNN (2005) reported that "...most managers accept the benefits blogging can bring." Examples include, establishing a company as a thought leader in its sector, providing tips and insights on potential new products, facilitating feedback on existing products, and allowing an outlet for good company news, as well as a chance to ease bad news into the ether. The most obvious and compelling reason to start a corporate Weblog is "...to establish a direct relationship with customers in a context that can build trust over time; something all the advertising in the world can struggle to accomplish." (CNN, 2005)

Marketers need to understand the risks and rewards of communicating in such open spaces as the Internet. Another important issue is the measurement of weblog performance. Most measurements are still in their infancy. (Fry, 2006) Yet Oster (2005) suggests that organizations need to be tuned into what customers and non-customers are saying about their company, and their products. Oster believes that many companies do not really know the many negative remarks being made about their brands. Clearly then, marketers considering using weblogs, or advertising on blogs, should monitor the tenor and the tone of the site; then make a decision about the extent of their participation; if any. Many mainline companies have made the decision that the rewards of the Internet are worth the risks. Baker and Green (2005) report that Gawker Media, a daily Manhattan media news and gossip Weblog, sells ads for everything from Nike to Absolute Vodka, commanding up to $25,000 per month for a sponsorship. There is evidence of continued technological development in the future of weblogs, and, despite some predictions of its demise, there is evidence that blogging will be increasing—at least until it is replaced by new technology (which is very likely considering the history of technological development). Weblog software is becoming easier to use, thereby expanding the number of organizational and consumer users. (*Business Week* 2006) Eventually, it will become easier to incorporate more media and more mobile capabilities into Weblogs to bring in more mainstream users.

Regardless, CGM usage is growing and may provide value to both consumers and marketers. Therefore, marketing practitioners must continue to scan the environment for new developments that may impact the creation and use of marketing programs that include CGM. Given the rapid growth of CGM worldwide, academicians and practitioners need to consider identifying monitoring, measuring, and interpreting the consumer-generated media websites that are relevant to their industry, their company, and their brands.

MEASURING DIGITAL ADVERTISING AND MEDIA

Web Analytics and Metrics

Digital technologies have opened the door to new possibilities in data collection and analysis of business processes; including customer behavior. As a consumer travels in the virtual, or digital world, everywhere he or she goes, and everything he or she does, leaves a trail of bits of information because almost all actions and activities are recorded. Marketers can and should analyze the rich data that is generated. Marketers can then use the resultant consumer behavior information to help optimize the network infrastructure and improve website architecture. Marketers can also use it to measure the effectiveness of website design as well as any associated marketing tactics used on a site or its affiliated sites, and search engines.

For marketers, Web analytics can almost surely improve business results. For example, specific metrics can obtain the complete picture of a company's website's performance. This should help firms acquire, convert, and retain customers, develop strategies to deliver greater value, measure and improve customer satisfaction, identify drivers of customer pain and delight, and create win-back programs for lost customers. Additionally, these metrics can explore other important types of customer research such as market segments, best new product concepts, pricing, and best promotion practices.

CONCLUSION

One of the most appealing qualities of digital advertising and digital media is the opportunity for marketers to explore and evolve with along with the digital marketing capabilities they work with. Naturally, marketers want digital capabilities that truly work to deliver relevant messages to a defined market in the time and space desired by the customer. This chapter covered the breadth of digital media as it relates to marketing and advertising; beginning with a historical overview of the Internet followed by various types of emerging digital media, and various types of digital advertising.

This chapter explained how a website should be developed and managed in order to accomplish marketing and advertising objectives. It also offered a broad scope of tactics for driving traffic to a website and stimulating ecommerce and digital relationships. This chapter provided the foundation for introducing new digital elements into traditional marketing and advertising programs. Such innovations in digital media and advertising can improve marketing strategy formulation and execution. Each day brings advances in knowledge, and new applications of new technologies. Sometimes these changes are occurring so rapidly that it is challenging to understand them, let alone apply them effectively.

What we do know, however, is that using the Internet effectively can help companies better interact with their customers and potential customers, deliver information, deliver goods and services, and build ongoing relationships (relationship marketing). Academics and marketers need to continue to research how consumers behave in digital spaces, and their ever-changing use of digital media. Only then will they be able to effectively incorporate digital media and advertising into their marketing programs.

Finally, Web analytics are readily available and should be at the core of the development, implementation, and evaluation of all digital media advertising and marketing programs. (Helm and Kiley 2009) Experimentation with almost all forms of digital media and advertising will continue because companies need to determine how to effectively connect with consumers in the digital age. This will lead to many opportunities for future research on the productive use of various types of digital promotions. The key challenge for is not only to master digital media and advertising, but to stay abreast of technological advances and industry trends.

REFERENCES

Aaker, D. A. (1996). *Building Strong Brands*. New York: The Free Press.

Aaker, J. L. (1997, August). Dimensions of brand personality. *JMR, Journal of Marketing Research*, 347–356. doi:10.2307/3151897

Anckar, B., Walden, P., & Jelassi, T. (2002). Creating customer value in online grocery shopping. *International Journal of Retail & Distribution Management*, *30*(4), 211–220. doi:10.1108/09590550210423681

Baker, C. (2006). What's all the Blog about? *The Washington Times*. Retrieved May 6, 2008, from http://www.washingtontimes.com/specialreports/20040814-114043-3023r.htm

Baker, S., & Heather, G. (2005, May 2). Blogs will Change Your Business. *Business Week*, 57-67.

Bakos, Y. (1997). Reducing buyer search costs: Implications for electronic marketplaces. *Management Science*, *43*(12), 1676–1692. doi:10.1287/mnsc.43.12.1676

Bakos, Y., & Brynjolfsson, E. (1999, December). Bundling information goods: Pricing, profits, and efficiency. *Management Science*, *45*, 1613–1630. doi:10.1287/mnsc.45.12.1613

Beal, B. (2004). Are RSS Feeds the Next Great Marketing Tool? *SearchCRM.com*. Retrieved May 14, 2008, from http://searchcrm.techtarget/com/originalcontent/0,289142.sid//gcil017317,00.html

Bierma, N. (2002). Our Online Diarist Finds it Easy to Get Lost in the Blog. *Chicago Tribune*. Retrieved May 2, 2008, from http://www.chicagotribune.com/search/dispatcher.front?Query=weblogs&target=article

Blackshaw, P. (2005, June 25). The Pocket Guide to Consumer-Generated Media. *The ClickZ network*. Retrieved June 20, 2008, from http://www.clickz.com/showPage.html?page=3515576

Bradlow, E. T., & Schmittlein, D. C. (2000). The little engines that could: Modeling the performance of World Wide Web search engines. *Marketing Science, 19*(1), 43–62. doi:10.1287/mksc.19.1.43.15180

Brandt, M., & Johnson, G. (1997). *Power Branding: Building Technology Brands for Competitive Advantage*. Newtonville, MA: International Data Group.

Brown, D. R. (2000). Editor's note. *GAIN: AIGA Journal of Design for the Network Economy, 1*(1), 2–3.

Brown, S. L., Tilton, A., & Woodside, D. M. (2002). The case for online communities. *The McKinsey Quarterly, 1*, 11.

Business Week. (2006). The Future of the Blog. *Business Week Online*. Retrieved February 18, 2008, from http://www.businessweek.com/print/innovte/content/feb2006/id20060224_155318.html

Byrn, E. (1999). *Altavista History*. Retrieved from March 13, 2008, http://www.clubi.ie/webserch/engines/altavist/history.htm

Carlin, D. (2006, November 14). Can Daily Motion Challenge YouTube? *BusinessWeek.com*. Retrieved April 1, 2008, from http://www.businessweek.com/globalbiz/content/nov2006/gb20061114_086712.htm?chan=search

Changchien, W. S., Lee, C.-F., & Hsu, Y.-J. (2004, July). On-line personalized sales promotion in electronic commerce. *Expert Systems with Applications, 27*(1), 35–52. doi:10.1016/j.eswa.2003.12.017

Charles, G. (2006, September 27). Audi Hunts Music Ties for Podcasts to Support TT. *Marketing*, 5.

Chatterjee, P., Hoffman, D. L., & Novak, T. P. (2003). Modeling the clickstream: Implications for web-based advertising efforts. *Marketing Science, 22*(4), 520–541. doi:10.1287/mksc.22.4.520.24906

Cho, Y. S., Yong-Sauk, H., & Jae-Chase, P. (2002). The DN Grid Model for E-Positioning in E-Business Environment. In *International Academy of E-Business Conference Proceedings*, Las Vegas, NE (pp. 46-49).

CNN. (2005). The Rise and Rise of Corporate Blogs. *CNN.com*. Retrieved June 22, 2008, from http://www.cnn.com/2005/BUSINESS/12/20/company.blogs/index.html

Converse. (n.d.). Retrieved March 8, 2009, from http://www.converse.com/index.aspx?mode=c1&bhcp=1#CATEGORYC1

deChernatony, L. (2001, February). Succeeding with brands on the Internet. *Brand Management, 8*(3), 186–193. doi:10.1057/palgrave.bm.2540019

Deliso, M. (2006, August 28). RSS, Podcasts are Worthwhile Investments. *Advertising Age, 77*(35), 4.

Dickey, I. J., Lewis, W. F., & Siemens, J. C. (2007). The evolution of Internet weblogs: History, current trends, and projections of usage in marketing strategy. *Journal of Business and Behavioral Sciences, 19*(1), 91–102.

Direct Marketing Association. Email Delivery Best Practices for Marketers and List Owners, http://www.the-dma.org/antispam/EmailBP-FINAL.pdf October 2005, pp.2-10. Retrieved March 1, 2009]

Donada, C. (2002). E-Business and the Automotive Industry: What Stakes for the European Dealers? *International Academy of E-Business Conference Proceedings*, International Academy of E-Business, Las Vegas, NE, 76-79.

Farmer, M. A., & Sandoval, G. (2001, July 9). Webvan Delivers its Last Word: Bankruptcy. *CNET News*. Retrieved March 12, 2009, from http://news.cnet.com/2100-1017-269594.html

Farrelly, G. (1999). *Search Engines: Evolution and Revolution*. Retrieved May 18, 2008, from http://webhome.idirect.com/~glenjenn/search/history1.htm

Fry, J. (2006). Blog Epitaphs? Get Me Rewright! *The Wall Street Journal Online*. Retrieved February 27, 2008, from http://online.wsj.com/article_print/SB114072068850081570.html

Gardner, B., & Levy, S. J. (1955, March). The product and the brand. *Harvard Business Review*, 33–39.

Google Zeitgiest Archive. (2002). Retrieved April 22, 2008, from http://www.google.com/press/zeitgeist/archive.html

Grannis, K., & Davis, E. (2008 April 8). Online Sales to Climb Despite Struggling Economy. *Forrester Research*. Retrieved January 13, 2009, from http://forrester.com

Hart, C., & Blackshaw, P. (2006 January). Internet Inferno. *Marketing Management*, 19-25.

Haubl, G., & Trifts, V. (2000). Consumer decision making in online shopping environments: The effects of interactive decision aids. *Marketing Science*, *19*(1), 4–21. doi:10.1287/mksc.19.1.4.15178

Hauseman, A. V., & Siekpe, J. S. (2008). The effect of web interface features on consumer online purchase intentions. *Journal of Business Research*, *62*, 5–13. doi:10.1016/j.jbusres.2008.01.018

Hlem, B., & Kiley, D. (2009, January 12). Edgy advertising in a tenuous time. *Business Week*, 48.

Hodder, C. (2002). *God and Gap: What has Asda got to do with Jerusalem? Branding and being a Christian in the 21st century—some Reflections*. Retrieved January 21, 2008, from http://wwwinstitutefor brand leadership.org/Chris_HodderBrands_and_Theology.htm

Hoffman, D. L., & Novak, T. P. (1996). Marketing in hypermedia computer-mediated environments: Conceptual foundations. *Journal of Marketing*, *60*(July), 50–68. doi:10.2307/1251841

Hoffman, D. L., Novak, T. P., & Chatterjee, P. (1995). *Commercial Scenarios for the Web: Opportunities and Challenges*. Retrieved May 24, 2008, from http//slum.huji.ac.il/Vol1/issue3/hoffman.html

Hoffman, D. L., & Patrali, C. (1995). Commercial Scenarios for the Web: Opportunities and Challenges. *Journal of Computer-Mediated Communication*, *1*(3). Retrieved May 6, 2008, from http://www3.interscience.wiley.com/journal/120837666/abstract?CRETRY=1&SRETRY=0

Hrastnik, R. (2005). The Full Circle of RSS Marketing Power. *RSS-Specifications.com*. Retrieved November 16, 2007, from http://www.rss-specifications.com/full-circle-rss.htm

Human Factors Engineering. (n.d.). Retrieved March 8, 2009, from http://reliability.sandia.gov/Human_Factor_Engineering/human_factor_engineering.html

Jesdanun, A. (2008). Cell Phones Represent a New Media for Companies. *Single Touch*. Retrieved March 1, 2009, from http://www2.singletouch.net/content/view/86/109/

Kaferer, J. N. (1992). *Strategic Brand Management: New Approaches to Creating and Evaluating Brand Equity*. London: Logan Page.

Kahney, L. (2000). The web the way it was. *Wired News*. Retrieved June 23, 2008, from http://www.wired.com/news/culture/0,1284,34006-2,00.html?tw=wn_story_page_next1

Kalaignanam, K., Kushwaha, T., & Varadarajan, P. (2008). Marketing operations efficiency and the Internet: An organizing framework. *Journal of Business Research, 61*(4), 300–308. doi:10.1016/j.jbusres.2007.06.019

Kalakota, R., & Robinson, M. (2001). *E-Business 2.0: Roadmap for Success*. Reading, MA: Addison-Wesley.

Kalyanam, K., & McIntyre, S. (2002). The e-marketing mix: A contribution of the e-tailing wars. *Journal of the Academy of Marketing Science, 30*(4), 487–499. doi:10.1177/009207002236924

Klaassen, A. (2007). Real Revolution isn't Facebook's Ad Plan: Zuckerberg makes Big Claims, but Future Lies in Power of Peer-to-Peer. *Adage.com*. Retrieved November 19, 2007, from http://adage.com/digital/article?article_id=121929

Krishnamurthy, S. (2003). *E-Commerce Management*. Mason, OH: South-Western.

Lal, R., & Sarvary, M. (1999). When and how is the Internet likely to decrease price competition? *Marketing Science, 18*(4), 485–503. doi:10.1287/mksc.18.4.485

Lenhart, A., Madded, M., & Smith, A. (2007). Teens and Social Media: The Use of Social Media Gains a Greater Foothold in Teen Life as they Embrace the Conversational Nature of Interactive Online Media. *The Pew Internet & American Life Project*. Retrieved May 12, 2008 from http://www.pewInternet.org/PPF/r/230/report_display.asp

Little, J. D. C. (1979). Decision support systems for marketing managers. *Journal of Marketing, 43*, 11. doi:10.2307/1250143

Macgill, A. R. (n.d.). Parent and Teen Internet use. *Pew Internet & American Life Report*. Retrieved May 16, 2008 from http://www.pewInternet.org/PPF/r/225/report_display.asp

MacMillan, D. (2009, January 12). Online Video Ads: A Bag of Tricks, the five most common types of ads you'll see in videos on the Web, and how they're used. *Businessweek*. Retrieved March 13, 2009, from http://www.businessweek.com/technology/content/jan2009/tc20090126_305941.htm

Madsen, H. (1996 December). Reclaim the Deadzone. The Beleaguered Web Banner can be Zapped into an Effective and Eye-Popping Advertising Shingle, but Radical Surgery Awaits. *Wired, 4*(12). Retrieved June 24, 2008, from http://www.wired.com/wired/archive/4.12/esmadsen.htm

Markillie, P. (2004, May 15). A perfect market. *Economist, 371*(8375), 3.

McEnallhy, M. R., & deChernatony, L. (1999). The evolving nature of branding: Consumer and managerial considerations. *Academy of Marketing Science Review, 2*, 1–26.

McMillan, D. (2009). What Works in Online Video Advertising. *Business Week*. Retrieved March 8, 2009, from http://www.businessweek.com/technology/content/jan2009/tc20090126_341533.htm

McTaggart, J. (2004). Fresh direct. *Progressive Grocer, 83*(4), 58–60.

Menon, S., & Soman, D. (2002). Managing the power of curiosity for effective web advertising strategies. *Journal of Advertising, 31*(3), 1–14.

Metcalfe's Law. (n.d.). searchnetworking.com. Retrieved March 8, 2000, from http://searchnetworking.techtarget.com/sDefinition/0,sid7_gci214115,00.html

Moore, R. E. (2003). From genericide to viral marketing: on brand. *Language & Communication, 23*, 331–357. doi:10.1016/S0271-5309(03)00017-X

Mulpuru, S. (2008, May 7). The State of Online Retailing 2008: Marketing Report. *Forrester Research, Inc.* Retrieved January 9, 2009, from http://www.forrester.com

Oser, K. (2005, August 8). Marketers wrestle with hard–to-control content. *Advertising Age*, 20.

Owen, D. (2000). Using Search Engines and Portals. In G. J. Swinfen (Ed.), E-Media (pp. 89-96). Henley-on-Thames, UK: Admap Publications.

Palser, B. (2005). News a la carte. *American Journalism Review, 27*(1). Retrieved June 4, 2008, from http://www.questia.com/googleScholar.qst,jsessionid=LlbL4QxyLTqRhFdrwJ9hTpHQcnnG3yd2kpvtWpzyJSnffhLlCycG!-553604554?docId=5008837690

Parasraman, A., & Zinkhan, G. M. (2002). Marketing to and serving customers through the internet: An overview and research agenda. *Journal of the Academy of Marketing Science*, *30*(4), 286–295. doi:10.1177/009207002236906

PR Newswire US. (2006, September 21). *Free Podcast Tours Give Visitors an Insider's Look at Philadelphia, New Downloadable Audio Tours Offer Yet Another Way for Visitors to Explore the City*. Retrieved May 18, 2008, from http://www.gophila.com/Go/PressRoom/pressreleases/Free_Podcast_Tours_Give_Visitors_an_Insiders_Look.aspx

Report, M. A. (2008). *Limbo-GfK, produced in conjunction with GFK/NOP research. Q2 2008.* Retrieved March 1, 2009, from http://mmaglobal.com/uploads/Limbo_MAR_Report_Q2_2008.pdf

Rubenstein, H., & Griffiths, C. (2001). Branding matters more on the Internet. *Brand Management*, *8*(6), 394–404. doi:10.1057/palgrave.bm.2540039

Shocker, A. D., Srivastava, R. K., & Ruekert, R. W. (1994, May). Challenges and opportunities facing brand management. *JMR, Journal of Marketing Research*, 149–158. doi:10.2307/3152190

Siegal, C. (2004). *Internet Marketing. Foundations and Applications*. Boston, MA: Houghton Mifflin Company.

Smith, J. W. (2006 January). A Marketplace of Social Engagement. *Marketing Management*, 52.

Sonnenreich, W. (1997). A History of Search Engines. Retrieved July 12, 2008, from http://www.wiley.com/legacy/compbooks/sonnenreich/history.html

Travis, D. (2001). Branding in the digital age. *The Journal of Business Strategy*, *22*(3), 14–18. doi:10.1108/eb040166

Trudell, G., & Kolkin, E. (1999, September 27). Traditional Values in a High-Tech World. *InformationWeek*, 233-238.

Varadarajan, Y. (2002). Marketing strategy and the internet: An organizing framework. *Journal of the Academy of Marketing Science*, *30*(4), 296–312. doi:10.1177/009207002236907

Vikas, A., Manz, C. C., & Glick, W. H. (1998). An organizational memory approach to information management. *Academy of Management Review*, *23*(4), 796–809. doi:10.2307/259063

Watson, R. T., Leyl, F., Pitt, P. B., & Zinkhan, G. M. (2002). U-commerce: Expanding the universe of marketing. *Journal of the Academy of Marketing Science*, *30*(4), 332–347. doi:10.1177/009207002236909

West, D. (2005). Editorial. *Journal of Advertising Research, 24*(3), 267-268. Retrieved May 16, 2008, from http://www.businessweek.com/magazine/content/07_40/b4052072.htm?campaign_id=nws_insdr_sep21&link_position=link3

Wikipedia. (n.d.). *Blogosphere*. Retrieved June 15, 2008, from http://en.wikipedia.org/wiki/Blogosphere

Winer, D. (1999). *The History of Weblogs*. Retrieved May 17, 2008, from http://newhome.weblogs.com/history of Weblogs The Wall Street Journal. (2006, August 2). *McDonald's Seeks Young Adults in Their Realm – Podcasts, Bars*. Retrieved May 2, 2008, from http://www.cattle-network.com/content.asp?contentid=56797

Yang, Y. (2004). *New Data Mining and Marketing Approaches for Customer Segmentation and Promotion Planning on the Internet*. Retrieved July 10, 2008, from http://en.scientificcommons.org/7595063

Chapter 2
Media Evolution and the Advent of Web 2.0

Laura F. Bright
Texas Christian University, USA

ABSTRACT

In today's marketplace, new technology innovations and the changing media environment offer endless opportunities to consumers: seemingly infinite amounts of information via the internet, a plethora of broadcast stations and channels, and higher functionality and control through such technologies as online content aggregators and digital video recorders. These technological changes have redefined the media landscape and thus the role of advertising in new media consumption. As interactive media markets become increasingly segmented, it is vital for advertisers to examine effective techniques for communicating with consumers via such customized and controlled channels. This chapter will examine how media has evolved over the last several decades and the impact Web 2.0 technologies are making within the interactive advertising space.

INTRODUCTION

In today's marketplace, new technology innovations and the changing media environment offer endless opportunities to consumers: seemingly infinite amounts of information via the internet, a plethora of broadcast stations and channels, and higher functionality and control through such technologies as online content aggregators and digital video recorders. These technological changes have redefined the media landscape and thus the role of advertising in new media consumption. As interactive media markets become increasingly segmented, it is vital for advertisers to examine effective techniques for communicating with consumers via such customized and controlled channels.

Media fragmentation, consumer interactivity, and greater ability to personalize content are all products of recent technology advancements leading to one outcome – the empowerment of the consumer. Shapiro (1999) claims that technology

DOI: 10.4018/978-1-60566-792-8.ch002

has brought with it a reduction of institutional control resulting in an increase of individual control, both in terms of program selection and advertising exposure. Further, Shapiro (1999) asserts that we live in an environment that fundamentally allows us a higher level of control; this is not the age of narrowcasting where someone else prepares packaged content for you, but you can prepare a whole media content package for yourself and limit your exposure to advertising accordingly.

To this end, the emergence of Web 2.0 technologies, including personalized content delivery services, has created an abundance of niche markets online, attracting more than 69 million users in 2006 and generating $450 million plus in advertising revenues in the same year (Verna, 2007). The personalized, or customized, media environments made available to consumers through such services have the potential to decrease information overload by tailoring content to the consumers specifications as well as provide a sense of perceived control to the consumer. The availability of these services has increased in recent years with personalization services at most major search engine sites, including Google and Yahoo as well as being available via desktop applications (i.e., NetNewsWire, RSS Bandit, Apple Mail RSS, etc.). As such, a customized online environment would be defined as any type of web-based content aggregation application that allows a user to customize his or her content per their specifications. The consumer benefits of customized online environments, coupled with their projected growth in popularity, make them a potentially rich advertising outlet within the interactive niche. (Godek & Yates, 2006; Liang, et al., 2006)

The availability of highly customized information spaces allows consumers to tailor their exposure to specific content needs and desires (Liang, et al., 2006). The tailoring of such exposure has been made possible by web-based applications that aggregate content per the consumer's specifications. This further allows media exposure to be more tailored or "consumer-centric" rather than "publisher-centric" (Morrissey, 2005). As the consumption, creation and distribution of web-based content continues to evolve, content aggregation tools and Web 2.0 applications that utilize Really Simple Syndication (RSS) technology will become more usable and accessible to consumers, helping to create manageable information spaces that are personalized, customized and relevant. These types of information spaces provide a conduit for exposing consumers to context relevant advertising in a less cluttered environment, thereby potentially leading to increased cognitive involvement and liking, or attitude. As the effectiveness of traditional interactive advertising continues to decline, customized online environments could provide an arena that allows advertisers to connect with consumers during moments of peak user satisfaction.

Although the creation and dissemination of media content has been a constant in our world for hundreds of years, the potential for an ordinary consumer to communicate with and influence a mass audience has just recently been achieved with the advent of Web 2.0 technologies. Examples of prominent Web 2.0 websites and web-based applications that support the creation, distribution and consumption of CGC include, but are not limited to, YouTube, MySpace, Facebook, Wikipedia, StupidVideos, Flickr, Blogger, and personal Web pages, among others. Amidst the plethora of both traditional and digital media choices today, the Internet has revealed itself to be an outlet where traditional forms of media entertainment can also converge and be offered to consumers in a time and place that is most convenient for them. While traditional media are nowhere near extinction, it is clear that trends are changing such that consumers are in more control of their media consumption than ever before in history and have the freedom because of technology to create quality media content. This media content creation sphere continues to shift towards a 'user-centric model' led by CGC and away from the past model that has been characterized as 'publisher-centric' (Morrissey, 2005). Beginning in 2004 with the explosion of the Web 2.0 market, CGC has formed a plethora of niche markets within the media landscape generating more than $450 million in advertising revenues (Verna, 2007, p.2). As a result of this changing paradigm and expanding advertising channel, top television networks are integrating blogs, podcasts, and news feeds into their current media strategies, reflecting the importance of CGC in communicating with today's consumers. Certainly the exhilarated growth of this nascent area presents both significant problems and opportunities for marketing researchers to better understand consumer motivations, consumption, creation, and effectiveness of CGC.

The widespread consumption and creation of Web 2.0 technologies in recent years has confirmed the emergent trend of increased consumer control over media exposure. Consumers are beginning to rely less on media being pushed at them through traditional channels, and instead are focusing on creating a media environment that revolves around them. To compete in this environment, advertisers must learn how to both gain exposure via customized media environments as well as use these in an advantageous way to drive consumers to their websites. If used properly, advertisers can not only expose consumers to their brand in highly context relevant situations, but also prime consumers for further content and advertising interactions via their websites.

From a theoretical perspective, several approaches apply to the investigation of consumer response to customization in online environments. As identified by Liang, et al. (2006), information overload, uses and gratifications and user involvement are three frameworks typically applied when empirically investigating consumer response to personalization, or customization, in media environments. In this case, information overload theory implies an increase in user satisfaction as personalization increases, while the uses and gratifications theory provides the motivational underpinnings of media selection. Additionally, user involvement theory "implies that users prefer content recommended by a process in which they have explicit involvement" (Liang, et al., 2006, p. 2). It has been shown that uses and gratifications theory provides a bridge between the psychological characteristics of consumerism and mass media consumption. According to the expectancy-value approach to uses and gratifications (see Palmgreen, Wenner & Rayburn, 1980), consumers' compare between the gratifications sought and obtained. Based on past media experiences, they develop their future media exposure patterns in a never-ending circular process (Rubin, 2002, p.533). Past research linking general media use and various gratifications from the media is well established (e.g. Donohew et al. 1987; Palmgreen, Wenner & Rayburn, 1980). Accordingly, it is a logical approach to apply what is a well-known paradigm in traditional media to the use of customized online environments and their advertising related behaviors.

As content exposure through Web 2.0 technologies further penetrates the market, more research must be done to better understand how consumers are interacting in such environments, and thus what types of interactive advertising will be most beneficial to reach such consumers therein. The 'control revolution' (Shapiro, 1999) represents a vast population of new consumers, sometimes characterized as 'digital natives', whose ability to process information in media environments is 'fundamentally different than their predecessors' (Prensky, 2001, p.1). It is this fundamental difference that warrants further investigation with regard to how consumers respond to content within customized online environments depending on their desire for control.

For more than three decades, scholars have sought to understand why people use certain media content and its impact on their experience, the gratifications they obtained and how it impacts future behavior or consumption. As the delivery mechanisms for mass media continue to evolve, it is vital to better understand how consumers are controlling their media environments and how they perceive advertising delivered through such outlets. Although the potential benefits of customized online environments are clear, they have not received due attention as an upcoming, niche interactive advertising vehicle. Currently, exposing consumers to advertising in the online environment via standard websites typically involves a combination of interactive banner advertising, sponsored search, rich media, email marketing and pop-up ads – all of which have staggeringly low response rates (Endicott, et al., 2007). As such, this study will provide insight into consumers perceptions of advertising within customized online environments as well as how the act of customization impacts their media enjoyment, attitude toward advertising, and behavioral intention for future use.

MEDIA EVOLUTION

Mainstream media, including television, radio, and print publications, have moved through an evolutionary lifecycle since their inception and are continuing to evolve into ever more fragmented media offerings. Similarly, the online media landscape has evolved into a robust information space that provides both marketers and consumers an outlet for efficient, timely communication as well as entertainment, information seeking and commerce. As increasing numbers of consumers direct their attention away from traditional media and instead toward interactive media, marketers are being challenged to integrate their offerings with those created by consumers themselves as well as make advertising offerings available through increasingly customized online environments. The last several decades have shown a continued decline in newspaper readership and magazine circulation, and, while it continues to show growth in overall viewership, the television market is plagued by a proliferation of program offerings leading to fragmented audiences and decreasing overall program ratings. This shift toward greater engagement with interactive media presents a promising new wave of advertising outlets for marketers to have at their disposal.

The Internet has shown itself to be an outlet where traditional forms of media entertainment can converge and be offered to consumers in a time and place that is most convenient for them (Tauder, 2006). With usage expanding on a yearly basis, the Internet has come to serve as a media outlet for an overwhelming majority of American adults (71%). Amongst these consumers, an increasing amount of online content is being made available via Web 2.0 applications, such as the customized new environments available via Google Reader (Verna, 2007). While traditional media are nowhere near extinction, it is clear that trends are changing such that consumers are more in control of their media consumption in both the interactive and traditional realms. Not only have media evolved to distribute a diverse collection of news and information, they have also enabled consumers with a greater capability to contribute their thoughts, opinions, and personal media through websites that support user-generated content and social networking (Daugherty, Eastin & Bright, 2007). This shift toward greater consumer control coupled with a dramatic increase in the amount of content available online as the potential to reward consumers with feelings of control while also causing information overload. It is this dichotomy that makes customized online environments fertile ground for experimentation regarding the effectiveness of content delivery and interactive advertising.

Never before throughout human history have we experienced the level of media evolution currently encompassing our daily lives. Mainstream media, including television, radio, and print publications, have moved through evolutionary lifecycles since their inception. Similarly, the online media landscape has evolved into a robust information space that provides both marketers and consumers with an outlet for efficient, timely communication. As increasing numbers of consumers direct their attention away from traditional media and toward interactive media, marketers confront the challenge of integrating their offerings with those created by consumers themselves. The past several decades reveal a steady decline in newspaper readership and magazine circulation, and though the television market continues to grow in terms of overall viewership, it also suffers a proliferation of program offerings, leading to fragmented audiences and decreasing program ratings (Anderson, 2006).

Today, television, radio, newspapers, magazines, the Internet, movies, music, and more, represent an information society created by technology ultimately converging around the media audience. These technologies have redefined the media environment and thus media consumption as a seemingly infinite number of offerings are connecting and empowering audiences through communication channels. Media scholars acknowledge that traditional media models of communication may no longer adequately represent digital media, for which "convergence" may serve as an increasingly more accurate representation (Perry, 2002). As a result, the convergence of media through technology continues to shift power toward an audience centric model of media control and away from the past model that has been characterized as 'publisher-centric'. In other words, the advancements of technology have lead to one outcome–the empowerment of the consumer.

CUSTOMIZATION IN WEB 2.0 ENVIRONMENTS

Over time, the Internet has become a dynamic, highly personalized information space where consumers can tailor their media exposure to their specific needs and motivations (Liang et al., 2006). Tailoring of media exposure has become a reality for consumers as technologies have advanced in recent years, including the advent of such consumer control based technologies as the DVR, user-generated content websites (e.g., YouTube, Blogger, Flickr, etc.) and online content aggregation services (e.g., Google Reader). As consumers continue to desire greater control over media environments and advertising exposure, the use of such technologies will no doubt expand beyond the niche markets they now serve. Customized online environments make media exposure more consumer-centric rather than publisher-centric and thus provide a natural choice for consumers who have a high desire for control as these types of environments allow them to control their content stream (Morrisey, 2005).

For much of the 20th century, humans have consumed information and advertising through a standard set of media outlets, including television, newspapers, magazines and radio. Within these media, advertising is typically pushed toward the consumer in an effort to interrupt their media viewing experience and attract attention toward the product or service being advertised (Godin, 1999). As new media outlets, such as the Internet, have emerged, this tactic of interruption marketing via traditional channels has become ever more disruptive for consumers leading to increased levels of advertising annoyance and avoidance. To put this into an interactive context, the use of such push strategies online, such as banner ads and spam e-mail, are perceived by consumers as annoying, disruptive and intrusive (Li et al, 2002), while ads that are congruent with website content have been shown to generate more positive brand attitudes (Cho, 2003). Consumers, with their combined sense of increased media control and ad avoidance mechanisms, are extremely difficult to reach with traditional push marketing strategies. Thus, it is imperative for advertisers to devise new methods for interacting with consumers via customized media channels, such as those being investigated with this study.

Pull marketing strategies are a potentially effective way to communicate with online consum-

Figure 1. Examples of current Web 2.0 applications

ers as they are rooted first and foremost with the consumer, thereby allowing for a high perception of content and media control during exposure. The ability to push advertising content in the online environment has been possible since the inception of the Internet as such exposure mechanisms are inherent in the structure of this information space. Indeed, the ability for consumers to pull advertising content into their media landscape, such as opt-in email newsletters, has also been available since the inception of the Internet, however, Web 2.0 based content aggregation services have streamlined this process in such a way that consumers can pull relevant content into their lives with little effort beyond subscribing to an RSS feed on a given website. With such a vast amount of content available online, it is not uncommon for consumers to be overloaded with information; this overload severely limits one's capacity to process information (Lang, 2000). To combat this information fatigue, content customization applications allow consumers to pull desired content into a centralized location (e.g. a web-based or desktop application) where they can peruse the information at their leisure in a time and place that is most conducive to them (Garcia and Valdes, 2004).

Content customization applications, among them NewsFire, Feedster, Bloglines, NetNewsWire, RSS Bandit, and Google Reader, can be customized by the consumer to comb the web for specific content (i.e. keyword searches) or media content from websites that they visit regularly, such as blogs, newspapers, or photo feeds (See Figure 1). Once customized, the content aggregation tool will then automatically refresh media content per the consumer's specifications; similar to checking email, news feed applications typically check for new content several times a day. This continuous feeding of information to the consumer via customized online environments has the potential to provide benefit to both consumers and interactive advertisers. Consumers could potentially see a decrease in information overload and advertisers could have a new niche for interacting with traditionally hard to reach consumers. Figure 1 displays an example such an application (NetNewsWire)

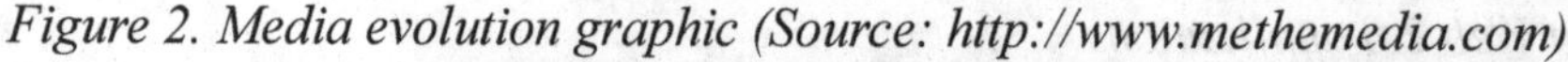

Figure 2. Media evolution graphic (Source: http://www.methemedia.com)

Figure 3. Screenshot of a content aggregator with advertising present

that contains both media content and a traditional banner advertisement (480 x 60 pixels).

Content aggregation tools continue to gain standing in the online market and are becoming increasingly integrated into web browsing applications thereby expanding consumer access (Vickers, 2007). With this increase in accessibility to content, consumers are allowed to pull desired content into their media landscapes making for a more cohesive and manageable information exchange for those who publish online content as well as the advertisers that utilize such outlets to communicate a message. As a result, content aggregation applications are an important tool for both advertisers and media to be aware of because they facilitate the delivery of messages alongside relevant, customized media content. In addition to web and personal computer based applications, content aggregators can also transfer to mobile devices such as Palm pilots or iPhones, thereby further increasing the availability of content.

Given that customized online environments are an emergent technology, little academic research has been completed to empirically investigate the effects of customization, or control, on this type of media experience. As the creation and distribution of content via Web 2.0 technologies continues to evolve, content aggregation tools will become more usable and accessible to consumers, helping to create a manageable information space that is customized and relevant. Moving forward, advertisers and marketing professionals must shift their thinking from a traditional push strategy to one that enables consumers with the desire to pull their content into self-defined media environments (Tauder, 2007).

News aggregation applications are an important tool for advertisers to be aware of because they facilitate the delivery of advertising messages to the desktop of the target's computer via relevant media content. As evidenced by the associative link theory, this is a positive way to deliver advertising content to consumers. In addition to personal computer based applications, news aggregators powered by RSS also run on mobile devices such as Palm pilots. This allows for endless possibilities for advertising exposure and context relevance both online and on the go. Put simply, 'RSS is the next wave of real estate the network (ad) builders are going to go after' (Morrissey 2005).

In essence, using content aggregation applications compatible with RSS technologies, consumers are enabled to pull relevant content into their media landscape, as opposed to having irrelevant messages pushed at them during their information seeking process. With this increase in perceived control over their content exposure, consumers could potentially have more cognitive capacity to process information as well as be exposed to advertising with increased relevance and personalization. Current forms of available advertising in RSS feeds include banner ads, keyword ads, sponsorships, and product placement. To compete in today's convergent media landscape, advertisers must adapt their communication strategies to customization and control parameters, such as 1) addressability, 2) interactivity, 3) time-shifting, and 4) interoperability (Tauder, 2006). Web 2.0 environments have the potential to help advertisers communicate within these new information parameters.

THE PSYCHOLOGY OF CONSUMER CHOICE IN WEB 2.0 ENVIRONMENTS

At the most fundamental level, the advent of customizable technologies has given consumers a greater choice in their exposure to media and advertising content. While established control technologies allow consumers to record multiple television stations, skip advertising and time-shift programming to their needs, customized online environments provide a similar function in that they tailor news content to make it more addressable, customized and informative for consumers while saving them time, providing information value and ease of information overload (Tauder, 2006). To operationalize the construct of consumer choice as it applies to customized online environments, for the purposes of this research, consumers will be exposed to a stimulus that primes the customization category and sets expectations accordingly. Hence, it is imperative to better understand the impact of priming and choice on consumer psychology within the cognitive, affective and behavioral realms.

According to Herr (1986), an "individual's expectations indeed affect the nature of a behavioral interaction" – regardless of whether this expectation was set by the consumer or someone independent of the consumer, such as a lab researcher (p. 1106). Empirical research has also confirmed that when consumers are primed with a given category, they are more likely to use that category as a reference when evaluating information (Higgins and King, 1981; Srull and Wyer, 1978). While Herr's (1986) work focuses primarily on the judgmental and behavioral consequences of priming in social interactions, his findings suggest that expectations have a considerable impact on behavioral intention. To further delineate the process that occurs when consumers are primed with categorical information, Higgins and King (1981) describe the process of priming, or framing of information, as an energy cell process whereby consumers will apply priming elements to the evaluation of new information (i.e. the experiment stimulus) so long as the stimulus is relative to the category. Alternatively, Srull and Wyer (1981) look at priming effects using a storage bin model. In their model, when consumers are primed with a given category, for example customization of media content, the category is placed atop the mental storage bin and used as the primary point of evaluation for subsequent incoming information. Thus, if the incoming information is congruent with the primed category, the preceding experience will be catalogued within the primed category for future use. It is important to note that both of these models are constructed on the tenet that the primed category, in this case 'customized online environments', will be invoked when evaluating incoming information. As such, affective dimensions, such as attitude and enjoyment, could be impacted depending upon how well the incoming information maps to the primed category (Herr, 1986).

According to Kardes (2002), the priming effect is a common tactic used in mass media to influence consumers across a variety of subjects and concepts – often times priming consumers with information that they rarely think about. Given the novelty of customization in the online environment, it is possible that consumers rarely consider their options concerning customization of news content; in fact it could present an ambiguous category target for some consumers. Based on data presented by Herr (1986), the ambiguity of the target has some impact on a consumers interaction with the stimulus, however most are unaware of the "subtle influence" that priming provides for a given experience (Kardes, 2002, p. 68).

CONSUMERS' DESIRE FOR CONTROL IN THE WEB 2.0 WORLD

Humans strive to be causal agents; the source of their behavior and their own environment (DeCharms, 1968). Shapiro (1999) notes "our interest in personal control is motivated as much by a survival instinct as by narcissism. It is key to our sense of self-esteem and confidence" (p. 23). Accordingly, recent studies suggest that our desirability of control emanates from biological determinants as well as social ones (Declerck, Boone, & De Brabander, 2006). Due to the natural prevalence of control in our lives, it has been studied in different forms, scales, and terminologies. For example, control has been examined in the literature as a desire for control (Burger and Cooper, 1979), a locus of control (Rotter, 1966), actual control (Cramer & Perreault, 2006), perceived control (Godek and Yates, 2005), behavioral control, cognitive control (Faranda, 2001), decisional control, and feeling in control (Declerck, Boone, & Brabander, 2006).

Desirability of control is defined as "a stable personality trait reflecting the extent to which individuals generally are motivated to control the events in their lives" (Burger 1985, p. 1520). According to Burger and Cooper (1979), desirability of control is a motivational trait, which measures how sought-after the personal control trait is for a person. Clearly there is a motivation in our nature to control life's events, however, as with other personality traits it ranges on a scale across different individuals. People vary and thus demonstrate different propensities toward control, which could help explain our different behaviors. According to its operational definition, a person who exhibits a high desirability of control is a leader, assertive, active, decisive and manipulative in situations to create desired outcomes. Conversely, a person who exhibits low desirability of control is more influenced by others, nonassertive, uncertain, doubtful and passive (Burger & Cooper, 1979). Studies that have used the desirability of control construct demonstrate how differences in a consumer's desirability of control explain daily behaviors and decisions such as achievement-related behaviors (see Burger, 1985 and also Burger, 1992) and proneness to depression (see Burger 1984).

Directly related to the current research, past work has connected the control construct with media use (Schutz, 1966). For instance Schutz suggests, "three interpersonal needs - inclusion, affection, and control - influence all aspects of communication between people" (in Rubin, 1993, p.161). Further, Rubin (1993) has linked external control (related to the belief of fate and chance occurrence) with passive audiences and internal control (related to the belief of self-determinism) with active media audiences. Summarizing research into the latter construct, Rubin states that people with strong external control are fearful of society, indiscriminant or ritualistic media consumers, are not motivated by freedom to choose, and tend to be persuaded more easily by media content. Conversely, people with strong internal control demonstrate the opposite tendencies. In the field of interactive media, Wu (2006) demonstrated that control, as an individual/personality trait, is related to media use. Alpert et al. (2003) examined the environment of e-commerce and note that the issue of control is pivotal to consumers in the media experience: "the clearest result to emerge from our studies is users' fervent desire to be in control" (Alpert et al., 2003, p.385).

Althaus and Tewksbury (2000) probe the use of the Internet as a surveillance medium that helps gratify two needs while consuming political news contents: the need for information and the desirability of control. Their findings suggest that desirability of control is a strong predictor of news exposure — at least as strong as traditional political knowledge as a predictor. They also claim that the control construct is positively related to surveillance with the media. That is, the greater a person's desirability of control, the more they will expose themselves to the media. The literature provides evidence which links control and general media use (e.g. Althaus & Tewksbury, 2000; Auter & Ray, 1999; Rubin 1993). Moreover, research supports the notion that desirability of control is positively related to media use. Accordingly, it is expected that desire to control will positively predict the use of customized online environments as well as the interaction with advertising therein.

In marketing, an increase of perceived control was linked to pleasantness in service and consumption experiences (Faranda 2001). Rubin (1993) has further demonstrated a positive correlation between control and communication motivation for pleasure. Within the context of interactive media, Liu and Shrum (2002) have developed a theoretical model for interactivity and found that desirability of control is a key factor in obtaining satisfaction from the interactive process. They suggest that people who have a high desirability of control will be more satisfied with interactivity than people who have a low desirability of control.

Thus, it is anticipated that consumers with a high desire for control will experience greater media enjoyment when exposed to a customized online environment. Along with creating a perception of control, customized online environments also have the potential to increase consumer enjoyment by decreasing information overload. The following section will review information overload as an independent construct and how it can potentially impact a consumer's media experience.

INFORMATION OVERLOAD IN ONLINE ENVIRONMENTS

Despite existing for a mere 5,000 or so days, the commercial Internet contains an incredibly vast amount of information that can easily overwhelm even the most adept consumer of information (Kelly, 2007). As information loads become greater, the ability of a consumer to process cognitive stimuli in a reasonable manner becomes increasingly difficult. In many cases, this excessive stimulus can lead to consumers becoming overwhelmed and unable to focus on their target goal – be it related to entertainment, information seeking, or social motivations. With new technologies, such as content aggregators, the glut of information available online has become more manageable and palatable for consumers who elect to engage with such media experiences. Given the existing reciprocal linkage between information load and user satisfaction (Liang, et al., 2007), it is intuitive that consumers with high levels of perceived information overload may experience greater media enjoyment when given the capacity to customize, or tailor, their media exposure to topics of interest. As such, it is imperative to examine a consumer's perceived information overload as a potential factor during exposure to customized online environments.

Across all types of media, information overload can be caused by a variety of factors, including but not limited to information quantity, quality, format (Ho and Tang, 2001) as well as the number of ideas present, idea diversity, time constraints, and topic area (Grise and Gallupe, 2000). When compared to traditional media, online environments provide a level of interactivity and expanse of available information that creates an interesting paradox. Today's consumers have more information available to them than ever before, however due to the glut of information available as well as the variety of interactive formats it is available in, information overload is prevalent. Once overloaded with information, few if any consumers will be able to process auxiliary information, such as advertising, leading to a loss for both consumers and advertisers (Lang, 2000). Customized online environments could help compensate for this loss by creating a niche environment for advertisers to communicate with less overloaded, and more cognitive available, consumers.

Advertising abounds across all aspects of today's interactive marketplace and is often described as an impediment for consumers as they seek goal fulfillment online while undoubtedly contributing to feelings of information overload as well (Cho and Cheon 2004; Li, Edwards and Lee 2002). With this glut of information, consumers can be overwhelmed, given their limited capacity for processing information. In advertising and media effects research, the limited capacity model (LCM) of mediated message processing provides a framework for examining how consumers explicitly process media content delivered through various media vehicles (Lang, 2000). The LCM is rooted in the information processing aspects of cognitive psychology.

The LCM is based upon two primary tenets, 1) consumers are information processors by nature, and 2) consumers have relatively limited resources available to process information at any given time. As humans, one of the primary tasks that consumers do is process information, including media content and advertising. According to Lang (2000), the act of processing information can be divided into three sub-processes that are conceptually more tenable in a linear fashion, but whom occur in an iterative, continuous and oft times simultaneous way within a consumer's cognitive realm. The three sub-processes are, 1) encoding, 2) storage, and 3) retrieval. During the encoding phase of information processing, a consumer creates an "idiosyncratic representation of the message" based upon controlled and automatic selection processes (Lang, 2000, p49). While controlled selection processes are a reflection of a consumer's goals, motivations and expected outcomes, automatic selection is activated as a stimulus presents information that is relevant to the consumer's goal fulfillment (i.e., ad relevance) or as the information environment encounters an unexpected change due to the presence of a stimulus (i.e., ad intrusiveness) (Graham, 1997; Ohman, 1997). The storage process begins after the initial encoding phase and involves transferring the information from short-term storage to long-term storage to become part of an associative memory network. The last phase, retrieval, involves searching the associative networks in long- term memory and reactivating information into working memory as needed (Lang, 2000).

As it relates to media content, the LCM provides explanatory power as to why certain messages may be encoded while others are not. Simply put, the information processing components of encoding, storage and retrieval typically work simultaneously; as such, if a consumer decides to allocate resources to a primary task (i.e. reading news through a content aggregator) thereby limiting the resources available to secondary tasks (i.e., processing advertising in such environments) the encoding of such secondary information will suffer. Thus, as the LCM dictates, processing resources can be increasingly allocated to a single sub-process, resulting in a failure of optimal performance amongst the remaining two sub-processes.

In sum, the LCM provides a framework for testing a consumer's ability to process information under a variety of cognitive loads. In a customized online environment, consumers encounter fewer advertisements and are instead exposed to articles and news items they have self-selected or personalized. While traditional news websites are typically cluttered with a plethora of advertising messages, RSS feeds offer advertisers a place to reach niche markets of consumers amongst far less advertising clutter. Consumers will ultimately carry their ability to avoid interactive advertising ("banner blindness") into customized media environments, however, these environments present an arena where highly customized and controlled content can be brought to consumers.

Based on current growth in Web 2.0 environments and online information in general, consumers will continue to deal with information overload as they navigate the various information spaces upon which they have come to rely (Verna, 2007). The LCM provides explanatory power for how customized online environments can help consumers deal with information overload – such environments could potentially aide consumers information processing by providing relevant and personalized content in an uncluttered interface. Similar to desire for control, a consumer's perceived information overload level will be considered as a potential factor in the relationship between customization and the cognitive, affective and behavioral components of a consumer's experience.

MEDIA ENJOYMENT AND WEB 2.0

The term *enjoyment* has been conceptualized in media studies to "indicate a general positive disposition toward and liking of media content" (Nabi and Kremar, 2004, p. 290). Several scholars have attributed an increase in information processing capabilities in interactive environments to states of media enjoyment within consumers (Sherry, 2004; Sicilia and Ruiz, 2007). In a recent study by Sicilia and Ruiz (2007), a state of enjoyment within a consumer was found to "enhance, rather than impede favorable information processing" when navigating a standard web environment, such as a corporate website. Additionally, Hoffman and Novak (1996) have found that an enjoyable experience will increase learning, provide a more positive subjective experience, and promote exploratory behavior. Finally, Huang (2003) notes that more intense enjoyment states within consumers indicate higher perceived performance of interactive environments, in terms of usefulness and pleasantness, while Webster, Trevino and Ryan (1993) confirm that the flow experience is directly related to expected future technology use, or behavioral intention. As this relates to customized media environments, Sicilia and Ruiz (2007) show empirical evidence that interactive environments can be used by consumers to "aid in making decisions" and "enhance online processing and enjoyment" (Sicilia and Ruiz, 2007, p15).

It is well documented in the uses and gratifications research that consumers use media for enjoyment. As such, there are a variety of factors that will contribute to a consumer's sense of media enjoyment. As this relates to control, consumers who feel more in control of their media environment may receive more media enjoyment because they can customize a content package that is relevant to their needs thereby reducing the amount of time it takes to achieve their goals. Additionally, as documented by Liang, et al. (2007), decreases in information overload can increase user satisfaction with personalized media environments.

Feelings of enjoyment can easily be associated with those of satisfaction – for example, a consumer may be satisfied with and find enjoyment in a given media experience. As such, Palmgreen and Rayburn's (1985) discussion of media satisfaction offers an important perspective on the construct of media enjoyment. Although satisfaction is a key concept in other areas of social science, little attention as been paid to this concept in the area of media studies. As it pertains to this chapter, the concept of satisfaction has been defined as pleasure / displeasure, consumption experience (i.e. navigation experience in customized online environment), and evaluation of the benefits of consumption (Palmgreen and Rayburn, 1985). In addition to it's association with satisfaction, media enjoyment can also be linked with attraction, liking, and preference (Nabi and Kremar, 2004). However, the most poignant conceptualization of media enjoyment is as an attitude that allows researchers to "broaden our understanding not only of the precursors of enjoyment but its behavioral outcomes as well" (Nabi and Kremar, 2004, p. 292).

ATTITUDES AND BEHAVIOR IN WEB 2.0 ENVIRONMENTS

A consumer's attitude can best be described as a positive or negative disposition toward a given object, person, or event. The study of attitude and attitude change has long been a vital component of advertising research as consumer attitudes are considered to be a direct pre-condition, or antecedent, to consumer behavior. Over the last century, the study of attitudes has evolved from the initial theories of Hovland, Festinger, Abelson, and Heider to a robust set of theories and models that predict attitude change based upon dual processes and multiple routes to persuasion (Petty and Cacioppo 1983; MacInnis and Jaworski, 1989). As such, attitudes are seen as derivatives of both personal (micro) and social (macro) factors that determine both how we react to persuasive messaging and integrate it into our lives.

A person's attitude represents a psychological tendency that is expressed by evaluating a particular object and can serve various motivations (Eagly and Chaiken, 1993, p.479). Katz's (1960) seminal work on functional theory is considered by many essential for understanding the complex motivational underpinnings and functions of attitudes. Functional theory states that attitudes may serve various motivations depending on the purpose and that one's behavior is a function of their attitude toward that behavior (O'Keefe, 2002, p.29). The basis of this theory centralizes around the view that in order to impact behavior you must understand the motivational source of the attitude. For instance, a person's willingness to interact with customized online media environments using Web 2.0 technologies will be determined by his or her attitude toward such media exposure and level of perceived control. However, because people's motivations can vary greatly, consumers may decide to create and interact with customized media environments for different reasons.

Overall, functional theory has been widely accepted among theorists as a robust framework for recognizing the diverse motivational patterns of attitudes (Abelson & Prentice, 1989; Herek, 1987; Locander and Spivey, 1978). In particular, Katz's (1960) typology posits that any given attitude held by any given individual will serve one or more of four distinct personality functions: a utilitarian function, a knowledge function, an ego-defensive function, and a value-expressive function. The utilitarian function acknowledges that people are motivated to gain rewards and avoid punishment from their environment. Specifically, this function represents attitudes based on self-interest. In terms of self-defined media environments, consumers served by this motivational function would create such environments for personal incentives. In contrast, the knowledge function recognizes that people are driven by the need to gain information in order to organize and understand one's environment. We are motivated by the need to understand and make sense out of our experiences. Users of customized media environments served by this function would engage in such behaviors because it helps them understand their environment, the topic at hand, and/or ultimately themselves because they feel a sense of intrinsic wisdom. Subsequently, the value-expressive function is served by attitudes that allow individuals to express or relate with their self-concepts and values. This function is perceived as enhancing one's image in the eyes of the world through matching their moral beliefs. Thus, consumers of customized media content motivated by this function would feel inherently gratified with self-esteem for creating content and being a member of an online community that shares the same principles they consider important. It validates and helps them feel good for who they are and what they believe about the world. Finally, the ego-defensive function represents motivations that are designed to protect people from internal insecurities or external threats. They serve the internal function of defending one's self-image. Consumers motivated by this function would participate in order to minimize their own self-doubts, to feel a sense of belonging, and possibly reduce guilty feelings of not contributing.

While these four functions remain the core constructs for understanding attitudinal motivations, contemporary researchers have continued to clarify and explore additional contributions. For instance, Smith (1973) proposed an extension of the value-expressive function focused on the motivation for social adjustment in expressing attitudes or behavior that are agreeable to others. The function has since evolved to include motivations concerning relationships with others and recognizes the distinction between internal beliefs and the desire for external relationships independent of moral values. In particular, this social function compels people to seek opportunities to be with friends or to participate in activities perceived favorably by important others (Clary, et. al. 1998). Within the realm of customized online media environments, the social function would be a strong motivator as the concepts of sharing and interacting socially are widespread. Creators of customized media environments would be motivated by this function because of how important reference groups would perceive their membership in such an online community. Even though each of the functional sources are capable of making independent motivational contributions to the formulation of one's attitude, the theoretical assertion remains that attitude is served by a multitude of origins and more than likely driven by a combination of sources (Katz, 1960).

In the domain of advertising, much focus has been devoted to the investigation of how consumers react to commonplace types of advertising on the Web, ranging from banner ads to sponsorships, and pop-up ads. While dynamic and interactive advertisements were found to be more effective than static ads in producing positive consumer responses (Coyle and Thorson, 2001), recent research suggests that consumers' overall response to advertising on the Web is increasingly negative as they become more savvy and sceptical about the values of such advertisements (Cho and Cheon,

2004; Coutler et al., 2001). In fact, the online landscape has become congested with advertising in its more intrusive forms and consumers strive to avoid advertising as much as possible because such advertising is likely to interfere with the tasks or interests they are pursuing online (Cho and Cheon, 2004; Li, Edwards and Lee, 2002). Moreover, it has been shown that while Web searchers consider sponsored search advertising as less relevant than organic search results, they are essentially equally relevant (Jansen and Resnick, 2006). Taken together, the literature suggests that interactive advertising features that enhance consumers' understanding of relevance without actually interfering with their intended tasks should be successful in eliciting their favorable attitudes. Advertising via RSS feeds is an advertising medium that fits this description, and due to its informative and (mostly) non-intrusive nature is not likely to be perceived as annoying or irrelevant by users of customized media environments.

Among the variety of factors influencing consumer response to advertising on the Web, congruity between the ad and the website content in which the ad is placed appears to be a significant factor in advertising perception (Cho, 2003; Moore, Stammerjohan and Coutler, 2005; Shamdasani, Stanaland and Tan, 2001). In Cho's (2003) study of banner ads, advertising content that was congruent with the editorial content was more effective as it was less likely to interrupt the consumer's primary task or focus. Similarly, the higher level of congruity between the product category advertised in a banner ad and the context of the website in which the ad was embedded resulted in more favorable consumer responses than low relevance between the ad and the website context (Moore, Stammerjohan and Coutler, 2005; Shamdasani, Stanaland and Tan, 2001). This bodes well for advertising via customized media environments because the ability to deliver highly customized and relevant content is inherent.

Alternatively, research by Li, et al. (2002) suggests that as online consumers become increasingly goal oriented, online advertising techniques that are interactive and non-congruent shall become substantially more intrusive because they will stand between consumers and their goal actualization. Their research identified three causes of ad irritation: (1) content, (2) execution, and (3) placement. Among these, ad placement online is considered to be the primary indicator as to whether an ad is considered intrusive or not. This focus on the location of an ad ties back to the previously discussed findings confirming that increased ad congruency in an online environment leads to a higher click through rate and more favorable consumer attitudes (Cho, 2003). Thus, content congruent advertising perceived as useful in this context should elicit less irritation amongst consumers upon exposure.

Taking the above findings into account, this chapter seeks to better understand how consumers react to customized online environments, and, in turn what impact that has on their media enjoyment, attitudes toward advertising and behavioral intention for using customized online environments. As technology advances continue to open niche markets for interacting with online consumers, it is imperative to gain a more robust perspective of how consumers are interacting with advertising in this arena. More so than ever before, consumer attention is illusive and advertisers must be always mindful of effective methods for communicating their marketing messages. Customized online environments could provide a potentially effective outlet for reaching such consumers.

CONCLUSION AND IMPLICATIONS FOR FUTURE RESEARCH

As media continue to adapt to the changing technology needs of today's consumers, it is imperative to gain insight into the effects of Web 2.0 technologies on media experiences. Current research in this area has focused primarily on content personalization and recommendation systems as they relate to user satisfaction. To further expand this research into the realm of Web 2.0 technologies, future research should examine how consumers interact with Web 2.0 technologies in terms of their motivations and expected outcomes of such technology use. Recent online research involving Social Cognitive Theory (LaRose & Eastin, 2004; LaRose, et al., 2002; Eastin & LaRose, 2000) has emerged to offer explanatory power for consumer Internet use and could provide a better understanding of the Web 2.0 phenomenon.

In the last several years, Web 2.0 technologies have empowered consumers and enabled them to connect with one another in the broad online information space. In this regard, it is imperative for marketing researchers to begin to gain a better understanding of the impact of Web 2.0 technologies and the underlying reasons consumers use such applications to experience media content and connect with other consumers. To date though, little research has been undertaken on Web 2.0 and its perceptions amongst both the consumers and creators of this type of media content. Thus, this chapter has focused on how consumers interact with Web 2.0 technologies in terms of their media enjoyment, attitudes and behaviors in such online environments. Because consumer perceptions are capable of being influenced by media messages, the effective understanding of the expectations sought and the outcomes obtained from the use of Web 2.0 technologies are important to both academic scholars interested in theoretical research as well as marketing professionals focused on branding online.

As Web 2.0 technologies becomes more prevalent, understanding why consumers are drawn to consume content via such media vehicles becomes increasingly important, especially as the media industry moves toward a user-centric model of consumption. As a result, it is imperative to gain an understanding of how individuals behave according to expected outcomes for the use of Web 2.0 technologies in order to recognize how such content might benefit the media. While consumption of any new consumer technology requires a certain level of technical knowledge, we expect positive prior media experience and attitude effectively lead consumers toward consuming media content via Web 2.0 technologies. At the same time, desire of media control is another prerequisite for Web 2.0 technology use. Compared to other media, and primarily traditional media, Web 2.0 technologies, and beyond, enable consumers to be extremely flexible allowing for maximum control over media content.

Through the integration of desirability of control, attitude and the social cognitive construct of prior experience, this chapter advances current understanding of how and why people are using Web 2.0 technologies. As consumers adopt an active approach when experiencing media content, they strive toward self-expression by engaging in behaviors that provide them with a voice or showcase their individual thoughts (e.g., blogs, forums, personal Web sites). Future research should explore the impact of individual skill or self-efficacy on this process. For example, the creation of videos, production of music, and acquisition of necessary knowledge to post a wiki require more aptitude than simply using a computer keyboard (i.e., as required by an online discussion forum). Investigating the differences in different types of Web 2.0 activities could provide a more in-depth insight. Therefore, a thorough understanding of the psychological makeup of Web 2.0 consumers is even more critical because the consumption and delivery of communication messages might be refined for maximum impact. By providing consumers with a forum in which they may use Web 2.0 technologies, media technology professionals might enhance the value of information they present online by engaging consumers in an active media experience.

The Web 2.0 market likely will expand greatly during the next decade as more users migrate toward consuming media content through customized vehicles. Opportunities abound for media technology and marketing communication professionals in this burgeoning information space, as evidenced by the forecasted $4.3 billion in advertising revenues by 2011 (Verna 2007). Industries thus must seize this opportunity to communicate relevant content to audiences through this channel. As the digital information society continues to evolve, identifying key individual characteristics that lead to expected outcomes could help clarify media consumption online. While Web 2.0 technologies present a promising outlet for advertisers, they must also be used wisely when integrated with traditional media content in order to provide the most relevant and positive experience for online consumers.

REFERENCES

Abelson, R. P., & Prentice, D. A. (1989). Beliefs as possessions: A functional perspective. In A. R. Pratkanis, S. J. Breckler, & Ag. G. Greenwald (Eds.), Attitude Structure and Function (pp. 361-381). Hillsdale, NJ: Erlbaum.

Alpert, S. R., Karat, J., Karat, C.-M., Brodie, C., & Vergo, J. G. (2003). User attitudes regarding a user-adaptive ecommerce web site. *User Modeling and User-Adapted Interaction*, *13*, 373–396. doi:10.1023/A:1026201108015

Althaus, S. L., & Tewksbury, D. (2000). Patterns of internet and traditional news media use in a networked community. *Political Communication*, *17*, 21–45. doi:10.1080/105846000198495

Auter, P. J., & Lane, R. Jr. (1999). Locus of control, parasocial interaction and usage of TV ministry programs. *Journal of Communication and Religion*, *22*(1), 93–120.

Burger, J. M., & Cooper, H. M. (1979). The desirability of control. *Motivation and Emotion*, *3*(4), 381–393. doi:10.1007/BF00994052

Cho, C. (2003). Factors influencing the clicking of banner ads on the WWW. *Cyberpsychology & Behavior*, *6*(2), 201–215. doi:10.1089/109493103321640400

Cho, C.-H., & Cheon, H. J. (2004). Why do people avoid advertising on the Internet? *Journal of Advertising*, *33*(4), 89–97.

Clary, E. G., Snyder, M., Ridge, R., Copeland, J., Stukas, A., Haugen, J., & Miene, P. (1998). Understanding and assessing the motivations of volunteers: A functional approach. *Journal of Personality and Social Psychology*, *74*(6), 1516–1530. doi:10.1037/0022-3514.74.6.1516

Coulter, R. A., Zaltman, G., & Coulter, K. S. (2001). Interpreting consumer perceptions of advertising: An application of the Zaltman metaphor elicitation technique. *Journal of Advertising*, *30*(4), 1–21.

Coyle, J. R., & Thorson, E. (2001). The effects of progressive levels of interactivity and vividness in web marketing sites. *Journal of Advertising*, *30*(3).

Cramer, K. M., & Perreault, L. A. (2006). Effect of predictability, actual controllability, and awareness of choice on perceptions of control. *Current Research in Social Psychology*, *11*(8), 111–126.

Daugherty, T., Eastin, M., & Bright, L. F. (2008). Exploring Consumers Motivations for Creating User-Generated Content. *Journal of Interactive Advertising*.

DeCharms, R. (1968). *Personal Causation*. New York: Academic Press.

Declerck, C. H., Boone, C., & De Brabander, B. (2006). On feeling in control: A biological theory for individual differences in control perception. *Brain and Cognition*, *62*, 143–176. doi:10.1016/j.bandc.2006.04.004

Donohew, L., Palmgreen, P., & Rayburn, J. D. II. (1987). Social and psychological origins of media use: A lifestyle analysis. *Journal of Broadcasting & Electronic Media, 31*(3), 255–278.

Eagly, A. H., & Chaiken, S. (1993). *The Psychology of Attitudes*. Fort Worth, TX: Harcourt Brace Janovich College Publishers.

Eastin, M. S. (2005). Teen internet use: Relating social perceptions and cognitive models to behavior. *Cyberpsychology & Behavior, 8*(1), 62–71. doi:10.1089/cpb.2005.8.62

Elliot, M. T., & Speck, P. S. (1998, January). Consumer perceptions of advertising clutter and its impact across various media. *Journal of Advertising Research*, 29–41.

Faranda, W. T. (2001). A scale to measure the cognitive control form of perceived control: Construction and preliminary assessment. *Psychology and Marketing, 18*(12), 1259–1281. doi:10.1002/mar.1052

Garcia, D., & Valdes, R. (2004). Blogs Present Unique Challenges and Opportunities for Advertisers. *Gartner Report*.

Godek, J., & Yates, J. F. (2005). Marketing to Individual Consumers Online: The Influence of Perceived Control. *Online Consumer Psychology*, 225-244.

Graham, F. K. (1997). Afterward: Pre-attentive processing and passive and active attention. In Lang, P. J., Simons, R. F., & Balaban, M. (Eds.), *Attention and Orienting: Sensory and Motivational Processes* (pp. 417–452). Hillsdale, NJ: Erlbaum.

Grise, M., & Gallupe, B. (2000). Information overload: Addressing the productivity paradox in face-to-face electronic meeting. *Journal of Management Information Systems, 16*(3), 157–185.

Herek, G. M. (1987). Can functions be measured? A new perspective on the functional approach to attitudes. *Social Psychology Quarterly, 50*(4), 285–303. doi:10.2307/2786814

Herr, P. M. (1986). Consequences of priming: Judgment and behavior. *Journal of Personality and Social Psychology, 51*(6), 1106–1115. doi:10.1037/0022-3514.51.6.1106

Higgins, E. T., & King, G. A. (1981). Accessibility of Social Constructs: Information Processing Consequences of Individual and Contextual Variability. In Cantor, N., & Kihlstrom, J. F. (Eds.), *Personality, Cognition and Social Interaction*. Hillsdale, NJ: Erlbaum.

Ho, J., & Tang, K. (2001). Towards an Optimal Resolution to Information Overload: An Infomediary Approach. In *Proceedings of the 2001 International ACM SIGGROUP Conference Supporting Group Work* (pp. 91-96). Boulder, CO: ACM Press.

Hoffman, D. L., & Novak, T. P. (1996). Marketing in hypermedia computer- mediated environments: Conceptual foundations. *Journal of Marketing, 60*, 50–68. doi:10.2307/1251841

Huang, M.-H. (2003). Designing Website Attributes to Induce Experiential Encounters. In *Computers in Human Behavior* (Vol. 19, pp. 425-442). Retrieved April 25, 2003, from http://www.elsevier.com/locate/comphumbeh/

Jansen, B. J., & Resnick, M. (2006). An examination of searchers' perceptions of non-sponsored and sponsored links during ecommerce Web searching. *Journal of the American Society for Information Science and Technology, 57*, 1949–1961. doi:10.1002/asi.20425

Kardes, F. R. (2002). *Consumer Behavior and Managerial Decision Making* (2nd ed.). Upper Saddle River, NJ: Pearson Education, Inc.

Katz, D. (1960). The functional approach to the study of attitudes. *Public Opinion Quarterly*, *24*, 27–46. doi:10.1086/266945

Kelly, K. (2007). Predicting the Next 5,000 Days of the Web. *TED: Ideas Worth Spreading*. Retrieved October 1, 2008, from http://www.ted.com/index.php/talks/kevin_kelly_on_the_next_5_000_days_of_the_web.html.

Lang, A. (2000). The limited capacity model of mediated message processing. *The Journal of Communication*, 46–70. doi:10.1111/j.1460-2466.2000.tb02833.x

LaRose, R., & Eastin, M. S. (2004). A social cognitive explanation of internet uses and gratifications: Toward a new model of media attendance. *Journal of Broadcasting & Electronic Media*, *48*(3), 358–377. doi:10.1207/s15506878jobem4803_2

LaRose, R., Mastro, D., & Eastin, M. S. (2001). Understanding internet usage: A social-cognitive approach to uses and gratifications. *Social Science Computer Review*, *19*(4), 395–413. doi:10.1177/089443930101900401

Li, H., Edwards, S., & Lee, J. (2002). Measuring the intrusiveness of advertisements: Scale development and validation. *Journal of Advertising*, *31*(2), 37–47.

Liang, T.-P., Lai, H.-J., & Ku, Y.-C. (2006). Personalized content recommendation and user satisfaction: Theoretical synthesis and empirical findings. *Journal of Management Information Systems*, *23*(3), 45–70. doi:10.2753/MIS0742-1222230303

Liu, Y., & Shrum, L. J. (2002). What is interactivity and is it always such a good thing? Implications of definition, person, and situation for the influence of interactivity on advertising effectiveness. *Journal of Advertising*, *31*(4), 53–64.

Locander, W. B., & Spivey, W. A. (1978). A functional approach to attitude measurement. *JMR, Journal of Marketing Research*, *15*(4), 576–587. doi:10.2307/3150627

MacInnis, D. J., & Jaworski, B. J. (1989). Information processing from advertisements: Toward an integrative framework. *Journal of Marketing*, *53*, 1–23. doi:10.2307/1251376

Moore, R. S., Stammerjohan, C. A., & Coulter, R. A. (2005). Banner advertiser-web site context congruity and color effects on attention and attitudes. *Journal of Advertising*, *34*(2), 71–84.

Morrissey, B. (2005). *Advertisers Try to Reach Users With Different Buying Behavior*. Dateline New York.

Nabi, R. L., & Kremar, M. (2004). Conceptualizing media enjoyment as attitude: implications for mass media effects research. *Communication Theory*, *14*(4), 288–310. doi:10.1111/j.1468-2885.2004.tb00316.x

O'Keefe, D. J. (2002). *Persuasion: Theory & Research* (2nd ed.). Thousand Oaks, CA: Sage Publications, Inc.

Ohman, A. (1997). As fast as the blink of an eye: Evolution preparedness for preattentive processing of threat. In Lang, P. J., Simons, R. F., & Balaban, M. (Eds.), *Attention and Orienting: Sensory and Motivational Processes* (pp. 165–184). Hillsdale, NJ: Erlbaum.

Palmgreen, P., & Rayburn, J. D. II. (1985). A comparison of gratification models of media satisfaction. *Communication Monographs*, *52*, 334–346. doi:10.1080/03637758509376116

Palmgreen, P., Wenner, L. A., & Rayburn, J. D. II. (1980). Relations between gratifications sought and obtained: A study of television news. *Communication Research*, *7*, 161–192. doi:10.1177/009365028000700202

Perry, D. (2002). Theories of Media Audiences. In *Theory and Research in Mass Communication* (2nd ed., pp. 70–92). Mahwah, NJ: Lawrence Erlbaum Associates.

Petty, R. E., & Cacioppo, J. T. (1986). *Communication and Persuasion: Central and Peripheral Routes to Attitude Change*. New York: Springer Verlag.

Prensky, M. (2001). Digital natives, digital immigrants. *On the Horizon. NCB University Press, 9*(5), 1–9.

Rubin, A. M. (1993). The effect of locus of control on communication motivation, anxiety, and satisfaction. *Communication Quarterly, 41*(Spring), 161–171.

Rubin, A. M. (2002). The uses-and-gratifications perspective of media effects. In Bryant, J., & Zillmann, D. (Eds.), *Media Effects: Advances in theory and research* (2nd ed., pp. 525–548). Mahwah, NJ: Lawrence Erlbaum.

Schutz, W. C. (1966). *The Interpersonal Underworld.* Palo Alto, CA: Science and Behavior Books.

Shamdasani, P. H., Stanaland, A. J. S., & Tan, J. (2001, July). Location, location, location: Insights for advertising placement on the web. *Journal of Advertising Research*, 7–21.

Shapiro, A. L. (1999). *The Control Revolution: How the Internet is Putting Individuals in Charge and Changing the World We Know*. New York: Public Affairs.

Sherry, J. L. (2004). Flow and media enjoyment. *Communication Theory, 14*(4), 328–347. doi:10.1111/j.1468-2885.2004.tb00318.x

Sicilia, M., & Ruiz, S. (2007). The role of flow in website effectiveness. *Journal of Interactive Advertising, 8*(1). Retrieved on February 29, 2008 from http://www.jiad.org/vol8/no1/ruiz/index.htm

Smith, M. B. (1973). Political attitudes. In Knutson, J. (Ed.), *Handbook of political psychology* (pp. 57–82). San Francisco: Jossey-Bass.

Srull, T. K., & Wyer, R. S. (1978). Category accessibility and social perception: some implications for the study of person memory and interpersonal judgments. *Journal of Personality and Social Psychology, 37*, 841–856.

Tauder, A. R. (2006). Getting ready for the next generation of marketing communications. *Journal of Advertising Research*, 1–4.

Verna, P. (2007 June). User-Generated Content: Will Web 2.0 Pay Its Way? *eMarketer*, 1-31.

Vickers, A. (2007). Smart Growth in an Era of Digital Disruption. *Avenue A | Razorfish Insight*, Retrieved July 1, 2007, from http://www.avenuea-razorfish.com

Webster, J., Trevino, L. K., & Ryan, L. (1993). The dimensionality and correlates of flow in human-computer interactions. *Computers in Human Behavior, 9*(4), 411–426. doi:10.1016/0747-5632(93)90032-N

Wu, G. (2006). Conceptualization and measuring the perceived interactivity of websites. *Journal of Current Issues and Research in Advertising, 28*(Spring), 87–104.

Chapter 3
Economic Issues in Media Regulation:
An EU and US Perspective

Geraldine Ryan
University College Cork, Ireland

Edward Shinnick
University College Cork, Ireland

ABSTRACT

Changes in technology bring new challenges and opportunities for every industry, and the media industry is no different. Today people use mass media, and in particular the Internet, to participate in discussions and debate, to advertise and sell their products, to collect and store knowledge and to interact with the global community on the information super-highway. Given both the fast pace of innovation in the media industry and consumer demands for ever greater media content regulatory authorities are faced with challenging times. In this chapter, the authors examine how vertical mergers, vertical restraints, regulations, and competition policy are impacting on the European and American media industries. The authors examine how the internationalisation of the industry, increased merger activity, and the move towards cross media ownership are impacting on market concentration and diversity. The authors conclude that a balance must be struck between encouraging greater capital flows into the industry to help develop innovation, and the need to protect the public's long term interest through ensuring competitive markets.

INTRODUCTION

Up to 120 years ago, the only means of communicating with large numbers of people was through the spoken word and the printed page. The development of radio in 1896 and television in 1928[1] changed the way people communicate. Today, mass media is used to debate political and social issues on a world scale. Nowadays, most people can use mass media, and in particular the Internet, to participate in discussions and debate, to advertise and sell their products, to collect and store knowledge and to interact with the global community on the information super-highway. The emerging online players are not subject to substantive limitations on content, ownership, or geography; they can pick and choose the audiences they target, the content they buy, and the way

DOI: 10.4018/978-1-60566-792-8.ch003

they provide it (Samuel, 2005). The combination of digital convergence, personal computing, and global networking has ratcheted up the pace of development and is giving rise to radical shifts in the media industry.

The internet, and more recently broadband internet, has had a major impact on the way people communicate. The most recent OCED data shows that over 247 million OECD consumers have internet access (OECD, 2008), while data from Internet World Statistics shows that over 1,463,632,361 currently use the internet (Internet World Statistics, 2008). As the speed at which information gets sent to us increases, and the capacity of telecommunication networks to deliver greater volumes of information grows, so too does the range of uses to which these technologies can be applied. Consumers' demand for speed, convenience, and quality will continue to rise as each new development raises their level of expectation. Tomorrow's media providers will help drive technological progress across a range of fronts. Consumer choice will be facilitated through advances in packet-switching technology, higher bandwidths, greater digital storage capacity and enhanced buffering and compression technologies (Samuel, 2005).

The internet changes the cost structure, scope of products and services, and geographic shape of media, creating an entirely different set of regulatory challenges. It caters to individualised rather than local, state or country institutions. It is pretty clear that it will be a key driver of the next wave of competition and the markets we have traditionally defined as 'media' will change. This development is likely to put greater demands on the regulatory regime as it tries to keep abreast of such developments. The legal and administrative regulation of media structure, delivery, and content, though still largely a matter of national law, is increasingly becoming an international one. For example, European institutions, such as the Council of Europe and the European Union are progressively playing crucial roles in the determination of media law, policy and regulation, often seeking diversity both in content and in economic ownership. However the convergence of various electronic methods of content delivery across borders threatens to undercut any attempts at regulation.

In this chapter, we examine the economic regulation of the media industry both in the EU and the US and demonstrate the importance of this issue in fully understanding the industry. We also examine how the internet continues to change the media industry and the way it is regulated. Our focus is on the economic regulation of this industry and the economic theory that underpins much of this regulation. We also look at how the EU and US have attempted to apply regulation in this fast changing industry. An outline of the regulatory environment in both jurisdictions is provided and cases are analysed to illustrate the different approaches taken by the EU and US authorities. A full understanding of media industry regulation is crucial for both policy makers and industry players as advances in the economic theory of vertical integration and vertical restraints point to potential unforeseen benefits of such arrangements. A brief outline of the economic costs and benefits of vertical arrangements will therefore be outlined.

The remainder of this chapter is structured as follows. Section 2 describes the challenges facing the media industry and this is followed in Section 3 by a brief introduction to the economic theory of vertical integration along with a description of the role of regulation and competition policy. Section 4 outlines the regulation of the media industry in the EU and Section 5 does the equivalent for the US. Section 6 concludes by describing the challenges facing the media industry and its regulation.

THE CHANGING FACE OF MEDIA

When we think of media, we generally tend to think of it in its traditional forms–radio, television, cinema, newspapers and magazines. However, our communications environment is changing and today, many of us also think of the internet as a key media component. We are living in an age in which decisions made about information access will have a profound impact on our lives and that of the media industry. Emerging new developments in information and communication technologies are already affecting the ways we organize our work, seek information and develop innovations. Nonetheless, by and large we have differentiated these various silos, and defined them as different markets within the overall media industry.

Like any business, the media industry has evolved over time. Since Marconi sent and received his first radio signal in Italy in 1896, we have seen the introduction of media such as the television, cable and satellite television, video recorders, mobile phones, the internet and the World Wide Web. Since the introduction of privately run Internet Service Providers in the 1980s, and its expansion into popular use, the Internet has had a drastic impact on culture and commerce.[2] Its impact on the media industry is on-going. The industry is currently in a period of rapid economic and technological change, with sector boundaries and core technologies undergoing fundamental transitions. For example, traditional telephone companies are now merging with cable television firms to create facility-based broadband companies while underlying technologies are shifting from telephony to internet protocol and wireless systems.

The driving force behind the phenomenal growth in the internet has been the recognition by businesses and individuals of the power of the World Wide Web to reach customers and each other. This has led to significant advances in the industry through the use of online media. With internet usage and download speeds increasing throughout the world, the delivery of print, audio and video media has been dramatically transformed. Now consumers can access all forms of media content through one delivery mode. In addition consumers can contribute content by uploading material in a way that was not possible with traditional delivery methods. Other advances have occurred in the print media, where most newspapers have developed their own websites where content can be updated and supplemented by audio or video content. In radio, podcasting has become a new form of media that has enabled these providers to keep up with changing consumer habits. In television markets, the introduction of satellite technology combined with the internet, allow consumers to control their TV's remotely such that programmes can be set to record via a mobile telephone or computer.

Along with changes in delivery modes we are also witnessing a convergence among the different media modes. The internet is the single biggest contributing factor to this convergence by becoming the common access point for media content. Your newspaper, television station and favourite book publishers can all now be accessed through the internet rather than the more traditional and distinct 'hard' copy versions. This brings the different forms of media into much more direct competition with each other and this benefits consumer choice. However the effects may not all be positive, since new entrants face a possible barrier to entry through the need to reach a large scale in order to compete with the big incumbent firms and through the need to break through consumer loyalty to their existing media suppliers.

Another development in online media is the emergence of a new phenomenon: social networking sites. The idea behind these sites is to connect individuals and businesses around the world. These sites support the maintenance of pre-existing social networks while many also help strangers connect based on shared interests, political views, and activities. The first site, SixDegrees.com, was launched in 1997. This site allowed users to create profiles, list their friends and surf their friends lists. The success of this site was short lived and in 2000 SixDegrees.com failed. Users of the site argued, that while the idea of the site was excellent, many of their friends did not have internet access and so the site served little purpose (Kiehne, 2004).

In 2001, a new type of social networking site called Ryze.com debuted. The aim of this site was to help people leverage their business networks. Nowadays social networking sites such as MySpace and Facebook attract millions of users, many of whom have integrated these sites into their daily practices.[3,4] MySpace, established in 2003, differentiated itself by regularly adding new features and by allowing users to personalise their pages. In July 2005, News Corporation purchased MySpace for $580 million (BBC, 2005), attracting massive media attention. Today, MySpace has the second highest membership with 117 million worldwide members (Dalrymple, 2008). The most popular site today is Facebook. This site began in early 2004 as a Harvard only social networking site (Cassidy, 2006). By the end of its first year, membership expanded to include students from Stanford, Columbia, and Yale and by September 2006, anyone, over the age of 13, with a valid e-mail address was permitted to use the site. In 2007, Facebook permitted users to decorate their profiles using HTML and Cascading Style Sheets and since then (i.e. June 2007–June 2008) its membership has grown from 52 million to 132 million worldwide (Dalrymple, 2008).[5]

Social network sites also benefit entrepreneurs' and small businesses which are looking to expand their contact base. Companies use these sites for advertising in the form of banners and text adverts. Since businesses operate globally, social networks can make it easier to keep in touch with contacts around the world. One of the most popular business networking sites is LinkedIn. All 500 of the Fortune 500 corporate members and more than 25 million individuals in 150 countries build their personal networks through LinkedIn (LinkedIn, 2008). It helps users to find employees, industry experts, jobs, and make deals. In the last few years, many media sharing sites have implemented social networking features. For example, the photo-sharing site Flickr, now owned by Yahoo, lets people comment on others' photos, join groups and add friends, while video-sharing site YouTube, now owned by Google, has became a huge phenomenon partly because it lets people create user profiles, comment on videos and collect 'subscribers' for their videos.

Current Challenges for the Media Industry

Changes in technology bring new challenges and opportunities for every industry, and the media industry is no different. For example when television arrived, it was widely predicted that it would devastate radio, and perhaps movies and newspapers. Yet nothing like this has happened. Similarly, when the CD-ROM appeared on the scene, people predicted the demise of the printed book. In the past new technologies have not led to the demise of the old technologies, however they have changed the type of service delivered by these services. The feared substitution between television and newspapers did not happen, instead newspapers adapted. Broadsheets, for example, while no longer the first to report on news stories; now provide comment and analysis (see Naughton, 2006). In a similar way it is expected that the internet, while not wiping-out older technologies, will force them to adapt to their new environment.

One notable challenge faced by the media industry is to adapt to changes in the way it is funded. Traditionally, all mass media was funded in the same way; large multinational companies, such as Procter and Gamble, Coca Cola and Ford, paid high prices to radio and TV stations for the privilege of getting access to large audiences. Taplin (2006) argues that this relationship was based on the law of scarcity. This was especially true for markets where product groups were very similar, for example in the drinks market, and the only way producers could differentiate themselves and grow their market was through TV and radio advertising. With relatively few local channels, and even fewer prime time TV and radio advertising slots companies were willing to pay extraordinary amounts of money for peak airtime. Consumers also benefited, as long as they were willing to put up with the commercials then they did not have to pay for the programmes. This relationship worked well until about 10 yrs ago. Since then the internet, broadband, digital television and mobile devices have given consumers more mobility and control. Consumers are now less willing to listen to radio adverts or watch television adverts and as a result, producers are less willing to pay for them. A recent IAB advertising report shows that internet advertising ($21.2 billion), surpassed radio advertising ($19.8 billion) and cable television advertising ($20.9 billion) in the United States in 2007 (PricewaterhouseCoopers, 2008). Social networking sites have become acceptable among advertisers. United States social network advertising expenditure is expected to be $1,430 million in 2008 (eMarketer, 2008), with Facebook receiving the largest share of that spend ($755 million). Advertisers are attracted to these sites for their ability to draw a massive audience of hard-to-reach young consumers.

Similarly, newspapers and magazines have experienced a drop in advertising revenue in the last few years. In 2007, newspapers share of the world advertising market fell to 27.5% from 28.7% in 2006. At the same time, internet advertising was up 32.45%.[6] Despite this newspapers and magazines remain the world's largest advertising medium, with a 40% share (WAN, 2008).[7] A recent survey by the World Association of Newspapers shows that paid daily newspaper circulations were up or stable in nearly 80% of countries. The five largest markets for newspapers are China with 107 million copies sold daily, India (99 million), Japan (68 million), US (nearly 51 million) and Germany (20.6 million). In places where paid-for circulation is declining, notably the US and some of Western Europe, newspapers continue to extend their reach through a wide variety of free and niche publications and through their rapidly developing multi-media. The number of newspaper on-line sites grew by 51% from 2003 to 2007.

Another major challenge facing the media industry is the way in which it regulates itself. The purpose of media regulation is to ensure existing players are not allowed to use their market power to close down new forms of competition, and that, as far as possible, consumers decide what form this revolution takes and what services and content they wish to access. The internet poses new challenges to regulators as it changes the cost structure and geographic shape of media. A brief description of the economic theory underpinning regulation of media markets, along with the role of regulation and competition policy in media markets are outlined in the next section.

ECONOMIC THOERY AND THE ROLE OF REGULATION

The economic theory most relevant to the regulation of media markets is that of vertical integration. This concerns the linkages between the various stages in the value chain with an industry, for example, between buyers and sellers of media content. The approach taken by the industrial organisation strand of this theory studies how vertical integration affects the exercise of market power.[8]

There are two related issues in this literature. The first is vertical mergers. Here some issues of concern are, control and ownership, exclusive contracts, mergers and state aid and how these issues may change the balance of market power in the industry to the determinant of consumers and, in relation to media markets in particular, to the diversity of opinion. Initially, vertical integration was seen as promoting market foreclosure.[9] This, along with the extension of monopoly power argument, was used initially to block many vertical mergers, despite some potential efficiency effects. The second issue is that of vertical restraints, that is business practices that can accomplish some of the same objectives as vertical integration through contractual means rather than by merging, for example, exclusive dealing (contracts), tying,[10] and territorial restraints.[11]

The bias against such vertical arrangements was later relaxed when studies showed there were no anticompetitive effects, unless pre-existing market power occurred at one level or both.[12] This literature identified previously unrealised potential benefits of vertical integration such as technological economies, transaction costs such as, coordination costs, economies of scale and scope, efficiencies and reduction of the double marginalisation effect.[13] Along with these potential benefits, the issue of state aid was added. In particular such aid can potentially lead to a distortion of market power, aggravate issues of control and ownership, and create potential for market foreclosure through subsidising otherwise unprofitable ventures.

The regulation of media markets is an attempt to address some of these problematic issues associated with vertical arrangements and the evolution of such markets. Regulation has transformed the role of government and business through establishing a series of rules and guidelines that aim to balance consumer and producer interests. Many markets are subject to regulation including air transport, utilities and the media. Originally, government regulation was perceived as achieving public interest goals. Legislators were assigned the role of developing regulation to help achieve collective goals, which would not otherwise be achieved due to a failure of the market, such as monopoly power, inadequate information and externalities, leading to high prices, high profits, misleading information and both allocative and productive inefficiencies. The solution to many of these problems was to develop output regulations (e.g. standards of performance) and input regulations (e.g. rules of conduct) and introduce a regulatory regime to oversee these regulations.

Any negative effects of regulation, such as impeding economic growth, competitiveness, innovation, price competition, entry, investment and efficiency, can be compounded if the regulatory system becomes overly bureaucratic, if vested interest groups seek regulation in order to block competition or if existing regulations become obsolete. This correction of market failure became the central theme of the public interest theory. The private interest theory later challenged this notion and maintained that regulation benefits groups of people which it may not have initially been set up to benefit. That is, private interest groups can use the political process to achieve (or re-direct) regulatory benefits for themselves at the expense of the public. Therefore government regulation can fail when it does not achieve its desired initial objective(s). This creates another form of market failure, that of regulatory failure.

It is important to distinguish between what may be called 'restrictive' regulations that have the potential to reduce competition and beneficial regulations that can protect consumers. Some restrictive agreements, anti-competitive practices and distributional practices may result when firms decide to collude rather than compete with each other. The traditional neo-classical theory in economics, which portrays the two extremes of perfect competition and monopoly, is often used to gauge the effect of such practices and is also used as a benchmark for policy prescription. Using this framework, it is generally believed that collusive practices tend to work against the interests of consumers and result in an inefficient use of resources. These inefficiencies occur both in terms of productive inefficiency (firms not operating at minimum average cost) and allocative inefficiency (price not equal to marginal cost) (Carlton and Perloff, 2005).

Competition policy is often introduced in order to avoid such inefficiencies, where competition policy is an instrument of public policy that monitors the behaviour of individual firms. It must be flexible enough to allow firms to grow and benefit from economies of scale in production, while also ensuring that the economy in general and consumers in particular do not suffer as a result of too few firms competing with each other in a particular market. This highlights an inherent conflict that exists in competition policy. That is, what size must a firm reach in order to benefit from economies of scale and how does competition policy react to large firms who by exploiting economies of scale are capable of dominating the industry by taking over or closing down rival firms. Competition policy therefore has the difficult task of creating an environment that allows firms to expand to their efficient size while at the same time guaranteeing that barriers do not exist that would inhibit the emergence of new firms in the same market.

Competition legislation that attempts to achieve this balance between firm growth and market dominance exists in many countries. The United States was one of the first countries to introduce restrictions on firm behaviour (in the form of legislation) due to the public discomfort with large amounts of economic power being held by a few private institutions. The government introduced the *Sherman Act 1890*, and this was followed by the *Clayton and Federal Trade Commission Acts 1914*.

The European Union introduced competition policy in its founding document, the Treaty of Rome. One objective set out in this document is to ensure that competition affecting member states is not distorted. Articles 81 and 82, in particular, outline EC policy with regard to competition. One feature of this policy was that the domestic laws of each country in the EU were to be brought into line with these. Articles 81 prohibit the prevention, restriction or distortion of competition in trade in any goods or services and Article 82 prohibits the abuse of a dominant position in trade in any goods or services.

The European Commission is empowered by the Treaty to apply these rules and can do this through its investigative powers and the imposition of fines on undertakings who violate EU antitrust rules. Since 1 May 2004, all national competition authorities are also empowered to apply fully the provisions of the Treaty in order to ensure that competition is not distorted or restricted.

MEDIA REGULATION IN EUROPE

Characteristics of European media markets today indicate a fast growing and evolving market structure where old and once dominant incumbents compete with smaller, and in some cases niche, players in a marketplace where technology is changing both the production and delivery of media products and services. The existence of incumbent players, who were once public monopolies, has resulted in the use of regulation along with market forces of competition in an attempt to achieve the effective operation of media markets in the public interest.

The structure of media markets has greatly influenced the delivery of new products and services across new geographic markets. Structural issues such as vertical integration and market power have an impact on consumer protection through regulation, concentration of ownership through merger activity and the competitive effect of state aid.

Nowadays the structure of media markets has become more complex, involving many new players made possible through developments in technology. Figure 1 illustrates a simple, aggregate, version of what a typical media industry chain may look like. The first component of the chain is material owners, that is, those who hold the legal rights to material such as book, music, sporting events etc. The second component is the producers of content, such as film and television producers, book publishers and music producers. Broadcasters constitute the third component and these include the traditional outlets such as public service television, pay TV operators and increasingly the internet service providers are becoming more important in this group due to the importance of the internet. The fourth component is the distributors who transport the product

Figure 1. A vertically integrated media market

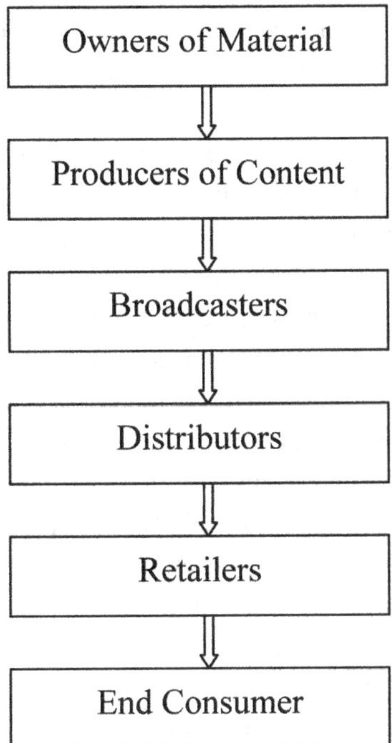

through networks such as cable, satellite, mobile, and books. Retailers who sell content to the final consumer make up the fifth component, while the final consumer constitutes the last component in this chain.

Many of today's larger media companies have come about as a result of vertical integration, that is ownership of more than one of the stages in the media chain depicted in Figure 1. McChesney (1999) identified vertical integration in the media industry as a means by which companies can increase market power by promoting cross-selling media products or brands. For example, making a film and then cross promoting it over different media can be very profitable. McChesney gives the example of Disney's *The Lion King* which generated a profit of over $1 billion, through developing a Broadway show, a TV series and an array of media spin-offs. In addition it led to 186 items of merchandising.

Changes in technology and increasing competition brought about by privatisation and deregulation of former state broadcasters in Europe has led to the consolidation of this media industry chain, where firms have increasingly become involved in more than one component. One consequence of this is the way in which it significantly alters how competition works in the market. As the boundaries between these components become less obvious the emphasis in competition analysis may shift away from how information is delivered to the products offered by companies. Such products can include advertising space, the supply of content from broadcasters to distributors, retailers and to consumers, premium content such as sporting events and the delivery of news and information.

Since the 1980s there have been an increasing number of mergers of media companies and as a result the industry has become more concentrated. Alongside this trend, the influence of advertisers and owners has increased significantly. In some places media companies are owned by major multinational corporations where revenue from advertising is a crucial component of profits. The reliance on advertising has resulted in questions being raised on the impartially of content from these media stations and whether they are overly influenced by corporate interests. The fear here is that stories may be biased or dropped altogether in order not to offend advertisers or owners. If this were to occur the ability of the public to make informed decisions is likely to be affected. Increased concentration also brings with it the traditional fears associated with oligopolies and monopolies, in terms of price, quality and choice. The issue of choice is also important in the context of a desire to have a wide diversity of opinion in such an important market as media. Therefore ownership and in particular the concentration of ownership is a major issue in the analysis of modern media markets (Bagdikian, 2000).

Vertical integration was once looked upon as bad for consumers and governments subsequently treated it with suspicion fearing the creation of dominant companies and a lack of innovation within the industry. Nowadays vertical integration is seen as a necessary way for companies to compete effectively in global markets. In the media industry one of the most common activities is for distribution companies and content providers to seek out alliances with each other. One of the primary benefits to vertical integration is on efficiency grounds arising from both economics of scale and\or scope. Other potential benefits include, improvement in products, the development of new products, and streamlining distribution channels. Potential negative effects of vertical integration are based around the issue of market power and can include the exclusive rights to products, using market power in one market to restrict output, thereby rising price, in another market, creating a barriers to entry, and strengthening of a dominant position (see, for example, Iosifidis, 2005; Coates and Sauter, 2007).

These structural issues pose challenges to regulators in trying to achieve a balance between competitive market behaviour on the one hand and protection of the consumer or the public interest on the other hand. In fast moving markets such as media, these challenges are even greater.

Regulatory Measures in the EU

Since mid 1980 all European Union (EU) member states have gradually tailored their individual national media regulatory regimes to bring them in line with a central European view. In 1990 EU member states implemented the Television Without Frontiers (TWF) Directive. Initial implementation of this directive was poor. However, pressure exerted by the European Institutions was substantial, such as the enforced implementation of the TWF requirements throughout member states by the European Court of Justice. In parallel with the actions of the Court, the Commission's Merger Task Force was active in moulding Europe's commercial broadcasting markets through the application of competition law.

Coates and Sauter (2007) note how the regulatory framework of the telecommunications and broadcast industries are different and plans to integrate these frameworks across the EU did happen at the transmission infrastructure level but not at the content level. Telecommunications was initially considered to be monopolistic in nature, where national government would own such companies to achieve public service objectives such as universal service. With breakthroughs in technology and increased access to capital, the monopolistic approach was no longer deemed essential. The result was a progressive liberalisation of telecommunications markets beginning in 1990. Full liberalisation was achieved, in principle, in 1998 even though five countries (Greece, Ireland, Luxembourg, Portugal and Spain) were given a temporary derogation from the liberalisation timetable on the basis that the telecommunications networks were small and under developed. These derogations have now expired.

The issue of joint ownership of telecommunication and cable networks was also considered by the Commission on the basis that cable networks can be used as local communication services and are therefore potentially competing networks. The Commission ruled that any telecoms operator that also owned a cable network must, in most cases, keep the two operations legally separate. The key issue guiding the reasoning of the Commission in devising its regulatory framework is that of access, as many of the companies in this market were once state-owned natural monopolies who were in a position to build up strong dominant positions in markets in advance of liberalisation.

In comparison to telecommunication, there is little regulation of the media industry across the EU. Two examples are, first the Television Without Frontiers Directive gives Member States the power to prevent pay television operators from acquiring exclusive rights to events that are deemed to be of 'major importance for society', where each Member Sates defined what is of major importance. The second example, is that of exclusive rights, where exclusivity itself is not considered to restrict competition. The landmark case law on this goes back to the *Coditel I*[14] case of 1980, where the Court of Justice considered that exclusivity is inherent in copyright and exclusive rights contracts do not necessarily breach EC competition law.

A later case *Coditel II*[15] in 1981 outlined three issues where exclusive contracts may breach competition law. These were, (i) duration and scope of exclusivity, (ii) the appreciability of its impact on competition between broadcasters in the acquisition of rights and on downstream television markets, and (iii) its effect on trade between Member States (see Coates and Sauter, 2007). The Commission subsequently sought to limit the duration and scope of exclusive contracts so as to achieve a competitive market and avoid such agreements becoming a barrier to entry and resulting in market foreclosure. Recent cases concerning the merger of two telecommunication companies *Telepiu/Stream*[16] and the sale of football rights by leagues would indicate that the Commission is concerned with both the accumulations of exclusive rights and exclusive rights being in the hands of a single purchaser.

The regulation of the Internet is far more problematic. Johnson and Post (1996) outline the problems of using the more traditional regulatory models for the Internet. For example, applying territorially based rules are difficult given the non-geographic nature of this market. Physical location is often irrelevant or else cannot be established which results in a lack of control over content, ownership and competition issues. Some attempts have been made to address these issues. For example, in the area of e-commerce, the EU typically focuses on issues of jurisdiction, national rules and the protection of national interests. In terms of privacy issues, the EU has laws governing the collection, use and dissemination of personal information. Finally in relation to content, the EU regulates content on the basis of protecting public opinion which includes national cultures, languages and identities.

In 2007, the European Commission announced a new directive, which revised the legislation put in place in the 1990's and covered all audiovisual media services, ranging from traditional TV broadcasts to emerging on-demand TV services. This directive should be implemented by EU member states by the end of 2009. The new rules relax restrictions on TV advertising and for the first time will permit 'product placement' - the placement of a specific product in TV programmes for commercial purposes. Product placement has been common in the US since the 1970s, creating, what some say is, an unfair competitive advantage for US productions. Under the new EU rules, product placement will be permitted, but not in informative programmes–such as news, documentaries and children's programmes.

Merger Regulations

EU competition policy tries to ensure that competition effects are achieved in markets, excessive market power is curtailed and any anticompetitive practices that may allow firms to achieve excessive market power or create barriers to entry are prevented. At the same time competition policy tries to achieve a balance between encouraging technological innovation, price competition and wide consumer choice. Open and free competition is seen as the most effective way of achieving this balance. In the media sector EU competition rules have been applied more frequently over the past number of years because of an increase in the number and complexity of merger cases. Of particular concern is to identify what is an acceptable level of consolidation for this sector given how technology has dramatically changed the business model of media companies.

In assessing the merger of two media companies, the Commission must decide whether the proposed merger would result in a substantial lessoning of competition in the market, based on all available evidence. This decision process can be made more difficult in media markets due to the rapidly changing business environment brought about by advances in technology. For example convergence of technologies across the media sector has resulted in an increased degree of overlap between what were once considered distinct markets. For example, advertising and content can be distributed across many different media with the advances made in broadband technology and availability. The print and radio media, for example, were once considered distinct markets, however the content of both can now be accessed through a third media device, the mobile telephone. Indeed it is this drive by the 'old' media companies to reinvent themselves in the face of technological advances that has resulted in an increase in merger activity in this industry. Many of these companies are concerned about the large number of viewers using online media sites such as YouTube and Yahoo, such that 'old' companies are proposing to merge with 'new' companies so as not to become redundant in this sector. Hence we have a diversified media sector with overlapping media components in all the large media companies. This is best illustrated by News Corporation's large bid of $5 billion for Dow Jones, which valued the publishers of the *Wall Street Journal* at a higher price-to-earning multiple than Google.

On the issue of the influence of technology on merger regulation, one thing for sure is that it is very difficult to predict how technology will evolve and shape future markets. It is quite possible that technology will help to increase competition in some markets and decrease competition in other markets, but it is unlikely that we can know beforehand the impact with any degree of certainty. This has important implications for media regulation since a merger between, for example, a print and radio firm was once considered to be safe, because these markets were considered to be distinct. If these markets become interlinked, a merger may now be less safe from a competition viewpoint. Once again, in the media sector there is also the issue of diversity, where differing viewpoints is considered desirable so that any one media organisation cannot assert undue influence on society.

The EU implemented the Merger Regulations in 1990 to complement EU competition policy and it gave the Commission preemptive powers to deal with mergers. In 2003 the EC adopted a series of merger control guidelines to appraise mergers. These guidelines detail how a merger will only be challenged if it is considered to increase the market power in such a way that it is likely to harm consumers' interests, such as lead to higher prices, poorer quality or reduced consumer choice (Levy, 2005). The Merger Regulations cover only large mergers, that is, those mergers between firms with an aggregate turnover of at least €5 billion and a turnover within the European Economic Area of more than €250 million. As a consequence of these thresholds, many mergers have been allowed to proceed without analysis (Just and Latzer, 2000). An analysis of some of the merger cases blocked under the Merger Regulations provides some indication of what guides the Commission's decisions in media mergers. The creation of a dominant position was a critical factor in many of these decisions. For example, the MSG Media Services case in 1994, the proposed merger of WorldCom and Sprint in 2000 and the blocking of the AOL-Time Warner merger with EMI in 1999 were all prohibited on the grounds that they would have created a dominant position in the relevant market with negative consequences for consumers.

State Aid

One final issue to look at in the EU context is that of state aid. Current policy in the EU centres on The Broadcasting Communication[17] first adopted in 2001. In this policy a set of principles applicable to the financing of public service broadcasting were outlined. These principles give the Member States' wide discretion to define public service broadcasting and outline the Commission's task to preserve fair competition. By this it means a clearly defined public service mission along with limiting state aid to what is necessary to achieve this mission. In particular, overcompensation and any possible cross subsidisation of commercial activities are strictly prohibited.

In January of 2008 the Commission launched a public consultation on the future framework that will apply to state funding of public service broadcasting. This is an attempt to improve transparency and legal certainty in addition to allowing public service broadcasters fulfil their mission in the new media environment.[18] Over the years the Commission has used the existing guidelines to assess several complaints lodged by private competitors against the financing of public service broadcasters. Approximately 20 decisions have been taken by the Commission where it has further clarified it's the application of State aid rules to the broadcasting sector.[19]

Several of these decisions related to the broadcasting sector in Germany. For example, in 2007 the Commission rules against German government's plans to part finance (up to €6.8 million over 5 years) the fees commercial broadcasters pay for the transmission of their programs on the digital terrestrial television network on the basis that the proposals failed to fully identify the problem that required state aid and the failure to choose appropriate and non-discriminatory means of funding. This is an example of how technology is changing media markets and how such innovation is not automatically granted state subsidies, despite the obvious benefits to consumers. The Commission's point was that State support must target specific areas where the free market does not provide solutions and must not discriminate between competing services, in this case between terrestrial, cable and satellite transmission. Furthermore, the Commission considered the proposals to have the effect of potentially distorting competition between these three transmission platforms as the proposal only supported transmission over one platform, thereby disregarding the principle of technology neutrality.

MEDIA REGULATION IN UNITED STATES

With the advent of electronic communications technologies in the United States, governmental control moved to a system of regulation. Soon after the first commercial broadcast in 1920, Congress introduced the first set of broadcasting regulations, known as the Radio Act[20] (Alexander *et al.*, 2004). These regulations were superseded in 1934 by the Communications Act. This act saw the introduction of the Federal Communications Committee (FCC), which was created to protect and represent the public interest. The committee was established to regulate 'interstate and foreign commerce in communication by wire and radio so as to make available, so far as possible, to all the people of the United States, without discrimination on the basis of race, colour, religion, national origin, or sex, a rapid, efficient, nation-wide and world-wide wire and radio communication service ..."(FCC, 2008).

The regulatory structure was specifically designed to be flexible and adaptive to the changing shape of the industry, so much so that Congress left the regulatory standard open and allowed the FCC to fill in the details over time (Corn-Revere and Carveth, 2004). By 1938, the FCC used the 'public interest' standard to place harsh restrictions on ownership concentration in broadcast stations and they outlawed most local cross-ownership of different types of media entities (Baker, 2007). In addition, in spite of the prohibition against censorship in the 1934 Communications Act, the commission used the 'public interest' standard to place restrictions on the content of the program ming which a station may broadcast (Oregon Bar Press Broadcasters Council, 2000). These included restrictions on political editorials, obscene and indecent programming, lotteries, contests and promotions, children's programming on television, recorded telephone conversations, prohibited advertising on broadcast stations.

The FCC have tried to structure a media market that is competitive enough to satisfy their customers while, at the same time, is diverse enough to provide a range of information and viewpoints necessary for informed public debate (Shelanski, 2006). Since its inception, the committee has been responsible for preserving competition in the media industry and consequently it has set many boundaries on media ownership. For example, in the context of a merger, the FCC only allowed an entity to control two television stations in a single market if at least one of the stations was not among the top four stations in the market and at least eight independently owned television stations remained in the market after the transaction was completed (Mitra, 2001). For a long time, the FCC justified these boundaries by arguing that, there was a direct relationship between democracy and a communications system of diverse sources. For example, in 1947, the Hutchins report argued that media concentration undermined the presses crucial roles as conveyer of information, government watchdog and educator. Horwitz (2005) argued that the logic of government policy generally derived from the combination of antitrust laws and regulatory practice with free speech jurisprudence. Until 1980 the FCC enforced the 'fairness doctrine' which compelled licensed broadcasters to provide balanced coverage of public issues, thereby allowing diverse voices to the airwaves (Magarian, 2008).

In 1983, Congress expanded the remit of the FCC to include the encouragement of new technologies and services. This new provision created a presumption favouring increased competition in the communications marketplace (Corn-Revere and Carveth, 2004). In 1996, Congress introduced the Telecommunications Act and made a clear move to deregulate the media industry and increase the level of competition. Immediately after the Act, there was a substantial increase in retail video competition, especially for new technologies such as satellite broadcasting and broadband internet service and this competition continues to grow (Owen, 2008). The Act eliminated most cross-market entry barriers and relaxed concentration and merger rules. The Act also overruled all state restrictions on competition on local and long distance telephone services. The Bell Operating Companies (Baby Bells) were freed to provide long distance service outside and inside their regions (Alexander *et al.,* 2004). All nationwide limits on radio-station ownership were repealed, but local limits on concentration were maintained.[21] In addition, the Act eliminated the twelve station television and raised the national cap to thirty-five percent, while also encouraging the deployment of advanced telecommunications capability on a reasonable and timely basis.

The aim of the Telecommunications Act was to produce more competition, more diversity of opinion, lower prices for consumers and more wealth for the economy. The FCC reacted very quickly after the act. For example, the day the act was signed the FCC granted several waivers to the Walt Disney Company to help facilitate its merger with Capital Cities/ABC (McConnell, 1996). Within a month, the commission implemented new rules on TV and radio station ownership and by April has proposed to extend the license terms for television and radio to 8 years (Corn-Revere and Carveth, 2004). However, many argue that the Act did not live up to expectations. For example, between 1996 and 2003 over 4,000 radio stations were bought out by larger corporations. By 2003, one company, Clear channel Inc., owned more than 1,200 radio stations across the country (Copps, 2003). Similarly, the raising of the cap on television to 35% spurred huge media mergers and greatly increased media concentration. The Common Cause Education Fund argued that "just five companies–Viacom, the parent of CBS, Disney, owner of ABC, News Corp, NBC and AOL, owner of Time Warner, now control 75% of all prime-time viewing" (Common Cause Education Fund, 2005: 5). Many cable companies also decided to cash in, for example AT&T bought TCI for $48 billion in 1998 (Warf, 2003), while AT&T announced its $58 billion takeover of MediaOne in 1999 (Labaton, 2000).

The proposed merger of three giants of the cable television industry: Time Warner, Turner Broadcasting System, and TCI resulted in a more assertive antitrust policy in the US. This case is an example of how a vertical merger brought about fears of foreclosure between cable programming (the upstream industry) and cable service (the downstream industry). TCI was at the time the largest cable service provider with 27% of the market, followed by Time Warner with 17%. Furthermore Time Warner owned several cable networks and Turner provided cable channels. Time Warner and Turner were allowed to merge, with some restrictions, but TCI was not allowed to have any direct interest in the newly merger company.[22]

The mega-merger between America Online and Time Warner in 2001, valued at around $100 billion, changed the regulatory environment of the media industry. According to Yoo (2002) the merger re-opened discussion about open access to high-speed broadband systems. Around the time of this merger, consumers in the US were switching to broadband internet, which allowed customers to employ a proprietary Internet Service Provider (ISP). This raised concerns among competitors that such exclusivity arrangements had the potential to reduce consumer choice and harm competition. Corn-Revere and Carveth (2004) showed that the top four multiple systems operators, in 2002, served around 64% of US households. As a result the FCC were asked to "impose an open-access requirement that would require cable modem systems to make their transmission lines available to other, non-proprietary ISPs on a reasonable and non-discriminatory terms" (Yoo, 2002: 175). While the FCC had previously rejected calls for imposing open access as a condition to approving AT&T's acquisition of TCI and MediaOne, they conditioned their approval of the AOL-Time Warner merger on the merged company's willingness to negotiate access arrangements with at least three unaffiliated ISPs. In 2001, Time Warner also appealed and overturned the FCC's 1992 rule limiting the reach of cable systems to 30% of potential subscribers nationwide. The D.C. Circuit court found that the FCC had set the level of ownership arbitrarily and without sufficient justification in the administrative record.

By 2003, the FCC recognised the many of its regulations were either irrelevant or insufficient in the changing media marketplace. Rulings in the Time Warner v. FCC and Fox Television v. FCC case[23] in 2001 and the Sinclair Broadcast Group v. FCC case[24] in 2002, highlighted that in future the FCC's media ownership rules would need to be carefully justified on the basis of actual market evidence (Curwen, 2005). While it had been argued in 1996 that the Communications Act would "save consumers $550 billion, including $333 billion in lower long-distance rates, $32 billion in lower local phone rate and $78 billion in lower cable bills" within 10 years, "cable rates have surged by about 50 percent, and local phone rates went up more than 20 percent" (Common Cause Education Fund, 2005: 5). In addition, between 1996 and 2003, the market value of companies in the telecommunication industry fell by about $2 trillion and these companies shed around half a million jobs. Shelanski (2006) highlights the extent to which the media industry had changed by showing that, "In 1980, for example, there were 9,278 radio stations and 1,011 television stations, about 19.2 million household cable subscribers receiving approximately twenty nationally distributed, non-broadcast program networks, 1,745 daily newspapers, and no mass-market internet. By 2003, there were 13,450 radio stations' and 1,747 television stations, more than 900 million US household cable and satellite subscribers receiving 388 nationally distributed, non-broadcast program networks, 1,456 daily newspapers and more than 60 million household internet subscribers" Shelanski (2006: 372-373).

Over the last 25 years we have witnessed a dramatic consolidation in the US media market. Bagdikian (2000) notes that in 1983, 50 corporations dominated the media industry, by 1987 these

50 companies had decreased to 29 and by 1990 the number has further decreased to 23. At the end of the 1990s McChesney (1999) identified 9 corporations that dominated the media world, these were AOL-Time Warner, Disney, Bertelsmann, Viacom, News Corporation, TCI, General Electric, Sony and Seagram. The scale of these mergers also increased dramatically with the AOL Time Warner $350 billion merger in 2000 was more than 1000 times larger than the biggest deal of 1983 (Bagdikian, 2000). Further consolidation ensued such that by the end of 2006 only 8 corporations dominated the US media industry, these were; Disney, AOL-Time Warner, Viacom, General Electric, News Corporation, Yahoo, Microsoft and Google. This latest list demonstrates the advances made by internet-based companies who take up 3 positions on this top 8 list. This consolidation in the media industry can lead to concerns about diversity of information as well as competition concerns.

By 2003, the regulations were considered to have no longer met the objectives of the committee, that is to foster competition, diversity, and localism. After completing their biennial review, the FCC modified and relaxed many of the regulations governing ownership of mass media outlets. The order permitted media mergers to be controlled by antitrust law rather than by industry-specific regulations. The order also repealed the ban on newspaper/broadcast and broadcast/radio cross-ownership and retained the ban only in markets with three or fewer television stations in markets with four to eight television stations, the order permitted cross-ownership between a daily paper or a television station, as well as cross-ownership between either a daily paper or a television station and a limited number of radio stations. In markets with nine or more television stations, there are no cross-media limits applied, although the individual radio and television limits apply. The order raised the national television ownership cap from 35% to 45% (Yoo, 2002).

Reducing restrictions on media mergers produced a storm of protest, from all sides. Public opposition was greater than for any other FCC action. In June 2004, one year after the FCC ruled in favour of unrestricted media ownership in the US, a federal appeals court reversed the FCC rule. Further deregulation of media ownership is prohibited for now and the national television ownership cap has been dropped to 39% (Labaton, 2004). The most recent review was completed in December 2006 and is known as The Quadrennial Review Order[25]. Following this review the following rules were adopted:

(1) ***Newspaper/Broadcast Cross-Ownership*** is permitted when a daily newspaper seeks to combine with a radio station or when a daily newspaper seeks to combine with a television station in a top 20 designated market and (a) the television station is not ranked among the top four stations in the DMA and (b) at least eight independent 'major media voices' remain in the DMA.

(2) ***Local Television Ownership Limit***–a single entity may own two television stations in the same local market if (a) the so-called 'Grade B' contours of the stations do not overlap; or (b) at least one of the stations in the combination is not ranked among the top four stations in terms of audience share and at least eight independently owned and operating commercial or non-commercial full-power broadcast television stations would remain in the market after the combination.

(3) ***Local Radio Ownership Limit*** -one entity may own (a) up to five commercial radio stations, not more than three of which are in the same service (i.e., AM or FM), in a market with 14 or fewer radio stations; (b) up to six commercial radio stations, not more than four of which are in the same service, in a market with between 15 and 29 radio stations; (c) up to seven commercial radio stations, not more than four of which are

in the same service, in a radio market with between 30 and 44 radio stations; and (d) up to eight commercial radio stations, not more than five of which are in the same service, in a radio market with 45 or more radio stations.

(4) ***The National Television Ownership Limit*** - In 2004, Congress enacted legislation that permits a single entity to own any number of television stations on a nationwide basis as long as the station group collectively reaches no more than 39% of the national TV audience. The statute also excluded the national television cap from the ownership rules required to be reviewed in the quadrennial review proceedings. Accordingly, the national television cap was not under review in the 2006 quadrennial review proceeding.

(5) ***Radio/Television Cross-Ownership Limit***– one company may own in a single market: one TV station (two TV stations if permitted by the local TV ownership rule) and one radio station regardless of total market size; or if at least 10 independent media voices (i.e., broadcast facilities owned by different entities) would remain after the merger, up to two TV stations and up to four radio stations; or if at least 20 independently owned media voices would remain post-merger, up to two TV stations and up to six radio stations or one TV station and up to seven radio stations. Parties must also comply with the local radio ownership rule and the local TV ownership rule.

(6) **Dual Network Ban**–This rule permits common ownership of multiple broadcast networks but prohibits a merger of the "top four" networks, i.e., ABC, CBS, Fox, and NBC. Multiple challenges to the *Quadrennial Review Order* currently are pending in the U.S. Court of Appeals for the Ninth Circuit, which will decide which court will ultimately hear these challenges.

CHALLENGES FOR POLICY MAKERS AND REGULATORS

Traditionally vertical integration and vertical restraints were seen to be against the consumer's interests. More recently, the potential benefits of such arrangements have materialised. This highlights the need for a comprehensive cost-benefit analysis of all such arrangements. In media markets such analysis is of added importance when the issue of reducing diversity of opinion is considered, along with the potential anticompetitive effects in upstream or downstream markets through increasing market power. Added to this are the ambiguous efficiency effects, which all lead to the importance of case-by-case analysis so that one can fully understand the economics of vertical integration and how mergers, contracts and state aid in the media industry effect how this industry operates. Added to these is the issue of advances in technological innovation that are changing this industry, all of which demonstrate the importance of a rigorous economic analysis of the industry and which provides policy makers and economists with considerable challenges in the years ahead as they weigh up the costs and benefits of vertical arrangements in an ever changing media industry.

One of the challenges facing policy makers is a risk that the exclusive acquisition of rights for new and emerging services will allow the rights-holders to shut out competition across a range of services delivered over new networks. This could deprive consumers of choice and quality and could determine the success or failure of a new competitor. For example, a report by the European Commission[26] in 2005 on 3G sporting content noted that mobile operators expect that access to sports content will become a significant demand driver for 3G services and a key branding element given its high profile and relevance with regard to marketing.

Other new media such as IPTV (internet protocol television) also pose new challenges to policy makers and regulators. These services began by offering telephone services, they then extended to offer data services and are now starting to offer television in countries such as France, Germany, Italy, Spain, and the UK. Due to the large financial investments required by new broadcasting technologies, media companies have engaged in mergers and acquisitions. National governments have aided industry concentration by relaxing media ownership rules, including those restricting cross media ownership. In an attempt to improve their market positions, media companies have combined merger and acquisition strategies with those of internationalisation and diversification. As media companies are also expanding into adjacent communications markets, the definition of media markets is becoming more difficult, making regulation problematic. Indeed, without specific rules for the media industry, the European Commission is often accused of unreasonable arbitration and competition decisions on the media industry often face appeal.

As the forms of media communication adapt to the new available technologies, the regulators are starting to play a larger role in monitoring media mergers. The Commission prevents mergers or changes in ownership between two or more entities that would result in a substantial lessening of competition. This should continue to prevent undue concentration or accumulation of market power in the media, which would result in higher prices or lower quality service for consumers. However, a possible downside to this may be to negatively affect innovation in media services. Therefore regulation and merger analysis has to balance these two potentially conflicting outcomes.

While the internet has become the dominant platform for individuals and organisations to exchange information, the regulation of the Internet in which laws and technology interact have never reached an international common ground. In many respects, national borders have dissolved. Location, for all practical purposes, no longer exists. Countries must cope with the changes brought about by new technologies and adjust to the new realisation that the control they once exercised over business, citizens and information have been greatly reduced. In addition, Internet jurisdiction law is still in its infancy and this presents new challenges to regulators who must encourage innovation, foster growth and protect the public interest in this 'cyberspace' free from geography.

A further challenge is how to measure market concentration and address the related issue of diversity. Whether you consider media markets to be concentrated or not, depends very much on how you define the relevant product and geographic market. One point of view is that media markets are concentrated and the number of merger deals that have occurred in this industry are used to support their point of view. In particular, the big mergers over the past two decades have significant effects on the type and diversity of information available. Bagdikian (2000) argues that a smaller number of owners have possession of larger numbers of media properties and these owners have exercised strong influence over national legislation and government agencies. In addition the large prices paid for media firms create heavy financial pressures on all aspects of the business including news and journalism divisions. The widely noted cutbacks in broadcast news divisions and instances of commercial conflicts of interest at even quality newspapers in the 1990s would appear to confirm this (Downie and Kaiser, 2002).

Others argue that even though there have been a notable number of large mergers in the media industry there has also been very significant growth in the sector, which reduces the potentially negative effects of large mergers. Noam (2006), for example contrasts the early 1980s, when 3 television networks collectively controlled 92% of TV viewers, one company (AT&T) controlled 80% of local telephone service and nearly 100% of the long distance market, and another company (IBM) accounted for 77% of the computer market, to the mid 1990s when, after the deregulation of cable television and the break-up of AT&T, the networks accounted for barely more than 50%

of TV viewers, AT&T served 55% of the long distance market and virtually no local customers, and no computer manufacturer supplied more than 12% of the microcomputer market. Therefore while there has been significant merger activity, Noam's argument is that the huge overall growth of the industry has alleviated any dangers of concentration.

Changes in delivery systems brought about by the nature and growth of the Internet blurs the lines between traditional media and further complicates the traditional antitrust thinking about geographical markets. Therefore there is a need to move toward evaluating the media industry as a whole. This will also have implications on how we assess diversity in addition to how we devise and evaluate media regulations. Economic models show that as the number of substitutes for any product or service increases, the market fragments and minority-interest products becomes economically viable. In the new media industry of today, where we have witnessed greater substitutability than ever, such fragmentation has occurred and this has increased the viability of 'marginal' products, resulting in many more media players in the industry. Therefore when analysing the issue of diversity regulators should take a much broader view of the market and include all substitutable media.

Given both the fast pace of innovation in the media industry and consumer demands for ever greater media content regulatory authorities are faced with challenging times. A balance must be struck between encouraging greater capital flows into the industry to help develop innovation and protecting the public's long term interest through ensuring competitive markets. In particular regulatory authorities must resist the temptation to increase the regulatory burden each time a new media delivery method is introduced. In addition, consistency in applying the existing regulations and a possible harmonisation of regulatory rules across the EU and US would go a long way towards encouraging the development of this industry to the overall advantage of the consumer.

REFERENCES

Alexander, A., Owers, J., Carveth, R., Hollifielf, C. A., & Greco, A. N. (Eds.). (2004). *Media Economics, Theory and Practice*. Hillsdale, NJ: Lawrence Erlbaum Associates Inc.

Bagdikian, B. H. (2000). *The Media Monopoly*. Boston: Beacon Press.

Baker, C. E. (2007). *Media Concentration and Democracy: Why Ownership Matters*. Cambridge, MA: Cambridge University Press.

BBC. (2005). *News Corporation in $580m Internet Buy*. Retrieved on September 1, 2008, from http://news.bbc.co.uk/1/hi/business/4695495.stm.

Boyd, D. M., & Ellison, N. B. (2007). Social network sites: Definition, history and scholarship. *Journal of Computer-Mediated Communication, 12*(1). Retrieved from http://jcmc.indiana.edu/vol13/issue1/boyd.ellison.html.

Carlton, D. W., & Perloff, J. M. (2005). *Modern Industrial Organization* (4th ed.). New York: Addison-Wesley.

Cassidy, J. (2006). Me media: How hanging out on the Internet became big business. *New Yorker (New York, N.Y.), 82*(13), 50.

Coates, K., & Sauter, W. (2007). Communication: Telecoms, Media and Internet. In Faull, J., & Nikpay, A. (Eds.), *The EC Law of Competition* (2nd ed.). Oxford, UK: Oxford University Press.

Common Cause Education Fund. (2005). *The fallout from the Telecommunications Act of 1996: Unintended Consequences and Lessons Learnt, Common Cause, Holding Power Accountable*. Washington, DC: Common Cause Education Fund.

Copps, M. (2003, January 16). Crunch Time at the FCC. *The Nation*. Retrieved on September 18, 2008, from http://www.thenation.com/doc/20030203/copps

Corn-Revere, R., & Carveth, R. (2004). Economics and Media Regulation. In Alexander, A. (Eds.), *Media Economics: Theory and Practice*. Hillsdale, NJ: Lawrence Erlbaum Associates Inc.

Curwen, P. (2005). Consolidation in the USA: Does Bigger Mean Better. *Rearview, 7*(5). Retrieved from http://www.emeraldinsight.com/Insight/ViewContentServlet?Filename=Published/NonArticle/Articles/27207eab.001.html

Dalrymple, J. (2008). *Facebook Continues to Dominate Social Networking Sites*. Retrieved on August 21, 2008, from http://www.networkworld.com/news/2008/081208-facebook-continues-to-dominate-social.html?fsrc=rss-webservices.

Downie, L., & Kaiser, R. G. (2002). *The News About the News: American Journalism in Peril*. New York: Random House.

eMarketer. (2008). *Social Networking Marketing: Where Too Next*. Retrieved on August 19, 2008, from http://www.emarketer.com/Report.aspx?code=emarketer_2000433

FCC. (2008). *The FCC and its Regulatory Authority*. Retrieved on August 23, 2008, from http://www.fcc.gov/aboutus.html

Horwitz, R. B. (2005). On media concentration and the diversity question. *The Information Society, 21*(3), 181–204. doi:10.1080/01972240490951908

Internet World Statistics. (2008). *Internet Usage Statistics, the Big Picture*. Retrieved August 19, 2008, from http://www.internetworldstats.com/stats.htm

Iosifidis, P. (2005). The Application of EC Competition Policy to the Media Industry, *International Journal on Media Management,* 7(3\4), 103-111.

Johnson, D. R., & Post, D. (1996). Law and Borders: The Rise of Law in Cyberspace. *Stanford Law Review, 48*(1), 13–67.

Just, N., & Latzer, M. (2000). EC competition policy and market power control in the Mediamatics Era. *Telecommunications Policy, 24*, 395–411. doi:10.1016/S0308-5961(00)00035-5

Kiehne, T. P. (2004). *Social Networking Systems: History, Critique, and Knowledge Management Potentials. Mimeo*. School of Information, The University of Texas at Austin.

Labaton, S. (2000, June 6). AT&T's Acquisition of MediaOne Wins Approval by FCC. *The New York Times*.

Labaton, S. (2004, June 23). Senate Votes to Restore Media Limits. *The New York Times*.

Levy, N. (2005). Mario Monti's legacy in EC merger control. *Competition Policy International, 1*(1), 99–132.

LinkedIn. (2008). *About LinkedIn*. Retrieved on August 19, 2008, from http://www.linkedin.com

Magarian, G. P. (2008). Substantive Media Regulation in Three Dimensions. *Villanova Public Law and Legal Theory Working Paper Series*. Working Paper No 2008-05.

McChesney, R. W. (1999). *Rich Media Poor Democracy: Communication Politics in Dubious Times*. Champaign, IL: University of Illinois Press.

McConnell, C. (1996, February 12). Mega-Merger gets FCC Nod. *Broadcasting and Cable*.

Milgrom, P., & Roberts, J. (1992). *Economics, Organization and Management*. Englewood Cliffs, NJ: Prentice Hall.

Mitra, S. (2001). The death of media regulation in the age of the Internet. *Legislation and Public Policy, 4*, 415–438.

Naughton, J. (2006). *Our Changing Media Ecosystem in Communications: The Next Decade, a collection of essays prepared for the UK Office of Communications* (Richards, E., Foster, R., & Kiedrowski, T., Eds.). London: Ofcom.

Noam, E. M. (2006, June). Deregulation and market concentration: An analysis of post-1996 consolidations. *Federal Communications Law Journal*, *58*, 539–549.

OECD. (2008). *OECD Statistics*. Retrieved from http://www.oecd.org/

Ordover, J., Saloner, G., & Salop, S. (1990, March). Equilibrium vertical foreclosure. *The American Economic Review*, *80*, 127–142.

Oregon Bar Press Broadcasters Council. (2000). *Media Handbook on Oregon Law and Court System*. Retrieved on September 25, 2008, from http://www.open-oregon.com/New_Pages/media_handbook/toc.html

Owen, B. M. (2008). The temptation of media regulation. *Regulation*, 8–12.

PricewaterhouseCoopers. (2008). *Interactive Advertising Bureau Internet Advertising Revenue Report*.

Samuel, G. S. (2005, November 10). *Australian Communications and Media Authority, 1st Annual Conference*.

Shelanski, H. A. (2006). Antitrust law as mass media regulation: Can merger standards protect the public interest? *California Law Review*, *94*, 370–421. doi:10.2307/20439038

Taplin, J. (2006). The IP TV Revolution. In Castells, M., & Gustavo, C. (Eds.), *The Network Society: From Knowledge to Policy*. Washington, DC: Johns Hopkins Center for Transatlantic Relations.

Viscusi, K., Harrington, J., & Vernon, J. (2005). *Economics of Regulation and Antitrust*. Cambridge, MA: MIT Press.

WAN. (2008). World Press Trends: Newspapers are a Growth Business. *World Association of Newspapers*. Retrieved August 23, 2008, from http://www.wan-press.org/print.php3?id_article=17377

Warf, B. (2003). Mergers and acquisitions in the telecommunications industry, growth and change. *Journal of Urban and Regional Policy*, *34*(3), 321–344.

Yoo, C. S. (2002). Vertical Integration and Media Regulation in the New Economy. *Vanderbilt Public Law and Legal Theory.* Working Paper 2002-01.

ENDNOTES

1 The idea behind television was made earlier. However, in 1928, Philo Farnsworth made the world's first working television system with electronic scanning of both the pickup and display devices.

2 The internet started out as a US military funded project in the late 1960's called the Advanced Research Project Agency Network (ARPANET) which was a secure computer communications network that could survive a nuclear attack. It evolved into a vehicle which was used solely by academic and researchers to communicate and collaborate. However, over the past two decades it has been embraced by the corporate world and has evolved into a mainly commercial entity whose rapid expansion is fuelled by online advertising and selling.

3 For more details on the development of social networking sites see Boyd and Elisson (2007).

4 Other popular social networking sites include Bebo, Skyrock Blog, StudiVZ, Youmeo, Hi5, Orkut, Friendster, and Cyworks.

5 Internationally, Facebook's growth is huge. In Europe the company saw 303% growth, Asia Pacific 458%; Middle East–Africa 403% and Latin America 1055%.

6 Interestingly, the United Kingdom has nearly 40% of all internet advertising revenues generated in Europe, while Germany has 23% and France has 14%. If the US and

European markets are combined, the US would have a 62% share, followed by the UK with 15% and Germany with 8%.

7 Globally television is still the largest advertising medium.

8 For an extensive treatment of the industrial organisation approach to vertical integration Milgrom and Roberts (1992) and Viscusi *et al.* (2005).

9 Where a vertical arrangement can reduce the vigour of competition which existed in these previously competitive segments.

10 The practice where a supplier agrees to sell its customer one product, only if the customer agrees to purchase all of its requirements of another product from the supplier.

11 See Viscusi *et al.* (2005) for an extensive treatment of these issues.

12 See Ordover *et al.* (1990).

13 The double marginalisation effect refers to the case where the price of an input is marked up twice as a result of market power in both input markets. A vertical merger of the firms in both of these markets may help to reduce the size of this mark-up.

14 1980/881/EC

15 1982/3381/EC

16 2004/311/EC.

17 See IP/01/1429

18 See IP/08/24

19 See http://ec.europa.eu/competition/sectors/media/decisions_psb.pdf for an overview of these decisions.

20 The Radio Act was introduced in 1927.

21 The new law permitted one company to own as many as eight stations in the nation's largest local markets, up from a local limit of four stations per market.

22 See Viscusi *et al.* (2005: 255) for a more detailed discussion of this case.

23 D.C. Circuit court found that the FCC failed to provide any basis for retaining either the national television station ownership limit or the cable/ broadcasting ownership cap.

24 D.C. Circuit court found that FCC had failed to justify its remaining local broadcast station ownership limits.

25 See http://www.fcc.gov/ownership/

26 EC, Concluding report on the Sector Inquiry into the provision of sports content over third generation mobile networks, Brussels, 21/09/2005.

Chapter 4
Advertising in Virtual Worlds:
Facilitating a Hierarchy of Engagement

Paul R. Messinger
University of Alberta, Canada

Xin Ge
University of Northern British Columbia, Canada

ABSTRACT

This chapter describes how virtual worlds can be used for advertising and other communications to consumers. To help conceptualize how virtual worlds enable enhanced forms of communications to consumers, the authors introduce a conceptual framework which they call a hierarchy of engagement in advertising communications. They argue that virtual worlds facilitate deeper levels of engagement in this hierarchy. The authors then describe, from a practical standpoint, how to manage the traditional elements of advertising campaigns—message, media, timing, intensity, and budget—in the context of virtual worlds to help achieve deeper levels of engagement, which they argue lead to greater brand recall and loyalty. To put these points in context, they begin with a short history of gaming and social computing. To assist with selection of virtual worlds in which to conduct communication campaigns, the authors present a typology of virtual worlds and provide a description of some extant virtual worlds using this typology. The chapter concludes with a description of needed future work to harness virtual worlds for customer engagement.

INTRODUCTION

Virtual worlds constitute an increasingly prominent communications and entertainment medium in the lives of many adults, teens, and children. As such, virtual worlds constitute an important new vehicle for advertising and customer communications. According to one estimate, 20 to 30 million people regularly participated in virtual worlds in 2006, spending an average of almost twenty-two hours per week within these spaces (Balkin & Noveck, 2006). For those who participate in them, the names of these worlds are household words, including adult worlds, such as Second Life, World of Warcraft, Kaneva, and Entropia Universe; children's worlds, such as Webkinz, Neopets,

DOI: 10.4018/978-1-60566-792-8.ch004

Club Penguin, Habbo, Whyville, TyGirlz, and RuneScape; community-specific worlds, such as Cyworld and HiPiHi; media-focused worlds, such as vSide; and educational worlds, such as ActiveWorlds, there.com, and Forterra Systems. The challenge for businesses and other organizations is to learn to harness this new communications medium.

A key distinguishing feature of virtual worlds is that people interact with each other through digital 3D anthropomorphic characters called avatars. In any given virtual world, thousands of people can interact simultaneously within the same three-dimensional environment. Through their avatars, people can play, explore, communicate, join group activities, design objects, write code to animate objects, trade things, make money, and take classes. Indeed, virtual worlds are believed to have implications that go beyond how we play, to also include how we buy, work, and learn (Bartle, 2006; Balkin & Noveck, 2006). According to a research firm Gartner, Inc., "by the end of 2011, 80 percent of active Internet users (and Fortune 500 enterprises) will have a 'second life'" (i.e., an avatar or presence in a virtual community like Second Life; Gartner, 2007). And generally, since participation is inherently characterized by rich, multifaceted interaction (through avatars) with other people and organizations, virtual worlds afford the possibility of communicating with consumers by interacting with them. Consumers can learn about a company and its products through a process of learning-by-doing and relationship building, rather than through mere exposure to traditional advertising messages in non-interactive media.

Sensing the emergence of a new interactive medium, companies have started to harness virtual worlds for various marketing activities including running in-world virtual stores, promoting virtual and real products, and fostering customer communities. Examples of the early corporate entrants in virtual worlds include Honda, Coca-Cola, Starwood Hotels, and the NBA. In fact, some authors even suggest that virtual worlds and the 3D Internet will become as important to companies in five years as the Web is now (Driver et al., 2008).

Purpose of this Chapter

Given the rapid development and significant potential of virtual worlds as a venue for targeted, interactive marketing communications, companies need to learn to avail themselves of the new communication opportunities that virtual worlds offer. Yet, because of their newness, the study and application of the medium of virtual worlds for advertising and communications is still in its infancy. The purpose of this chapter is to inform media professionals and scholars of the potentialities of virtual worlds to disseminate communications to a target audience, to glean consumer feedback, to enhance audience engagement, and to create consumer value and experiences. In particular, we discuss how companies can use virtual worlds to better achieve the following communications objectives:

- Advertising–pertaining to disseminating traditional communications to customer segments about products or services.
- Customer feedback–pertaining to receiving communications from customers (this includes formal market research).
- Customer engagement with a company's services–pertaining to consumers utilizing a company's products or services in-world (typically on an on-going basis).
- Creation of customer communities–pertaining to fostering rich interactions among groups of customers around particular leisure, learning, or work activities through avatar interaction.

Along these lines, this chapter contains two intended contributions.

First, at a strategic conceptual level, this chapter helps media professionals and academics to better understand and realize the potential of virtual worlds to expand the scope of communications. In particular, we argue that there are various stages of engagement of consumers associated with a communication campaign. Successively greater levels of engagement include consumers (1) receiving company communications, (2) receiving and sending communications, (3) participating with a company in service co-creation, and (4) interacting with a community of consumers to enhance service co-creation. Unlike traditional mass media, which are most suited to one-way communications, the Internet constituted an improved vehicle for consumer engagement. The thesis of this chapter is that 3D virtual worlds go a step further by promoting a synchronous avatar-based social computing context for deeper consumer engagement. That is, virtual worlds constitute a space in which a company can further interact with consumers at all four levels of the proposed "hierarchy of engagement."

Second, at a tactical implementation level, we describe how to manage the traditional elements of a communication campaign—message, media, timing, intensity, and budget—and how these are aligned with key features of virtual worlds. To do this, we first introduce a five-element typology that describes key features of virtual worlds; these elements consist of purpose, population, platform, place, and profit model. We then discuss how the traditional elements of a communication campaign are influenced by considerations associated with these five typology elements.

The remainder of this chapter is organized in five main parts. First, we trace the history of virtual worlds back to its antecedents in electronic gaming and on-line social networking. Second, we describe a typology of worlds with implications for advertising and communications (we will later discuss this typology in relation to traditional elements of a communication campaign in the section "Tactical Considerations: Communication Campaign Elements"). Third, we describe the proposed hierarchy of engagement and how companies can use virtual worlds to facilitate each level of engagement described in the hierarchy. Fourth, we describe new considerations brought into play when managing communications in the realm of virtual worlds. Finally, we conclude and suggest open questions for future consideration.

HISTORICAL PROGRESSION OF VIRTUAL WORLDS

Open or unstructured virtual worlds represent a blending of the elements of immersive 3D gaming environments, developed in the gaming industry over the last 25 years, together with elements of online social networking. This conclusion can be seen by tracing the development of electronic gaming since the 1970s. (For a historical treatment including periods prior to the 1970s, see Castronova, 2002.)

Arcade Games

The video game industry is widely believed to have been launched when *Pong* was released by Atari Interactive in November 29, 1972 (Wiki/pong, 2008). While not the first entrant into this emerging market, it became the first highly successful coin-operated arcade video games (Herman et al., 2008), and was soon followed by *Tank*, *Indy 500*, *Space Invaders*, and *Pac-Man* (Winter, 2008). These games added the element of real-time video interactivity, which enhanced reflexes and provided the excitement of real activity, to the key elements of earlier games which involved (a) strategic and tactical objective-oriented problem-solving (e.g., chess, go, bridge, and poker; see Castronova, 2002, Figure 1) or (b) thematic and fantasy role-playing (e.g., Parker Brothers Co.'s *Monopoly*), or some combination of these (e.g., historic battle simulations, including *D-Day*, *Midway*, *Bismarck*, *Stalingrad*, and sports simulations, including *Stratomatic Baseball* and *Football*). Many of the earliest video games were single-player games played against the computer.

Console Systems

In 1986, the Nintendo Entertainment System was released across the U.S. (previously released as Famicom in Japan), featuring popular characters like Mario, Donkey Kong, Zelda, and Popeye (Herman et al., 2008). Many of these games were initially for a single player, but subsequent generations of games permitted players to compete against each other. Sporting games had been a major success with users of the early console systems; popular fighting games subsequently elevated home console gaming to a new level with such releases as *Street Fighter II* and *Mortal Kombat*. Some modern forms of console systems, such as the Nintendo Wii system, include dynamic user interfaces for various physical games and electronic sports.

LAN Games

LAN (Local Area Network) parties provided yet another venue for experiencing social interaction through gaming. The games in these events were computer-based instead of console-based. LANs required everyone present to load the same software, but then allowed for an essentially unlimited number of participants. Most of the games used in these sessions were first-person shooter (FPS) games, where the objective was to simply, and often (electronically) barehanded, wreak havoc (Jansz & Martens, 2005).

Internet Connectivity

In the mid-1990s, Nintendo, Sega, and Sony introduced more powerful consoles that used compact discs and 32- and 64-bit systems (Herman et al., 2008). With time, Sega would drop out of the console race and focus solely on software development for the different gaming platforms. The next stage of modern gaming consoles took shape with the start of a new millennium. As Personal Computer (PC) and Internet technology grew at a rapid pace, so too did the video game consoles' capabilities. Releases of the PlayStation 2 and Microsoft Xbox offered gamers the ability to connect to the Internet and play against and talk with other gamers. This completely redefined what types of games would be popular in the home. With a network of users able to join in on a game, the landscape of video games became much more expansive, not only geographically, but also in terms of the nature of the social interaction they enabled.

Unstructured Games

Subsequent game forms permitted freedom for the player to roam around a large world, rather than proceed along preset paths only. One particular genre of "god games" afforded the player an omnipotent role. Some games also introduced shared player contributions through the Internet. "Sandbox," "open," or "unstructured" games introduced freedom into gaming that did not previously exist. The *Grand Theft Auto* series, though controversial, serves as an excellent example. These expansive settings and freedom of movement coupled with injections of realism into the surroundings—such as progression of daily time in a 1 second to 1 minute ratio—creates an immersive environment unlike structured gaming (Murray, 2005).

Games with Player Generation of Content

Some games took this trend one step further and presented the gamer with near-total freedom within the game environment, if not always total control over its behaviors. Peter Molyneux introduced the "god game" in 1989, where the player is quite literally near-omnipotent (Au, 2001). The massively successful *The Sims,* its sequels *The Sims*

Online, The Sims 2, and the upcoming *Spore,* provided the player a certain amount of control of their environment and the ability to generate their own content (Kelly, 1994), including "skins" for the avatars, new types of decor for the homes, and new pieces of furniture. Indeed, Electronic Arts (the producer of *Sims* games) claims that over 80% of the game's content is made by users (Ondrejka, 2006). (This alone was not new; in 1996, *Quake* became the first multiplayer, free-form game that provided open standards which allowed for user contributions; Hinton, 2006). Nevertheless, despite the user-generated content, in these environments players are still playing a game with online components; they do not exist in a virtual world. New entrants changed this and took the potential of such Internet frameworks beyond the entertainment realm.

Worlds with Designer-Provided Objectives

In worlds such as *World of Warcraft, Everquest, Lord of the Rings Online*, *City of Heroes/Villains*, and *Age of Conan,* avatars can wander where they wish, but also gain certain skills and strengths by earning experience points (Lastowka & Hunter, 2006). Some of these worlds are beautifully rendered, and players' avatar identities are maintained and develop over time, responding, in part, to significant interaction with other people's avatars. These massively multiplayer on-line role-playing games (MMORPGs) offer small "quests," or designer-provided objectives that serve as games within the larger game (Song & Lee, 2007). Some of the worlds have become very large in their scope and number of participants; *World of Warcraft*, for example, has over 10 million subscribers (Blizzard, 2008). Nevertheless, these MMORPGs reflect the designer-intended gaming tradition which also influenced earlier electronic games.

Social Networking Sites

Although not gaming, *per se*, social networking sites influenced the development of virtual worlds. These environments support members pursuing their own objectives of socializing and sharing of textual and pictorial content (and, increasingly, audio and video content). The first instance of a social networking platform was SixDegrees.com, launched in 1997 (according to Boyd & Ellison, 2007). These platforms allow members to (a) easily create "profiles" with information about themselves, and (b) support the differentiation of public vs. private information on members' profiles, with authorized access to the private aspects of the members' profiles only to their "trusted" circle of friends. Other common features include communication media such as blogging, instant messaging and chat, notifications when the profiles of one's friends have been updated, introductions to friends of friends, reviewing of content and tagging with general comments, and content recommendations based on the members' comments and reviews. The sites can be *geographically-based* assuming a particular language and cultural etiquette (e.g., Cyworld was initially launched in South Korea in 1999), *demographically-based* (e.g., neopets.com is for children, nexopia.com is for teens, and Facebook was originally for Harvard students), or *activity-based* (e.g., LinkedIn for professional introductions, YouTube for video sharing; Dogster and Catster to exchange pet information; hisholyspace.com for faith-based exchange). These environments bring together most elements that have come to be considered under the heading of "web 2.0" technologies in simple, highly usable ways for people who have little to no technical expertise. (For a thoughtful survey of the various social networking sites, together with a historical overview, see Boyd & Ellison, 2007).

Open Virtual Worlds

The distinctive feature of open virtual worlds is the social interaction among people and their avatars that occurs in a 3D immersive shared environment with user-chosen objectives, user-generated content, and social networking tools. In these worlds, people can form relationships as friends, romantic partners, virtual family members, business partners, team members, group members, and online community members. They can also create things, and save, give, or sell what they created to other people. And, as the objects that are created might be desired by others, they suddenly have value in the real-world economy (Lederman, 2007; Lastowka & Hunter, 2006). These various features make virtual worlds as desirable virtual spaces for collaborative play, learning, and work. According to Bartle (2006, page 31), "[f]rom their humble beginnings, virtual worlds have evolved to become major hubs of entertainment, education, and community." And further, according to Balkin & Noveck (2006) "[a]lthough the development of these virtual worlds has been driven by the game industry, by now these worlds are used for far more than play, and soon they will be widely adopted as spaces for research, education, politics, and work."

Overall, purely as a popular form of entertainment, gaming has grown to compete in size with the movie industry. By 2007, the computer and video game industry alone was able to generate $18.85 billion dollars in global sales, including $9.5 billion in game sales and $9.35 billion in console sales (Bangeman, 2008). And, if the predictions for future growth within the industry are correct, this number should more than double by 2010 (Kolodny, 2006).

But beyond entertainment, much activity in virtual worlds is growing in the realms of business, education, and culture. Concerning advertising and promotions, Barnes (2007) provides a list of 126 prominent real life brands in the prominent virtual world Second Life as of August 31, 2007. Concerning retailing and service businesses, in February 2007, there were 25,365 business owners in Second Life (DMD, 2007), most of whom owned stores, rented real estate, or managed clubs. Concerning education, well over 150 universities have a presence in Second Life, and some of them actually conduct classes and other educational activities (Graves, 2008). Business, public organizations, and cultural groups are using the environment for conferencing, public meetings, delivering informational services, and performances or exhibits. As activity grows in virtual worlds, such as Second Life, it is increasingly important for us to understand the implications of these worlds for advertising and customer communications.

TYPOLOGY OF VIRTUAL WORLDS

Turning to the current state of virtual worlds, we provide a compact overview of some of the popular virtual worlds in Table 1 using a five-element typology. This typology also shows the relationship of virtual worlds to electronic gaming and social network sites. We adopt this typology from C. Porter's (2004) analysis of virtual communities (see Messinger et al., 2008).

The typology consists of five elements: purpose (content of interaction), population (participants in interaction), platform (design of interaction), place (location of interaction), and profit model (return on interaction). This is a new "5 P's"–describing virtual communities and virtual worlds. *Purpose* varies according to whether the objective of the activity is strategic, thematic, self-determined (open), educational, media sharing, age focused, or other content focused. *Population* describes the size of the group (two players, a few players, or many players) and distinguishing characteristics of the target user market. *Platform* (or technology platform) describes whether interaction is asynchronous or synchronous, avatar-mediated, and occurs through the Internet, a LAN, a con-

Table 1. Typology applied to selected games, online social networking sites, and virtual worlds*

	Purpose	Population	Platform	Place	Profit Model
Games					
Chess	Strategic Objective	Two Player	Board Game	Collocated	Fixed Fee
Monopoly	Thematic Objective	2–6 Players	Board Game	Collocated	Fixed Fee
FPS - Console	Tactical Objective	1–4 Players	Console Systems	Collocated	Fixed Fee + Extras
FPS–LAN	Tactical Objective	1–1,000+ Players	LANs	Collocated	Fixed Fee + Extras
Internet Scrabble	Strategic Objective	2–6 Players	Synchronous	Dispersed	Variable Fee
The Sims Online	Thematic Objective	Mass Market	Synchronous	Dispersed	Free + Extras
World of Warcraft	Tactical/Thematic Objective	Mass Market	Avatar Mediated Sync.	Dispersed	Fixed Fee + Subs + Extras + Ads
Online Social Networking Sites					
LinkedIn	Themed Network	Businesspeople	Asynchronous	Dispersed	Free+Ads+Extras
Hisholyspace.com	Themed Network	Religiously Affil.	Asynchronous	Dispersed	Free+Ads+Extras
Dogster, Catster	Themed Network	Children	Asynchronous	Dispersed	Free+Ads+Extras
Flixter	Themed Network	Interest Group	Asynchronous	Dispersed	Free+Ads+Extras
YouTube	Themed Network	Interested in Video	Asynchronous	Dispersed	Free+Ads+Extras
MySpace	Open Network	Young Adults–Creative	Asynchronous	Dispersed	Free+Ads+Extras
Facebook	Open Network	Young Adults	Asynchronous	Dispersed	Free+Ads+Extras
Virtual Worlds					
ActiveWorlds	Education	Mass Market	Avatar Mediated Sync.	Dispersed	Subs+Extras+Ads
Forterra Systems	Education	Mass Market	Avatar Mediated Sync.	Dispersed	Subs+Extras+Ads
HiPiHi	Self-Determined	Chinese	Avatar Mediated Sync.	Dispersed	Subs+Extras+Ads
Sony PlaySt. Home	Teen Play	Plays &.Owners	Avatar Mediated Sync.	Hybrid	Subs+Extras+Ads
Vside	Media Sharing	Young People	Avatar Mediated Sync.	Dispersed	Subs+Extras+Ads
Webkinz	Child's Play	Children	Avatar Mediated Sync.	Hybrid	Ancillaries +Extras
Second Life	Self-Determined	Mass Market	Avatar Mediated Sync.	Dispersed	Subs+Extras+Ads

*We apply C. Porter's (2004) typology of virtual communities to games, online social networking sites, and virtual worlds, using our own descriptors for each of the five typology elements.

FPS = First Person Shooter Game Subs–Subscriptions

Ads–Advertising Hybrid–Both Collocated and Dispersed Sync–Synchronous

sole system, phone-based, or face-to-face. *Place* describes whether participants are collocated or geographically dispersed; whether they engage in the world from home, work, their automobiles, or their cell-phones; and whether the interaction is completely or only partially virtual. *Profit model* describes whether the business model associated with the platform is based on a fixed user-fee, subscriptions, fee per use, advertising from sponsors, virtual extras sold to users, or real-world ancillaries.

At this point in the chapter, we include this table as a current "snapshot" of some virtual worlds. The table also describes how some virtual worlds differ from each other, and how they can be seen as related conceptually and historically to the electronic-game industry and to social network sites. Later, we will use the typology as an organizing principle for consideration of tactical issues involving message, media, timing, intensity, and budget. Now, we turn to development of the "hierarchy of engagement."

STRATEGIC CONSIDERATIONS: HIERARCHY OF ENGAGEMENT

From a strategic perspective, we propose that there are four levels of engagement with consumers, as described in Figure 1. While we believe that these four levels of customer engagement apply generally to the "real world," we argue in this section that virtual worlds are particularly suited to engagement with consumers at all four levels of this hierarchy.

In particular, the proposed hierarchy of engagement works progressively as follows. First, a company can send one-way communications. Such communications characterize advertisements in traditional media that expose consumers to particular messages. Second, a company can engage consumers in two-way communications. Such communications can include feedback being sought by the company, possibly as formal market research or less formal measures of customer satisfaction (to which the company may respond over time by enhancing its product or service offering). Alternatively, the consumer may seek assistance in utilizing or benefiting from the company's products or services, and the company may respond with advice. Third, the company and consumer can work together toward service co-creation. This takes two-way communication beyond just dialog to a process of joint activity whereby a collaborative relationship is established that provides customized service-value for the consumer, and both the company and the consumer help to co-create this value. Fourth, the company can foster an environment that supports the emergence of consumer communities revolving around the company's products and services. In these customer communities, individual can share information about how to make best use of the service and they may even interact socially or professionally in related activities that add social value to the company's services. We hypothesize that deeper levels of engagement in this hierarchy result in greater brand recall, purchase incidence, and loyalty to the firm. We leave it to future research to verify this hypothesis.

Figure 1. Hierarchy of engagement

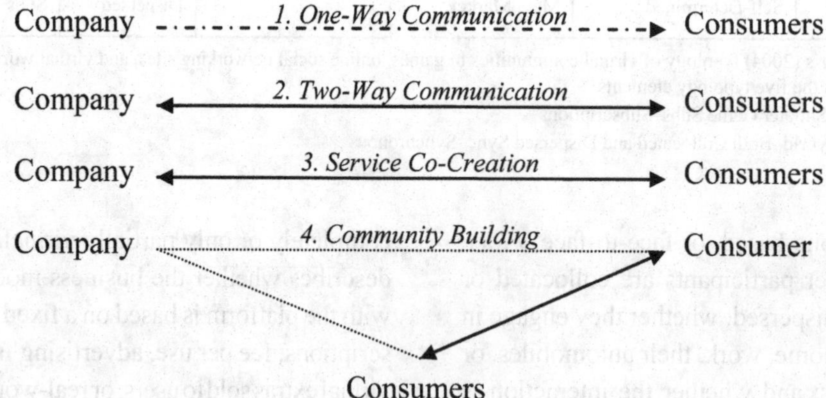

To put our hierarchy in context, we first compare it with the well-known "hierarchy of effects" models proposed by practitioners and researchers. Consumer psychologists would describe hierarchy of effects models as a three-stage process underlying consumer purchase behavior: cognition–affect–behavior (or "C-A-C" for "cognitive-affective-conative"). This is occasionally described more evocatively as "think-feel-do." The most influential formulations of the hierarchy of effects models include (1) St. Elmo Lewis's sales funnel (1898; see ProvenModels), and Strong's related AIDA model (1925), both of which describe a four-step strategy for selling: ensure attention - arouse interest - create desire - get action; (2) Daniel Starch's proposition regarding advertising in 1923: "To be effective, an advertisement must be. .. seen - read - believed - remembered - acted upon"; (3) Lavidge and Steiner's expanded model: ignorance - awareness - knowledge - liking - preference - conviction–action (1961); and (4) Colley's DAGMAR (i.e., acronym for Defining Advertising Goals for Measured Advertising Results) model designed for measurement: unawareness - awareness - comprehension - conviction - action (1961).[1] All of these treatments involve stages of consumer reactions to marketing stimuli from product unawareness to actual purchase.

Unlike the hierarchy of effects models that focus on the internal psychological processes of consumers, the framework described in this chapter identifies different forms of social engagement that potentially influence the consumer. This includes (a) one-way communication, (b) two-way communication, (c) value co-creation around a product or service, and (d) collaborative community building surrounding an activity. Traditional advertising is limited to the first of these and personal selling generally involves elements of the second as well. The proposed hierarchy of engagement, by contrast, puts these two in context and notes two deeper forms of engagement arising from a range of interaction with the service provider and with the surrounding social context in which the consumer is embedded. Thus, the hierarchy of engagement helps one identify (and potentially make use of) different forms of social interaction and influence in virtual worlds communications.

We should acknowledge past work on engagement, but this work has also tended to come from the perspective of the internal psychological processes of consumers, rather than considering different forms of social interaction and influence. Thus, engagement has been considered in terms of (a) enhancing the effectiveness of advertising processing (Wang, 2006; Green, 2007), (b) storage of the message in memory (White, 2007), and (c) measures of attentiveness to brand messages (Plummer et al., 2006; Plummer et al., 2007).

We also should acknowledge work categorizing social computing behaviors, including (a) inactives, (b) spectators (read blogs; watch video from other users; listen to podcasts; read online forums; read customer ratings/reviews), (c) joiners (maintain profile on a social networking site; visit social networking sites), (d) collectors (use RSS web feeds; add "tags" to web pages or photos; "vote" for Web sites online), (e) critics (post ratings/reviews of products/services; comment on someone else's blog; contribute to online forums; contribute to/edit articles in a wiki), and (f) creators (publish a blog; publish your own Web pages; upload video you created; upload audio/music you created; write articles or stories and post them). This categorization, termed the "Social Technographics™" by Forrester Research, is based on surveys of 4,475 US adults in December 2006 and 4,556 youth in October 2006 to learn about their use of social computing technology adoption (Li et al, 2007). This categorization works at the individual consumer and market segment level, unlike our hierarchy of engagement which works at the level of the type of engagement (one-way, two-way, value co-creation, and community value reinforcement).[2]

Having placed the hierarchy of engagement in the context of related past work, we now discuss how virtual worlds facilitate the four levels of engagement of the proposed hierarchy.

One-Way Communication

The simplest use of virtual worlds is to target consumer populations with commercial messages and other activities to build brand loyalty, just as is done with traditional advertising and public relations. This can be done in several ways, including (1) simple brand presence in the form of a named store or island; (2) selling or giving free samples through vending machines or some other means; (3) using in-world 3D hyperlinked objects that open up a pop-up window to a company's 2D Internet website upon being touched by a user's avatar (a process called "tunneling"); (4) banner ads on virtual billboards (containing virtual landmarks); (5) in-world advertising can be disseminated via instant messaging capabilities; (6) sponsorship of in-world cultural events, such as plays, fashion shows, races, parties; (7) product placement in thematic games such as Grand Theft Auto, and (8) advertising in in-world newspapers, newsletters, radio, or video shows. For example, Figure 2 provides screenshots of three companies with presence in Second Life (Dell Island, the Nissan car trial facility, and the offices of PA [management] Consulting services). Figure 3 shows examples of retail presence in Second Life. Figure 4 lists prominent real life brands with a virtual presence in Second Life as of August 31, 2007.

Figure 2. Examples of corporate presence in Second Life

Figure 3. Examples of retail presence in Second Life

Figure 4. Prominent brands in Second Life (Barnes, 2007)

Adidas, Amazon, AMD, AOL, Bain & Company, Banton Dell Books, BBC Radio 2, Best Buy Co. Inc, BMD, Calvin Klein, Circuit City, Cisco, CNET, Coca-Cola, Coldwell Banker, Comcast, Crayon, Daily Telegraph, Dell, Fiat, H&R Block, Heineken, IBM, ING, Intel, Leo Burnett, Major League Baseball, Mazda Europe, Mercedes Benz, Microsoft, MTV, NBA, NBC, Nissan, Phillips, Playboy, Pontiac/GM, Random House/Bantam, Reebok, Renault, Reuters, Sears, Sony, Sprint, Starwood-Loft Hotels, Sun Microsystems, Talis, Thompson NETg, Toyota, Visa Europe, Warner Bros Music, Wired Magazine, Xerox, and Yankee Stadium

Firms are still experimenting to learn which forms of mass communication and merchandising work best. "We are there for a learning experience," said Doug Meacham, Circuit City's manager of infrastructure services, during an interview with Direct magazine. "In the near future this is going to be a fairly seamless extension of the web that you deal with today." (DMD, 2007). In addition, virtual activities have occasionally been picked up by traditional press, creating a crossover effect whereby a company's virtual presence can lead to news stories and public relations impressions in traditional medial (see Figure 5).

Overall, the effectiveness of virtual worlds in one-way communications is reflected in the following quote: "Just as the web replaces and extends the capabilities of traditional print media, Second Life is extending the capabilities

Figure 5. Media impressions after appearing in Second Life (* Mentions of Second Life in relation to the company name multiplied by total impressions for that medium (includes online, print, and broadcast), January--May 2007. Source: DMD, 2007)*

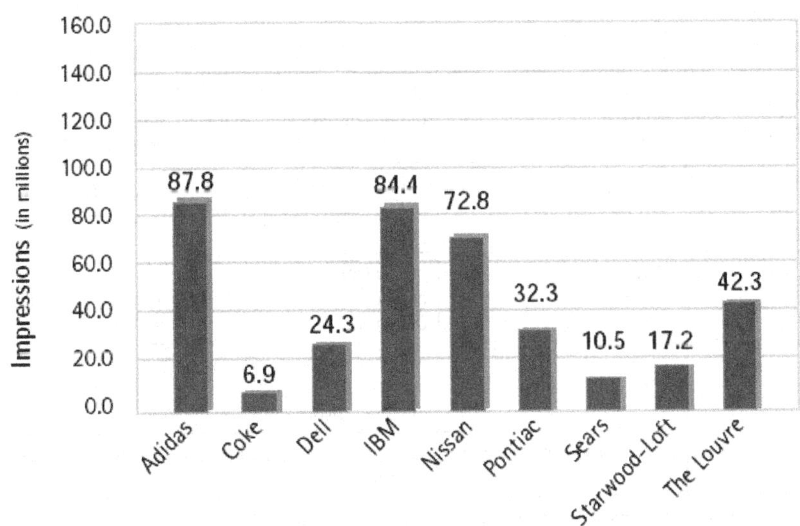

of broadcast media and chat. Second Life now surpasses the intensity of broadcast advertising at an even more favorable price point than print" (Source: *MediaPost*).

Two-way Communication

The next level of consumer engagement involves also attending to informal customer feedback and formal market research. Informal customer feedback can be elicited in several ways, including (1) instant messages or emails to the company (prompted when an avatar touches an in-world 3D hyperlink), (2) in world comment logs (using various platforms in-world and with pop-up Internet windows), and (3) in-world conversations between service avatar staff and customers. Formal market research techniques that harness virtual worlds for customer feedback are summarized in Table 2. For each technique, the table indicates practices before the Internet, how the Internet changed them, and how application of technologies in synthetic worlds will likely lead to further changes in the future.

As indicated in the table, with the advent of the Internet, focus groups began to be carried out using chat forums, online conferencing, and learning systems. Now with virtual worlds, avatars can sit in a virtual room (possibly inspecting virtual prototype products), or they can participate in a virtual field trip to, for example, examine a new retail concept or a proposed real estate development. In addition, both Internet methods and virtual worlds can show panels of head shots of the avatars, or the participants themselves, in conjunction with the other views. Such focus group services are already available in Second life (Terdiman, 2007),[3] and some managers state that "Second Life is great to get very honest feedback, more honest than in any focus group, because in a focus group, you sort of know what's expected from you. Second Life residents are more extroverted and honest about their feelings" (according to a statement in a conference in Second Life from Achim Muellers, head of brand relations and co-operations at BMW).

Concerning survey collection, the Internet has greatly facilitated computer mediated data collection, using adaptable webforms that input information directly into a database. In virtual worlds, the survey can be taken in an immersive field setting, possibly with the support of field avatars acting as lab assistants, or in the process of touring a building or natural site. These sur-

Table 2. Market research techniques: changes associated with virtual worlds

Market Research		Standard Methods	2-D Internet	Virtual Worlds
Data Type	Focus Groups & Depth Interviews	conference rooms; living rooms; & field meetings	chat forums; online conferencing; learning systems	room view (of avatars); virtual field trips; head-shots; hybrids
	Surveys	mail; phone; mall-intercept; hybrid	Adaptable webforms input to a database; email or web panels	immersive field setting; avatar support; in-world panels
	Test Markets	very expensive	online stores; chat forums and blog discussion	in-world roll-out of virtual products
	Observation	human observation	webpage clicks; email openings; in-store sensors	usage patterns of personal objects & specially-oriented structures; in-store kiosks
	Ethnographic Consumer Research	social context of consumption	netnography: social context of virtual communities	moves netnography from analysis of text to a range of virtual interactions

(See Messinger and Ge, 2009 for further background on market research and virtual worlds.)

veys can be taken in-world through scripts that provide the questions through a sequence of chat lines or instant messages, or by having one's avatar touch an in-world hyperlink (that is part of a survey ATM) that calls a pop-up menu with a website containing various webforms. In Second Life, there is even an island devoted to offering such survey-taking opportunities to residents for (generally small amounts of) Linden Dollars. Two large survey websites that can be accessed in this way are www.gameATM.com, a privately run site, and www.MyLindens.com, an official site of Linden Lab promoted on Money Island in Second Life. To help with ongoing collection of data on Second Life, there is even a "First Opinions Panel in Second Life," consisting of a sample of consumers being tracked periodically by a market research firm to monitor common behaviors and attitudes of residents.

Concerning test markets, the Internet made possible online product distribution and facilitated online reviews and word-of-mouth on chat forums and blog discussions. In virtual worlds this can be expanded to roll-out of virtual products to ascertain the satisfaction of users and the adoption rates, and possibly evidence of carry-over as indicators or influencers of success in the real world. Starwood Hotel, the international lodging chain, has used Second Life to enable collaboration with potential customers to test their ideas involving large investments. In this way, the Aloft brand of Starwood Hotels and Resorts was released in Second Life just before it was launched in the real world (Wasserman, 2007). Mazda has also ventured into designing an experiential marketing vehicle, and the car's designers even appear in virtual form to launch the new model. Nissan also sells cars from an eight-story vending machine as a form of test market. Toyota also sells customizable virtual Scions and offers "how-to" classes for residents wishing to make customizations. Adidas even allows customers to design their own sneaker in Second Life, helping Adidas to design more remarkable "first life" sneakers.

Concerning direct observation, with the advent of the Internet, methods have moved from examination of human activities to webpage clicks, email openings and in-store sensors. With virtual worlds, this has expanded to examination of in-world usage patterns, including utilization of in-store kiosks. Ethnography also moved first to the Internet in the form of "netnography" to study the social context of virtual communities (Kozinets, 2002). With virtual worlds, netnography can also involve a range of virtual interactions in virtual worlds, including avatar-to-avatar interviews, focus groups, analysis of virtual artefacts, and more participative methods of data collection that utilize the range of methods from ethnography. These methods can go far beyond the earlier methods of netnography that mostly used textual processing and analysis from chat room and discussion boards.

Overall, attentiveness to customer feedback and market research serve a dual function. In the first instance, these activities generate valuable data useful for modifying the design of products and services. In addition, these activities engage the consumer more deeply with the firm. Consumers become a part of an extended "design team" and may feel greater identification with a firm's products and services.

Service Co-Creation

The third step of customer engagement involves co-creating service with the firm. The key to offering such service is to build a combined service delivery platform with multiple points of contact that include (1) in-world service interface, (2) Internet service, information, and e-commerce connectivity, and (3) real human service delivery, all of which connect to a (4) centralized database that keeps track of (a) customers' consumption history and patterns, (b) inventory, and (c) resource management used to create inventory. This, presumably, is a deeper form of interaction than the previous two steps. (For background on dealing with these issues, see Messinger et al., 2009a).

Several firms are actively offering in-world service delivery: As noted in a report about Second Life, "Brands that score most highly on the [brand impact] metric tend to go beyond showing their products, provoking virtual versions and web links. They provide opportunities for deeper engagement by making a brand-relevant contribution to the community and creating opportunities for interaction such as co-creation and customization of products" (DMD, 2007).

Appendix 3 provides an extensive lists of services offered on Second Life (together with the location therein), including consumer services, media services, government services, tourism services, public relations and marketing services, educational services, and training activities. Service delivery can involve customizing and downloading digital content, education and training, remotely accessing government or business office services, or ordering real-world physical products. For example, Thomson's NetG corporate training division, which provides custom training solutions for corporate clients on Microsoft and Cisco products, reportedly makes \$10,000 a month by providing training, mentoring, and customized podcasts for their corporate clients in Second Life. Similarly, the University of California, Davis, has created a virtual hallucination simulator to give psychiatry residents a better understanding of what schizophrenic patients actually experience. And universities like Harvard Law School use Second Life to host virtual classes and conferences complete with video, sound, and PowerPoint presentations. (As examples, Figure 6 shows a typical outdoor classroom environment, an interactive 3D tutorial, and an indoor meeting location.) Other services involve customization. For instance, Sears, in partnership with IBM, is working on allowing customers to create a virtual version of a kitchen, complete with exact dimensions and layout.

Figure 6. Examples of educational and training service facilities in Second Life

Panel A. Outdoor Classroom

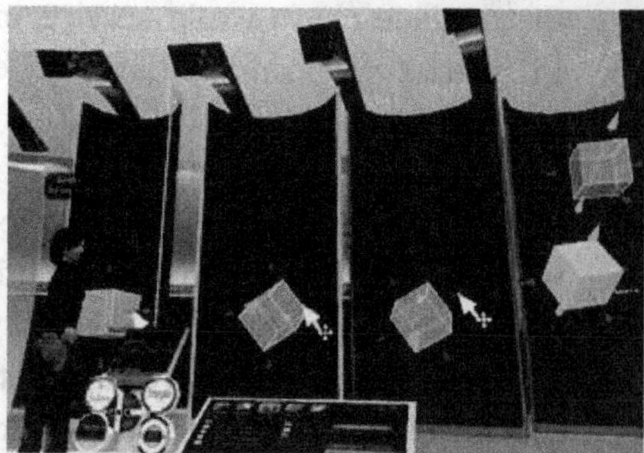

Panel B. Interactive 3D Tutorial

Panel C. Indoor Meeting Location

Challenges to offering such services involve thoughtful adaptation of a company's "real-world" services to virtual worlds recognizing the special characteristics and limitations of the medium. In particular, we note the following: (1) It is helpful to make stores and products relevant to the virtual lives of people in-world; (2) it is important to educate "newbies" and to make the interface as user-friendly as possible; (3) it is essential, even after creating a sim (i.e., a simulated environment or real estate development), store, or product, to promote it to residents; and finally, (4) one must recognize the technological constraints of the new medium. In particular, locations often have capacity limitations, so that no more than forty to sixty residents can be engaged at a time in retail environments or sponsored events, such as fashion shows. In addition to generating avatar traffic, it is necessary for virtual businesses to use the same tactics that e-commerce sites use to generate web traffic. These tactics include in-world promotions, appealing to the in-world search engine, listing firms' special offerings and activities on event boards, word-of-mouth, offering "freebies" (one of the biggest draws for people to virtual stores in Second Life), and locating stores in high trafficked areas such as virtual malls.

Overall, offering services in virtual worlds involves kinesthetic (dynamic) participative creative collaboration of customers with a firm. This is deeper engagement with customer than sending messages and listening to customer feedback and market research. This engagement may also carry over to greater loyalty to a firm's non-virtual services.[4]

Community Building

The deepest level of engagement goes beyond a customer interacting with the product or service provider, to also interact with other enthusiasts by participating with a community of like-minded individuals using a product or service. This is a deeper level of engagement because interacting with a firm, in the first place, to get the products or services is a prerequisite to interacting with other customers in user communities. Firms can facilitate such user communities by creating community enablers in virtual worlds of various types.

A virtual community depends on combining communication and content to foster exchange of information. By its nature, the information exchange allows people to learn about each other as they learn more about the focal topics of the community. The commercial application is to have people engage in an activity revolving around a company's products or services. This can happen for sports (running, soccer, ice skating, parachuting), dance-sport, matchmaking, music, drama, and various other activities. Hagel and Armstrong (1997) identify various motivations for consumers joining online communities, including (1) shared interest, (2) relationship building, and (3) transaction. Building on these thoughts, Rothearmel and Sugiyama (2001) describe several types of associated communities, including (a) communities of interest (composed of individuals who share a common interest, hobby or skill set), (b) communities of relationship (composed of individuals who share some intense life experience, such as a disease diagnosis), (c) communities of exchange (composed of individuals who share information to facilitate economic exchange–such as, a group of boat owners), and (d) communities of practice (composed of individuals who work, learn, and innovate together). Perhaps the community of interest and community of practice models seem to offer the greatest commercial potential.

These communities have been argued (Wegner et al., 2002) to develop, as described by Figure 7, with people of shared interests finding each other in Stage 1, coming together to participate in online forums beginning in Stage 2, and becoming increasingly active in Stage 3. The communities then become more dispersed in Stage 4 and are still remembered by participants in Stage 5. To play a formative role, the key thing for a sponsoring organization to do is to see that the people come together in online forums in Stage 2.

Figure 7. Stages of development of communities of practice (Level of activity is shown on the vertical axis)

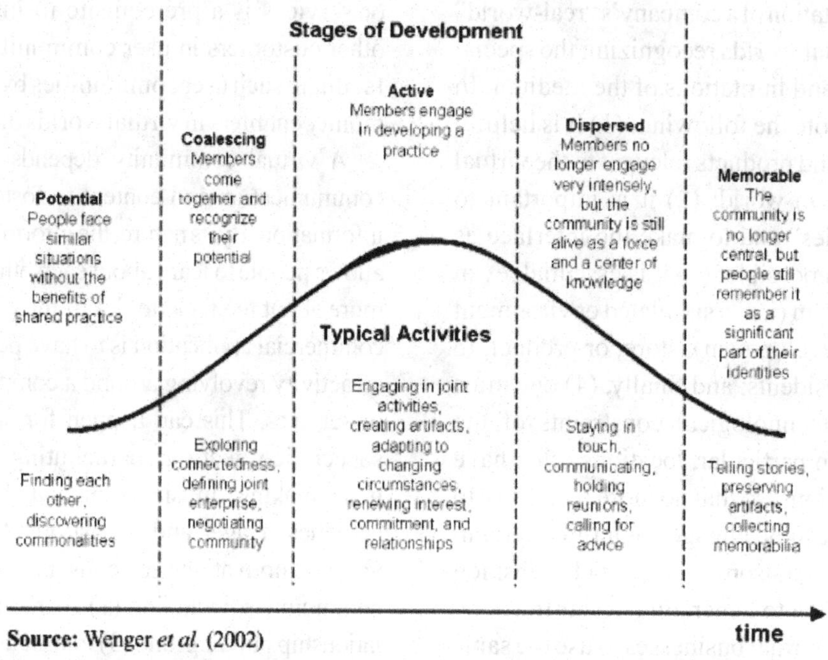

Source: Wenger *et al.* (2002)

A community of practice revolves around a shared domain of interest, shared membership (where members form relationships to engage in joint activities, help each other, and share information), and shared practice (consisting of repertoires of resources: experiences, stories, tools, and ways of addressing recurring problems). Some communities of practice are quite small; some are very large, often with a core group and many peripheral members. Some are local, and some cover the globe. Some meet mainly face-to-face, and some mostly online. Some are within an organization, and some include members from various organizations. Some are formally recognized, often supported with a budget; and some are completely informal and even invisible. Communities develop their practices through a variety of activities, including problem solving, gathering of information, seeking experience, reusing assets, coordinating synergistic activities, discussing developments, documentation of projects, mapping knowledge, and identifying gaps. The concept of community of practice has found a number of practical applications in business, organizational design, government, education, professional associations, development projects, and civic life (Wenger et al., 2002; Wenger & Snyder, 2000; Wenger, 2004, 2001, and 20042004).

To facilitate a community of users, the firm can (1) host discussion boards, (2) organize expert or consumer reviews and recommendations, (3) organize user events, including practices, competitions, user exhibitions, and social outings, (4) provide expert advice and a wiki knowledge system for shared information, and (5) create a second-hand market or auction site for products and for sharing resources inexpensively. Each activity is different and requires a slightly different bundle of supporting activities.

In virtual worlds, there already are numerous examples of communities of interest, relationship, exchange, and practice users. One interesting aspect of virtual worlds is that the community can go beyond sharing ideas to also sharing virtual experiences. For example, individuals in the premier virtual world, Second Life, share virtual interactions, as evidenced by comments such as virtual friends saying, "We met at Reuters" or "We boogied at Pontiac" or even "we dined on Chicken Kiev at Sublime." An example of a periodically organized activity is that every two weeks a local resident hosts a "girls' night out" inside Second Life with a group of avatars who congregate at the iVillage loft. Other group activities include virtual champagne parties and participation in a fashion show, as well as mingling with celebrities like Arianna Huffington (DMD, 2007). Other activities include dating clubs for residents of each U.S. state; people acting out Shakespeare plays; groups associated with particular virtual locations such as Venice (consisting of renters and frequent visitors to that virtual location); organization for gay and lesbian people, and numerous others. Indeed, there is a separate search facility in Second Life for groups, with thousands to choose from. Similar groups exist in Kaneva and other virtual worlds, as well as on Facebook and other social computing websites.

In all of these cases, virtual worlds go beyond facilitating one-way communications, collecting market research information, and delivering services, to foster ongoing social activity around shared interests, experiences, set of relationships, or work practices. While the computer mediated environments involve virtual interaction, the people who interact with each other are real–and so are their shared experiences. If an organization can stimulate such social engagement around its services or products, this goes far beyond sending messages by traditional media.

TACTICAL CONSIDERATIONS: COMMUNICATION CAMPAIGN ELEMENTS

We now turn to the tactics of managing the traditional elements of a communication campaign–the objective, message, media, timing, intensity, and budget—for virtual worlds. Following Table 3, these match up with the five typology elements of virtual worlds: purpose, population, platform, place, and profit model.

Message

When choosing worlds as a vehicle for one-way communication (as well as deeper levels of engagement), a desirable criterion for world selection, building on a general principle of traditional media selection, is to match the communication message with the purpose of the world in question. That is, it is desirable to achieve a "message-world fit." Obvious examples are advertising toys, school supplies, and Sega DS systems on children's worlds, or advertising software and books on education-focused worlds.

As enumerated in Appendix 1, there are numerous different types of virtual worlds, including (1) self-determined virtual worlds (e.g.,

Table 3. Advertising and customer communications in virtual worlds

Communications Elements	*Virtual World Elements*	*Principle*
Message	Purpose	Message-World Fit
Media	Population	Demographic & Psychographic Targeting
Timing	Platform	Synchronous or Asynchronous Communication Company or Consumer Initiated Mediated by Avatar, Web Page, Audio, or Video
Intensity	Place	At Home, Work, Auto, or Cell
Budget	Profit Model	Up-Front or "Pay as You Go"

Second Life, Kaneva, Entropia Universe), (2) education-focused worlds (e.g., Forterra systems, ActiveWorlds), (3) community self-determined worlds (e.g., Cyworld, HiPiHi), (4) media-focused (e.g., vSide), and (4) children-focused worlds (e.g., Webkinz, Whyville, Habbo, Club Penguin, RuneScape). One can promote products in self-determined worlds by linking the advertising message with particular themes or groups active within particular virtual worlds.

Media

Media selection should generally be done to target suitable demographic and psychographic segments. As relates to most virtual worlds, the international composition of participants is both a blessing and a curse. The reach is potentially global, but, for many worlds, geographic targeting is much less possible than in such media as newspapers, radio, local television, or even Facebook. Thematic targeting to consumers of particular lifestyles, however, is quite feasible, by focusing on particular themed virtual worlds and electronic games.

Appendix 2 provides a cross-section of various current virtual worlds varying in several dimensions. A basic challenge for advertising agencies concerning target market selection will be to become acquainted with the demographic, psychographic, and geographic characteristics, as well as the membership sizes and participation levels, of the various extant virtual worlds and electronic games for media placement. Manuals, electronic guides, and other services that provide this kind of information are likely to grow to assist with future in-world advertising.

As an example, Second Life, the premier self-determined world, has grown in residents from 1 in 2001 to 8.3 million by August 2007, 2 million of which had been active in the last 60 days, and during the same time period, around 20,000-35,000+ users were in-world at any given time (Messinger et al., 2009b). In April 2010, 488,694 customers spent money in-world (Second Life, 2010).The average age of the adult SL world is 33 and the average age of the teen SL world is 15, with 41.1% of all residents female. There is global participation including residents from the U.S. (31.2%); France (12.7%); Germany (10.5%); U.K. (8.1%); the Netherlands (6.6%); Spain (3.8%); Brazil (3.8%); Canada (3.3%); Belgium (2.6%); Italy (1.9%); Australia (1.5%); Switzerland (1.3%); Japan (1.3%); Sweden (1.0%), and many other countries (Second Life Economic Statistics, 2008). In our own survey of 197 SL residents, we found that nearly 75 percent of participants made less than $60,000 annually, while only two percent earned over $100,000. Most participants had completed high school, completed their undergraduate degree, or at least spent some time in university or college (87%), while only five percent had graduated with their Masters or PhD degree.

The segment size of children's worlds is also large and growing. According to *The NY Times* (October 28, 2007), the number of unique monthly visitors to Club Penguin more than doubled in the previous year, to 4.7 million from 1.9 million, while the traffic on Webkinz.com grew to 6 million visitors from less than 1 million, citing as a source Media Metrix, an online-usage tracking company.

Some worlds, especially fantasy ones (such as World of Warcraft), offer virtual environments quite separate from the real world in which people can *immerse*. Other worlds, for example the ones focusing on education and training, offer opportunities for people to *augment* their real-world activities and social networks with their virtual world activities and online social networks.

Timing

As compared to traditional communications, communications timing in virtual worlds differs in a fundamental way when customer interaction takes the multifaceted engagement forms shown in the hierarchy of Figure 1. For traditional communications, timing is asynchronous, planned, and initiated by the firm. For virtual worlds, however, timing is often synchronous, more spontaneous, and initiated by consumers. In addition, communication with customers is frequently mediated by avatar representatives.

To illustrate this point, Figure 8 shows the schedule of timing and intensity of a traditional advertising campaign. This schedule shows the media categories used, the exact communications vehicle (e.g., newspaper name or television or radio station), the cost per appearance of an ad, the general scheduling of the ad appearances over a 12 period (month) time-frame, the total number of ad appearances in each communications vehicle, the cost for each communications vehicle, and the total cost.

For one-way communications carried out in virtual worlds (see Figure 1), this same type of schedule should be constructed. The only difference is that the media categories would include chosen virtual worlds (e.g., from among those listed in Appendices 1 and 2) as well as types of communications vehicles in each virtual world.

For two-way communications, the firm or its customers may initiate the process. For market research, for instance, timing is still similar to traditional advertising campaigns, often done asynchronously and initiated by the firm. When surveys are used, contact is typically initiated in-world using instant messages and emails; possibly coupled with virtual advertisements. Test markets are also planned in advance and initiated by the firm, often in conjunction with an elaborate traditional advertising campaign. Focus groups, by contrast, are carried out synchronously and mediated by field avatars. In this context, it is important to manage the style of interaction and the impression created by field avatars (analogous to management of interaction with moderators in real focus groups). Direct observation and ethnographic observation are also carried out synchronously, and ethnographic observation, in particular, also requires management of field avatars. More informal feedback may be initiated by the consumer or, after a service encounter, initiated by the firm.

Figure 8. Traditional advertising campaign schedule

	Cost	1	2	3	4	5	6	7	8	9	10	11	12	#	$
General Publications															
Wall Street Journal	27,972	2	1	2	1					2	3	1	2	13	391,608
Business Week	11,920	1	1	1	1					1	1	1	1	8	95,360
Sports Illustrated	20,290	1		1	1					1			1	5	101,450
Vertical Publications															
Advertising Age	5,200	1	1		1					1	1	1		6	31,200
Journal of Marketing	520	1			1					1			1	4	2,080
Insurance Magazine	725	1			1					1			1	4	2,900
The Secretary	950	1			1					1			1	4	3,800
Television Prime Time															
Dallas	2,200	2	1	2	2					1	2	1	1	12	26,400
New York	6,050	2	2	1	1					2	2		2	12	16,500
Boston	1,500	2	2	2	2					2		2	1	13	19,500
Television—Late															
Dallas	550	2	1	1	1					2	1	1	2	11	6,050
New York	1,500	1	1	2	2					1	1	2	1	11	16,500
Boston	750	1	2	1	1					1	2	1	2	11	8,250
Newspapers															
San Francisco	8,211	2	2	2	2					2	3	1	3	17	139,587
Los Angeles	9,840	2	2	2	2					3	1	2	2	16	157,440
Chicago	10,769	2	2	2	2					2	2	3	1	16	172,304
Totals		24	18	19	22					24	19	16	22	164	1,247,029

Source: Messinger (1995)

For service co-creation, communication and engagement is quite a bit different. For a multi-modal service delivery system including human, automated, and hybrid points of contact, the communications are typically synchronous. The firm can use automation for certain points of contact, with planning of an automated response, but typically it is necessary to have a human backup response in the form of a telephone/skype/audio conversation or an email/instant message response. Some firms make a point of responding to emails within 24 hours, which is good, but other firms have instantaneous response through a chat system or a call centre. Managing the queue is an important consideration, of course, to avoid customer frustration with the process. Often, customer delivery may be mediated by an avatar, as it is in in-world

E-Commerce Settings

In this case, attending to impression and exception management and working out scripts of communication messages for various contingencies is very important. Here the service delivery system is part of the communications package. One should engage in service blueprinting to work out the likely paths that consumers take through the process and the resources devoted to the various stages. Things are really quite different in so many ways from a traditional advertising campaign, because customers may have contact with many different people within an organization. The organization becomes the communication delivery vehicle, but the consumer is typically the initiator of the process. And along with any messages intended by the company is a subtext to the effect "this employee/organization is/is not efficient and caring." Since the customer must co-create the process, it is critical for the customer to be educated about his or her role in overall service delivery. This takes us into the service management literature, applying the principles to virtual worlds.

Related to community building, communications occur between customers in various forms of word-of-mouth. Timing for this level of engagement differs most from the timing of traditional advertising because engagement occurs synchronously, is initiated mostly by the customers, and may well occur between field avatars or other forms of computer mediated communications, like Facebook or YouTube sites. The firm can influence communications by advertising in a virtual world like Second Life, or on social network sites like Facebook, but typically that is not enough. The firm must go considerably further by organizing events, hosting or sponsoring chat networks. Everyone knows that the firm has an economic interest in sponsoring or helping to mediate these activities, but the firm should make an effort to appear to be objective. Formal dispute resolution protocols are desirable to avoid the appearance of any firm bias in the process. At the same time, the firm must have a business model which involves being paid for some form of supporting service or ancillary products. Managing the process is similar to service delivery since the process may require process blueprinting and managing points of contact. At the same time, the firm is the facilitator, and the interaction may not involve the firm directly at all, which requires a more subtle hands-off management approach, in setting up social resources for the community and the virtual ecosystem as a whole. At the same time, a quick response from the firm may be needed when it is asked for. This is an art–to some extent, each industry has different technological features, structure, and historical patterns of behavior. Commonalities and convergent best practices should be learned across industries, but some improvisation and customization of the interaction and role within the virtual community is typically required, and perhaps quite profitable.

Intensity and Budge

Concerning message intensity, traditional communications can be received at various points of contact–at home, work, and on the road, and in particular geographical localities on a cell-phone. The same can be said for virtual communications. One difference is that the consumer must go to and open up the virtual world on his or her machine. Traditional advertisements often interrupt consumers from their other planned activities; it is not yet known whether most consumers feel equally interrupted by promotional messages in virtual worlds. In Second Life, people have more latitude of choosing where they wish to visit, whether it be environments where scripts and promotions are not permitted, or environments where promotions are encouraged.

As for budget, a difference is that most traditional communication must be budgeted before beginning the campaign. Common methods of setting the advertising budget are (1) setting the advertising/sales ratio, (2) matching the competitors' absolute spending or spending ratio, and (3) using an objective and task method. The last involves setting specific measurable objectives, such as a percent aided and unaided brand and advertising recall, or trial and repeat rates, at a particular instant in time, and then determining the timing, sequence, and number of tasks needed to attain these objectives. While the last approach is the most conceptually appealing, the first approach is easiest to carry out since a traditional income statement already contains the needed information. For virtual worlds, the budget is typically more "pay as you go," the cost may be based on the number of clicks or on a percentage of some measurable outcome. While the same three approaches are relevant to setting a virtual world budget, one should adjust the budgeting approach to ratio forms (similar to the first approach above) in order to allow for more communication automatically if sufficient revenues are being generated. To "cap" or limit communications spending in a period, when sales and profits continue to be generated would be a mistake in such a case.

In sum, this section has described how to adapt the tactics of a communications program to virtual worlds by considering the purpose of the targeted virtual worlds, the population of consumers reached, the virtual world platform, the place of reaching the customers, and the profit model. These considerations match the traditional considerations of advertising campaigns involving choice of the message, media, timing, intensity and budget (see Table 3).

CONCLUSION

Virtual worlds represent a 3D extension of the Internet combined with social computing functionality. As perhaps the most multifaceted of new media, virtual worlds engender both high potential and high learning cost for companies utilizing them.

This chapter describes a four-element hierarchy of progressively deeper levels of communication and engagement with consumers, involving one-way communication, two-way communication (including market research), service co-creation, and community building. This hierarchy, together with the point that the virtual worlds permit multi-faceted communication across all four elements of the hierarchy, is offered as a conceptual academic contribution.

This chapter goes on to describe current effective practices by which companies achieve all four levels of engagement in the hierarchy. In particular, we discuss forms of one-way and two-way communications commonly used by companies in virtual worlds. We also discuss practices that firms have used to engage consumers in service-co-creation and to foster community building. Lastly, the chapter describes the tactics of carrying out communications campaigns in virtual worlds in terms of managing the message, media, timing, intensity, and budget. This discussion of effective practices, together with consideration of the tactics of managing campaign elements in virtual worlds, is offered as a more tangible contribution for practitioners.

We discuss the above topics after we first provide background on the recent history of electronic gaming and social networking that led to the evolution of virtual worlds. We also put the various worlds in perspective by summarizing a five-element typology of virtual worlds, whose elements–purpose, population, platform, place, and profit model–happen to also match up generally with the five elements of a communications campaign–message, media, timing, intensity, and budget.

Many issues remain for future consideration. These include (a) continued work developing applications of virtual worlds for advertising and communications; (b) enhancements of communication technologies; and (3) future research topics concerning advertising and communications utilizing the various new media, including virtual worlds.

Applications

Future applications of virtual worlds for advertising and communications include (1) improved integration of traditional advertising and public relations with communications that use the new media, including virtual worlds and social networking; (2) increased connectivity between different virtual worlds and forms of social computing; (3) exploration of new payment models, rather than a fixed fee, and (4) development of rating metrics and manuals to help firms choose in which worlds to promote, advertise, engage in other communications, or sponsor community-building activities. Because we are still in the "early days" of virtual worlds, we must continue to develop new best practices to utilize these worlds for each of the four elements of the proposed hierarchy of engagement.

Technology

Important issues involve identifying and developing future technologies that will continue to enhance communications and social computing in electronic gaming, online social networking, and virtual worlds. These new technologies should make the linkages more seamless between existing communications forms and between devices (including computers, telephones, cell-phones, televisions, car navigation systems, stereos, home alarm systems, other sensing devices, radios, cameras, camcorders, and musical instruments). Improvements in sensing devices and the non-verbal gesturing capabilities of avatars would also be desirable (and likely).

Research

A key research question that requires further examination will involve establishing the link between deeper levels of engagement according to our proposed hierarchy and such outcome variables as brand recall (aided and unaided), purchase intentions, product trial, and brand loyalty. A second area for future research will be to elaborate on ways to best manage each of the four engagement forms of the proposed hierarchy. This would describe which different communications media, technologies, social computing sites, and virtual worlds are most amenable to each of the four types of engagement. In addition, research should be done to learn (1) how to harness these new media generally, (2) what effects the new media have on consumer behavior, (3) the new roles of consumer communications in service delivery, and (4) the best way to design and manage field-research avatars and virtual-service representatives.

Figure 9. First author's Avatar

Communications managers and researchers are still learning how to talk to consumers in online environments. We are still learning how well-established advertising practices transfer to virtual worlds and electronic games. Recognition of the importance of this issue is shown by the theme "Virtual Social Identity and Consumer Behavior" of an advertising conference held in May 2008 (*27th Annual Advertising and Consumer Psychology Conference*). Our hope is that the hierarchy of engagement described in this chapter will aid in the future development and application of virtual worlds for advertising and customer engagement.

ACKNOWLEDGMENT

This research was supported by the Social Sciences and Humanities Research Council of Canada, through its Initiative on the New Economy Research Alliances Program (SSHRC grant 538-02-1013) and by faculty research grants from the University of Alberta School of Business and School of Retailing (the latter funded by Walmart) and from the University of Northern British Columbia. For much help, the authors would like to thank Kristen Smirnov, Eleni Stroulia, Kelly Lyons, Run H. Niu, Michael Bone, and Stephen Perelgut. The work has also significantly benefitted from comments of participants of the 2009 Advanced Research Techniques (ART) Forum in Whistler, B.C., Canada and of the University of Alberta Marketing Seminar. Lastly, the authors thank co-editors Terry Daugherty, Matt Eastin and two anonymous reviewers for very constructive suggestions.

REFERENCES

Adrian, A. (2007). I™: Avatars as trade marks. *Computer Law & Security Report*, *23*(5), 436–448. doi:10.1016/j.clsr.2007.07.002

American Marketing Association Conference Proceedings: 2006AMA Winter Educators' Conference (Vol. 17, pp. 226-231).

Anderson, C. A., & Bushman, B. J. (2001). Effects of violent games on aggressive behavior, aggressive cognition, aggressive affect, physiological arousal and prosocial behavior: a meta-analytic review of the scientific literature. *Psychological Science*, *12*(5), 353–359. doi:10.1111/1467-9280.00366

Au, W. J. (2001). Playing God. *Lingua Franca: The Review of Academic Life*, *11*(7), 12–13.

Balkin, J. M., & Noveck, B. S. (Eds.). (2006). *The state of play: Law, games, and virtual worlds*. New York: New York University Press.

Bangeman, E. (2008, January 24). Growth in gaming in 2007 far outpaces movies, music. *ARS Technica*. Retrieved May 30, 2008, from http://arstechnica.com/news.ars/post/20080124-growth-of-gaming-in-2007-far-outpaces-movies-music.html

Barnes, S. (2007). Virtual worlds as a medium for advertising. *The Data Base for Advances in Information Systems*, *38*(4), 45–55.

Bartle, R. A. (2006). Why governments aren't gods and gods aren't governments. *First Monday*. Retrieved March 1. 2008. from http://firstmonday.org/issues/special11_9/bartle/

Blizzard.com. (2008). *World of Warcraft reaches new milestone: 10 million subscribers*. Retrieved January 22, 2008, from http://eu.blizzard.com/en/press/080122.html

Boulos, K. M. N., Lee, H., & Wheeler, S. (2007). Second Life: An overview of the potential of 3-D virtual worlds in medical and health education. *Health Information and Libraries Journal*, *24*, 233–245. doi:10.1111/j.1471-1842.2007.00733.x

Boyd, D. M., & Ellison, N. B. (2007). Social network sites: Definition, history, and scholarship. *Journal of Computer-Mediated Communication*, *13*(1). Retrieved from http://jcmc.indiana.edu/vol13/issue1/boyd.ellison.html.

Bronack, S., Riedl, R., Tashner, J., & Greene, M. (2006). Learning in the zone: A social constructivist framework for distance education in a 3D virtual world. In. *Proceedings of Society for Information Technology and Teacher Education International Conference*, *2006*, 268–275.

Castronova, E. (2002). On virtual economies. *CESifo Working Paper No. 752. Category 9: Industrial Organization (July),* 1-39. Retrieved from http://ssrn.com/abstract_id=338500

Christ, P. E., & Peele, C. A. (2008). Virtual worlds: Personal jurisdiction and click-wrap licenses. *Intellectual Property & Technology Law Journal*, *20*(1), 1–6.

Cole, H., & Griffiths, M. D. (2007). Social interactions in massively multiplayer online role-playing gamers. *Cyberpsychology & Behavior*, *10*(4), 575–583. doi:10.1089/cpb.2007.9988

Colley, R. (1961). *Defining Advertising Goals for Measured Advertising Results*. New York: Association of National Advertisers.

Dickey, M. J. (2005). Three-dimensional virtual worlds and distance learning: Two case studies of active worlds as a medium for distance education. *British Journal of Educational Technology*, *36*(3), 439–451. doi:10.1111/j.1467-8535.2005.00477.x

DiPaola, S., Dorosh, D., & Brandt, G. (n. d.). *Ratava's line: Emergent learning and design using collaborative virtual worlds*. Retrieved March 1, 2008, from http://ivizlab.sfu.ca/research/colabdesign/dipaolaF1.pdf

DMD. (2007). Diversified media design, combined storey, and market truths limited. In *The virtual brand footprint: The marketing opportunity in Second Life.*

Driver, E., Jackson, P., Moore, C., & Schooley, C. (2008, January 7). Getting Real Work Done In Virtual Worlds. *Forrester Research*. Retrieved April 30, 2008, from http://www.forrester.com/Research/Document/Excerpt/0,7211,43450,00.html

Edery, D. (2006). Reverse product placement in virtual worlds. *Harvard Business Review*, *84*(12), 24–24.

Edwards, C. (2006). Another world. *Engineering and Technology*, *1*(9), 28–32. doi:10.1049/et:20060904

Farkas, M. G. (2007). *Social software in libraries: Building collaboration, communication, and community online*. Medford, NJ: Information Today.

Fawkes, P. (2008 February). *Initial thoughts on mind-control gaming, electronics & gadgets, gaming & virtual worlds*. Retrieved May 29, 2008, from *http*://www.psfk.com/category/gaming-virtual-worlds/page/2

Gartner, Inc. (2007, April 24). *Gartner says 80 percent of active Internet users will have a second life in the virtual world by the end of 2011*. Retrieved May 29, 2008, from http://gartner.com/it/page.jsp?id=503861

Goel, L., & Mousavidin, E. (2007). vCRM: Virtual customer relationship management. *The Data Base for Advances in Information Systems*, *38*(4), 56–60.

Grabowski, A., & Kruszewska, N. (2007). Experimental study of the structure of a social network and human dynamics in a virtual society. *International Journal of Modern Physics*, *18*(10), 1527–1535. doi:10.1142/S0129183107011480

Graves, L. (2008). A second life for higher Ed. *U.S. News & World Report*, *144*(2), 49–50.

Green, A. (2007 March). Are viewers engaged with advertising? Does it matter? *WARC Media FAQ*. Retrieved October 25, 2008, from http://www.warc.com/LandingPages/Generic/Results.asp?Ref=76

Hans, H. B., Neumann, M. M., Haber, T. E., & Mader, F. (2006). Virtual sales agents. In

Hemp, P. (2006). Avatar-based marketing. *Harvard Business Review, 84*(6), 48–56.

Hendaoui, A., Limayem, A., & Thompson, C. W. (2008, January). 3D social virtual world: Research issues and challenges. *IEEE Internet Computing*, 88–92. doi:10.1109/MIC.2008.1

Herman, A., Coombe, R. J., & Kaye, L. (2006). Your Second Life? Goodwill and the performativity of intellectual property in online digital gaming. *Cultural Studies, 20*(2/3), 184–210. doi:10.1080/09502380500495684

Herman, L., Horwitz, J., Kent, S., & Miller, S. (2008). The history of video games. *Gamespot*. Retrieved February 10, 2008, from http://www.gamespot.com/gamespot/features/video/hov/

Hinton, A. (2006). We live here: Games, third places and the information architecture of the future. *Bulletin of the American Society for Information Science and Technology, 32*(6), 17–21. Retrieved May 30, 2009, from http://www.asis.org/Bulletin/Aug-06/hinton.html

Holzwarth, M., Janiszewski, C., & Neumann, M. M. (2006). The influence of avatars on online consumer shopping behavior. *Journal of Marketing, 70*(4), 19–36. doi:10.1509/jmkg.70.4.19

Hugues, J. (2007). From virtual sex to no sex? *Ethical Technology*. Retrieved March 1, 2008, from http://ieet.org/index.php/IEET/more/hughes20070228/

Hunt, S. D. (1991). *Modern marketing theory: Critical issues in the philosophy of marketing science*. Cincinnati, OH: South-Western Publishing Co.

Jansz, J., & Martens, L. (2005). Gaming at a LAN event: the social context of playing video games. *New Media & Society, 7*(3), 333–355. doi:10.1177/1461444805052280

Jin, S. A., & Bolebruch, J. (2008). *Effects of Apple's spokes-avatar on iPhone advertising in Second Life*. Working paper presented at the 27th annual Advertising and Consumer Psychology Conference of the Society for Consumer Psychology, Philadelphia, 2008.

Jin, S. A., & Sung, Y. (2008). *Effects of brand personality on advertising in Second Life*. Working paper presented at the 27th annual Advertising and Consumer Psychology Conference of the Society for Consumer Psychology, Philadelphia, 2008.

Kadavasal, M. D., Dhara, K. K., Wu, X., & Krishnaswamy, V. (2007). Mixed reality for enhancing business communications using virtual worlds. In *Proceedings of the 2007 ACM symposium on Virtual reality software and technology* (pp. 233-234).

Kelly, K. (1994 January). Will Wright: The mayor of SimCity. *Wired*.

Kim, H., Lyons, K., & Cunningham, M. A. (2008, January). Towards a Theoretically-Grounded Framework for Evaluating Immersive Business Models and Applications. In *Proceedings of the 41st Annual Hawaii International Conference on System Sciences*.

Kozinets, R. V. (2002). The field behind the screen: Using netnography for marketing research in online communities. *JMR, Journal of Marketing Research, 39*(1), 61–72. doi:10.1509/jmkr.39.1.61.18935

Lastowka, F. G., & Hunter, D. (2006). Virtual worlds: A primer. In Balkin, J. M. (Ed.), *The state of play: Law, games, and virtual worlds*. New York: New York University Press.

Lavidge, R. J., & Steiner, G. A. (1961). A model for predictive measurements of advertising effectiveness. *Journal of Marketing*, *25*(4), 59–62. doi:10.2307/1248516

Leblebici, H., Salancik, G. R., Copay, A., & King, T. (1991). Institutional change and the transformation of interorganizational fields: An organizational history of the U.S. radio broadcasting industry. *Administrative Science Quarterly*, *35*, 333–363. doi:10.2307/2393200

Lederman, L. (2007). Stranger than fiction: Taxing virtual worlds. *New York University Law Review*, *82*(6), 1620–1672.

Li, C., Bernoff, J., Fiorentino, R., & Glass, S. (2007, April 19). Social technographics: Mapping participation in activities forms the foundation of a social strategy. *Forrester Research*. Retrieved June 11, 2008, from http://www.forrester.com/Research/Document/Excerpt/0,7211,42057,00.html

Lohr, S. (2007, October 10). Free the Avatars. *The New York Times*. Retrieved May 29, 2008, from http://bits.blogs.nytimes.com/2007/10/10/free-the-avatars/

MacInnes, I. (2006). Property rights, legal issues, and business models in virtual world communities. *Electronic Commerce Research*, *6*(1), 39–56. doi:10.1007/s10660-006-5987-8

Maher, L., Liew, M., Gu, P., & Lan, N. D. (2005). An agent approach to supporting collaborative design in 3D virtual worlds. *Automation in Construction*, *14*(2), 189–195. doi:10.1016/j.autcon.2004.07.008

Mayer-Schonberger, J., & Crowley, J. (2006). Napster's second life?: The regulatory challengers of virtual worlds. *Northwestern University Law Review*, *100*(4), 1775–1826.

Melby, T. (2008). How Second Life seeps into real life. *Contemporary Sexuality*, *42*(1), 1–6.

Mennecke, B. E., Terando, W. D., Janvrin, D. J., & Dilla, W. N. (2007). It's just a game, or is it? Real money, real income, and real taxes in virtual worlds. *Communications of the Association for Information Systems*, *20*, 134–141.

Messinger, P. R. (1995). *The marketing paradigm: A guide for general managers*. Cincinnati, OH: Southwestern College Publishing.

Messinger, P. R., & Ge, X. (2009). The Future of the Market Research Profession. In Smith, C., Kisiel, K., & Morrison, J. (Eds.), *Working through Synthetic Worlds* (pp. 15–44). Burlington, VT, USA: Ashgate Publishing Company.

Messinger, P. R., Li, J., Stroulia, E., Galletta, D., Ge, X., & Choi, S. (2009a). Seven challenges to combining human and automated service. *Canadian Journal of Administrative Sciences*.

Messinger, P. R., Stroulia, E., & Lyons, K. (2008). A typology of virtual worlds: A historical overview and future directions. *Journal of Virtual Worlds Research, 1*(1). Retrieved May 30, 2009, from http://journals.tdl.org/jvwr/article/view/291/222

Messinger, P. R., Stroulia, E., Lyons, K., Bone, M., Niu, A., Smirnov, K., & Perelgut, S. (2009b, June). Virtual worlds—past, present, and future: New directions in social computing. *Decision Support Systems*, *47*(3), 204–228. doi:10.1016/j.dss.2009.02.014

Methenitis, M. (2007). A tale of two worlds: New U.S. gambling laws and the MMORPG. *Gaming Law Review*, *11*(4), 436–439. doi:10.1089/glr.2007.11404

Murray, S. (2005). High art/low life: The art of playing Grand Theft Auto. *PAJ a Journal of Performance and Art, 27*(80), 91–98. doi:10.1162/1520281053850866

Nebolsky, C., Yee, N. K., Petrushin, V. A., & Gershman, A. V. (2003). Using virtual worlds for corporate training. In *Proceedings of the 3rd IEEE International Conference on Advanced Learning Technologies (ICALT'03)*.

Nobel, N. (2006). *Aesthetics and gratification: Sexual practices in virtual environments*. Working Paper. Trinity University, San Antonio, TX

Ondrejka, C. (2006). Escaping the gilded cage: User-created content and building the metaverse. In Balkin, J. M. (Ed.), *The state of play: Law, games, and virtual worlds*. New York: New York University Press.

Pilieci, V. (2008, February 18). *Video game is free -- just watch onscreen ads*. Winnipeg Free Press. Retrieved March 1, 2008, from http://www.winnipegfreepress.com/canada/story/4127803p-4721275c.html

Pitta, D. A., & Fowler, D. (2005). Online consumer communities and their value to new product developers. *Journal of Product and Brand Management, 14*(5), 283–291. doi:10.1108/10610420510616313

Plummer, J., Cook, B., Diforio, D., Schachter, B., Sokolyanskaya, I., Korde, T., & Heath, R. (2007). *Measures of engagement: Volume II*. Advertising Research Foundation, White Paper (March).

Plummer, J., Cook, B., Diforio, D., Sokolyanskaya, I., & Ovchinnikova, M. (2006). *Measures of engagement*. Advertising Research Foundation, White Paper (June).

Pong. (2008). Retrieved May 30, 2008, from http://en.wikipedia.org/wiki/Pong

Porter, C. E. (2004). A typology of virtual communities: A multi-disciplinary foundation for future research. *Journal of Computer-Mediated Communication, 10*(1).

ProvenModels. (n. d.). *AIDA sales funnel*. Retrieved May 30, 2009, from http://www.provenmodels.com/547/aida-sales-funnel/lewis

Ragusa, J. M., & Bochenek, G. M. (2001). Collaborative virtual design environments. *Communications of the ACM, 44*(12), 40–43. doi:10.1145/501317.501339

Rosenman, M. A., Smith, G., Maher, M. L., Ding, L., & Marchant, D. (2007). Multidisciplinary collaborative design in virtual environments. *Automation in Construction, 16*(1), 37–44. doi:10.1016/j.autcon.2005.10.007

Roy, U., & Kodkani, S. S. (1999). Product modeling within the framework of the World Wide Web. *IIE Transactions, 31*(7), 667–678. doi:10.1080/07408179908969867

Schumann, D. W., & Thorson, E. (2007). *Internet Advertising: Theory and Research*. San Francisco: Lawrence Erlbaum Associates.

Second Life. (2010), Monthly customer spending distribution. Retrieved May 4, 2010, from http://secondlife.com/statistics/economy-data.php

Sherry, J. L. (2001). The effects of violent video games on aggression: a meta-analysis. *Human Communication Research, 27*(3), 409–432.

Sipress, A. (2006, December 26). Where real money meets virtual reality, the jury is still out. *Washington Post*. Retrieved March 1, 2008, from http://www.washingtonpost.com/wp-dyn/content/article/2006/12/25/AR2006122500635.html

Smythe, J. M. (2007). Beyond self-selection in video game play: An experimental examination of the consequences of massively multiplayer online role-playing game play. *Cyberpsychology & Behavior, 10*(5), 717–721. doi:10.1089/cpb.2007.9963

Song, S., & Lee, J. (2007). Key factors of heuristic evaluation for game design: towards massively multi-player online role-playing game. *International Journal of Human-Computer Studies, 65*(8), 709–723. doi:10.1016/j.ijhcs.2007.01.001

Strong, E. K. (1925). Theories of selling. *The Journal of Applied Psychology, 9*, 75–86. doi:10.1037/h0070123

Subrahmanyam, K., Greenfield, P. M., & Tynes, B. (2004). Constructing sexuality and identity in an online teen chat room. *Journal of Applied Developmental Psychology, 25*(6), 651–666. doi:10.1016/j.appdev.2004.09.007

Swanson, K. (2007). Second Life: A science library presence in virtual reality. *Science & Technology Libraries, 27*(3), 79–86. doi:10.1300/J122v27n03_06

Wang, A. (2006). Advertising engagement: A driver of message involvement on message Effects. *Journal of Advertising Research, 46*(4), 355–368. doi:10.2501/S0021849906060429

Wenger, E. (2004). Knowledge management is a donut: shaping your knowledge strategy with communities of practice. *Ivey Business Journal* (January).

Wenger, E., McDermott, R., & Snyder, W. (2002). *Cultivating communities of practice: a guide to managing knowledge*. Harvard Business School Press.

Wenger, E., & Snyder, W. (2000). Communities of practice: the organizational frontier. *Harvard Business Review*, (January-February): 139–145.

Whang, L. S., & Chang, G. (2004). Lifestyles of virtual world residents: Living in the on-line game Lineage. *Cyberpsychology & Behavior, 7*(5), 592–600.

White, R. (2007, October). Engagement, involvement and attention. *Admap, 487*, 23–24.

Winter, D. (2008). *Arcade Pong*. Retrieved February 10, 2008, from http://www.pong-story.com/arcade.htm

Yee, N. (2006). The demographics, motivations, and derived experiences of users of massively multi-user online graphical environments. *Presence (Cambridge, Mass.), 15*(3), 309–329. doi:10.1162/pres.15.3.309

Yee, N., & Bailenson, J. (2007). The Proteus Effect: The effect of transformed self-representation on behavior. *Human Communication Research, 33*(3), 271–290. doi:10.1111/j.1468-2958.2007.00299.x

Yee, N., Bailenson, J., Urbanek, M., Chang, F., & Merget, D. (2007). The unbearable likeness of being digital: The persistence of nonverbal social norms in online virtual environments. *Cyberpsychology & Behavior, 10*(1), 115–121. doi:10.1089/cpb.2006.9984

ENDNOTES

1. Related work is the association model (Preston and Thorson, 1984), adoption of innovations (Rogers, 1962) and information processing (McGuire, 1969). Some treatments emphasize what advertisements are designed to achieve while others emphasize the desired audience response. Also related are descriptions of extensive problem solving including five activities (arousal of need – information search – evaluation– purchase decision – repurchase decision) with an associated cognitive culmination for the decision maker of each of these five activities

(need awareness – knowledge – preference – trial – post-purchase evaluation).

2 A related idea consists of Ross Mayfield's Power Law of Participation (2006) with levels of engagement including the following range of activities: read, favorite, tag, comment, subscribe, share, network, write, refactor, collaborate, moderate, and lead. Disproportionately fewer people contribute disproportionately more to higher levels of participation. http://ross.typepad.com/blog/2006/04/power_law_of_pa.html

3 An early provider of such services, Market Truths, won a business plan competition sponsored in SL by Linden Lab.

4 Along these lines, Edery (2006) suggests that an interesting commercial opportunity has gone relatively unnoticed: reverse placement or the commercial translation of fictional brands or products from virtual worlds into the real world.

APPENDIX 1

Table 4. Virtual World Types with Prominent Examples

Self-Determined
Second Life. The premier virtual world with beautiful rendering of avatars and the physical environment; navigation through walking, running, flying, teleporting; and vehicles; elaborate scripting language for movement of avatars and building; communication through digital chat and shout, voice communication (for members), instant messaging and distributing note cards; in-world content created by residents through a computer aided design system and uploading; objects and land are tradable with varied property rights; in-world monetary system exchangeable for U.S. dollars, and social networking facilitates that support the creation and maintenance of groups. Launched in 2001; currently more than 7 million residents. (**secondlife.com**)
Kaneva. With a name that stands for "canvas", this world supports creativity through a blend of virtual-worlds technology, 2D social networking, and a YouTube player through Kaneva TV sets wherein each registered member has an avatar, a profile (like in 2D social-networking sites), and a home (which they can decorate by importing content they may have in other sites); and groups are endowed with an open space to develop as they wish. Launched in 2004, with approximately 600,000 members currently. (www.kaneva.com)
Entropia Universe. Science-fiction world, set on a distant planet named Calypso, a cross between SL and World of Warcraft, with fantasy-like avatars, popular activities including hunting and mining, free membership, and a local currency PEDs (Project Entropia Dollars) to buy things, convertible back to real-world currencies through public auctions (Crews 2007). In March 2007, Entropia was the first western virtual world to expand into China, partnering with Cyber Recreation Development Corp. (CRD), an online entertainment company supported by the Beijing Municipal People's Government to create a cash-based virtual economy for China (VWN 2007a). Launched in 2003, with over 580,000 registered accounts. (www.kaneva.com)
Education Focused
Forterra Systems. There.com was founded in 1998 and went on to develop Forterra Systems and There, which was subsequently sold to Makena. The Forterra virtual worlds provide training-through-simulation for e-learning, military, healthcare, and entertainment industries based on the OLIVE (Online Interactive Virtual Environment) platform (Kusher 2008). (www.forterrainc.com)
ActiveWorlds. Released in 1995 by Worlds Inc and merged with Vanguard Enterprises, Inc in January 21, 1999, after which the company's name was changed to Activeworlds.com, Inc. and, later, Active Worlds, Inc. Several worlds dedicated to education in the main Active Worlds Universe; this company also launched the Active Worlds Educational Universe (AWEDU), which is targeted only to educational institutions; and, in addition, discounts are offered to educational institutions that want to conduct educational activities in the world. (www.activeworlds.com)
Community Self-determined
Cyworld. Cyworld is a 2D/3D social-networking site that was originally launched in 1999 in South Korea and was subsequently acquired in 2003 by SK Communications (SKU), Korea's largest wireless service provider, since substantially expanded with Chinese, Japanese, Taiwanese, and US versions. Similar to MySpace or Facebook, Cyworld members create their own home pages, with photos, documents, and other media, but Cyworld homepages are 3D and can be decorated with digital furniture, art, TVs and music. The service itself is free, but homepage customizations are paid for with the world's digital currency, called dotori (Korean for "acorns"), which cost 10 cents each. Cyworld is now reported to be larger than YouTube in terms of daily video uploads and second to iTunes with number of songs sold (Ewers 2006 and Ihlwan 2005). 18 million members, with 90% of all Koreans in their 20s having a Cyworld account (http://en.wikipedia.org/wiki/Cyworld). (www.nate.com)
HiPiHi. Recently-formed Chinese counterpart of SL, with a more "Eastern aesthetic," launched for private Beta testing in March 2007, including an English interface (http://www.hipihi.com/ news/trends_placard010e.html). Now partnering with Origami Frontiers and others to expand into mobile virtual-world services across Asia Pacific. Offer more prefabricated items than SL so that users can more rapidly customize their environment (and during Beta testing, users are offered a free 100m x100m tract of real estate). The founders say that subscriptions will be free and revenue will be generated by advertisements, similar to those the 2D web, and extras (products and services) for sale within the world, but no currency yet in existence.. 60% of the HiPiHi members are now female (Roger 2007). (www.hipihi.com)
Media Focused
vSide. Focused on media and entertainment, vSide members can go to virtual clubs, corresponding to over 40 different music channels, where they can socialize and enjoy their favorite music provided by vSide partners which include Interscope, Kitsons, Rocawear, StarStyle, eDoc Laundry, and Downtown Records. A rich variety of avatars may be created; avatars can earn "Respekt" by discovering interesting details hidden in the world's architecture, making friends or visiting stores. They can also buy "Creds" from in-world ATMs in order to buy clothes and other items. As a members' Respekt increases, they can have an apartment, where members can tune into his or her chosen channels without having to navigate and make selections in the channels area, as well as other special privileges (like buying specially restricted clothing for example) in the socially stratified vSide world. All content is provided by professional artists. Once a member has an apartment in the world. A streaming-video capability is planned for the near future (Doppelganger 2007 and Wilson 2007). Members spend 11 hours per month in the world, compared with an average of two hours per month for typical social networks. (www.vside.com)

continued on following page

Table 4. continued

Children's Worlds
Webkinz. Targeted to children aged 4 -13 who, upon purchasing a Webkinz plush toy in real stores, receive a secret code which they use to log onto the virtual world of Webkinz and get (a) a matching virtual pet. After "adopting" the Webkinz virtual pet, (b) a free 2D+ room in which the virtual pet can live, (c) a free virtual "extra" consisting of some virtual item the virtual pet can use, and (d) two thousand units of Kinzcash, the Webkinz World virtual money. The virtual world also includes games, places to purchase extras for the pets with Kinzcash, and social networking features such as email to friends (for security purposes, the content is limited to just 16 predetermined messages, such as "my pet seems sick"), and, upon sharing a password with a friend in the real world, the ability to coexist and interact in the same virtual environment with a friend's pet avatar. Purchase of real accessories also provide a code for a similar virtual item for their virtual pet. The "buzz" among children at school and play includes Lil'Kinz in birthday party "lootbags." (www.webkinz.com)
Whyville. Children's world focuses on education along with fun, founded by Numedeon Inc. Membership is free. When children log on they get 200 "clams," the Whyville currency. Initially, children have to take a "chat license test" before they are allowed to chat with other members of the world. Children under 13 can take the test, only after their parent approves their membership with a fax. Whyville citizens can earn clams by engaging in activities such as restaurant clean up and educational plots, including tracing the origin of a "whypox" epidemic or participating in a WhyEat(Right) challenge, for example. All income-earning activities are recorded in the member's salary ledger. Recently, a Spanish bank, Bankinter, opened a virtual branch in this world–after a week, users had deposited 90 million clams into certificates of deposits and 21 million into interest bearing savings accounts. Whyville also introduces children to civic life and politics. Whyville citizens can participate (run for office and vote for a representative) in senate elections. The senate members are supposed to hear issues from citizens and try to resolve them or forward them to city workers (company employees). The Whyville avatars are simply faces; children make their face with parts made by other Whyville citizens who have part-designing licenses. Face parts cost clams although there are also free face parts in a special location, Grandma's house. Without a paid membership, face parts disappear after three months. population of over 3 million (VWN 2007b). (www.whyville.net)
Habbo. Launched in 2000 by Sulake, a Finnish company, and targeted to teens between 13 and 18 years old with 80 million accounts (50/50 male/female ratio), 100,000 concurrent users at any point in time, and 7.5 million unique active users per month. Membership is again free but to join special clubs and furnish their Habbo hotel rooms, members need to pay with "Habbo Coins" which they can buy through a phone land line or a text message from a mobile (http://www.crunchbase.com/company/habbohotel). In addition to memberships, another source of revenue for Habbo are advertisements, which come in two forms: web-style ad banners and branded furniture and clothes by providers such as Target and PepsiCo. According to the company, the in-world items had a total market value of around $550,000,000 in 2007, and the company reported $30 million in revenues in 2006 (Nutt 2007). (www.habbo.com)
Club Penguin. Recently acquired by Disney Corporation and popular with children 6–14, players can choose several games and activities to participate in through their virtual penguin. There are free accounts that provide limited access, and monthly subscriptions, which allow players to purchase clothes for their penguin, items for their igloo, and offer additional choices through colors and backgrounds. Member players earn coins by playing games and use their coins to purchase items. Players are able to interact with other players' penguins in the games and through chat. With Club Penguin, parents choose if players can chat freely or only through a small selection of chat texts. If they choose free chat, monitors exist who watch for abuse and players can report inappropriate behavior with a click of their mouse (Narravo 2007). (www.clubpenguin.com)
RuneScape. This 3D MMORPG is operated by Jagex, Ltd. and targets a wider range of ages, including teems 13 years and older, teens, and even adults. It offers free accounts or monthly paid memberships, which provide access to additional features (new areas, quests, and items). Players customize their avatars and set their own goals. RuneScape has 158 "worlds" (each exactly the same) in order to manage the fact that there are millions of registered players and only two thousand players may be active in any one world at a time. Players interact with other players through chatting, trading items (produced using skills or by collecting raw materials), fighting each other or game monsters, and collaborating on quests. Quests are story lines that players can choose to complete. In addition to quests, players engage in activities to enhance their skill levels in a variety of ways. A player's skill level determines their chance of success in battles and other non-combat activities. Unlike Webkinz and other games for younger players, Runescape players have full freedom in the content of their chats, which are, by default, public. Players can have a list of "friends" with whom they engage in private chat. A player can also compile a list of "ignores": people who cannot engage in chat with that player. In Runescape's economy, players trade items earned through non-combat activities and sell them for "gold pieces" or "gp" or collect gold by killing other players, taking their possessions and selling them for gold, successfully completing quests, killing monsters, or finding gold pieces on the ground. Unlike other worlds described in this section, Runescape game items and gold cannot be sold or exchanged for real money (real-money trading is prohibited). Runescape also interjects random events to reduce the chance that players are using automated programs (macros) to complete repetitive tasks, which earn players skill level and / or gold pieces. (www.runescape.com)

APPENDIX 2.

Table 5. Comparative statistics for a sample of virtual worlds (Sources: Examination of each world, Virtual Worlds Management http://www.virtualworldsmanagement.com, and DMD, 2007)

World Name	Company	World Focus	Currency	User Gen Content	Target Audience	Ad Supported	Initial Cost	Virt Item Sales	3d/2d	URL
Entropia Universe	Mindark-2003	Public	PED	Yes	18 +	Yes	Free	yes	3d	http://www.entropiauniverse.com
	World of Warcraft	Public	WoW Gold		teens and adults					
	Forterra Systems-1998	Private			Enterprise	n/a	n/a	n/a	3d	http://www.forterrainc.com/
ProtoSphere	ProtonMedia	Private			Enterprise	n/a	n/a	n/a	3d	http://www.protonmedia.com/
Alphaworld	Activeworlds Inc.	Both		Yes	13 +	Unknown	n/a		3d	http://www.activeworlds.com/
Qwaq Forums	Qwaq	Private			Enterprise	n/a	n/a	n/a	3d	http://www.qwaq.com
Google Earth-2005	Google, Inc.	Public		Yes	everyone	n/a currently	Free	No	3d	http://earth.google.com/
Microsoft Virtual Earth-2006	Microsoft	Public		Yes	everyone	None	n/a			http://maps.live.com/
Imvu	Imvu-2004	Public		Yes	18 +	Credits	Free	yes	3d	http://www.imvu.com
Kaneva	Kaneva-2004	Public	Kaneva credits	Yes	Public	Yes	Free	not yet	3d	http://www.kaneva.com
Multiverse	Multiverse-2004	Both	defined by world		defined by world	defined by world	n/a			http://www.multiverse.net/
3B	3B International	Public		Yes		Yes	Free	No	3d	http://3b.net
vSide (Lounge)	Doppelganger, Inc.	Public	Reskpekt, Creds	No	older teenagers		Free		3d	http://www.themusiclounge.com/
Flowplay	Flowplay	Public	yes		older teenagers		planned 5.99		unknown	http://www.flowplay.com/
Second Life	Linden Lab	Both	Lindens	Yes	18 +	Yes	free, 5.99	yes	3d	http://secondlife.com/
HiPiHi	HiPiHi-2005	Public	?	Yes	Public	Unknown	free, in beta	not yet	3d	http://www.hipihi.com/
Cyworld	Cyworld, Inc.	Public	Acorns	Yes, limited	13 +	Yes	Free	yes		http://us.cyworld.com/
there.com	Makena Technologies, Inc.	Both	Therebucks	yes, limited	13 +	Yes	free, $9.95 once	yes	3d	http://www.there.com
3B International	3B	Public	none	Yes	Unknown	yes	-	No	3d	http://3b.net

continued on following page

Table 5. continued

World Name	Company	World Focus	Currency	User Gen Content	Target Audience	Ad Supported	Initial Cost	Virt Item Sales	3d/2d	URL
TEENS and TWEENS										
Teen Second Life	Linden Lab	Public	Linden $	Yes	13 – 18	yes			3d	http://teen.secondlife.com/
Dubit	Dubit Ltd.	Public			13 – 18	yes	Free	No	2d+	http://www.dubitchat.com
Multiple worlds	MTV / Viacom	branded	MTV$	Yes	tweens +teens	yes	Free	yes	3d	http://www.vlb.mtv.com/
Stardoll	Stardoll AB	Public	StarDollars	No	7 – 17	yes	Free	yes	2d	http://www.stardoll.com/en/
Habbo	Sulake Corporation	Public	HabboCoins	no, limited coming	13 – 16	yes	Free	yes	2d	http://www.habbo.com/
CCMetro	Coke	branded	Therebucks	No	13+	yes	Free	yes	3d	http://www.mycoke.com/
Gaia Online	Gaia Interactive, Inc.	Public	Gaia Gold	No	Public	yes	Free	yes		http://www.gaiaonline.com
Zwinktopia	IAC	Public	Zbucks	No	13+	yes	free and can purchase Zbucks	yes	2d + 3d	http://www.Zwinky.com
Runescape	Jagex Limited	Public	Gold Pieces	No	13+	no	free or $5/month	yes	3d	http://www.runescape.com/
CHILDREN										
Ty Inc	Ty Girlz	branded	TyDollars	No	6 – 13	yes	free with purchase	yes	2d	www.tygirlz.com
Club Penguin	New Horizon Interactive	Public	virtual coins	No	6 – 14	no	free or $5.95/month	yes	2d	http://www.clubpenguin.com/
Webkinz	Ganz	Public	Kinzcash	No	6 – 13	for real-worldwebkinz items	free with purchase	yes	2d	http://www.webkinz.com/
Barbie Girls	Mattel	branded	B-Bucks	No	6 – 13	yes	free + extras with purchase	yes	2d	http://www.barbiegirls.com/
Nicktropolis	Viacom	branded	NickPoints	No	6 – 13	yes	Free	yes -- swap for points	3d	http://www.nick.com/nicktropolis
Multiple worlds	Corus Entertainment	branded	Botanickels	yes (storyline)	tweens	yes	Free	yes	2d+	http://thebigrip.com/

continued on following page

APPENDIX 3

Table 5. continued

World Name	Company	World Focus	Currency	User Gen Content	Target Audience	Ad Supported	Initial Cost	Virt Item Sales	3d/2d	URL
Neopets	Viacom	Public	Neopoints	yes (email, video, etc.)	children	yes	Free	yes	2d + 3d	http://www.neopets.com/
Virtual Magic Kingdom	Disney	branded	credits	yes (mashups)	8 – 14	yes	Free	yes	3d	http://vmk.disney.go.com/vmk
Whyville	Numedeon	Public	Clams	yes, limited	8 – 15	no	free or purchas pass for priority	yes	2d	http://www.whyville.net
Gopets	gopets	Public	Shells	No	children	no	free and can purchase gold shells	yes	3d	http://www.gopetslive.com
Millsberry.com	General Mills	branded	Millsbucks	No	children	yes	Free	yes	2d	http://www.millsberry.com/

Table 6. Various Services, Universities, Brands, and Other Entities in Second Life

Consumer Services and eCommerce		Thompson NetG: Thompson 182, 123, 35
ABN AMRO: ABN AMBR 238, 15, 22		Toyota: Scion City 44, 40, 23
Adidas: Adidas 104, 183, 55		Vodafone: Vodafone Island 128, 128,0
AMD: AMD Dev Central 124,151,31		**Media Companies**
AOL Pointe: AOL Pointe 128, 128, 0		AOL Pointe: AOL Pointe 128, 128, 0
Autodesk: Autodesk 128, 125, 54		Bantam Dell Publishing (Random House): Sheep Island 123,28,25
BMW: BMW New World 195, 66, 23		BBC Radio 1: BBC Radio 1 128, 127, 32
Circuit City: IBM 10 136, 38, 22		Choc Hebdo: La Plaine 59, 140, 37
Cisco Systems: Cisco Systems 128, 127, 30		CNET: Millions of Us 226, 30, 38
The Connected Home: The Connected Home		MTV Laguna Beach Laguna Beach 63, 218, 25
Dell Computer, Main Island: Dell Island 43, 162, 24		NBC Universal Headquarters: NBC 2 131, 123, 43
H&R Block: HR Block 113,48,37		Northsound Radio Scotland: Fusion Unity 204, 131, 22
IBM Sandbox: IBM 121, 154, 33		Popular Science, PopSci Future Lounge: Millions of Us 193, 133, 24
IBM 1 Virtual Universities Community. Theater I: IBM 1 128, 128, 23		Reuters: Reuters 127, 99, 25
IBM 2: IBM 2 128, 128, 22		Sundance Channel: Sundance Channel 55, 173, 38
IBM 3: IBM 3 243, 105, 23		The Infinite Mind: Infinite Mind 209, 76, 46
IBM4 IBM05 / Recruitment Project: IBM 4 130, 183, 22		Wired: Millions of Us 203, 228, 23
IBM 6: IBM 6 128, 126, 22		**Government/Public Entities**
IBM 7 Greater IBM Connection:		U.S. Congress (Democratic Party) Capitol Hill 128, 128, 0
IBM 8 SOA Hub: IBM 8 104, 106, 23		Swedish Consulate
IBM 9: IBM 9 128, 129 22		**Politicians**
IBM 10 Theater M, Circuit City: IBM 10 139, 42, 22		Mrs Ségolène Royal, French socialist candidate to the 2007 presidency, Comité 748 : Désirs d'avenir: Bretton 175, 233, 102
iVillage: Sheep Island 42, 150, 25		Mrs. Hillary Clinton, U.S. Democratic candidate 2008 presidency: Isles of Intrigue2 133, 137, 604
Major League Baseball: Baseball 214, 129, 27		Mr. Barack Obama, U.S. Democratic candidate 2008 presidency: Silicon Island 222, 217, 32 (unofficial)
Mercedes-Benz: Mercedes Island 128, 128,0		Mr. John Edwards, U.S. Democratic candidate 2008 presidency: Onnuri 169, 25, 87 ; Laguna Beach 219, 113, 23
Nissan: Nissan 19, 129, 26		**Agencies**
PA Consulting: PA Consulting 116, 119, 27		Centers for Disease Control and Prevention: Juwangsan 218,223,0
Pontiac Main Island: Pontiac 179, 96, 24		Homeland Security Synthetic Environments for Emergency Response Simulation
Reebok: Reebok 111, 100, 97		National Oceanic & Atmospheric Administration Meteroa 246, 244, 309
Reuters: Reuters 127, 98, 25		**Various Non-Profit Organizations**

continued on following page

Table 6. continued

Sears: IBM 10 95, 32, 23		**Tourism Boards** of Intoscana, Tuscany and Galveston, Texas, both launching soon.
Sony|BMG: Media Island 108, 111, 21		**Marketing and Public Relations Firms,** fifteen
Starwood Hotels: Aloft Island 68, 69, 27		Leo Burnett: Millions of Us 193,80,23
Sun Microsystems: Sun Pavilion 182, 144,55		**Market Research Companies**, two
Sundance Channel: Launching January 2007		**Various universities**, not necessarily offering classes, and some not open to the public, including Ball State University, Center for Media Design: Middletown 196, 179, 31; Harvard Extension School and Law School: Launching soon; New York University: Launching soon; Ohio University, Ohio University Without Boundaries SL Campus: Ohio University 20,36,24; Pepperdine University: Malibu Island; University of Illinois at Urbana Champaign: Cybrary City 220, 138, 24 (Partial list).
TELUS: Shinda 187, 72, 22		

Source: DMD (2007) and Business Communicators of Second Life. A comprehensive list of Institutions and Organizations in Second Life is kept at the Simteach wiki (simteach.com/wiki).

Chapter 5
The Influence of Immersion on Product Placement Effectiveness:
A Synthesis and Review of Product Placement in Traditional and Digital Media

Tamara L. Ansons
University of Manitoba, Canada

Fang Wan
University of Manitoba, Canada

Jason P. Leboe
University of Manitoba, Canada

ABSTRACT

With a focus on the factors that determine the effectiveness of product placements, we compare the use of product placements in traditional and digital media. Despite the enthusiastic use of product placements in both forms of media, research has not provided conclusive results as to the effectiveness of this form of marketing. After reviewing the factors that alter product placement outcomes, we present a conceptual model designed to highlight the processes that we perceive as altering the consequences of product placements. We presume that whether or not a product placement results in positive consequences for an embedded brand depends on a combination of influences that stem primarily from the degree of a consumer's immersion within the media experience. The highly stimulating and self-directed nature of digital media is predicted to produce profitable consequences for embedded brands, making it a prosperous venue for marketers to utilize to feature their brands.

DOI: 10.4018/978-1-60566-792-8.ch005

INTRODUCTION

Brands have been integrated within culture narratives for non-promotional purposes as early as Charles Dickens' *The Pickwick Papers* (1837), within which the *Pickwick* carriage line was featured (Newell, Salmon and Chang 2006). Now, brand integration, or product placement, has become an increasingly popular alternative to conventional advertising. The expectation is that global investment in product placement marketing strategies will increase from $3.46 billion in 2004 to an estimated $6.94 billion in 2009 (PQ Media 2005).

The source of this trend toward rapidly increasing investment in the placement of brands within entertainment media is both due to a change in marketing strategy and new developments in media technology. The more subtle appearance of a brand within entertainment narratives effectively circumvents consumers' resistance to the influence of advertising on their brand preferences and brand choices. Such resistance is more likely to occur in response to more overt forms of advertising (Balasubramanian, Karrh, and Patwardhan 2006). Moreover, recent technological advancements (e.g., *TiVo*; the availability of television programs online) have given viewers the opportunity to avoid traditional forms of marketing, such as advertisements that are broadcasted during television commercial breaks (PQ Media 2005). As a consequence of these developments, there has been a proliferation of product placement in contexts ranging from motion pictures and television programs to children's learning books (e.g., *The M&M's Brand Counting Book*; Neer 2003), best-selling novels (e.g., *Bulgari*, the Italian jewelry company, sponsored Fay Weldon to feature the brand in the title of her novel, *The Bulgari Connection*; Neer 2003), and video games (e.g., in *CSI 3: Dimensions of Murder*, *Visa*'s fraud-protection service alerts players to a stolen credit card, providing an essential clue for solving a murder mystery; Brown 2006).

Accompanying this growing ubiquity of product placements is the lack of a comprehensive understanding as to its effectiveness at increasing consumers' choice of a brand over its competitors. Indeed, in some cases, product placements have been controversial enough to negatively influence consumers' attitude toward a brand, without any corresponding influence on their actual purchasing behavior. For example, the authors of the best-selling novel, *Cathy's Book: If Found Call 650-266-8233*, recently disclosed that they described characters as wearing specific makeup lines by *Cover Girl* in exchange for promotional ads for the book on *beinggirl.com*, a website aimed at adolescent girls and owned by *Cover Girl*'s parent company. However, pressured by the public and media's criticism of both the brand sponsor and the book's publisher, the book's authors removed all product placements from the book in its newer release. Nevertheless, there was no evidence that the public's negative reaction to this instance of product placement translated into lower sales either of the book or of *Cover Girl* products (Rich 2008). Despite the staggering amount of money spent globally on the embedding of products within entertainment media, this type of incident raises questions as to whether such marketing strategies necessarily translate into changes in consumer behavior.

A growing body of literature reveals that brand placements do not inevitably convey a benefit to the brand with respect to the most relevant outcome variables; consumers' evaluation of a brand over its competitors (i.e., brand attitude) and their actual choice of the brand among competing alternatives (i.e., brand choice; e.g., Cowley and Barron 2008; Law and Braun 2000; Russell 2002). Furthermore, measures of product placement effectiveness commonly rest upon the presumption that a product placement is effective if the experience of encountering a brand within entertainment media is memorable. That is, marketing experts often use success in later remembering a product placement event as a surrogate for the effectiveness of that event in promoting increases in actual purchasing behavior. If the viewer remembers having encountered the brand within some entertainment medium, the assumption is that the brand will reap the benefits and the viewer will be more likely to select that brand in the future (Babin and Carder 1996; Gupta and Lord 1998). Contrary to this assumption, the evidence suggests that the memorability of product placement experiences do not consistently translate into enhancements of either consumers' brand attitudes or their tendency to select a brand amongst its competitors. In some studies, enhanced memory for a product placement event was found to have a positive relationship with brand attitude (e.g., Russell 2002; Vollmers and Mizerski 1994), whereas, in other studies, enhanced memory for a product placement event was found to have either a negative effect on brand attitude or had no influence on brand attitude at all (Bhatnagar and Wan 2009; Cowley and Barron 2008; Law and Braun 2000; Matthes, Schemer, and Wirth 2007). Clearly, complex associations exist between characteristics of a product placement experiences, the memorability of product placement experiences, and the critical outcome measures of consumers' brand attitudes and brand choices. Consequently, marketers cannot reasonably justify the vast resources currently spent on product placements prior to achieving a sophisticated understanding of how these critical factors relate to one another.

In this chapter, with a primary focus on the factors that determine the effectiveness of product placements, we provide a comparison of traditional and digital media. We define traditional media as media that has been presented in the form of "text and pictures in books and magazines and on radio and TV stations in a way that allowed audience members to attend to a presentation or not" (Vorderer 2000, p. 22). In contrast, we define digital media as media that utilizes new technology (i.e., computers) and "offers their users an opportunity to not only select specific content and respond to it, but also to modify the content that is presented to them" (Vorderer 2000, p. 22). A critical difference between traditional media and digital media experiences is the degree of consumers' involvement and immersion. We posit that consumers' level of interaction with traditional media generally takes the form of passive involvement and is less absorbing compared to their level of interaction with digital media. As a consequence of the relatively high level of viewer-directed interaction with digital media, we suspect that consumers' attention may be more distracted from product placement events that occur in that context than product placements embedded within more traditional media (see also Glass 2007; Vorderer 2000; Yang, Roskos-Ewoldsen, Dinu, and Arpan 2006). In turn, our expectation is that viewers' distraction from product placement events within digital media would impair their future ability to explicitly recall details of those product placement events. As counterintuitive as it may seem, we suggest that the failure to explicitly recall details of product placement events will often convey more benefits to the featured brand than product placement events that are more explicitly memorable.

During exposure to digital media, the viewer may experience this higher level of immersion most strongly while engaged in online games. Even so, we suggest that other forms digital media, such as browsing content-driven or community-building websites (e.g., blogs, *YouTube* videos, and *FaceBook* pages), are uniquely immersive as well. Hence, an understanding as to how the processing of product placements differ when presented in the context of traditional versus digital media must accommodate for this difference in the viewers' level of engagement. The effectiveness of a single product placement event may well depend on which of these two media categories acts as host to that event. Before turning our attention to the use of product placement in digital media, we will first discuss the use of product placements in traditional media and the evidence that has demonstrated the effectiveness of these product placements.

PRODUCT PLACEMENT IN TRADITIONAL MEDIA

Up to now, the most common method for evaluating the effectiveness of product placements within traditional media have focused on the memorability of the brand featured in the product placement event. Such research often reveals that product placements do enhance future recall of information related to the embedded brand (e.g., Babin and Carder 1996; Gupta and Lord 1998). Nevertheless, a number of studies also reveal that only a tenuous and inconsistent association exists between product placements' role in enhancing memory for brand-related information and enhancement of viewers' evaluation and/or actual choice of the brand among competing alternatives. Research indicates that the association between viewers' future success in remembering a product placement experience and their subsequent evaluation and/or choice of the brand can be negative (Law and Braun 2000), positive (Weaver and Oliver 2000), mixed (Russell 2002; Yang and Roskos-Ewoldsen 2007), or absent altogether (van Reijmersdal, Neijens, and Smit 2007).

For example, research by Law and Braun (2000) emphasized the complexity of using memory measures as a gauge of the effectiveness of product placements. In their study, participants were presented with short video clips that contained products that were seen-only, heard-only or audiovisual (both seen and heard). Their results revealed that the presentation of audiovisual products led to the best performance on subsequent memory measures (recall and recognition measures), but unfavorable outcomes in the brand choice task. In contrast, the presentation of seen-only products led to the poorest performance on the recognition task, but the most favorable choice outcomes. Supporting Law and Braun's initial findings, other researchers have confirmed that factors promoting enhanced success in remembering a product placement experience can result in negative outcomes for the brand, both with respect to the viewers' attitude toward the brand and their likelihood of choosing the brand among alternatives (e.g., Auty and Lewis 2004; Matthes et al. 2007).

Despite these observations demonstrating that a negative association can exist between the memorability of a product placement event and the viewers' brand evaluations and/or brand choices, other studies suggest that this association can be positive in some instances. Weaver and Oliver (2000), for example, found that exposure to a product placement event both improved recognition scores and enhanced attitude ratings for a brand that appeared in a clip from a television show. Russell (2002), however, found both a positive and negative relationship between memory measures and attitude ratings for embedded brands. In her study, Russell explored the impact of product placement modality (audio vs. visual presentation) and the degree of association between the product placement event and the plot of the sitcom in which the event occurred. The outcome was that both of these factors interacted in complex ways when contributing to both memory and attitude ratings. For auditory placements, the product placement was more likely to be remembered later than for visual placements, regardless of the placement's connection with the plot. Moreover, these auditory placements resulted in the most favorable brand evaluations when the product was highly connected with the plot. In contrast, visual placements resulted in the least favorable brand evaluations when the product placement was highly connected with the plot. Notwithstanding these findings, a recent study by van Reijmersdal et al. (2007) obtained no evidence of an association between memory measures of a product placement event and the favorability of participants' evaluations for the featured brand.

Together, these investigations of the consequence of product placement events within traditional media contexts suggest that a complex relationship exists between characteristics of the product placement event, later success in remembering that event, and the consequences of the product placement for viewers' brand evaluations and purchasing choices. Later in this chapter, we will closely examine the role that various factors play in determining the effectiveness (or lack of effectiveness) of product placement events. In the next section, however, we will provide a brief overview of current industry trends and previous research that has examined the use and effectiveness of product placements in digital media.

PRODUCT PLACEMENTS IN DIGITAL MEDIA

Although inconsistent results as to the effectiveness of product placements in traditional media makes it difficult to formulate a unified conceptual model of product placement that could be applied to product placements embedded within digital media, we speculate that digital media may be a more consistently effective outlet for product placements. Already, product placements are on the rise in digital media outlets, having been increasingly embedded within blogs, *YouTube* videos, *FaceBook* pages, and online games. Kuchinskas (2004) has reported that *Marqui* recruited bloggers to mention their brand in exchange for a substantial monetary incentive. A new software application, *SplashCast*, allows members of *FaceBook* to post videos on their page that advertisers can modify by placing their brand. Viewers of the video may then select the featured product from a link, which brings them into contact with more information about the brand or to pages that provide the viewer with an opportunity to buy the product (Shields 2008). *Sprint Nextel* has reportedly offered $20 for the first 1,000 *YouTube* videos that somehow incorporates their new *Samsung* phone (Admin 2008). A recently developed website, *PayPerPost.com*, provides a means for advertisers to contact bloggers that they wish to insert product placements within their websites. Similarly, *brandfame.com* offers a service that both producers and advertisers can use to promote consumers' access to their marketing videos on video-sharing websites, like *YouTube*. Such efforts to take advantage of the product placement opportunities that exist within digital media environments are likely to continue, or even accelerate, in the future.

Given the highly stimulating and self-directed nature of digital media consumption, we expect that consumers tend to become more absorbed and engaged into the media consumption, compared to when merely passively viewing traditional media. In this way, we expect that the immersive processing that occurs when interacting with digital media will promote a basic similarity between viewers' experience of product placements within digital media and their experience with more conventional advertising campaigns that employ a narrative. Marketing a brand by building an engaging story around it, rather than engaging directly in arguments as to the strengths of the brand, has been found to promote forming an association between the brand and positive affect (Green and Brock 2000; Sujan, Bettman, and Baumgartner 1993) and reduces the consumers' engagement in critical thoughts about claims made about the brand (Green and Brock 2000, Escalas 2004, 2007). Presumably, the viewers' engagement into the story stimulates positive emotional responses that can be transferred onto the brand and distracts viewers from developing criticisms of the brand's quality and desirability. Likewise, our expectation is that the immersive quality of consumers' interactions with digital media will convey similar positive outcomes for product placements embedded within those media. In particular, due to the viewers' active engagement in digital media experiences, product placements within those contexts should generally benefit from: 1) positive associations generated by the viewers' interactions and 2) a reduction of the amount of resources that the viewers has available. As with narrative forms of advertising, enjoyment of the digital media experience itself may convey some positive affective associations onto the brand that appears in that context. At the same time, the high level of mental resources demanded by active engagement with digital media ought to minimize the resources available for viewers to become aware of the marketing strategy embodied by the product placement and should reduce their capacity to engage in negative thoughts either about the brand or about the product placement strategy (Li, Daugherty and Biocca, 2001, 2002, 2003; Nicovich 2005; Wirth et al. 2007; Wright 2002).

In support of these predictions, Lee and Faber (2007) found that the level of immersion influenced the effects of product placements that occurred within online games. When online game players were required to allocate more cognitive resources to playing the game, these players showed low levels of recall for brands that appeared in the online game. That is, players who were inexperienced showed lower levels of recall for the embedded brand, compared to players who were experienced. Moreover, when experienced players where highly involved with the online game, they also performed poorly on a subsequent brand recall task. Unfortunately, evaluative and choice measures were not collected for this study, so the impact of immersion on these measures still needs to be specified. Nevertheless, product placements that are embedded within highly immersive environments, such as digital media, ought to produce more positive evaluative and choice outcomes for embedded brands than product placements embedded within more passively-viewed environments, such as traditional media. Given these predictions, product placements within digital media may provide a most promising venue for marketers to feature their products. In contrast, decisions about whether to pursue product placements within some form of traditional media ought to follow considerations about the viewers' level of engagement within that media experience.

Although we suspect that product placements within digital media will be more consistently effective at enhancing consumers' brand attitudes and the likelihood of choosing a brand among alternatives, these ideas have yet to be rigorously tested. In consequence, we perceive the research literature on the effectiveness of product placements within both traditional and digital media to be quite sparse, particularly when considering the enthusiasm and extravagance with which companies pursue costly product placement initiatives. In the next section, we seek to provide a theoretical foundation for future research on the factors that promote effective product placement events. Our approach treats a single product placement event as not necessarily valuable either for increasing sales of a brand or increasing consumers' positive evaluation of a brand. Instead, we presume that whether or not a product placement event will result in positive consequences for the profitability of a brand will depend on a combination of influences that stem primarily from the degree of a consumers' immersion within the media experience. In subsequent sections of this chapter, we identify several factors that are known to be important in determining the consequences of a product placement event for brand memorability, brand evaluations, and brand choices. What this review of the literature reveals is that factors that enhance memorability of a product placement event will also tend to reduce consumers' evaluations and likelihood of choosing the featured brand. In combination, this research also reveals that high levels of immersion in a media experience will also tend to lower the memorability of a product placement event, producing benefits for a brand on the dimensions of consumers' evaluations of the brand and their choice of the brand among alternatives. We end the chapter by describing a conceptual model designed to highlight the processes that we perceive as giving rise to this negative association between product placement memorability and brand evaluations/choices. In particular, we use this conceptual model to illustrate our expectations as to why product placements that occur within digital media should tend to be more effective at enhancing sales of a featured brand than product placements that occur within traditional media.

FACTORS THAT DETERMINE THE CONSEQUENCE OF PRODUCT PLACEMENTS

The Role of Consumer Presence on Product Placement Outcomes

Presence refers to the psychological feeling of being located and acting within a mediated environment, rather than the true environment in which an individual is located (Grigorovici and Constantin 2004; Li et al. 2001, 2002, 2003; Nicovich 2005; Wirth et al. 2007). In other words, presence is loosely defined as the perception of being in the media in which an individual is viewing. Although presence occurs, to some extent, for all forms of media, presence is expected to be highest for digital media experiences. Presence will be enhanced for digital media because of the immersive nature of this type of media. That is, digital media provides viewers with the opportunity to interact with the media (i.e., actively search the internet for particular websites) and incorporates a number of senses (i.e., visual, auditory and kinesthetic sensations may be involved when playing an online game), which contribute to enhancing a sense of presence when exposed to product placements that occur within this type of media (Wirth et al. 2007).

Research that has examined the impact of immersion within digital media has found support for the importance of this factor in influencing brand evaluative and choice outcomes. Li et al. (2002) found favorable outcomes for products that were advertised using immersive digital 3D advertising. These favorable brand outcomes were found to be driven by the increased sense of presence that occurred for products that were presented using 3D advertising. Furthermore, the highly immersive nature of digital media environments has been found to also impact the outcomes of product placements. Grigorivici and Constantin (2004) examined the effectiveness of product placements that occurred within a 3D world that induced a feeling of presence in the viewer. Although Grigorivici and Constantin found that viewers performed poorly on recognition and recall tasks, they did show a more favorable preference rating after brand exposure.

Similarly, research by Nicovich (2005) found the participants who were involved with an interactive computerized video game reported positive ratings of advertisements that occurred during the video game.

Thus, although the feeling of presence may interfere with brand-memory performance, presence appears to produce positive brand-evaluative outcomes for product placement that occur within both traditional and digital media. We suspect that immersion and the feeling of presence results in poor memory performance for featured brands, but favorable evaluative outcomes because of the cascading affect that presence has on persuasion knowledge and memory. That is, to maintain the feeling of presence, cognitive resources are allocated to the processing of information that enhances the media experience. As a consequence, cognitive resources that may have been otherwise used to elaborate upon the brand and activate persuasion knowledge are not available; hence, the memorability of the brand will be low, but the evaluative and choice outcomes are expected to be favorable. We elaborate upon this notion by describing how persuasion knowledge and memory processes are influenced by the feeling of presence in the sections that follow.

Persuasion Knowledge

According to the Persuasion Knowledge Model (PKM; Friestad and Wright 1994), an event is perceived as being a persuasion attempt if the target (i.e., the viewer or the consumer) has accumulated sufficient persuasion knowledge to identify an agent (i.e., a marketer or a salesperson) as engaging in a persuasion tactic. Given that product placements are being used more frequently as a deliberate strategy by marketers, it is likely that viewers are becoming more aware of product placement events as a form of a persuasion attempt. As a result, viewers may discount the use of the brand within the media context as a motive for purchasing that brand in the future or they may discount the character that is using the product as a true endorser of it. Moreover, they may allocate cognitive resources to processing the brand and become disengaged, frustrated, or annoyed with the medium in which the placement occurs (Bhatnagar and Wan 2009; Friestad and Wright 1994). Recent studies provide evidence for the negative impact that persuasion knowledge has product placement outcomes (Cowley and Barron 2008; Matthes et al. 2007; Russell 2002). Although such product placement events that attract cognitive resources in this way may be memorable, the viewer can react by punishing the brand with lower evaluations and a lower likelihood of purchasing the brand in the future.

Providing more direct evidence of the impact of activating persuasion knowledge, Wei, Fischer, and Main (2008) found that, within a radio broadcast, awareness of a product placement event tended to produce less favorable evaluations for the featured brands. However, listeners' evaluations of brands that were high in familiarity or that were highly congruent with the content of the radio broadcast were not negatively affected by the activation of persuasion knowledge. Moreover, when the product placement event was stated as being a deliberately paid placement by the brand, listeners evaluated the brands more favorably than when listeners were aware of product placement events that were more subtle. This result suggests that negative brand evaluations are most likely to occur when consumers become aware of a product placement event that is meant to be subtle. Presumably, persuasion knowledge activation is most damaging to brand evaluations when it occurs during what consumers perceive as covert instances of product placement.

We suggest that the level of presence is critical in determining whether or not the activation of persuasion knowledge occurs. Just as narrative processing in advertising has been found to increase positive affect (Green and Brock 2000; Sujan et al. 1993) and reduce critical thoughts (Green and Brock 2000, Escalas 2004, 2007), we expect that the high sense of presence generated by an immersive media experience will minimize viewers' awareness of the persuasion tactics represented by a product placement event (see also Campbell and Kirmani 2000). Due to constraints on cognitive processing, immersion within a media experience will make processing resources less available for becoming aware of persuasion tactics. Consequently, media experiences that are highly immersive will be more immune to the negative consequences commonly associated with persuasion knowledge activation, resulting in comparatively more positive consequences of the product placement event for enhancing consumers' brand evaluations and their tendency to choose the brand over its competitors (Campbell and Kirmani 2000; Friestad and Wright 1994; Wright 1974). As discussed above, digital media experiences ought to be particularly suited for maximizing the effectiveness of product placements, because such experiences generally demand a higher level of consumer immersion and promote a greater sense of consumer presence than traditional media experiences.

Memory

Although past research indicates a complex relationship between the impact of a product placement on brand-related memory and brand evaluative and choice outcomes, we maintain that memory plays a critical role in influencing the relationship between exposure to a product placement and brand evaluations and choice. We speculate that the nature of the relationship between memory outcomes and evaluative and choice outcomes is dependant on the content of the information that is remembered. By considering how the content of the information remembered from a product placement event alters brand evaluations and selections, we deviate from the approach used in prior research, which has focused on brand-related memory outcomes as being independent from evaluative and choice outcomes. When the medium is not highly immersive, viewers will elaborate upon and remember brand-related information. This allocation of cognitive resources will, therefore, carry forward to negatively impact evaluative and choice outcomes (Auty and Lewis 2004; Law and Braun 2000; Matthes et al. 2007). However, when the media is highly immersive, viewers will experience an enhanced feeling of presence (Grigorivici and Constantin 2004), and will, accordingly, be more inclined to process information related to enhancing their media experience. As a consequence, memory for media-related information will be enhanced, which has been found to positively affect brand attitude and choice (Escalas 2004, 2007). Digital media experiences are expected to result in poor remembering if brand-related information (Grigorivici and Constantin 2004) accompanied by good remembering of media-related information, making them apt for producing positive brand evaluations and selections.

The Role of Product Placement Prominence on Product Placement Outcomes

Another factor that has been previously shown to play an important role in impacting the effectiveness of product placement in traditional media is the prominence of the brand in the media in which it appears. A fairly consistent finding from traditional media is that more prominent brands placements result in better performance on memorability measures, but less favorable brand attitude ratings (Cowley and Barron, 2008; Matthes et al. 2007) or a lower likelihood of choosing the brand among alternatives (Auty and Lewis 2004; Law and Braun 2000). However, other studies suggest product placement prominence produces mixed memory and attitude results (Russell 2002; Yang and Roskos-Ewoldsen 2007), or positive results for both product placement memorability and attitude ratings (Weaver and Oliver 2000). Thus, the prominence of a product placement event can produce different outcome matrices, composed of measures of brand memory, brand evaluations, and brand choices.

Initial research within a digital media context by Grigorovici and Constantin (2004) found that brands that were presented obtrusively in the form of billboards within a virtual reality scene were more likely to be remembered, compared to brands that were presented as integrated product placements within the scene. Adding to and qualifying these findings, Lee and Faber (2007) found that memory for brands that appeared focally within an online game were more likely to be remembered, compared to brands that appeared more peripherally. However, this finding was qualified by the interaction between the prominence of the placement, the players' level of experience and involvement. That is, prominently displayed brands were more likely to be remembered by all groups of players, except for experienced players who were highly involved with the game. The authors suggested that this finding indicates that experienced players who were highly immersed in the experience were intensely focused on completing the game, and, therefore, did not have cognitive resources available to process even prominent, centrally-displayed brands.

Despite the frequently poor future remembering of brands featured in digital media product placements, as reported by Lee and Faber and others (e.g., Chaney, Lin, and Chaney 2004; Grigorovici and Constantin 2004; Nelson 2002), memorability of the featured brands improve when the brand is highly integrated into the digital medium, as with online advergames in which the brand plays an integral role in the game (Winkler and Buckner 2006). Thus, the memory outcomes that result from the impact of the prominence of the product placement support the propositions outlined in our conceptual model. Mainly, when brands are integrated with the media that a viewer is exposed to, viewers tend to remember the brands, which may lead to less favorable evaluative and choice outcomes. In contrast, when brands are presented peripherally, viewers are less likely to remember those brands, which may lead to more favorable evaluative and choice outcomes. Given the different impact that prominence has on brand memorability, evaluative and choice outcomes, it is essential that marketing practitioners deliberately specify the wanted outcomes of using a product placement in order to eschew outcomes that may not be the goal of the product placement.

The Role of Product Placement Modality on Product Placement Outcomes

Another factor that has demonstrated its role in determining the effectiveness of product placements within traditional media is the modality in which the brand appears in the placement. In line with Paivio's (1986) dual coding theory, Law and Braun (2000) found that audiovisual items were best remembered. This advantage was thought to arise because the information was stored as both visual and auditory information. However, the relationship between memorability outcomes and evaluative and choice outcomes appears to be qualified by the congruence between the modality and the prominence of the placement (Russell 2002). That is, since auditory information perpetuates the development of the plot, subtle product placements are incongruent and prominent auditory product placements are congruent with this type of placement. In contrast, since visual information provides the background information for the plot, prominent product placements are incongruent and subtle visual product placements are congruent with this type of placement. As a consequence of the match between modality and prominence, incongruent information would be expected to receive an atypically high amount of cognitive processing, where as congruent information would not be expected to receive any additional cognitive processing. Indeed, Russell (2002) found results that supported these hypotheses. Mainly, prominent auditory product placements were found to be remembered and to be more favorable evaluated by the viewers. However, prominent visual product placements were found remembered well also, but to be less favorably evaluated by the viewers. These findings emphasize the importance of considering how various factors may interact with one another and, in turn, determine the effectiveness of the product placement event. Nevertheless, the underlying factor that appears to determine product placement effectiveness is the manner in which cognitive resources are allocated. Allocation of cognitive resources away from the product placement event will reduce the memorability of brand, but, ultimately, lead to more favorable evaluative and choice outcomes.

With respect to digital media, to date, there have not been any studies that have examined the specific impact of modality on the effectiveness of product placements. Despite this gap in the literature, the propositions that are outlined in our conceptual model may provide a guideline for practitioners and researchers who are interested in examining the moderating role of modality in the effectives of product placement in digital media. That is, product placements that attract a high amount of cognitive resources would be expected to result in improved memory performance, but lead to less favorable brand evaluations and less favorable outcomes regarding consumers' tendency to choose a brand among alternatives. Of course, given the difference in the way a user interacts with digital media, the relationship that has been found for modality with traditional media may not be found for digital media. Since many forms of digital media utilize visually rich media, perhaps visual information is treated as more integral to digital media experiences, compared to auditory information. As a consequence, the interaction between modality and the prominence of the product placement may be found to vary depending on the type of media in which the product placement is embedded. Since this proposition has not been tested, investigating the role of product placement modality in digital media would be insightful for both consumer psychology researchers and marketing practitioners.

The Role of Product-Medium Fit on Product Placement Outcomes

The extent to which a product fits within the content of a media experience is known to be an important factor that determines effectiveness of product placements. Lee and Faber (2007), for example, found that inexperienced online game players were more likely to remember product placements that were irrelevant to the tasks required by an online game than were experienced game players. Lee and Faber suspected that inexperienced players are relatively less able to selectively process only information that is related to performing well in the game. As a result, game-irrelevant product placements will be processed by these players, but will tend not to be processed by experienced game players, who are more proficient at selectively attending to only game-relevant information. Findings from other research by Nelson (2002) also supports the notion that incongruent or atypical product placements tend to be better remembered than congruent, or typical, product placements. Despite the greater memorability of incongruent product placements, based on the conceptual model developed in this chapter, this outcome is expected to translate into less favorable evaluation and choice outcomes for the featured brand.

The Role of Consumers' Past Brand Experience on Product Placement Outcomes

Consumers' preconceived notions about brands that appear as product placements may impact the effectives of product placements. Nelson (2002), for example, found that recall for brands embedded within a video game differed depending on the player's previous experience with the brand. Specifically, brands that were relatively novel were more likely to be recalled, compared to more familiar brands. More recently, Wei et al. (2008) presented participants with a clip from a radio broadcast that was manipulated to contain either a familiar or unfamiliar brand. Wei et al. found that evaluations of the familiar brand were favorable, even when participants were aware of the persuasion tactics that were being employed. Thus, the negative effects of activating persuasion knowledge were reduced when consumers had some preexisting knowledge about a brand that appeared as a product placement.

In combination, Nelson's (2002) and Wei et al.'s (2008) findings suggest that although familiar brands that appear in a product placement might be less likely to be remembered, these brands appear to be protected from negative outcomes that may result from activating persuasion knowledge. Possible reasons that highly familiar brands are more effective candidates for product placements is that they are less likely to be remembered by the consumer and may be more integrated with the content of the media experience than less familiar brands (Balasubramanian et al. 2006). In consequence, brand evaluations and choice of a brand will be enhanced for familiar brands even while memorability for the product placement experience is relatively poor. Nevertheless, whether a product placement strategy will be useful for an unfamiliar brand may depend on the objectives of the marketing campaign.

Returning to a recurring theme in this chapter, marketing practitioners should weigh the value of making a product placement event memorable against the potential cost of consumers' awareness of the product placement causing the activation of persuasion knowledge. In turn, this persuasion knowledge could have negative consequences for other key measures of product placement effectiveness. If the main objective of a product placement is to enhance brand awareness, featuring a less familiar brand in that way might be useful, since memorability of the brand will tend to be higher than for brands that the consumer has less familiarity. Even so, featuring a less familiar brand in a product placement event poses some risk that enhanced memorability of the product placement event will also be associated with lower brand evaluations and a suppressed tendency to actually purchase the brand.

CONCEPTUAL MODEL OF PRODUCT PLACEMENT EFFECTIVENESS: TRADITIONAL VERSUS DIGITAL MEDIA

Throughout this chapter we have provided a review of the literature that describes various outcomes of product placements in both traditional and digital media. The overwhelming finding from this review is that factors that enhance the memorability of a product placement event will also tend to reduce consumers' evaluations and likelihood of choosing the featured brand. In our conceptual model (see Figure 1), we attempt to integrate these findings by outlining factors that alter the manner in which a product placement event is perceived by a viewer.

Foremost among these factors is the degree of consumers' immersion within the media experience. When consumers are highly immersed with the media, as with digital media, we expect that cognitive resources will be allocated to processing information related to enhancing their media experience. In contrast, when consumers are passively viewing media, as with traditional media, we expect that consumers will have cognitive resources available to process brand-related information. The consequence of the availability of cognitive resources when viewing immersive versus non-immersive media influences whether consumers elaborates upon and remembers media-related or brand-related information. The difference between the content of the product placement event that is

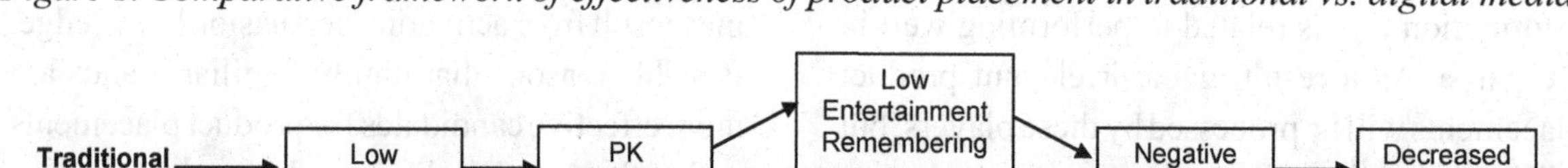

Figure 1. Comparative framework of effectiveness of product placement in traditional vs. digital media

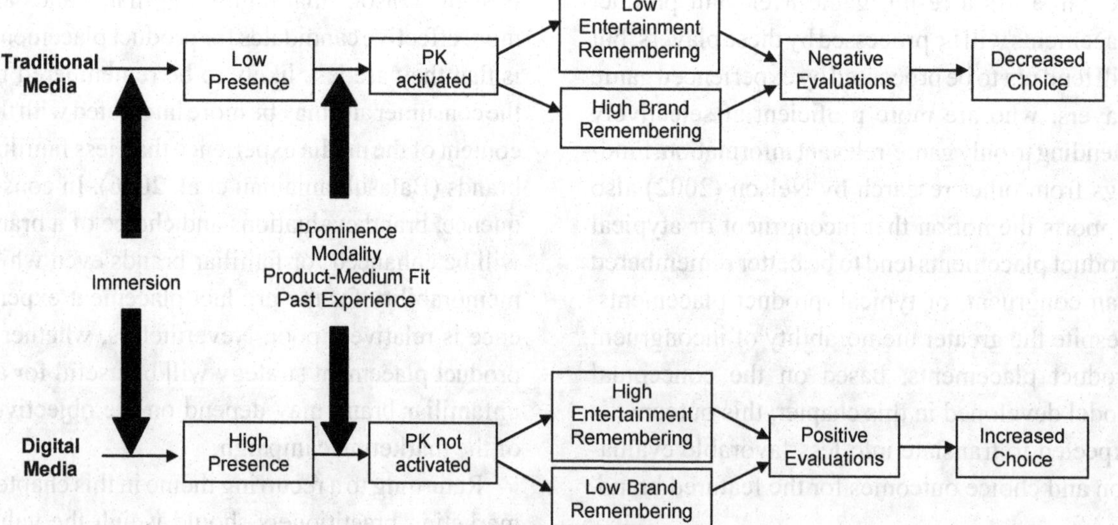

remembered by the consumer after viewing immersive versus non-immersive media ultimately affects the consumers' evaluations of and choice of the featured brand.

In addition to the impact that immersion has on moderating the effectiveness of product placements, the impact of other factors were discussed in the preceding section. Across these additional factors, the underlying cognitive processes that influence the effectiveness of the product placement event are expected to remain the same. Mainly, when cognitive resources are available and allocated to processing brand-related information, evaluations and choice of the featured brand will suffer. However, when cognitive resources are not available and allocated to processing media-related information, evaluations and choice of the featured brand will be prosperous.

Based on our conceptual model, product placements that occur within digital media are expected to produce particularly positive brand evaluations and increase the likelihood of consumers selecting the featured brand. Mainly, consumers who view digital media are expected to become more immersed with the media experience. This increased immersion is expected to induce the feeling of presence and the processing of information related to enhancing the media experience, which, in turn, depletes the consumer of cognitive resources that may have been used to activate persuasion knowledge. Consequently, consumers' will display poor memorability for the brands that are featured during a product placement event. Importantly, however, this poor memorability of the embedded brand is expected to lead to more favorable brand evaluations and increase consumers' choice of the brand. Given the potential profitable outcomes that are predicted by our conceptual model, presenting brands within digital media offers a promising venue for marketing practitioners to pursue to increase the profitability of their brand.

REFERENCES

Admin. (2008). *Product Placement on Youtube: A New Advertising Approach?* Retrieved from http://payperclickoffer.com/product-placement-on-youtube-a-new-advertising-approach/

Auty, S., & Lewis, C. (2004, September). Exploring children's choice: The reminder effect of product placement. *Psychology and Marketing, 21*, 697–713. doi:10.1002/mar.20025

Babin, L. A., & Carder, S. T. (1996). Viewers' recognition of brands placed within a film. *International Journal of Advertising, 15*(2), 140–151.

Balasubramanian, S. K., Karrh, J. A., & Patwardhan, H. (2006). Audience response to product placements: An integrative framework and future research agenda. *Journal of Advertising, 35*(3), 115–141. doi:10.2753/JOA0091-3367350308

Bhatnaghar, N., & Wan, F. (2009). *Dual Impacts of Self-Character Similarity: The Moderating Role of Narrative Immersion on Product Placement Effects*. Working paper, Asper School of Business, University of Manitoba.

Brown, E. (2006). *Product Placement on the Rise in Video Games: Marketers Desperate to Engage well-to-do market of 132 Million Gamers*. Retrieved from http://www.msnbc.msn.com/id/13960083/

Campbell, M. C., & Kirmani, A. (2000, June). Consumers' use of persuasion knowledge: The effects of accessibility and cognitive capacity on perceptions of an influence agent. *The Journal of Consumer Research, 27*, 69–83. doi:10.1086/314309

Chaney, I. M., Lin, K.-H., & Chaney, J. (2004). The effect of billboards within the gaming environment. *Journal of Interactive Media, 5*(1), 54–69.

Cowley, E., & Barron, C. (2008). When product placement goes wrong: The effects of program liking and placement prominence. *Journal of Advertising, 37*(1), 89–98. doi:10.2753/JOA0091-3367370107

Dickens, C. (1837). *The Posthumous Papers of the Pickwick Club*. Oxford, UK: Chapman and Hall.

Escalas, J. E. (2004). Imagine yourself in the product: Mental simulation, narrative transportation, and persuasion. *Journal of Advertising, 33*(2), 37–48.

Escalas, J. E. (2007, March). Self-referencing and persuasion: Narrative transportation versus analytical elaboration. *The Journal of Consumer Research, 33*, 421–429. doi:10.1086/510216

Friestad, M., & Wright, P. (1994). The persuasion knowledge model: How people cope with persuasion attempts. *The Journal of Consumer Research, 21*(1), 1–31. doi:10.1086/209380

Glass, Z. (2007). The effectiveness of product placement in video games. *Journal of Interactive Advertising, 8*(1). Retrieved from http://www.jiad.org/article96.

Green, M. C., & Brock, T. C. (2000). The role of transportation in the persuasiveness of public narratives. *Journal of Personality and Social Psychology, 79*(5), 701–721. doi:10.1037/0022-3514.79.5.701

Grigorovici, D. M., & Constantin, C. D. (2004). Experiencing interactive advertising beyond rich media: Impacts of ad type and presence on brand effectiveness in 3D gaming immersive virtual environments. *Journal of Interactive Media, 5*(1), 31–53.

Gupta, P. B., & Lord, K. R. (1998). Product placement in movies: The effect of prominence and mode on audience recall. *Journal of Current Issues in Research and Advertising, 20*(1), 47–59.

Kuchinskas, S. (2004). *Marqui Product Placement in Blogs.* Retrieved from http://www.internetnews.com/ec-news/article.php/3440401

Law, S., & Braun, K. A. (2000). I'll have what she's having: Gauging the impact of product placements on viewers. *Psychology and Marketing, 17*(12), 1059–1075. doi:10.1002/1520-6793(200012)17:12<1059::AID-MAR3>3.0.CO;2-V

Lee, M., & Faber, R. J. (2007). Effects of product placement in on-line games on brand memory: A perspective of the limited-capacity model of attention. *Journal of Advertising, 36*(4), 75–90. doi:10.2753/JOA0091-3367360406

Li, H., Daugherty, T., & Biocca, F. (2001). Characteristics of virtual experience in electronic commerce: A protocol analysis. *Journal of Interactive Marketing, 15*(3), 13–30. doi:10.1002/dir.1013

Li, H., Daugherty, T., & Biocca, F. (2002). Impact of 3-D advertising on product knowledge, brand attitude, and purchase intention: The mediating role of presence. *Journal of Advertising, 31*(3), 43–58.

Li, H., Daugherty, T., & Biocca, F. (2003). The role of virtual experience in consumer learning. *Journal of Consumer Psychology, 13*(4), 395–407. doi:10.1207/S15327663JCP1304_07

Matthes, J., Schemer, C., & Wirth, W. (2007). More than meets the eye: Investigating the hidden impact of brand placements in television magazines. *International Journal of Advertising, 26*(4), 477–503.

Media, P. Q. (2005). *Product Placement Spending in Media 2005*. Retrieved from http://www.pqmedia.com/product-placement-spending-in-media.html

Neer, K. (2003). *How Product Placement Works.* Retrieved from http://money.howstuffworks.com/product-placement.htm

Nelson, M. R. (2002, March). Recall of brand placements in computer/video games. *Journal of Advertising Research*, *42*, 80–92.

Newell, J., Salmon, C. T., & Chang, S. (2006). The hidden history of product placement. *Journal of Broadcasting & Electronic Media*, *50*(4), 575–594. doi:10.1207/s15506878jobem5004_1

Nichovich, S. G. (2005). The effect of involvement on ad judgment in a video game environment: The mediating role of presence. *Journal of Interactive Advertising*, *6*(1). Retrieved from http://www.jiad.org/article67.

Paivio, A. (1986). *Mental Representativeness: A Dual Coding Approach*. New York: Oxford University Press.

Rich, M. (2008). In Book for Young, Two Views on Product Placement. *New York Times*. Retrieved from http://www.nytimes.com/2008/02/19/books/19cathy.html?_r=1&oref=slogin

Russell, C. A. (2002, December). Investigating the effectiveness of product placements in television shows: The role of modality and plot connection congruence on brand memory and attitude. *The Journal of Consumer Research*, *29*, 306–318. doi:10.1086/344432

Shields, M. (2008). *SplashCast Launches Product Placement Platform: The Startup Produces Mini, Multimedia Applications That Users Can Add to Their MySpace and Facebook Pages*. Retrieved from http://www.mediaweek.com/mw/content_display/esearch/e3i90cbbc45ee5b571635f598a25fc68192.

Sujan, M., Bettman, J. R., & Baumgartner, H. (1993). Influencing consumer judgments using autobiographical memories: A self-referencing perspective. *JMR, Journal of Marketing Research*, *30*(4), 422–436. doi:10.2307/3172688

van Reijmersdal, E. A., Neijens, P. C., & Smit, E. G. (2007). Effects of television brand placement on brand image. *Psychology and Marketing*, *24*(5), 403–420. doi:10.1002/mar.20166

Vollmers, S., & Mizerski, R. (1994). A Review and Investigation into the Effectiveness of Product Placements in Films. In K. Whitehill King (Eds.), *Conference Proceedings of the 1994 Conference of the American Academy of Advertising* (pp. 97-102). Athens, GA: American Academy of Advertising.

Vorderer, P. (2000). Interactive Entertainment and Beyond. In Zillmann, D., & Vorderer, P. (Eds.), *Media Entertainment: The Psychology of Its Appeal* (pp. 21–36). Mahwah, NJ: Lawrence Erlbaum.

Weaver, D. T., & Oliver, M. B. (2000 June). *Television Programs and Advertising: Measuring the Effectiveness of Product Placement within Seinfeld*. Paper presented to the Mass Communication Division at the 50th annual conference of the International Communication Association (ICA), Acapulco, Mexico.

Wei, M.-L., Fischer, E., & Main, K. J. (2008). An examination of the effects of activating persuasion knowledge on consumer response to brands engaging in covert marketing. *Journal of Public Policy & Marketing*, *27*(1), 34–44. doi:10.1509/jppm.27.1.34

Winkler, T., & Buckner, K. (2006). Receptiveness of gamers to embedded brand messages in advergames: Attitudes towards product placement. *Journal of Interactive Advertising*, *7*(1), 37–46.

Wirth, W., Hartmann, T., Bocking, S., Vorderer, P., Klimmt, C., & Schramm, H. (2007). A process model of the formation of spatial presence experiences. *Media Psychology*, *9*, 493–525.

Wright, P. (1974, October). The harassed decision maker: Time pressures, distractions, and the use of evidence. *The Journal of Applied Psychology*, *59*, 555–561. doi:10.1037/h0037186

Wright, P. (2002, March). Marketplace metacognition and social intelligence. *The Journal of Consumer Research*, *28*, 677–682. doi:10.1086/338210

Yang, M., & Roskos-Ewoldsen, D. R. (2007). The effectiveness of brand placements in the movies: Levels of placements, explicit and implicit memory, and brand-choice behavior. *The Journal of Communication*, *57*, 469–489. doi:10.1111/j.1460-2466.2007.00353.x

Yang, M., Roskos-Ewoldsen, D. R., Dinu, L., & Arpan, L. M. (2006). The effectiveness of 'in-game' advertising: Comparing college students' explicit and implicit memory for brand names. *Journal of Advertising*, *35*(4), 143–152. doi:10.2753/JOA0091-3367350410

Chapter 6
Evolving Media Metrics from Assumed Attention to Earned Engagement

Martha G. Russell
Stanford University, USA

ABSTRACT

This chapter stems from recent discussions with academic, advertising and channel researchers.[1] *In this review, four types of issues relevant to new agendas for advertising research are highlighted: the legacy of metrics based on the interrupted narrative model of advertising and assumed attention; real advertising campaigns as a source of innovations in developing new metrics for earned engagement; the interdisciplinary theoretical foundations for studying engagement and persuasion in advertising; and the need for advertisers, media developers and academicians to collaborate and expedite the creation of metrics to rationalize the monetization of new media used for advertising. Measuring engagement and persuasion in the current media ecology requires metrics that consider simultaneous media exposure and continuous partial attention in the context of a participatory culture and multifaceted objectives for advertising campaigns.*

INTRODUCTION

New technologies, consumer control, media fragmentation, and business pressures are contributing to a media culture of continued partial attention (Brint, 2001). This trend has produced renewed interest in understanding the dynamics of engagement and using them to execute successful, persuasive advertising campaigns. The changes produced by this trend have important implications for the questions, methods and metrics of advertising research.

The field of advertising has traditionally differentiated purchased media (space in the media is purchased by advertisers) and earned media (space in the media is acquired without payment through journalistic and public relations efforts.) In a like manner, a distinction can be made between assumed engagement, in which audience metrics count the number of people who could

DOI: 10.4018/978-1-60566-792-8.ch006

potentially pay attention to a message, and earned engagement, in which the audience engages with the message in a real or imagined way because the message is perceived to merit interaction.

Legacy audience media metrics, such as CPM (cost per thousand), CPP (cost per person), and CPI (cost per insertion), arose from the desire of channel developers, advertisers and their clients to quantify cost/benefit of media purchases. When they were developed, these legacy metrics assumed that each media channel was delivered to its audiences (individuals, family, etc.) in a singular fashion. In recent years, the range of media that advertisers can purchase has expanded. The ability to personalize messages and integrate them across media is rapidly evolving. The participatory media culture has spread globally. In short, media and its use have changed. The old metrics–although widespread in their use–are simply not sufficient for today's advertising delivery methods and the multi-tasking and multi-channel involvement taking place.

The evolution of those metrics has already begun. The traditional language of measured media measurement is being expanded with new metrics–POI (point of influence), POP (point of purchase), POC (point of consumption), buzz, and social channel indicators. Some of these are experimental; some are becoming accepted; others have yet to be invented and defined. The hope of advertisers and their clients, channel developers and researchers is that new metrics will provide actionable measures of the impact by persuasive messages on intended attitude and behavioral changes. With valid and actionable metrics, new media channels can be appropriately priced and advertisers will have a rational basis for recommending advertising strategies and media buys for their clients.

The vested interests of advertisers, their clients, channel developers, and academic researchers are somewhat different, yet all may benefit from valid and actionable new metrics. Academicians are exploring new constructs that help to explain engagement and persuasion processes in the context of continuous partial attention and a participatory media culture. Channel developers are looking for pricing models that reflect the value of audience engagement they can deliver. The agency business is in the midst of an urgent shift to realign with the cultural and business environments. With limited time available for research and reflection, practitioners make generalizations based on anecdotal evidence.

Establishing new metrics requires time and involves intellectual and operational challenges. The process is multidimensional and complex. Collaboration across these different perspectives is required if the new metrics are to be relevant across the industry.

In this time of change, collaboration among practitioners, channel and technology developers and academicians is urgently needed to accelerate the co-creation and migration of metrics from a model that assumes the engagement of an individual in an interrupted narrative to a model of earned engagement in an always-on, multi-tasking environment. In this collaboration, academicians can leverage case studies of real advertising campaigns to generate new, testable hypotheses. Practitioners can deploy academic insights to shortcut trial and error processes as they design and implement campaigns.

EVOLVING MEDIA USE AS CONTEXT

For several decades, broadcast advertising and media metrics have been based on the interrupt model of traditional narrative media, in which advertisements–persuasive messages that were intended to inform and persuade–interrupted the audiences who were engaged in the broadcast narrative. When there were only a handful of broadcast channels–e.g., radio in '30s and '40–writers initially wrote those shows (such as Fibber Magee and Molly) in order to give their sponsors an opportunity to promote their products. Writers of these shows used the interrupted narrative model for the timing of their commercial messages, and advertising agencies developed around the commissions earned from these media placements.

In those days, there were roughly a dozen markets, each with millions of persons, bringing both a receptive attitude and an expectancy of relevance, along with their undivided attention to the media experience. Now the more likely scenario includes millions of markets with approximately a dozen persons in each (Anderson, 2006). Attention to the constructed, linear narrative has evolved to periodic and partial engagement across multiple and simultaneous media that are user-centric, user-defined, and often user-generated. The objective of the old broadcast model was to reach an aggregated audience. Objectives for new media emphasize identifying and engaging niches of fragmented markets with each fragment expecting relevancy in a media ecology that includes personalized narrowcasting.

The growing use of digital technologies, personalized media and participatory expectations has had a significant impact on legacy media (newspapers, broadcast TV and radio) and their metrics of reach and frequency. In 1988 television channels reached 67% of all TV viewers. In the early 90s, channel cumulative viewership dropped to 53%. In 2003, it dropped to a 38 share, and a channel needed a minimum 12 share rating to keep a show on the air. In 2007, the top ten news websites had a larger share of audience than legacy media in the United States (Burns, 2008). In 2008 a major channel won the primetime ratings war with an 8 share rating, roughly 17 million viewers (Russell, 2008a).

Simultaneous media use by multi-tasking consumers is a fact in today's marketplace. In a landmark 2003 study, significant use of TV and Internet simultaneously was documented, also showing significant generational differences in whether people attend to each medium equally or to one more than the other (Pilotta, Schultz & Drenik, 2004). Younger consumers in the Millennial generation, born between 1978 and 1996, use media differently than people born earlier. The use patterns of this cohort have had a significant impact on media (Ito, 2009). Studies have documented that Millennials used media for an average of 10.5 hours a day in 2008, compared to 7 hours a day in the '90s, and that they used different media than previous generations (Lenhart et al., 2007).

Consumer-generated media–such as blogs, wikis and social channeling sites–have gained wide use and credibility by this segment, which has essentially defined social channels–41% use MySpace, Facebook, or similar channels daily. Millennials prefer the computer screen–the 2nd screen–to the TV screen. Many users text message regularly on what is now called the 3rd screen–the mobile device, and forty percent said they IM–instant message–every day (Lenhart et al., 2007). Millennials multi-task at an almost biological level, and their media engagement represents a complex periodicity.

Additionally, multi-channel marketing strategies have become standard practice; and permission marketing, Internet selling practices, and social media have been integrated into many strategies and campaigns. Spending on alternative media hit $73.43 billion in 2007, a 22% increase over 2006, and was forecast in 2008 to increase 27% over 2007 levels of spend (Stevenson, 2007). In the four years between 2005 and 2008, audience engagement in user-generated video grew from slightly over 3 billion in 2005 to 35 trillion views in 2008 (AccuStream, 2008).

Although the world has become more transparent to both channels and advertisers, it has also raised the bar in terms of understanding engagement, impact and value. Previous media metrics and their measurements assumed that each media exposure occurred in isolation. A more accurate understanding of the current media environment requires that measurements of attention, engagement, receptivity, persuasion, influence, and effectiveness acknowledge simultaneous media exposure.

Advertising has been described as "the art of getting a unique selling proposition into the heads of the most people at the lowest possible cost" (Reeves, 1961). It has been described as an activity that "increases people's knowledge and changes people's attitudes" (Jones, 1990). Advertising is a meaning-generating discipline and industry; advertising gives meaning to products and services. Over time, changes in both media and advertising practices reflect the cultural moment and how that changes over time. Additionally, changes in the way advertising messages are consumed reflect changes in how people relate to each other and to their media, as well as to their brands, products and services.

FIELD EXPERIENCES AND INNOVATIONS IN NEW METRICS

Advertising planners, creative professionals and media buyers are hired to devise and implement advertising campaigns that change consumer behaviors and attitudes, in the context of cultural milieu and business objectives. Their professional reputations are at stake as they work within time and budget to develop insights and integrate them into campaign strategy on behalf of their clients.

The responsibility of gathering insights and developing strategy to guide the development of creative expressions, as well as the choice of channels and media, is often assigned to advertising account planners. Planners strive to identify the right message–what to say and how to say it, the right time–when to communicate, and the right place–where to say it. They evaluate various aspects of the decision process, the media, the influencers, and the brand that are critical to producing better targeting, messaging and results for products and brands (Burns, 2008).

It's not surprising, then, that the metrics used in developing these insights and recommending strategy reflect the values held by these and other practitioners –channel developers, creative developers, media planners, brand managers, and marketers. Innovations in metrics used by these professionals in real campaigns also reflect the expectations and growing demand for accountability in the field. The evolution of new metrics provides early clues about how the advertising industry is changing.

Field examples of real advertising campaigns, shared by workshop participants, described new metrics for new media and included the research that was conducted to guide planning, as well as assessments to document effectiveness of the campaign objectives. The methods and metrics used by practitioners in these field experiences reflected the clients' and campaigns' objectives, time and budget. Results of these evaluations were intended to provide prescriptive feedback–results and insights that could be used in making the next round of decisions to reduce the risk of financial expenditures and improve the effectiveness of results. The intent to prescribe decisions that align with business objectives differentiates the research conducted by practitioners from the research conducted by academic researchers, which has a more descriptive intent and seeks to explain phenomena in the context of a field of knowledge.

Some practitioners reported that their campaigns relied on a single, well-defined metric to demonstrate success, but most used several different indicators, according to the campaigns' objectives and the media used. Developers of new media channels, for example, added awareness metrics to prove the effectiveness of new channels. Retailers, on the other hand, only believed those measures when they saw they were consistent with sales uplifts.

A single, focused objective can sometimes be documented with a single, focused metric. For example, a retail coupon program the key metric was coupon redemption (Stinson, 2008). The key metric in a sustainability and energy utilization program is behavior change, evidenced through a reduction in energy use (Armel, 2008).

However, for campaigns with more complex objectives such as loyalty or brand building, evidence of success requires several metrics that each address an aspect of the customers, their contexts, the media used, and the scope of changes sought. The more complex the objectives of the campaign, the more complex are the metrics needed to assess interim results and overall success. Suites of metrics, as well as individual metrics, gain greater meaning when changes are measured over time.

When the Mojito Party campaign for Barcardi resulted in a seven percent uplift in off-premise sales, marketers named it the "social butterfly effect," referring to Lorenz' concept in Chaos Theory (Gleick, 1987), and recognizing the channel effect of influencers in the social context. Invited to a local party by friends, consumers sampled a rum drink, called a Mojito, learned how to make it, and received the supplies they needed to introduce it to others. The active ingredient of this campaign was personal recommendation, supported by new media with collateral print and online information. The trusted metric was increased sales (Hayden, 2008).

However, new metrics for new media are emerging. They reflect variety in both campaign objectives and the use of new media. Campaign objectives continue to include awareness, familiarity, affinity, recall, preference, purchase and repeat purchase, but they also include social channel effects, recommendations and influence. New social media, mobile media, ubiquitous media, and the participatory context - surveys, polls, contests, elections, sales, redemption, requests, recommendations, and advocacy - have contributed to both the ability to measure interim results and the requirement for doing so.

Several innovative measurements have been pioneered as measures of the success of advertising in influencing the consumer decision pathway; they address one or more elements of the media, the consumer, or the context. Since many of these new approaches have been introduced in the context of real advertising, it is not surprising that they reflect the business value of actionability–the ability to apply results of those studies (or insights generated because of them) in order to prescribe strategy or make decisions. For example, the traditional change model of smoking cessation has, for many years, included the phases of precontemplation, contemplation, action, and maintenance. Based on qualitative research with smokers who were trying to quit, account planners modified this model with a middle step of building resolve (desire, acceptance, and confidence). A communication campaign was designed around the key element of resolve–re-learning triggers. The registration of smokers intending to quit at www.becomeanex.com was used as an indication of campaign success and used to document that the campaign generated resolve (Giles, 2008).

In another campaign, developed by the GSD&M agency in Austin, Texas, the account planners responsible for the Air Force recruitment campaign introduced changes into the traditional recruitment model of lead generation, career exploration and enlistment. To increase the pool of persuadable youth, the agency used experience marketing to first inspire youth and their mothers, changing the way both thought and felt about the Military, then followed with career exploration to the stimulate questions about enlistment, before any of the conversations with recruiters who affirmed interest and guided enlistment. Pre and post attitudinal measures documented the effectiveness of the inspiration-oriented experiences. A higher proportion of enlistments resulted from inquiries, presumably because the youth experienced less resistance from their mothers. The client called it a success and renewed their contract with the agency for a second 10-year period (Giles, 2008).

When over 250,000 unique visitors logged into the online Dell Lounge twice or more, following experiential marketing at Austin City Limits, advertisers and clients called it a success. Rights to the Justin Timberlake Tour at the Austin City Limits Music Festival had been purchased by BBDO with the expectation that 12,335 people in the audience every night would have the potential of hearing an advertisement. Under a promotional services agreement with Dell, the objective was identified of getting the message out into crowd. Street teams mingled through the audience and surrounding areas to hand out fliers encouraging SMS (text messaging) to get backstage, enter an arena surrounding the stage, or enter contests related to his music. Before his concert, a large video-taped image of Timberlake on the Jumbo screen promoted the importance of Dell computers in his life, and the audience was encouraged to go to the online Dell Lounge to register to win an autographed computer. Page views on the blogs of invited bloggers reflected the viral spread of news of the concert and the contest. The primary objective of the campaign was to help make Dell Computers a lifestyle brand; however, since Dell computers are sold online, the audience multiple of nearly 200 times the concert attendance commanded great respect (Hayden, 2008).

Digital technologies give advertisers greater opportunities to automatically collect information about audience exposure and response to the media delivered. They provide greater options for the creation, delivery and adaptation of communications campaigns; and tracking can be specific to the user, event and product. For example, digital screens with context-aware advertising have been introduced into waiting rooms, elevators, bars, stores and gas stations. Sensors and feedback to database-driven content systems allow advertisements on these media to dynamically change price or message (Russell, 2008b; Russell, 2009), personalize content (Cox, 2008), reflect changes in individuals' social channels (Madhok, 2008), and conform to the context (Cox, 2008) in real-time. These adaptive media have the capacity to engage and persuade consumers either in tiny bursts of on-the-go time or while consumers are waiting in the retail establishment. They can be used to deliver advertising at the point of purchase, the point of influence and the point of consumption.

Narrow-casting, the ability to send a specific message to a specific location, allows customized messages to be delivered to individual screens in public (store, bars, elevators) or private (mobile phones, automobiles) places. Both quantitative and qualitative methods have been used to measure the effectiveness of out-of-home narrowcast advertising. At the time of this writing, many of the narrow-casting channels are still in pilot or preliminary stages. Channel equipment providers have cited studies using measures of awareness and recall to document that people noticed video messages inside bars (Burns, 2008), convenience stores (Russell, 2008c) and outside at the fueling stations (Cox, 2008). They have used those measures to claim that ads placed in the new out-of-home channels worked. However, claims became believable to retailers only as increased sales of the advertised products were observed at the locations testing the channel and its ads.

Digital technology also brings narrow-casting to individuals–to their personal spaces (cars and homes) and their personal devices (computers and mobile phones). User-influenced content and events, such as contests, polls, sweepstakes, games, privileged access, and challenges, have been implemented, with quantitative measures of consumer participation used to measure their effectiveness. Experiential involvement that invites online consumer dialogue has been paired with media buys, with results showing that user-influenced and generated dialogue trails (and tracks) the scripted dialogue of media buys. Among the pairings of media buys and user involvement, online voting in response to real events and online media has been observed to generate the very strong results. (Hayden, 2008).

The metrics that track assumed attention are evolving and are now specific to particular aspects of engagement. Measures of reach (cost per thousand or CPM) continue to be used for online communications in which awareness is the primary objective. Page views and click through rates (CTR) have become accepted metrics for evaluating audience attention in online channels, and cost per click (CPC) is considered by some to be a reasonable way to evaluate ad effectiveness. Website visits and page views can be useful in comparing lift versus control markets. These metrics are easily tracked by practitioners through dashboard views that are updated on a real-time basis. Alternative creative expressions (tag lines and copy) have been tested for their effectiveness, and results have been used to optimize active ad campaigns by suspending the laggards and giving greater visibility to the winners. But if the objective of the ad goes beyond attention (and many campaigns are built on objectives that include entering the competitive set) brand-building, or affirming brand choice, other considerations are needed.

If advertising strategy includes test and control (for example with DMA or other market clusters) or seeks to compare exposed versus unexposed consumers or if the advertising objective is engagement or conversion, a number of other emerging metrics can be used to evaluate success. Search behaviors, incremental navigations, and customer signups are becoming acceptable measures to evaluate engagement and conversion. Standard reports of these include the identification of the highest and fastest gainers, changes in the frequency of queries quarter by quarter and year to year, as well as comparisons of how queries have changed - by geography and over time (Konar, 2008). Queries can also be used as an online measure of an offline campaign. The 2006 Pontiac TV ad campaign, for instance, included a call to action for online search (Hayden, 2008).

Additionally, search terms have been used to document consumer requests for information and reflect persuasion by indicating the evolution from awareness to investigation to conversion. Query volume is continuous, so search analysis can provide a flow of metrics to reflect audience engagement and inform campaign decisions. Interactive online dashboards provide advertisers with continuous metrics and multiple levels of analyses to pinpoint opportunities during the course of campaigns. New functionality in metrics dashboards allows planners to share both the metrics and their perspectives on its meaning (Konar, 2008).

Other interim measurements used to document the effectiveness of advertising in promoting consideration are based on recommendations–advocacy and word of mouth. For example, an advertising campaign conducted for MiniCooper created a website on which owners were encouraged to communicate with each other and on which they were able to direct of the conversation. A sense of community with other owners developed and drove online advocacy, measured using the online promoter score. An online promoter score was calculated by plotting measures developed from coded language and online conversations of CGM (consumer-generated media, also known as consumer generated content or user-generated content) and against sales data. At a two month lag, this metric of advocacy was shown to be a predictor of sales (Hayden, 2008).

Earned engagement is reflected in the power of online social channels to create influential recommendations. While there have been fundamental challenges to the analysis of CGM, buzz–a form of engagement and a result of engagement–can identify engaged individuals, indicates the degree of engagement, and predicts consumer response, given that engagement. Using every message as a valid data point, taking place in the context of their online social selves and social channels (their public profiles, wallpaper, group memberships, and friends), the text of blog posts and their associated comments reflect consumers' engagement. Buzz reach is a more complex metric than the traditional reach measures; it includes not only the number of eyeballs potentially exposed to content on a given page, but also on how much of that page is relevant to a product or brand, and how many people are tracking that page. Caution is needed in interpreting buzz as engagement, however, because engagement is multidimensional. Buzz relies on open data and reflects conversation–inherently complicated with slang, irony, nicknames, and jargon. Using buzz metrics demands a constant balance between precision and ambiguity. Language offers many ways of referring to one thing, and language is easily misinterpreted (Niederhoffer, 2008).

Analyzing buzz–in corporate communications (Veda, 2008) as well as at the consumer level–requires provisions for managing data quality and insight for interpretation–first becoming intimate with the data, drilling down, and taking different perspectives before making interpretation. Data for analysis can become multidimensional with methods such as weighting the source (influence), attaching metadata from traffic (how many people are viewing, how much talking, unique audience, audience growth rate), and measures of how many people are linking into the messages (authority), how quickly people are citing, and average time between linking. Insightful analysis further requires consideration of the dynamics under the buzz–the valence of the discussion, intentions, and peaks (Niederhoffer, 2008).

Many of the new buzz metrics are descriptive. To get deeper, more diagnostic clues about engagement, linguistic analysis can be added to the analysis of buzz. By measuring the types of words used, analysis reveals how individuals and groups of people, events, products and brands are related to each other. Linguistic style is closely tied to individuals' psychological and social states. In fact, studies have shown relationships of linguistic style to emotion (depression, deception), biological states (testosterone), personality (neuroticism), cognitive style (complex thinking), and traditional age, gender and class demographics (Pennebaker, Booth, Francis, 2007).

Another method of studying linguistic markers is sentiment analysis. Sentiment analysis requires highly nuanced interpretations and represents a complex set of evaluations and uses indicators such as pronoun use (shared reality and social connection), verb use (particularly emotionally-valenced or recommendation verbs), syntactical references, and style (immediacy–short words, first person pronouns, low number of articles, positive emotion, verbs more than nouns). Sentiment analysis of buzz and recommendations provides important indicators of engagement, intimacy and social connection to brands, products or services (Niederhoffer, 2008). Linguistic markers and sentiment analysis can be used to diagnose engagement in online conversations and evaluate the customer context (Pennebaker & Niederhoffer, 2003).

Prescriptive metrics are also needed to monitor the performance of campaign communications. In a multi-tasking and multi-media ecology, evaluating a campaign's effectiveness in engaging and persuading the audience requires a corresponding complexity in the metrics used. Managing the customer context involves reaching the right audience at moments of relevance, integrating and reinforcing across media and across time, creating and using interactive, engaging ad formats, and measuring and optimizing to deliver performance. Several early innovations in measuring aspects of this complexity include Reach-through-relevance, Screen-consumption-quotient, Power-Score, and Serios. "Reach-through relevance" is an approach that takes advantage of market fragmentation by crafting an advertising platform that provides multiple (and possibly simultaneous) contact with consumers who are multi-tasking across channels. Identification of these practices has been guided by a combination of old and new metrics, measuring both assumed and earned engagement along the persuasion process, as well as by its ultimate objective. The experience of one leading online channel suggests that two practices are indicative of effectiveness in achieving reach-through relevance in online advertising (Konar, 2008).

The first of these practices addresses multi-tasking. It integrates complementary content and formats across media with messages that reinforce relevance and desirability. A call to action in the Heinz campaign, based on engagement with the brand, drove the submission of qualified CGM contest video entries, hours spent watching submissions and interacting with the branded media, as well as a visible lift in ketchup sales.

The second practice, interactive and engaging ad formats, uses context-aware gadget ads to display content differently depending on the site on which it appeared. The content of the ad is synched to the content of the site and is presented on the basis of search, as well as the sequence and pages visited prior to the ad site (Konar, 2008).

The third practice, Screen Consumption Quotient, is an index for variable pricing of media space based on the number of people potentially exposed to the ad and qualified by the business value of an individual customer (Madhok, 2008) or of a particular audience (Burns, 2008). It has been developed to measure a mixture of media across a number of different market segments.

A forth practice, known as the Power Score (Giles, 2008), is a constructed metric derived for each channel at each stage of a specified decision pathway. Computation of the Power Score includes a report of exposure, influence, valence of influence, and hierarchy of influence at a particular inflection point in the defined communication architecture. Using a combination of qualitative and quantitative insights and measures, a purchase decision model is developed to: describe the desired think, feel and do outcomes intended for an advertising campaign; quantify the decision process elements–the stage relevance, the task importance, and the mindset salience; quantify brand priorities–brand equity by stages and task; and message testing and channel indices (expectation and passion) by stages and by tasks. This decision model is then transformed into a communication architecture (the connection opportunities that exist across influential interactions that are depicted as a dialogue map, a message architecture, and media roles). Using quantitative data from original and syndicated sources, a derived Power Score is constructed to assess the potential of a channel to drive awareness, top of mind, shape an opinion (Giles, 2008).

Finally, a fifth innovative perspective called Serios, relates to a monetary-based message prioritization system, which provides each user a dashboard view of their recognition by co-workers for attention to and responsiveness on highest priority team objectives. Driven by an appreciation for the economics of user attention for the approximately two billion people who use email and the estimate that in 2009 the average corporate email user will spend 41% of the workday managing email messages, Serios enables both the sender and the receiver to learn what is important to each other and to quantify the value of reading and responding (Radicati, 2007). Although developed for the work environment, value clarification in one-to-one relationships and dashboard metrics of those measures warrants consideration as relevant metrics for advertising. Advertisers, as well as corporate communication managers, acknowledge the fluidity of digital media across work time and leisure time, as well as across devices and media. Attention and engagement metrics for corporate communications have potential application for advertising communications–and vice versa.

Advertising practitioners, whether they are clients, account planners or channel developers, view the desired results of advertising according to their objectives. For each, engagement and persuasion are evaluated in the context of business objectives. Innovations in metrics for these evaluations must be influenced by the media used, and it is not unusual for innovative campaigns to include new as well as old. Practitioners want the metrics of their advertising campaigns to evaluate how well the campaign has accomplished intentional changes in the relationships between customers and their products and brands. The conundrum facing practitioners is that a single, established metric is easier to communicate, use, and manage; yet, multiple measures (often new and not fully understood) are needed to accurately reflect the engagement of audiences in today's multimedia advertising campaigns and the extent to which they are persuaded. This represents a new level of complexity for practitioners and for researchers and calls for creativity in developing new metrics that will measure engagement and persuasion across the liquidity of ubiquitous media (Russell, 2009).

ENGAGEMENT AND PERSUASION IN ADVERTISING

The traditional advertising/marketing funnel was based on discrete media exposures to individuals and focused on a pathway of building awareness, generating demand, and building brands. Early constructs were borrowed from mass communication theory to provide a basis for understanding message diffusion and distribution (Schramm & Roberts, 1961). Later, the Hierarchy of Effect model hypothesized that consumers went through a series of steps–awareness, knowledge, preference, conviction and purchase–and that they were receptive at any stage to conversion through demand fulfillment and direct response. The notion that repetitive exposure to messages improved the persuasiveness of the messages was extensively studied and became accepted (Metheringham, 1964; Krugman, 1962).

Broadcast advertising often took advantage of narrative content, with the benefit of engagement and a typically positive mood, on which an advertiser could build engagement with a brand. The notion that emotional involvement with the narrative content in the broadcast increased attention and consequently memory for the ads, was widely accepted (and disputed) by both academicians and practitioners (Doyle, 1994; Du Plessis, 2005). The interrupted narrative practices of broadcast advertising at that time were a good match for this linear model. But, assumptions of linear processing and the power of the narrative in the early narrative model have been challenged by recent trends in consumers' multi-tasking, multi-media use patterns. Attention focused on a single medium has given way to the noise of multi-tasking, escalating the challenge of creating effective engagement in an environment of partial attention (Opir et al.). Reach and frequency metrics, which were appropriate for targeting market segments in the interrupted narrative model of advertising, have been joined by clicks and conversions–metrics that reflect interaction, the choice of self-interruption, and individualized online search behaviors. The concept of earned, rather than assumed, engagement is increasingly part of advertising planning. As the objective of advertising has evolved from capturing a market to building a market, the importance of consideration–and the engagement on which it rests–has become much more important (Konar, 2008).

Today, advertising experience designers study the triggers of consumer engagement and purchase decision processes in order to identify new opportunities for the right message, time and place. One cross-channel consumer-centric approach used by advertising strategists, for example, maps the dynamics of consumer decision cycles across triggers, stages and transitions against the mindset, emotions, decision criteria, and media used by those consumers. In this approach, strategic considerations of which media to use (and how) still requires an understanding of consumer perceptions about the brand, against winners and losers in the category. But strategy also rests on an understanding of consumers' media habits and the role that media play in the context of the decision cycle on engagement and persuasion–whether those are newly encountered media, passively used media or actively sought media.

The concept of engagement is seen differently by media channel professionals, advertisers and academics. Channel professionals want to count the connections consumers have with their media so they can more convincingly say: "Buy my property. Your customers watch it. . .all the time. And they really like it!" (Hayden, 2008). This is a prescriptive objective. Advertisers and their agencies want to understand how to engage consumers in order to gain their attention and influence what they want, love and buy. Many advertising practitioners think of engagement as a multidimensional and holistic concept that is influenced by context. This context includes the many roles the media and engagement play in a consumer's life and the decision making pathway that is called into play for a specific category of goods and services. Creating a campaign requires using this as a prescription.

Academic researchers, on the other hand, generally have a descriptive objective for their studies. They use a variety of constructs and methods to understand engagement and persuasion–some holistic and integrated, some very specific and finely defined. Anthropology, ethnography, psychology, social psychology, education, and sociology–each discipline has constructs, methods and perspectives that are particular to the way engagement and persuasion are viewed. A complete and holistic understanding of a complex phenomenon, such as advertising engagement and persuasion, requires a synthesis of perspectives.

Anthropology, the study of the webs of meaning and significance that guide behavior and actions in our culture, helps provide insights for developing deeper consumer connections by providing an understanding of what's happening beneath the surface. Ethnographic researchers strive to illuminate the meaning that lies behind observed and reported behavior, providing contextual insights that help translate behavior so that its significance is clear to those on the outside (Stinson, 2008). This level of understanding, considered "thick description" (Geertz, 1974), helps practitioners to drive product/brand connections deeper, by mitigating the risks of connecting with consumers on only a shallow level and for only a very brief time.

An ethnographic approach, partially derived from anthropological perspectives on culture and meaning, is based on two fundamental assumptions. The first assumption is that consumer connections are based on symbolic properties attributed to products, services and brands; these properties vary with time, culture, location, and other factors. The second assumption is that these connections are mutable; they're subject to change by either consumers and the brand–or both. The implication of this is that both consumers and producers have power over the meaning given to brands and products; both have the ability to change (Stinson, 2008).

Psychologists have traditionally studied engagement in terms of how people relate to each other, situations and markets. They focus on one or more psychological components of engagement: cognitive (resonance–"get it"–speaks to me), emotional (totally immersed, absorbed, the opposite of indifference), social (interactive, participative and involved), and longevity–a time factor, a commitment to the future, seeing a long term relationship (Niederhoffer, 2008).

The field of psychology has proposed several different ways to think about persuasion. Persuasion, as a companion to engagement, is seen by some as a rational, active thinking process, "to cause someone to believe, convince." Others focus on the role that feelings or emotions play, "to induce, lure, attract, entice" (Oxford, 1996). In advertising, the construct of persuasion has undergone several theoretical shifts over time and across the disciplines of psychology, anthropology, and social psychology. Early explanations were based on main effects (McGuire, 1969)–such as learning theory (Hovland, Janis & Kelly, 1953; Kelman, 1958) or cognitive response theory (Greenwald, 1968). Main effects studies described the influence of persuasion variables (distraction, emotion, source credibility) on increased or decreased persuasion as a single process.

Other psychological theories attempting to explain persuasion have been based on dual process models in which information is processed by either central or peripheral routes: the Elaboration Likelihood Model (Petty & Cacioppo, 1981, 1986); the Hedonic Experiential Model (Holbrook & Hirschman, 1982); the Hierarchical Processing Model (MacInnis & Jawroski, 1989); and the Experiential Processing Model (Meyers-Lee & Malaviya, 1999). The dual process models acknowledge that multiple effects are possible for the same variable, that any one effect could be caused by different processes, and they accept the possibility that any one variable could operate differently in different situations. The dual process models differ in terms of which effects, processes and situations they use to describe those processes and effects.

Psychologists' studies also often focus on the extent to which physiological and neurological changes occur when people are engaged. Using measures of skin conductance and heart rate, their measures reflect the physical dimensions of emotional engagement (Ahn et al., 2009). Research has also shown that different regions of the brain are activated when people believe they are interacting online with real people, as opposed to with a computer-automated application, a finding with significant impact on audience engagement in online media (Chen et al., 2009). These finely-focused perspectives come together with holistic concepts, such synchrony–the matching of behaviors, the adoption of similar behavior rhythms, the manifestation of simultaneous movement and the interrelatedness of individual behaviors in studies that show synchrony (Bernieri, Reznick & Rosenthhal, 1988) and synchronicity (Nass & Moon, 2000) are related to positive affect in interactions, to interpersonal liking and smoothness of interactions, and to linguistic style matching (Niederhoffer & Pennebaker, 2000). In other words, synchrony and synchronicity aid engagement.

Other factors influence engagement as well. Applying foundational research that studied massively multiplayer games to identify critical influences in the juiciest media of its time, Reeves and Read (2009) have identified the ten ingredients for great games, and for creating engaging immersive experiences in both work and leisure environments.

The field of social psychology has also made important contributions to the understanding of persuasion. Some social psychological constructs, such as interpersonal communication (Watzlawick, Bavelas & Jackson, 1967) or the self-validation model (Bailenson et al., 2007; Petty & Brinol, 2008), focus on metacognitive processes to understand how an individual's thoughts about the content, source or process of communication may help to explain attention, relevance, and engagement with media in the human experience. "Focusing on the processes by which variables have their impact is important because it is informative about the immediate and long-term consequences of persuasion" (Petty & Brinol, 2008). Others focus on the environments–ambient as well as stationary–in which people experience environmental, social and media cues (Kaptein et al., 2010.)

Both psychologists and social psychologists have studied the influence of emotions on persuasion and decision making (Zajonc & Marcus, 1982; Mittal, 1994; Shiv & Fedhorikhin, 1999; Damasio, 2004; Bailenson et al., 2008). The notion that emotion increases attention and memory (Biel, 1990; Doyle, 1994; Du Plessis, 2005) has received acceptance by both academicians and practitioners. Nass, however, argues that moods, which last from minutes to hours, should be the focus of such studies, rather than emotions, which last only for seconds. Moods, he argues, are the emotional lenses through which people experience their worlds. Some key persuasive goals that are influenced by mood and may benefit from different mood strategies include trust, memory, persuasion, acquisition, and continued use (Nass, 2008).

Sentiments are anticipated moods, judgments that predict the ways stimuli will induce moods. Sentiments may be conscious or unconscious. The sentiments created by anticipating moods use the mechanism of transference to attach valence and arousal to products that would otherwise not elicit those responses. For example, the anticipation that "If I use this product, I will feel confident" or "This product will makes me feel happy" is based on sentiments rather than on emotion in its physiological definition.

Sentiments, according to Nass, are dominated by two dimensions: the arousal continuum that ranges from calm to excited; and the valence continuum that ranges from negative to positive. Arousal reflects a readiness for action and involves dimensions that are more physical that cognitive. Valence refers to the positive or negative content of the mood. Interesting differences have been noted in the extent to which arousal or valence dominates mood and sentiment in older and younger age cohorts, the younger being dominated by arousal, the other dominated by valence. Media psychologists have noted a secular trend across age groups such that people are becoming more arousal oriented, leading to an arousal culture that embraces constant change and abhors boredom (Nass, 2008).

Psychological theories fall short of a holistic explanation in that they do not acknowledge that people may process both central arguments and peripheral cues. Using constructs from the field of education, Woods and Murphy propose that new insights on how perception–the active part of cognition and the tools and filters through which we absorb our environment–is involved in persuasion (modifying or altering the knowledge of an individual) may require constructs of both philosophy and psychology (Woods and Murphy, 2002). In the field of philosophy, on the other hand, persuasion is framed in terms of rhetoric and often does not acknowledge conceptual change. They propose that constructs of conceptual change may be useful in understanding how organized knowledge structures change. Although Woods and Murphy focus on how people "come to believe" (i.e., are persuaded to new beliefs) in educational settings, these concepts have application in other situations in which conceptual change is the objective.

Sociologists have also embraced the question of audience engagement–using concepts of social channels and epidemiology–to study, for example, audience engagement in YouTube videos. Applying two constructs of epidemiology (a power-law distribution of waiting times between cause and action and an epidemic cascade of actions becoming the cause of future actions), the relaxation response of a social system after endogenous and exogenous bursts of activity was documented by studying the time series of daily views of YouTube videos (Crane & Sornette, 2008). Results showed fast gainers were prompted by particular events as well as by quality of the content.

In sum, current academic approaches to studying and understanding engagement and persuasion include concepts and tools sanctioned by a variety of academic colleagues and their disciplines. Each discipline has its unique perspective. For many the objective of the research has been to expand understanding, to contribute to a pool of knowledge. Some applications of these results to "real advertising" are described in the literature, but in general, these studies by academicians are intended to describe phenomena rather than to inform planning or evaluate campaign results. The constructs and tools used by practitioners for studying engagement and persuasion, on the other hand, while they may include descriptive components, are intended to be prescriptive–to guide decisions.

Just as for practitioners, there is a conundrum for academic researchers in the expectation that new measures can be developed to truly reflect engagement in new media and measure its persuasive impact. While disciplinary deconstruction of engagement and persuasion may facilitate intellectual precision in developing theoretical constructs and making logical explanations more defensible, the complexity of life outside the laboratory relegates the precision of academic measurements to research problems that are less urgent. Additionally, the requirement that academic research make new contributions to the intellectual domain means that academicians often use promising innovations as a stepping stone to the next granular insight, rather than stitching them together and refining an integrated framework.

Both academicians and practitioners are confronted with yet another conundrum for developing metrics that measure engagement and persuasion. There are some factors for which we do not yet have means to measure (yet these factors are believed to be true). There are also factors that can be measured but which are not fully understood. Professional wisdom and seasoned judgment include understanding the individual constructs as well as the metrics that integrated them. An integrated and holistic understanding is essential for the descriptive analysis of engagement and persuasion processes. An integrated and holistic understanding is also essential for the prescriptive analyses that inform strategic decisions in real campaigns. It is the synchrony of these two requirements that makes collaboration between academicians and practitioners vital to the development of metrics in the field of advertising.

RESEARCH COLLABORATION NEEDED AMONG ADVERTISERS, CHANNEL DEVELOPERS AND ACADEMICS

Theorists, analysts, and practitioners are making great strides to close the gap between old metrics and new media by developing new measures for both old and new media. These measurements and the methods by which they are obtained vary across specializations in advertising: product/brand design; out of home advertising; mobile advertising; online advertising; and experiential advertising. Methods and measurements in academic studies vary by discipline. Some measure assumed engagement; others measure earned engagement.

The challenge–and the opportunity–for channel developers, channel managers and media planners of both old and new media today–is to co-evolve new metrics that reflect the new media, the new patterns of media use, the new content, and the new mindset of exposure that will help to justify pricing, based on today's objectives for advertising effectiveness. The requirements for understanding advertising impact have now evolved beyond exposure as the primary indicator, and beyond awareness and recall as advanced levels.

The current cultural context suggests that measuring the return on advertising expenditures must reflect the consumer's relationship with the brand–across media and over time. The initial CPM metrics were created because advertisers wanted to establish a basis for pricing the opportunity to interrupt listeners' and viewers' attention to a narrative. Generally speaking, it quickly became clear to those wanting to advertise that the use of mass media was a relatively inexpensive way to do so. CPM helped justify a larger expenditure for media that had the potential to reach a larger audience in a single task, single medium environment. Measures of effectiveness, defined by metrics, were the basis of the value on which pricing was determined.

Value-defined pricing continues to be relevant today. In an environment of limited resources, media planners use metrics to evaluate the cost and benefit of potential media buys; they want to reduce the risks and increase the returns on their media spend. The desire for new metrics by practitioners necessarily reflects the accountabilities of their professions and their employers. Current cultural shifts in the scope and definition of markets, the durability of brand loyalties and the epidemiology of influence mandate the evolution of CPM toward metrics that capture the interaction between the consumer and the communication, as well as its impact on the consumer's relationship with the product or band.

In a like manner, significant opportunities exist for academic researchers to enrich theory testing, generate new hypotheses and validate new metrics through attention and engagement with real advertising campaigns–contributing to their disciplines with expanded scope. New academic research agendas in engagement and persuasion can be stimulated by the field experiments conducted by advertising planners and practitioners, and many new intellectual frontiers can be identified for advertising research. Engagement and persuasion are multidimensional phenomena that require interdisciplinary approaches to develop a full understanding; and new media are continually evolving.

The influence of emotion, moods and sentiment on happiness, confidence and trust has important academic and practical implications. The meaning of convenience–instant gratification, ease of use, and access–and its relevance to various phases of consumer purchase decision processes has both immediate and long term considerations. It is imperative to understand the relevance and role of community in empowerment, sharing, and leadership for communication and influence. The interplay of background and foreground in simultaneous media usage is foundational to understanding attention, receptivity and messaging in simultaneous media use. Further understanding of these issues may help to create metrics and also to guide their use.

Given the importance of personal context to create the relevance that earns engagement, today's planners must also study authenticity, credibility and relationship trajectories in the brand experience, in decision pathways, and in cultural context. They need earned engagement metrics that are relevant to today's self-interruptive multi-tasking, multi-media consumer-generated media environment.

Measurements of effectiveness are vital to the business propositions of new media, and parsimony is advantageous in developing metrics and standards. Definitions and standards are evolving, but at this time are treated on a situational basis. At this time, it is important to consider all innovations in measuring effectiveness and investigate their potential. But, as mentioned earlier, the choice of measurement must be closely tied to the advertiser's objectives.

Media metrics are used by clients to judge the effectiveness of campaign: sales, overall traffic, earned media, and directional data. Assessment metrics inform the "refresh" of the media and guide product design and development. Metrics are also needed by advertisers and channel developers. Advertisers need metrics to determine priorities, to decide on conflicting arguments and to resolve competing values in organizations and systems. Channel developers need metrics to demonstrate to investors–and to clients–that there is a return on the investment of resources. Decisions often cannot wait for more research. In the absence of proven metrics, experience shows that the void will be filled. Either faulty metrics will be used or best guesses will prevail.

Practitioners' integrative and iterative experiments in the field offer rich opportunities for advertising researchers to test theory, methods and conclusions and describe those in the context of the holism of real life. Collaboration and transparency between academics and practitioners in the development of constructs and strategies can allow more rapid iterations in testing new measurement concepts and methods and can reduce the risks in selecting those to scale for broader use.

SUMMARY AND CONCLUSION

There is a need to develop robust metrics appropriate to measure advertising effectiveness in earned engagement of today's multi-media environments in which consumers interrupt their own multi-tasking as their attention shifts between background and foreground media experiences. Engagement is emotional, intimate, immediate and experiential. Persuasion is complex and includes processes and effects that can operate differently in various situations. Current research and analytics are better at diagnosing than prescribing.

The current state of knowledge and tools are not yet sufficiently developed to provide formulaic guidelines for how to generate engagement and persuasion in new media. Rather, they are better used for analyzing consumers' responses and learning about their relationships to issues, products and brands. Even while they are evolving, new metrics have a strong role to play as thinking, planning tools–to illuminate relative differences to be considered in setting advertising and media strategies.

Advancing the state of metrics for advertising in new media requires collaboration among advertisers, channel developers, channel managers, and academicians. All of these interested parties have a renewed interest in disambiguating engagement, identifying and measuring the active ingredients of persuasion, and understanding how to leverage new media to accomplish their separate but related objectives.

REFERENCES

AccuStream iMedia Research. (2008, January). *Professional and UGV Market Size 2005 - 2008: Views, Category and Brand Share Analysis.*

Ahn, S. J., Bailenson, J., Fox, J., & Jabon, M. (in press). Using automated facial expression analysis for emotion and behavior prediction. In Doeveling, K., von Scheve, C., & Konijn, E. A. (Eds.), *Handbook of Emotions and Mass Media*. New York: Routledge.

Anderson, C. (2006). *The Long Tail: Why the Future of Business is Selling Less*. New York: Hyperion Press.

Armel, K. C. (2008). *Changes in energy usage as indicators of audience engagement in sustainability messaging*. Retrieved from http://www.archive.org/details/ChangesInEnergyUsageAsIndicatorsOfAudienceEngagement.

Bernieri, F., Davis, J., Rosenthal, R., & Knee, C. (1994). Interactional synchrony and rapport: Measuring synchrony in displays devoid of sound and facial affect. *Personality and Social Psychology Bulletin*, *20*, 303–311. doi:10.1177/0146167294203008

Brint, S. (2001). Gemeinshaft revisited: A critique and reconstruction of the community concept. *Sociological Theory*, *12*(1).

Burns, N. (2008). *Barfly Channels: Media engagement and measurement at the point of consumption*. Retrieved from http://www.archive.org/details/Media_Engagement_And_Measurement

Chen, J., Shohamy, D., Ross, V., Reeves, B., & Wagner, A. D. (in press). The impact of social belief on the neurophysiology of learning and memory. *Journal of the Society for Neuroscience.*

Cook, W. (2007, February 20). *First opinion. An ARF research review for integration marketing and communication limited's market contact audit ™ methodology.*

Cox, T. (2008). *Convergence of digital media and convenience retailing*. Retrieved from http://www.archive.org/details/ConvergenceOfDigitalMediaAndConvenienceRetailing.

Crane, R., & Sornette, D. (2008). Robust dynamic classes revealed by measuring the response function of a social system. *Proceedings of the National Academy of Sciences of the United States of America*, *105*(41), 15649–15653. doi:10.1073/pnas.0803685105

Damasio, A. R. (2004). *Looking for Spinoza*. London: Random House.

Doyle, P. (1994). *Marketing Management & Strategy*. Upper Saddle River, NJ: Prentice-Hall.

Du Plessis, E. (2005). *The Advertised Mind*. London: Kogan Page.

Geertz, C. (1974). Myth, symbol and culture. *Proceedings of the American Academy of Arts and Sciences*, *101*, 1.

Giles, M. (2008). *Customer centricity: monetizing authentic customer connections across the consumer journey*. Retrieved from http://www.archive.org/details/CustomerCentricity

Gleick, J. (1987). *CHAOS: Making a New Science*. New York: Penguin Books.

Greenwald, A. G. (1968). Cognitive learning, cognitive response to persuasion, and attitude change. In Greenwald, T. B., & Ostrom, T. (Eds.), *Psychological Foundations of Attitudes* (pp. 147–170). New York: Academic Press.

Hayden, T. (2008). *Successfully executing integrated experiences in today's alternative reality*. Retrieved from http://www.archive.org/details/SuccessfullyExecutingIntegratedExperiencesInTodaysAlternativeReality

Heath, R. (2007). *Emotional persuasion in advertising: a hierarchy-of-processing model*. Working Paper 2007.07, School of Management, University of Bath.

Heath, R. G. (2000). Low involvement processing–a new model of brands and advertising. *International Journal of Advertising*, *19*(3), 287–298.

Holbrook, M. B., & Hirschman, E. C. (1982). The experiential aspects of consumption: consumer fantasies, feelings, and fun. *The Journal of Consumer Research*, *9*(2), 132–140. doi:10.1086/208906

Hovland, C., Janis, I., & Kelley, H. (1953). *Communication and Persuasion*. New Haven, CT: Yale University Press.

Ito, M., & Daisuke, O. (2009). Technosocial Situations: Emergent Structurings of Mobile Email Use. In Ito, M., Matsuda, M., & Okabe, D. (Eds.), *Personal, Portable, Intimate: Mobile Phones in Japanese Life*. Cambridge, MA: MIT Press.

Kaptein, M. C., Markopoulos, P., de Ruyter, B., & Aarts, E. (2009). Persuasion in ambient intelligence. *Journal of Ambient Intelligence and Humanized Computing*, *1*(1), 43–56. doi:10.1007/s12652-009-0005-3

Kelman, H. C. (1958). Compliance, identification, and internalization: Three processes of attitude change. *The Journal of Conflict Resolution*, *2*, 51–60. doi:10.1177/002200275800200106

Konar, E. (2008). *Integrating engagement across the customer context*. Retrieved from http://www.archive.org/details/IntegratingEngagementAcrossTheCustomerContext

Kover, A. J., Stephen, M. G., & James, W. L. (1995). Creativity vs. effectiveness? An integrating classification for advertising. *Journal of Advertising Research*, *6*, 29–38.

Krugman, H. E. (1962). An application of learning theory to TV copy testing. *Public Opinion Quarterly*, *26*, 626–634. doi:10.1086/267132

Lenhart, A., Madden, M., Rankin, M. M., & Smith, A. (2007). *Teens and social media, Reports: Family & Friends*. Retrieved from http://pewinternet.org/PPF/r/230/report_display.asp

MacInnis, D. J., & Jawroski, B. J. (1989). Information processing from advertisements: toward an integrative framework. *Journal of Marketing*, *53*(4), 1–23. doi:10.2307/1251376

Madhok, A. (2008). *The invited conversation: personalized and integrated communication platform*. Retrieved from http://www.archive.org/details/TheInvitedConversationPersonalizedAndIntegratedCommunicationPlatform

McGuire, W. J. (1969). The nature of attitudes and attitude change. In Lindzey, G., & Aronson, E. (Eds.), *Handbook of Social Psychology* (*Vol. 3*, pp. 136–314). Reading, MA: Addison-Wesley.

Metheringham, R. (1964, December). Measuring the net cumulative coverage of a print campaign. *Journal of Advertising Research*.

Meyers Levy, J., & Malaviya, P. (1999). Consumers' processing of persuasive advertisements: An integrative framework of persuasion theories. *Journal of Marketing*, *63*, 45–60. doi:10.2307/1252100

Mittal, B. (1994). Public assessment of TV advertising: faint and harsh criticism. *Journal of Advertising Research*, *34*(1), 35–53.

Nass, C. (2008). *Understanding and leveraging emotional engagement*. Retrieved from http://www.archive.org/details/UnderstandingAndLeveragingEmotionalEngagement

Nass, C., & Moon, Y. (2000). Machines and mindlessness: Social responses to computers. *The Journal of Social Issues*, *56*(1), 81–103. doi:10.1111/0022-4537.00153

Niederhoffer, K. (2008). *Measuring engagement in social media and new online media: new perspectives on measuring involvement*. Retrieved from http://www.archive.org/details/MeasuringEngagementInSocialMediaAndNewOnlineMedia

Nuyens, G. (2008) *Engaging avatars and their operators*. Retrieved from http://www.archive.org/details/EngagingAvatarsAndTheirOperators

Ophir, E., Nass, C. I., & Wagner, A. D. (2009). Cognitive control in media multitaskers. *Proceedings of the National Academy of Sciences of the United States of America*, *106*(37), 15583–15587. doi:10.1073/pnas.0903620106

Oxford Dictionaries. (2008). *Concise Oxford English Dictionary* (11th Ed. Revised). Oxford, UK: Oxford University Press.

Pennebaker, J. W., Booth, R. J., & Francis, M. E. (2007). Linguistic Inquiry and Word Count (LIWC2007), a text analysis program. Austin, TX: LIWC.net.

Pennebaker, J. W., Mehl, M. R., & Niederhoffer, K. (2003). Psychological aspects of natural language use: Our words, our selves. *Annual Review of Psychology*, *54*, 547–577. doi:10.1146/annurev.psych.54.101601.145041

Petty, E. P., & Brinol, P. (2008). From single to multiple to metacognitive processes. *Perspectives on Psychological Science*, *3*(2), 137–147. doi:10.1111/j.1745-6916.2008.00071.x

Petty, R. E., & Cacioppo, J. T. (1981). *Attitudes And Persuasion: Classic And Contemporary Approaches*. Dubuque, IA: William A. Brown.

Petty, R. E., & Cacioppo, J. T. (1986). *Communication And Persuasion: Central And Peripheral Routes To Attitude Change*. New York: Springer-Verlag.

Pilotta, J. J., Schultz, D. E., & Drenik, G. (2004). Simultaneous media usage: a critical consumer orientation to media planning. *Journal of Consumer Behaviour*, *30*(3).

Point of Purchase Advertising International (POPAI). (2003, January). *In-store advertising becomes a measured medium*. Convenience Channel Study.

Reeves, B., & Read, J. L. (2009). *Total Engagement: Using Games and Virtual World in Change the Way We Work and Play*. Cambridge, MA: Harvard Business Press.

Reeves, R. (1961). *Reality in Advertising*. New York: Alfred A. Knopf.

Roush, W. (2005). August) Social machines. *Technology Review*.

Russell, M. G. (2008a). Engagement Pinball. In *3rd Annual Customer Engagement Survey, Report 2009, cScape | eConsultancy 2008*. Retrieved March 1, 2009, from http://www.cscape.com/features/Pages/customer-engagement-register.aspx

Russell, M. G. (2008b). *Wait marketing in fast-paced retail settings*. Retrieved from http://www.archive.org/details/WaitMarketingInFast-pacedRetailSettings

Russell, M. G. (2008c). Benevolence and effectiveness: persuasive technology's spillover effects in retail settings. In Oinas-Kukkonen, H. (Eds.), *Persuasive 2008* (pp. 94–103). Berlin: Springer-Verlag. doi:10.1007/978-3-540-68504-3_9

Russell, M. G. (2009). Narrowcast pricebook-driven persuasion: Engagement at point of influence, purchase and consumption in distributed retail environments. *Journal of Software*, *4*(4). doi:10.4304/jsw.4.4.365-373

Russell, M. G. (2009). The call for creativity in new metrics for liquid media. *Journal of Interactive Advertising*, *9*(2).

Schramm, W., & Roberts, D. F. (1961). *The Process and Effects of Mass Communication*. Urbana, IL: University of Illinois Press.

Senser, R. (2008). *New media engagement as a virtuous process*. Retrieved from http://www.archive.org/details/NewMediaEngagementAsAVirtuousProcess.

Shiv, B., & Fedhorikhin, A. (1999). Heart & mind in conflict: the interplay of affect and cognition in consumer decision making. *The Journal of Consumer Research*, *26*(3), 278–292. doi:10.1086/209563

Stevenson, V. S. (2007). *VSS Communications Industry Forecast 2007-2011*.

Stinson, T. (2008). *Consumer understanding as a foundation for creating audience engagement*. Retrieved from http://www.archive.org/details/ConsumerUnderstandingAsAFoundationForCreatingAudienceEngagement

The Radicati Group, Inc. (2007). *Addressing information overload in corporate email: the economics of user attention*. Whitepaper by The Radiciati Group, Inc. Palo Alto, CA. Retrieved from http://www.seriosity.com/downloads/Seriosity%20White%20Paper%20-%20Information%20Overload.pdf

Veda, Q. (2008). *Engaging Enterprise Audiences In New Media*. Retrieved from http://www.archive.org/details/EngagingEnterpriseAudiencesInNewMedia

Watzlawick, P., Bavelas, J. B., & Jackson, D. D. (1967). *Pragmatics of Human Communication*. New York: Norton & Co.

Wierville, C. (2008) *Customer engagement and product/service innovation*. Retrieved from http://www.archive.org/details/CustomerEngagementAndProductServiceInnovation.

Woods, B. S., & Murphy, P. K. (2002). Separated at birth: the shared lineage of research on conceptual change and persuasion. *International Journal of Educational Research*, *35*(7-8), 633–649. doi:10.1016/S0883-0355(02)00007-1

Zajonc, R. B., & Marcus, H. (1982). Affective and cognitive factors in preferences. *The Journal of Consumer Research*, *9*(2), 123–131. doi:10.1086/208905

ENDNOTE

1 Including a two-day workshop, "Monetizing Engagement in New Media," sponsored by Media X at Stanford University August 2008. This chapter draws upon presentations and discussions in this workshop, in which agency, channel and academic researchers met to collaboratively understand the dynamics of continuous partial engagement in multi-tasking environments, to exchange strategies that leverage relevance across media, and

to share insights on how actionable metrics can monetize the value of engagement in personalized media across mass markets.

The author thanks Dr. Kate Niederhoffer, Dachis Consulting, for her participation as co-leader of this workshop.

Section 2

Consumer Generated Content:

Applications And Impact

Chapter 7
Expectancy-Value:
Identifying Relationships Associated with Consuming User-Generated Content

Terry Daugherty
The University of Akron, USA

Matthew S. Eastin
The University of Texas at Austin, USA

Laura F. Bright
Texas Christian University, USA

Shu-Chuan Chu
DePaul University, USA

ABSTRACT

Consumers today have more control over media consumption than ever before, with interactive media helping to transform the industry away from a traditional publisher-centric focus towards a new dynamic user-centric model. Examples of prominent Web 2.0 media environments that support the creation, distribution and consumption of user-generated content (UGC) include YouTube, MySpace, Facebook, Wikipedia, StupidVideos, Flickr, Blogger, and personal Web pages, among others. In addition, recent media research involving Social Cognitive Theory has emerged to offer explanatory power for Internet use and could provide a better understanding of the UGC phenomenon. Therefore, a theoretical model grounded in Social Cognitive Theory was tested examining the relationships between media experience, desirability of control, attitude and the consumption of UGC. A survey was administered to an opt-in online panel (N=325) recruited for Web-based research with the findings confirming the hypothesized model.

INTRODUCTION

Over the last several decades, the media landscape has evolved into a complex and dynamic conglomeration of both traditional and interactive media that seek to serve the needs of today's fast-paced lifestyles. While traditional media are struggling under the weight of increased segmentation, the interactive environment has shown the capacity to capitalize on this fragmented market by offering media alternatives that provide consumers a

DOI: 10.4018/978-1-60566-792-8.ch007

voice amidst the whirlwind of information and advertising. In the online world, these new media options are being driven increasingly less by publishers and more so by consumers empowered to consume, create, and distribute media, often referred to as user-generated content (UGC). User-generated content refers to media that is created or produced by the general public rather than by paid professionals and is primarily distributed via Web 2.0 technologies online. In fact, the Internet has come to serve as an outlet for an overwhelming majority of American adults (71%) with creators of UGC expected to climb to 95 million by 2011 (Verna, 2007). Given these numbers, it is evident that UGC must be strongly considered by marketing technology professionals as both a means to disseminate brand friendly information, through both the delivery and creation of media content, but also as a means of keeping a finger on the pulse of their consumers.

Although the creation and dissemination of media content has been a constant in our world for hundreds of years, the potential for an ordinary consumer to communicate with and influence a mass audience has just recently been achieved with the advent of Web 2.0 technologies. Examples of prominent Web 2.0 websites and web-based applications that support the creation, distribution and consumption of UGC include, but are not limited to, YouTube, MySpace, Facebook, Wikipedia, StupidVideos, Flickr, Blogger, and personal Web pages, among others. Amidst the plethora of both traditional and digital media choices today, the Internet has revealed itself to be an outlet where traditional forms of media entertainment can also converge and be offered to consumers in a time and place that is most convenient for them. While traditional media are nowhere near extinction, it is clear that trends are changing such that consumers are in more control of their media consumption than ever before in history and, because of new media technologies, have the freedom to create as well as disseminate content. This media content consumption sphere continues to shift towards a 'user-centric model' led by UGC and away from the past model that has been characterized as 'publisher-centric' (Daugherty, Eastin, & Bright, 2008). Beginning in 2004 with the explosion of the Web 2.0 market, UGC has formed a plethora of niche markets within the media landscape generating more than $450 million in advertising revenues (Verna, 2007, p.2). As a result of this changing paradigm and expanding media channel, top television networks are integrating blogs, podcasts, and news feeds into their current media strategies, reflecting the importance of UGC in communicating with today's consumers. Certainly the accelerated growth of this nascent area presents both significant problems and opportunities for media technology researchers to better understand consumer motivations for consumption and the effectiveness of UGC.

Recent online research involving Social Cognitive Theory (LaRose & Eastin, 2002, 2004; Eastin & LaRose, 2000) has emerged to offer explanatory power for consumer Internet use and could provide a better understanding of the UGC phenomenon. Specifically, social-cognitive theory is a framework that explains human actions along three combined areas: individuals, environments and behavior. Within SCT, behavior is an observable act and the performance of behavior is determined, in large part, by the expected outcomes of the behavior. These expectations are formed through our own direct experience or mediated by vicarious reinforcements observed through others. Ultimately, individuals act according to expected outcomes and learning experiences organized around six basic types of motivations for human behavior: novel sensory, social, status, monetary, enjoyable activity, and self-reactive incentives (Bandura, 1986).

User-generated content has empowered consumers and enabled them to connect with one another in the broad online information space. In this regard, it is imperative for media technology researchers to begin to gain a better understanding of the impact of UGC and underlying reasons consumers use such content. To date though, little research has been undertaken on UGC and its perceptions amongst the consumers of this type of media content. Therefore, the proposed chapter will focus on detailing the role of UGC within the media landscape by using a social cognitive framework while presenting results of a recent study examining the expected outcomes associated with the amount of time spent consuming UGC. The principal research proposition is that a positive relationship exits between expected values gained from an action and the behavior itself with future behavior capable of reinforcing motivational states. Because consumer perceptions are capable of being influenced by media messages, the effective understanding of the expectations sought and the outcomes obtained from consuming UGC are important to both academic scholars interested in theoretical research as well as media technology professionals focused on branding online.

MEDIA EVOLUTION AND CONSUMER CONTROL

Never before throughout human history have we experienced the level of media evolution currently encompassing our daily lives. Mainstream media, including television, radio, and print publications, have moved through evolutionary lifecycles since their inception. Similarly, the online media landscape has evolved into a robust information space that provides both marketers and consumers with an outlet for efficient, timely communication. As increasing numbers of consumers direct their attention away from traditional media and toward interactive media, marketers confront the challenge of integrating their offerings with those created by consumers themselves. The past several decades reveal a steady decline in newspaper readership and magazine circulation, and though the television market continues to grow in terms of overall viewership, it also suffers a proliferation of program offerings, leading to fragmented audiences and decreasing program ratings (Anderson, 2006).

Today, television, radio, newspapers, magazines, the Internet, movies, music, and more, represent an information society created by technology ultimately converging around the media audience. These technologies have redefined the media environment and thus media consumption as a seemingly infinite number of offerings are connecting and empowering audiences through communication channels. Media scholars acknowledge that traditional media models of communication may no longer adequately represent digital media, for which "convergence" may serve as an increasingly more accurate representation (Perry, 2002). As a result, the convergence of media through technology continues to shift power toward an audience centric model of media control and away from the past model that has been characterized as 'publisher-centric'. In other words, the advancements of technology have lead to one outcome–the empowerment of the consumer.

Recently, Andrew Heyward, former president of CBS news, emphasized "the most important invention in Television in the last century was not the satellite or computer; it is the remote control" (Page, 2006, p. 18). According to Heyward, consumers create their own media environment and "watch what they want when they want" (Page, 2006, p. 18). Audiences face the opportunity to make media content choices themselves rather than rely on traditional gatekeepers (Perry, 2002). Designating this phenomenon as the 'the control revolution,' Shapiro (1999) claims that technology has brought with it a reduction of institutional control resulting in an increase of individual control. Further, Cover (2006) defined the control revolution in terms of a war. He describes this war as a "push-and-pull of author versus (intended) audience control over the text" (p.153).

Human nature suggests that we strive to be causal agents over our environment and the source of our own behavior (DeCharms, 1968). A desire for personal control is motivated as much by survival instinct as well as our sense of self-esteem and confidence (Shapiro, 1999). In fact, research reveals that desirability of control emanates from both biological and social determinants (Declerck, Boone & De Brabander, 2006) and has been investigated throughout the social science literature as locus of control (Rotter, 1966), actual control (e.g., Cramer & Perreault, 2006), perceived control (e.g., Klein & Helweg-Larsen, 2002), behavioral control, cognitive control (Faranda, 2001; Haidt & Rodin, 1999), decisional control, feeling in control (Declerck, Boone & Brabander, 2006), and the illusion of control (Thompson, Thomas & Armstrong, 1998; Wolfgang, Zenker & Viscusi, 1984). Furthermore, the emerging concept of media control, defined as the audience's ability to consume media content when, where, and how consumers choose, is pivotal for understanding audience behavior given the new media technologies specifically designed to provide control over media consumption, namely UGC on Web 2.0 websites.

The Emergence of UGC and the Power of Media Distribution

Many scholars believe that media fragmentation, consumer interactivity, and personalization are the product of technology advancements. The emergence of the Internet, by its very nature, has enhanced content and file sharing applications, which in turn have shaped the consumption and distribution mechanisms for UGC. Over time, the Internet has become a highly personalized information space in which consumers can tailor their media exposure to their specific needs and desires (Liang, Lai & Ku, 2006). Tailored exposures become possible through Web-based applications that aggregate information and UGC according to subscriber's specifications, which again indicates consumer-centric media exposures rather than publisher-centric ones. As the consumption of UGC continues to evolve, content aggregation tools and Web 2.0 applications built on Really Simple Syndication (RSS) technology will become more usable and accessible to consumers, helping create a manageable information space that is both customized and relevant. The ability to publish content in the online environment has been possible since the inception of the Internet, because personal publication mechanisms are inherent to the structure of this information space. However, constant, organic growth and change is what leads to an information explosion online and the consumption of UGC. Ultimately, a balance of power between message producers and media audiences has been lacking for years, and UGC potentially represents a power shift within the industry. The trend toward greater control means media theorists must focus more on understanding audience motivations for consuming media content as users are confronted with more choices today than ever before (Severin & Tankard, 1992). Furthermore, examining relationships associated with consuming UGC through the Social-Cognitive Theory (SCT) framework allows academic researchers and media professionals to understand how individuals develop behavioral patterns over time and how individuals act according to expected outcomes stemming from prior experience and personal traits (Bandura, 2001). In the context of UGC consumption, individual psychological traits, media experience and personal beliefs (i.e., attitude) about such media technology are all essential antecedents of behavior.

SOCIAL COGNITIVE THEORY

SCT and How it Relates to UGC

For more than three decades, scholars have sought to understand why people use certain media content within the uses and gratifications paradigm. It has been shown that the uses and gratifications framework provides a bridge between the psychological characteristics of consumerism and media consumption. According to the expectancy-value approach to uses and gratifications (see Palmgreen, Wenner & Rayburn, 1980), consumers' compare between the gratifications sought and obtained. Based on past media experiences, they develop their future media exposure patterns in a never-ending circular process (Rubin, 2002, p.533). Past research linking general media use and various gratifications from the media are well established (e.g. Babrow & Swanson, 1988; Donohew et al. 1987; Palmgreen, Wenner & Rayburn, 1980). Accordingly, it is a logical approach to apply this well-established paradigm to the consumption of UGC.

From the traditional perspective of uses and gratifications, LaRose and Eastin (2004) have taken a complimentary approach toward understanding media consumption through social-cognitive theory. Social-cognitive theory is a framework that explains behavior while combining three components: individuals, environments and behavior. The theory discusses how individuals acquire their behavior "through evaluations of personal experiences and self assessments of their thought processes, they employ a self-reflective capability that helps them better understand themselves, their environments, and variations in situational demands" (LaRose et al., 2001, p.397). Ultimately, individuals act according to expected outcomes and learning experiences. Guided by Bandura (2001), LaRose and Eastin (2004) emphasize the importance of prior experience as an explanation to behavior. In addition, personal attitude is also an important predictor of behavior. In the context of the media, prior media experience and attitude toward the media (i.e., UGC) are extremely relevant to the explanation of consumers' UGC behaviors. To examine the relationship between individual characteristics, behavior and outcomes, a theoretical model is presented in Figure 1.

Individual characteristics that users bring into media consumption contribute toward their determined use of a medium (Eastin & Daugherty, 2005). As mentioned, the concept of control is extremely pivotal to human behavior, and media consumers in particular, especially in light of new media technologies that allow for more control by consumers with regard to content consumption. Desirability of control is defined as "a stable personality trait reflecting the extent to which individuals generally are motivated to control the events in their lives" (Burger 1985, p. 1520). According to Burger and Cooper (1979), desirability of control is a motivational trait, which measures how sought-after the personal control trait is for a person. Clearly there is a motivation in our nature to control life's events, however, as with other personality traits it ranges on a scale across different individuals. People vary and

Figure 1. Media use model

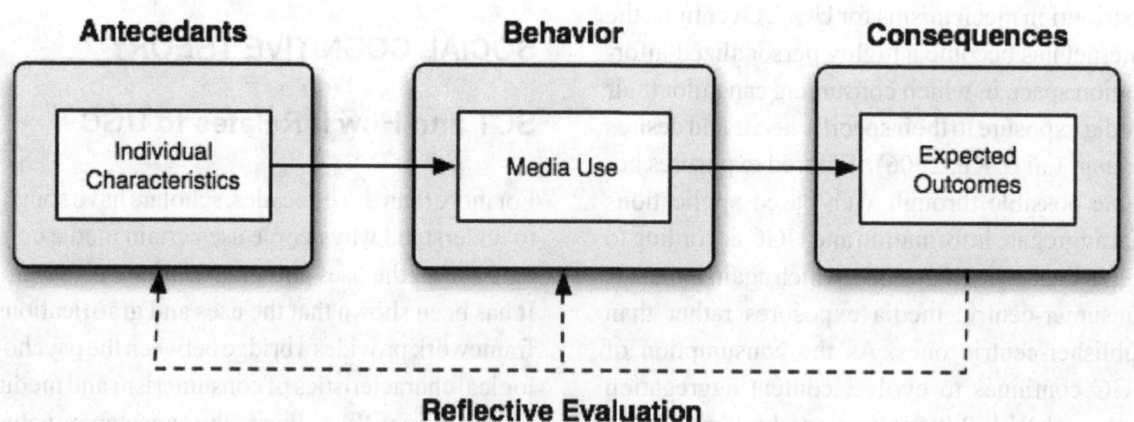

thus demonstrate different propensities toward control, which could help explain our different behaviors. According to its operational definition, a person who exhibits a high desirability of control is a leader, assertive, active, decisive and manipulative in situations to create desired outcomes. Conversely, a person who exhibits low desirability of control is more influenced by others, nonassertive, uncertain, doubtful and passive (Burger & Cooper, 1979). Studies that have used the DC construct demonstrate how differences in the desirability of control explain daily behaviors and decisions such as achievement-related behaviors (see Burger, 1985 and also Burger, 1992) and proneness to depression (see Burger 1984).

Past work has connected the control construct with media use (Schutz, 1966). For instance Schutz (1966) suggests, "three interpersonal needs- inclusion, affection, and control- influence all aspects of communication between people" (in Rubin, 1993, p.161). Further, Rubin (1993) has linked external control (related to the belief of fate and chance occurrence) with passive audiences and internal control (related to the belief of self-determinism) with active media audiences. In the field of interactive media, Wu (2006) demonstrates that control, as an individual/personality trait, is related to media use. Furthermore, Alpert et al. (2003) examined the environment of e-commerce and notes that the issue of control is pivotal to a consumer's media experience: "the clearest result to emerge from our studies is users' fervent desire to be in control" (Alpert et al., 2003, p.385). Althaus and Tewksbury (2000) probe the use of the Internet as a surveillance medium that helps gratify two needs while consuming political news contents: the need for information and the desirability of control. Their findings suggest that desirability of control is a strong predictor of news exposure—at least as strong as traditional political knowledge as a predictor. They also claim that the control construct is positively related to surveillance with the media. That is, the greater a person's desirability of control, the more s/he will expose him/herself to the media. Thus, the literature provides evidence which links control and general media use (e.g. Althaus & Tewksbury, 2000; Auter & Ray, 1999; Cover, 2006; Rubin, 1993; Wober & Gunter, 1982). Moreover, research supports the notion that desirability of control is positively related to media use. Accordingly, it is expected that desire to control will positively predict UGC consumption.

Klein and Helweg-Larsen (2002) found, through meta-analysis, a strong relationship between optimistic bias and perceived control. Simply, the more people believe that they have control over future events the more optimistic they are about their sequence of life and events. In marketing communication, an increase of perceived control was linked to pleasantness in service and consumption experiences (see Chandran & Morwitz, 2005; Faranda, 2001). Rubin (1993) has further demonstrated a positive correlation between control and communication motivation for pleasure. Within the context of interactive media, Liu and Shrum (2002) have developed a theoretical model for interactivity and found that the desirability of control variable is a key factor in obtaining satisfaction from the interactive process. They suggest that people who have a high desirability of control will be more satisfied with interactivity than people who have a low desirability of control. In the case of UGC, it is logical to believe a positive linkage exists between desire of control, use, and expected outcomes (e.g., enjoyment) when consuming these forms of media technology. As being hypothesized in this study, this increase in desire of control and expected outcomes may be linked to the ability to consume content in a social setting through UGC behaviors, such as posting videos and pictures.

Previous experience with media also represents and individual characteristic each user maintains that is strongly associated with future media consumption. The reason is because when a user chooses to consume media they are making a decision how to allocate a scarce resource –time.

Numerous studies have dealt with understanding the way people make use of their time resources, make time allocation decisions and choose time consuming activities (McKechnie, 1974; Duncan, 1978; Gronau, 1977) Within consumer psychology, the generally accepted belief is that time allocation decisions are governed by the combination of the temporal activity itself, psychological characteristics, and situational factors (Feldman and Hornik 1981).

Undeniably, an expenditure of time is involved each instance media is consumed and as a result this "experience" is an important factor in understanding media consumption. In fact, the reality facing everyone is that time is a scarce resource and both a precursor and result of media consumption. However, because of the number of media choices today, coupled with limited time, audiences have begun to seek additional control and consume more than one form of media at the same occasion (Croteau and Hoynes 2003).

Finally, a user's attitude toward UGC stemming from prior experience is also an individual characteristic considered as a causal antecedent that reinforces and leads to future behavior. For example, a positive interaction with a certain medium, in our case the UGC, should influence future patterns of UGC use. Conversely, a negative experience (i.e. difficulty of use) should affect UGC use in different ways, and perhaps cause complete media abstention. The more positive an experience with UGC, the more likely people will consume and produce positive expectancies for future use leading to behavior.

A person's attitude represents a psychological tendency, expressed by evaluating a particular object, and can serve various motivations (Eagly & Chaiken, 1993). According to Eastin and Daugherty (2005), media consumption constitutes a deliberate, active behavior in which audiences seek content according to their internal motivations. These internal motivations represent functional sources designed to meet specific consumer needs and serve as the foundation for attitude formation, ultimately influencing behavior (O'Keefe, 2002). In terms of media use, a consumer's willingness to experience UGC depends on his or her attitude toward the consumption of UGC. However, because individual motivations can vary greatly, consumers may decide to consume UGC for different reasons.

Katz's (1960) seminal work on functional theory is considered by many essential for understanding the complex motivational underpinnings and functions of attitude. Functional theory states that attitudes serve various motivations, depending on the purpose, such that one's behavior becomes a function of their attitude toward that behavior (O'Keefe, 2002). The basis of this theory centers on the view that to influence behavior, we must understand its motivational source (i.e., attitude). As noted earlier, the motivational sources driving media consumption depend on the formation of positive or negative attitudes toward a medium. However, because virtually everyone in the United States engages in daily media consumption, media researchers often end up comparing attitudes and experiences with media (i.e., behavior) using a reciprocal relationship perspective (Perry, 2002). According to Myers (1998), the attitude→behavior relationship can range from nonexistent to very strong, such that attitude about a given object determines the person's interactions with that object. As it relates to UGC, a consumer's attitude derives from both the perceived value of the content and how it relates to his or her existing beliefs and feelings (i.e., motivational sources). Behavior ultimately is influenced by the attitude of the consumers who experience UGC. To this end, we expect attitude toward UGC consumption to be positively related to UGC behavior, which subsequently influences expected outcomes.

To parse out the development of attitude and its relationship to behavior, Fazio and Towles-Schwen (1999) present an integrated framework based on either spontaneous or deliberative processing. The deliberative processing route lends itself well to the consumption of UGC, whereas the spontaneous processing of attitude objects applies better to the creation of UGC. Spontaneous processing of attitudes relies on personal theories of action associated with environmental triggers that cue memories, which suggest an attitude and course of action needed. The act of creating UGC in turn depends on attitude toward both previous experiences with UGC and the immediacy of the situation that involves its creation. In this regard, consumers must have positive attitudes toward UGC in general to prompt their positive reaction to a situation in which they can create their own UGC. Provided a positive cue exists, the likelihood of UGC creation increases as positive exposure to UGC increases.

Ultimately, a user's attitude may affect both the creation and consumption of UGC independently, though we know little about how attitude may explain this relationship. Behavior ultimately is influenced by the attitude of the users who experience it; therefore, we must explicate a more complete conceptualization of the elements of such attitudes. Understanding how a user's attitude influences his or her behavior may have significant explanatory power in distinguishing the relationship between the consumption and creation of UGC. Furthermore, examining relationships associated with creating UGC through the SCT framework allows academic researchers and media technology professionals to understand how individuals develop behavioral patterns over time, as well as how individuals act according to expected outcomes stemming from personal traits and prior experience (Bandura 2001).

While understanding key motivational antecedents that influence behavioral mechanisms in an important process, it unfortunately only represents the first half of the media equation and does not adequately explain the media consumption process fully. To this end, a primary goal of media technology researchers is also to understand behavioral outcomes or effects of media use. The social cognitive approach frames expected outcomes (gratifications) as influencing but also resulting from behavioral incentives (needs). These concepts indeed have the potential to expand our understanding of media and the impact on behavior, in this case, UGC usage. According to Bandura (1986), expected outcomes are organized around the basic motivations for human behavior, such as novel sensory, social, status, enjoyable activity, and self-reactive incentives (see LaRose & Eastin, 2004 for a new media perspective).

Using previous research as a guide, two of the six expected outcomes outlined by Bandura (1986) are applicable within the hypothesized model of UGC consumption and their outcomes. For the purposes of this research, the following theoretically defined expected outcomes are examined, 1) social interaction and 2) enjoyment. Social and enjoyment incentives are directly inline with sensory dimensions used by Bandura (1986) as UGC can be seen as a mechanism to enable social interaction through the use of applications provided by UGC, such as YouTube and Facebook. For example, consumers may enjoy posting amusing clips for friends in social settings, which facilitates enjoyment from the experience.

Developing a Model for Understanding the Consumption of UGC

To examine how prior media experience, desirability of control and attitude toward using UGC influence the decision to consume UGC, a theoretical model (Figure 2) is proposed. In order to test these theoretical relationships, variables from the model were examined using an online survey. While distinct hypotheses were posited from the literature, the principal research proposition was that a positive relationship exists between expected outcomes gained from an action and the behavior itself, with individual characteristics capable of influencing behavior.

Figure 2. Antecedants and consequences of user-generated content consumption

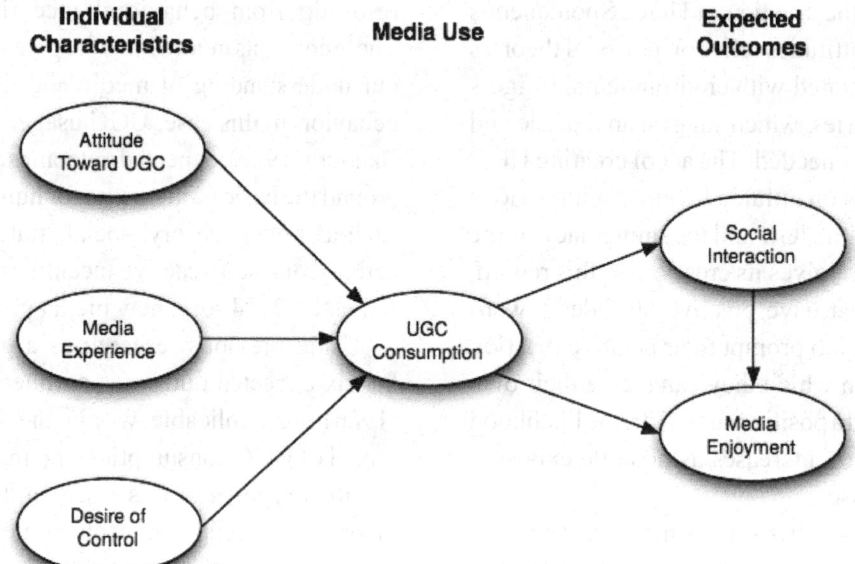

PRIMARY RESEARCH

A survey was administered to an opt-in subject pool recruited for Web-based research (i.e., online panel). Data were gathered from 325 participants over a seven-day period with 1,000 e-mail invitations sent on day one, 1,500 on day three, and 500 on day 5. The survey was closed once 325 completed surveys were recorded (day seven). Because a purposive sample was selected based on sample size, response rate was not calculated since the survey was closed after being open for the designated duration. However, the completion rate, defined as those who completed the survey divided by those who accessed it, was 77%. The average age of participants was around 44 years old. Fifty-one percent of respondents were male with 49% female. Further, the majority of respondents classified themselves as Caucasian (47%) while attending some college (32.9%) with a household income ranging from \$20,001 to \$40,000 (28.3%).

At the beginning of the survey, participants were provided a conceptual definition of UGC as a reference to interpret the questionnaire. Specifically, participants read "User-generated content (UGC) refers to media content that is created or produced by the general public rather than by paid professionals and is primarily distributed on the Internet. This includes such online content as digital video, blogging, podcasting, mobile phone photography, wikis, and user-forum posts, among others." After reading the conceptual definition of UGC, participants completed a questionnaire that asked about their overall media experience (e.g., TV and radio), desire of control, attitude toward UGC, as well as their UGC consumption and expected outcomes through using UGC technologies. In addition, their basic demographic variables were also assessed.

Media experience (M = 824.1, SD = 478.6) and UGC consumption (M = 237.2, SD = 205.1) were recorded via self-reported 'average time spent per day' items. To assess the type of media most commonly experienced, prevalent categories previously identified were selected (i.e., TV, newspaper, radio, magazine, and Internet). Established seven-point semantic differential scales were used to test other proposed variables with reliability assessment conducted on desire of control, attitude and expected outcomes using Cronbach's Alpha (desire of control $M = 4.8$, $SD = .65$, $\alpha = .86$; attitude toward UGC $M = 4.7$, $SD = 1.24$, $\alpha = .93$; social interaction $M = 4.6$, $SD = 1.15$, $\alpha = .95$; enjoyment $M = 4.8$, $SD = 1.15$, $\alpha = .93$), with all exceeding the generally accepted guideline of .70 (Hair, Anderson, Tatham, & Black, 1998, p.118). Composite measures for each of the scales were then constructed to represent the multiple items and used in the subsequent analysis to reduce measurement error.

Overall, the data fit the model shown in Figure 2, χ^2 (6) = 22.58, $p < .01$; CFI = .91; GFI = .93; RMSR = .10. From this model, experience with media ($\beta = .37$), desire of control ($\beta = .26$), and attitude toward UGC ($\beta = .33$) significantly predicted UGC consumption, which significantly influences the social interaction ($\beta = .41$) and enjoyment outcomes ($\beta = .22$). In addition, there is also a strong relationship between social interaction and enjoyment outcome ($\beta = .61$). From these relationships, 44% of the variance is explained within UGC, 17% of the variance in the social interaction outcome, and 53% of the variance in the enjoyment outcome was predicted. Figure 3 illustrates the model with the path analysis results.

CONCLUSION AND FUTURE IMPLICATIONS

As UGC becomes more prevalent, understanding why consumers are drawn to consume content becomes increasingly important, especially as the media industry moves toward a user-centric model of consumption. As a result, it is imperative to gain an understanding of how individuals behave according to expected outcomes for the consumption of UGC in order to recognize how such content might benefit media technology. The current chapter presents a framework of understanding the effect of three individual characteristics, prior media experience, attitude toward UGC and desire of control, on individuals' UGC consumption and their expected outcomes of social interaction and enjoyment. While consumption of any new consumer technology requires a certain level of technical knowledge, we expect positive prior media experience and attitude effectively lead consumers toward consuming UGC content. At the same time, desire of media control is another prerequisite for UGC consumption. Overall, this chapter provides some evidence that there is a positive relationship between media

Figure 3. Relationships between individual characteristics, media use, and expected outcomes

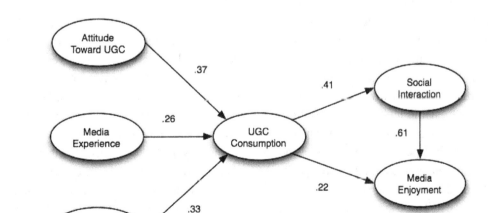

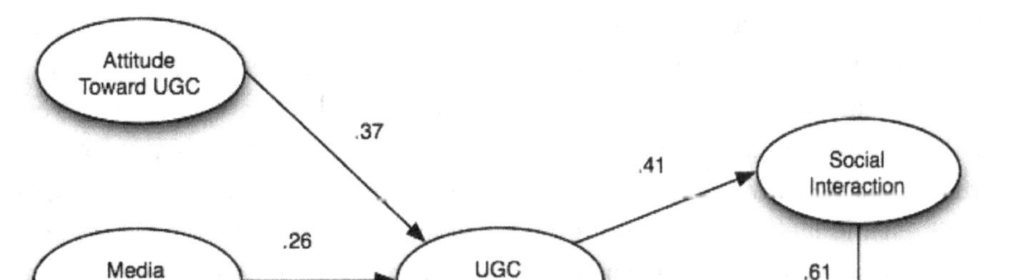

experience, desirability of control, attitude and UGC consumption, which provides insight and predictive power for the outcomes of enjoyment and social interaction. In other words, individuals who experience media positively, maintain favorable attitudes toward such media technology, and seek to control content based on psychological tendencies, are more likely to visit and/or create blogs, construct Web sites, and visit wiki sites, which stimulate positive outcome expectancies of UGC consumption. These findings confirm the relationship between a consumer's attitude and behavior toward a given attitude object (i.e., consumption of UGC). Determining this positive relationship is critical as we attempt to investigate the effects of the consumption of UGC on both consumer behavior and marketing communication efforts. This relationship suggests that as a consumer's attitude toward UGC strengthens, the consumption of such content increases, which further is positively associated with social interactivity and enjoyment incentives. This finding spotlights the importance of creating positive customer experiences with UGC, in terms of both products offered and content provided by media technology professionals to promote goods and services through UGC.

In addition, desirability of control also displayed a positive relationship with UGC consumption and the expected outcomes. This is hardly surprising considering the desirability of control construct represents the aspiration of a person to be in control (behaviorally speaking) (see Burger, 1984; Burger, 1992). Compared to other media, and primarily traditional media, Web 2.0 technologies, and beyond, enable UGC to be extremely flexible allowing for maximum control over media content. Accordingly, a person who perceives the "state" of being in control as desirable would probably use such media technologies more often, as our findings suggest. These are important results as they add to the scarce literature on psychological trait influences and media technology. Within the framework of media studies, our findings are even more relevant and pioneering. To the best of our knowledge, Althaus and Tewksbury (2000) were the only researchers who have examined the desirability of control within the realm of media studies. The authors, as mentioned, applied the scale to Internet use in a political communication environment and concluded that the desirability of control construct is positively related to surveillance with the media. These findings line up with the current UGC consumption findings. Hence, we can begin to observe a solid pattern emerging in regards to the relationship between desirability of control and media technology.

Through the integration of desirability of control, attitude and the social cognitive construct of prior experience, this chapter advances current understanding of how and why people are consuming UGC. As UGC users adopt an active approach when experiencing UGC, they strive toward self-expression by engaging in behaviors that provide them with a voice or showcase their individual thoughts (e.g., blogs, forums, personal Web sites). Future research should explore the impact of individual skill or self-efficacy on this process. For example, the creation of videos, production of music, and acquisition of necessary knowledge to post a wiki require more aptitude than simply using a computer keyboard (i.e., as required by an online discussion forum). Investigating the differences in different types of UGC activities could provide a more in-depth insight. Therefore, a thorough understanding of the psychological makeup of UGC consumers is even more critical because the consumption and delivery of communication messages might be refined for maximum impact. By providing consumers with a forum in which they may consume or use UGC, media technology professionals might enhance the value of information they present online by engaging consumers in an active media experience.

The UGC market likely will expand greatly during the next decade as more users migrate toward consuming UGC. Opportunities abound for media technology and marketing communication professionals in this burgeoning information space, as evidenced by the forecasted $4.3 billion in advertising revenues by 2011 (Verna 2007). Industries thus must seize this opportunity to communicate relevant content to audiences through this channel. As the digital information society continues to evolve, identifying key individual characteristics that lead to expected outcomes can help clarify media consumption online. The current chapter sides with the idea that a positive relationship exits between expected values gained from an action (i.e., UGC consumption) and the behavior itself. Of course, this single examination represents just a first step in a new and unexplored area of online consumer behavior, and continued work must verify and validate these results to provide a full understanding of the impact of UGC.

REFERENCES

Abdullatif, H. I., & Hamadah, L. N. (2005). The factorial structure of the desirability of control scale among kuwaiti subjects. *Social Behavior and Personality*, *33*(3), 307–312. doi:10.2224/sbp.2005.33.3.307

Alpert, S. R., Karat, J., Karat, C.-M., Brodie, C., & Vergo, J. G. (2003). User attitudes regarding a user-adaptive ecommerce web site. *User Modeling and User-Adapted Interaction*, *13*, 373–396. doi:10.1023/A:1026201108015

Althaus, S. L., & Tewksbury, D. (2000). Patterns of internet and traditional news media use in a networked community. *Political Communication*, *17*, 21–45. doi:10.1080/105846000198495

Anderson, C. (2006). *The Long Tail: Why the Future of Business is Selling Less of More*. London: Random House Business Books.

Auter, P. J., & Lane, R. Jr. (1999). Locus of control, Parasocial interaction and usage of TV ministry programs. *Journal of Communication and Religion*, *22*(1), 93–120.

Babrow, A. S., & Swanson, D. L. (1988). Disentangling entecedents of audience exposure levels: Extending expectancy-value analyses of gratifications sought from television news. *Communication Monographs*, *55*, 1–21. doi:10.1080/03637758809376155

Bandura, A. (1986). *Social Foundations of Thought and Action: A Social Cognitive Theory*. Englewood Cliffs, NJ: Prentice Hall.

Bandura, A. (2001). Social cognitive theory of mass communication. *Media Psychology*, *3*, 265–299. doi:10.1207/S1532785XMEP0303_03

Burger, J. M. (1984). Desirability of control, locus of control and proneness to depression. *Journal of Personality*, *52*, 71–89. doi:10.1111/j.1467-6494.1984.tb00551.x

Burger, J. M. (1985). Desirability of control and achievement-related behaviors. *Journal of Personality and Social Psychology*, *48*(6), 1520–1533. doi:10.1037/0022-3514.48.6.1520

Burger, J. M. (1992). Desirability of control and academic performance. *Canadian Journal of Behavioural Science*, *24*(2), 147–155. doi:10.1037/h0078716

Burger, J. M., & Cooper, H. M. (1979). The desirability of control. *Motivation and Emotion*, *3*(4), 381–393. doi:10.1007/BF00994052

Chandran, S., & Morwitz, V. G. (2005, September). Effects of participative pricing on consumers' cognitions and actions: A goal theoretic perspective. *The Journal of Consumer Research*, *32*, 249–259. doi:10.1086/432234

Cover, R. (2006). Audience inter/active: Interactive media, narrative control and reconceiving audience history. *New Media & Society*, *18*(1), 139–158. doi:10.1177/1461444806059922

Cramer, K. M., & Perreault, L. A. (2006). Effect of predictability, actual controllability, and awareness of choice on perceptions of control. *Current Research in Social Psychology, 11*(8), 111–126.

Croteau, D. R., & Hoynes, W. (2003). *Media and Society: Industries, Images and Audiences*. Thousand Oaks, CA: Pine Forge Press.

Daugherty, T., Eastin, M. S., & Bright, L. (2008). Exploring consumer motivations for creating user-generated content. *Journal of Interactive Advertising, 8*(2). Retrieved from http://www.jiad.org/.

DeCharms, R. (1968). *Personal Causation*. New York: Academic Press.

Declerck, C. H., Boone, C., & De Brabander, B. (2006). On feeling in control: A biological theory for individual differences in control perception. *Brain and Cognition, 62*, 143–176. doi:10.1016/j.bandc.2006.04.004

Donohew, L., Palmgreen, P., & Rayburn, J. D. II. (1987). Social and psychological origins of media use: A lifestyle analysis. *Journal of Broadcasting & Electronic Media, 31*(3), 255–278.

Duncan, D. J. (1978). Leisure types: Factor analyses of leisure profiles. *Journal of Leisure Research, 10*, 113–125.

Eagly, A. H., & Chaiken, S. (1993). *The Psychology of Attitudes*. Fort Worth, TX: Harcourt Brace Janovich College Publishers.

Eastin, M. S., & Daugherty, T. (2005). Past, Current, and Future Trends in Mass Communication. In Kimmel, A. (Ed.), *Marketing Communication: Emerging Trends and Developments*. Oxford, UK: Oxford University Press.

Eastin, M. S., & LaRose, R. L. (2000). Internet self-efficacy and the psychology of the digital divide. *Journal of Computer-Mediated Communication, 6*. Retrieved from http://www.ascusc.org/jcmc/vol6/issue1/eastin.html.

Faranda, W. T. (2001). A scale to measure the cognitive control form of perceived control: Construction and preliminary assessment. *Psychology and Marketing, 18*(12), 1259–1281. doi:10.1002/mar.1052

Fazio, R. H. (1986). How Do Attitudes Guide Behavior? In Sorrentino, R. M., & Higgins, E. T. (Eds.), *Handbook of Motivation and Cognition* (pp. 204–243). New York: Guilford.

Fazio, R. H., & Towles-Schwen, T. (1999). The MODE Model of Attitude-Behavior Processes. In Chaiken, S., & Trope, Y. (Eds.), *Dual Process Theories in Social Psychology* (pp. 97–116). New York: Guilford.

Feldman, L. P., & Hornik, J. (1981, March). The use of time: An integrated conceptual model. *The Journal of Consumer Research, 7*, 407–419. doi:10.1086/208831

Gebhardt, W. A., & Brosschot, J. F. (2002). Desirability of control: Psychometric properties and relationships with locus of control, personality, coping, and mental and somatic complaints in three Dutch samples. *European Journal of Personality, 16*, 423–438. doi:10.1002/per.463

Gronau, R. (1977, December). Leisure, home production, and work: The theory of the allocation of time revisited. *The Journal of Political Economy, 85*, 1099–1123. doi:10.1086/260629

Haidt, J., & Rodin, J. (1999). Control and efficacy as interdisciplinary bridges. *Review of General Psychology, 3*(4), 317–337. doi:10.1037/1089-2680.3.4.317

Hair, J. F., Anderson, R. E., Tatham, R. L., & Black, W. C. (1998). *Multivariate Data Analysis* (5th ed.). Upper Saddle River, NJ: Prentice Hall.

Katz, D. (1960). The functional approach to the study of attitudes. *Public Opinion Quarterly, 24*, 27–46. doi:10.1086/266945

Klein, C. T. F., & Helweg-Larsen, M. (2002). Perceived control and the optimistic bias: A meta-analytic review. *Psychology & Health, 17*(4), 437–446. doi:10.1080/08870440220000004920

LaRose, R., & Eastin, M. S. (2002). Is online buying out of control? Electronic commerce and consumer self-regulation. *Journal of Broadcasting & Electronic Media, 46*(4), 549–564. doi:10.1207/s15506878jobem4604_4

LaRose, R., & Eastin, M. S. (2004). A social cognitive explanation of Internet. Uses and gratifications: Toward a new model of media attendance. *Journal of Broadcasting & Electronic Media, 48*(3), 358–377. doi:10.1207/s15506878jobem4803_2

LaRose, R., Mastro, D., & Eastin, M. S. (2001). Understanding internet usage: A social-cognitive approach to uses and gratifications. *Social Science Computer Review, 19*(4), 395–413. doi:10.1177/089443930101900401

Liang, T.-P., Lai, H.-J., & Ku, Y.-C. (2006). Personalized content recommendation. *Management Information Systems, 23*(3), 45–70. doi:10.2753/MIS0742-1222230303

Liu, Y., & Shrum, L. J. (2002). What is interactivity and is it always such a good thing? Implications of definition, person, and situation for the influence of interactivity on advertising effectiveness. *Journal of Advertising, 31*(4), 53–64.

McKechnie, G. E. (1974). The psychological structure of leisure: Past behavior. *Journal of Leisure Research, 6*, 27–35.

Myers, D. G. (1998). *Social Psychology* (9th ed.). New York: McGraw-Hill.

O'Keefe, D. J. (2002). *Persuasion: Theory & Research* (2nd ed.). Thousand Oaks, CA: Sage Publications.

Page, R. (2006, November 11). General Session Summary: Andrew Heyward on the Power of the Remote and the Rise of New Media. *Public Relations Society of America.*

Palmgreen, P., Wenner, L. A., & Rayburn, J. D. (1980). Relations between gratifications sought and obtained: A study of television news. *Communication Research, 7*, 161–192. doi:10.1177/009365028000700202

Perry, D. K. (2002). *Theory and Research in Mass Communication: Contexts and Consequences* (2nd ed.). Mahwah, NJ: Lawrence Erlbaum Associates.

Robinson, J. (1977). *How American Use Time: A Social-Psychological Analysis of Everyday Behavior*. New York: Praeger.

Rotter, J. B. (1966). Generalized expectancies for internal versus external control of reinforcement. *Psychological Monographs, 80*, 9–28.

Rubin, A. M. (1993). The effect of locus of control on communication motivation, anxiety, and satisfaction. *Communication Quarterly, 41*(Spring), 161–171.

Rubin, A. M. (2002). The uses-and-gratifications perspective of media effects. In Bryant, J., & Zillmann, D. (Eds.), *Media effects: Advances in theory and research* (2nd ed., pp. 525–548). Mahwah, NJ: Lawrence Erlbaum.

Schutz, W. C. (1966). *The Interpersonal Underworld.* Palo Alto, CA: Science and Behavior Books.

Severin, W. J., & Tankard, J. W. Jr. (1992). *Communication Theories: Origins, Methods, and Uses in the Mass Media* (3rd ed.). White Plains, NY: Longman Publishing Group.

Shapiro, A. L. (1999). *The Control Revolution: How the Internet is Putting Individuals in Charge and Changing the World We Know*. New York: Public Affairs.

Smith, R. A., Wallston, B. S., Wallston, K. A., Forsberg, P. R., & King, J. E. (1984). Measuring desirability of control of health care processes. *Journal of Personality and Social Psychology*, *47*, 415–426. doi:10.1037/0022-3514.47.2.415

Thompson, S. C., Thomas, C., & Armstrong, W. (1998). Illusion of control, underestimations, and accuracy: A control heuristic explanation. *Psychological Bulletin*, *123*(2), 143–161. doi:10.1037/0033-2909.123.2.143

Verna, P. (2007 June). User-Generated Content: Will Web 2.0 Pay Its Way? *eMarketer*, 1-31.

Wober, M., & Gunter, B. (1982). Television and personal threat: Fact or artifact? A British survey. *The British Journal of Social Psychology*, *21*, 239–247.

Wolfgang, A. K., Zenker, S. I., & Viscusi, T. (1984). Control Motivation and the Illusion of Control in Betting on Dice. *The Journal of Psychology*, *116*, 67–72.

Wu, G. (2006). Conceptualization and measuring the perceived interactivity of websites. *Journal of Current Issues and Research in Advertising*, *28*(Spring), 87–104.

Chapter 8
Race-Specific Advertising on Commercial Websites:
Effects of Ethnically Ambiguous Computer Generated Characters in a Digital World

Osei Appiah
The Ohio State University, USA

Troy Elias
University of Florida, USA

ASTRACT

Avatars and anthropomorphic characters by marketers are becoming more commonplace on commercial web sites. Moreover, a trend among marketers is to use ethnically ambiguous models in advertising to appeal to specific consumer segments. This study helps our understanding of not only how best to segment and appeal to racially diverse consumers but how people interact with virtual human agents in relationship to the literature on audience response to real humans. It was predicted that Blacks would respond more positively to a Black agent, than they would to either a White agent or an ethnically ambiguous agent. It was also expected that Whites would show no difference in their response based on the race of the computer agent. The findings demonstrate that Blacks had more positive attitudes toward a computer agent, had more positive attitudes toward a web site and recalled more product information from a site when the site featured a Black agent vis-à-vis a White agent. Whites showed no significant response difference concerning the agent, the brand or the site based on the racial composition of the computer agents. Interestingly, the ethnically ambiguous character was overall just as effective in persuading both White and Black browsers as were the same-race agents.

Technological advancements in computing, communication technologies and information management have significantly altered the nature of mass media within the last two decades (Chaffee & Metzger, 2001). The establishment of a virtually limitless wave of channels through increasing broadband connectivity and new technological developments has ultimately led to the 'demassification' of the media (Chaffee & Metzger, 2001; Tharp, 2001). The enhanced bi-directionality of communication by virtue of the new information age, has provided users with

DOI: 10.4018/978-1-60566-792-8.ch008

significantly enhanced capabilities to transmit and retrieve information, especially when compared to the mass society era. Individuals now have access to information from a wide array of sources and amplified interactive access (Papacharissi & Rubin, 2000). In addition to this, however, users also have improved capabilities to create and contribute content themselves. Users have more control in the way content is disseminated and received, all at less financial and temporal costs than ever before (Chaffee & Metzger, 2001). In the ongoing march toward media convergence the enhanced ability of users to share information with each other has led to a significant increase in interpersonal influence (Subramani & Rajagopalan, 2003). Particularly in today's current commercial media framework, media outlets, advertisers, and marketers are well advised that they no longer sell goods and services to individual consumers, but are actually in the business of selling goods and services to networks of customers (Rosen, 2000). Other problems faced by mass marketers in today's media environment include the resultant shrinking of traditional mass audiences, and the inability of traditional marketing efforts to capture and hold the attention of their audience.

With ever-increasing informational and interactive access (Papacharissi & Rubin, 2000), consumers are becoming increasingly difficult to reach and their attention equally difficult to attain much less to hold (Rosen, 2000). With so many offerings and available channels, consumers are hardly able to differentiate one company's offerings from another, particularly in e-commerce settings. This has motivated advertising agencies to develop new and innovative ways to capture the attention of their audiences.

Companies are increasing using digital media like the Internet, which offer unique features that may enhance the persuasive effects of advertising and other strategic communication efforts by allowing information to be presented in a multimodal format that takes advantage of animation and instantly playing audio and video—*rich media*. Companies utilizing their web sites to promote their brand can benefit from the multi-sensory interaction of sight, sound, and motion. Unlike simple text-only or text-picture appeals, commercials and video clips on the web can be better used to "convey a mood or image for a brand as well as to develop emotional or entertaining appeals that help make a dull product appear more interesting" (Belch & Belch, 2001, p. 354). The perceptually pleasing ability of digital, rich, and vividly presented information on a commercial web site may be inherently interesting, attention-getting, thought-provoking, image producing, emotionally arousing and easy to elaborate upon (Appiah, 2006; Kim, Kardes, Herr, 1989; McGill & Anand, 1989).

A particularly important way to capture audiences' attention and increase the entertainment value and customer satisfaction in virtual shopping environments is to use computer-generated characters or "avatars" on digitally rich commercial web sites (Holzwarth, Jaiszewski, & Neumann, 2006).

Computer-Generated Anthropomorphic Agents: Avatars and Agents

Computer-generated anthropomorphic characters are computer agents or avatars that have been provided human traits or qualities, such as computer generated faces (Gong & Nass, 2007). Computer-generated anthropomorphic characters are frequently imbued with the ability to speak through either computer-generated speech or prerecorded natural speech (Gong & Nass, 2007). These virtual humans are a new and increasingly prominent type of digital communicator, and are being used in many capacities. For instance, virtual humans have been utilized as computer interface agents (Gong & Nass, 2007; Lee & Nass, 2002), as avatars or virtual representations of self in video games (Eastin, 2006), in virtual environments (Bailenson, Beall, Loomis, Blascovich, & Turk, 2005), and for the purposes of computer-mediated communication (Lee, 2004). Computer-generated anthropomorphic characters are usually categorized as being one of two types, either agents, which are computer-controlled characters, or avatars, which are user-controlled (see Nowak, 2004; Eastin, Appiah, & Cichirillo, in press; Gong & Nass, 2007). Computer-generated characters are being used as digital communicators on websites as well as in computer games and applications with increasing frequency (Gong & Nass, 2007). A major overlooked effect of the proliferation of virtual human characters is that individuals who interact with them are increasingly being exposed to racial entities that are not real humans or real-human representations (Gong, Appiah & Elias, 2007).

Computer-generated anthropomorphic characters are often imbued with basic social identities that frequently include race (Baylor & Kim, 2003; Gong, Appiah, & Elias, 2007). As a result, an important theoretical consideration establishes how ethnicity operates in virtual contexts between source and viewer as opposed to the more traditional communication contexts involving real humans or humans interacting with mediated real-human entities and representations. Simply, do virtual human representations stimulate traditional racial responses of ingroup and outgroup members as often found with real-human entities (Gong, Appiah, & Elias, 2007)? Answers to this and similar questions hold significant implications for individuals of all ethnicities, particularly Blacks.

Ostensibly, Blacks have made significant inroads with respect to their representations in advertisements in traditional media, most notably television and print (Wilkes & Valencia, 1989; Zinkhan, Qualls & Biswas, 1990). Subsequent studies have revealed, however, that Blacks in advertisements are still being utilized in restricted roles (Entman & Rojecki, 2000), for short time periods (Greenberg & Brand, 1994), and in racially-integrated groups (Wilkes & Valencia, 1989). Additionally, Blacks who do not have expert qualifications or who are not recognizable celebrities have been disproportionately used to advertise low-end, inexpensive products (Bang & Reece, 2003). Ironically, despite a common perception of Blacks living in the U.S. being destitute, they currently have more disposable income than they did in the past, and outspend non-Black consumers in several high margin categories (Cooper, 2004). Continued failure to acknowledge the importance of this demographic could be to the detriment of many organizations. Additionally, a lack of understanding of how race affects consumer attitudes and communication of individuals of all ethnicities in today's current information society could also prove deleterious.

In today's online environment consumers are ever-exposed to racial entities that are computer-generated in a multitude of digital communication environments. There exists, however, limited insight as to the impact of virtual race and ethnicity, particularly in e-commerce settings. Additionally, research has yet to examine ethnic ambiguity as a key predictor of consumer attitudes toward products featured on commercial websites. What the research has shown, however, is that people automatically and unconsciously follow the same social rules when they interact with computers as when they interact with humans (Nass & Moon, 2000; Reeves & Nass, 1996). Nass and colleagues, in the media equation discourse community, have established that social rules such as displays of ingroup favoritism, politeness, reciprocity, gender stereotypes, and personality are applied in much the same way when humans interact with computers as when they interact with other humans (Gong, Appiah, & Elias, 2007). Moreover, with respect to race and ethnicity, Nass and colleagues (2000) have found that agents that are the same ethnicity as participants tend to elicit more positive ratings of social attraction and trustworthiness, as well as greater conformity than agents of a different ethnicity. A noticeable trend that has been identified by the scant research is an ingroup preference for same-race computer agents. This seems to follow the same pattern of results as that found among the growing body of studies examining real humans (for review see Gong, Appiah, & Elias, 2007). For instance, Baylor and Kim (2003) found that among computer-generated Black and White virtual pedagogical agents, users rated the same-race agents as more engaging and affable. Baylor, Shen, and Huang (2003) also found same-race preference in direct choice-making among Black and White virtual pedagogical agents. However, since the latest cultural trend among marketers is to use ethnically ambiguous models in advertising (Arlidge, 2004), the question arises, how might this process work for agents that are neither White nor Black but racially or ethnically ambiguous?

Ethnically Ambiguous Characters

Marketers are increasingly using ethnically ambiguous models in advertising to appeal to specific consumer segments (Arlidge, 2004). Given nearly seven million Americans identified themselves as members of more than one race in the 2000 census, there appears to be an emerging call in advertising and marketing for the use of ethnically neutral, diverse or ambiguous characters to reach consumers (La Ferle, 2003). A number of marketing experts perceive that character ambiguity in an advertisement is effective because there is a current fascination, particularly among young consumers, with racial-hybrid-looking models (Arlidge, 2004). This attraction by young consumers may be due in part to census data that indicate audiences 25 and under are twice as likely as older adults to identify themselves as multiracial (La Ferle, 2003). For young Blacks 18-29, forty-four percent of them no longer believe it is appropriate to consider Black people as one race (Williams, 2007)

This apparent trend has led some marketers to assume that it may be time to dismiss the use of a specific race as a consumer segmentation indicator (Arlidge, 2004). In fact, some critics argue that the infrequent use of ethnic-specific models in lieu of ethnically ambiguous models is not a recent phenomenon. Sengupta (2002) argues that mixed-raced models have long been casts in advertisements that would generally call for the presence of Black models, and have frequently been used by advertisers as the prototype of ethnic beauty.

This noticeable increase in the use of ethnically ambiguous models in consumer advertising suggests an implicit assumption within the advertising industry that ethnically ambiguous models are more effective than Black models in persuading Black consumers (Sengupta, 2002). Out of this concern, and the prevailing evidence that computer generated characters by marketers are becoming more commonplace on commercial web sites, it seems reasonable to examine the effect that Black, White, and ethnically ambiguous computer-generated agents on a commercial web site may have on Black and White consumers' evaluations of brand sites.

Theoretical Framework

The available research on audiences' responses to ethnically ambiguous characters is less than conclusive. Research indicates that some people neither perceive racially ambiguous characters as a member of their ingroup nor do they perceive them as a member of a relevant outgroup (see Willadsen-Jensen & Ito, 2006). Other research, on the other hand, points to a tendency for audiences to categorize ethnically ambiguous characters as members of an outgroup (Willadsen-Jensen & Ito, 2006). Social identity theory and the distinctiveness principle should provide a better understanding of how audiences process information from both ethnically ambiguous and unambiguous sources.

Social Identity Theory of Inter-group Behavior

A social identity is defined as "that part of an individual's self-concept that is derived from his knowledge of his membership in a social group (or groups) together with the emotional significance attached to that membership" (Tajfel, 1974, p. 69). Social identity theory asserts that a positive social identity is generally desired and is based on comparisons made between individual's ingroup and a relevant outgroup (Tajfel, 1974; Tajfel & Turner, 1986). Individuals are motivated to view ingroup members more favorably as a means to maintain or enhance self-esteem (Hogg, 2004; Tajfel & Turner, 1986). Within the social identity theoretical framework, people are assumed to have a fundamental need to achieve and maintain positive social identity for social groups to which they belong.

Research on group identities demonstrates that ingroup-outgroup social comparisons are based on a specific social identity that is both salient to and valued by the ingroup (Hogg, Terry, & White, 1995; Tajfel & Wilkes, 1963). The salience of a distinctive trait determines its accessibility and meaningfulness for group members (Vignoles, Chryssochoou, & Breakwell, 2000). The greater the salience of the specific social category such as race (Mastro, 2003) the greater one's ingroup identification and favoritism (Appiah, 2001; Espinoza & Garza, 1985). Race, in particular, may be the most salient social category among minority members (Fujioka, 2005; Phinney, 1990) due in part to their numeric composition in society. According to the theoretical framework associated with the distinctiveness principle (Breakwell, 1986; Brewer, 1991), a person's sense of belonging and identification is generally strengthened by a group's unique size in a particular community (Appiah, 2007; Brewer, 1991; Vignoles et al., 2000). The smaller the group's size the more likely they are to distinguish themselves from other groups (Brewer, 1991). For instance, Black people are a numeric minority in society; therefore, as a group they should be highly aware and mindful of their race in personal and mediated situations. In contrast, as a numeric majority in society race is not salient or necessarily valued by Whites and may not grow in importance until they are no longer in the majority in specific settings (Phinney, 1992). As a given ethnic group becomes numerically more dominant in a social environment, ethnicity becomes progressively less salient and less valued in the self-concept of its members (McGuire et. al., 1978). This is evident by research that demonstrates majority Whites are less likely than minority Blacks and Hispanics to mention their ethnicity when asked to list characteristics that are important in defining themselves (McGuire et al., 1978; Phinney, 1992).

As a result of race being more salient and valued, numeric minorities express more ingroup favoritism than those members who are apart of a numeric majority (see Elias, 2008). In fact, advertising studies on race suggest Whites have no ingroup preference for same-race characters vis-à-vis different-race characters whereas Blacks' consistently show ingroup favoritism towards same-race characters (Appiah, 2001, 2003, 2007). Specifically, Black audiences are attracted to and more likely to select Black characters (Knobloch-Westerwick, Appiah, & Alter, 2008), rate Black characters more positively (Whittler, 1991; Appiah, 2007), develop more favorable attitudes towards Black-targeted media and its content (Aaker et al., 2000; Appiah, 2001, 2002), and show an increased likelihood of purchasing products promoted by Black characters (Whittler, 1989). These studies suggest that, unlike Whites, when Blacks encounter a same-race computer-generated agent on a commercial web site they should respond more positively than they would to a different-race computer-generated outgroup member such as a White agent or an ethnically ambiguous agent. Therefore, it is predicted that Black Internet surfers will respond more positively to a Black computer-generated character, than they will to either a White character or an ethnically ambiguous character whereas Whites will demonstrate no response difference based on the race of the computer-generated character. This is further supported by work on social categorization, which is derived from the same metatheorethical framework as social identity theory (Hogg, Hardie, & Reynolds, 1995).

Social identity theorists, and by extension self-categorization scholars, view social groups as being categories of people, such as ingroup and outgroup members for instance, that are consistently "perceptually homogenized" (Hogg, 2004). Outgroups tend to be homogenized more so than ingroup members (Hogg, 2004). During self-categorization, individuals depersonalize their perception of self and others in terms of a group prototype. Depersonalization, then, facilitates inter-individual attitude or 'liking' towards others based on the prototypicality of their group membership, as opposed to evaluating them based on individual idiosyncrasy (Hogg, Hardie, & Reynolds, 1995). As a result, it is not difficult to imagine that Blacks will evaluate individuals that meet the prototypical standards of Black exemplars more favorably than they will a source that is less prototypical and which might be more easily classified with outgroup members. This has been supported by the work of Hogg, Hardie, and Reynolds (1995) who found that while attraction in interpersonal relationships relates to overall similarity, attraction among group members is based on prototypical similarity. Black participants, therefore, should respond more favorably to a source that is more prototypically Black. As a result, the following hypotheses have been developed:

- H_1: Blacks will perceive themselves more similar to the Black agent than they will to either the White or ethnically ambiguous agent.
- H_2: Blacks will identify more with the Black agent than they will to either the White or the ethnically ambiguous agent.
- H_3: Blacks will have more positive attitudes toward the Black agent than they will either the White or the ethnically ambiguous agent.
- H_4: Blacks will have more positive attitudes toward the brand after viewing the website featuring the Black agent than they will after viewing the website featuring either the White or the ethnically ambiguous agent.
- H_5: Blacks will have more positive attitudes toward the Acura website featuring a Black agent than they will towards a website featuring either a White or an ethnically ambiguous agent.
- H_6: Blacks will recall more information from the Acura website featuring the Black agent than they will the Acura website featuring either a White or an ethnically ambiguous agent.

It should be noted, that a major assumption that is being made for this study is that a stimulus featuring an animated, young, Black female character with a congruent Black female voice is more prototypically Black than an ethnically ambiguous character or a White character with a similarly racially congruent voice.

METHOD

Participants and Design

One hundred seventy-one undergraduate students (53 Black and 118 White) from a large Midwestern university participated in the study. Fifty-nine percent of the participants were female and forty-one percent were male with a mean age of 21. Participants were recruited from courses in the School of Communication, Black Cultural Center, and the Office of Minority Affairs. The study utilized an experimental method to examine the effects of using Black, White and ethnically ambiguous agents on participants' evaluations of a commercial web site. The experiment used a 3 (computer-generated agent: Black, White or ethnically ambiguous) x 2 (participants' race: White or Black) between-subjects design. The study examined the extent to which the race of agent and race of the user affected evaluations of the brand displayed on the website. The six dependent variables include: 1) perceived similarity to agent; 2) identification with the agent; 3) attitude towards the agent; 4) attitude towards the brand; 5) attitude towards the web; and 6) recall of product information.

Stimuli

A version of the Acura car web page was re-created by a professional Web designer. Acura is a luxury brand from the Japanese automaker Honda Motor Company. An automobile site was used because cars tend to represent a product class of general interest and usage among a broad cross-section of the student collegiate population. Three versions of one of its commercial pages were created, each with identical images and accompanying text related to Acura cars. For each condition a talking, female, computer animated product spokesperson was used. The computer spokespersons' used were SitePal generated characters. SitePal is an Internet-based subscription service that allows users to create animated speaking characters that can be incorporated onto a website. The same female character was used for the study; however, the character's race was modified across the three experimental conditions. That is, the only difference among the three web pages was the ethnicity of the agent (i.e., Black, White, or ethnically ambiguous). Figures 1-3 present the images of the Black, White, and ethnically ambiguous animated characters that were used.

Figure 1. Condition 1: Black female agent

Figure 2. Condition 2: White female agent

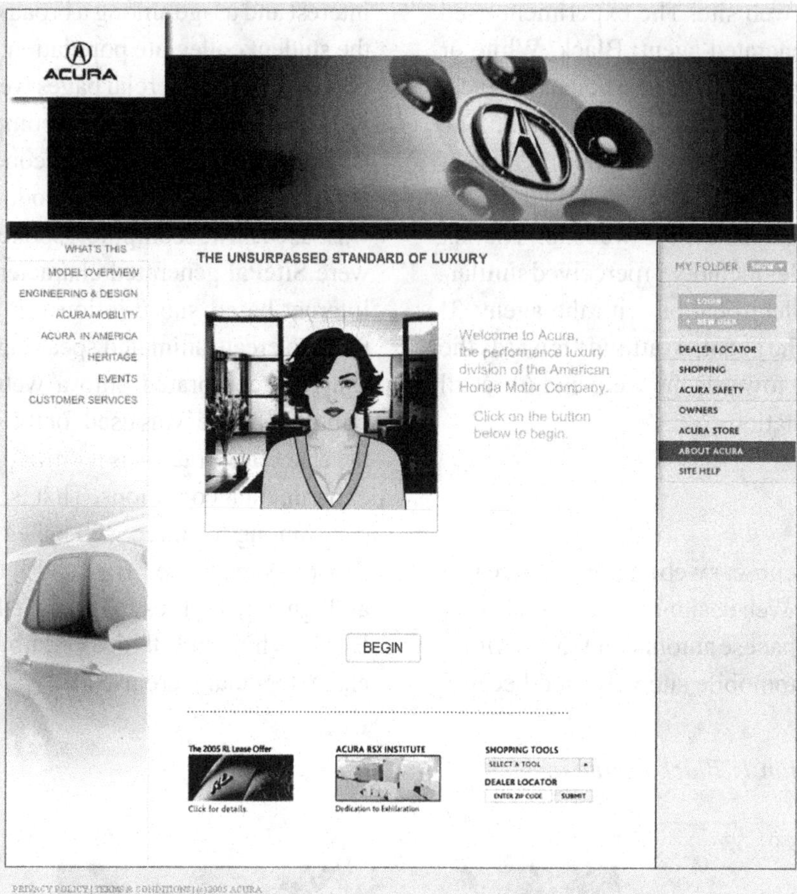

The first condition was the talking, Black animated female agent condition. For this condition a 210 x 315 pixel, animated Black female agent with Black eyes was placed on the left hand side of the screen. This computer-generated anthropomorphic agent used a prerecorded ethnically congruent (i.e., Black female), natural voice, which was synchronized to the lip and facial movements of the character. The second condition was exactly the same as the first condition except that the agent used was a White female with blue eyes. An ethnically congruent (i.e., White female), prerecorded natural voice was used for condition two. The third condition followed the same format, except that the computer-generated character used in this condition was an ethnically ambiguous female with Black eyes. The voice used for this character was again an ethnically congruent (i.e., mixed-race female), prerecorded natural voice.

The computer-generated female agents were used as spokespeople on the Acura website. Each agent greeted the user and provided instructions concerning how to browse the Acura Web page. For example, the character greeted the participants with the following: "Hello. Welcome to Acura Right Ride! My name is Angie, and I'll be your personal guide today. Based on your responses to just a few questions, we'll help you find a car that best suites your lifestyle." In order to create interaction between the participant and the spokesperson, the agent engaged the user in a number of questions—that were not recorded—

Figure 3. Condition 3: ethnically ambiguous female agent

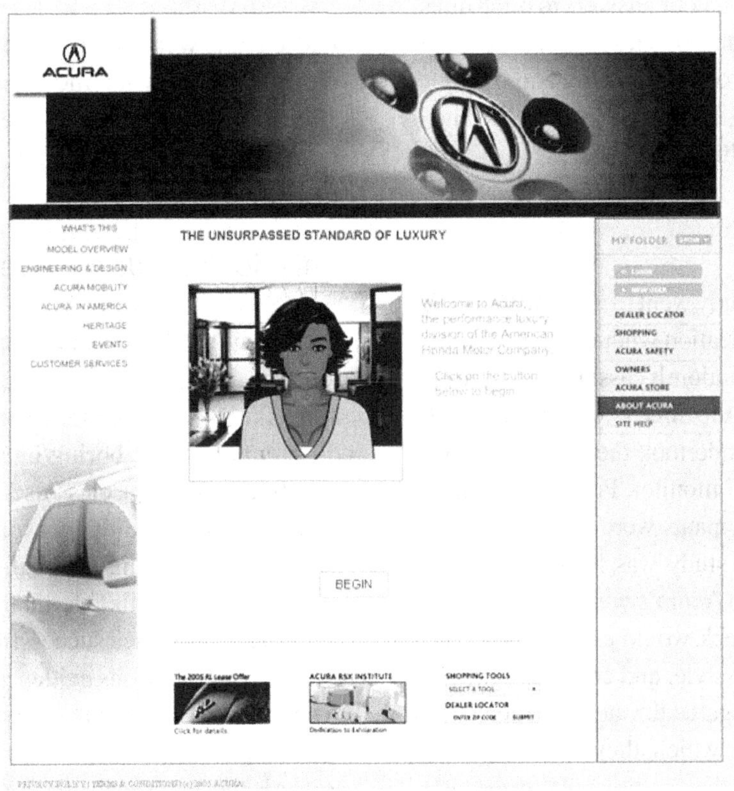

to which the user responded. Each response by the user activated the agent, leading the agent to provide another statement or ask another question. Each agent asked the user eight questions. Viewers responded to each question by clicking one of five options available for each question. The spokesperson was positioned on the left side of the page, and on the right side of the page were the same questions asked by the female agents (in Word format) along with five mutually exclusive answer options. It should be noted that the questions asked by the agents were merely used to get the participants to interact with the agents in a commercial environment. No data was saved from these questions. Oncc participants sclected an answer the agent would respond in a reassuring way. For example, one question that the agent asked was, "You like clothes that are?" The response options were: trendy, vintage, sporty, classic, or whacky. When participants selected their answer the agent verbal reply was always, "I don't know about you but I like to mix it up a little." Another question asked by the agent was, "What is your favorite form of entertainment?" The response options were movies, comedy, theatre, sports, or music. After selecting a response option, the agent would always reply with, "Those all sound like fun." Other questions included: "What is your favorite type of food?" "What activity would you prefer to do on vacation?" and "What genre of music do you prefer most?" After each question the user would then click on the "next" button to take them to the next question.

After responding to the eight questions, the agent generated a picture of three cars (Acura RSX, Acura TSX, and Acura MDX) that were supposed to represent cars that fit the lifestyle and personality of the participants based on their responses to the eight questions. The same three cars always appear at the end of the session for each condition. The agent concluded the session by stating: "Based on your answers to our 8 questions, we feel that any of these 3 cars would be an ideal match for your personality and lifestyle. Thanks for stopping by, and good luck! We know you'll make the right choice!"

Procedure

Participants in the study went to a lab located in the School of Communication where each was seated in a cubicle and randomly assigned to browse through only one of the three experimental conditions. Participants undertook the experiment on a computer with a 17" monitor. Prior to navigating the Web page, participants were told that the purpose of the Internet study was for researchers to test some changes to Acura's web site. They were told that their feedback would enable researchers to improve the look, style, and content of the site. All participants navigated through the 8 questions on the Web site, after which, they then answered a questionnaire. Once they completed the questionnaire, participants were debriefed and asked not to tell anyone about what they had seen in the study.

Measurement Instrument

The measurement instrument collected information for the six dependent variables: 1) perceived similarity to the agent; 2) identification with the agent; 3) attitude towards the agent; 4) attitude towards the brand; 5) attitude towards the website; and 6) recall of product information.

Perceived Similarity

Participants rated their degree of similarity to the agent in terms of overall lifestyle, cultural background, dress, appearance, and basic values (Whittler, 1989). A similarity scale was created by averaging the mean scores from each of the five scales. For this scale a coefficient alpha was computed ($\alpha = .86$).

Identification with the Agent

Participants were asked to indicate how strongly they identified with the agent (Aaker, et. al., 2000) on the Acura web site on a seven-point Likert scale ranging from not at all (one) to very strongly (seven).

Attitude Towards the Agent

Participants were asked to provide their attitude towards the agent. An index was created by averaging the mean scores of eleven, 7-point semantic differential scales: boring/interesting, bad/good, negative/positive, useless/useful, worthless/valuable, poor/outstanding, not for me/for me, weak/strong, not appealing/appealing, not attractive/attractive, and not likable/likable. Although these items have been used successfully in other studies and have shown strong evidence of reliability (e.g., Appiah, 2001; Deshpandé & Stayman, 1994), a reliability analysis was conducted. For the attitude towards the agent scale, the coefficient alpha was computed ($\alpha = .93$).

Attitude Towards the Brand

Participants were asked to provide their attitude towards Acura the brand. An index was created by averaging the mean scores of eleven, 7-point semantic differential scales: boring/interesting, bad/good, negative/positive, useless/useful, worthless/valuable, poor/outstanding, not for me/for me, weak/strong, not appealing/appealing, not attractive/attractive, and not likable/likable. For the attitude toward the brand scale, the coefficient alpha was computed ($\alpha = .96$).

Attitude Towards the Website

Participants were asked to provide their attitude towards the Acura website. An index was created by averaging the mean scores of eleven, 7-point semantic differential scales: boring/interesting, bad/good, negative/positive, useless/useful, worthless/valuable, poor/outstanding, not for me/ for me, weak/strong, not appealing/appealing, not attractive/attractive, and not likable/likable. For the attitude toward the website scale, the coefficient alpha was computed ($\alpha = .92$).

Recall

The questionnaire assessed aided recall of specific visual and verbal aspects from the Acura web site and the spokesperson. Aided or cued recall is a commonly used technique in media research (e.g., Beattie & Mitchell, 1985; Gunter, Furnham, & Frost, 1994) and is mentioned as an effective way to measure attention and comprehension of specific media (Beattie & Mitchell, 1985). The recall procedure used in this study was modeled after that used by Appiah (2002) and Gunter and colleagues (1994). This procedure cued participants with verbal and nonverbal aspects of the stimuli to probe recall of media content. There were 8 questions in total that assessed aided recall. These questions included: "Name the models of the 3 Acura cars shown at the end of your session on the web site?" "Where on the site was the following logo located?" "What was the name of the animated female character?" "What color were the 3 Acura cars shown at the end of your session on the web site?" "The slogan located above the animated character read: The Unsurpassed Standard of ___." Participants were given one point for a correct reply, and zero points for an incorrect answer. Thus, a total score of 8 points could be achieved.

Race of Participants

Participants were given a list of racial and ethnic groups from which to choose. Only subjects who indicated their identification with Black/African American or White/European American were included in the analysis.

RESULTS

Manipulation Check

A pretest was conducted whereby twenty Black and twenty White undergraduates were exposed to fifteen female computer-generated characters with varying skin complexion. Among the fifteen characters were the three experimental characters, which were randomly mixed in with the group. Each participant was asked to indicate the race/ ethnicity of the female character from a list of racial/ethnic groups (e.g., Asian/Asian American, Black/African American, White/Caucasian, Hispanic, etc.). Among this list participants also had the option of selecting "biracial/multiracial" or "can't tell/don't know." One hundred percent of the Blacks identified the Black character as "Black/ African American," one hundred percent identified the White character as "White/Caucasian" and seventy-five percent (15) of the participants identified the ethnically ambiguous character as either "biracial/multiracial" or "can't tell/don't know." Similarly, one hundred percent of Whites identified the Black character as "Black/African American," one hundred percent identified the White character as "White/Caucasian" and sixty-five percent (13) of the participants identified the ethnically ambiguous character as either "biracial/ multiracial" or "can't tell/don't know."

A pretest was conducted on eight different voices (3 Black voices, 2 White voices, and 3 mixed-raced voices) that were from people representing Black, White, and mixed-race ethnic groups. Sixteen Black and Sixteen White undergraduates individually listened to each of the human voices. After each voice they were asked to indicate the speaker's race/ethnicity. The voice that was identified as most closely representing each race was chosen for the study. The Black voice that was selected was identified by all 16 Black participants and 14 White participants as a Black voice. The White voice that was selected was identified by all 16 Black and 16 White participants as a White voice. The ethnically ambiguous voice that was selected was identified as either "biracial/multiracial" or "can't tell/don't know" by 10 (63%) of the Black participants, while 4 (25%) participants identified the person as White and 2 (13%) participants identified the person as Black. Eleven (69%) of the White participants identified the voice as either "biracial/multiracial" or "can't tell/don't know."

Hypotheses Testing

A series of two-way analyses of variance were conducted to test the hypotheses. Follow-up analyses were conducted to examine significant findings. The same analyses were conducted for all six dependent variables.

Perception of Similarity

It was hypothesized that Blacks would perceive themselves more similar to the Black agent than they would to either the White or ethnically ambiguous agents. It was also expected that Whites would respond no differently to the agents based on the race of the agents. A significant interaction between participants' race and agents' race was found (F (2, 168) = 43.56, $p < .001$). Further examination of the means using one-way ANOVA (see Table 1) showed that Blacks overall perceived themselves more similar to the Black agent (M = 5.02, SD = 1.34) than they did the White agent (M = 2.24, SD = .89, $p < .001$), and the ethnically ambiguous agent (M = 4.31, SD = 1.16, $p < .05$). Moreover, Blacks perceived themselves more similar to the ethnically ambiguous agent (M = 4.31, SD = 1.16) than they did the White agent (M = 2.24 SD = .89, $p < .001$). White participants perceived themselves more similar to the White agent (M = 4.25, SD = 1.07) than they did either the Black agent (M = 3.36, SD = .87, $p < .001$) or the ethnically ambiguous agent (M = 3.44, SD = .95, $p < .001$, see Table 2). The findings provide support for H1.

Identification

It was hypothesized that Blacks would identify more with the Black agent than with either the White or the ethnically ambiguous agents. A significant interaction between participants' race and agent's race was found (F (2, 170) = 12.22, $p < .001$). Further examination of the means using one-way ANOVA indicated that Blacks identified more strongly with the Black agent (M = 4.56, SD = 1.79) than they did with the White agent (M

Table 1. Means for Black participants' responses to race-specific computer-generated female agents with race-specific voice

	Black Internet Browsers		
	Black Female Agent	White Female Agent	Ethnically Ambiguous Agent
Similarity to Agent	5.02[a]	2.24[c]	4.31[b]
Identification with Agent	4.56[a]	2.06[b]	4.41[a]
Attitude Towards Agent	4.76[a]	3.45[b]	4.84[a]
Attitude Towards Brand	4.90	5.16	5.53
Attitude Towards Web	4.79[a]	4.05[c]	5.41[a]
Recall of Product Information	9.50[a]	4.33[c]	6.80[b]

Note. Means with different superscripts differ significantly from each other at $p < .05$.
$\underline{N}$ = 53.

Table 2. Means for White participants' responses to race-specific computer-generated female agents with race-specific voice

	White Internet Browsers		
	Black Female Agent	**White Female Agent**	**Ethnically Ambiguous Agent**
Similarity to Agent	3.36[b]	4.25[a]	3.44[b]
Identification with Agent	3.28	3.41	3.32
Attitude Towards Agent	4.69	4.43	4.25
Attitude Towards Brand	5.21	5.43	5.31
Attitude Towards Web	4.75	4.95	4.64
Recall of Product Information	7.40	7.88	8.33

Note. Means with different superscripts differ significantly from each other at $p < .05$.
$N = 118$.

= 2.06, *SD* = 1.26, p < .001). Moreover, Blacks identified more with the ethnically ambiguous agent (*M* = 4.41, *SD* = 1.58) than they did with the White agent (*M* = 2.06, *SD* = 1.26, p < .001). However, Blacks showed no difference in identification based on whether the agent was Black or ethnically ambiguous. White participants showed no significant difference in their identification based on the race of the agents. These findings provide partial support for H2.

Attitude Towards the Agents

A significant interaction between participants' race and agents' race was found (*F* (2, 168) = 5.68, *p* < .01). An examination of the means using one-way ANOVA indicated Blacks have more positive attitudes toward the Black agent (*M* = 4.76, *SD* = 1.41) than they did toward the White agent (*M* = 3.45, *SD* = 1.34, *p* < .01). Moreover, Blacks had more positive attitudes towards the ethnically ambiguous agent (*M* = 4.84, *SD* = 1.08) than they did towards the White agent (*M* = 3.45, *SD* = 1.34, *p* < .01). However, Blacks demonstrated no difference in their attitude towards the Black agent vis-a-vis the ethnically ambiguous agent. Whites demonstrated no significant difference in their attitude towards the agents based on the race of the agents. These findings provide partial support for H3.

Attitude Towards the Brand

No significant interaction or main effects were detected for participants' race and agents' race. These findings do not support H4.

Attitude Towards the Website

It was predicted that Blacks would have more positive attitudes toward the website featuring a Black agent than they would the web site featuring a White or an ethnically ambiguous agent. A significant interaction between participants' race and agents' race was found (*F* (2, 170) = 9.39, *p* < .001). As shown in Table 1, the examination of the means indicated Blacks had more positive attitudes toward the Acura web site when it featured a Black agent (*M* = 4.79, *SD* = 1.09) than they did when the web site featured a White agent (*M* = 4.05, *SD* = 1.29, *p* < .05). Moreover, Blacks had more positive attitudes toward the web site when it featured an ethnically ambiguous agent (*M* = 5.41, *SD* = .95) than they did when it featured a White agent (*M* = 4.05, *SD* = 1.29, *p* < .001). White participants displayed no difference in their attitude towards the web site based on the race of the agents featured on the site. These findings provide partial support for H5.

Recall

It was predicted that Blacks would recall more information from the Acura website featuring the Black agent than they would the website featuring the White or ethnically ambiguous agent. A significant interaction between participants' race and agents' race was found ($F(2, 104) = 7.60, p < .01$). As shown in Table 1, the examination of the means indicated Blacks recalled more information from the Black agent ($M = 9.50$, $SD = .71$) than they did from the White agent ($M = 4.33$, $SD = 2.30$, $p < .01$) or the ethnically ambiguous agent ($M = 6.80$, $SD = .84$, $p < .05$). Moreover, Blacks recalled more information from the ethnically ambiguous agent (M = 6.80, $SD = .84$) than they from the White agent ($M = 6.80$, $SD = 2.30$, $p < .05$). White participants demonstrated no recall difference based on the race of the agent. The findings support H6.

DISCUSSION

Early communication theorists have argued that the analysis of consumer behavior "goes far beyond its commercial implications into general patterns of human behavior" (Katz and Lazarsfeld, 1955, p. 7). Katz and Lazarsfeld (1995) posit that through an understanding of advertising and its effects on consumers, one can more effectively empirically study human action and develop systematic knowledge. As Elias (2008) articulates, some of the implications of segmenting a market based on race and ethnicity are immense. This study helps academics as well as practitioners understanding of not only how best to segment and appeal to racially diverse consumers but how people interact with virtual human agents in relationship to the literature on real humans. Moreover, the study contributes to the literature by examining the combined effects of web-based computer agents and ethnically ambiguous agents on Black and White web users' consumer attitudes. Previous research has failed to adequately examine ingroup and outgroup members' evaluations of e-commerce websites featuring racially diverse computer agents, particularly ethnically ambiguous agents.

The results demonstrate that Blacks' perceived themselves more similar to, identified more strongly with, and had more positive attitudes toward the Black computer agent than they did the White computer agent. Moreover, Blacks had more positive attitudes toward the web site and recalled more product information from the site when the brand site featured a Black agent vis-à-vis a White agent. These findings support social identity theory and the distinctiveness principle. Blacks, due to their numeric minority status in society that makes their race more salient and valued to them, responded more favorably to ingroup members (Black agents) than to outgroup members (White agents).

In contrast, despite perceiving themselves more similar to the White agent, Whites showed no significant response difference concerning the agent, the brand or the site based on the racial composition of the computer agents. This seems to support one component of the distinctiveness principle. That is, the greater (less) the salience of a specific social category such as race the greater (less) one's ingroup favoritism (Appiah, 2001; Espinoza & Garza, 1985). Given their majority status in society, Whites may be unaware of their "Whiteness" and place little value on race when making evaluative judgments concerning products.

These findings also seem to confirm that audiences use similar social rules when interacting with computer agents as they do when interacting with real humans. In support, these findings mirror research examining human-to-human interaction with White and Black characters on e-commerce websites (e.g., Appiah, 2003, Appiah, 2007).

A particularly interesting finding in this study is that the ethnically ambiguous character was overall just as effective in persuading both White and Black browsers as were same-race agents. It is possible that neither Blacks nor Whites perceived ethnically ambiguous characters as a member of their ingroup and were unable to seamlessly link them to a member of a relevant outgroup (see Willadsen-Jensen & Ito, 2006).

These results have important implications for marketers struggling to best understand how to effectively advertise to racially diverse consumers in the digital world. The findings suggest that there may no longer be a pressing need to use same-race endorsers to appeal to consumers when ethnically ambiguous characters have the potential to appeal to a broad spectrum of ethnic consumers. Ethnic ambiguous agents may cross ethnic and racial lines that in the past prevented advertising campaigns from being effectively standardized to mass audiences. For instance, the use of ethnically ambiguous characters in ads directed at young racially diverse consumers may quickly become the norm given consumers 25 and under are twice as likely as older adults to identify themselves as multiracial (La Ferle, 2003). Given the possible universal appeal of ethnically ambiguous agents, future research should test these agents alongside same-race agents on Hispanic, Asian, and multiracial consumers. Also, future research should examine the impact of selective exposure methodology on audiences' character preferences. This technique would allow users to select the type of ethnic agent they would like to interact with on the site and give the researcher the ability to unobtrusively measure the persuasive effect of this selection.

These findings may fuel the debate concerning whether advertisers should use targeting strategies based on the race of the consumer (Arlidge, 2004), particularly when using computer-generated agents in virtual e-commerce environments. Computer-generated virtual human entities are becoming prevalent in a variety of digital communication environments because their technological nature makes them a feasible choice of representation and a natural fit with the computer platform (Gong, Appiah & Elias, 2007). For example, Gong, Appiah and Elias (2007) contend that it is significantly more challenging to program representations of real people into the flow and motion of a virtual world compared to seamlessly embedding digital characters in a virtual world. Also, virtual characters are ubiquitous in computer games and virtual environments, and are also commonly used in Web applications and stand-alone computer applications, such as virtual online news anchors (e.g., http://www.ananova.com/video), e-commerce agents (Tanaka, 2000), and virtual educators (Lester, Stone, Converse, Kahler, & Barlow, 1997). Thankfully, communication researchers are beginning their journey in examining the growing phenomenon of virtual human entities and ethnically ambiguous agents.

REFERENCES

Aaker, J., Brumbaugh, A., & Grier, S. (2000). Non-target market effects and viewer distinctiveness: The impact of target marketing on attitudes. *Journal of Consumer Psychology*, *9*(3), 127–140. doi:10.1207/S15327663JCP0903_1

Ahrens, F. (2006). The nearly personal touch: Marketers use Avatars to put an animated face with the name. *The Washington Post*. Retrieved December 7, 2007, from http://www.washingtonpost.com/wp-dyn/content/article/2006/07/14/AR2006071401587.html

Appiah, O. (2001). The effects of ethnic identification on Black and White adolescents' evaluation of ads. *Journal of Advertising Research*, *41*(5), 7–22.

Appiah, O. (2002). Black and White viewers' perception and recall of occupational characters on television. *The Journal of Communication, 52*(4), 776–793. doi:10.1111/j.1460-2466.2002.tb02573.x

Appiah, O. (2003). Americans online: Differences in surfing and evaluating race-targeted web sites by Black and White users. *Journal of Broadcasting & Electronic Media, 47*(4), 534–552. doi:10.1207/s15506878jobem4704_4

Appiah, O. (2006). Rich media, poor media: The impact of audio/video vs. text/picture testimonial ads on browsers' evaluations of commercial web sites and online products. *Journal of Current Issues and Research in Advertising, 28*(1), 73–86.

Appiah, O. (2007). The effectiveness of typical-user testimonial ads on Black and White browsers' evaluations of products on commercial web sites: Do they really work? *Journal of Advertising Research, 47*(1), 14–27. doi:10.2501/S0021849907070031

Arlidge, J. (2004, January 4). The new melting pot: Forget Black, forget White. The future is generation EA. *The Observer,* 19.

Bailenson, J. N., Beall, A. C., Loomis, J., Blascovich, J., & Turk, M. (2005). Transformed social interaction, augmented gaze, and social influence in immersive virtual environments. *Human Communication Research, 31*, 511–537. doi:10.1111/j.1468-2958.2005.tb00881.x

Bang, H., & Reece, B. B. (2003). Minorities in children's television commercials: New improved, and stereotyped. *The Journal of Consumer Affairs, 37*(1), 42–67.

Baylor, A. L., & Kim, Y. (2003). *The role of gender and ethnicity in pedagogical agent perception.* Paper presented at the E-Learn (World Conference on E-Learning in Corporate, Government, Healthcare, & Higher Education), Phoenix, AZ. Retrieved July 8, 2004 from http://pals.fsu.edu/publications.html.

Baylor, A. L., Shen, E., & Huang, X. (2003). *Which pedagogical agent do learners choose? The effects of gender and ethnicity.* Paper presented at the E-Learn (World Conference on E-Learning in Corporate, Government, Healthcare, & Higher Education), Phoenix, AZ.

Beattie, A. E., & Mitchell, A. A. (1985). The relationship between advertising recall and persuasion: An experimental investigation. In Alwitt, L. F., & Mitchell, A. A. (Eds.), *Psychological processes and advertising effects* (pp. 129–155). Hillsdale, NJ: Erlbaum.

Belch, G. E., & Belch, M. A. (2001). *Advertising and promotion: An integrated marketing communications perspective* (5th ed.). New York: McGraw-Hill Irwin.

Breakwell, G. M. (1986). *Coping with threatened identities*. London: Methuen.

Brewer, M. B. (1991). The social self: On being the same and different at the same time. *Personality and Social Psychology Bulletin, 17*, 475–482. doi:10.1177/0146167291175001

Chaffee, S. H., & Metzger, M. J. (2001). The end of mass communication? *Mass Communication & Society*, *4*(4), 365–379. doi:10.1207/S15327825MCS0404_3

Desphande, R., & Stayman, D. (1994). A tale of two cities: Distinctiveness theory and advertising effectiveness. *JMR, Journal of Marketing Research, 31*, 57–64. doi:10.2307/3151946

Eastin, M., Appiah, O., & Cicchirillo, V. (in press). Identification and the influence of cultural stereotyping on post game play hostility. *Human Communication Research*.

Elias, T. (2008). *A tale of two social contexts: Race-specific testimonials on commercial web sites and their effects on numeric majority and numeric minority consumer attitudes*. Paper presented at the Advertising Division of the Annual Convention of the Association for Education and Journalism and Mass Communication, Chicago, IL., August 2008.

Entman, R. M., & Rojecki, A. (2000). Advertising Whiteness. In Entman, R. M., & Rojecki, A. (Eds.), *The Black Image in the White Mind*. Chicago: University of Chicago Press.

Espinoza, J., & Garza, R. (1985). Social group salience and interethnic cooperation. *Journal of Experimental Social Psychology*, *21*, 380–392. doi:10.1016/0022-1031(85)90037-X

Fujioka, Y. (2005). Emotional TV viewing and minority audience: How Mexican Americans process and evaluate TV news about in-group members. *Communication Research*, *32*(5), 566–593. doi:10.1177/0093650205279210

Gong, L., Appiah, O., & Elias, T. (2007). *See minorities through the lens of ethnic identity: Reflected onto racial representations of real humans and virtual humans*. Paper presented at the annual convention of the National Communication Association.

Gong, L., & Nass, C. (2007). When a talking face computer agent is half-human and half-humanoid: Human identity and consistency preference. *Human Communication Research*, *33*, 163–193. doi:10.1111/j.1468-2958.2007.00295.x

Greenberg, B. S., & Brand, J. E. (n.d.). Commercials in the classroom: The impact of channel one advertising. *Journal of Advertising Research*, *34*(1), 18–27.

Gunter, B., Furnham, A., & Frost, C. (1994). Recall by young people of television advertisements as a function of programme type and audience evaluation. *Psychological Reports*, *75*, 1107–1120.

Hogg, M., Terry, D., & White, K. (1995). A tale of two theories: A critical comparison of identity theory with social identity theory. *Social Psychology Quarterly*, *58*, 255–269. doi:10.2307/2787127

Hogg, M. A. (2004). Social categorization, depersonalization, and group behavior. In Brewer, M. B., & Hewstone, M. (Eds.), *Self and social identity*. London: Blackwell Publishing.

Hogg, M. A., Hardie, E. A., & Reynolds, K. J. (1995). Prototypical similarity, self-categorization, and depersonalized attraction: A perspective on group cohesiveness. *European Journal of Social Psychology*, *25*(2), 159–177. doi:10.1002/ejsp.2420250204

Holzwarth, M., Janiszewski, C., & Neumann, M. M. (2006). The influence of avatars on online consumer shopping behavior. *Journal of Marketing*, *70*, 19–36. doi:10.1509/jmkg.70.4.19

Kim, J., Kardes, F. R., & Herr, P. H. (1989). Consumer expertise and the vividness effect: Implications for judgment and inference. *Advances in Consumer Research. Association for Consumer Research (U. S.)*, *18*, 90–93.

Knobloch-Westerwick, S., Appiah, O., & Alter, S. (2008). News selection patterns as a function of race: The discerning minority and the indiscriminating majority. *Media Psychology*, *11*(3), 400–417. doi:10.1080/15213260802178542

La Ferla, R. (2003, December 28). *Generation E. A.: Ethnically Ambiguous*. Retrieved December 28, 2003, from http://www.nytimes.com/2003/12/28/fashion/28ETHN.html

Lee, E.-J., & Nass, C. (2002). Experimental tests of normative group influence and representation effects in computer-mediated communication: When interacting via computers differs from interacting with computers. *Human Communication Research, 28*, 349–381. doi:10.1093/hcr/28.3.349

Mastro, D. (2003). Social identity approach to understanding the impact of television messages. *Communication Monographs, 70*(2), 98–113. doi:10.1080/0363775032000133764

McGill, A. L., & Anand, P. (1989). The effect of vivid attributes on the evaluation of alternatives: The role of differential attention and cognitive elaboration. *The Journal of Consumer Research, 16*, 188–196. doi:10.1086/209207

McGuire, W., McGuire, V., Child, P., & Fujioka, T. (1978). Salience of ethnicity in the spontaneous self-concept as a function of one's ethnic distinctiveness in the social environment. *Journal of Personality and Social Psychology, 36*(5), 511–520. doi:10.1037/0022-3514.36.5.511

Nass, C., & Moon, Y. (2000). Machines and mindlessness: Social responses to computers. *The Journal of Social Issues, 56*(1), 81–103. doi:10.1111/0022-4537.00153

Nowak, K. L. (2004). The influence of anthropomorphism and agency on social judgment in virtual environments. *Journal of Computer-Mediated Communication, 9*(2).

Oakes, P. J., Haslam, S. A., & Turner, J. C. (1994). *Stereotyping and social reality*. Oxford, UK: Blackwell.

Papacharissi, Z., & Rubin, A. M. (2000). Predictors of Internet use. *Journal of Broadcasting & Electronic Media, 44*(2), 175–196. doi:10.1207/s15506878jobem4402_2

Phinney, J. S. (1990). Ethnic identity in adolescents and adults: Review of research. *Psychological Bulletin, 108*, 499–514. doi:10.1037/0033-2909.108.3.499

Phinney, J. S. (1992). The multigroup ethnic identity measure: A new scale for use with diverse groups. *Journal of Adolescent Research, 7*(2), 156–176. doi:10.1177/074355489272003

Reeves, B., & Nass, C. (1996). *The media equation: How people treat computers, television, and new media like real people and places*. New York: Cambridge University Press.

Rosen, E. (2000). *The anatomy of buzz: How to create word-of-mouth marketing*. New York: Doubleday.

Sengupta, S. (2002). In the eyes of the beholder: The relevance of skin tone and facial features of African American Female models to advertising effectiveness. *Communication Reports, 16*(2), 210–220.

Snyder, C. R., & Fromkin, H. L. (1980). *Uniqueness: The human pursuit of difference*. New York: Plenum.

Subramani, M. R., & Rajagopalan, B. (2003). Knowledge-sharing and influence in online social networks via viral marketing. *Communications of the ACM, 46*(12), 300–307. doi:10.1145/953460.953514

Tajfel, H. (1974). Social identity and intergroup behaviour. *Social Sciences Information. Information Sur les Sciences Sociales, 13*(2), 65–93. doi:10.1177/053901847401300204

Tajfel, H., & Turner, J. C. (1986). The social identity theory of intergroup behavior. In Worchel, S., & Austin, W. G. (Eds.), *Psychology of intergroup relations* (pp. 7–24). Chicago, IL: Nelson-Hall.

Tajfel, H., & Wilkes, A. (1963). Classification and quantitative judgments. *The British Journal of Psychology, 54*, 101–114.

Tharp, M. C. (2001). *Marketing and consumer identity in multicultural America*. Thousand Oaks, CA: Sage Publication.

Vignoles, V., Chryssochoou, X., & Breakwell, G. M. (2000). The distinctiveness principle: Identity, meaning, and bounds of cultural relativity. *Personality and Social Psychology Review*, *4*(4), 337–354. doi:10.1207/S15327957PSPR0404_4

Whittler, T. E. (1989). Viewers' processing of actor's race and message claims in advertising stimuli. *Psychology and Marketing*, *6*, 287–309. doi:10.1002/mar.4220060405

Whittler, T. E. (1991). The effects of actors' race in commercial advertising: Review and extension. *Journal of Advertising*, *20*(1), 54–60.

Wilkes, R. E., & Valencia, H. (1989). Hispanics and Blacks in television commercials. *Journal of Advertising*, *18*(1), 19–25.

Willadsen-Jensen, E. C., & Ito, T. A. (2006). Ambiguity and the timecourse of racial perception. *Social Cognition*, *24*(5), 580–606. doi:10.1521/soco.2006.24.5.580

Zinkhan, G. M., Qualls, W. J., & Biswas, A. (1990). The use of Blacks in magazine and television advertising: 1946 to 1986. *The Journalism Quarterly*, *67*(3), 547–553.

Chapter 9
Social Impact of Digital Media and Advertising: A Look at Consumer Control

Gregory O'Toole
Pennsylvania State University, USA

ABSTRACT

Around the world today we have convenient, fingertip access to continual, informational content. At first the free flow of information seems convenient, empowering, and endlessly beneficial for those world citizens with access to it. This chapter takes a closer look at this relationship in terms of today's consumer and the mediated information they are exposed to and asks the question of whether or not this is necessarily a good thing. The chapter looks at the historical relationship of power and information for guidance in this examination while considering active and inactive audience, corporate and independent media texts, and the possible relationships between Victor Frankl's 'existential void' and mediated messages today.

People can be very moral, but they are acting within institutional structures, constructed systems which only certain options are easy to pursue, others are very hard to pursue. -Noam Chomsky

We shape our tools, and then our tools shape us. -Marshall McLuhan

DOI: 10.4018/978-1-60566-792-8.ch009

THE INTRODUCTION: SETTING THE STAGE

Theoretical Cultivation Analysis

Everything is information. The good news is that in our current information age we have convenient, fingertip access to continual, global content; the bad news is that in our current information age we have convenient, fingertip access to continual, global content. At first the free flow of information seems convenient, empowering, and endlessly beneficial for those citizens with access. We take great pains to bridge the social agency and access digital divides. Companies are continuously inventing and marketing smaller pocket-sized devices with which can communicate instantaneously and in a variety of ways. We spend vast amounts of money every day for more connections, faster networks, and ubiquitous wifi. All of this can only be a good thing, right? Not so fast. Upon a closer look, we have to wonder if more content can ever be too much content. Are we mentally, emotionally, critically, politically, and techno-psychologically prepared to deal with the amount of information that comes at us once the flood gates are opened wide, and continue to open ever wider? Who is in control? What are the consequences of information overload and how do we deal with this properly?

Historically, information production and distribution has always equaled a certain amount of power for those in control of these processes: in the one-to-many relationship of mass media producers control what the *inactive* viewers see, hear, and read. It has been shown that through the event of broadcast, news outlets have had the power to shape the relative importance a viewer may apply to certain content (Gerbner, 1969). This process can even influence which issues are thought to be most serious and most important to the viewing public. This historic imbalance between the agencies of media producers and those of media consumers is changing as a result of our available media communication technology, creating a new type of media consumer: the *active* viewer. As a result of this influx, as media consumers in the Internet age, we are in need of a critical regiment to control and understand what we choose to digest as part of our own media diets. Through experience we know that too much of anything is not a good thing. As with the over-consumption of sugar, fat, cholesterol, and salt for our bodies, today, as media consumers, we have the individual responsibility of our media diets and in dealing with the potential for information glut.

Further, there is a media outlet available for every point of view that exists. Sure, we can find a blog entry on just about any topic, including posts that fall on both sides of any story. How do we know where to find the facts that the American media is supposed to provide for us in order that we become and remain informed, knowledgeable citizens? Where is the objectification that the media is supposed to lend us in order that we make informed decisions on our own? There is any number of bloggers out there, but which one is correct? CNN runs their content distribution twenty-four hours a day, but is what they are pouring into our living rooms, our computers, our cell phones really important for us to know? If not all of it, how much of it? Today, in the Internet age, these are the questions that can only be answered by each individual as a living member of planet Earth. Gone are the days of a "good," informed citizen needing only to subscribe and read the local newspaper each morning, and the evening edition at night. In our current information epoch we have many more decisions to make, and the power to make the right ones. With a little thoughtfulness and effort, we can do this to the benefit of ourselves and our communities: The good news is that in the information age we have continual, global information content at our fingertips. The bad news is that in the information age we have continual, global content available at our fingertips.

In our contemporary media-rich world, there is now, more than ever, the need for an applicable theoretical investigation on these questions which involve the ideas of past thinkers like Karl Marx, renowned psychiatrist Dr. Victor Frankl, self-educated sociologist Eric Hoffer, and other writers whose work on the nature of media, power, information and mass movements contribute to an advanced academic foundation in media theory and can help us to understand the effects of the prevailing condition of our world today.

Our cultural condition, as it is, certainly is a difficult one to navigate. Known to be in a Post Modern era, as individuals in a larger community, we can no longer rely on the grand narratives we once could to show us the way. When the nuclear family has broken up, where do young people turn for guidance? When our religions cause wars and endless controversy where do we turn for spiritual guidance? When our community leaders, politicians, and company CEOs spend more time defending themselves from fraudulent and other illegal charges, who can we trust? When a daily avalanche of consumerist messages point us toward consumption as the way to happiness from where do we find the strength to resist?

As Professor Sut Jhally of the University of Massachusetts at Amherst points out that "today's hyper-consumerism is driven by ever more sophisticated advertising and public relations techniques. The specific product is secondary. What they're really selling is lifestyle (and) ideology…" (n.d.). It is essential for us in these investigations to look at the wide potential for acceptance of the messages of mass media texts. It is equally important to inquire into how, as a culture, we have the potential, consciously or otherwise, to allow these mediated messages to actually, in many ways, become at least part of the significance of our daily existence, and to keep in mind that ultimately we the citizen need to remain in control of the information we access, how we react to it, and what we hold dear and true. One might warn the audience member to do their best to think critically on every topic they consider and do their best not to be swayed in any way by beautiful actors, big budgets, slick graphics, or political agendas: a task that is much easier said than done to be sure. The objective of this chapter is to offer these thoughts as theory and as a catalyst to a larger discussion.

THE HISTORIC CONDITION: POWER STRUCTURES, MEDIA, AND THE INACTIVE AUDIENCE

Information is Power

In a subsection called "Ruling Class and Ruling Ideas" of *The German Ideology*, Karl Marx held that "the class which is the ruling material force of society is at the same time its ruling intellectual force" (Marx, 1975). Historically, those members of a society that retain the means (i.e. money, power, ability) to create and distribute intellectual content hold influence and sway over those who do not. Simply put, historically, a class struggle has always existed between two entities: media producers and media consumers. The consumers, most of us, are those readers and viewers who are subject to the intellectual force of the other, the production class. Today, we may witness the truth in this theory when examining cultural hegemony in the context of mass media messages and their production processes. Further we see that "the class which has the means of material production at its disposal has control at the same time over the means of mental production, so that thereby, generally speaking, the ideas of those who lack the means of mental production are subject to it" (Marx, 1975).

Within this historic context we cannot help but wonder if it is possible that the messages – the shows, advertisements, and news – of mass media conglomerates have become so prevalent today that they are influencing their viewers to the point of affecting what is and what is not an important and significant part of viewers' lives? Can the omnipresence and wide-ranging establishment of a message in turn affect its own relevance? Is it true that "the mass media in general, and especially the electronic news media, are part of a 'problem-generating machine' geared to entertainment, voyeurism, and the 'quick fix'" (Altheide,

1996) and not necessarily as a tool for distributing truth and fact, and as means of generating social change? And finally, in the Internet age, does the advent and availability of today's media communication technology obliterate Marx's ability to define a class which lacks the means of material production?

Culture Industry and the Existential Void

Altheide and Grimes authored that the "Iraq War challenges sociological theorizing about social change and policy, and raises fundamental questions about the role of knowledge and critique in social life when public discourse and agendas are partially shaped and communicated through entertainment-oriented mass media" (2005). An industry of culture arises out of this type of environment and in the end, audience and viewer control may be at risk. Theodore Adorno writes that "the power of the culture industry's ideology is such that conformity has replaced consciousness" (Adorno, n.d.). Every day in the United States these distractions come to us via mass media in the form of television shows, entertainment-news channels, multimedia advertising, the Internet, radio, mobile telephones, personal media, and film. This creates what Adorno and co-writer Max Horkheimer refer to as a culture industry in their

Figure 1.

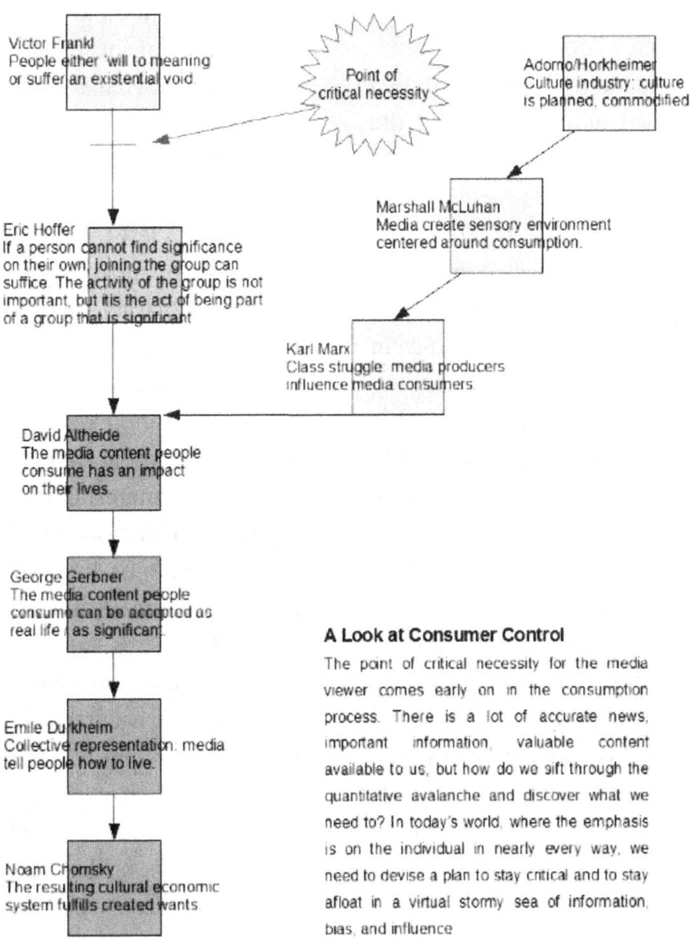

Dialectic of Enlightenment. The culture industry is a sociological condition where reification, or the commodification of everything, has set in and culture is bought and sold as is any other commodity. Uniquely, the process is one which "fuses the old and familiar into a new quality. In all its branches, products which are tailored for consumption by masses, and which to a great extent determine the nature of that consumption, are manufactured more or less according to plan" (Adorno, n.d.). It is through such a process that the content of media enters into our daily lives. Through such an assessment of historic, cultural-sociological studies we see that "media contribute to (…) people's perceptions and interests in everyday life" (Altheide, 1996).

Victor Frankl and his renowned Logotherapy posit that the *existential void* is only filled by the will to meaning, that all persons have an inherent need to feel significance of some kind (Frankl, 1959). At the same time, self taught sociologist Eric Hoffer, who studied and wrote about the nature of mass movements, suggests that in order to satisfy basic human social needs we may need to be a part of a social movement – regardless of the ways in which the movement is constituted (Frankl, 1959). This participation can substitute for a lack of personally developed significance in our lives. This replacement is key to this chapter, and shows that when individuals are not capable of satisfying themselves, that their existential void can be, and often times is, filled by joining the movement in order to give them not only hope, but substance. Spoon fed ideologies across hundreds of television channels, magazine ads, billboards, newspapers, personal media, and all types of Internet web sites can be pretty convincing to the individual, especially the individual who is susceptible to mass movements or one who is not satisfied with their own results in the ongoing philosophical pursuit to fill their own existential vacuum.

George Gerbner's cultivation analysis in the late 1960s turned out a Cultivation Theory based on human reaction to prolonged television consumption. The theory states that, after time, a person will begin to perceive the actual, real, experiential world around them more and more like the world they see on TV (Hoffer, 1951). That is, the ways in which these media outlets portray the world, are accepted to viewers as the way things in the world really are. Gerbner's theory only strengthens the idea that the messages transmitted by our mass media have great influence on their audiences. This phenomenon cannot any longer be denied.

Additionally, it is agreed by research scholars David Croteau and William Hoynes that "the ideological influence of media can be seen in the absences and exclusions just as much as in the content of the messages" (Croteau & Hoynes, 2003). Thus we see the strong and ever present influence of media texts not only in what is presented to us, but what may not be presented as well. All of these ideas combined show great influence of what we see and read in the media can have a great effect on our lives.

Theodore Adorno's warnings of the authenticity of culture – mediated culture – comes into play now, as we view these less active mass audiences as groups of individuals who are pummeled by and hence distracted by the consumerist messages we are bombarded with every hour of our days. Corporations and private sector think tanks are formulating their own agendas, year after year, while the people are numbed with twenty-four hour coverage of material goods, pop stars, television heroes, various social phenomena, conceptual national enemies, unending talk of every frazzled end of a natural disaster, or a kidnap victim in Aruba. It is in this state of distraction, Adorno says, that the inactive, non-critical viewer is duped into consent. When current ideologies are presented through mass media as hegemony there is little discourse about what is right and wrong, about what is significant and what is not.

Karl Marx's idea that the dominant class is the ruling class, which is the class that defines, is also important. Because corporations are the powerfully influential force in global commerce today, the American corporation is not only a part of, but largely makes up Marx's dominant class of the current day. If CNN is of this description, which it is, than the CNN television channels and their Internet news site are their clarions. It is both relevant and important, then, to examine how these news outlets convey meaning of ideas to their audiences.

Collective Representation

If cultural sociologist Emile Durkheim is correct, CNN has the power and very well may be utilizing their potential to inform the general public on how to live, on how to understand, and in what ways they may be successful in their pursuit of happiness. According to Durkheim, this collective representation followed by a mediated identity-forming process informs us of what to wear, what to eat, how to speak, how to spend our time, how to spend our money, and even what to believe is important. From birth we are enmeshed within a "whole system of representations by means of which men understand each other" (University of Chicago, n.d.). And if, time after time, we are told by CNN, MSNBC, Fox, HBO, Hollywood, NBC, and People.com what it is we need to know, and -- according to these producers of media content -- how we are to feel about what we are being told, does this not influence our daily lives? Kinder and Iyengar show that media "news shapes the relative importance Americans attach to various national problems" and that media outlets for news "powerfully influence which problems viewers regard as the nation's most serious" (1987). The question then must be asked: Can the same affective empowerment be attributed to the advertisements these media outlets run?

The same premises that Adorno outlines in "On Popular Music" (1941) are not only applicable to popular music but to all mass media today, including American corporate owned Internet web sites as sources for news and the high paying advertisements they project. As structure for this argument, we look here at how Adorno outlined the negative effects of pop music in three main points. One, the music, once it reaches an audience, has been highly standardized, and gives off an ideal of pseudo-individualism where the art of the process, the creativity that makes art unique, i.e. the individuality, has been removed. Second, the popularity element promotes what Adorno calls *passive consumption* and *consent* to adhere without critical thought on the part of the consumer or listener. Third, the negative psychological consequences: *rhythmic obedience* and *emotionality*. Rhythmic obedience, as Adorno explains it is the distraction of the rhythm of the music, not paying attention to the words, not caring what the actual message of the media text even is, or if it contains a message at all. Emotionality is the distractive qualities of the text, an obsession with the impassioned drama, tugging on the heart strings, and a replacement of the state of affectivity in place of critical examination. This process creates "a society of children who are only concerned with their own immediate, emotional, and physical gratification" (Ahlkvist, 2006).

What is important to keep in mind is that the media industry and the marketing firms of American corporations work together as a highly profitable business relationship, and the top players in these corporations are the ones making the rules, doing the distracting, and pulling the proverbial wool over consumer America's eyes. Is it possible then that the result is a nation largely constituted by Adorno's ill-advised sheep?

Because it claims to be a hard news and trustworthy journalism-based organization, without being critical of its content, viewers can and will accept what is playing on the major media outlets as an important event; and act, speak, and live accordingly. The National Leadership Index completed each year at Harvard University shows dramatically steep decline for 2007 and 2008 in the trust viewers have toward the journalism of American media (John F. Kennedy School of

Government, 2007; John F. Kennedy School of Government, 2008). Often times we don't even trust the news we're getting, however, it still has an impact on our lives. What we are talking about here is the content being broadcast and how, by default, it becomes fodder for our daily thoughts. Radio research has shown that in the United States 72% of mass media audience members will take the content they are given as valid information as to what is going on in the world; 11% will seek out independent sources, look for a more fair media environment, construct their own content, or self program; and 17% will self program eventually (Davis, 2006). Based on this study then the numbers are largely in favor of mass media audience members accepting whatever content their favorite stations, channels, or sites are supplying. Finally, with the lines in place, private sector think tanks and other corporation-based profiteers on all levels are capable of carrying out their agendas: to make profit via mass consumption.

Created Wants

Professor Noam Chomsky of MIT points out that ideally, for the corporation, the population has to be "turned into completely mindless consumers of goods that they do not want" let alone need. In developing what are called *created wants* the corporation's goal is to impose on people a "philosophy of futility," to "focus them on the insignificant things of life, like fashionable consumption" (Achbar, Abbot, & Bakan, 2003) in order that they desire these things for life's improvement and, in turn, purchase these products for this reason.

McLuhan posited that media aid in creating a "sensory environment that produced Western capitalist societies – an environment that was bureaucratic and organized around mass production" (Croteau & Hoynes, 2003). This process suggests a great influence of social structure and some but very little human agency. It is not to say that this theory falls into the realm of technological determinism, that "people exist only as rational employers of technology or pieces of the proverbial chessboard who will be moved by the requirements of the technologies" (Croteau & Hoynes, 2003), but a moral life, outside of the grasp of these influential media messages is difficult to attain. Chomsky makes it clear that "people can be very moral, but they are acting within institutional structures, constructed systems which only certain options are easy to pursue, others are very hard to pursue" (Achbar, Abbot & Bakan, 2005).

Today, we see accessibility, influential power, and God-like omnipresence of mass media, which, to the unsuspecting mind can provide Hoffer's necessary ingredients required to "satisfy the desire for self-advancement" in those who "find a worth-while purpose in self-advancement." Additionally, those "who see their lives as irremediably spoiled cannot find a worth-while purpose in self advancement. The prospect of an individual career cannot stir them to a mighty effort, nor can it evoke in them faith and a single-minded dedication." To these individuals, the counterfeit meaning of mass media offers its ability to quench the underlying "passion for self-renunciation," or the potential to be "reborn to a new life" (Hoffer, 1951). We can see from Professor Altheide's "fear" paper that "from the standpoint of media content as cause, researchers ask whether news reports can "cause," or "lead" people ... including the extent to which relevant values and perspectives may be "cultivated" (Altheide, 1996). From this perspective, the mass media play a large role in shaping public agendas by influencing what people think about (Altheide, 1996), and "encourage, perhaps even dictate, particular ways of talking and thinking" (Croteau & Hoynes, 2003).

Indeed it seems that it is the media and the ensuing onslaught of messages which are somehow falsely filling Victor Frankl's existential vacuum – an existential-psychological phenomenon which he describes as the void which occurs in the absence of an individual's will to meaning. A new web site, recent "reality" television, another record-breaking attempt at the next fascinating PlayStation2™ game are easily accessible, but highly temporal filler for the void, and therein lies the samsaric distress, and the instamatic placebo elixir for Frankl's existential vacuum. From the advertisers perspective, ideally we as media consumers will constitute a society made up of "individuals who are totally disassociated from one another. Who's conception of themselves, the sense of value, is just how many *created wants* can I satisfy?" To counteract this process, we must be mindful of what we read, critical of what we watch.

Images and Reality

Historian Daniel Boorstin studied the effects and relationships of media images to the viewing audience who regularly interacted with these media. He found that the "pervasiveness of visual images was changing the very meaning of "reality." That news and entertainment images are becoming "so embedded in our consciousnesses" (Croteau & Hoynes, 2003) that it is repeatedly difficult to discern between image – what we are given by media producers as reality – and the reality we know to be actual: Reality.

Emile Durkheim's collective representation idea may perpetuate this now-embedded system, allowing for a cultural practice that unites its practitioners. We want to feel – some scholars say we have to feel – that we belong to a community, like we are a part of something. This collective memory (*How are we to be good Americans in our global society?)* of how we are supposed to act, feel, speak, and carry on furthers the idea, and the difficulties, of what Durkheim calls fragmented identities. We are living in a postmodern, post journalistic society where mass media formats and information technology make it difficult not only to distinguish between journalist and event (Altheide, 1996), but even more so to retain our own identities.

News of the Day

In accessing news of the day we have to deal with "spin," the added layer of subjectivity to fact. In accessing news, spin is the killer and everyone denies having a hand in it. Then there is "hype." How do we navigate through the hottest story of the day? The more you look into Post-modern information theory, the more you see that at this late stage of the game, there are no centers from which to stand and make an objectively informed judgment.

Today's news organizations are posters for exploiting the spectacle. During the O.J. Simpson "white Bronco" event of 1994, as an example, 95 million viewers tuned in (Kim, 1994). When the trial was over 142 million people listened on radio and watched television as the verdict was delivered, an astounding 91% of viewers (Jones, n.d). Some say this was the event that took television news shows and magazines from the role of news informer to news maker and created a new genre of television content: Infotainment. Although this may make the news more fun to consume, in considering our dilemma, this type of news coverage overloads the viewer with content.

What some of these shows are good for is having an obsessive operation of posting and broadcasting a high amount of coverage on what is happening around the world, and using new and innovative methods of dissemination and delivery. This high quantity of data is not all bad, all of it is information, it's just that there is an outlet for everyone nowadays, no matter what your point of view is. There is a lack of, or absence of what philosophers like Fredrick Jameson call the "meta narrative," meaning there is no big picture by which to structure our observations and assessments.

In the past we've had our world religions for moral and spiritual guidance. Today we have enough information to inform us of all the wars and endless controversy religions have caused. Where do we turn for this moral and spiritual guidance? In the past we've had our community leaders, politicians, and maybe even business executives to offer political and economic advisement. Today are bombarded daily with stories breaking of these so-called leaders' who seem to spend more time defending themselves from fraudulent and other illegal charges than they do being leaders. In this type of environment, who can we trust? These are some of the meta narratives which we once had as a resource on how to get by and how to live happily. Now we see the emphasis on the self and the only meta narrative that we are offered on a mass scale is consumerism. When a daily avalanche of consumerist messages point us toward consumption as the way to happiness, it becomes increasingly difficult to sort through the content and find real significance, after all, it seems we are unable even to agree on what really matters.

So what happens? We find ourselves floating around taking in all of this information. And what Fox says might be somewhat factual, and what CNN posts is somewhat factual, but another issue is the angle they choose, the words they use, their terminology. For example: Considering the conditions in the Middle East, a major news network was found to use the word "terrorist" when talking about the deaths caused by Palestinian militants. When talking about the deaths caused by Israel militants the same network used words (i.e. euphemisms) such as "fighters," "soldiers," "army," etc. When a news broadcast acts in this way, it is skewing the data. The question we have to ask is why are they doing this? Is it for their own interests? Are they being influenced by national hegemony?

To get a more complete set of facts one must go outside mainstream media. Today, often times, this can be as easy as turning on the television as long as you know which channel to dial in. *Democracy Now!*, the television and radio current events and news shows produced by the Corporation for Public Broadcast can be far more informative and, simultaneously, far less biased in their content and delivery. For example, I often cite Professor Chomsky who has appeared many times on the *Democracy Now!* network. Chomsky explains the law of concision on mainstream media news. To be concise is very important to commercial media. Because of the advertising time that pays the show's bills, the content a show airs must fit well between commercial time slots. In most mainstream media outlets in the United States, this can mean anywhere from two to ten minutes. Within that two to ten minutes a story, weather forecast, sports update, or guest speaker must be able to introduce their topic, make their point, and conclude clearly before it is time for another commercial break. That is why, Chomsky points out, you see over and over again these news stories and reporters "towing the party line." I don't believe that it is ABC who sets out to fool anyone, or to neglect an important point of view on a controversial topic, but it is what McLuhan refers to as our mediated sensory environment and Western capitalist rules of the free market that help to create this bureaucratic system which results in this way. Viewers miss out on the full story on commercial media. This is an important difference between commercial media and public media. Because public media are not reliant on commercial breaks, they are not restricted from reporting more of a longer-winded, discussion format account of news events.

If a news outlet has the time to tell the full story viewers have a much better chance of getting the full story. It is from Noam Chomsky which we learned that George H.W. Bush, for example, sold Saddam Hussein the chemicals he used on the Kurds, one the deeds, according to the George W. Bush administration, which Saddam was vilified for and which served as catalyst to invading Iraq. Etc. This important information was not talked about on and of the major media outlets in the United States. But this is key information. They will start their reporting after the fact, stating the administration wants to declare war on Iraq and Saddam in order to save the Kurdish people from this villain, which could be true, but which is only part of the whole story. But, with only part of the story, the "good" part, people think "Yes, this is good. War is necessary. Saddam is a killer." And maybe he is. He was. But the problem with American corporate media as we witnessed over the second half of the 20th century is that they won't tell you how Saddam became a killer: he was a killer in part because the United States leadership sold him the weapons to do so, to carry out his plan. The entire story lacks concision and cannot be told between commercial breaks.

We see this over and over and over and over with US corporate media news and issues they cover. It's a business plan. They say they give you what you need to be informed, but they give you what you need to be informed unless it could be bad for their profit margin. How many United States citizens are aware of the fact that the United States Department of Defense has over 200 military bases in foreign countries? That is incredible, considering there are roughly the same number of countries in the world. Left leaning entertainment talk shows are starting to use the term "empire" in referring to what has historically been referred to in other Presidential administrations as our campaign of responsibility which works hard to spread Democracy around the world.

That is what we are dealing with: multiple points of view and a media outlet for anyone who cares to listen. That is the difficulty in getting the "whole story." With the outlets we are bombarded with every minute, you will not ever get the whole story. The whole story lacks concision, and if the story does not fit nicely in between commercial breaks, you won't see it aired. That is one reason you see all the talking heads up there towing the party line: their arguments have concision.

THE CURRENT RESPONSE: POWER STRUCTURES, MEDIA, AND THE ACTIVE AUDIENCE

Thanks in large part to Web 2.0 we are living currently in a world which is growing in its numbers of active audience members. However, we still can imagine, within an ever-increasing population, a large group of less active individuals who are not taking advantage of these more personalized and useful media platforms to create and transmit and share information, but sit back and take what is handed them.

The traditional mass media format of conventional newspapers online offers an example of the more passive one-to-many relationship of transmitting information much the same way television and radio have functioned for decades. The blog, on the other hand, and many other applications of the Internet, are examples of the many-to-many relationship of information transference widely available on the new media platform. It is a central thesis to this chapter that a more open exchange of information occurs as a result of the Internet, new methods of journalism, and personal media development, particularly the attributes of Web 2.0. The Internet is the first widely used communication technology to provide two-way interaction on a truly mass scale. The one-to-many relationship of radio, television, film, and newspapers that has been enjoyed for so many decades by business and its advertisers is coming to an end. This is not to say that these media will go away, in fact, I don't think they ever will, but there is now a strong alternative which has been and will continue to influence these other media, their producers, and audiences in significant and fundamental ways.

This multi-directional flow of communication is the blueprint for the success of a coming democratization of information. This movement includes the combined uses of emerging personal media communication technologies by individuals, grassroots organizations and independents. These processes are applied across the World Wide Web and the Internet largely on web sites and personal mobile media devices instituting all-media blogs, podcasts, and geographic information systems to allow for what Dan Gilmore calls "Citizen Media" or "Citizen Journalism." We see this emergent from the youth of the global culture.

Currently, through educational institutions across (but not limited to) the United States and Europe, and emerging media studies departments, we are experiencing a growth in education to promote a new generation to retain the skills required to contribute to the new media landscape of blogs, photo blogs, podcasts, vlogs and other emerging forms of personal multimedia production, interaction, and delivery. Specifically, the integration of wireless, mobile hardware such as cell phone capture and publishing, Palm, Blackberry devices, video cams, still cams, laptops, Wiki's, and XML formatting RSS 2.0 broadcast are changing the vary formats in which individuals can and do receive their information about the world around them. These numerous digital devices and services are now changing the ways in which individuals express themselves and participate in their communities. Through these changes, we see the impact of personal media on the fields of journalism, publication, mass media broadcasting, and alternative media. We are witnessing first hand a new mode of citizenship and participatory politics.

As Marx wrote in 1845, "the class which has the means of material production at its disposal has control at the same time over the means of mental production, so that … the ideas of those who lack the means of mental production are subject to it … therefore, as they rule as a class … (they) rule also as thinkers, as producers of ideas, and regulate the production and distribution of the ideas of their age: thus their ideas are the ruling ideas of the epoch." Perhaps we are seeing the transformation of "the class which has the means of material production," of who really has the power "as producers of ideas … and distribution of the ideas" of our age. What we still refer to as "new" media, it is the current and emerging media communication technologies which enables this transference of the power of the voice.

THE CONCLUSION AND SOLUTION: CRITICAL NECESSITY

In Buddhist philosophy, the word *samsara* is defined as "the total pattern of successive earthly lives experienced by a soul" (Saiva Siddhanta Church, 2006) and is supplemented often with the idea of the individual's experience of daily life harboring this "cycle of ignorance and suffering" (Smith, 1999) without the relief of enlightenment, a significant reason for being, and a break from the purposeless circuit. It is the goal of a Buddhist to achieve enlightenment and to escape from samsara. "The Vipassana meditator uses his concentration as a tool by which his awareness can chip away at the wall of illusion and cuts him off from the living light of reality. It is a gradual process of ever-increasing awareness into the inner workings of reality itself…It's called Liberation…the goal of all Buddhist systems and practice" (Jones, n.d.). It is my thought that this idea of samsara, well studied by Buddhists and scholars around the world, and documented for millennia in Eastern texts, which characterizes the progression of an overwhelmingly large percentage of Americans today. Today, as media consumers with endless resources at our fingertips, it is the content with the highest distribution budget, the loudest audio, and the most famous celebrities that garner our attention. It is constant and it is nearly absolute in the ways it consumes our attention. This is the cycle that needs to be broken. We are thinking individuals who have the means to do just this.

There is a lot of accurate news, important information, valuable content available to us, but how do we sift through the quantitative avalanche and discover what we need to? How can we function most efficiently in our data rich environment without allowing for all the content of the Internet; television characters and shows; mp3 players and podcasts; magazine, web, and television ads; and mobile message soliciting into our lives to act as "substitutes either for the whole self or for the elements which make life bearable and which the individual cannot evoke out of their individual resources" (Hoffer, 1951).

I am convinced that there is just too much information in the world: far too much ease of production and distribution, too much easy access to some of it, and too much with mediocre, time-consuming access to it, to make much of a good judgment call on any of it. We know that even "the most trusted name in news" needs to be examined closely before we take what it says to heart. In today's world, where the emphasis is on the individual in nearly every way we need to devise a plan to stay critical and to stay afloat in a virtual stormy sea of information, bias, and influence.

I suggest taking the time to seek out those scholars, institutions, and organizations that you feel are being straight. Always ask yourself "who might benefit?" from a story or news cast and what the relationship might be to those paying the bill.

The Internet is loaded with easy access methods to good, informative information. Many site now employ a "what's new" type of data feed. RSS makes it easy load in widely used Web browsers like Firefox. Also, people have to listen to NPR more, *Democracy Now!* more, Robert McChesney at the University of Illinois is doing tireless work on issues such as media and democracy, something we all need to know more about. His web site offers book links, articles, and the updated podcast to his weekly radio talk show "Media Matters" in which he holds discussions with leading cultural, intellectual, political, and business figures from around the globe. Find these resources, be critical of why you choose them, and be creative in how you access them. For example, I usually listen to McChesney's audio podcast while running.

Additionally, my suggestion to everyone is to never think of TV (especially the news shows) as anything but pure entertainment. Read a big newspaper a few times a week, regularly, and use the Internet to look into issues using university domains, Amnesty International, the UN, on and on. That is what I meant about some outlets being "Mediocre" in accessibility and time-consuming as well. It is very time consuming to get the whole story and most people cannot do it, or don't know how to do it. I know how, now you know how, and I spend a lot of time researching this for Ph.D., but I still don't have a lot of time for it. That is a big, big factor on why the current model continues to pervade. And, I think it is only going to get worse. Obama cannot do anything about this.

Does a mass media machine like CNN and its constant bombardment of these types of messages have an effect on the culture which is subject to it twenty-four hours a day? Many scholars would say it does, in the form of mass movements, and that to satisfy basic human social needs joining the movement – no matter what the movement is – can substitute for other personally developed significance in our lives. Instead of seeking out religion, community, or moral sustainability, today's individual far more easily acquires the corporations created wants. This replacement of what is of value is a key to the premise of this theory. Hoffer states, and I question in the context of mass media, when individuals are not capable of satisfying themselves, that their "existential void" – their drive to find reason for being – can be, and often times is, filled by joining the movement in order to give them not only hope, but substance. Spoon fed ideologies across hundreds of television channels, magazine ads, billboards, newspapers, personal media, and all types of Internet web sites can be pretty convincing to the individual, especially the individual who is susceptible to mass movements or one who is not satisfied with their own results in the ongoing philosophical pursuit to fill their own existential vacuum.

We can hope that this somewhat blind consumption is not the case, and that people of the world purchase and consume only the things they need to live a simple and content life. However, simple observation will show that, with a limited number of exceptions to the rule, this is not how American society operates. With the advent of the Internet, it may be the best of times and the worst of times for the accessibility and importance placed on information. Perhaps a new socialization is evolving as a result of this emphasis and the mass media devices available to us. In an environment that contains such omnipresent media – and their messages – turning up the personal information filter is not an option, but a requirement, where the individual needs to be highly critical to keep afoot of a search for truth in a vastly hypertext – and image-based – world.

REFERENCES

Achbar, M., Abbot, J., & Bakan, J. (Directors). (2005). *The Corporation* [Motion Picture]. USA: Zeitgeist Films.

Adorno, T. (1941). *On Popular Music.*

Adorno, T. (n.d.). *Culture Industry Reconsidered.* Retrieved February 26, 2009, from http://libcom.org/library/culture-industry-reconsidered-theodor-adorno

Ahlkvist, J. (2006). *Sociology of Mass Media.* USA: Unpublished Lecture, University of Denver.

Altheide, D. (1996). The news media, the problem frame, and the production of fear. *The Sociological Quarterly*, *38*(4), 647–668. doi:10.1111/j.1533-8525.1997.tb00758.x

Altheide, D. L., & Grimes, J. N. (2005, September). War programming: The propaganda project and the Iraq War. *The Sociological Quarterly*, *46*(4), 617–643. doi:10.1111/j.1533-8525.2005.00029.x

Croteau, D., & Hoynes, W. (2003). Media Society (3rd ed.). Thousand Oaks, CA: Pine Forge Press. Davis, M. (2006). Current Radio Topics. Unpublished Lecture, University of Denver, USA.

Frankl, V. (1959). *Man's Search for Meaning.* New York: Simon & Schuster.

Gerbner, G. (1969). *Towards 'Cultural Indicators': The Analysis of Mass Mediated Public Message Systems.*

Hoffer, E. (1951). *The True Believer*. New York: Harper & Row Publishers, Inc.

Iyengar, S., & Kinder, D. M. (1987). *News that Matters*. Chicago, IL: University of Chicago Press.

Jhally, S. (n.d.). *Advertising and the End of the World.* Lecture. Retrieved February 26, 2009, from http://www.sutjhally.com/audiovideo

John, F. Kennedy School of Government, Harvard University. (2007). *A National Study in Confidence in Leadership, National Leadership Index 2007.* Retrieved from http://www.hks.harvard.edu/leadership/images/CPLpdf/cpl_index%20 2007%20(3).pdf.

John, F. Kennedy School of Government, Harvard University. (2008). *A National Study in Confidence in Leadership, National Leadership Index 2008 Draft.* Retrieved from http://content.ksg.harvard.edu/leadership/images/CPLpdf/nli%20report.pdf

Jones, T. L. (n.d.). The O.J. Simpson Murder Trial: Prologue. *True TV*. Retrieved on February 25, 2009, from http://www.trutv.com/library/crime/notorious_murders/famous/simpson/index_1.html

Kim, A. (1994). Pulp Nonfiction. *Entertainment Weekly*. Retrieved on February 25, 2009, from http://www.ew.com/ew/article/0,302832,00.html

Marx, K. (1975). The German Ideology. London: Lawrence & Wishart. (Original manuscript published in 1845).

Saiva Siddhanta Church. (2006). *Saiva Siddhanta Church.* Retrieved June 1, 2006, from http://www.himalayanacademy.com/

Smith, E. J. (1999). *Radiant Mind* (1st ed.). New York: Riverhead Books.

University of Chicago. (n.d.). *The Society for Social Research.* Retrieved February 26, 2009, from http://ssr1.uchicago.edu/PRELIMS/Theory/durkheim.html

Chapter 10
Consumer Reviews on Retail Websites:
A Marketing and Social Phenomenon

Sung-Yeon Park
University of Wisconsin-Madison, USA & Bowling Green State University, USA

Gi Woong Yun
University of Wisconsin-Madison, USA & Bowling Green State University, USA

ABSTRACT

Consumer reviews on retail websites are now established as a common type of user-generated marketing communication online. To provide a comprehensive and well-defined framework for researchers and marketers who are interested in its implementation and evaluation, a synthetic review of existing studies on the consumer reviews are conducted here. More specifically, the prevalence and popularity of consumer reviews of retail websites, the motivations behind the review activities, and the effects are examined in detail. Three important message characteristics of the reviews - volume, valence, and value - are also identified and discussed. After this assessment of the current status is completed, the focus is shifted to a more existential question about the consumer reviews: Whether the reviews posted by consumers are essentially "commons," an entity created by members of a wide open community and amendable to exploitation by consumers and marketers alike, or "intellectual properties" of the online retailers who collect and manage them. Subsequently, a view that regards the consumer reviews as social capital is presented, followed by a discussion concerning moderation and reputation systems as quality control mechanisms.

INTRODUCTION

Consumer reviews on retail websites are now established as a common type of user-generated marketing communication online. Most major online retailers have adopted the review features on their websites and consumers often name the reviews as the most desired element on retail websites. Some consumers even consult the online reviews before going out to buy products in brick-and mortar stores.

In spite of their high values for consumers and marketers alike, however, consumer reviews on retail websites have not been studied well.

DOI: 10.4018/978-1-60566-792-8.ch010

Although the unique form of user-generated content has received some attention from both industry analysts and academic researchers, the investigations have not provided a comprehensive and yet well-defined framework for researchers and marketers who are interested in its implementation and evaluation. Market reports have often been too narrowly focused on the impact of consumer reviews on purchase decisions, whereas most academic studies have shown interest in consumer reviews on retail websites only as part of online word of mouth (WOM), which includes communications taking place in other online consumer platforms such as discussion forums, chat rooms, electronic mailing lists, Weblogs, instant messages, and personal emails. Consumer reviews on retail websites are also differentiated from consumer reviews on such sites as *epinion.com* and *Angie's list*. These review sites base their existence on independent and unbiased information about products and services and thus no known connection to commercial interests such as online retailers is crucial for their credibility. On the other hand, consumer reviews on retail websites serve a similar function in spite of their obvious relationship to the retailers who will be directly affected by the reviews.

Indeed, it is important to understand the influence of retail website consumer reviews on purchase decisions. Consumer reviews on retail websites are also similar to other consumer-generated online information in terms of the functional characteristics and features. At the same time, consumer reviews on retail websites merit a more focused and systematic inquiry into the communication phenomenon itself. Out in the field, consumer review features have rapidly evolved due to the developments in technology to accommodate well structured databases, user-friendly interfaces, and various recommendation or reputation systems. The availability and affordability of the review function implementation services, in turn, enabled online retailers to adopt the features easily. Furthermore, the expansion of global information networks has facilitated cross-national connectivity, and the social network aspect of the Internet has imbued social and cultural significance to this new form of consumer-to-consumer communication.

Therefore, it is very timely to assess the current status of research on consumer reviews on retail websites and raise some important issues that have been overlooked by practitioners as well as researchers. To achieve this overarching goal, the first part of this chapter will be devoted to a synthetic review of existing studies on the consumer reviews. More specifically, the prevalence and popularity of consumer reviews on retail websites, the motivations for consumer reviewers, and the marketing effects of the reviews will be examined in detail. Three important message characteristics of the reviews – volume, valence, and value – that affect consumer attitudes and behaviors will be also identified and discussed, followed by a cautionary note on ethical issues related to consumer reviews.

After completing these tasks, in the second part, we will turn the readers' attention to a more fundamental question of whether the consumer reviews are commons shared by all the participants or the properties of the online retailers. Subsequently, we will present a view that regards the consumer reviews as social capital and also discuss moderation and reputation systems as quality control mechanisms. Although this second part may not seem as tactically important to marketers as the first part of this chapter, understanding this debate will strengthen their strategic position in implementing and managing consumer reviews on their websites. It is hoped that the commons vs. property debate will also attract some interest from researchers who study various user-generated content on the Web.

Prevalence and Popularity of Consumer Reviews on Retail Websites

From the early days of the online retail industry, a few marketers encouraged customers to rate and/or comment on products sold on their websites. For instance, *Amazon.com* integrated consumer reviews as an essential tool of its marketing communication with the launch of the website. Across all their product offerings, the online retailer displayed consumer reviews in addition to their expert reviews and expanded the review options over time. On the other hand, the practice was not fully embraced by the vast majority of US online retailers until recently. By 2004, only 16% of 100 leading US online retailers were found to have adopted some form of consumer review feature (Yun, Park, & Ha, 2008). The reluctance on the part of online retailers was understandable, considering the many potential management problems and ensuing costs.

Today, however, it appears that consumer reviews on retail websites have become more widely available. According to an industry statistic, one third of the top 300 retail websites have consumer review features. An industry analyst also predicted that every major e-commerce site will have some form of review system within a year (Sullivan, Feb. 15, 2008). A quick visit to popular retail websites such as *Walmart.com* and *Sears.com* also validates this prediction. These heavy-weight mass merchandisers, who used not to have any consumer review feature in 2004, have now fully adopted the practice. Furthermore, some marketers like *Petco* reportedly utilized consumer reviews to enhance their official marketing messages by incorporating them into outbound emails to their loyal customers (Magill, March 1, 2006).

Typically, a consumer review feature is clearly marked by a heading "Customer/Guest Reviews" and comprised of an open-ended commenting function and a rating function. The former usually presents a text box to customers to write a review about the featured product while the latter asks customers to rate the item on a 4 or 5-point scale. While virtually all consumer reviews on retail websites are located on the bottom of a product page, many retail websites also display the average score of customer ratings and a hyperlink to the open-ended customer reviews on the top of the page.

Some review features also include multi-attribute ratings. For example, *Zappos.com*, an online fashion clothing/accessories retailer, asks customers to rate their products on the specific dimensions of "Comfort" and "Look," in addition to the overall rating commonly found on retail websites. In the consumer electronics category, *Dell.com* uses the three criteria of quality, features, and values. Still, *Amazon.com* is considered a leader in the innovation of consumer review features. In addition to the standard text reviews, the website encourages multi-modality reviews such as video and audio. Recently, the online marketer also created a discussion forum on each product page to facilitate more free discussion about the featured product amongst its customers. Although not as sophisticated as *Amazon.com*, consumer review features on *Walmart.com* are also notable because of the quick shift from having no review feature in 2004 to being equipped with a set of detailed questions by the summer of 2007. Besides the standard rating and open-ended comments, consumer reviewers on *Walmart.com* can rate the product on the attributes of "Value for price paid" and "Meets expectations." They can also provide a summative evaluation by choosing between "recommend" and "don't recommend." Furthermore, the review features solicit from the reviewers information about the age and gender of the buyers, the duration of owning the product reviewed, and the frequency of product usage, which enables a more thorough evaluation of the consumer review as well as the product.

While this rapid and widespread adoption of consumer review features by online retailers may be one indicator of their popularity, industry reports directly support the view that consumer reviews are widely accepted and utilized by online shoppers. Consumers actively look for review features when they navigate websites to purchase products online. In one report, 75% of online shoppers said that it is extremely or very important to read customer reviews before making a purchase (Creamer, July 23, 2007). Consistent with this report, approximately two thirds of consumers actually read consumer-generated product reviews online, and more than 80% of readers said that the reviews directly impacted their purchase decisions. (Sullivan, February 15, 2008).

Amongst various sources of product and service information, peer reviews were preferred over expert reviews by a margin of 6-to-1 (Creamer, July 23, 2007) and trusted more than television and radio advertising (Sullivan, February 15, 2008). These mostly positive views on consumer reviews were reiterated in academic studies as well. Peer consumers were evaluated to be more trustworthy than either human experts who review various products for retail websites or expert systems that make recommendations based on consumer profile data (Senecal & Nantel, 2004).

Motivations for Consumer Reviewers

While the findings above clearly illustrate that consumer reviews are highly valued and respected by online shoppers, they do not explain the motivation to participate in the review process which takes some time and effort to create the review content. In most cases, a reviewer also has to surrender personal information to register and log-in before submitting a review. On some retail websites, it is not very difficult to find consumer-provided product images and extensive video clips offering tips on how to use the products. Considering the fact that these activities are completely voluntary and rarely rewarded financially, these high-effort consumer review activities can be quite puzzling without understanding the motivations behind them.

One way to find out why people post product reviews on retail websites is to survey individuals. Although there is no published study that posed the exact question, Hennig-Thurau and his colleagues investigated consumer motivations for sharing opinions on goods and services on consumer online platforms such as *epinions.com*. In the study (Hennig-Thurau, Gwinner, Walsh, & Gremler, 2004), the researchers identified eight motivations for consumer reviewers: venting negative feelings, concern for other consumers, social benefits ("chat among like-minded people is a nice thing," "fun to communicate this way with other people in the community," "meet nice people this way"), economic incentives, helping the company, advice seeking, platform assistance ("believe the platform operator knows the person in charge within the company and will convey my message," "the platform operator will stand up for me when speaking to the company," "has more power together with others than writing a single letter of complaint"), and extraversion/positive self-enhancement ("my contributions show others that I am a clever customer," "express my joy about a good buy," "feel good when telling others about my buying success"). In subsequent analyses, the researchers also revealed that social benefits, concern for other consumers, extraversion/positive self-enhancement, and economic incentives were related to the online platform visit and comment writing frequencies.

Since retail websites are different from the consumer community websites, this finding may not be directly relevant to the motivations of consumer reviewers on retail websites. In particular, the social benefits and economic incentives motivations are deemed irrelevant to consumer reviewers on many retail websites because the consumers are unlikely to consider the retail sites as a community and also online retailers in the US do not provide financial incentives for consumer reviews (Yun, Park, & Ha, 2008). The rest of the aforementioned motivations, however, appear to be as relevant to retail websites as they are to the online consumer-opinion platforms. Also, it should be noted that *Amazon.com* has made efforts to make the social benefits motivation relevant to its users by creating a consumer review discussion forum on many of its product pages.

If they want, online retailers could also motivate consumers to write reviews by providing economic incentives. However, doing so will have serious ramifications for the whole review system. First, the presence of a financial incentive may cast a serious doubt on the validity of the reviews. Second, being offered a financial reward, consumers may feel obligated to return the favor by posting positive reviews or understate their dissatisfaction with the product. Third, some consumers may regard the financial reward as an insult to their benevolent intention and feel discouraged rather than encouraged to submit a review.

Indeed, there is an economic psychological theory called "motivation crowding theory" that exactly predicts this scenario (Frey & Jegen, 2001). The theory is based on the assumption that there are two types of motivations for human behaviors: extrinsic vs. intrinsic. Intrinsic motivations stem from an innate desire for pleasure or personal satisfaction whereas extrinsic motivations are imposed on individuals from the outside in the form of either offers of reward or punishment for noncompliance. When either the reward or punishment is present, the extrinsic motivation "crowds out" or replaces the intrinsic motivations because it impairs self-determination or self-esteem. Because this theory has not yet been tested in the context of consumer reviews on retail websites, its applicability remains to be seen. But, this is a research topic that will be theoretically meaningful and practically helpful. In the meantime, marketers will be prudent to be mindful about this possibility and adopt strategies that address their weaknesses without jeopardizing current strengths.

Marketing Benefits of Consumer Reviews on Retail Websites

Increased Sales

Available evidence suggests a strong influence of online consumer opinions on purchase decisions. An experiment demonstrated that, in comparison with recommendations made by other sources such as human experts and expert systems, recommendations by peer consumers were more effective in swaying the final product choice (Smith, Menon, & Sivakumar, 2005). Consumer reviews and ratings were often quoted as the functionality consumers want most on retail websites. A majority of online consumers (63%) responded that they were more likely to buy from sites with ratings and reviews (Burke, May 1, 2008). A survey revealed that, especially for first-time buyers, consumer reviews on retail websites were effective in turning them from browsers to actual buyers (Freed, March 1, 2007). An analysis of book sales data from *Amazon.com* also reported a consistent finding: The number of consumer reviews was a positive predictor of sales rank (Li & Hitt, in press).

Customer Satisfaction and Loyalty

Aside from the increased sales, cultivation of customer satisfaction and loyalty can be a distinct purpose of consumer review features. In a survey (Freed, March 1, 2007), consumer product reviews were found to increase customer satisfaction and loyalty. Retail websites with consumer review features scored consistently higher than the ones without the features in terms of customer satisfaction with the website and the retailer. The likelihood of return was also higher for consumers who visited an online retailer featuring consumer reviews. In terms of post-purchase satisfaction and site loyalty among people who made a purchase on retail websites, consumer reviews increased post-purchase satisfaction and site loyalty as much as by 21% and 18%, respectively. A model based on a large set of online customer data also confirmed that community features including consumer reviews had a significant impact on customer loyalty to online retailers (Srinivasan, Anderson, & Ponnavolu, 2002).

Increased Traffic and Time Spent on the Website

Since consumer reviews have become a standard feature on many retail websites, some people surf a number of retail websites solely for the purpose of reading consumer reviews in them. Once consumers come into a retail website, they are also likely to spend more time there if the website has the consumer review features because it takes a significant amount of time to read and weigh consumer reviews for the product of interest. In addition, some reviews can lead consumers to other product pages that also have a set of reviews.

Besides its potential to generate sales, website traffic has also emerged as a yardstick of marketing success on its own due to its ability to generate revenues. Many retail websites are now linked to other online retailers. When a consumer on a retail website clicks on a link to another retail website and makes a purchase on that linked website, the original retail website receives a commission. A heavy traffic on a retail website can also turn into financial revenue when the website has the *Google Adsense* style advertising network sections because the website is paid every time a consumer clicks through the *Adsense* links.

4. Boost in Search-Engine Rankings

One big difference between online and offline retailing is that online shoppers can afford to be more flexible about where to shop than offline shoppers. In traditional retail shopping, the choice of store often precedes the choice of products. In other words, a decision on the type of store and its location is an important part of planning and consumers sometimes adjust their shopping list based on product availability within the store that they are already in. Online shoppers, on the other hand, can start from a product and then choose among many retail websites that carry the exact product. In this scenario, it is extremely important that a retail website has a high ranking on popular search engine results.

Because consumer reviews add a lot of data to retail websites that can be indexed by major search engines, it can improve the standing of an online retailer on the list of websites generated from a keyword search and thus can increase the number of unique visitors. Consumer reviews are also more effective in boosting the rankings than other marketer-generated product information because unique content such as the reviews are usually regarded more favorably by search engines (Creamer, July 23, 2007)

Security Assurance

In addition to the other benefits, consumer reviews on retail websites serve an important function that is unique to the online environment. The issue of online security has been the source of consumer anxiety from the dawn of online retailing and news items concerning identity theft are constant reminders of the lurking danger. Regardless of their valence and quality, the mere presence of consumer reviews can address this critical concern of consumers by signaling to visitors that the website is a safe place to shop. The logic behind this is as follows: When many other people visit, shop, and/or leave reviews, this website is not an unpopulated dangerous corner of the cyberspace. Rather, it can give an impression that the retail website is at least secure and reliable.

Volume, Valence, and Value of Consumer Review Messages on Retail Websites

Based on the evidence presented thus far, one can reasonably draw a conclusion that having review features is almost always better than not having them at all. It appears that the online retail industry as a whole has also grasped the reality and fully embraced consumer reviews in their practices. Therefore, now is the time for researchers to ask questions about which particular attributes of consumer reviews are crucial in generating better results. This inquiry opens up fertile ground for more theory-driven research that can also inform marketers how to design and manage their consumer review features strategically. To date, three attributes of consumer reviews have received some attention in the research community.

Volume is one of them. Overall, a higher volume of consumer reviews was found to result in better outcomes. Using the *Amazon.com* book sales data, Li and Hitt (in press) illustrated that a higher number of reviews yielded higher sales rank. Although not in the retail context, the volume of consumer reviews was also found to be a significant predictor of box office revenue for Hollywood movies. Using online review metrics, researchers repeatedly demonstrated that a higher volume of consumer reviews on *Yahoo! Movies* website was related to increased box office sales (Dellarocas, Zhang, & Awad, 2007; Liu, 2006). In yet another study conducted in a discussion group context, the number of product reviews on a discussion forum was positively related to consumers' attitudes toward the brand, especially for a brand that was highly regarded from the beginning (Chiou & Cheng, 2003). Since the review features are open to virtually all consumers and there is no limit in the number of reviews that a consumer can post, the volume of reviews can vary from zero to thousands. For most online retailers, the primary task concerning the reviews may be simply to attract as many as they can. There are too many places that consumers can go and post their reviews, and online retailers have to compete for the reviews not only with other retailers, but with other consumer opinion platforms as well.

Another important attribute of consumer reviews is valence. In general, more positive reviews were found to increase the likelihood of purchase. In the model constructed by Li and Hitt (in press), the average rating of a book was a significant predictor of its sales rank. In the movie industry context again, the valence of consumer reviews was found to be one of the significant and positive predictors of box office sales (Dellarocas, Zhang, & Awad, 2007).

Then, how common are negative reviews on retail websites and should they be necessarily considered to be a "red flag" for online retailers? According to an industry report, on average, positive reviews outnumber negative reviews by the ratio of 8-to-1. For example, negative reviews were found to comprise approximately 16% of 4,000 consumer reviews on *Amazon.com*. In terms of rating, industry observers also noticed a trend that they called "the J-curve." There are not many one-star ratings and even fewer two- and three-star ratings, followed by a huge leap in the number of four- and five-star ratings (Burke, May 1, 2008).

The impact of negative reviews on consumer decisions is more complicated. Macro-level analyses demonstrated that positive reviews led to a higher sales volume (Dellarocas, Zhang, & Awad, 2007; Li & Hitt, in press). Accordingly, online markers would want more positive product reviews that can lead to product sales. Furthermore, research on traditional WOM has established a "negativity effect" stating that negative WOMs exert stronger influence on purchase decisions than positive WOMs (Weinberger & Dillon, 1980). Therefore, it is plausible that negative reviews may override positive reviews and persuade potential customers not to buy a product.

At the same time, there are other factors to consider. Whereas the immediate increase in sales may be more strongly influenced by positive reviews, long-term satisfaction and loyalty may be more closely related to negative reviews. Indeed, negative reviews are more often considered to be helpful and honest (Burke, May 1, 2008). Industry experts also noted that most online shoppers buy products regardless of negative reviews (Sullivan, February 15, 2008). These seemingly contradictory reports can be reconciled when we consider the reality of product choices. In mass-merchandized markets, it may be unrealistic to expect a product to be satisfactory in every aspect, especially when the price is introduced into the equation. Therefore, in many purchase decision processes, negative reviews may allow consumers to deliberately weigh all the pros and cons about the product rather than chasing away potential buyers. When a consumer has realistic expectations about a product, the consumer is less prone to experience buyer remorse and, thus, more likely to come back to the retailer next time. Last but not least, negative reviews can save money for retailers by reducing product returns. Negative reviews keep consumers from buying the "wrong products" in the first place, which leads to significant savings in operation costs (Sullivan, February 15, 2008).

Indeed, a few studies that investigated the effects of valence along with other factors illustrated the complicated nature of the consumer decision process. In a study that examined the interaction between review valence and product type, Sen and Lerman (2007) found that consumers of utilitarian products took negative reviews more seriously by assuming the reviewers' motivations favorably while consumers of hedonic products tended to ignore negative reviews by assuming the negative review irrelevant to the actual product quality. Susceptibility to negative consumer reviews was also found to be dependent on pre-existing attitudes toward the brand or retailer. When a brand had a high initial reputation, the brand image was not affected by negative consumer opinions on a discussion group. When a brand had a low reputation, on the other hand, the brand image was further damaged by negative consumer opinions (Chiou & Cheng, 2003). Similarly, consumers who patronized a retail website based on familiarity were less likely to be affected by negative consumer reviews than consumers who shopped primarily based on price (Chatterjee, 2001).

The third and the least studied attribute of consumer reviews is value, which is interchangeable with the term "quality." Although a retail website has a lot of positive reviews, the retailer would not be able to use the reviews as leverage against their competitors in the long term, if the reviews are of little value to consumers. A group of researchers identified relevance, objectiveness, understandability, and sufficiency as the criteria for review quality. Accordingly, they also defined that reviews with low values are emotional, subjective, and vacuous, with no information except expressions of subjective feelings or simple interjections of affirmation or disapproval (Park, Lee, & Han, 2007).

Subsequently, the same researchers conducted an experiment that examined the effects of review quality and volume based on the level of situational consumer involvement. Consistent with the framework provided by the elaboration likelihood model, quality of the reviews was a significant predictor of purchase intention for highly involved consumers while the quantity was not. For consumers with low involvement, on the other hand, quantity, or volume, of the reviews was more important than the quality. Although the research on the value of consumer reviews is still in preliminary stages, this topic has a great potential to generate useful knowledge on consumer reviews. For instance, future research can address the question of what makes consumers appreciate certain reviews and not others. Or, the differences in the value criteria, based on the demographic or psychographic characteristics of consumers, can be an interesting topic to explore. The following Figure 1 provides an overview of the online retail consumer review process.

Figure 1. An overview of the online retail customer review process

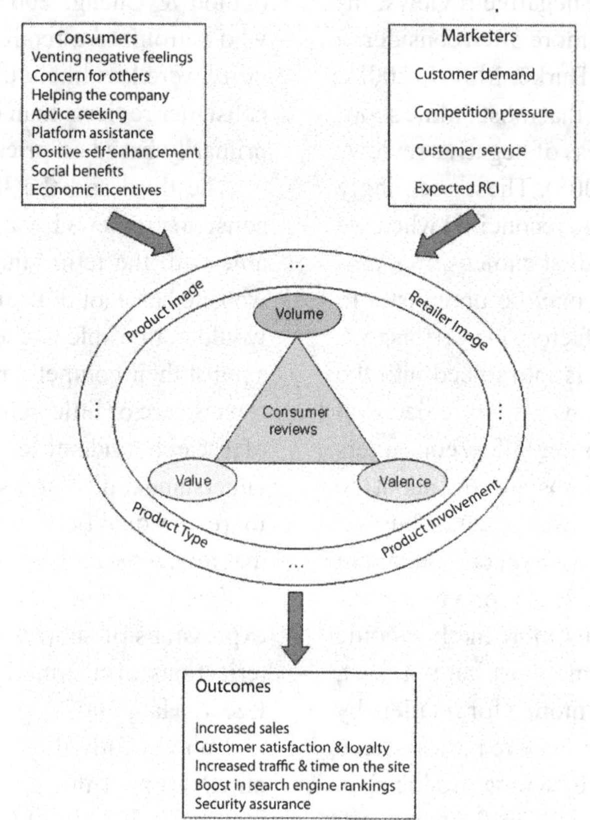

Ethical Considerations Regarding Consumer Reviews on Retail Websites

All these discussions about consumer product reviews on retail websites rest on one important principle: The reviews are truthful opinions of consumers who had some experience with the product. Although this is the most fundamental assumption underlying all the review-related activities, one shouldn't be surprised to find out that this principle is not always observed.

First, the principle can be infringed when the reviews are not written by consumers. Marketers have become increasingly aware of the power of user-generated contents on various Internet outlets such as video sharing sites, social networking sites, and product and service review sites. Although stealth tactics to sneak in positive reviews and delete or neutralize negative reviews are not unheard of in the online marketing circle, it shocked a lot of people when a company was actually sued for posting self-serving reviews on an independent product and service review website (Davis, March 10, 2008). Although an industry expert estimated that paid fake reviews account for less than 10% of all consumer reviews on the Internet, the concerns are real and justified (Sullivan, February 15, 2008). Even within the online marketing industry, practitioners started to call for standards for "buzz" or "viral" marketing (Snyder, 2004) and, as a response, the Word of Mouth Marketing Association has developed a Code of Ethics that emphasizes honesty and respect for the rules of communication venues (Miller & Associates, 2007).

Second, a violation of the principle is made if the reviews are not truthful, even when written by peer consumers. One caveat in the all-voluntary doctrine of consumer reviews is the possibility that a consumer can write a review voluntarily, but with a little encouragement by marketers, often in the form of material incentives. However, it will be very difficult and time-consuming to gather intelligence on which marketers are engaging in such tactics and it will be even harder to tell whether a consumer review is influenced by the effort. Therefore, most review sites delegate the responsibility of identifying fake reviews to individual consumers who use the websites. *TripAdvisor*, an independent review site for the travel industry, on the other hand, has a firm policy that prohibits marketers from providing incentives to their customers in exchange for the reviews. When identified, the website eliminates those consumer reviews (Graham, May 21, 2008). Although news reports on unethical behaviors are rare, a recent story involving fake consumer reviews for *Belkin* products on *Amazon.com* illustrates how easy it is to manipulate the consumer review systems. An online sales representative of the company reportedly posted highly positive reviews about Belkin products under pseudonyms. He was also accused of recruiting people to post positive product reviews for $.65 per piece (Pogue, January 19, 2009).

Although may not be as clear-cut as those cases, some other behaviors by both consumers and marketers push the ethical boundaries of consumer reviews as well. While not on the payroll of a marketer, a consumer can be provided with a product for test trial. If the person writes a review about the product on retail websites, it can be considered a violation of the principle unless the reviewer discloses that the product was offered free by the marketer. On the other hand, online retailers can also violate their customers' right to access information by unnecessarily imposing too many restrictions on the content of reviews. It is debatable whether it is fair to ban any comment on special offers available in other places, other products, and competing retailers, which are commonly restricted on many retail websites. Although the intention on the part of marketers is understandable, these comments can be beneficial for consumers.

Consumer Reviews on Retail Websites: Commons or Properties?

The confusion about what is allowed and what is not and the blatant violations of ethical guidelines can be partially attributed to the lack of a general consensus regarding the fundamental nature of the consumer reviews. Consumer reviews on retail websites are user-generated content produced for the purpose of communicating to other consumers. In terms of the participant dynamics, consumer reviews on retail websites have a few characteristics distinct from any other forms of consumer-to-consumer communications about products or services. First, consumers can read and comment on product reviews posted by other consumers who they have never met, whereas the flow of traditional consumer-to-consumer communications takes place in a closed social network (Brown & Reingen, 1987). Second, a consumer who posts a review has to assume his or her audiences and address them whereas a consumer expressing his or her view usually knows exactly to whom he or she is talking, which may render the review content more general than other consumer opinions mostly shared in interpersonal contexts.

Whereas these two characteristics are applicable to most consumer opinions available online, there are other characteristics that are unique to consumer reviews on retail websites. First of all, the communication forums can only be enabled by online retailers who adopt consumer review features to their websites. Also, unlike other consumer-to-consumer communications which take place outside of the marketers' domain (e.g., independent review sites and chat rooms), online product reviews are displayed within the retail websites. In addition, once posted by consumers, the reviews can be read by other consumers visiting the product site anytime and anywhere, which makes them more referable than other online consumer opinions available elsewhere on the Internet (Schindler & Bickart, 2005).

Considering these characteristics, one may conclude that consumer reviews on retail websites are part of marketing communication rather than organic consumer communication. Indeed, this perspective is supported by the fact that the availability and format of consumer reviews are completely dependent on the marketers' decisions. This view is also widely shared by marketers who make a substantial amount of investment in installing and managing review systems. Marketing researchers and industry analysts also reinforce the belief that consumer reviews are part of marketing communication by producing research that situates consumer reviews in a wider context of marketing communication and compares consumer reviews with other marketer-generated messages.

Before accepting this prevalent view, however, it may be useful to examine consumer reviews in the framework of an emerging economic model called "commons-based peer production." (Benkler, 2006) "Commons" refers to an institutional form of structuring the rights to access, use, and control of resources and is characterized by shared rights over any resource in the commons among its members. It is the opposite of "property" that recognizes the authority of one person or a particular group of people over any resources controlled by the organization.

Commons, in turn, can be classified into four types based on two criteria (Benkler, 2006). First, depending on the exclusivity of membership, some commons are open to anyone (open commons) whereas others are limited to a defined group (limited-access commons). Second, some commons, especially the limited-access ones, have more or less elaborate rules governing its resources whereas others don't.

Certainly, retail websites are the properties of the marketers and the review features are also installed and maintained by marketers at their expense. But it is not clear whether the contents of the consumer reviews are also "properties" of the website owners. Rather, from the perspective of membership and regulation, consumer reviews on retail websites operate fairly similarly to the open commons. There is no barring circumstances for entry. Although some retail websites limit the privilege of review writing to consumers who have used the product before, there is no way to cross-validate the claim of product experience. Other than this, anyone can join other consumer reviewers as long as they register and log-in. In some retail websites, even the registration and log-in steps are not required. As a rule, consumer reviews are very loosely regulated in terms of the governance of the review contents as well. Most retail websites have a published review guideline and reserve the right to block or remove reviews that are deemed to have violated either laws or others' rights. Other than these instances, however, anyone can contribute their opinions in the form of consumer reviews. The usage of the consumer reviews is also hardly constrained in that anybody visiting a retail site can view the reviews and use them in any way that they want within legal bounds. In addition, consumer reviews are the outcome of peer production in that there is no hierarchy and people participate in the creation and consumption of the reviews mostly on their own terms. Even though there is little to none monetary reward for their input, a great number of people participate in the production of consumer reviews.

Then, what are the roles and rights of retail websites over the consumer review process? According to Benkler (2006), an act of communication is comprised of three distinct functions. First, people, whether professional or amateurs, should create a meaningful content. Second, the content should be put in a context where it is considered relevant and credible. Third, the content or information should be distributed to others who can make use of it. In the mass-mediated world, all three functions were often carried out by one organization. In a network-based economy, however, Benkler (2006) claims, this process is much more disaggregated. The most prominent example is the user-generated content (UGC) on the Internet. The importance of UGC in the marketing context has notably increased (Cheong & Morrison, 2008). Unlike other UGCs found in consumer community sites and social networking sites, however, consumer reviews on retail websites entirely depend on the site owners for the distribution function and the function of assigning relevancy and credibility.

Unfortunately, the legal rights and responsibilities of consumer reviewers and online marketers over the consumer reviews are not well defined yet. Although many online retailers provide guidelines detailing what renders a review unpublishable on their websites, most of the guidelines are not explicit on who owns the reviews and what the rights of both consumer reviewers and the retailers are. One rare exception is found on *Amazon.com* that states that consumer reviewers, by posting content or submitting material, grant *Amazon* a "nonexclusive, royalty-free, perpetual, irrevocable, and fully sublicensable right to use the content in any form in any media."

Obviously, this contractual statement was carefully crafted to maximize the benefits that the retailer may reap from the review activities while protecting itself from any liability caused by the reviews. At the same time, the statement clearly recognized consumer reviewers' ownership over their comments and also allowed consumers to use their comments in other contexts by claiming the retailer's right to be nonexclusive. On *Amazon.com*, consumer reviewers can also modify or delete their reviews at will.

Consumer Reviews as Social Capital

Whether one views the consumer reviews as commons or properties of retailers, it is indisputable that consumer reviews illustrate what people can achieve through collective collaboration. The seemingly unproductive activities at the individual level such as surfing and posting created a significant amount of information as social capital. Accumulation of quality information about products and services can contribute to consumer welfare to a great extent. Furthermore, the presence of high-quality reviews, as opposed to low-value ones, can encourage others to do the same. In the end, this process may trigger a positive feedback loop that nurtures an environment where people voluntarily provide useful information to other consumers. This perspective is theorized by a social scientific analytic framework known as the social identification and deindividuation (SIDE) model (Lee & Nass, 2002). According to the SIDE model, the activities of participants on an online forum are influenced by identification and general group norms. Honest and useful information contributed by a large number of individuals will make the general online social environment prone to social co-operation rather than harmful social scathing.

Aggregation of trustworthy information by general online users can be potentially crucial for the further proliferation of online economic activities. It has been known that trust among the users of an online platform is very fragile due to the anonymous nature of online communication. People can easily opt out when they feel that the communication is not worth their time or meaningful. Or, some people intentionally engage in deceitful and hurtful communication behaviors when expressing their views or dealing with others online. Without trust, the online retail industry will become a market for "lemons" (Akerlof, 1970) and online business transactions are very likely to be limited to the exchange of cheap and low quality products.

Along with other measures such as an institutional seal of approval, consumer reviews can be a solution to the shortage of trust. Despite the difficulties of building trust online, aggregated credible and useful information by anonymous peer consumers can facilitate an environment where people will be engaged in exchanges of opinions and, eventually, persuade one another to buy products and services online. From this view, the aggregated consumer reviews comprise important social capital that can be crucial in the further advance of an economy in which the abundance of high-quality information benefits honest and responsible marketers as well as consumers.

Moderation and Reputation Systems as the Quality Safeguards of Consumer Reviews

Considering this significance of consumer reviews as social capital, it becomes all the more important that we find ways to protect the quality and integrity of consumer reviews in the interest of everybody involved. Fortunately, there are useful evaluation mechanisms available online such as moderation and reputation systems.

Online moderation systems are very similar to their off-line counterparts. Moderators command and control consumer reviews. They can set up guidelines for reviewers to follow and have the authority to remove or edit consumer reviews that are deemed to have violated the guidelines. Most of these moderation activities occur either during or immediately after a consumer submits a review. Online reputation systems, on the other hand, become effective over time after a review has been posted. Once a consumer review becomes public, other consumers can rate the review based on how helpful it is. Although a study reported that only 5 out of 100 retail websites had this reputation system in 2004 (Yun, Park, & Ha, 2008), it appears that a lot of online retailers have adopted this function since then. Additionally, some online retailers have features that allow consumers to evaluate the reviewers, the source of information, as well.

For both the moderation and reputation systems, reviewer log-in and registration are necessary. A consumer who submits a review should be identifiable, though not necessarily by his or her real name, to be sanctioned for either irrelevant or inflammatory reviews and to get a proper recognition for good reviews. A majority of the consumer review systems require consumers to register and log-in before using the review features (Yun, Park, & Ha, 2008). During the registration process, site administrators can collect personal information including email, home address, phone numbers, and, sometimes, a demographic profile. And the information collected during the registration can be used for the purpose of controlling the quality of consumer reviews.

In practice, a significant proportion of retail websites have adopted the moderation system. Upon submission, more than half of 100 leading online retail websites displayed the consumer reviews after a delay ranging from a day to a week (Yun, Park, & Ha, 2008). Indeed, the filtering can be an effective quality control mechanism. But, there are caveats against the moderation system. For instance, it makes submitted consumer reviews vulnerable to the biases of the moderator or moderating system (Stromer-Galley, 2000; Jensen, Farnham, Drucker, & Kollock, 2000). The biases of a small group of moderators and the fear of being punished by the moderators can discourage message posting (Jensen et al., 2000). In the case of consumer reviews on retail websites, the threat is more obvious because retailers would welcome positive reviews while being wary of negative ones. Even if the website administrators do not reject negative reviews categorically, they may examine negative reviews closer than positive reviews and thus find more of them in violation of their consumer review guidelines.

Furthermore, a lack of moderator resources can leave a hole for flaming and unreliable postings (Wright, 2000). It takes a lot of time and effort to monitor the postings constantly, especially when there is a lot of review activity on the website. When the website is small and deals with a limited number of customers, the task of moderating the reviews may be manageable. But, for many retail websites that carry thousands of products targeting a mass market, the task can become overwhelming very quickly. The evolution of a recommendation system on an online discussion forum called *Slashdot* (www.slashdot.org) clearly illustrates this problem. At the opening of the site, a relatively small number of *Slashdot* moderators were able to maintain the website by deleting abusive messages when the number of postings was not very high. But, as the website grew increasingly popular, the moderators were quickly overwhelmed. Eventually, the website developed a sophisticated system in which the duty and authority of moderation was efficiently and evenly distributed among its members. The system picked moderators amongst candidates who were registered to the website and then the chosen moderators had the authority for a limited term, only to pass down the power to other members when theirs expired (CmfrTaco, 1999). However, it is questionable whether this model will be applicable to online retailers because retail websites are different from online community sites. Currently, most online retailers do not pay close attention to all consumer reviews on their websites. Although they delay postings of submitted reviews, a lot of them even do not screen the reviews at all, whereas some outsource Web application service providers to screen reviews (Parks, April 2008). This reality may discourage smaller online retailers from implementing a moderation system for fear of losing control.

The other control mechanism, the reputation system, has both strengths and weaknesses as well. Kollock (1999) posited that previous behaviors can predict future behavior and this can be conceptualized as a reputation. In other words, when someone has a good reputation, we can expect a similarly good behavior from the same person in the future. People frequently employ a reputation system in their daily encounters with others by basing their credibility judgments on the reputation of the others. One's credibility can be founded on various factors such as academic credentials, occupation, experience, and appearance, to name a few. In online environments, however, reputation as defined as a behavioral pattern is more relevant and readily applicable because the other information is not as salient as in off-line contexts.

A clear advantage of the reputation system vis-à-vis the recommendation system is that it is free from the concerns about the moderator biases and the limited moderator resources that were identified as the weaknesses of the latter. Users of a website can participate, knowingly and unknowingly, in the quality control process. Their contribution is explicit if the participation occurs by actively evaluating or rating others' postings. If one does not engage in the evaluative activities but conducts quantifiable activities like clicking on a particular review, the person implicitly contribute to the reputation system by adding a number to the access frequency. Besides the simple frequency of review access, a consumer review can also be ranked based on other activities such as the frequency of replies, the number of threads, and the frequency of page access (Jensen et al., 2000).

Ironically, these strengths also expose the reputation system to a potential threat of insolvency. The reputation system, especially the explicit kind, requires active participation in large numbers. When there are not many people participating in the rating of consumer reviews, the reputation system may not function properly (Terveen & Hill, 2001). Review ratings conducted by a small number of consumers can be unreliable and cannot command trust of other consumers. Another important issue, if not necessarily a drawback, of the reputation system is concerned with how to implement it. A reputation system can be set up to provide positive reinforcements, to impose sanctions, or to do both. In other words, a consumer review may receive a positive rating point only, a negative point only, or both positive and negative rating points, depending on the reputation system.

Overall, negative reputation systems that allow negative rating of *reviewers* are considered to be less productive. Some researchers pointed out that negative reputation systems may promote blacklisting and discourage review posting in the whole community. In addition, blacklisted users can easily create multiple identities to bypass the negative reputation system, if necessary (Kollock, 1999). However, negative reputation systems applied to *posted reviews,* as opposed to the reviewers, may serve some purposes. For one, the fact that the reviews are subject to peer evaluation can alert potential consumer reviewers to be more mindful of the quality of their postings. For the users of the reviews, a negative rating on a posted review can signal that the review may not merit their consideration. Hence, it can save time and effort of consumers and enable them to focus on high-value reviews.

CONCLUSION

As examined throughout this chapter, consumer reviews on retail websites serve multiple functions for consumers, marketers, and the wider society. Therefore, it is in the interest of everyone in society to protect the integrity of the communication process and further refine the configurations to solicit more active and open participation from various members of the consumer community. It will be wise of online retailers to align their interest with the interest of consumers and society in their efforts to achieve this goal. Consumers, on their part, also need to fulfill their responsibilities by contributing honest and thoughtful reviews while keeping a watchful eye on the activities of fellow consumers and marketers that may depreciate this important social capital.

This chapter did not intend to single out particular online retailers as good or bad examples of consumer review management. At the same time, it is hard not to notice that *Amazon.com* has been mentioned many times for innovative review features and policies that also make sense from the theoretical perspective. Although the consumer review features are only part of what has made them so successful, their dominant position in the online retail industry certainly serves the lesson to other online retailers to invest more on research and intelligence to stay on the frontline of customer relationship management.

Empowered consumers are often considered to be the biggest change in the advertising and marketing field brought about by the interactive media. What is equally significant, however, is the change in the way marketers communicate with their customers. Consumer empowerment does not necessarily lead to the crippling of marketers' power and influence. The only certain change is the mode of communication from being unidirectional to becoming more and more bidirectional. In this paradigm shift, consumer reviews should be regarded by online retailers as a powerful tool in their arsenal that they can deploy to nurture a mutually beneficial relationship with their customers. The research community should also play an important role during this transitional period by providing strategies that can contribute to the proliferation of online businesses as well as consumer welfare.

REFERENCES

Akerlof, G. (1970). The market for 'Lemons': Quality uncertainty and the market mechanism. *The Quarterly Journal of Economics, 84*, 488–500. doi:10.2307/1879431

Benkler, Y. (2006). *The wealth of networks: How social production transforms markets and freedom*. New Haven, CT: Yale University Press.

Brown, J. J., & Reingen, P. H. (1987). Social ties and word-of-mouth referral behavior. *The Journal of Consumer Research, 14*(November), 350–362. doi:10.1086/209118

Burke, K. (2008, May 1). E-commerce link: Humanizing the Web. *Target Marketing*. Retrieved August 6, 2008, from http://www.targetmarketingmag.com/story/reprints.bsp?sid=95879&var=story

Chatterjee, P. (2001). Online reviews: Do consumers use them? *Advances in Consumer Research. Association for Consumer Research (U. S.), 28*, 129–133.

Cheong, H. J., & Morrison, M. A. (2008). Consumers' reliance on product information and recommendations found in UGC. *Journal of Interactive Advertising, 8*(2). Retrieved July 30, 2008, from http://www.jiad.org/article103

Chiou, J., & Cheng, C. (2003). Should a company have message boards on its websites? *Journal of Interactive Marketing, 17*(3), 50–61. doi:10.1002/dir.10059

CmdrTaco. (1999, September 9). *Slashdot Moderation*. Retrieved April 17, 2003, from http://slashdot.org/moderation.shtml

Creamer, M. (2007, July 23). At last, the reviews are In Wal-Mart wakes up to the power of the people. *Advertising Age*.

Davis, W. (2008, March 10). Company accused of posting self-serving reviews. *Media Post Publications*. Retrieved August 6, 2008, from http://www.mediapost.com/publications/index.cfm?fuseaction=Articles.showArticleHomePage&art_aid=78101

Dellarocas, C., Zhang, X., & Awad, N. F. (2007). Exploring the value of online product reviews in forecasting sales: The case of motion pictures. *Journal of Interactive Marketing, 21*(4), 23–45. doi:10.1002/dir.20087

Freed, L. (2007, March 1). Customer product reviews: Key to driving satisfaction, loyalty and conversion. *Foresee Results*. Retrieved on August 1, 2008, from http://www.ForeSeeResults.com

Frey, B. S., & Jegen, R. (2001). Motivation crowding theory. *Journal of Economic Surveys, 15*(5), 589. doi:10.1111/1467-6419.00150

Graham, J. (2008, May 21). Online reviews can help grow a business: More consumer prowl Web looking for recommendations. *USA Today*.

Hennig-Thurau, T., Gwinner, K. P., Walsh, G., & Gremler, D. D. (2004). Electronic word-of-mouth via consumer-opinion platforms: What motivates consumers to articulate themselves on the Internet? *Journal of Interactive Marketing, 18*(1), 38–52. doi:10.1002/dir.10073

Jensen, C., Farnham, S. D., Drucker, S. M., & Kollock, P. (2000 April). *The effect of communication modality on cooperation in online environment.* Paper presented at the CHI, Hague, Netherlands.

Kollock, P. (1999). The production of trust in online markets. In Lawler, E. J., Macy, M., Thyne, S., & Walker, H. A. (Eds.), *Advances in Group Processes* (*Vol. 16*). Greenwich, CT: JAI Press.

Lee, E. J., & Nass, C. (2002). Experimental tests of normative group influence and representation effects in computer-mediated communication. *Human Communication Research, 28*(3), 349–381.

Li, X., & Hitt, L. M. (in press). Self selection and information role of online product reviews. *Information Systems Research.*

Liu, Y. (2006). Word-of-mouth for movies: Its dynamics and impact on box office receipts. *Journal of Marketing, 70*, 74–89. doi:10.1509/jmkg.70.3.74

Magill, K. (2006, March 1). Petco tests product reviews. *Direct*. Retrieved July 24, 2008, from http://directmag.com/disciplines/email/marketing_petco_tests_product/

Miller, R. K. (2007). *The 2007 entertainment, Media & advertising market research handbook (RKM1471789)*. Loganville, GA: Richard K. Miller & Associates.

Park, D., Lee, J., & Han, I. (2007). The effect of on-line consumer reviews on consumer purchasing intention: The moderating role of involvement. *International Journal of Electronic Commerce, 11*(4), 125–148. doi:10.2753/JEC1086-4415110405

Park, S., & Ha, L. (2005). Interactivity in consumer commenting functions: A comparison of Korean and U.S. leading retail websites. In *Proceedings of the American Academy of Advertising Asia-Pacific Conference*, Hong Kong.

Parks, L. (2008 April). Peer reviews drive online buyers: Bath & Body Works kicks up conversion rate using customer comments. *Stores*. Retrieved August 4, 2008, from http://www.stores.org/Current_Issue/2008/04/edit8/index.asp

Pogue, D. (2009, January 19). Belkin employee paid users for good reviews. *New York Times*. Retrieved February 16, 2009, from http://pogue.blogs.nytimes.com/2009/01/19/belkin-employee-paid-users-for-good-reviews/?scp=1&sq=belkin%20employee%20&st=Search

Schindler, R. M., & Bickart, B. (2005). Published word of mouth: Referable, consumer-generated information on the Internet. In Haugtvedt, C. P., Machleit, K. A., & Yalch, R. (Eds.), *Online consumer psychology: Understanding and influencing consumer behavior in the virtual world* (pp. 35–61). Mahwah, NJ: LEA.

Sen, S., & Lerman, D. (2007). Why are you telling me this? An examination into negative consumer reviews on the Web. *Journal of Interactive Marketing, 21*(4), 76–94. doi:10.1002/dir.20090

Senecal, S., & Nantel, J. (2004). The influence of online product recommendations on consumers' online choices. *Journal of Retailing, 80*(2), 159–169. doi:10.1016/j.jretai.2004.04.001

Smith, D., Menon, S., & Sivakumar, K. (2005). Online peer and editorial recommendations, trust, and choice in virtual markets. *Journal of Interactive Marketing, 19*(3), 15–37. doi:10.1002/dir.20041

Snyder, P. (2004, June 28). Wanted: Standards for viral marketing. *Brandweek, 45*(26), 21.

Srinivasan, S. S., Anderson, R., & Ponnavolu, K. (2002). Customer loyalty in e-commerce: An exploration of its antecedents and consequences. *Journal of Retailing, 78*(1), 41–50. doi:10.1016/S0022-4359(01)00065-3

Stromer-Galley, J. (2000). On-line interaction and why candidates avoid it. *The Journal of Communication*, (Autumn): 111–132. doi:10.1111/j.1460-2466.2000.tb02865.x

Sullivan, E. A. (2008, February 15). Consider your source: As e-commerce sites add consumer-generated review systems, marketers and consumers hope truth trumps disingenuousness. *Marketing News*, 16-18.

Terveen, L., & Hill, W. (2001). Beyond recommender systems: helping people help each other. In Carroll, J. (Ed.), *HCI In The New Millennium*. Reading, MA: Addison-Wesley.

Weinberger, M. C., & Dillon, W. R. (1980). The effects of unfavorable product information. In Olson, J. C. (Ed.), *Advances in Consumer Research* (*Vol. 7*, pp. 528–532). Ann Arbor, MI: Association for Consumer Research.

Wright, K. (2000). Perceptions of on-line support providers: an examination of perceived homophily, source credibility, communication and social support within on-line support groups. *Communication Quarterly, 48*(1), 44–59.

Yun, G. W., Park, S., & Ha, L. (2008). Influence of cultural dimensions on online interactive review feature implementations: A comparison of Korean and U.S. retail websites. *Journal of Interactive Marketing*, *22*(3), 40–50. doi:10.1002/dir.20116

Chapter 11
Electronic Word of Mouth and Consumer Generated Content:
From Concept to Application

Ye Wang
Missouri School of Journalism, USA

Shelly Rodgers
Missouri School of Journalism, USA

ABSTRACT

With the Internet, even ordinary Web users can conveniently create and disseminate media content. The notion of User-Generated Content (UGC) or Consumer-Generated Content (CGC) captures the user-as-producer feature and refers to content that is not generated or published by professionals on the Internet, unlike traditional media. An important type of online advertising that makes use of CGC is eWOM (electronic word-of-mouth) advertising. Defined in terms of situations where consumers refer products or services to other consumers on the Internet, eWOM is closely related to CGC and can be applied to many online forums for UGC and CGC. With this in mind, this chapter seeks to define and categorize eWOM based on different online platforms of CGC, review existing research in eWOM, and, finally, extend the use of eWOM to health promotion by examining characteristics of eWOM in an online breast cancer bulletin board.

INTRODUCTION

Web 2.0 and other online applications have transformed mass communication from a one-way to a two-way communication system. With the Internet, even ordinary Web users can conveniently create and disseminate media content. The notion of User-Generated Content (UGC), or Consumer-Generated Content (CGC), captures the user-as-producer feature. Since UGC and CGC are more trusted by consumers - and more persuasive - than traditional advertisements (Bickar & Schindler, 2001; Goldsmith & Horowitz, 2006; Okazaki, 2008), marketers are trying to become part of the communication process and engage consumers by making use of CGC to accomplish advertising goals. For example, online retailers like Amazon.com and Walmart.com invite consumers to write product reviews, whether positive or negative, to assist other consumers with buying decisions.

DOI: 10.4018/978-1-60566-792-8.ch011

Ebay.com builds its business on a reputation ranking system based on buyers' and sellers' comments. To engage consumers, Oscar advertiser Cottonelle toilet paper asked Oscar viewers to vote and chat online about whether they install their rolls "under or over" (Horovitz, 2010). Many companies upload their TV commercials to YouTube.com, provide a Facebook fan page, or subscribe to a Twitter account, all of which are driven by peer-to-peer communications. These examples suggest that CGC can occur in a variety of online formats (e.g., a corporate website versus a Facebook fan page), and can consist of a multitude of features or characteristics.

Closely related to the application of CGC in the digital advertising "mix" is the concept of eWOM. Despite the popularity of this emerging tool, few studies have systematically examined the literature on eWOM via CGC. The definitions of eWOM often overlap to include viral advertising, eWOM, and CGC (Hennig-Thurau et al., 2004). Additionally, research on eWOM ranges from seeking- and providing- behaviors of eWOM to (e.g., Fong & Burton, 2006; Lieberman & Goldstein, 2005; Nelson & Otnes, 2005), eWOM motivations (e.g., Goldsmith & Horowitz, 2006; Sun, Youn, Wu, & Kuntaraporn, 2006), eWOM types and format (e.g., Thorson & Rodgers, 2006), features of eWOM advertising (e.g., Bickar & Schindler, 2001; Evans et al., 2001; Okazaki, 2008), and consumers' psychological responses to eWOM advertising (e.g., Benedicktus & Andrews, 2006; Senecal & Nantel, 2004). Despite the growing number of studies on eWOM, it clear unclear what may be missing in the bigger eWOM picture, and what (if anything) should be examined further in research to offer a more comprehensive understanding of eWOM. In other words, the bulk of literature on eWOM needs to be organized under an integrated model, which can be tested and developed by researchers and practitioners for the purpose of maximizing this new form of advertising.

Since the Interactive Advertising Model (IAM) was proposed with features of interactive advertising in mind, andresearch has drawn upon several paradigms or schools of thoughts (Rodgers and Thorson, 2000), this chapter chose to apply the Interactive Advertising Model (IAM) to categorize existing literature on eWOM. The three paradigms used in the IAM are the functional school, the structural school, and the school of information processing. The functional school examines interactive advertising as a function of advertising effectiveness; the structural school investigates the structural features of eWOM; and, the information processing school deals with the underlying psychological processing of eWOM messages (Rodgers & Thorson, 2000).

Using this theoretical framework, this chapter fulfills three major goals: 1) define and categorize eWOM based on different online platforms of CGC; 2) review and contrast existing research on eWOM; and, 3) extend the use of eWOM to health promotion by examining characteristics of eWOM in an online breast cancer bulletin board.

DEFINITION AND TYPES OF EWOM

CGC and eWOM are two closely related concepts. CGC is defined as Internet content that is generated and published by everyday consumers, not media or communications professionals. In turn, eWOM is characterized as "any positive or negative statements made by potential, actual, or former customers about a product or company, which is made available to a multitude of people and institutions via the Internet" (Henning–Thurau et al., 2004, p. 39). From the definitions we can see that, eWOM is a specific type of CGC about products or companies.

Marketers intentionally initiate various types of eWOM, such as viral marketing, viral advertising, and online testimonials, to influence consumers' attitudes and behaviors (Golan & Zaidner, 2008;

Stauss, 1997). Therefore, eWOM is often simply characterized as a form of advertising. At the same time, public relations companies have added eWOM to their product offerings to deal with negative online reviews of brands (Rosenwald, 2010). As such, eWOM also fits within the realm of public relations. However, this chapter chose the angle of eWOM as advertising because this perspective best captures various types of eWOM and reveals the influence of eWOM on consumer attitudes and behaviors–which is perhaps more amenable to advertising.

Unlike traditional Business-to-Consumer (B2C) advertising models, an important feature of eWOM is that *consumers* control and create the marketing communication about a given product or service, to a large extent. For commercial groups or companies, changing or influencing eWOM opens up new opportunities for marketing. For example, eWOM within social media is one important type of eWOM. A recent survey by Marketingsherpa showed that most advertising and public relations professionals believe that online discussion among consumers through social media is an effective tool for achieving branding goals, building reputation, and enhancing awareness (Odden, 2009). For example, the Cloud Cult Campaign is one example of how to successfully implementat CGC. Through their E-surance campaign, Cloud Cult utilized Facebook to reach consumers and allow them to view content about their insurance brand, discuss the brand with other consumers, and build online communities (Vorro, 2009). Since the online discussions were essentially about the product and the company, a considerable proportion of CGC was in the form of eWOM throughout the entire advertising campaign, and emotional bonds were created among consumers as the result.

Drawing from this as well as other examples, the authors extend current eWOM definitions to include the emotional as well as the structural aspects of eWOM by proposing this definition: any degree or combination of positive, negative, or neutral comments, recommendations, or any statements about companies, brands, products, or services discussed or shared among consumers in digital or electronic formats. In this sense, the proposed definition modifies the current definition of eWOM presented earlier in two important ways. First, positivity and negativity are two important aspects of eWOM, but the valence values of eWOM are often beyond a simple dichotomy. Some eWOM could be a mix of positive and negative valences, and some could be essentially neutral, as in the case of a reviewer who writes only facts about the product without any introduction of negative or positive valence. Second, with the wide applications of eWOM in various communication areas, we felt the definition must expand to include these the multitude of applications. For example, in health promotion the consumer is generally a patient and products are typically medical treatments or procedures. These would not typically fall within the traditional definitions of eWOM, yet more diverse forms and understandings should be taken into consideration to gain the broadest possible understanding of eWOM in a variety of contexts and applications as well as with a variety of products, services and consumer types. To illustrate these two modifications, this chapter presents the results of a content analysis of eWOM on a breast cancer bulletin board later in this chapter.

However, it is important to point out that eWOM could be further classified into two broad categories based on different platforms of CGC: eWOM in online feedback systems and consumer review sites, and eWOM on electronic discussion boards, online communities, and online social networking sites. Previous studies have shown that eWOM on these two types of CGC platforms differ in terms of features and roles in the marketing communications mix.

The first type of eWOM is often generated in online feedback systems and consumer review websites. An online feedback system is specifically designed for consumers to exchange their opinions about products and services. For example, many online e-commerce sites, such as Amazon.com, eBay.com, and Walmart.com invite consumers to write a product comment after a purchase. In addition to consumer comments on retailers' websites there are also third party review websites such as TripAdvisor.com, which claim to provide "unbiased" reviews for hotels and vacations.

Since the major purpose of online feedback systems and review websites is to provide information to consumers for product evaluation, most CGC in this form is considered eWOM. As such, consumer comments are directly linked to the marketing of products and services and closely relate to the influence of eWOM on brand reputation (Dellarocas, 2003), trust (Benedicktus & Andrews, 2006), attitudes toward products (Bickar & Schindler, 2001), and consumer decision-making (De Bruyn & Lilien, 2008), to name a few.

A second type of eWOM occurs on electronic discussion boards, online communities, and online social networking sites. Electronic discussion boards and online communities are considered online platforms, which facilitate communications among consumers with shared interests and experiences. Social networking sites are designed for particular segments of the population (like business professions or working moms) to maintain and expand interpersonal relationships with friends and relatives. For example, although the average age of an individual user is increasing, Facebook.com was originally designed for young people to share pictures and life experiences through connections. LinkedIn.com helps professionals to maintain business relationships. Given the growing popularity of these social networking sites, this style of content as well as its social connectivity format is reaching users beyond the initially planned target segment.

Electronic discussion boards, online communities, and online social networking sites create a more natural setting for eWOM advertising. Researchers have identified several basic and important aspects of eWOM for these contexts, which include an informational aspect, an emotional aspect, and valence value of informational and emotional eWOM (Dillard & Nabi, 2006; Evans et al., 2001; Fong & Burton, 2006; Lieberman & Goldstein, 2005). For example, upon returning from a vacation, people may want to share their experience with friends on Facebook. They may post photos and talk about the details of their trip, including the hotel they stayed at, restaurants they ate at, activities they participated in, and so on. Informational eWOM could express how clean the hotel was, whether the staff was courteous, whether they liked the swimming pool, etc. Emotional eWOM may demonstrate how the individual felt when they were enjoying the sunset in the café, how happy they were when they danced with friends at a local bar, or how funny a cab driver was during the trip. Emotional eWOM could also be negative (Dillard & Nabi, 2006; Lieberman & Goldstein, 2005) and can have degrees of negativity as well as positivity.

As is shown in the above examples, since personal experience is frequently exchanged on electronic discussion boards, in online communities, and online social networking sites, emotion is an important part of eWOM on those platforms. Unlike the first type of eWOM, which is largely information-oriented, the influence of emotional eWOM on consumers' attitudes and behaviors is a significant issue for the second type of eWOM. Therefore, looking for features that are informational eWOM, emotional eWOM, and their valence value is the foremost task of marketers who want to influence eWOM in a more natural setting for eWOM advertising (Dillard & Nabi, 2006; Evans et al., 2001; Fong & Burton, 2006; Lieberman & Goldstein, 2005).

To summarize, eWOM is a type of CGC. Based on different features and roles of eWOM in the marketing communication mix, there are two major types of eWOM: informational-oriented contexts, such as consumer reviews on online feedback systems and review websites, and more emotionally-oriented contexts in which consumer opinions and comments are shared with friends and family on electronic discussion boards, in online communities, and on social networking websites. The latter type of eWOM appears in a more natural setting of online communication, and therefore is often a mixture of positive and negative emotions as well as information. If marketers want to use eWOM as an efficient marketing tool, understanding how consumers talk about their products and services is the first and most important step to understanding eWOM, its components, its features, and any potential effects of those components and features. Before undertaking this task, however, it is essential to gain a fundamental understanding of the existing literature on eWOM and to do this, we have organized eWOM studies into the three schools of thought outlined by the IAM, as noted earlier. This next section provides a brief summary.

A REVIEW OF THE EWOM LITERATURE: THREE SCHOOLS OF THOUGHT

In this section, we organize the eWOM literature into three categories by applying the Interactive Advertising Model (IAM). We should point out that studies may overlap categories because studies sometimes use more than one approach or school of thought and, as shown by the IAM, the three schools of thought used here are interralated. Thus, the purpose of the categorization is not to provide a mutually exclusive taxonomy, but to help readers obtain an overall understanding of existing research on eWOM across these schools of thought in an effort to identify potential gaps and opportunities for research in this area.

The IAM perspective is a useful guideline for organizing components and features of eWOM and any related studies. First, different from integrated models of traditional advertising, the IAM includes unique features of interactive advertising such as users' motivations of searching information (Rodgers & Thorson, 2000). Second, the IAM incorporates three schools of thoughts, which have been used by studies on interactive advertising (Rodgers & Thorson, 2000). Third, the IAM is a model that allows empirical testing, replication, and theoretical development of research on interactive advertising, including eWOM (Rodgers & Thorson, 2000). Thus, we use the IAM as our organizing schema to offer further insights into the eWOM literature.

As shown in Table 1, the three schools of thought that the IAM draws on are information processing and structuralism. The functionalist approach views Internet usage as a function of fulfilling certain purposes and satisfying needs (Rodgers & Thorson, 2000). The functionalist approach to interactive advertising consists of two components: Internet motives and modes (Rodgers & Thorson, 2000). Internet motives refer to the inner "drive" of carrying out an online activity (Rodgers & Thorson, 2000). Internet mode assesses the extent to which an online activity is goal oriented (Rodgers & Thorson, 2000). Under the larger umbrella of the functional approach, lies the uses and gratifications (U&G) approach, which is frequently used in mass communication to identify motives of using the Internet (Rodgers & Thorson, 2000). In addition, LaRose, and Eastin (2004) propose a model of Internet use based on Social Cognitive Theory, which contains motivational factors and other psychological constructs (LaRose & Eastin, 2004). Closely related to the functionalist approach is the second school, which is information processing (Rodgers & Thorson, 2000). The information processing approach examines consumers' psychological responses to interactive advertising, including attention, memory, and attitudes (Rodgers & Thorson, 2000). While both the functionalist and information processing approaches answer the questions of why and how people use the Internet, the third school of thought, structuralism, examines the physical features of interactive advertising (Rodgers & Thorson, 2000). For instance, the structural approach looks at types, formats, and features of interactive advertising (Rodgers & Thorson, 2000)

Table 1. Functionalism, information processing, and structuralism

Functionalism	H. Chiu, Y. Hsieh, Y. Kao, and M. Lee (2007) M. Eastin, and R. LaRose (2003) J. Fong, and S. Burton (2006) R. E. Goldsmith, and D. Horowitz (2006) D. Gremler (2004) T. Hennig-Thurau, K. P. Gwinner, G. Walsh, and D. C. Huang, Y. Shen, H. Lin, and S. Chang (2007) K. O. Jones, B. E. Denham, and J. K. Springston (2006) R. V. Kozinets (1999) R. LaRose, and M. Eastin (2004) S. Rappaport (2007) T. Smith, J. Coyle, E. Lightfoot, and A. Scott (2007) A. Steyer, R. Garcia-Bardidia, and P. Quester (2006) T. Sun, S. Youn, G. Wu, and M. Kuntaraporn (2006)
Information Processing	R. L. Benedicktus, and M. L. Andrews (2006) B. Bickart, and R. M. Schindler (2001) C. Dellarocas (2003) J. Graham, and W. Havlena (2007) K. Hung, and S. Yiyan Li (2007) J. Nail (2007) K. Niederhoffer, R. Mooth, D. Wiesenfeld, and J. Gordon (2007) S. Okazaki (2008) C. Riegner. (2007) S. Senecal, and J. Nantel (2004) K. S. Thorson, and S. Rodgers (2006)
Structuralism	P. Mason, and B. Davis (2007)

Functional Aspects of eWOM

Turning again to Table 1, we learn that the functionalism approach to eWOM addresses two questions: "how" or "why" do people write, share or use eWOM advertising? How do Internet users generate and disseminate eWOM? Why do Internet users generate and disseminate eWOM? The first group of studies in this area investigates the "how" questions: opinion seeking- and providing- behaviors on the Internet, and the flow of information in online networks.

Information giving- and seeking- behaviors are defined as producing and eliciting eWOM (Fong & Burton, 2006). When consumers offer their opinions on products or services, eWOM is created. Sometimes consumers voluntarily offer their opinions, and sometimes they are replying to requests for information and recommendation. For example, when one looks for recommendations for cameras on an online discussion forum of photography, most of the feedback is eWOM. Information seeking and providing is an essential part of activities within online communities and online discussion groups. Nelson and Otnes (2005) examined the content on wedding message boards and found that brides-to-be often obtain wedding advice from trusted online communities. Fong and Burton (Dellarocas, 2003) examined two online discussion boards about photography and digital cameras. They found that most of the posts on the American discussion board were recommendation giving, whereas most of the posts on the Chinese discussion board were recommendation seeking posts. They concluded that Americans are more willing to generate opinions about products, namely eWOM, while Chinese consumers are more frequently seeking eWOM opinions. Jone, Denham, and Springston's (2006) study also connected information seeking with demographic features. They found that young women look for breast cancer screening information online more frequently than did middle-aged women.

Electronic word-of-mouth studies have also examined the inner structure of online networks and have examined how eWOM is disseminated among Internet users. First, the importance of opinion leaders in online social networks has been emphasized repeatedly by previous studies (Allsop, Bassett, & Hoskins, 2007; Fong & Burton, 2006; Kozinets, 1999; Stauss, 1997; Sun, Youn, Wu, & Kuntaraporn, 2006). Opinion leaders are participants who have a lot of knowledge on a subject matter and have strong ties with the online community. They frequently participate in online discussions, and can influence the opinions of online community members. People who are willing to try new products, who are experienced with the Internet, and who have strong ties with other online community members are more likely to be opinion leaders and more likely to generate eWOM (Sun, Youn, Wu, & Kuntaraporn, 2006).

Second, distribution of eWOM within an online community is highly concentrated and not randomly distributed among participants with a small number of members posting as much as 20% of the eWOM messages (Steyer, Garcia-Bardidia, & Quester, 2006). These findings suggest that marketers should identify those critical individuals who serve as opinion leaders in the online communities to which they belong, and start a conversation with these leaders to foster a relationship (Steyer, Garcia-Bardidia, & Quester, 2006) that can be used to benefit the brand and brand users.

In addition to answering questions about how eWOM is produced and disseminated, a fairly large proportion of research has sought to understand "why." Why do people seek and provide eWOM? What are their motives? Generally, there are four types of Internet motives: search, communicate, shop, and surf (Rodgers, Wang, Rettie, & Alpert, 2007). Motives for eliciting and producing eWOM identified by previous studies can be broadly broken down into the four categories. Table 2 provides some examples of motives of eliciting and producing eWOM.

Many specific types of motives have been identified by previous studies. Goldsmith and Horowitz (Goldsmith & Horowitz, 2006) revealed motivations for seeking eWOM. People seek eWOM from other consumers when they want to reduce risk, secure lower prices, get information easily, get pre-purchase information, or when they accidentally get or seek (unplanned) eWOM. People may also search intentionally for eWOM because others do it, because it is as much entertaining as it is informative, or because of offline promotions in traditional media such as TV or newspapers (Goldsmith & Horowitz, 2006). Hennig-Thurau and colleagues (2004) outlined five types of motivations underlying CGC and eWOM articulation: focus-related utility, consumption utility, approval utility, moderator-related utility, and homeostasis utility. Focus-related utility is the utility a consumer receives when adding value to the community through his or her eWOM contribution. Approval utility is consumers' satisfaction that comes from other members' approval. Moderator-related utility is derived from third-party interventions. Homeostasis utility refers to the function of virtual life that rebuilds psychological balance. Antecedents of eWOM-articulation were also identified. The willingness to experiment with new products, experience with the Internet, and Internet social connections are significant predictors of eWOM-articulation (Sun, Youn, Wu, & Kuntaraporn, 2006). Studies also examined motivations of a specific eWOM-related online activity. For example, by interviewing bloggers, Huang, Shen, Lin, and Chang (Huang, Shen, Lin, & Chang, 2007) identified five major motivations for blogging: self-expression, life documenting, commenting, forum participating, and information searching.

Information Processing and eWOM

Turning now to information processing, this category of research has focused on audience effects of eWOM, or how eWOM as a form of CGC influences consumers' attitudes and behav-

Table 2. Motives of eliciting and producing eWOM

Search	Communication	Shopping	Surfing
• Get information easily • Reduce their risk • Get pre-purchase information • Secure lower prices	• Focus-related utility • Approval utility • Internet social connection • Forum participating	• Consumption utility	• By accident/unplanned information seeking

iors (see Table 1). Findings show that eWOM is different from traditional WOM, and is more persuasive than business-to-consumer communication. For instance, Dellarocas' (2003) review of research on online feedback systems argues that an online feedback mechanism is different from traditional WOM since it has the potential to construct large-scale WOM networks. Therefore, it may have greater influence on brand reputation than traditional WOM. Bickart and Schindler (2001) compare the persuasive ability of CGC and corporation-generated product information. Their findings indicate that an online discussion is more persuasive than corporation-generated product information (Bickar & Schindler, 2001).

However, eWOM can influence attitudes in two-ways, positive and negative. For example, Thorson and Rodgers' (2006) study on eWOM within political blogs showed that simply the appearance of a feature, which enables the creation of eWOM and CGC was enough to form positive attitudes toward the political blog (Thorson & Rodgers, 2006). A recent study by Okazaki (2008) involving a mobile-based referral campaign showed that teenagers who heard about a mobile-based campaign from an eWOM source had more positive attitudes toward the campaign than those who learned about it from a website. Graham and Havlena (2007) by measuring the role of eWOM in an integrated promotion with online and offline strategies, argued that an integrated marketing plan should include online strategies, such as eWOM (Graham & Havlena, 2007).

However, as early as in 1997, Stauss (1997) pointed out that eWOM is a double-edged sword. Negative comments as a form of people's collective forces to protest can ultimately hurt a product and a company. For example, after examining the effects of an electronic feedback system on consumer trust, Benedicktus and Andrews (2006) found that several service failures could spread quickly in an electronic feedback system, and as a result consumers lose trust in the company rather quickly. Hung and Li's (2007) study also showed that the dual dynamics of eWOM posed both opportunities and challenges to marketers since consumers could become more critical toward products, services, and commercial promotions through peer-to-peer communications in online communities.

In addition to attitudes, eWOM may also influence purchase intention. For example, online comments and reviews were found to influence purchase intent for high-involvement products but not for low-involvement products (Riegner, 2007). High "buzz" levels on blogs can drive sales, and therefore are used as an indicator of sales forecasting in the consumer package goods (CPG) industry (Niederhoffer, Mooth, Wiesenfeld, & Gordon, 2007).

To summarize the previous two sections, studies from the functionalism and information processing perspectives add to our knowledge on motives for eliciting and providing eWOM, dissemination of eWOM, and influence of eWOM on consumers' responses. What is still missing from the bigger picture of eWOM is what eWOM "looks like" specifically the types, formats, and features of eWOM. Since knowing structural features of eWOM is the first step for marketers to learn how consumers are creating and talking about their products and services (Buroker, 2009), the structural approach is useful in that enables examination of the specific components, aspects, and features that are present in eWOM communication.

Structural Features of eWOM

The major structural aspects of eWOM include: types, formats, and features. Type refers to the general orientation of the communication about the eWOM product or service discussed. For instance, our earlier review showed that there are political and health-oriented types of eWOM. Format refers to the particular way that eWOM advertising is created or disseminated, as in the form of an online testimonial or a consumer online review. A feature refers to the distinguish characteristic or characteristics of an eWOM advertising messages. Just as advertisements contain a multitude of features or distinguishing characteristics (like emotional appeals or provocative visuals), eWOM could contain any number of structural features. In this chapter and consistent with our earlier summary, we chose to focus on three structural features: valence features, informational feature, and emotional features of eWOM. Given that so little is known about the particular features that consumers use to write or create eWOM advertising, we chose to focus the remainder of this chapter on examining the presence and practical usage of these three eWOM features.

First, we should note that unlike other forms of interactive advertising (like banner ads or commercial websites) where message structure has been frequently examined (Rodgers & Thorson, 2000), the structural school of thought is less popular among studies on eWOM. Some studies of the functional school of thought have examined the structural features of eWOM as a complement to their major studies (e.g., Hardey, 2001; Lieberman & Goldstein, 2005; and Nelson & Otnesm 2005). However, studies with a primary focus on the structural features of eWOM are few in number and appear much less frequently in the eWOM literature than studies within the information processing and functional schools of thought. An example of one study solely devoted to examining structural features of eWOM is Mason and Davis (2007) who focused on message features that reveal how participants of online discussions positioned and re-positioned themselves in interpersonal communication (Mason & Davis, 2007).

Because of the lack of studies on structural features of eWOM and the significance of such studies in areas where researchers and marketers have limited access (such as a breast-cancer online bulletin boards), this chapter attempts to fill the gap by presenting a case study of eWOM in an online breast cancer bulletin board. Medical topics such as breast cancer are sensitive, and commercial intervention into breast cancer online bulletin boards may introduce ethical issues, such as conflicts of interest. Because of these restrictions, the existing literature on health-related online bulletin boards focuses on the psychological support aspect and lacks a promotional perspective (Fogel, Albert, Schnabel, Ditkoff, & Neugut, 2002; Gustafson, Hawkins, Pingree, McTavish, Arora, Mendenhall et al., 2001; Hersh, 2006; Lieberman & Goldstein, 2005). However, an analysis of structural features from a promotional perspective can help to determine the features or specific characteristics used by individuals in describing their positive or negative attitudes toward various products and services, which can subsequently used to inform the literature on the various features that may be effective in disseminating eWOM as an effective tool for health promotion and other commercial promotions.

In addition to the value of exploring structural features of eWOM, there is another important reason to present this case study. As pointed out earlier, this focus is consistent with our earlier recommendation to modify the current definition of and extend existing studies on eWOM by focusing on non-traditional marketing contexts–such as health–and by looking at specific informational and emotional aspects of eWOM.

Thus, by analyzing eWOM on a breast cancer online bulletin board, we can extend existing studies in areas that are currently under-researched to enhance knowledge about not only eWOM in a traditional commercial context but also in non-traditional contexts where eWOM is occurring in a more naturalistic environment. Because of the special nature of health issues, the amount of information and the valence of emotion in health-related persuasion are two important aspects of health-related eWOM. First, eWOM provides opportunities to share personal experiences from the everyday consumers' perspective. Previous studies on health-related online discussions showed that emotions once aroused, set up a general tone for the message, which can also frame information conveyed during the online discussion (Dillard & Nabi, 2006; Lieberman & Goldstein, 2005). Therefore, health-related online discussion provides an excellent case study for examining emotional valence of eWOM occurring in a more natural setting to gain a better understanding of its components and features. Second, since personal stories are used to tell how a treatment or medication impacted an individual's life, we argue here that emotion is often more complex in a health-related eWOM context than in a commercial product and service-related eWOM context. Our case study, therefore, provides an opportunity to examine emotional valences beyond simply being negative or positive, but rather takes into consideration the various degrees and types of negativity or positivity as well.

To orient the reader, our analysis of structural features of eWOM on a breast cancer bulletin board concentrated on four structural features: the proportion of informational and emotional eWOM, to what extent eWOM was emotionally positive, negative, neutral, or mixed, what product types were mentioned in eWOM, and to what extent information-seeking and –providing was prevalent in those online discussions.

In addition to the three theoretical values mentioned above, a very important practical value of such an analysis is that online bulletin boards represent important outlets for gathering data about segmented audiences who share a common interest or bond. Potentially, marketers can make use of eWOM within online bulletin boards, and learn about their consumers, instead of using expensive data collection means such as focus groups and surveys. This could be especially useful for health communication professionals since they always need to plan and implement research-based health promotions with low budget.

EWOM ON A BREAST CANCER BULLETIN BOARD

Online breast cancer bulletin boards are virtual platforms used for sharing eWOM messages about breast cancer-related medical information and personal experiences. In the past, marketers have not been allowed in health-related online communities, and most studies to date have examined these environments from a non-commercial perspective (Godes & Mayzlin, 2004; Gustafson, Hawkins, Pingree, McTavish, Arora, Mendenhall et al., 2001; Hersh, 2006). While these studies serve to inform the present example and establish that people need online communication for health-related issues, the present research adds to existing literature by examining the promotional potential of the interactive forums. Drawing on the structural aspects of the IAM–and as outlined in this chapter - the purpose of this example is to explore the presence of structural features of eWOM to better understand the specific features and characteristics of eWOM occurring in a context in which breast cancer patients discuss products in the natural flow of conversation. The chosen method of investigation was a content analysis of 50 women's "life stories" randomly sampled from an online bulletin board, resulting in 2,166 instances of eWOM.

eWOM, Information, and Emotion

In the traditional model of health, doctors monopolized the medical information market (Hardey, 2001). The emergence of online communications, however, changed the traditional doctor-patient relationship (Hardey, 2001). Compared with professional recommendations from doctors, consumer-initiated communication is of less accuracy and quality. Therefore, accurate information is not the sole consideration of patients who participate in consumer-initiated communication. Emotion plays an important role in the conveyance of information (Lieberman & Goldstein, 2005). Emotion is regarded as important as cognition in achieving the goals of cancer communication (Dillard & Nabi, 2006). Since emotion is an important factor that can potentially impact the persuasive influence of health communication, it is worthwhile to examine the composition and valence of eWOM to determine the extent of its use in an online bulletin board. Therefore, the first two research questions in the current study are:

- RQ1: What is the proportion of emotion and information in eWOM?
- RQ2: What is the valence of emotions in eWOM?

When exchanging eWOM, cancer patients and survivors may also directly encourage people to purchase (or not purchase) certain products or services. So far, few previous studies show how frequently cancer patients offer direct recommendations in online consumer-to-consumer (C2C) communication. The current study takes a preliminary look at the frequencies of direct recommendations in eWOM and poses the research question:

- Q3: What are the features of direct recommending?

eWOM and Product Types

Product type may also influence persuasive techniques used in cancer-related communication. Cancer-related products are considered risk-driven since they are closely associated with cancer, a deadly disease (Lang, 2006). There are cancer prevention products, cancer detection products, and cancer therapies. Additionally, patients are also interested in non-medical products and services, which are frequently used in patient's daily life, such as wigs and bras. These products have different levels of risk. Research has shown that different cancer products are affected by persuasive information in different ways (Jones, Denham, & Springston, 2006). Therefore, another purpose of this content analysis is to examine the relationship between cancer product types and structural features of eWOM. In terms of product types, the current study has a larger scope than earlier studies in that product types range from ones about cancer prevention to non-medical products and services. At the same time, the present example also looks carefully at the subcategories under cancer prevention products, leading to the fourth and final research question.

- Q4: What, if any, are the differences of eWOM across product types?

Content Analysis

In this content analysis, the context was an online breast cancer bulletin board. We obtained a demographic profile of users that were coded as well as all the postings of 50 women who were randomly selected from the universe of individuals who use this particular bulletin board. In this way we were able to obtain each woman's "life story" that includes a timeframe of a few months to several years, depending on when the individual first visited the online community. Frequencies were calculated for the demographic information of the selected women. Most participants were cancer patients (95%) and the rest were adult children and/or spouses of cancer patients (5%). Participants were 31-65 years in age, with 22% under 40, 50% between 40 and 50 and 28% above 50. Only 20% of participants reported that they had children. Forty-four percent of participants reported that they were employed; 96% were married, and 4% were divorced.

Two graduate students individually coded the postings for eWOM, resulting in 2,166 separate instances of eWOM (excluding the "can't tell" category). The intercoder reliability, measured by Scott's Pi, was .80 based on 20% of the sample (Scott, 1955). The variables included: 1) types of eWOM appeals, 2) product types, 3) attitude, 4) informational valence, 5) emotional valence, and 6) recommending behaviors.

Types of eWOM Appeals

Types of eWOM appeals were defined as the type of persuasive techniques the eWOM uses to refer to the product. There were four sub-categories: emotional, informational, both, and can't tell. Emotional eWOM was defined as eWOM that arouse the feeling of fear, guilt, anger or happiness; informational eWOM was defined as eWOM about facts, data or numbers; the category of "both" meant that both emotional and informational eWOM appeared in one post. "Can't tell" was used when only the name of a product was mentioned, without any further information or comments, and coders could not decide whether it was informational or emotional or both. Such as, "my doctor gave me Effexor."

Product Types

Product type had six categories: cancer prevention products, cancer detection products, cancer therapeutic products, physical products, services, and others. Cancer prevention products were further divided into minerals, vitamins, food and vegetables, drinks, physical activity, and other.

Attitude

Attitude was defined as a participant's general views associated with the product/brand. Attitudinal valence is reflected by the global tone of the message containing products/brands and could be positive, negative, neutral (neither positive nor negative), mixed (both positive and negative).

Informational Valence and Emotional Valence

We also examined the valence of informational and emotional elements in the eWOM. The possible valence values for informational and emotional elements were positive, negative, neutral or mixed. To differentiate attitude, emotion, and information, an example is offered: a user wrote that she thought a cancer treatment was good for controlling her cancer, but she suffered from heart burning and poor appetite, which made her depressed. The post showed that the overall evaluation of the treatment was positive, which means the attitude toward the treatment was positive. At the same time, she offered negative information about the side effects of the treatment, and negative emotion associated with the treatment.

Recommending Behaviors

A direct recommendation refers to advice given about the brand or product (e.g., "try" this brand or this product). Participants used recommending behaviors to show a strong preference for certain products at the expense of others. Both recommendation-seeking and -giving behaviors were coded. Coders also evaluated the valence of recommendation behavior, coded as positive, negative or mixed (both positive and negative).

The unit of analysis was the individual posting. Both the name (pseudonym provided by the participant) of individuals who posted the message and the time of posting were coded to identify each post.

Statistical Analysis

After deleting the "can't tell" category for all variables (eWOM that only mentioned the name of a product), the resulting N of eWOM was 2,166, which the remainder of the analysis is based upon. This means that, on average, each woman wrote an average of 43 eWOM messages. As for the proportion of eWOM (RQ1), there were nearly three times as many informational (n = 1,371) as emotional (n = 409) appeals. Looking specifically at informational appeals, there were fewer negative (n = 606) and mixed (n = 272) messages and nearly equal numbers of neutral (n = 646) and positive (n = 642) ones.

For emotional appeals (RQ2), there were far more neutral (n = 1,377) than positive (n = 355), negative (n = 250) or mixed (n = 184) tones. However, when emotionality was shown, it tended to be more positive (n = 355) than negative (n = 250) ($\chi^2 = 511.798$, $p < .01$).

We also examined direct recommendations of eWOM (RQ3). First, the results show that direct recommending is common among participants. On average, every woman made six direct recommendations, and every 12.6 posting had a recommendation. Among these messages, 234 were recommendation seeking and 308 were recommendation giving. Direct recommendations were positive (n = 244) more so than negative (n = 23) or mixed (n = 41), which means that participants were inclined to encourage use of a product rather than discourage it.

To address RQ4, a cross-tabulation was calculated for emotional and informational appeals across product types. Cancer therapies were the predominant topic (n = 1,245) followed by discussions about physical products (n = 515), services (n = 178), cancer detection (n = 170), and cancer prevention (n = 58).

As shown in Table 3, the cross product comparison indicated that there was more informational than emotional eWOM for every product type ($\chi^2 = 21.87$, $p < .01$).

Table 4 shows that neutral emotion is the dominant type of emotional eWOM for all product categories, but each product type slightly differed from the rest on positive and negative emotional eWOM, proportionally. As shown in Table 4, there were more negative than positive emotions for cancer detection products, and more positive than negative emotions for cancer therapeutic treatments, physical products, and services ($\chi^2 = 76.71$, $p < .01$).

In contrast, there was almost equal numbers of neutral, positive, and negative informational eWOM in general, while eWOM with mixed informational valence value was the smallest category for all product types (Table 5). However, there were differences in valence value for specific product types. There was more neutral information about cancer detection products and cancer treatments than negative information or positive information. There was more positive information than negative information of physical products and services ($\chi^2 = 377.697$, $p < .01$).

In addition, product attitudes were also measured for eWOM in relation to product types. Results show that participants more frequently held positive attitudes toward cancer prevention products than negative attitudes (see Table 5). However, the reverse is true for cancer therapeutic

*Table 3. Product type * eWOM type*

		eWOM			Total
		Emotion	Information	Both	Total
Product	Cancer prevention product	7	44	7	58
	Cancer detection treatment	50	94	26	170
	Cancer therapeutic treatment	239	772	234	1245
	Physical product	88	340	87	515
	Service	25	121	32	178
Total		409	1371	386	2166

*Table 4. Product type * emotional valence*

		Emotion				Total
		Positive	Negative	Neutral	Mixed	
Product	Cancer prevention product	5	1	52	0	58
	Cancer detection treatment	26	32	90	22	170
	Cancer therapeutic treatment	186	168	783	108	1245
	Physical product	89	44	333	49	515
	Service	49	5	119	5	178
Total		355	250	1377	184	2166

*Table 5. Product type * information valence*

		Information				Total
		Positive	Negative	Neutral	Mixed	
Product	Cancer prevention product	34	9	13	2	58
	Cancer detection treatment	28	34	87	21	170
	Cancer therapeutic treatment	229	458	383	175	1245
	Physical product	219	100	129	67	515
	Service	132	5	34	7	178
Total		642	606	646	272	2166

products in that there were more negative than positive attitudes (χ^2 = 305. 471, p < 0.01). In contract to emotional valence, attitudes, i.e. the general tones of eWOM were most of the time positive rather than neutral.

Discussion of Content Analysis Results

The major findings of our study showed that eWOM predominantly took the form of informational (versus emotional) appeals. When emotion was revealed, eWOM was neutral most of the time, and there was more emotionally positive eWOM than emotionally negative eWOM. In other words, emotional negativity was not that common on the discussion board. This finding differed depending on which product type was examined.

The analysis of the structural features reveals several insights into eWOM on the breast cancer discussion board. First, it seems that eWOM in the breast cancer discussion forum have complex emotional valence values. There was a large proportion of emotionally neutral eWOM, and a considerable number of eWOM with mixed emotional valence. Second, eWOM in the breast cancer discussion forum was most of the time emotionally neutral. When emotionality was shown, eWOM was most of the time positive than negative for most product categories except cancer detection treatment. Based on the two observations, we can infer that the neutrality in emotion may be a result of avoidance of emotional negativity associated with cancer-related treatments, products, and service. A possible explanation of avoidance of negativity is that such online discussion forums are considered a place to reduce pressure from inflicting its deadly disease. Meaning, negativity may very well have been intentionally avoided by participants. This finding is in line with human nature avoiding pain and danger suggested by theories (Lang, 2006).

*Table 6. Product type * attitude valence*

		Attitude				Total
		Positive	Negative	Neutral	Mixed	
Product	Cancer prevention product	35	3	20	0	58
	Cancer detection treatment	48	38	55	29	170
	Cancer therapeutic treatment	349	434	310	152	1245
	Physical product	254	104	75	82	515
	Service	147	7	12	12	178
Total		833	586	472	275	2166

As pointed out in the previous paragraph, emotion associated with cancer detection treatments was most of the time neutral or negative. However, at the same time, people's attitudes toward cancer detection products were more frequently positive or neutral than negative. This seeming contradiction is understandable. Because cancer detection products are associated with high-risk consequences, i.e. having cancer, it is natural that cancer detection products are associated with negative emotion. However, at the same time, because of the usefulness of information provided by cancer detection products, the rational part of a human being leads people to form positive attitudes toward those products. Theoretically, this finding implies that the risk associated with certain health-related messages or behaviors leads to negative emotion, but it does not necessarily lead to negative attitudes toward the health-related messages or behaviors. The influence of cognition seems to play a more influential role than emotion in attitude-formation in cancer communication. Practically, the contradictory results imply that marketers may be better off emphasizing positive attitudes toward cancer screening in an attempt to avoid priming women's anxiety.

While participants may intentionally avoid negativity, a positive trend to encourage others to take actions was also observed. Participants also provided direct recommendations where they explicitly asked another participant to "try" a product or service, and this recommending behavior occurred most often in positive ways such that encourage use of a product/service versus discourage not using a product or service—again, emphasizing positive over negative information. Rationally, taking actions to cope with this medical condition increases the possibility of a cure rather than doing nothing. Appreciating the merit of taking actions, participants may consciously facilitate behavioral changes. This trend of emphasizing positive actions can also explain the phenomenon that there was much more emotionally neutral eWOM and slightly more emotionally positive eWOM than emotionally negative eWOM about cancer treatment products. Taking treatments most of the time introduces the possibility of getting better, and therefore, should be encouraged and facilitated. Theoretically, this finding implies that the processing of eWOM is a conscious and rational process, to a larger extent, and negative emotion is intentionally controlled. Instead, the rational mind of the participants created large amounts of emotionally neutral and positive eWOM of cancer treatments to facilitate this behavior among each other.

From the above discussion, we can see that analysis of structural features can provide useful information for both theoretical research and practical investigation. In addition, the results also demonstrated that the definition of eWOM should be modified in two ways as mentioned when defining eWOM. First, the understanding of products and brands should be extended. Over two thousand eWOM were identified on the breast cancer bulletin board, which showed that even health-oriented online discussions could generate large amount of eWOM. Besides eWOM about ordinary products such as wigs and bras, there were a lot of eWOM about cancer detection, treatment, and prevention procedures, services, and products. Those product types are different from the traditional concept of products and brands, but are of great importance to understand eWOM in the context of health promotion. Second, the definition of eWOM should be broadened to include more versatile classification of valence values. The case study presented here showed that neutral eWOM was a significant proportion of eWOM in the breast cancer online bulletin board. Neutral eWOM also provides useful information for theoretical explanations of eWOM and practical applications of eWOM. Specifically, since the frequency differences between emotionally positive and negative eWOM were most of the time small (most of the time < 50) in this case, the tendency of avoiding emotional negativity may be less unclear solely by simply looking at emotionally positive and negative eWOM. However, by incorporating emotionally neutral eWOM into the analysis, the large number of emotionally neutral eWOM made it evident that emotional negativity was avoided most of the time. Supposing that emotionally neutral eWOM were small in number, we would come to the conclusion that positive and negative emotions are generally balanced in the online discussion. From the above discussion, we can see that predominant neutrality existed in eWOM for a reason. In summary, the definition of eWOM should be extended to include consumer statements about more diverse products and brands, ranging from positive, negative, to neutral and mixed eWOM. eWOM should be further refined as "comments, recommendations, or any statements about products and services on the Internet."

SUMMARY

This book chapter sought to define and categorize electronic word-of-mouth (eWOM) based on different online platforms of consumer-generated content (CGC), review existing research in eWOM, and extending the use of eWOM to health promotion by examining characteristics of eWOM in an online breast cancer bulletin board. We began our chapter by situating eWOM within the broader CGC context and argued that the current definition of eWOM needs to be modified in two ways: by expanding the contexts within which eWOM occurs, for instance, health-related and non-commercial contexts versus traditional commercial contexts online; and by examining valence in terms of degree of positive versus negative eWOM as well as recognizing the role of informational versus emotional information conveyed in eWOM advertising. Relating eWOM to different online CGC platforms, this chapter describes two primary contexts, i.e., informational contexts such as online feedback systems and consumer review sites, and emotionally-oriented contexts in which strong connections and ties are formed with friends and family members who share similar interests, hobbies, values, etc., such as electronic discussion boards, online communities, and online social networking sites. Our chapter describes how these two contexts differ in terms of features and roles in the marketing communications mix.

In the second section of this chapter, we outlined a schemata based on Rodgers and Thorson's (2000) Interactive Advertising Model that helps to organize existing literature on eWOM in terms of three schools of thought: functionalism, information processing, and structuralism. Studies from the functional approach consisted of descriptive results based on consumers' eliciting and producing eWOM, patterns of dissemination, and motives of eliciting and producing eWOM. Studies from the perspective of information processing examined influences of eWOM on consumers' psychological response to eWOM including influences of eWOM on consumers' attitudes and purchase behaviors. Last, we examined structural features, including studies on types, formats, and features of eWOM, We argued that the structural features of eWOM is the least frequently examined area in the scholarly literature on eWOM and therefore requires additional research to provide greater understanding on eWOM is structured and what specific features are used in creating and disseminating eWOM.

From the review of eWOM this book chapter identifies two gaps in the eWOM literature: the lack of analysis of structural features in areas where researchers and practitioners have limited access, and the extension of the current definition of eWOM to include more valence values and product types, which is more realistic of how eWOM occurs. To address this, a case study of eWOM on a breast cancer online discussion board was presented in the third and final section of this chapter. The results revealed two trends: avoidance of emotional negativity, and encouragement of positive actions with regard to specific products and services. We discussed both theoretical and practical implications of these results. Since the neutrality of eWOM can also provide useful information we argued that the definition of eWOM should be extended to include more diverse categories of valence values. The large volume of eWOM created and shared by the women in the sample—especially eWOM about cancer detection, prevention, and treatment—indicates that the definition of eWOM should also take into account those types of "non-traditional" product types.

We hope that after reading this chapter, a clearer understanding of the concepts of eWOM and CGC can be gained. By pointing out the current definition of eWOM within the broader CGC literature, and by extending this definition, specifying types of eWOM, organizing the literature into the three schools of thoughts, and demonstrating the practical and theoretical uses of examining eWOM features within the context of a non-traditional consumer-generated forum, this book chapter offers readers a comprehensive summary of existing (and needed) eWOM studies to pursue new directions in research.

ACKNOWLEDGMENT

The authors wish to thank Petya Eckler, Doctoral Candidate, Missouri School of Journalism, for her assistance in editing this manuscript.

REFERENCES

Allsop, D., Bassett, B., & Hoskins, J. (2007). Word-of-Mouth research: Principles and applications. *Journal of Advertising Research, 47*(4), 398–411. doi:10.2501/S0021849907070419

Benedicktus, R. L., & Andrews, M. L. (2006). Building trust with consensus information: The effects of valence and sequence direction. *Journal of Interactive Advertising, 6*(2), 17–29.

Bickart, B., & Schindler, R. M. (2001). Internet forums as influential sources of consumer information. *Journal of Interactive Marketing, 15*(3), 31–40. doi:10.1002/dir.1014

Buckler, G. (2009). Businesses tap new markets with social media: Twitter, blogs and Facebook are becoming enterprise tools in their own right. *Special small business, business, Technology.* Retrieved from http://www6.lexisnexis.com/publisher/EndUser?Action=UserDisplayFullDocument&orgId=101735&topicId=101800040&docId=l:952641936&start=5

Buroker, J. (2009, April 1). Use online social networks to market your company. *Wisconsin State Journal,* 22.

Chiu, H., Hsieh, Y., Kao, Y., & Lee, M. (2007). The determinants of e-mail receivers' disseminating behaviors on the Internet. *Journal of Advertising Research, 47*(4), 524–534. doi:10.2501/S0021849907070547

De Bruyn, A., & Lilien, G. L. (2008). A multi-stage model of word of mouth through electronic referrals. *International Journal of Research in Marketing, 25*, 151–163. doi:10.1016/j.ijresmar.2008.03.004

Dellarocas, C. (2003). The digitization of word of mouth: Promise and challenges of online feedback mechanisms. *Management Science, 49*(10), 1407–1424. doi:10.1287/mnsc.49.10.1407.17308

Dillard, J. P., & Nabi, R. L. (2006). The persuasive influence of emotion in cancer prevention and detection message. *The Journal of Communication, 56*(S1), S123–S139. doi:10.1111/j.1460-2466.2006.00286.x

Eastin, M., & LaRose, R. (2003). *A social cognitive explanation of Internet uses and gratifications: Toward a new theory of media attendance.* Paper presented at the annual meeting of the International Communication Association, Marriott Hotel, San Diego, CA.

Evans, M., Wedande, G., Ralston, L., & Hul, S. (2001). Consumer interaction in the virtual era: Some qualitative insights. *Qualitative Market Research: An International Journal, 4*(3), 150–159. doi:10.1108/13522750110393053

Fogel, J., Albert, S. M., Schnabel, F., Ditkoff, B. A., & Neugut, A. I. (2002). Internet use and social support in women with breast cancer. *Health Psychology, 21*(4), 398–404. doi:10.1037/0278-6133.21.4.398

Fong, J., & Burton, S. (2006). Electronic word-of-mouth: A comparison of stated and revealed Behavior on electronic discussion boards. *Journal of Interactive Advertising, 6*(2), 61–70.

Godes, D., & Mayzlin, D. (2004). Using online conversations to study word-of-mouth communication. *Marketing Science, 23*(4), 545–560. doi:10.1287/mksc.1040.0071

Golan, G. J., & Zaidner, L. (2008). Creative strategies in viral advertising: An application of Taylor's six-segment message strategy wheel. *Journal of Computer-Mediated Communication, 13*(4), 959–972. doi:10.1111/j.1083-6101.2008.00426.x

Goldsmith, R. E., & Horowitz, D. (2006). Measuring motivations for online opinion speaking. *Journal of Interactive Advertising, 6*(2), 1–16.

Graham, J., & Havlena, W. (2007). Finding the missing link: Advertising's impact on word of mouth, Web searches, and site visits. *Journal of Advertising Research, 47*(4), 427–435. doi:10.2501/S0021849907070444

Gustafson, D. H., Hawkins, R., Pingree, S., McTavish, F., Arora, N. K., & Mendenhall, J. (2001). Effect of computer support on younger women with breast cancer. *Journal of General Internal Medicine, 16*(7), 435–445. doi:10.1046/j.1525-1497.2001.016007435.x

Hardey, M. (2001). 'E-health': The Internet and the transformation of patients into consumers and producers of health knowledge. *Information Communication and Society, 4*(3), 388–405.

Hennig-Thurau, T., Gwinner, K. P., Walsh, G., & Gremler, D. D. (2004). Electronic word-of-mouth via consumer-opinion platforms: What motivates consumers to articulate themselves on the Internet? *Journal of Interactive Marketing, 18*(1), 38–52. doi:10.1002/dir.10073

Hersh, A. (2006). *I know how you feel: A person-centered approach to supportive messages in online breast cancer groups.* Paper presented at the annual International Communication Association, New York, NY.

Horovitz, B. (2010, March 5). Oscar advertisers hope to build buzz on Twitter, Facebook. *USA Today*. Retrieved March 5, 2010, from http://www.usatoday.com/money/media/2010-03-05-oscarsocial05_ST_N.htm

Huang, C., Shen, Y., Lin, H., & Chang, S. (2007). Bloggers' motivations and behaviors: A model. *Journal of Advertising Research*, *47*(4), 472–484. doi:10.2501/S0021849907070493

Hung, K. H., & Li, S. Y. (2007). The influence of eWOM on virtual consumer communities: Social capital, consumer learning, and behavioral outcomes. *Journal of Advertising Research*, *47*(4), 485–495. doi:10.2501/S002184990707050X

Jones, K. O., Denham, B. E., & Springston, J. K. (2006). Effects of mass and interpersonal communication on breast cancer screening: Advancing agenda-setting theory in health contexts. *Journal of Applied Communication Research*, *34*(1), 94–113. doi:10.1080/00909880500420242

Kerlinger, F. H. (1986). *Foundations of Behavioral Research* (3rd ed.). New York: Holt, Reinhart & Winston.

Kozinets, R. V. (1999). E-tribalized marketing?: The strategy implications of virtual communities of consumption. *European Management Journal*, *17*(3), 252–264. doi:10.1016/S0263-2373(99)00004-3

Lang, A. (2006). Using the limited capacity model of motivated mediated message processing to design effective cancer communication messages. *The Journal of Communication*, *56*(S1), S57–S80. doi:10.1111/j.1460-2466.2006.00283.x

LaRose, R., & Eastin, M. (2004). A social cognitive theory of Internet uses and gratifications: Toward a new model of media attendance. *Journal of Broadcasting & Electronic Media*, *48*(3), 358–377. doi:10.1207/s15506878jobem4803_2

Lieberman, M. S., & Goldstein, B. A. (2005). Self-help on-line: An outcome evaluation of breast cancer bulletin boards. *Journal of Health Psychology*, *10*(6), 855–862. doi:10.1177/1359105305057319

Mason, P., & Davis, B. (2007). More than the words: Using stance-shift analysis to identify crucial opinions and attitudes in online focus groups. *Journal of Advertising Research*, *47*(4), 496–506. doi:10.2501/S0021849907070511

Nail, J. (2007). Visibility versus surprise: Which drives the greatest discussion of Super Bowl advertisements? *Journal of Advertising Research*, *47*(4), 412–419. doi:10.2501/S0021849907070420

Nelson, M. R., & Otnes, C. C. (2005). Exploring cross-cultural ambivalence: A netnography of intercultural wedding message boards. *Journal of Business Research*, *58*(1), 89–95. doi:10.1016/S0148-2963(02)00477-0

Niederhoffer, K., Mooth, R., Wiesenfeld, D., & Gordon, J. (2007). The origin and impact of CPG new-product buzz: Emerging trends and implications. *Journal of Advertising Research*, *47*(4), 420–426. doi:10.2501/S0021849907070432

Odden, L. (2009, April 1). Comprehensive guide to social media marketing from marketingsherpa. *Wisconsin State Journal*, 22.

Okazaki, S. (2008). Determinant factors of mobile-based word-of-mouth campaign referral among Japanese adolescents. *Psychology and Marketing*, *25*(8), 714–731. doi:10.1002/mar.20235

Peters, E., Lipkus, I., & Diefenbach, M. A. (2006). The functions of affect in health communications and in the construction of health preferences. *The Journal of Communication*, *56*(S1), S140–S162. doi:10.1111/j.1460-2466.2006.00287.x

Rappaport, S. (2007). Why we talk: The truth behind word-of- mouth: Seven reasons your customers will or will not talk about your brand. *Journal of Advertising Research, 47*(4), 535–536. doi:10.2501/S0021849907070560

Riegner, J. C. (2007). Word of mouth on the Web: The impact of Web 2.0 on consumer purchase decisions. *Journal of Advertising Research, 47*(4), 436–447. doi:10.2501/S0021849907070456

Rodgers, S., & Thorson, E. (2000). The interactive advertising model: How users perceive and process online. *Journal of Interactive Advertising, 1*(1).

Rodgers, S., Wang, Y., Rettie, R., & Alpert, F. (2007). The Web motivation inventory: replication, extension, and application to Internet advertising. *International Journal of Advertising, 26*(4), 447–476.

Rosenwald, M. (2010, March 29). Reputations at stake, companies try to alter word of mouth online. *Washington Post.* Retrieved March 31, 2010, from http://www.washingtonpost.com/wp-dyn/content/article/2010/03/28/AR2010032802905.html?hpid=sec-tech

Rothman, A. J., Bartels, R. D., Wlaschin, J., & Salovey, P. (2006). The strategic use of gain and loss framed messages to promote healthy behavior: How theory can inform practice. *The Journal of Communication, 56*, S202–S220. doi:10.1111/j.1460-2466.2006.00290.x

Scott, W. A. (1955). Reliability of content analysis: The case of nominal scale coding. *Public Opinion Quarterly, 17*, 321–325. doi:10.1086/266577

Senecal, S., & Nantel, J. (2004). The influence of online product recommendations on consumers' online choices. *Journal of Retailing, 80*, 159–169. doi:10.1016/j.jretai.2004.04.001

Shimp, T., Wood, S., & Smarandescu, L. (2007). Self-generated advertisements: Testimonials and the perils of consumer exaggeration. *Journal of Advertising Research, 47*(4), 453–461. doi:10.2501/S002184990707047X

Smith, T., Coyle, J., Lightfoot, E., & Scott, A. (2007). Reconsidering models of influence: The relationship between consumer social networks and word-of-mouth effectiveness. *Journal of Advertising Research, 47*(4), 387–397. doi:10.2501/S0021849907070407

Stauss, B. (1997). Global word of mouth, service bashing on the Internet is thorny issue. *Marketing Management, 6*(3), 28–30.

Steyer, A., Garcia-Bardidia, R., & Quester, P. (2006). Online discussion groups as social networks: An empirical investigation of word-of-mouth on the Internet. *Journal of Interactive Advertising, 6*(2), 51–60.

Sun, T., Youn, S., Wu, G., & Kuntaraporn, M. (2006). Online word-of-mouth (or mouse), An exploration of its antecedents and consequences. *Journal of Computer-Mediated Communication, 11*(4), 1104–1127. doi:10.1111/j.1083-6101.2006.00310.x

Thorson, K. S., & Rodgers, S. (2006). Relationships between blogs as eWOM and interactivity, perceived interactivity, and parasocial interaction. *Journal of Interactive Advertising, 6*(2), 39–50.

Vilpponen, A., Winter, S., & Sundqvist, S. (2006). Electronic word-of-mouth in online environments: Exploring referral network structure and adoption behavior. *Journal of Interactive Advertising, 6*(2), 63–77.

Vorro, A. (2009). Building the network: Recognizing the potential for relationship building, a number of insurers turn to social media. *Insurance Networking News: Executive Strategies for Technology Management, 4*(12), 1542–4901.

Chapter 12
Does *Second Life* Mark the Beginning of a New Era of Online Shopping?
Exploring the Avatar-Based Shopping Experience in Virtual Worlds

Jang Ho Moon
The University of Texas at Austin, USA

Yongjun Sung
The University of Texas at Austin, USA

Sejung Marina Choi
The University of Texas at Austin, USA

ABSTRACT

In this chapter, the authors explore the unique social dimension of shopping in virtual worlds, namely Second Life, by examining the role of avatar-based interactions in determining consumer shopping experience. To this end, an overview of Second Life, and other similar virtual worlds, is provided. This chapter then introduces the concept of social presence and offers a conceptual discussion of how avatar-based shopping in virtual environments is distinctive from shopping in other Web environments. Next, the authors present the preliminary findings of the ongoing research study investigating how consumers' interactions with salespersons and peer consumers via avatars influence their shopping experience in Second Life. This chapter concludes with a future prospect of virtual worlds and directions for future research.

INTRODUCTION

One of the most recent internet trends are virtual worlds. Just like the hugely successful web-based social networking sites, such as MySpace and Facebook, virtual worlds have emerged as "the next big thing" (Olga, 2007). Following the vast popularity of *Second Life*, a number of other virtual worlds have been created, and currently attract a wide range of people from around the

DOI: 10.4018/978-1-60566-792-8.ch012

world. According to a market research study by Kzero (2008), over 70 virtual worlds, including beta-test versions, are currently accessible. Many multinational corporations including Google, IBM, McDonalds, and Disney have leaped on the virtual world bandwagon and created virtual worlds of their own. Gartner, a technology analytical firm, predicts that 80 percent of the active internet users and Fortune 500 companies will participate in some type of virtual world by the end of 2011 (Gartner, 2007).

The mounting popularity of virtual worlds opens up new doors for marketers, and numerous real life companies, such as Coca-Cola, Dell, Nike, and NBC, have established their presence to appeal to their current and potential customers in the various virtual worlds. Moving beyond their initial attempt to create a mere presence through billboards and kiosks, marketers have begun more proactive efforts to explore the full potential of virtual worlds as a venue for marketing communications and interactions with consumers. Another promising business application of virtual worlds reflects the fast-growing number of consumers engaging in e-commerce in these virtual environments. For example, e-commerce transactions taking place in *Second Life* currently numbers in the thousands and generates significant real world revenue. Transactions involve numerous virtual items tailored for avatars, ranging from clothing to real estate.

From a consumer's standpoint, virtual worlds provide a unique online shopping experience. In virtual stores, consumers are able to obtain detailed product information, as well as try the 3D products. Real-time interactions with salespersons and other shoppers enhance the realism and social sense of the shopping experience. Most distinctive of shopping in a virtual world is that the avatar is the consumer. Avatars serve as a surrogate for consumers in virtual worlds. For this reason, it is expected that consumer behavior in virtual worlds is different from that in the brick-and-mortar real world or the traditional online shopping environments. Nevertheless, little is known about the unique characteristics of consumer behavior in virtual settings and the potential of the virtual worlds as an effective e-commerce venue.

The purpose of this chapter is, therefore, to explore the unique dimension of marketing and e-commerce in the virtual world, namely *Second Life* (SL), with an emphasis on the role of avatar-based social interactions in determining the consumer shopping experience. First, we present an overview of virtual worlds as an emerging marketing and shopping venue. In doing so, we discuss two notable marketing cases to illustrate the potential of virtual worlds in engaging consumers to shop and consume. Second, we introduce the concept of social presence and provide a conceptual discussion of how avatar-based shopping in multi-user virtual environments is distinctive from shopping in other Web environments, or the offline world. Next, we report our preliminary findings of on-going research that investigates how consumer interactions with salespersons and peer consumers via avatars influence their shopping experience in SL. This chapter concludes with a future prospect of shopping in virtual worlds and directions for future research.

MARKETING IN VIRTUAL WORLDS

There are two primary types of virtual worlds. The first type is called the Massively Multiplayer Online Role-Playing Games (MMORPGs). MMORPGs include games such as Lineage, World of Warcraft, and EverQuest. MMORPG is essentially a genre of computer role-playing games in which a multiple number of players simultaneously control their own game characters in a virtual fantasy world. The second type of virtual world consists of non-game virtual environments such as SL, There, Kaneva, and vSide. The latter tends to include game-like elements, but virtual environments in this category primarily offer a cyber hangout place for many people, wherein they engage in a multitude of activities with no geographic or time constraints. Users can enjoy a variety of socializing activities in these virtual environments such as clubbing, dating, taking educational courses, attending music concerts, and shopping, which are less purposive, but more social in nature than those found in MMORPGs.

Among the virtual worlds currently available, *Second Life*, which began in 2003, is perhaps the most popular. As of September 2008, *Second Life* had over 14 million users from around the world.

Several factors characterize SL, the first of which is social interactions. Social interactions are one of the major activities among SL users; they meet new people, converse and do things together in real time. Within the virtual world of SL, individuals have the opportunity to form and maintain virtual friendships and become involved in various communities and organizations. Therefore, SL is essentially a social medium that integrates a number of advanced communication technologies, such as chat rooms, video games, user-generated contents and instant messaging, thereby enabling its users to enjoy a variety of online activities with others, ranging from social networking to virtual shopping (Siklos, 2006).

Second, users of SL encompass a more general population, unlike other virtual worlds, such as typical MMORPGs for gamers that are targeted at a specific population. As shown in Figure 1, as of January 2008, approximately 35% of SL users are between the ages of 25 - 34, followed by the age groups of 18 - 24 (25%) and 35 - 44 (24%), respectively. Interestingly, 15% of SL users are over the age of 45. As for gender, the SL user population is quite balanced: 59% of its users are male and 41% are female. In addition, SL is internationally diversified. Users log in from over 105 countries including the United States (35%), Germany (8%), United Kingdom (8%), Japan (6%), and France (5%). These demographic characteristics suggest that SL can be a cost-effective marketing channel for marketers to reach a wide range of adult consumers across the globe.

Third, SL has its own currency, called Linden Dollars. Linden Dollars are freely tradable with real money. As of August 2008, one U.S. dollar was equivalent to 270 Linden Dollars. Although people buy and sell virtual goods in SL, the money involved in the transactions is real. According to the Linden Lab, the inventor of SL, economic activities in SL averaged over 1.5 million U.S.

Figure 1. Second Life Monthly Active Users by Age (Second Life, 2008)

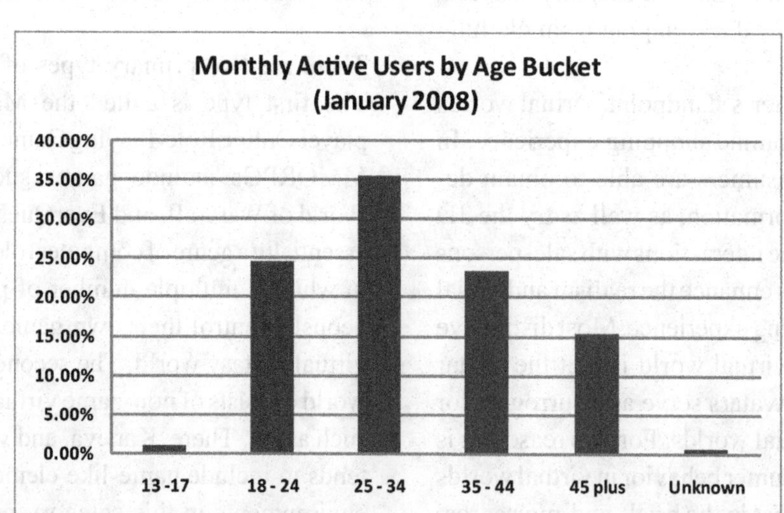

$ per day in 2007 (Linden Lab, 2007). This suggests the strong potential of SL as an e-commerce venue, wherein marketers can look after a lucrative market with unconventional communication strategies and promotional ideas.

With the growing realization of the abovementioned unique characteristics of SL, and its upside potential, marketers have progressively entered into this virtual world and embarked on various ventures. Table 1 presents a list of corporations that have established a virtual presence in SL. We will discuss two of the corporations in detail: the American Apparel and Toyota Scion.

The Case of American Apparel

American Apparel, a Los Angeles-based clothing company known for its provocative advertising and sweatshop-free products, is a pioneering marketer in SL. With the recognition that SL users are similar to its primary target market in the real world, American Apparel decided to market itself in the SL. American Apparel opened its virtual store in SL in June 2006 and became the first real-world retailer to have a store in SL. At this virtual store, SL users can buy American Apparel products for their avatars. These products typically cost less than $1. In a deliberate effort to convey its consistent brand image to SL users, American Apparel's virtual store aesthetically matched its "real-world" stores (Figure 2).

Table 1. Examples of Product and Service Brands in Second Life

Product/ Service Category	Brand
Automobiles	Toyota, BMW, Mercedes Benz, Pontiac, Mazda, Nissan
IT	Intel, Cisco, AMD, IBM, Sun Microsystems, Microsoft
Media	Reuters, BBC, Sky News, AOL, Channel 4
Entertainment	MTV, Sony BMG, Sundance
Retail	Armani, Adidas, Reebok, American Apparel, Circuit City, Sears
Telecoms	Vodafone, Sony Ericcson

The company's most interesting and innovative promotion for their virtual store was the "Be Your Own Twin" campaign. That is, when consumers buy a virtual product with their avatars from American Apparel's SL store, they receive a 15% discount on the same item for themselves in real life. For example, if a consumer purchases a virtual Pom-Pom Beanie for his/her avatar, the consumer will receive a 15%-off coupon for the purchase of a real Pom-Pom Beanie at American Apparel's "real" online store. This unprecedented marketing strategy was successful in that it comprehended and capitalized on the unique, dual-identity experience of consumers in SL. While avatars perform all activities in SL, real people create and control the avatars. They can therefore enjoy a vicarious experience in SL through their avatars. Due to the close connection between a virtual identity and a real identity, consumers might consider purchasing the same products for themselves, especially if they see their avatars benefitting from using the products.

Case of Toyota Scion

Scion is a youth-focused compact automobile manufactured by Toyota. Scion's marketing strategy is to maintain a special, cool, and cutting-edge brand identity. To successfully accomplish this, Scion has reduced its advertising budget for traditional mass media and has undertaken non-traditional marketing efforts via experiential events, branded entertainment, and social networking sites. This wasn't always the case. In 2006, MySpace.com was considered too mainstream for Scion. Scion then decided to establish a virtual presence in SL to successfully reach the young, trend-setting, and tech-savvy population.

In November 2006, Toyota launched "Scion City," a gigantic virtual automotive dealership in SL (Figure 3). Toyota was the first automotive manufacturer to initiate marketing communica-

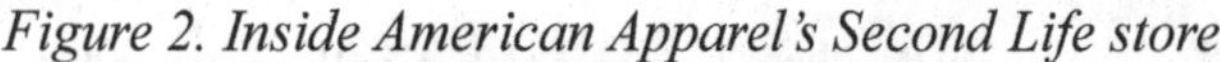

Figure 2. Inside American Apparel's Second Life store

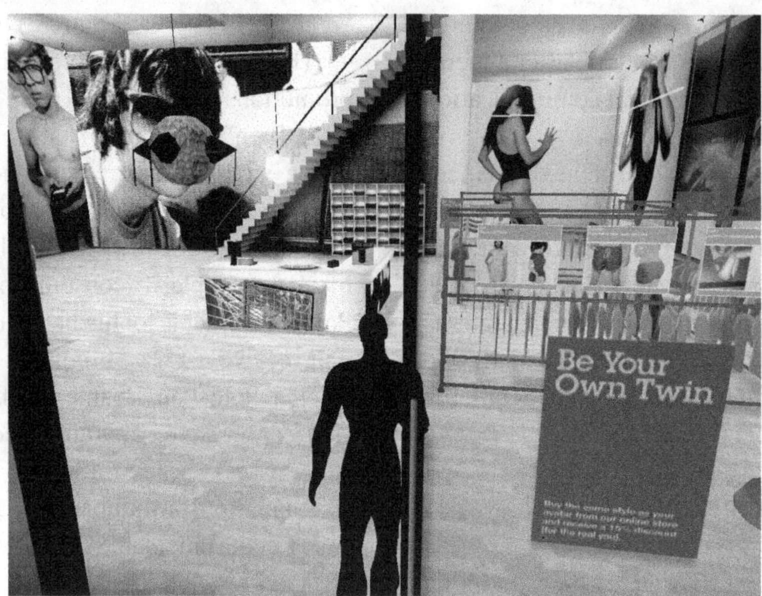

tions in SL. When their avatars climb into a virtual Scion, SL users can view and experience expertly rendered interior details, such as the dashboard, steering wheel, and seats. The users can also have their avatars test-drive various Scion models. If they like the car after test-driving it, they can buy a virtual Scion for their avatars for 300 Linden Dollars, which translated to about $1 at that time frame.

Virtual driving cannot compare to driving a car in real life, and virtual automobiles are not necessary for SL avatars, as they are able to freely

Figure 3. Scion's Second Life Dealership

teleport and fly anywhere. Yet, this virtual driving experience provides users with an opportunity to actively participate with the product, rather than passively obtain product information from seeing advertising, reading news articles or visiting the website. In this way, virtual consumption can generate stronger consumer interest and consumer-brand connection, which may result in real-world purchases.

Lessons from the Cases

The above two cases of brand marketing in SL provide the reader with a snapshot of the current state of virtual worlds for business applications and illustrate the potential of SL and other similar virtual worlds, as an effective venue for nurturing consumer-brand relationships and generating revenues for marketers. The essential element of the two cases is the smart adaptation of the concept of virtual shopping for their marketing communication strategies in the avatar-based environments.

A study by Li, Daugherty, and Biocca (2003) revealed that marketers can increase the values of product information they present to consumers, by creating compelling virtual experiences with their products. In this way, American Apparel and Scion have successfully provided a venue wherein consumers could virtually experience company products through their avatars and promotional campaigns, which, in turn, can draw consumers to the virtual establishments.

While the aforementioned marketing campaigns shed some light on the successful business applications of virtual worlds, they have not fully capitalized on the distinctive nature of communal cyber places and have neglected the most essential aspect of consumer behavior in such environments. Central to the uniqueness of consumer behavior in the virtual world is the real-time based, social interactions via the form of avatars. For instance, what if the virtual Scion dealership was staffed by salesperson avatars that greeted and assisted every visitor? What if consumers shopped with their friends in the virtual store of American Apparel? Adding such a social dimension to the virtual experience may enhance the effectiveness of the marketing campaigns.

In the following sections, we bring a theoretical lens to our understanding of consumer behavior in the emerging virtual worlds and recommend a systematic stream of research models that empirically investigates the topic that is focused on the social dimension of the avatar-based, virtual experience. More specifically, a conceptual framework for explicating the virtual consumer behavior in a shopping context will be presented and the preliminary findings in support of the theoretical notion will be discussed.

VIRTUAL SHOPPING AND SOCIAL PRESENCE

Shopping in Virtual Worlds

The literature has suggested that virtual reality technology presents promising potential for e-commerce applications, since it simulates physical goods in a realistic manner (Walsh & Pawlowski, 2002). Virtual product simulation permits consumers to virtually experience products (Jiang & Behbasat, 2002; Ryan, 2001). A virtual reality experience, such as this, can improve consumer product knowledge, brand attitude and purchase intention (Klein, 2003; Li, Daugherty, & Biocca, 2002). However, prior studies suggest that virtual reality alone is not sufficient to create consumer satisfaction. Even web-based online shopping lacks social interactivity (Hou & Rego, 2002) and does not allow for consumer interaction with a salesperson (Ernst & Young, 1999). Research findings indicate that the most significant inhibitor of web-based online shopping is the absence of pleasurable experiences, social interaction, and personal consultation by a sales representative (Barlow, Siddiqui, & Mannion, 2004).

In summary, prior research suggests that both interpersonal interaction and social experiences are the two key dimensions in which the current web-based online shopping can improve. In this view, SL-like, multi-user, virtual worlds combined with their avatar features can serve as an ideal setting for virtual shopping that enables social interaction and experiences which are currently lacking in other virtual environments.

Avatar-Based Social Interaction in Virtual Worlds

SL and other similar virtual worlds appear to be a promising venue for online shopping, because they add a rich social dimension to the typical one-way shopping experience through avatar-based interpersonal communication. An avatar is defined as "a general graphic representation that is personified by means of computer technology" (Holzwarth, Janiszewski, & Neumann, 2006, p. 20), or put more simply, it is "a representation of the user as an animated character in virtual worlds" (Loos, 2003, p. 17). Avatars have the potential to enrich interpersonal communications and bonds by allowing consumers to engage in more dynamic, intimate, and meaningful conversations (Vasalou, Joinson, & Pitt, 2007). In this regard, avatars can fulfill a consumers' desire for interpersonal communications and social experience in their virtual shopping experience. In the form of avatars, consumers can undertake a variety of shopping activities (e.g., browsing, window-shopping) in a vivid manner. Social encounters and interactions during shopping are visually manifested in a similar way as they do in real life (e.g., seeing and meeting other shoppers and shopping with friends) that are not obtainable in traditional web-based shopping (Papadopoulou, 2007).

In essence, consumer avatars in virtual worlds can communicate with salespeople and peer consumer avatars in real time, while browsing and shopping. Such social interactions allow consumers to enjoy a more realistic, credible, and attractive shopping experience. Given that the lack of one-on-one interaction is a major weakness of traditional online shopping, virtual worlds present a breakthrough to online shopping, by providing a socially fulfilling shopping experience. For this reason, avatars, and the social interaction among them, should be considered the most significant features of the consumer shopping experience in the virtual world.

Social Presence in Virtual Worlds

The concept of social presence provides a useful theoretical framework for understanding the unique social aspect of consumer behavior in virtual worlds, expressed in the form of avatars. Social presence is one crucial dimension of presence, the sense of "being with others" in a mediated environment (Biocca, Harms, & Burgoon, 2003). Originating from the incipient work by Short, Williams and Christie (1976), social presence has been studied as an important construct in understanding individuals' experiences in various mediated environments. At the outset, social presence was conceptualized as a quality of the communication medium and defined as "the degree of salience of the other person in [an] interaction and the consequent salience of the interpersonal relationships" (Short, Williams, & Christie, 1976, p. 65). More recently, Heeter (1992) referred to social presence as "the extent to which other beings in the world appear to exist and react to the user" (p. 265). Similarly, other scholars have described social presence as a feeling of "co-presence" (Mason, 1994) or "virtual togetherness" (Durlach & Slater, 2000). In summary, social presence is an individuals' sense of "being together" with others in a mediated environment.

Several studies have demonstrated the impact of social presence on an individuals' experience in a mediated environment. The social presence perception generated by an avatar at a web-based shopping site was found to increase consumer satisfaction with the retailer, attitude toward the product and purchase intention (Holzwarth, Janiszewski, & Neumann, 2006). Prior studies also suggest that anthropomorphic agents, such as virtual salespeople, enhance social presence in virtual environments (e.g., Nowak & Biocca, 2003; Sivaramakrishnan et al., 2007; Skalski & Tamborini, 2007). Furthermore, individuals experience greater social presence when perceiving an avatar as a digital representation of another human being, than when viewing the avatar as a computer-controlled agent (Guadagno et al., 2007).

In SL, avatars can easily interact with each other via an instant messaging type of chatting tool, or a voice chatting function. In this way, people can network with their existing friends, make new friends, and form various types of social groups. Therefore, in SL, and other virtual worlds, people can experience a strong social presence through avatar-based social behaviors. Given the sound social aptitude of virtual worlds like SL, consumers can shop in a more socially engaging fashion by communicating with peer consumers and salespeople in real time while shopping. The following section discusses these interactions with the two most important parties involved in the shopping experience: the peer shoppers and the salespeople.

Interaction with Peer Shoppers

A notable social interaction while shopping in virtual worlds is the "shopping with friend" experience. A friend that provides aid to a shopper's decision making process is identified in the literature as a "purchase pal" (Bell, 1967; Furse et al., 1984; Hartmen & Kicker, 1991; Midgely, 1983). Purchase pals are formally defined as "individuals who accompany buyers on their shopping trips in order to assist them with their on-site purchase decisions" (Hartman & Kiecker, 1991, p.462). The role of purchase pals varies. Purchase pals structure decision problems, provide information, evaluate products and alternatives, negotiate prices, and help make final decisions with the buyers. Real world examples of purchase pal use includes inexperienced automobile purchasers relying on their fathers in their evaluation of products (Furse, Punj, & Stewart, 1984), husbands obtaining assistance from their wives in their suit purchasing decisions (Midgley, 1983), and shoppers turning to friends or relatives who assist them in negotiating prices (Bell, 1967).

Previous research suggests that shopping with purchase pals is an enjoyable activity. Both adults and teen shoppers reported that having "fun" was an important motivation for shopping with others (Hartman & Kicker, 1991; Mangleburg et al., 2004). Previous findings also indicate that the enjoyment of shopping with friends favorably influences the shopper's behavior. Consumers tend to spend more money when shopping with their friends, than when shopping alone (Granbois, 1968; Mangleburg et al., 2004; Sommer et al., 1992; Woodside & Sims, 1976). Furthermore, shopping with a friend reduces the perception of risk and uncertainty that buyers associate with a big purchase decision and increases the buyers' confidence in that a wise purchase decision was made (Kiecker & Hartman, 1994).

In summary, shopping with others, and social interactions with them, at the point of purchase can influence a consumers' actual purchase decisions. Based on the existing literature of real life shopping experiences, it is reasonable to believe that the virtual shoppers' shopping experience and their purchase decisions could be influenced by the peer shoppers accompanying them. As discussed previously, SL enables users to engage in social functions and manifests these social interactions in vivid 3D graphical images. In this virtual environment, consumers can enjoy the "shopping with others" experience in a similar way as they enjoy a co-shopping experience in real life.

Interaction with Virtual Salespersons

Another significant feature enhancing the shopping experience in virtual worlds is the presence of salespeople, more precisely, salesperson avatars. A number of virtual stores in SL employ virtual salespersons to assist customers and improve their shopping experience by providing a socially engaging environment. Previous studies suggest that interactive agents, such as virtual salespersons, enhance social presence (Sivaramakrishman et al., 2007; Skalski & Tamborini, 2007). Consumers experience greater social presence in response to anthropomorphic agents that are visually represented (Nowak & Biocca, 2003).

Salesperson avatars can also enhance trust in e-commerce. Nowak and Rauh (2005) indicate that consumers perceive anthropomorphic avatars as more credible than non-anthropomorphic avatars. Similarly, a virtual personal advisor, which is another type of salesperson, can enhance trust (Cassell & Bickmore, 2000; Urban et al., 2000). Retailing literature has also proposed that virtual sales agents can increase the pleasure of the shopping experience, similar to offline shopping encounters (Reynolds & Beatty, 1999). Taken together, the previous research findings suggest that shopping in virtual worlds, wherein salesperson avatars are available and interactions between consumer avatars and the salesperson avatars are visually represented, can exceedingly enhance the consumer shopping experience in terms of social presence, store and product attitudes, satisfaction, and purchase intentions.

Preliminary Research

In light of the previous conceptual discussion, SL-like virtual worlds can be understood as a socially interactive and fulfilling shopping environment with a strong social presence. Unlike conventional web-based shopping, shopping in these virtual worlds provides a unique opportunity for consumers to observe the presence of others, including sales personnel and peer shoppers, in visual format and communicate with them. While such interactions take place via avatars, shopping experiences in virtual worlds are similar to those in the real world, as consumers in virtual worlds perceive avatars as representations of real human beings. In addition, virtual worlds, like SL, enable avatars to take the form of sophisticated 3D-graphic anthropomorphic representations. These avatar forms further enhance the realism of the interactions in virtual environments. As a result, consumers are believed to experience a strong sense of social presence while shopping in virtual worlds.

The preliminary findings of an ongoing research project have provided empirical evidence in support of the aforementioned role of avatars, in determining consumer shopping experiences in the virtual world. More specifically, the first part of the study addresses the question of how interactions with other avatars, particularly those of salespersons and peer shoppers, influence the consumers' sense of social presence, as well as store and brand evaluations. To assess the impact of the presence of salesperson and peer consumer avatars, a 2 (salesperson vs. no salesperson) × 2 (peer consumer vs. no peer consumer) between-subjects experimental design was employed. A virtual retail store of a fictitious clothing brand (i.e., MOON) was created in SL as an experimental setting (Figure 4). A total of 80 subjects (28 males and 53 females) participated in the study. The subjects were randomly assigned to one of the four experimental conditions. They were given instructions that they were invited to do a beta test of the virtual store for a new apparel brand being introduced. After reading the instructions, the subjects were asked to shop around in the virtual store for 5 minutes and then answer a series of questions gauging their social presence perception and product and store evaluations. The subjects were then debriefed and dismissed.

Results of a series of two-way analysis of variance (ANOVA) showed positive effects on the presence of both salesperson and peer consumer avatars on the subjects' responses to the shopping experience. That is, subjects who interacted with salespersons or peer consumer

Figure 4. The virtual retail store used in the experiment

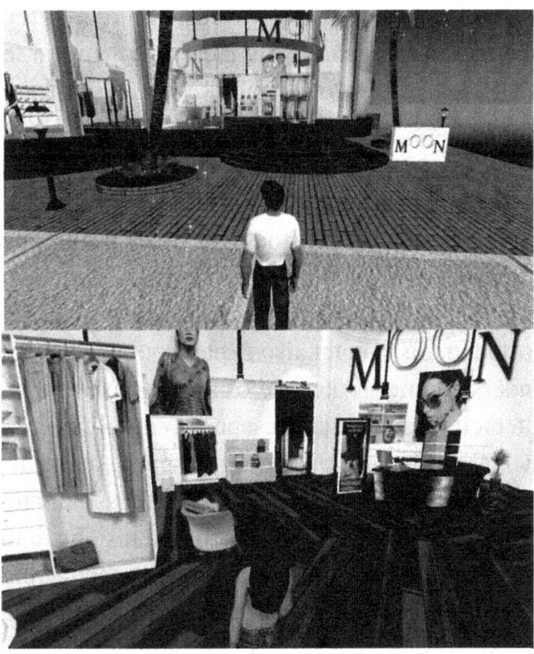

avatars, exhibited higher levels of social presence, store trust, store enjoyment, store attitude, brand attitude, and purchase intentions, than did those who had no interactions with either salesperson or peer consumer avatars. Overall, the findings of this preliminary study lend empirical support for the hypothesized positive role of social interactions with both salespersons and peer consumer avatars in the virtual shopping environment. In light of these findings, creating a strong sense of social presence via social interactions among avatars should be a primary strategic focus of virtual shopping.

FUTURE RESEARCH DIRECTIONS

In his interview with *Business Week in 2007*, Bob Moore, a virtual world researcher at Palo Alto Research Center predicted that three-dimensional virtual worlds will become the pervasive interfaces in the near future (Hof, 2007). Many other researchers and experts of virtual worlds further envisage the prosperity of virtual worlds in a far more realistic, interactive and social form (Hof, 2007). Avatars are predicted to continue to be a key element of the upcoming internet renovation, but only in a different type. In their effort to integrate virtual worlds into the current World Wide Web and create an interoperable 3D internet, IBM and Linden Lab have decided to collaborate on the invention of "universal" avatars, which will enable the exploration of multiple virtual worlds and other traditional Websites that permit a single avatar identity.

Virtual world shopping is also predicted to expand. While business in virtual worlds mainly targets avatars, marketers have begun to develop virtual shopping stores for real-life consumers with real goods. Companies such as View22 and Kinset have constructed 3D virtual stores for major marketers including Brookstone, Kohler, and GE, to name a few. In the future, the conventional online shopping environment will be transformed to a SL type of virtual shopping milieu. This conversion will change how consumers shop online. To illustrate, one could shop at the Gap virtual store with his/her friends even if they are physically miles apart. Their avatars meet and converse with each other via voice messaging, while they walk through the aisles together searching for new clothing. They can try on clothing that is set to their body measurements and spin around to show their friends. In addition, if they have questions or need assistance, they can easily find the virtual salesperson. This is the embodiment of real life shopping in a virtual manner, which leads to consumer satisfaction through a realistic, enjoyable, and social shopping experience.

Research in this area is still in its early stages, and several issues appear to warrant future research attention, in light of the future prospect of virtual worlds for business applications. First, the nature of social presence consumers experience during a virtual shopping experience is something that needs further investigation. Interactions with salesperson and peer shopper avatars might lead to differing levels of social presence. Second, the unique vicarious experience through the surrogates of avatars in virtual worlds calls for careful examination. It would be interesting to see if the consumer decision-making process and their influencing factors vary with their shopping needs. That is, consumers purchase products for themselves, or for their avatars, in virtual worlds, and social presence and other environmental factors might have differential impacts in these two situations. Another issue for future research to delve into is the interplay of real life relationships, and virtual world interactions, in affecting consumers' social presence perception and shopping experience. While this study has explored the impact of the presence of other unfamiliar shoppers, it is not known if co-shopping with their existing purchase pals, perhaps their real-life friends, exerts a greater influence on consumers' shopping experiences in the virtual shopping context. Findings of future studies on these topics should significantly advance our theoretical knowledge in this area and assist scholars in identifying additional research agendas.

CONCLUSION

In the present chapter, we discussed and examined the impact of avatar-based consumer interactions in determining their shopping experience in virtual worlds, namely, the SL. In the view of the literature and empirical findings of our preliminary study, virtual worlds open up a new door for shopping and begin a novel era of online shopping by providing a socially engaging environment. Unlike conventional web-based commerce, shopping in virtual worlds enables consumers to observe the presence of others, including sales personnel and peer shoppers, in a visual format and freely interact with them. While such interactions occur via avatars, shopping experiences in virtual worlds are decidedly similar to those found in the real world. Since the lack of one-on-one interactions has been noted as a major obstacle to current online shopping, virtual worlds, wherein social interactions are manifestly incarnated, appear to be an ideal setting for socially fulfilling shopping experiences.

To our knowledge, the present chapter offers the first formal discussion of the social dimension of shopping in virtual worlds by presenting empirical evidence in support of the theoretical notion. The findings of the preliminary study reported in this chapter also expand our conceptual understanding of the role of avatar-based social interactions and social presence in virtual environments, particularly in virtual shopping contexts. Managerially, the theoretical discussion and empirical findings together provide insights into the design of effective approaches to persuading consumers in emerging virtual worlds. Promoting social presence and a socially engaging shopping environment should be of vital importance to marketers in their efforts to attract and retain customers, and to establish desirable relationships with them in virtual worlds.

REFERENCES

Barlow, A. K. J., Siddiqui, N. Q., & Mannion, M. (2004). Developments in information and communication technologies for retail marketing channels. *International Journal of Retail & Distribution Management*, *32*(2/3), 157–163. doi:10.1108/09590550410524948

Bell, G. D. (1967). Self-confidence and persuasion in car buying. *JMR, Journal of Marketing Research*, *4*(1), 46–52. doi:10.2307/3150163

Biocca, F., Harms, C., & Burgoon, J. K. (2003). Toward a more robust theory and measure of social presence: Review and suggested criteria. *Presence (Cambridge, Mass.)*, *12*(5), 456–480. doi:10.1162/105474603322761270

Cassell, J., & Bickmore, T. (2000). External manifestations of trustworthiness in the interface. *Communications of the ACM, 43*(12), 50–56. doi:10.1145/355112.355123

Durlach, N., & Slater, M. (2000). Presence in shared virtual environments and virtual togetherness. *Presence (Cambridge, Mass.), 9*(2), 214–217. doi:10.1162/105474600566736

Ernst & Young. (1999). *The Second Annual Ernst & Young Internet Shopping Study: The Digital Channel Continues to Gather Steam*. Ernst & Young Publication, Ernst & Young LLP.

Furse, D. H., Punj, G., & Stewart, D. W. (1984). A typology of individual search strategies among purchasers of new automobiles. *The Journal of Consumer Research, 10*(4), 417–431. doi:10.1086/208980

Gartner. (2007, April 24). *Gartner Says 80 Percent of Active Internet Users Will Have A Second Life in the Virtual World by the End of 2011*. Retrieved May 5, 2008, from http://www.gartner.com/it/page.jsp?id=503861

Granbois, D. H. (1968, October). Improving the study of customer in-store behavior. *Journal of Marketing, 32*, 28–32. doi:10.2307/1249334

Guadagno, R., Blascovish, J., Bilenson, J., & Mccall, C. (2007). Virtual humans and persuasion: The effects of agency and behavioral realism. *Media Psychology, 10*, 1–22.

Hartman, C. L., & Kiecker, P. L. (1991). Marketplace influencers at the point of purchase: The role of purchase pals in consumer decision making. In *1991 AMA summer educators' conference proceedings* (pp. 461–469). Chicago: American Marketing Association.

Heeter, C. (1992). Being there: the subjective experience of presence. *Presence (Cambridge, Mass.), 1*(2), 262–271.

Hof, R. (2007, April 16). The Coming Virtual Web. *Business Week*. Retrieved June 15, 2007, from http://www.businessweek.com/technology/content/apr2007/tc20070416_780263.htm

Holzwarth, M., Janiszewski, C., & Neumann, M. M. (2006). The influence of avatars on online consumer shopping behavior. *Journal of Marketing, 70*, 19–36. doi:10.1509/jmkg.70.4.19

Hou, J., & Rego, C. (2002). *Internet Marketing: an Overview*. University of Mississippi Working Paper. Retrieved June 15, 2007 from http://faculty.bus.olemiss.edu/crego/papers/hces0802.pdf

Jiang, Z., & Benbasat, I. (2002). *Virtual Product Experience: Effects of Visual & Functionality Control of Products on Perceived Diagnosticity in Electronic Shopping*. University of British Columbia.

Kiecker, P., & Hartman, C. L. (1994). Predicting buyers' selection of interpersonal sources: The role of strong and weak ties. In Allen, C. T., & John, D. R. (Eds.), *Advances in consumer research* (*Vol. 21*, pp. 464–469). Provo, UT: Association for Consumer Research.

Klein, L. R. (2003). Creating virtual product experiences: the role of telepresence. *Journal of Interactive Marketing, 17*(1), 42–55. doi:10.1002/dir.10046

Kzero. (2008). *The virtual worlds universe*. Retrieved August 30, 2008, from http://www.kzero.co.uk/blog/?page_id=2092

Li, H., Daugherty, T., & Biocca, F. (2002). Impact of 3-D advertising on product knowledge, brand attitude, and purchase intention: The mediating role of presence. *Journal of Advertising, 31*(3), 43–57.

Li, H., Daugherty, T., & Biocca, F. (2003). The role of virtual experience in consumer learning. *Journal of Consumer Psychology, 13*(4), 395–407. doi:10.1207/S15327663JCP1304_07

Linden Lab. (2007). *Economics.* Retrieved May 2008, from http://lindenlab.com/pressroom/general/factsheets/economics

Loos, P. (2003). *Avatar, in lexicon electronic business* (Schildhauer, T., Ed.). Munich, Germany: Oldenbourg.

Mangleburg, T. F., Doney, P. M., & Bristol, T. (2004). Shopping with friends and teens' susceptibility to peer influence. *Journal of Retailing, 80*(2), 101–116. doi:10.1016/j.jretai.2004.04.005

Mason, R. (1994). *Using communications media in open and flexible learning.* London: Kogan Page.

Midgley, D. F. (1983). Patterns of interpersonal information seeking for the purchase of a symbolic product. *JMR, Journal of Marketing Research, 20*(1), 74–83. doi:10.2307/3151414

Nowak, K. L., & Biocca, F. (2003). The effect of the agency and anthropomorphism on users' sense of telepresence, copresence, and social presence in virtual environments. *Presence (Cambridge, Mass.), 12*(5), 481–494. doi:10.1162/105474603322761289

Nowak, K. L., & Rauh, C. (2005). The influence of the avatar on online perceptions of anthropomorphism, androgyny, credibility, homophily, and attraction. *Journal of Computer-Mediated Communication, 11*(1), 153–178. doi:10.1111/j.1083-6101.2006.tb00308.x

Olga, K. (2007, May 22). Virtual World Gold Rush. *BusinessWeek.com.* Retrieved June 15, 2007, from http://www.businessweek.com/technology/content/may2007/tc20070522_380944.htm

Papadopoulou, P. (2007). Applying virtual reality for trust-building e-commerce environments. *Virtual Reality (Waltham Cross), 11*(2), 107–127. doi:10.1007/s10055-006-0059-x

Reynolds, K. E., & Beatty, S. E. (1999). Customer benefits and company consequences of customer–salesperson relationships in retailing. *Journal of Retailing, 75*(1), 11–32. doi:10.1016/S0022-4359(99)80002-5

Ryan, C. (2001). Virtual reality in marketing. *Direct Marketing, 63*(12), 57–62.

Second Life. (2007). Economy Statistics. *Second Life.* Retrieved June 15, 2007, from http://blog.secondlife.com/2006/12/12/growth-of-second-life-community-and-economy/

Short, J., Williams, E., & Christie, B. (1976). *The social psychology of telecommunications.* London: John Wiley and Sons.

Siklos, R. (2006, October 19). A Virtual World but Real Money. *The New York Times.* Retrieved June 15, 2007, from http://www.nytimes.com/2006/10/19/technology/19virtual.html?ex=1183521600&en=9370daefa88875de&ei=5070

Sivaramakrishnan, S., Wan, F., & Tang, Z. (2007). Giving an e-human touch to e-tailing: The moderating roles of static information quantity and consumption motive in the effectiveness of an anthropomorphic information agent. *Journal of Interactive Marketing, 21*(1), 60–75. doi:10.1002/dir.20075

Skalski, P., & Tamborini, R. (2007). The role of social presence in interactive agent-based persuasion. *Media Psychology, 10,* 385–413.

Sommer, R., Wynes, M., & Brinkley, G. (1992). Social facilitation effects in shopping behavior. *Environment and Behavior, 24*(3), 285–297. doi:10.1177/0013916592243001

Urban, G. L., Sultan, F., & Qualls, W. (2000). Making trust the center of your Internet strategy. *Sloan Management Review, 1,* 39–48.

Vasalou, M., Joinson, A. N., & Pitt, J. (2007). Constructing my online self: avatars that increase self-focused attention. In *Proceedings of the SIGCHI conference on Human factors in computing systems* (pp. 445-448). New York: ACM Press.

Walsh, K. R., & Pawlowski, S. D. (2002). Virtual reality: a technology in need of IS research. *Communications of the Association for Information Systems, 8*, 297–313.

Woodside, A. G., & Sims, J. T. (1976). Retail sales transactions and customer 'purchase pal' effects on buying behavior. *Journal of Retailing, 52*(3), 57–64.

ADDITIONAL READING

Argo, J. J., Dahl, D. W., & Manchanda, R. V. (2005). The Influence of a Mere Social

Bagozzi, R. P., & Dholakia, U. M. (2002). Intentional social action in virtual communities. *Journal of Interactive Marketing, 16*(2), 2–21. doi:10.1002/dir.10006

Bailenson, J. N., & Yee, N. (2006). A longitudinal study, of task performance, head movements, subjective report, simulator sickness, and transformed social interaction in collaborative virtual environments. *Presence (Cambridge, Mass.), 15*(6), 699–716. doi:10.1162/pres.15.6.699

Bailenson, J. N., Yee, N., Merget, D., & Schroeder, R. (2006). The effect of behavioral realism and form realism of real-time avatar faces on verbal disclosure, nonverbal disclosure, emotion recognition, and copresence in dyadic interaction. *Presence (Cambridge, Mass.), 15*(4), 359–372. doi:10.1162/pres.15.4.359

Fiore, A. M., Kim, J., & Lee, H. (2005). Effect of image interactivity technology on consumer responses toward the online retailer. *Journal of Interactive Marketing, 19*(3), 38–53. doi:10.1002/dir.20042

Gerhard, M., Moore, D., & Hobbs, D. (2004). Embodiment and copresence in collaborative interfaces. *International Journal of Human-Computer Studies, 61*(4), 453–480. doi:10.1016/j.ijhcs.2003.12.014

Hassanein, K., & Head, M. (2006). The impact of infusing social presence in the Web interface: An investigation across different products. *International Journal of Electronic Commerce, 10*(2), 31–55. doi:10.2753/JEC1086-4415100202

Hemp, P. (2006). Avatar-based marketing. *Harvard Business Review, 84*(6), 48–56.

Hof, R. (2006, May 1). My Virtual Life. *Business Week*. Retrieved June 15, 2007, from http://www.businessweek.com/magazine/content/06_18/b3982001.htm

Holbrook, M. B., & Hirschman, E. C. (1982). The experiential aspects of consumption: Consumer fantasies, feelings and fun. *The Journal of Consumer Research, 9*, 132–140. doi:10.1086/208906

Huang, S., & Lin, F. (2007). The design and evaluation of an intelligent sales agent for online persuasion and negotiation. *Electronic Commerce Research and Applications, 6*(3), 285–296. doi:10.1016/j.elerap.2006.06.001

Hyman, P. (2007, October 15). More Virtual Worlds: Yes, Really. *Business Week*. Retrieved October 30, 2007 from http://www.businessweek.com/innovate/content/oct2007/id20071015_036882.htm

Kim, J., & Forsythe, S. (2007). Hedonic usage of product virtualization technologies in online apparel shopping. *International Journal of Retail & Distribution Management*, *35*, 501–514. doi:10.1108/09590550710750368

Kim, J., & Forsythe, S. (2008). Adoption of Virtual Try-on technology for online apparel shopping. *Journal of Interactive Marketing*, *22*(2), 45–59. doi:10.1002/dir.20113

Lee, K. M. (2004). Presence, explicated. *Communication Theory*, *14*(1), 27–50. doi:10.1111/j.1468-2885.2004.tb00302.x

Li, H., Daugherty, T., & Biocca, F. (2001). Characteristics of virtual experience in electronic commerce: A protocol analysis. *Journal of Interactive Marketing*, *15*(3), 13–30. doi:10.1002/dir.1013

Lo Priore, C., Castelnuovo, G., Liccione, D., & Liccione, D. (2003). Experience with VSTORE: Considerations on presence in virtual environments for effective neuropsychological rehabilitation of executive functions. *Cyberpsychology & Behavior*, *6*(3), 281–287. doi:10.1089/109493103322011579

McConnon, A. (2007, August 13). Just Ahead: The Web As A Virtual World. *Business Week*. Retrieved December 15, 2007, from http://www.businessweek.com/magazine/content/07_33/b4046064.htm?chan=technology_technology+index+page_best+of+the+magazine

(n.d.). Presence in a retail context. *The Journal of Consumer Research*, *32*(2), 207. doi:10.1086/432230

Riva, G. (1999). Virtual reality as communication tool: A socio-cognitive analysis. *Presence (Cambridge, Mass.)*, *8*(4), 462–468. doi:10.1162/105474699566341

Sallnas, E. L. (2005). Effects of communication mode on social presence, virtual presence, and performance in collaborative virtual environments. *Presence (Cambridge, Mass.)*, *14*(4), 434–449. doi:10.1162/105474605774785253

Schlosser, A. E. (2003). Experiencing products in the virtual world: The role of goal and imagery in influencing attitudes versus purchase intention. *The Journal of Consumer Research*, *30*, 184–197. doi:10.1086/376807

Schroeder, R. (2002). Social Interaction in Virtual Environments: Key Issues, Common Themes, and a Framework for Research. In Schroeder, R. (Ed.), *The Social Life of Avatars: Presence and Interaction in Shared Virtual Environments* (pp. 1–18). London: Springer.

Takahashi, D. (2007, October). Investment in virtual worlds tops $1 billion in past year. *The Mercury News*. Retrieved October 30, 2007 from http://blogs.mercurynews.com/aei/2007/10/investment_in_virtual_worlds_tops_1_billion_in_past_year.html

Whitney, S. L., Sparto, P. J., Hodges, L. F., Babu, S. V., Furman, J. M., & Redfern, M. S. (2006). Responses to a virtual reality grocery store in persons with and without vestibular dysfunction. *Cyberpsychology & Behavior*, *9*(2), 152–156. doi:10.1089/cpb.2006.9.152

Yee, N. (2006). The demographics, motivations and derived experiences of users of massively-multiuser online graphical environments. *Presence (Cambridge, Mass.)*, *15*, 309–329. doi:10.1162/pres.15.3.309

KEY TERMS AND DEFINITIONS

Avatar: 2D or 3D animated digital representation of the user in the virtual world. They are typically customized by their user.

Second Life: *Second Life* is one of the most widely known non-game virtual worlds, where over 14 million internet users (as of September 2008) from around the world are registered.

Social Presence: Social presence is the users' visual and emotional sense of being in the same space with other users, which is evoked by an experience of real-time communication activities or social interactions with other users in virtual worlds.

Virtual Co-Shopping: Virtual co-shopping is a "shopping together" experience in thc virtual world where multiple avatars shop together in the same virtual store in real-time.

Virtual Salesperson: Virtual salesperson is an employee avatar of the virtual store that helps virtual shoppers by providing product information and recommending products. These virtual salespersons are controlled by a real human being.

Virtual Shopping: Virtual shopping is an online consumer shopping activity in a virtual world, where a shoppers' avatar can see and interact with other avatar shoppers and salespersons while they are shopping in the digital replica of a real world brick-and-mortar store.

Virtual World: A virtual world is a computer-mediated online environment combining either 2D or 3D graphics with the text-based or voice message-based communication system. This environment allows multiple avatars to interact with each other at the same time.

Chapter 13
Consumer Generated Advertising in Blogs

Dilip Mutum
University of Warwick, UK

Qing Wang
University of Warwick, UK

ABSTRACT

Blogs are the newest and potentially most attractive online media available to marketers. This chapter discusses the unique nature of blogs and the growing power of consumer generated content. This raises a number of questions as well as new opportunities. As the authors point out that existing literature on blog marketing only discusses the possible advantages of using blogs as a marketing tool and the addition of blogs into the marketing mix. However, the problem is that these studies totally ignored consumers' perception towards blogs that carry advertisements. The rise of advertising companies that have stepped in to fill the gap between companies and bloggers, are discussed. Some examples of successful blog advertising campaigns are also provided. This chapter also presents a conceptual model that examines the salient factors that are likely to influence consumer attitude towards blogs and towards advertising in blogs, and more specifically on sponsored posts on blogs. It is hoped that this chapter would encourage other researchers to take a look at this unique media which in turn will help shed new light on how blogs are enabling a new model of consumer collaboration and consumer generated advertising.

INTRODUCTION

The Advent of Blogs as a New Online Media

Of the various online media available to marketers, "Blogs" are the newest and potentially the most attractive. They have become a part of what Deighton and Kornfeld (2007) describes as a "digital interactive transformation in marketing." This revolution shows no signs of slowing down and according to a report by Universal-McCann (2009) on the impact of social media, 71 percent of active internet users read blogs. Blog participation has also increased with more people leaving comments (an increase to over 50 percent in 2009). The

DOI: 10.4018/978-1-60566-792-8.ch013

report also shows that over 29 percent of Internet users have blogged about a product or brand. Furthermore, according to Technorati's State of the Blogosphere 2008 report, approximately 133 million blogs (Winn, 2009) were indexed by Technorati, as compared to approximately 70 million blogs in 2007 (Sifry, 2007). Interestingly, the 2008 Technorati report also mentions that a majority of bloggers (54 percent) had advertising on their blogs (White, 2009). Another report by the Pew Internet and American Life Project in 2008 (Smith, 2008), reveals that 12 percent of internet users have created or work on their own online journal or blog, while about 33 percent of all American internet users read blogs. In Europe, around three percent or four million Internet users actively write blogs (Forrester, 2006). Blogging has also gained wide acceptance in Asia. Take a look at Malaysia for example. A survey by Microsoft Malaysia revealed that nearly half (41 percent) of people online are actively blogging (Microsoft, 2006). While in China, the number of bloggers is expected to cross the 100 million mark (SinoCast, 2006). It is no wonder that the word "Blog" was chosen as the top word of 2004 by Merriam-Webster (BBC, 2004).

The term "weblog", was first coined by Jorn Barger on his *Robot Wisdom* website on 17 December 1997 (Kottke, 2003). A few years later, in the mid of 1999, Peter Merholz, came up with the word "blog" after breaking the word weblog into the phrase "we blog" in the sidebar of his blog Peterme.com (Kottke, 2003). Though some authors argue that the word is not a *portmanteau* of the word web and log, the terms 'blog', 'weblog' and 'web log' are often used interchangeably (Economist, 2006; Kottke, 2003). Various authors have also defined the word 'blog' differently. The popular belief that blogs are "personal online journals" (BBC, 2004) may not be accurate as most blogs are "public" and interactive in nature (Adamic & Glance, 2005; Kelleher, 2006; Marken, 2005). A number of blogs focus on specific topics ranging from politics and sports to entertainment and technology. It is also not uncommon for bloggers (person who write blogs) to have more than one blog with multiple themes. Some of the well-known blogs like Slashdot (http://slashdot.org/), Engadget (http://www.engadget.com/) and Boing Boing (http://boingboing.net/), have multiple contributors as well.

A better definition of the word 'Blog' was given by Wright (2006) who defines it as a web page that contains regularly posted inlays that are archived and arranged in reverse chronological order. *The Oxford Dictionary of Modern Slang* defines it as 'an Internet website containing an eclectic and frequently updated assortment of items of interest to its author' (Ayto & Simpson, 2005). Our definition of blog recognises their interactive nature and the fact that there may be more than one author. Thus, we define a blog as an "interactive website with posts that are updated frequently and may contain links, images, video or music clips, of interest to its author or authors that are archived and arranged in reverse chronological order."

Brad L. Grahamon was the first person to use the term "Blogosphere" on his blog on September 10, 1999. It was re-coined by William Quick later in 2002. He wrote "I propose a name for the intellectual cyberspace we bloggers occupy: the Blogosphere." It later gained popular usage and is now commonly used to refer to the community of blogs, bloggers and blog posts (Wright, 2006).

The fact that a huge number of companies including Google, General Motors and a host of others, have started their own corporate blogs, is an indication of this growing realisation of the importance of blogs (Lee, Hwang, & Lee, 2006; Moulds, 2007). Blogging among CEOs have also becoming increasingly popular and the list includes Jonathan Schwartz, CEO of Sun Microsystems (http://blogs.sun.com/jonathan/) and Guy Kawasaki, CEO of Fog city Software (http://blog.guykawasaki.com/). It is estimated that 58 (11.6%) of the Fortune 500 companies have business blogs (Socialtext.net, 2008).

Most previous blog studies have focussed on bloggers and their motivations for blogging (Kumar, Novak, Raghavan, & Tomkins, 2004; Trammell & Keshelashvili, 2005). Other studies have focussed on the credibility of blogs as a source of information, especially with reference to news blogs, while others look at ways in which companies can set up and the benefits of having a corporate blog.

Though online advertising has been researched extensively, especially in the Western countries, very limited lifestyle or attitudinal studies, has been carried out on consumers concerning their perception of advertising on blogs. Some of the literature that exists on blog marketing only discusses the possible advantages of using blogs as a marketing tool and the addition of blogs into the marketing mix (Koeppel, 2007; Ron & Tasra, 2007). However, the problem is that these studies totally ignore the perception of consumers towards blogs that carry advertisements and sponsored posts. There is still not sufficient evidence to show that blogs are better or worse than other media concerning their effectiveness as an advertising medium.

Businesses are naturally wary of investing in such a new medium when its long-term development prospect remains largely unknown. The existing research has not addressed the issue of the motivations that drive consumers to visit blogs nor linked it to the consumer attitudes towards blogs. Furthermore, credibility of blogs that carry sponsored posts, promoting a company, their products and/ or services remain largely un-researched.

Consumer Generated Advertising

Blogs are consumer generated, digital 'word of mouth' transmission of information. They are also interactive in nature allowing bloggers and visitors to exchange ideas. This conversational nature of blogs makes them ideal for building and maintaining computer-mediated relationships (Kelleher, 2006; Marken, 2005). Most scholars recognise the importance of interpersonal influence and word-of-mouth (WOM) communications in this process (Litvin, Goldsmith, & Pan, 2008). Looking at it from the marketing perspective, WOM was initially defined as "face-to-face communication about products or companies among those people who were not commercial entities" (Litvin et al., 2008). Later Westbrook (1987) differentiated WOM from other mass-media channels to define it as: "all informal communications directed at other consumers about the ownership, usage, or characteristics of particular goods and services or their sellers." WOM is one of the mechanisms that customers use to evaluate alternatives in the overall consumer decision process. Review of literature indicates that, WOM might actually be the major driver of the diffusion or adoption of new products or services (Bass, 1969; Hu, Pavlou, & Zhang, 2006).

The advent of the Internet and computer-mediated communication has given rise to what is known as electronic word-of-mouth or eWOM (Gruen, Osmonbekov, & Czaplewski, 2006) and bloggers are part of this. Research has indicated that eWOM may be a more credible source of information to customers than other sources of information created by marketers (Bickart & Schindler, 2001). Bloggers are opinion leaders and they recommend products when they like them – "almost 70% of them tell their friends" (Forrester, 2006). This conversational nature of blogs makes them ideal for building and maintaining computer-mediated relationships (Kelleher, 2006; Marken, 2005).

All these developments have given rise to some issues of concern. Despite the rapid growth of blogs and their potential to revolutionise the media and advertising industry, many conflicting views exist as to whether and how such potential, if any, may be realised. People's attitudes towards using blogs for commercial activity also differ vastly, some believe that it enables the shift of locus and control of marketing communication from companies to consumers, facilitates open participation and hence is a positive progress towards democratisation. On the other hand, others believe that using blogs for any form of commercial activity like consumer generated advertising will destroy the blogosphere's credibility (Kirkpatrick, 2006). Therefore, the objective of this chapter is not only to provide a relatively comprehensive review of the advent of blogs as a new online media, but more importantly to conceptually examine the salient factors which are likely to influence consumer attitude towards blogs and towards advertising in blogs, i.e. the "consumer generated advertising."

A NEW MODEL OF MARKETING COMMUNICATION

Consumer Decision Making Model

When we talk about marketing communications, we need to firstly consider the classic hierarchy-of-effects (HOE) model. The model is widely-used to explain consumer decision making process. The classic traditional hierarchy framework asserts that a consumer goes through a three-stage process: *cognitive*, which refers to the awareness or learning something new; *affective*, when they develop feeling, interest or desire; and finally *behavioural*, when the customer takes action. There are so many different HOE models in marketing literature but the most cited is the one that was initially developed by Lavidge and Steiner (1961) who stated that advertising effects occur over a period of time and in specific stages. According to them, consumers go through six steps before the actual purchase, namely, 1) Awareness, 2) Knowledge, 3) Liking, 4) Preference, 5) Conviction and finally 6) Purchase. This traditional hierarchy of advertising effects models has been widely debated and even attacked by a number of scholars (Barry, 2002; Barry & Howard, 1990; Weilbacher, 2001), with some questioning the linear progression as well as the sequence of steps. Despite these criticisms, this model does provide a framework for marketing academics and practitioners to understand consumer's responses to marketing communication.

The advent of consumer generated content including blogs raises a number of questions as well as new opportunities. There is a need to examine how consumers react to different advertising formats in this new medium. The results of an experiment by Bruner & Kumar (2000) indicate that the advertising hierarchy-of-effects as seen in the traditional media can be transferred to websites as well. However, it is still unclear as to how the concept of online interactivity can be readily incorporated into this model.

In the traditional consumer decision making model, consumers are assumed to go through five stages in decision process in a linear fashion (Blackwell, Miniard, & Engel, 2001). This involves an increase in complexity as you go along the steps in the decision process and in the process needing more cognitive effort. Thus, they start with 'problem or need recognition' followed by 'search'. Consumers would then evaluate the available alternatives and finally make a choice. They will then go for an evaluation of their decision (Schiffman & Kanuk, 1994:566-580; Solomon, 1996:268). There have been a number of alternative models that are extensions or modifications of the traditional linear model. However, the problem with this model was that it assumes the consumer as living in a vacuum and looks at them as problem solvers. The fact is that consumers live in a community and interact with other consumers. With the advent of online communities including blogs, such communication and interaction become not less but more prominent and are in real time. For example, consumers may suddenly come across a new gadget that has just been launched on a gadget blog. While going through the specifications and deciding whether to buy it, the reviews and comments or other customers regarding this gadget is readily available and can be used to help make the decision there and then.

On the other hand, traditional marketing communication is mostly one way information flow from the companies to the customers. Advertising agencies usually plan, create and implement advertising campaigns or other forms of promotion for their clients. The clients dictate their objectives and usually have a role in shaping the campaign. However, the creative work is left up to the agencies. Now, with online media such as blogs, companies can interact directly with customers in their corporate blogs or by providing incentives for bloggers to review or write about their products and services. This may be in line with McKenna's (1991) strategic view of relationship marketing where the customer is placed first and which involves genuine customer involvement. Blogs are enabling a new model of consumer collaboration, and in turn, they are affecting the locus of control of marketing communication. In other words, consumer generated advertising has created a new commercial path for business to consumers.

Marketing Communication in Blogs

The earliest forms of advertising to appear on blogs were the graphical banner or text ads. In this respect, Google or more specifically the Google adsense program is the market leader for contextual advertising solutions, whereby targeted advertisements are automatically displayed based on the content on the blog. A few companies later started to sponsor content on blogs to create awareness and/or to promote their products and services. This led to the growth of a new branch of marketing communication known as 'Consumer Generated Advertising' (Walker 2006), which refers to sponsored content on blogs, wikis, forums, etc. Based on the presence of advertising, blogs can be broadly categorised into those with graphical advertisements and those with sponsored content. The differentiation between the graphical advertisements and sponsored content is quite important. As opposed to the graphical ads which have been around on websites for quite some time, sponsored content on blogs is a relatively new development in online advertising. It refers to blog entries or posts and may be in the form of feedbacks, reviews, opinion, videos, etc. and usually contain a link back to the desired site using a keyword.

Two main questions arise, namely how would the blog visitors react to these posts and whether carrying the advertisements and/ or sponsored posts would lower the credibility of the blogs carrying them. Researchers have just begun to examine these issues.

As mentioned earlier, one of the major implications of the advent of consumer generated advertising has been the reduction of intermediaries between companies and their customers. Companies that traditionally used advertising agencies to reach out to their customers can now instead approach consumers directly using corporate blogs or via bloggers, who are consumers themselves (see Figure 1).

To some, the idea that bloggers would take over campaigns normally run by ad agencies with million dollar budgets, may seem like pipe dream but some companies have actually gone ahead and are actively working with bloggers. This disintermediation has resulted in the breakdown of the traditional advertising model where the advertising agencies were usually the only interface with the customer. For instance in the UK, when British mobile company Hutchison 3G UK Limited launched the 3 Skypephone, the company contacted prominent bloggers throughout the country. The bloggers were given free samples and then asked to review the mobile phones. News and reviews of the phones around the web were then carried on the 3mobilebuzz blog (http://www.3mobilebuzz.com). This could have backfired if the bloggers had written negative reviews but it was a calculated risk. As it turns out, most of the reviews were positive. Boeing is another example of a company that used blogs to create a dialogue with their potential customers. During

Figure 1. Advertising routes and emergence of consumer generated advertising

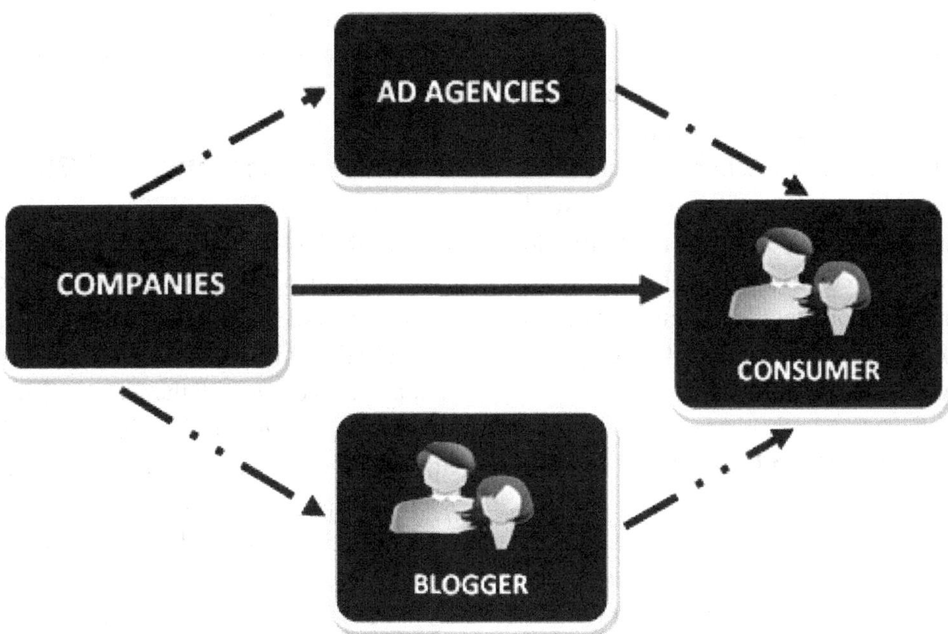

the development of their 787 Dreamliner plane, they actively used blogs to spread information about the plane mainly through the blog of Randy Baseler, the vice president of marketing (http://boeingblogs.com/randy/). He also responded to posts about the plane on other blogs as well.

Of course, it would be wrong to assume that there has been a complete disintermediation between businesses and the consumers. Despite the fact that traditional advertising firms have been slow to adopt this new medium, several start-up companies specialised in consumer generated advertising on blogs have stepped in to fill this vacuum. Blogitive, which started in early 2006, was the first online service to pay bloggers on a per-post basis (Shull, 2006). However, the present market leader for consumer generated advertising is Izea (formerly known as PayPerPost.com), an Orlando based startup. The company has been going from strength to strength (Hof, 2006) and have even secured funding from investors. This is a clear indication that some companies have realised the importance of the role that blogs play in the new model of marketing communication (Economist, 2006; D. Kirkpatrick & Roth, 2005; Wright, 2006).

CONSUMER ATTITUDE TOWARDS BLOGS AND ADVERTISING IN BLOGS: TOWARDS A CONCEPTUAL MODEL

Before we can even start to understand the consumers' attitude toward sponsored posts or what is called "consumer generated advertising", we need to understand why they like to visit blogs in the first place and in particular, why they prefer some blogs more than others. According to Chang & Wang (2008), consumer attitude and behavioural intention toward online media is affected by users' internal and external motivation and perceived interactivity, such as ease of use, usefulness and flow experience. In an experimental study looking at perceived interactivity of three websites, the need for cognition was shown to be an antecedent of perceived interactivity and it was the significant predictor that influenced perceptions of high or low interactivity of websites (Jee & Lee, 2002). In addition, credibility perceptions with regards to the blogger are likely to moderate the effect of perceived interactivity on consumer attitude toward blogs. Consumer attitude toward the blogs in turn is likely to affect their attitude toward the sponsored posts carried by the blogs. Next we provide more detailed discussion of the factors as the drivers of consumer attitude toward consumer generated advertising.

Motivations for Blog Usage

As already discussed, blogs are a relatively new development on the web involving a different way in which people interact with each other online. The fact that a large number of internet users read blogs (Lenhart & Fox, 2006) indicates that, there are some underlying motivations for blog usage. Korgaonkar and Wolin (1999) showed that consumers used the web for a number of reasons besides retrieving information and *intrinsic motivations* play a greater role than demographic factors in web usage behaviour. Their research further indicates that individuals' need for cognition may be one of the reasons why people seek out and visit blogs. The need for cognition (NFC) scale was developed by Cacioppo & Petty (1982) and reflects the extent to which people engage in and enjoy effortful cognitive activities. It is defined as an individual's tendency to engage in and enjoy cognitive endeavours. Studies have shown that individuals with a high NFC are intrinsically motivated while those with lower NFC require extrinsic motivation to involve in cognitive activities. Those with a lower NFC are sometimes referred to as cognitive misers (Taylor, 1981). While describing motivations of consumers to using information services in the Internet, Kaynar & Amichai-Hamburger (Kaynar & Amichai-Hamburger, 2008) showed that there was a correlation between NFC and professional services use, with people high in NFC using information services in the Internet relatively more than those low in NFC.

Perceived Interactivity of Blogs

Despite the fact that various authors acknowledge the importance of the concept of interactivity, a clear and valid framework is still lacking (Jee & Lee, 2002). While some authors use it to mean the human interaction with the web, such as speed of interaction (Campbell & Wright, 2008; Novak et al., 2000; Steuer, 1992), others focussed on the social exchanges (Deighton & Kornfeld, 2007).

Deighton & Kornfeld (2007) categorised three types of interaction in social exchange of relevance to marketing. These are, communal, instrumental and voyeuristic.

Communal interaction refers to those active participants in the online community while instrumental interaction refers to the use of the community for some temporary advantage. Finally voyeuristic interaction refers to observing others participants' communal activities. It was pointed out that most of those interactions involved in digital communities are voyeuristic, while communal and instrumental interactions are only present to a small extent. Considering the fact that blogs are a form of digital community, it would be important to see whether this holds true for blogs as well.

In marketing literature, most authors have focussed on perceived interactivity rather than the actual interactivity facilitated by interactive technologies (Wu, 1999, McMillan and Hwang, 2002, Sohn and Lee, 2005). Perceived interactivity is thus subjective or experiential and differs from the actual, objective or structural interactivity (Wu, 2006). In the context of the conceptual framework that we are developing in this paper, we use the construct of perceived interactivity developed and verified by Liu (2003). Liu developed this scale to measure the interactivity of websites, which is thus more relevant to blogs than other existing interactivity measures. This construct is composed of three correlated but distinct dimensions: active control, two-way communication, and synchronicity. Even though it leads to affective or behavioural responses, it is separated from those consequences and the fact that it considers the interactivity of websites. Perceived interactivity of the blogs should be an important driver for blog usage, because bloggers are early adopters of technology; are active, multitasking Internet surfers, they trust other bloggers and are more open-minded than the average online consumer does (Forrester, 2006). Having discussed the effect of perceived interactivity on blog users' attitude toward blogs, next, we will discuss the effect of credibility perceptions of the blogs/bloggers on blog users' attitude toward blogs.

Credibility of Blogs and Attitude Towards Blogs

The conversational and interactive nature of blogs makes them ideal for building and maintaining computer-mediated relationships and trust (Kelleher, 2006). However, the few studies that have examined blogs have focused mainly on them as sources of news, especially politics (Adamic & Glance, 2005; Johnson, Kaye, Bichard, & Wong, 2007; Yang, 2007), little is known about how consumers perceive the credibility of blogs and how their credibility perceptions may interact with perceived interactivity of blogs to influence their attitude towards blogs. Bloggers and their users become part of a community and form bonds. The question is whether the trust that develops between members of this digital community translates into credibility of the blogs.

Regarding the concept of credibility itself, there exists a debate among various scholars in literature who view the concept of credibility from different perspectives (Flanagin & Metzger, 2000; Metzger, Flanagin, Eyal, Lemus, & McCann, 2003). Most authors define credibility of a source or information as believability (Fogg et al., 2001; Fogg & Tseng, 1999) and seen as a perceived quality (Fogg & Tseng, 1999; Self, 1996). Fogg and Tseng (1999) identified trustworthiness and expertise, as the two components of credibility. In other words, highly credible sources are perceived to have high levels of trustworthiness and expertise. It should be noted that recent studies have empirically shown that information credibility is distinct from trust (McKnight & Kacmar, 2007). An increase in the perceived credibility of a source or information will ultimately lead to trust by the receivers of that information.

In addition, there have been a number of studies on media credibility (Hardin, 2002; Metzger et al., 2003). Walther et al., (2004) identified three dimensions of credibility, namely, safety, trustworthiness, and dynamism. Related to trustworthiness, site authorship and sponsorship were also identified as important criteria of web site credibility (Lynch, Vernon, & Smith, 2001). They showed that the attributes and trustworthiness of the source author relates to source credibility.

Among the various scales used to measure source credibility in marketing communication, Harmon and Coney's (1982) credibility scales have been among the most widely adapted. They measured credibility of a source using adjectives with seven point semantic differential scales. The adjectives were: trustworthy/not trustworthy, good/bad, open- minded/close-minded, trained/untrained, experienced/ not experienced, and expert/not expert. More recently, '*webelievability*' is another term that has been introduced into the credibility literature. Johnson and Kaye (2002) coined the term to refer to "the degree to which people judge online information as credible." This differs from source credibility as it looks at the information presented. So the question is how the uptake of information presented by a blogger is affected by their perceived credibility?

Attitude Towards Advertising in Blogs

If a blog/blogger is perceived as credible, will this perceived credibility be transferred to products and services recommended by that blog/blogger? Credibility as conceptualised by Flanagin & Metzger (2000) have assessed it in three ways, namely, *message credibility*, which is the perceived credibility of information presented on the website; *sponsor credibility*, the perceived credibility of the blogger and finally, *site credibility*, the perceived credibility of the blog as a whole.

A experimental study of students in the US and Korea (Ko, Cho, & Roberts, 2005) investigating the motivations and consequences of interactivity in the online context and found that different types of interaction had a positive effect on attitude towards site, which in turn leads to a positive attitude towards brand and purchase intentions. Relating this to blogs, it remains to be tested whether consumers who have a positive perception towards blogs would have a positive attitude towards sponsored posts as well. Nevertheless, we have reason to believe that attitude towards blogs is closely correlated to attitude towards sponsored posts carried in that blogs. This is because that bloggers ultimately get to decide what to post, and they are keenly aware that whatever they post will affect their credibility and ultimately their popularity. Therefore they act as the guardian for the type of posts put on their blogs to ensure that their own credibility is not adversely affected.

The fact that bloggers "don't pretend to be neutral" may be another reason why their credibility is closely linked to the credibility of the sponsored posts they carry in their blogs. In fact blog users may even view the biased tone of bloggers positively (Johnson & Kaye, 2004). Research has shown that bloggers are opinionated and open people, often revealing personal information on their blogs, even revealing intimate details of their life (Herring, Kouper, Scheidt, & Wright, 2004; Nardi, Schiano, & Gumbrecht, 2004; Nowson & Oberlander, 2006). Blog users judged blogs to be even more credible than traditional media (Johnson & Kaye, 2004). They point out that "users may find weblogs more credible because they are independent rather than controlled by corporate interests."

Based on the discussion in this chapter, Figure 2 presents the conceptual model of consumer attitude towards blogs and sponsored posts, which can be further tested empirically.

DISCUSSION

Blogs have the potential to change the competitive landscape and companies who understand the impact of such new technologies are likely to dominate the industry and the future marketplace. For marketers, blogs are the "non-marketing" communication paths, or new traffic lanes not built for "the convenience of marketers but for consumers" (Deighton & Kornfeld, 2007). This

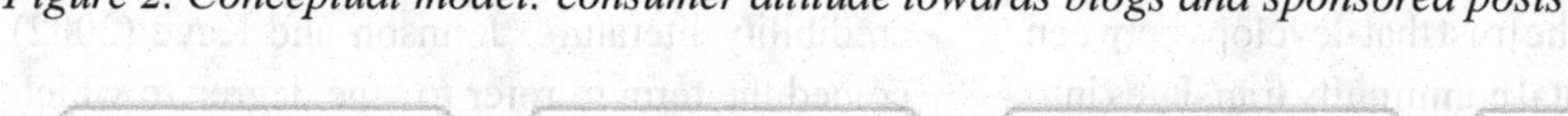

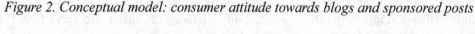

Figure 2. Conceptual model: consumer attitude towards blogs and sponsored posts

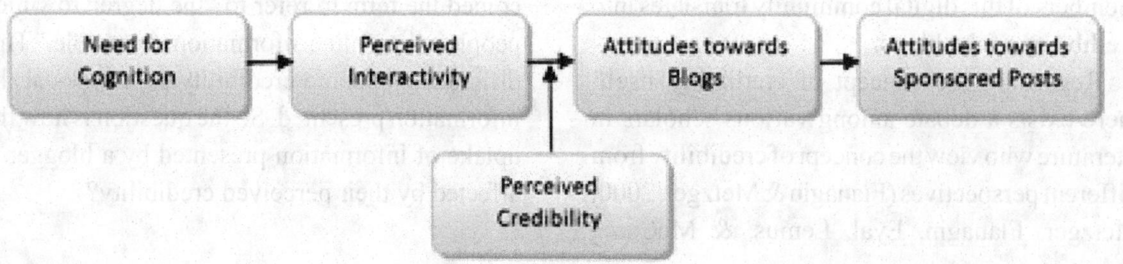

has created new and unexpected challenges and opportunities for marketers to influence, participate or even fit in the social world of consumers. However, given the profound implication of blogs for consumers and for company, it is surprising that there exist very little theoretical and empirical studies, if any, on this emerging social phenomenon. Understanding such radically new technologies is extremely difficult for the users themselves due to the high uncertainty regarding cost and benefit trade-offs, which in turn makes it hard for marketers to measure adequately the potential impact of these new technologies for the business. This chapter sets out the first step to meet this challenge by conceptually examining factors that may influence consumer attitude towards blogs as well as advertising in blogs.

Our conceptual development as presented in the model identified consumer motivation, particularly need for cognition, perceived interactivity of blogs and perceived credibility of blogs as the salient factors that are likely to influence consumer attitude towards blogs and advertising in blogs. The transferability of attitude towards blogs to attitude towards sponsored content in blogs is also proposed, although empirical study will be required to test this proposition. The implication of this proposed transferability of attitude from blogs to advertising in blogs for the companies is that they need to understand the concerns of the bloggers and the ways they can be active players in the emerging environment of "consumer generated advertising." This is because in the new model of marketing communication, the concerns of the bloggers become the concerns of the companies as well.

This chapter attempts to gauge the potential that blogs offers as a marketing and communication tool by understanding how blog users engage with blogs and how they perceive blogs as an advertising medium. Empirical testing of the conceptual model developed in this chapter would help shed some light on how blogs are enabling a new model of consumer collaboration, and in turn, how this new model of consumer collaboration affects the locus of control of marketing communication.

REFERENCES

Adamic, L. A., & Glance, N. (2005). The Political Blogosphere and the 2004 US Election: Divided They Blog. In *Proceedings of the 3rd international Workshop on Link Discovery* (pp. 36-43).

Ayto, J., & Simpson, J. (Eds.). (2005). *The Oxford Dictionary of Modern Slang*. Oxford, UK: Oxford University Press.

Barry, T. E. (2002). In defense of the hierarchy of effects: A rejoinder to weilbacher. *Journal of Advertising Research, 42*(3), 44–47.

Barry, T. E., & Howard, D. (1990). A review and critique of the hierarchy of effects in advertising. *International Journal of Advertising, 9*(2), 121–135.

Bass, F. M. (1969). A new product growth model for consumer durables. *Management Science, 15*(January), 215–227. doi:10.1287/mnsc.15.5.215

BBC. (2004). *'Blog' Picked as Word of the Year*. Retrieved September 18, 2007, from http://news.bbc.co.uk/1/hi/technology/4059291.stm

Bickart, B., & Schindler, R. M. (2001). Internet forums as influential sources of consumer information. *Journal of Interactive Marketing, 15*(3), 31–40. doi:10.1002/dir.1014

Blackwell, R. D., Miniard, P. W., & Engel, J. F. (2001). *Consumer Behavior*. Ft. Worth, TX: Harcourt College Publishers.

Bruner, G. C., & Kumar, A. (2000). Web commercials and advertising hierarchy-of-effects. *Journal of Advertising Research, 40*(1/2), 35–42.

Cacioppo, J. T., & Petty, R. E. (1982). The need for cognition. *Journal of Personality and Social Psychology*, *42*(1), 116–131. doi:10.1037/0022-3514.42.1.116

Chang, H. H., & Wang, I. C. (2008). An investigation of user communication behavior in computer mediated environments. *Computers in Human Behavior*, *24*(5), 2336–2356. doi:10.1016/j.chb.2008.01.001

Deighton, J. A., & Kornfeld, L. (2007). Digital Interactivity: Unanticipated Consequences for Markets, Marketing and Consumers [Electronic Version]. *HBS Working Papers*. Retrieved from http://www.hbs.edu/research/pdf/08-017.pdf

Economist. (2006). *It's the Links, Stupid*. Retrieved September 26, 2007, from http://www.economist.com/surveys/displaystory.cfm?story_id=6794172

Flanagin, A., J., & Metzger, M., J. (2000). Perceptions of Internet information credibility. *Journalism & Mass Communication Quarterly*, *77*(3), 515–540.

Fogg, B. J., & Tseng, H. (1999). The Elements of Computer Credibility. In *Proceedings of the SIGCHI Conference on Human Factors in Computing Systems: The CHI is the Limit* (pp. 80-87).

Forrester. (2006). *Profiling Europe's Bloggers: What Marketers Need to Know before Entering the Blogosphere*. Retrieved July 15, 2008, from http://www.forrester.com/ER/Press/Release/0,1769,1112,00.html

Gruen, T. W., Osmonbekov, T., & Czaplewski, A. J. (2006). eWOM: The impact of customer-to-customer online know-how exchange on customer value and loyalty. *Journal of Business Research*, *59*(4), 449–456. doi:10.1016/j.jbusres.2005.10.004

Hardin, R. (2002). *Trust and Trustworthiness*. New York: Russell Sage Foundation.

Harmon, R., & Coney, H. (1982). The persuasive effects of source credibility in buy and lease situations. *JMR, Journal of Marketing Research*, *19*(May), 255–260. doi:10.2307/3151625

Herring, S. C., Kouper, I., Scheidt, L. A., & Wright, E. L. (2004). Women and Children Last: The Discursive Construction of Weblogs. *Into the Blogosphere: Rhetoric, Community, and Culture of Weblogs*. Retrieved August, 23, 2008, from http://blog.lib.umn.edu/blogosphere/women_and_children.html

Hof, R. (2006 October). *Unrepentant PayPerPost Gets Funding*. Retrieved September 26, 2007, from http://www.businessweek.com/the_thread/techbeat/archives/2006/10/unrepentant_pay.html

Hu, N., Pavlou, P. A., & Zhang, J. (2006). Can Online Reviews Reveal a Product's True Quality? Empirical Findings and Analytical Modeling of Online Word-of-Mouth Communication. In *Proceedings of the 7th ACM Conference on Electronic Commerce* (pp. 324-330).

Jee, J., & Lee, W. N. (2002). Antecedents and consequences of perceived interactivity: An exploratory study. *Journal of Interactive Advertising*, *3*(1), 1–26.

Johnson, T. J., & Kaye, B. K. (2002). Webelievability: A path model examining how convenience and reliance predict online credibility. *Journalism & Mass Communication Quarterly*, *79*(3), 619–642.

Johnson, T. J., & Kaye, B. K. (2004). Wag the blog: How reliance on traditional media and the Internet influence credibility perceptions of weblogs among blog users. *Journalism & Mass Communication Quarterly*, *81*(3), 622–642.

Johnson, T. J., Kaye, B. K., Bichard, S. L., & Wong, W. J. (2007). Every blog has its day: Politically-interested Internet users' perceptions of blog credibility. *Journal of Computer-Mediated Communication*, *13*(1), 100–122. doi:10.1111/j.1083-6101.2007.00388.x

Kaynar, O., & Amichai-Hamburger, Y. (2008). The effects of need for cognition on internet use revisited. *Computers in Human Behavior*, *24*(2), 361–371. doi:10.1016/j.chb.2007.01.033

Kelleher, T. a. M., B. M. (2006). Organizational blogs and the human voice: relational strategies and relational outcomes. *Journal of Computer-Mediated Communication*, *11*(2), 395–414. doi:10.1111/j.1083-6101.2006.00019.x

Kirkpatrick, D., & Roth, D. (2005). Why there's no escaping the blog. *Fortune*, *151*(1), 32–37.

Kirkpatrick, M. (2006, June 30). PayPerPost.com Offers to Sell Your Soul. *TechCrunch.com.* Retrieved September 24, 2007, from http://www.techcrunch.com/2006/06/30/payperpostcom-offers-to-buy-your-soul/.

Ko, H., Cho, C. H., & Roberts, M. S. (2005). Internet uses and gratifications: A structural equation model of interactive advertising. *Journal of Advertising*, *34*(2), 57–70.

Koeppel, P. (2007). Use today's web technologies to connect with your customers. *Agency Sales*, *37*(9), 28–29.

Korgaonkar, P., & Wolin, L. (1999). A multivariate analysis of web usage. *Journal of Advertising Research*, *39*(2), 53–68.

Kottke, J. (2003). *It's Weblog Not Web Log*. Retrieved September 30, 2007, from http://www.kottke.org/03/08/its-weblog-not-web-log

Lavidge, R. J., & Steiner, G. A. (1961). A model for predictive measurements of advertising effectiveness. *Journal of Marketing*, *6*(October), 59–62. doi:10.2307/1248516

Lee, S., Hwang, T., & Lee, H. H. (2006). Corporate blogging strategies of the Fortune 500 companies. *Management Decision*, *44*(3), 316–334. doi:10.1108/00251740610656232

Litvin, S. W., Goldsmith, R. E., & Pan, B. (2008). Electronic word-of-mouth in hospitality and tourism management. *Tourism Management*, *29*(3), 458–468. doi:10.1016/j.tourman.2007.05.011

Liu, Y. (2003). Developing a scale to measure the interactivity of websites. *Journal of Advertising Research*, *43*(2), 207–216.

Lynch, D., Vernon, R. F., & Smith, M. L. (2001). Critical thinking and the web. *Journal of Social Work Education*, *37*(2), 381–386.

Marken, G. A. (2005). To blog or not to blog, that is the question. *Public Relations Quarterly*, *50*(3), 31–33.

McKenna, R. (1991). *Relationship Marketing: Successful Strategies for the Age of the Customers*. Reading, MA: Addison-Wesley Publishing Company.

McKnight, D. H., & Kacmar, C. J. (2007). Factors and Effects of Information Credibility. In *Proceedings of the Ninth International Conference on Electronic Commerce* (pp. 423-432).

McMillan, S. J., & Hwang, J. S. (2002). Measures of perceived interactivity: An exploration of the role of direction of communication, user control, and time in shaping perceptions of interactivity. *Journal of Advertising*, *31*(3), 29–42.

Metzger, M. J., Flanagin, A. J., Eyal, K., Lemus, D. R., & McCann, R. M. (2003). Credibility for the 21st century: Integrating perspectives on source, message, and media credibility in the contemporary media environment. *Communication Yearbook*, *27*, 293–335. doi:10.1207/s15567419cy2701_10

Microsoft. (2006, November 29). *Women Rule in Malaysian Blogosphere*. Retrieved from http://www.microsoft.com/malaysia/press/archive2006/linkpage4337.mspx

Moulds, J. (2007, September 14). *Blogs: The Latest Tool in Decision-Making*. Retrieved September 24, 2007, from http://www.telegraph.co.uk/money/main.jhtml?xml=/money/2007/09/14/bcnblogs114.xml

Nardi, B. A., Schiano, D. J., & Gumbrecht, M. (2004). Blogging as Social Activity, or, Would You Let 900 Million People Read Your Diary? In *Proceedings of the 2004 ACM Conference on Computer Supported Cooperative Work* (pp. 222-231).

Nowson, S., & Oberlander, J. (2006). *The Identity of Bloggers: Openness and Gender in Personal Weblogs*. Paper Presented at the AAAI Spring Symposium - Technical Report.

Ron, D., & Tasra, D. (2007). Effective marketing with blogs. *EventDV*, *20*(10), 26.

Self, C. S. (1996). *Credibility. An Integrated Approach to Communication Theory and Research*. Mahwah, NJ: Erlbaum.

Shull, E. (2006, October 26). *Welcome to Blogitive*. Retrieved September 29, 2007, from http://www.blogitive.com/2006/10/26/welcome-to-blogitivewelcome-to-blogitive/#more-3

Sifry, D. (2007). *The State of the Live Web*. Retrieved September 11, 2008, from http://technorati.com/weblog/2007/04/328.html

SinoCast. (2006). *China's Blog User Base Expected to Approach 100mn Next Year*. Retrieved July 18, 2008, from http://findarticles.com/p/articles/mi_hb5562/is_200607/ai_n22733639?tag=artBody,col1

Smith, A. (2008). New Numbers for Blogging and Blog Readership. Retrieved March 16, 2009, from http://www.pewinternet.org/Commentary/2008/July/New-numbers-for-blogging-and-blog-readership.aspx/.

Socialtext.net. (2008). *Fortune 500 Business Blogging Wiki*. Retrieved August 19, 2008, from http://www.asia.socialtext.net/bizblogs/index.cgi

Sohn, D., & Lee, B. (2005). Dimensions of Interactivity: Differential Effects of Social and Psychological Factors. *Journal of Computer-Mediated Communication*, 10(3), article 6. Retrieved July 18, 2008 from http://jcmc.indiana.edu/vol10/issue3/sohn.html

Taylor, S. E. (1981). The Interface of Cognitive and Social Psychology. In Harvey, J. (Ed.), *Cognition, Social Behavior, and the Environmen* (pp. 189–211). Hillsdale, NJ: Erlbaum.

Universal-McCann. (2009).Wave 4. Retrieved March 2010, from http://universalmccann.bitecp.com/wave4/Wave4.pdf/.

Walther, J. B., Wang, Z., & Loh, T. (2004). The effect of top-level domains and advertisements on health web site credibility. *Journal of Medical Internet Research*, *6*(3), e24. doi:10.2196/jmir.6.3.e24

Weilbacher, W. M. (2001). Point of view: Does advertising cause a hierarchy of effects? *Journal of Advertising Research*, *41*(6), 19–26.

Winn, P. (2009). State of the Blogosphere 2008. Retrieved March 16, 2010, from http://technorati.com/blogging/article/state-of-the-blogosphere-introduction/.

Wright, J. (2006). *Blog Marketing: The Revolutionary New Way to Increase Sales, Build Your Brand, and Get Exceptional Results*. New York: McGraw-Hill.

Wu, G. (1999). Perceived interactivity and attitude toward web sites. In Marilyn, S. Roberts, E. (Eds.) Proceedings of the American Academy of Advertising Conference, 254-262.

Wu, G. (2006). Conceptualizing and measuring the perceived interactivity of websites. *Journal of Current Issues and Research in Advertising*, *28*(1), 87–104.

Yang, K. C. C. (2007). Factors influencing internet users' perceived credibility of news-related blogs in Taiwan. *Telematics and Informatics*, *24*(2), 69–85. doi:10.1016/j.tele.2006.04.001

Chapter 14
Motivations for Social Networking Site Adoption

Harsha Gangadharbatla
University of Oregon, USA

ABSTRACT

Social networking sites (SNSs) are being increasingly used by businesses to add value to companies as well as consumers. Yet, very little is known as to why individuals adopt and use SNS. The current chapter reviews literature on uses and gratification and technology acceptance model (TAM) to propose a framework for SNS adoption. Six main motivational factors are identified from literature and are expected to influence SNS adoption: need to belong, entertainment, communication, information, commercial value, and self-expression. Further, two main barriers to SNS adoption, technology and privacy, are expected to hinder adoption. The proposed theoretical framework is a first step toward understanding SNS adoption and both managerial and theoretical implications are drawn.

INTRODUCTION

Social networking sites (SNS) provide a means for millions of users to communicate and network with friends and strangers. According to Nielsen, online social networking sites have surpassed email in terms of reach by the end of 2008 (Ostrow 2009). The number of people using SNS has increased rapidly from 10 percent of all U.S. households belonging to at least one SNS in 2007 (Lewis 2007), to over 35% by the end of 2008 (Lenhart 2009). The number of unique visitors to MySpace increased from 50 million in May 2006 (comScore 2006), to 117 million in June 2008 (comScore 2008). According to Boyd and Ellison (2007), the first social networking site, SixDegrees.com, was launched in 1997, which allowed users to create profiles and list their friends. In the following years, several SNSs like AsianAvenue, BlackPlanet, MiGente, LiveJournal, Ryze, Friendster, Linkedln, MySpace, Hi5, Orkut, Flickr, Yahoo! 360, Bebo, Facebook, Twitter, and MyChurch were launched in that chronological order (for an excellent history of SNSs, please see boyd and Ellison (2007)).

DOI: 10.4018/978-1-60566-792-8.ch014

Boyd and Ellison (2007) define SNS as "web-based services that allow individuals to (1) construct a public or semi-public profile within a bounded system, (2) articulate a list of other users with whom they share a connection, and (3) view and transverse their list of connections and those made by others within the system" (p. 2). SNSs differ from AIM, ICQ, chat, or for that matter an address book in that there is an added networking component to SNSs. Other people can not only see who is on your friend list but also communicate with them and add them as their friends. As one might imagine, there are many types of SNS users. For instance, a recent Simmons Research study identified 38 consumer personalities, with common classifications such as socially isolated, approval seekers, health and image leaders, smart loyal, smart green, brand loyal, stay-at-home moms, upscale grays, first-time home buyers, and divorced (Bulik 2008).

There are two broad types of networking sites: business-oriented (such as Ecademy, LinkedIn, or Spoke) and social-oriented (Facebook, MySpace, Meetup, Orkut, or Tribe). Some networks such as Ryze serve both purposes. Members can join SNSs in one of the two ways—via registration or via connection. In the registration-based model, individuals sign in with a valid email address and the site is open to everyone without any sort of approval or moderation whereas in the connection-based model, individuals can only become members if they know someone who is already a member of that SNS (Murchu, Brestlin, and Decker 2004). Irrespective of the type of SNS, these sites are being increasingly used by both businesses and nonprofit organizations.

Social Networking Site Usage by Organizations

With more people using SNSs, businesses, non-profit organizations, churches, and even political candidates are looking at leveraging the power of these existing networks. SNSs are being used to mobilize support for political candidates, causes, services, and even brands. During the 2008 presidential elections, both the Democrat and Republican presidential candidates have used SNSs to organize and raise money online. For instance, Barack Obama has over 500 groups on Facebook.com at the time of writing this chapter with as many as 500,000 members in them. He also has many applications and events in his name that are being used by users to organize rallies, meetings, fundraising activities, and even protests. SNSs provide for a quick way to mobilize people and rally them for a cause and many organizations are doing just the same.

Apart from political and non-profit organizations using SNS to rally people, several media outlets are also relying on them for news and networking. For instance, in the sex scandal involving Gov. Elliot Spitzer, New York Times identified the alleged call girl by linking to her MySpace page in their online article. Within hours several thousand user-created groups were formed on MySpace and Facebook that ensued a heated debate about the scandal (Simon 2008). Media outlets even reported that she was on Facebook till the wee hours in the morning deleting and responding to comments on her profile page (Simon 2008). Media organizations are forming alliances with SNSs in order to gain publicity, deliver content, and boost their ratings. MSNBC teamed up with MySpace to deliver coverage of "Decision '08" just as ABC did with Facebook.com (McIntyre 2008).

Businesses are also using SNSs today to target consumers and create value for their brands. SNSs represent investments in establishing electronic gateways—as content aggregators or as web portals—for efficient access to information and services online for consumers (Murchu, Breslin and Decker, 2004). According to BusinessWeek, Nike in collaboration with Google created joga.com, an Orkut-like SNS for soccer fans, that runs in 140 countries and 14 different languages (Christopher 2008). Business owners and the PR professionals use SNSs to create content, promote products, services and events, educate and entertain users through blogs, and use them for search engine optimization (Klein 2008). Organizations also use SNSs for recruiting purposes. For instance, LinkedIn is considered one of the best sites for networking and human resources purposes (Klein 2008).

Finally, usage of SNSs as advertising vehicles is something that is growing in importance. Companies have come to realize the potential of SNSs as advertising vehicles and a total of $865 million was spent last year on advertising on SNSs in the U.S. (eMarketer 2006a). Most of this money was spent on SNSs that are often visited by teens and young adults. MySpace, with 55 million unique visitors just in the month of September of 2006, accounted for $525 million of the overall spending (Advertising Age 2007). This is because SNSs are particularly useful in targeting young consumers who grew up with the Internet and are experts in ignoring banner ads, blocking popups, and deleting spam (Christopher 2008). Companies are turning to SNS with campaigns such as "*The Fantanas*" for Fanta® created by Starcom Media Group (SMG) to tap into the immense potential these sites have for reaching a target that no longer watches television or pays any attention to advertising in other media. In order to reach today's youth whose attention is divided among the Internet, television, videogames, texting, and talking on cell phones, technology savy companies, like Toyota, Coca Cola and Wells Fargo, are relying heavily on SNSs (Christopher 2008).

Worldwide advertising spending on SNSs was $1.2 billion in 2007 and is expected to rise to $4 billion by 2011 (Christopher 2008). Usage of SNSs for advertising and marketing is only expected to increase given that in a recent survey by eMarketer (2006b) almost half of the respondents claimed they would actively seek out shopping information, coupons, and discounts on SNSs if they were made available to them. SNSs provide for means of targeting individuals by interests, how often they comment, upload photos and videos, and by what networks and groups they belong to (Klaassen 2008). According to Facebook.com, advertisers can leverage the power of SNSs by precisely targeting individuals with Social Ads, relevant stories about their friends engaging with different businesses. Users learn about brands and businesses from trusted friends on Facebook rather than from businesses. There are three ways to use SNSs like Facebook for marketing: build pages to connect with audiences, use Social Ads that spread relevant messages virally, and gather information about people, their interests, and activities on SNSs (Christopher 2008). Social ads are made possible in part by programs like Beacon (Klaassen 2007), which allows users to display the items they rent or buy on sites like Blockbuster.com to their friends, thereby recommending them to their friends (Gangadharbatla 2008).

The success of SNSs as advertising vehicles depends mainly on the number of people using them. The more people registered with a SNS, the more revenue it generates in terms of advertising or subscription fees. Unfortunately, very little research has been done to understand the motivations for SNS adoption (Gangadharbatla 2008). The purpose of this chapter is to review literature and propose a conceptual framework that outlines the motivations for and barriers to SNS adoption. Theoretical and practical implications are drawn from the proposed framework and future research directions are suggested.

LITERATURE REVIEW

Research on SNS is a relatively new area with the majority of it focusing on impression management in online communities (Watts, Dodds, and Newton 2002), friendship performance, network structure, online/offline connections, and privacy issues (Gross, Acquisti, and Heinz 2005; boyd and Ellison 2007). Typology of online communities (Hagel and Armstrong 1997), classification of members (Preece et al. 2004; Franz and Wolkinger 2003), and recently, consequences of SNS usage (Ellison, Steinfield, and Lampe 2007) have also received some attention from academic researchers. The focus of the current chapter is limited to understanding the motivations for why individuals join and use SNSs. Drawing from Uses and Gratification (U&G) literature and the Technology Adoption Model (TAM), a conceptual framework explaining both motivations for and barriers to SNS adoption is proposed.

MOTIVATIONS

A Uses and Gratification approach examines what people do with media more so than what media do to people (Katz 1959), which is a good approach when understanding the motivations for SNS adoption that are of interest rather than the effects or consequences of doing so. Uses and Gratifications literature suggests that individuals use media to gratify their needs and wants (Katz, Blumler, and Gurevitch 1993; Rubin 1983) and it operates under the basic assumption that individuals' communication choices are purposive and goal-directed (Katz et al. 1974). Several researchers have adopted a U&G approach to explain why people use newspapers, radio, television, and recently the Internet (Ruggiero 2000). For instance, Pompper, Kinnally, and McClung (2005) suggest that listeners use radio primarily for entertainment followed by other reasons such as habit, pass time, and escape. Similarly, in the realm of television several researchers examined why individuals consume television content and concluded that pass time/habit, relaxation, companionship, entertainment, escape, social interaction, information, and arousal are chief reasons among others (Rubin 1983). Ferguson and Perse (2000), LaRose and Eastin (2004), Papacharissi and Rubin (2000), Perse and Greenberg Dunn (1998), and others have employed U&G to understand the antecedents and consequences of computer-mediated communication. Apart from most of the reasons why people use television, one important factor that emerges with computer-mediated communication is the aspect of interactivity (Shin and Kim 2007). Interactive function of the Internet such as email, chat rooms, listservs, IM, and SNSs are not found in television (Kaye and Johnson 2002).

Research examining the uses and gratifications of social media is new and at the time of writing this chapter only one article (Raacke and Bonds-Raacke 2008) that took a U&G approach to SNS was found. In the absence of studies that examine SNS directly, some of the literature on computer-mediated communication is used as a basis for the conceptual framework proposed. In identifying the factors that motivate SNS usage, Raacke and Bonds-Raacke (2008) suggest that the vast majority of college students use SNS for reasons such as making new friends and locating old friends. Uses and gratification literature suggests that media can serve functions like "connecting people...with different kinds of others (self, family, friends, nation, etc.)" (Katz et al 1974, p.63). Consistent with that, Raacke and Bonds-Raacke (2008) suggest that for college students SNSs fulfills not only communication needs but also social needs, such as a desire to be part of a larger community. The desire to stay in touch and make new friends stems from a more basic need to belong. In understanding why individuals join virtual communities and discussion forums, Watson and Johnson (1972) and Ridings and Gefen (2004) identified need to belong as a primary reason. Other researchers also point to make plans with friends, make new friends and stay in touch with old friends, and to flirt with someone as common reasons why young people use SNSs (Lenhart and Madden 2007). The desire to belong results in increased communication and SNS fills the gap by providing additional access points to stay in touch with friends and family. Several users join groups and communicate with people that have common interests. For instance on Facebook, users can join their college network, city network, organization, sorority, and fraternity networks, fan clubs for television shows, celebrities, and athletes. Papacharissi and Rubin (2000) suggest that individuals sometimes use the Internet to communicate with others as an alternative to face-to-face contact. This may be true with SNS as well, which illustrates the first two propositions.

- **P1:***Individuals' desire to belong drives SNS adoption.*
- **P2:***Individuals' desire to communicate with others motivates SNS adoption.*

The third factor underlying SNS adoption is entertainment, which is often mentioned as one of the primary reasons why individuals use television (Rubin 1983) and computers (LaRose and Eastin 2001; Stafford, Stafford, and Schkade 2004) in U&G literature. Many users can join and use SNSs as a means of recreation, passing time, procrastination of homework, fun, and escapism. All of these fit under the description of entertainment (Blumler and Katz 1974). The entertainment motive for SNS adoption is different from traditional media in that computer-mediated communication is personal and one-on-one, yet similar in that collective consumption such as friends getting together in an apartment to browse profiles and entertainment themselves as a group is also possible.

- **P3:***Individuals' desire for entertainment drives SNS adoption.*

The fourth factor, information, stems from individuals' desire to seek information, find out about events, learn about new things, and satisfy curiosity, all of which are frequently cited as motives for consumption of traditional media (McQuail, Blumler, and Brown 1972). SNSs provide for a way to keep tabs on friends, check on others' status on profiles (e.g., twitter.com) and exchange information through bulletin boards, personal emails, wall posts, uploading audio and video files, posting links, writing online journals and blogs, getting notifications and broadcasting their relationship status. The role of information seeking becomes all the more important in an online context especially when seeking political (Kaye and Johnson 2002) and commercial information (Eighmey 1997; Korgaonkar and Wolin 1999). While television can also be used for information seeking, the nature of the Internet where individuals actively search for product information, research for work, download software, create and post content on user-generated content sites such as YouTube makes it different (Ferguson and Perse 2000). In this sense, the web (and therefore, SNS) might be more tuned to gratifying users' informational needs more so than television, which predominantly driven by entertainment, escape, and social interaction needs (Kaye and Johnson 2002). The higher the need for information in individuals the higher the likelihood they adoption SNS

- **P4:***Individuals' need for information motivates SNS adoption.*

Similar to usage of Internet for information needs is the use of Internet for commercial purposes. SNSs are often used to satisfy commercial needs such as searching for product information, posting classified ads, buying and selling items, posting resumes and searching for jobs. For instance, Facebook.com has a Marketplace application where users can post items for sale, find roommates, advertise moving sales, and buy items like furniture and even cars. Eastin (2002) and LaRose and Eastin (2002) note the adoption of Internet for commercial purposes. The commercial aspect of SNSs is something that has never been examined before. Given the usage of Internet for commercial activities, it is logical to expect that some individuals derive some motivation to adopt SNS for commercial purposes. If individuals perceive SNSs as ideal channels for commercial activities, they are more likely to adopt and use SNSs.

- **P5:** *The perceived commercial value of SNSs motivates SNS adoption.*

Lastly, self-expression is another use of SNSs, which is similar to the person identity motive often mention in uses and gratification literature (Blumler and Katz 1974; McQuail, Blumler, and Brown 1972). Several users adopt SNSs for self-promotion as prospective job candidates (LinkedIn.com), dates (eHarmony.com), and friends (Facebook.com and MySpace.com). The idea of self-expression on SNSs is unique in that the consequences are less permanent than, say, getting a tattoo. Nonetheless, self-expression on SNSs is considered an integral part of how individuals, especially youth, define themselves and is often taken seriously.

- **P6:** *Individuals' desire for self-expression motivates SNS adoption.*

Barriers

Raacke and Bonds-Raacke (2008) in their survey of 116 college students identified several reasons why individuals might not use social networking sites. From a U&G perspective, some of the reasons mentioned for non-usage of SNSs are "they have no desire to have an account" (70.3%), "they are too busy" (63.4%), "they think it is a waste of time" (60.4%), "they feel intimidated" (5.9%), and "they think others would not be interested in their accounts" (5.0%). Barriers to SNS adoption can be classified into two categories: technology-related and privacy concerns.

The Technology Adoption Model (TAM) can be used to explain some of the barriers to SNS adoption. TAM suggests that the ultimate adoption of any technology depends on two factors, perceived usefulness and perceived ease of use (Davis, Bagozzi, and Warshaw 1989). Many of the motivational factors discussed earlier such as entertainment, fulfilling the need to belong and need for information, commercial activities, and self-expression relate to the perceived usefulness of SNS. The second factor, perceived ease of use, is related to the barriers presented by SNS adoption. Eastin (2002) and Eastin and LaRose (2000) term this perceived ease of technology as self-efficacy or Internet self-efficacy. The adoption of computer-mediated communication, e-services, and other Internet technologies is positively linked to individuals' levels of Internet self-efficacy (Eastin 2002; Daugherty, Eastin, and Gangadharbatla 2005). When it comes to SNS adoption, these barriers are reflected in Raacke and Bonds-Raacke's (2008) survey of college students where 51.5% of respondents thought nonusers do not have Internet access at home and 34.7% thought nonusers were not good at using technology. Technical difficulties such as no access to Internet, slower connection speeds, interface and usability issues, difficulty in joining, inviting others, and adding friends, photos, and other multimedia files all contribute to less usage and in some cases total rejection.

Along the same lines of technological difficulties, problems arising from viruses and third-party applications on SNSs that store and collect personal information might also present barriers to adoption. Online privacy has been extensively researched (Caudill and Murphy 2000; Sheehan 2002) and has been identified as a major barrier to Internet and digital media adoption (Lin 1999; Ko, Cho, and Roberts 2005; Sheehan 2002). For instance, SNSs make collecting and transmitting personal information for marketing purposes easier. SNSs collect and display tremendous amounts of personal information such as full names, email addresses, gender, birthdays, age, phone numbers, networks users belong to, sexual orientations, political and religious leanings, AIM and chat ids, hobbies and activities, favorite music, television shows, movies, books, athletic teams, favorite quotes, conversations with friends and strangers, friend lists, and other applications installed on their profiles. With so much information stored on SNSs servers, individuals might be apprehensive about joining SNSs to begin with. Lastly, the growing number of sexual offenders and child predators on SNSs such as MySpace could also potentially impede SNSs adoption.

- **P7:** *Both technology and privacy concerns present barriers to SNS adoption.*

To sum up, six U&G and two barriers to SNS adoption have been identified in the literature review. These motivations and barriers have been put in a conceptual framework in figure 1 to explain SNS adoption. The perceived uses and gratifications along with barriers presented for adoption form the basis for individuals' attitudes toward a particular medium or technology. For instance, if an individual sees SNSs as high in entertainment value, his or her attitude toward SNSs is expected to be more favorable. In other words, the six factors identified, need to belong, communication, entertainment, information, commerce, and self-expression are all antecedents to SNS adoption with two main barriers, technology and privacy.

CONCEPTUAL FRAMEWORK

The motivating factors identified in the literature and included in this framework are expected to influence SNS adoption via individuals' attitudes toward SNSs. Attitude is often defined as "a mental and neural state of readiness which exerts a directing influence upon the individual's response to all objects and situations with which it is related" (Allport 1935, p.810). While attitude is not the same as overt behavior, a disposition toward some action or object does influence behavior. The issue of whether attitude and behavior are related has been the subject of serious debate among psychology researchers for many years. The general conclusion is that attitude toward an action and the subjective norms influence an individual's intention to perform an action, which in turn influences the actual behavior (Ajzen and Fishbein, 1980, Ajzen, 1988). The reader is advised to see Ajzen and Fishbein (1980) for the seminal work on the substantial relations amongst the key constructs, attitudes, behavioral intentions, and actual behav-

Figure 1. Framework of SNS adoption

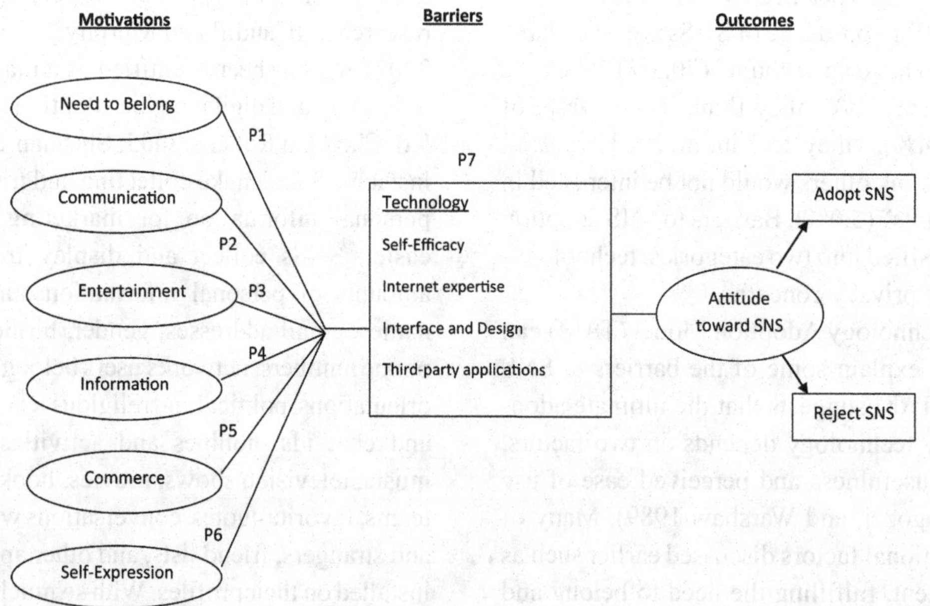

ior. Another approach to attitude-behavior study is the functional approach. A functional approach to understanding attitudes provides some insight into what motivates individuals to use SNSs. Katz's (1960) seminal work on functional theory is considered by many essential for understanding the complex motivational underpinnings and functions of attitudes. Eagly and Chaiken (1993) suggest that a particular object can serve various motivations. Functional theory states that attitudes may serve various motivations depending on the purpose and that one's behavior is a function of their attitude toward that behavior (O'Keefe, 2002, p.29). The basis of this theory centralizes around the view that in order to impact behavior you must understand the motivational source of the attitude. Therefore, a person's adoption of SNSs will be partly determined by his or her attitude toward SNS in particular.

CONCLUSION

Social networking sites are a multi-billion dollar business with their role in adding value to companies and consumers and their usage as advertising vehicles is only expected to gain in importance. In reviewing the literature on uses and gratifications and Technology Adoption Model, it can be concluded that SNS adoption stems from six basic motivations: need to belong, communication, entertainment, information, commerce, and self-expression. Each of the motives identified present interesting insights into understanding how individuals negotiate their "space" within a social network, and why that is important. While entertainment and information motivations are commonly mentioned in literature for uses and gratifications of traditional media usage, the other factors are unique to computer-mediated communication. Two major hurdles to SNS adoption have also been identified: technology-related and privacy. Technology-related barriers include Internet expertise, attractiveness of SNS interfaces, third-party applications, and usability of the site itself. Given the wealth of information that individuals carry on their profile, privacy is a big concern. Terms and conditions as to how this information will be used by the site and how accessible it is to potential sex offenders, child predators, and marketers will determine how easily people adopt SNSs or not. The framework proposed is essential to understanding SNS adoption. It presents opportunities for further empirical research but nonetheless has some limitations.

Limitations

Individual-level differences in adoption do exist that have not been included in the framework proposed. These differences could be based on demographics such as gender, age, income, and location. For instance, "women are more likely to engage in online communication to maintain personal connections with family, friends, and coworkers, whereas men use online communication for pursuing sexual interests and romance." (Weiser 2004 in Raacke and Bonds-Raacke 2008, p. 169). Individuals may also differ in their levels of Internet self-efficacy, need to belong, and need for cognition that might influence their adoption of SNS (Gangadharbatla 2008). Next, the proposed framework for SNS adoption is purely theoretical and lacks empirical support. However, it does present a starting point for numerous studies that could be undertaken to test the proposed framework and better understand SNS adoption. The purpose of the current chapter is not to generalize findings but to provide an initial step toward understanding all the antecedents and consequences of SNS usage.

Implications

From a theoretical standpoint, the current framework is a first step toward understanding the motivations for SNS adoption. The role of entertainment value, information value, and social needs in traditional media usage has been studied extensively in uses and gratification literature. SNS adoption presents new motivational factors in communication value, commercial value, and self-expression. These factors are new in that traditional media such as television or radio may not be ideal for any of these. The Internet, however, has changed how people communicate, transact, shop, bank, and express themselves online. SNSs being an integral part of the Internet includes these plausible additional motivations for adoption and presents opportunities for researchers interested in understanding these motives from a theoretical perspective. These motivations are consistent with studies that examine computer-mediation communication and Internet adoption. SNS adoption is similar to other media adoptions in some ways (motives such as entertainment, escapism, information, and identity) and yet, different and unique is some ways (motives such as self-expression and commercial aspect). In other words, the current study extends uses-and-gratification theory to explain and predict SNS adoption.

From a managerial perspective, the study presents some implications for increasing membership and activity on SNS. This is important because the revenue generated by SNSs is directly linked to the number of users that are signed up. The motives and barriers to SNS adoption identified in this study each signify an implication for SNS owners, policy makers, and advertisers that use SNSs. For instance, sites that tap into individuals' need to belong have a greater chance of increasing membership. Site design and interface seem to influence users' perception and motivation to become a member. Other implications relate to providing value in terms of information and entertainment to users. Advertisers can create viral content and let members link to other sites with the possibility of exponential scaling. Furthermore, SNSs may be perfect vehicles for targeted advertising given the large amounts of valuable data these sites contain in terms of profile information. User profiles often include information about individual's choice of movies, books, television shows, radio stations, hobbies, political leanings, and music. Some sites also display users' demographics in terms of income level, location, education, and work information. Lastly, the presence of sex offenders and privacy issues do present some barriers in SNS usage but policy makers need to frame policies that control or closely monitor such unwanted entities on SNS and pay close attention to how the information is being shared and distributed.

Future Research

The proposed framework is a good starting point for testing and answering various research questions. All the propositions mentioned in the conclusion section need to be tested with rigorous qualitative and quantitative analyses. For instance, a focus group would help investigate and fill in gaps in the framework by identifying additional motivations that might not have been identified in the literature review. These additional motivations and barriers need to be included in the framework to ultimately develop a robust model that completely explains SNS adoption. After developing a model for SNS adoption, it could be put to the rigors of quantitative testing through structural equation modeling or similar tools. A simple survey could measure the variables in the model and these variables could be used to test both measurement and structural models that explain SNS adoption. Another approach to understand SNS adoption is using actual data from an SNS like Facebook.com. If actual data of user behavior and browsing patterns can be obtained, it could be used to better understand SNS usage. However, it may not be useful in determining initial adoption, as it would not include data from nonusers. For that, a survey methodology might be the most appropriate approach.

Apart from testing the proposed framework with empirical data, the area of privacy in social networking sites merits more attention. The traditional definition and meaning of privacy are slowly changing on SNS. If privacy means the right to be left alone, in an online context, one's privacy is only as good as their network and friends. For instance, one may choose to not participate actively on SNS but there is little control over what his or her friends post about them. When a friend posts pictures from a late night party that you went to but did not want everyone to know what does that mean to your privacy? How does one define privacy in a social network? These are some questions that can be answered with further research on SNS.

REFERENCES

Advertising Age. (2007). *Digital Marketing and Media Fast Pack.*

Ajzen, I. (1988). *Attitudes, personality, and behavior.* Chicago: Open University Press.

Ajzen, I., & Fishbein, M. (1980). *Understanding Attitudes and Predicting Social Behavior*. Englewood Cliffs, NJ: Prentice-Hall.

Allport, G. W. (1935). Attitudes. In Murchison, C. (Ed.), *Handbook of social psychology* (pp. 798–844). Worcester, MA: Clark University Press.

Blumler, J. G., & Katz, E. (1974). *The uses of mass communications: Current perspectives on gratifications research.* Beverly Hills, CA: Sage.

Boyd, D. M., & Ellison, N. B. (2007). Social network sites: Definition, history, and scholarship. *Journal of Computer-Mediated Communication, 13*(1). Retrieved March 5, 2008, from http://jcmc.indiana.edu/vol13/issue1/boyd.ellison.html

Bulik, B. (2008, May 5). Is your consumer using social media? [from Communication & Mass Media Complete database.]. *Advertising Age, 79*(18), 12–13. Retrieved September 4, 2008.

Caudill, E. M., & Murphy, P. E. (2000). Consumer online privacy: Legal and ethical issues. *Journal of Public Policy & Marketing, 19*(1), 7–19. doi:10.1509/jppm.19.1.7.16951

Christopher, L. (2008, March 20). Advertisers Go Net Native. *Seybold Report: Analyzing Publishing Technologies, 8*(6), 5-14. Retrieved September 4, 2008, from Academic Search Premier database. comScore. (2006). *Social networking sites continue to attract record numbers as Myspace.com surpasses 50 Million U.S. visitors in May.* Retrieved March 13, 2008 from http://www.comscore.com/press/release.asp?press=906

comScore. (2008). *Social Networking Explodes Worldwide as Sites Increase as Sits Increase their Focus on Cultural Relevance.* Retrieved June 26, 2009, from http://www.comscore.com/index.php/Press_Events/Press_Releases/2008/08/Social_Networking_World_Wide/(language)/eng-US

Daugherty, T., Eastin, M., & Gangadharbatla, H. (2005). e-CRM: Understanding Internet Confidence and Implications for Customer Relationship Management. In I. Clarke III & T. B. Flaherty (Eds.), Advances in Electronic Marketing. Hershey, PA: Idea Group Publishing, Inc.

Davis, F. D., Bagozzi, R. P., & Warshaw, P. R. (1989). User acceptance of computer technology: A comparison of two theoretical models. *Management Science, 35*(8), 982–1003. doi:10.1287/mnsc.35.8.982

Eagly, A. H., & Chaiken, S. (1993). *The Psychology of Attitudes.* Fort Worth, TX: Harcourt Brace College Publishers.

Eastin, M. S. (2002). Diffusion of e-commerce: An analysis of the adoption of four e-commerce activities. *Telematics and Informatics, 19*(3), 251–267. doi:10.1016/S0736-5853(01)00005-3

Eastin, M. S., & LaRose, R. L. (2000). Internet Self-Efficacy and the Psychology of the Digital Divide. *Journal of Computer-Mediated Communication, 6*. Retrieved August 29, 2007, from http://www.ascusc.org/jcmc/vol6/

Eighmey, J. (1997, May). Profiling user responses to commercial websites. *Journal of Advertising Research*, 59–67.

Ellison, N. B., Steinfield, C., & Lampe, C. (2007). The benefits of Facebook friends: Social capital and college students' use of online social network sites. *Journal of Computer-Mediated Communication, 12*(4). Retrieved January 22, 2008, from http://jcmc.indiana.edu/vol12/issue4/ellison.html

eMarketer. (2006a). *Brands to Spend $1.8 Billion on Social Networking Sites by 2010*. Retrieved August 29, 2007 from http://www.emarketer.com/Article.aspx?id=1004085

eMarketer. (2006b). *Social networking online boosts bottom line*. Retrieved August 29, 2007, from http://www.emarketer.com/Article.aspx?id=1004313

Ferguson, D. A., & Perse, E. M. (2000). The World Wide Web as a functional alternative to television. *Journal of Broadcasting & Electronic Media, 44*, 155–194. doi:10.1207/s15506878jobem4402_1

Franz, R., & Wolkinger, T. (2003). Customer Integration with Virtual Communities. Case Study: The online community of the largest regional newspaper in Austria. In *Proceedings of the Hawaii International Conference on System Sciences*, January 6-9, 2003, Big Island, Hawaii.

Gangadharbatla, H. (2008). Facebook Me: Collective self-esteem, need to belong, and Internet self-efficacy as predictors of the iGeneration's attitudes toward social networking sites. *Journal of Interactive Advertising, 8*(2). Retrieved September 4, 2008, from http://www.jiad.org/article100

Gross, R., Acquisti, A., & Heinz, A. (2005). Information Revelation and Privacy in Online Social Networks. In *Proceedings of the 2005 ACM workshop on Privacy in electronic society* (pp. 71-80).

Hagel, J., & Armstrong, A. G. (1997). *Net gain: Expanding markets through virtual communities*. Boston: Harvard Business School Press.

Katz, E. (1959). Mass communication research and the study of popular culture: An editorial note on a possible future for this journal. *Studies in Public Communications, 2*, 1–6.

Katz, E., Blumer, J. G., & Gurevitch, M. (1974). Utilization of mass communication by the individual. In Blumer, J. G., & Katz, E. (Eds.), *The uses of mass communications: Current perspectives on gratification research* (pp. 19–32). Beverly Hills, CA: Sage.

Katz, E., Blumler, J. G., & Gurevitch, M. (1973). Uses and gratification research. *Public Opinion Quarterly, 37*(4), 509–523. doi:10.1086/268109

Kaye, B., & Johnson, T. (2002, March). Online and in the know: Uses and gratifications of the Web for political information. [from Communication & Mass Media Complete database.]. *Journal of Broadcasting & Electronic Media, 46*(1), 54. Retrieved September 4, 2008. doi:10.1207/s15506878jobem4601_4

Klaassen, A. (2007, November 26). Facebook's Bid Ad Plan: If Users Like You, They'll be Your Campaign. *Advertising Age*. Retrieved February 1, 2008, from http://adage.com/digital/article?article_id=121806&search_phrase=%22social+ads%22

Klaassen, A. (2008, April 7). Actions louder than words on social nets. [from Communication & Mass Media Complete database.]. *Advertising Age, 79*(14), 3–33. Retrieved September 4, 2008.

Klein, K. (2008, August 7). Are Social Networking Sites Useful for Business? *Business Week Online*. Retrieved September 3, 2008, from Academic Search Premier database.

Ko, H., Cho, C., & Roberts, M. S. (2005). Internet uses and gratifications: A structural equation model of interactive advertising. *Journal of Advertising*, *34*(2), 57–70.

Korgaonkar, P. K., & Wolin, L. D. (1999, March). A multivariate analysis of Web usage. *Journal of Advertising Research*, 53–68.

LaRose, R., & Eastin, M. (2001). Understanding Internet Usage: A social-cognitive approach to uses and gratifications. *Social Science Computer Review*, *19*(4), 395–413. doi:10.1177/089443930101900401

LaRose, R., & Eastin, M. (2004). A social cognitive theory of Internet uses and gratifications: Toward a new model of media attendance. *Journal of Broadcasting & Electronic Media*, *48*(3), 358–377. doi:10.1207/s15506878jobem4803_2

LaRose, R., & Eastin, M. S. (2002). Is online buying out of control? Electronic commerce and consumer self-regulation. *Journal of Broadcasting & Electronic Media*, *46*(4), 549–564. doi:10.1207/s15506878jobem4604_4

Lenhart, A. (2009, January 14). Adult and Social Networking Websites. *Pew Internet & American Life Project, 2009*. Retrieved June 27, 2009, from http://www.pewinternet.org/~/media//Files/Reports/2009/PIP_Adult_social_networking_data_memo_FINAL.pdf.pdf

Lenhart, A., & Madden, M. (2007, January 7). Social Networking Websites and Teens: An Overview. *Pew Internet & American Life Project, 2007*. Retrieved August 25, 2007, from http://www.pewinternet.org/PPF/r/198/report_display.asp

Lewis, J. (2007). *Social Networking: Examining User Behavior*. Retrieved August 29, 2007, from http://www.webpronews.com/topnews/2007/04/10/social-networking-examining-user-behavior

Lin, C. A. (1999). Online service adoption likelihood. *Journal of Advertising Research*, *39*(2), 79–89.

McIntyre, T. (2008). *MSNBC joins MySpace to combat the Facebook-ABC alliance*. Retrieved September 3, 2008, from http://tech.blorge.com/Structure:%20/2008/04/24/msnbc-joins-myspace-to-combat-the-facebook-abc-alliance-2/

McQuail, D., Blumler, J., & Brown, R. (1972). The television audience: a revised perspective. In McQuail, D. (Ed.), *Sociology of Mass Communication*. London: Longman.

Murchu, I. O., Breslin, J., & Decker, S. (2004). *Online Social and Business Networking Communities*. DERI Technical Report, August 2004.

O'Keefe, D. J. (2002). *Persuasion: Theory and Research* (2nd ed.). Thousand Oaks, CA: Sage Publications, Inc.

Ostrow, A. (2009). *Social Networking Sites More Popular than Email*. Retrieved June 27, 2009, from http://mashable.com/2009/03/09/social-networking-more-popular-than-email/

Papacharissi, Z., & Rubin, A. M. (2000). Predictors of internet use. *Journal of Broadcasting & Electronic Media*, *44*(2), 175–196. doi:10.1207/s15506878jobem4402_2

Perse, E., & Greenberg Dunn, D. (1998). The utility of home computers and media use: Implications of multimedia and connectivity. *Journal of Broadcasting & Electronic Media*, *42*, 435–456.

Pompper, D., Kinnally, W., & McClung, S. (2005, May 26). *Appealing to Abandoning Adolescents: Radio Use Motivation Factors and Time Spent Listening*. Conference Papers -- International Communication Association. Retrieved September 4, 2008, from Communication & Mass Media Complete database.

Preece, J., Nonnecke, B., & Andrews, D. (2004). The top five reasons for lurking: improving community experiences for everyone. *Computers in Human Behavior*, *2*(1).

Raacke, J., & Bonds-Raacke, J. (2008). MySpace and Facebook: Applying the uses and gratifications theory to exploring friend-networking sites. *Cyberpsychology & Behavior*, *11*(2), 169–174. doi:10.1089/cpb.2007.0056

Ridings, C., & Gefen, D. (2004). Virtual Community Attraction: Why People Hang Out Online. *Journal of Computer-Mediated Communication, 10*(1). Retrieved August 29, 2007, from http://jcmc.indiana.edu/vol10/issue1/ridings_gefen.html

Rubin, A. M. (1983). Television uses and gratifications: The interaction of viewing patterns and motivations. *Journal of Broadcasting*, *27*, 37–52.

Ruggiero, T. (2000). Uses and gratifications theory in the 21st century. [from Communication & Mass Media Complete database.]. *Mass Communication & Society*, *3*(1), 3–37. Retrieved September 4, 2008. doi:10.1207/S15327825MCS0301_02

Sheehan, K. B. (2002). Toward a typology of Internet users and online privacy concerns. *The Information Society*, *18*(1), 21–32. doi:10.1080/01972240252818207

Shin, D., & Kim, W. (2007). *Uses and Gratifications of Digital Multimedia Broadcasting: What People Do with Digital Multimedia Broadcasting?* Conference Papers -- International Communication Association, Retrieved September 4, 2008, from Communication & Mass Media Complete database.

Simon, M. (2008). Dupre's MySpace page evolves with scandal. *CNN online*. Retrieved March 14, 2008 from http://www.cnn.com/2008/US/03/13/ashley.myspace/index.html

Stafford, T. F., Stafford, M. R., & Schkade, L. L. (2004). Determining uses and gratifications for the Internet. *Decision Sciences*, *35*(2), 259–285. doi:10.1111/j.00117315.2004.02524.x

Watson, G., & Johnson, D. (1972). *Social psychology: Issues and insights*. Philadelphia: J.B. Lippincott.

Watts, D. J., Dodds, P., & Newman, M. (2002). Identity and search in social networks. *Science*, *296*(5571), 1302–1306. doi:10.1126/science.1070120

Weiser, E. (2000). Gender differences in Internet use patterns and Internet application preferences: a two-sample comparison. *Cyberpsychology & Behavior*, *4*, 167–178. doi:10.1089/109493100316012

Chapter 15
Convergence, Contradiction and Collaboration:
Case Studies on Developing Creative Strategies for Digital Components of Integrated Campaigns

Brian Sheehan
Syracuse University, USA

Antony Young
Optimedia, USA

ABSTRACT

This chapter explores the profound impact of the digital revolution on the advertising business. Specifically, it looks at how advertisers and their agencies are changing the ways they plan media, create advertising ideas, and integrate their campaigns using digital and traditional media. Three key themes are explored: 1) the critical importance of context, which challenges advertisers to fundamentally re-evaluate the relationship between media placement and messaging; 2) the challenge of fragmentation to goals of integration: in the digital scenario, the ability to manage complexity has become a key competitive advantage; 3) the need for a new process to ensure the creative development process is in tune with context and focused on simplicity: this process is called the contextual creative brief. A number of case studies are provided of advertising campaigns that have pioneered in these areas. They are: Mitsubishi's "Which Car?" campaign, Lexus' "Mosaic" campaign, Toyota's "Best in Jest" and "Sketchies" campaigns, Ambien CR's "Points of Stress" campaign, and the Simpsons Movie launch campaign.

INTRODUCTION

The purpose of this chapter is to highlight the key dynamics in developing digital creative strategies for integrated campaigns. We will explore three basic themes: convergence, contradiction and collaboration. In doing so, we will consider how the creative objectives of digital and mainstream media converge. This framework will establish recommended steps to deliver effective digital creative approaches, and strategies that integrate into the overall marketing communication mix. We

DOI: 10.4018/978-1-60566-792-8.ch015

believe these steps have significance for clients and agencies who are increasingly challenged by the proliferation of digital media and the goal of integration.

Creativity and Media Forms: An Evolution

While creativity has always been at the heart of the advertising business, the industry has found it necessary to evolve due in part to the development of new media forms. When NW Ayer & Son the first full service advertising agency opened its doors in 1869, newspaper and poster advertising was the main advertising form. For over half a century ad agencies and brands built their reputation on their ability to create print ads. However, between 1923 and 1930, 60% of American families acquired a radio set (Carter, 2006), which launched the golden age of radio advertising and with that a new set of creative skill-sets were called on.

Television in the 50's and 60's opened a new era for advertising agencies and creativity. Initially, television advertising was a crude form of radio with pictures, but as advertising agency techniques developed and as audiences became more sophisticated, a creative renaissance of branding and slogans materialized. Coca-Cola wanted to teach the world to sing and Michael Jordon in his Nikes urged consumers to *Just Do It*.

While direct marketing had been well established since the Second World War, it really picked up momentum in the 70's, coinciding with an oil crisis and a recession, which led to increased demand for more sales responsiveness from advertising. This marketing channel continued its steady climb in the 80's with the growth of cable television. During this time, advertising that delivered results, and a higher degree of measurability, formed an entirely different set of creative rules.

Enter the Internet in the 90's. In the same way that television advertising evolved, the general ad industry started with their equivalent of "a radio with pictures," which was essentially putting brochure pictures and copy online. Independent digital marketing specialists led the way, initially combining creative skills with technological savvy and data competencies. A new creative order was established. In addition to a growing list of new media options, the existing *old* media adapted and evolved to attract new audiences. For example, 125 year-old institution, *The Wall Street Journal* is pushing its content beyond its newspaper readership base across cable television, its website, email pushes, a color magazine and mobile. Radio stations are broadcasting on the web, via satellite and through podcasts; while the nation's major broadcasters are investing or acquiring digital platforms. These developments are forcing advertisers and their agencies to adapt and demand creative concepts that can 'live' across multiple digital and traditional media forms.

The Internet Is No Longer a Niche Medium: It Is Mainstream

According to a recent IDC study (2008), Internet advertising will grow 8 times as fast as the advertising industry at large and is expected to be the #2 medium in the US by 2012, outpacing newspapers, cable TV and broadcast TV; to be second in spending only to direct marketing. The IDC report also went on to say that video advertising would be the biggest disrupter of Internet advertising, with advertisers expected to shift advertising online from national broadcast. According to a survey by Netpop|U.S. (2006), four of the top six sources used for influencing purchase decisions are found online, with "browsing in retail stores" only slightly edging out search engines as the most important influencer. Marketers are quickly feeling it is uncomfortable to manage their mass advertising media channels separate from other specialized communication channel disciplines, in particular, digital, but also in-store, sponsorship, marketing PR and trade efforts. Developing digital creative in isolation of other advertising efforts is now far less attractive than establishing digital's role within the collective strategy and overall advertising mix.

Digital Has Caused the Advertising Business to Re-Evaluate Its Processes

The objectives of advertising do not change just because of the emergence of new media. Advertising remains an important channel for marketers to drive sales. However, it does change *how* they communicate. Traditional mass media broadcast and print advertising tended to center around brand awareness and brand building as the primary strategy. At the core of this chapter is the belief that most digital media, like web advertising, *functions* differently than traditional media and is able to add further dimension to existing strategies. Three major reasons for this are:

The Capability to Measure Consumer Response

In some respects, digital media has set higher standards of evaluating consumer reaction and creative engagement. Tracking and optimization tools can provide granular and near real time response to creative material. This invokes not just a higher degree of accountability but the ability to be more sophisticated about influencing buyer behavior.

The Level of Interactivity

The interactive functionality the Internet affords enables a more personalized experience. Users are able to get the information how they want it, when they want it. This means the Internet has become the information medium of choice and a significant factor in *influencing* a purchase decision.

The Peer to Peer or Social Media Factor

According to research undertaken by the Kelsey Group, one in four Internet users use online reviews prior to paying for a service delivered off line in key categories that include restaurants, travel, hotels, legal services, medical, automotive or home services (comScore/The Kelsey Group study, 2007). A Keller Fay Group survey revealed that among teens, 39% of word of mouth about a brand happens online, via text, email, IM, chats and blogs (Hein, 2007).

As a result, consumer's relationship with their digital media presents more powerful opportunities in combination with other traditional media to communicate a brand.

What This Chapter Sets Out to Do

We introduce three clear steps that need to be incorporated into the creative development process to ensure creative strategies are: 1) rooted in relevant consumer use of the digital channels; 2) not just included but integral into marketing communications campaigns; and 3) delivering against business and brand objectives. These are covered under the headings: *Consumer Control and the Importance of Context; Conflict: Digital and Integration; and Context and Content: Conflict or Collaboration?* We will use five case studies to demonstrate the importance of these points. Our experience is that these can be applied universally across business categories, from large considered purchases to fast moving consumer package goods or services. They are applicable whether the work is developed in a full-service advertising agency or across a combination of specialist agencies working on behalf of a marketer. And they can be used as a template to evaluate the quality of a creative strategy.

To this end, this chapter provides a practical framework for advertisers and agencies to improve their marketing effectiveness in a time of revolutionary change driven by the digital revolution. One of the fundamental impacts of digital media has been the vast increase in fragmentation. In a fragmented media world, it becomes critical to match advertising content to the most effective placement or context. Further, given the current pressures on all marketers of downward economic trends, it becomes critical—often a question of economic survival—to insure maximum return on marketing investment (ROMI). We believe our framework for matching content to context is a pragmatic strategy for improving ROMI.

Below we discuss the theoretical foundation of this chapter, *the uses-and-gratifications model*, which emphasizes consumer control of media. Our recommendations are the result of exploring a simple, increasingly urgent, question as it relates to the intended uses and the gratifications that consumers seek. Namely, in a world of increasing consumer control of digital media, can digital advertising be integrated seamlessly into multi-faceted campaigns?

THEORETICAL FOUNDATION

The theoretical foundation for this chapter is the *uses-and-gratifications* model. Uses-and-gratifications posits that people choose specific media in order to gain specific gratifications, and that different individuals can use the same media messages in very different ways depending on their purposes or needs. It emphasizes that people are in control of their usage and their relationships with various media. A medium's ability to meet a person's needs—or gratifications sought, including desires for escapism, personal relationships, personal identity, and observation of the world around them, will dictate whether a person uses that specific medium (Blumler & Katz, 1974). Uses and gratifications has sometimes been described as "optimistic" or "humanistic" because it emphasizes each person's power of choice, and therefore the media's subservience to individual control.

Although we are using this model as the foundation of our analysis, it is only fair to mention that there continues to be a lot of controversy about whether uses and gratifications is actually robust enough to be deemed a full-blown theory. Those who believe in the insidious power of media to influence ordinary people in ways they don't always recognize (e.g., media hegemony advocates) fault uses and gratifications for being naïve in attributing complete freedom of choice and interpretation to individuals as they relate to media. Some detractors believe it is a sociological theory that is not supported by a strong psychological theory (Severin & Tankard, 1997). On the other hand, uses-and-gratifications proponents, like Thomas Ruggiero (2000), argue forcefully that the uses and gratifications model has never been more relevant than it is today in relation to digital media. He asserts: "…the emergence of computer-mediated communications has revived the significance of uses and gratifications. In fact, uses and gratifications has always provided a cutting-edge theoretical approach in the initial stages of each new mass communications medium: newspapers, radio and television, and now the Internet" (p.3).

Whether uses-and-gratifications is a complete theory or not, we believe it provides a strong and relevant framework within which to analyze the role of digital media as it relates to the advertising creative strategy process. Ruggiero makes a strong point: the initial stages of any new medium lead to strong levels of engagement between people and that new medium. In the early stages, people are less passive about the new medium: they explore it, play with it, and master it, making strong choices about what they watch, read, or hear. Malcolm Gladwell (2002), in his bestselling book *The Tipping Point*, likens this process to catching a virus: communities of people "infect" each other with an excitement for the new medium. In the case of the Internet for example, the infection has taken a deep hold because it has actually strengthened the connection between the people who created the virus through e-mail, blogs, chat rooms, etc.

We believe that uses and gratifications is specifically relevant for digital media, not only because it is newer than other media, but because of its unique nature. As Rayburn (1996) suggests, the Internet is consumed "intentionally," with people making very purposeful choices about which content they view. They move from site to site, and move within sites, based largely on a mixture of pre-determined and spontaneous needs. In short, digital interactive media engages people in ways more traditional media cannot. Two-way communication creates a stronger sense of on-going engagement. The Internet, for example, allows active participation and a unique level of control over the process of persuasion as consumers can limit and/or change the order of presentation of marketing information at any time based on their preferences or needs (Hoffman & Novak, 1996). Importantly, the engagement is not just intellectual: it is physical as well. People are physically involved to a unique degree in interactive media, whether they are navigating a web site with mouse movements and finger clicks, using a joystick for gaming online, pressing a touch-screen kiosk, or just rolling the wheel on their Blackberry.

Paul Ratzky, Senior Director of Agency Development at Yahoo, sees the difference between digital and traditional media as fundamental: "Digital interactive media can be viewed as 'lean forward' media, while traditional media can be viewed as 'lean back.' The former is usually a very active experience, while the latter is usually very passive." Teen usage of the Internet exemplifies this proactive approach with more than half of online teens creating content on the Internet (Lenhart & Madden, 2005). For marketers and advertising agencies, taking an approach to digital advertising that emphasizes consumer control, like uses and gratifications, recognizes that digital media is a two-way street where the consumer engages the media in at least equal proportion to the media engaging the consumer.

The uses-and-gratifications model is also relevant to our analysis because digital media compresses the hierarchy of effects (McMillan, 2007). Hierarchy of effects models (Lavidge & Steiner, 1961; Palda, 1996) propose that advertising works in a step-by-step fashion, first providing awareness (i.e., cognition), then providing a feeling or emotion about the product (i.e., affect), and finally persuading the consumer to action (i.e., behavior). In the digital realm a consumer's action—such as an inquiry or purchase—is often available much closer in time to the points of initial cognition and affect of a marketer's message. Action is just a click away, not next Friday's trip to the mall. While this allows advertisers an opportunity to turn messaging into swift action, it also gives the consumer a stronger level of understanding about, and control over, the relationship between persuasion and action. The relationship is clearly recognized by consumers, and digital advertising messages are frequently activated by the user based on their relevance to the user's immediate needs sought.

Uses-and-Gratifications may give too much credit to the control people have over the media they encounter; however, there is a clear consensus that the consumer has more control over media in the digital realm than ever before. As a testament to this newfound level of control, TIME magazine's 2006 person of the year was "You." TIME specifically recognized the power of ordinary people to shape the world around them using digital media. In the words of Time Editor Lev Grossman, "It's about the many wresting power from the few... and how that will not only change the world but also change the way the world changes." In the case of Marketing, the many are everyday consumers; the few are advertisers, their agencies, and media owners. As if to underscore this sea change, recent books and marketing trade publications have started calling the current marketing era "The Era of Consumer Control." In our analysis of the relationship between digital media and the creative process, it seems only fitting for us to start with a theoretical model that emphasizes consumer control as its basis.

Consumer control in digital space is critical for another powerful reason. As we've seen, roughly 40% of brand "buzz" now takes place online and this number promises to get even larger. Digital and traditional advertising messages are only the beginning. Increasingly, consumers actively connecting to other consumers online are deciding the success or failure of the multitude of products and services advertised. In the case studies to be reviewed, creating buzz was essential to success for the Simpsons movie, the Lexus IS, and Mitsubishi's Galant. Control is no longer just about what people choose to see, it is about what they choose to pass on, and how they choose to comment on it, in their virtual communities.

CONSUMER CONTROL AND THE IMPORTANCE OF CONTEXT

One of the most significant changes in the advertising landscape resulting from the growth of digital media has been the increasing importance of *context*. On a simplistic level, context is nothing more than *where* your message appears. Advertisers and agencies have long been interested in analyzing the places where their message appears. For over half a century, advertising agencies and media agencies have poured over viewer data regarding television and radio programs, readership data regarding newspapers and magazines, etc. Their focus has been to find a relevant audience for advertisers' messages. Generally, once that audience was found, it didn't matter which show, program, magazine or newspaper they saw the message in. As long as the message was seen, it was considered a rating point or impression with an equal amount of value to any other rating point or impression. As long as the audience saw the message a certain number of times, the message was considered delivered. In this fashion, context can be seen as having been important to marketers and advertisers as a means of demographic or psychographic segmentation.

Context on the Internet

With the advent of digital media—particularly the emergence of the Internet—context has taken on a new, exciting and more complex meaning. Context has become a search not only for a target audience that is *relevant to the advertiser*, but also a search for places and experiences where the advertisers' messages will be particularly *relevant to the consumer*. Because the web gives consumers the ability to zero-in on narrowly defined areas of interest, advertiser messages are more often successful or unsuccessful based on whether they have specific relevance to the specific media context within which they are imbedded. In other words, they are more successful if they are directly related to consumers' desired uses and the gratifications. Therefore, in theory, ads for a new medicine should be more effective in a health and wellbeing website like webmd.com or menshealth.com. Cosmetic ads should be more effective when placed in sites that women go to for beauty advice like makeupalley.com.

Research in offline media has also shown that context influences ad effectiveness (Plummer, Rappaport, Hall, Barocci, 2007). Unfortunately, an advertiser's ability to match specific product messages to the broad content that people are turning to for information or entertainment is significantly limited in traditional media versus the online environment. Digital environments are more finely tuned to help marketers pinpoint consumers' specific uses and gratifications for media consumption. However, the imperative to take advantage of greater contextual relevance in the online space is not absolute. Shamdasani & Stanaland (2001) tested internet banner ads for two types of products—one considered high involvement (a car) and the other considered low involvement (a sports drink)—on attitude to the ad, attitude to the brand, intention to click on the ad, and intention to purchase. The results were very different for the two ads. For the high involvement product, the effectiveness of the ad was related strongly to contextual relevance (i.e., strong link between the ad message and the site content) on all of the measures. For the low-involvement product, contextual relevance mattered much less (Dou & Krishnamurthy, 2007). Therefore, according to these results, it might be okay to just look for quality sites for low involvement products (i.e., sites where their audience is concentrated), like advertisers look for quality TV shows. For high-involvement products on the other hand, there is a significant opportunity to match message to media placement, and a creative imperative to construct messaging that makes the most of the context within which the message appears.

The importance of context can be highlighted by the increasing importance of the once lowly online search ad. Search now commands 41% of all money spent on Internet advertising, compared to just 19% for Internet display advertising(IAB, 2006), and it is expected to stay at that percentage through 2010 (eMarketer, 2006). Why is search now described as the "King Kong" of digital media? It is because of the power of its relationship with searchers. "Beyond 'everyday research' more than 90% of people find or launch websites through search, even when they know the URL" (Plummer, et. al., 2007, p.101). Search has a special relationship with consumers. Its context is almost pure. It brings people the exact content they seek in the exact place they want it. In addition, it provides the information in a way that makes the searcher feel comfortable and in control. When a consumer searches for a specific car, for example, and they get results for that car, the results are highly relevant to an extraordinary degree. Historically, search placement was something brands just did. Today, search placement strategy is one of the most demanding, creative and competitive areas of marketing. Search seems simple, but the special contextual place it holds with consumers make it a one of the most hard-fought battlegrounds in marketing today. Unfortunately, even today, for some marketers and agencies, search is seen as a technical specialty as opposed to a core marketing function.

Consumer control and the importance of context in digital media require us to *fundamentally re-evaluate the relationship between the way media is planned and the way the message is developed.* This affects the creative strategy process, the creative development process, and ultimately, the process for evaluating creative effectiveness. Based on the research noted above, it would be quite easy to jump to the conclusion that this re-evaluation need only be considered for high-involvement products like cars or golf clubs, but that would be a mistake. As noted, the very nature of digital media—its interactivity and its compression of the hierarchy of effects—means that creative messaging in the digital realm is a very different proposition than creative messaging in traditional media. Simply, when developing creative for digital media, context matters: it really matters.

These observations directly support the implications of the uses and gratifications model. Context represents the end result of consumer control of digital media. The consumer starts with their usage intent then search—usually through a search engine—for the most relevant context. As more media become digital, search becomes more important as consumers continue to drive the specific context within which they see their advertising and consider it for relevance.

CONFLICT: DIGITAL AND INTEGRATION

Digital media is by no means as new as it is made out to be. Although it is commonly referred to as "new media," it is a proverbial babe in swaddling clothes compared to its more mature stable-mates, such as television and magazines. In fact, digital media has been utilized by major marketers and agencies for the best part of the last decade. It is now quite decidedly in the mainstream of marketing efforts. Agencies and clients who have not developed interactive capabilities are considered nothing short of dinosaurs. In that case, you might rightly ask yourself, "Is this chapter really so important?" or "Is the relationship between digital marketing and the creative strategy process really such a groundbreaking subject?" We think the answer to both questions is a resounding "yes." The reason it is so important and groundbreaking has little to do with the nature of digital media or consumer behavior; it has a lot to do with the structural transformation that is taking place in the advertising industry, within client organizations, and media owners. It's about where clients and agencies have been, where they are going, and where they are now. It has a whole lot to do with the industry's biggest single goal: *integration*.

Fragmented Messaging

As media and messaging have multiplied in the last decade, advertisers and their agencies have realized there is an urgent need to manage the consistency of their messaging. Not so long ago, when an advertiser produced a few TV ads or print ads a year, consistency was relatively easy. Today it is normal for a single brand to have television, print, outdoor ads, websites, online display ads, email campaigns, direct marketing campaigns, experiential marketing events, PR releases and stunts, community outreach and cause-related marketing programs all running simultaneously. Within each of these messaging channels, it is not uncommon for there to be multiple communications approaches modified to reach different demographic and psychographic targets. With different marketing groups within clients—and different agencies—handling various aspects of the brand's messaging, the core message can become hopelessly fragmented. It is not unheard of for there to be so many messages and programs going on for one brand that no one person on the client side or agency side has actually seen all of the messages until after they appear in the marketplace, much less tried to manage them all.

In this world of fragmentation, driven in part by the most fragmented of all media—the Internet—the idea of integration has become an ideal. In fact, advertising agencies now often eschew the very idea that they do "advertising," preferring to label themselves as purveyors of Integrated Marketing Communications (IMC). Not surprisingly, advertising agencies are trying very hard to convince their clients they have not only the capabilities to develop every area of messaging, but also the discipline and processes to manage a brand's portfolio of messages in an integrated way. In the world of integrated marketing, the whole is significantly bigger than the sum of its parts. This is sometimes called the "marketing multiplier principle," where one plus one can equal three. Advertisers for their part value integration with equal fervor, whether they allow one agency to lead it for them or whether they choose to manage integration themselves by bringing a number of advertising agencies and suppliers together to achieve a common goal.

The Establishment of Specialist Agencies

Where integration gets tricky is not necessarily between one medium and another, but rather between media planning and creative development processes on the one hand and between digital creative development and traditional creative development on the other. The reasons for both situations are surprisingly similar. In each case, organizational silos develop over time around areas of very specific organizational expertise. In the case of media and creative, a split in expertise was created within advertising agencies. Based on market forces in the 1990s, the media expertise within big advertising agencies was recognized as having a higher market value outside of those agencies. Media departments moved out of advertising agencies and were re-born as media agencies. With the help of advertising agency consolidation into larger holding companies, they were able to create a level of scale that made their purchasing power—and their subsequent investment in research and media tools—immense. The focus was decidedly on media buying. Clients perceived big purchasing to be a strong benefit. In an environment where media supply was increasing, stand-alone companies that planned and bought media made sense. As a result, agency holding companies created new independent media companies *within* their overall organizations. Omnicom's agencies created companies like OMD and PhD, and Publicis' agencies created companies like Starcom and Zenith.

In the case of creative development, the explosion of the Internet created a need for technical expertise that traditional agencies did not possess, and which they could not develop quickly. Small technical, entrepreneurial companies in places like Silicon Valley understood the Internet better; and they already had the digital expertise traditional agencies coveted and were racing to acquire. Here a new silo was being created entirely outside the traditional advertising agency structure. Significantly, the work these companies were doing was in direct competition with agency hegemony over the creative development process. For many brands this would be the first time that any aspect of their brand's advertising creative would be developed by someone other than their "agency." Likewise, for many brands this would be the first time that multiple pieces of creative developed by different companies or creative groups would be in the market simultaneously. Today, the landscape has become extremely complex with many advertising agencies offering media planning and digital expertise to clients in addition to working in collaboration with stand-alone media agencies and digital companies. In some cases all of these agencies may be owned by the same holding company, and in some cases not. An agency with 20 different clients may have 20 different combinations of resources, both internal and external. To further confuse matters, many client marketing departments are now struggling to regain control of digital media, which they had handed to their e-commerce or technical groups because the marketing department either didn't know how to handle it or misunderstood its potential.

The Need to Manage Complexity

As we can see there are many divisions and complications when looking at ways to improve the effectiveness of digital media advertising. To help simplify matters, this chapter focuses specifically on ideas for managing media strategy development and creative development for digital media used in integrated campaigns.

Over the past few years, the dynamic changes highlighted above have led to a variety of different ways for brands to manage the creative strategy process. In some cases, different creative strategies are developed for different marketing messages with the client managing their integration to the brand's equity or a brand's over-riding mission statement. In some cases, the traditional agency acts as a "brand navigator" making sure all the brand's marketing agencies are working to the same creative strategy for any given campaign. No matter how many agencies an advertiser uses, whether it is one or ten, the goal is the same: to drive the creative messaging as consistently as possible in a complex world where many messages and messengers are employed.

Poor management of integration leads to fragmentation of message, which in a world of fragmented media can be a recipe for disaster. In an industry where integration is creating a centripetal force in relation to advertising creative development and the proliferation of media and messages is creating a centrifugal force, a practical approach to creative strategy that reconciles the two forces is essential. We will propose just such a practical approach which we hope will be significant for optimizing creative development in an advertising environment that needs to be both digital and integrated. Measuring the success of such an approach over time will form the basis of further meaningful study.

CONTEXT AND CONTENT: CONFLICT OR COLLABORATION?

So far we have looked in detail at the importance of context when presenting a message to consumers and the challenges of integration in a world where many hands touch the creative process. Now we will look at how these things relate to each other in the real world of developing digital advertising creative. We will make the assumption that for most brands the digital advertising campaign is part of their overall advertising campaign and that integration of their overall message is desired. Based on what we've reviewed so far, an obvious goal for creative strategies that include digital elements would be to infuse them with a thorough understanding of how consumers interact with and even control particular digital media. Further, they would include an appreciation of what is unique about the specific context of the digital media being used in the campaign.

The Traditional Briefing Process

Before we talk about how the creative strategy can be improved today, it might be helpful to review how creative strategies were traditionally developed within advertising agencies. Historically, there were two important briefs for any campaign: the creative brief and the media brief. These two briefs were developed by the account service or planning group and then presented to the respective creative and media personnel who would do the actual work of developing the creative ideas and media plan. Unfortunately, it was not uncommon for the two teams to be working in complete isolation from each other. The creative would often be developed without any knowledge of what the media team was doing—a rating point being just a rating point after all. Likewise, the creative executions would often be developed and go to air or press without the media team ever seeing them before they were finished. The team developing the brand's media plan might see the brand's ad while watching TV at home before ever seeing it in the agency.

Given the great changes in the media landscape over the past decade, you might guess that media departments and creative departments working to separate briefs is no longer the case, and you would be right. You would also be wrong. Already, there is strong movement towards greater integration and communication between media and creative groups. There is a growing consensus about the importance of recognizing consumer control of digital media and the context of specific digital platforms like websites and mobile phone applications. However, integrating media expertise and creative development expertise is not always easy, even in the strategy development stage. The explosion in the number of new media types leads to complexity. Today, media planners have to consider a plethora of digital options as well as shopper media, experiential media, and ambient media, just to name a few. Another reason is that creative agencies and media agencies look at things differently and often have different ideas about how to solve specific marketing problems. In the cases where a separate digital agency is doing the digital creative development, the link between the digital agency and the creative agency can be even weaker than the one between creative agencies and media agencies: old habits die hard.

To complicate matters further, media owners with digital capabilities now work routinely with media agencies to develop and produce specific digital creative ideas that can get approved, produced and executed without the creative agency's creative director ever being involved. At one end of the spectrum, the creative strategy process for integrated campaigns with digital elements can result in creative developed with no insight into the specific media context that makes the message relevant to consumers. At the other end of the spectrum, it can result in contextually relevant executions that fall flat conceptually because the best creative talent was not employed. That's the worst case. Now let us talk about the best case.

The Contextual Creative Brief

Integration is increasingly becoming a coordinated way of working (i.e., an integrated working process), versus just coordinating all of the various pieces of an advertising campaign. Maximizing the effectiveness of digital advertising starts with the creative briefing process. We believe that creative briefs should be transformed into ***Contextual Creative Briefs*** in order for digital advertising to be most effective. We recommend that *Contextual Creative Briefs* adhere to three simple guidelines provided in Table 1.

These are simple, but important requirements for delivering more engaging and effective digital messaging. For digital advertising to succeed as part of integrated campaigns, media expertise must become part of the creative development process, and digital creative strategy must be unified with creative strategy for the rest of the campaign. By following the steps above, integration is improved, while flexibility to execute different media differently within the campaign is enhanced. Ultimately, this process ensures that consumers' increasing control over the relevance of their digital context, through such things as search engines, is matched by advertisers' ability to embed a relevant message in that context, as outlined in Figure 1.

The left side of Figure 1 illustrates that each consumer now has an unprecedented tool at their disposal for gathering relevant digital information and/or entertainment: their search engine. The information and/or entertainment gathered by Google, for example, is the specific context within which an advertisement may appear. Because the results of the consumer's search are so granular (i.e., finely sifted by the search engine's algorithm, from among millions of potential contexts, to be specifically what the consumer is looking for), it makes it vital that the advertising message fit that finely-tuned context to be seen as relevant by the consumer. Relevance of the message, therefore, becomes a key determinant of potential success. On the right side of Figure 1, consumer complexity and media fragmentation have led to the potential for many different types of messages for the same product or brand. The *Contextual Creative Brief* process helps insure these messages are both well matched to the specific context within which they will appear and consistent with each other across a variety of contexts.

Table 1.

1. Digital elements should be included in a single Integrated Communications Plan (ICP)–There should be only one communications strategy. Every person working on the campaign—whether they are developing creative executions, media plans, promotions, etc., or whether they work at the creative agency, media agency, interactive agency, etc.—should be working from a single comprehensive brief. The ICP should include a single, ***unified messaging objective*** as well as the specific role of each medium being used.
2. The ICP should call out the ***contextual media insight***–The unique context of an individual medium may call for a very different creative execution to maximize that media opportunity. Contextual insights are vitally important for digital media given consumers' level of control, but they can also be useful for traditional media when the product or message lends itself to leveraging a medium's context. The contextual insight, as opposed to the more common consumer insight, asks: "In what unique way does the consumer relate to this specific medium?" Consumer insights are still vital: they tell us how consumers relate to the product, category or benefit. The contextual insight does not replace the consumer insight, it adds to it.
3. The digital executions should be a seamless part of the campaign's organizing creative idea, yet be as executionally unique as they need to be–Every element of the creative campaign should clearly be part of the campaign's core creative idea. The core creative idea is defined by message, tone, and character. Digital executions should not be allowed to create their own creative platform. However, to properly use contextual media insights to enhance the effectiveness of digital media within an integrated campaign, flexibility in execution is required. Without flexibility, integrated campaigns can become the equivalent of a matched set of luggage, where every execution, in every medium, looks and acts exactly the same. This can be comforting to marketers, who at the very least can claim successful integration of many elements. But this can also mean the digital components of such campaigns are woefully underdeveloped, and eventually under-perform, because "lean back" messaging didn't engage people in a "lean forward" environment.

Figure 1. Content meets context: a model for creating contextually relevant digital advertising campaigns in an era of increasing consumer control

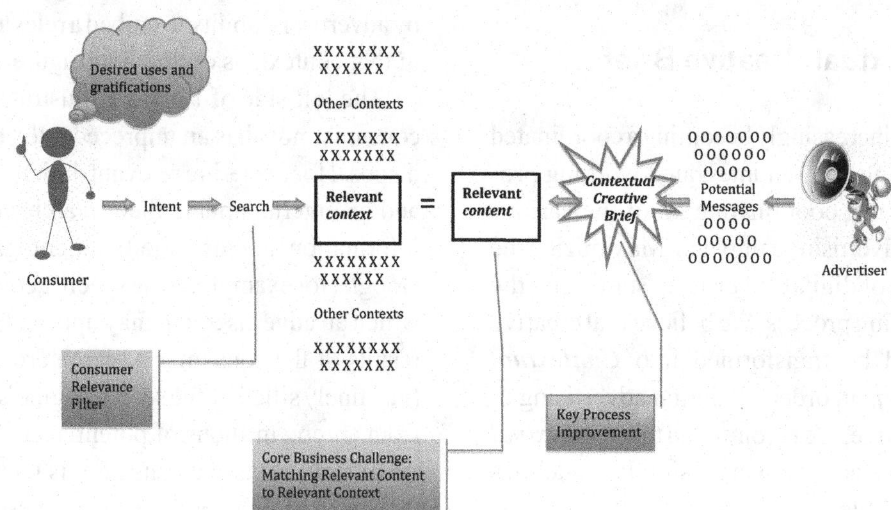

CASE STUDIES

In order to demonstrate the power of a ***contextual creative brief***, we will look at a number of case studies where following the rules noted above led to outstanding digital campaigns that were seamless parts of outstanding integrated campaigns. Each of these examples demonstrates an outstanding use of media context to enhance creative effectiveness. The first three cases come from the automotive industry. The automotive industry was one of the first to invest in big digital advertising programs. The automotive category is consistently ranked as one the biggest categories in total media spending (in 2007 auto marketers spent over $12 billion), so the auto companies were also among the first to have the financial resources to invest heavily in digital. Automotive is also a high interest category, which means they have a lot to gain by creating engaging and interactive experiences.

Mitsubishi Crashes the Super Bowl

During the 2004 Super Bowl, Mitsubishi took a chance, actually two chances. First, a brand that did not have the budget firepower of automotive big boys like Ford or Toyota decided to take advantage of a discount on a still very expensive Super Bowl spot. These are the sort of decisions that can make or break a marketing director. Just ask Ian Beavis, who was Mitsubishi's senior vice president of marketing at the time. He knew that using that big a percentage of his budget to drive awareness alone was a bad bet. He knew they had to use the opportunity to do something for their brand that would generate an unprecedented level of interest and excitement. He, and his advertising agency, Deutsch, gambled that they could use the highest profile media space a company can buy as a teaser whose job it was to drive viewers to the web for the payoff. With these two gambles dancing in his head, Beavis may not have slept very well the night before the Super Bowl. After the spot ran—and the gamble had paid off—Mitsubishi had created something that, in the words of one reporter, "was enough to make people want to get back into advertising again" (Jaffe, 2004, ¶3). The reporter noted that it had "more drama, intrigue and suspense" than an episode of 2004's most popular TV show, "Survivor."

The Mitsubishi spot was simple and effective. It featured a comparison test between a Mitsubishi Galant and the best-selling Toyota Camry. As the two cars drove side-by-side at high speeds, each was preceded by an18-wheel truck that started dropping hazards in their way. The cars swerved to avoid such flying obstacles as bowling balls and garbage cans. But the big surprise came when two full-sized sedans came rolling out of the trucks, landed on the road in front of the speeding Galant and Camry, and started rolling and flipping in front of the two cars. It seemed as if a NASCAR-style chain-reaction pile-up was just about to begin. Which car would avoid the tremendous collision? Both of them? One of them? Neither of them? Just as the viewer was about to see, the film froze and a superimposed headline simply said: "SeeWhatHappens.com." Beavis and his agency believed that if they could create enough suspense they could drive millions of viewers to their website to see how the cliffhanger was resolved. While they were there, Mitsubishi believed that they could get enough people who would never have been interested in a Galant to take a closer look and ultimately buy one. Their faith was strong because they knew that 70% of people buying a Mitsubishi went to the web first. As a smaller manufacturer, they also knew that people had to learn more about a Mitsubishi before buying one, and the web was the perfect place to give them more information in an engaging way. This expensive, high profile commercial was merely a tool to do that on a tremendous scale.

So how well did it work? From a marketing point of view it worked extremely well, far exceeding its objectives. According to Ian Beavis, who is a colorful and straight-talking Australian, "It bloody near blew the back off the servers!" He notes people spent an inordinate amount of time on the website and the campaign had what he calls a "long tail effect," with a consumer pass-along component that went on for weeks after the initial campaign ran. The numbers were staggering: 31 million visits to SeeWhatHappens.com between the Super Bowl and August 2004; 11 million visits within six hours of the broadcast; 8 million unique visitors; two-thirds of visitors watched the full commercial two times or more; and web leads to its dealers tripled. The ad generated more web traffic in 24 hours than Mitsubishi.com generated in an average month.

What was it that made this campaign so powerful that it moved 31 million people to do something they probably never would have done: visit a site for the Mitsubishi Galant? Obviously a great, suspenseful creative idea had a lot to do with it. But the Super Bowl is chock full of great creative ideas that make us laugh, make us cry or make us sit on the edge of our couches. They rarely make us do anything, and with rare exception do they make us—on the basis of one spot alone—have a different relationship with a company that we may have had no relationship with before. Such breakthrough success is the domain of Apple's "1984" commercial and the stuff of advertising legend. Mitsubishi's success was based on something very simple, and at the time, in 2004, still quite novel: an appreciation for media context.

The contextual insight that drove the Mitsubishi idea at every stage was that people go to the Internet to get quick answers. When there is something a person wants to know or a dilemma that they need to resolve, the quickest answer is to go to the web; they are looking for quick usage to deliver immediate gratification. Mitsubishi simply created a dilemma on television where the only way to see for yourself what happened was to go to their website. It sounds painfully simple. Yet it is the difference between what Mitsubishi did and a typical creative brief that results in a simple side-by-side demonstration on TV where everything gets resolved in 30 seconds. Such a spot would not get consumers to take the step that Mitsubishi desperately needed: to get more engaged with a smaller brand that might disappear from consciousness the minute the spot ends—Super Bowl spot or not. Mitsubishi and Deutsch appreciated the contextual difference between a "lean forward" medium such as the web, and a "lean back" medium, such as television, and integrated them perfectly into a seamless, powerful campaign. This understanding permeated the entire creative development process. When we asked Ian Beavis how they coordinated the media brief with the creative brief, he said, "The web people, the media people, and the creative people were always on one page. There was only ever one brief: drive people to the web."

Lexus Lives in Many Dimensions

In 2005, Lexus was a brand on a roll. For five years running Lexus had been the number one selling luxury automotive brand in the USA. Lexus had cemented its reputations on a car and SUV line-up that included sedate and elegant sedans such as the LS 400 and the ES 300, as well as the wildly popular RX 300, which dominated the segment that it had virtually created in the late 1990's, the entry-level luxury SUV. Lexus had also cemented its brand image with the stolid promise of "The Relentless Pursuit of Perfection."

Despite Lexus' seeming dominance of the luxury space it had some chinks in its armor. Lexus had fewer younger luxury buyers (buyers in their 30's and early 40's) than their key competitors Mercedes Benz and BMW. Lexus also trailed far behind both brands in the minds of consumers on performance attributes. Lexus had launched a product in 2001 aimed squarely at both the youth market and its performance image. The product was the IS 300. Although a moderate success initially, sales of the car had dropped to only about 8,000 units by 2005. It had not brought in as many young buyers as Lexus wanted and it had not significantly improved Lexus' image for performance.

For the newly re-vamped 2006 model, Lexus had big plans. They overhauled the product completely offering two engine options and a level of performance that would challenge the segment leader, BMW 3-Series, head on. They added the level of luxury on the interior that made the car feel like a true Lexus (the original model being a bit Spartan for a luxury car), and they gave the car a sleek and aggressive exterior that would please Lexus stalwarts as well as people who turned their nose up at the first generation IS. Lexus set a sales target that was no less aggressive: 40,000 units. Considering that the first IS in its heyday never exceeded 25,000 units per year, this was a tall order.

When Lexus and its agency, Team One Advertising, began researching the car with thirty-somethings, they realized two things. First, the car was a winner. It had attractive styling, a terrific interior package, and impressive performance. Second, they realized that younger buyers had changed significantly since they last launched the IS 300 five years earlier. The biggest change was their lifestyle, which had been revolutionized by the emergence and proliferation of digital technology and digital media. Younger luxury car buyers were now living their lives in a constant state of multi-tasking. Multi-tasking was not just a phenomenon for younger luxury buyers: people all over society, and just about every businessperson with a laptop or PDA, were multi-tasking. What made this group unique was that they loved it; they felt that multi-tasking added value to their lives. Digital devices, websites and the like made their lives better and more fulfilling. This was a far cry from fifty-something consumers who bemoaned multi-tasking as a necessary evil.

It did not take the agency long to see a connection between the strengths of the new IS and the values of younger luxury car buyers. The new car performed well in a number of dimensions (e.g., styling, luxury, technology, performance) as opposed to its key competitor, BMW 3-Series, which was seen as doing one thing (i.e., performance) very well. At the same time, digital technology was seen as increasing the number of positive dimensions of their lives. They could do more, experience more, and have more stimulation in any finite amount of time. The campaign theme "Why Live in One Dimension" was born. On top of being a rallying cry that connected a new lifestyle and a new car, it was a not so subtle swipe at BMW.

Lexus and Team One quickly realized that by embracing their new campaign idea they had a tiger by the tail. Their advertising campaign had to walk the talk. In order to be relevant and credible, the new IS campaign had to be present in the dozens of dimensions of the target audience's life, most of them driven by digital devices and technology. That meant a fully-integrated campaign where the digital components were in the driver's seat and the traditional components were passengers. And the digital components needed to be everywhere the audience was multi-tasking: on the web, on mobile phones, on digital outdoor, and especially experimental media. It would be even better yet if the campaign could invent some new form of digital media and create a new dimension.

Ultimately, Lexus created a massive integrated campaign that included television, print, outdoor, websites, e-mail, online ads, brochures, special events, and even cool mobile phone applications. But where the campaign really stood out was with two ideas that elevated the IS by breaking new ground in digital media and delivery. By their very existence, Lexus communicated that it not only understood the many dimensions of the lives of young luxury buyers, but that they could add to those dimensions. The two ideas were called the "Mosaic" and the "Hologram."

The Mosaic

The Mosaic was an ambitious idea from the start. Lexus Vice President of Marketing, Deborah Wahl Meyer, had called all of her marketing people and all the key players from Team One and her other marketing partners together for a working session. The session was designed to build teamwork, generate new ideas, and make sure all the players touching this unprecedented launch were on the same page. The Mosaic idea came out of a breakout session in the meeting and was met with immediate, enthusiastic, and unanimous excitement. It was a great idea and everyone knew it.

The idea was that Lexus would create a special website for the IS where people could share personal pictures of the many dimensions of their lives. The pictures would be uploaded to the site and become components of a mosaic picture of the IS online. This would be the first view people would have of the car's new styling. Imagine a modern-day Georges Seurat painting where every colored point that makes up the image of the car is really a photograph contributed by someone over the internet. The site was very sophisticated. When people revisited the site, they would see the mosaic picture of the car and then zoom in to their specific pictures to reveal exactly what part of the mosaic their pictures comprised. It had a viral component making it a fun and surprising way to share your pictures with friends. The site was very deep, offering a personalized "IS Experience" which was like a virtual test drive where you set the car's color, the weather, the road conditions and even the music. There were also mobile phone downloads allowing you to get information on your phone from Lexus or a number of your favorite sites, like Fox Sports.

Lexus wanted to go far beyond just having a viral, fun, and interactive website. This idea had to live in many dimensions. So Lexus rented a huge billboard in Times Square to broadcast the mosaic live. At regular intervals the billboard would show the mosaic of the car and then zoom in to show some of the specific pictures that comprised it; so anyone's humble pictures could be featured in Times Square. This feature became a big incentive to get involved with the site.

To make things even more interesting and multi-dimensional, Lexus hired street teams to roam Times Square sporting digital cameras. The street teams would take pictures of the people, their families and friends, many of them tourists who were thrilled to be in Times Square. Through a special program, the street teams were able to upload the pictures to the mosaic and feature them on the giant billboard within minutes. For many it was the thrill of a lifetime to see their picture on a four-storey electronic billboard in one of the busiest and most famous intersections in the world. Life even imitated art with many people taking pictures of the billboard featuring their likeness to show their friends at home or even re-load onto the site.

In this case, Lexus created new modes of relevant usage to provide unexpected gratifications that engaged and delighted their audience.

The Hologram

Lexus added yet another interesting dimension to the Times Square experience by renting a storefront on the corner of 42nd Street and Broadway and using it to create a new type of media experience. Lexus had recently been exposed to a new technology from Europe that they found interesting, and they were looking for just the right project to use it. The IS launch was it. The technology involved a battery of high-tech projectors that could create an incredibly lifelike 3-D hologram of the new IS. Kiosks allowed the Lexus team to bring the idea to the next level by allowing pedestrians walking by on the street to control the hologram. People walking by could rotate the car, looking at its different angles. They could change its color. They could even drive it in and out of the storefront.

The hologram had all the best features of a cutting-edge automotive website; but instead of being limited to one laptop it was in the middle of one of the world's busiest intersections for large crowds to see, interact with, and enjoy. In fact, the 42nd Street storefront got so much pedestrian attention that New York City police officers had to regularly move the crowds on to avoid jamming the intersection. After its New York premiere, the hologram was featured in other big cities like Los Angeles, and a smaller version of the hologram was used at events and large dealerships.

The results of the "Why Live in One Dimension" campaign were astounding. Lexus ran past their sales targets, selling over 50,000 units in the first 10 months. They brought in significantly more young buyers to the brand, and the campaign drove up all of the Lexus brands' key image attributes, with the largest increase being in the area of performance. At the end of 2007, the IS series was still selling over 50,000 units annually. By taking advantage of breakthroughs in digital technology, Lexus was able not only to claim relevance to younger drivers' multidimensional, multitasking lives, but also to deliver a new multidimensional experience. The IS 300 walked the talk, not an easy task for a staid brand with little previous connection to younger luxury drivers.

The key to the success of the campaign was the combination of new technology, smart contextual insight, and creative thinking. As Deborah Meyer noted: "The best aspects of the campaign, for example the Mosaic, were things we worked on together. There were no silos. The creative people, media, interactive, client, and agency were all working to the same strategy. There was a simple and shared vision." Team One's creative director, Chris Graves, believes success came from a new type of insight: "We are always looking at insights about how consumers relate to our products. What made the IS launch so successful was that we had a deep insight about the way our consumers related to digital media and technology. This put our media experts and interactive experts right in the middle of our traditional creative-development process. We learned a lot from this."

Toyota Laughs It Up with YouTube

For the launch of the 2008 model Corolla, Toyota was also trying to court youth, but unlike Lexus "youth" meant young adults in their late teens and early twenties. Marketers know that this group is hard to reach at the best of times. With the emergence of digital media, this job is even tougher. As one of the USA's top television spending brands,

Toyota knows that television viewing by late teens and twenty-somethings has been plummeting in recent years. One solution has been to shift more money for youth-oriented products like the Toyota Yaris to online advertising and events. Yet, the problem with advertising strategies that "push" the message over the web is the tremendous number of sites available to youth. The audience is finely fragmented and many sites don't lend themselves to the kind of relevant, non-interruptive messaging that younger audiences value.

Toyota, and its agency, Saatchi & Saatchi Los Angeles, solved this problem with a neat combination of consumer insight, contextual insight and good old-fashioned media planning basics. The first insight was clear: if you wanted to reach a young audience, you needed to be on the web. Whether you were on the web or on TV, you needed to find broad reach channel. Toyota was trying to sell hundreds of thousands of Corollas; it had its sights clearly set on making Corolla the best-selling car model in the USA in 2008. On the web, there are few sites that offer this kind of reach. Examples are sites like Face Book and YouTube. But these are not the kind of sites where users want to be interrupted by lots of advertising. The key was to find a way to work with such broad-reach sites to enhance the users experience instead of detracting from it. This was particularly important for Corolla, a car with a boring heritage, but which now offered a model that was perfectly styled, optioned and price for young people. That's where the contextual insights came in.

John Lisko, Executive Communications Director at Saatchi & Saatchi LA, set his team to the task. They quickly came up with a simple, powerful contextual insight: what made YouTube different than television was that the content people were looking at were predominantly short, funny films. With this thought in mind, they realized that they could do a lot more than just push a digital advertisement on YouTube. They could use it as a "pull" medium, offering young viewers a chance to see the best of the best of what they were looking for, and a chance get involved in the comedy content that they loved. From this insight, two YouTube/Toyota Corolla initiatives were born: "Best in Jest" and "Sketchies."

"Best in Jest" was launched in March of 2008 and was a new destination powered by YouTube and custom designed for Toyota. It was a repository for the funniest videos of the week. It is sponsored by Corolla and also features funny videos of Corolla for those who wish to view them. "Best in Jest" adds value to the YouTube experience, allowing people to see the funniest videos quickly without having to find them via countless hours of searching.

"Sketchies" is a YouTube-powered site that Corolla sponsored. The site allows the YouTube viewing community to submit short comedy sketch videos to be judged for cash and prizes. The videos had to include a road trip (for obvious reasons) and a musical instrument (just for fun). "Best in Jest" and "Sketchies" allowed Corolla to be relevant when advertising in YouTube because they understood the context and made the most of it for YouTube users.

The results were outstanding. Saatchi & Saatchi LA reported that recent research on the campaign showed significant increases in brand favorability, purchase consideration, and a variety of Corolla product attributes for respondents who had visited the sites. Impressively, 55% of the "Sketchies" contest visitors said they would consider purchasing a Corolla.

Saatchi's Lisko attributes the success to the power of the original media insight: "This campaign was the difference between advertising on YouTube and creating a new YouTube experience that was relevant to a young audience and a perfect fit for Corolla. Corolla was adding value, not taking away. Working with new media is about understanding three things: context, context, and context. When media insights get a seat at the creative table amazing things can happen."

In the case of Toyota, a savvy advertiser aligned their message directly to their consumers' desired usage and the specific gratifications sought. Content met context.

TWO CASES THAT GO DIGITAL AND BEYOND

In this chapter we have been emphasizing the importance of contextual insights to maximize the effectiveness of the digital components of integrated campaigns. However, contextual insights are important for every medium and every element. We emphasize their importance for digital media because, as we have seen, digital media has a fundamentally different relationship and interaction with consumers. When an integrated campaign is done right all media are maximizing their specific context within the lives of consumers. Ambien CR and The Simpsons Movie are two good examples

Ambien CR–Advertising at the Point of Need

Adweek described it as a wake-up call for one of the country's most popular prescription sleep aids. For the first time since it went on the market, the Ambien brand would be facing new competitors as its base brand went generic. Its maker, Sanofi-Aventis, needed a marketing plan to launch its new formulation *Ambien CR* a new 2-layered sleep-aid that is "controlled released." The first layer puts you to sleep while the second layer helps you stay asleep through the night. It promised "A good night's sleep from start to finish." Its lead competitor, Sepracor's Lunesta, was planning to spend some $200 million on a media marketing blitz, more than double its annual budget.

Ambien CR's media agency, Optimedia US, immediately recognized the importance of having both a consumer emotional insight and a consumer contextual insight. According to John Potenzano, Communications Planning Director at Optimedia: "For the advertising to resonate, it needed to work at both a creative and a media environment level."

Consumer groups uncovered two telling insights. The first insight to be uncovered was the emotional one: Insomnia sufferers know they don't get enough sleep, but they tend to tough it out. It is not until they are suffering from stress that they become more receptive to messaging from products like Ambien CR. That insight was important as it helped lead to the second insight which was contextual. This insight was in answer to the question: What kind of relationship do insomniacs have with various media when they are under stress? The answer was striking.

Insomnia sufferers have a very different relationship with all kinds of media when they are under stress. They actively seek out media to help keep them occupied and calm them down. They watch late night and early morning TV more than non-sufferers. They are more likely to up watching TV or on-line on Sunday nights before the start of the workweek. They are more likely to be visiting travel websites, thinking they need a holiday. They watch TV to relax and use the web to keep occupied.

The agency reasoned, if we could tap into the *points of stress* consumers would be more receptive to the advertising messages. This simple question about context gave Optimedia plenty of clues about when to advertise, where to advertise, and how to advertise. Ambien CR combined television and online in a complementary way, where TV built awareness of the benefits and online gave the detailed explanation of how it worked.

Late night and early morning became important times to advertise. As did Sunday night/Monday morning. Monday became the day most would see an Ambien CR ad on TV or be served an ad online. To reach people who lose sleep Sunday night, the agency ran a heavy concentration of Ambien CR commercials during the "morning papers" segment in NewsNight with Aaron Brown on CNN on Monday nights. Ambien CR sponsored the prime-time movie slots on Sunday and Monday nights. They sponsored travel websites.

Their media plan also targeted business travelers who experience time-zone changes.

Daylight saving weekend (i.e. when the clocks shift forward an hour) is a reminder that people are going to lose an hour of sleep and the media gives extra attention to insomnia issues. Ambien CR sponsored a CBS Healthwatch feature about clock change and sleep awareness. They also sponsored Lifetimetv.com's fourth quarter 2005 "Holiday De-stress" minisite, which featured music, aromatherapy, yoga, games and astrology. On-air promos on Lifetime TV drove viewers to the site. Ambien CR also sponsored programming around the New Year's Day marathon.

Search was also an integral part of the media mix as search campaigns were maximized around high awareness peaks driven by the television and print advertising. Sanofi-Aventis realized that search strategy was vital: it is where consumers express their specific usage intent in the hope that what returns to them, in both editorial and advertising content, will achieve their gratification needs.

Without focusing on media context, it would have been very easy to just do a demographic analysis of insomnia sufferers and run media based on research as to where those demographic audiences could be reached. Ambien CR would have missed a huge opportunity to send highly targeted messages when and where their potential buyers were most engaged with the specific media being used.

In the end, Optimedia came up with a plan for Ambien CR that cost half of what its new competitor spent. Ambien was able to maintain the lion's share of the sleep aid market while exceeding the client's goals of converting Ambien's base brand to Ambien CR.

The Simpsons Movie: Blurring Media and Reality

There is no more hotly contested market than the box office. New big budget movies from Hollywood's largest production companies slug it out every week to see which movies will have a big opening weekend and which will be also-rans. Being number one for an opening weekend can be the difference between making $100 million and losing $100 million. Few movies survive long after a weak opening. The Simpsons movie had one advantage: a big pre-existing base of loyal fans. Yet the franchise was almost 20 years old and it had no guarantee that its popular 30-minute format would entice fans to pay eight dollars to watch a full-length movie.

20th Century Fox Studios realized that relying on advertising that focused on the popularity of the show or its characters to drive ticket sales would be a mistake. Had they done that, a simple television campaign on high-rated shows would have given them all the reach they needed to get the word out. Instead, they took advantage of the special opportunities created by emerging media. Their goal was to create a level of involvement with the Simpsons that went way beyond awareness of a new movie launch. By carefully manipulating the contextual opportunities presented by both digital and experiential media, Fox made the launch of the Simpsons movie less like a typical movie launch and more like a cultural event.

For starters, Fox created fun TV commercials and an engaging website. The site had lots of cool stuff ranging from the usual (e.g., wallpapers & screen savers) to some silly yet surprisingly addictive games, complete with lots of "D'oh" & Aye Carumba! sound effects. It had a virtual tour of Springfield and a tool that let you create your own Simpsons avatar. Just the sort of thing to get Simpsons fans engaged. But understanding context often means understanding the people you want to reach will not necessarily go to your site. So, Fox created a cross-promotion on Burger King's site where people could submit a photo and "Simpsonize" themselves. This was a viral application that was fun do and share whether you were a Simpsons fanatic or not. Where the campaign really shined, however, was when it used the web and even went out into the real world to turn context on its head.

Three ideas really stand out as outstanding examples of reinventing the way people relate to media in its broadest sense. The first was an online contest that pitted 14 different American cities named Springfield for the honor of being named "the" Springfield of Simpsons fame, giving the winner the right to hold the movie's premiere. The contest got not only the populations of these cities engaged, but became a public relations extravaganza with the contest and results covered by sponsor USA Today and various news organizations around the country. When little Springfield, Vermont beat the likes of sizeable Springfield, Illinois, the residents of the winning town were described by USA Today as being in a Simpsons "Frenzy." The second idea was an online campaign in partnership with JetBlue Airways. As one might expect, different Simpsons became spokespersons for different JetBlue destinations. But the campaign started to bend reality by having mogul Montgomery Burns take over the regular blog that had been set up by Jet Blue's chairman. The hijacked blog led off as follows: *"Hi I'm Montgomery Burns, Here's my newest attempt at robbing a man of his livelihood. I have temporarily taken over David Neeleman's blog as I believe I have more efficient ways to run this airline. I could crush him like an ant."*

The third, and perhaps most spectacular, contextual idea was a joint promotion with 7-Eleven. Eleven 7-Eleven stores around America were physically transformed into Kwik-E-Marts (patterned after the show's convenience store helmed by Apu Nahasapeemapetilon), complete with loads of Simpsons-based products. All of the signage inside and out was changed. For people on the street, or stopping by for their morning cup of coffee, the world was just a little bit different. The line between fantasy and reality had been crossed. They not only knew there was a movie coming out, but they were deeply engaged in the Simpson's experience. People didn't have to be Simpsons fanatics to be caught up in the amusement and to feel that life would be a little more fun if they went to the movie.

Fox's creativity in challenging the usual uses of media, and even reality, led to tremendous results. The film earned over $30 million on its opening day and $74 Million for its opening weekend. It was the third highest non-sequel opening of all-time. For a July opening of a non-sequel, it was number one all-time. Had this animated movie, with its quirky sense of humor, looked at media the traditional way, or even used digital media in a non-creative way, there is a good chance that only Simpsons fans would have shown up, with the Simpsons movie relegated to the list of big-time money losers.

CONCLUSION

We began this chapter with a reminder that consumers' control over their media choices has never been more important. They have unprecedented control over what advertising messages they choose to see. Due to this increasing control, advertisers and markets need to be far more cognizant of the specific media context within which their messages appear. On a simplistic level, this will allow them to better match their message to its environment.

The proliferation of messages for brands, the history of how brands developed their advertising and the emergence of media and interactive agencies that are vying with traditional creative agencies to control messaging have combined to create a crisis for many marketers and agencies. Our research and our personal experience lead us to recommended three essential steps to help improve the situation:

- Digital elements should be included in a single Integrated Communications Plan (ICP).
- The ICP should call out the contextual media insight.
- The digital executions should be a seamless part of the campaign's organizing cre-

ative idea, yet be as executionally unique as they need to be.

The purpose of these recommendations is to help increase integration while simultaneously taking advantage of the opportunities created by understanding the unique context of each medium. We believe that such contextual insights have never been more important than they are now with the explosion of digital media. A simple way to think about the difference is to think of emotional insights as the answers to questions like "How does the brand fit uniquely in the lives of the people who use it?" or "How does this category of product improve people's lives?" A contextual insight on the other hand can be seen as an answer to a question like "How do people interact with this medium in a way that's different than other media?" Both types of insight are necessary to develop great campaigns, but unfortunately the creative departments of many agencies don't explore contextual insights when developing campaigns. Our advice above is intended to place these media-based insights right in the middle of creative development. Nowhere is the integration of these contextual insights more important than with digital media, which are as diverse as they are increasingly plentiful.

We highlighted five case studies. They are excellent examples of campaigns that have a single, integrated creative thought across media, as well as outstanding contextual insights. Each case shows that when advertisers and their agencies respect consumers' increasing control of media, and also respect each medium's ability to engage consumers in ways unique to that medium, great things can happen. The centripetal force of integration and the centrifugal force of digital media proliferation can be brought into equilibrium. What it takes is the right balance of emotional and contextual understanding throughout the creative development process. We believe that this balance can in part be achieved by the following our recommendations above.

Our suggestions are more about process than creativity. When people who work on great campaigns—like the ones we've outlined in this chapter—talk about what led to success, the most common themes we heard were "Everyone was on the same page," "There was only one brief," or "We had a different kind of insight." One unified brief, one over-riding creative idea, and meaningful contextual insights combining for success.

Malcolm Gladwell provides us a word of warning in the Tipping Point that we ignore at our peril. When he talks about "social epidemics," like the emergence of websites, blogs, and email as forms of social networking, he notes that like any real epidemic, signs of immunity can start to grow. He tells a story we can all relate to:

I remember when I first got e-mail, back in the mid-1990s. I would rush home with great anticipation and dial in on my 4800-baud modem and I would have...four messages from four very good friends. And what would I do? I would immediately compose four long, elegant responses. Now, of course, I get up in the morning and go to my computer and I have sixty-four messages, and the anticipation I once felt has been replaced by dread.... So how do I respond? I compose very, very short e-mails...and I often take two or three days to get back to people.... (p. 274)

The warning for advertisers is clear. When new media stops being new and becomes overloaded with unwanted and irrelevant messages, consumers stop participating as actively. The best way to avoid this fate is to make sure our messages are as relevant as possible: relevant in content, relevant in approach, and most importantly, relevant in context.

Theoretically, one of the oldest ideas about media usage is turning out to be one of the best. Observations of increasing levels of consumer control validate the uses-and-gratification model. More specifically, the digital revolution has allowed consumers to communicate their desired usages, and their gratifications sought, directly to advertisers. They communicate these by the content they pull in through search engines and the context within which the content is embedded. When advertisers observe closely, they can create the equivalent of advertising nirvana: a relevant advertising message in a relevant context that matches, exactly, the consumers' initial usage and gratification demands.

SUGGESTIONS FOR FURTHER STUDY

We have reviewed a number of case studies where contextual insights at the creative brief stage led to a successful nexus between advertising content and context. A natural area for further study would be to take an experimental view towards the *Contextual Creative Brief*. Comparing the effectiveness and ROMI of a random sample of campaigns developed to the criteria of the *Contextual Creative Brief* to a control sample of campaigns developed using a traditional creative briefing process would be instructive. Our prediction is that, over time, agencies and clients who adopt the *Contextual Creative Brief* will show significant improvements in effectiveness and ROMI vs. traditional creative briefing approaches.

REFERENCES

Blumler, J. G., & Katz, E. (1974). *The uses of mass communications: current perspectives on gratifications research*. Beverly Hills, CA: Sage.

Carter, S. (Ed.). (2006). In Historical statistics of the United States (Millennial Ed.). Cambridge, UK: Cambridge University Press.

Dou, W., & Krishnamurthy, S. (2007). Using brand web sites to build brands: A product vs. service brand comparison. *Journal of Advertising Research*, 47, 2. eMarketer. (2006). *Search marketing: Players and problems.*

Gladwell, M. (2002). *The tipping point: how little things can make a big difference*. New York: Little, Brown & Company.

Grossman, L. (2006, December 13). Time's person of the year: you. *TIME*. Retrieved July18, 2008, from http://www.time.com/time/magazine/article/0,9171,1569514,00. html? cnn=yes

Hein, K. (2007, August 6). Teen talk is, like, totally branded. *Brandweek*. Retrieved August, 1, 2008, from http://www.kellerfay.com/?page_id=123

Hoffman, D. L., & Novak, T. P. (1996, January). A new marketing paradigm for electronic commerce. *The Information Society*, *13*, 43–54.

IAB. (2006). Interactive advertising revenues grow 30% to a record $12.5 billion in '05. *Interactive Advertising Bureau*. Retrieved April 12, 2006, from http://iab.printthis.clickability.com/pt/cpt?action=cpt&title=IAB+Press+Release&expire=&urlID=17977334&fb=Y&url=http://www.iab.net/news/pr_2006_04_20.asp&partnerID=297

IDC. (2008May). U.S. Internet Advertising 2008–2012 Forecast and Analysis: Defying Economic Crisis.

Jaffe, J. (2004, February 18). Case study: See what happens. *iMedia Connection.* Retrieved July 17, 2008, from http://www.imediaconnection.com/printpage/printpage.aspx?id=2821

Lavidge, R. J., & Steiner, G. A. (1961). A model for predictive measurements of advertising effectiveness. *Journal of Marketing*, *26*(6), 59–62. doi:10.2307/1248516

Lenhart, A., & Madden, M. (2005). Teen content creators and consumers. *Pew Internet and Life Project*. Retrieved June 25, 2006 from http://www.pewinternet.org/pdfs/PIP_Teens_ Content_Creation.pdf

McMillan, S. J. (2007). Internet advertising: one face or many? In Schuman, D. W., & Thorsen, E. (Eds.), *Internet advertising: theory and research*. Mahwah, NJ: Lawrence Erlbaum Assoc, Inc.

Netpop/U.S. (2006). *Study of purchase influencers.*

Palda, K. S. (1966). *The measurement of cumulative advertising effects*. Englewood Cliffs, NJ: Prentice-Hall.

Plummer, J., Rappaport, S., Hall, T., & Barocci, R. (2007). *The online advertising playbook: proven strategies and tested tactics from the advertising research foundation*. Hoboken, NJ: John Wiley & Sons, Inc.

Rayburn, J. D. (1996). Uses and gratifications. In Salwen, M. B., & Stacks, D. W. (Eds.), *An integrated approach to communications theory and research* (pp. 97–119). Mahwah, NJ: Lawrence Erlbaum Associates, Inc.

Ruggerio, T. E. (2000, February). Uses and gratifications theory in the 21st century. *Mass Communication & Society*, *3*(1), 3–37. doi:10.1207/S15327825MCS0301_02

Severin, W. J., & Tankard, J. W. Jr. (1997). *Communications theories: origins, methods, and uses in the mass media* (4th ed.). White Plains, NY: Langman.

Shamdasani, P., & Stanaland, A. J. S. (2001). Location, location, location: Insights for advertising placement on the web. *Journal of Advertising Research*, *41*, 4.

APPENDIX

Table 2. Campaign summaries

Mitsubishi Campaign Summary	
Unified Messaging Objective:	*Demonstrate that Galant handles better than the best-selling Camry*
Contextual Insight:	*The internet is where people go for immediate answers*
Organizing Creative Idea:	*See What Happens!*
Lexus Campaign Summary	
Unified Messaging Objective:	*Communicate that the new Lexus IS offers much more than just great performance*
Contextual Insight:	*Digital media offers the connectivity to create multi-dimensional experiences and the technology to create entirely new ones.*
Organizing Creative Idea:	*Why Live in One Dimension?*
Toyota Campaign Summary	
Unified Messaging Objective:	*Communicate that Corolla's style, features and price fit young people's lives.*
Contextual Insight:	*Interrupting Young consumers with ad messages on entertainment sites like YouTube do more harm than good.*
Organizing Creative Idea:	*Corolla appreciates what's funny, like it being the perfect car for you.*
Ambien CR Campaign Summary	
Unified Messaging Objective:	*Communicate Ambien CR's unique controlled release properties that provide a more effective sleep aid.*
Contextual Insight:	*Insomniac sufferers have a very different relationship with their media, and when stressed are more receptive to advertising messaging*
Organizing Creative Idea:	*A good night's sleep from start to finish.*
Simpsons Campaign Summary	
Unified Messaging Objective:	*Create engagement and buzz beyond simple awareness that engages non-Simpson's fanatics.*
Contextual Insight:	*Digital and experiential media offer opportunities to immerse people into their own real-life Simpsons' experiences.*
Organizing Creative Idea:	*The Simpsons movie is REALLY here!*

Section 3
Digital Engagement And New Metrics

Chapter 16
Point of Involvement, Purchase and Consumption:
The Delivery of Audience Engagement

Neal M. Burns
The University of Texas at Austin, USA

ABSTRACT

Advertising effectiveness and its measurement has characteristically been a subject of concern and debate and with the availability and access of the Internet and digital technology the issue is still elusive and complex. This chapter provides a review of the measures that were frequently used to determine the audience that was impacted with traditional media resources as well as those media and message processes generally called new or "alternative" - in that they are different than the traditional electronic, print and out-of home that have been used by advertisers and their agencies for more than 100 years. The chapter reviews and discusses which measures are simply cost indices and which are measures of effectiveness. The emphasis reflects the interests of both those working in the field as practitioners as well as those involved in its research and instruction. In a profession in which decisions in the past were built upon cost per thousand (CPT or CPM), cost per point (CPP) and the challenges of ROI and share fight, the metrics for new media must be precisely defined, valid and reliable. Assessing advertising effectiveness is–as has been said–challenging. The need to inform, persuade and sell in a global marketplace with a technological base that incorporates all we have used in the past plus the networks and mobile delivery now available have already served to make this aspect of communication a compelling set of opportunities. Digital media and delivery are revolutionary and their impact will be profound. Ideally, the problems to be solved will bring those doing the research and those in practice closer than they have been in the past. The metrics to be developed and the narratives that will follow will reflect the ways in which we relate to products and services and to each other in the 21st Century.

DOI: 10.4018/978-1-60566-792-8.ch016

INTRODUCTION

Advertising delivery has always been characterized by the rapid adoption of available technology in the hope of reaching the desired audience in new–sometimes surprising–and effective ways. Wonderful histories of advertising's development have been written (e.g. Presbrey, 1929; Wallechinsky, & Wallace, 1975-1981), but a brief recap here may help frame this chapter. Somehow, given the excitement of new technology, innovative metrics and the joy and frequency with which so many of us send 140 character messages - it seemed reasonable to start at the very beginning.

HISTORY, MEDIA AND MEASUREMENT

There are stories–perhaps apocryphal–about early messages (circa 900 AD) carved in the steps leading up from the sea in the Greek islands that advertised various houses of prostitution for the benefit of those sailors that had just landed. Town criers in the marketplace during Greek and Roman times announced the goods and bargains offered by mall merchants–demonstrating the value of a loud voice in the market place and the value of delivering advertising messages close to the point of purchase.

The birth of print advertising is generally attributed to ads for health and beauty aids appearing among some British newspapers in the 1600's (British Library)–as well as occasional requests for the return of lost horses. Posting offices, where one could write and place help wanted or information about lost wagons and animals, were fairly common in British cities and co-existed for a time with newspapers. The superiority of the newspaper in terms of distribution and targeted ownership enabled the medium to flourish and in the late 1600's published newspapers were inundated with ads. Printing, distribution and improvements in the manufacture of paper enabled magazines to soon join the genre of print media (Fleming, 1976) and content and resulting popularity served to define special interests. Magazines were quickly realized to be an excellent vehicle for the placement of ads primarily intended for the readership of the particular publication. Combined with the introduction of these advertising resources, normally delivered directly to the residence of the intended recipient, a desire to reach the audience where they worked, played and traveled developed.

The Brits again are often referenced as the introductory source of outdoor advertising signs (Fleming, 1976). In a short period of time England was so over-saturated with pasted-up notices and posters that Charles II, feeling the need for advertising regulation, pronounced, "No signs shall be hung across the streets shutting out the air and the light of the heavens" (Wallechinsky, & Wallace, 1975-1981). Yet, the apparent ease with which these outdoor messages could be posted and the rapid rate at which they proliferated were considered proof of their popularity–and for some–their effectiveness. Yet, American advertising history (Applegate, 1998) and that nation's love of their cars and the open road certainly requires a mention. The road-side presence of Burma Shave's small, outdoor poster boards and their windshield height, were part of almost any road trip in America. The signs came in groups of four and in sequential fashion presented a humorous rhyme–or advertising jingle/haiku - that always ended with the words "Burma Shave". These signs preceded the widespread erection and rental of roadside billboards in the USA, and they demonstrated the appeal and recall of well designed, well placed outdoor ads (Margolin, Brichta, I., & Brichta, V., 1979). In time these developments and the importance of outdoor advertising would create the category referred to as out-of-home - OOH.

The advent of electronic media, however, provided the opportunity of reach rarely imagined by the originators of print and outdoor advertising vehicles. With the availability of radio and the opportunity to create product supportive messages (i.e., advertising), agencies who were now accepted as part of the capitalist economic engine conceived and wrote stories that could be enacted within the total purchased time segment and serialized so that continued interest with the characters and the saga itself was maintained. These broadcasts served as vehicles for the agency's client's advertisements–with the show often being the exclusive domain or vehicle for a single product or advertiser and also served as one of the early models for television programming. Television became an instant resource for network and spot ads–as well as infomercials–and the use of electronic media combined with print became the model for integrated advertising campaigns–and at times outdoor was used for extending presence and memorability. Clearly the addition of sight with sound was expected to produce a message with more impact and engagement value than had previously been experienced.

The business models developed to make these methods of delivering mediated messages financially rewarding were complex and incorporated a number of critical dimensions. The notion of time and space as inventory to be sold, and its value depending on day part and seasonal issues, was understood fairly early. The concept of engagement–finding some way of capturing the nature and value of the interaction that existed between the message being delivered and its intended audience–also began to surface, although establishing those relationships in a definitive and financially meaningful way proved difficult.

Delivering the opportunity for a message to be seen led to ways of defining the reach and frequency (R & F) a delivery mechanism or medium possessed–and pricing based upon those numbers led to the emergence of a relatively standard and widely adopted metric pricing determinant known as CPM (the cost for the advertiser to reach one thousand persons, i.e., Cost of Ad / Audience Delivered x1000). Given the acceptance of a set of assumptions, by the emerging national publications and by the electronic media, analysts allowed reach and frequency estimates of audience size and share to dominate reports concerning the success of placement in a particular medium. It also enabled planners and buyers to compare costs of alternative media and the "R & F" metric became the organizing framework for defining the advertising mix. Firms like Arbitron and Nielsen emerged to realistically provide the best estimates of the impact of the advertising placed.

The well established language (CPM, CPP, CPI and related metrics) of media buyers and planners— as well as that of broadcasters and advertisers would need to adapt to properly reflect the alternative media being used in the delivery of marketing communications in the 21st Century. With broadband access and the rising importance of mobile and in-place digital communication, revisions in the thinking about cost and effectiveness of media delivery were needed. The efficiencies delivered at new alternative digital and experiential brand touch points, in terms of both audience reach and desired impact, were not adequately reflected when analyzed using traditional metrics (Harris Interactive, 2009; Passikoff, Keys, & Schultz, 2007).

The business itself was constantly driven by a desire to understand if the advertising was working. Both those paying for the message development and its placement as well as those who created the work and determined its exposure strategy (media planning and buying) wanted to know what was producing results and what was not. And, shortly thereafter the media itself -- stations, networks, magazines -- wanted evidence of the superiority of their delivery as a way of maintaining price point and proving their value over competitive entries. Key questions begging for answers included: Did the ads result in more traffic in the stores? Were more products sold when the advertising ran? Did the ads help build brand loyalty? Were the ads well liked? Did the intended audience hear or see the material–and if so, how would we know the value of the ads that were placed/viewed? In short, was the audience "engaged"? And, of course, as Western commercialization developed and the United States took a "leadership" role in the development of advertising and marketing strategies and tactics, questions about our culture and value system also became fair game.

THE RESEARCH PROCESS

As one prepares a chapter on advertising and in the process assembles a supportive bibliography on advertising and on advertising research there is–sadly–an inescapable conclusion; advertising research is the cause of statistics (and you probably thought it was baseball - or smoking). The primary emphasis of most advertising research has focused–as mentioned above - on the impact of advertising on the consumer (Gerdes, Stringam, & Brookshire, 2008; Walker, 2008). Did they like it, did they understand it, did they remember it, did they buy it, would they consider buying it. There are clearly giants in advertising research - Daniel Starch, Arthur Nielsen, Charles Osgood (1957) and others (Applegate, 1998)–whose work has served to define the category and bring new tools to help answer these questions as well as framing new issues.

In addition to some historical review and an examination of marketing analytics, this chapter also considers advertising in the context of social expression since that point of view supports a better understanding of media technology and the ways in which people relate to it - which is the substance of this article. In one way or another the nature of the audience's involvement with the advertising calls for a descriptive terminology; ideally, a description that helps establish the intellectual, emotional and behavioral actions the message produced–as well as support for the pricing structure upon which the time or space sold is based. Such a representation must also include an understanding of the attitudes and behavior of the audience. Such consideration allows us a brief excursion to consider the relationship between contemporary media and the postmodern era as used and reflected in the work of the advertising profession (Ewen, 1976).

Jean-Francois Lyotard (1979), the French philosopher, has written extensively on the impact of postmodern attitude and execution in art and literature and it is tempting and instructive to consider its impact on advertising as well. For example, Lyotard wrote that postmodernism has brought an ending to the "Grand Narrative", a term he introduced in his book *The Postmodern Condition* (Lyotard, 1979). Lyotard believed that these accepted narratives provided the rationale for myths and historical events that established the power relationships within society and also made them "legitimate" and believable. Today, he suggested, postmodern society is surrounded by a plethora of "small narratives" all representing different points of view and all, presumably of equal value.

As examples of small narratives in advertising, consider campaigns like "Mikey likes it", "You deserve a break today" or "Got milk" (all of which may be found at www.youtube.com) among many, many others. These almost personal and often non-supported points of view are accepted by their audience and are considered of value. They are worthy of expression, in large part, since the sense and earlier belief that there exists a moral and ethical–perhaps even religious - standard that assigns importance and value–i.e., the grand narrative - has been replaced. Society at large accepts a number of different perspectives, and incorporates them as part of our culture. The creative product of the ad agencies heralded the postmodern era. Even in a short period of time the shift from an Ogilvy-agency ad to the Bernbach look and feel was unmistakable. It represented the shift from the established, almost "Protestant-like" values to highly idiosyncratic behavior and redefining or totally ignoring the "rules" for typography, white space and the rest–"doing your thing".

With the technological advances that have essentially ushered in digital media and defined it, postmodern thought and new values were enabled. When combined with the fracturing of the social contract and with the end of (or certainly diminished) trust in leadership it was clear the relationship between the audience and the media was to be redefined. Along with new media, new authoritative voices sprang up introducing a new cohort of entrepreneurs and thought leaders–e.g., Jeff Bezos of Amazon, Sergey Brin and Larry Page of Google and Jeff Skoll of eBay - who understood the monetization of their new products and services and the viral spread that would occur to those widely dispersed audiences using the Internet, e-mail text messaging and blogs.

The ways in which the audience of the 21st Century relates to the media options with which they are presented differs significantly from the previous and well - established delivery and participatory behavior of earlier populations. Audience share, as measured by the number of households and CPM, has slipped dramatically (Heaton, 2009; Klaassen, 2009), and the consequences have been apparent in the economic crisis of 2008-2009. Newspapers in spring of 2009 reported cutting more than 31,000 jobs, while the broadcast industry (radio and TV) at the same time reported reducing employment by 13,000 jobs. Advertising agencies were comparably affected with BNET reporting more than 30,000 jobs lost during that same period (Edwards, 2009). In part, these staffing changes were all related to the new viewing habits of the American audience.

The range of available media and the amount of time spent with the media selected have changed–not necessarily across the board but within particular segments (Eastin, Yang, & Nathanson, 2006). The rigor with which television audiences watch their favorite shows and the times at which they watch them have changed dramatically. In the Solution Research Group Consultants' Digital Life Study (Solution Research Group Program, 2009) respondents who had seen one of the leading 20 prime time shows during the past 24 hours were asked to identify the source of their viewing. Among all respondents 25% of prime time viewing was time shifted using a DVR, broadband, mobile or similar device. In those households with DVR respondents preferred using it as a means of time-shifting and reported that they regularly skipped viewing the commercials compared to only half the viewers doing so in the study one year earlier.

The "rules" developed and adopted during the 1980's for media participation by the audience have been transformed as a function of available technology and lifestyle (McLuhan, M., Hutchon, & McLuhan, E., 1978). In attempting to answer questions of current media participation the advertising research and measurement discipline–and industry–grew, charged with determining the effectiveness and comparative cost benefits of alternative media buys and strategies. The surprise in the midst of the revised emphasis on judging the effectiveness of advertising was the growing decline in viewership, readership and overall participation with traditional media. As the topic of declining viewership became one which moved from off-handed comments among media planners to topics at national meetings to best-selling business books, two major dimensions were identified that helped frame the discussion: attitudes and values of the viewing audience and the accessibility of broadband communications. Every audience cohort studied reported that the source of viewing has time shifted through the use of a DVR, broadband, mobile device or similar technology. Almost simultaneously, the importance of social networks and the amount of time key age cohorts allocated to their usage grew.

Clearly the use of DVR and time-shifting regarding television alters the relationship between the share of audience that has their sets tuned to the show as opposed to the audience actually exposed to the advertiser's commercial. Ideally, clear cut, well-defined measures would be welcomed by both the advertiser and the venue or retail outlet that houses the signage. Yet, settling on a standard to express value delivered is far more complex than appears at first blush. Advertisers, for example, now have the ability to answer the famous "Wanamaker query" (paraphrased as 'half my advertising is worthless–I just don't know which half') and examine store sales as a measure of the effectiveness of the ads placed. Sales is, for many advertisers, the most important measure of success. The retailer's perspective, however, may be more focused on other indices of message effectiveness–for example - dwell time in the establishment or data demonstrating that the messages and content displayed resulted in a larger register ring are two frequent concerns.

In assessing media effectiveness researchers and practitioners have rather consistently looked at four key parameters. Reach - normally understood as the number of persons (sometimes households, etc.) that will read/hear/see the advertisement; frequency - usually considering two dimensions–how often the ad appears in the medium and the number of times that a member of the desired audience sees it; impact–is a shorthand way of describing position, look or length of the ad (e.g., four color as opposed to black and white); and finally, continuity–knowing that the pattern of ad insertions over time, while it may not increase costs, can increase ad effectiveness.

Generally speaking, ad agency media planners and buyers, as well as their client counterparts, consider the exposure their expenditures will produce and look closely at Gross Rating Points (GRPs)–the accepted measure of how much advertising exposure will be delivered to a particular population on a per capita basis. GRPs are the mathematical product of reach and frequency: if the reach is 80% and the average frequency is 2.5, then the GRPs total 200. GRPs thus provide a comparative measure of per capita advertising exposure. They incorporate both how much advertising exposure potentially exists and how many of a particular population may have viewed that exposure (Wikipedia).

LOOKING AT ENGAGEMENT AND DIGITAL MEDIA

In studying CPM and GRP comparisons it is important to realize that the numbers are, "generalized averages"; CPM varies by market as well as media selected and time of day or issue. The orientation that the digital signage industry promotes goes beyond these metrics and claims to deal more with effectiveness than price indices. What then, should serve as the metric that helps compare advertiser's purchases in these new media with traditional media expenditures? And, which measures are really simply cost indices and which are measures of effectiveness? In a profession in which decisions in the past were built upon cost per thousand (CPT or CPM), cost per point (CPP) and the challenges of ROI and share fights, what should the operative criteria for new media and experiential advertising expenditures be?

As the dynamics of consumer and communication channels change, marketers seek new and better ways to measure the effectiveness of their programs and justify their marketing spend. The notion of "engagement" is considered by some (e.g. Appelbaum, 2001; Burns, 2009; Haven, 2007) to be a particularly valuable analytic measurement of content effectiveness, of customer value and brand strength. The Advertising Research Foundation (ARF) gave strong visibility to the importance of engagement in its conference in 2006 and the associated and widely circulated white paper "Measures of Engagement" (Plummer, Cook, Diforio, Sokolyanskaya, & Ovchinnikova, 2006). The ARF defined engagement as "an integrative concept that has to span engagement with the brand, engagement with the idea or 'creative' and engagement with the media or context." A "turned-on" customer, they continued, results from stimulating co-creation (i.e., additional ideation, personal associations, future visions, etc), which in turn, leads to a more personal, deeper relationship with the brand and product.

Engagement with the message(s) being delivered is a complex measure and as has already been discussed is not simply defined by a single dimension (Eastin, Yang, & Nathanson, 2006). The level of engagement that occurs and is demonstrable is a function of the perceived relevance of the message to the audience market. The brand evangelists for the product being promoted find that the content speaks to them about their life style and the important role played by the product or service. There is also a segment of the audience–often identified as non-users or rejectors (members of this segment may have been users in the past but have stopped) - for whom the message has little, if any, value. Another group however - often called "persuadables"– (a notion introduced to the author in the mid 1980's by Jack Supple, then Executive Creative Director at the Minneapolis advertising agency Carmichael Lynch)–represents an opportunity to build share, and messages encouraging their engagement can be particularly effective.

It is important to note the behavioral or emotional engagement sought is not limited to purchase. For segments like those identified above there are several levels of interaction that can suggest building a brand relationship or having the consumer enter the "franchise". These may include visiting the brand's web site, responding to a relevant blog, downloading information, agreeing to receive additional e-mail, or serving to strengthen the feelings about a product or brand already purchased. Clearly the engagement of those receiving the message and the level of subsequent participation varies as a function of the personal relevance of the message, its content and tone of voice and the place in which it was delivered.

The benchmark for many has been the presence and the level of engagement–emotional, intellectual and behavioral - in some ways reminiscent of the concept of "**flow**," an experience that is at once demanding and rewarding, which Mihaly Csikszentmihalyi has described so well in his work (Csikszentmihalyi, 1997). Yet, the ways in which consumption of media occurs today reflects a shift from attending solely to "major" broadcasts or narratives to being open to and presented with a more diverse set of shorter episodes, varying in length and content, many of which occur simultaneously. Thus, an agreed upon set of measures defining engagement has been elusive. Today, in an over-saturated, multimedia, multitasking world, the effectiveness of message delivery and shifting attention challenges notions of deep emotional and behavioral engagement. An emerging literature (Davenport, & Beck, 2001; Eastin, Yang, & Nathanson, 2006) on the level of comprehension occurs with multi-channel stimuli and the ability of the central nervous system to attend to simultaneous delivery is also an important aspect of engagement but beyond the scope of the present paper.

Almost every current study on media usage reports that the source of viewing has changed through the development and adoption of the DVR, broadband, mobile device or similar technology. For example, Nielsen has reported that the heaviest users of the Internet are also among the heaviest viewers of television: the top fifth of Internet users spend more than 250 minutes per day watching television, compared to 220 minutes of television viewing by people who do not use the Internet at all (Nielsen Reports, 2008). Nielsen found the reverse is true as well - the lowest consumers of television have the lowest usage levels for the Internet.

Further, the Nielsen study showed that almost one-third of in-home Internet activity occurred while the user was watching television, demonstrating that there is a significant amount of simultaneous Internet and television usage; an example, perhaps, of the plethora of "small narratives," in Lyotard's terms, with which we are surrounded as well as consumer multi-tasking behavior (Foehr, 2006). Nielsen's ratings now include DVR watchers, as well as time shifting among the audience not only through their own recording devices but through the use of services like HULU (a free online video service that offers hit TV shows with altered short commercials that cannot be deleted from the transmission) - another example of the kind of control desired by the audience of their media exposure .At the same time, describing the precise relationship between the exposure to the message and the viewer's/ customer's behavior remains quite complex. In today's media environment the relationships among the different channels, and their collective impact on a customer's buying decision, are far more difficult to gauge (and influence) than they once were. Yet, basic to the decision to advertise and place the ad is the ability of the network and/ or the agency to provide some evidence that the message was, in fact, seen.

Two major influences are responsible for a re-examination of advertising effectiveness metrics. The current consumption of media reflects a shift from attending to "major" presentations –e.g., viewing 30 minutes plus of TV (followed and interrupted by commercials) in the style of the grand narrative - to being presented a more diverse set of shorter episodes, varying in length and content, many of which are presented simultaneously. One way of looking at the change is the movement from a single channel narrative model of particular content to one of sequential engagement with a variety of content–and in the presence of multiple channels. Although the phenomenon is not particularly new, interest in simultaneous exposure to multiple channels of information has again captured the interest of behavioral scientists studying the relationship between attention and effectiveness of advertisements (Max, 2008; Passikoff, Keys, & Schultz, 2007). The current multi-channel, multi-media environment raises the competitive advertising effort to gain audience attention. And, with the end (or clearly the diminution) of interruptive advertising methods, the production and display of interactive user generated content is likely to prevail. Yet in the complexity of the media presented "prevail" is very likely a transient phenomenon and represents the period of time that a dominant message may emerge as "figure" in a shifting figure-ground relationship (Jordan, 1968). In media environments that encompass in-place and mobile digital presentations, the goal is to devise or encourage content that captures audience attention and participation and then to 1) demonstrate positive economic outcomes to the advertiser and 2) build messaging programs around the goal of stimulating more engagement behaviors.

It's important to note that attention and engagement, when used to describe the degree of interaction between one exposed (e.g., the audience) to content/ or message is not limited to a purchase of a product or service; it encompasses all the interactions that a prospect or customer may have in relation to a brand. There are a number of pre- or post-sale activities that can be (directly or indirectly) predictive of a future purchase or re-purchase; they include visiting a Web site, downloading a whitepaper, calling customer service, recommending a product, or commenting on a blog.

Some of the newer metrics, like Net Promoter® and several other services and applications on the web, continually seems to demonstrate the effectiveness of word-of mouth (W-O-M) as the primary advertising techniques. (Google–and Microsoft's newcomer Bing–are in that context little more than aggregations of what others say about the topic, person, brand, product or service–a technologically compiled W-O-M.) A Net Promoter® score analyzes customers' responses to a website query roughly concerning satisfaction and categorizes them based upon the likelihood that the respondent will recommend the product or service to others (Keiningham, 2007). The "net" score is essentially an arithmetic value arrived at by subtracting the values attributed by those somewhat negative or detracting points of view from those respondents with positive points of view. Generally, three groups are identified ranging from enthusiasts to unhappy customers; Promoters, Passives and

Detractors. Thus, while the metric is simple and straight-forward, the question itself (Would you refer a friend?) may be considered as "leading" by some and is not applicable across all commercial categories. And the net score provides little suggestion for remedy –improved sales training, cleaner rest rooms, competitive pricing, etc. Yet, its ease of administration and computation may be an example of the great desire on the part of advertisers to possess a "marker"–an indication of advertising effectiveness–from data that can be easily collected and understood.

MEASURING AND EVALUATING ENGAGEMENT

The research tools available for measuring engagement have been in use for the past 50 years with varying levels of success and for the most part do an adequate job. Brand recognition and recall studies with varying distance from initial exposure, association techniques, customer satisfaction surveys, all give some indication of how customers feel about a product, service, or brand. Consider the intricate relationship between just two channels: the Internet and a retail store. A consumer can visit a store to look at a product, purchase it, and bring it home. Or, she may look at the product in the store, then go home to compare prices on the Internet, and purchase from a lower-priced competitor. Alternatively, she may do her homework first on the Internet (e.g., comparing prices and features or reading customer reviews), buy the product from a trusted vendor, and then have it shipped to her house or pick it up at one of the retailer's local outlets. Two channels, with multiple behaviors and multiple types of engagement.

As the dynamics of consumer and communication channels change, marketers are seeking new and better ways to measure the effectiveness of their programs and justify their marketing spend. Brian Haven of Forrester Research has proposed a metric that defines engagement as "the level of involvement, interaction, intimacy, and influence an individual has with a brand over time". The metric–Forrester's estimate of audience engagement–described in Brian Haven's 17 page report is built from both online and offline data, using quantitative and qualitative measures and what Forrester calls "the fuzzy areas in the middle best characterized by social media"

Major advertisers and measurement firms have tried to add a level of precision to in-store metrics in an attempt to provide a measure that would satisfy both the advertiser and the retail establishment. One such attempt called PRISM (Pioneering Research for In-store Metrics) focused upon the in-store traffic and the level of support or compliance with the promotional efforts at the retail level by store management (In-Store Marketing Institute). PRISM suggested and tested the premise that the likelihood of the store's patrons seeing the message was a function of two variables; in-store traffic and store compliance with advertiser marketing instructions. While the system had promise, costs of installation, management and analysis became larger and more complex than initially planned and Nielsen suspended the effort in early 2009 (The Market Research Industry Online, 2009).

The PRISM approach reflected the importance of accurate measurement of in-store customer traffic and understood and valued the active participation of store management in supporting the media. Yet, the development of behavioral targeting and the realization of the differential value of certain segments to an advertiser was not an integral part of the equation. The inclusion of the quality of the audience viewing the digital media was a key part of the approach of vJive Networks, an advertising-driven digital signage network that was founded in 2004 (www.vjivenetworks.com). Currently vJive reports being in more than 1,000 venues across the top 25 metropolitan areas in India. Looking for a way to quantify the value of their screens to potential advertisers, vJive chose not to focus on merely measuring traffic, footfall or "opportunities to see"–essentially Reach and Frequency metrics typical of existing electronic and print media. Instead, they looked to the retailers themselves to supply these data, or to existing organizations that provide census data–and elected to supplement those indices with data describing the value and purchasing power of the establishment's audience or patrons. The increased marketing segmentation and the differential value of retail shoppers in India helped to underscore the value of this new measure.

Thus, vJive - as opposed to only reporting the quality of engagement with on-screen content - also focuses on the geo-demographic descriptors, e.g., household income, education level, frequency of dining out and other variables that help define the value of the advertisements that appear on screen. Rather than non-differential pricing of the available network inventory of advertising time and space, vJive developed the Screen Consumption Quotient (SCQ) metric, an overall location value score based in part on foot traffic in the establishment, but heavily influenced by evaluating the descriptors listed above. Seventy percent of the SCQ score incorporated by vJive is based on the Household Potential Index data published by the Media Research Users Council, India and 30% on the revenue is based upon estimates of in-store traffic. The SCQ score incorporates a value for customer quality over quantity. Screens in stores with high SCQ scores have their ad inventory priced accordingly and reflect the value to the advertiser of the relevance and behavior of the audience being reached (Gerba, 2008).

Whether other network owners will follow vJive's lead remains to be seen. If so, one might expect a similar metric to start appearing in U.S. digital signage networks. By instituting standard rates and values ascribed there will be one less barrier to adoption for advertisers still hesitant to spend money on a new in-store digital advertising medium. The author believes that digital network owners and management will, in all likelihood, institute measures similar to vJive's. Related approaches have been launched as may be seen in the media planning business of Handshake Marketing and Business Development (http://www.handshakemarketing.com), SeeSaw Media (www.seesawnetworks.com), by the Barfly/Touchtunes bar and restaurant penetration (http://www.touchtunes.com/barfly.html), Captivate Networks [1] (http://www.touchtunes.com/barfly.html), ADCENTRICITY (and their partnership with Impact Mobile) (http://www.adcentricity.com), and a host of other special purpose digital screen advertisers. The Nielsen/Arbitron metric leaders are, at the time of this writing, also examining this approach as well as monitoring the impact and effectiveness of in-store digital screen advertising. In the short term, adding the customer value component to the pricing equation is likely to help stimulate adoption of the new metric by advertisers and their agencies and establish the full value of in-place digital signage (Burns, 2008).

With broadband the new networks have had the ability to launch digital out of home displays with some ease–although fully implementing digital-out-of-home (DOOH) for consumer input and texting is more challenging. Representing an advertising medium that in some cases goes beyond the point of purchase to the point of consumption, digital displays are gaining a portion of the advertising spend and offer measurement opportunities that are accessible and quantifiable. These in-place media listed above include digital and programmable displays at beer and wine coolers in groceries and convenience stores, specialty channels in pharmacies and doctor's' waiting rooms, flight information displays at airports, hotel in-room screens, elevators, corporate communications screens in conference rooms and lobbies and in bars and restaurants (e.g., the Handshake or SeaSaw capabilities). While the business models for these applications differ, they illustrate the convergent and pervasive influence of this medium as an advertising vehicle.

Behavioral engagement metrics such as Forrester's can give advertisers a window into not only which stage individuals are at in their progression from prospects to customers, but also the velocity at which they are moving toward the end goal. Not unlike websites on the Internet, a number of measurements can be obtained from the attentiveness and interaction encouraged by DOOH. These include measures of interaction via SMS with the screen and good estimates of screen attention and when the attention occurs generated by eye cameras. Such insights into the value of all stages of the customer "pipeline" can help marketers determine the impact that marketing efforts may have on increasing that value. The measured result, however, does not have to be a sale (i.e., a direct (or immediate) economic transaction). Equally important are the many indirect methods for increasing value, such as a referral that leads to a new customer, or a white-paper download that educates a prospect and influences a future product decision. The web provides us with sufficient data to track how customers or prospects are engaging with a company; the key is to synthesize it into a clear model for demonstrating either short- or long-term economic benefit (Keiningham, 2007). And, the current emphasis for the metrics used is for output related effects rather than the "input" measurements that have been so closely associated with traditional media planning in the past.

WRAPPING UP

As those of us in advertising and marketing explore, begin to understand and use media and message processes generally called new or "alternative" - in that they are different than the traditional electronic, print and out-of home that have characterized the business for the past 125 years - we struggle to develop an appropriate analysis of their effectiveness. What should serve as the metric that helps us compare advertiser's purchases in these new media with traditional media expenditures? And, which measures are simply cost indices and which are measures of effectiveness? In a profession in which decisions in the past were built upon cost per thousand (CPT or CPM), cost per point (CPP) and the challenges of ROI and share fight, what should the operative criteria for new media and experiential advertising expenditures be (Heaton, 2009; Klaassen, 2009)?

For example, while we may know that the likelihood of purchase increases among those in the audience that download a whitepaper, the precise gain in sales (and thus ROI) is still a reasonable estimate and not quite as "quantitative" as many would like. Similarly, positive word-of mouth increases the product interest and significant transaction likelihood of many of those in the communication network but an index that describes the gain and is accepted by advertisers and their agencies is needed.

New metrics that are precisely defined and are both valid and reliable, will be critical for the monetization of alternative media, as well as helping us understand the ways in which we relate to mediated content delivered in accordance with contemporary technology and life style. Time shifting for example, frequently used (and enjoyed) by younger age group is a consequence of the availability of DVR, mobile technology and web sites like hulu (www.hulu.com) mentioned earlier. Yet, the growth of these alternative viewing sources for movies and TV shows is also an indication of a desire to avoid exposure to the advertisements that essentially have formed the economic platform for commercial television and radio broadcasts of the last century. Internet advertisers and their agencies are also finding that the "pop-ups" and musical inserts they are currently using conform to the definition of advertising as initially put forward by Roy Spence, one of the founders of the Austin, Texas advertising agency GSD&M; his term "the uninvited guest" continues to represent a valid view of the ways in which ads are used to interrupt the narrative and are often perceived by the intended audience. Harris Interactive (2009) recently reported that many US consumers are "very frustrated" by the number, frequency and style of many common types of internet ads. In contrast the effectiveness and use of social networks in promoting interest and sales of products is increasing. A recent report of consumer reviews for movies was found to be a significant predictor of box office revenue for Hollywood movies (Dellarocas, Award, & Zhang, 2004). Using online review metrics, it was shown that a higher volume of consumer reviews on *Yahoo! Movies* Web site was related to increased box office sales. Absolut Vodka as part of its aggressive campaign for market share has a frequently visited Facebook page called Top Bartender (http://www.facebook.com/AbsolutTopBartender?ref=search), Dell Computer's blog "Direct2Dell" (http://en.community.dell.com/blogs/direct2dell/) is an important source of information supported by well established users and loyal customers. And, a well-targeted use of twitter by Burton Snow Boards (http://www.burton.com) can be seen at their site storedotburton (http://twitter.com/storedotburton).

Assessing advertising effectiveness is–as has been said–challenging. The tools of advertising research must meet the standards that are applied to all contemporary research; such tools are expected to be statistically reliable, the studies in which they are used should involve representative samples that will be considered projectable by others in the field and they need to have been vetted by the industry as relevant to the task at hand–i.e., measuring what they purport to measure. New media and their relationship to technology will be for the next several decades a source of discovery and enlightenment for both the industry and the academy. The need to inform, persuade and sell in a global marketplace with a technological base that incorporates all we have used in the past plus the networks and mobile delivery now available have already served to make this aspect of communication a compelling set of opportunities. As Bob Garfield so elegantly points out in the Chaos Scenario (Garfield, 2009) the changes in place today as well as those that are, in a sense, moments away are not merely innovative nor are they on the same continuum as newspapers, magazines, radio and television. Digital media and delivery are revolutionary and their impact will be profound. Ideally, the problems to be solved will bring those doing the research and those in practice closer than they have been in the past. The metrics to be developed and the narratives that will follow will reflect the ways in which we relate to products and services and to each other in the 21st Century.

REFERENCES

Absolut Top Bartender on Facebook. (n.d.). Retrieved from http://www.facebook.com/AbsolutTopBartender?ref=search

Adcentricity. (n.d.). Retrieved from http://www.adcentricity.com

Appelbaum, A. (2001, June). The Constant Customer. *Gallup Management Journal*.

Applegate, E. C. (1998). *Personalities and Products: A Historical Perspective on Advertising in America*. London: Praeger.

British Library. (n.d.). Retrieved from http://www.bl.uk/reshelp/findhelprestype/news/index.html

Burns, N. M. (2008). *Establishing cost and effectiveness rationale for digital out of home media* (White Paper). Barfly Networks.

Burns, N. M. (2009, April). *In-store Persuasive Technologies*. Presented at Persuasive Technology 2009 Meeting, Claremont College, USA.

Burton Snowboards. (n.d.). Retrieved from http://www.burton.com

Captivate. (n.d.). Retrieved from http://www.captivate.com

Compared to Last Year, Advertisers Rely Less on Print Ads and More on Internet and Digital. (2009, July). Harris Interactive.

Csikszentmihalyi, M. (1997). *Finding flow: the psychology of engagement with everyday life.* New York: Basic Books.

Davenport, T. H., & Beck, J. C. (2001). *The attention economy: understanding the new currency of business.* Harvard Business School Press.

Dellarocas, C., Award, N., & Zhang, X. (2004). *Exploring the Value of Online Reviews to Organization: Implications for Revenue Forecasting and Planning.*

Digital Life America. (2009, May). Solution Research Group Program. Retrieved from http://www.srgnet.com/us/programs.html

Direct2Dell. (n.d.). Retrieved from http://en.community.dell.com/blogs/direct2dell/

Eastin, M. S., Yang, M.-S., & Nathanson, A. I. (2006, June). Children of the net: An empirical exploration into the evaluation of internet content. *Journal of Broadcasting & Electronic Media, 50*(2), 211–230. doi:10.1207/s15506878jobem5002_3

Edwards, J. (2009, July 29). *BNET's Ad Agency Layoff Counter: 34,828 Jobs Lost.* Retrieved from http://industry.bnet.com/advertising/1000433/bnets-ad-agency-layoff-counter/

Ewen, S. (1976). *Captains of Consciousness.* New York: McGraw-Hill.

Fleming, T. (1976). *How it was in advertising: 1776-1976.* Mandan, ND: Crain Books.

Foehr, U. G. *Media Multitasking among American Youth: Prevalence, Predictors, and Pairings.* Menlo Park, CA: The Henry J. Kaiser Foundation.

Garfield, B. (2009). *The Chaos Scenario.* Stielstra Publishing.

Gerba, B. (2008, January 1). Media Metrics: Finding the Darjeeling Limit. *MediaPost Magazines.*

Gerdes, J. Jr, Stringam, B. B., & Brookshire, R. G. (2008). An integrative approach to assess qualitative and quantitative consumer feedback. *Electronic Commerce Research, 8*(4), 217–234. doi:10.1007/s10660-008-9022-0

Handshake Marketing and Business Development. (n.d.) Retrieved from http://www.handshakemarketing.com

Haven, B. (2007, August). *Marketing's New Key Metric: Engagement.* Forrester Research Report.

Heaton, T. (2009, July 20). *CPM rates are falling (Thank God).* Message posted to http://www.thepomoblog.com/

Hulu. (n.d.). Retrieved from http://www.hulu.com

In-Store Marketing Institute. (n.d.). Retrieved from http://www.instoremarketer.org

Jordan, N. (1968). *Themes in Speculative Psychology.* London: Tavistock Publications.

Keiningham, T. L. (2007). A longitudinal examination of net promoter and firm revenue growth. *Journal of Marketing, 71*(3). doi:10.1509/jmkg.71.3.39

Klaassen, A. (2009, January 29). Online CPM Prices Take Tumble. *Advertising Age.*

Lyotard, J.-F. (1979). *The Postmodern Condition.*

Margolin, V., Brichta, I., & Brichta, V. (1979). *The promise and the product: 200 Years of American advertising posters.* New York: Macmillan.

Max, K. (2008, June). *Media engagement - developing consistent measures across multiple media channels.* Budapest, Hungary: ESOMAR Worldwide Multi Media Measurement (WM3).

McLuhan, M., Hutchon, K., & McLuhan, E. (1978). Multi-media: The laws of the media. *English Journal, 67*(8). doi:10.2307/815039

Nielsen Shutters, P. R. I. S. M. *Initiative*. (2009, January 26). The Market Research Industry Online. Retrieved from http://www.mrweb.com/drno/news9467.htm

Osgood, C. E., Succi, J. G., & Tannenbaum, T. H. (1957). *The Measurement of Meaning*. Chicago: University of Illinois Press.

Passikoff, R., Keys, B., & Schultz, D. E. (2007, October). Cross-media Engagement Evaluations. *Admap Magazine*.

Plummer, J., Cook, B., Diforio, D., Sokolyanskaya, I., & Ovchinnikova, M. (2006, June). *Measures of Engagement* (White Paper). Advertising Research Foundation.

Presbrey, F. (1929). *The History and Development of Advertising*. New York: Doubleday.

SeeSaw Network. (n.d.). Retrieved from http://www.seesawnetworks.com

Storedotburton on Twitter. (n.d.). Retrieved from http://twitter.com/storedotburton

Target Rating Point. (n.d.). Wikipedia. Retrieved from http://en.wikipedia.org/wiki/Target_Rating_Point

Touchtunes. (n.d.). Retrieved from http://www.touchtunes.com/barfly.html

TV Viewing and Internet Use are Complementary. (2008, October). New York: Nielsen Reports.

vJive. (n.d.). Retrieved from www.vjivenetworks.com

Walker, R. (2008). *Buying In the secret dialogue between what we buy and who we are*. New York: Random House.

Wallechinsky, D., & Wallace, I. (1975-1981). *History of Advertising: Ancient History, Middle Ages and the Early Days*. Retrieved from Trivia Library website: http://www.trivia-library.com/a/history-of-advertising-ancient-history-middle-ages-and-the-early-days.htm

ENDNOTE

1 The Captivate Network, owned by Gannett Media is an example of conventional media companies reaching out and acquiring or entering the digital and alternative media space.

Chapter 17
Digital Metrics:
Getting to the Other 50 Percent

Michelle R. Nelson
University of Illinois at Urbana-Champaign, USA

Helen Katz
Starcom Mediavest Group, USA

ABSTRACT

This chapter reviews measures of advertising effectiveness in research and practice from the pre-digital to the digital era. A focus on efficacy and ethics in terms of measurement and consumer privacy issues associated with collecting, monitoring and learning from digital metrics is discussed. Research questions related to persuasion knowledge and digital privacy are posed.

"Half the money I spend on advertising is wasted; the trouble is I don't know which half." John Wanamaker, (attributed) U.S. department store merchant (1838–1922)

INTRODUCTION

These famous (or infamous) words are still cited today as marketers try to determine how to reach their desired target audiences with the right message in the right medium at the right time to inspire those consumers to purchase (more of) the marketers' brands. Media measurement has undergone vast transformation since Wanamaker's time. For example, in 1906 radio broadcasters simply asked, "Is anybody out there?" suggesting listeners should write a letter to inform them. More than one hundred years later, planners have access to cross-measurement and fusion media data collecting media habits and linking them to actual buyer behavior (Sass 2007). Yet, one of the most basic research questions–who is the audience -- is still being discussed (Webster, Phalen & Lichty 2006).

Today, marketers want and need to know much more than that, however. With the explosion in media choices, and the desire for consumers to have greater control over their media and ad exposure, marketers are challenged to gain more precise and accurate information, not only on who is the audience, but where they are and how receptive

DOI: 10.4018/978-1-60566-792-8.ch017

they might be to ad messages. ***Digital metrics*** (audience measurement of digital media) present a great opportunity to collect, gather and use a remarkable amount of audience information. Such information offers advertisers new micro-targeted means of reaching audience members. Yet, with great data also comes great responsibility for the ethical management of that information to protect consumer privacy. In this chapter, we review the transition from old to new metrics, discuss what works today, and what is needed tomorrow in terms of measurement and consumer privacy issues associated with collecting, monitoring and learning from digital metrics.

The IDC Digital Marketplace Model and Forecast predicts that total worldwide Internet advertising will be as much as $51.1 billion in 2012. Although still a relatively small proportion of overall ad spending, the number is growing faster than all other forms of media. Despite this industry growth, as well as an increasing focus among lawmakers and regulators on behavioral targeting and online advertising, research has yet to fully address these important issues. We provide an overview of the key concepts along with a number of future research questions in the hopes of spurring more attention in this area.

METRICS: ADVERTISING EFFECTIVENESS THEN: THE EYEBALLS (AND EARS) HAVE IT

Measurement of advertising effectiveness–whether digital or not–should conform to advertising objectives (Li & Leckenby 2007). So if the objective of an advertising campaign is to increase brand awareness, then a direct response behavioral metric, such as how many times someone clicked on a banner ad, may not be the most appropriate measure. Indeed, our contemporary thinking about advertising objectives and measurement goes back more than one hundred years. The earliest model of advertising effectiveness, created in 1898 by Elmo St. Lewis, focused on 'attention, interest, desire, and action' (AIDA) (Barry 1987). Subsequent academic models of effectiveness, such as the "hierarchy of effects" model by Lavidge and Steiner (1961), also focused on cognition (thinking), affection (liking) and conation (behavior). Although Ray (1973) found some evidence for the existence of cognition, affection, and conation, there have been critiques of such hierarchical models of advertising effectiveness (see Robertson 1970; Weilbacher 2001). Measures of advertising effectiveness in academic studies have largely followed these hierarchies–including advertising recall or recognition (for cognition), attitude toward the ad and ad liking (for affection) and conation (usually purchase intent).

Real-world metrics of traditional media have also relied on advertising attention and recall, employing active techniques of measurement by asking people questions. For example, in 1923 Dr. Daniel Starch began analyzing print advertisements by interviewing people and asking them whether the ad was "noted" (reader remembers seeing ad), "associated' (reader remembers seeing name of advertiser) and "read most" (reader actually read at least half of the ad). Similarly, for broadcast media, the first ratings service ("Crossley ratings") telephone interviewed potential radio listeners in the mid-late 1930s asking them to recall their own radio listening during the past 3-6 hours. However, even those early researchers noticed that people did not or could not always remember what they had listened to. This active measurement technique was flawed. In addition, the metric focused on media exposure and not advertising exposure. A competitor at that time, pollster George Gallup, devised a method that concentrated not on recall but on current listenership ("coined telephone coincidental"). Questions focused on what programs audiences were listening to at the time of the call, what station they were tuned to, and the name of the sponsor of the program. Demographic information (age, gender) was also collected. This method was instituted into a syndicated ratings practice by Clark-Hooper in 1934. The service began reporting audience shares, percent of listeners and demographic information–thus "by the end of the 1930s the basic pattern of commercial audience research for broadcasting was set" (Webster et al. 2006, p. 98). Subsequent measures included "aided recall" where respondents were given a roster of programs and asked in a personal interview which programs they listened to and in radio diaries to write down radio listening.

All of these measurement techniques required audience members to remember what media they were exposed to either in the past or the present. Such methods have been criticized because people either do not remember or they over-report or under-report certain kinds of programs (Webster et al. 2006). However, more passive forms of measurement were developed to circumvent some of these problems. These are reviewed next.

METRICS: TECHNOLOGY DRIVES TRANSITIONS

So why the changes? In a word - Technology. The shift to bits and bytes from dots and spots has resulted in many changes not only in how media audiences are being measured and reported, but also in marketers' expectations of what these media can do for them.

It has been a gradual but ongoing transition. The first shifts were seen as far back as 1942 when the A.C. Nielsen Company, which had acquired and then perfected an audiometer device, used it to record when the radio set was turned on (Webster et al. 2006). The company launched the Nielsen Radio index and combined it with an inventory of each household's pantry (purchase data). Then in the 1960s, Nielsen moved its television audience measurement away from paper diaries to TV set meters (a technology that it still relies on). That made the measurement electronic, removing some of the 'burden' on consumers to remember and relay their media (and advertising) exposure.

It was not until the 1980s, and under the threat of competition, that Nielsen introduced additional electronic measurement in the form of the People Meter. This device, similar to a TV remote control, enabled viewers in the national Nielsen sample to punch in and out when they were watching TV, at the time they were doing so, rather than recording on paper every 15 minutes of their TV day. Today, there are 18,000 homes participating in the national People Meter service, with several hundred People Meters also measuring viewing activity in the top 25 local markets.

In the 1990s, Arbitron went down a similar, and in some ways more advanced, technological path in the quest to enhance audience measurement metrics. Its introduction of the Portable People Meter (PPM) removed the need for any kind of button pushing or active participation. By wearing a pager-like device that automatically picks up radio (and TV) signals embedded in the media content, a panelist can provide that data passively to Arbitron. But it is the introduction, growth, and development of the Internet as an advertising medium that has truly changed the metrics involved in audience measurement.

THE INTERNET: ADVERTISING AND METRICS

By virtue of the fact that the Internet is able to passively collect every click of the computer mouse, to follow the user wherever they go on the Web, and to see explicitly which ads are clicked on, the world of audience measurement has been decisively changed. In traditional media forms, what has usually been measured is the audience's 'opportunity to see' an ad–their exposure to a TV program or radio quarter hour or magazine or newspaper issue. With the Internet (and digital measurement in general), the greater level of data granularity enables marketers to capture exposure to the ad within the medium. What they are measuring and how they measure depends to some extent on the advertising format. Each of these will be reviewed next within a general discussion of Internet ad measurement.

Advertising formats have changed since the first simple banner ads were created in 1997, which provided a billboard, or display ad similar to a static newspaper image. As video, sound, and movement were added, the ads became far more dynamic, and were called rich media. But perhaps the biggest change has been the growth of search advertising, using keywords. In 2008, more than 33% of ad spending worldwide was allocated to keyword ads, 20% to display ads, and 19% to classified ads ("Internet ad growth," 2008).

Keywords

Under the name "search marketing," keyword ads are also referred to as Textual Ads (short textual messages usually marked as sponsored links) (Chakrabarti, Agarwal, & Josifovski 2008). They work in two ways: (1) sponsored search/paid search where ads are placed on pages on a web search engine based on the search query. In this case, all the major search engines (e.g., Google) act as search engine and advertising agency combined; (2) contextual advertising or context match where ads are placed within a generic, third-party web page (usually through an 'ad network' intermediary). As the name suggests, these ads are placed according to the semantic similarity of the content and the ads (key word matches) as well as click-through feedback.

The two main ways to measure Internet ad effectiveness are by click through rates and conversion rates. *Click–through rates (CTRs)* are obtained by dividing the number of users who clicked on an ad on a web page by the number of times the ad was delivered (impressions), while *conversion rates* are the percentage of search-generated visitors who make a purchase or answer a call to action). Although these numbers are typically low in sponsored search (about 1-2%, the same response rate, on average, as direct mail), other potential benefits such as cross-selling and advertising brand-specific keywords (Ghose & Yang 2008) are offered. For example, retailers can pair the searched-for product with other products that sell well on the same web site and 'direct' searchers to other popular products.

Classified Ads

Classified ads–where individuals find the right buyers for their products–have found new forms on the Internet beyond local newspapers (Diaz 2007). For the first time in almost 100 years, newspapers are losing revenue from classified advertising to specialized classified sites such as Craigslist or classifieds on Facebook. Indeed, online traffic to such sites has grown to 42.2 million unique visitors a month, according to March 2009 figures ("Online classified," 2009). Forty-five percent of all Internet users have used online classified sites. As a result, the classified industry is in a time of transition–but buyers and sellers themselves have more options to find one another.

Display Ads

Display ads, (often called banner ads) come in many forms and sizes in digital media. They can be text, graphics, static or animated, and even interactive, with more than 14 different sizes (Li & Leckenby 2007). Rich media display ads allow users to interact with the content or even with marketers or other customers. For example, Volvo piped Twitter into its ad units as a way to respond directly with customers (Morrisey 2009). Advertisers are also experimenting with live video and 3D technology within its display ads. Visa's global campaign featured real-time scenes from cities around the world in their display ads (Morrisey 2009).

Although banner ads were one of the first forms of advertising on the Internet, their share of Internet advertising budgets has fallen in recent years from 1999 when they accounted for 56%

of the market (IAB) to just 20% in 2008, even as the actual money spent on display ads has risen. In 2008, growth in elaborate display ads slowed down (Clifford & Helft 2008). This was due, in part, to the economic downturn, but also because ad dollars have shifted into search-based ads, reflecting that "advertisers are becoming more performance, ROI-focused," according to an analyst at Jeffries & Company.

Display ads can be measured in a number of ways. Traditionally, they were viewed as a direct response tactic, thus click-through rates were the primary measure. However, perhaps due to falling click-through rates (i.e., from their high of a 3% in the 1990s to less than 0.5% in recent years (Li & Leckenby 2007), additional measures are now employed, such as *impressions,* which can show display ad views–i.e., the number of times an ad is viewed, where they are viewed, demographics of those exposed to ads, and frequency. A "cost-per-engagement" pricing model only charges marketers when the consumer interacts with the ad (Steel 2009). The use of impressions as a digital metric also enables media planners to make more direct comparisons to traditional media forms, such as television or print, where the same metric can be calculated.

Within academic research, effectiveness of display ads has been addressed in both experimental (e.g., Li and Bukovac 1999) and field-based (e.g., Rosenkrans 2009) studies. This relatively small body of research has demonstrated that increased interactivity (e.g., Chandon, Chtourou, and Fortin 2003), banner size (e.g., Li and Bukovac 1999), color-contrast (Dreze and Hussherr 2003), and rich media capability (Rosenkrans 2009) contribute to higher click-through rates. However, click-through is a behavioral metric that requires conscious attention on the part of the audience. With increasing advertising clutter, it is likely that audiences do not or cannot attend consciously (or click through) all of the advertising on a web page. Yet, the display ad may still impact the audience in a manner not captured by click-through rates. Indeed, an early study by Briggs and Hollis (1997) found that banner ads were able to increase ad awareness, brand perceptions, and favorable attitudes–even without click-throughs, thus pointing out the potential for image building or brand equity through display ads. Further, in a more recent experimental study, Yoo (2008) manipulated various levels of consumer attention and then measured recall, attitudes toward the advertised brands, and placement of advertised brand into consideration sets. The findings suggest that even when consumers did not consciously process the ad and could not explicitly recall the brand, the ads had some positive effects on consumers' brand attitudes. Further, those with exposure to the brands but not *conscious* exposure were more likely to place the advertised brand into their consideration sets than those who were not exposed to the brand at all. Yet despite some promise of branding offered in a handful of academic studies, the majority of marketers still question the viability of brand-building online (Morrissey 2009). Such beliefs relate to the metrics most commonly used in industry to measure effectiveness. Results of a 2009 survey of top marketers by Forbes.com found that only 31 percent of marketers regarded brand building as a viable metric for digital advertising as compared with 51% who used click-through rates (Morrissey 2009).

Some studies have also compared web-based measures with more traditional measures (e.g., attitude toward the brand). The results are, however, not conclusive. For example, a study by media agency Starcom, behavioral targeting network Tacoda, and ComScore–revealed that there were no correlations/statistical relationships between display ad clicks and brand metrics (attitude toward brand/click-thru rate) (ComScore, 2008). Further, the study showed that "heavy clickers" (those who accounted for 50% of all display clicks) made up only 6% of those online; thus, clickers were by no means representative of the general or online public. However, another study conducted by ComScore for the pharmaceutical industry showed that the impact of banner (display) ads, search marketing and visits to the branded Web site all resulted in increased brand awareness and favorability. Such positive effects were especially true for prospective users of the products ('prospects'). Results showed greater aided brand awareness when audience members interacted with a rich media ad (The Center for Media Research, 2008). Clearly, given the inconclusive evidence, more research is needed in this area. Ideally, the research could employ theoretical models of audience involvement and new understandings of implicit persuasion from psychology (e.g., Petty et al. 2009) to better understand measures such as engagement and impressions and discern how the various metrics fit together.

MORE METRICS: DATA COLLECTION & TARGETING

Beyond click-throughs and impressions, other metrics that are routinely captured for Internet audiences include:

- **Time spent viewing**: how much time was spent on a particular website or web page
- **Reach and frequency:** traditional media metrics showing the percent of a target group reached by a website and/or campaign. The reach represents the unduplicated audience for that site/page, while frequency shows how often that group is reached by the site/page
- **Behavioral target activity:** viewing behavior/activity among a group defined based on their web activity (as opposed to demographics)
- **Retention rate:** percent of a group visiting a given website last month who also visited the site this month.
- **Conversations:** amount and type of 'talk value' about an advertisement
- **Registrations:** number of people who sign up or register on the website as a result of an ad
- **Conversion Rates:** percent of those who clicked on an ad that results in a sale.

All of these metrics vary depending on how they are defined. For most traditional media, they either rely on active reporting of behavior (such as the Nielsen people meter, where panelists have to press a button every time they start and stop watching TV), or on consumer recall ("do you remember seeing this particular magazine in the past 30 days?"). For the Internet, the measurement is passive. For syndicated measurement companies, once someone has agreed to be part of the panel, all the company needs to do is load special software onto panelists' computers and all computer activity is passively captured. Websites can collect most of that even without panelist permission. This is called Behavioral Tracking or Behavioral Targeting and it provides advertising to Internet users based on their Web surfing habits.

The way that the behavior is captured is through the use of **cookies**. Originally referred to as "magic cookies"–named after tokens with mystical powers in role-playing games (Wildstrom 1996) - they are "placement of small text files on a consumer's hard drive that are then offered back to the Web site during subsequent visits by the consumer " (Miyazaki 2008, p.20). The Web site itself provides the cookie, and then the browser installs the cookie on the computer's hard drive (Davidson 2007). A range of data can be collected from behavioral data tracking user movements–including time, duration, and sequence of movements; user information such as demographics; passwords; and media tracking–(i.e., how many times a banner ad appeared). The total collection of data that is captured on the computer is referred to as *clickstream data* (Erickson 1996). The Internet measurement companies tie that data to audience behavior–who has been exposed, and for how long. That, in turn, can be classified into consumer behaviors–any shopping or commerce conducted over the web. And they can deep-dive into online-specific behaviors, including instant messaging, email, gaming, or streaming media (audio and video). The data are then projected from the panel to the total online universe.

Unlike spyware, which offers no real value to consumers (Davidson 2007), cookies can be useful. For example, because certain types of information are stored on Web sites, consumers do not need to re-enter personal data (such as a mailing address) when visiting certain Web sites, their password is stored in a cookie - such as the *New York Times* web site (Berg 1997). Or they are able to pay for items in a virtual shopping cart at the end of their online shopping (rather than separately for each item). Interestingly, even the legal definition of cookies focuses on positive aspects, "Cookies are computer programs commonly used by Web sites to store useful information such as user names, passwords and preferences, making it easier for users to access Web pages in an efficient manner" (see Davidson 2007, p. 447). However, the downside occurs when the data collected are more than a consumer wants to share or when the information is being used for a purpose for which s/he did not consent.

From a marketer's standpoint, the behavioral information gained from cookies can be used to create user profiles for more effective segmenting and targeting in advertising and products, and the data do not usually provide any personally identifiable information. Segmenting, the "process of dividing the market into more manageable submarkets or segments" (Urban 2004), is typically based on consumer factors, product factors or media factors (see Rodgers, Cannon & Moore 2007). Once consumers have been segmented into demographic or passion groups (e.g., dog lovers)–advertisers can use the information to make sure advertising gets the 'right' message to the 'right consumer'–reducing the financial waste of paying to reach everyone (Beane & Ennis 1987). This is where targeting comes in. Targeting, "the process of delivering content or ads to segments or visitors based on their known attributes" (Phillips 2008), allows advertisers to tailor message content to fit particular aspects of the consumer when and where they are the most receptive. Tailored messages are attended to (Pechmann & Stewart, 1990), more persuasive (Ariely 2000), better liked (Kern et al. 2008) and show a greater chance of being 'clicked on' (Chatterjee, Hoffman & Novak 2003) than general messages.

What digital metrics can provide, beyond the traditional ways to segment and target audiences (e.g. demographics - age, gender, ethnicity), is the ability to do behavioral targeting - the 'technology and process in which an ad or content is shown to a visitor based on their past actions and behaviors' (Phillips 2008). For example, advertising practitioners are already creating multiple versions of messages for different audience members (up to 20,000 versions of an ad for a single brand; see Story 2007, also Morrisey 2009). The goal is a more personalized message for each customer.

Personalization is a "specialized flow of communication that sends different recipients distinct messages tailored to their individual preferences or characteristics" (White et al. 2008, p.40). Personalization in the broader online world can be based either on explicit data collection (demographics, product ratings, opt-in information provided by consumer) or implicit data collection (inferred about user–based on cookies that collect information related to search queries, purchase history/ browsing history; Cranor 2003). For example, if a consumer is looking for airline tickets to San Francisco online, an ad may appear for spas in the area or San Francisco sights or restaurants. Personalization, however, can also be profile-based-- whereby cookies are used to recognize returning visitors. When a consumer visits Amazon.com and the website welcomes him by name and even offers recommendations based on his past purchase behavior, it does so by analyzing his prior Internet activity as well as the personal information it has stored from his previous visits to that site. Such personalization offers relevant information to benefit the consumer; however, the line between "personal enough to be useful" and "so personal it freaks me out" is a fine one (Mediapost, July 28, 2008). For example, Facebook's personalization included a travel ad directed to a media blogger that read, "Hey Jew…", which was promoting "adventure travel that's worth the schlep!" (Berkowitz 2008) and another ad was targeted to an engaged woman that read, "Do You Want to be a Fat Bride?" (Beckman 2008). While such ads can certainly capture attention, it is questionable as to whether they are effective or offensive.

Indeed, this level of personalization can have a detrimental effect when the message is deemed "too personal." An experimental study by White et al. (2008) showed that consumers had a negative response to 'highly personalized' e-mail solicitations, especially when the offer in the message was not directly related to the personal information offered (i.e., personalization was not justified). For marketers, then, the challenge is to use information to target (by media) and by message–with just the right combination of relevance and personalization.

The availability of all these data has transformed the way that marketers think about media. For once metrics became available that could link consumers' exposure to an advertising message to their subsequent action, marketers realized that the Internet had leapfrogged over most other media forms to become the most accountable medium at their disposal (the exceptions being direct mail and direct response messages on TV or radio). Thus, the drive for accountability has helped speed up the development of digital metrics for other media. In TV, for example, the digital data coming off the cable set top box (STB) or from a digital video recorder (such as TiVo) provides a 'clickstream' of viewing activity at the household level that can report on second-by-second behavior in the household. From this, marketers can gain access to several new metrics. Included in these are:

- **Commercial ratings:** percent of households viewing an individual commercial
- **Commercial retention:** percent of households viewing the program who remained tuned during the commercial
- **Tuneaway:** among homes tuned to a channel prior to a commercial, the percent that tuned away at some point during that commercial
- **Timeshifting**: in Digital Video Recorder (DVR) households, the amount of time that is viewed at a time later than when the program or commercial first aired

Although for some in the industry, the return to household-based measures from the demographic (age and sex) viewer groups available in the syndicated 'currency' measures is considered a step backwards, others believe it is in fact a liberating move. There is increased skepticism that the traditional age/sex segments are in fact discriminating enough to show meaningful differences in the viewing behavior. Then, and perhaps more importantly, the household STB data can be readily matched up to more discrete target groups, including a marketer's proprietary database of customers. This is the promise of addressable TV advertising, whereby different ad messages are sent simultaneously to different homes, based on the known characteristics of those homes. For example, dog food ads would only be sent to homes known to own a dog. Households with children could receive an ad for a minivan while the single young male living next door would, at that exact same moment, see an ad for a sports car. The data to create such matches come from third party companies such as Acxiom or Experian, that collect data on all households as part of their credit reporting services. Although, as of 2009, there are no nationwide technical standards, addressable advertising is being tested at regional levels (Helm 2009). Eventually, the ad viewing may be connected directly to purchase: consumers will be able to obtain information or buy a product using their remote controls. It is also possible that the targeted devices could be used for copytesting several versions of an ad or for commercial delivery that is linked to prior ad exposure. If a home has seen one particular McDonald's ad 20 times, it would then get switched, and a different piece of creative could be sent to that household, thereby reducing the likelihood that the target viewers would be tired of seeing it and tune it out.

Despite the advantages for creating targeted advertising, thereby eliminating advertising waste, the questions raised by digital media and metrics are many. In a world where one's Internet or TV activity can be tracked down to the second, many fear a 'big brother' scenario where someone (or some company) could use that information to ill effect. If a consumer is searching on the web for information about diabetes, would her insurance company find out and raise her premiums? Could a parent's heavy viewership of 'trashy' television be used against them in divorce proceedings? And does the fact that a person watched an ad for a particular car (or beer or shoe) mean that he is then going to be bombarded by other messages from that same marketer because they believe he is more interested in their offering?

What all of this comes down to is the issue of consumer privacy. Who owns the data that is tracking consumers' media movements? Who should have access to that data? Can the data even be collected if one has not expressly and overtly given his or her permission in advance? And are there various levels of acceptability? That is, is it tolerable to collect and report aggregated household information but only after a set minimum of homes have been included? Once consumers opt in to a panel, is everything that they are doing reportable, or are there still limits on the data that can be collected? All of these issues are currently being debated and investigated. A focus on privacy issues is presented next.

PRIVACY

"The same technological advances that have made the Internet a potent marketing tool have also multiplied the threats to user privacy" (Lwin, Wirtz, & Williams 2007, p. 572).

In offline environments, consumers are generally willing to forego a certain amount of privacy to take advantage of benefits from marketers. For example, retail-shopping cards collect details about individuals' shopping behaviors. In exchange for providing a certain amount of personal information, the consumer receives coupons or other incentives for products targeted to her. Even if privacy is a concern, consumers feel they can control the amount of information provided and weigh the benefits of doing so. However, technology has changed the scope and nature of information gathering (Ashworth & Free 2006). The scope of data available is seemingly infinite. For example, Yahoo! "collects 10 terabytes of user data a day, not including content, email or images"... (Conti & Sobiesk 2007, p.112). Although these data are used to segment and target messages more effectively to the consumer, the concern persists that information is gathered online in such a way that the audience cannot detect or avoid it (Ashworth & Free 2006). Further, as Milne (2000) points out, consumer information is stored "on a database platform that is potentially accessible to the entire Internet world" (p.1).

Clearly, the scope and methods of data gathering and storage can pose greater risk to consumers. For instance, in 2006 America Online (AOL) inadvertently released their dataset containing 20 million web searches for 657,426 of their members. The data included search queries–some containing potentially sensitive information related to medical or financial issues. Although the data were in fact anonymous (numbers were used, not names), it was apparently fairly easy to work backwards from the "anonymous" cluster of web searches to identify real-world users (Barbaro & Zeller 2006). This privacy leakage was related to how the company stored the information, yet issues arise with all facets of digital metrics. Here, we review consumers' view of privacy issues and then discuss the issues with respect to collecting, monitoring and learning from digital metrics. In so doing, we outline future directions and questions for research. See Figure 1 for a conceptual diagram.

CONSUMER PRIVACY: KNOWLEDGE, CONTROL AND CONCERN

Consumer privacy has been conceptualized in academic research as "the consumer's ability to control (1) presence of other people in the environment during a market transaction or consumption behavior; and (2) dissemination of information related to or provided during such transactions or behaviors to those who were not present" (Goodwin 1991, p. 152). With digital media, other people may not be physically present, but the method of measurement can mean data are being collected, stored, and perhaps disseminated without a consumer's knowledge or control.

Two important dimensions of privacy include ***consumer knowledge*** (high/low) and ***consumer control*** over information collection and use (high/low; Milne 2000). In order to exert some form of control over data, consumers should have some knowledge about data collection and use procedures in general–i.e., a "general online marketing literacy"–perhaps best captured by the Persuasion Knowledge Model (PKM) (e.g., Friestad & Wright 1994, 1995, 1999). The PKM examines the general set of beliefs that lay people hold about how persuasion "agents" (e.g., marketers, PR practitioners, advertisers) operate, including

Figure 1. Conceptual model of privacy concern: antecedents and consequences for digital advertising

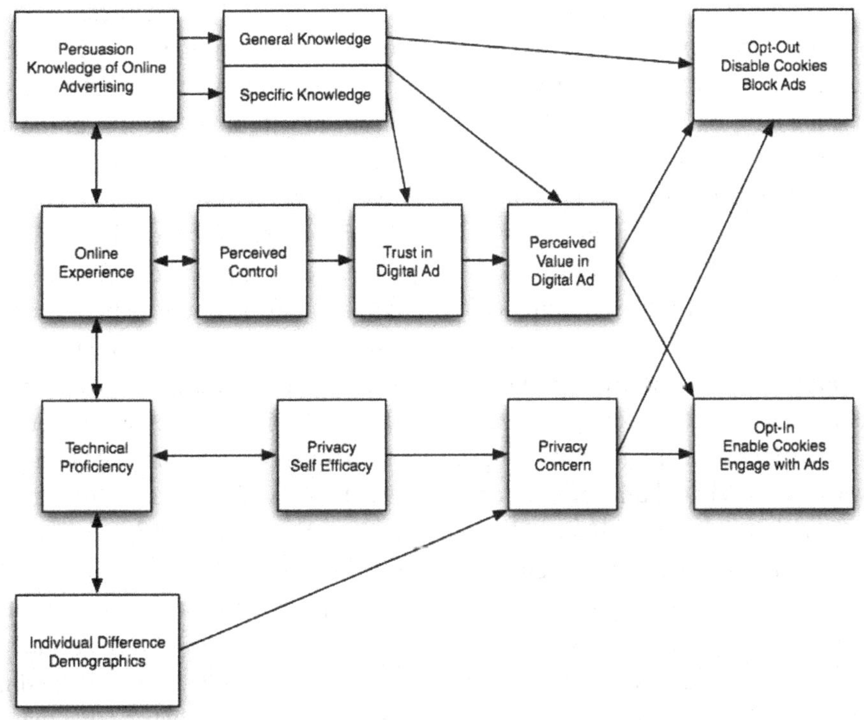

perceptions of agents' goals and tactics, evaluation of the effectiveness or appropriateness of persuasion attempts, and self-reflections of agents' own ability to cope with these attempts. It is essentially a 'folk model' of how persuasion attempts work. People may learn about persuasion tactics such as online advertising from many sources, including discussions with family and friends, direct experiences with persuasion agents, and commentary in the media (Friestad & Wright 1994). In addition, what people believe they know (perceived persuasion knowledge) and their actual knowledge may differ.

Research has shown that people *believe* that they learn about privacy issues from privacy seals and privacy notices, yet their 'actual' knowledge is very low (Rifon et al. 2005; Turow et al. 2008). It is believed that consumers are generally unaware of cookie practices or show overconfidence in their perceived knowledge as compared to real knowledge about such data collection procedures (Miyazaki 2008). For example, whereas 83% of respondents from a nationally representative U.S. sample correctly believed that "companies today have the ability to follow activity across many websites on the Web," 25% *in*correctly believed that "when a website has a privacy policy, it means the site will not share information with other Web sites or companies" (Turow et al. 2008, p.416). These findings led the researchers to conclude that only "a small proportion of Internet-using American adults have a highly sophisticated knowledge framework regarding marketplace privacy" (p.419). This survey offers some insight into persuasion knowledge about privacy–but a more detailed approach to understanding the level of persuasion knowledge about online advertising or metrics is warranted. What characteristics or tactic knowledge is essential for consumers? For example, what is the level of knowledge related to the terminology and functionality of various advertising forms, as implied by the deputy general counsel for Google, Nicole Wong's question: "... would the user really understand what a behaviorally targeted ad is compared to a contextual ad?" (Hansell 2009).

There is also media literacy related to the potential risks and benefits associated with specific information collection (Rifon et al. 2005) and with privacy rules in general (Turow, Hennessy, & Bleakley 2008). When the online world is constantly shifting, how might everyday consumers gain persuasion literacy? Who has the responsibility for online literacy? Are there demographic or psychographic factors related to levels of media literacy on these issues? Future research might address these questions.

- **RQ 1:** What is general tactic "persuasion knowledge" in the context of digital media? (i.e., what exactly do consumers need to know?)
- **RQ 2:** What is the level of persuasion knowledge about online advertising, digital metrics, and behavioral targeting?

Research has shown that most people suspect their data are being used, but they don't know how (Turow 2003). Further, despite the vast media coverage surrounding the AOL leakage, a majority of university students and middle-aged adults surveyed within six months of the incident were not aware of it (Conti & Sobiesk 2007). In addition to general online literacy, consumers should also have *specific* knowledge about particular company practices with regard to data collection and use, gained through experience and by reading companies' privacy statements or other notices. The information can give consumers ***control***–they can decide whether they wish to provide information or even visit the web site (Culnan & Milberg 1998). Although most companies now have online privacy statements (Adkinson, Eisenach, & Lenard 2002), a survey by TRUSTe' revealed that only 20% of people read privacy statements "most of the time." Reasons for not reading statements include perceived difficulty of understanding the notice (Good et al. 2005), distrust that the company will adhere to policies, and a general apathy or lack of concern about privacy (Milne & Culnan 2004). To combat these issues, researchers advocate creating standard, readable notices or even opt-in policies on web sites (Milne 2000).

Opt-in policies would give the consumer the most control over collection and use of their information. Indeed, this position was advocated (but not mandated) by Federal Trade Commission Chairman Jon Leibowitz (Davis 2009b). However, some experts suggest there is no practical structure or format available in the ad industry as of 2009 (Kalehoff 2009). Instead, researchers advocate standardized "iconic representations" that offer easily recognizable and specific communication about privacy practices of the web site (Rifon et al. 2005; Turow et al. 2008). Yet, even readable notices–up front and not buried within a privacy notice -- are uncommon. Also, given that any web site likely contains multiple advertisements with each one of them collecting, storing and sending different types of information about the viewers–it is difficult to create a standard notice (Hansell 2009). In response, however, Google instituted a policy for its behavioral tracking system whereby the phrase, "Ads by Google" is placed on each ad. If a user clicks on the phrase, she will receive some information about tracking and how to 'turn off' some of the tracking functions. Turow, privacy expert and professor at the Annenberg School for Communication, recommended a more comprehensive system (Hansell 2009). This system places the letter "T" for targeting on each ad to alert users that ad is collecting information about them. If users click on the ad, they are directed to a 'privacy dashboard,' where they could learn exactly which information was used to target the user and how to edit the information or opt out. In 2009, at least one web publisher experimented with providing specific knowledge to its readers (Kalehoff 2009). A banner ad on the "All Things Digital" blog web site of the *Wall Street Journal* included a notice that read, "A note about tracking cookies" (Kalehoff 2009). The notice went on to inform the viewer of the existence of tracking cookies on the web site and how to get rid of the tracking cookies. Further, if viewers clicked on links within the notice, they discovered additional educational materials about cookies.

Yet, research to date has not investigated the influence of these various labeling practices on consumer knowledge or behavior.

- **RQ 3:** How might general persuasion knowledge about online advertising and behavioral targeting influence self-efficacy and audience response?
- **RQ4:** How might specific persuasion knowledge of a particular advertisement - gained through 'notice' - influence audience response?

Several studies suggest that as consumers gain knowledge of online procedures in general, they demonstrate more accurate knowledge about data collection practices (Turow et al. 2008) and are able to more critically evaluate and control their own behavioral choices (Good et al. 2007; Miyazaki 2008). Indeed, simple disclosure of specific cookie use to customers before they visited a web site significantly diffused their negative reactions (Miyazaki 2008).

Perhaps those with high knowledge and high control have a higher sense of ***privacy self-efficacy*** (Rifon et al. 2005). Self-efficacy is the "beliefs in one's capability to organize and execute a particular course of action to achieve important attainments" (Bandura 1997, p. 3) and privacy self efficacy is the confidence in one's ability to protect one's privacy. Those who score higher on privacy self-efficacy were found to provide less information on a website (Rifon et al. 2005). Yet, those with high knowledge and control are sometimes also willing to accept some personal data collection to benefit from incentives (Lwin, Wirtz, & Williams 2007) perhaps because they feel they can control the information.

- **RQ 5:** How might privacy self-efficacy influence audience response to online advertising and privacy?

The response to privacy measures and issues in general is not standard across audiences. Older people and women have been shown to be more concerned than men about online information gathering and ramifications for personal privacy (Milne et al., 2004; Sheehan 1999). In a survey of younger people (university students), the concern over digital privacy was not prevalent (Conti & Sobiesk 2007). Users felt they had adequate knowledge and control over their own information–and the majority felt it was their own responsibility to protect privacy. In other studies, years of schooling and those with more online experience were more likely to generate more accurate beliefs about online data collection (Turow et al. 2008) and to report that they engage in 'protective behavior' (Milne et. al 2004).

Beyond demographic variables, there is a standard Privacy Segmentation Index (PSI) created by market-research firm, Harris Interactive, which queries people about their attitudes toward privacy and then categorizes them into three "privacy-sensitive groups": (1) privacy fundamentalists–who feel strongly about privacy; (2) privacy pragmatists (who have strong feelings over privacy related to information misuse, yet allow information collection if reasons for use are provided); and (3) "privacy unconcerned"–those with no real concerns (Taylor 2003). Yet, the implications of these individual-difference variables for privacy behaviors have not been fully explored.

- **RQ 6:** How do individual differences in attitudes toward privacy (or privacy concern) influence subsequent behaviors?

Some research has examined relationships between attitudes or concerns over privacy and subsequent behaviors (e.g., Rifon et al. 2005; Celsi & Olson 1988). Yet this literature has revealed mixed results in part due to the problems with inconsistent terminology and measurement of the construct "concern for privacy" and the potential for social desirability in responses (Rifon et al. 2005). In one such study, university students claimed to perform various behaviors to protect their online identity such as encrypt email, use anonymous re-mailers, and use anonymizers while browsing, yet their responses also correlated positively with a social desirability index (Milne et al. 2004). The authors comment that "students might have overstated their technical abilities" (p.225). Indeed, no perceived or actual knowledge was assessed in the study.

Celsi and Olson (1988) suggest that greater concern for privacy might motivate information processing and behaviors related to privacy, such as seeking out privacy related information. Other studies have also shown links between attitudes or concern over privacy and self-reported behaviors. For instance, in an Internet survey, Sheehan and Hoy (1999) noted that concerns over privacy were related to users' subsequent behaviors–such as not registering for a web site, providing incomplete information, requesting removal from a mailing list and even 'flaming' (sending highly negative responses). Similarly among Australian and South African Internet users, Dolnicar and Jordan (2007) found that privacy concerns exist and that such concerns are related to self-reported 'protective' behavior. Despite these findings, other researchers suggest there may be no such relationships (Rifon et al. 2005). What is needed is a standard definition of the key concepts (e.g., privacy concern) and empirical research to assess behavioral intentions and actual behaviors. For example, would concern over privacy influence whether or to what extent consumers choose to interact with digital advertising?

- **RQ 7:** How does concern for privacy influence consumer behaviors and responses to online advertising?

Concerns over data collection usually fall into one or more of the following categories; collection of personal information, internal and external unauthorized use of secondary use of information, error in personal information, and improper use of information (Smith et al. 1996). Another taxonomy (Wang et al. 1998) shows that people are worried about improper data acquisition (access, collection or monitoring), improper use (analysis or transfer), privacy invasion (unwanted solicitation), and improper storage. Indeed, data retention or storage is rarely discussed, but "anecdotal evidence suggests that every interaction with these companies is scrupulously logged and stored indefinitely" (Conti & Sobiesk 2007, p.112). The database is one of the most valuable assets of online companies. Despite the potential for leakage of the AOL variety, a survey of university students revealed little concern over data storage (Conti & Sobiesk 2007). Indeed, 94% of respondents indicated that "indefinite search retention" would not change their surf habits. The issue with such retention relates to company changes in the future or loss of control of that valued database.

Advertisers and consumers alike need to understand privacy issues related to methods of data collection and use. One of the most popular social network web sites, Facebook, has faced a number of privacy issues with respect to data collection and use. Thus, it serves as an apt case study to analyze consumer privacy concern and policies.

CASE STUDY: FACEBOOK

Beacon Blunder and Beyond

Facebook is a social networking web site that was founded by Mark Zuckerberg and friends at Harvard University in 2004. What began as a pilot project for use by Harvard students expanded to high school and university students and finally to anyone with a valid email address. As of 2009, the web site boasts a user base of 200,000,000 active users worldwide. Although the primary function may be for users to connect to one another and share information, its use as a marketing device through the use of banner ads and other products and services such as 'branded groups' (e.g., Apple) is noteworthy. Yet, in its relatively short lifetime, the web site has faced a number of challenges to privacy.

An early Facebook service "Techmeme" was based on the power of "word of mouth" and friend referrals. The service was essentially a 'social ad,' which worked by broadcasting to users the name and photo of their friends who like or used a certain brand, product, or service (Hansell 2008). The service, launched in November 2007, used to discern which products users like was called Beacon, which gathered information about what you like (or bought) from other Beacon-affiliated web sites. According to a company press release, the service would allow users to perform various actions related to the participating web sites, including "posting an item for sale, completing a purchase, scoring a high score in an online game or viewing of video." Although the idea of sharing branded information with friends related well to the overall use of Facebook, the problem occurred largely because the service was initially *opt-out*, and users' friends received updates and status feeds, sometimes related to their own gifts! As a result, advocacy group Moveon.org organized a petition and facebook group with the following message just a couple weeks after the Beacon launch:

"Matt in New York already knows what his girlfriend got him for Christmas... Why? Because a new Facebook feature automatically shares books, movies, or gifts you buy online with everyone you know on Facebook. Without your consent, it pops up in your News Feed--a huge invasion of privacy. Can you sign the petition to facebook today? Then invite friends to this group! Petition: "Facebook must respect my privacy. They should not tell my friends what I buy on other sites—or let companies use my name to endorse their products—without my explicit permission." Apparently, within 10 days, more than 50,000 people joined this group and as a result, Facebook changed the service from opt-out to an opt-in service (Farber 2007) with a public apology and new privacy controls announced by Mark Zuckerberg in December 2007 (Zuckerberg 2007).

In addition to privacy issues surfacing from Beacon, Facebook has come under scrutiny for the ability of hackers to download users' profiles through data mining (Jones & Soltren 2005) and when users were unable to completely remove their profiles (Aspan 2008). At stake was the ownership of user data–would Facebook retain the information that users uploaded even after the users deleted their profiles? According to a terms of service agreement, it appeared that Facebook owned users' data 'indefinitely.' After this policy came to the attention of the media and Facebook users by an article in *The Consumerist* (Walters 2009), Facebook agreed to change its terms of service agreement. As a result of these various privacy issues, in February 2009, Facebook involved its users in the creation of policy and principles of its web site. According to the company's press release: "Users will have the opportunity to review, comment and vote on these documents over the coming weeks and, if they are approved, other future policy changes." In essence, the popular web site evolved from publisher-centered information ownership and control to a more consumer-centric and democratic model of data ownership control and policy. Despite the growing popularity of the web site, questions surrounding its value and future related to advertising revenue are still raised. The future of Facebook and the monetization of social networking and advertising remains a mystery.

PRIVACY SUMMARY

Digital metrics offer an enormous amount of information about "the audience"–explicit information provided willingly by the consumer through web site registrations, profiles (such as on Facebook) as well as implicit information collected by cookies. Clearly, the lines between what digital measurement can provide and what consumers are willing to have collected about them are still being clarified. There will be more consumer education needed, to explain the benefits and value to the consumer of passive digital measurement, and the possible threats that a loss of personal data can create. Turow et al. 2008 suggest, for example, that without a unified national philosophy of marketplace privacy–"the best approach for educating Americans on the subject may well be to streamline the discussion of regulations"–especially through schools, community organizations, and the media (p. 421). Marketers will keep focused on the former, while privacy advocates and consumer groups will likely emphasize the latter. It is in the industry's interests to educate consumers about online data and how it is and should be used. Websites should all post their privacy statements in clear and accessible ways, including the presence and use of cookies. For the inclusion of a discrete amount of useful information at the time when the data are actually being collected would help consumers' knowledge acquisition and control (Cranor 2003).

FUTURE RESEARCH AND CONCLUDING THOUGHTS

There has never been a more exciting time to be dealing with audience measurement and media usage. Consumers work and play with digital media, advertisers are increasingly turning to digital forms for their messages, and regulators are considering the ethical and legal ramifications of the digital media. Yet, academic research has not yet fully embraced research in digital media. We hope that this chapter will serve as a catalyst to move research forward in this area.

The growth and development of digital media forms have provided consumers with more choice and control over their media consumption, at the same time as they offer marketers more accurate and granular information on which to base their spending decisions. We have outlined some common digital metrics used today, but what will the future of digital media look like? Will advertising remain a key revenue model for web sites? In 2009, some advertisers are experimenting with new 3D forms. For example, Carmichael Lynch created a 3-D Sasquatch character for Jack Link's that users could print out and play with in front of a webcam to interact with a 3D digital environment (Klaassen 2009). Marketers are also increasingly interweaving marketing material with editorial content (Hessel 2009). For example, *The New York Times* offered a web advertising campaign for the television series, *Mad Men*, which included a "mini-archive of Times articles about the show within the ad unit." Said the Vice President of Research & Development, Michael Zimbalist, "We have to give advertisers an opportunity to market through the content, not just around it." Further, as mobile technology catches up, digital media has finally moved beyond the laptop into mobile opportunities where geo-targeting is not uncommon. Each of these new forms offers new avenues for exploring ad effectiveness and social issues. Are the ads more likely to be accessed if integrated into content? If targeting the consumer where she lives and plays? What has happened to the so-called Chinese Wall separating editorial and advertising in a digital age? Questions such as these offer promising areas for future consideration in academic research and professional practice.

In fact, digital media are changing *all* media. By offering marketers greater accountability for their media dollars, these new media forms have set a new standard for marketers' understanding of and expectations for the role that all media play in the marketing mix. As the research director at one large media agency put it, "There is more and more emphasis by advertisers for greater return-on-objectives in campaigns, particularly in the digital space where the accountability data is so readily available" ("New Study Shows"...2008). Indeed, as Jack Klues, president of Publicis Groupe, has noted, marketers increasingly will want and need to begin the media planning process with digital (online) media, rather than adding them in as an afterthought to a television-based plan [Klues 2008].

If this is, indeed, the path that marketers take, the need for even more digitally-based audience measurement will grow. There will be continued experimentation, for example, with multi-screen measures (TV + PC + Mobile) now being tested by companies such as Nielsen, as well as continued work in data fusion. Media data will increasingly be combined with purchase information to provide a more holistic view of how all the elements truly work together to achieve a marketer's ultimate objective, to increase sales. At the same time, we will inevitably see the development of industry standards to ensure that the measurement services continue to provide reliable and valid data, and do so in ways that do not infringe on consumers' rights in any way. The debate over privacy is bound to get louder and will likely involve legislators and regulators along the way. For example, Representative Rick Boucher (D-VA.) publicly stated he will introduce privacy legislation in 2009–while FTC Chairman Leibowitz appears to side with consumers' rights (advocating an opt-in policy). Yet, at the highest level, Supreme Court Justice Antonin Scalia warns that privacy laws may conflict with the First Amendment (Davis 2009a).

In the end, what we hope and expect the development of digital metrics to do is give John Wanamaker, and all the marketers that followed him, a better answer to the question of 'which half' is wasted. And in doing so, help them determine ways to avoid that waste altogether.

REFERENCES

Adkinson, W. F., Eisenach, J. A., & Lenard, T. M. (2002). *Privacy Online: A Report on the Information Practices and Policies of Commercial Web Sites*. Washington, DC: Progress & Freedom Foundation. Retrieved July 15, 2008, from http://www.pff.org/publications/privacyonlinefinalael.pdf

Ariely, D. (2000). Controlling the information flow: Effects on consumers' decision making and preferences. *The Journal of Consumer Research*, *27*(2), 233–248. doi:10.1086/314322

Ashworth, L., & Free, C. (2006). Marketing dataveillance and digital privacy: Using theories of justice to understand consumers' online privacy concerns. *Journal of Business Ethics*, *67*, 107–123. doi:10.1007/s10551-006-9007-7

Aspan, M. (2008, February 11). How Sticky Is Membership on Facebook? Just Try Breaking Free. *The New York Times*. Retrieved from http://www.nytimes.com/2008/02/11/technology/11facebook.html?_r=2&ref=business&oref=slogin.

Bandura, A. (1997). *Self-efficacy: The Exercise of Control*. New York: W.H. Freeman.

Barbaro, M., & Zeller, T. (2006, August 9). A Face is Exposed for AOL Searcher No. 4417749. *The New York Times*. Retrieved June 15, 2009, from http://www.nytimes.com/2006/08/09/technology/09aol.html?ex=1312776000

Barry, T. (1987). The Development of the Hierarchy of Effects, An Historical Perspective. In Leigh, J. H., & Martin, C. R. (Eds.), *Current Issues and Research in Advertising* (pp. 251–295). Ann Arbor, MI: University of Michigan.

Beane, T. P., & Ennis, D. M. (1987). Market segmentation: A review. *European Journal of Marketing*, *21*(5), 20–43. doi:10.1108/EUM0000000004695

Beckman, R. (2008, September 3). Facebook Ads Target You Where it Hurts. *Washington Post*, CO1. Retrieved from http://www.washingtonpost.com/wp-dyn/content/article/2008/09/02/AR2008090202956.html

Berg A. (1997, January 17). op. cit., NPR, Talk of the Nation Science Friday, Transcript # 97011702-211, available on Lexis/Nexis computerized database service.

Berkowitz, D. (2008, July 17). The Chutzpah of Facebook's 'Jewdar. www.mediapost.com. Retrieved June 15, 2009, from http://www.mediapost.com/publications/?fa=Articles.showArticle&art_aid=86800

Briggs, R., & Hollis, N. (1997). Advertising on the Web: Is there response before click-through? *Journal of Advertising Research*, *3*(2), 33–45.

Chakrabarti, D., Agarwal, D., & Josifovski, V. (2008). Contextual Advertising by Combining Relevance with Click Feedback. In *Search: Ranking & Retrieval Enhancement, International World Wide Web Conference Committee (IW3C2)*, April 21–25, 2008, Beijing, China.

Chandon, J. L., Chtourou, M. S., & Fortin, D. R. (2003, June). Effects of configuration and exposure levels on responses to Web advertisements. *Journal of Advertising Research*, 217–222.

Chatterjee, P., Hoffman, D. L., & Novak, T. P. (2003, October). Modeling the clickstream: implications for Web-based advertising efforts. *Marketing Science*, *22*(4), 520–541. doi:10.1287/mksc.22.4.520.24906

Clifford, S., & Helft, M. (2008, May 19). Online Search Ads Faring Better than Expensive Displays. *The New York Times*. Retrieved from http://www.nytimes.com/2008/05/19/technology/19online.html

ComScore. (2008, February 12). *New Study Shows that Heavy Clickers Distort Reality of Display Advertising Click-Through Metrics*. Retrieved from http://www.comscore.com/press/release.asp?press=2060

Conti, G., & Sobieski, E. (2007). An Honest Man Has Nothing to Fear: User Perceptions on Web-based Information Disclosure. In *Symposium On Usable Privacy and Security (SOUPS) 2007*, July 18-20, Pittsburgh, PA, USA.

Cranor, L. F. (2003, October 30). 'I Didn't Buy it for Myself' Privacy and Ecommerce Personalization. In WPES '03. Washington, DC: ACM.

Culnan, M. J., & Milberg, S. J. (1998). *The Second Exchange: Managing Customer Information in Marketing Relationships*. Unpublished Working Paper, Georgetown University.

Davidson, S. (2007). From Spam to Stern, Advertising law and the Internet. In Schumann, D. W., & Thorson, E. (Eds.), *Internet Advertising, Theory and Research* (pp. 427–471). Mahwah, NJ: Lawrence Erlbaum Associates.

Davis, W. (2009a, May 1). Free Speech Trumps Privacy Online. *Daily Online Examiner*. Retrieved June 15, 2009, from http://www.mediapost.com/publications/?fa=Articles.showArticle&art_aid=105258

Davis, W. (2009b, May 12). FTC's Leibowitz Opts for BT Opt-In. *Daily Online Examiner*. Retrieved June 15, 2009, from http://www.mediapost.com/publications/?fa=Articles.showArticle&art_aid=105954

Diaz, S. (2007, August 31). On the Internet, A Tangled Web Of Classified Ads With So Many Sites, Sifting Is Difficult. *Washington Post*, D01. Retrieved July 30, 2008, fromhttp://www.washingtonpost.com/wp-dyn/content/article/2007/08/30/AR2007083002046_pf.html

Dolnicar, S., & Jordaan, Y. (2007). A market-oriented approach to responsibly managing information privacy concerns in direct marketing. *Journal of Advertising*, *36*(2), 123–149. doi:10.2753/JOA0091-3367360209

Drèze, X., & Hussherr, F.-X. (2003). Internet advertising: Is anybody watching? *Journal of Interactive Marketing*, *17*(4), 8–23. doi:10.1002/dir.10063

Erickson, J. (1996, June 30). Are Those Who Go Online To Send Junk Mail Out of Line? Growth of Unsolicited Direct Mail on Internet Raises Questions of Privacy. *Star Tribune*, 3D.

Farber, C. (2007, November 29). Facebook Beacon Update: No Activities Published Without Users Proactively Consenting. *ZDnet.com*. Retrieved June 1, 2009, from http://blogs.zdnet.com/BTL/?p=7188

Friestad, M., & Wright, P. (1994). The persuasion knowledge model: How people cope with persuasion attempts. *The Journal of Consumer Research*, *21*(1), 1–31. doi:10.1086/209380

Friestad, M., & Wright, P. (1995). Persuasion knowledge: Lay people's and researchers' beliefs about the psychology of persuasion. *The Journal of Consumer Research*, *22*(1), 62–74. doi:10.1086/209435

Friestad, M., & Wright, P. (1999). Everyday persuasion knowledge. *Psychology and Marketing*, *16*(2), 185–194. doi:10.1002/(SICI)1520-6793(199903)16:2<185::AID-MAR7>3.0.CO;2-N

Ghose, A., & Yang, S. (2008). Analyzing Search Engine Advertising: Firm Behavior and Cross-Selling in Electronic Markets. In *Internet Monetization–Sponsored Search, International World Wide Web Conference Committee (IW3C2)*, April 21–25, 2008, Beijing, China.

Good, N., Dhamija, R., Grossklags, J., Thaw, D., Aronowitz, S., Mulligan, D., & Konstan, J. (2005). Stopping Spyware at the Gate: A User Study of Privacy, Notice and Spyware. In *Symposium on Usable Privacy and Security (SOUPS),* July 6-8, 2005, Pittsburgh, PA.

Goodwin, C. (1991). Privacy: Recognition of a consumer right. *Journal of Public Policy & Marketing, 19*(Spring), 149–166.

Hansell, S. (2009, March 19). An Icon That Says They're Watching You. *Bits Blog - The New York Times*. Retrieved June 15, 2009, from http://bits.blogs.nytimes.com/2009/03/19/an-icon-that-says-theyre-watching-you/

Helm, B. (2009, April 7). Will Targeted TV Ads Justify Higher Fees? *Business Week*. Retrieved June 15, 2009, from http://www.businessweek.com/magazine/content/09_16/b4127000389178.htm

Hessel, E. (2009, May 28). Gray Lady Juicing up Digital Ads. *Forbes.com*. Retrieved June 15, 2009, from http://www.forbes.com/2009/05/28/new-york-times-business-media-advertising.html

IDC. (2008, May 30). *IDC Finds Internet Advertising Keeps Growing Fast Despite Economic Difficulties*. IDC Press release. Retrieved from http://www.idc.com/getdoc.jsp?containerId=prUS21260308

Jones, H., & Soltren, J. H. (2005). *Facebook: Threats to Privacy.* Cambridge, MA: Massachusetts Institute of Technology. Retrieved on April 30, 2008 from http://www.swiss.ai.mit.edu/6095/student-papers/fall05-papers/facebook.pdf

Kalehoff, M. (2009, April 3). A Note About Tracking Cookies, MediaPost Publications, Onelinespin@mediapost.com. Retrieved from http://www.mediapost.com/publications/?fa=Articles.showArticle&art_aid=103459.

Kern, D., Harding, M., Storz, O., Davis, N., & Schmidt, A. (2008). Shaping How Advertisers See Me: User Views on Implicit and Explicit Profile Capture. In CHI 2008, April 5-10, 2008, Florence, Italy, ACM.

Klaassen, A. (2009, April 27). Speaking of Augmented Reality, Here's a 3-D Sasquatch: Latest Ad From Jerky Maker Jack Link's Uses Webcam to Create Image. *AdAge.Com*. Retrieved June 15, 2009, from http://adage.com/digitalnext/article?article_id=136287

Klues, J. (2008, April 11). *Media Today.* Presentation to University of Illinois at Urbana-Champaign Department of Advertising Faculty, Illini Center, Chicago.

Lavidge, R., & Steiner, G. (1961, October). A model for predictive measurements of advertising effectiveness. *Journal of Marketing*, 59–62. doi:10.2307/1248516

Li, H., & Bukovac, J. I. (1999). Cognitive impact of banner ad characteristics: An experimental study. *Journalism and Mass Communication, 76*(2), 341–354.

Li, H., & Leckenby, J. D. (2007). Examining the Effectiveness of Internet Advertising Formats. In Schumann, D. W., & Thorson, E. (Eds.), *Internet Advertising, Theory and Research* (pp. 203–224). Mahwah, NJ: Lawrence Erlbaum Associates.

Lwin, M., Wirtz, J., & Williams, J. D. (2007). Consumer online privacy concerns and responses: A power-responsibility equilibrium perspective. *Journal of the Academy of Marketing Science, 35*, 572–585. doi:10.1007/s11747-006-0003-3

Milne, G. R. (2000). Privacy and ethical issues in database/interactive marketing and public policy: A research framework and overview of the special issue. *Journal of Public Policy & Marketing, 19*(1), 1–6. doi:10.1509/jppm.19.1.1.16934

Milne, G. R., Bahl, S., & Rohm, A. (2008). Toward a framework for assessing covert marketing practices. *Journal of Public Policy & Marketing, 27*(Spring), 57–62. doi:10.1509/jppm.27.1.57

Milne, G. R., & Culnan, M. J. (2004). Strategies for reducing online privacy risks: Why consumers read (or don't read) online privacy notices. *Journal of Interactive Marketing, 18*(Summer), 15–29. doi:10.1002/dir.20009

Milne, G. R., Rohm, A. J., & Bahl, S. (2004). Consumers' protection of online privacy and identity. *The Journal of Consumer Affairs, 38*(2), 217–232.

Miyazaki, A. D. (2008). Online privacy and the disclosure of cookie use: Effects on consumer trust and anticipated patronage. *Journal of Public Policy & Marketing, 27*(1), 19–33. doi:10.1509/jppm.27.1.19

Morrissey, B. (2009, May 25). Real Time: The Web's New Prime Time. *Adweek.com*. Retrieved from http://www.adweek.com/aw/content_display/news/digital/e3i15f4e2b3b4a-487b3b5cd5347ebd07cbf

Online Classified Use Soaring in US. *Pew Survey*. (2009, May 22). Retrieved from http://www.pewinternet.org/Media-Mentions/2009/Online-classified-use-soaring-in-US-Pew-survey.aspx

Pechmann, C., & Stewart, D. W. (1990). The effects of comparative advertising on attention, memory, and purchase intentions. *The Journal of Consumer Research, 17*(September), 180–191. doi:10.1086/208548

Petty, R. E., Fazio, R. H., & Briñol, P. (Eds.). (2009). *Attitudes: Insights From the New Implicit Measures*. New York: Psychology Press.

Phillips, J. (2008, July 2). Performance, Performance, Performance. *Metrics Insider*. Retrieved June 15, 2009, from http://www.mediapost.com/publications/index.cfm?fa=Articles.showArticle&art_aid=85886

Ray, M. (1973). Marketing Communication and the Hierarchy of Effects. In Clarke, P. (Ed.), *New Models for Communication Research* (*Vol. 2*, pp. 146–175). Beverley Hills, CA: Sage.

Rifon, N. J., LaRose, R., & Choi, S. M. (2005). Your privacy is sealed: Effects of Web privacy seals on trust and personal disclosures. *The Journal of Consumer Affairs, 39*(2), 339–362. doi:10.1111/j.1745-6606.2005.00018.x

Robertson, T. S. (1971). *Innovation and the Consumer*. New York: Holt, Rinehart & Winston.

Rodgers, S., Cannon, H. M., & Moore, J. (2007). Segmenting Internet Markets. In Schumann, D. W., & Thorson, E. (Eds.), *Internet Advertising, Theory and Research* (pp. 149–183). Mahwah, NJ: Lawrence Erlbaum Associates, Publishers.

Rosenkrans, G. (2009). The creativeness and effectiveness of online interactive rich media advertising. *Journal of Interactive Advertising, 9*(2). Retrieved from http://www.jiad.org/article114.

Sass, E. (2007, August 13). Overview: Cross-Media Measurement Takes Off. *Media Daily News*. Retrieved from http://www.mediapost.com/publications/index.cfm?fa=Articles.showArticle&art_aid=65499

Sheehan, K. B. (1999). An investigation of gender differences in online privacy concerns and resultant behaviors. *Journal of Interactive Marketing, 13*, 24–38. doi:10.1002/(SICI)1520-6653(199923)13:4<24::AID-DIR3>3.0.CO;2-O

Sheehan, K. B., & Hoy, M. G. (1999). Flaming, complaining, abstaining: How online users respond to privacy concerns. *Journal of Advertising, 28*(3), 37–51.

Smith, H. J., Milberg, S. J., & Burke, S. J. (1996). Information privacy: Measuring individuals' concerns about organizational practices. *Management Information Systems Quarterly, 20*(2), 167–196. doi:10.2307/249477

Steel, E. (2009, May 6). Sprucing up Online Display Ads. *Wall Street Journal.com*. Retrieved from http://online.wsj.com/article/SB124156876159389809.html

Story, L. (2007, August 6). It's An Ad, Ad, Ad, Ad World. *The New York Times*. Retrieved July 15, 2008, from http://www.nytimes.com/2007/08/06/business/media/06digitas.html

Taylor, C. R. (2003). Consumer privacy and the market for customer information. *The Rand Journal of Economics*, *35*(4), 631–650. doi:10.2307/1593765

The Center for Media Research. (2008, July 15). *Internet Ad Growth Percentage High, But Traditional Ad Dollars Higher*. Research Brief. Retrieved from http://www.mediapost.com/publications/index.cfm?fa=Articles.showArticle&art_aid=86497

The Center for Media Research. (2008, August 1). *Online Advertising Shows Significant Impact on Brand Awareness*. Research Brief. Retrieved from http://www.mediapost.com/publications/?fa=Articles.showArticle&art_aid=87420

Turow, J. (2003). *Online Privacy: The System is Broken*. Report from the Annenberg Public Policy Center of the University of Pennsylvania. Retrieved from http://www.asc.upenn.edu/usr/jturow/internet-privacy-report/36-page-turow-version-9.pdf

Turow, J., Hennessy, M., & Bleakley, A. (2008). Consumers' understanding of privacy rules in the marketplace. *The Journal of Consumer Affairs*, *42*(3), 411–424. doi:10.1111/j.1745-6606.2008.00116.x

Urban, G. L. (2004). *Digital Marketing Strategy*. Upper Saddle River, NJ: Prentice-Hall.

Walters, C. (2009, February 15). Facebook's New Terms Of Service: 'We Can Do Anything We Want With Your Content. Forever.' *The Consumerist*. Retrieved from http://consumerist.com/5150175/facebooks-new-terms-of-service-we-can-do-anything-we-want-with-your-content-forever

Wang, H., Lee, M., & Wang, C. (1998). Consumer privacy concerns About internet marketing. *Communications of the ACM, 41*(3), 63–70. doi:10.1145/272287.272299

Webster, J. G., Phalen, P. F., & Lichty, L. W. (2006). *Ratings Analysis: Theory and Practice of Audience Research* (3rd ed.). Mahwah, NJ: LEA Lawrence Erlbaum Associates.

Weilbacher, W. W. (2001, November). Point of view: Does advertising cause a 'hierarchy of effects'? *Journal of Advertising Research*, 19–26.

White, T. B., Zahay, D. L., Thorbjornsen, H., & Shavitt, S. (2008). Getting too personal: Reactance to highly personalized email solicitations. *Marketing Letters*, *19*, 39–50. doi:10.1007/s11002-007-9027-9

Wildstrom, S. (1996, November 11). They're Watching You Online. *Business Week*. Retrieved from http://www.businessweek.com/1996/46/b350141.htm

Yoo, C. Y. (2008). Unconscious processing of Web advertising: Effects on implicit memory, attitude toward the brand, and consideration set. *Journal of Interactive Marketing*, *22*(2), 2–18. doi:10.1002/dir.20110

Zuckerberg, M. (2007, December 5). *Thoughts on Beacon*. Message posted to http://blog.facebook.com/blog.php?post=7584397130

Chapter 18
Virtual Identities from Virtual Environments

Melvin Prince
Southern Connecticut State University, USA

ABSTRACT

The creation of identities in immersive online digital environments has become commonplace in consumer behavior. Consumers frequently enter into socially networked, computer mediated environments (CME's) as avatars. A user can design his or her avatar by choosing typologies of facial features, body types and clothing styles. The chapter concerns Avatar analysis as a system for generating and analyzing consumer information of practical value to marketers. Avatar analysis enhances understanding of brand perceptions and meanings, discovers new ways of positioning and differentiating brands, and provides insights for improving the effectiveness of brand communications. Using websites such as Second Life to draw avatars, consumer identity projections are elicited based on consumers' perceptions and interpretations of their own digital figure drawings i.e., virtual social identities of consumers and brands. These identity projections disclose their real and ideal selves, brand-as-a-person, and imagery of a typical brand user.

AVATARS AND PSYCHOLOGICAL PROFILES

Avatars serve to mirror their creator's self-identity and serve as a medium for self-disclosure. Self-identity may be defined as the unique character of one's self, as distinguished from others. Forms by which self-identity is disclosed may be either realistic or imaginary. Self-disclosure of one's identity may relate to a hobby, opinion, capability, or personal attractiveness. Self-disclosure is relatively consistent regardless of the form in which self-identity is presented (Kang and Yang, 2006). Self-identity as portrayed by an avatar may consciously reference the actual self, the ideal self, or an unconscious self-image. Gender and age affect the style and focus given to self-identity disclosure. Females are prone to express imaginary identities when they are unfamiliar with parties viewing their avatars. Age affects self-disclosure

DOI: 10.4018/978-1-60566-792-8.ch018

i.e., people in their 20's and 30's in discussing their avatars are more likely to disclose opinions about such matters as public affairs issues.

A study by Vasalou et al (2008) provides rich insights for the interpretation of person and lifestyle profiles. Avatars show how a face is personalized, linking special facial features and hair color and styling to the physical identity. Personality, taste and object cathexis are represented by fashion expressions e.g., individual clothes, taste in coordinating clothing outfits, special signature items displayed on the person. Avatars are a means of understanding a subject's values including group affiliations, accepted cultural norms, emotional attachments, and response to environmental experiences.

AVATARS AND CONSUMER INSIGHTS

Perceptions of Avatars' traits have been studied under conditions of experimental manipulation. Nowak and Rauh (2006) used a static context for presentation of digitally created, experimenter-produced, avatars to which participants responded. Participants' perceptions of anthropomorphism, androgyny, credibility, homophily, attraction and likelihood of choice for interaction were obtained in response to experimental avatars to which they were exposed. Participants were found to choose perceived attractive and credible avatars to represent themselves. They voiced a preference for avatars that matched their own gender and regarded female avatars as more attractive than male avatars.

Avatars have also been used for applications in clinical psychology. Clinical applications include using avatars to diagnose and treat phobias, anxiety disorders, eating disorders, sexual disorders, and neurological damage. In a framework for future research in the area (Gaggioli, Mantovani, Castelnuovo, Wieberhold, and Riva, 2003), three levels of analysis involving avatars have been identified: (1) identification of salient physical features, (2) simulation of the virtual human's behavioral realism, and (3) relational or interactional potentialities.

The fields of consumer marketing and buyer behavior have increasingly

focused on avatars. This is evidenced by recent research into the influence of virtual identities for online shopping, the impact of avatars as online customer service representatives, and even as virtual human branded product introductions available on the web. Avatars have been found to serve as effective online sales agents generating higher levels of retailer satisfaction, more positive product attitudes and stronger purchase intentions. Characteristics mediating these effects include perceptions of the avatar's attractiveness and expertise, as these interact with levels of product involvement (Holzwarth, Janiszewski and Neuman, 2006).

In one study, it was found that animated avatars do not heighten consumer trust of a product. However, the authors recommend that future studies present avatars with increased vividness, facial expressions and better synchronization with online marketing communications (Qiu and Benbasat, 2005). Intention to use avatar-related products was successfully predicted in another study (Chung, 2005). Ease of use of the avatar, its perceived usefulness, and attitudes toward the avatar were key determinants of the intention to use the avatar-related product.

SELF-CONGRUITY AND VIRTUAL IDENTITIES

Covering a broad spectrum of approaches to self-congruity avatar analysis is expected to become fertile ground for future work in psychological aspects of consumption. The present work, discussed in this chapter, is interdisciplinary and has profound implications not only for marketers and marketing academicians, but also for economists and psychologists.

Self-congruity is a motive for maintaining consistency of the self. Components of self-congruity are self-esteem, self-consistency and self-knowledge. Self-image congruity is a state where a consumer's cognitive self-image matches impressions of product attributes. Self-congruent buyer behavior includes product attitudes, choices and usage in the context of various situations. A recurring theme in the literature is the issue of actual and ideal self-congruity. The relationship between self-concept/product image congruity and consumer behavior has been well established for some time (Sirgy 1982).

The moderating roles of, (a) product conspicuousness, (b) product personalization, or strong symbolic associations, and (c) personality variables has been similarly demonstrated. Product congruity with the actual and ideal self has been found to be additive in consumer choice behavior outcomes (Sirgy 1985), but also to vary in relative importance with the cultural context (Quester et al 2000).

In the past, work on self-congruity was based largely on quantitative techniques to measure and correlate self-image and product images. Typically these studies employed Q-Sort methodology, semantic differential, adjective checklists or Likert scale approaches.

Examples of self-image traits measured quantitatively might include a scale of self-concept person concept and product concept (Malhotra 1981). Another psychological trait that might be quantitatively measured and mapped to products is self-esteem. Self-esteem measurement would involve the use of the State Self-Esteem scale which is comprised of twenty five-point statements used to gauge the state measure of self-esteem at a particular point of time (Heatherton and Polivy, 1991).

Recent work by Zaltman (2003) demonstrates that innovative qualitative interview techniques probe deep and unconscious meanings that more standard quantitative techniques fail to elicit. However, Zaltman in his Metaphor Elicitation approach does not make the leap to self-congruity—the fit between consumer and brand personalities. While Zaltman recognizes the phenomenon, the emphasis in his ZMET methodology is on consumer thinking processes in relation to brand meanings. Rather than placing the initial focus on the consumer's psychological makeup, the ZMET method begins with the consumer's selection of images that metaphorically communicate product meanings which are ultimately linked to the consumer's memory and affect systems. A complementary system for explaining consumer choice warrants exploration and testing.

Extending self-congruity theory to explain and predict consumer choice by the use of other qualitative methods, such as figure drawings as projective device, patently makes sense. However, to date, qualitative approaches employing human figure drawings seem not to have been brought into play to analyze self-congruity and consumer preferences.

Avatars are a modern version of figure drawings, which have a venerable history in psychological research. Pre-Avatar figure drawings had more flexibility, in terms of the size of the figure, its location, unique features, omission of major parts, etc. Avatars also differ from hand-drawn figures in that they allow coloring i.e., skin, eye and hair color, and clothing colors. Avatars can be esthetically drawn by people with varying artistic skills, and the options employed can be recorded.

On the other hand, there is considerable overlap between characteristics of hand-drawn figures and avatars. Avatars enable participants to construct their own personalities through which they interact with other people (Fetscherin & Latteman 2007). Participants design their own virtual characteristics and appearance, including body proportions, sexual differentiation, facial features, clothing and skin color.

Examination of the literature on figure drawings suggests the concept of an avatar analyzer (see Appendix: A Digression on the History of Figure Drawings). Unlike classical figure drawing analysis, self-congruity analysis from avatar figure drawings relies on the consumer's projections of self images and brand personality, using his or her own drawings as a projection stimulus. That is, the consumer identifies personality characteristics in avatar figure drawings, the self-congruities connecting self and brand, together with the behavioral consequences of such connections (see Figure 1).

From an applied perspective, marketers stand to benefit from research on this new tool by learning about the most important traits specifically associated with buying perceptions and preferences. This research should improve marketing strategies with respect to psychologically defined market segmentation and product positioning. Tactically, by learning more about how personality traits affect consumer behavior, marketers can improve product designs and communications programs.

SELF-CONGRUITY PROJECTION

Self-congruity is a process that compares beliefs about a perceived consumer self image and a product (referent) image. Self-image refers to actual self-image, ideal self-image or to brand user profile image. Person and product image comparisons made by consumers are based on criteria of valence, strength and salience (Sirgy 1986). The self-esteem motive moderated by self-consistency effects underlies evaluative self-congruity. Self-congruity may be viewed as positive or negative. The valence of the perceived self-image combined with that of the referent self image determines the self-congruity condition.

From an applied perspective, evaluative self-congruity processes result in predictable consumer outcomes such as brand preference (attitude) and brand purchase intention (behavioral intention). These derive, in large measure, from anticipation of a purely personal self evaluation or the social image consequence of a brand preference or purchase.

RESEARCH QUESTIONS

Some questions for the research are:

- RQ1: Which characteristics of avatar drawings project particular aspects of self?
- RQ2: How do self-image traits relate to buyer behaviors?
- RQ3: What dynamic processes account for self and product congruence?

Figure 1. Virtual identities: brand personality and behavioral outcomes

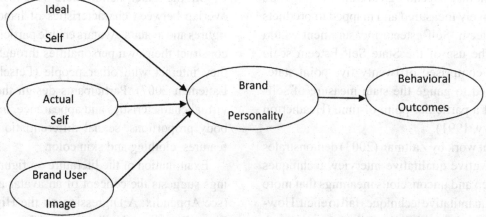

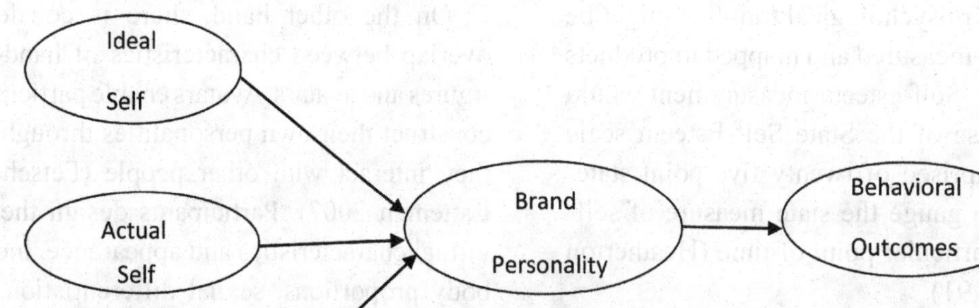

Based on quantitative studies, some self-image traits that may be evidenced in avatar analysis are conventionality, emotionality, excitability, and ruggedness.

Tables 1 and 2 illustrate the *theoretical* associations made by the analyst between personal traits and Avatar indicators on one hand, and buyer behavior preferences on the other. In the actual research, projected personal traits are obtained from consumers' associations and the list of traits that fit self-congruence theory and data is refined and expanded.

Past quantitative research into aspects of the self-concept as determinants of buying preferences has yielded far less than anticipated. This is due to the failure to (a) employ appropriate concepts that are specific to buyer behavior, and (b) use appropriate projective methodologies for assigning traits to individual consumers.

PRELIMINARY RESEARCH PROTOCOL

Techniques for the analysis of Avatar drawings were developed and refined over the course of a year. During this time, interviews relating to such drawings were conducted. Continual feedback from interviewers on the interview experience and substantive data analyses led to methodological refinements and the current research protocol.

Table 1. A hypothetical measurement system

Personal Traits	Avatar Indicators
Conformity motivation	Modest clothing
Arousal	Motioning of arms
Self-confidence	Facial expressiveness
Masculinity	Solid physique

Table 2. A theoretical causal system

Personal Traits	Buyer Behavior Preferences
Conformity motivation	Skirts and jackets
Arousal	Furs and jewelry
Self-confidence	Speculative investments
Masculinity	Pick-up trucks

Before any drawing is made, the interviewer records identifying data and preliminary answers to questions about demographic characteristics and buyer behavior for a specified category. Demographics include: gender, age, income, education, occupation. Buyer behaviors obtained include: brands tried, brands currently used, length of time used, frequency of use, usage occasions, favorite brands. The technique of administration of the projective section involves simply asking the subject to draw individual avatars that represent actual self, ideal self, brand user profile and the brand or product personality that is the focus of the research. The subject does the drawings in a computer mediated environment, such as *Second Life*.

After each drawing is reviewed in the presence of the interviewer, consumers describe the avatars in terms of physical characteristics, personality traits and life style patterns. In each case, the subject is asked to make up a story about the avatar drawing. Probes would include questions such as "Who is the story about?" "How do I differ from others to whom I might be compared?" "Who wants to associate with me?" "What am I thinking?' "How do I feel about myself?" "What are some meaningful experiences that I have had?" "How do I interact with others?"

After each story, the subject is probed for a series of associations to the figure. Finally, the subject is intensively probed about the overall congruence between the actual self and the brand, as well as the congruence between the ideal self and the brand. In both cases the subject will be asked about the meaning and evaluation of specific facets of self and brand congruence.

ILLUSTRATIVE IDENTIFICATION OF SELF-CONGRUITY IN CONSUMER BEHAVIOR

The Avatar Analyzer technique is used to isolate salient attribute dimensions that describe states of agreement or disagreement between perceived self-image and referent images. Perceived self-images may be about either the actual self or the ideal (desired) self. Referent self images may be about either brand personality images or brand user profile impressions.

An example of Avatar analysis is given to show the variable numbers and types of personal and referent attribute dimensions involved.[1] The mix of attribute dimensions depends on individual traits and lifestyles, demographic groupings and the nature of the product category.

Self-Congruity: Sallie and Abercrombie Jeans. Sallie is a forty year old married stay at home mom with four children. Her self-congruity with Abercrombie jeans was explored, using the Avatar drawings she was asked to create. Sallie's avatar portrayed a blue-eyed smiling woman with blonde short hair and a blue knitted woolen ribbed ski hat with white-rimmed ski goggles attached. She also wore a pink down ski parka with a mandarin neckline, open at the neck, and a charcoal gray turtleneck sweater. She was seated on a green snowmobile on an ice blue curvy road. She was only visible from the waist up in her snowmobile. It looked like a clear day, and the background consisted of snow-covered, high-peaked mountains.

Sallie was asked to describe her avatar and the person it represented. She said the avatar was around 140 pounds and five feet nine inches. The avatar was a professional married woman with children. Traits ascribed to the avatar were adventurous, caring, nurturing and competitive. The avatar was athletic, especially with respect to winter sports. She is a careful, value-oriented shopper.

Sallie's wardrobe includes comfortable and sporty jeans. She views straight-legged Abercrombie jeans as boyish and she, herself, has a boyish figure. She is not happy with her body. She feels that Abercrombie jeans are used primarily by younger women, and her desire is to look younger in these jeans. She describes the jeans as rugged, and her athletic bent classifies her as rugged, as well. The Abercrombie brand is economical, as is Sallie.

Salient congruent attribute dimensions found in this analysis include comparisons between the consumer self and the referent brand on ruggedness, economical, youth-oriented, boyish-ness.

CONCLUDING REMARKS

The foregoing exposition on avatar analysis provides unique insights into aspects of the self-concept as determinants of buying preferences. Past research in this area has yielded far less than anticipated. This is due to the failure to (a) employ appropriate concepts that are specific to buyer behavior, and (b) use appropriate projective methodologies for assigning traits to individual consumers. From an applied perspective, marketers will benefit from this frame of reference by learning about the most important traits associated with specified buying preferences. This will lead to improved market segmentation and product positioning strategies. Tactically, by learning how these traits operate, marketers can improve product designs and communications programs. Additionally, marketers will benefit by learning about a brand's perceived personality and its most important associated traits. At the same time, consumer personalities that parallel those of the brand will surface through future research. This will lead managers to develop strategic insights about the customer and brand relationships. Additionally, the special nature of the brand-consumer relationships may be a basis for successful brand differentiation.

Avatar analysis is a promising new tool for basic research. With this tool, a graphical nexus is described between self-image and product image and is linked to consumer preferences. This opens up new vistas for streams of basic and applied academic research. The technology of consumer avatar drawings opens up rich opportunities for theory-building and methodological innovations.

The approach outlined in this chapter opens a new mind-set. Based in self-congruity thinking, the new frame of reference constrains marketers to have a dual focus on the interplay of people and products. The result of this dual focus is a stronger and more positive consumer-brand engagement. Adoption of the Avatar Analyzer will bring greater understanding and control of brand preference, customer satisfaction and brand loyalty.

REFERENCES

Abell, S. C., Harkheimer, R., & Nguyen, S. E. (1998). Intellectual evaluations of adolescents via human figure drawings: An empirical comparison of two methods. *Journal of Clinical Psychology, 54*, 811–815. doi:10.1002/(SICI)1097-4679(199810)54:6<811::AID-JCLP8>3.0.CO;2-J

Abell, S. C., Heiberger, A. M., & Johnson, J. E. (1994). Cognitive evaluations of young adults by means of human figure drawings: An empirical investigation of two methods. *Journal of Clinical Psychology, 50*, 900–904. doi:10.1002/1097-4679(199411)50:6<900::AID-JCLP2270500614>3.0.CO;2-3

Abell, S. C., Von Briesen, P. D., & Watz, L. S. (1996). Intellectual evaluations of children using human figure drawings: An empirical investigation of two methods. *Journal of Clinical Psychology, 52*, 67–74. doi:10.1002/(SICI)1097-4679(199601)52:1<67::AID-JCLP9>3.0.CO;2-T

Adler, P. T. (1970). Evaluation of the figure drawing technique: Reliability, factorial structure, and diagnostic usefulness. *Journal of Consulting and Clinical Psychology, 35*, 52–57. doi:10.1037/h0029645

Adler, P. T. (1971). Ethnic and socio-economic status differences in human figure drawings. *Journal of Consulting and Clinical Psychology, 36*, 344–354. doi:10.1037/h0031125

Aikman, K. G., Belter, R. W., & Finch, A. J. Jr. (1992). Human figure drawings: Validity in assessing intellectual level and academic achievement. *Journal of Clinical Psychology, 48*, 114–119. doi:10.1002/1097-4679(199201)48:1<114::AID-JCLP2270480116>3.0.CO;2-Y

Chung, D. (2005). Something for nothing: Understanding purchasing behaviors in virtual environments. *Cyberpsychology & Behavior, 8*, 538–554. doi:10.1089/cpb.2005.8.538

Fetscherin, M., & Lattemkmann, C. (2007). *User Acceptance of Virtual Worlds: An Explorative Study about Second Life*. Winter Park, FL: Rollins College.

Gaggioli, A., Mantovani, F., Castelnuovo, G., Wieberhold, B., & Riva, G. (2003). Avatars in clinical psychology: A framework for the clinical use of virtual humans. *Cyberpsychology & Behavior, 6*, 117–125. doi:10.1089/109493103321640301

Heatherton, T. F., & Polivy, J. (1991). Development and validation of a scale for measuring state self-esteem. *Journal of Personality and Social Psychology, 60*, 895–910. doi:10.1037/0022-3514.60.6.895

Holzwarth, M., Janiszewski, C., & Neuman, M. (2006). The influence of avatars on online consumer shopping behavior. *Journal of Marketing, 70*, 19–36. doi:10.1509/jmkg.70.4.19

Kang, H. S., & Yang, H. D. (2006). The visual characteristics of avatars in computer-mediated communication: Comparison of internet relay chat and instant messenger as of 2003. *International Journal of Human-Computer Studies*, *64*, 1173–1183. doi:10.1016/j.ijhcs.2006.07.003

Machover, K. (1953). *Personality Projection in the Drawing of the Human Figure*. Springfield, IL: Charles C. Thomas.

Malhotra, N. K. (1981). A scale to measure self-concept, person concepts, and product concepts. *JMR, Journal of Marketing Research*, *18*, 456–464. doi:10.2307/3151339

Nowak, K. L., & Rauh, C. (2006). The influence of the avatar on online perceptions of anthropomorphism, androgyny, credibility, homophily, and attraction. *Journal of Computer-Mediated Communication*, *11*, 153–178. doi:10.1111/j.1083-6101.2006.tb00308.x

Qiu, L., & Benbasat, I. (2005). Online consumer trust and live help interfaces: The effects of text-to-speech voice and three-dimensional avatars. *International Journal of Human-Computer Interaction*, *19*, 75–94. doi:10.1207/s15327590ijhc1901_6

Quester, P. G., Karunaratna, A., & Goh, L. K. (2000). Self-Congruity and product evaluation. *Journal of Consumer Marketing*, *17*, 525–537. doi:10.1108/07363760010349939

Sirgy, M. J. (1982). Self-Concept in consumer behavior: A critical review. *The Journal of Consumer Research*, *9*, 287–295. doi:10.1086/208924

Sirgy, M. J. (1985). Using self-congruity and ideal congruity to predict purchase motivation. *Journal of Business Research*, *13*, 195–206. doi:10.1016/0148-2963(85)90026-8

Sirgy, M. J. (1986). *Self-Congruity: Toward a Theory of Personality and Cybernetics*. New York: Praeger.

Swensen, C. H. (1968). Empirical evaluations of human figure drawings: 1057-1966. *Psychological Bulletin*, *70*, 20–44. doi:10.1037/h0026011

Swenson, C. H. (1957). Empirical evaluations of human figure drawings. *Psychological Bulletin*, *54*, 431–463. doi:10.1037/h0041404

Vasalou, A., Joinson, A., Banziger, T., Goldie, P., & Pitt, J. (2008). Avatars in social media: balancing accuracy, playfulness and embodied messages. *International Journal of Human-Computer Studies*, *66*, 801–811. doi:10.1016/j.ijhcs.2008.08.002

ENDNOTE

1 For their interviews, respondents supplied paper copies of their Avatar images and no electronic files were maintained. Furthermore, permission to reproduce respondent Avatars for later publication was not obtained. Therefore, the reader will have to be content with my personal case description of an avatar drawing.

APPENDIX

Digression on the History of Figure Drawings

Early landmark work on figure drawings traces to Karen Machover (1949). Her figure drawing test was based on extensive studies of hospital and clinical patients exhibiting psychological disorders. The figure drawing was interpreted by a trained technician, in the context of other case materials. The interpretation was augmented by questions directed at the subject about the person represented in the drawn figure. The subject was directed to make up a story about the figure and was probed as to whether the person was smart, good looking, nervous, sad, a loner, trustworthy, etc.

In Machover's test, personality assessment by the clinician was based on a number of features in the figures drawn by subjects, including: a) the head, b) social features: parts of the face, facial expression, mouth, lips, chin, eyes, eyebrows, ear, hair, nose, neck, Adam's apple, c) contact features: arms and hands, fingers, legs and feet, toes, and d) miscellaneous body features: trunk, breast, shoulders, hips and buttocks, waistline, joints e) clothing: conspicuous buttons, pockets, tie, shoe and hat f) structural and formal aspects: theme, action or movement, drawing sequence, symmetry, mid-line, size and placement, stance, perspective, type of line g) conflict indicators: erasures, shadings.

Interpretation of figure drawings led to such personality diagnoses as perfectionist, reclusive, anxiety-ridden, sexual identity conflict, evasive, compensation, other-directed, narcissist, power-driven, introverted, high aspirations, emotionally immature, self-preoccupied, retreatist, obsessive, serious.

Most of the subsequent published research on figure drawing diagnostics has focused on detection of psychiatric syndromes, cognitive maturity, or intelligence testing. Distinct populations studied have been children, adolescents and adults.

In a review of figure drawing studies from 1957-1966, it was concluded that figure drawing is a useful clinical tool. Overall global interpretations proved most reliable and valid. Individual signs from the drawings varied considerably in their reliability and validity for clinical diagnoses. There was need to control for the quality of the drawings (Swenson 1968).

Adler (1970, 1971) in his basic research on figure drawings found one primary factor—cognitive maturity, or sophisticated representation of body image-- that explained most of the variance in test interpretation. In his conclusion the test had a limited function i.e., assessing cognitive staging. Additionally, the reliability and validity of such interpretations on an individual basis was somewhat uncertain. Drawing ability was also suggested as a confounding variable in diagnostic interpretation. Ethnic, social class backgrounds and sex affect cognitive maturity scores. These conclusions were based on differences in drawing size, placement and subject drawing interpretations. Middle class were more likely than lower class to show mature body image concepts in figure drawings. Minority groups showed less cognitive maturity in their figure drawings. Adler found that men and women tested similarly on figure drawings. However, for a small segment, men were somewhat more prone to display bizarre representations. Further, diagnostic group predictions of psychological presenting symptoms were prone to failure.

Figure drawing scores have been correlated with standard IQ tests (Abell et al 1994). Figure drawings as measures of cognitive ability were found to have strong inter-rater reliabilities but modest correlations with IQ among young adults. Abell et al (1996, 1998) also found similar results in samples of children and adolescents. In general, it was concluded that figure drawings are a relatively weak proxy for standard IQ tests.

The possible confounding influence of psychopathology was introduced as a possible explanation for the modest correlations. It was further noted that figure drawings were time-bound, especially with regard to changing clothing fashions.

Another study of the relationship between figure drawing interpretation and intellectual level or academic achievement showed a lack of predictive validity (Aikman 1992).

Chapter 19
The "Digitalisation" of Youth:
How Do They Manage and Integrate Digital Technologies?

Pedro Quelhas Brito
Universidade do Porto, Portugal

ABSTRACT

The digitalization of youth signifies their complete immersion, active participation and involvement in the production, consumption and sharing of digital content using various interconnected/interfaced digital devices in their social network interactions. A prerequisite to successful commercial communication with young people is having a good understanding of new media, along with their social and psychological framework. The behaviour, motivation and emotions of youth in general and in relation to digital technologies, especially the meaning attached to mobile phones, the Internet (mainly social network sites) and games (computer-based and portable) should also be addressed if advertisers aim to reach this target group.

WHY FOCUS ON YOUTH?

Babies, children, adolescents and young adults are all relatively dependent on their parents. Nevertheless, they are consumers and potential or active consumers. There is consensus recognising children's influence on family decision-making. This influence varies according to the mother's attitudinal dimensions (Roberts, Wortzel, & Berkeley, 1981) and the children's influence on family purchases. Moreover, the likelihood of any given purchase being achieved depends on the collaborative interaction between parent and child (Darian, 1998). The relative influence of each family member varies by product, by stage of the decision-making process, and by various judgment criteria, such as point-of-purchase decisions, the brand, or style in durable goods (Belch, Ceresino, & Belch, 1985). More recently, the increasing expertise of youth with computing and digital media-related tasks turns many parents into becoming learners from their own children (Ekström, 2007). However, such a "new media-savvy" profile expresses a construction of

DOI: 10.4018/978-1-60566-792-8.ch019

competence to counteract the discourse made by adults under which kids are permanently exposed to the risk of digital media (MacKeogh, 2001). Compared with previous generations the consumer status of today's youth occurs at an early age. The statement, "kids grow older younger" sums up that process of becoming the decider and consumer quicker and sooner (Mitchell & Reid-Wash, 2005; Siegel, Coffey, & Livingstone, 2001).

Moreover, the youth represent an interesting research area because:

- they are a "market"–relevant by its size (over 200 million citizens are under 16 years-old in the EU and North America) and economic power;
- they can provide indications of trends of how digital technologies may be exploited in the future (e.g.: Lenhart, Madden, Macgill, & Smith, 2007);
- they are generally (and traditionally) considered a difficult target to access and communicate with (e.g.: Oates & Gunter, 2002; Mangleburg & Bristol, 1998);
- they are a truly global segment since they share similar tastes and preferences in terms of brands, sites and gizmos worldwide (eg.: Larson & Wilson, 2004; Lindstr∅m & Seybold, 2004; Tsai, 2006);
- they are used to getting what they want–in this materialistic world their wishes become mandatory (Bee-Gates, 2006; Lindstrom & Seybold, 2003);
- they are challengers and pioneers, early adopters of technology and eager to change/re-invent the rules (e.g.: Drotner, 2005; Kim, 2008; Lenhart, Madden, & Hitlin, 2005);
- the current Net-generations will be the future leaders/deciders/buyers–e.g. the young Japanese adults who grew up in the digital era maintain their digital technological habits and use patterns (Miyata, Boase, & Wellman, 2008);
- although evocative the term net generation or digital natives is too simplistic to describe youth - it is more realistic to consider many minorities with distinct and specific relation with new technologies rather than an homogeneous group (Jones, Ramanau, Cross & Healing, 2010).

NATURE OF DIGITAL MEDIA

The attraction for digital media among young people derives from intrinsic characteristics of digital technology. Before looking at the "digital" aspect, the ideological debate concerning the dialectic nature of media should be considered. The "new" media can be understood by contrasting it with the former format and then exploring the specifics of new media technology.

Ideological Debate

Although the growing influence of the Internet became particularly evident during the nineties, the ideological roots of the new media lay in the debate between two media theorists during the sixties. Williams (1961, 1976) stressed the complex role of social, cultural and economic dimensions in shaping technologies. Here, human affairs ascertain the pace and scale of how a specific technology is mobilized. Depending on the social use of technology it may be converted into a medium (of communication). To reach this status, it may provide information, express an idea or represent some content or form of the world. Far from considering the development of the media as a human agency, McLuhan (1964, 1969) held that technology is an extension of human capacity. In his conception, (media) technology structures peoples' lives in the manner they pursue their activities, and in particular it affects and changes social arrangements and relationships. The (new) media technology (electronic broadcasting) aesthetically mediates our relationship with the world since it is multidirectional in all senses–physical and mental. Insisting on the power of (media) technologies, McLuhan envisaged networked communication systems and anticipated the "coupling" of people and machines with an interweaving of technology into peoples' lives. Radically, he stood for the notion that new media is more than a simple tool; it becomes an environment in itself. Thus, it quantitatively and qualitatively impacts our everyday life of work and entertainment, our human relationships, as well as human-machine interactions.

For those who were born at the end of eighties and later, Williams/McLuhan's discussion is, at best, too intellectual, distant, or not even relevant. Since they never (fully) experienced the "old media", they are unable to draw a distinction between "the before" and "the new". Besides, what is labelled as "old media" is very likely to be viewed by tweens as museum-like stuff, and seen through the lens of their only available media, the new one (Brito, 2008). Before turning back to the world of today's youth, the characteristics of the new media in contrast with the old media should be considered.

Analogue vs. Digital World

Based on Thompson's (1995) contribution, Lister, Dovey, Giddings, Grant, & Kelly (2003) defined communication media as "the institutions and organizations in which people work (the press, cinema, broadcasting, publishing, and so on) and the cultural and material products of those institutions (the forms and genres of news, road movies, soap operas which take material form in newspapers, paperback books, films, tapes and disks)" (p. 9). Clearly this definition points to an institution where media production takes place. The model under which a few "institutions" framed by law, politics, culture, financial/corporation and educational systems convey their control and exert their influence over the "mass" of the public still epitomizes the hegemonic configuration of mass media (Watson, 2008). The glue that cements such a powerful structure is ideology–the public dimensions of beliefs/values and manifestation of an ideal through cultural, social and political discourses (Watson, 2008). The audience's attention continues to be selective but simultaneously depends upon media for (Rokeach & DeFleur, 1976): guidance, clarification of values, attitude formation, ambiguity/uncertainty reduction, agenda-setting and opening up of people's belief systems. Access to world-wide information transforms the local citizen into a cosmopolite engaged in a constant process of self-formation (Thompson, 1995).

Those audiences are not passive receivers of media messages. They use, exchange and modify the message, not necessarily in a linear or top-down direction but also with some degree of social mediation. Their significant others–relatives, friends and colleagues–and opinion leaders reprocess and retransmit the message, undergoing further mediation (McQuail & Windahl, 1993).

The mass media model depicted earlier did not disappear at once. Mergers and acquisitions have made production centres more concentrated but also vulnerable to global competition. Still, the technological ease of producing or capturing (not necessarily editing) allows users to distribution information, and thus, creating non-professionals to have an uncontrolled role (Thurman, 2008). For example, in a dictatorial regime a human-rights demonstration activist can witness and record the police using excessive force for repression, then send a short digital movie to someone or upload it to YouTube.com, making the incident instantly accessible to a worldwide audience.

There is no purely technological revolution (Toffler, 1980). Regardless of how big the change is, it always includes and involves an ideological, social and experiential range of different phenomena. As we consider the technological determinism advocated by McLuhan (1964) it is more effective to look firstly at the characteristics of new media, then explore the "uses" and the social implications. The term "new media" may include both the Internet and any computer-mediated communication such as TiVo or digital games, which makes it quite general and abstract (Lister, Kelly, Dovey, Giddings, & Grant, 2003). That is, the word "media" suggests a continuity and connection with the past industry devoted to broadcast news, whereas "new" implies progress, novelty, or at least a difference and in some way a break with the past.

New Media Dimensions

'New media' includes Digital, Interactive and Virtual media.

Digital Media

First, digital is a mathematical problem. In the late thirties Alan Turing developed it conceptually. In order for his binary machine concept to be workable, three attributes had to be present: complete, consistent and decidable (Gere, 2002). The simple numerical representation of data into discrete elements of 0's and 1's in computing (and programming) and storage capabilities gave rise to the following benefits (Manovich, 2001; Negroponte, 1995):

(1) Digitalisation–this is the most distinct feature, as opposed to analogue: the physical properties of the input data are not converted into a similar/analogous object but into abstract symbols which are available whenever and wherever the user wants, in a seemingly perfect replica.
(2) Modularity–Data or media elements (such as sounds, images and video) can be re-assembled in different scales without losing their separate identities;
(3) Automation–The combination of computer programs, numerical coding and modular structures allows for automatic operation;
(4) Variability and flux–Contrary to analogue media where any change implies having to deal with the entire physical object, digital media makes it easy to produce an almost infinite number of variations with only partial editing;
(5) Transcoding–is better understood under the logic of computing than under the perspective of new media. This is about translating a code into another format. It requires both database management to organize and access data, and interfaces designed for easy connections between web-sites, games, virtual spaces and software.
(6) Miniaturization–Since these technology inputs large quantities of data, the access speed as well as rate of exchange (or conversion) has to be also very high.

Interactivity

Interactivity is perhaps the one most widely associated with digital (new) media. To fully map out its distinguishing features several dimensions should be taken into consideration (Huhtamo, 1999; Jensen, 1999; Lister et al., 2003; Shultz, 2000):

(1) *Ideological level*–Interactivity represents a value-added quality since it maximises consumer choices in relation to media sources/outputs. The neo-liberal idea of personalization is now made real.
(2) *Instrumental level*–The audience intervenes. They become active media users instead of just "reading" or "viewing". Their engagement goes beyond the text-based experiences. They play, experiment and explore. Ultimately, they communicate with others under a certain base of relationship reciprocity;
(3) *Hypertext*–This lexical computing term is especially relevant to understanding new media. Thanks to this dynamic method of

data retrieval any user can access successive nodes (of text/data) within a multilinear mode, linked together according to an organization of database knowledge-management logic.

(4) *Decentralization* - Standardization and uniformity characterize the content, production, distribution and consumption of cinema, radio programmes and newspapers of mass media. The digital technologies or computer-mediated communications established a network-based distribution, blurring the consumer and production tasks. Today anybody, depending on their skills, may publish and broadcast their own "news," or simply, thoughts. There are many forms of user-generated content and citizen-produced media including blogs, vlogs, podcasts, digital storytelling, participatory video, wikis, etc.

Virtual Reality

This is the most emblematic, science-fiction driven and utopian (Flichy, 1999) concept of the digital world. Basically, reality is simulated to generate fantasy under an immersive computer-generated environment. Virtual reality aims to produce a scenario/community (cyberspace) where we are independent of spatial location, transcending geographic and social frontiers. This process also involves our identity. Who is to stop us from inventing another persona? (e.g. Secondlife.com)

The logical consequences of this new era are twofold:

- Globalization - Access to digital media is available almost anywhere and anytime, as long as economic/financial, social/political (e.g. censure) and Internet access constraints permit;
- Convergence–Two technological evolutionary steps occurred almost simultaneously: (1) technological convergence between media, telecommunications and the Internet; (2) the World Wide Web gradually took over the Internet. Originally a network of computers globally linked together based on a common language protocol (IP) and also supporting communications using the Transmission Control Protocol (TCP) and the Internet Protocol (IP), the Internet embraced email services, Usenet, IRLs or chat rooms, and MUD (multi-user domains). Now the Internet is synonymous with www.

Activities such as shopping, banking, gaming, inter-personal communication and entertainment can be performed with the same platform. The user benefits from having more channels (TV, radio and newspapers) to choose from, and from having full control over the media menu. Furthermore, portability and personalization have made multimedia and personal communications readily available everywhere.

The 'Web' of Theories and Digitalisation of Youth

In order to understand to what extent digital technologies are so attractive to the young and to explain the specific meaning they attach to them, an overview of some relevant theories is a useful step before considering their integration and management of these technologies. Good starting points are the biological (physical and cognitive) and social development of youngsters. Although social network theories are not specifically suited to any age group, they are strongly endorsed as a way of framing people's online relationships. Finally in this section, the question of why the Internet is so attractive (even seductive) is addressed and tentatively tackled.

Biological and Psychological Development

Pre-teens gradually comprehend the world's complexities thanks to the progressive use of concrete operational thought, expressed in their ability to apply logical principles such as identification, reversibility and reciprocity (Piaget, 1952). However, such processes do not occur in a vacuum. The socio-cultural context can enhance or hinder children's learning (Vygotsky, 1978). Parallel with this, neurological maturation takes place, increasing their memory capacity, processing speed (Kail, 2000) and knowledge base (Berger, 2006). The latter mechanism makes further learning and remembering easier. Iteratively reinforcing previous knowledge acquisition allows some degree of mental automatization, which saves processing time and cognitive resources (Demetriou, Christou, Spanoudis, & Platsidou, 2002). Following Berger (2006), the systematization and integration of memory, processing speed and knowledge forms the control process. Under selective attention this mechanism regulates emotion and internal cognitive monitoring (metacognition) of information flow within the system. Age and culture influence the control process, its accuracy and efficiency.

Teenagers undergo deep transformations, some of which are visible in their physical growth (height and weight) and hormone production, which induces changes in body rhythms and biological stress (Belsky, Steinberg, & Draper, 1991). We can summarise puberty changes by their relevance to the use of digital technologies:

- Sexual maturation–beyond biology, girls and boys invest more in their appearance (e.g. hairstyles, cloths and cosmetics) and become more interested in each other (flirting, hand-holding, dating,...romance) (Berger, 2006);
- Thrill seeking–emotions overcome reason. Teens tend to rush and perform according to their immediate feelings and excitement instead of planning or reflecting. While almost ready to control the limbic system, the pre-frontal cortex lags behind to offset strong and immediate sensations. They strive for intensity, excitement and arousal and are drawn by music, movies and other high-stimulation experiences (Dahl, 2004; Steinberg, 2004);
- Intuitive versus deductive thinking–by the age of 14, teens can easily engage in hypothetical-deductive reasoning. That is, they are able to analyse and think logically. However, the intuitive cognition, also referred to as heuristic or experiential thoughts driven by feelings and memories, and counterbalances analytic thought. (Keating, 2004; Moshman, 1999);
- Adolescent egocentrism–teens tend to regard themselves as unique, special and more socially significant to others. They may experience three characteristic beliefs/myths: invincibility (being immune to harm or defeat), personal fable (fated to be heroic and endowed with a legendary life) and public self-centred position (absolutely admired by an imaginary audience where they are at centre stage) (Elkind, 1979).

Socialization Theories–Identity Formation

Being social is not an innate state, it is a human product. Socialization is the process through which people learn to be social beings and acquire specific rules, skills and cultural knowledge by interacting and communicating with others (Fulcher and Scott, 2007). The self-consciousness of themselves as an autonomous independent reflective entity represents one of the most remarkable psychosocial achievements resulting from the adolescent crisis (Erikson, 1968). The central process of self-conception or awareness of self as a person/individual is called social identity, and it is likely one of the most meaningful outcomes of socialization. Who am I? We are a blend of what we want to be, what we make, and what we feel about how others describe us, which includes a sort of a label indicating social positions and occupational roles, real and imagined. Primary socialization takes place at home, led by parents or caregivers, where children learn the basic paradigms of our society encapsulated by language, gender and culture. In the second step of (secondary) socialization, a child has to face the outside world along with his/her formal education (Fulcher and Scott, 2007). The teenager seeks to keep a stable personality immune to changing circumstances, in which their behaviour remains consistent over time (Chandler, Lalonde, Sokol, Bryan, & Hallet, 2003). However, the need for a sense of continuity with the past as claimed by Chandler et al, (2003) does not imply the development of unique identity. Teens may try out different possible selves and test them realistically or imaginatively (Markus & Nurius, 1986). Even when we stop questioning almost everything, we end up accepting multiple identities because we simultaneously share several social types: gender, ethnicity, family role, worker/job and religion Fulcher & Scott, 2007). Therefore, far from being pathological, such identity flexibility expresses an adaptation to our contemporary society. We simply explore different narratives by selectively drawing on the reconstruction of our own biographies in response to the varying and complex situations of our life (Bauman, 1995).

Three theories are in accord explaining the same phenomena of socialization and identity formation: the Role–learning theory, rooted in sociology traditions associated with the structural-functionalist approach; the Symbolic Interactionism theory, offering a social psychological perspective and focus on cognitive meanings; the Psychoanalytical theory, which as the designation suggests is ingrained in psychological traditions and stresses emotional meaning (Fulcher & Scott, 2007). Although conceptually distinct, each theory proposes a complementary contribution that is particularly helpful to interpreting the way youth live with digital technologies.

Role-Learning Theory

Role-learning theory (Bales, 1950; Johnson, 1961; Parsons, 1951) suggests people are constrained to learn social roles, which is seen as an institutionalized form of social relations. The formal means of training, as well as the rewards of conformity and punishment of deviation, are not enough to guarantee and perform such social roles, people have to internalize them. That is to say, they make socially approved expectations part of their self. They automatically act according to and completely committed to social roles. Their own social identity becomes a natural and normal corollary of the basic ingrained social scripts that structure their society/culture. The over-socialized standpoint was criticized and replaced by a more social/cultural institutional relativistic approach: instead of being socially programmed, people analyze the existing social frameworks and take up roles, sometimes conflicting ones, and assume those that with some degree of freedom partially fit their social expectations (Giddens, 1976; Turner, 1962; Wrong, 1961).

Symbolic Interactionism

Symbolic interactionism (Goffman, 1959; Mead, 1934) holds that everything is a social construction. An objects' (social) existence depends on the attribution of meaning. That process is in itself a social construction, built up through communication and negotiation between groups sharing similar goals. Children don't learn about material objects, but the manipulation of symbols, and representations of objects. The best way to discover the cognitive meaning of an interaction partner is to imitate. Playing other roles and observing their reactions favours children's understanding of social roles. Their social identity results from the interplay of two conceptions of self: the "I" is the source of action for the authentic self, but what everybody witnesses and reacts against is the "me". The latter is the social self. It reflects others' attitudes. Playing or pretending to be someone else is an instrumental activity even for adults. Whatever our job, position or social role, in our process of self-presentation we may chose to perform as a "person" who is more of an imputation of that self or product of the social interaction performance than the exact "I". We can act out multiple identities but whether the final outcome conforms or not, the social expectations depend on the audiences.

Psychoanalitical Theory

Psychoanalitical theory (Freud, 1962) - Following Freudian tradition, the "true self" is hidden and submitted to the pleasure-seeking/sexual forces of "id". What arises on the surface of the social arena is the "ego," previously domesticated by the "super-ego". The construction of the social identity is the tension process of morality, social conventions and parental prohibitions aimed at controlling the irrational "beast". Youth's experience of satisfaction and frustration help to define the limits of what can be culturally appropriate within an expression of their biological nature. To avoid anxiety, youth try to balance their deeply emotional energy with the drive for group acceptance, sense of belonging and social recognition (Sullivan, 1947). Their particular self-conception or identity is a permanent motivational weight scale.

Social Network Theory

Cooley (1998) characterized two principal types of groups: primary and secondary. The former is composed of persons who know one another well, seek one another's company, and are emotionally closed. Their members have a "we" feeling and enjoy being together (Shepard, 2007). The secondary group is instrumental, impersonal and goal oriented (Cooley, 1998). Both types of groups require some degree of social interaction. The process of mutual influence (Turner, 2002) may be expressed through five possible modalities: co-operation, conformity, social exchange, coercion and conflict (Nisbet, 1970). The first three basic social interaction modes are more typical of the primary group scenario than the remaining two.

The social network concept goes beyond social interaction and group development dynamics. It embraces, at a broad level, an ecological environment dimension adding up to the social relationship web (Cotterell, 2007). To better understand the functions of social networks, especially if applied to an adolescent context, another theoretical insight is particularly useful: Attachment theory. Although conceptualized to describe a child's relationship with significant others, the four features of attachment expression (Bowlby, 1969) remain relevant even into adulthood (Thomson, 2005): proximity seeking, separation distress, safe haven and secure base. These attachment representations provide a structure that shapes peoples' attitudes, regulates their behaviour and moderates their emotional expectations toward their peer relations (Carlson, Sroufe, & Byron, 2004). Ultimately, adolescent friendships under a social network paradigm partly extend the psychological process that regulates personal feelings and behaviours to the actions and feelings that similarly regulate it within groups (Nickerson & Nagle, 2005; Smith, Murphy, & Coats, 1999).

Technically, a social network does not overlap the primary and even the secondary group. It also does not necessarily involve close or continuous social interaction. The total set of a web of social relationships covers links of all kinds among individuals (Mitchell, 1973). Moreover, each individual can be connected to others through direct or indirect social ties with varying levels of strength, reciprocity and order linking several social environments (Cotterell, 2007). Socialization implies social interaction, and that is built upon social networks. In childhood the first extended (beyond family and relatives) social network experience arises from peer relationships. Social acceptance is instrumental to social cognition (Haselager, Cillessen, Lieshout, Riksen-Walraven, & Hartup, 2002). More than peer acceptance and popularity, children value friendship. The effect of friends teaching social skills and the effective contribution to emotional regulation lasts until adulthood (Bagwell, Schmidt, Michelle, Newcomb, & Bukowski, 2001). As children grow older friendships become more selective, intense, stable, intimate and also hurtful (Erwin, 1998). Close friendships among youth means the sharing of common interests, values and emotional needs, which involves choosing and being chosen by others having similar socioeconomic status and demographical characteristics (age and ethnicity) (Aboud & Mendelson, 1996, Reynolds, 2007). In general, social and psychological influences exerted by peers and friends can be summarized as follows (Berndt and Murphy, 2002; Dishion & Owen, 2002; Erwin, 1998; Lahelma, 2002; Pahl, 2000; Tarrant, MacKenzie & Hewitt, 2006):

- Participation and social companionship–"we are not alone";
- Reciprocity, trust, confident ("we share our secrets") and mutual acceptance without being (too) judgmental;
- Emotionally supportive. Validates feelings and reinforces self-esteem;
- Counterculture - against adult standards;
- Group pressure–membership implies rule conformity–sometimes they induce collective deviancy and even destructive behaviours: e.g. drug use initiation, alienation from school, aggressive behaviour, and sexual activity.

Young People and Digital Technology

Finally, assuming these characteristics and most of those theories existed during the old media age, why are digital technologies so attractive (even seductive) to youth? We not only borrow that question from Rosen's (2007) book, but also part of the answer.

1) **Happiness**: Valkenburg and Peter (2007) found that Instant Messaging usage is positively associated with adolescents' well-being, provided that the moderating influence of the time spent with friends and quality of this friendship were also present.
2) **Control**: the 'buzz' of exploring without direct adult supervision makes youth quite active in deciding what, when and how they use the Internet. For young people the huge amount of possibilities/content/interfaces (e.g. gaming, surfing, IMing, e-mailing and blogging) stimulates their interaction with others and with the machine (e.g.Turkle, 1995 and 2004);
3) **Freedom**: it allows anonymity and favours disinhibition and intimacy;
4) **Psychological absorption**: expressed by a sense of escape from reality and disruption of time perception (Csikszentmihalyi, 1998, Young, 2001);
5) **Psychological gratification**: Song, Larose, Eastin, & Lin (2004) described seven Internet gratification factors–virtual community, information seeking, aesthetic experience, monetary compensation, diversion, personal status and relationship maintenance. Although it was applied to analyzing Internet addiction tendency components, it is still valid in other contexts.

Integration and Management of Digital Technologies

There are no reasons to believe the social and psychological development processes of youth radically suffer from their involvement with digital technologies. Similarly, most theories should still be valid. However, new problems may require additional intellectual investment to theorize.

Today's teens and children were born in the digital age. Therefore, at least for the affluent part of the world, since most of the technology is no longer analogue they are by default digitally interactive. Today's youngsters are digital natives; they do not know any other language than the digital language of the Internet, computers and video games (Prensky, 2001). They are totally wired (Goodstein, 2007). They are so virtually exposed that they live online (Rosen, 2007). As was defined previously, digitalisation of youth represents a complete emersion, active participation and involvement in production, consumption and sharing of digital content by using various interconnected/interfaced digital tools in their social network interaction process. Through digitalisation, the scope goes beyond the status of being online, but also encompasses the creation/manipulation of data off-line (using appropriate software and other digital technologies) to be used online, or to "copy" data online to be transformed and consumed off-line. For example, taking a digital picture, digitally enhancing it, posting it online in a social network site, or downloading podcasts, music and videos and sharing them online too.

It is well known that adolescents can easily integrate the following digital technologies and underlying activities:

- capturing images–digital cameras;
- listening to, watching and sharing music and videos - MP3/4 and iPod players;
- connecting to their social network–e.g. IM/Messenger, Myspace, Facebook, Twitter, or Hi5;
- editing, participating and forecasting news/opinions/comments–web-blogs;
- designing and updating their own web-pages;
- entertaining–alone or with the community–e.g., PSP, Gameboy, Playstation, Xbox, MMUOG
- imagining and creating virtual realities–e.g. Secondlife;
- publishing and "broadcasting" personal relevant "news" using mobile phones–SMS, MMS.

The process of integration digital technologies to an adolescent's daily life implies: the planning of activities, interconnectedness among devices, functional specialization, coordination of tasks among peers, and expertise. Regardless of the purpose, whether mostly hedonic (having fun) or somewhat utilitarian (e.g. academic tasks) for that integration to succeed requires management skills, and management purports decision-making. Young people have to decide what, where, when, how and for how long they use such technologies/devices. Some of the variables taken into consideration in this management task can be summarized as follows: (e.g. Andersen, Tufte, Rasmussen & Chan, 2007; Buckingham, 2007; Boneva, Quinn, Kraut, Kiesler, & Shklovski, 2006; Haythornthwaite, 2000; Ishii, 2006; Kim, Kim, Park, & Rice, 2007; Lenhart, Rainie & Lewis, 2001; Licope & Smoreda, 2005; Oksman & Turtianen, 2004):

- Social network dimensions and diversity;
- Social network quality (nature of the ties: strong/weak);
- Size of the message–length of text;
- Degree of intimacy, closeness of acquaintances;
- Type/format of file to transmit;
- Physical distance;
- Nature of the content and publicizing implications for both the sender and receiver;
- Urgency;
- Cost;
- Locale of transmission: home, street or travelling/commuting;
- Purpose: educational or non-educational/entertainment;

- Cultural setting: e.g. Asian youth tend to devote more time to educational use of digital media than Europeans;
- Type and number of receivers/audience willing to reach–private/public

All the variables presented in the previous list may not be enough to accurately predict the likelihood of a youth's use of a given digital technology in a specific context. An iPod or mobile phone carries an intrinsic symbolic dimension relevant only to the one who possesses it (Belk, 1988). *Symbolic Interactionism* theory indicates that what really matters to users is not necessarily the nature of the object but the meaning they attach to it. In the remainder of this section we look at the meaning of three specific digital technologies among youth: mobile phones, the Internet (mainly social network sites) and games (portable devices and on/off-line computer based).

Mobile Phone

When we presented several groups of tweens and teens with a hypothetical scenario forbidding the use of mobile phones at school they almost panicked, exhibiting emotional opposition to such an infringement of their constitutional rights of communicating (Brito, 2008). Such reactions showed the extent to which, for them, the mobile phone is absolutely essential communication tool.

Apparently (Brito, 2008), many children want to own a cell phone. However, their knowledge about the product's attributes and their awareness of benefits and values differ. Martensen (2007) identified four segments of tweens (8 to12 years old) crossing over gender and age. Two different segments share the same age range: "*Segment 2–the identity making freaks–use mobile phone as a signal of value and as a means of achieving social status among friends, and Segment 4–the passive–mobile phones don't have any functional or psycho-social consequence nor any influence on social recognition and self-esteem*" (pp.119 and122).

Several authors characterized the motivations, gratifications and purposes sought through ownership of mobile phones:

• Aoki and Downes (2003)–to feel safe, to manage time efficiently, to keep in touch with friends and family, image, dependency and for financial benefits;
• Leung & Wei (2000)–fashion/status, affection/sociability, relaxation, mobility, immediate access, instrumentality and reassurance;
• Martensen (2007)–to make children reachable; it is a flexible way to contact them since they are busy in many different activities and constantly on the move; it promotes social recognition, ego-actualization and self-image;

One of the salient features of cell phones is their portability. Kakihara & Sorensen (2002) proposed three interrelated mobility dimensions: spatial, temporal and contextual. From the contextual dimension, portable media/telecommunication enables access free from constraints such as situation, mutual recognition and mood. Teenagers develop their personal space, defining the boundaries for or against the relationship with friends and relatives (Oksman & Turtiainen, 2004), hence the mobile phone clearly has an instrumental role in their lives.

Youngsters may pursue private conversations without the direct interference of their parents, regardless of whether they are present or not. And that represents freedom. Freedom to contact anyone, anywhere, anytime they choose, and freedom to control incoming calls. Often for the first time they feel the power of being in control. The ritual of emancipation (Wilska, 2003) is influential in the process of socialization. In addition, not owning a mobile phone could be a prerequisite for social exclusion (Charlton, Panting, & Hannan., 2002; Ling, 2000). There are several types of institutionalized social discourses concerning cellular phones: the parental discourse highlights danger and safety, whereas the youth discourse stresses self-determination and sociability. The media discourse focuses on image and independence fed by advertising messages portraying friendship, style and individuality (Campbell, 2006). Parental and adolescent discourses collide at the contradictory needs of teen autonomy and the parents' need to maintain contact with them. Therefore the control is bidirectional. Turkle (2008) points to the other side of the coin: "Just as always-on/always-on-you connectivity enables teens to independently postpone managing their emotions, it can also make it difficult to assess children's level of maturity, conventionality defined in terms of autonomy and responsibility. Tethered children know that they have a backup" (p.128).

The symbolic nature of mobile phones is better captured by analyzing the unambiguous meaning youngsters attach to some specific (technical) characteristics/features.

The following Figure 1 provides an overview on mobile phone functionality and meaning.

Digital Games

We use the term "digital games" irrespective of the platform: on a PC, the Internet, handheld, video console or specialized game console. They can be played alone or in-group, against virtual players or in a co-presence community. The game interaction

Figure 1. Mobile phone functionality and meaning

Multipurpose device (1)

Voice telephony, Calendar, Watch, Music platform, Alarm clock, Calculator, Game player, Internet navigation, Payment/debit, TV viewer/Mobisodes, Social date-finder service, Medical data center, Health monitoring, RFID, Advertising portal, Geolocational, ...

Voice/text based mode switching

- The synchronic (voice) or asynchronic (text messaging) depends on the preference for the conversational nature of the interaction or control over the time and hiatus in order to think and compose it (Madell & Muncer, 2007).
- The social skills and the degree of receiver/ sender intimacy determine the choice between the voice or text mode (Ishii, 2006);
- Texting SMS is a very discrete communicational mode, hardly censored, and ideal for romantic interactions (Dietmar, 2005; Ito & Okabe, 2005);
- Text composition requires linguistic (including bizarre forms of punctuation) and manual dexterity skills (Ling, 2007). Strong user ability and sense of personal control gives incentive for mobile texting and reduces anxiety (Mahatanankoon & O'Sullivan, 2008);
- *"In general, the telegraphic text message quickly communicates a state, rather than opening a dialogue*

Ringtones and social exchange

The personalization of musical ringtones favors immediate caller identification and eventual adjusted reaction. Rather than just a summons to answer, everybody near the receiver can experience those sounds. *"The choice of musical ringtones is a form of self-expression, a projection of personal*

Wearable technology

The highly personal nature of mobile phones and the personalization tools incorporated in them make mobile phones a potential fashion object. With the aesthetization of the mobile phone it becomes a self-expressive and symbolically communicates a

Mobile gaming

Although more limited than other portable (specialized) game players, the games stored in mobile phones produce a similar effect: they provide entertainment, multiply emotional striving among players, generate a new landscape transcending their "normal" life, uphold a community feeling (e.g. Katz & Acord 2008; Steinkuehler & Williams, 2006). Convenience – the possibility of being used anytime, anywhere – outperforms the enjoyment

Private soundscape

Digital music players contribute both to isolating the listeners from their ambient environment and to creating/controlling their personal atmosphere. Among youth such options enhance social collaboration by sharing musical tastes and it confers status

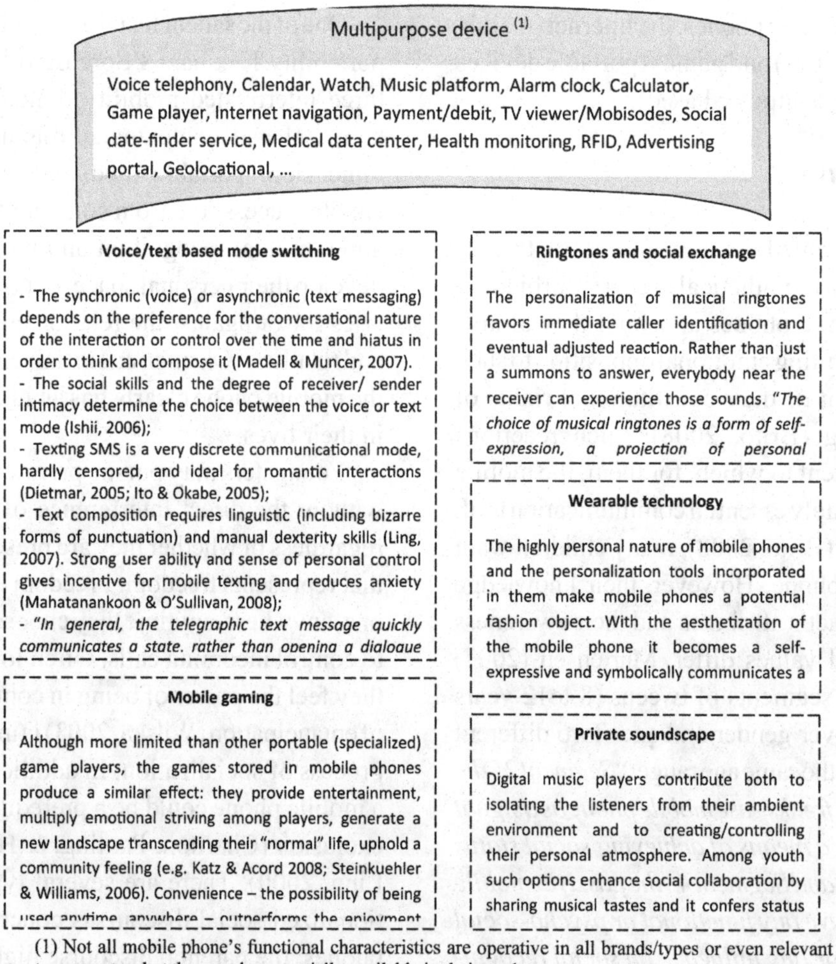

(1) Not all mobile phone's functional characteristics are operative in all brands/types or even relevant to youngsters but they can be potentially available in their pocket.

can also be managed online or off-line. Games can also be categorized as strategy/problem solving; racing; fighting (Walkerdine, 20007). Ultimately games are also framed within the concept of control, thus power (McLeod & Lin, 2010). Digital and Video Games are surrounded by controversy; their influence on behaviour and values; the real or virtual nature of digital games; and contradictory evidence which feeds and promotes divisive/ hot positions. We now look at the digital games through scrutinizing these dichotomies.

Internet

The focus of this section is on social network sites (SNSs). Their growth indicates increasing attractiveness, especially amongst youth. Furthermore, those sites integrate several technical features/ interfaces which stimulate the users' creative participation and control. Boyd & Ellison (2007) defined SNSs as "web-based services that allow individuals to (1) construct a public or semi-public profile within a bounded system, (2) articulate a list of other users with whom they share a connection, and (3) view and traverse their list of connections and those made by others within the system"(p. 211). According to Boyd and Ellison, two characteristics make SNSs unique: the public display of connections and (the volunteer) visibility of the users' profile. This concept is not consensual; Beer (2008) categorizes most of SNSs under an umbrella type: Web2.0. Not all SNSs are alike.

Figure 2.

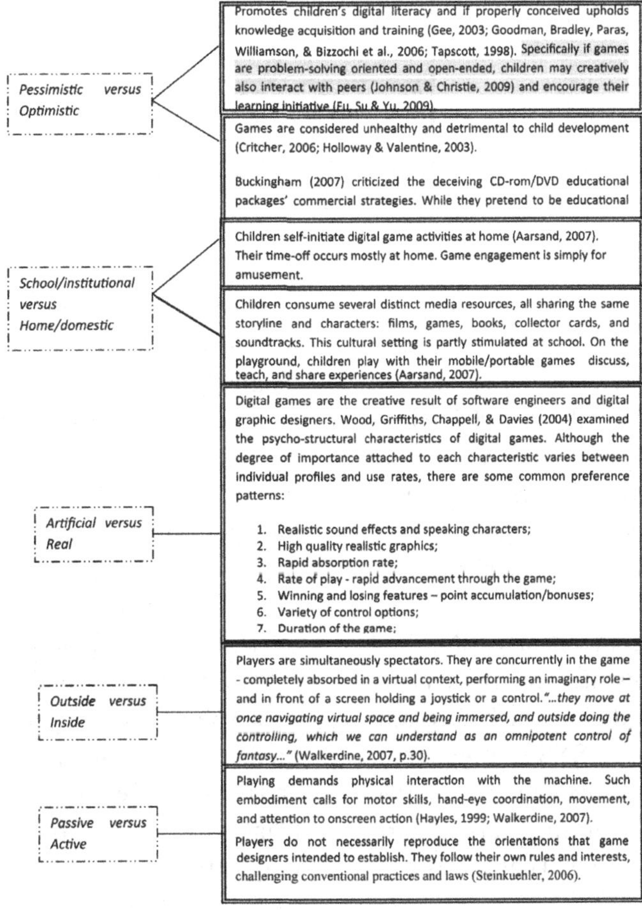

Figure 3.

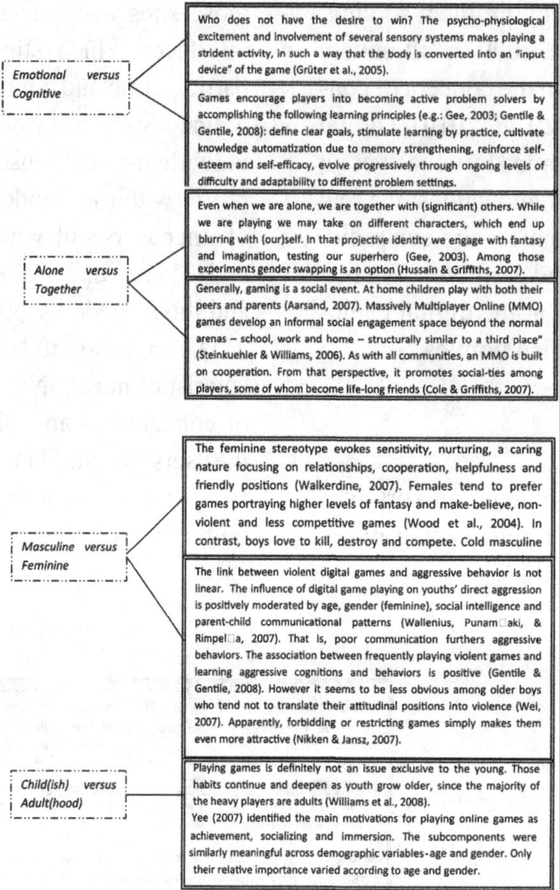

Some requires bi-directional confirmation, others just one-directional definition of proposed ties. Some are anonymous; others favour an implicit self-presentation (Boyd & Ellison, 2007; Zhao, Grasmuck, & Martin, 2008). None of the more than 35 SNSs available were universally popular. They were regionally adopted, suggesting SNS membership mirrors the users' social network background (Hargittai, 2008).

Before looking at the components of SNSs and how they work, it is worthwhile to briefly consider two separate Internet "products" which were later conceptually integrated into SNS configuration: personal home-pages and chat rooms. How do we want the world to see us? What aspects of ourselves would we like to communicate? Those two questions could be answered by developing a personal home page. Dominick (1999) found that in more than 94% of personal pages' the content includes a feedback mechanism and links to other sites. Lists of preferences such as likes/dislikes and personal data account for 72% of situations, and 55% post their personal photos. Chat rooms are wide open, public, anonymous, informational settings organized by topics, without any traditional frames or regulations and basically reflecting the long-established anarchy of the Net. The term "chat" is misleading, since conversation assumes a writing mode with an oral style. Quickness, redundancy and linguistic flexibility characterize this medium (Tingstad, 2003). Formally, a codified pattern of pragmatic communication tactics idiosyncratically conveys a group-specific meaning (Baym, 1998). In particular, two moments/situations seem intensely relevant in the chat process (Tingstad, 2003): (1) introducing themselves–greeting rituals loaded with meaning, where the nickname plays a structural role; (2) maintaining the talk going on–fast replies, no pauses, humour and irony are valuable resources. In Tingstad's (2003) ethnographic research, kids described chat rooms as "places to meet people and talk". The definition along with the insider knowledge approach (i.e, proposed by Baym, 1998), calls for a sense of community. Community is essentially a dynamic setting focus on what people do rather than what people are, thus boundaries are developed through social relationships representing structural markers (e.g. Cohen, 2000; Rheingold, 2000; Tingstad, 2003). In the context of chat rooms, the community boundary markers are: language, status, hostility topics, friendliness, greeting rituals, interests, humour and teaching (Tingstad, 2003).

The following schema depicts the interconnection among three topics regarding SNSs: (1) components (how does it work?); (2) effects and consequences of those technical/social elements; (3) players and their goals (members' characteristics and motivation to join):

Finally, when looking at the predictors of Internet use patterns–informational, social and entertainment - in teens' demographics, Eastin (2005) demonstrated is "that people use the Internet differently, for different reasons, and with different influences" (p. 72). In this section we only stress the social use.

Figure 4. Social network sites

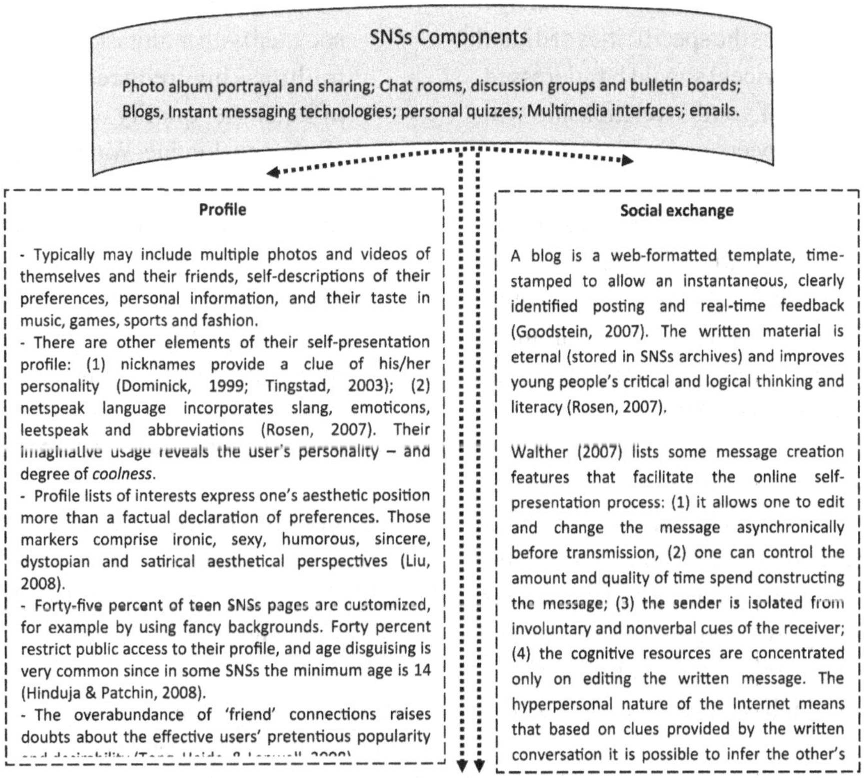

SNSs Components

Photo album portrayal and sharing; Chat rooms, discussion groups and bulletin boards; Blogs, Instant messaging technologies; personal quizzes; Multimedia interfaces; emails.

Profile

- Typically may include multiple photos and videos of themselves and their friends, self-descriptions of their preferences, personal information, and their taste in music, games, sports and fashion.
- There are other elements of their self-presentation profile: (1) nicknames provide a clue of his/her personality (Dominick, 1999; Tingstad, 2003); (2) netspeak language incorporates slang, emoticons, leetspeak and abbreviations (Rosen, 2007). Their imaginative usage reveals the user's personality – and degree of *coolness*.
- Profile lists of interests express one's aesthetic position more than a factual declaration of preferences. Those markers comprise ironic, sexy, humorous, sincere, dystopian and satirical aesthetical perspectives (Liu, 2008).
- Forty-five percent of teen SNSs pages are customized, for example by using fancy backgrounds. Forty percent restrict public access to their profile, and age disguising is very common since in some SNSs the minimum age is 14 (Hinduja & Patchin, 2008).
- The overabundance of 'friend' connections raises doubts about the effective users' pretentious popularity

Social exchange

A blog is a web-formatted template, time-stamped to allow an instantaneous, clearly identified posting and real-time feedback (Goodstein, 2007). The written material is eternal (stored in SNSs archives) and improves young people's critical and logical thinking and literacy (Rosen, 2007).

Walther (2007) lists some message creation features that facilitate the online self-presentation process: (1) it allows one to edit and change the message asynchronically before transmission, (2) one can control the amount and quality of time spend constructing the message; (3) the sender is isolated from involuntary and nonverbal cues of the receiver; (4) the cognitive resources are concentrated only on editing the written message. The hyperpersonal nature of the Internet means that based on clues provided by the written conversation it is possible to infer the other's

Table 1.

Why Here?
"Behind the screen" is a very powerful metaphor used to illustrate the anonymous, distant and safe presence of others who facilitate – make easier and faster – personal self-disclosure (Joinson, 2001; Turkle, 1995). Self-disclosure does not necessarily mean that people reveal their "true self"; it is rather a consequence of online disinhibition effect. Suler (2004) explored the conjoint factors underlying the creation of the online disinhibition effect: anonymity, invisibility, asynchronicity, solipsistic introjections (in a participant's mind their feelings merge with others), dissociative imagination, minimization of status and authority. As the SNSs designation suggests, the users' goals is to interact, whether locating old friends or making new ones (Raacke & Raacke, 2008). Bryant, Jackson, & Smallwood, (2006) showed that adolescents create quantitatively and qualitatively similar ties on/offline. That does not imply that they are indifferent to the tone of feedback from their exhibited profiles. Positive reactions enhance teens' social self-esteem and psychological well-being (Valkenburg, Peter & Schouten, 2006) especially among those experiencing low life-satisfaction (Ellison, Steinfield & Lampe, 2007). Youth's offline life, in terms of trouble and parental communication, affects the likelihood of a close online relationship (Wolak, Mitchell, & Finkelhor, 2003). Online dating develops quicker than off-line (Rosen, Cheever, Cummings & Felt, 2008). Nevertheless, the effect of self-disclosure on the romance process was moderated by age, education and ethnicity. However, the authors concluded that lower levels of self-disclosure were preferred when choosing a date partner…, some degree of mystery was welcome. Finally, McKenna, Green & Gleason's (2002) experiments proved that participants' ties intensified more following an initial Internet interaction compared with an initial face-to-face meeting.

CONCLUSION

Youth and the New Media

To understand how youngsters use, live with, integrate and manage digital technologies the concept of digital media had to be analyzed as well as the underlying theoretical explanations rooted in the spheres of psychology and sociology. Ultimately it is about technology, thus the specificities of digital intermediaries (the devices) should be addressed. The scope and limits of youth's relationship with the world, with their peers and with themselves are also determined by the technological features of various digital devices/platforms such as the Internet, mobile phone and digital games.

In this section we schematically depict a synthesis of the analysis of the various topics scrutinized previously. However, a practical and managerial dissection of that analysis is still missing.

It is not accurate to ascribe the association of digital media use with its instrumental (utilitarian view) and emotional (attachment, symbolic meaning and dependency) attributes exclusively to youngsters. In fact, other age groups share similar relationships with digital technology and completely assume both of these attributes.

What makes youth special in regard to this new media?

1. Their limited or lack of experience with the analogue world. For them the "new" (media) is already "old" media;
2. The 'others' (Friends & friends) are always with "me". That omnipresence or state of "perpetual contact" (Katz & Aakhus, 2002) is made possible by portable digital devices;
3. Intensity of usage expressed by time length, frequency and diversity of contacts, all associated with multitasking. Notwithstanding multitasking reduces performance and affects the quality of learning process (Bowman, Levine, Waite & Gendron, 2010).
4. Expertise and sophistication. Some of them are better equipped than their parents. Nevertheless, they are far more capable than the past generation to live with, deal with and manage life under an overwhelmingly digital future environment.

Communication vs. Advertising

The information processing of advertising is age-dependent, and even among youngsters it is not uniform. Like adults, young ad viewers do not engage both central and peripheral routes for changing attitudes. Their attitudes are similar regardless of their involvement level (Harari, Lampert & Wilzig, 2007). Children's rudimentary and simple

Figure 5. Schema: aspects and context of youngsters' digitalisation process

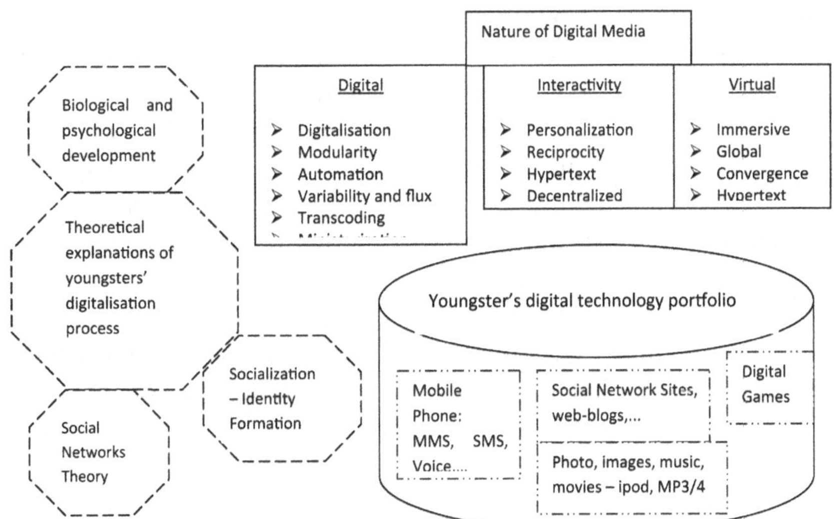

cognitive elaboration style hinders distinguishing between advertising and surrounding program content. They have difficulty understanding the underlying sales, persuasion, stereotypical and even deceptive intentions of advertising (Bakir, Blodgett & Rose, 2008; Moses & Baldwin, 2005). At age 12 they have not yet acquired an adult-like understanding of advertising (Rozendaal, Buijzen, & Valkenburg, 2008). With further experience coping with ads older children recognize and frame the interpretation of subsequent brand usage and evaluate the brand positively if the ad is appreciated (Moore and Lutz, 2000; Wright, Friestad, & Boush, 2005). As children develop, their susceptibility to advertising in terms of liking, desire and intention to request advertised products can be mediated by adult commentary during the exposure to commercials (Buijzen & Mens, 2007). Along with household purchasing participation, shopping skills, and product and brand knowledge enhancement, children also develop an understanding of advertising tactics and appeals. The latter indicates that mature kids become less trustful and entertained concerning ads, and more skeptical and discerning (John, 1999). In this transition the way socialization agents interact with youngsters–family communication orientation, susceptibility to peer influence and advertising exposure - determines the degree of skepticism toward advertising (Mangleburg & Bristol, 1998).

Transposing the topic of adolescent consumer socialization to online advertising and e-marketing practices, Youn (2008) studied the role of family communication patterns (concept-oriented versus socio-oriented) on persuasive online practices. Here, Youn found pluralistic (low socio and high concept oriented) and consensual teens (high on both orientations) tended to be more concerned with privacy issues and exhibited more negative attitudes toward online advertising than laissez-faire (low on both orientations) and protective teens (high socio- and low concept-oriented). In spite of typically being very analytical and voicing negative opinions toward advertising in general, adolescents also enjoy discussing and sharing their savvy positions with peers about some of the more creative advertisement approaches (Ritson & Elliott, 1999). Advertising is a resource for youngsters–for diversion, inspiration and as a pretext to enter dialogues–a vehicle for recognition and success, a tactic for overcoming shyness and to showing parents evidence of their expertise (Lawlor, 2008).

From a managerial perspective what really matters is how we can make things work effectively. At first glance, there are some obvious formulas when using new media:

- Don't act only according to the rules of old media.
- Thinking and acting fast was always a competitive advantage, but now speed is a survival issue.
- Be humble and keep learning, since what was sure and true yesterday is often useless today.

Putting together the dimensions of digital technology, young people's socio-psychological characteristics and companies' goals (e.g. expansion, profit, youth segment penetration), the following reflect thoughts about the how to communicate with young people:

- Apparently nonconformity advertising has worked well among teens (Bao & Shao, 2002). However, it is not wise to deliberately be cool. Ultimately it is the youth who will label it as cool or not. Otherwise it will be classified as pretentious or ridiculous. Product endorsement with celebrities or characters who are popular among children is equally as effective as using unknown and inexpressive characters due to the status of cognitive information elaboration process (Harari, et al., 2007).
- Lindgaard, Fernandes, Dukek, & Brown (2006) found that university students were able to make an impression of a web page within 50 milliseconds before deciding to stay. This impressive record challenges web designers to conceive sites with high visual appeal, as well as showing the users' expertise in judging what is worthwhile, or not. Furthermore, they are a merciless demographic. Once irritated, they simply ignore and avoid a web page, or worse, they spread negative information through word-of-mouth. Therefore, it is worth testing ideas and concepts and constantly updating these analyses.
- Rappaport (2007) outlined three new models centred on relevance to consumers. The "on demand model" (e.g. TiVo) allows a person to decide, filter, and schedule what they wish to watch or listen to. In the 'engagement model' instead of focusing on transactional relationships, a brand's emotional connection with the consumer is emphasized. Finally, the notion of "advertising as a service" refocuses a managers' approach to consumers on identifying the information and the types of services consumers really need by using ads as a vehicle. In this view, the best way to attract youth is by giving them power:
- Allow them to share some control over the brand and give some branding elements away.
- Invite them to participate in adjusting, modifying or building communicational tools.
- Stimulate them to discuss and disseminate creative/imaginative solutions among their peers by promoting viral marketing networks. Traditionally sports and music sponsorships provided endless opportunities to link sport or music "stars" with their fans through a specific popular brand. Furthermore, the Internet makes those "stars" even more and permanently accessible.
- Online advertising can build brand equity in similar ways as traditional media (Hollis, 2005). However, if the brand managers' intention is to entail a relationship–hopefully loyalty–with their young customers, the appropriate approach is not to concentrate exclusively on advertising but on communication (in a broad sense). The examples above call for sales promotion–e.g. con-

tests–and public relations–e.g. sponsorship along with advertisements. To strategically manage the relationship with your customers the integrated marketing communication (e.g. Lee & Park, 2007) allows not only efficiently articulating online/offline investments but also reaching that difficult target pragmatically. Finally, online business models inspired by SNSs do not wait for academic considerations. For instance, fast food companies successfully developed prepaid credit cards and instant store credit (virtual cards) delivered online and which were very handy/convenient to youth lifestyles (Macsai, 2008).

Kids and teens always will be kids and teens! Their structural (biological nature) and fundamental psychological features under a maturation process have been and will be (fairly) explained by the theories presented here. Regardless of the technologies available, it is very likely that kids and teens will keep playing, sharing their feeling and thoughts with their peers, learning and interacting with each other and with machines in the future as their parents and grand-parents did in the past. What have been changing are those (technological) intermediaries and those tools. Such endless process set "new" problems and challenges to researchers and managers as well as to parents and educators. As always, the winners in this game will be those who understand the appetites and aspirations of the current digital generation, and who are able to lead the market with ever-evolving products and services.

REFERENCES

Aarsand, P. A. (2007). Children's consumption of computer games. In Katz, J. E. (Ed.), *Handbook of Mobile Communication Studies* (pp. 47–62). Cambridge, MA: MIT Press.

Aboud, F. E., & Mendelson, M. J. (1998). Determinants of friendship selection and quality: developmental perspective. In W. M. Bukowski, A. F. Newcomb & W. W. Hartup (Eds.), The company they keep: Friendship in Childhood and adolescence (pp. 87-112). NY: New York: Cambridge University Press.

Acar, A. (2007). Testing the effects of incidental advertising exposure in online gaming environment. *Journal of Interactive Advertising*, *8*(1), 1–36.

Andersen, L. P., Tufte, B., Rasmussen, J., & Chan, K. (2007). Tweens and new media in Denmark and Hong Kong. *Journal of Consumer Marketing*, *24*(6), 340–350. doi:10.1108/07363760710822927

Aoki, K., & Downes, E. J. (2003). An analysis of young people's use of and attitudes toward cell phones. *Telematics and Informatics*, *20*(4), 349–364. doi:10.1016/S0736-5853(03)00018-2

Bagwell, C. L. Schmidt, Michelle. E., Newcomb, A. F. &., & Bukowski, W. M. (2001). Friendship and peer rejection as predictors of adult adjustment, In. In W. Damon, (series Ed.) and D. W. Nangle & C. A. Erdley (vol.Eds.)., New directions for child and adolescent development: no.91. The role of friendship in psychology adjustment (pp. 25-49). SF: San Francisco: Jossey-Bass.

Bakir, A., Blodgett, J. G., & Rose, G. M. (2008, June). Children's responses to gender-role stereotyped advertisements. *Journal of Advertising Research*, (June): 255–266. doi:10.2501/S002184990808029X

Bales, R. F. (1950). *Interaction process analysis. MA*. Reading, MA: Addison-Wesley.

Bao, Y., & Shao, A. T. (2002, June). Nonconformity advertising to teens. *Journal of Advertising Research*, (June): 56–65.

Bauman, Z. (1995). *Life in fragments: essays in postmodern morality*. Oxford, UK: Basil Blackwell.

Baym, N. (1998). The emergency of online community. In Jobes, S. G. (Ed.), *Cybersociety 2.0*. Thousand Oaks, CA: Sage.

Baym, N. K., Zhang, Y. B., & Lin, M. C. (2004). Social interactions across media. *New Media & Society*, *6*(3), 299–318. doi:10.1177/1461444804041438

Bee-Gates, D. (2006). *"I want it": navigating childhood in a materialistic world*. London: Palgrave-MacMillan.

Beer, D. (2008). Social Network(ing) sites…revisiting the story so far: a response to danah boyd & Nicole Ellison. *Journal of Computer-Mediated Communication*, *13*, 252–275. doi:10.1111/j.1083-6101.2008.00408.x

Belch, G. E., Ceresino, G., & Belch, M. A. (1985). Parental and teenage child influences in family decision making. *Journal of Business Research*, *13*, 163–176. doi:10.1016/0148-2963(85)90038-4

Belk, R. W. (1988, September). Possessions and extended self. *The Journal of Consumer Research*, *15*(September), 139–168. doi:10.1086/209154

Belsky, J., Steinberg, L., & Draper, P. (1991). Childhood experience, interpersonal development, and reproductive strategy: an evolutionary theory of socialization. *Child Development*, *62*, 647–670. doi:10.2307/1131166

Berger, K. S. (2006). The developing person: through childhood and adolescence (7th ed.). N.Y.: New York: Worth Publishers., 7th ed.

Berndt, T. J., & Murphy, L. M. (2002). Influences of friends and friendships: myths, truths, and research recommendations. In R. V. Kail (Ed.), Advances in child development and behavior, (vVol. 30, (pp. pp. 275-310). San Diego, CA: Academic Press.

Boneva, B., Quinn, A., Kraut, R., Kiesler, S., & Shklovski, I. (2006). Teenage communication in instant messaging era, In. In R. Kraut, M. Brynin and & S. Kiesler (Eds.). Computers, Phones and the Internet: domesticating information Technology (pp. 201-218). NY: New York: Oxford University Press.

Bowlby, J. (1969). *Attachment and loss: Attachment. (vVol. 1)*. Harmondsworth, UK: Penguin.

Bowman, L. L., Levine, L. E., Waite, B. M., & Gendron, M. (2010). Can students really multitask? An experimental study of instant messaging while reading. *Computers & Education*, *54*, 927–931. doi:10.1016/j.compedu.2009.09.024

boyd, d. m. and ., & Ellison, N.B. (2007). Social network sites: definition, history, and scholarship., *Journal of Computer-Mediated Communication*, 13, 210-230.

Brito, P. Q. (2008). *Conceptualizing and illustrating the digital lifestyle of youth*. Working Paper no. 300. Faculdade de Economia - Universidade do Porto. Portugal.

Bryant, J. A., Jackson, A. S., & Smallwood, A. M. K. (2006). IMing, text messaging, and adolescent social networks. *Journal of Computer-Mediated Communication*, *11*, 577–592. doi:10.1111/j.1083-6101.2006.00028.x

Buckingham, D. (2007). That's edutainment. New media, marketing and education in the home, In. In K. M. Ekström and & B. Tufte. (Eds.), Children, media and consumption (pp. 33-46). Gothenburg, Sweden: Nordicom.

Buijzen, M., & Mens, C. (2007). Adult mediation of television advertising effects: a comparison of factual, evaluative, and combined strategies. *Journal of Children and Media*, *1*(2), 177–191. doi:10.1080/17482790701339233

Campbell, R. (2006). Teenage girls and cellular phones: discourse of independence, safety and 'rebellion.'. *Journal of Youth Studies*, *9*(2), 195–212. doi:10.1080/13676260600635649

Campbell, S. (2008). Mobile technology and the body: apparatgeist, fashion, and function. In Katz, J. E. (Ed.), *Handbook of Mobile Communication Studies* (pp. 153–164). Cambridge, MA: MIT Press.

Carlson, E. A., Sroufe, L. A., & Byron, E. (2004). The construction of experience: a longitudinal study of representation and behavior. *Child Development*, *75*, 66–83. doi:10.1111/j.1467-8624.2004.00654.x

Chandler, M. J., Lalonde, C. E., Sokol, B. W., Bryan, W. & ., & Hallet, D. (2003). Personal persistence, identity development and suicide: a study of native and non-native North American adolescents. Monographs of the Society for research. *Child Development*, *68*(2), serial n°273.

Charlton, T., Panting, C., & Hannan, A. (2002). Mobile telephone ownership and usage among 10- and 11 year-olds: participation and exclusion. *Emotional & Behavioural Difficulties*, *7*(3), 152–163.

Cole, H., & Griffiths, M. D. (2007). Social interactions in massively multiplayer online role-playing gamers. *Cyberpsychology & Behavior*, *7*(1), 575–583. doi:10.1089/cpb.2007.9988

Cooley, C. H., & Schubert, H. J. (1998). *On self and the social organization*. Chicago: University of Chicago Press.

Cottrell, J. (2007). *Social Networks in youth and Adolescence* (2nd ed.). London: Routledge.

Critcher, C. (2006). *Critical readings: moral panics and the media*. London: Open University Press.

Csíkszentmihályi, M. (1998). *Finding flow: the psychology of engagement with everyday life*. New York: Basic Books.

Dahl, R. E. (2004). Adolescent brain development: a period of vulnerabilities and opportunities, Keynote address. *Annals of the New York Academy of Sciences*, *1021*, 1–22. doi:10.1196/annals.1308.001

Darian, J. C. (1998). Parent-child decision making in children's clothing stores. *International Journal of Retail and Distribution Management*, *26*(11), 421–428. doi:10.1108/09590559810246377

Demetriou, A., Christou, C., Spanoudis, G. & ., & Platsidou, M. (2002). The development of mental processing: efficiency, working memory, and thinking. *Monographs of the Society for research in Child Development*, *67*(1), serial n°268.

Dietmar, C. (2005). Mobile communication in couple relationship. In Nyiri, K. (Ed.), *A sense of place: the global and local in mobile communication* (pp. 201–208). Vienna, Austria: Passagen Verlag.

Dishion, T. J., & Owen, L. D. (2002). A longitudinal analysis of friendship and substance use: bidirectional influence from adolescence to adulthood. *Developmental Psychology*, *38*, 480–491. doi:10.1037/0012-1649.38.4.480

Dominick, J. R. (1999). Who do you think you are? Personal home pages and self-presentation on the World Wide Web. *Journalism & Mass Communication Quarterly*, *76*(4), 646–658.

Drotner, K. (2005). Mediatized childhoods: discourses, dilemmas and directions. In Qvortrup, J. (Ed.), *Studies in Modern Childhood* (pp. 39–58). London: Palgrave-MacMillan.

Eastin, M. S. (2005). Teen Internet use: relating social perception and cognitive models to behavior. *Cyberpsychology & Behavior*, *8*(1), 62–75. doi:10.1089/cpb.2005.8.62

Ekind, D. (1979). *The child and society: essays in applied child development. NY*. New York: Oxford University Press.

Ekström, K. M. (2007, July). Parental consumer learning or 'keeping up with the children.'. *Journal of Consumer Behaviour*, *6*(July-August), 203–217. doi:10.1002/cb.215

Ellison, N., Steinfield, C., & Lampe, C. (2007). The Benefits of Facebook "Friends:" Social Capital and College Students' Use of Online Social Network Sites. *Journal of Computer-Mediated Communication*, *12*, 1143–1168. doi:10.1111/j.1083-6101.2007.00367.x

Erikson, E. H. (1968). *Identity: youth and crisis. NY*. New York: Norton.

Erwin, P. (1998). *Friendship in childhood and adolescence*. London: Routledge.

Flichy, P. (1999). The construction of new digital media. *New Media & Society*, *1*(1), 33–38. doi:10.1177/14614448990010010006

Freud, S. (1962, original 1923). The ego and Id., London: Hogarth Press. (Original manuscript published in 1923).

Fu, F. L., Su, R. C., & Yu, S. C. (2010). EGameFlow: A scale to measure learners' enjoyment of e-learning games. *Computers & Education*, *52*, 101–112. doi:10.1016/j.compedu.2008.07.004

Fulcher, J., & Scott, J. (2007). Sociology, (3rd ed.), NY: New York: Oxford University Press.

Gee, J. P. (2003). *What video games have to teach us about learning and literacy. NY*. New York: Palgrave MacMillan.

Gentile, D. A., & Gentile, J. R. (2008). Violent video games as exemplary teachers: a conceptual analysis. *Journal of Youth and Adolescence*, *37*, 127–141. doi:10.1007/s10964-007-9206-2

Gere, C. (2002). *Digital Culture*. London: Reaktion Books.

Giddens, A. (1976). *New rules of the sociological methods*. London: Hutchinson.

Goffman, E. (1959). *The presentation of self in everyday life*. Harmondsworth, UK: Penguin.

Goodman, D., Bradley, N. L., Paras, B., Williamson, I. J., & Bizzochi, J. (2006). Video gaming promotes concussion knowledge acquisition in youth hockey players. *Journal of Adolescence*, *29*, 351–360. doi:10.1016/j.adolescence.2005.07.004

Goodstein, A. (2007). *Totally wired: what teen and tweens are really doing online. NY*. New York: St.Martin's Press.

Grüter, B., Mielke, A., & Oks, M. (. (2005). Mobile gaming–experience design. In *Proceedings from pervasive: The 3rd International Conference on Pervasive Computing*, Munich.

Harai, T. T., Lampert, S. I., & Wilzig, S. L. (2007). Information processing of advertising among young people: The elaboration likelihood model as applied to youth. *Journal of Advertising Research*, *47*(3), 326–340. doi:10.2501/S0021849907070341

Hargittai, E. (2008). Whose space? Differences among users and non-users of social network sites. *Journal of Computer-Mediated Communication*, *13*, 276–297. doi:10.1111/j.1083-6101.2007.00396.x

Haselager, G. J. T., Cillessen, A. H. N., Van Lieshout, C. F. M., Riksen-Walraven, J. M. A., & Hartup, W. W. (2002). Heterogeneity among peer-rejected boys across middle childhood: developmental pathways of social behaviour. *Developmental Psychology*, *38*, 446–456. doi:10.1037/0012-1649.38.3.446

Hayles, N. K. (1999). *How we became posthuman: virtual bodies in cybernetics, literature, and informatics*. Chicago: University of Chicago Press.

Haythornthwaite, C. (2000). Online personal networks. *New Media & Society*, *2*(2), 195–226. doi:10.1177/14614440022225779

Hinduja, S., & Patchin, J. W. (2008). Personal information of adolescents on Internet: a quantitative content analysis of MySpace. *Journal of Adolescence, 31*, 125–146. doi:10.1016/j.adolescence.2007.05.004

Hollis, N. (2005, June). Ten years of learning on how online advertising builds brands. *Journal of Advertising Research,* (June): 255–268. doi:10.1017/S0021849905050270

Holloway, S. L., & Valentine, G. (2003). *Cyberkids: children in the information age*. London: Routledge.

Huhtamo, E. (1999). From cybernation to interaction: a contribution to an archeology of interactivity. In Lunenfeld, I. P. (Ed.), *The Digital Dialectic: New Essays on New Media* (pp. 96–110). Cambridge, MassMA: The MIT Press.

Hussain, Z., & Griffiths, M. D. (2008). Gender swapping and socializing in cyberspace: an exploratory study. *Cyberpsychology & Behavior, 11*(1), 47–53. doi:10.1089/cpb.2007.0020

Ishii, K. (2006). Implications of mobility: the uses of personal communication media in everyday life. *The Journal of Communication, 56*, 346–365. doi:10.1111/j.1460-2466.2006.00023.x

Ito, M., & Okabe, D. (2005). Intimate connections: contextualizing Japanese youth and mobile messaging. In R. Harper, L. Palen and & A. Taylor (Eds.). The inside text: social, cultural and design perspectives of SMS (pp. 127-146). Dordrecht, The Netherlands: Springer.

Jensen, J. F. (1999). Interactivity–tracking a new concept in media and communication studies. In Mayer, I. P. (Ed.), *Computer and Media Communication* (pp. 25–66). Oxford, UK: Oxford University Press.

John, D. R. (1999, December). Consumer socialization of children: a retrospective looks at twenty-five years of research. *Journal of Advertising Research,* (December): 183–213.

Johnson, H. M. (1961). *Sociology: a systematic introduction*. London: Routledge & Keegan Paul.

Johnson, J. E., & Christie, J. F. (2009). Play and digital media. *Computers in the Schools, 26*, 284–289. doi:10.1080/07380560903360202

Joinson, A. N. (2001). Self-disclosure in computer-mediated communication: the role of self-awareness and visual anonymity. *European Journal of Social Psychology, 31*, 177–192. doi:10.1002/ejsp.36

Jones, C., Ramanau, R., Cross, S., & Healing, G. (2010). Net generation or digital natives: Is there a distinct new generation entering university? *Computers & Education, 54*, 722–732. doi:10.1016/j.compedu.2009.09.022

Kail, R. (2000). Speed of information processing: development change and links to intelligence. *Journal of School Psychology, 38*, 51–61. doi:10.1016/S0022-4405(99)00036-9

Kakihara, M., & Sørensen, C. (2002). Mobility: An Extended Perspective, *IEEE. Published iIn the Proceedings of the Hawai'i International Conference on System Sciences*, January 7-10, Big Island, Hawaii.

Katz, J. E., & Aakhus, M. A. (Eds.). (2002). *Perpetual contact: Mobile communication, private talk, public performance*. Cambridge, UK: Cambridge University Press. doi:10.1017/CBO9780511489471

Katz, J. E., & Acord, S. K. (2008). Mobile games and entertainment. In Katz, J. (Ed.), *Handbook of Mobile Communication Studies* (pp. 153–164). Cambridge, MA: MIT Press.

Katz, J. E., Lever, K. M., & Chen, Y. F. (2008). Mobile music as environmental control and prosocial entertainment. In Katz, J. E. (Ed.), *Handbook of Mobile Communication Studies* (pp. 367–376). Cambridge, MA: MIT Press.

Katz, J. E., & Sugiyama, S. (2005). Mobile phones as fashion statements: the co-creation of mobile communication's public meaning. In R. Ling and & P. Pedersen (Eds,), Mobile communications: re-negotiation of the social sphere (pp. 81-63), London: Springer.

Keating, D. P. (. (2004). Cognitive and brain development. In R. M. Lerner and& L. D. Steinberg (Eds.), Handbook of Adolescent Psychology (2nd ed., pp. 45-84) 2nd ed., NJ: Hoboken, NJ: Wiley.

Kim, H., Kim, G. J., Park, H. W., & Rice, R. E. (2007). Configurations of relationships in different media: FtF, email, instant messenger, mobile phone, and SMS. *Journal of Computer-Mediated Communication, 12*, 1183–1207. doi:10.1111/j.1083-6101.2007.00369.x

Kim, M. (2008). The creative commons and copyright protection in the Digital Era: uses of creative commons licenses. *Journal of Computer-Mediated Communication, 13*, 187–209. doi:10.1111/j.1083-6101.2007.00392.x

Koskinen, I. (2008). Mobile multimedia: uses and social consequences. In Katz, J. E. (Ed.), *Handbook of Mobile Communication Studies* (pp. 241–257). Cambridge, MA: MIT Press.

Lahelma, E. (2002). School is for friends: secondary school as lived and remembered. *British Journal of Sociology of Education, 23*(3), 367–381. doi:10.1080/0142569022000015418

Larson, R., & Wilson, S. (2004). Adolescence across Place and Time: Globalization and the Changing Pathways to Adulthood. In Lerner, R., & Steinberg, L. (Eds.), *Handbook of adolescent psychology* (pp. 299–330). New York: Wiley.

Lawor, M. A. (2008), What do children do with advertising?–a uses and gratifications' perspective, In *Child and Teen Consumption 2008 Conference*, Trondheim, Norway.

Lee, D. H., & Park, C. W. (2007, September). Conceptualization and measurement of multidimensionality of integrated marketing communications. *Journal of Advertising Research*, (September): 222–236. doi:10.2501/S0021849907070274

Lenhart, A., Madden, M., & Hitlin, P. (2005). *Teens and Technology: youth are leading the transition to a fully wired and mobile nation*. Retrieved from http://www.pewinternet.org/

Lenhart, A., Madden, M., Macgill, A. R., & Smith, A. (2007). *Teens and social Media*. Retrieved from http://www.pewinternet.org/PPF/r/230/report_display.asp

Lenhart, A., Rainie, L., & Lewis, O. (2001). *Teenage life online: the rise of the instant-message generation and the internet's impact on friendship and family relationship*. Retrieved from http://www.pewinternet.org/

Leung, L., & Wei, R. (2000). More than just talk on the move: uses and gratifications of cellular phones. *Journalism & Mass Communication Quarterly, 77*(2), 308–320.

Licope, C., & Smoreda, Z. (2005). Are social networks technologically embedded? How networks are changing today with changes in communication technology. *Social Networks, 27*, 317–335. doi:10.1016/j.socnet.2004.11.001

Licoppe, C. (2008). The mobile phone's ring. In Katz, J. E. (Ed.), *Handbook of Mobile Communication Studies, (pp* (pp. 139–152). Cambridge, MA: MIT Press.

Lindgaard, G., Fernandes, G., Dukek, C., & Brown, J. (2006). Attention web designers: you have 50 miliseconds to make a good first impression! *Behaviour & Information Technology, 25*(2), 115–126. doi:10.1080/01449290500330448

Lindstrøm, M. & ., & Seybold, P. B. (2004). *Brand Child: remarkable insights into the minds of today's global kids and their relationship with brands*. USA. New York: Kogan Page.

Ling, R. (2000). "We will be reached": the use of mobile phone telephony among Norwegian youth. *Information Technology & People, 13*, 102–120. doi:10.1108/09593840010339844

Ling, R. (2007). Children, youth, and mobile communication. *Journal of Children and Media, 1*(1), 60–67. doi:10.1080/17482790601005173

Lister, M., Dovey, J., Giddings, S., Grant, I., & Kelly, K. (2003). *New Media: a critical introduction*. London: Routledge.

Liu, H. (2008). Social network profiles as taste performances. *Journal of Computer-Mediated Communication, 13*, 252–275. doi:10.1111/j.1083-6101.2007.00395.x

MacKeogh, K. (2001). National Strategies for the Promotion of On-Line Learning in Higher Education. *European Journal of Education, 36*(2), 223–236. doi:10.1111/1467-3435.00061

Macsai, D. (2008, August 22). Marketing to millennials. *Business Week*, August 22.

Madell, D. E., & Muncer, S. J. (2007). Control over social interactions: an approach for young people's use of the Internet and mobile communications? *Cyberpsychology & Behavior, 10*(1), 137–140. doi:10.1089/cpb.2006.9980

Mahatanankoon, P., & O'Sullivan, P. (2008). Attitude toward mobile text messaging: an expectancy-based perspective. *Journal of Computer-Mediated Communication, 13*, 973–992. doi:10.1111/j.1083-6101.2008.00427.x

Mangleburg, T. F., & Bristol, T. (1998). Socializations of adolescents' skepticism toward advertising. *Journal of Advertising, 28*(3), 11–20.

Manovich, L. (2002). *The Language of New Media*. Cambridge, MA: MIT Press.

Markus, H., & Nurius, P. (1986). Possible selves. *The American Psychologist, 41*, 954–969. doi:10.1037/0003-066X.41.9.954

Martensen, A. (2007). Mobile phones and tweens' needs, motivations and values. Segmentation based on means-end chains. In Ekström, K. M., & Tufte, B. (Eds.), *Children, media and consumption* (pp. 107–126). Gothenburg, Sweden: Nordicom.

McKeanna, K. Y. A., Green, A. S., & Gleason, M. E. J. (2002). Relationship formation on the Internet: what's the big attraction? *The Journal of Social Studies, 58*(1), 9–31.

McLeod, J., & Lin, L. (2010). A child's power in game-play. *Computers & Education, 54*, 517–527. doi:10.1016/j.compedu.2009.09.003

McLuhan, M. (1969). *Connterblast*. London: Rapp & Whiting.

McLuhan, M. (2001,original 1964). Understanding Media. London: Routledge.

McQuail, D., & Windahl, S. (1993). *Communication models for the study of mass communication* (2nd ed.). London: Longman.

Mead, G. (1934, original 1927). Mind, self and society. Chicago: University of Chicago Press. (Original manuscript published in 1927).

Mitchell, C., & Reid-Walsh, J. (Eds.). (2005). Seven going on seventeen–tween studies in the culture of girlhood. N.Y.: New York: Peter Lang Publ. Inc.

Mitchell, J. J. (1973). Networks, norms and institutions. In J. Boissevain & J. J. Mitchell (Eds)(Eds.), Network analysis: studies in human interaction (pp. 15-35). The Hague, Netherlands: Mouton.

Miyata, K., Boase, J., & Wellman, B. (2008). The Social Effects of Keitai and Personal Computer Email in Japan. In Katz, J. E. (Ed.), *Handbook of Mobile Communication Studies* (pp. 209–222). Cambridge, MA: MIT Press.

Moore, E. S., & Lutz, J. R. (2000, June). Children, advertising and product experiences: a multi-method inquiry. *Journal of Advertising Research*, (June): 31–48.

Moses, L. J., & Baldwin, D. A. (2005). What can the study of cognitive development reveal about children's ability to appreciate and cope with advertising? *Journal of Public Policy & Marketing*, *24*(2), 186–201. doi:10.1509/jppm.2005.24.2.186

Moshman, D. (1999). *Adolescent psychological development: rationality, morality and identity*. Mahwah, NJ: Eribaum.

Negroponte, N. (1995). *Being digital*. New York: Vintage.

Nikerson, A. B., & Nagle, R. J. (2005). Parent and peer attachment in late childhood and early adolescence. *The Journal of Early Adolescence*, *25*, 223–249. doi:10.1177/0272431604274174

Nikken, P., & Jansz, J. (2007). Playing restricted videogames: relations with game ratings and parental mediation. *Journal of Children and Media*, *1*(3), 227–243. doi:10.1080/17482790701531862

Nisbet, R. A. (1970). The social bond., N.Y.New York: Knopf.

Oates, C. J., Blades, M., & Gunter, B. (2002). Children and television advertising. *Journal of Consumer Behaviour*, *1*(3), 238–245. doi:10.1002/cb.69

Okazaki, S., Skapa, R., & Grande, R., I. (2008). Capturing global youth: mobile gaming in the U.S., Spain, and the Czech Republic. *Journal of Computer-Mediated Communication*, *13*, 827–855. doi:10.1111/j.1083-6101.2008.00421.x

Oskman, V., & Turtiainen, J. (2004). Mobile communication as a social stage. *New Media & Society*, *6*(3), 319–339. doi:10.1177/1461444804042518

Pahl, R. (2000). *On friendship. Cambridge*. Cambridge, MA: Polity Press.

Parsons, T. (1951). *The social system. NY*. New York: Free press.

Piaget, J. (1952, original 1936). The origins of intelligence in children. Oxford, UK: International University Press. (Original manuscript published in 1936).

Prensky, M. (2001). *Digital Natives, Digital Immigrants*. Retrieved from http://www.marcprensky.com.

Prensky, M. (2004). *The emerging online life of the digital native: what they do differently because of technology, and how they do it*. Retrieved from http://www.marcprensky.com.

Raacke, J., & Raacke, J. B. (2008). MySpace and Facebook: applying the uses and gratifications theory to exploring friend-networking sites. *Cyberpsychology & Behavior*, *11*(2), 169–174. doi:10.1089/cpb.2007.0056

Rappaport, S. D. (2007). Lessons from online practice: new advertising models. *Journal of Advertising Research*, *47*(2), 135–141. doi:10.2501/S0021849907070158

Reynolds, T. (2007). Friendship networks, social capital and ethnic identity: researching the perspectives of Caribbean young people in Britain. *Journal of Youth Studies*, *10*(4), 383–398. doi:10.1080/13676260701381192

Ritson, M., & Elliott, R. (1999). The social uses of advertising: an ethnographic study of adolescent advertising audiences. *The Journal of Consumer Research*, *26*(3), 260–277. doi:10.1086/209562

Roberts, M. L., Wortzel, L. H., & Berkeley, R. L. (1981). Mother's attitudes and perceptions of children's influence and their effect on family consumption. *Advances in Consumer Research. Association for Consumer Research (U. S.)*, *8*, 730–735.

Rokeach, S. J. B., & DeFleur, M. L. (1976). A dependency model of mass-media effects. *Communication Research*, *3*(1), 3–21. doi:10.1177/009365027600300101

Rosen, L. D. (2007). *Me, MySpace, and I: parenting the net generation. NY*. New York: Palgrave-MacMillan.

Rosen, L. D., Cheever, N. A., Cummings, C., & Felt, J. (2008). The impact of emotionality and self-disclosure on online dating versus traditional dating. *Computers in Human Behavior*, *24*, 2124–2157. doi:10.1016/j.chb.2007.10.003

Rozendaal, E., Buijzen, M., & Valkenburg, P. (2008). Comparing children's and adults' cognitive defenses to television advertising. In *Child and Teen Consumption 2008 Conference*, Trondheim, Norway.

Shepard, J. M. (2007). *Sociology*. New York: Thomson Wadsworth.

Shutz, T. (2000). Mass media and concept of interactivity: an exploratory study of online forums and reader email. *Media Culture & Society*, *22*(2), 205–221. doi:10.1177/016344300022002005

Siegel, D. L., Coffey, T. J. & ., & Livingstone, G. (2001). *The great tween buying machine–marketing to today's tweens*. N.Y.: New York: Paramount M.P. Inc.

Smith, E. R., Murphy, J., & Coats, S. (1999). Attachment to groups: theory and management. *Journal of Personality and Social Psychology*, *77*, 94–110. doi:10.1037/0022-3514.77.1.94

Song, I., Larose, R., Eastin, S. M., & Lin, C. A. (2004). Internet gratifications and Internet addiction: on the uses and abuses of new media. *Cyberpsychology & Behavior*, *7*(4), 384–394. doi:10.1089/cpb.2004.7.384

Steinberg, L. (2004). Risk taking in adolescence: what changes, and why? *Annals of the New York Academy of Sciences*, *1021*, 51–58. doi:10.1196/annals.1308.005

Steinkuehler, C. A. (2006). Why game (culture) studies now? *Games and Culture*, *1*(1), 97–102. doi:10.1177/1555412005281911

Steinkuehler, C. A., & Williams, D. (2006). Where everybody knows your (screen) name: online games as "third places". *Journal of Computer-Mediated Communication*, *11*, 885–909. doi:10.1111/j.1083-6101.2006.00300.x

Suler, J. (2004). The online disinhibition effect. *Cyberpsychology & Behavior*, *7*(3), 321–326. doi:10.1089/1094931041291295

Sullivan, H. S. (1947, original 1939). Conception of modern psychiatry, NY: New York: W.W. Norton. (Original manuscript published in 1939).

Tapscott, D. (1998). *Growing-up digital: the rise of the net generation., NY*. New York: McGraw-Hill.

Tarrant, M., MacKenzie, L., & Hewitt, L. A. (2006). Friendship group identification, multidimensional self-concept, and experience of developmental tasks in adolescence. *Journal of Adolescence*, *29*, 627–640. doi:10.1016/j.adolescence.2005.08.012

Thompson, J. B. (1995, original 1971). The media and Modernity: social theory of media. Cambridge: Polity Press. (Original manuscript published in 1971).

Thompson, R. A. (2005). Multiple relationships multiply considered. *Human Development*, *48*, 102–107. doi:10.1159/000083221

Thurman, N. (2008). Forums for citizen journalists? Adoption of user generated content initiatives by online news media. *New Media & Society, 10*(1), 139–157. doi:10.1177/1461444807085325

Tingstad, V. (2003). *Children's chat on the net: a study of social encounters in two Norwegian chat rooms*. Trondheim, Norway: NOSEB/NTNU.

Toffler, A. (1980). *The third wave*. New York: Bantam.

Tong, S. T., Heide, B. V. D., & Lanwell, L. (2008). Too much of a good thing? The relationship between number of friends and interpersonal impressions on Facebook. *Journal of Computer-Mediated Communication, 13*, 531–549. doi:10.1111/j.1083-6101.2008.00409.x

Tsai, C. (2006). What is the Internet? Taiwanese high school students' perceptions. *Cyberpsychology & Behavior, 9*(6), 767–771. doi:10.1089/cpb.2006.9.767

Turkle, S. (1995). *Life on the screen: identity in the age of the Internet. NY.* New York: Simon and Schuster.

Turkle, S. (2004). Whither psychoanalysis in computer culture? *Psychoanalytic Psychology: Journal of the Division of Psychoanalysis, vol. 21*(no. 1), pp. 16-30.

Turkle, S. (2008). Always-on/always-on-you: the tethered self. In Katz, I. J. (Ed.), *Handbook of Mobile Communication Studies* (pp. 121–137). Cambridge, MA: MIT Press.

Turner, J. H. (2002). *Face-to-face: toward a sociological theory of interpersonal behavior*. Stanford, CA: Stanford University Press.

Turner, R. (1962). Role-taking. Process versus conformity. In Rose, A. (Ed.), *Human behaviour and social process*. London: Routledge & Kegan Paul.

Valkenburg, P. M., & Peter, J. (2007). Preadolescents' and adolescents' online communication and their closeness to friends. *Developmental Psychology, 43*(2), 267–277. doi:10.1037/0012-1649.43.2.267

Valkenburg, P. M., & Peter, J. (2007). Online Communication and Adolescent Well-Being: Testing the Stimulation Versus the Displacement Hypothesis. *Journal of Computer-Mediated Communication, 13*, 1169–1182. doi:10.1111/j.1083-6101.2007.00368.x

Valkenburg, P. M., Peter, J., & Schouten, P. (2006). Friend networking sites and their relationship to adolescents' well-being and social self-esteem. *Cyberpsychology & Behavior, 9*(5), 584–590. doi:10.1089/cpb.2006.9.584

Vygotsky, L. S. (1978, original 1935). Mind in society: the development of higher psychological processes. Cambridge, MA: Harvard University Press. (Original manuscript published in 1935).

Walkerdine, V. (2007). *Children, gender and video games. NY.* New York: Palgrave-MacMillan.

Wallenius, M., Punamäaki, R. L., & Rimpeläa, A. (2007). Digital game playing and direct and indirect aggression in early adolescence: the roles of age, social intelligence, and parent-child communication. *Journal of Youth and Adolescence, 36*, 325–336. doi:10.1007/s10964-006-9151-5

Walther, J. B. (2007). Selective self-presentation in computer-mediated communication: Hyperpersonal dimensions of technology, language, and cognition. *Computers in Human Behavior, 23*, 2538–2557. doi:10.1016/j.chb.2006.05.002

Watson, J. (2008). *Media Communication: an introduction to theory and process* (3rd ed.). London: Palgrave-MacMillan.

Wei, R. (2007). Effects of playing violent videogames on Chinese adolescents' pro-violence attitudes, attitudes toward others, and aggressive behavior. *Cyberpsychology & Behavior, 10*(3), 371–372. doi:10.1089/cpb.2006.9942

Williams, D., Yee, N., & Caplan, S. E. (2008). Who plays, how much, and why? Debunking the stereotypical gamer profile. *Journal of Computer-Mediated Communication, 13*, 993–1018. doi:10.1111/j.1083-6101.2008.00428.x

Williams, R. (1961). *Long revolutions*. London: Penguin.

Williams, R. (1976). *Keywords: a vocabulary of culture and society*. Glasgow, UK: Fontana.

Wilska, T. A. (2003). Mobile phone use as part of young people's consumption styles. *Journal of Consumer Policy, 26*, 441–463. doi:10.1023/A:1026331016172

Wolak, J., Mitchell, K. J., & Finkelhor, D. (2003). Escaping or connecting? Characteristics of youth who form close online relationships. *Journal of Adolescence, 26*, 105–119. doi:10.1016/S0140-1971(02)00114-8

Wood, R. T. A., Griffiths, M. D., Chappell, D., & Davies, M. N. O. (2004). The structural characteristics of video games: a psycho-structural analysis. *Cyberpsychology & Behavior, 7*(1), 1–10. doi:10.1089/109493104322820057

Wright, P., Friestad, M., & Boush, D. M. (2005). The development of marketplace persuasion knowledge in children, adolescents, and young adults. *Journal of Public Policy & Marketing, 24*(2), 222–233. doi:10.1509/jppm.2005.24.2.222

Wrong, D. (1961). The oversocialized concept of main in modern sociology. *American Sociological Review*, 26.

Yee, N. (2007). Motivations to play online. *Cyberpsychology & Behavior, 9*(6), 772–775. doi:10.1089/cpb.2006.9.772

Youn, S. (2008). Family communication influences on teens' online consumer socialization. In, *Child and Teen Consumption 2008 Conference*, Trondheim, Norway.

Young, K. S. (2001). *Caught in the net: how to recognize the signs of Internet addiction and winning a strategy recover., NY*. New York: Wiley.

Zhao, S., Grasmuck, S., & Martin, J. (2008). Identity construction on Facebook - Digital empowerment in anchored relationships. *Computers in Human Behavior, 24*, 1816–1836. doi:10.1016/j.chb.2008.02.012

Chapter 20
Consumption and Marketing in A 3D Virtual Space:
The Second Life Experience

Gülnur Tumbat
San Francisco State University, USA

Lisa Bennett
San Francisco State University, USA

ABSTRACT

Second Life (SL) established itself in 2003 as a virtual world where people can create an alternate life as an avatar (www.secondlife.com). It provides a fertile ground for real-world businesses to market their products to a tech-savvy and brand-conscious group of potential consumers. The goal of this exploratory chapter is to gain an understanding about the SL experience for these consumers and provide examples of some of the marketing practices. The authors conclude that while SL does provide an alternative for businesses for building, maintaining, and extending their real world brand presence, it remains primarily as a 3-dimension (3-D) virtual social space for people to connect and communicate with like-minded others.

SECOND LIFE AS A COMMERCIAL SPACE

Users of SL are free to make their *second life* whatever they want it to be and the only real limitation is their creativity. As residents in SL, avatars can own homes, lead a life of luxury and even pick and choose what they want their physical features to look like. The term avatar refers to the users' virtually constructed onscreen graphic characters. Some tech-savvy users can learn how to build their own items in SL or trade goods with other users. Others may opt to purchase real world brands using the SL currency, Linden dollars, which can be exchanged for real-world currency through the exchange service provided by Linden Labs, the creators of SL. The exchange rate offered for Linden dollars allows SL to hover on the cusp between the virtual and real worlds. News agencies like Reuters are taking this new economy seriously and have created an in-world news center (http://reuters.secondlife.com) to "contribute objective financial news and data to help a growing economy, and to experiment with

DOI: 10.4018/978-1-60566-792-8.ch020

an important new medium" (Harris, 2007, p.1). SL's currency exchange puts real-world monetary value on user-created virtual products that may or may not exist in the real world. In fact, SL introduces a whole new twist to lifestyle marketing.

According to the constantly updated statistics on the SL website (http://blog.secondlife.com), as of January 2008, the population of SL is more than 12 million. The majority of the (active) residents (38%) are from the US although there are inhabitants from more then a hundred other countries. Among these avatars, 41% of them are female and 59% male. The total number of hours spent online has increased drastically since SL's introduction in 2003. These inhabitants spend a good portion of their day in SL (more than 20 hours a week). Furthermore, Table 1 shows the numbers and distribution of active users by age in January 2008. The average resident is 33 years old. Big crowds in SL also result in increasing money exchanges. Accordingly, Lindex virtual currency exchange has reached $744,564.

According to a non-profit Dutch think-tank EPN, the possibility of earning money is not the main motivation for the majority of inhabitants although remains as a motive for some (de Nood and Attema, 2006). EPN found that the main motivations to enter into SL are to have fun, to make friends, or to experience things which are difficult or impossible in real life (de Nood and Attema, 2006).

Table 1. Monthly active users by age category for January 2008 (Source: http://blog.secondlife.com)

Age	%Avatar Count	Total Hours	%Total Hours
13-17 (Teen Grid)	0.96%	129,992.02	0.46%
18-24	24.50%	4,559,714.15	16.20%
25-34	35.43%	9,735,769.83	34.59%
35-44	23.35%	7,915,295.92	28.12%
45 plus	15.25%	5,676,036.23	20.17%
Unknown	0.51%	126,910.58	0.45%
		Total: 28,143,718.73	

Not only consumers, but also companies, various organizations, and even government institutions started to show great interest in this alternative public space. Starbucks has coffee stores, Swedish Embassy has a branch, Harvard University offers lessons, and numerous brands are part of the virtual malls of SL. Since SL is a virtual reality, its residents can create whatever lifestyle they want to experience–this can serve huge advantage to clever marketers who are able to unwrap the desires, feelings, and imagery that might be motivating this new breed of consumers, often referred to as "Consumer 2.0." However, these clever marketers might be surprised to find that their new breed of consumers isn't so new after all. They are the same consumers that existed before SL; this space is just a new medium with which to connect to them. In other words, SL communities are "formed primarily around personal interests and activities" and "for this reason, the best entry point for outside companies is often through brands and products that already attract Second Life users" (Au 2008, p.1).

It may be true that real-world brand and product preferences carry over into SL, but it does not reveal much about *which* brands and products are associated with the different in-world communities or *how* these brands and products are being consumed in the virtual space. After all, SL has been around for about five years and has received mixed reviews on the potential opportunities it offers to the real world. After a rush to the virtual world of Second Life, marketers followed the crowd without knowing what to do when they arrived (von Hoffman, 2007). Unable to experience the visibility and strategic benefits they had originally hoped for, many have since shutdown or abandoned their in-world efforts.

However, there are still some who have not counted the virtual space out as a potential marketing channel. In fact, Mark Kingdon (former

CEO of Organic Omnicom), recently took over the Linden Labs. He believes that "despite the fact that Madison Avenue went and left, Second Life is thriving" because "it is the only social media property where the business model is central to the user experience" (Hansell, 2008, p. 5). This might mean those who attempted to advertise and market within SL without understanding the dynamics of this space may have failed because they did not consider the nuances of the virtual world platform and how it is held together by its communities of consumers. Are users interested in the same products, services, and experiences in the virtual world as they are in the real world? Should companies consider SL as a new marketing channel and platform through which they can increase their market share and brand awareness? In order to answer these questions and more, companies should evaluate SL with the same discipline they use when considering any other integrated marketing communications tool to understand whether or not their target audience is represented and within reach.

STARTING A SECOND LIFE

An exploratory virtual ethnography can help companies understand consumption and marketing dynamics in this virtual environment. Observational data can be collected using a cyberethnographic (Sayre, 2001) or netnographic (Kozinets, 2002) approach to gain an understanding of the research field and to identify and analyze business practices and community dynamics in SL. Netnography is an adaptation of ethnographic methods used in cultural anthropology applied to the study of online and cyberspace communities (Kozinets 1997, 1998, 2002; Nelson and Otnes, 2005).

As part of our own efforts to understand the opportunities SL has to offer, we, the authors, created online characters (avatars) and stepped into SL. We spent considerable time in SL observing and recording interactions among other avatars, capturing personal experiences, and noting the practices of companies with virtual branches within the SL community. In order to embed ourselves in this virtual world and its cyberculture, our avatars moved through SL first as residents and then as the owners of an in-world market research firm within this virtual community. With the latter, we aimed to attract SL avatars and to understand their perspectives on the SL experience. We also actively followed the blogs of the SL residents. By living in and interacting with the community, we were able to make observations in order to learn more about in-world and real world consumption practices. We wanted to understand and explore marketing opportunities in SL and if so, how marketers can improve their efforts to reach this unique virtual audience.

In the next section, we will provide an overview of the SL experience. Then we will describe avatar experiences in this virtual world and provide examples of business practices that are uniquely relevant to the SL environment followed by their implications on marketing and consumption.

THE SECOND LIFE ENVIRONMENT

The first challenge for businesses considering entry into SL is to identify how they will utilize the platform. Potential uses include provision of meeting places, e-commerce, advertising, and product and brand placement. A company may also aim simply to build organizational experience that will help them determine the best way to connect with consumers via this new medium.

After registering for a free account at the website, users choose their avatar's name and download the free program to their computer. This program is very robust and as such, requires a considerable amount of memory and a strong graphics card in order to run properly. In fact, the cost of the required needed hardware might dissuade some consumers from downloading and running the program. Marketers should be aware of how the program's technical constraints might shape user characteristics within the virtual space. From the outset, marketers might assume the users have fairly current computer systems and are willing to commit a good portion of their system's memory to using SL.

SL is a dynamic and a changing world where users literally build the space as they go. Although the virtual world's appearance and concept is similar to a massive multi-player online role-playing game (MMORPG), it should not be mistaken for one. Actually, it would be too much of a stretch to call what is going on in Second Life as a game. Researchers have noted that SL players tend to use the world more as an elaborately designed chat room (Townsend, 2008, p.28). However, the rich graphics that bring the world to life require robust computer systems, similar to those required for MMORPG gaming environments. This makes it easier and more likely for "gamers," who already have their computers set-up to SL specifications, to join. Given that they are also already familiar with what to expect from a virtual environment, gamers are likely to make the shift to SL and could make up a substantial group for marketers to consider. It is important to note that for the users who typically have their computer for day-to-day Internet browsing and word processing, joining the SL community might not come so easily.

User Interface

SL residents can and does create a world that mimics their "first" life–the real world. Running streams are accompanied by the sounds of rushing fresh water, and birds chirping; squirrels even run through parks unannounced. Anything is possible in this world; the only major limitation is the user's own technical skills. However, once in SL, users may struggle to navigate through the virtual environment (beyond using basic arrow strokes) and may require additional instructions. For example, users might not initially be aware that they can choose to explore the world through their avatar's eyes or from a more voyeuristic perspective by placing the camera view directly behind their avatar. Instead, they might stumble around at first until they discover the camera angle feature. This is just one example of some of the navigation issues that Claus Nehmzow, a noted virtual world consultant, might have been referring to as "some of the nitty-gritty idiosyncratic details of SL we have to overlook to some degree because it's not as good as it could be" (Donahue 2007, p. 10). Although the user interface offers plenty of menu options, most are technically sophisticated, with names that are not intuitive, like "recompile scripts in selection" and "show HUD attachments" (see Figure 1).

Figure 1. User interface with sophisticated menu options

While these cues might make more sense after a visit to the help menu or an online message board, new users may find it difficult to fully understand what to do and how to manipulate the display. The user interface could be a hurdle that companies (and SL itself) will need to address in order to keep their virtual doors open for business. Consumers who are uncomfortable with the interface or cannot customize it to add value to their experience might become disinterested, representing a lost opportunity for SL and its marketers.

Orientation and Help Islands

Linden Labs seems to be aware of the difficulties new users face and has crafted a solution for them. The company requires all new avatars to visit "Orientation Island" when they connect to SL for the first time. The island provides several stations for avatars to learn how to perform tasks like picking up items, chatting, and changing their appearance. The island is also a good place to meet other new users. Although helpful, visiting the island can be time-consuming and new users should expect to spend considerable time visiting the required learning stations before being allowed to dive into their own SL experience. Although it is a helpful feature; however, SL allows users to visit the island only once. The reason for this rule is unclear; perhaps the rule is in place to encourage users to reach out to the SL community to ask for help or to minimize traffic volume on the island. Luckily, there are several Help Islands residents can visit as much as they want after they've left the safety of Orientation Island. The Help Island is a great resource for new SL residents because they have access to self-appointed SL mentors. These mentors are simply other avatars who make themselves available to newer or less knowledgeable residents in order to welcome them and serve as a resource for essentially anything they might need in-world. The island is also a helpful place to visit if residents need a "refresher course" for getting around SL.

Communities

The amount and variety of communities available for residents to explore are endless. If they are not able to find something they are interested in, they can create a forum and build whatever it is they want. Within these communities, there are some accepted and implied standards of behavior set by their members. In fact, some communities are private and access can be denied by red and transparent walls that say "Do Not Enter." Some in-world homeowners put this type of security system around the homes they've created so others do not have access to their land.

There are plenty of virtual public places to explore–many of which resemble their real world counterparts. For example, there are clubs, beaches, and shopping malls, each with different themes and personalities. The rules of each community are usually posted as reminders, but even if they aren't, the avatars will politely remind people who are breaking the rules to abide or leave. These in-world communities are similar to those of chat rooms and the same type of rules and behaviors are expected. Annoying advertisers, obscenities, and hateful subject matter are typically not acceptable in these communities, just as they are not usually welcome in chat rooms. SL very much operates like a 3-D chat room and residents can expect the conduct within such communities to be consistent with what they are used to experiencing in regular online chat rooms.

However, one area within SL is very different from anything found in an online chat room. These are "sandboxes," or creative spaces where avatars can go to practice building objects, such as homes, boats, vending machines, and shoes (see Figure 2). The sandboxes offer an open building space to meet other avatars and learn the skill that is most valued within this virtual world–building. Building is a useful skill in SL because it allows avatars to contribute to the creation of the surrounding virtual world. Avatars that can build can usually sell their goods to other avatars that lack building skills. Given the importance of building within SL, the sandboxes serve as one of the most important places within the virtual world. Even if a resident cannot build or is not interested in building anything, he or she can go to the sandboxes to meet people and get help with acquiring or developing almost any item. Sandboxes serve as one of the main hubs of SL and it is no surprise in-world advertisers and freelance builders have caught on and have begun to place billboards in them.

THE SECOND LIFE EXPERIENCE

To get a true sense of the SL experience and how it might apply to a company's specific use of the tool, marketers might try forming their experience within this virtual world around the target consumer they seek to understand. Our observations and conversations with other avatars within SL provided insight into understanding the potential this platform can have for both consumers and marketers. For example, one of our avatars was named "Michelle." Michelle was attractive, down to earth, and approachable. She wore jeans and a simple black top. Michelle had brown hair and brown eyes and appeared to be in her 20s. Michelle was a regular resident in SL, who was interested in shopping, meeting people in the different social venues, and exploring everything the virtual world had to offer. Michelle also identified herself as a graduate student interested in consumer behavior and business practices within SL while interviewing other avatars to get a sense of their virtual consumer experiences. Avatars were generally accepting and for the most part helpful in showing her around and even bringing her with them to different in-world events.

Companies can rest easier knowing that beyond socializing, avatars are also heavily involved in shopping. Similar to the real world, SL has both malls and stand-alone stores. To find out what kinds of products are available in SL, users can search for malls and explore several different places. However, one major difference that is noticeable right away is that unlike real malls, SL's shopping areas are lacking a major component: people.

There are several possible explanations for the lack of "visible" consumers. First, purchases are made by pointing at a desired product and then by clicking the "buy" prompt. It's a fairly easy and quick process that does not require a long physical presence in commercial areas. The ease of the process also benefits those who wish to sell products–simply develop a script for the item and post a picture of it for customers to click on. A second possible reason for the lack of customer volume is the sheer quantity of malls and places to purchase goods. This also makes it difficult for users to identify the best places to purchase specific items. Searches conducted with the SL user interface pull up the most popular places that

Figure 2. Advertising at SL sandboxes

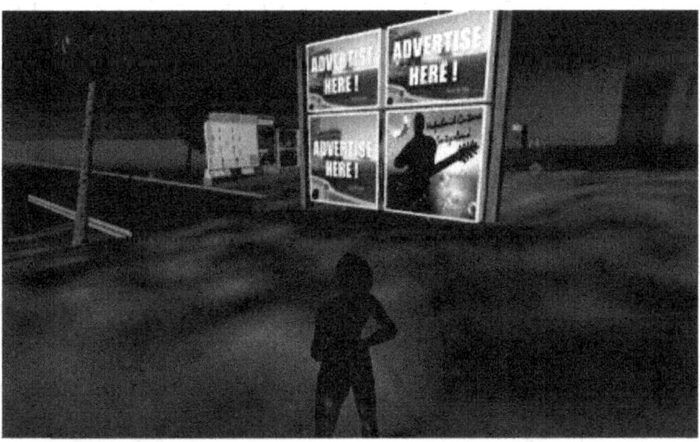

match the search, based on reported traffic. If there is no traffic in a particular shopping area, it will rank very low on the search list, regardless of the quality of the stores, and decrease the number of new visitors. Simply put, businesses need people in order to bring in more people (Surowiecki, 2005). Lastly, many people purchase items, like sandboxes, from friends or people they meet in SL. Most people still use SL primarily as a social networking tool and either visit stores recommended by their SL friends or buy directly from the people they meet. Rather than congregating in malls, people frequent other popular social areas within SL–bars, dance clubs, public courtyards, help islands, and beaches.

ESTABLISHING A BUSINESS IN SECOND LIFE

The consumer experience in a virtual world is much different compared to the kind of market implications businesses might face. Although the motivations and desires between the two experiences might be mutually aligned, it is important to recognize the unique challenges businesses face in this virtual environment in terms of their consumer base.

To get a sense of the types of challenges businesses face in-world and to embed ourselves in our field site more, we established a virtual market research firm. First, we started thinking about what kind of image we wanted our company to have in SL. We wanted our market research firm to be professional, accessible, and comfortable for visitors; not stiff and corporate. We started exploring business districts to see if we could find suitable office space, but we didn't see anything that we believed would get traffic. We considered that if we were in a standard office building, passersby would not be able to see our office from the street; they would have to enter the building first. Instead, we decided we wanted to lease office space in an upscale, trendy area surrounded by boutique shops with retail storefronts. Although it was not our intent to sell anything, we wanted to establish a corporate presence as much as possible.

Unsure of how to find a space that matched our preferences, we began speaking with people in the malls we were visiting and asking them if they knew of such a place in SL. People were more than willing to help us. It seemed as if the avatars in SL were always available and approachable. We had the sense they were roaming around SL because they really didn't have anything else to do–almost as if they were so bored, they were happy to be tasked with helping us set-up our market research office and were proud to give referrals to their friends who are in-world real estate agents and developers.

We kept our office design simple and only put up a sign that said "Participate in Market Research." During the one month we were there, we rarely saw any other avatars in the mall vicinity and when we asked people we met in other places to stop by or join us at our place of business, the common response was a lack of interest in leaving their friends where they were already hanging out, especially because they were unfamiliar with where our office was located.

When considering a presence in SL, it is important for businesses to recognize a point they often take into consideration in the real world: Location is still a priority for success. However, in SL, the best place for businesses to have a presence is wherever their target consumers spend most of their time. In other words, to succeed in SL, businesses need to go out of their way to bring their products or services directly to their consumers. That's the focus of the next section.

LOCATING VIRTUAL CONSUMERS

As a pure function of its existence, SL's landscape is constantly changing. This isn't much unlike the environment businesses encounter in the real world, but it certainly does offer unique challenges to companies trying to identify and collect research about their consumers in SL. Our own efforts to obtain a variety of consumer perspectives within the virtual world brought us to several different places in search of avatars willing to have a conversation about their life and consumption practices in SL. The examples below represent the diverse range of consumers that can be found in SL. Avatar names have been removed to maintain privacy.

Avatar A: Splurger in SL

Whether it's a virtual campus or a meeting place for online courses, universities have a strong presence within SL. Similar to the real world, we can rely on these institutions and the communities they support for uninhibited interest and participation in consumer research. Finding the virtual university communities in SL is as easy as conducting a quick in-world search for the keyword "university."

Our search brought us to the Princeton University SL campus. The campus was welcoming and had an immediate sense of an old ivy-league university. We were impressed by how the builders were able to convey the prestige and tradition that Princeton's real campus has to the virtual space. There were even squirrels snacking on nuts on the virtual grass lawn. We found it interesting that our real world imagery of the school matched what we saw as we moved through the SL campus.

While exploring the campus, we met a 45-year-old male from Arizona. In the real world, he is an Instructional Technology Specialist for a community college. He shared that he was in SL to research how he could get his school involved with in-world classroom instruction. He currently teaches classes online and is involved in distance education as an instructor, so he is looking into the possibility of creating virtual classrooms that can help to engage his distance learners more by having them participate in a classroom setting.

He is very active in SL for his work and has in-world friends who are also technology instructors. Beyond education, he and his friends call themselves "techies" and they enjoy hanging out in SL, because they live far away in real life. They meet in SL to teach each other how to build things and they also enjoy chatting over beers at virtual pubs. Sometimes, he said, they go to dance clubs for a "guys' night out" and will try to meet women on SL, even though he is married with a family in real life.

To prepare for these dance nights, they purchase dance animations, clothing, shoes, and hairstyles on a fairly regular basis. Rather than going to the virtual mall or stand-alone stores, he gets almost everything he buys from his friends or their friends. He likes to stay within his network because he knows he can trust the script and he knows he can get items for free or at a very low cost. If he does go to stores, he was proud to share that he is very loyal and will only go to stores that sponsor the in-world classes he participates in when he does choose to spend money in SL. He attends free SL technology classes on a regular basis and wishes to support their continued sponsorship.

Compared to the real world, he considers himself someone who allows his avatar to splurge. In real life, he rarely purchases new shoes or clothing and doesn't get expensive haircuts. However, in SL, because the prices are so cheap and things are so easy to build or find for free, he finds that he really enjoys being fashionable because he can afford to do so, whereas in the real world, he considers himself to be a "penny pincher."

He has also participated on the business side of SL by building furniture and selling it to other avatars. It's an enjoyable hobby for him, so after hearing from avatars in the sandboxes liked his work, he decided he would sell it for a small fee. His intent was to make money he could use for purchasing the fun items, like clothes, that he likes to buy. He indicated that most of his business and learning transactions take place in the sandboxes. Avatar A's consumer behavior in SL is different from his real-world consumption because he feels he can afford to do more in the virtual world. This consumer example demonstrates how SL offers people more than the pure value of the product. Consumers are also gleaning satisfaction from being involved in their experience by receiving notoriety from other consumers for the items they can build and sell. Furthermore, compared to the real world, these types of consumers believe they have much more buying power to essentially live what they consider to be a comfortable second life.

Avatar B: The Entrepreneur

Another type of consumer thriving in SL is a testament to the old adage, "build your own destiny." Quite literally, these consumers are creating a satisfying virtual experience by building SL. They are the consumers who are technically savvy and interested in using the virtual world as a place to fine tune their programming skills and make a profit while doing it. We met one such individual on one of our visits to the public sandboxes where we found her practicing building large, colorful objects and transforming them into different shapes. We soon learned that in real life, she is an older female, over 50, living in Central Canada. Along with her partner, she owns a business that develops SL experiences for companies trying to make a presence in SL. She is also a professor at a university and is in the process of implementing SL at her school.

She typically buys clothes, shoes, furniture, building supplies and textures in SL. She enjoys buying expensive brand names for her shoes because she never buys them in real life. However, for her clothing and furniture, she tries to buy the same styles in-world that she buys in real-life because she enjoys them and finds her taste to be consistent. She doesn't think of her virtual experience as a place where she can be someone else, but rather, she sees it as her extended self (Belk, 1988). Our observation from interacting with her is that her real life is so embedded in SL, the two worlds have in fact become blended for her, which has allowed her to maintain consistent consumption choices in both worlds.

Since she enjoys the same brands in-world as she does in the real world, we asked her whether or not she's able to find all of the same brands in here that she can in real life. For the most part, whether the places are legitimate or not (*i.e.,* if it's the real business or a SL posing as the real business), she has been able to find the same brands. She thinks it's great because the brand name represents quality to her, so she likes her avatar to stick to the same quality that she enjoys in real life. She mentioned the only negative thing she's seen from real-life stores coming to SL is that their "sims" (stores) remain empty and without any traffic–not even employees nor service customers present.

Overwhelmingly, the lack of personal presence by companies is the most common criticism of SL. In fact, more than 70 percent of SL residents are disappointed in the presence that marketers have established in SL and they view that presence as simple "extensions of existing, traditional advertising efforts and not something that taps into the world's unique power" (von Hoffman, 2007, p.1). The SL entrepreneur's insight on why she believes traditional advertising can't work in SL is due to the social aspect of the community within the SL platform. People do not want to leave their friends and go outside of their community to learn about a new product, they want to be able to interact with the product and integrate it into their communities. Her perception was consistent with what we found in our own experience and the experiences of the other avatars we met in SL.

Her experience with the virtual event hosted by a building company was positive because the builder was able to target a network of avatars that are connected by their mutual interests in construction and owning virtual real estate. This type of consumer experience reinforces how important it is in SL for businesses to bring their brand, their products, and their reputation directly to their target market and how doing so can connect them to entire networks of users via the community's primary virtual space.

Avatars C and D: A Virtual Valentine and A Virtual Bride

In addition to shopping, romance is another motivator for people to become involved with the virtual world. Although online romance is not unique to virtual reality, the ability to bring a 3-D experience to these relationships does provide those with an SL romance an added sense of reality. For businesses that profit from supporting romance, this means there's plenty of opportunity within the virtual world.

We spoke with avatars who purchased or received extravagant luxury items from their in-world significant others. The luxury items they referred to were consistent with the typical courting artifacts that are exchanged in the real world. A particular consumer, Avatar C, noted he has both a first life girlfriend and a SL girlfriend, but only receives jewelry from his SL partner.

Just as in the real-world, people exchange expensive gifts in SL to impress a potential mate (Sherry, 1983). However, SL allows most avatars access to a luxurious lifestyle they are not able to afford in the real world. Most of the people we spoke with mentioned they would never be able to give these expensive gifts in real life and said it felt good to be able to live the "good life" in SL and see what it's like to be seen as a successful, wealthy individual. Courting rituals from the real world crossed over and maintained their place SL relationships. So, it would seem the virtual world provided these users with a real-world sense of satisfaction and accomplishment in being able to provide for their partners. Marketers should pay attention to a consumer reaction this strong.

One visit to any mall within SL and users will notice just how heavily romance is being marketed to consumers. Bridal gowns, honeymoons, event coordinators–everything an avatar would need to get married is just one click away. One such example is of an 18-year-old woman from Sweden, Avatar D. We met her in a jewelry store looking at wedding bands in one of the popular malls in SL. We soon found out she was finalizing the last minute to-do items on her list in preparation for her virtual wedding, which was to occur at the end of that week.

To our surprise, she and her real-life fiancé met in SL and were now living together. Because their shared network of friends were for the most part online, they wanted to share their special day with their SL life friends before tying the knot in real life. They also saw SL as an opportunity to see what it would be like to be virtually married before making it official in real life. She shared that because both she and her fiancé had committed so much of their time and life to the community within SL, they almost held more value in the virtual nuptials than they expected to hold to the real-life nuptials. There was also a sense of commitment they felt to the network of friends they had established together online to bring their relationship to the next level in-world.

Although the cost of her virtual wedding was far less than she was planning to spend in real life, she still felt she was trying to stay within a set budget while planning the wedding of her dreams. She booked caterers, a venue, a DJ, and was planning on wearing the dress of a lifetime that she was having built by an in-world designer. She considered every detail one would arrange for a real-life wedding during her virtual "big day," even the same level of stress. Although she was trying to stay within a set budget, she shared that if it came down to getting something she likes and staying within her budget, she would get what she wants.

Romance is a major component of life in SL, where "reality and unreality brush up against one another uncomfortably" and even though "the site essentially revolves around users adopting an identity and an avatar that may, or may not, bear some relationship to who they are in real life" (Stanage, 2007, p.1; see also Schau and Gilly,

2003), one thing seems to be true–consumption is as much a part of online courtship as it is offline.

ADVERTISING PRACTICES

The presence of advertising billboards and note card spamming is common in SL. Land owners are free to ban such activities, but in order to lease space and make the most of the land they have, most owners allow advertisements. Still, a lot of ad spaces are unsold (see Figure 3). We asked a few business owners why they thought this was the case. For the most part, business owners do not spend money on renting ad space because they do not believe enough traffic pays attention to the ads.

According to one informant we spoke with, Avatar E, the business owners are right. In-world consumers do not want to have to stop what they're doing in order to pay attention to advertisements. The dilemma is two-pronged. First, walking or flying by a billboard keeps the consumer mobile and they're likely to ignore the ad if it is non- engaging. Second, if the billboard ad is engaging, it will likely have a link that teleports the avatar to the advertiser's location. Avatar E indicated his dislike of these links because, teleporting away from his location distracts him from what he was doing.

Figure 3. Unused advertising space in SL

Avatar E's story is consistent with a lot of criticism surrounding SL. Residents want to be engaged, but they do not want to be taken away from what they're doing in their preferred community in order to view a marketing campaign. They would rather stay with their SL life friends and learn from other people about the products and services they are using than to venture out on their own.

Business owners reported the same phenomenon indicated by Avatar E. Most of their business comes from word-of-mouth referrals from their friends. Some of them have friends who are SL mentors and have passed along their names to the new users that come to the mentors for help as they try to set up their SL avatar, home, or business.

Again, this follows the trend that social networking is the driving force behind how business is conducted in SL.

One intriguing finding is that real-life businesses may benefit from virtual brand loyalty without even realizing it. In most dance clubs, malls, and pubs within SL, avatars are regularly exposed to real world brand names and products (see Figure 4). In some cases, companies have paid to place their products in SL, but more frequently, SL users who are fans of particular products, like Guinness and Abercrombie and Fitch, have incorporated brand images into their virtual space. Some businesses have raised legal issues with these practices because they have not given explicit permission for their brand images to be reproduced in SL, but it does stand to reason that the companies might be

gaining brand awareness within these pockets of the virtual world without a single penny of investment. On the other hand, companies like Ben and Jerry's and Reuters have invested considerable assets into their SL Sims, and because they have not found a way to bring their product into the SL communities, it is unlikely they are increasing their brand awareness. Again, the best way to connect with the SL community is to inject products and services into the communities, rather than build a highly sophisticated virtual space that fails because it does not receive any traffic. Once access to brands is made easier, then people enact relationships with brands (Fournier, 1998) through their avatars since becoming a resident of SL is a heavily consumption oriented phenomenon.

EXAMPLES OF SOME COMPANIES IN SL

American Apparel

While exploring SL, we were continually told how popular American Apparel's SL presence once was in the virtual world. When we tried to go check out the store, the doors were locked. It's not clear why it failed, but it is temporarily shut down. We found a link that took us to a website with the following information:

"Needless to say, it's been quite a year. We've had thousands of visitors from all over the world and made a ton of new friends, seen some interesting things from furry folks to virtual terrorism, caused a bit of a clamor, and sold some virtual t-shirts and it's been great. But we feel like our time is up here. So we're closing our doors on Lerappa Island for now. This doesn't mean we're finished with the virtual world. Stay tuned to see what we do next."

BMW

We did not find a lot of interest or interaction on the BMW island. The island's theme was "clean energy," and in support of this, BMW had posted information about sustainable energy in addition to creating a futuristic design. They have built a theatre where avatars can sit, but there is nothing to watch–the view is simply two clean energy cars, which avatars can also sit in. The island is at least maintained; when we visited it had an advertisement (in March 2008) mentioning that BMW will be at the Geneva International Motor Show. Nonetheless, the site seems to have been abandoned, as there are no visitors, no upcoming events, and nothing to become involved with.

Figure 4. A non-affiliated pub proudly displaying the Guinness logo

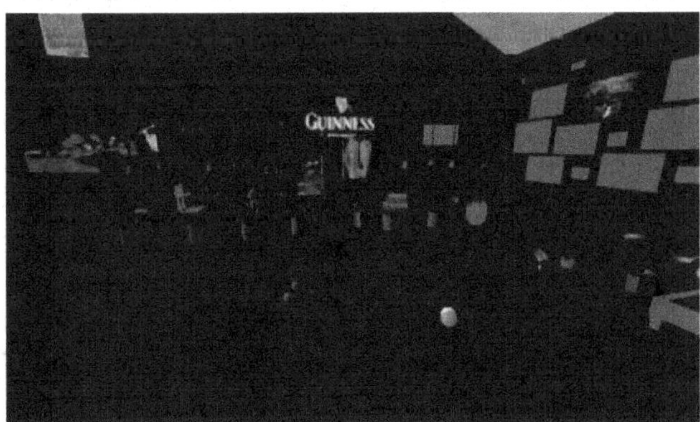

Cisco

When we visited Cisco's Island, there were no avatars present. A "Cisco home" shows how all of Cisco's products can be used in a personal residence and prompts invite users to explore each room. Every mouse click opens a link to Cisco's web page. There isn't much interaction–most of it is like a museum in that you can look but can't really touch. The site appears to be deserted and doesn't seem up to date. There's a sign advertising their "Connected Life Contest" but it's dated October 30, 2007 (about two years old).

Dell

The computer company Dell created a fairly complex island featuring places of interest such as the Dell Museum, Michael Dell's dorm room (most likely modeled after the company's original headquarters), a travel center, and city corridors available for avatars to explore. The company clearly attempted to create an "experience" as it is designed to be somewhat of an attraction–complete with souvenir and coffee shops to relax in after looking around. It seems as though Dell is struggling to attract visitors to its island, however, since there were no avatars present when we visited. Part of the problem is that although the island features areas to explore, it still does not offer much interaction with the consumer. There were few items to click on and not much direction to guide the user through the island. The items we found that were clickable teleported us to different areas of the island. We quickly became lost and couldn't find our way back. As a result, we were forced to teleport back to Dell's entry point landmark just to start over–a frustrating experience that does not encourage visitors to stay. There were no signs of any recent activity, which led us to believe the company is not actively using the island anymore. Like an abandoned ghost town, no events or activities were posted and nothing connects consumers to the Dell products.

Microsoft

Although one might assume a computer company would be more in tune with the virtual consumer, Microsoft's island was empty and unimpressive. Like most of the other commercial sites we visited, the island had no avatar traffic, no current events posted, and very little connection offered to the consumer.

Geek Squad

Among all these high-tech companies, only Geek Squad had an active presence. Geek Squad had an online avatar that was solely responsible for the company in SL. He told us he has 10-20 avatar customers per day. Geek Squad believes their approach provides more interaction, which they believe has been successful. They are planning to provide training seminars in SL, in which they believe they have a chance to network with people all around the world. They believe that they have to be an active community participant to survive long term in SL. The Geek Squad avatar explained the company's view that "developments that are well under way will make this a suitable business platform over the next few years." The avatar told us about the importance of getting a feel for what people in SL want. He says that lack of research is one of the most important reasons why businesses just dive in and fail shortly afterwards in SL. "Most people who've been in SL as long as I have tend to have a strong sense of community," he said, emphasizing the importance of the community dynamics.

Domino's Pizza

Domino's Pizza announced it would implement a long-term strategy to use SL as a platform to reach its 18-35 year old target audience by "opening multiple franchises across SL and increasing its online branding presence" by offering "money-off codes and coupons through its Second Life stores, to be redeemed online and in-store" according to Marketing Week (October 2007, p. 14). We did a quick search to find its in-world franchises, with hopes of stopping by to see how its long-term strategy for virtual expansion is coming along. Unfortunately, we were only able to find one franchise in-world and as we half expected, it was completely empty. The in-world store offers very little interaction with avatars. It resembles its real-world storefronts and once inside, there are only two things for avatars to do: click on the pizza to get a free SL pizza that goes straight into the avatar's inventory (no customization of toppings or size) or click on the link to the Domino's website to place an online order for a real pizza. Domino's likely halted the long-term strategy it announced in October due to lackluster results from its in-world store. The company failed to recognize that real-world marketing strategies and business models can't be implemented in the exact same way in SL. Their fizzled in-world franchise strategy is another example of why marketers need to involve the audience to create a quality experience and develop imaginative ways to drive traffic, increase interaction and provide fresh, regularly updated content in order to integrate their consumers' experiences in both the real and virtual worlds.

SECOND CHANCE IN SECOND LIFE

The initial rush to SL was led by innovators and early-adopter marketers who were anxious to establish a presence in the virtual world. In their haste to gain visibility within this new platform, they may have made some assumptions about how their business would achieve success within virtual reality (Laroche, Yang, McDougall, and Bergeron, 2005). Many seem to have quite literally taken the name "Second Life" to heart and simply replicated what they knew was successful in the real world to their efforts in the virtual world. However, as we've observed, many of these companies struggled to recognize one very important fact about SL: It's not for everyone.

Out of the seven companies we discussed earlier, what was Geek Squad able to identify about SL as a business platform that large, high-tech companies like Cisco, Microsoft, and Dell missed? Rather than jumping into SL with the intention of replicating their real-world marketing plan or setting up a virtual storefront, Geek Squad invested time into researching the virtual space in order to gain a better understanding of how SL could add value to their business. Based on their research, they created a virtual space where there is always a company representative in-world who attends community events and serves as a resource to those who need help navigating SL. They learned that SL was driven by (1) community, and (2) interaction, and (3) involvement as our consumer data also suggested. Next, we will discuss these aspects as they relate to consumption.

Consumption Communities

It is well-known that alternative forms of communities such as those that are not geographically bound but rather centered around forms of consumption such as brands (Muniz and O'Guinn, 2001; Muniz and O'Guinn, 1996) have changed the marketing landscape. These take the form of brand communities, subcultures of consumption (Schouten and McAlexander, 1995; Wheaton, 2003), tribes (Cova and Cova, 2002; Maffesoli, 1996), marginal subcultures (Hebdige, 1979) and include geographically concentrated (Holt, 1995) or dispersed communities (Boorstin, 1974), which include Internet and various virtual communities (Fischer, Bristor, and Gainer, 1996; Rheingold 1993; Tambyah, 1996) and have been of interest to consumer researchers and marketers. Through this exploratory study, we add to this existing body of research that with the growth of Web 2.0 and the advent of businesses dabbling in the virtual space, there is one point that will determine a business's success in SL. That is the extent to which the company realizes SL is a social networking tool and adopts a strategy that works with users' expectations and habits. The people who live in this virtual world are first and foremost there to socialize and, are interested in maintaining their sense of connectedness within this virtual community. Even if they are moving through SL alone, they are still interested in connecting with people wherever they go to explore, build items, or meet people.

Geek Squad's story is a precise example of how research can be a competitive advantage for a company considering a presence in the virtual world. Although it serves as somewhat of a virtual role model for success in SL, the company's virtual success is relative to its intended use of the platform. The company isn't trying to make a quick profit in SL. Instead, they're building connections within communities of unique consumers, through which they rely on word-of-mouth to undoubtedly increase brand awareness and brand loyalty. They're also likely to be obtaining a great deal of direct consumer learning, which they otherwise would need to the help of a third party to collect.

Similar to our example above, other companies looking to establish a presence in SL should consider doing some baseline research of their own (see the 2008 special issue of Journal of Virtual Worlds on consumer behavior in virtual worlds). The very first question a company should investigate is whether or not their target consumers are present within the virtual world. Because SL is primarily driven by its community, it's necessary to understand if there is an established community within the world that has a consumption need the company can satisfy. Although it's exciting for marketers to create consumption needs for potential consumers by tapping into their emotions and motivations, the infinite nature of virtual reality demands that companies involve their consumers with their products or messages quickly (avatars can teleport away with a quick click) and directly.

Consumer Involvement

In addition to exploring community dynamics, understanding consumer involvement is the key (Greenwald and Leawitt, 1984; Celsi and Olson, 1998; Zaichkowsky, 1985). There are various antecedents that trigger involvement which can be personal, object-related, or situation-specific (Zaichkowsky, 1985). Consumer involvement is a motivational construct, in other words it reflects how motivated consumers are to process information. It can range form simple processing, where one considers only the basic features of a message all the way to elaboration where she links this information to her preexisting knowledge system (Greenwald and Leawitt, 1984). In our context, preexisting knowledge system may comprise real-life consumption experiences that are now carried over to SL.

When consumers are truly involved, they enter a flow state (Csikszentmihalyi, 1991). Flow is an optimal experience with characteristics such as a sense of playfulness; a feeling of being in control, concentration and highly focused attention. There are two important antecedents for flow experience to occur. One, the activity has to be challenging. Second, consumers have to have necessary skills to be able to engage in it. In other words, they must perceive a balance between their skills and the challenges of the interaction. If the activity is not sophisticated and consumer is over-skilled, s/he would be bored. In the opposite situation where the activity is super challenging and consumer has no skills at all, s/he would feel anxiety (Csikszentmihalyi, 1991). Flow is especially a useful construct in the context of SL. As Hoffman and Novak (1996) notes, in hypermedia environments such as SL, the key consequences of the flow experience for consumers are increased learning, exploratory and participatory behaviors, positive subjective experiences, and a perceived sense of control over their interactions.

Interaction

The pure basis of SL requires not only a high level of involvement and but also interaction from the consumers. One might also remember the earlier discussion about the highly technical SL user interface. These two factors can be barriers to entry for some consumers, which may indirectly create a tech-savvy consumer environment. This means the avatars within SL are likely to be comfortable with, and expect, a highly interactive experience that is closely tied to their specific desires and interests within the comforts of their own community.

Traditional communication models have long been modified to include interaction between company and consumer and also interaction among consumers. Consumers today have many more choices available to them and greater control over which messages they choose to process. Unlike most commercial virtual worlds such as World of Warcraft and EverQuest, SL is mostly user created and managed. Consumers are also becoming co-producers in the communication process (Vargo and Lusch, 2004, 2006; Arnould and Thompson, 2005). The idea of co-production is directly related to the concept of customer experience. It suggests that consumers can't be seen as passive audiences anymore. They instead need to be regarded as collaborators in co-producing the consumption and/or service experience and co-creating the value for their brands (Lusch, Vargo, and O'Brien, 2005, Bendapudi and Leone, 2003; Prahalad and Ramaswamy, 2004). Co-production of value occurs as a consequence of extending the range and depth of communicative interaction (Ballantyne and Varey 2006), in our case, into virtual worlds.

DISCUSSION

Technology and the Web 2.0 craze have quickly changed the way business is conducted across the globe. The scope of competition has long been shifted from being local or even regional, it is now global. In fact, whether a business is service-based or manufactures a physical product no longer matters–technology makes it possible for every business to compete around the world by the click of a mouse. In order to be successful, businesses not only need to be prepared to compete globally, they need to position themselves to compete in what lies beyond the global economy and understand that no matter how much technology advances, at the core of business lies the fundamental need for people to connect and socialize in order to communicate effectively. Businesses looking to be involved with SL or other 3D social spaces need to understand that even as opportunities for business grow; even as this virtual environment can be better manipulated to give real-world businesses a competitive advantage; it is still a social network at its core.

Most businesses moving to the virtual setting are interested in setting up a storefront because they see it as a cost-saving opportunity compared to the real world. All of the sales can be transacted by the point and click of the consumer 24 hours a day. Though this business model works in the online world of Amazon and eBay, it is a proven failure on SL. For success on SL, the business should consider a strategy using a customer service avatar or other features that will engage the consumers when they visit the sim or the store. Without an avatar on site, the store is less likely come up in search results, so the business will not receive any traffic. Additionally, avatars that visit stores are looking for something other than a simple business transaction. Providing customer service or some other form of interaction that taps into the visitors' SL experience will keep them from going to another competitor and will increase future business by establishing a loyalty base. Thus, to be successful in the virtual world, businesses need to have avatars present in their sims to not only generate traffic, but to service those visitors that do come.

Businesses looking to market on SL should also be prepared to go to the customers. As we found, avatars like to stay with their social group and will seldom stray to explore without their friends. Therefore, companies need to consider other ways to reach these avatars. They need to create or sponsor events that provide visibility to the consumers. Once the community becomes familiar with what the business is about or sees that the business supports an event they're interested in, they're more likely to develop an interest in the company's brand or product.

For some, understanding what SL consumers really want can be challenging for a couple reasons. First, most avatars are capable of building whatever objects they want in their world. If they don't know how to build it, they likely know someone who does or can reach out to their network to acquire what they need. Second, the virtual world makes it possible for anyone to have the life they've dreamed of living. For some, this means sitting in a lecture at the Princeton sims to feel the prestige of an Ivy League education. For others, this means owning a mansion in the clouds with plenty of waterfalls to create a zen-like escape. In SL, understanding the intangible factors that might motivate avatars' consumption is more challenging because these factors could potentially be rooted in the real world or the virtual world. Recognizing the added complexity virtual reality introduces to traditional consumer behavior models is essential to understand this new era of consumption.

Whether a company is interested in using SL for a lead generation tool, virtual retail storefront, or simply a way to generate brand presence, one thing is certain–the consumers in this virtual world exist to create (whether it be a house or an identity), explore, and most of all, socialize. Second Life is still a social network and for businesses to succeed in this virtual community, they will need to focus their communication strategies on bridging social experiences to their products and brands.

REFERENCES

Arnould, E. J., & Thompson, C. J. (2005). Consumer culture theory (CCT): Twenty years of research. *The Journal of Consumer Research*, *31*(4), 868–883. doi:10.1086/426626

Au, W. J. (2008). *Second Life marketing: Still strong*. Retrieved on 05/07/08 from http://www.businessweek.com/technology/content/may2008/tc2008054_665274.htm

Ballentyne, D., & Varey, R. J. (2006). Creating value-in-use through marketing interaction: The exchange logic of relating, communicating, and knowing. *Marketing Theory*, *6*(3), 335–348. doi:10.1177/1470593106066795

Belk, R. W. (1988). Possessions and the extended self. *The Journal of Consumer Research*, *15*(2), 135–168. doi:10.1086/209154

Bendapudi, N., & Leone, R. P. (2003). Psychological implications of customer participation in co-production. *Journal of Marketing*, *67*(1), 14–28. doi:10.1509/jmkg.67.1.14.18592

Boorstin, D. J. (1974). *The Americans: The Democratic Experience*. New York: Vintage.

Celsi, R. L., & Olson, J. C. (1988). The role of involvement in attention and comprehension processes. *The Journal of Consumer Research*, *15*(2), 210–224. doi:10.1086/209158

Cova, B., & Cova, V. (2002). Tribal marketing: The tribalisation of society and its impact on the conduct of marketing. *European Journal of Marketing*, *36*(5), 595–620. doi:10.1108/03090560210423023

de Nood, D., & Attema, J. (2006). *Second Life: The Second Life of virtual reality*. EPN Report.

Donahue, M. (2007). Setting up shop on Second Life. *Pharmaceutical Executive*, *27*(11), 8–10.

Fischer, E., Bristor, J., & Gainer, B. (1996). Creating or escaping community? An exploratory study of Internet consumers' behaviours. *Advances in Consumer Research. Association for Consumer Research (U. S.)*, *23*, 178–182.

Fournier, S. (1998). Consumers and their brands: Developing relationship theory in consumer research. *The Journal of Consumer Research*, *24*(4), 343–353. doi:10.1086/209515

Greenwald, A. G., & Leavitt, C. (1984, June). Audience involvement in advertising. *The Journal of Consumer Research*, *11*, 581–592. doi:10.1086/208994

Hansell, S. (2008). *A second leader for Second Life*. Retrieved on 05/07/08 from http://bits.blogs.nytimes.com/2008/05/05/a-second-leader-for-second-life/

Harris, P. (2007). Inside out: The realities of virtual business. *J@pan Inc.*, *74*(Nov/Dec).

Hebdige, D. (1979). *Subculture: The Meaning Of Style*. London: Routledge. doi:10.4324/9780203139943

Hoffman, D. L., & Novak, T. P. (1996). Marketing in hypermedia computer-mediated environments: Conceptual foundations. *Journal of Marketing*, *60*(3), 50–69. doi:10.2307/1251841

Holt, D. B. (1995). How consumers consume: A typology of consumption practices. *The Journal of Consumer Research*, *22*(1), 1–25. doi:10.1086/209431

Journal of Virtual Worlds. (2008). *Consumer Behavior in Virtual Worlds*. Special Issue, 1(November). (http://www.jvwr.com).

Kozinets, R. V. (1999). E-Tribalized marketing? The strategic implications of virtual communities of consumption. *European Management Journal*, *17*(3), 252–264. doi:10.1016/S0263-2373(99)00004-3

Kozinets, R. V. (2002). The field behind the screen: Using netnography for marketing research in online communities. *JMR, Journal of Marketing Research*, *39*(1), 61–72. doi:10.1509/jmkr.39.1.61.18935

Laroche, M., Yang, Z., McDougall, G. H. G., & Bergeron, J. (2005). Internet versus bricks-and-mortar retailers: An investigation into intangibility and its consequences. *Journal of Retailing*, *81*(4), 251–267. doi:10.1016/j.jretai.2004.11.002

Lusch, R. F., Vargo, S. L., & O'Brien, M. (2007). Competing through service: insights from service-dominant logic. *Journal of Retailing*, *83*(1), 5–18. doi:10.1016/j.jretai.2006.10.002

Maffesoli, M. (1996). *The Time of the Tribes: The Decline of Individualism in Mass Society*. London: Sage.

Muniz, A., & O'Guinn, T. (1996). Brand community and the sociology of brands. In Corfman, K. P., & Lynch, J. G. (Eds.), *Advances in Consumer Research*. Provo, UT: Association For Consumer Research.

Muniz, A., & O'Guinn, T. (2001). Brand communities. *The Journal of Consumer Research*, *27*(4), 412–432. doi:10.1086/319618

Nelson, M., & Otnes, C. (2005). Exploring cross-cultural ambivalence: A netnography of intercultural wedding message boards. *Journal of Business Research*, *58*(1), 89–95. doi:10.1016/S0148-2963(02)00477-0

Prahalad, C. K., & Ramaswamy, V. (2004). *The Future Of Competition: Co-Creating Unique Value With Customers*. Cambridge, MA: HBS Press.

Rheingold, H. (1993). *The Virtual Community: Homesteading on the Electronic Frontier*. New York: Addison Wesley.

Sayre, S. (2001). *Qualitative Methods for Marketplace Research*. Thousand Oaks, CA: Sage.

Schau, H. J., & Gilly, M. C. (2003). We are what we post? Self□presentation in personal web space. *The Journal of Consumer Research, 30*(3), 385–404. doi:10.1086/378616

Schouten, J., & McAlexander, J. (1995). Subcultures of consumption: An ethnography of the new bikers. *The Journal of Consumer Research, 22*(1), 43. doi:10.1086/209434

Sherry, J. F. Jr. (1983). Gift giving in anthropological perspective. *The Journal of Consumer Research, 10*(2), 157. doi:10.1086/208956

Stanage, N. (2007). *From Second Life to second-degree murder*. Retrieved on 04/18/08 www.guardian.co.uk/commentisfree/2007/jan/16/fromsecondlifetoseconddegr

Surowiecki, J. (2006). *The Wisdom of Crowds*. New York: Anchor.

Tambyah, S. K. (1996). Life on the net: The reconstruction of self and community. In Corfman, K. P., & Lynch, J. G. (Eds.), *Advances in Consumer Research*. Provo, UT: Association for Consumer Research.

Townsend, J. (2007). Second Life is just the first step for brands in virtual worlds. *Marketing Week, 30*(26), 28.

van Dolen, W. M., Dabholkar, P. A., & de Ruyter, K. (2007). Satisfaction with online commercial group chat: The influence of perceived technology attributes, chat group characteristics, and advisor communication style. *Journal of Retailing, 83*(3), 339–358. doi:10.1016/j.jretai.2007.03.004

Vargo, S. L., & Lusch, R. F. (2004). Evolving to a new dominant logic for marketing. *Journal of Marketing, 68*(1), 1–7. doi:10.1509/jmkg.68.1.1.24036

Vargo, S. L., & Lusch, R. F. (2006). Service-dominant logic: Reactions, reflections, and refinements. *Marketing Theory, 6*(3), 281–288. doi:10.1177/1470593106066781

Von Hoffman, C. (2007). *Are marketers dying on Second Life?* Retrieved on 05/07/08 www.brandweek.com/bw/news/recent_display.jsp?vnu_content_id=1003563242&imw=Y

Wheaton, B. (2003). A subculture of commitment. In Rinehart, R. E., & Sydnor, S. (Eds.), *To The Extreme: Alternative Sports, Inside And Out*. Albany, NY: State University of New York.

Zaichkowsky, J. L. (1985). Measuring the involvement construct in marketing. *The Journal of Consumer Research, 12*(3), 341–352. doi:10.1086/208520

Chapter 21
Teaching Taboo Topics Through Technology

Piya Sorcar
Stanford University, USA

Clifford Nass
Stanford University, USA

ABSTRACT

Solving the problem of how to provide effective health education on diseases subject to social taboos is an immediate need. The social stigma of HIV/AIDS is particularly prominent in the developing world, where 95 percent of all HIV-infected persons live. Millions of people risk death from HIV/AIDS while cultures and laws resist change. New approaches must be created to provide education despite whatever social, structural, cultural, and legal barriers exist. Fortunately, the emergence of new media and information and communication technologies (ICT) has provided new ways to help bypass social taboos and provide effective education. This chapter discusses these challenges and presents criteria for evaluating the efficacy of educational campaigns aimed at promoting awareness relating to taboo topics using a specially designed HIV/AIDS curriculum—Interactive Teaching AIDS—as an exemplar. It incorporates key pedagogical and communication theories and approaches in order to maximize its efficacy. To provide psychological comfort and promote coherent understanding, this ICT-based application couples the presentation of biological aspects of transmission with culturally-familiar euphemisms and metaphors to communicate ideas about prevention measures. Created using a rigorous, iterative, and research-based process, the 20-minute application provides detailed yet accessible culturally-appropriate explanations of all key aspects of HIV/AIDS prevention. For people living in areas that cannot easily access explicit HIV/AIDS materials due to social, cultural or other constraints, the positive results of the authors' study suggest that it is possible to design curricula that are socially-acceptable and accurate, that promote significant gains in learning, retention, and changes in attitudes. Furthermore, these materials can encourage learners to proactively seek more information regarding the taboo topic and share prevention information with others. Educators who are reticent to teach about such subjects due to embarrassment or lack of health expertise can utilize similar approaches to educate students.

DOI: 10.4018/978-1-60566-792-8.ch021

INTRODUCTION TO TEACHING ABOUT TABOO TOPICS

This chapter discusses the challenges of providing education about topics that are considered taboo but must be taught to protect public health and welfare. A conceptualization of taboos is presented, and various ways through which technology can enable one to address taboo subjects while respecting social and cultural norms and values is discussed. Drawing on theoretical and empirical literature, advantages and disadvantages of various information and communication technologies (ICT)[1] and other strategies for providing the requisite information and persuasion necessary to address taboo topics effectively are analyzed. Criteria are presented for evaluating the effectiveness of such educational campaigns and curricula. Following this, the procedures one should employ to develop appropriate messages for ICT are discussed, using a recent AIDS campaign—*Interactive Teaching AIDS*—as an exemplar. *Interactive Teaching AIDS* is an ICT-based application designed by the *TeachAIDS*[2] organization to provide evidence-based, culturally-appropriate HIV/AIDS prevention education to audiences for whom discussing topics related to sexual practices is considered taboo.

Laws and Norms

Virtually all societies have formal rules of behavior, called laws, which are defined by the state and enforced by a formal governmental apparatus. Even in democratic societies aiming to maximize individual freedom, laws are enforced independent of whether the individual members of the society believe that the rules reflect extant value systems or not (Maine, 2004). Even the most unpopular laws must be enforced to ensure the legitimacy of the entire legal system (Weber, 1978).

All societies also have informal rules of behavior, called norms, which are defined by culture and traditions. While many norms are embodied in and enforced by laws, there are also norms that simply set expectations of behaviors. That is, norms are enforced by general societal pressure (sometimes in addition to that of the state) or the collective infliction of non-legal sanctions on deviants, those who disobey the norms, subjecting them to stigmatization, criticism, ostracism, or even non-state force (Posner, 2002).

In addition to the distinction between laws and norms, there is also an important distinction between positive versus negative laws and norms. Positive laws and norms prescribe behaviors that individuals are required or pressured to perform. For example, almost all nations have laws requiring children to attend at least some school, some nations have laws requiring military service, and a few legally compel voting. Similarly, there are negative laws and norms, defining what people must not do: murder is illegal in virtually all societies, theft is illegal in most societies, and gum chewing is banned in a few societies, for example. In democratic societies, laws are primarily negatively stated—anything that is not expressly forbidden is permitted—while in totalitarian societies, laws are often positively stated—and anything that is not expressly permitted may be forbidden. Societies also have positive norms which are not related to their laws: virtually all cultures encourage age-based rituals, many cultures have words that are supposed to be spoken to elders, and a few specify markers that should be placed on homes.

Taboos

The focus of this research is on *taboos*—negative norms that involve actions, practices, or states that carry a strong social stigma[3]. The word *taboo* comes from the Tongan word *tabu* (Webster's Dictionary, 2003), for "forbidden" or "banned". Capitan Cook defined the notion of taboo during his third voyage around the world (Allan & Burridge, 2006) and introduced it into English in 1784, through a publication accounting his trip to Tahiti (Thody, 1997).

Taboos are social prohibitions created over time. They depend on, and are reinforced by, communitywide complicity (Douglas, 2002). They are inextricably linked to culture and thus vary significantly across the world; what is taboo in one culture may be completely acceptable in another.

Societies create taboos for a number of reasons, including:

Supporting the Legal System

Laws reflect individuals' covenants with the greater society. That is, to the extent that laws are legitimate, they reflect the society's norms. Thus, with few exceptions (e.g., driving a few miles over the speed limit), violating the law is a taboo in all societies. The stronger the norm in which a law is grounded (e.g., murder vs. copyright violations), the greater the taboo against violating that law.

Supporting Religion and Other Belief Systems

Religious prohibitions are often more strict than legal ones. While an activity may be legal, violating a prohibition of one's religion, particularly in very pious cultures, is taboo. Nearly every religion and culture has one or more foods or drinks that may not be consumed (sometimes under certain circumstances). For example, for Muslims, eating pork is taboo while eating beef is perfectly acceptable, while for many Hindus, the opposite is the case. However, in India, where Islam and Hinduism represent the vast majority of the people, neither is banned by law. In many cases, violating religious prohibitions can actually be considered more taboo than violating laws that prohibit such activities.

Relation to Other Taboos

In some cases, if an action or state is a direct consequence of, or related to, another taboo, then it becomes taboo by this association. Often, the taboo persists even if it is not actually related to the other taboo action or state. For example, the Old Testament forbids the eating of a calf in its mother's milk. This taboo has now been extended such that it is taboo for Orthodox Jews to eat any kind of meat in any kind of milk. Another example is the use of a wet nurse or milk-bank. Since wet nurses are allowable in cases where an HIV-positive mother wants to avoid passing the virus to her newborn, in some communities mothers that do not breastfeed may be thought to be seropositive. This exposes them to stigma associated with an HIV-infection (Population Reports, 2009). In areas where community members are aware of vertical transmission and breastfeeding is a cultural norm, a mother opting out of breastfeeding for any reason can lead to a taboo by association, even if it is not the reason she chose to forgo breastfeeding (Abiona, Onayade, Ijadunola, Obiajunwa, Aina & Thairu, 2006).

Protection Against Harm

A large number of taboos, arguably the vast majority, evolve from a need to protect against real or perceived harms. Laws against murder or drunk driving fall under this category. However, there are also taboos which have evolved within some groups to protect against harms which are not de jure illegal. Cigarette smoking, for example, is an activity which is generally legal, allowed by most religions, and unrelated to any other significant taboo. Nonetheless, a taboo against it has evolved in many sectors of society due to the fact that anyone in the smoker's immediate vicinity is subject to potential harm via second-hand inhalation of smoke. Some taboos are applied only to special categories of people. For example, some activities, words, and ideas are considered acceptable for adults but harmful to children, either because they are believed to adversely affect a child's development or threaten their "innocence." Thus, in the United States, the movie rating system identifies movies that might be taboo for children ("PG"), those that are particularly taboo for children under 13 ("PG-13"), and those which may not be seen by children under 17 ("NC-17"). Similarly, there are taboos with respect to minorities. These types of taboos most commonly apply to words and symbols which are considered offensive. The most extreme example of this is hate speech. Inciting hatred against a specific group is a form of speech which is illegal in Canada and numerous other countries, but is protected in the United States under the First Amendment of the U.S. Constitution. However, not only are negative characterizations of any minority group taboo in the United States; associating with individuals who make these characterizations is also considered taboo. Taboos that stem from the desire to protect against harm can take other forms as well. The desire to protect animals commonly kept as pets—e.g., dogs, cats, and horses—leads to taboos that make them inappropriate for consumption. Because pets are often anthropomorphized to a certain extent by their owners, as well as by society at large, using these animals as food may feel to many groups "as if you are eating your own children" (Thody, 1997).

Reinforcement of Power Relations

In some cases, dominant persons or groups define certain topics or behaviors taboo as a way of controlling the actions of others in a population. Just as Newspeak in George Orwell's *Nineteen Eighty-Four* eradicated dangerous ideas by eliminating certain words from a language, so too may some individuals or groups be oppressed or controlled by making certain topics forbidden. Leading members of society and controllers of opinion have the power and influence to make taboos as repressive as they would like them to be (Douglas, 2002). In such cases, criticism is punished or suppressed, and entire topics may become unspeakable and unthinkable (Douglas, 2002). In China, for example, the government takes an active role in censoring not only information, but also certain topics of discussion: Internet searches on terms such as "freedom," "democracy," and "Falun Gong" consistently turn up no results, as these concepts are actively filtered from search engines (Kurtenbach, 2005; Thompson, 2006). What is particularly striking about the Chinese example of censorship is that individual members of society not only play a key role in preventing access to this information, they are openly proud of the fact that they are protecting their society (Thompson, 2006). In many parts of the world, certain power relations have become institutionalized as part of the culture. Criticism of these power relations, or activities which could lead to their criticism or erosion, are often considered taboo. One example is the historical relationship between monarchs in numerous European nations and their countries' citizens. The doctrine of royal absolutism, once common in many nations, dictated that a monarch's word and judgment were beyond contestation. While this took on religious overtones and justifications, this was ultimately a belief system designed to reinforce the power of monarchs over their subjects. While the taboos against criticizing monarchs might have been strong, the taboos concerning actions against monarchs were obviously much stronger. In most countries in the world, crimes of treason still carry some of harshest penalties, and these originate historically from crimes against monarchs themselves. Another example of taboos concerning power relationships is found in the caste system in India. It has traditionally been verboten (and in many circles, still is) for individuals of different castes to intermarry. As with other taboos in this category, while there are protections against harm which provide the ostensible justification for the existence of these taboos, the real origin of the taboo is the preservation of pre-existing power relations. In the case of the caste system, wealth, education, and social status were stratified according to caste, and members of higher castes needed to intermarry in order to preserve that social order. As such, the taboo against marrying someone of a lower caste was much stronger than the taboo against marrying someone of a higher caste. Overall, these sorts of taboos are only discredited, ameliorated, or lifted when leading members of society choose to modify, enrich, or eliminate them (Douglas, 2002).

CHALLENGES IN TEACHING ABOUT TABOO TOPICS

Comparing Teaching Difficulties

There are two broad categories in which one can place the vast majority of taboos: 1) taboos against actions or states (e.g., divorce, incest, cannibalism, food prohibitions, or trespassing, and 2) communication taboos, including taboos against words, symbols, and topics (e.g., profanity, swastikas, and sex education). The critical difference between action/state and communication taboos is that it is simple and straightforward to instruct individuals to not perform or assume taboo actions or states, or to discuss the efficacy and motivations for the existence of those taboos. However, by definition, it is extremely difficult or even impossible to directly express or discuss taboo words, symbols, or topics.

This difference becomes critical when taboos become unhelpful or anachronistic. For example, in the United States during the 1950s, the action of breastfeeding was taboo among the middle and upper classes because baby formula was viewed as more healthful. However, once there was scientific consensus that breastfeeding was healthier than formula for babies, through extensive deliberation, the previous norm could be discussed, evaluated, and overturned.

Conversely, openly discussing issues related to race and diversity can be extremely difficult, particularly in racially mixed settings (Benton & Daniel, 1996). In many schools and communities, which are comprised of diverse groups, teachers are encouraged to help students talk about their similarities and differences. However, determining the best mechanism to openly discuss such issues and further encourage students to feel safe and communicative remains a challenge for educators (Benton & Daniel, 1996). Some scholars argue that not talking about race at all—"artificial color-blindness" or being "colormute"—is just as harmful as discussing it in an inappropriate way (Benton & Daniel, 1996; Pollock, 2005). Teachers aim to foster comfortable and open environments in order to support a healthy exchange and communication of ideas, but communication taboos are extraordinarily difficult or impossible to even discuss, let alone overcome.

Figure 1 below presents a set of taboo topics and the (arguable) relative level of difficulty in discussing them. This diagram was developed for illustrative purposes only in order to more easily discuss issues around teaching such topics. The location of the taboo topics will differ greatly based on time, culture, and contexts. However, the point remains that there are highly taboo topics and learning how to effectively teach about them, while respecting social and cultural norms and values, is critical.

Home Economics is a basic topic around the world, with few or no taboos associated with it. Hence, teaching it openly is straightforward. *Poetry* is somewhat different, as it is a broader category whose position may vary on the taboo scale based on its content; however, it too is not structurally difficult to teach.

Censorship (in China) may be relatively low on the taboo scale, in that people in China know that available information is censored, and many openly support this as a benevolent action by the government to protect its people. However, it may be difficult to teach fully about the concept and subject of censorship in China without being able to directly address which topics are censored and why.

The topic of *Racial Diversity* is taboo in many communities in the United States because of the country's history relating to slavery and civil

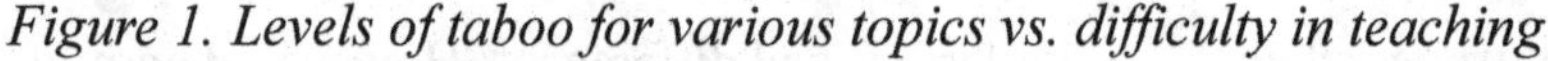

Figure 1. Levels of taboo for various topics vs. difficulty in teaching

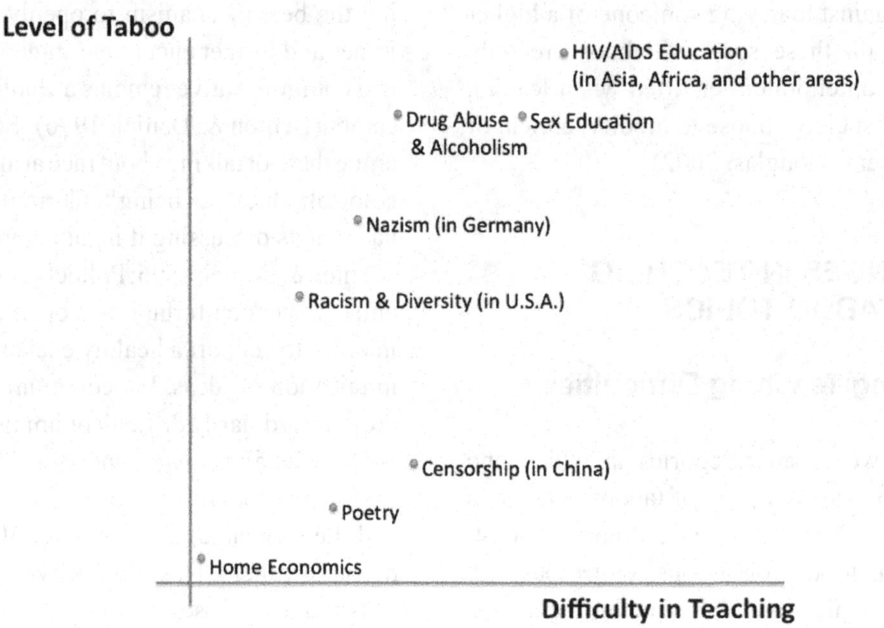

rights, and the complex nature of race relations that have evolved over time.

Sex Education for youth, although not an illegal topic in most countries, is often still a taboo topic, of varying intensity. It is linked to premarital sex and premarital pregnancy, both of which often violate religious beliefs. The association of sex education to these other taboo topics elevates its position on the taboo scale. Many parents and teachers advocate abstinence-based education because they believe that comprehensive sex education promotes promiscuity among young people (Dhillon, 2006, Smith, Kippax, Aggleton & Tyrer, 2003), which they wish to discourage. Additionally, students may feel uncomfortable openly discussing sex-related topics with their instructors, making the subject even more taboo. In order to enhance comfort during such lessons, some schools separate children by their gender or have outside organizations give specialized talks on these issues.

Why is HIV/AIDS More Difficult to Teach About?

Educating a population on *HIV/AIDS* is in a somewhat different and arguably more challenging category than educating about other taboo topics. Most importantly, it may rank very high on the taboo scale, because it is a compound of many taboos. This makes it extremely difficult to teach in certain socially conservative contexts. Many Asian countries in particular historically tend to be socially conservative regarding topics relating to human sexuality. Comprehensive HIV/AIDS education in these countries generally requires teachers to discuss numerous sensitive and highly taboo topics that are associated with the transmission of HIV (e.g., premarital sex, adultery, commercial sex work, homosexuality, intravenous drug use, and death). One ministry official in Southeast Asia said the following with regards to teaching sex education in their schools:

"...sex education (or sexual education or sexuality education) in its liberal sense is not taught in any of the topics in the science syllabus developed by the Curriculum Development Department at any level of education in Brunei Darussalam as this is contrary to the teachings of Islam. Sex [education] that explicitly mentioned the encouragement] use of condoms and other forms of contraceptives including IUDs, sex enhancement devices and drugs including orally taken pills, masturbation, forms of intercourse (oral, anal, vaginal), 'free' sex, multiple partners, exchanging spouses, free intermingle among men and women for pleasure as a pastime, or communal marriage, polyandry, infidelity, the likes of any unnatural forms of sex (including homosexuality and lesbianism) is strongly condemned in Islam. Unlawful and immoral sex practices including premarital sex are all forbidden (haram) in Islam." (Smith, et. al., 2003)

The case of HIV/AIDS has been identified as "dual stigma"—not only is the syndrome itself stigmatized because it is perceived as a threat to health and safety, but, furthermore, it is associated with groups that were already highly stigmatized before the global outbreak (Herek & Glunt, 1988; Derlega & Barbee, 1998). In India, where homosexual acts were de jure illegal until the July 2009 ruling and commercial sex work is still de jure illegal, health care workers are in many cases unable to provide appropriate education on treatment and counseling to these groups at all (Agoramoorthy & Minna, 2007). Taboos relating to discussing issues like race can also come into play, since it is important to dispel misconceptions held by many people that certain groups are more susceptible to the disease. Hence, it is extremely difficult in many socially conservative societies to teach about HIV/AIDS prevention and treatment.

Finally, an unusual challenge in HIV/AIDS education is that even a presentation of the salient information may directly challenge social norms of power or gender relations. For example, the taboo concerning the discussion of issues relating to gender power relations in many parts of the world is in this category. In societies where men are afforded more sexual freedom than women (which has historically been most societies in the world, though the extent varies considerably), confronting issues such as whether a husband is faithful, can be difficult to the point of being unacceptably offensive. To the degree that governments and public education systems allow the perpetuation of these taboos reinforcing such power relations, curricula, such as HIV/AIDS education materials, which challenge these social mores, may not be approved.

Previous and Existing Educational Approaches to Teaching about Taboo Topics

When a subject is too taboo or difficult to address, there is a strong temptation to avoid the subject entirely. When taboo topics are confronted, a range of pedagogical strategies have been employed:

Metaphors, Euphemisms and Humor

By employing specific metaphors, educators can illustrate a concept without directly mentioning the sensitive subject. Similarly, through euphemisms, educators may rely on subtle and, thus, less offensive expressions to communicate similar messages. It is often difficult to find metaphors or euphemisms that accurately communicate particular concepts clearly. Hence, the validation of the clarity, accuracy, and acceptability of these mechanisms within the target group is essential to their efficacy.

Technical Terms

Some curricula and/or educators utilize technical jargon in place of more commonplace words. This is a common technique to educate about sexuality or more generally the human body (e.g., using the words "myocardial infarction" instead of "heart attack"). The use of technical terminology may mask or distance the subject, making it more comfortable for both educators and learners to communicate about an issue. However, it may be unclear how well learners are able to understand, let alone absorb the materials.

Direct Approach

Some educators believe the best way to absolve a topic of its taboo status is to talk openly and directly about it, regardless of the resulting discomfort levels among participants. The assumption is that with open discussion, individuals will become more comfortable and, in time, the taboo will diminish or even cease to exist. However, this strategy is not viable when the taboo is reified through law.

Localization

Creating culturally-appropriate versions of curricula, which reflect the local context, is another way to appeal to individual communities. Although customization may be challenging, and in some situations more expensive, it may help learners to further identify with the particulars of a subject. Incorporating feedback from individuals who are familiar with the ground realities, rather than using a one-size-fits-all methodology, can make the materials more acceptable and comfortable for the learners.

Below are two examples that demonstrate the use of existing approaches to educating about taboo topics. Since research indicates that most taboos around the world are related to the human body and its various transformations (e.g., sexuality, disease and death) (Allan & Burridge, 2006), the examples selected below fall within this category. Furthermore, topics that are both taboo and relate to improving human health are especially important to address because they represent tremendous opportunities and challenges for the population; only through accurate education can individuals inform and protect themselves.

Existing Campaign Exemplars

Example 1: Breast Cancer Education in Native American Communities

There are significant public health efforts to educate women about breast cancer in the United States. Accurate and timely information is provided through multiple sources, including personal doctors, newspapers, magazines, and scholastic resources. However, open discussion about breast cancer is strictly forbidden in certain Native American communities, significantly hindering early detection and appropriate treatment. In the Navajo language, the word "cancer" literally means "the sore that does not heal" and, therefore, conjures a sense of hopelessness, preventing early cancer detection in these communities. Furthermore, it is culturally taboo to talk about cancer because the community believes that to discuss cancer means to invite it (Robinson, Sandoval, Baldwin & Sanderson, 2005).

After being diagnosed with breast cancer, Nellie Sandoval, and her oncologist Frances Robinson, developed a nine-minute pilot informational video to present accurate and valuable information (e.g., early detection, self-examination) to more than 100 Native Americans across several states. To connect with the target population, the video was narrated by a Native American health healer and included a "message of permission" for learners to seek information and accept a new tribal tradition. In the pilot study, 100 percent of the respondents said they received information they needed. The success of the first video triggered the need for a second one based on breast cancer treatment modalities. Researchers associated with this project have plans to conduct a longitudinal study on the efficacy of the culturally-sensitive learning materials (Robinson et al., 2005).

Example 2: Maternal Health in Mali

As late as the 1990s, pregnancy was considered a taboo topic among certain communities in Mali and was rarely discussed even between husbands and wives. Couples associated issues relating to pregnancy and maternal health with shame and embarrassment (Clemmons & Coulibaly, 2000). The strong social prohibition made it difficult for women to receive the additional care and proper nutrition needed during pregnancy. Even in cases where women wanted to seek maternal health services, their emotions inhibited them from discussing such needs with their partners (Clemmons & Coulibaly, 2000). The lack of direct and open communication was a contributing factor to Mali suffering from one of the highest maternal and infant mortality rates in the world[4] (Singhal & Rogers, 2003).

In 1989, research through the Dioro Child Survival Project revealed the cultural and social barriers to women seeking maternal health services. Researchers built directly on Malian tradition to promote behavioral change. Traditionally, Malian married women wore a white cloth, called the *pendelu*, which symbolized marital roles and duties. The Dioro Project authorities used local *griots* (Malian educators who are also entertainers) to introduce a tacit cultural symbol to represent the change in status. The married Malian women were encouraged to wear a green pendelu (instead of the traditional white) when they became pregnant. Instantly, the people around the pregnant woman, including her husband, knew of her status and could support her appropriately, without any discussion needing to take place. This tacit symbol dramatically increased transparency, knowledge, and communication between husbands and wives while maintaining sensitivity to the context of cultural change. Three months after the campaign, survey results demonstrated that communication about maternal health rose from 3 percent to 65.5 percent among married couples (Clemmons & Coulibaly, 2000). Also, 41.7 percent of the husbands interviewed said they lightened their wife's workload during her pregnancy and 49.6 percent said they made sure she received good nutrition (Clemmons & Coulibaly, 2000).

The above examples employ different combinations of the techniques described earlier to teach about taboo topics as illustrated below:

Framework for Evaluation of Curricula Relating to Taboo Topics

Providing education materials is only the first step in the learning process. It is equally important to evaluate whether the learners are absorbing the target messages after the content has been delivered to them. There are multiple dimensions to consider when evaluating the effectiveness of a given curriculum or approach to educating on taboo topics. Below are four questions that should be addressed while evaluating any attempt to teach a taboo topic:

How Socially Acceptable Is the Approach?

Being able to coexist with cultural norms is of critical importance in educating about a taboo topic. There are many advocates of addressing taboos "head-on" by providing materials which

Table 1. Techniques for teaching about taboo topics

	Avoidance (Indirect Discourse)	Metaphors & Euphemism	Technical Terms	Direct Approach	Localization
Example 1: Breast Cancer Among Native Americans			X	X	X
Example 2: Child and Maternal Health in Mali	X	X			X

themselves become taboo. This approach will limit whether the materials will ever be used in the contexts in which they are most needed. Later in this chapter, ways to promote social acceptability are discussed, for instance, integrating images that are acceptable to learners.

How Accurate/Complete Is It?

This is normally not a consideration for evaluating curricula in general because it is assumed that all materials within a competently designed curriculum will be accurate. However, in educating about taboo topics, there are often tradeoffs that must be made, for example, between social acceptability and accuracy. If a curriculum is accurate to the point of being blunt about a topic whose discussion is taboo, then it will fail the social acceptability test. In other cases, the curriculum may be accurate but incomplete, leaving out the most taboo details in order to provide education on related but less taboo ones. This dimension includes the level of inclusion of specific information about a topic and not simply what is covered being accurate. The best curricula will find a way to present accurate and relatively complete information using an alternate vocabulary, medium, conceptual model, or other approach, in order to keep the materials socially acceptable.

How Effective Is It?

It is not sufficient for a curriculum to be socially acceptable and accurate/complete—it must also be effective and result in learning and retention (and where appropriate, attitude and behavior change). An educational approach may be too technical, foreign, esoteric, or otherwise ineffective, and that will override any advantages in other domains it may have.

How Easy Is It to Deploy?

The greatest theoretical educational approach in the world will not produce results unless it can actually be deployed in the real world. Infrastructure, language, and cost considerations are examples of the additional dimensions along which a curriculum must be evaluated.

The last two criteria—efficacy and ease of deployment—are the typical dimensions upon which general curricula are evaluated. Social acceptability and accuracy are unique dimensions for curricula on taboo topics. The following table illustrates how different approaches to teaching taboo topics have advantages or disadvantages along these four dimensions.

Based on Table 2, there are two important observations which should be made. The first is that it is possible (and in fact typical) for different approaches to be combined in any given curriculum. For example, for certain sections of the curriculum, metaphors may be used, while for others technical terms or a direct approach may be used. The second observation is that a localized curriculum has the potential to fulfill all of the key requirements that have been identified, so in contexts where taboos around a topic are prevalent, localization will almost certainly be a required feature of the curriculum.

Drawing on the previous conceptualizations and evaluation criteria is a case study which provides a detailed description of the development of a new curriculum to teach about a highly taboo topic–HIV/AIDS–in India. Its goal was to maximize the various categories introduced in the framework on evaluation and ground them in pedagogical techniques and communication strategies to create materials appropriate for learners.

The remainder of this chapter will provide background for the HIV/AIDS case study, review literature and strategies to combat and educate around HIV/AIDS in India, and present arguments for a technological solution appropriate for particular taboo contexts. Next, pedagogical techniques and communication strategies needed to create materials appropriate for learners will be presented. These techniques ground a consideration of the various categories introduced in

Table 2. Advantages and disadvantages of framework for evaluation

	Social Acceptability	Potential Accuracy/ Completeness	Potential Efficacy	Ease of Deployment
Avoidance	**High** No education is being provided	**Low** No education is being provided	**Low** No education is being provided	**High** No education is being provided
Metaphors & Euphemism	**Medium** Depends on the nature of the taboos and the metaphors and euphemisms	**Medium** Depends on the nature of the taboos and the metaphors and euphemisms	**Medium** Depends on the nature of the taboos and the metaphors and euphemisms	**High** Deploying alternate curriculum based on context
Technical Terms	**Medium** Depends whether the designer/ educator can find appropriate ones to fit context	**High** Technical terms can actually be more precise	**Medium** May be hard to understand and challenging to train instructors	**High** Deploying alternate curriculum based on context
Direct Approach	**Low** You cannot address the taboo subjects directly	**High** Implies that effectively anything can be said	**Medium** Being overly blunt about taboo topics can distract from what is being taught	**Medium** There may be resistance from instructors and channel owners
Localization	**High** Materials are culturally-appropriate, enhancing acceptability within the local community	**High** Depends on how complete the materials are presented	**High** Depends on context and application of localization methods	**High** Deploying alternate curriculum based on context

the framework by demonstrating both design and evaluation based on them.

CASE STUDY BACKGROUND: HIV/AIDS EDUCATION IN INDIA

In India, HIV/AIDS is one of the most challenging taboo topics and contexts for educators. The taboo around openly discussing topics like sexual practices, among other sensitive ones, has made addressing HIV/AIDS either taboo or extremely difficult. The fact that this single subject matter compounds several taboo topics into a single discussion (e.g., commercial sex work, homosexuality, adultery, premarital sex, intravenous drug use and death) presents unique and particularly difficult challenges. If a sound educational approach can be created to effectively address such a complex topic, similar approaches may be employed to tackle relatively less taboo topics.

The following sections provide more detailed information on the particular context in India and previous attempts to education on HIV/AIDS education. Following this will be a detailed description of how the technological solutions employed to address these challenges, while incorporating key communications and pedagogical theories and approaches to promote efficacy of the application.

The Challenge and Opportunity

One of the greatest public health challenges facing the world today is how to provide effective health education in Asia. With more than 60 percent of the world's people residing in Asia, the provision of effective prevention and awareness of communicable diseases in this region has direct benefits for the rest of the world, just as not doing so has direct negative consequences. As witnessed during the near pandemic of Severe Acute Respiratory Distress Syndrome (SARS) originating in China in 2002, deadly diseases can now spread within days around the world. So, prevention is far more important and achievable than containment. The primary global example of this today is HIV/AIDS, with which 33.2 million people worldwide currently live (UNAIDS, 2007). Asia has

14.4 percent of all HIV/AIDS infected people in the world, and India has the world's third-largest national infected population, after South Africa and Nigeria (UNAIDS, 2007).

Disease prevention and management is facilitated when modes of disease transmission can be discussed openly, as was the case for SARS. Historically, illnesses like leprosy, cholera and syphilis, have also been stigmatized (Herek & Glunt 1988; Pradhan, Sundar & Singh, 2006; Valdiserri, 2002). Diseases such as HIV/AIDS that are transmitted sexually, including via commercial sex workers and intravenous drug use, present significant challenges because social stigma often precludes such open discussion (Pradhan et. al., 2006; Valdiserri, 2002). Last year, various organizations spent ten billion USD on HIV/AIDS programs through private donations and government funding in developing countries alone (Sharma, 2008), in hopes of, among other things, raising awareness and curbing stigma.

Solving the problem of how to provide effective health education on diseases subject to social taboos is an immediate need. The social stigma of HIV/AIDS is particularly prominent in the developing world, which has 95 percent of all HIV-infected persons (Noble, 2007). One study comprised of 433 students, faculty and technical staff of public health services in South India found that 42 percent of respondents believed seropositive individuals should be quarantined, 31 percent said that infected students should be kept out of classes, and 36 percent stated that it would be better for everyone if persons with AIDS killed themselves (Ambati, Ambati, Rao, 1997). This kind of stigma not only makes it difficult to provide awareness and prevention-related education, but it also complicates estimates of societal levels of high-risk behaviors and disease prevalence. In fact, nine out of ten people infected worldwide do not know they are seropositive for HIV (Singhal & Rogers, 2003). In Asia, the challenge is significantly exacerbated by the social stigma associated with discussing sexual practices or anything at all related to sex (Bennett, 2000; Reuters, 2006; Sharma, 2005; Solomon & Chakraborty, 2004; Wong, Lee & Tsang, 2004;). In many states of India[5], the National AIDS Control Organization (NACO)-issued sex education curriculum[6]—which included the official HIV/AIDS education curriculum—has been banned entirely from public schools (Chadha, 2007; Gentleman, 2007; Sabha, 2007 ; Sify News, 2007; Zaheer, 2007). This is despite reports showing that pre-marital sex is increasingly common among young people (Abraham & Kumar, 1999; Bio-Medicine, 2005; Biswas, 2003; Sachdev, 1998; Sharma, 2005). One study, which Sharma (2001) notes was suppressed by India's Health Ministry, found that a quarter to a third of India's young people (ages 15-24) living in slums in Delhi and Lucknow are engaging in premarital sex (Sharma, 2001). In a 2002 survey by *The Week Magazine*, 69 percent of unmarried young males and 38 percent of young females admitted to premarital sex in India (The Week, 2002, as cited in Sharma, 2005; The HIV Update International, 2002).

India also presents a unique opportunity to explore and deliver innovative methods of HIV/AIDS prevention education. Many agencies have predicted India will be the next hot zone for HIV/AIDS, shifting the epidemic's center from South Africa (Padma, 2005; Perry, 2005; Sudha, Vijay & Lakshmi, 2005; Yang, 2003). With approximately 2.5 million infected individuals (UNAIDS, 2007), it is imperative to provide effective prevention education as the virus continues to spread. However, India's socially conservative culture often prevents open communication of transmission-related information. Furthermore, India's diverse population, consisting of dozens of distinct cultures, over 200 languages and dialects, and significant class-related issues, presents daunting challenges. Any form of education must consider the complex culture, history, and regional differences in order to raise awareness and promote change in knowledge, attitudes, and beliefs.

With the increasing number of HIV-positive individuals and the current ban on sex education by several state governments (Chadha, 2007; Gentleman, 2007; Sabha, 2007; Sify News, 2007; Zaheer, 2007), it is clear that an alternative method of delivering prevention education is required in order to delay the spread of the virus. According to the National AIDS Control Organization in India, the primary mode of transmission is via sexual fluids. Sexual transmission accounts for 86 percent of HIV infections in India today, followed by other means such as injection drug-use (2.4 percent), blood transfusion and through blood products (2.0 percent)—iatrogenic transmission—and vertical transmission (3.6 percent) among other unspecified routes (6.0 percent) (National AIDS Control Organization, 2005, as cited in, Correa & Gisselquist, 2006; UNAIDS, 2007).

Several recent studies indicate that Indians generally lack accurate knowledge about transmission and tend to be unaware of health-related resources, even in relatively well-educated circles (Perry, 2005; Pramanik, Chartier & Koopman, 2006). For example, a recent survey found that 59 percent believed there is a cure for HIV available (Medical News Today, 2007). Another study found that although college students were more open to premarital relationships and sexually active, they were "ignorant" of issues around sexual anatomy and functions (Sachdev, 1998). The virus is also no longer limited to high-risk populations, such as commercial sex workers and truck drivers, and has spread throughout the general urban and rural populations with presence in all states and union territories (Avert, 2009; Noble, 2007; Solomon, Kumarasmy, Ganesh & Amalraj, 1998; UNAIDS, 2007). In fact, most seropositive individuals fall outside of the high-risk groups (Avert, 2009), including the rich and poor, with infection rates among young people and women progressing at an alarming rate (Cichocki, 2007; Sharma, 2008; UNAIDS, 2007).

As a result of all of these factors, there is clearly a need to develop new means of providing effective prevention education for the general population in India. Although the estimated prevalence (0.2–0.5 percent)[7] among adults (15-49) living with HIV is low relative to other countries (UNAIDS, 2008), with such a large population in India, a mere 0.1 percent increase in prevalence will result in an estimated more than half a million additional infections (Avert, 2009).

The official numbers may underestimate the true infection rate, since a large number of HIV/AIDS cases go unreported (National AIDS Control Organization (NACO), 2006; Avert, 2009). There are several reasons for this. First, individuals may not know they are seropositive since a characteristic of the disease is an ability to live for many years without any AIDS-defining clinical symptoms (Derlega & Barbee, 1998). Early symptoms are similar to the influenza and HIV is asymptomatic (Ambati et al., 1997; Porter, 1993).

Second, although there has been a vast increase in HIV sentinel surveillance sites (176 in 1998 to 1134 in 2007) (NACO, 2007), individuals may avoid getting tested or reporting their infection for fear of being stigmatized and/or ostracized by their family, healthcare officials and the community at large. Singhal and Rogers (2003) describe HIV/AIDS patients and their families as a new class of 'untouchables'. In fact, the stigma is so strong in India that unlike nearly every Western nation, no famous Indian personality has ever publicly disclosed their HIV-positive status even though several have been infected (Singhal & Rogers, 2003).

Third, according to many experts, some officials may have downplayed the crisis and/or exaggerated the positive effects of its educational efforts (Padma, 2005). In 2005, the Indian government announced that, in one year alone (2003 to 2004), it was able to reduce the rate of new infections by 95 percent (Perry, 2005); the Health Minister claimed that India reduced the 520,000 new infections in 2003 to a low 28,000 in 2004 (Mukherjee, 2005). Furthermore, some states previously said to have had hundreds of thousands of HIV-infected people were deemed AIDS-free (Perry, 2005). The figures were met with mass disbelief from various international agencies and health experts working in the field, claiming that they were misrepresentative of the underlying data and that the ground realities were different (Padma, 2005).

Identifying the Source of the Taboo Topic

Designing an effective solution requires first understanding the primary source of the taboo and discussing the possible reasons for its existence. Specifically, for this case study, is the dearth of sex education or HIV/AIDS education in Indian schools related to a desire to oppress the weaker members of Indian society in some way? In other words, is HIV/AIDS education withheld as a form of intentional repression or is it a desire to reinforce certain power relationships?

Systematic and intentional repression based on power relations does not appear to account for the HIV/AIDS stigma in Indian society. India is a relatively conservative society, where members of the opposite sex holding hands or kissing in public may lead to fines or worse[8]. These penalties are applied equally to men and women. In 2006, conservatives asked Vasundhara Raje, the Chief Minister of Rajasthan, to resign after she offered a ceremonial kiss on the cheek to welcome a businesswoman friend at the World Economic Forum (Dhillon, 2006; Sappenfied, 2007). Bollywood actors generally cannot kiss in movies, and the limits of what is considered indecent is much lower than in occidental societies. Shailendra Dwivedi, a lawyer in Madhya Pradesh, filed a criminal case against a kiss between two actors in the movie *Dhoom 2* (released November, 2006) accusing "the stars of lowering the dignity of Indian women and encouraging obscenity among India's youth" (Dhillon, 2006). Perhaps one of the most controversial public displays of affection was in April 2007 between Hollywood actor Richard Gere and Indian actress Shilpa Shetty. Gere embraced Shetty and kissed her several times on the cheek at an AIDS awareness rally in New Delhi. Following this event, protestors shouted "death to Shilpa Shetty," while demonstrators burned effigies of Gere (BBC News, 2007). News of the public kiss was carried on the front page of numerous Indian newspapers. Gere publicly apologized numerous times and according to BBC News, Shetty said, "[Richard Gere] especially told me to tell the media that he didn't want to hurt any Indian sensibilities" (BBC News, 2007). A court in Jaipur, Rajasthan issued a warrant for Gere's arrest on charges of indulging in an obscene act (BBC, 2007; Hindustan Times, 2007; Singh, 2007), however, he was cleared of the charges, and the case was thrown out by the Supreme court (BBC, 2008). As such, there is a strong taboo against public displays of affection and discussing topics around sexual practices openly, which is directly related to these cultural values.

While many taboos around ideas or topics are relaxed when presented in professional (e.g., medical, governmental, or educational) settings, the taboo against discussing sex openly, in many Indian classrooms, is just as strong. There is a widespread belief amongst Indian parents that open discussions of sex and related topics–even in the classroom–is obscene and may lead to higher incidences of pre-marital sex and other indecent behavior (Dhillon, 2006; Smith et. al., 2003).

This point of view is not unique to India. It is shared by proponents of abstinence-based sex education even in the United States. In fact, this view is so strong among certain groups in the United States that the federal government, which has not had any set initiative for comprehensive sex education, has increased funding for abstinence-only programs from $9 million in 1997 to $176 million in 2007 (Howell, 2007; Masters, Beadnell, Morrison, Hoppe & Gillmore, 2008), despite the government's own federally-funded evaluation of numerous abstinence-based programs indicating they do not delay sexual initiation, reduce teen pregnancy or sexually transmitted infections (Avert, 2009; Howell, 2007; Mathematica, 2009). Although some reports suggest positive effects of abstinence-only or "abstinence until marriage" initiatives, experts claim these studies are not methodologically sound or do not provide robust empirical evidence indicating a strong case (Oakley, Fullerton, Holland, Arnold, France-Dawson, Kelley & McGrellis, 1995). The Society for Adolescent Medicine has stated that, although abstinence should be included as one of the many options within comprehensive sex education programs, funding towards abstinence-only programs should be replaced with funding for medically-accurate comprehensive sex education (Masters, 2008; Society for Adolescent Medicine, 2006).

Empirical research has shown that comprehensive sex education is actually more effective than abstinence-only programs in delaying sexual initiation and other perceived negative sexual outcomes (Kirby, 2002; Masters, 2008; Santelli, Ott, Lyon, Rogers, Summers & Schleifer, 2006; Sharma, 2005). Moreover, sex and HIV/AIDS education programs do not increase sexual behavior either in the United States (Kirby, 2002) or in the developing world (Kirby, Obasi & Laris, 2006; Kirby, Laris, Rolleri, 2007). However, this is generally not believed by conservatives throughout the United States and certainly not by many parents in India.

As a result of this skepticism, numerous state governments across India (e.g., Maharashtra, Gujarat, Madhya Pradesh, and Karnataka among others) have banned sex education in public schools altogether. However, it is important to note that this is limited exclusively to school curricula and does not mean these topics are censored for adults. Thus, banning sex education among students does not fit the typical pattern of oppressing groups in order to dehumanize them in some way, because of course, children will eventually become adults and be immune to such control. Instead, it is more typical of the social and legal limits that all societies set for young people in the belief that it will protect them from harm and allow them to grow in the desired way.

An alternate explanation for the state of HIV/AIDS education in Indian society is that the government is not interested in actually providing these resources since the disease disproportionately affects lower social classes. Similar to criticisms and conspiracy theories relating to the U.S. government, this hypothesis seems to have no basis in fact. The National AIDS Control Organization (NACO) operates under the division of the Ministry of Health & Family Welfare to manage the AIDS epidemic in India. NACO has established 35 HIV/AIDS control societies across all Indian states and Union Territories to respond more appropriately to spread of the virus and coordinate a national response (Avert, 2009; NACO, 2008). NACO has been given an extremely large budget by Indian standards. Launched in 1992, Phase I of the National AIDS Control Program received $99.6 million USD to, among other things, establish and strengthen management capacity in the country, promote public awareness, improve blood safety (Claeson & Alexander, 2008). Phase II included a budget of $460 million included activities around providing prevention interventions for at-risk groups and the general population as well as AIDS care initiatives (Claeson & Alexander, 2008; NACO, 2009). [9] For Phase III, which takes place between 2007-2011[10], the Indian government budgeted a 2.5 billion USD dollar response[11] to the epidemic, with 70 percent earmarked towards prevention efforts (Araujo, 2008; Avert, 2009). This phase includes targeting high-risk groups with evidence-based prevention methods (e.g., condom promotion, peer education), among other activities (Claeson & Alexander, 2008). In addition, there are more than 1000* NGOs, many of which are funded by NACO, working on HIV/AIDS prevention and treatment issues across the country. NACO has also partnered with other organizations to launch campaigns like the Red Ribbon Express, which is a seven-coach train filled with health materials travelling to 166 districts across 23 states in the country (Avert, 2009; NACO, 2007). Public billboards and public service announcements are not difficult to find.

Overall, the taboos surrounding HIV/AIDS relate directly to either the taboos around discussing sexual topics or taboos relating to actions or states which are either illegal, highly controversial, or both.

It should be noted that there is a significant difference between merely mentioning, or using the phrase, HIV/AIDS, and actually discussing it. As long as none of the taboo elements relating to it are mentioned, a simple message along the lines of "think about AIDS" is acceptable in many circumstances in which full discussion would not be acceptable. The conflicts with taboos inevitably arise when one attempts to engage in a more comprehensive discussion about the topic, especially about prevention.

A distinction should also be made between taboos concerning actions or states and communications taboos relating to HIV/AIDS. For example, drug-use is taboo, but there is no communications taboo associated with it, as there is universal agreement on what the message should be—"say no to drugs". On the other hand, homosexuality is considered a taboo state by many in India, but it also has communications taboos associated with it. This is because it falls into the category of actions or states relating to HIV/AIDS that are not discussed in schools due to their political divisive nature. That is, there is no clear popular consensus on what the overall message relating to that topic should be. While everyone can agree on drug-use being harmful, homosexuality on the other hand is an issue which takes on a political nature in India—as it does in many countries—and, as a result, there are those who would oppose a message of acceptance as well as those who would oppose a message of condemnation. Considering that homosexual acts were de jure illegal until July of 2009 in India, this is not surprising. Even in the United States, most public schools do not teach about homosexuality because of this similar political divide (Jan, 2006; Newsom, 2008).

Discussions of HIV/AIDS can likely be had without choosing sides, either advocating or denouncing the associated activities or states which are considered controversial. Of course, there are some people and groups who perpetuate the mistaken belief that HIV/AIDS only affects minorities, or even that HIV/AIDS is a form of divine punishment for what they consider to be immoral acts (Kopelman, 2002; Redjimi & Lert, 1993). For them, the provision of HIV/AIDS education to the general population is not only unnecessary but would constitute tacit approbation of those activities or states, and thus they would oppose HIV/AIDS education itself. Fortunately, that mistaken viewpoint is in the extreme minority, and most people recognize the public and personal benefit of teaching others to protect themselves against an incurable, transmissible, and fatal disease.

Thus, the question which remains is how to provide complete, accurate, and effective HIV/AIDS prevention education without using methods, messages, or language which automatically trigger societal rejection due to conflict with the aforementioned taboos. It is precisely these challenges and opportunities that lead researchers to ponder whether a curriculum could be devised to improve knowledge and change attitudes, despite these barriers (Sorcar, 2009).

Previous Attempts at HIV/AIDS Education

In many cases, laws and social norms prohibit the delivery of sexual health information through the standard educational, medical, or public health systems. Numerous studies have documented stigma and discrimination faced by patients from medical professionals (Kurien, 2007; Leary & Schreindorfer, 1998). In fact, although the National AIDS Control Organization (NACO) in India advocates confidentiality, one study presented at the 2002 International Conference on AIDS revealed that 95 percent of patients registered for surgical procedures were not only involuntarily tested for HIV, but their surgeries were cancelled if they tested seropositive (Malavade, Shah, Shah, Shah, 2002; United Nations Population Fund, 2009). Hence, there has been heavy emphasis in India in launching HIV/AIDS awareness campaigns through the mass media (e.g., messages on billboards, posters, television spots, radio ads) in order to reach large populations. There have been large-scale combined efforts by news organizations, foundations, and the Indian government to spread awareness through the mainstream media (James, Hoff, Davis & Graham, 2005). Although this method is capable of simultaneously reaching a large number of people to raise awareness, there are many reasons why its exclusive or primary use is incapable of stemming the HIV/AIDS epidemic.

Educational campaigns via mass media have been constrained by cost. Because advertising is priced according to time and space used, educational advertisements are dispersed in terse segments (e.g., television spots are approximately thirty seconds to two-minutes, billboards usually carry one or two messages). Examples of these include the Buladi campaign launched by the West Bengal AIDS Control Society, and the Balbir Pasha campaign launched by the Population Services International. It may be difficult for learners to build knowledge based on these brief presentations, as these campaigns involve limited durations of exposure.

Second, depending on the type of media, there are intrinsic limitations on the impact on key sub-populations. For example, television ads are only accessible to homes with television sets. Going one step further, television sets are only available to homes with electricity. Thus, individuals who see television ads at home, tend to have a significantly higher socioeconomic standing. However, the groups most lacking in basic HIV/AIDS education are often of lower socioeconomic standing. HIV/AIDS messages on billboards are usually expressed in written text, which limits their impact to the 62.5 percent of the population that is literate (Census of India, 2001). Even more problematic, women who are in remote villages are less likely to be exposed to any kind of HIV/AIDS media campaigns at all. A 2006 survey, conducted by the National Family Health Survey (NHFS), found that 70 percent of women in rural Bihar had not even heard of HIV/AIDS (Mishra, 2007).

Finally, mass media campaigns only allow for one-way communication—learners receive the messages but are not able to ask questions or immediately follow-up in any way. It is, therefore, difficult to gauge whether the correct messages are being acquired and spread through these channels. It is also difficult to isolate the effects of particular messages, making it impossible to identify and study targeted improvements from one campaign to the next.

Because there is no cure for HIV, and antiretroviral medications are out of reach for most of India's population (in that they are too expensive and must be taken for an infected person's entire life), prevention is critical in curbing the spread of the epidemic. Although numerous educational materials and interventions are available throughout the world, many are developed by medical personnel, who while having the best intentions and being well-versed in diagnosis and treatment, are less familiar with developing pedagogically-grounded and effective curricula (Singhal & Rogers, 2003). When educating about communicable diseases, being able to adapt curricula to pre-existing notions of behavior is imperative for content to be assimilated in a coherent fashion. The ability to understand and apply HIV prevention strategies properly, especially in high-risk situations, is vital to preventing transmission. At a minimum, properly understanding prevention strategies could significantly curb stigma and fear-related issues associated with the subject. Hence, the development of highly effective education messages should be based on formative assessments, pedagogically sound messages, and culturally appropriate materials. The framework for evaluation can be used to determine whether curricula relating to taboo topics, is likely to be effective for the target group.

Cultural Challenges

Many activists argue that the socially conservative nature of many Asian cultures put vulnerable populations at extreme risk. In their view, it is the responsibility of the government to help change those cultures to make them more progressive and capable of openly discussing sexual practices (Medical News Today, 2007; Mukherjee, 2007; Sundaram, 2007). Changing ingrained cultural norms, however, is difficult and is obviously opposed by many conservative groups. In addition, democratically elected governments are generally not eager to tell their constituents that their cultural values are in any way incorrect or outdated. [In India, for example, homosexuality is considered a taboo topic by many and a was de jure criminalized until June 2009:

Whoever voluntarily has carnal intercourse against the order of nature with any man, woman, animal shall be punished with imprisonment for life, or with imprisonment of either description for a term which may extend to 10 years, and shall be liable to fine. (Section 377, Indian Penal Code, 1860)

This provision deterred certain marginalized populations from getting tested for HIV out of fear of being ostracized or even imprisoned for their behavior (Agoramoorthy & Minna, 2007). There is also the issue of paternalism: it is difficult to justify an intervention that labels a culture as flawed.

Mass media campaigns aimed at promoting educational messages that do not properly stress evidence-based prevention strategies may actually have devastating effects on society. Decision-makers of each state may continue to ban sex and HIV/AIDS education in schools, claiming that the media campaigns, albeit ineffective, are providing enough education. As such, these mass media campaigns are mere band-aid solutions that do not address many of the root causes of the problem. Moreover, these campaigns do not adequately address many of the underlying issues, such as gender-based inequalities, which promote the spread of the virus through the population.

Why Technology and Not Teachers

Although open discussions between students and educators would be an ideal method of imparting accurate knowledge and correcting myths and misinformation, many teachers across India do not feel comfortable addressing the topics of sex or HIV/AIDS in the classroom. Since HIV/AIDS is directly related to other sensitive subjects its relationship to these taboos makes it even more challenging to discuss openly. Numerous studies dealing with prevention education have found teachers reticent and uncomfortable to discuss sexual matters with their students (Kirby et al., 2006; Nayak & Bose, 1997; Smith et al., 2003; Verma, Sureender & Guruswamy, 1997). In 2007, teachers in Uttar Pradesh publicly burned materials in bonfires to protest sex education (India Together, 2008).

Waiting for a country's culture and laws to change, or even trying to change it, is not a viable means of warding off a possibly immediate pandemic. New approaches must be created to provide education despite whatever social, structural, cultural, and legal barriers exist. Fortunately, the emergence of new media and ICT has provided possibilities for innovative ways to help bypass social taboos and provide effective messages in ways that were simply not possible in the past. Self-guided learning mechanisms, whether book, audiotape, or a computer application, allow learners to assimilate information in a private learning spaces, free from public scrutiny and embarrassment. This freedom from embarrassment also applies to teachers, who often choose neither to teach about taboo subjects nor emphasize curricula with which they themselves are not comfortable. Additionally, ICT is superior to books and tapes from a monitoring perspective because ICT is inherently trackable—one can know exactly how many learners completed the application, how long it took them to answer particular questions, as well as whether they were able to answer questions correctly. Powerful insights can be gained from granularly tracking how learners interacted with individual modules, enabling one to rapidly improve the efficacy of the applications. Furthermore, Internet applications are amenable to a multitude of functions, for example, providing and exchanging information, use of simulation-based modules, facilitating decision-making and action planning, promoting specific behaviors and self-care, providing social support, and managing demand for health services (Nguyen, Carrieri-Kohlman, Rankin, Slaughter & Stulbarg, 2004; Nguyen, Cuenco, Wolpin, Benditt & Carrieri-Kohlman, 2007; Orlandi, Dozier & Marta, 1990; Sampson & Krumboltz, 1991), which are essential to improving health outcomes. Finally, ICT allows designers to both standardize best practices and readily adapt content to local needs (e.g., adaptation for language, ethnicity, gender differences as well as differing levels of familiarity with the subject).

In some cases, providing education via ICT can actually be more effective than other more traditional means, and hence have been advocated in public health circles (Burnett, Magel, Harrington & Taylor, 1989; Lightfoot, Comulada & Stover, 2007; Orlandi et al., 1990). A recent computer-based HIV prevention intervention, targeted towards delinquent youths in the United States, found that youth exposed to the computer-based intervention were significantly less likely to engage in sexual activity, relative to the non-computer-based group and control group (Lightfoot et al., 2007). Also, the computer-based group reported fewer partners in the follow-up three months later (Lightfoot et al., 2007).

As new forms of ICT have been created, so too have learning applications utilizing those technologies. Some of these applications are for big-screen (projection) formats, while others are for smaller formats such as mobile devices. These types of applications can be used to communicate a message to large groups or one person at a time. Each approach has advantages and disadvantages. Furthermore, some educators choose to use ICT as a form of "edutainment" to enhance comfort or in cases when the teachers may not be as familiar with a subject. The use of technology-based learning has enabled new forms and formats for learning beyond the traditional model of in-person, linear, real-time instruction.

Given the structural, political, legal and cultural constraints in providing effective and yet accessible prevention materials, an interdisciplinary team of experts was assembled to explore these daunting challenges and work towards building an educational approach which could be accessed more openly by the Indian society.

CONSTRUCTING A TECHNOLOGICAL SOLUTION

Foundation for Educational Software

While working with an interdisciplinary team of experts at Stanford (spanning the fields of public health, communications, human computer interaction and education), Piya Sorcar designed and authored an interactive HIV/AIDS prevention application to specifically avoid the taboos and other cultural barriers that have impeded AIDS education and resulting changes in behavior. The software provides detailed, yet accessible and acceptable, discussions of all aspects of HIV/AIDS and hence had the potential for widely altering the knowledge and associated risk behaviors of Asian youth and adults (Sorcar, 2009).

With various bans on sex education, access to AIDS education is limited in many Indian communities (BBC News, 2007; Mukherjee, 2007). Since HIV/AIDS is a taboo subject in India, a major design consideration for this tutorial was to maximize comfort levels among learners while they were interacting with the software.

After learning that despite hundreds of millions of dollars spent on HIV/AIDS prevention in India, basic knowledge of transmission was still limited, further investigation was needed. Several first-generation Indian undergraduate and graduate students who had recently migrated to the United States from India were interviewed about these issues. Because of the deeply sensitive nature of topics relating to sexual practices, researchers had to build trust with students before asking them questions relating to their personal experiences.

Based on IRB-approved research conducted on several hundred young adults in India, a team of interdisciplinary experts and researchers at Stanford University were recruited to develop an application to bypass Asian cultural sensitivities and yet provide highly effective prevention education (Sorcar, 2009). *Interactive Teaching AIDS* was an ICT-based application aimed to provided research-based, culturally-appropriate HIV/AIDS prevention education to audiences where discussing topics related to sexual practices is often considered taboo. The pilot application, which took two years to develop, test, and optimize, was initially designed only for an Indian audience and targeted young adults, but has since been adapted for learners throughout the world.[12]

The application used a question-driven approach. The questions in the animated tutorial were based on: 1) the most frequently asked questions by learners in the design phase and 2) the most misunderstood facts about HIV/AIDS transmission and prevention. Furthermore, unlike other curricula which is either purely scientific (e.g., HIV transmission discussed in the context of virology or infectious disease) or teaches learners to avoid the questionable activity entirely (e.g., "Just Say No" and other abstinence-based sex education campaigns), this method utilized an entirely different approach. To maximize comfort and promote coherent understanding, it coupled biological aspects of transmission with culturally familiar euphemisms and metaphors to communicate ideas around prevention measures, utilizing numerous education and communication theories. Entertainment education has been documented as being a powerful tool to bring sensitive subjects, such as HIV/AIDS, into public discourse (Piotrow, Kincaid, Rimon & Rinehart, 1997; Singhal & Rogers, 1999).

The ITA tutorial was based on numerous pedagogies and theories explored in the following section. It focused solely on knowledge gain and bypassed taboos by carefully avoiding challenging cultural norms or making normative statements. The tutorial was also designed to be highly flexible because it used animations rather than live actors. There were separate male and female versions of the application, incorporating both male and female doctor and student characters for various target groups.

Developing a Coherent Conception: The Fan Effect

Media campaigns about HIV/AIDS that are limited in scope (e.g., billboards carrying one or two main messages, or television ads of 30 seconds to 1 minute) can cause misconceptions if the learner does not have a firm grasp of the basic concepts. Learning about HIV/AIDS protective measures is in some ways analogous to learning to drive. If a student learns about using the car mirrors from a billboard, turning the wheel from a television commercial, and utilizing the car breaks from a radio ad, it would be challenging for them to piece all the concepts together to drive a car properly. Imagine this difficulty coupled with the inability to ask those around you open questions about driving because it was a sensitive or taboo subject. Similarly, learners receive fragmented data about HIV/AIDS transmission through various mass media campaigns in India, making it difficult for them to create a coherent overall picture for prevention and understanding. Furthermore, the misunderstandings may become even more convoluted when they are coupled with the reticent behavior of individuals of all ages around this subject.

Research shows that expert knowledge centers on concepts that are connected and assembled in an organized fashion (Bransford, Brown & Cocking, 1999). Usable knowledge is, therefore, quite different from a large set of disconnected facts.

Fan Effect learning theory shows that the more individual facts that a person learns about a single concept, the more difficult it is for them to retrieve particular facts from memory (Anderson, 1974; Anderson & Reder, 1999). This retrieval mechanism is especially difficult when the set of facts do not have an internal cohesiveness or integration (Spoehr, 1994). Furthermore, connecting facts in a coherent fashion allows learners to build patterns and relationships leading to a deep understanding as well as greater transfer to novel situations (Bransford et al., 1999).

One common way educators present health education in a cohesive manner is through a list of "DOs" and "DON'Ts" (e.g., do take steps to protect yourself, don't engage in risky behaviors). Previous research on effective methods to promote HIV prevention has shown that this presents "superficial knowledge" and is therefore unlikely to translate into actionable prevention methods and may even increase fear among learners (Au & Romo, 1996; Au, Roma & DeWitt, 1999). When teaching about HIV/AIDS prevention to young people, it is imperative to avoid fragmented knowledge (e.g., "dos"and "don'ts") and focus on creating a coherent conception (e.g., teaching concepts around bodily fluids, fluid transmission). This allows students to organize considerable information, as well as to learn to reason through novel settings (Dooling & Lachman, 1971).

Since sex and reproductive health education is not mandatory in India, it is unclear how individuals piece together the disparate bits of information they might receive. For instance, promoting the popular ABC campaign (<u>A</u>bstinence, <u>B</u>e Faithful, Use <u>C</u>ondoms) among people who do not understand the basics of fluid transmission can make understanding the underlying message more difficult. However, a person with limited knowledge, who follows this campaign blindly, may be especially at risk. For instance, the 'B' in 'Be Faithful' is in reference to having a monogamous faithful relationship with their partner. Consider a case where a man is having relationship with a female commercial sex worker and he is "being faithful", in the sense that he is visiting the same commercial sex worker (CSW) and, therefore, abstains from using a condom. Although he is following the advice of the ABC campaign literally, he is still at risk if the CSW is having sexual relations with other clients.[13] Similarly, a faithful wife may follow the ABC campaign verbatim; however, if her husband is having an extramarital affair, she is still at risk. Being able to simply repeat rules and campaign messages is not good enough. Individuals must understand the underlying concepts underlying these messages are grounded in. In both the above scenarios, all individuals involved are at risk of an HIV infection. With little knowledge of transmission, blindly following the advice of a public campaign can have ill effects. Due to these sorts of misunderstandings, organizations such as Population Services International have launched campaigns to improve comprehension of exactly this sort of transmission-related issue (Population Services International, 2003).

The baseline surveys coupled with the one-on-one interviews with first-generation Indians revealed several misunderstandings among the target group, such as the belief that HIV can be transmitted through kissing, hugging, or water. Several students knew that HIV could be transmitted through blood and noted they had seen ads about such educational messages. However, when asked "how" one could get HIV from blood (e.g., touching blood, licking blood), it was evident the learners had superficial knowledge about the topic. The ITA curriculum therefore, did not rely heavily on prior knowledge in order to understand fundamental concepts of transmission. Rather it introduced a broad description of how bacteria and viruses work within the body, through an analogy of soldiers within a country. It then progressed to the concept of body fluids–reviewing high-risk and no-risk fluids in the body. Next, the application facilitated learners to understand that high-risk fluids must literally enter the human body to create a risk of infection. Finally, the application helpd learners identify and connect various actions (e.g. coughing, hugging) with bodily fluids and transmission modes. This entire sequence was developed, through an iterative design approach based on testing, to give learners a coherent conception of how the virus survives in the human body and to provide the learner with a way of assessing whether he or she is at risk. Furthermore, providing visual representations of the concepts help to orient learners and have shown to facilitate retention (Pinsky & Wipf, 2001).

Balancing Social Acceptability with Accuracy and Efficacy

Although research indicates that fear-based approaches, in specific cases, can increase information processing and associated gains in learning (Kim, Sorcar, Um, Chung, Lee, 2008; Lee & Ferguson, 2002), teaching about taboo topics requires particular sensitivity to maintaining comfort for both students and administrators. Fear-based interventions tend to be highly graphic and disturbing. With the ban on sex education in India and sensitivity around subjects like HIV/AIDS, they would likely not be acceptable to traditional institutions, regardless of their efficacy.

Selecting images that are both comfortable and efficacious is both important and extremely challenging. On the one hand, communicating sensitive messages via simple representations, like stick figures, would maintain higher levels of overall comfort. However, the abstract nature of the representation might hinder accurate message communication, and thus learning. On the other hand, designers can use highly graphic and explicit images, which would communicate exact actions to best understand transmission. However, these sorts of images would be uncomfortable for learners. Feeling comfortable with the materials may further ensure that learners share information

Figure 2.

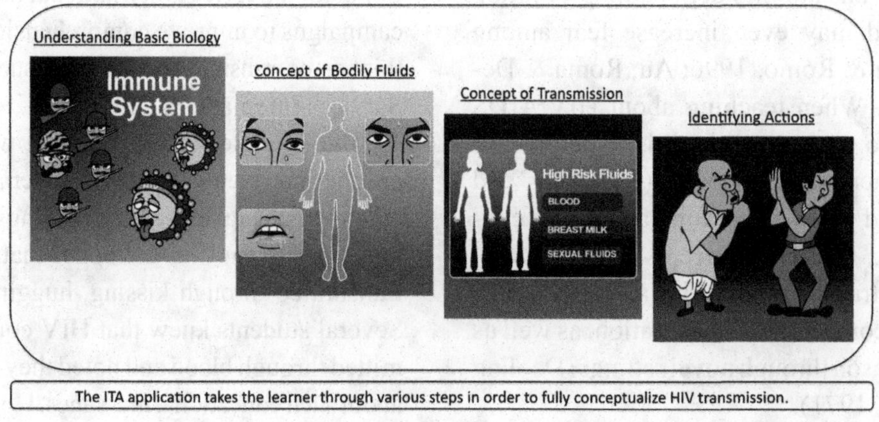

The ITA application takes the learner through various steps in order to fully conceptualize HIV transmission.

with others. The goal was to identify images that would be both clear and effective but also maximize comfort and social acceptability.

Identifying Socially Acceptable Graphics

A Stanford IRB-approved anonymous survey was conducted on 200 undergraduate students in New Delhi, India to better understand the mindset of young adults, assess their baseline knowledge, and understand what types of pictures could be utilized to communicate messages and maximize comfort and learning. School officials restricted the kinds of pictures that could be tested on the students, limiting the range of the data. However, this negotiation process was highly informative, as it allowed the researchers to further grapple with the kinds of images and information allowed within the scholastic environment. The survey was rejected several times before schools finally agreed to run it on their students. With each survey iteration, questionable and uncomfortable materials were removed and resubmitted the survey for approval.

It is likely that most HIV/AIDS curricula will need to contain facts about breastfeeding, child delivery and sexual intercourse, since these are all common modes of transmission. The pictures in the survey were all simple black and white drawings from existing HIV/AIDS curricula used by local NGOs[14]. Below is a subset of pictures from the survey depicting these methods of transmission. The numbers associated with each picture (36 percent breastfeeding, 52 percent child delivery, 59 percent intimacy) represent the percentage of students that indicated that they were unsure, uncomfortable or very uncomfortable with the associated graphics. After reviewing these results, it was necessary to identify other images to communicate the correct messages and maximize comfort levels.

Researchers worked with the target group and identified culturally-sensitive pictorial depictions which communicated the concept of bodily fluids and transmission. They also explored varying degrees of humor with images, which when used appropriately, can be an effective mechanism to overcome a taboo topic (Fennell, 1993; Singhal & Rogers, 2003).

Below are a few examples of the types of pictures[15] the focus groups felt most comfortable with while communicating issues of transmission. These are a few examples used to devise a socially acceptable approach, which was discussed as part of the framework for evaluation. The pictures on the left were tested and replaced with the pictures on the right in the ITA applications.

For the representation of breastfeeding, learners indicated that simply exposing less of the

Figure 3. Selected results from baseline survey. The numbers associated with each picture (36% breastfeeding, 52% child delivery, 59% intimacy) represent the percentage of young adults that responded to the baseline survey who were either unsure, uncomfortable or very uncomfortable with the associated graphics

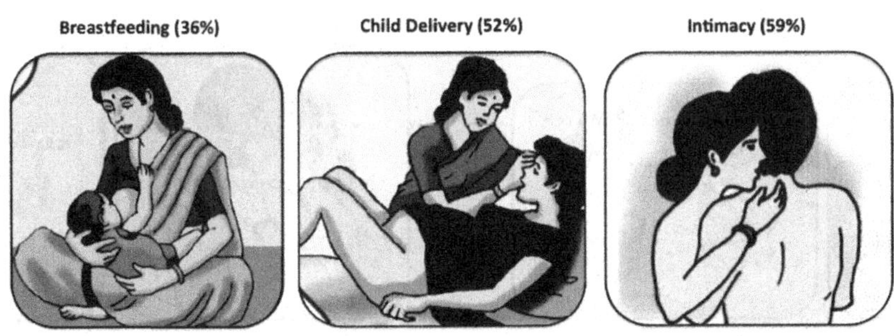

Figure 4. Representation of breastfeeding. To maximize comfort, the picture (on left) representing breastfeeding was replaced by the picture (on right) exposing less skin

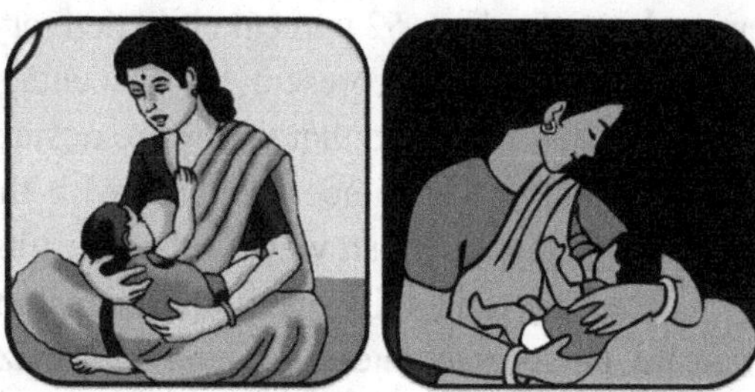

woman's breast increased overall comfort with the image and communicated the same message. The final pictures were also less detailed in that less volumetric shading was used to flatten the image further. The picture on the right was used in the final animation.

The final application included a simple animated sequence to convey delivery. Instead of showing a half exposed body, as in the picture (left), it featured a woman fully clothed (wearing an *Indian sari*) and then, through animation, a baby appears in her arms. The learners understood this woman to be euphemistically delivering a baby and found this imagery comfortable and even entertaining. With regards to providing information on vertical transmission, it was not the explicit knowledge of how infants are delivered that was central to creating a conceptual understanding, rather connecting the concepts related to transmission of the virus.

Figure 5. Representation of child delivery. The picture (on left) representing child delivery was replaced by the image (on right). Through animation, the pregnant woman morphs into one holding a baby

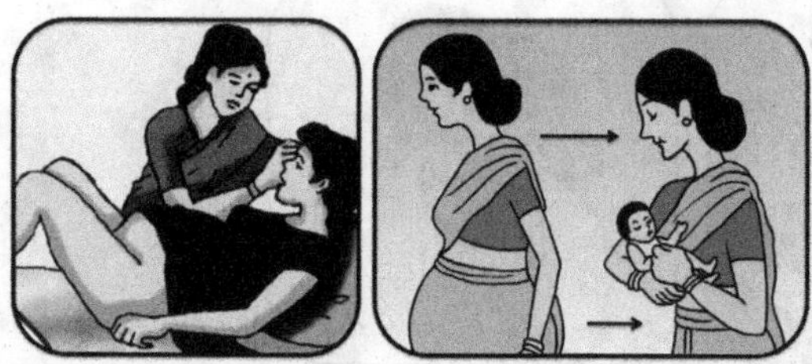

In order to represent intimacy, the animation incorporated ideas from old Bollywood movies from the 1960s and 1970s, which are viewed comfortably by masses in India.

In the picture above, instead of showing a couple publicly kissing (which is taboo in India), the animation showed a couple coming very close to kissing and then the camera panned up a tree (away from the couple) and the lovebirds kiss instead (picture on top right). This is an example of a culturally-appropriate use of a euphemism. The target group clearly understood the concept, especially since this sequence parallels love scenes from old Bollywood movies.

Figure 6. Representation of intimacy #1. The picture (on left) representing intimacy was replaced by a euphemistic image (on right) showing a close-up of the lovebirds kissing instead

Figure 7. Representation of intimacy #2. The picture (on left) representing intimacy was replaced by a culturally-appropriate image (on right) of a bride, sitting on her honeymoon bed, decorated by ceremonial flowers, representing a sexual connection

While discussing sexual intercourse (picture on top right), the animation included cultural elements from Bollywood movies and Indian traditions.

In order to maximize comfort, instead of showing a man and woman intimate with one another, the animation displayed an image of a woman in her wedding gown sitting on a bed decorated with flowers. This sort of floral arrangement (the tradition is called "suhag raat") takes place on the bed where a husband and wife will honeymoon on their wedding night.

Application of the Media Equation

The curriculum draws on the following principle based on 35 studies described in *The Media Equation* (Reeves & Nass, 1996): people apply the same social rules and heuristics when interacting with media as they do when interacting with actual people and places. Furthermore, these responses were true of all the segments they were tested on including children, college sophomores, business people, and technology experts. These social responses to media are unconscious and automatic.

Due to the sensitive nature of this subject and discomfort among young adults to discuss it openly, ICT was chosen to deliver the ITA curriculum. *The Media Equation* suggests that students should be able to learn from the animated characters in a similar way to learning from humans, with the added benefit of knowing they are only interacting with technology. This should help diminish embarrassment or discomfort as the interaction is with a completely non-threatening technological device as opposed to a human. However, one important difference (and benefit) that was discovered through the focus groups was that learners felt less embarrassed about sensitive topics when interacting with technology instead of with other people.

While designing the animated characters and discussing their features, it was discovered that students in the focus groups felt even more comfortable if the characters did not have names associated with them. Originally, primary characters in the animation were given generic names (e.g. Raja, Rani). However, being that these names were generic, the users inevitably knew someone with those names and said they thought about them during their interaction with the curriculum. Suddenly, the students' experience did not feel "private" anymore, consistent with the ideas from *The Media Equation*. Removing character names from the curriculum had the added benefit of avoiding religious or caste classifications.[16] Other HIV/AIDS initiatives have encountered problems with selecting names for campaign characters specifically due to the religious associations (Shah, 2006).

Mnemonic Devices as Learning Tools

Mnemonic devices, which use visual image links, have been shown to enhance retention of difficult concepts (Lorayne & Lucas, 1974; Luria, 1968). They are essentially memory aids designed to help the learner create associations between various constructs.

The ITA application reinforces primary concepts through various pictorial mnemonic devices. These devices were used to help students retain novel concepts. For instance, students learn about the *Three Point Mantra* (left), which outlines the high-risk transmission fluids (top left). Every time the doctor says *Three Point Mantra*, he/she (depending on the version) holds up his/her three fingers, which are used as a symbol or icon throughout the animation.

- **3-Point Mantra** (High-Risk Fluids)
  1) Blood
  2) Breast Milk
  3) Sexual Fluids

Another example of a mnemonic device is the concept of the *Triangle Test*, which helps the learner assess whether he or she is at risk in a

Figure 8. Mnemonic device to facilitate learning about fluid transfer. The ITA application uses mnemonic devices to help learners better understand the most important concepts. Above is are examples of the 3-point mantra and the Triangle Test

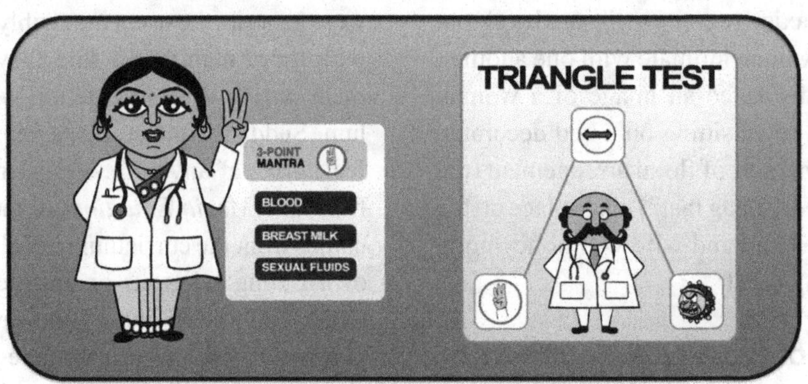

particular situation. There are three parts to the *Triangle Test*, arranged on the three corners of a triangle. The memory aid reinforces that there are three steps for considering the risk of an infection. The doctor character uses his or her pointer to show the learner the direction to properly use this learning tool. See below for the mnemonic strategy.

- Triangle Test
  - *Step One:* Is there a HIGH RISK FLUID?
    - If no, stop here. There is no HIV risk.
    - If yes, proceed to STEP 2.
  - *Step Two:* Is there DIRECT TRANSFER?
    - If no, stop here. There is no HIV risk.
    - If yes, proceed to STEP 3.
  - *Step Three:* There is a POSSIBLE HIV INFECTION.
    - Go see a doctor.

Voice Properties and Gender Concurrence

Nass and Brave demonstrate the applicability of social psychological principles of similarity attraction to the design of computer agents (Nass & Brave, 2005). They discuss the concept of homophily—similars attract—which essentially means that people are attracted to other people who are most similar to them. Participants rated

Figure 9. Mnemonic devices for learning about risky behaviors. Above is the example of the Triangle Test. This use of a mnemonic device helps the learner assess whether he or she is at risk of an HIV infection

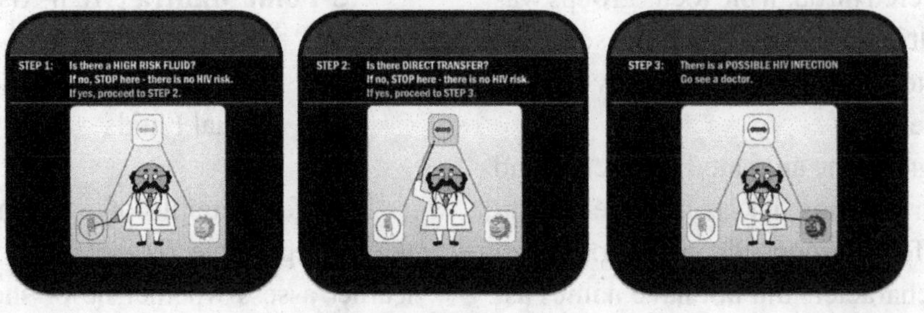

agents similar to themselves as the most credible, trustworthy and friendly. Based on these findings, male and female characters with voices similar to the target audience were chosen. Because this animation was aimed towards young adults in India, voice actors with similar accents and pronunciations within the appropriate age groups were recruited.

The current animations features voices selected directly by young people in the target audience. The development team first selected five to six candidate voice actors and then uploads sample clips using an online survey tool. The students in the target group then vote on the voice choices, advocating which ones they like best, given the context. The winning voice actors then record the entire script for the animation. This is an interesting way to incorporate a participatory design approach in order to secure a better local fit for such educational tools.

The animation itself consists of a discussion between a student and his/her physician through which basic HIV/AIDS-related questions and concepts are explored in order to better understand transmission and prevention methods. Separate versions for males and females (the male version has a male doctor and male student while the female version has a female doctor and female student) were also developed. This decision was based on the evidence that gender concordance is important while discussing sensitive issues (e.g. sex education), particularly among female patients (Fang, McCarthy & Singer, 2004).

Cultural Embeddings

"If culture is a factor in transmission and impact, it follows that prevention and care require a cultural approach"–Healthlink Worldwide, 2007

Experts say that cultural embeddings are an integral component to designing HIV/AIDS materials (Commission for Africa, 2005). Integrating values, beliefs and traditions into educational materials helps to build trust and engagement at the community level (Healthlink Worldwide, 2007) and has lead to greater overall program acceptance and sustainability (UNFPA, 2004). It is particularly important to use culturally sensitive materials while designing messages for highly stigmatized subjects as not to offend the learners (Singhal & Rogers, 2003). Some individuals may be interacting with the materials in order to protect themselves and their loved ones. Others may either be seropositive or know someone (e.g. family member, friend, co-worker) who is infected with the virus. Culturally-appropriate approaches have shown greater impact on promoting awareness, changes in attitudes (stigma reductions) and further inclusion of those living with HIV and AIDS (Healthlink Worldwide, 2007). It is particularly important to develop appropriate materials as life threatening illnesses, such as HIV and AIDS, can present tremendous physical and psychological distress on those infected as well as others within their social network (Derlega & Barbee, 1998).

There are several cultural elements embedded into the ITA application in order to make it familiar and appropriate for the learners. Throughout the development process, numerous individuals with expertise in India related social and cultural issues were consulted. A professional award-wining artist[17], with decades of experience, was engaged to illustrate all the Indian animated characters.

The ITA application also utilizes ideas from experts who have studied India-related social and cultural issues. Several brainstorming sessions in and around Stanford were conducted, targeting Indians who had recently migrated from India, to learn about cultural sensitivities and necessities in designing further outreach of the application. In order to be consistent with the expectations of young learners, the materials incorporated ideas from popular Bollywood films, including trends, costumes choices, cultural icons, and analogies through the animated characters.

Figure 10. Cultural embeddings. The ITA application incorporates many cultural embeddings. Above are pictures of some of the characters in the animation

Figure 11. MS&E 17SI course at Stanford University. MS&E 17SI: Stanford undergraduate and graduate students brainstorming ideas for the India Interactive Teaching AIDS application through a Management Science and Engineering course

Based on feedback from the focus groups, several words, phrases and metaphors were tested and altered to be more culturally-appropriate and appear more colloquially. Interaction with experts and the focus groups revealed the importance of using particular phrases correctly to further ensure acceptance of the program. Below are some examples:

a. The proverb "*an ounce of prevention is worth a pound of cure*" is more commonly said and written in India simply as "*prevention is better than cure*". Since the baseline survey revealed that young people had many questions around a cure for HIV/AIDS, the title for the animation became "*Prevention is Better than NO CURE*".
b. Instead of saying "*appearances can be deceiving*", the application uses a more popular Indian derivation, "*appearances are deceptive*".
c. The chapter describing viruses included a list of the most typical viruses affecting Indians (e.g., polio, chicken pox, and measles)

The learning and communication theories summarized in this chapter were carefully examined and tested piecemeal in the focus groups before combining them into the ITA application. In particular, they were used to maximize cultural appropriateness and promote acceptance of the prevention education.

DISCUSSION AND ANALYSIS

Comparison of Case Study to Framework for Evaluation

Table 3 summarizes the ITA application using the framework for evaluation described earlier in the chapter. It demonstrates how the application ideally fits into the various categories for the framework.

Success of Interactive Teaching AIDS

A large-scale study was conducted using the *Interactive Teaching AIDS* application in September, 2007 on 386 young adults in India. The study found statistically significant gains in learning ($p<.001$), retention ($p<.001$), and changes in attitudes (greater acceptance of HIV/AIDS-related issues and people) ($p<.001$). Furthermore, 98.6 percent of the participants felt comfortable

Table 3. Comparison of case study to framework for evaluation

	Social Acceptability	Potential Accuracy/ Completeness	Potential Efficacy	Ease of Deployment
Interactive Teaching AIDS (by TeachAIDS organization)	*Why it is socially acceptable:* Curricula presents HIV/AIDS prevention material while decoupling it from traditional sex education (may enter into areas where sex education is banned or considered sensitive). Campaign materials based on both what public health officials consider important as well as needs identified by target population (through baseline surveys). Characters designed to suit cultural likes and dislikes (e.g. costumes). Character voices selected to reflect Indian accents (selected by target audience). Script adapted to incorporate colloquial phrases (piloted and iterated based on feedback from target audience). Culturally-appropriate metaphors and euphemisms (piloted and iterated based on feedback from target audience). Male and female specific version to accommodate gender preferences and empowerment. Materials available in multiple languages to suit local audiences.	*Why it is accurate/ complete:* ICT-based curriculum delivers exactly the same information every time. Materials vetted by numerous medical and health professionals. Cultural euphemisms and metaphors tested on target population to ensure they are communicating the correct messages. Alternate and novel concepts around teaching about HIV/AIDS prevention materials tested on students to ensure efficacy in learning.	*Why it is effective:* Learners can utilize the materials in private or semi-private contexts, and control the pace and flow of information. Detailed information can be provided in a full-tutorial context, as opposed to piecemeal approaches of most mass media campaigns. Materials developed based on iterative design process (piloted on hundreds of students in India) to test the learning, retention, comfort and overall efficacy of the learning materials. Summative and formative based on target audience were developed and used. Use of pedagogically-grounded strategies and communications theories to improve learning and retention (e.g. mnemonic devices, voice interfaces)	*Why it's easy to deploy:* Free software has zero marginal distribution cost when used through the Internet, and minimal cost of production on CD. Materials from CDs can be installed on numerous computers. May be administered regardless of teacher's previous knowledge. Learning materials can be deployed using various technologies, depending on local context (computers, mobile devices, project with large screen). May be viewed regardless of Internet connectivity. Materials can be used in conjunction with other materials or as a stand-alone mass communications tool. Materials scalable to small or large audiences (use of computer or PDA for one-on-one interaction or projected to numerous people at the same time, which may be most useful in resource-poor locations. Animations contain subtitles for hearing impaired and audio for preliterate learners to ensure greater access to the materials.

learning from this tool and 94.5 percent said that they learned more about HIV/AIDS through this animated tutorial than any other communication method, including television or school. Perhaps the most remarkable result was that, although it was related to numerous taboo subjects, almost all of the young adults were willing to forward the tutorial to others and wanted to learn more about HIV/AIDS. One month after initial exposure to the tutorial, students were rapidly seeking out and educating others about HIV/AIDS prevention through peer networks, with nearly all of them sharing information learned from the tutorial with someone else (Sorcar, 2009).

The success of *ITA* led to the development of TeachAIDS, a California-based nonprofit aimed at providing research-based, culturally-appropriate HIV/AIDS materials for learners around the world. The theory, methodology, and development process outlined have been extended to create learning applications for people of diverse cultures. TeachAIDS has partnered with numerous governmental agencies and non-governmental organizations, and research institutions to develop and launch customized applications. Outside of India, TeachAIDS has had great success in launching interactive animated materials in around the world including South Korea, Rwanda, South Africa and China, among others. The campaigns have been so compelling that in 2009 numerous A-list celebrities (e.g., Shabana Azmi, Amol Palekar, Akkineni Nagarjuna, among others) joined the TeachAIDS efforts and gifted their voices to the animated works to expand the reach even further.

Theoretical, Empirical, and Methodological Contributions

With the success of this approach, there is great potential to change the way educators think of addressing and delivering this form of education entirely. Regardless of the ban on sex education throughout India and the cultural sensitivities around discussing this across the globe, a way to provide education for all was discovered, regardless of their cultural norms and social contexts. This same methodology can be, and already is being, extended to other contexts where taboo topics hinder the effective dissemination of education for potentially life threatening conditions.

Theoretical Contributions

Determining effective methods to openly discuss and educate about sensitive issues, while encouraging learners to feel safe and communicative, remains a tremendous challenge for communication experts (Benton & Daniel, 1996). Research indicates that most taboos are inextricably linked with the various transformations of the human body (e.g., disease, death) (Allan & Burridge, 2006), making

Figure 12. Left: The Canadian International Development Agency (CIDA) uses TeachAIDS.org materials for their Rural Health Education Project in Goa, India. Right: High school students at Oakland International High School in California, United States, using TeachAIDS.org materials as part of their comprehensive lessons on HIV/AIDS awareness and prevention strategies

Figure 13. Left: Students at Central Johannesburg College (CJC) in South Africa working on TeachAIDS.org baseline study. Right: Youth at Stepping Stones International in Botswana interacting with TeachAIDS.org applications

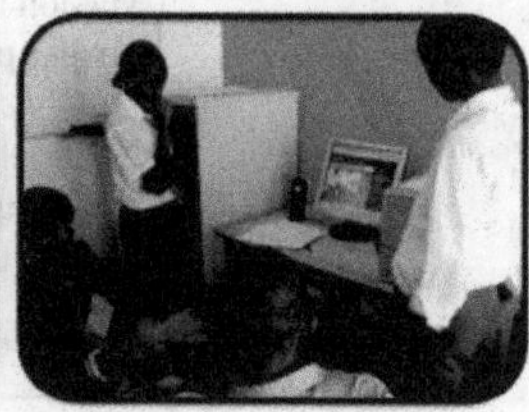

these issues particularly difficult about which to educate. Numerous studies have shown that teachers themselves can be reticent and uncomfortable providing sexual education to their students (Nayak & Bose, 1997; Verma et al., 1997). Although these challenges exist, there is little, if any, guidance on how to develop effective materials for taboo topics. This research will significantly contribute to the literature around best practices to teach about sensitive subjects. The theoretical framework identifying the challenges in teaching about communication taboos has been coupled with the framework for evaluating multiple dimensions and efficacy of such targeted curricula with a successful exemplar that future researchers can draw and build-upon to enhance effective communication, particularly in education and public health related fields.

Communicating learning from this new approach is especially important since evidence shows that it is possible to effectively teach about sensitive issues without disrespecting or challenging cultural beliefs and norms. Unlike other HIV/AIDS curricula, which are based on biomedical approaches (highly technical) or teach avoidance of particular activities to prevent danger (e.g. "Just Say No" campaigns, abstinence-based sex education), this method incorporates the pedagogical and cultural advantages of each. On one side, students are receiving the scientific knowledge in a way they understand and are able to build on prior knowledge, furthermore extend it to novel contexts. On the other side, stakeholders remain highly comfortable with the message itself and its delivery. If the results from this study are any indication of future possibilities, a theoretical framework has been unveiled, which researchers, communications experts, and educators can extend to other challenging and sensitive contexts (e.g., Hansen's disease, formerly known as leprosy).

Empirical Contributions

The empirical findings will contribute to the literature around the complex relationship between knowledge and attitudes. Furthermore, they will help in understanding the differences between these relationships for different cultures, socio-economic classes etc. Using a similar pattern to develop rigorous measures, outcomes can be determined in other Asian and African countries, which face similar challenges as India around discussing HIV/AIDS issues publicly.

Furthermore, porting this curriculum to other contexts and media (e.g. mobile devices, flip-charts, cartoon books, video) to measure the efficacy of using these platforms to spread awareness can be explored. This is especially important since, despite obvious need for this education, not all communities have equal and unlimited access to technology. Alternate media and distribution channels have differing advantages and disadvantages in terms of access, ease-of-development, ease-of-use, cost, efficacy, and other factors (see Table 4). Further research will need to be conducted in order to determine the true cost/benefit analysis of these models.

Methodological Contributions

Arguably one of the most significant contributions of this work is its provision of an understanding of the process of development of such a tool. Using the framework and following the documented step-by-step process will help experts extend these lessons to other contexts.

This chapter outlines two tiers of methodologies that can be followed. First, there are the more broad concepts. These would include lessons such as conducting assessments to identify the source of the taboos, understanding the cultural challenges, assessing various methods to deliver curricula, and iterative testing and development, among others. The second tier includes more specific strategies to appropriate an application, including selection of proper voices, suitable graphics, culturally appropriate analogies, mnemonic devices, and colloquial passages. Together, these strategies can inform the design of more effective interventions.

Table 4. Advantages and disadvantages of different media

Medium / Channel	Description	Advantages	Disadvantages
Flash	PC, advanced mobile device-based distribution	Interactivity, Internet-based tracking, rich user interface	Access limited to those with funds and access to PCs and Internet or very sophisticated mobile devices
Java	Intermediate mobile distribution	Improved access over Flash version, private learning environment	Limited UI, difficult to port animation, most mobile devices in India and other developing nations not supported
SMS	Widespread mobile distribution	Universal mobile access, private learning environment	Requires reimagining of curriculum to work through an SMS UI, SMS costs money
Audio	Mobile / landline telephone distribution	Universal telephone access, private learning environment	Requires reimagining of curriculum to work through audio UI, calls cost money
Book	Cartoon books, textbooks, flip-charts	Near-universal access (assuming literate and preliterate versions), storyboard will generally translate well to a book	No interactivity or trackability, high distribution costs

Scalability and Diffusion of Innovation

The diffusion of innovations theory (Rogers, 1995) concerns how new technology spreads through cultures. With the success of this exemplar, curricula like the ITA application can be disseminated through informal and formal learning environments. Informal learning environments would include museums, Internet, mobile devices, or by NGOs or other outreach organizations developing HIV awareness campaigns.

Formal learning environments would include school-like facilities. Scholastic environments are ideal vehicles for dissemination of accurate and comprehensive HIV/AIDS related information and have been identified by experts as appropriate places to undertake such activities (Kirby, Short, Collins, Rugg, Kolbe, Howard & Miller, Sonenstein & Zabin, 1994; SIECUS, 1999).

First, involvement in and attachment to school and plans to attend higher education are all related to less sexual risk-taking and lower pregnancy rates. Second, students in schools with manifestations of poverty and disorganization are more likely to become pregnant. Third, some school programs specifically designed to increase attachment to school or reduce school dropout effectively delayed sex or reduced pregnancy rate, even when they did not address sexuality. Fourth, sex and HIV education programs do not increase sexual behavior, and some programs decrease sexual activity and increase condom or contraceptive use. Fifth, school-based clinics and school condom-availability programs do not increase sexual activity, and either may or may not increase condom or contraceptive use. Other studies reveal that there is very broad support for comprehensive sex- and HIV-education programs, and accordingly, most youth receive some amount of sex or HIV education. However, important topics are not covered in many schools. (Kirby, 2002)

Because this tutorial does not incorporate explicit images or educate via traditional sex education, its likelihood of acceptance among Indian schools and other informal structures is greater. Also, locating critical information within ICT allows educators to comfortably facilitate and/or augment the learning process and alleviates pressure to deliver accurate medical content and feelings of embarrassment or uneasiness. Outside of these physical environments, it can also be disseminated via the Internet, including social networks like Facebook and Orkut, popular among young learners.

The next stage in scaling this solution is to create a collaborative system to allow participants from around the world to contribute to developing new curricula. This would be a web-based system much like Wikipedia, except with structured data and processes to allow for staged development and high levels of quality control. High quality, verified content is a requirement for any health-related curriculum. The creation of this system will not only allow for the creation of more effective curricula, but it will also allow those curricula to be developed and iterated upon more quickly than ever before. This is particularly advantageous in dealing with possible future public health outbreaks along the lines of conditions like SARS.

CONCLUSION

The successful outcomes of the Interactive Teaching AIDS intervention on hundreds of young adults in India, and the subsequent launching of the highly successful TeachAIDS nonprofit, has demonstrated that it is possible to create an effective communication messages despite the challenges in educating about taboo topics. Tools like the ITA application can be disseminated through formal and informal learning environments, depending on where it is most suitable. Because these applications do not incorporate explicit images or educate through traditional approaches, they have been acceptable in various institutes and other organizations around the world. Using these lessons, reticent educators can more comfortably facilitate the learning process without the pressure of delivering accurate medical content, while minimizing feelings of embarrassment or uneasiness. Furthermore, such applications can be administered as a standalone learning tools or used as a supplement to an existing curriculum. Experts can use canned versions irrespective of their previous knowledge or extend modules using the similar methodologies.

Building on previous theoretical and empirical literature, a framework of evaluation, outlining critical issues to consider has been introduced, while designing effective materials to best educate on taboo topics. Combining the flexibility of ICT-based applications with culturally-appropriate learning materials, experts can develop tools which both maximize learning and simultaneously work within existing cultural norms and traditions. Through the dissemination of effective and carefully crafted messages, TeachAIDS? hopes to provide open access to prevention materials and improve the lives of individuals around the world.

REFERENCES

Abiona, T. C., Onayade, A. A., Ijadunola, K. T., Obiajunwa, P. O., Aina, O. I., & Thairu, L. N. (2006). Acceptability, feasibility and affordability of infant feeding options for HIV-infected women: A qualitative study in south-west Nigeria. *Maternal and Child Nutrition*, *2*, 134–144. doi:10.1111/j.1740-8709.2006.00050.x

Abraham, L., & Kumar, A. (1999). Sexual experiences and their correlates among college students in Mumbai City in India. *International Family Planning Perspectives*, *25*(3), 139–146. doi:10.2307/2991963

Agoramoorthy, G., & Minna, J. H. (2007). India's homosexual discrimination and health consequences. *Revista de Saude Publica*, *41*(4), 657–660. doi:10.1590/S0034-89102006005000036

Allan, K., & Burridge, K. (2006). *Forbidden Words: Taboo and the censoring of language*. Cambridge, UK: Cambridge University Press. doi:10.1017/CBO9780511617881

Ambati, B. K., Ambati, J., & Rao, A. M. (1997). Dynamics of knowledge and attitudes about AIDS among the educated in southern India. *AIDS Care*, *9*(3), 319–330. doi:10.1080/09540129750125118

Anderson, J. R. (1974). Retrieval of propositional information from long-term memory. *Cognitive Psychology, 6*, 451–474. doi:10.1016/0010-0285(74)90021-8

Anderson, J. R., & Reder, L. M. (1999). The fan effect: New results and new theories. *Journal of Experimental Psychology. General, 128*(2), 186–197. doi:10.1037/0096-3445.128.2.186

Araujo, P. D. (2008). *Is India's population at risk of contracting HIV?* Retrieved January 20, 2009, from http://www.voxeu.org/index.php?q=node/1651

Au, T. K., Roma, L. F., & DeWitt, J. E. (1999). Considering children's folk biology in health education. In Siegal, M., & Peterson, C. (Eds.), *Children's Understanding of Biology and Health* (pp. 209–234). Cambridge, UK: Cambridge Studies in Cognitive and Perceptual Development.

Au, T. K., & Romo, L. F. (1996). Building a coherent conception of HIV transmission: A new approach to AIDS education. In Medin, D. (Ed.), *The Psychology of Learning and Motivation* (pp. 193–237).

Avert. (n.d.). *Abstinence*. Retrieved January 26, 2009, from http://www.avert.org/abstinence.htm

Avert. (n.d.). *Overview of HIV and AIDS in India*. Retrieved January 26, 2009, from http://www.avert.org/aidsindia.htm

Bennett, L. R. (2000). Sex talk, Indonesian youth and HIV/AIDS. *Development Bulletin Australian Development Studies Network, 52*, 54–57.

Benton, J. E., & Daniel, P. L. (1996). Learning to talk about taboo topics: A first step in examining cultural diversity with preservice teachers. *Equity & Excellence in Education, 29*(3), 8–17. doi:10.1080/1066568960290303

Better Breastfeeding, Healthier Lives: Women with HIV Face Crucial Breastfeeding Decisions. (n.d.). Population Reports. Retrieved February 18, 2009, from http://www.infoforhealth.org/pr/l14/7.shtml

Bio-Medicine. (2005). *Youth becoming sexually active at a younger age*. Retrieved January 20, 2009, from http://www.bio-medicine.org/medicine-news/Youth-Becoming-Sexually-Active-At-A-Younger-Age-5886-1/

Biswas, R. (2003). India's youth programs to combat AIDS must be diverse and widespread. *Population Reference Bureau*. Retrieved January 20, 2009, from http://www.prb.org/Articles/2003/IndiasYouthProgramstoCombatAIDSMustBeDiverseandWidespread.aspx

Bransford, J., Brown, A. L., & Cocking, R. R. (Eds.). (1999). *How people learn: Brain, mind, experience, and school*. Washington, DC: National Academy Press.

Burnett, K. F., Magel, P. E., Harrington, S., & Taylor, C. B. (1989). Computerized assisted behavioral health counseling for high school students. *Journal of Counseling Psychology, 36*(1), 63–67. doi:10.1037/0022-0167.36.1.63

Census of India. Census Data. (2001). *Literacy Rate: India–Part 3.* Retrieved from http://www.censusindia.net/ results/provindia3.html

Chadha, M. (2007 April). Indian state bans sex education. *BBC News*. Retrieved January 20, 2009, from http://news.bbc.co.uk/2/hi/south_asia/6523371.stm

Cichocki, M. (2007). HIV Around the World–India. *About.com*. Retrieved March 14, 2009, from http://aids.about.com/od/clinicaltrials/a/india.htm

Claeson, M., & Alexander, A. (2008, July). Tackling HIV In India: Evidence-based priority setting and programming. *Health Affairs, 27*(4), 1091–1102. doi:10.1377/hlthaff.27.4.1091

Clemmons, L., & Coulibaly, Y. (2000). Turning the ordinary into the extraordinary: The green pendelu and maternal health in Mali. *Dioro Approach Project Report*. Retrieved January 20, 2009, from http://www.comminit.com/ drum_beat_55.html

Correa, M., & Gisselquist, D. (2006). Routes of HIV transmission in India: assessing the reliability of information from AIDS case surveillance. *International Journal of STD & AIDS*, *17*, 731–735. doi:10.1258/095646206778691194

Court issues warrants against Shilpa Shetty, Richard Gere. (2007, April 26). *Hindustan Times*. Retrieved January 13, 2007, from http://www.hindustantimes.com/StoryPage/ StoryPage.aspx?id=b307da1b-cec7-419f-9e65-6108d797dbb3&ParentID=eda501ca-affe-4d4d-a93f-05a591421050&,amp,amp,amp,amp, amp,amp, amp,amp,amp,amp,amp,amp,&Head line=Court+issues+warrants+against+Shilpa% 2C+Gere

Derlega, V., & Barbee, A. P. (Eds.). (1998). *HIV and social interaction*. Thousand Oaks, CA: Sage Publications.

Dhillon, A. (2006). The land of Kama Sutra chokes on a kiss. *The Age*. Retrieved January 20, 2009, from http://www.theage.com.au/news/ entertainment/the-land-of-kama-sutra-chokes-on-a-kiss/2006/12/15/1166162320089.html

Dooling, D. J., & Lachman, R. (1971). Effects of comprehension on retention of prose. *Journal of Experimental Psychology*, *88*(2), 216–222. doi:10.1037/h0030904

Douglas, M. (2002). *Purity and Danger*. London: Routledge & Kegan Paul.

Evaluation of Abstinence Education Programs Funded Under Title V. Section 510. (n.d.). *Mathematica Policy Research, Inc*. Retrieved January 26, 2009, from http://www.mathematica-mpr.com/ welfare/abstinence.asp#reports

Fang, M. C., McCarthy, E. P., & Singer, D. E. (2004). Are patients more likely to see physicians of the same sex? Recent national trends in primary care medicine. *American Journal of Public Health*, *117*(8), 575–581.

Fennell, R. (1993). Using humor to teach responsible sexual health decision making and condom comfort. *Journal of American College Health*, *42*(1), 37–39.

Gentleman, A. (2007, May). Sex education curriculum angers Indian conservatives. *International Herald Tribune| ASIA-Pacific*. Retrieved January 20, 2009, from http://www.iht.com/ articles/2007/05/24/africa/letter.php

Gere faces Indian arrest warrant. (2007, April 27). *BBC News*. Retrieved January 13, 2009, from http://news.bbc.co.uk/2/hi/entertainment/6596163.stm

Gere kiss sparks India protests. (2007, April 16). *BBC News*. Retrieved January 13, 2009, from http:// news.bbc.co.uk/2/hi/entertainment/6560371.stm

Goffman, E. (1963). *Stigma: Notes on the management of spoiled identity*. Englewood Cliffs, NJ: Prentice Hall.

Herek, G. M., & Glunt, E. K. (1988). An epidemic of stigma: Public reactions to AIDS. *The American Psychologist*, *43*(11), 886–891. doi:10.1037/0003-066X.43.11.886

Howell, M. (2007). The history of federal abstinence-only funding. *Advocates for Youth*. Retrieved March 15, 2009, from http://www. advocatesforyouth.org/publications/factsheet/ fshistoryabonly.pdf

India Together. (2008 September). *Their secret status and a risky schooling*. Retrieved January 20, 2009, from http://www.indiatogether.org/2007/ sep/chi-aidskids.htm

India's Shyness towards Sexual Education Fuelling AIDS. (2002, November 1). *The HIV Update International, 2*(37).

James, M., Hoff, T., Davis, J., & Graham, R. (2005). Leveraging the power of the media to combat HIV/AIDS. *Health Affairs, 24*(3), 854–857. doi:10.1377/hlthaff.24.3.854

Jan, T. (2006). *Parents rip school over gay storybook*. The Boston Globe. Retrieved March 16, 2009, from http://www.boston.com/news/local/articles/2006/04/20/parents_rip_school_over_gay_storybook/

Kim, P., Sorcar, P., Um, Sujung, Chung, H., & Lee, Y. (2008). Effects of episodic variations in web-based avian influenza education: influence of fear and humor on perception, comprehension, retention and behavior. *Health Education Research.* Retrieved from doi:10.1093/her/cyn031

Kirby, D. (2002). The impact of schools and school programs upon adolescent sexual behavior. *Journal of Sex Research, 39*(1), 27–33. doi:10.1080/00224490209552116

Kirby, D. (2002). Effective approaches to reducing adolescent unprotected sex, pregnancy, and childbearing. *Journal of Sex Research, 39*(1), 51–57. doi:10.1080/00224490209552120

Kirby, D., Laris, B. A., & Rolleri, L. A. (2007). Sex and HIV education programs: Their impact on sexual behaviors of young people throughout the world. *The Journal of Adolescent Health, 40*(3), 206–217. doi:10.1016/j.jadohealth.2006.11.143

Kirby, D., Obasi, A., & Laris, B. A. (2006). The effectiveness of sex education and HIV education interventions in schools in developing countries. *World Health Organization Technical Report Series, 938*, 103–150.

Kirby, D., Short, L., Collins, J., Rugg, D., Kolbe, L., & Howard, M. (1994). School-based programs to reduce sexual risk behaviors: A review of effectiveness. *Public Health Reports (Washington, D.C.), 109*(3), 339–360.

Kopelman, L. M. (2002). If HIV/AIDS is punishment, who is bad? *The Journal of Medicine and Philosophy, 27*(2), 231–243. doi:10.1076/jmep.27.2.231.2987

Kurien, M., Thomas, K., Ahuja, R. C., Patel, A., Shyla, P. R., Wig, N., & Mangalani, M., Sathyanathan, Kasthuri, A., Vyas, B., Brogen, A., Sudarsanam, T. D., Chaturvedi, A., Abraham, O. C., Tharyan, P., Selvaraj, K. G., Mathew, J., & India CLEN HIV Screening Study Group. (2007). Screening for HIV infection by health professionals in India. *The National Medical Journal of India, 20*(2), 59–66.

Kurtenbach, E. (2005 June). 'Freedom,' 'democracy' taboo words on Chinese Internet. *The Associated Press.* Retrieved January 20, 2009, from http://www.usatoday.com/tech/news/2005-06-14-chineseInternet_x.htm

Leary, M. R., & Schreindorfer, L. S. (1998). The stigmatization of HIV and AIDS: rubbing salt in the wound. In Derlega, V. J., & Barbee, A. P. (Eds.), *HIV and Social Interaction* (pp. 12–29). Thousand Oaks, CA: Sage Publications.

Lee, M., & Ferguson, M. (2002). Effects of anti-tobacco advertisements based on risk-taking tendencies: Realistic fear vs. vulgar humor. *Journalism & Mass Communication Quarterly, 79*(4), 945–963.

Lightfoot, M., Comulada, W., & Stover, G. (2007). Computerized HIV preventive intervention for adolescents: Indications of efficacy. *American Journal of Public Health, 97*(6), 1027–1030. doi:10.2105/AJPH.2005.072652

Lives in Focus. (2008). *Living with HIV/AIDS in India*. Retrieved January 20, 2009, from http://www.livesinfocus.org/aids/2006/

Lorayne, H., & Lucas, J. (1974). *The memory book*. New York: Ballantine.

Luria, A. R. (1968). *The mind of the mnemonist*. New York: Avon.

Maine, H. (2004). *Ancient Law*. New Brunswick, NJ: Transaction Publishers.

Malavade, J. A., Shah, S. R., Shah, J. J., & Shah, R. M. (2002). *Ethical and legal issues in HIV/AIDS counseling and testing, 2002 International Conference on AIDS* (Abstract No. ThPeE7902). Retrieved on January 28, 2009, from http://gateway.nlm.nih.gov/MeetingAbstracts/ma?f=102250984.html

Masters, T. N., Beadnell, B. A., Morrison, D. M., Marilyn, J. H., & Gillmore, M. R. (2008). The Opposite of sex? Adolescents' thoughts about abstinence and sex, and their sexual behavior. *Perspectives on Sexual and Reproductive Health, 40*(2), 87–93. doi:10.1363/4008708

Medical News Today. (2007 May). *Sex education bans hinder India's efforts to curb spread Of HIV, NACO official says*. Retrieved January 20, 2009, from http://www.medicalnewstoday.com/articles/71487.php

Medical News Today. (2007 November). *MAC AIDS Fund survey of people in nine countries finds misconceptions, stigma.* Retrieved September 2, 2008, from http://www.medicalnewstoday.com/articles/89000.php

(2003). *Merriam-Webster's collegiate dictionary* (11th ed.). Springfield, MA: Merriam-Webster.

Ministry of Home Affairs, Government of India. (1860). *The Indian Penal Code, Section 377.* Retrieved January 20, 2009, from http://www.mha.nic.in/

Mishra, A. (2007 March). India: 70% rural women in Bihar not aware of HIV/AIDS: survey. *Hindustan Times.* Retrieved February 14, 2009, from http://www.hindustantimes.com/news/181_1926931,000900030002.htm

Mukherjee, K. (2005 June). Indian, Pakistani prostitutes discuss AIDS lessons. *Reuters NewMedia*. Retrieved January 20, 2009, from http://www.aegis.com/news/re/2005/RE050641.html

Mukherjee, K. (2007 July). Sex education creates storm in AIDS-stricken India. *Washingtonpost.com*. Retrieved on January 20, 2009, from http://www.washingtonpost.com/wp-dyn/content/article/2007/07/14/AR2007071401390.html

Myths and Facts about HIV/AIDS. (n.d.). *Global strategies for HIV prevention, rural education and development*. Sahaya International, International Training and Education Center on HIV. Retrieved on January 20, 2009, from http://go2itech.org/pdf/p06-db/db-50922-02.pdf

Nass, C., & Brave, S. (2005). *Wired for speech: How voice activates and advances the human-computer relationship*. Cambridge, MA: MIT Press.

National AIDS Control Organization. (2007). *HIV Sentinel Surveillance and HIV Estimation 2007: A Technical Brief.* Retrieved on March 16, 2009, from http://www.nacoonline.org/upload/Publication/M&E%20 Surveillance.% 20Research/HIV%20Sentinel%20Surveillance%20and%20HIV%20Estimation%202007_A%20Technical%20Brief.pdf

National AIDS Control Organization. (n.d.). *Monthly updates on AIDS*. Retrieved August 2006, from http://www.nacoonline.org/NACO

National AIDS Control Organization. (n.d.). *Organisational Structure.* Retrieved September 2008, from http://www.nacoonline.org/About_NACO/Organisanal_Structure/

National AIDS Control Organization. (n.d.). *About NACO*. Retrieved September 2008, from http://www.nacoonline.org/About_NACO/

National AIDS Control Organization. (n.d.). *Funding of the National AIDS Control Programme Phase-II*. Retrieved January 25, 2009, from http://www.nacoonline.org/About_NACO/Funds_and_Expenditures/

National AIDS Control Organization. (n.d.). *Health Minister Launches Third Phase of NACP*. Retrieved January 25, 2009, from http://www.nacoonline.org/NACO_Action/Media__Press_Release/

Nayak, J., & Bose, R. (1997). Making sense, talking sexuality: India reaches out to its youth. *SIECUS Report*, *25*(2), 19–21.

Newsom, G. (2008). Prop 8 battle rages over whether gay marriage would be taught in schools. *Los Angeles Times*. Retrieved March 16, 2009, from http://articles.latimes.com/2008/oct/19/local/me-gayschools19

Nguyen, H. Q., Carrieri-Kohlman, V., Rankin, S. H., Slaughter, R., & Stulbarg, M. S. (2004). Internet-based patient education and support interventions: A review of evaluation studies and directions for future research. *Computers in Biology and Medicine*, *34*(2), 95–112. doi:10.1016/S0010-4825(03)00046-5

Nguyen, H. Q., Cuenco, D., Wolpin, S., Benditt, J., & Carrieri-Kohlman, V. (2007). Methodological considerations in evaluating eHealth interventions. *Canadian Journal of Nursing Research*, *39*(1), 116–134.

Noble, R. (2007). *Worldwide HIV & AIDS statistics commentary*. Retrieved March 15, 2009, from http://www.avert.org/worlstatinfo.htm

Oakley, A., Fullerton, D., Holland, J., Arnold, S., France-Dawson, M., Kelley, P., & McGrellis, S. (1995). Sexual health education interventions for young people: A methodological review. *British Medical Journal*, *310*, 158–162.

Orlandi, M. A., Dozier, C. E., & Marta, M. A. (1990). Computer-assisted strategies for substance abuse prevention: Opportunities and barriers. *Journal of Consulting and Clinical Psychology*, *558*(4), 425–431. doi:10.1037/0022-006X.58.4.425

Padma, T. V. (2005 May). *Experts dispute Indian claims of huge drop in HIV cases*. Retrieved March 15, 2009, from http://www.scidev.net/en/news/experts-dispute-indian-claims-of-huge-drop-in-hiv.html

Parlato, M., & Seidel, R. (Eds.). (1998). *Large Scale Application of Nutrition Behavior Change Approaches: Lessons from West Africa*. Arlington, VA: Basic Support for Institutionalizing Child Survival (BASICS) Project. Retrieved February 10, 2009, from http://www.pronutrition.org/files/Large%20Scale%20BCC%20Approaches.PDF

Perry, A. (2005). When silence kills. *TIME ASIA*. Retrieved January 15, 2009, from http://www.time.com/time/asia/ covers/501050606/story.html

Pinsky, L. E., & Wipf, J. E. (2001). Innovations in education and clinical practice. *Journal of General Internal Medicine*, *15*, 805–810. doi:10.1046/j.1525-1497.2000.05129.x

Piotrow, P., Kincaid, D. L., Rimon, J. G., & Rinehart, W. (1997). *Health Communication: Lessons from family planning and reproductive health*. Westport, CT: Praeger.

Pollock, M. (2005). *Colormute: Race talk dilemmas in an American school*. Princeton, NJ: Princeton University Press.

Population Services International (PSI). (2003). *Balbir Pasha: HIV/AIDS Campaign is the talk of Mumbai.* Retrieved January 20, 2009, from www.psi.org/resources/pubs/balbir-pasha.pdf

Porter, S. B. (1993). Public knowledge and attitudes about AIDS among adults in Calcutta, India. *AIDS Care, 5*(2), 169–176. doi:10.1080/09540129308258597

Posner, E. A. (2002). *Law and Social Norms.* Cambridge, MA: Harvard University Press.

Pradhan, B. K., Sundar, R., & Singh, S. K. (2006). Socio-Economic Impact of HIV and AIDS in India. *United Nations Development Programme.* New Delhi, India: New Concept Information Systems Pvt. Ltd. Retrieved January 28, 2009, from http://data.undp.org.in/hivreport/India_Report.pdf

Pramanik, S., Chartier, M., & Koopman, C. (2006). HIV/AIDS stigma and knowledge among predominantly middle-class high school students in New Delhi, India. *The Journal of Communicable Diseases, 38*(1), 57–69.

Redjimi, G., & Lert, F. (1993). Images of AIDS among teenagers and young adults. *AIDS Care, 5*(4), 449–465. doi:10.1080/09540129308258014

Reeves, B., & Nass, C. (1996). *The media equation: How people treat computers, television, and new media like real people and places.* New York: Cambridge University Press/CSLI.

Report Card HIV Prevention for Girls and Young Women. (n.d.). *United Nations Population Fund.* Retrieved January 28, 2009, from www.unfpa.org/hiv/docs/report-cards/india.pdf

Report of the Commission for Africa. (n.d.). *Commission for Africa.* Retrieved January 29, 2009, from http://www.commissionforafrica.org/english/report/thereport/english/11-03-05_cr_report.pdf

Reuters. (2006 March). *Asia-Pacific countries must end cultural taboos about sex, discrimination, to curb HIV/AIDS epidemic, advocate says.* Retrieved January 20, 2009, from http://www.kaisernetwork.org/daily_reports/ print_report.cfm?DR_ID=36203&dr_cat=4

Richard Gere cleared of obscenity. (2008, March 14). *BBC News.* Retrieved January 13, 2009, from http://news.bbc.co.uk/2/hi/south_asia/7295797.stm

Robinson, F., Sandoval, N., Baldwin, J., & Sanderson, P. R. (2005). Breast cancer education for Native American women: Creating culturally relevant communications. *Clinical Journal of Oncology Nursing, 9*(6), 689–692. doi:10.1188/05.CJON.689-692

Rogers, E. M. (1995). *The Diffusion of Innovations* (4th ed.). New York: Free Press.

Sabha, R. (2007). Sex Education in Curriculum. *National AIDS Control Organization.* Retrieved January 25, 2009, from http://www.nacoonline.org/NACO_Action/Media__Press_Release/

Sachdev, P. (1998). Sex on campus: A preliminary study of knowledge, attitudes and behaviour of university students in Delhi, India. *Journal of Biosocial Science, 30*(1), 95–105. doi:10.1017/S0021932098000959

Sampson, J. P., & Kruboltz, J. D. (1991). Computer assisted instruction: A missing link in counseling. *Journal of Counseling and Development, 69*(5), 395–397.

Santelli, J., Ott, M. A., Lyon, M., Rogers, J., Summers, D., & Schleifer, R. (2006). Abstinence and abstinence-only education: A review of U.S. policies and programs. *The Journal of Adolescent Health, 38*, 72–81. doi:10.1016/j.jadohealth.2005.10.006

Sappenfield, M. (2007). In India, A Public Kiss is Not Just a Kiss. *The Christian Science Monitor*. Retrieved September 17, 2008, from http://www.csmonitor.com/2007/0430/p01s03-wosc.html

Sex education runs into trouble. (2007, August). *BBC News*. Retrieved January 20, 2009, from http://news.bbc.co.uk/1/hi/world/south_asia/6949714.stm

Shah, S. P. (2006). Visibility in Mumbai producing the spectacle of Kamathipura: The politics of red light. *Cultural Dynamics, 18*(3), 269–292. doi:10.1177/0921374006071615

Sharma, B. (2008 September). Making inroads. *Tehelka*. Retrieved January 20, 2009, from http://www.tehelka.com/story_main40.asp?filename=Ws130908makinginroads.asp

Sharma, P. (2005 December). Sex education still off the charts. *India Together*. Retrieved January 20, 2009, from http://www.indiatogether.org/2005/dec/edu-notaboo.htm#src

Sharma, R. (2001). More than a quarter of India's youngsters have premarital sex. *British Medical Journal, 322*(7286), 575. doi:10.1136/bmj.322.7286.575

Shetty defends Richard Gere kiss. (2007, April 17). *BBC News*. Retrieved January 13, 2009, from http://news.bbc.co.uk/1/hi/entertainment/6563425.stm

SIECUS. (1996). Issues and answers. Fact sheet on sexuality education. *Sexuality Information and Education Council of the United States Report, 24*(6), 1–4.

Sify News. (2007 March). *No sex education in Madhya Pradesh schools*. Retrieved January 20, 2009, from http://sify.com/news/fullstory.php?id=14412544

Singh, B. P. (2007). Rajasthan court issues warrant against Gere. *Hindustan Times*. Retrieved January 13, 2009, from http://www.hindustantimes.com/storypage/storypage.aspx?id=3307c846-cfce-489d-b220-1b399b9759ee&ParentID=eda501ca-affe-4d4d-a93f-05a591421050&&Headline=Rajasthan+court+issues+warrant+against+Gere

Singhal, A., & Rogers, E. M. (1999). *Entertainment-education: A communication strategy for social change*. Mahwah, NJ: Lawrence Erlbaum Associates.

Singhal, A., & Rogers, E. M. (2003). *Combating AIDS communication strategies in action*. New Delhi, India: Sage Publications.

Smith, G., Kippax, S., Aggleton, P., & Tyrer, P. (2003). HIV/AIDS school based education in selected Asia-Pacific countries. *Sex Education, 3*(1), 3–21. doi:10.1080/1468181032000052126

Society for Adolescent Medicine. (2006). Abstinence-only education policies and programs: A position paper of the Society for Adolescent Medicine. *The Journal of Adolescent Health, 38*(1), 83–87. doi:10.1016/j.jadohealth.2005.06.002

Solomon, S., & Chakraborty, A. (2004). A review of the HIV epidemic in India. *AIDS Education and Prevention, 12*(3A), 155–169. doi:10.1521/aeap.16.3.5.155.35534

Solomon, S., Kumarasamy, N., Ganesh, A. K., & Amalraj, R. E. (1998). Prevalence and risk factors of HIV-1 and HIV-2 infection in urban and rural areas in Tamil Nadu, India. *International Journal of STD & AIDS, 9*, 98–103. doi:10.1258/0956462981921756

Sorcar, P. (2009). *Teaching Taboo Topics Without Talking About Them: An Epistemic Study of a New Approach to HIV/AIDS Prevention Education in India*. Published Doctoral Dissertation, Stanford University.

Spoehr, K. T. (1994). Enhancing the acquisition of conceptual structures through hypermedia. In Kate, M. (Ed.), *Classroom lessons: Integrating cognitive theory and classroom practice* (pp. 75–101). Cambridge, MA: MIT Press.

Sudha, R. T., Vijay, D. T., & Lakshmi, V. (2005). Awareness, attitudes, and beliefs of the general public towards HIV/AIDS in Hyderabad, A capital city from South India. *Indian Journal of Medical Sciences*, *59*(7), 307–316. doi:10.4103/0019-5359.16506

Sundaram, V. (2007 December). Let's NOT talk about sex, baby. *New America Media*. Retrieved September 1, 2008, from http://news.newamericamedia.org/news/view_article.html?article_id=e5589d57e3d6e65b0e17efb1fd28bba4

Thody, P. (1997). *Don't Do IT! A dictionary of the forbidden*. New York: St. Martin's Press.

Thompson, C. (2006 April). Google's China problem (and China's Google Problem). *The New York Times*. Retrieved January 20, 2009, from http://www.nytimes.com/2006/04/23/magazine/23google.html?_r=1&pagewanted=print

UNAIDS. (2004). *Action Against AIDS Must Address Epidemic's Increasing Impact on Women, Says UN Report*. Retrieved January 20, 2009, from http://www.unifem.org/news_events/story_detail.php?StoryID=130

UNAIDS. (2007). *AIDS epidemic update*. Press Release. Retrieved January 20, 2009, from http://www.unaids.org/en/HIV_data/2007EpiUpdate/default.asp

UNAIDS. (2007). *2.5 million people living with HIV in India*. Retrieved March 28, 2008, from http://www.unaids.org/en/KnowledgeCentre/Resources/FeatureStories/archive/2007/20070704_India_new_data.asp

UNAIDS. (2007). *Annex 1: HIV and AIDS estimates and data, 2007 and 2001*. Retrieved January 21, 2009, from http://data.unaids.org/pub/GlobalReport/2008/jc1510_2008_global_report_pp211_234_en.pdf

UNFPA. (2004). Working with Communities and Faith-based Organizations. *Culture Matters*. Retrieved January 29, 2009, from http://www.unfpa.org/upload/lib_pub_file/426_filename_Culture-Matters_2004.pdf

Valdiserri, R. (2002). HIV/AIDS stigma: An impediment to public health. *American Journal of Public Health*, *92*(3), 341–342. doi:10.2105/AJPH.92.3.341

Verma, R. K., Sureender, S., & Guruswamy, M. (1997). What do school children and teachers in rural Maharashtra think of AIDS and sex? *Health transition review: The cultural, social, and behavioural determinants of health*, S7, 481-486.

Vijian, P. (2009). India Targets 3.5 Billion Free Condoms To Curb HIV/Aids. *Bernama.Com Malaysian National News Agency*. Retrieved February 18, 2009, from http://www.bernama.com.my/bernama/v3/news.php?id=389722

Vlahov, D., & Junge, B. (1998). The role of needle exchange programs in HIV prevention. *Public Health Reports (Washington, D.C.)*, *1*(113 Supplement), 75–80.

Weber, M. (1978). *Economy and Society, Vol. 1*. Berkeley, CA: University of California Press.

What's culture got to do with HIV and AIDS? Why the global strategy for HIV and AIDS needs to adopt a cultural approach. (2007). *HealthLink Worldwide*. Retrieved January 29, 2009, from http://www.healthlink.org.uk/PDFs/findings7_hiv_culture.pdf

Wodak, A., & Cooney, A. (2006). Do needle syringe programs reduce HIV infection among injecting drug users: a comprehensive review of the international evidence. *Substance Use & Misuse*, *41*(6-7), 777–813. doi:10.1080/10826080600669579

Wong, W. C., Lee, A., & Tsang, K. K. (2004). Correlates of sexual behaviors with health status and health perception in Chinese adolescents: A cross-sectional survey in schools. *AIDS Patient Care and STDs*, *18*(8), 470–480. doi:10.1089/1087291041703656

Yang, S. (2003 June). Researchers warn that AIDS in India could become as dire as in Africa. *UC Berkeley News.* Retrieved January 20, 2009, from http://www.berkeley.edu/news/media/releases/2003/06/19_india.shtml

Zaheer, K. (2007 May). Get real and save Indian youth from AIDS–official. *Reuters UK.* Retrieved January 20, 2009, from http://uk.reuters.com/article/healthNews/idUKDEL6968520070517?feedType

ENDNOTES

1 ICT is defined as any form of digital technology (e.g. Internet, personal computers, mobile devices and other wireless communications) that helps transmit and receive information and aid communications.

2 TeachAIDS (www.TeachAIDS.org) is a California-based nonprofit founded through Stanford University and operating worldwide.

3 According to Erving Gofman, the Greeks originated the term stigma and it can be defined as "an attribute that is deeply discrediting" (Goffman, 1963).

4 During this time in Mali, infant mortality (170 per 1000 live births) and maternal mortality (2000 per 100,000 live births) were extremely high (Fishman, Gottert, Kanté, Parlato, Anthony, 1998, as cited in Parlato & Seidel, 1998). For children between 3-36 months old, 11 percent showed signs of acute malnutrition and 25 percent for chronic malnutrition (National Demographic and Health Survey, 1987, as cited in Parlato & Seidel, 1998).

5 The states of Gujarat, Madhya Pradesh, Maharashtra, Karnataka, Rajasthan Chhattisgarh and Kerala have banned or refused the use of the official curriculum (Gentleman, 2007; Zaheer, 2007).

6 The official curriculum called the Adolescence Education Programme was developed through the Ministry of Human Resource Development and NACO together (Sabha, 2007).

7 Estimates based on 1122 sentinel sites and the National Family Health Survey, a country-wide community based household survey (NACO, 2007).

8 There is a fine of $12 for kissing in public in Delhi (Sappenfied, 2007).

9 This includes funding from the Government of India, World Bank, USAID, CIDA, United Nations Development Program (UNDP), AusAID, Global Fund and DFID.

10 Minister for Health & Family Welfare, Dr. Anbumani Ramadoss launched the Third Phase of the National AIDS Control Program in July of 2007 (NACO, 2007)

11 Phase III funding is from a combination of resources including, the Government of India, non-governmental organizations, international non-governmental organizations, industry and other agencies (e.g., World Bank, Bill and Melinda Gates Foundation) (Avert, 2009).

12 The *Interactive Teaching AIDS* applications can be accessed at www.TeachAIDS.org.

13 Note, that an average commercial sex worker in Mumbai services approximately seven clients each night (Singhal & Rogers, 2003).

14. Image Sources: Global Strategies for HIV Prevention, Rural Education and Development, Sahaya International, International Training and Education Center on HIV, Global Strategies for HIV Prevention and Lives in Focus.
15. The Indian illustrations in the Interactive Teaching AIDS software were developed by Manick Sorcar Productions and were animated by a medical animation team through the Medical Research Information Center and Care and Visual Ltd.
16. Most Indian names tend to be associated with a particular religion or caste of the individual.
17. Culturally-appropriate illustrations were developed by Manick Sorcar Productions (www.manicksorcar.com).

Section 4
Advertising Tactics in Gaming, Sports and Politics

Chapter 22
Advertising:
It's in the Game

Paul Skalski
Cleveland State University, USA

Cheryl Campanella-Bracken
Cleveland State University, USA

Michael Buncher
Cleveland State University, USA

ABSTRACT

The diffusion of digital media technologies since the 1990s has opened many new channels through which advertisers may reach consumers. This chapter examines the manifestations and effects of advertising in video games. Although early video games rarely and purposefully included advertising, its presence in many contemporary game genres (particularly sports and racing titles) is impossible to ignore. In-game advertising has become a more than $60 million dollar industry (Gaudiosi, 2006) and is expected to grow to almost $2 billion by 2010 (Shields, 2006). The present chapter covers the history and types of advertising in video games before shifting to a discussion of research on its effectiveness. The chapter concludes by highlighting the potential of advertising in games, from both applied and research perspectives.

A BRIEF HISTORY...

In-game advertising has a history almost as old as video games themselves, and like the medium in which they take place, games have gone through considerable changes over time. This section chronicles the history of in-game ads and touches on some of the reasons for its recent explosion in popularity. This is not meant to be an exhaustive history[1], but simply an overview noting key events of in-game advertisement history and providing some perspective on its recent developments.

In-game advertisements did not originate solely in early video games, but can be traced back to the coin-operated devices that preceded video games, including pinball. In 1964 there was a *Mustang* pinball machine that feature artwork resembling the car that Ford released that year, but it is not known if the brand name was licensed (Vedrashko, 2006). This may not be the very first example of gaming-related advertising, but it is certainly similar to some of the early and current

DOI: 10.4018/978-1-60566-792-8.ch022

instances of advertising in video games where the goal is not so much to sell a product unrelated to the game, but to incorporate a real product into a game environment to enhance the believability and authenticity of the experience.

Many examples of video game advertisements were brand placements fairly unrelated to the game content, however. A graphical version of the 1973 text game *Lunar Lander*, for example, included an element where the player could make a McDonalds appear by landing in a certain location (Lunar Lander, 2008). After the restaurant appears, the astronaut is shown ordering a Big Mac to go. Similar to *Mustang,* this example illustrates how real world brands can make it into virtual environments and games without the owner of the brand necessarily paying for the "advertisement." Some early game ads were for other products from the game company or designer. For instance, *Adventureland*, a game by Scott Adams released in 1978, featured an ad for an upcoming game of his called *Pirate Adventure* (In-game advertising, 2008).

Besides these early examples, of which there are too many examples to cover completely, one type of in-game advertisement, the advergame, really captures many of the early attempts at integrating advertisements into video games. Here, the term *advergame* is used to describe those games developed or modified primarily for the purpose of advertising, branding or promotion. Although many past and current games have product placements or billboards that are analogous to the real world, those advertisements are generally added for either additional revenue or to enhance the authenticity of the experience. True advergames in the purest sense are not subtle and started to appear in the early 1980s. A prime example is 1982's *Tooth Protector,* which was a mail order game from Crest Toothpaste producers Johnson & Johnson. In this game, the player controls a character known as the "Tooth Protector" who protects a row of teeth from food particles dropped by the "Snack Attackers." The Tooth Protector bounces the particles back at the Attackers; otherwise three hits to the same tooth causes it to decay and the player must save it with a toothbrush, dental floss, and rinse (Bogost, 2007). Another early and very rare example is a game called *Pepsi Invaders*, which was a clone of the popular *Space Invaders* produced by Atari for Coca-Cola in 1983. The game looked and played similarly to *Space Invaders*, but instead of shooting aliens the player's ship shot at letters spelling Pepsi and a Pepsi logo which replaced the original game's command ship that soared across the top of the screen. The game is notable for adopting the unusual in-game advertising strategy of the "attack ad," since the Pepsi name and logo were included in a negative context with no mention of the sponsoring brand (Vedrashko, 2006). A final advergame of this era that deserves mention is *Chase the Chuck Wagon*, produced by Spectravision for the Atari 2600 to promote Ralston Purina's Chuck Wagon Dog Food. Like *Tooth Protector*, this game was only available by mail. Its rarity has led some video game collectors to refer to searching for rare games as "chasing the chuck wagon" (Cassidy, 2002).

Advergames like these were produced during a relatively short period of time before the video game industry crash of 1983, which essentially put an end to their development for awhile. At least one game released before the golden age came to an end, however, transcended the standard definition of an advergame. For the arcade game *Tapper*, developers Bally-Midway came to Budweiser with the idea for a game featuring a bartender with the goal of serving drinks and picking up empty glasses. The Budweiser brand would be used for various bar items and on the arcade machine's artwork. The marketers of the game hoped this would make it easier to get the game into bars serving Budweiser, thereby increasing sales of the machine. This game was not developed solely to advertise Budweiser, but also to make a good game and sell arcade machines. The addition of the Budweiser brand was done to increase sales in bars, and the brand also worked in the context of the game to make it seem more authentic. For this reason, *Tapper* is not a true advergame, since it does not meet the definition requirement of being developed solely to advertise the product. *Tapper's* ability to stand on its own without the branding was demonstrated clearly after some of the machines found their way into dedicated video game arcades. This created controversy, however, since minors had access to the game and there was a fear that it would promote underage drinking. To eliminate this problem, the company took out all Budweiser references and changed the name of the game to the generic *Root Beer Tapper* (Fox, 2006).

In the late 80s, video games had a massive resurgence in popularity due to the success of the Nintendo Entertainment System (NES) (Kent, 2001), and a new generation of advergames followed. One notable example is *Avoid the Noid*, which was released in 1989 for personal computers. The game was part of an advertising campaign by Domino's Pizza that included TV commercials featuring the Noid, a mischievous character who desired to make pizzas cold with a freeze ray. In the game, the player controlled a delivery boy who needed to get pizzas delivered to the top of an apartment building within 30 minutes or lose his job. During the trek, the player was confronted by the villainous Noid, who was subsequently featured in an NES game called *Yo! Noid* ("Yo! Noid Shrine," n.d.). Other games utilizing this model included *Cool Spot* and *Too Cool to Fool* featuring the 7-Up spot and the Frito-Lay character Chester Cheetah, respectively (Vedrashko, 2006). As in the golden age, there were also games like *Tapper* that might not be considered pure advergames but certainly contained their fair share of product placement. *Zool*, for example, was a platform game released for the Amiga in 1992 that featured Chupa Chups lollipops heavily in the first three "Sweet World" levels which looked like candy fantasy lands (Zool, 2008).

Today, the world of advertising in-games is not so simple, as there are a multitude of manifestations. For instance, banner advertisements on websites sometimes look like "games" encouraging web surfers to "swat the fly" or "punch the monkey" or engage in some similar action just to get a hit and transport them to a product site (usually). There are also numerous, simple advergames on websites for brands like M&M's and General Mills. An early example was a flash game on the M&M's site where the player used virtual M&M's to draw pictures that were judged in a weekly contest (Lindstrom, 2003).

Current generation graphics allow game characters and avatars to be dressed and accessorized with products for real brands that can be purchased in stores, like Gibson guitars in *Guitar Hero III* or Nike shoes in the NBA 2K6 basketball game (Burns, 2005). Due to the online capabilities of modern consoles, virtual billboards and movie posters can also be changed and updated throughout the life of a game. Entire virtual worlds like *Second Life* have their own markets complete with currencies and products in addition to advertising. Amidst all of these new dynamic changes, however, the tried and true advergame is still being developed and made available to consumers. A promotional effort by Burger King in 2006, for example, resulted in the King Games, three titles developed by Blitz Games for the Xbox and Xbox 360. The games, *Sneak King*, *Pocketbike Racer*, and *Big Bumpin'*, were available for an additional $3.99 with the purchase of a value meal. All together more than 3.2 million of the games were sold in the U.S. and Canada over a six week period (Nuttall, 2007).

One especially noteworthy example of a modern advergame is *Americas Army (AA)*. *AA* was developed for the purpose of recruiting by the United States Army. Since it was created for this purpose, as opposed to sell game units, it fits the definition of an advergame. *AA* is a tactical shooter in which the player controls a soldier in the Army (America's Army, 2008). The player must complete training missions before going on to further levels, similar to the training they would receive in the real army. *AA* is owned by the U.S. government and is distributed for free online or on free DVDs at recruitment centers. It has gone through multiple updates and is available on platforms ranging from PC to mobile phone. *AA* is superior to most advergames which are generally simple, short and derivative. The game features 3-D environments, multiple soldier classes, and numerous training levels. *AA* takes advergaming to the next level and it remains to be seen where this type of advertising goes next.

These are merely a few examples of a much larger phenomenon. Advertising in and through video games is now quite common and expected to become even more widespread in coming years (Shields, 2006). There are many reasons for this spike in popularity, according to Nelson (2002), including increasing horizontal integration of media industries and resulting opportunities for cross promotion, unique characteristics of games like interactivity along with their shift toward greater realism, and the increasing appeal of games to diverse segments of the population. Games may now be the best advertising vehicle to reach young males in particular, in fact, given recent reports suggesting they now spend more on games than on other forms of media (Slocombe, 2005). To better understand contemporary in-game advertising and provide further examples, this chapter now shifts to a detailed discussion of types or categories of in-game advertising.

TYPES OF IN-GAME ADVERTISEMENTS

To date, little work has been done on attempting to comprehensively categorize the various types of advertising in games. As with any topic that spans more than one industry, attempts made come from multiple perspectives that often fail to acknowledge competing views. A more encompassing consideration of the many kinds of in-game advertising will help advance knowledge of this topic. This section will try to cover the different forms of in-game ads from a non-theoretical perspective, given the small amount of existing literature in this area. Distinctions between forms will be made simply if they seem different and not be based on whether or not they have a different impact. This can provide a foundation for future research examining the effects of in-game ads.

Some categorizations describe in-game ads in ways that borrow from advertising terms generally applied to other forms of media. Bogost (2007), for example, describes three approaches to advertising in general, including (1) demonstrative, (2) illustrative, and (3) associative, that may be applied to games. *Demonstrative* ads would showcase the use of a product's features and functions directly. This type can been seen in racing games like *Gran Turismo*, in which a driver may have to select between different vehicles based on their performance specifications approximating their real world abilities. *Illustrative* ads are more indirect than demonstrative ads and usually provide a context for the product while promoting its use. Using the same example, the incremental benefit of choosing a car with better specifications will be illustrated to the player through their performance in a race. *Associative* advertising seems to be the most prevalent form of in-game ad, especially in advergames, and it tries to make a connection between the product and niche market, lifestyle, or abstract ideal (like "being cool"). An example of this type of advertising is the snowmobile game *Arctic Racer 3D* on Nabisco's website. The game does little to demonstrate the features or illustrate the benefits of the product but instead tries to associate Nabisco products with snowmobiling and the attitudes people have toward that activity (e.g., it being fun, exciting, cool, etc.). Taken as a whole, this categorization scheme offers some insight into how in-game advertising can be used, but since it applies to all forms of advertising it does not address the unique qualities of in-game ads.

One of the first attempts at differentiating between types of in-game ads specifically breaks them down into two categories, giveaways and integral games (Gardner, 2001). *Giveaways* are described as games which have little to do with the brand being advertised and tend to be short, simple, and derivative of other classic games. A couple of examples would include the flash games *Invaders* and *Whipround* that were once featured on Pilsner Urquell's website (Bogost, 2005). *Invaders* is an obvious *Space Invaders* clone (like *Pepsi Invaders*) that replaces the space ship the player controls with a bottle of Pilsner Urquell beer. *Whipround* is a *Pac-Man* clone that features Pilsner Urquell beer bottles as energizer pellets allowing Pac-Man to temporarily eat his ghost enemies. These examples use a similar formula and feature a product placed in a game in an unnatural context for the product. *Integral games* vary from giveaways in that the game play requires the brand, product, or service being advertised. One example of an integral game is *Ericsson Ground Zero* in which the player needs to utilize an Ericsson mobile phone to track down items in a scavenger hunt. These two types are a good starting point for understanding how in-game ads can differ. However, they miss some types of advertising in games that are better explained through additional categories.

Another categorization outlines four approaches to video game advertising including (1) standard mainstream video games as a platform for advertising or product placement, (2) games as a part of a larger cross-media strategy, (3) custom-built advergames, and (4) edge cases (Maragos, 2005). This categorization approaches game advertising by focusing on the ways a company could attempt to advertise with a game as opposed to how necessary they are for the game play, like the previous categorization. The first way listed, *standard mainstream video games*, are non-advergames that are developed as games in and of themselves and include advertising. This may be too broad of a category because it would include both in-game product placement and more traditional advertising like billboards advertisements in racing games. *Games that are a part of a larger cross-media strategy*, the second category, includes instances when a movie and a game based on the movie are released simultaneously. The movie and the game for *Spiderman*, for instance, work as advertisements for each other. Although this is a common occurrence today, it is a borderline in-game advertisement since the whole game could be considered an advertisement. Third, *custom built advergames* are games designed around a product. Again, this may be too broad as it does not address whether the ads are, borrowing from the previous categorization, giveaways or integral. The final type listed, *edge cases,* seem to refer to advertising that does not fit into the other categories. Some of the examples given include the Pepsi-branded Nintendo DS released in Japan and *Virtual Magic Kingdom* which is a virtual re-creation of Disneyland. This type of advertising certainly takes place, but it is difficult to observe where in the game, if at all, the advertising takes place. This categorization adds some breadth to the previous classification scheme, however, due to the inclusion of games other than advergames.

A third categorization expands on outlining types of in-game ads and includes (1) advergames, (2) product placement, (3) real-world analogs, and (4) cross-promotion (Horwitz, 2004). *Advergames* have already been discussed, and here the term is used similarly to describe games that are sponsored by advertisers and developed as stand-alone games with branding messages. The main difference between this definition and the one listed in the first section of the chapter is that this one allows for games like *Tapper* to be considered an advergame. This is because the definition only states the game is sponsored by advertisers which allows for the game to be developed in order to sell games instead of just the product or brand. *Product placement* refers to appearance branded objects in a game, like name brand cars in the *Gran*

Turismo series. The *real-world analogs* category is the one that really expands on previous categorizations and includes virtual ads that would appear in the real world, without which the game may lose authenticity. This includes stadium boards covered with ads in sports games or billboards in racing games, which almost all new titles in these genres have. The fourth format, *cross-promotion*, is similar to the cross-media advertising type mentioned in the previous categorization but extends to product lines of a non-media nature. The example given by Horwitz is the use of the Diesel clothing line in the game *Devil May Cry 2*. The game featured a few sets of clothing for the playable characters featuring the Diesel logo, while Japanese Diesel stores featured the games characters in promotional material (IGN Staff, 2003). Cross-promotion advertising goes beyond product placement because the company that has its products featured within the game reciprocates by advertising for the game.

Nelson (2002), finally, adds more breadth to the above categorization schemes by discussing seven types of brand/product placements in video games: (1) sponsorship, (2) brands as major part of gameplay, (3) characters as branded images, (4) background images as self promotion for a game or game publisher's games, (5) background advertisements and product placements, (6) game players create own advertisements/brands through character customization, and (7) background—licensed music uses well known groups, sports commentators. *Sponsorship* refers to "cross selling" of a league, network, etc. such as a basketball game promoting the NBA. *Brands as major part of game play* is pretty much the same as integral games described above. C*haracters as branded images* seem like a borderline case that includes the use of real athletes in sports games. The next two types integrate background images in games that promote either the game/publisher (category 4) or other brands/products (category 5). The sixth type, *game players create own advertisements/ brands through character customization*, seems borderline again and would include creating sponsors (possible in some NASCAR games) or selecting/attracting sponsors. The final *background* category refers to selling music, groups and other audio through a game by having it play during the game or be a major part of gameplay.

The categorizations above offer a fairly complete picture of the forms an in-game advertisement can take, but more must be said about their necessity, state, interactivity, and potential to be a part of larger online communities, which are important potential distinguishing features of ads in games compared to those in traditional media like television and film.

AD PROMINENCE

The first game-specific categorization was focused on the prominence of the brand featured in advergames and outlined giveaways versus integral game ads (Gardner, 2001). This categorization may be important to remember when investigating the effects of advergames on the player. For example, prominent integral ads such as having real brands of rackets in a tennis game that affect outcomes through varying properties and qualities may have a stronger effect on consumers than a brand or product that merely appears in the background of a game environment for associative purposes.

Static vs. Dynamic Ads

Another factor to keep in mind with in-game advertising is whether the ad is static or dynamic. A static in-game ad will not change over time, whereas a dynamic ad may. This feature is made easier today due to the Internet capabilities of modern consoles and personal computers. Static ads appear to be the most prominent form, but more dynamic ads may make an appearance as technology and the in-game advertising industry grow. The examples listed throughout this chapter so far have been static ads, but technology has allowed for games that once featured static ads to be updated in order to accommodate dynamic advertisements. *SWAT 4*, for example, is a game that originally featured static ads, but if players downloaded the 1.1 patch (an update to a game), the game presented dynamic ad posters (Smith and Wood, 2005). The posters (for game rental services, TV show premieres, and soft drinks) did not display the same ad in the same place but rather altered the content and location of posters when a level was replayed. In a fascinating new twist on dynamic ad placement, U.S. President Barack Obama purchased space on billboards appearing in the racing video game *Burnout: Paradise* during his presidential campaign (Pigna, 2008).

Both product placement and real-world analog ads could be either static or dynamic. A good example of an integral product placement in an advergame is a basketball game designed to advertise Nike Shox as discussed by Chen and Ringel (as cited in Bogost, 2007). The game demonstrated the qualities of different shoes in the Shox lineup by having them impact how high a player could jump. This type of advertising is static as the shoe lineup was set at the game's release and did not change. However, a dynamic approach could be used in a more advanced basketball game such as one of the *NBA Live* or *NBA 2K* titles. This approach would allow the shoes featured in the game to be updated throughout the game's life to match any new styles released after the game. Similar to the posters in *SWAT 4*, the same dynamic model can be applied easily to billboards in video games so that they always feature a product that matches the player's profile (Gaudiosi, 2006). This consideration may seem to be of minor importance, but it could moderate an advertisement's impact since it can directly affect the number of exposures to the ad and whether the ad is customized or targeted to the player.

Ad Interactivity

One vitally important consideration is the interactivity of an in-game advertisement, given that interactivity is perhaps the most important feature distinguishing games from other forms of media entertainment. There are real-world analog billboards that players see as part of the environment and then there are billboards that the player can crash through or repel down like the Axe deodorant billboard in *Splinter Cell: Chaos Theory* (Jana, 2006). The same goes for product placements, which could be used by the player as a health source, a weapon, or in some other way. Jeep used an interactive product placement in *Tony Hawk's Pro Skater 2*, for example, that featured a Jeep vehicle in which the player could perform rail tricks for points (Wong, 2004). The game could have easily featured a Jeep the player could not interact with but the developers instead chose to include an interactive model. Considerations such as these have potential implications for the effects of in-game ads.

Ads in MMO Games

The presence of advertising in online multiplayer virtual worlds should also be considered. The most prominent example of an online virtual world with ads is *Second Life*, which probably would not fit most definitions of a video game but still functions as a game-like multiplayer online world. These types of virtual worlds can reach new heights of in-game advertising that includes future product promotion. The aloft Hotel being planned by Starwood Hotel & Resorts Worldwide, for example, was first built in *Second Life*, which allowed users to visit the hotel and give feedback to the developers before the completion of its real-world counterpart (Siklos, 2006). The potential for ads in online virtual worlds is vast, and massively multiplayer online role playing games (MMORPGs) are beginning to incorporate them. One borderline example is the Pizza Hut command line available in *Everquest II* that allows players to order food from the restaurant's menu (Svennson, 2005). This is more of a feature than an advertisement, since players are not confronted by any kind of message but rather decide to type in the command of their own volition. However, if more of these borderline examples crop up, or if they begin to expand in their capabilities, it may be necessary to add them to a typology of in-game ads.

Clearly, there are many types of in-game advertisements. The most prominent forms seem to be advergames and product/brand placements, and the latter may include virtual objects, real-world analogs, and even characters and music in games. Each type of in-game ad can also be more or less necessary to gameplay (integral vs. giveaways), static or dynamic, and interactive or non-interactive. The dizzying number of forms in-game advertisements can take does not address one vitally important consideration for advertisers, however—the impact in-game ads have on consumers. What does the research evidence on this say?

RESEARCH EVIDENCE

Paralleling the rise of in-game advertising in this decade, several recent studies have been conducted on its effectiveness. Almost all of these studies have focused on brand placement using memory as the primary dependent variable. Research on memory of game ads parallels similar research that has been conducted on film and television (e.g., Karrh, 1998; McCarty, 2004; Yang, Roskos-Ewoldsen, & Roskos-Ewoldsen, 2004) and findings in these traditional media areas have been mixed, depending on factors such as story placement and brand type (Yang, Roskos-Ewoldsen, Dinu, & Arpan, 2006). Video games introduce several new considerations into this mix, chiefly interactivity. This section reviews research on advertising in games beginning with memory-related findings, given the important role of memory in past product placement research and in the process of persuasion (Perloff, 2007).

MEMORY/RECALL/ RECOGNITION EFFECTS

In one of the first published research articles on in-game advertising effects, Nelson (2002) explored how brand placement impacts recall through two experiments. In study one, she had 20 subjects play the console auto racing game *Grand Turismo 2* for 15 minutes. The game was selected because it contains an average of 10 advertisements per game in the form of billboards and sideboards (e.g., for Goodyear tires, Penzoil motor oil). Immediately following exposure to the game, subjects were given a free recall measure asking them to list any brands remembered from the game and it revealed that, on average, 4.53 brands were remembered. Additionally, all but one of the participants remembered the brand of car they chose, suggesting that brands that are a major part of game play are more highly recalled. A follow-up survey five months later revealed that many of the brands were forgotten, which points to a possible lack of long-term effects. In study two, Nelson used the same procedure but had subjects play a computer "racing game demo" that was selected because the content could be manipulated. She varied whether the ads were for local brands (e.g., Mad Dogs Sports Bar and Pizzeria) or national brands (e.g., Pepsi) and asked participants (N = 16) how many they recalled following exposure. On average, 30 percent of ads were remembered. The most remembered ads, interestingly, were for local/novel brands and brands personally relevant to the participants, with the local brands even being remembered by some after a delay. This suggests the potential value of localizing ads in video games, a practice that was once difficult given static programming but may now be possible given the rise of gaming over online connections. Overall, Nelson's (2002) work offers some support for in-game advertising impacting memory and suggests two potential moderating variables: level of game play integration (major vs. minor) and type of brand (local/novel vs. national).

Nelson, Yaros, and Keum (2006) extended this initial research to include additional variables, including a slightly different brand type manipulation (fictional vs. real) and media context (playing vs. watching). Sixty-two participants in this study either played or watched a racing game in which they were exposed to two real brands (Coca-Cola, Gap Jeans) and two fictional brands (Crank Cola, Gem Jeans) a total of 24 times each. They then completed a free recall measure as in the previous study, and results indicated that real brands were more remembered than fictitious ones, though the authors believe this effect could diminish over longer game playing times or with dynamic in-game ads that change. Findings also revealed that playing impeded recall, as players recalled significantly fewer ads than watchers. The authors speculate that the cognitive resources required for active control of a video game may inhibit learning of embedded brands. While this might suggest that games are a less effective advertising vehicle than passive media due to their interactivity, Nelson et al. believe they can be similarly effective if ads are integrated through non-interactive "cut scenes" or in games in which players take turns, which are fairly common now. Players and watchers did not differ in game liking or perceived persuasion in this study, suggesting that watching does not negatively impact the experience of a game. The findings of this study address the crucial variable of interactivity and further advance understanding of brand type as a determinant of in-game advertising effectiveness.

In another racing game study involving brand placement and memory, Schneider and Cornwell (2005) explored the effects of ad prominence, game experience and flow on recall. Flow is a psychological state thought to be common during game play that involves focused attention, a sense of complete control, a distortion in sense of time passing, and lack of self consciousness (Csikszentmihalyi, 1990). For their study, Schneider and Cornwell had 46 players fill out a questionnaire that included measures of flow (multiple-item scale), brand recall (as in the previous two studies), and prior game experience after completing five laps in the PC racing game *Rallisport Challenge*. A content analysis conducted before the study coded the ads in the game according to whether they were subtle or prominent, depending on their size, color, attractiveness and position in the game environment. Results indicated that, as expected, prominent placements had higher recall and recognition levels than subtle placements. This suggests that not all placements are the same and points to the value of emphasizing certain brands, perhaps even as a part of gameplay. Expert players were also found to have higher recall levels than novices, perhaps because they can see more or do not have to focus as much on central action, allowing them to take in more peripheral content such as brands. Contrary to expectations, the authors found no relationship between flow and brand recognition/recall. They speculate that this may have been due to the game not being challenging enough for players to enter a flow state and recommend using different games and genres in future research.

MEMORY AND NON-RACING GAMES

A few recent studies have looked at memory of in-game advertising in genres other than racing. Chaney, Lin, and Chaney (2004) had 42 participants play an online first person shooter game that included billboards for fictional products (e.g., soda, pizza, digital camera) placed by the researcher. Each ad appeared once in separate high action areas of the game environment. After 15 minutes of play, participants completed unaided recall measures. Even though players remembered seeing ads, half could not remember any specific products or brands, and only one participant remembered all of the information. The authors attribute this recall inability to the players' allocation of their mental resources to the game instead of peripheral details, which could be a function of limited information processing capacity and/or entering a "flow" state. Open-ended comments from players seem to support the latter explanation more than the first. Reasons for not remembering uncovered in this study included "too busy killing," "too focused," and "in the zone." Overall, these findings suggest a lack of recall effectiveness of in-game ads in atypical genres such as FPS games, where product placement may seem forced and unnatural.

In the most ambitious scholarly study of memory and in-game advertising to date, Yang, Roskos-Ewoldsen, Dinu, and Arpan (2006) examined the effectiveness of in-game ads in sports and racing titles. The researchers had 153 participants play either a soccer game (*FIFA 2002*) or driving game (*Formula 1 2001*) with comparable numbers of embedded ads for 20 minutes. Participants then completed either an implicit (word fragment task) or explicit (recognition task) memory measure. The implicit memory measure was a novel contribution of this study and was designed to get at unintentional or unconscious recognition of in-game advertising. Results indicated that participants had low levels of explicit memory but relatively high implicit memory of brands. This is important considering that prior research on in-game advertising had only used explicit measures. Yang et al.'s findings suggest that, although the interactive nature of games may distract players from explicitly remembering ads, they may still be remembered implicitly and have an effect on implicit brand attitude and later purchasing decisions. This obviously has important implications for scholars and practitioners and suggests the value of adding both explicit and implicit memory measures in future studies.

Recently, Skalski and Bracken (2008) adapted the above methodology and examined how implicit memory would be impacted by media *vividness*, defined as "the ability of a technology to produce a sensorially rich mediated environment" (Steuer, 1995, p. 41). Vividness (also called *media richness*) has already received attention in research on 3-D Web advertising (e.g., Li, Daugherty, & Biocca, 2003) and was examined in the context of video games by Skalski and Bracken by having ad content displayed in High Definition (HD) or Standard Definition (SD). Specifically, they had 110 participants either play or watch a basketball game (*NBA 2K8*) or a hockey game (*NHL 08*) in either HD or SD and then take an implicit recall test. Results indicated there was a difference in the raw number of ads recalled, as hockey players/viewers remembered significantly more ads. When the findings were broken down by the proportion of ads recalled, however, participants in the basketball condition remembered a higher percentage than those in the hockey condition (30% versus 21%). This is interesting considering the hockey game had more ads than the basketball one. It suggests that not only genre (e.g., sports) but type of game within a genre (e.g., basketball vs. hockey) can affect reactions to in-game advertisements. Having too many ads, as the hockey game perhaps did, may decrease the probability of a given ad being remembered. Contrary to predictions, however, experiencing a game ad in HD had no effect on recall beyond that of SD.

In sum, the scholarly research in this area reveals low to moderate but still noteworthy effects of in-game advertising on memory, and these findings parallel those of the game industry. A phone survey by Nielsen Entertainment and Activision, for example, indicated that more than a quarter (27%) of active male gamers could recall in-game advertising from the last game they played (Activision, 2004). The studies reviewed above identify several variables that may moderate this general effect, including interactivity, brand type, and game type. Two other variables of potential importance from research will also now be considered—attitudes toward in-game advertising and the experience of presence.

ATTITUDES TOWARD IN-GAME ADVERTISING

Both Nelson (2002) and Chaney, Lin, and Chaney (2004) asked participants about their attitudes toward product placement in games. Nelson's findings indicated that players were generally favorable toward the practice of product placement in games, noting that it could add to realism. Open-ended comments showed these positive attitudes may not extend to certain genres and situations, however, such as having real brands in a fantasy world. While ads along a racetrack or in a stadium make sense, they do not make sense in a medieval forest, for example. As one gamer in the Nelson study put it: "Sports are ok—but it would be weird to see a Pepsi in *Mario Brothers.*" Findings from the Chaney, Lin, and Chaney study on billboards in a first person shooter game (atypical genre) echo this sentiment. The vast majority of participants who recalled any products or brands were either neutral or unfavorable toward the idea that billboards enhanced the experience of a game. The results of these studies have clear implications for practitioners and underscore the importance of exercising caution in deciding what games to place ads in.

Findings from industry and commercial sources seem to conflict somewhat with the scholarly research above, however, and suggest that players are much more accepting of in-game ads. A 2006 advice column by a market research professional advises that players are tolerant of in-game advertising when the brand placement enhances the gaming experience by being both relevant and a part of the game experience (Kennish, 2006). While this seems to support academic knowledge, more recent industry research does not. Nielsen Games, for example, reported that 82% of 1,300 gamers reported that the gaming experience was as enjoyable with ads as without (Sandburg, 2008). While this may indicate that gamers are becoming more accepting of in-game ads, some question the validity of industry-commissioned reports, which are typically communicated through short press releases that do not include a full reportage of methods or results. As Anderson (2006) points out, "statements such as 'gamers like the realism advertising brings' are [often] trotted out uncritically, usually by those with ads to sell." As evidence for this claim, he examined a report by comScore Media Metrix that seemed to indicate that gamers don't mind in game ads and found that, actually, the findings showed that 63 percent of hard core gamers and 73 percent of casual gamers disagreed with the statement that "ads make games more realistic." Despite bold claims by industry sources, there appears to be resistance to at least some forms of in-game advertising among gamers, and a number of critics are suggesting that industry research be treated with a degree of skepticism (e.g., Sandburg, 2008).

THE ROLE OF PRESENCE

The psychological experience of presence (the "perceptual illusion of nonmediation," Lombard & Ditton, 1997) may also be an important determinant of the effectiveness of in-game advertising. Presence does positively influence outcomes associated with persuasion in general (Daugherty, Gangadharbatla, & Bright, in press) and 3-D advertising specifically (Li, Daugherty, & Biocca, 2002), and this effect should extend to games. In the previously described Nelson, Yaros, and Keum (2006) study, telepresence (specifically the sensation of "arrival" in the media environment) was found to positively mediate the relationship between game liking and perceived persuasion. Another study by Grigorovici and Constantin (2004) exposed participants to a game-like virtual environment with 3D billboards and product placements and found that presence (engagement) was negatively associated with brand recall. This finding echoes those of the Chaney, Lin, and Chaney (2004) study reported earlier, which looked at experience of flow, and suggests that states such as presence and flow may distract from memory of certain content, which has also been shown in evidence from non-gaming contexts (e.g., Skalski, Tamborini, Glazer, & Smith, 2009). This does not mean that persuasion is negatively affected by those states, however—it may simply be that persuasion works through different mechanisms when users are highly immersed. Given that video games are perhaps the most likely of all popular media to create a sense of presence due to the combination of interactive control and increasingly realistic graphics and sounds they offer players (Tamborini & Skalski, 2006), telepresence and related concepts such as flow seem to be especially important considerations for future research on in-game advertising.

FUTURE DIRECTIONS FOR SCHOLARSHIP ON IN-GAME ADVERTISING

The above review of research literature on in-game advertising suggests several directions for future scholarship, and these and other considerations will be elaborated upon in this final section, including the value of using more direct outcome measures, the potential for modifying or "modding" game environments, and the importance of considering multiple forms of in-game ads and related technological changes.

Outcome Measures

As the above review suggests, most research thus far has focused on recall as the primary dependent variable. While recall is important, it does not exactly get at what ultimately interests many advertisers, i.e., persuading consumers to purchase products or at least have more favorable brand and product attitudes. Few investigations to date have considered outcomes beyond memory of products in games, however. The Nelson, Yaros, and Keum (2006) study did ask participants about "perceived persuasion," or the extent to which they believed each brand in the game affected their own brand attitudes, and their findings revealed greater perceived persuasion from real brands than fictitious brands. Yet this type of outcome measure only scratches the surface of what can and should be done in future research on in-game advertising effectiveness. The promise of implicit memory measures points to one intriguing avenue for future research. Yang, Roskos-Ewoldsen, Dinu, & Arpan (2006) point out that implicit memory can lead to implicit attitudes, which have been shown to be a good predictor of the related behavior (Fazio & Olson, 2003). Measuring and accounting for these attitudes will help in predicting behavior. The attitude-behavior relationship has been the subject of numerous theories and models in the persuasion literature, and as Perloff (2007) points out, the more researchers know about when and how attitudes influence behavior, the more useful their recommendations can be to real-life persuaders, including advertisers. The rise of online gaming has opened up the possibility for even more direct assessment of outcomes, such as "click throughs" based on user behavior toward ads (similar to what has been done in Web research), and these and other effectiveness measures should all be considered by researchers.

Ad "Modding"

Video games also open up unprecedented possibilities for researchers to manipulate how ads appear. Many titles now come with tools for "modding" or changing aspects of the game, and this can be accomplished with relative ease. The first author of this chapter, for example, modded the first-person shooter game *Unreal* for a summer grant project (Skalski, 2007). In a short time and with no experience, he successfully added several realistic-looking signs onto the walls to one of the game's 3-D environments (including for Mountain Dew and his host university) using standard images found online (e.g., .jpg, .bmp files). Importantly, the signs responded realistically to actions in the game world due to the game's extant "engine" or core software—shooting a gun or firing a rocket at the signs, for example, left marks on them in expected ways without having to do any new programming. Chaney, Lin, and Chaney (2004) used a similar procedure to add the billboards in their study, and there are many other exciting possibilities for this type of modding. Researchers could, for example, manipulate brand frequency (e.g., placing different numbers of ads within a game environment) or type (e.g., changing a sign in a game to one of several different versions), to address issues raised in existing research as well as to explore new possibilities for advertising. As Blascovich et al. (2002) argue, virtual environment technology can overcome many deficiencies of traditional experiments, including lack of control. Video games are currently the most popular form of virtual environment technology and they open up a world of possibilities for advancing scholarship on advertising even beyond the video game context.

The Role of Types and Technologies

The review of types of in-game ads from earlier in this chapter calls attention to one obvious gap in the research literature: the lack of studies on new forms of advertising in games. The research thus far has followed the approach of studies on movies and television focusing on product and brand placement, but what about advergames or interactive in-game products or dynamic ads? These new forms of advertising have been given scant attention in the literature to date, but there are some signs that they are capturing the attention of scholars. Garau (2008), for example, did an experiment on the influence of advergames on player behavior and found a relationship between flow experienced during play and frequency of brand purchases as well as communicating about the advergame to others. Issues related to specific forms of in-game advertising should continue to be addressed.

Finally, the importance of considering technology in in-game advertising research cannot be understated. The history section in this chapter highlights advances that have occurred in in-game advertising over time due largely to technology, and these should continue into the future. Specific technologies to look out for, both at the hardware and software level, include:

- ***HDTV*:** The ongoing diffusion of High-Definition Television (HDTV) promises to bring highly vivid visuals to viewers and players. Microsoft has even dubbed the newest generation of gaming the "HD Era" (Cross, 2005). Although Skalski and Bracken (2008) found HD to have no effect on recall of brands in sports games, there is some evidence of its potential. In a study of television ads, Bracken (2007) found that viewers had more favorable attitudes towards brands presented in HD than the same brands presented in standard definition. This suggests that HD can increase ad effectiveness, and future work on HD games should focus on outcomes beyond recall (such as attitude and purchase intention) as well as ad placement in other game genres.
- ***3-D*:** Just as they came to movie theaters in the 1950s, stereoscopic 3-D visuals are coming to a game console near you. Sony recently announced that 3-D PlayStation 3 games will be released in 2009, and film director James Cameron has stated that he believes true 3-D is the future of gaming (Faylor, 2008). The implication for game advertising is that players may soon have brands and products seemingly jumping

off the screen and into their living rooms (with the help of special glasses, of course). Research into this development can extend existing work on 3-D interactive advertising effects (e.g., Li, Daugherty, & Biocca, 2002) by examining the additional impact of stereoscopy, which creates an even greater illusion of depth than conventional 3-D graphics.

- ***New interfaces***: The controllers players use to interact with games have recently become a major focus of the game industry due to the success of the Nintendo Wii, the *Guitar Hero* series, Sony EyeToy games, and other titles controlled using lifelike movements. These types of interfaces hold tremendous potential from an advertising standpoint. It is not difficult to imagine future game experiences being designed around realistic control devices with a marked effect on performance, such as a branded Wiimote or club interface that positively affects a player's golf swing. At a more fundamental level, game controllers give players the ability to interact with objects in the game, possibly including brands and products. The extent to which games do this and the persuasive effects of this type of interaction is an important consideration for researchers.
- ***Custom characters and virtual products***: A key development highlighted in the types section of this chapter is the ability of games to not only show products but to have consumers actually experience them in virtual form, through the types of interfaces just discussed. Gaudiosi (2006) speculates about the persuasive effects of driving the latest Porsche, outfitting one's character in Rocawear, or even wearing a real brand of sneakers in a game that increases the dexterity of one's avatar. These are empirical questions, and avatar creation programs are diffusing widely, both in games and at the console level. Sony's PlayStation Network and Microsoft's Xbox Live service recently added customizable avatars, for example, to compete with Nintendo's popular Miis, and both plan to make branded clothing available for outfitting the characters (Lovison, 2009). Future research should examine the effectiveness of these types of initiatives along with the persuasive effects of virtual product use.
- ***Virtual reality (VR)***: The technology with the ultimate telepresence-inducing potential is undoubtedly virtual reality (VR), which promises to completely isolate media users from their surrounding environment using goggles, gloves, and other immersive hardware (Tamborini et al., 2004). Although VR was a buzzword in the early 1990s, the hype surrounding it has been tempered by the poor performance and failure of VR initiatives (Ebersole, 1997). Even if it never diffuses widely, VR still represents a way for game and advertising researchers to create a strong manipulation of "being there" for theory testing. And if VR does take off, it has the potential to make players feel closer than ever to brands and products.
- ***Mixed reality (MR)***: Mixed reality systems are emerging technologies that combine virtual images with images of the real world (Freeman, Steed, & Zhou, 2005). As with VR, MR users typically wear goggles, but instead of only seeing a virtual environment they see virtual objects in their physical environment. In other words, MR goggles are like eyeglasses with the capability of displaying computer imagery in selected areas. A gaming application of this technology developed at the University of Singapore is *Human Pacman,* which superimposes graphics from the classic arcade game *Pac-Man* (such as dots and power-ups) onto city streets and buildings.

Players then choose to be either Pac-Man or a ghost and physically walk the streets playing the game (Sandhana, 2005). The potential for these games is both amazing and frightening (imagine, for example, seeing gamers running around the streets "shooting at" virtual foes that only they can see), but it has obvious benefits for advertisers. It would allow them to place gamer-targeted messages such as virtual billboards in real-world settings.

- ***Mobile devices*****:** Gaming on cell phones and other mobile devices is expected to grow rapidly in coming years, due to factors such as the increasing technological ability of phones to deliver quality games and the general affordability of mobile titles (Perez, 2008). Mobile games have the potential to deliver advertisements "on the go," and the vast capabilities of contemporary cell phones are being put to even more innovative advertising uses. One example is a game called *Zhouma 101* developed by researchers in Taipei. To take part in this multiplayer experience, gamers with a camera phone stand outside of a large city building with video screens at a specified time and are given a topic to photograph. They then have a set amount to rush around the city and shoot the best image they can find of it. The results are displayed prominently on the building when time is up, and both players and spectators are given the opportunity to vote on a winner (Jehmlich, 2007). The advertising connection is that players are given brands to shoot (e.g., 7-11 in one contest), which forces them to attend to ads and then engagingly shows their photos of the ads or brands to a mass audience at the end. This type of "pervasive gaming" experience could be extended to getting players to go to particular stores or to take part in other behaviors beneficial to advertisers.
- ***Online gaming*****:** Gaming over the Internet, finally, intersects with many of the new advertising technologies previously discussed. It can be used to dynamically update ads in a game, as mentioned earlier, and also to bring players together online in social and collaborate ways, perhaps even through the types of custom avatars discussed in this section. The *Second Life* community illustrates much of the potential inherent in online advertising. Virtual stores with regularly updated merchandise and the capability for users to purchase virtual and real products may be incorporated into games just as they are in *Second Life.* The continuing diffusion of broadband Internet access will only increase the advertising possibilities inherent in online gaming as well as its importance to gaming in general.

All of the above innovations hold great promise for future advertising and promotion. They are looming on the horizon, if not here already, and demand the attention of researchers. This chapter has reviewed the history and types of advertising in games along with study findings and considerations for future research. There is still much to be learned about this burgeoning area and researchers must answer the call, to increase understanding and aid future development. As Nike's famous slogan says, "Just Do It."

REFERENCES

Activision. (2004). *Activision and Nielsen Entertainment team to provide standardized measurement metrics for video game audiences.* Press release. Retrieved October 1, 2008 from http://investor.activision.com/ReleaseDetail.cfm?releaseid=149231

America's Army. (2008). In *Wikipedia, The free encyclopedia.* Retrieved August 24, 2008 from http://en.wikipedia.org/wiki/America's_Army#cite_note-Turse-33

Anderson, N. (2006). Most gamers do not agree that advertising makes games more realistic. *Ars Technica.* Retrieved October 5, 2008 from http://arstechnica.com/news.ars/post/20061002-7879.htm

August 19, 2008, from http://nationalcheeseemporium.org/

Blascovich, J., Loomis, J., Beall, A., Swinth, K., Hoyt, C., & Bailenson, J. (2002). Immersive virtual environment technology as a research tool for social psychology. *Psychological Inquiry, 13*, 103–125. doi:10.1207/S15327965PLI1302_01

Bogost, I. (2005, June 11). Beer, nudity, and Pac-Man. *Water Cooler Games.* Retrieved August 20, 2008 from http://www.watercoolergames.org/archives/000416.shtml

Bogost, I. (2007). *Persuasive games: The expressive power of videogames*. Cambridge, MA: The MIT Press.

Bracken, C. C. (2007). *That was a great ad: The impact of high definition television commercials on audiences' attitudes toward brands*. Presented to the second annual Persuasive Conference, Stanford, CA.

Burns, E. (2005). Nike iD steps into NBA 2K6. *The ClickZ Network.* Retrieved August 12, 2008 from http://www.clickz.com/showPage.html?page=3552726.

Cassidy, W. (2002, December 17). Top 10 gaming grails. *GameSpy.* Retrieved August 18, 2008, from http://archive.gamespy.com/top10/december02/grails/

Cross,J.(2005).HDEracomingtogaming.ExtremeTech. Retrieved January 15, 2006 from http://www.extremetech.com/article2/0,1558,1774523,00.asp?kc=ETRSS02129TX1K0 00532

Daugherty, T., Gangadharbatla, H., & Bright, L. (in press). Presence and persuasion. In Bracken, C. C., & Skalski, P. (Eds.), *Immersed in media: Telepresence in everyday life*. New York: Routledge.

Ebersole, S. (1997). A brief history of virtual reality and its social applications. *Encyclopedia of interactive media.* Retrieved February 3, 2009 from http://faculty.colostate- pueblo.edu/samuel.ebersole/336/eim/papers/vrhist.html

Faylor, C. (2008). PlayStation 3 getting true 3D visual support in 2009, claims developer. *Shacknews.* Retrieved February 3, 2009 from http://www.shacknews.com/onearticle.x/56514

Fazio, R. H., & Olson, M. A. (2003). Implicit measures in social cognition research: Their meaning and use. *Annual Review of Psychology, 54*, 297–327. doi:10.1146/annurev.psych.54.101601.145225

February 11, 2009, from http://www.informationweek.com/news/mobility/business/showArticle.jhtml?articleID=208801005

Fox, M. (2006). *The video games guide*. London: Boxtree Ltd.

Freeman, J., Steed, A., & Zhou, B. (2005). Rapid scene modelling, registration, and specification for mixed reality systems. In *Proceedings of ACM virtual reality software and technology* (pp. 147-150), Monterey, CA.

Garau, C. (2008). The influence of advergames on players' behaviour: An experimental study. *Electronic Markets, 18*(2), 106–116. doi:10.1080/10196780802044859

Gardner, P. (2001, June 1). Games with a day job: Putting the power of games to work. *Gamasutra*. Retrieved August 18, 2008 from http://www.gamasutra.com/features/20010601/gardner_01.htm

Gaudiosi, J. (2006). Product placement to die for. *Wired*. Retrieved April 25, 2008 from http://www.wired.com/wired/archive/14.04/gads.html.

Grigorovici, D. M., & Constantin, C. D. (2004). Experiencing interactive advertising beyond rich media: Impacts of ad type and presence on 3D gaming immersive virtual environments. *Journal of Interactive Advertising, 5*(1). Retrieved September 23, 2008, from http:/jiad.org/article53

Horwitz, J. (2004, September 23). Advertising and cross-promotion. *Jupiter Research*. Retrieved August 19, 2008 from http://www.jupiterresearch.com/bin/item.pl/research:concept/111/id=95647/

In-game advertising. (2008). In *Wikipedia, the Free Encyclopedia*. Retrieved April 25, 2008 from http://en.wikipedia.org/wiki/In-game_advertising#cite_note-adweek-0

Jana, R. (2006). Is that a video game—or an ad? *Business Week*. Retrieved October 1, 2008 from http://www.businessweek.com/innovate/content/jan2006/id20060124_792815.htm

Jehmlich, D. (2007). Gamevertising: An interactive advertising experience. *Trendburo*. Retrieved February 11, 2009 from http://www.trendbuero.de/index.php?f_articleId=1880&f_categoryId=155

Karrh, J. A. (1998). Brand placement: A review. *Journal of Current Issues and Research in Advertising, 20*(2), 31–49.

Kennish, F. (2003, March 3). In-Game advertising do's and don'ts. *iMedia Conncection*. Retrieved on September 30, 2008 from http://www.imediaconnection.com/content/8489.asp

Kent, S. L. (2001). *The ultimate history of video games*. New York: Three Rivers Press.

Li, H., Daugherty, T., & Biocca, F. (2002). Impact of 3-D advertising on product knowledge, brand attitude, and purchase intention: the mediating role of presence. *Journal of Advertising, 31*(3), 43–57.

Lindstrom, M. (2002, July 23). Brand games: your move. *The Clickz Network*. Retrieved August 18, 2008, from http://www.clickz.com/showPage.html?page=1430331

Lombard, M., & Ditton, T. (1997). At the heart of it all: The concept of presence. *Journal of Computer Mediated Communication, 3*(2). Retrieved April 20, 2005 from http://jcmc.indiana.edu/vol3/issue2/lombard.htm

Lovison, B. (2009). A tale of two avatars. *Gaming Insider*. Retrieved February 10, 2009 from http://www.mediapost.com/publications/?fa=Articles.showArticle&art_aid=99894

Lunar Lander. (2008, April 4). In *Arcade-History*. Retrieved August 18, 2008 from http://www.arcade-history.com/index.php?page=detail&id=1417

Maragos, N. (2005, March 7) Serious games summit: Advergaming for private and public interests. *Gamasutra*. Retrieved August 18, 2008, from http://www.gamasutra.com/view/feature/2209/postcard_from_gdc_2005_serious_.php

McCarty, J. A. (2004). Product placements: The nature of the practice and potential avenues of inquiry. In Shrum, L. J. (Ed.), *The Psychology Of Entertainment Media: Blurring the Lines Between Entertainment and Persuasion*. Mahwah, NJ: Lawrence Erlbaum.

Nelson, M. R. (2002). Recall of brand placements in computer/video games. *Journal of Advertising Research, 42*, 80–92.

Nelson, M. R., Yaros, R. A., & Keum, H. (2006). Examining the influence of telepresence on spectator and player processing of real and fictitious brands in a computer game. *Journal of Advertising, 35*(4), 87–99. doi:10.2753/JOA0091-3367350406

Nuttall, C. (2007, January 30). Burger King's whopping games sales. *Financial Times*. Retrieved August 18, 2008 from http://blogs.ft.com/techblog/2007/01/burger-kings-whhtml/

Perez, M. (2008, June). Mobile gaming revenue to hit $4.5 billion. *Information Week*. Retrieved

Perloff, R. M. (2007). *The dynamics of persuasion*. New York: Lawrence Erlbaum Associates.

Pigna, K. (2008). Presidential candidate ads appear in Burnout Paradise. *1Up.com*. Retrieved October 14, 2008 from http://www.1up.com/do/newsStory?cId=3170635

Sandburg, A. (2008). 82% positive to in-game ads, someone call Ripley's! *That video game Blog*. Retrieved September 30, 2008 from http://www.thatvideogameblog.com/2008/06/18/82-react-positively-to-in-game-advertisement/

Sandhana, L. (2005). Pacman comes to life virtually. *BBC News*. Retrieved February 3, 2009, from http://news.bbc.co.uk/2/hi/technology/4607449.stm

Schneider, L. P., & Cornwell, T. B. (2005). Cashing in on crashes via brand placement in computer games: The effects of experience and flow on memory. *International Journal of Advertising*, *24*(3), 321–343.

Shields, M. (2006). In-game ads could reach $2 billion. *Adweek*. Retrieved April 25, 2008, from http://www.adweek.com/aw/national/article_display.jsp?vnu_content_id=1002343563

Siklos, R. (2006, October 19). A virtual world but real money. *The New York Times*. Retrieved August 18, 2008 from http://www.nytimes.com/2006/10/19/technology/19virtual.html?_r=1&oref=slogin

Skalski, P. (2007). *Game modding. Presentation delivered to Visualization and Digital Imaging Lab*. University of Minnesota Duluth.

Skalski, P., Tamborini, R., Glazer, E., & Smith, S. (2009). Effects of humor on presence and recall of persuasive messages. *Communication Quarterly*, *57*(2), 136–153. doi:10.1080/01463370902881619

Slocombe, M. (2005). Men spend more money on video games than music: Nielsen report. *Digital-Lifestyles*. Retrieved November 1, 2006 from http://digital-lifestyles.info/display_page.asp?section=cm&id=2091

Smith, A., & Wood, P. (2005, July 1). *Online advertising for the gamer generation*. Retrieved

Staff, I. G. N. (2003, January 10). Dante, meet Diesel. *IGN*. Retrieved February 11, 2008 from http://ps2.ign.com/articles/382/382175p1.html

Steuer, J. (1995). Defining virtual reality: Dimensions determining telepresence. In Biocca, F., & Levy, M. R. (Eds.), *Communication in the age of virtual reality* (pp. 33–56). Hillsdale, NJ: LEA.

Svensson, P. (2005, February 24). Sony builds pizza-order function into 'Everquest II'. *USA Today*. Retrieved August 19, 2008 from http://www.usatoday.com/tech/products/services/2005-02-24-sony-pizza_x.htm

Tamborini, R., Eastin, M., Skalski, P., Lachlan, K., Fediuk, T., & Brady, R. (2004). Violent virtual video games. *Journal of Broadcasting & Electronic Media*, *48*(3), 335–357.

Tamborini, R., & Skalski, P. (2006). The role of presence in the experience of electronic games. In Vorderer, P., & Bryant, J. (Eds.), *Playing video games: Motives, responses, and consequences*. Mahwah, NJ: Lawrence Erlbaum Associates.

Turcotte, S. (1995). *Gimme a Bud! The feature film product placement industry*. Unpublished Master's thesis, Austin, Texas, University of Texas.

Vedrashko, I. (2006). *Advertising in computer games*. Unpublished master's thesis, Massachusetts Institute of Technology, Cambridge.

Wong, M. (2004, October 18). Advertisments inserted into video games. *redOrbit.* Retrieved August 19, 2008 from http://www.redorbit.com/news/technology/94730/advertisements_inserted_into_video_ga mes/#

Yang, M., Roskos-Ewoldsen, B., & Roskos-Ewoldsen, D. R. (2004). Mental models of for brand placement. In Shrum, L. J. (Ed.), *The psychology of entertainment media: Blurring the lines between entertainment and persuasion*. Mahwah, NJ: Lawrence Erlbaum Associates.

Yang, M., Roskos-Ewoldsen, D. R., Dinu, R., & Arpan, L. M. (2006). The effectiveness of in game advertising: Comparing college students' explicit and implicit memory for brand names. *Journal of Advertising, 35*(4), 143–152. doi:10.2753/JOA0091-3367350410

Yo! Noid Shrine. (n.d.). Retrieved September 12, 2008 from http://www.nesplayer.com/yonoid/noids.htm

Zool. (2008, October 10). In *Wikipedia, the Free Encyclopedia.* Retrieved October 12, 2008, from http://en.wikipedia.org/wiki/Zool

ENDNOTE

1 For a more exhaustive history, see the advergames chapter in *Persuasive Games: The Expressive Power of Video Games* (Bogost, 2007).

Chapter 23
Online Gaming:
Demographics, Motivations, and Information Processing

Vincent Cicchirillo
The University of Texas at Austin, USA

ABSTRACT

Online gaming has become a major part of our culture. In order to understand this new media in our society we must examine the motivations for playing these types of games and how that impacts individuals processing of information. This book chapter sets out to examine those motivations and how motivational processing influences in-game content during game play. More importantly how individuals recognize, process, and evaluate information relative to their motivations for playing an online game. Furthermore, this chapter not only explores the product-related segmentation variables, but also demographic segmentation variables. Thus, taken together variables such as motivations, demographics, and game features allows us to paint a clearer picture of the: who, how, and why of online gaming.

INTRODUCTION

Video and computer games are big business. In fact, it was estimated by the Entertainment Software Association (ESA) that sales for computer and video game software reached about $11.7 billion in 2008. Blizzard Entertainment, the developers behind the game *World of WarCraft* announced in 2007 that they had recruited over 9 million subscribers to that particular game (van Lent, 2008). Not only do individuals have to pay a one time fee to purchase the game ($50-$60), but they also must pay a monthly subscription fee to play that game online. According to van Lent if you do the math that's nearly $1.5 billion dollars annually! The success of online games has even spawned console systems (i.e., X360 & PlayStation 3) and video games that allow users to connect to the internet and compete or play with other users in a multiplayer format.

The gaming industry certainly takes it sales figures seriously. A person only need to look at the amount of money developers spend upon marketing their games, which is usually about

DOI: 10.4018/978-1-60566-792-8.ch023

the same amount of money it takes to produce that game (Nussenbaum, 2004). Thus, if a game takes anywhere from $12 million to $20 million to create, then this same amount needs to go into marketing that game through multiple advertising campaigns in order to ensure that the game makes a profit. According to Nussenbaum the increase in costs has game developers seeking secondary revenue streams through online subscription fees and in-game advertising. Gaming industry leaders speculate that the amount of money spent on in-game advertising could reach $2 billion dollars by the year 2010 (Shields, 2006). In fact there is an advertising corporation called Massive (http://www.massiveincorporated.com) that caters solely to advertising within video games or in-game advertising. This trend was not lost on the part of politicians. For instance, newly elected President Barack Obama spent roughly $44,000 on in-game advertising between October 6th and November 3rd in 2008 for multiple Xbox 360 games (Miller, 2008). The advertisements sponsored voting early and were featured within 17 video games for the Xbox 360 (Sinclair, 2008). The amount spent on these advertisements seems relatively small in comparison to the entire amount put towards running a presidential campaign. However, the return on the investment would seem to be worthwhile, especially if you asked John McCain.

The increase of in-game advertisements certainly brings up important questions related to how individuals process information while playing a video game. Even more important is how that information is processed when it occurs simultaneously with game content. Audience analysis certainly could give us some insights into the answers to the previous questions. According to Livingstone (1999) “As audiences become less predictable, more fragmented or more variable in their engagement with media, understanding the audience is even more important for theories of social shaping, design, markets and diffusion than, perhaps, was true for older media” (p. 62). Thus, understanding the audience and their motivations for play is the first step in gaining knowledge about how content within a video or online game is processed. As academics and industry professionals we need to understand a) what is online gaming, b) who plays online games, and c) what are individual’s motivations for playing online games. In order to suggest new directions in gaming research we need to understand the phenomenon that we are studying. Furthermore, the demographic characteristics of online gamers may not be as easily presumed as once thought and therefore not as easily targeted as predicted. Therefore, this chapter will integrate what online gaming is along with player demographics in order to better understand motivations behind playing online games. Once these motivations are understood we can get a clearer picture of how individuals process information during game play.

WHAT IS ONLINE GAMING?

Online games have been referred to as MMORPG’s, which stands for Massively Multiplayer Online Role-Playing Games. However, online games have also been referred to as massively multiplayer/multiuser online (MMO’s), massively multiplayer online game (MMOG’s), or massively multiplayer online persistent world (MMOPW’s) (Chan & Vorderer, 2006). MMORPG’s have been defined as “a persistent world… that exists independent of the user” (Yee, 2005, p. 4). Users create their own graphical avatars and interact in an online world with other users and their avatars. Users can login or logout anytime, but the world still exists online and is open to numerous users. In fact, an interesting aspect of these games is the fact that most MMORPG’s include a minimum of about 2,000 users (Yee). Thus, these virtual environments at any one point in time can house numerous avatars and characters.

Long before the word MMORPG was a part of our vernacular; games played over the internet were referred to as MUD’s (Multiple User Domains/Dungeons) (Kent, 2003). The first MUD was developed in 1978 by Roy Trubshaw and was nothing more than a few interconnected chat rooms (Bartle, 1990). It should also be mentioned that Richard Bartle was also a developer who worked alongside Trubshaw to create these MUD's (Lawrie, 2002). MUD's have a longstanding connection to role-playing board games like Dungeons & Dragons (D&D), mainly because many of the developers like Bartle were avid fans of D&D (Stewart, 1996). This may help to explain why most of today's MMORPGs resemble D&D type fantasy worlds and role-playing aspects. According to Blackmon (1994) D&D is a fantasy game in which players pick a character and interact with other characters and obstacles (e.g. monsters). The game is purely face-to-face as players interact as they would when playing a game of monopoly on a game board. Character development and the outcome of battles are decided by a series of dice rolls (Blackmon). In games like D&D, a player acts as the Dungeon Master rolling the dice to decide these outcomes, in MUD's the server controls the outcome (Yee, 2005). MUD's are essentially D&D type role-playing, only in online chat rooms that are primarily text driven and lack graphical representations. Thus, players enter the room and read descriptions of what the room looks like, smells like, and contains. Players interact with other players and objects through typed commands. Although, this seems fairly primitive compared to today's online games, MUD's are still quite popular among multiple users.

However, one area that revolutionized the online gaming industry was the implementation of graphical representations. Instead of users reading what a room looked liked, they actually see this world come to life on their computer screens. According to Yee (2006b, p. 311):

On a simplistic level, MMORPGs could be thought of as a scenic chat room with a variety of interactive tasks. Users experience cities, jungles, and even the falling rain or snow in rich real-time 3D graphics, and communicate with each other using typed chat and templated gestures and expressions. They interact with the world through a combination of mouse-driven interfaces and typed commands, and partake of a large number of varied activities that increase in complexity, reward, and time involvement which typically operate on a random-ratio reinforcement schedule. These activities revolve around character advancement and translate into a functional advantage in terms of the mechanics of the world, whether this is combat capability, social status, avatar appearance, geographic knowledge, equipment quality, or even cooking skills. Whereas the first few MMORPGs focused heavily on combat-oriented advancement, recent MMORPGs have offered more diverse forms of advancement. For example, in Star Wars Galaxies, one can become a skilled musician, chef, hair stylist, animal tamer, or politician.

A game called *Meridian 59* was one of the first graphical online games developed, but failed to meet the criteria for the term "massively" because it could only host 250 users at one time (Kent, 2003). Although, developers often referred to *Meridian 59* as a massive multiplayer, the distinction of the first MMOG often goes to *Ultima Online* (Kent), which was developed in 1997 by Electronic Arts (EA). The debate of what was the first MMOG is still questioned; however it is not the purpose of this chapter to solve that argument. The inclusion of graphical representations was an important development in the history online gaming. The advent of graphical representations has expanded research into virtual environments with new and expanding opportunities. Furthermore, advancements in graphical technology allow MMORPG's to offer different factors and features that may give us an understanding of why certain individuals choose to play these types of games.

Chan and Vorderer (2006) outlined five aspects that differentiate MMORPG's from other online games. Aspects such as *persistence, physicality, social interaction, avatar-mediated play, verti-*

cal game play, and *perpetuity* all contribute to what makes an online game a MMORPG (Chan & Vorderer). *Persistence* often refers to the fact that the "virtual world" users inhabit exists continuously, whether or not that player is logged in or not. Other users can login and play anytime they wish and the number of individuals playing the game at any one time may fluctuate. Thus, events in this "virtual world" occur even when the person is not logged onto the server, these events are often driven by other users (Yee, 2006b). The persistence aspect may offer a few insights into the motivations behind playing online games. The worlds in which these users inhabit seem to resemble real worlds in terms of consistency. Thus, players of online games may do so to escape the real world into a fantasy world, but still require a level of consistency or persistence that real worlds or environments provide. Another form of *persistence* relates to a chosen players representation (avatar) that maintains the same identity and/or personality (Chan & Vorderer). Although, an individual's avatar may increase in abilities (e.g. physical, magical, stamina, etc…), they generally keep the same contacts and personal characteristics. A player's avatar is an important aspect of an online game. As will be discussed, individuals do not just spend time advancing or enhancing their avatars, they spend money on enhancements for that avatar.

According to Chan and Vorderer (2006), *physicality* indicates that these worlds are representations of material objects and environments. As Yee suggested, these locations can replicate anything from the jungle to frozen tundra and incorporate all of the processing capabilities of computers to create 3-D graphical environments. The fantastic nature of the avatars and the worlds would seem to infer that most games revolve around fantasy role-playing in distant castles and lands. However, some games such as *SecondLife* offer anything from playing games to partaking in virtual classrooms provided by educational institutions (http://secondlifegrid.net/programs/education). Thus, not all online communities and websites are dedicated to role-playing. The consistent fact is that regardless of the type of virtual world or community all provide opportunities to interact with objects and environments that symbolize tangible items. Virtual objects can be bought and sold by users across multiple types of online games for their avatars to use or profit from the sale. According to Natkin (2006) players have the ability to influence and interact with the virtual economy of the game, which may also have an impact on the real world economy. Individuals in the *World of WarCraft* can buy or trade for objects such as weapons, shields, potions, and even reputations (see www.guild-bank.com). In non-fantasy based games such as the *SIMS* furniture, clothing, and other items can be bought and sold online (Natkin). This virtual commerce aspect of the game means that individuals may not just see these games as enjoyment, but also economic opportunities. This may also add a different kind of motivation that has not been considered by researchers.

Chan and Vorderer (2006) further identify *social interaction* and *avatar-mediated play* as specific characteristics of an MMORPG. The simple fact that numerous individuals at any one point in time are playing online adds to the fact that individuals are likely to interact with other players. Many games offer the ability to join groups, clubs, and even have romantic relationships with other players. Ducheneaut, Moore, Nickell (2007) state that "unlike previous video games, MMOG's require players to exchange information and collaborate in real-time to progress in the game" (p. 129). Online games even offer different ways to interact with other players either through typed text or live audio between two or more players. Individuals may specifically seek out MMORPG's for the specific purpose of interacting with other players. Numerous researchers point to socializing as a major reason why individuals play online games (Bartle, 1990; Griffiths, Davies, & Chappell, 2004b; Kerr, 2006; Yee, 2006a). *Avatar-mediated play* is a characteristic that allows players to create their own characters or avatars within that game. In fact, the *World of WarCraft* offers ten playable races and numerous primary and secondary classes and professions (http://www.worldofwarcraft.com/info/races). Thus, individuals are offered unique opportunities to become whomever or whatever they wish within that online environment. Individuals may seek out online games in order to try a new profession, career, life-style, race, or even gender. Thus, experiencing what it might be like to live as another person with different characteristics and personalities could be motivating game play.

Finally, Chan and Vorderer (2006) identified both *vertical game play* and *perpetuity* as MMOG characteristics. Both of these characteristics are based upon how players define their achievement within play. Most online games are persistent worlds that continuously exist in virtual environments where there is no end or final completion to that game (*perpetuity*). Thus, players of MMOGs can never truly say they have beaten the game. Their level of success is measured by their characters attributes, wealth, reputation, and weapons/equipment (Chan & Vorderer). Success can also be measured by the level or rating of a players avatar. In fact, individuals may even purchase an avatar that has been advanced a few levels by another user or company that pays individuals to advance characters/avatars for sale. For instance, the web site *BuyMMOAccounts* (http://www.buymmoaccounts.com) offers individuals the chance to purchase a *World of WarCraft* character that has been advanced up a few levels from anywhere between $300 and $500 dollars. Natkin (2006) suggests that since there is no set concept of game length, attachment to the game follows certain social and material aspects for continuous, repeated game play. Goals and objectives within MMORPGs often change and are in no way static. The ability to offer players continuous game play with ever-changing plots, objectives, and goals can be a powerful motivating factor and addictive quality of online games.

One key aspect of MMOG's is the word "massive". Most if not all online games that want to be considered a true MMOG or MMORPG must have the ability to support thousands of players. Woodcock (2006) has been collecting subscription data to online games since 2002 based upon multiple sources (corporate data, press releases, news articles, anonymous sources, etc…). The results of this unique analysis have allowed researchers to gain valuable insights into how many individuals worldwide are playing MMOG's. Currently, the *World of WarCraft* is dominating the gaming market with over 10 million subscribers worldwide (Woodcock). Other games such as *Everquest II* and *City of Heroes/Villains* have over hundreds of thousands of players; however games such as *Sphere* and *PlanetSide* are estimated towards the lower end between fifteen & twenty-thousand players (Woodcock). Although, these estimates are not without error it does suggest that a great multitude of individuals have been and/or are starting to play MMOG's. It could be that sheer size of these worlds is a motivation in and of itself. Individuals may play simply because a multitude of different individuals from across the country and world are playing online.

SEGMENTING THE ONLINE AUDIENCE THROUGH DEMOGRAPHICS

In order to understand the motivations behind playing online games, we need to understand *who* plays these types of games. According to Oliver (2002) "the existence of certain individual characteristics may heighten or intensify media influences or may even provide a necessary condition for media influences to occur" (p. 518). Research conducted by Griffiths, Davies, & Chappell (2003, 2004a, 2004b) as well as extensive research conducted by Yee (2005, 2006a, 2006b) has provided excellent insights into the question of *who* plays online games. One assumption is that online game players are often younger socially withdrawn males.

However, research on the demographic characteristics of online game players questions this stereotypical image of online game players. Thus research that dispels commonly held assumptions about who plays online games needs to be understood before discussing how these demographics may influence the possible motivations of online game play.

Age

It is a common held assumption that most online gamers are teenagers. However, a recent demographic sample of MMOG players has disputed this widely held belief. Griffiths et al. (2003) conducted a secondary data analysis of demographic information from two fan websites dedicated to the massive online player game of *Everquest*. The results showed that out of 11,457 players from one website that approximately 72% were between the ages of 14 to 29 years (Griffiths et al.). The other website reported a larger age range between 10 and 30 years for 71% of the 12,538 sampled from that particular site (Griffiths et al.). Thus, evidence suggests that wide ranges of age groups are playing these types of games. This research paints quite a different picture in terms of the stereotypical image of an MMORPG player. Yee (2006b) examined the demographics of MMORPG players across a three-year span by recruiting them through multiple websites dedicated to online gaming. The results of this sample further challenged the youthful stereotype. The results showed that the average age of the respondents was 26.57 years, with only about 25% of the sample being teenagers (Yee). Thus, we can no longer assume that the market segments of online gamers are younger adolescents. Just like in real world environments different generations of individuals are interacting in online gaming environments.

Gender

Another stereotypical belief is that online gaming is a male dominated activity. Early research conducted on the examination of demographic characteristics of video game players suggested that only adolescent boys played video games (see McClure & Mears, 1984). This stereotype has been upheld in subsequent examinations of the effects of video game play (see Ballard & Lineberger, 1999). Lucas and Sherry (2004) noted that a random sample of college students who admitted to playing video games were more likely to be male (88.3%). However, a majority of the samples mentioned above were answering questions primarily about console games and not online games or MMOG's. Williams (2006) notes that this gender gap may occur because a majority of research aimed towards examining the effects of video game play has used adolescent samples. It is very possible that a majority of adolescent boys play console games and girls avoid such activities because they may have been deemed a male activity (Williams).

However, as mentioned before a majority of older individuals play MMOG's compared to adolescents. Thus, females may start to play MMOG's later on life because they provide activities in the gaming arena not typically male dominated, such as combat or killing. Griffiths et al. (2003, 2004b) found evidence suggesting an increasing number of females are starting to play online games (15%-20%). Although, not directly related to playing MMOG's, the Entertainment Software Association (ESA) released a news report on July 16, 2008 stating that 40% of computer and video game players are women. Yee (2007) found evidence to suggest that a large majority of female online gamers are between the ages of 23 and 40. Thus, it could be suggested that as females get older they are more likely to find reasons for playing online games than younger females. Although, the majority of MMOG players are male, female MMOG players should not be discounted.

Furthermore, motivations for playing an MMOG may be very different for male and female players.

Occupation/Yearly Income/ Marital Status

Yee (2007) found evidence to suggest that over 50% of MMORPG players work full-time. The slight majority of occupations goes to individuals in the information technology field (28.7%), however there seems to be great diversity when it comes to occupations that play MMOG's (lawyers, doctors, nurses, homemakers, office work, manual work, etc…) (Griffiths et al., 2004b). Griffiths et al. (2003) found that about 21% of online gamers make less than $35,000, 20% make between $35,000 and $60,000, and 14% make over $60,000 year. The above results make sense as most MMORPG's require a monthly fee and faster computer processing speeds, which cost money. The fact that individuals in the information technology and computer science fields are more likely to play MMOGs is also not surprising, as these individuals are more computer oriented. An interesting finding by Yee (2006b) relates to marital status of MMOG players. The results of demographic analysis reveal that most female players are married, while most male players are single. Evidence suggests that a majority of female players get involved because of a romantic partner (Yee). Thus, motivations may widely differ between men and women when deciding to start playing MMOG's. Finally, understanding these motivations may also help to predict how information is processed during game play. Individual's motivations for playing that online game may influence what in-game content is paid attention too and what is ignored.

MOTIVATION SEGMENTATION AND INFORMATION PROCESSING

Why are motivations important to information processing? The Uses and Gratifications perspective of media effects may add some insight on how to answer that question. The Uses and Gratifications approach to media effects was developed by Katz, Blumler, and Gurevitch (1973) to help explain individual's motivations for media use and selection. According to Rubin (2002) audience activity and media orientations are two essential concepts of uses and gratifications. Audience activity refers to the fact that individuals are not passive viewers of media, but rather, they are active participants who select and choose what they watch, hear, and read from media outlets. However, this activity is viewed on a continuum with individuals switching back and forth between passive and active viewers (Rubin). Thus, in terms of information processing, individuals often have different levels of cognitive involvement at any one point in time when processing a media message. The level of cognitive involvement is likely to influence what is remembered or recalled when playing an online game. For instance, an individual who is using a medium to gain knowledge or seek information (ex. watching a TV show about sharks) may have a different cognitive frameset than someone who is watching that show simply to alleviate boredom (Sherry, Lucas, Greenberg, & Lachlan, 2006). The amount of cognitive processing may be more effortful for people seeking to gain information than the person watching to pass the time. However, the person watching to pass time may be more susceptible to background features of the TV show because they are not as involved as the person with the information seeking motivation. If an individual is devoting a large amount of cognitive processing to completing a mission within an online environment or socializing with another player for information then it is likely that other sources of information are likely to be blocked out or passively processed. However, as will be discussed individuals may still recall in-game content passively through implicit associations.

Rubin (2002) further offers two distinct types of motivations about individuals' attitudes and expectations of their media use: ritualized and instrumental. In ritualized motivations individuals seek out media outlets to consume time or for diversionary purposes (Rubin). Instrumental motivations are more goal-directed such as seeking information about an object, environment, or individual. This may draw connections to economic perspectives about motivations because virtual objects may also be bought and sold between vendors and players (Natkin, 2006). Thus, utilitarian motivations of purchasing behaviors should be considered as a reason why individuals play online games. According to Mort and Rose (2004) utilitarian motivations relate to the functional purposes of outcomes produced by goods or products. This means that individuals may simply go online to purchase new clothing, weapons, or a means of transportation for their avatar. Any type of information related to these items would take cognitive processing priority over other aspects such as completing missions or socializing. Thus, these media orientations offer insights into audience activity when using a specific medium (Rubin). In terms of processing information during game play this means players may give cognitive processing priority to content that relates to their current motivations.

An important aspect of the uses and gratifications perspective is that it allows for the development of unique taxonomies of motives for using a specific type of media (Harris, 2004). Since online gaming offers opportunities for a multitude of interactions, events, and behaviors one needs to consider multiple motives for playing. Bartle (1990) was one of the first researchers to examine the motives for playing online games. Although, Bartle was addressing the motivations for playing MUD's, his research offers an entry point into the MMOG motivation literature. According to Bartle "a pattern emerged: people habitually found the same kinds of thing about the game 'fun', but there were several (four, in fact) sub-groupings into which opinion divided" (p. 2). The sub-groupings in which he refers to are four personality types that define individual's reasons for playing. The personality types are *Achievers*, *Explorers*, *Socialisers*, and *Killers* (Bartle). *Achievers* at the most basic level play the game in order to achieve game related goals, whether it is beating monsters or gaining points/ treasure (Bartle). *Explorers* play the game in order to discover new virtual worlds, in the case of MUD's this would be another virtual room. *Socialisers* play the game to interact with other players. Finally, *Killers* play in order to impose upon other players, thus to kill or inflict damage on other players in the game (Bartle).

Bartle (1990) further suggested that to maintain a proper working MUD, game administrators would need to find a delicate balance between these four personality types. Meaning, the MUD or "World" would need to emphasize certain aspects of the world or players, and the types of play (socializing or fighting) at any one point in time. For instance, Bartle mentioned that increasing the number of *Killers* in the game could drastically reduce the number of *Achievers* and *Socialisers*. However, Bartle's taxonomy of player types assumes that each personality is independent in terms of the individual (Yee, 2006a). Thus, a person can only be an *Achiever* and not a *Killer*, or a *Killer* and not a *Socialiser*. Players in most MMOGs may have multiple motivations for playing. Furthermore, graphical MUDs or MMOGs offer rules of engagement that already hamper killers from simply destroying every player in the environment. For instance, many MMORPGs like the *World of WarCraft* do not allow players to "duel" or engage in combat with another player unless both parties agree to this action (http://www.worldofwarcraft.com/info/basics/duels.html). Thus, MMOGs offer experiences and rules that are beyond what Bartle theorized would allow for a successful MUD. That said, Bartle's taxonomy does offer a beginning insight into some of the underlying motivations of online game play. Also, individuals who habitually play for certain reasons are more likely to attend to features with the online game that pertain to that style of play. Here, information processing is increased when an online game offers individuals the opportunities to play or interact in a virtual environment that meets the needs of different kinds of players.

Developer Perspectives

MUDs may offer a textual guide on how to design effective virtual environments. As mentioned, MUDs are primarily chat rooms with text describing the look and feel of the virtual room or environment. The effectiveness of a virtual environment may depend upon how that space meets individual's needs or motivations for playing and/or interacting in that space. Cheng, Farnham, and Stone (2002) conducted research into the designing and deploying of virtual environments by examining user feedback during the design process. The results suggest users and designers prefer 3-D environments with little abstraction that provide third-person points of view (Cheng et al.). Furthermore, users of these environments preferred environments that fostered social interaction and graphical representations that could present non-verbal cues similar to real-life interactions. Other design aspects have been found to influence enjoyment of video and computer games. For instance, Hsu, Lee, Wu (2005) examined the design features of action video games in order to assess what consumers of this type of media thought were fun and not fun. Hsu et al. asked participants to evaluate 28 different versions of the same game (*Pac Man*) and then describe why these games were evaluated positively or negatively. The results suggested that consumers favored aspects like novelty, interactivity, sense of control, and appealing presentation (Hsu et al.). At a structural level, players want to be able to customize their avatars and interact with them in new and changing environments that provide a certain level of control.

Individuals do not necessarily want total control, overcoming goals would be too simple and the game would be predictably easy if a player controlled everything that occurred in the environment. Players want a level of unpredictably and challenge, thus according to Klug and Schell (2006) they want the "illusion of control" (p. 92). For instance, it is noted by Salen and Zimmerman (2005) that for game play to be meaningful, players' actions must result in a system outcome. The game must respond to player's actions, because if this does not occur then a player has no control over what happens. A lack of control would likely hinder information processing for goals or objectives during game play because players would view the experience as a pointless endeavor. However, the reverse may also be said for total control, if players see objectives or goals within the game as too easily attainable it will likely result in diminished information processing of game play content. Thus, there must be a delicate balance of control in order facilitate higher levels of information processing.

Furthermore, a player's actions must be discernable to the extent that the game offers some form of feedback that something has occurred (Salen & Zimmerman, 2005). If a player acts upon an object or another player then the system should provide feedback in the form of visual or auditory responses in terms of the outcome of what occurred to that object or player. Although, this may seem to be fundamentally obvious, providing users with the appropriate feedback cannot be understated as a key to the success of a computer or video game. According to Garris, Ahlers, and Driskell (2002) appropriate game features that can be represented in the form of feedback increase individuals' interest and involvement during play. Cognitive processing may be increased through feedback that meets with the consistent visual or auditory response to an action within an online game. The implications are that proper feedback and means to achieve objectives highly influence the level of cognitive effort and focused attention a person gives when playing an online game.

Finally, it is suggested that individuals play in order to seek out romantic relationships in a safe environment. According to Klug and Schell (2006) "…if the game business can figure out a way to provide greater exploration of the kinds of fantasy relationships that men and women both want…that kind of content could really grow the industry exponentially" (p. 97). These types of interactions (not always romantic) have been taking place long before the introduction of graphical representations. As mentioned previously, researchers examining the motivations behind playing MMORPGs have consistently noted that socialization aspects are quite often the reason why people play.

Social Interaction

Griffiths et al. (2004b) examined the demographics and motivations of individuals who were online gamers of the popular MMOG *Everquest*. His research demonstrated that player's favorite aspects of the game were related to social interaction, while the least favorite aspect related to the immaturity of other players (Griffiths et al.). However, there were numerous other favorite aspects including: being able to group together, character advancement, tactics, trade skills, being part of guild membership, strategic thinking, taking on leadership roles, guild competition/politics, and the fact that there was no end to the game (Griffiths et al., see p. 483). Examples of their least favorite aspects included: helping inexperienced players, hand-to-hand combat, solo play, team play, and lack of customer service (Griffiths et al.).

Yee has provided the most detail in terms of motivations for playing online games. Yee's research began in 1999 through online surveys of MMORPG players and is called the Daedalus Project (http://www.nickyee.com/daedalus/). This research presents the most extensive and ambitious findings of online games. Yee (2006a) developed a taxonomy of MMORPG motivations through a factor analysis and social interaction was categorized as a main component of motivations for playing (p. 773):

- Social Component
  - Socializing—Having an interest in helping and chatting with other players
  - Relationship—The desire to form long-term meaningful relationships with others
  - Teamwork—Deriving satisfaction from being part of a group effort

Thus, the ability to socialize and interact is a common reason for playing online games (Yee; Griffiths et al., 2004b). Furthermore, the subcategories offer more insights into what kinds of interactions are taking place during game play. Thus, it can be seen that socialization taking place during game play goes beyond mere romantic interactions as suggested by Klug and Schell (2006). Interactions that involve helping other individuals or working as a team are common aspects that make MMOGs enjoyable. The more enjoyable an online game is the more likely a person will be involved within that gaming environment.

Cole and Griffiths (2007) examined the differences between social interactions that occurred online and those that occur off-line (face-to-face). The researchers reasoned that since social interaction is an important aspect of MMOGs, it may facilitate the development of friendships. Furthermore, this research suggests these online interactions offer qualities and characteristics that may be more positive and rewarding than offline interactions. Cole and Griffiths surveyed a large sample of both male and female MMORPG players about their online friendships. The results suggest a majority of male and female players have built friendships with individuals that they met during game play. Furthermore, over 80% of those sampled had mentioned that they enjoyed playing their chosen MMOG with real-life friends and family (Cole & Griffiths). The results also suggest there are differences to these interactions based upon gender of the player. For instance, female game players were more likely to discuss sensitive issue with online friends than real world friends.

It should also be noted that close to half of the participants had met online friends outside of the MMOG in real-life. Although offline relationships are often referred to as real-life friends, online friendships can be just as real. Kerr (2006) has suggested that "Social relationships may also be important in terms of understanding game preferences, duration, and frequency of play" (p. 125). From an information processing perspective, online game players may be more likely to cognitively focus on interactions with other players whom they have a long standing relationship than newly formed relationships. However, first time contacts within that game may initially receive a similar amount of attention, but have a shorter attention window. Finally, games that offer more opportunities for interactions with other players are more likely to gain cognitive efforts towards such endeavors.

Competition

As Bartle (1990) noted in his typology of MUD players, *Achievers* typically enjoy the game when they get chances to accomplish game-related goals such as finding/accumulating treasure and beating monsters or other players. This finding may have offered the first explanation of how competitive aspects of online game play (graphical or not) contribute to its overall experience. Furthermore, some individuals may find this aspect more enjoyable than others and may seek out instances of competition when playing. Vorderer, Klimmt, and Ritterfeld (2004) suggest that motives for the use of newer technologies are linked to competition and achievement because these technologies offer more interactivity than the rather passive traditional mediums. Thus, individuals may choose more interactive mediums because they offer more competitive situations. The achievement or goal-attainment of succeeding over another individual can elicit positive emotions that individuals routinely seek-out. According to Klug and Schell (2006), individuals compete in video games to experience positive emotions about themselves because they have out performed another individual.

To this end, Vorderer, Hartmann, and Klimmt (2003) explored the interactive and competitive aspects that make video and computer games enjoyable. These researchers conducted an experiment and an online survey in two separate studies to explore the enjoyment of competitive situations in computer games. Results support the hypothesis that higher levels of competition (more monsters) and more alternatives for action showed the highest levels of enjoyment (Vorderer et al.). Moreover, results suggest that individual's motivation to compete against others has more influence in the choice of a competitive computer game rather than an individual's self-efficacy to succeed in a computer game competition (Vorderer et al). Thus, even though individuals may not have confidence in their ability to succeed in competitions during game play they still choose computer games that are highly competitive.

Yee's (2006a) analysis of MMORPG motivations has shown that competition is a subcomponent of a larger structure related to achievement. As mentioned, even though online games may not offer rewards in the form of completion of a game, they can offer other forms of markers for success or achievement. Aspects like the accumulation of wealth and power (advancement), game optimization and analysis (mechanics), and challenging and dominating others (competition) all contribute to the higher component of Achievement (Yee). For instance, *World of WarCraft* (http://www.worldofwarcraft.com/wrath/features/gameplay/achievements) allows individuals through quests, events, world exploration, and player-to-player situations to advance their character in abilities and cosmetically (new armor, hair, clothes, etc…). Thus, competing against another individual offers the reward of winning, but there are also other achievements related to advancement of an individual's avatar.

Immersion

Yee's (2006a) factor analysis yielded four subcomponents of immersion. These include aspects such as exploration (discovery), story line and character history (role-playing), appearances and accessories (customization), and relaxation/escape (escapism) (Yee). Discovery was possibly one of the earliest aspects of immersion discussed. For instance, Bartle's (1990) taxonomy of MUD players identified *Explorers* as individuals who play games "to find out as much as they can about the virtual world" (p. 3). Role-playing involves the incorporation of a character with a unique background story or narrative. Schneider, Lang, Shin, and Bradley (2004) examined the effects of including a story narrative within a video game on identification, presence, emotional experiences, motivation, and physiological arousal. Recent video games, regardless of content, have come to include very intricate story lines (see any of the *Halo* or *Grand Theft Auto* series games) and character backgrounds. The results showed participants who played a story-based video game compared to non-story based video game reported greater levels of identification with their game characters and felt more presence within that game (Schneider et al.). Also, the story-based video game condition elicited more positive emotional valence than the non-story based condition (Schneider et al.). The inclusion of a story narrative along with a character/avatar narrative is likely to increase enjoyment and positive affect towards the game.

The third subcomponent of immersion relates to the ability to create and customize an avatar (Yee, 2006a). Most MMORPGs provide viewpoints from a third-person perspective. Why? First, many games take the customization of characters very seriously. As previously discussed, the *World of WarCraft* offers players the option of choosing their avatar representation from ten playable races and numerous primary and secondary classes and professions. Avatar-mediated play is also a main characteristic associated with most MMOG's (Chan & Vorderer, 2006). Cheng et al. (2002) noted that individuals prefer to have some control over the creation and appearance of their avatars. It would seem rather pointless to offer numerous customization options for the look and appearance of their characters, then not let them view that appearance within the environment. This may also influence other aspects related to identity formation and identification with avatars that first-person perspectives do not allow. Thus, third-person perspectives may offer an underlying motivation of character/avatar customization. In terms of cognitive processing individuals who are highly motivated to upgrade or change the appearance of their own characters maybe more likely to pay attention to such elements within the game that allow for such options. That is, players may be more likely to pay attention to other player's avatars for ideas about how to customization their own avatars. This likely plays a small, but significant factor of the socialization aspect of online gaming.

Finally, playing computer or video games allows users to participate in and perform activities they would not normally be able to do in real-life (Klug & Schell, 2006). Yee (2006a) referred to this subcomponent as escapism, which means that computer and video games have the ability to allow users to escape from the real-world. Furthermore, individuals can be transported to fictional locations that do not exist. As in most video games, the 3-D environments transport individuals to times and places that either do not exist or visit events in a historical sense (The Wild West, WII, Civil War, Medieval Times, etc…). Thus, not only do video and computer games offer experiences that individuals may only know as an observer, but they also allow users or consumers to take on personas and live vicariously in different times and places (Klug & Schell). In terms of processing information this means that individuals may be more likely to pay attention to features or aspects of the virtual environment that add to the consistency of that time period or location. For these individuals, socializing or competing is secondary to exploring the environment, which should present the most cognitive effort. Thus, background features are essential to a user who plays for escapism as the virtual environment is an important reason why they play video or computer games.

Gender Swapping

One unique aspect of online games that has not been discussed as a possible motivation is the ability to gender swap. Gender swapping refers to the phenomenon of "playing a different gendered character from oneself" (Hussain & Griffiths, 2008, p. 48). Differences in the demographics of who are and are not participating in this type of activity suggests important underlying motivations. For instance, Griffiths et al. (2004a) found that a majority of game players are likely to swap genders and that older male individuals are the most likely to engage in this activity. From here, Hussain and Griffiths explored the reasons behind gender swapping. Results suggest a majority of both male and female players gender swap, this is contrary to results found by Griffiths et al. However, the results also seem to suggest males and females gender swap for different reasons. Hussain and Griffiths note that females may gender swap in order to avoid male players soliciting them during game play. Thus, female users play as a male avatar in order to prevent male players from flirting or making sexual advancements towards them during online interactions. However, from a male user's perspective, it may be that "playing a female character meant that male gamers treated him far better" (Hussain & Griffiths, p. 52). Other motivations for gender swapping include enjoyment, curiosity, and because that particular gender was attributed certain sought after characteristics or skills.

Gender

Thus, there may be significant differences in motivations based upon gender. Cole and Griffiths (2005) found evidence that while both males and females enjoy socializing in MMOGs, male players may socialize for a sense of teamwork or camaraderie, while females may socialize for relational and intimacy purposes. Although, this may seem somewhat stereotypical of males and females the evidence does seem to point in this direction. For instance, Yee (2006a) found evidence to suggest significant gender differences in the relationship subcomponent of gaming motivations, but there were no differences in the socializing subcomponent. In a subsequent analysis, Yee (2006b) found that "female players prefer to relate to other players, while male players prefer to work together to achieve goals" (p. 319-320). Royse, Lee, Undrahbuyan, Hopson, and Consalvo (2007) investigated the uses and negotiation of women's usage of computer games from a feminist standpoint. The conclusions showed women who played more frequently did so for motivations of achievement and competition (Royse et al.). However, women who were deemed to be moderate game players were motivated by escapism and control.

Although, not specifically related to online gaming research has examined differences in information processing based upon gender. Hendriks-Vettehen, Schaap, and Schlosser (2004) argued that TV news is largely a masculine medium because it is typically created by men and is a stereotypically male profession. This aspect seems to be similar in relation to the creation and development of online games. An interesting finding from Hendriks-Vettehen et al. was that female participants expressed an overall lack of clarity with information presented in the news. Here, it could be suggested that females are not likely to process information related to stereotypical male endeavors such as competition and violence. In online games this may mean that female players are likely to focus upon and be more involved with stereotypical "feminine activities" such as socializing or relationship maintenance. However, this point should be warranted with caution as female players are still likely to enjoy competing against other players. Thus, there does seem to be some evidence to suggest that males and females may process certain kinds of content differently based upon the type of content. However, age of the game player may contribute significantly more than gender.

Age

It seems there may be large differences between males and females in terms of online game play. However, Yee has shown that age may be a factor that accounts for greater differences in motivations than gender. As discussed previously older individuals (20yrs +) make up the typical demographic of MMOG players (Griffiths et al., 2004b). Griffiths et al. (2004a) specifically compared adolescent and adult gamers for possible differences in motivations. The results indicate that while both adults and adolescents enjoyed the social aspects of online games, only adolescents enjoyed the violent aspects of online games (Griffiths et al., 2004a). Age of players may interact with gender for motivational differences. For instance, most female game players are older individuals (Yee, 2006b) meaning there is a considerable lack of adolescent female MMOG players. This may be due to the stereotypical image of video and computer games being a male activity especially among adolscent individuals. However, with male game players there seems to be a wider ratio in that both adolescent and adult males may be likely to play MMOG's. As Griffiths et al. (2004a) found, adolescents are more likely to play for violent purposes. Yee (2006b) has even found evidence that adolescents typically play for their own selfish reasons of personal gain. Although, both age and gender are worthy of consideration, together these two demographic characteristics offer greater insight.

IN-GAME PROCESSING

Motivations for online game play may affect individuals processing of events that occur during game play. In-game processing refers to individual's memory for events, content, and interactions that occurred during game play. Obviously, in a sense of consumer or player experiences, positive affect of game play is desired. This is not to say that individuals do not remember negative experiences of playing MMOGs. In terms of information retention, positive experiences should outweigh negative experiences. Certainly there are different aspects of video and computer games that establish the right conditions for involvement and enjoyment. These conditions are likely an interaction between multiple factors related to enjoyment, game experience, and player motivations. Thus, determining a player's motivation is a requisite to understanding involvement and enjoyment.

As discussed, there are numerous motivations for playing online games (Yee, 2006a, 2006b). Motivations for playing online games can take many forms, from playing simply to interact with other players (Cole & Griffiths, 2007), to competing or achieving goals (Vorderer et al., 2003), or to buying a coat or furniture for your avatar (Natkin, 2006). Also, there are factors related to *persistence*, *physicality*, *vertical game play*, *perpetuity*, and avatar development and creation (Chan & Vorderer, 2006) as well as immersion (Yee, 2006a) and gender swapping (Hussain & Griffiths, 2008). It has been suggested that different demographic segments have different motivations for playing online games. The larger questions is how can we understand the influence that motivations have on information processing for in-game content when there is a large variety of those motivations. A good starting point that may help clear up some of the confusion is too review similar research that has examined information processing (recall of content) of advertisements within video games and websites.

An important aspect that cannot be overlooked when it comes to content recall is *attention*. Meaning, the first step in understanding how individuals recall material of in-game content is through attention. According to Salisch, Oppl, and Kristen (2006) "attention governs the way in which information from the electronic game is taken up…Which information is selected depends on the salience and the affective valence of the figures on the screen in the sense that attractive protagonists are given more attention" (p. 160). Research examining the recall of advertisements within video games offers excellent insights into in-game processing. Although, this research has been somewhat limited, a few studies have examined individuals processing of advertisements within a video game. Yang, Roskos-Ewoldsen, Dinu, and Arpan (2006) examined college student's memory for brand advertisements placed within a sports video game. Yang et al. based their expectations upon the differences associated with explicit and implicit processing of message content. According to Rovee-Collier, Hayne, and Colombo (2001) explicit processing involves deliberative, effortful cognitive reflection of our memories. Thus, individuals who explicitly process information do so in a manner that puts forth cognitive effort on recall and recognition of that information. Conversely, implicit processing does not involve effort and is usually incidental in that it pops into the forefront of our minds (Rovee-Collier et al.). Yang et al. hypothesized that because individuals put forth a large amount of cognitive processing when playing a video game that there is less attention paid to the background features of that video game. It was assumed that implicit memory would be exhibited for brand names that were placed in the form of billboards within sports video games.

Yang et al. randomly assigned participants to one of three conditions. The first two conditions were sports games (*EA's Formula 1 2001*; *EA's FIFA 2002*), while the third condition was a control condition (Yang et al.). The researchers measured participants implicit (word completion task) and explicit (brand name recall) memory for the advertisements that appeared within the game after participants had finished playing. The word completion task requires participants to complete word fragments to create a word (i.e., E_P_; for "ESPN"). A total of 24 word fragments were included that could be completed as brand names from the two games (Yang et al.). Thus, some of the word fragments were for brand names that did not appear within that particular video game. According to the hypothesis, then individuals should complete more word fragments for brand names that appeared within the video game that they played. The results showed that participants were more likely to complete word fragments for brand names that appeared within the respective video game they had played. Yang et al. suggest implicit memory does influence recall of in-game content and that this may in fact be a more sensitive measure of influence for advertising recall. Explicit memory for brand names was only about 45-50% accuracy (Yang et al.). This is a relatively low estimate seeing that participants were explicitly asked to recall the brand names only half-hour after playing the video game. The results show that recall of content in a video game does not necessarily have to be based on effortful concentration upon that specific content. Memory for events or content may still be remembered even if that person is concentrating upon another aspect of the game. However, concentration may still be a key concept as will be discussed later.

Internet advertising is also an area that can help answer questions related to in-game processing as online media resembles the interactivity of online games. Research into banner advertisements may give us a clearer picture of how individuals process and retain attention to one aspect when there is virtual sea of information presented. Lohtia, Donthu, and Hershberger (2003) examined the content and design elements of banner advertisements on websites. Furthermore, the researchers compared business-to-business (B2B) and business-to-consumer (B2C) websites for their click-through rates. The researchers content analyzed numerous banner advertisements for color, interactivity, animation, emotional appeal, and incentives then analyzed each advertisements click-through-rate (CTR). Typically, clicking on an advertisement takes the user to another web page. The CTR is the number of times a banner advertisement is clicked on by the number of times it is served to the user's browser (Lohtia et al.). Results suggest the incorporation of interactivity and incentives actually lowered the CTR of B2B banner advertisements, whereas emotion and animation increased the CTR of B2C banner advertisements (Lohtia et al.). It seems that different design elements are more effective for B2B and B2C banner advertisements, with exception of medium color, which was successful for both types of advertisements. The differences in CTR rates based upon types of advertisements (B2B vs. B2C) could be attributed to differences in user motivations. Similar results have been generated from banner advertisements examined on online casino websites (see Robinson, Wysocka, & Hand, 2007). Thus, motivations for searching contributed to what information was recalled.

Rodgers and Thorson (2000) developed an integrated model of information processing for internet advertising based upon function and structure. Design elements (structure) and consumer's motivations (functions) for using the internet will influence their recall, attitude, and behavior towards those advertisements. In fact, "Probably most important to how interactive advertising operates are the motives and modes (serious versus playful) with which people enter cyberspace" (Rodgers & Thorson). Individuals who have goals (motives) in mind when they log onto the internet are more likely to pay attention to elements and features that relate to those goals. For instance, someone searching the internet to buy concert tickets may be more likely to pay attention to elements related to music or the purchasing of tickets rather than online dating-services or design elements (i.e., animation). However, when individuals search the web for entertainment purposes or no particular reason, elements of design such as color, animation, and trade characters are more likely to gain attention (Rodgers & Thorson). In relation to online gaming it is important to understand why an individual logged into the game. The purpose in any gaming session will likely influence what information gets cognitively processed.

Pravettoni, Leotta, and Lucchiari (2008) furthered examined the relationship between recall of banner advertisements based upon external factors and internal motivations. The researchers assumed that what is eye-catching to users depends upon their motive for use. According to Pravettoni et al., a person with an intended objective will give attention to features that relate to their motivations, however if a person has an exploratory (no specific objective) objective then banner stimuli will likely influence attention. The researchers conducted two experiments differing in the level of advertisement (banner vs. pop-ups) and objective (set objective vs. no objective). It was hypothesized that individuals with a goal-directed task (set objective) would be less likely to be influenced by external elements (design features) of both banner and pop-up advertisements. The results showed that individuals who were given a specific task had less recall of banner advertisements and pop-up advertisements (Pravettoni et al.). However, one interesting result was that when the pop-up advertisement was congruent with the task goal it was better remembered than if it was not congruent (Pravettoni et al.). Thus, factors of an online game may be paid attention to simply because they relate to that players goal or current mission.

Finally, repetition is likely to influence recall of banner advertisements. Yaveroglu and Donthu (2008) examined repetition strategies to banner advertisements in an online environment. Results from this study demonstrated that repetition of advertisements both single ads and varied ads for the same products created increased brand name recall and intentions to click (Yaveroglu & Donthu). Thus, repetitive content is more likely to influence recall. How does this relate to recall of content from MMOGs? Griffiths et al. (2004a; 2004b) have conducted research into the frequency and length of game play along with demographic characteristics. The results have showed that close to 25% of online gamers play for 10-20 hrs per week (Griffiths et al., 2004a). The low end of frequency of online gaming is somewhere around 5hrs per week. Yee (2006b) found a large majority of respondents spent close to 22 hours per week playing online and even more interesting was that 60% of the respondents reported playing for at least 10 hours continuously! Thus, there are greater chances of exposure to repetitive content due to the increased amount of time per week and time per game-play session that individuals give to MMOGs.

In the case of online games, information that relates to ones goals or motivations for playing are likely to be given priority over other types of information within the game. It could be suggested that content aspects related to the encouragement, development, and enhancement of motives for playing that online game would likely garner higher recall. However, effortful cognitive processing is not the only way information can be recalled from a video game. Yang et al. found evidence that implicit processing of information may also aid in the recall of content during video game play. As mentioned previously it may not just be the content itself, but the overall experience of playing an MMOG that contributes to content recall.

For instance, Choi and Kim (2004) examined features of online game play that contribute to an optimal experience and customer loyalty. Here, Choi and Kim constructed a conceptual model composed of social and personal interactions that may combine to influence an experience of *flow*, which then influences customer loyalty. The researchers invoked *flow* as the operationalization of an optimal experience. *Flow* can be attributed to the work of Csikszentmihalyi (1990), who characterized flow as an experience that results from immersion in ones actions. *Flow* has been defined as an interaction between an individual's skills and the challenge or difficulty of the task at hand. A difficult video or computer game may bring about frustration from an individual who cannot advance within the game to the next level. If the person can too easily advance it may likely result in boredom. The ultimate state of *flow* lies between frustration and boredom, such that a player may lose track of time and self-consciousness when trying to advance a level or complete a mission. However, *flow* has also been defined as "total concentration in an activity and the enjoyment which one derives from an activity" (Ghani & Deshpande, 1994, p. 382). Thus, *flow* results when a person feels immersed within a virtual environment through focused attention on goal attainment and an even interaction between skill and challenge.

Choi and Kim assumed that positive interactions between the system (game) and other users would contribute to the overall experience of playing an online game and thus flow would be experienced. The researchers differentiated between personal and social interactions. Personal interactions are based upon goals, operation, and feedback (Choi & Kim). Goals can be any type of objective or mission within that online game (i.e., collecting coins or beating a monster). Operation is based upon the means set out in order to achieve those goals, while feedback allows players to know that they have accomplished that goal (i.e., monster dies) (Choi & Kim). The results of the study showed that positive personal interactions (appropriate goals) and social interactions positively predicted individual's sense of flow during game play (Choi & Kim).

Flow is a construct that is likely to help explain the level of an individual's recall of content when motivation for playing is consistent with goals and objectives. The more individuals achieve a sense of *flow* the more likely that it will increase their concentration or attention for content within that online game. Sweetser and Wyeth (2005) conceptualized a concept of flow defined as "GameFlow" that combined eight elements or concepts as a model of computer game enjoyment. These concepts include concentration, challenge, skills, control, clear goals, feedback, immersion, and social interaction (Sweester & Wyeth). Thus, concentration is a likely condition that needs to be met in order for an individual to experience flow. However, there are other criteria that can establish increased concentration and flow. Weibel, Wissmath, Habegger, Steiner, and Groner (2008) examined differences in individuals' sense of flow and enjoyment within an online game based upon whether or not a user was playing against another user-controlled opponent or computer-controlled opponent. Most if not all MMOGs offer both options in terms of opponents. Weibel et al. reasoned that since a motivation of online gaming is social interaction that competition with another human opponent would increase an individual's sense of flow and enjoyment with that game. The results did show that participants who played against a user-controlled (human) opponent reported higher levels of flow and enjoyment. Also, Yee (2006a) had suggested that competition is a subcomponent of a larger motivation associated with achievement. Thus, a sense of *flow* may also be established if an individual can achieve certain objectives or goals, while playing that game.

Furthermore, those goals or objectives should be consistent in order to gain the most amount of concentration or attention to in-game content. As defined, implicit memory for background features and items may also benefit from increased concentration to aspects of the game during play. Flow within an online gaming environment can also be applied to recall of in-game advertisements. For instance, Nelsen (2002) examined the effectiveness of brand placements within video games in terms of recall and players attitudes towards the game and advertisement as outcomes. Nelsen differentiated the types of brand placements via passive (background features, ex. billboards) and active (characters & equipment, ex. name brand baseball bats) advertising. However, both types of brand placements seem to be similar in that neither are pertinent to the narrative or the game itself, but rather background props or items to be obtained. The results did suggest that game players were able to remember seeing brand names in the game they played across both short and long-term measures. Furthermore, these results suggest that when the item is a part of the game (e.g., using a Nike golf club) individuals have better short term recall of that object (Nelsen). Finally, Nelsen suggested brand placements within a video game resulted in increased perceptions of realism associated with that game. Thus, including advertisements in the forms of brand placements or billboards can enhance that video games realism. Although, not specifically related to flow, it can be suggested that this research points to aspects of recall that can be associated with the assumptions of flow. For instance, increased realism can lead to higher perceptions of immersion. Nelsen's research also showed that player's overall had positive perceptions of brand images within the video game. Enjoyment is a key aspect to the experience of flow and with an interaction between realism. This could suggest that individuals experienced a sense of flow. However, future research needs to be examined in order to provide evidence for this assumption.

Overall, research on advertising recall on the internet and in video games suggests that individuals who have goal-directed motivations (instrumental or utilitarian motivations) when using a medium are more likely to remember content that is related to those motives. User/player motives for playing online games are as diverse as the individuals who subscribe to such games. And there are different motivations for playing MMOGs and those motivations can be even further broken down based upon differences in demographics. Online gaming content that is congruent with user motives is more likely to establish higher user recall, than content that is incongruous with those motives. Thus, online game designers and administrators would be wise to develop in-game strategies that reinforce different individual motives for playing online games. Online games that involve social interaction in order to achieve goals along with appropriate operations (means to achieve objectives) are likely to generate higher content recall. Furthermore, suitable feedback is needed in order to gain and keep a player's attention. If online games can establish a sense of *flow* through meeting individual's needs for playing, it is more likely that in-game content will be remembered. However, it could be suggested that individuals may not always have an explicit motivation in mind when participating (e.g., ritualized motivations). Diversionary motives are more likely to be difficult to predict in terms of information processing. However, it is possible that past motives will influence what content is attended to and recalled.

FUTURE DIRECTIONS

It could be suggested that knowing before hand or addressing content that meets the needs of players will likely result in higher recall of content and overall a more enjoyable experience. The difficult task for researchers, designers, and marketers is knowing an individual's motivations for playing that game before that person logs into the game. This means that designers and marketers must think of new ways to establish in-game reinforcement of content related to the goals or motivations of users/players. Also, research needs to examine links between concepts of *flow* and recall of content. One assumption or criteria to establish *flow* is concentration (Sweetser & Wyeth). If concentration or effortful cognitive processing can aid in the recall of in-game content (Yang et al.) then it may be likely that the establishment of *flow* in an online game can increase individual's information processing of content during game play. Furthermore, it has been established that explicit and implicit memory constructs have shown to influence the recall of in-game content (i.e., Brand name recognition) (Yang et al.). This also needs to be further examined within online environments and the concept of *flow*. For instance, can increased concentration, enjoyment, social interaction, skill level, or competition aid in implicit memory for in-game content? If individuals are highly immersed within that virtual environment and focused upon the task at hand can players implicitly remember other aspects or background features during game play? Yang et al. did find evidence to suggest that implicit memory for name brand recognition was stronger via implicit measures than explicit measures. However, Yang et al. did not give participants instructions or goals when playing the video game. Would implicit memory still be as strong if participants were given a goal or objective when playing? Thus, which form of online game play motivation is likely to aid in implicit memory for in-game content: instrumental or ritualized motivations?

It has also been established that individuals play online games for various reasons. Features of online games from social interaction with other players (Chan & Vorderer), to gender swapping (Hussain & Griffiths), to the larger component of achievement (Yee) all contribute to individual's motives for playing these types of games. Understanding these motives is important to understanding enjoyment and customer loyalty as well as recall and attitudes towards in-game content. Certain features and aspects of online games are likely to garner more attention from individuals based upon their reasons for playing at that time. Furthermore, another motivation that may often be overlooked is that individuals play online games to purchase virtual objects or commodities (Natkin). Thus, utilitarian motivations related to the outcome of purchasing goods or services (new armor, weapons, clothing, etc…) such as in an increase in respect or advancement within that online game should be considered as a motivation.

This "commodity" motivation may bring up questions related to in-game recall of content related to product placements within virtual environments. Online games certainly have more than enough capabilities to incorporate features of product placements and virtual billboards. However, this should be warranted with caution, as Nelsen (2002) did find evidence to suggest that even though individuals thought brand placements within in a video game increased its realism, participants also suggested that this highly depends upon the context and story of the game. For instance, players suggested that if the placement of the advertisements within the game did *not* match real-life instances that it highly "deterred" from the overall gaming experience (Nelsen, p. 87). Thus, it could be suggested that an overload of gaudy advertising is likely to backfire in poor player evaluations of the game itself and lower player recall of content. Products within the game need to be more subtly presented to players/consumers in order for it to a) add to the realism of the game, b) not deter from the gaming experience, and c) increase recall of the content related to that product or service. Perhaps product placement might better serve in online games because it may not be so overt as a large virtual billboard in the Silvermoon City of the Eastern Kingdom! (*World of WarCraft*).

REFERENCES

Ballard, M. E., & Lineberger, R. (1999). Video games and confederate gender: Effects on reward and punishment given by college males. *Sex Roles*, *41*, 541–558. doi:10.1023/A:1018843304606

Bartle, R. (1990). *Early MUD history*. Retrieved from http://www.mud.co.uk/richard/mudhist.htm

Blackmon, W. D. (1994). Dungeons and dragons: The use of a fantasy game in the psychotherapeutic treatment of a young adult. *American Journal of Psychotherapy*, *48*, 624–632.

BuyMMOAccounts.com. (n.d.) Retrieved February 10, 2009, from http://www.buymmoaccounts.com

Chan, E., & Vorderer, P. (2006). Massively multiplayer online games. In Vorderer, P., & Bryant, J. (Eds.), *Playing video games: Motives, responses, and consequences* (pp. 181–194). Mahwah, NJ: Lawrence Erlbaum Associates, Inc.

Cheng, L., Farnham, S., & Stone, L. (2002). Lessons learned: Building and deploying shared virtual environments. In Schroeder, R. (Ed.), *The social life of avatars: Presence and interaction in shared virtual environments* (pp. 90–111). London: Springer Verlag.

Choi, D., & Kim, J. (2004). Why people continue to play online games: In search of critical design factors to increase customer loyalty to online contents. *Cyberpsychology & Behavior*, *7*, 11–24. doi:10.1089/109493104322820066

Cole, H., & Griffiths, M. D. (2007). Social interactions in massively multiplayer online role-playing gamers. *Cyberpsychology & Behavior*, *19*, 575–583. doi:10.1089/cpb.2007.9988

Csikszentmihalyi, M. (1990). *Flow: The psychology of optimal experience*. New York: Harper and Row.

Ducheneaut, N., Moore, R. J., & Nickell, E. (2007). Virtual third places: A case study of sociability in massively multiplayer games. *Computer Supported Cooperative Work*, *16*, 129–166. doi:10.1007/s10606-007-9041-8

Entertainment Software Association. (2007). *Computer and video game industry reaches $18.85 billion in 2007*. Retrieved on April 29, 2008, from http://www.theesa.com/archives/2008/01/computer_and_vi_1.php

Entertainment Software Association. (2008). *Essential facts about the computer and video game industry*. Retrieved on April 29, 2008, from http://www.theesa.com/facts/pdfs/ESA_EF_2008.pdf

Garris, R., Ahlers, R., & Driskell, J. E. (2002). Games, motivation, and learning: A research and practice model. *Simulation & Gaming, 33*, 441–467. doi:10.1177/1046878102238607

Ghani, J. A., & Deshpande, S. P. (1994). Task characteristics and the experience of optimal flow in human-computer interaction. *The Journal of Psychology, 128*(4), 381–391.

Griffiths, M. D., Davies, M. N. O., & Chappell, D. (2003). Breaking the stereotype: The case of online gaming. *Cyberpsychology & Behavior, 6*, 81–91. doi:10.1089/109493103321167992

Griffiths, M. D., Davies, M. N. O., & Chappell, D. (2004a). Online computer gaming: A comparison of adolescent and adult gamers. *Journal of Adolescence, 27*, 87–96. doi:10.1016/j.adolescence.2003.10.007

Griffiths, M. D., Davies, M. N. O., & Chappell, D. (2004b). Demographic factors and playing variables in online computer gaming. *Cyberpsychology & Behavior, 7*, 479–487. doi:10.1089/cpb.2004.7.479

Harris, R. J. (2004). *A cognitive psychology of mass communication* (4th ed.). Mahwah, NJ: Lawrence Erlbaum Associates.

Hendriks-Vettehen, P. G., Schaap, G., & Schlosser, S. (2004). What men and women think while watching the news: An exploration. *Communications: The European Journal of Communication Research, 29*, 235–251.

Hsu, S. H., Lee, F., & Wu, M. (2005). Designing action games for appealing to buyers. *Cyberpsychology & Behavior, 8*, 585–591. doi:10.1089/cpb.2005.8.585

Hussain, Z., & Griffiths, M. D. (2008). Gender swapping and socializing in cyberspace: An exploratory study. *Cyberpsychology & Behavior, 11*, 47–53. doi:10.1089/cpb.2007.0020

Katz, E., Blumler, J. G., & Gurevitch, M. (1973). Uses and gratifications research. *Public Opinion Quarterly, 37*, 509–523. doi:10.1086/268109

Kent, S. L. (2003). *Alternate reality: The history of massively multiplayer online games*. Retrieved July 20, 2008, from http://archive.gamespy.com/amdmmog/week1/

Kerr, A. (2006). *The business and culture of digital games: Gamework/Gameplay*. Thousand Oaks, CA: Sage.

Klug, G. C., & Schell, J. (2006). Why people play games: An industry perspective. In Vorderer, P., & Bryant, J. (Eds.), *Playing video games: Motives, responses, and consequences* (pp. 91–100). Mahwah, NJ: Lawrence Erlbaum.

Lawrie, M. (2002). *Parallels in MUD and IRC history*. Retrieved from http://www.ircnet.org/History/jarkko-mjl.html

Livingstone, S. (1999). New media, new audiences? *New Media & Society, 1*(1), 59–66. doi:10.1177/1461444899001001010

Lohtia, R., Donthu, N., & Hershberger, E. K. (2003). The impact of content and design elements on banner advertising click-through rates. *Journal of Advertising Research, 43*, 410–418.

Lucas, K., & Sherry, J. L. (2004). Sex differences in video game play: A communication-based explanation. *Communication Research, 31*, 499–523. doi:10.1177/0093650204267930

Massive Incorporated. (n.d.) Retrieved February 10, 2009, from http://www.massiveincorporated.com

McClure, R. F., & Mears, F. G. (1984). Video game players: Personality characteristics and demographic variables. *Psychological Reports*, *55*, 271–276.

Miller, R. (2008, October 30). Obama billed 44.5K for in-game advertising. *JoyStiq*. Retrieved January 14, 2009, from http://www.joystiq.com/2008/10/30/obama-billed-44-5k-for-in-game-advertising/

Mort, G. S., & Rose, T. (2004). The effect of product type on value linkages in the means-end chain: Implications for theory and method. *Journal of Consumer Behaviour*, *3*, 221–234. doi:10.1002/cb.136

Natkin, S. (2006). *Video games & interactive media: A glimpse at new digital entertainment*. Wellesley, MA: A. K. Peters, Ltd.

Nelsen, M. R. (2002). Recall of brand placements in computer/video games. *Journal of Advertising Research*, *42*, 80–92.

Nussenbaum, E. (2004, August 22). Video game makers go Hollywood. Uh-oh. *New York Times*, 5.

Oliver, M. B. (2002). Individual differences in media effects. In Bryant, J., & Zillmann, D. (Eds.), *Media effects: Advances in theory and research* (pp. 507–524). Hillsdale, NJ: Lawrence Erlbaum Associates, Inc.

Pravettoni, G., Leotta, S. N., & Lucchiari, C. (2008). The eye caught in the Net: A study on attention and motivation in virtual environment exploration. *The European Journal of Cognitive Psychology*, *20*, 955–966. doi:10.1080/09541440701804564

Robinson, H., Wysocka, A., & Hand, C. (2007). Internet advertising effectiveness: The effect of design on click-through rates for banner ads. *International Journal of Advertising*, *26*(4), 527–541.

Rodgers, S., & Thorson, E. (2000). The interactive advertising model: how users perceive and process online ads. *Journal of Interactive Advertising*, *1*(1). Retrieved on August 10, 2009, from http://jiad.org/vol1/no1/rodgers.

Rovee-Collier, C., Hayne, H., & Colombo, M. (2001). *The development of implicit and explicit memory*. Amsterdam: John Benjamins.

Royse, P., Lee, J., Undrahbuyan, B., Hopson, M., & Consalvo, M. (2007). Women and games: technologies of the gendered self. *New Media & Society*, *9*, 555–576. doi:10.1177/1461444807080322

Rubin, A. M. (2002). The uses-and-gratifications perspective of media effects. In Bryant, J., & Zillmann, D. (Eds.), *Media effects: Advances in theory and research* (pp. 525–548). Hillsdale, NJ: Lawrence Erlbaum Associates, Inc.

Salen, K., & Zimmerman, E. (2005). Game design and meaningful play. In Rasessens, J., & Goldstein, J. (Eds.), *Handbook of computer game studies* (pp. 59–80). Cambridge, MA: MIT Press.

Salisch, M. V., Oppl, C., & Kristen, A. (2006). What attracts children? In Vorderer, P., & Bryant, J. (Eds.), *Playing video games: Motives, responses, and consequences* (pp. 147–163). Mahwah, NJ: Lawrence Erlbaum.

Schneider, E. F., Lang, A., Shin, M., & Bradley, S. D. (2004). Death with a story: How story impacts emotional, motivational, and physiological responses to first-person shooter video games. *Human Communication Research*, *30*, 361–375. doi:10.1093/hcr/30.3.361

Secondlife. (2008). *Programs*. Retrieved on August 8, 2009, from http://secondlifegrid.net/programs/education

Sherry, J. L. (2004). Flow and media enjoyment. *Communication Theory*, *14*(4), 328–347. doi:10.1111/j.1468-2885.2004.tb00318.x

Sherry, J. L., Lucas, K., Greenberg, B. S., & Lachlan, K. (2006). Video game uses and gratifications as predicators of use and game preference. In Vorderer, P., & Bryant, J. (Eds.), *Playing video games: Motives, responses, and consequences* (pp. 213–224). Mahwah, NJ: Lawrence Erlbaum Associates, Inc.

Shields, M. (2006, April 17). Gaming's growth spurt. *MediaWeek, 16*, 7.

Sinclair, B. (2008, October 14). Obama campaigns in Burnout, 17 other games. *GameSpot*. Retrieved January 14 from http://www.gamespot.com/news/6199379.html

Snider, M. (2006, July 11). WWII shows no battle fatigue. *USA Today.*

Stewart, B. (1996). *Summary MUD history*. Retrieved from http://www.livinginternet.com/d/di_major.htm

Sweetser, P., & Wyeth, P. (2005). GameFlow: A model for evaluating player enjoyment in games. *ACM computers in Entertainment, 3*(3), 1-23.

van Lent, M. (2008, February). The business of fun. *Computer, 41*, 101–103. doi:10.1109/MC.2008.64

Vorderer, P., Hartmann, T., & Klimmt, C. (2003). *Explaining the enjoyment of playing video games: The role competition.* Paper presented to the ACM International Conference Proceeding of the second international conference on entertainment computing.

Vorderer, P., Klimmt, C., & Ritterfled, U. (2004). Enjoyment: At the heart of media entertainment. *Communication Theory, 14*, 388–408. doi:10.1111/j.1468-2885.2004.tb00321.x

Weibel, D., Wissmath, B., Habegger, S., Yves, S., & Rudolf, G. (2008). Playing online games against computer- vs. human-controlled opponents: Effects on presence, flow, and enjoyment. *Computers in Human Behavior, 24*, 2274–2291. doi:10.1016/j.chb.2007.11.002

Williams, D. (2006). Virtual cultivation: Online worlds, offline perceptions. *The Journal of Communication, 56*, 69–87. doi:10.1111/j.1460-2466.2006.00004.x

Woodcock, B. S. (2006). *MMOG chart*. Retrieved July 20, 2009, from http://www.mmogchart.com

World of WarCraft. *Player vs. player* (n.d.). Retrieved on August 4, 2009, from http://www.worldofwarcraft.com/info/basics/duels.html

World of WarCraft. *Character* (n.d.). Retrieved on August 5, 2009, from http://www.worldofwarcraft.com/wrath/features/gameplay/achievements.xml

Yahoo. Games. (2007). *Grand theft auto IV: Five reasons you want it*. Retrieved April 29, 2009, from http://videogames.yahoo.com/events/grand-theft-auto-iv/grand-theft-auto-iv-five-reasons-you-want-it/1199905

Yang, M., Roskos-Ewoldsen, D. R., Dinu, L., & Arpan, L. M. (2006). The effectiveness of in-game advertising: Comparing college students' explicit and implicit memory for brand names. *Journal of Advertising, 35*, 143–152. doi:10.2753/JOA0091-3367350410

Yaveroglu, I., & Donthu, N. (2008). Advertising repetition and placement issues in on-line environments. *Journal of Advertising, 37*, 31–43. doi:10.2753/JOA0091-3367370203

Yee, N. (2005). The Psychology of Massively Multi-User Online Role-Playing Games: Motivations, Emotional Investment, Relationships and Problematic Usage. In Schroder, R., & Alexson, A. (Eds.), *Avatars at Work and Play: Collaboration and interaction in shared virtual environments.*

Yee, N. (2006a). Motivations for play in online games. *Cyberpsychology & Behavior*, 9.

Yee, N. (2006b). The demographics, motivations, and derived experiences of users of massively multi-user online graphical environments. *Presence (Cambridge, Mass.)*, *15*, 309–329. doi:10.1162/pres.15.3.309

Yee, N. (2007). *The daedalus project*. Retrieved on August 5, 2009, from http://www.nickyee.com/daedalus/

Chapter 24
An Opportunity for In-Game Ad Placement:
The History of the Video Game Industry Interpreted Through the Meaning Lifecycle

Heather M. Schulz
The University of Texas at Austin, USA

Matthew S. Eastin
The University of Texas at Austin, USA

ABSTRACT

It is argued here that the potential connections video game advertisers can build with consumers makes this new medium a strong force in the digital media world. A meaning-based model is introduced to explain the fluctuation of meaning over time, which is caused by the individual and social interpretation and integration of signs and symbols. The history of video games will be comprehensively interpreted through this model to explain the active identification going on between consumers and video games.

INTRODUCTION

In-game ad placement, defined as the process of placing advertisements in video games, is a rapidly growing industry with $295 million spent in 2007, $403 million spent in 2008, and $443 million spent in 2009 (Verna, 2008; Verna, 2009). However, video game sales for 2008 were $22 billion, with $11.7 billion of that being in entertainment software sales, $8.9 billion in hardware console sales, over $2 billion in portable software sales, and $700 million in PC game sales (Hewitt, 2009). So there is still plenty of room for advertising growth. In the academic realm, in-game ad placement has been subjected to an increasing amount of research over the last decade (Nelson, 2002; Chaney, Lin, & Chaney, 2004; Grigorovici & Constantin, 2004; Nicovich, 2005; Yang, Roskos-Ewoldsen, Dinu, & Arpan, 2006; Lee & Farber, 2007; Wise, Bolls, Kim, & Venkataraman, 2008). It is argued here that the potential connections advertisers can build with consumers makes this new medium a strong force in the digital media world. The power of gaming rests in its high entertainment value, which is engaged in repeatedly by an active consumer. As outlined, each new wave of video game consoles

DOI: 10.4018/978-1-60566-792-8.ch024

and cartridges brings new opportunity for advertisers to engage in a meaning-based process of incorporation and consumption with the consumer.

Sherry (2004) points out that any medium may be sought out for entertainment purposes. However, in accordance with Csikszentmihalyi's (1997) concept of "flow," he argues that video games are uniquely suited for this purpose. Flow is characterized by the high level of engagement an individual displays while completing a task. Flow-inducing activities usually possess four traits: 1) clear rules and goals, 2) adaptable skill display, 3) feedback on results, and 4) few distractions. According to Sherry, "It is realized when there is a balance between the difficulty of the task and the skill of the participant" (p. 332). In the same way an individual builds his or her skills learning to play an instrument such as a saxophone or the piano, individuals also develop skills for media use over time. For example, children learn how to use books by developing their reading skills. Video games also require skill development, however, Sherry makes the argument that once even a rudimentary level of video game skill has been achieved, the process of flow can emerge.

In this chapter, a brief history of games (including the current era of video games) will be presented. Then, a review of the identity-building processes consumers participate in will be explored within the context of video game play. From here, a meaning-based model will be introduced to explain the fluctuation of meaning over time, which is caused by the individual and social interpretation and integration of signs and symbols. Finally, video games will be comprehensively interpreted through these models to explain the active identification going on between consumers and video games.

HISTORY OF GAMING

The history of games expands back to the beginning of recorded time. Games have functioned as tools to build social, analytical, and decision-making skills. As each game is passed from one generation to the next, they become contextualized into their immediate environment. Although many games have a core or basic premise that endures over the years, each consecutive version possesses an individualized significance for the timeframe and culture in which they are adopted. The inception of video games is no exception. Although the complexity and variety of video games continues to expand, video games as a whole are nothing more than digitalized versions of classic games, which have evolved over thousands of years. (Grunfeld, 1975; Botermans, Burrett, Van Delft, & Van Splunteren, 1989; Mohr, 1997).

For instance, many of the oldest games can be found in the recorded texts of Ancient Egypt, China, and India, starting around 2,000-3,000 B.C. (Mohr, 1997). Games such as mancala (Egypt), tic-tac-toe (Egypt), chess (India), snakes and ladders (India), go/wei ch'i (China), and checkers (China) were a socially acceptable practice to engage in because of their ties to religious and social functions such as mourning for the dead, learning "war" strategy, and understanding the moral differences between vices and virtues. These ancient games are still being played today and exist not only in their classic form, but also have been reinterpreted into "new" games. For example, chess is considered a war game because players develop offensive and defensive strategy skills as well as the concept of retaliation in a head-to-head match up. Territorial protections as well as aggressive capture-and-destroy techniques are common themes for this game. This conceptualization has been reinvented time and time again into other dueling strategy games such as Mortal Kombat, GoldenEye 007, Battleship, Command & Conquer, etc.

During the Medieval and Renaissance timeframe (400 A.D. – 1,600 A.D.), many of the games created were associated with Europe. During this time, one of the most dramatic shifts in terms of how games are played occurred with the development of cards. In fact, cards are a relatively recent style of game play. However, it is important to note that at this time, games possessed a notorious relationship with religion. Unlike the earlier era, instead of being utilized for religious instruction, cards were often denounced as a tool of Satan. But, it is important to remember that at this time of political instability, the national governments were being replaced by an economic feudal system which consisted primarily of nobility landholders and peasant-level serfs. The Christian church also became politically powerful, and every aspect of social life (laws, politics, ceremonies, etc.) began to be filtered through the lens of church and religion (Harper, 1979). Dominoes ("dotted cards"), dice, and darts also reached new heights of popularity at this time.

In the late 1800s, the first coin-operated entertainment devices began to appear in amusement parks, boardwalks, bars, and bowling alleys. These, often home-made, prototypes are some of the earliest versions of what will become video games. The most noted examples are pinball and foosball. During the first half of the 1900s, many of the modern classic board games appeared such as *Monopoly* and *Yahtzee*. However at this time, the electrification of gaming was also beginning to emerge as the first computer prototypes were created (Demaria & Wilson, 2004). During the late 1930s and early 1940s the first computers were being created on university campuses as well as governmental departments. Video game development on these new computers helped to usher in technological breakthroughs in computer programming. At this time, televisions were also being introduced to mass audiences.

The first known version of a video game appeared 1948. Called the Cathode-Ray Tube Amusement Device, the computer display was an oscilloscope, which utilized glass vacuum technology and electrons (Demaria & Wilson, 2004). Technically, this computer possessed analog circuitry instead of digital, so it was not the first official digital video game, but it was the first electric video game. The game itself consisted of a missile and target platform on a screen mimicking a radar display. In 1951, the NIMROD computer was the first digital computer to play a game (Lowood, 2006). Called *NIM,* it has roots in Ancient China, and consists of opposing players utilizing mathematical strategy as they take turns removing items from a pile. Soon after, in 1952, the EDSAC computer displayed a digital version of tic-tac-toe, and in 1958 a Ping Pong-type game, called *Tennis for Two*, was created for a computer with an oscilloscope.

During the late 1950s and early 1960s computers began to shrink from the size of a room to the size of a box. They also began to drop in price and therefore expand into the business sector. The first mass-produced video game was released in 1962 as a component of the PDP-1 computer. Titled *Spacewar!*, it was a head-to-head shooting game in outer space. During the 1970s and 1980s, additional home computers began to emerge in the market by companies such as Apple, Commodore, and Tandy. Arcade games such as *Galaxy Game* and *Computer Space* were some of the first mass-distributed arcade games. The creators of *Computer Space* would eventually establish Atari, the company who would subsequently be the leader in the video game arcade market.

In 1972, three important video game releases occurred: 1) the arcade game *Pong* by Atari, which pushed video games into mainstream culture, 2) the first hand-held electronic game (which simulated tic-tac-toe) was released by WACO, and 3) the first video game home console was released, titled the Magnavox Odyssey. During the late 1970s, other arcade games appeared with increasing popularity. Some of these games include: *Tank* (a dueling game), *Gran Track 10* (a car racing game), *Breakout* (a solitaire version of *Pong*), *Blockade* (a capture game), and *Space Invaders* (a missile-target game). The overwhelming leader of the arcade market at this time was Atari. Computer games were also released at this time, but they consisted primarily of textual combat games such as *DND*, a digital version of the tabletop game *Dungeon and Dragons*, or first-person shooter games such as *Maze War*. By the late 1970s, other home consoles were being introduced such as the Fairchild Channel F, the Atari 2600, and the 1978 Magnavox Odyssey[2].

During the early 1980s, the arcade market was at its height of popularity with the release of games such as *Pac Man* (a maze game), *Donkey Kong*, *Joust*, *Q*bert*, and *Donkey Kong Jr.* (all platform games). During this time, numerous other home consoles also emerged, including the Mattel Intellivision, the CBS ColecoVision, the Emerson Arcadia 2001, and the Smith Engineering Vectrex, among others. In fact, the arcade and home console markets quickly became saturated and then oversaturated as more and more low-quality, copycat games were created by third-party software developers (Demaria & Wilson, 2004; Shilling, 2006). At this time, since video game console (i.e., hardware) companies were unable to hold on to exclusive control of their gaming rights, the quality of many video games (i.e., software) during this era took a nosedive as companies focused on quantity over quality. In 1983, the overcrowded retail market caused the video game industry to momentarily collapse, forcing many console companies to fail. This crash also toppled Atari from its title as the leader of the arcade and home console markets.

The home console market reemerged in 1985 with the release of the Nintendo Entertainment System (NES), an 8-bit home console that included the game *Super Mario Brothers*. Other home consoles emerged in 1985, including the Atari ST and the Commodore Amiga, but the NES would dominate the market. One major factor in Nintendo's ability to obtain and sustain market dominance was its decision to strictly control game cartridge software licensing (Schilling, 2006). Other popular NES games at this time included the role-playing adventure games *DragonQuest*, *The Legend of Zelda*, and *Final Fantasy*. In 1989 Nintendo introduced an updated handheld console, Game Boy, which included the puzzle game *Tetris*. One year later, rival handheld consoles such as the Sega Game Gear and the Atari Lynx appeared.

The first formidable home console opponent of the NES appeared in 1989 with the 16-bit Sega Genesis, which featured the game *Sonic the Hedgehog*. In 1991, Nintendo responded with the release of the 16-bit Super NES (SNES). One of the most popular games for both consoles during this time was *Mortal Kombat* (a duel game). Now that the home console market was heating up again, the last major game in the arcade market during this time was *Street Fighter II* (a duel game). Eventually, many arcades were replaced by destinations such as Dave & Buster's and Chuck E. Cheese. The computer game market was able to stay afloat in this competitive market with games such as *Dune II* (a real-time strategy game - RTS), *Alone in the Dark* (a survival horror game), *Myst* (a puzzle game) and the immensely popular simulated-life series titled The Sims: *SimCity*, *SimEarth*, *SimAnt*, *SimLife*, *SimSafari*, *Simcity 3000*, etc.

The next wave of home consoles occurred from 1994-1996 with the 32-bit Sony PlayStation, the Atari Jaguar (64-bit), the Panasonic 3DO (32-bit), the Sega Saturn (32-bit) and the Nintendo 64, or N64 (64-bit). Many of these consoles began to utilize CD-ROM technology for their cartridges, which enabled the production of the first fully three-dimensional games such as *Super Mario 64* for N64, *GoldenEye 007* for N64, and *Tomb Raider* for PlayStation and Saturn. The Sony PlayStation was the clear market leader during this time, with the Nintendo 64 as the closest market challenger. However, a new wave of consoles was quickly around the corner and positioned to move video games from household entertainment to social phenomenon.

In 1996, with the introduction of the Internet to the public, Internet games for computers emerged. Then in 1999, Sega introduced the Dreamcast console which revolutionized home console video gaming by implementing an Internet modem and Web browser. Subsequent

Internet-capable consoles include the Sony PlayStation 2 (PS2), the Nintendo GameCube, and the Microsoft Xbox. At this time the PS2 was the market leader. Popular games during this time include *Grand Theft Auto III* for PS2, *Metroid Prime* for GameCube, *Halo 2* for Xbox, and *Guitar Hero* for PS2. The most recent wave of consoles released by the market's now three leading companies include: 1) the Microsoft Xbox 360, 2) the Sony PlayStation 3 or PS3, and 3) the Nintendo Wii. The Microsoft Xbox 360 was the market leader of its time until the release of the Nintendo Wii.

To this end, the process of game play has remained relatively stable over thousands of years. With the passage of time, new games emerge and are integrated into a society's culture. However, the basic function of games – as a form of entertainment – has remained intact. Now, with a firm understanding of how the gaming industry has developed, the discussion will transition to the consumer's side of game play. The following will explore how consumers build their identities through the process of integrating social meaning (and the items associated with this meaning such as video games) into their lives. Then, a meaning-based model is proposed which describes the fluctuation of meaning over time, portrayed in a meaning life cycle.

CONSTRUCTING MEANING THROUGH GAME PLAY

Meaning is constructed through the individual and social interpretation of signs and symbols. The interpretation of meaning is inherently subjective and identified by observing the interaction of objects, actions, and people (Morris, 1938; Levy, 1959; Csikszentmihalyi & Halton, 1981). Because both the individual and society must negotiate on the classification of meaning, the perception of meaning occurs on both a psychological and sociological level.

Individuals identify with the meaning that is attached to objects, social roles, and even other individuals. Therefore, an individual's identity is made up of two parts, the individual's evaluation of himself/herself which is called self-concept, and the individual's evaluation of how others view him/her. This notion could be summarized as group affiliation, or how the individual relates to the people around him/her. According to Burns (1979), this concept of a "dual consciousness" began to emerge in scholarly literature in the 1600s with Descartes (i.e., "I think, therefore I am") which emphasized the metaphysical phenomenon of self-awareness and split the self into a "self concept" and a "concept of self." During the 1700s, Immanuel Kant refurbished this idea into the "self as subject" and the "self as object." Then in the late 1800s, these concepts were again overhauled by William James into the "knower" and the "known".

During the 1950's Erving Goffman introduced the process of symbolic interactionism to describe the continual tension and interrelatedness of an individual to his or her society. Goffman (1959) used a dramaturgical (i.e., theatric) metaphor explaining how the individual puts on a show for others by managing one's impression. This "presentation of self" or "image projection" is communicated to others through the use of social cues. That way others, reading these cues, will know "who" he or she is. Items often studied during symbolic interactionism include setting, clothing, appearance, words, and nonverbal actions. As evident, here the process of communication through self-extension (Allport, 1961) is the underlying study of inquiry:

Objects serve as the set and props on the theatrical stage of our lives. They situate an individual's character or personality in a context. We use objects as markers to denote our character to others; we also use objects as markers to remind ourselves of who we are. In this sense we derive our self-concept from objects. That is, we use objects to convey and extend our self-concepts to others as well as to demonstrate the self-concept to ourselves. Objects convey our connection to others and help express our sense of self (Wallendorf & Arnould, 1988, p. 531).

In terms of mass communication, self-extension theory looks at the role of consumer products. People use the possession of specific brands in order to express their identity, in terms of both self-concept and group affiliation (Belk, 1988). Since brands possess symbolic meanings of culture, possession of that brand allows one to indirectly possess the cultural meaning (Aaker, Benet-Martinez, & Garolera, 2001; Douglas & Isherwood, 1978). Belk (1988) uses the metaphor of "positive contamination" to describe the process of obtaining meaning by being in physical proximity to something possessing a desired trait. The hope is that some of the cultural significance will magically rub off from the object to the individual.

Eastin, Appiah, and Cicchirllo (2009) provide an example of self-extension through video games in their analysis of racial identification with a video game character. When an individual is playing a video game where racial cues are signified, the symbolic meanings associated with a particular race may "contaminate" (via Belk) the individual. In this study, research participants who identified themselves as either White or Black were randomly assigned to play either a White or Black video game avatar in a make-believe, first-person shooting game. Another manipulation was the race of the opponent in the video game. Two post-play measures for this study were: 1) identification of the research participant to his/her avatar, and 2) aggressive thoughts experienced after playing the game. From this experimental design, Eastin et al. found that Black research participants had a higher identification score with Black video game avatars versus White avatars and White research participants had a higher identification score with White video game avatars versus Black avatars. Also, when a White participant was assigned a Black video game avatar, he/she exhibited higher levels of post-play hostility compared to the White participants assigned a White avatar. Finally, when a Black participant was assigned a White opponent, he/she exhibited higher levels of post-play hostility compared to the Black participants assigned a Black opponent.

In terms of self-extension, the higher levels of identification with one's own race for both Black and White research participants signifies that individuals allow an aspect of their personal identity to extend into their video game identity. In other words, a part of oneself extends into the daily activities of our lives. Also, in terms of the White participants, their higher levels of hostility arguably arose from their assignment as a Black video game avatar and the cultural stereotypes associated with this race. In other words, some of the identity from the video game extended back onto the real-world individual. Appiah (2004) brings attention to a similar phenomenon he calls "cultural voyeurism," and describes it as the acquisition of knowledge about another race and subsequent emulation of that culture through mass media, such as television shows, movies, music, and video games. In turn, the hostility exhibited for Black participants who played against White opponents also confirms the implicit self-extension of video game use onto the individual.

THE MEANING LIFECYCLE

Another way to understand the processes of symbolic interactionism, self-extension, and impression management would be to look at the shifts in meaning throughout time. As stated, the act of game play has remained relatively stable over thousands of years. The specific games played have varied, but only to the extent that they are a reinterpretation of the past. The same could be said of meaning as a whole. Meanings themselves often do no vary greatly over time. Yet, salience of meanings can vary greatly because over time society and the individual must continually reinterpret the world around them. The meaning-based model proposed here describes the fluctuation of meaning over time, portrayed in a meaning life cycle. In doing so, it moves from creation, to distinction, to identification, to application, to validation, and finally consumption.

Creation

Desire must exist before meaning can be created. The desire for the creation of a new meaning arises on both individual and social levels. Individually, a person participating in the creation of new meaning feels on some level a gap, deficiency, absence, want, need, craving, etc. If an individual felt completely fulfilled, then the creation of new meaning would become irrelevant. No one would need to attain new meaning in their life if they possessed full levels of personal fulfillment or self-actualization. On a social level, new meaning is not really created, but instead given salience or priority. Since society possesses the full spectrum of all the good and bad aspects of existence, then new meaning cannot really be created. Therefore, a gap does not become apparent in society as it does in the individual. Instead, the notion of scarcity drives the priority and salience of "new" meaning. Scarcity by definition describes a meaning that is no longer possessed by numerous individuals. Therefore, the gap felt in the individual's life is the realization that a meaning has become scarce in society.

Because video games possess the right mix of high entertainment value as well as high active participation by consumers, video game consumers may possess higher attention rates and therefore may be more willing to integrate the social messages communicated in video games because they feel part of the video game's community and culture. Therefore, with each new era of video game consumers, a newly desired level of meaning is created. For the individual, a desire arises for a new level of skill development through the entertaining nature of video games. This desire (i.e., gap) at the individual level highlights a level of scarcity in society. In other words, each new era of video games and/or consoles display what was scarce in society prior. An example of this can be found with the emergence of the Nintendo Entertainment System, as described above. The NES gained market dominance because it produced high-quality games with strict third-party licensing. This filled the need of consumers who were unhappy with the overcrowded prior home console market which offered hundreds of low-quality, copycat games (Schilling, 2006).

Distinction

Once meaning has been established, it must be distinguished from related topics. A newly created meaning must show what it is and what it is not. In other words, each meaning is at the same time connected to all other meaning, yet must stand on its own and carve out its own niche. Meaning is contextualized, and therefore the new meaning created does not exist in a vacuum and must show how it relates to other topics, both similar and dissimilar. As stated, many of the games and consoles released are just updated versions of games from the past (like dueling games, maze games, racing games, etc.), however each new version must display how it is similar and distinct from every game or console prior.

Identification, Application, Validation, and Consumption

Once meaning has been created and identified as distinct, it is then ascribed to something physical so that it can communicate what it represents. Since meaning itself is intangible, it is only when it is ascribed to a physical object does it become a symbolic representation that can be communicated between individuals and societies. Once meaning has been ascribed to an object, the use of that object implies the use of the related meaning. With the use of an object and therefore application of meaning, the individual and society negotiate on the acceptance of meaning transference to the individual. Through application, the individual is attempting to display their connection to the meaning, while society is determining whether or not this meaning will transfer to the individual.

The meaning created by both the individual and society is ascribed to a game or console through the purchase and habitual use by the consumers. The individual consumer perceives the game or console possesses a desired trait. The social agreement of this perception can often be studied by analyzing the "fads" or the games and consoles that reach mass heights of popularity. Often similar games and consoles are also available in the market at the exact same time. But, it is the connection of consumer and product on a mass level that underlines the shared meaning they possess. Therefore, the market leaders in terms of consoles and video games validate the individual and societal negotiation of what the new meaning represents.

The actual consumption stage is related to the idea of meaning being used or digested. At this stage, a certain amount of irony sets in for the individual. Now that he or she has obtained this meaning, the symbolic gap felt earlier should be filled. However it is often the case that a gap still exists, but has merely shifted. On a social level, the shifted gap felt by the individual is what is now deemed scarce. As one can see, new levels of scarcity appear in society through shifting levels of individual ownership of meaning. In terms of video games, the consumption of this meaning is often displayed during the end of a game or console era. After the fad passes, or perhaps because the fad was created, this creates a scarcity for each individual in a different aspect of their lives. Therefore, the meaning lifecycle starts anew, and a new era of available video games and video game consoles becomes available. The model shown in Figure 1 displays the full cycle of meaning from creation to consumption.

One can follow the fluctuation of meaning over time by studying the history of game play just described, looking at video games in particular. With the inception of technological advances such as television and computers, the creation of digital games appeared. The new meaning created for the individual was to utilize this new technology in fun and entertaining ways. The digital games created followed the same formats of classic game genres which have been played for thousands of years. Games such as *Tennis for Two* and *Spacewar!* (i.e., dueling games) fit into this new wave of meaning. However, it would be decades before computers were introduced to the home market. Therefore, arcade consoles were created that would play only one game. Examples of this era include *Pong* and *Space Invaders*, although soon even these were replaced by other games such as *Pac Man*, *Donkey Kong* and *Q*bert*. Each year, new games were being introduced in order to satisfy the individual craving for something different.

During the height of the arcade fad, the home console market was beginning to flourish. People now wanted to enjoy this gaming experience at home. However, the software for home consoles could not maintain market presence because copycat games were appearing all the time. Like stated above, this created an oversaturated market.

Figure 1. The meaning lifecycle

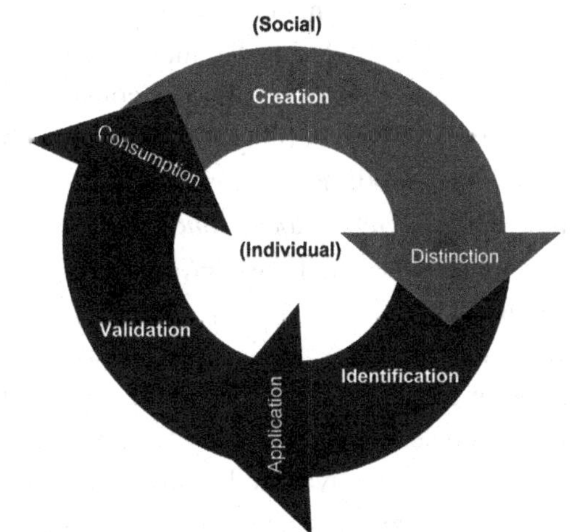

For a while, these copycat games filled the need for consumers to purchase many types of games at low prices. However, at the time of market saturation, on a societal level, the availability of good, high-quality games was missing. The 1983 video game market collapse signaled the shift of individual preference away from copycat games. In order to fill this new need of high-quality games, one company, Nintendo, developed strict software licensing deals. Individual consumers responded by purchasing the NES home console in order to meet this new need. Games popular during this time included *Tetris*, *Super Mario Brothers*, and *The Legend of Zelda*, which again were just updated versions of the classic puzzle and adventure game genres. By 1989, the domination of the NES console in the video game market once again displayed a new gap in society. Individuals no longer wanted one, strong home console with high-quality games. Now they wanted at least two to choose from. Individuals were craving choice once again. This manifestation was met with the rise in market popularity of the Sega Genesis.

Soon after, other rival consoles emerged, and now the new need being met was higher and higher picture resolution, from 8-bit to 16-bit to 32-bit to 64-bit, etc. Then, another technological revolution happened. With the arrival of the Internet, the concept of what video games were capable of producing shifted once again. Individual needs of graphic complexity and game complexity were being met by stronger and stronger consoles with Web capability. Today, the market has three main front runners in terms of home consoles: 1) Microsoft Xbox 360, 2) Sony PlayStation 3, and 3) the Nintendo Wii. Popular games at this time include *Guitar Hero*, *Rock Band*, *Halo 2*, and *Grand Theft Auto III*. However, this will soon be changing.

In terms of in-game ad placement, the cycling nature of meaning in general and video games in particular presents an opportunity for advertisers. Not only could an advertised brand obtain high levels of reach and frequency if it is connected to a video game or console that explodes into mass culture via mass acceptance (i.e., a fad or trend), but advertising could aid in the success of a video game or console. It is through advertising's success in ascribing meaning to products and services that provides any particular brand a measure of success. This same process can be applied to video games. Whether it is through creating a more realistic atmosphere in the video game environment, or by bringing in meanings from existing brands into a new game, advertising's knack for assigning meaning could create new levels of customer-brand relationships that have never existed before in any other medium. Again, this is because of the high entertainment value of the video game, which by nature is engaged in repeatedly by an active consumer. The cycling nature of the video game industry (and games as a whole) will continue on whether or not the advertising industry gets and stays involved in the process. However, an engaging prospect exists for advertisers to jump into a phenomenon of meaning creation, distinction, identification, application, validation, and finally consumption.

REFERENCES

Aaker, J. L., Benet-Martinez, V., & Garolera, J. (2001). Consumption symbols as carriers of culture: A study of Japanese and Spanish brand personality constructs. *Journal of Personality and Social Psychology*, *81*(3), 492–508. doi:10.1037/0022-3514.81.3.492

Allport, G. W. (1961). *Pattern and Growth in Personality*. New York: Holt, Rinehart and Winston.

Appiah, O. (2004). Effects of ethnic identification on web browsers attitudes toward, and navigational patterns on, race-targeted sites. *Communication Research*, *31*(3), 312–337. doi:10.1177/0093650203261515

Belk, R. W. (1988, September). Possessions and the extended self. *The Journal of Consumer Research, 15*, 139–168. doi:10.1086/209154

Botermans, J., Burrett, T., Van Delft, P., & Van Splunteren, C. (1989). *The World of Games: Their Origins and History, How to Play Them and How to Make Them*. New York: Facts on File, Inc.

Burns, R. B. (1979). *The Self-Concept: Theory, Measurement, Development, and Behavior*. New York: Longman.

Chaney, I., Lin, K., & Chaney, J. (2004). The effect of billboards within the gaming environment. *Journal of Interactive Advertising, 5*(1). Retrieved from http://www.jiad.org.

Csikszentmihalyi, M. (1997). *Finding Flow: The Psychology of Engagement with Everyday Life*. New York: Basic Books.

Csikszentmihalyi, M., & Halton, E. (1981). *The Meaning of Things: Domestic Symbols and the Self*. Cambridge, UK: Cambridge University Press.

Demaria, R., & Wilson, J. L. (2004). *High Score! The Illustrated History of Electronic Games*. Emeryville, CA: McGraw-Hill/Osborne.

Douglas, M., & Isherwood, B. (1979). *The World of Goods*. New York: Basic.

Eastin, M., Appiah, O., & Cicchirllo, V. (2009). Identification and the influence of cultural stereotyping on postvidogame play hostility. *Human Communication Research, 35*, 337–356. doi:10.1111/j.1468-2958.2009.01354.x

Goffman, E. (1959). *The Presentation of Self in Everyday Life*. Garden City, NY: Doubleday.

Grigorovici, D., & Constantin, C. (2004). Experiencing interactive advertising beyond rich media: Impacts of ad type and presence on brand effectiveness in 3D gaming immersive virtual environments. *Journal of Interactive Advertising, 4*(3). Retrieved from http://www.jiad.org.

Grunfeld, V. (1975). *Games of the World: How to Make Them How to Play Them, How They Came to Be*. New York: Holt, Rinehart and Winston.

Harper, N. (1979). *Human Communication Theory: The History of a Paradigm*. Rochelle Park, NJ: Hayden Book Company, Inc.

Hewitt, D. (2009, January 28). Computer and video game industry tops $22 billion in 2008 (press release). *Entertainment Software Association*. Retrieved September 27, 2009, from http://www.theesa.com/newsroom/release_detail.asp?releaseID=44

Lee, M., & Faber, R. J. (2007). Effects of product placement in on-line games on brand memory: A perspective of the limited-capacity model of attention. *Journal of Advertising, 36*, 75–90. doi:10.2753/JOA0091-3367360406

Levy, S. J. (1959, July). Symbols for sale. *Harvard Business Review, 37*, 117–124.

Lowood, H. (2006). A brief biography of computer games. In Vorderer, P., & Bryant, J. (Eds.), *Playing Video Games: Motives, Responses and Consequences* (pp. 25–42). Mahwah, NJ: Lawrence Erlbaum Associates.

Mohr, M. S. (1997). *The New Games Treasury*. New York: Houghton Mifflin Company.

Morris, C. W. (1938). *Foundations of the Theory of Signs*. Chicago: University of Chicago Press.

Nelson, M. (2002, April). Recall of brand placements in computer/video games. *Journal of Advertising Research*, 80–92.

Nicovich, S. G. (2005). The effect of involvement on ad judgment in a video game environment: The mediating role of presence. *Journal of Interactive Advertising, 6*. Retrieved from http://www.jiad.org

Schilling, M. A. (2006). Game not over: Competitive dynamics in the video game industry. In Lampel, J., Shamsie, J., & Lant, T. K. (Eds.), *The Business of Culture: Strategic Perspectives on Entertainment Media* (pp. 75–104). Mahwah, NJ: Lawrence Erlbaum Associates.

Sherry, J. L. (2004). Flow and media enjoyment. *Communication Theory*, *14*(4), 328–347. doi:10.1111/j.1468-2885.2004.tb00318.x

Verna, P. (2008 February). Video game advertising. *eMarketer*. Retrieved September 27, 2009, from http://www.emarketer.com/Reports/All/Emarketer_2000485.aspx

Verna, P. (2009 June). Digital entertainment meets social media. *eMarketer*. Retrieved September 27, 2009, from http://www.emarketer.com/Reports/All/Emarketer_2000580.aspx

Wallendorf, M., & Arnould, E. J. (1988). My favorite things: A cross-cultural inquiry into object attachment, possessiveness, and social linkage. *The Journal of Consumer Research*, *14*(4), 531–547. doi:10.1086/209134

Wise, K., Bolls, P. D., Kim, H., Venkataraman, A., & Meyer, R. (2008). Enjoyment of advergames and brand attitudes: The impact of thematic relevance. *Journal of Interactive Advertising*, *9*(1). Retrieved from http://www.jiad.org.

Yang, M., Roskos-Ewoldsen, D. R., Dinu, L., & Arpan, L. M. (2006). The effectiveness of in-game advertising: Comparing college students' explicit and implicit memory for brand names. *Journal of Advertising*, *34*(4), 143–152. doi:10.2753/JOA0091-3367350410

Chapter 25
Digital Media and Sports Advertising

John A. Fortunato
Fordham University, USA

ABSTRACT

Advertising and sponsorship in the area of sports continue to be a prominent way for companies to receive brand exposure to a desired target audience and obtain a brand association with a popular entity. The fundamental advantages of advertising and sponsorship in sports now combine with digital media to provide more extensive and unique opportunities for companies to promote their brands and potentially better connect with their customers. It is clear that digital media do not replace more traditional forms of sports advertising and sponsorship, but rather represent additional vehicles for promotional communication. This chapter begins by providing an explanation of the goals and advantageous characteristics of a sports sponsorship for a company. This review is necessary because developing an agreement with the sports property is required for sponsors to obtain exclusive rights to content (footage of that sport), and logos they could use on their product packaging or in their advertisements to better communicate a brand association. The chapter then offers four examples of companies using digital media to execute their sponsorships with sports properties: Sprite and the NBA, Verizon and the NFL, AT&T and the Masters Golf Tournament, and Wise Snack Foods and the Boston Red Sox and New York Mets. A fifth example looks at how sponsors are using another prominent media destination for the sports audience, ESPN. The chapter reveals the endless possibilities of what a sponsorship using digital media can include in the area of sports.

INTRODUCTION

It can be said that every time the technological communication environment changes and causes the mass media use of the audience to change, so too does the advertising industry. While the technology has changed, the ultimate goal of advertising has not. The most general objective of any advertisement is to persuade (e.g., Leckenby & Stout, 1985; O'Guinn, Allen, & Semenik, 2006; Tellis, 2004). However, understanding what

DOI: 10.4018/978-1-60566-792-8.ch025

determines the effectiveness of advertising as a persuasive form of communication continues to be an issue raised by many scholars (e.g.,Tellis, 2004; Till & Baack, 2005) and an obvious concern of all practitioners.

As audiences are provided with a multitude of communication vehicles to experience media content, advertisers simply need to be in the locations where their brands will be noticed by their desired target audiences. Bellamy and Traudt (2000) explain the necessity of brand exposure as "the fundamental concept is that a recognizable brand will more easily attract and retain customers than an unrecognizable one" (p. 127). In addition to the advertising placement to obtain brand exposure, some scholars indicate the message content of an advertisement can influence the audience's ability to better remember the brand name and to get them to think favorably about the advertised brand that can ultimately lead them to purchase the brand (e.g., Kelley & Turley, 2004; Till & Baack, 2005). The achievement of persuasion through advertising needs to combine the strategic placement and the proper message content to best create the desired effect. Fortunato and Dunnam (2004) thus describe any advertising strategy as having three specific goals: (1) obtaining exposure to the desired target audience, (2) increasing product brand recall, and (3) increasing consumer behavior (i.e., purchasing the brand).

Achievement of these persuasive advertising goals is, however, much more complicated in the current technological communication environment. Advertisers need to adapt to the technology and understand that digital media offer opportunities to better connect their brands with the consumer. For sports advertising digital media prominently include the Internet, both the company's own website and placement on the websites of leagues, teams, or sports media companies (i.e., ESPN or Sports Illustrated), hand-held wireless devices, and integration of advertising into video games. DeFleur and Dennis (2002) describe digital media as "the product of 'convergence,' the coming together of all forms of communication into a unified, electronically based, computer-driven system" (p. 215). They add digital media are interactive and involve "digital storage of information, its retrieval and dissemination" (p. 215). Bianco (2004) contends interactivity and a more precise measurement of the message's impact are the two advantages of advertising on the Internet instead of traditional mass media. He explains the interactive capability "enables marketers to gather reams of invaluable personal information directly from customers and adjust their sales pitch accordingly, in some cases in real time" (p. 65). O'Guinn, Allen, and Semenik (2006) summarize that prominent among the advantages for advertisers in using digital media are: target market selectivity, tracking, deliverability and flexibility, and interactivity (p. 572).

The area of sports remains a viable advertising vehicle to achieve brand exposure, especially to the desirable, and relatively hard-to-reach, male audience between the ages of 18 and 49 (e.g., Wenner, 1989). Wenner (1989) points out that "media organizations buy and sell sport much as they do any other news or entertainment commodity. The content per se is not what is being sold; rather it is the audience for that content that is being sold to advertisers" (p. 22). In speaking specifically about the advantage of advertising during sports television programming in relation to the competitive advertising environment, Bellamy (1998) adds that, "with a seemingly endless proliferation of television channels, sport is seen as the programming that can best break through the clutter of channels and advertising and consistently produce a desirable audience for sale to advertisers" (p. 73).

Another important variable in addition to the demographic characteristics in evaluating advertising in the area of sports is the nature of the sports audience. Sloan (1989) contends the term *fan*, short for fanatic, is more descriptive for people who watch sports, rather than describing them as merely spectators or viewers. For fans, experiencing sports has been shown to provide emotional satisfaction (Madrigal, 2000; Mullin, Hardy, & Sutton, 2007; Shank, 2009; Tutko, 1989; Underwood, Bond, & Baer, 2001; Wann, Royalty, & Roberts, 2000; Zillmann, Bryant, & Sapolsky, 1989). Tutko (1989) speaks to the emotional characteristic of being a sports fan, claiming that:

There can be little doubt that the athletic area has become a center for taking care of our emotional needs. We participate in and are spectators of the emotional charge. If athletics did not provide excitement it would be gone in a short period. We look forward to indulging in the joys of victory but all too often steep in the agony of defeat. Without the occasional emotional charge, life would be a little bit duller--a little bit less alive and perhaps even have less meaning (p. 113).

Because experiencing sports can satisfy emotional needs the sports audience has been described as very loyal in its behavior (Madrigal, 2000; Mullin, et. al., 2007; Underwood, et. al., 2001; Wann, et. al., 2000). Funk and James (2001) indicate the emotional and loyalty characteristics of the sports fan can result in consistent and enduring behaviors, including attendance and watching games on television. The emotion and loyalty characteristics certainly extend to behavior in other media forms such as print publication purchases, sports talk radio, and Internet or other digital media use to experience sports content.

SPORT SPONSORSHIP

In addition to traditional media advertising, particularly commercials during live games, and as the audience is increasingly being presented with multiple media options, sponsorship has become a viable strategy for many corporations to obtain the necessary brand exposure and achieve a better connection between the brand and the consumer (Fortunato & Dunnam, 2004; Meenaghan, 1991, 2001; Mullin, et. al., 2007; Pedersen, Miloch, & Laucella, 2007; Shank, 2009; Walliser, 2003). Savary (2008) explains the overall challenge in the current advertising environment, stating "brands must now forge an emotional connection with the consumer. Marketing messages must show how a product is relevant to a consumer. Campaigns need to evoke affinity and create a 'that brand is like me' sentiment. Brands need to show future customers not just how a product meets their needs, but how the product integrates into their life and how the brand reflects their values and reinforces their self-image" (p. 212). She argues, "the discipline of sponsorship and engagement marketing is ideally and perhaps uniquely suited to this challenge. Engagement marketing professionals know that this discipline surpasses other forms of marketing in inspiring passion and loyalty, creating a sense of shared values and turning fans into brand advocates" (p. 212). Corporations obviously believe that sponsorship of sports properties (i.e., leagues, teams, events, and athletes) is a valuable tool in the communication marketing mix as evidenced by the enormous financial investment in this strategy. The European Sponsorship Association estimated that over $30 billion was spent on sponsorships worldwide in 2005, with 85 percent of those expenditures with sports properties (Croft, 2006).

It should also be pointed out that sponsorship with the more popular sports properties (i.e., NFL, NBA, Major League Baseball, or the Olympics) can be cost prohibitive for many companies (Fortunato & Richards, 2007). For example, Adidas agreed to pay the NBA $400 million over 11 years to be the official uniform supplier for the league (Lombardo, 2006). T-Mobile agreed to pay the NBA $100 million over three years to be the official wireless communication brand for the league (Lefton, 2006). Molson Coors agreed to pay the NFL $500 million over five years to be the official beer sponsor for the league (Kaplan & Lefton, 2006). The Olympic Partner Program (TOP) has eleven worldwide sponsors that pay approximately $75 million per four-year cycle that includes both a Winter and Summer Olympic Games (Thomaselli, 2004).

What makes sponsorship such an attractive strategy for many corporations is that all of the parameters of the deal are negotiable and bound only by what the sponsor and the sponsored property can agree to (Fortunato & Dunnam, 2004). Although a sponsorship can take on many different forms, and therefore is difficult to define, researchers have identified the core components of a sponsorship agreement as an investment by the corporate sponsor in exchange for the exploitable commercial potential associated with the event or property (Meenaghan, 1991, 2001; Mullin, et. al., 2007; Ukman, 1996).

The benefits to the sports properties are obvious upon entering into sponsorship agreements as they add another major revenue stream. There are also benefits to the sponsoring brand, primarily the needed branded exposure. To assist with brand exposure through the sponsorship of a sports property there is the advantageous characteristic of communicating the brand to the audience during the context of the actual game or event – whether the audience is attending the game or experiencing it through the mass media. Stotlar (2001) explains that sponsorship can help reduce clutter and it can be more effective than traditional spot advertising by weaving elements of the brand into the actual game or event broadcast. The sponsorship communication during the broadcast of a game could include stadium naming rights, stadium signage that appears prominently on the television broadcast, sponsored scoreboards, halftime and pregame programs, and/or even having the announcer say the name of the brand. For some companies, particularly equipment manufacturers, the sponsorship features prominent athletes using the brand during competition (i.e., Tiger Woods and Nike).

In a sponsorship agreement this brand exposure often comes with the negotiated characteristic of exclusivity for the sponsoring corporation within its particular product category. Sports leagues and their teams sell exclusivity in a variety of product categories (i.e., airlines, automobiles, financial services). Exclusivity simply eliminates any competition that one company might receive from a rival within that product category at the sponsored event or location (e.g., Fortunato & Dunnam, 2004). Miyazaki and Morgan (2001) note that exclusivity avoids competitive interference that would be incurred in other media contexts (p. 10). For some industries, such as beer, soda, and credit cards, the characteristic of exclusivity provides not only brand exposure, but the additional advantage of stadium point-of-purchase of their brand products to an audience without competition. Through an exclusive sponsorship agreement with a team, a trip to the stadium might provide the consumer with only one brand option, either a Pepsi or a Coca-Cola depending on who is the team's sponsor. With some stadiums attracting millions of customers each year, these exclusive sponsorships are an extremely valuable commodity (e.g., Fortunato & Richards, 2007). In fact, Coca-Cola had pouring rights with four of the top five major league baseball teams in attendance in 2008 (New York Yankees, Los Angeles Dodgers, St. Louis Cardinals, and Philadelphia Phillies) giving it exclusive access to over 14.8 million consumers at those team's ballparks (http://sports.espn.go.com/mlb/attendance--It should be noted that Pepsi is the official soft drink of Major League Baseball and now also sponsors the New York Yankees as well as the New York Mets).

In addition to brand exposure and exclusivity, many authors indicate that developing and communicating a brand association between the sponsoring brand and the sponsored property is an objective that can be achieved through a sponsorship (e.g., Cornwell & Maignan, 1998; Dean 2002; Gwinner, 1997; Gwinner & Eaton, 1999; Irwin, Lachowetz, Cornwell, & Clark, 2003; Meenaghan, 2001; Pedersen, et. al., 2007; Shank, 2009; Till & Shimp, 1998; Walliser, 2003). Dean (2002) explains that "by associating itself with the sponsee, the sponsoring firm/brand shares in the image of the sponsee" (p. 78). Grohs and Reisinger (2005) suggest "the aim is to evoke positive feelings and attitudes toward the sponsor, by closely linking the sponsor to an event the recipient values highly" (p. 44). Stipp and Schiavone (1996) point out the sponsorship goals assume the target audience for the sponsorship will transfer their loyalty from the sponsored property or event to the sponsor itself.

To help achieve this transfer the sponsorship agreement allows the advertiser to communicate its association to the sports property by granting the sponsor rights to exclusively use content (footage of that sport), and logos that it could use on its product packaging or in its advertisements. For example, a Pepsi case or even an individual can or bottle, can have the image of the New York Mets logo. Or, McDonald's can have the Olympic rings logo on its bags and use that logo in its television commercials that also communicated to the viewer that McDonald's is a "Proud Partner" of the Olympic Games (Fortunato, 2008). The ideal outcome for the sponsor is that the popularity and the positive image and reputation of these sports teams and events can precipitate a similar favorable feeling by fans and consumers toward its brand. New York Met fans might think favorably about Pepsi because that company supports their favorite team. Shaw and Amis (2001) support that claim concluding sponsorships are an effective communication tool that can alter and enhance a company's image and reputation. Fortunato (2008) further states that some of the television commercials of Olympic sponsors during the broadcast of the Olympics games featured nothing more than an association with the event (i.e., Coca Cola having a commercial where people sat on a couch as if it was a bobsled or inviting viewers to "drink Coke, live Olympic," rather than speaking to any specific brand features). This use of the sport in the company advertisements also further promotes the league, team, or event. So sponsors are not only paying an upfront fee for an association and usage rights to content and logos provided by the league, they are promoting the league or team through their own advertising (i.e., Burger King as a sponsor of the NFL using NFL footage in its advertisements).

Researchers have indicated that sponsorship associations can be an effective way of differentiating one brand from its competition (e.g., Cornwell, Roy, & Steinard, 2001; Gwinner & Eaton, 1999; Irwin, et. al., 2003; Stipp & Schiavone, 1996). And, perhaps, most importantly, several researchers have even indicated that achieving a brand association transfer through sponsorship strategies could potentially influence consumer behavior, including an increase in purchasing the products of the sponsoring brand (e.g., Cornwell & Maignan, 1998; Cornwell, et. al., 2001; Dean, 2002; Harvey, 2001; Madrigal, 2000; Meenaghan, 2001; Miyazaki & Morgan, 2001). In examining college football fans, Madrigal (2000) points out that fan identification did extend from support of a team to support of companies that sponsor and are associated with that team. He states, "loyalty toward a preferred team may have beneficial consequences for corporate sponsors. Consistent with the idea of in-group favoritism, higher levels of team identification among attendees of a sporting event appear to be positively related to intentions to purchase a sponsor's products" (p. 21). Harvey (2001) adds "sponsorship changes the consumer's perception of a specific sponsor – which can rub off positively on brands that sponsor in terms of willingness to purchase those brands" (p. 64). Amato, Peters, and Shao (2005) found that NASCAR fans consciously make the decision to support and purchase the products of its sponsors. Other researchers have even found that sports sponsorships can enhance the stock price of the sponsoring corporation (e.g., Miyazaki & Morgan, 2001; Pruitt, Cornwell, & Clark, 2004).

That said, sponsorship is often only one component of a larger promotional communication strategy of a company. Researchers claim the best practice is to integrate event sponsorship and other forms of advertising and while each promotional communication method has its own specific strength, all advertising methods ultimately have the same goals (e.g., Cornwell & Maignan, 1998; O'Guinn, et. al., 2006; Quester & Thompson, 2001; Shrimp, 2003; Smolianov & Shilbury, 2005; Walliser, 2003). O'Guinn et. al., (2006) explain that "when marketers combine contests, a Web site, event sponsorship, and point-of-purchase displays with advertising, this creates an integrated brand promotion" (p. 12). Traditionally an integrated approach for sports properties meant a sponsorship agreement includes the purchase of broadcast commercial time (e.g., Fortunato, 2001). Buying commercial time is often, in fact, a necessary condition to becoming a league-wide sponsor. "For example, if Gatorade wanted to be the official sports drink of the NBA and have players drinking out of green cups with the Gatorade logo on them, Gatorade also had to buy commercial time on NBA television broadcasts" (Fortunato, 2001, p. 78). This integrated approach now includes the Internet and all forms of digital media.

In some aspects sports sponsorship has to be integrated, and not solely in digital media. An initial contractual agreement between the sponsor and the sports property still needs to be established to acquire content and logo rights and to have the league or team's footage be available on a digital media platform. Sports leagues might be resistant to completely altering the traditional television advertising environment as television remains the most lucrative revenue source for the most prominent sports leagues (e.g., Fortunato, 2001). For instance, in 2006 the NFL reached broadcast agreements with CBS, Fox, NBC, ESPN, and Direct-TV that pay the NFL revenue totaling over $3.75 billion per season.

The way people experience sports is also relevant to any evaluation of the advertising environment in this area. Experiencing sports continues to be driven by watching a game live on television. In describing the emotion of the sports fan, Wenner and Gantz (1998) claim the unknown outcome of the game is the motivation that generates the most interest and drives the behavior of watching. They point out the strongest motivation for watching sports on television deals with the resolution of ambiguity and identification with competitors, stating, "concerns with seeing 'who wins' and how one's 'favorite does' are among the strongest individual motivations for sports viewing. These tend to combine with the enjoyment that comes with experiencing the 'drama and tension' and the excitement of 'rooting' for a player or team to win" (p. 236). For sports, the outcome is unknown and fans can see the unscripted drama unfold live on television. The Super Bowl is arguably the greatest spectacle in American sports, and in some aspects for the field of advertising as well, viewed by more people every year than any other television program. Super Bowl XLIV played on February 7, 2010, between the New Orleans Saints and the Indianapolis Colts was the most-watched program in television history with an estimated average 106.5 million viewers (Best, 2010). Anheuser-Busch is the official, exclusive sponsor of the broadcast of the Super Bowl having reached agreements with all of the networks televising the game through 2011. The idea of sports leagues, and therefore advertisers, not having a presence on television still seems to be in the distant future.

EXTENDING SPORTS SPONSORSHIP TO DIGITAL MEDIA

For these reasons, the use of digital media has not replaced traditional advertising on sports events or traditional sponsorship strategies. However, once the relationship is established between the sponsor and the sports property it simply makes sense to establish an integrated promotional communication approach and to pull through all communication vehicles, including digital media. It is undeniable that digital media are already providing and will continue to offer an additional and valuable communication vehicle to connect with a highly desired target audience.

The advantageous characteristics of a sponsorship: negotiation of terms, exclusivity eliminating competition within a product category, and communication of association through the use of content or a logo, are all now extended to digital media initiatives. Just as sponsoring any team or league allows for the use of their logo on product packaging, the sponsorship allows for the sponsor's logo to appear on that league or team website. In many instances it is more than the appearance of the logo, but rather some interactive feature that is presented to online visitors, such as being linked to the company's website by clicking on the corporate logo or a longer form advertisement on the website using that league or team imagery to better communicate the brand association between the company and the property.

For example, on the New York Giants website, www.nygiants.com, the fan poll, which contains simple questions such as "how far will the Giants go this season," is presented by Dunkin Donuts with its logo clearly displayed. Beneath the response choices of the poll is a link to "view the Dunkin Donuts Joe 'The Cup' Dunkin Giants movie." This two minute, ten second video opens with Dunkin Donuts stadium signage and the plot has the main character, Joe "The Cup" Dunkin, being asked to kick the game winning field goal for the Giants. Joe "The Cup" Dunkin wears a Giants football helmet, but his uniform is a Dunkin Donuts cup. The movie ends with the ball resting between an upright and the cross-bar of the goal post with viewers not knowing if the ball goes over the cross-bar for the game winning kick before flashing to a screen showing the Giants logo and the Dunkin Donuts logo with its slogan "America runs on Dunkin."

The area of sports advertising and sponsorship becomes tailor made for digital media in allowing for better participation and interactivity in a number of scenarios. The following examples demonstrate how companies are effectively combining the advantageous characteristics of a traditional sponsorship agreement with the vehicles of digital media to provide an additional opportunity to promote their brands and potentially better connect with their customers.

SPRITE AND THE NBA

Sprite is the official soft drink sponsor of the NBA and is the presenting sponsor of the Dunk Contest during All-Star Weekend and the NBA Draft. On June 26, 2008, the NBA held its annual Draft of top collegiate and international players. Sprite used the traditional advertising methods of having signage at the location of the event, having commercials during the televised broadcast of the Draft on ESPN, having it mentioned by announcers during the broadcast that the NBA Draft was presented by Sprite, having it mentioned as the presenting sponsor in other broadcast outlets such as ESPN's SportsCenter, and having the Sprite logo appear in the official logo of the NBA Draft which was prominently displayed on the NBA and ESPN website.

In addition to this brand exposure there were extensive online endeavors coordinated between the NBA and Sprite. On the NBA website (www.nba.com) visitors on the day of the Draft went directly to what had been the NBA's Draft page (www.nba.com/draft2008/index.html). This opening page featured a picture of NBA stars Yao Ming and Lebron James on their respective Draft nights, various article links providing extensive coverage of the NBA Draft, and a banner headline that indicated the Draft was presented by Sprite with the official NBA Draft 2008 logo that included the Sprite logo. The website also featured the Sprite Fan Blog, where fans throughout the day could chat about Draft happenings, and the Sprite Draft Pick 'Em Challenge (www.nba.com/draft2008/nbapickem/home.jsp). In the Sprite Draft Pick 'Em Challenge contest fans predicted which players would be the top fourteen selected in the Draft with points being awarded based on the correct responses. The grand prize was a trip to the 2009

NBA All-Star Game in Phoenix. Two runner-up prizes were a $500 and a $100 gift card for the NBA's online store (www.nbastore.com).

The NBA benefited from this Draft contest sponsored by Sprite as participation required a person had to sign up online to be an NBA Fan Center Member and receive NBA All-Access materials (www.nba.com/allaccess/main.html). During registration a person would provide his or her demographic information and set up to receive e-mails from the league that featured weekly or daily headlines, merchandise discounts, ticket offers, or fantasy news. Once online registration was complete fans were sent a welcome to NBA All-Access e-mail that included 15 percent off your next purchase at the NBA's online store. The NBA Draft has long-been a marketing opportunity for the league beyond introducing its future stars (e.g., Fortunato, 2001). Once a player is selected at the Draft he is given the team's hat. Within one hour of the beginning of the 2008 Draft, NBA All-Access members received an e-mail offer to "get the same hat worn by the draftees of the 2008 NBA Draft" by going to nbastore.com. The e-mail also indicated "this message was sent to you because you subscribed to NBA offers e-mails."

Beyond the Draft, Sprite has furthered its association with the NBA by having extensive dealings with one of the league's preeminent stars, Lebron James. In 2003, James signed a six-year contract with Sprite. He has appeared in Sprite advertisements and his image has been on select cans of Sprite. In January 2007, Sprite introduced a new promotion as part of its subLYMONal campaign that invited consumers to create an exclusive theme song for Lebron James that would be part of the new Lebron23-23 promotion. At a newly created Lebron23-23.com website, fans had the opportunity to create their own music mix that could become the Lebron James theme song. The music tracks were posted on the website and visitors could vote for their favorite songs. During the voting period the music tracks, as well as video clips of Lebron James playing and subLYMONal images were posted on NBA.com/2323. Fans could choose their favorite Lebron James video clips and music mixes and combine them in creating their own music videos that they could digitally share with their friends.

At the end of the preliminary voting period, an expert panel reviewed the top 100 vote-getters and selected the best 23 music tracks. Of those 23 music track James, along with hip hop artists, Paul Wall and Al Fatz, selected the top three finalists. During the 2007 NBA All Star Weekend in Las Vegas, James and Sprite hosted an event at the Bellagio Hotel to unveil a new Lebron subLYMONal advertisement, announce the three finalists, and debut their music tracks. On February 17, the advertisement with the three different music tracks debuted on NBA All Star television programming with viewers prompted to vote up until March 2 for their favorite track through text messaging or visiting Lebron23-23.com. The winner of this fan voting would also get to join Paul Wall and Al Fatz in the studio to finish producing what would become Lebron James' theme song. Finally, during the promotion from January 1 through January 22, consumers could enter codes found under caps of specially marked bottles of Sprite and Sprite Zero at Lebron23-23.com and have a chance to win one of 23 prizes that included a signed Lebron James jersey, video iPods, and portable AM/FM stereo/CD players (http://nba.com/news/Lebron_song_070105.html).

In addition to these efforts, Sprite has a presence in the videogame *NBA Ballers: Phenom* for the Xbox and PlayStation 2 entertainment systems. *NBA Ballers: Phenom* is set in the neighborhoods of Los Angeles with the player controlling his or her own future in trying to become the next NBA phenomenon. Players can chart their own on-the-court and off-the-court future by deciding to either follow the Baller's dream of getting noticed as a basketball player and drafted into the NBA or choose to become a business mogul off-the-court by developing a clothing line, record label, or a movie deal. Sarah Mcllroy, director of in-game advertising and promotions for Midway Amusement Games, stated, "one of Midway's core in-game advertising strategies is to infuse games with cultural context and relevance through the integration of in-game product placements. The addition of key consumer brands such as Sprite, T-Mobile, and Spalding make the gameplay experience in *NBA Ballers: Phenom* organic and credible. We are very excited to be able to work with these companies and to give their brands the type of outreach and exposure that only interactive games can offer" (Midway Games Inc. Press Release, May 2, 2006; www.midway.com/us/mpr_4256.html).

Finally, the Sprite brand only represents one association between the NBA and Sprite's parent company, Coca-Cola. Since 1986, Coca-Cola and the NBA have been global marketing partners. The partnership includes digital initiatives such as The Finals Real Time, which provides fans photo and text updates to their wireless phones, or iCoke China, which offers exclusive content to its members in China. It is important to point out that these digital initiatives are supported with traditional advertising and sponsorship. Coca-Cola was a sponsor of the NBA Europe Live presented by EA Sports in 2006 and 2007 that featured four NBA teams conducting training camp in Europe and playing exhibition games against European teams in seven cities. Coca-Cola and its Sprite brand also support NBA events in several countries including China, Germany, Mexico, and Canada and have advertisements that appear in NBA international telecasts in 215 countries and 46 languages (www.nba.com/news/coca-cola_060616.html).

VERIZON AND THE NFL

In March, 2010, Verizon Wireless became the official wireless service of the NFL with a four-year deal estimated at a total of $720 million. Verizon replaced Sprint who was paying the NFL approximately $120 million per year (Ourand & Lefton, 2010). Through this sponsorship agreement Verizon offers its customers exclusive NFL content. The simple hope for Verizon is that this exclusive content will help attract and retain customers.

Through this sponsorship agreement the available programming through select mobile phones includes live streaming of NBC's Sunday Night Football games and the games on the NFL Network, the NFL RedZone Channel, which airs live look-ins of every key play and touchdown from Sunday afternoon games, and the NFL Network Channel. Other features of NFL Mobile on Verizon Wireless include: live streaming of the NFL Draft, live audio broadcasts of every regular season and playoff game, game highlights and an extensive collection of on-demand video featuring analysis and inside access from NFL Network and NFL Films. NFL Mobile from Verizon also allows for personalization and customization of content, including team or player alerts, ringtones, graphics, and fantasy information and statistics (NFL press releases, March 22, 2010, http://www.nfl.com/news/author?id=09000d5d8142ac0e). John Stratton, executive vice president and chief marketing officer for Verizon Wireless, stated, "this is an agreement that has, at its core, a mutual desire by both the NFL and Verizon Wireless to provide consumers with what they want on and off the field." Brian Rolapp, NFL senior vice president of media strategy, commented, "our fans have an insatiable appetite for football, and we will be able to keep them connected wherever they are on game day, but also throughout the year" (NFL press releases, March 22, 2010, http://www.nfl.com/news/author?id=09000d5d8142ac0e).

The individual NFL teams are still able to make their own telecommunication deals with wireless providers, which could include other programming such as coaches' shows as content. Verizon has sponsorship deals with fifteen NFL teams (Ourand & Lefton, 2010).

AT&T AND THE MASTERS GOLF TOURNAMENT

The Masters is one of the four annual major golf tournaments along with the United States Open, British Open, and PGA Championship. In 2008, the Masters Golf Tournament had its first two rounds televised on ESPN and its final two rounds televised on CBS. Direct-TV also featured four separate channels free for its subscribers: one channel showed the ESPN or CBS feed, the second was a highlight channel showing continuous coverage of that day's golf action, the third channel featured the action taking place live at Amen Corner, the famed 11th, 12th, and 13th holes of Augusta National, and the fourth channel showed live coverage of the 15th and 16th holes. In its broadcasts on ESPN and CBS in 2008, the Masters Golf Tournament coverage once again featured its long-standing tradition of having 56 minutes of every hour showing golf action, with only four minutes reserved for commercials.

Another long-standing policy of the Masters is that it only has two or three sponsors to avoid any advertising clutter. AT&T was one of the primary sponsors of the 2008 Masters Golf Tournament along with ExxonMobil and IBM. Each sponsor has its logo present on the Masters website (www.masters.org) and clicking on the logo leads the visitor directly to that company's website. In 2008 the Masters offered the audience three ways to visually experience the tournament: television, personal computer, and wireless device.

In 2008 content involving the Masters Golf Tournament was available through many AT&T media platforms. In addition to the ESPN and CBS television coverage AT&T customers through AT&T U-verse TV, AT&T Broadband TV, AT&T Mobile, as well as visitors online to the AT&T blue room, www.attblueroom.com/sports/events/masters.php, were able to access daily highlights and player interviews, a live feed of the Par 3 contest on the Wednesday before the start of the tournament, Masters Extra, one hour of live golf action before CBS or ESPN began their coverage, Amen Corner Live, and live coverage of the 15th and 16th holes. AT&T blue room visitors could also watch archived Masters Moments, a series of 24 highlight packages that showed past Masters tournaments, and daily coverage of the Masters driving range. Dan York, AT&T Entertainment Services head of content and programming, commented, "consumers today crave connectivity. They want to be able to access great content no matter where they are. Through our agreement with the Masters, we're able to deliver even more iconic footage to more people in more places than ever before" (April 2, 2008, AT&T Press Release, www.attblueroom.com/pressreleases).

WISE FOODS AND THE BOSTON RED SOX (DAVID ORTIZ)

WISE FOODS AND THE NEW YORK METS (JOSE REYES)

Wise Foods Incorporated produces potato chips, cheese doodles, and an assortment of other snack foods and has its products available in 20 of the eastern United States and Washington D. C.. Wise Foods is an official sponsor of the Boston Red Sox and New York Mets and has signage on the outfield wall at both Fenway Park in Boston and Citi Field in New York. Wise Foods also has a sponsorship agreement with one of each teams' star players, David Ortiz of the Red Sox and Jose Reyes of the Mets. As an official sponsor of both the team and the players in this specific example, Ortiz and Reyes appear on Wise product packaging in their respective team's uniform (by contrast, while Pepsi and its Aquafina bottled water brand are official sponsors of the New York Mets, David Wright, Mets all-star third baseman, has his own sponsorship deal with Aquafina competitor, Vitamin Water. In any advertisements for Vitamin Water, Wright cannot be seen wearing a Mets hat or uniform, but rather a generic baseball uniform).

On the front of the Wise product packages that feature a photo of Ortiz or Reyes there is a website for each player: www.wisesnacksquad.com/ortiz or www.wisesnacksquad.com/reyes. At these respective websites fans learn about the Wise Snack Squad, a traveling promotional caravan that made 18 visits to different locations in both the Boston and New York area in May and June of 2008. The website provided the Wise Snack Squad location appearance schedule. For instance, the Wise Snack Squad appeared at the specific location from 12:00 p.m., to 6:00 p.m., and finding it in Boston could lead to winning prizes such as Red Sox tickets, a meet-and-greet with David Ortiz, watching batting practice on the field at Fenway Park, or a road trip to see the Red Sox play the Yankees in New York. Finding the Wise Snack Squad in the New York area could lead to winning prizes such as Mets tickets, a meet-and-greet with Jose Reyes that included watching him take batting practice, throwing out the first pitch at a Mets game before watching that day's game from a luxury suite with 14 friends, or a road trip to see the Mets play the Phillies in Philadelphia.

Each website for the respective player also featured a "Swing for the Fences Home Run Derby" game. After providing general customer information, fans can play the online home run derby game acting as either Ortiz or Reyes, depending on which player's Wise Snack Squad website they visited. The video game stadium featured the centerfield scoreboard with a large Wise Foods logo surrounded by stadium like signage of Wise Foods potato chip and cheese doodle packages. Fans who sign up for the home run derby game are also eligible to win similar prizes as those who found the Wise Snack Squad.

ESPN

Sponsors not only have the option of associating with leagues, teams, or players, but media outlets that cover sports and are a destination for the sports audience certainly become a fruitful opportunity for advertisers to reach a desired demographic and incorporate digital media strategies. While companies have their own websites, they are not as popular as the websites of these sports leagues, teams, or a media outlet that offer valuable communication vehicles for brand exposure. No sports media entity is more prominent than ESPN. According to a Brand Research Study by Keleman and Associates Inc., ESPN has 97 percent brand awareness, is the number one media brand in sports, and is the number four leading name in sports, trailing only the NFL, Nike, and the NBA (ESPN Sales Media Kit, www.espncms.com). An SRI Knowledge Networks survey found that over 102 million people use an ESPN property in an average week, with 57% of men and 81% of avid sports fans using ESPN media, and 25 percent of all media time consumed by avid sports fans with an ESPN property (ESPN Sales Media Kit, www.espncms.com). The mission statement for ESPN is "to serve sports fans whenever sports are watched, listened to, discussed, read about or played" (ESPN Sales Media Kit, www.espncms.com). Beginning with the television network in 1979, ESPN now features multiple television networks (ESPN2, ESPN Classic, ESPN News, ESPNU, and ESPN Deportes), ESPN the Magazine, ESPN Radio, and several Internet and mobile offerings. The ESPN brand also has 34 international networks and distributes programming to 194 countries in sixteen different languages.

The ESPN empire still begins with the flagship network which earns approximately $4.00 per month from cable operators for the right to make the network available to their customers on their cable systems (Ourand, 2009). ESPN has the broadcast rights to the NFL, NBA, Major League Baseball, early round coverage of the Masters and golf's U.S. Open, tennis tournaments (including coverage of all four majors: Wimbledon, U.S. Open, French Open, and, Australian Open), college football (including the Bowl Championship Series games starting in 2011), college basketball, the college baseball World Series, and the X Games.

ESPN Radio has 725 affiliates and 325 branded affiliates that generate over an average of 20 million listeners per week. Over 55 percent of all sports radio listeners listen to an ESPN affiliate (Arbitron Nationwide DMA, ESPN Sales Media Kit, www.espncms.com). Most prominent on the radio network is the *Mike and Mike in the Morning* program (with hosts Mike Greenberg and former NFL player Mike Golic) which is also simulcast on ESPN2 and interviews from the show are archived on the ESPN website. ESPN the Magazine has over 14.6 million readers with a median age of 31.8 and a media income of $65,471. The magazine has seen its audience grow 17 percent from Spring 2007 to Spring 2008, with an over 130,000 audience increase in the male 18 to 34 demographic (ESPN Sales Media Kit, www.espncms.com).

In its digital media offerings ESPN's online website, www.espn.com, averages over 20 million monthly unique visitors and now represents the largest community of online sports fans, leading Yahoo! Sports by approximately half-million users (Comscore Media Metrix, rolling two month average, ESPN Sales Media Kit, www.espncms.com). ESPN online ranked number one in male composition and in 2007 1.2 billion videos were served and ESPN Fantasy had 3.2 billion page views with an average of 2.7 million unique users and 58 minutes per use. Online advertising opportunities include in-page video presentation, sponsorship of event sites, polls or scoreboards, rich media between page views including in a full screen format, and affiliation with fantasy contests, such as the NCAA Men's college basketball "Tournament Challenge." ESPN online also features an ESPN Insider program where subscribers receive exclusive content and ESPN 360, which features live sports online with up to ten games being broadcast simultaneously and viewers having the ability to pause, fast-forward, or rewind action and replay games for up to 48 hours after the event. Finally, ESPN Mobile has six million unique users and is the number one sports mobile website. It allows for advertising opportunities such as banners, sponsored links, or sponsored polls. ESPN Podcast has over eight million monthly downloads, with sponsorship opportunities including lead-ins to ESPN programming such as *Best of Mike and Mike*, *Pardon the Interruption*, and *Around the Horn*.

Companies sponsor with ESPN in a variety of ways with many using an integrated approach to reaching the audience through many of its communication touch points, including ESPN digital media. Pontiac Game Changing Performance represented one example of how a sponsor can coordinate its activities with ESPN. In this sponsorship deal fans went online and viewed the nominated plays and voted for their favorite college football Game Changing Performance. The nominees each week were reviewed on ESPN's College Gameday Program (which incidentally is "Built by the Home Depot") by announcers Lee Corso and Kirk Herbstreit and fans were invited to log onto the website and vote for their favorite play (www.espn.com/pontiac). The school responsible for the play selected by the fans in that given week was awarded a contribution to its general scholarship fund. That play was then included in voting at the end of the season for the Pontiac Game Changing Performance of the Year, with the school selected receiving an even more substantial award from Pontiac for its general scholarship fund.

There are multiple contests that companies sponsor through the ESPN brand. On the ESPN website there is heading for a link to all the contests. One such contest was ESPN's The Road to TitleTown presented by Wendy's. In the spring of 2008 fans nominated cities across the United States and argued their championship credentials. Twenty finalists were chosen and ESPN's SportsCenter visited each of those cities during July. The highlight package of each city was broadcast during SportsCenter and featured footage of that cities teams championship moments and interviews with prominent athletes of the city explaining why their city was indeed TitleTown USA (i.e., Derek Jeter, Yankees all-star shortstop, in the New York segment and Tim Tebow, University of Florida 2007 Heisman Trophy winning quarterback, in the Gainesville, Florida segment). Voting fans were also eligible to win a grand prize of a trip to any TitleTown finalist city.

At the main website for this promotion (http://promo.espn.go.com/espn/contests/wendys/), Wendy's had banner advertisements that featured a display of hamburgers and the slogan "Wendy's fresh, never frozen beef is waaaay better." Wendy's also had a store locator and clicking on to its logo on the ESPN website brought the visitor directly to the Wendy's website (www.wendys.com). There was also a pull down menu where fans can learn about each TitleTown city as well as view that cities feature that was televised on SportsCenter.

SUMMARY

Examples presented throughout this chapter reveal how some companies are incorporating digital media into their advertising and sponsorship in the area of sports. In addition to brand exposure, the opportunity for exclusivity within a product category and developing an association with a popular sports property continue to make sponsorship a viable promotional communication strategy. It is also clear that combining these characteristics with the capabilities of digital media can create a more powerful brand/consumer interaction and relationship. However, it should be understood that digital media do not replace traditional forms of sports advertising and sponsorship, but rather represent additional opportunities for advertising and marketing personnel to pursue. There still needs to be an initial agreement between the company and the property because the usage of content and logos whose rights are initially held by the league, team, or event is not possible without an agreement with the sports property. AT&T does not get to distribute the Masters Golf Tournament content or Verizon offer NFL content through their various digital media platforms without being official sponsors of those properties. In each of these examples digital media are only one part of a larger, more comprehensive advertising strategy that includes promotion through other media vehicles, including broadcast commercials during the live televised game, as well as face-to-face interactions with the brand.

Once a sponsorship agreement is reached an integrated promotional communication approach can be established. Sponsors can then use all media vehicles to promote their brands and potentially better connect with their customers. Just as negotiation makes anything possible in a more traditional sponsorship, digital media advertising in sports is only limited by what the creative personnel can develop and the parameters of what can contractually be agreed upon between the sponsor and the sports property. These examples are but a mere sampling of the many interesting and unique strategies that advertisers are executing in the area of sports and digital media. Future research on the subject of sponsors' use of digital media in the area of sports will provide more examples of how companies are using this technology and incorporating it into their promotional communication strategies.

REFERENCES

Amato, C. H., Peters, C. L. O., & Shao, A. T. (2005). An exploratory investigation into NASCAR fan culture. *Sport Marketing Quarterly, 14*(2), 71–83.

Bellamy, R. V. Jr. (1998). The evolving television sports marketplace. In Wenner, L. A. (Ed.), *Mediasport* (pp. 73–87). London: Routledge.

Bellamy, R. V. Jr, & Traudt, P. J. (2000). Television branding as promotion. In Eastman, S. T. (Ed.), *Research in media promotion* (pp. 127–159). Mahwah, NJ: Lawrence Erlbaum Publishing.

Best, N. (2010, February 9). Super Bowl new king of TV. *New York Newsday*, A5.

Bianco, A. (2004, July 12). The vanishing mass market: New technology. Product proliferation. Fragmented media. Get ready: It's a whole new world. *Business Week*, 61-68.

Cornwell, T. B., & Maignan, I. (1998). An international review of sponsorship research. *Journal of Advertising*, *27*(1), 1–21.

Cornwell, T. B., Roy, D. P., & Steinard, E. A. (2001). Exploring manager's perceptions of the impact of sponsorship on brand equity. *Journal of Advertising*, *30*(2), 41–51.

Croft, M. (2006, April 20). Sports sponsorship; Biggest is not always the best. *Marketing Week*, 45.

Dean, D. H. (2002). Associating the corporation with a charitable event through sponsorship: Measuring the effects on corporate community relations. *Journal of Advertising*, *31*(4), 77–88.

DeFleur, M., & Dennis, E. E. (2002). *Understanding mass communication* (7th ed.). Boston, MA: Houghton Mifflin.

Fortunato, J. A. (2001). *The ultimate assist: The relationship and broadcast strategies of the NBA and television networks*. Cresskill, NJ: Hampton Press.

Fortunato, J. A. (2008). Using message content to communicate a brand association: Olympic television advertising. *Journal of Sponsorship*, *1*(3), 248–257.

Fortunato, J. A., & Dunnam, A. E. (2004). The negotiation philosophy for corporate sponsorship of sports properties. In Pitts, B. G. (Ed.), *Sharing best practices in sports marketing* (pp. 99–111). Morgantown, WV: Fitness Information Technology, Inc.

Fortunato, J. A., & Richards, J. (2007). Reconciling sports sponsorship exclusivity with antitrust law. *Texas Review of Entertainment & Sports Law*, *8*, 33–48.

Funk, D., & James, J. (2001). The psychological continuum model: A conceptual framework for understanding an individual's psychological connection to sport. *Sport Management Review*, *4*(2), 119–150. doi:10.1016/S1441-3523(01)70072-1

Grohs, R., & Reisinger, H. (2005). Image transfer in sports sponsorships: An assessment of moderating effects. *International Journal of Sports Marketing & Sponsorship*, *1*, 42–48.

Gwinner, K. P. (1997). A model of image creation and image transfer in event sponsorship. *International Marketing Review*, *14*(3), 145–158. doi:10.1108/02651339710170221

Gwinner, K. P., & Eaton, J. (1999). Building brand image through event sponsorship: The role of image transfer. *Journal of Advertising*, *28*(4), 47–58.

Harvey, B. (2001). Measuring the effects of sponsorship. *Journal of Advertising Research*, *41*(1), 59–65.

Irwin, R. L., Lachowetz, T., Cornwell, T. B., & Clark, J. S. (2003). Cause-related sport sponsorship: An assessment of spectator beliefs, attitudes, and behavioral intentions. *Sport Marketing Quarterly*, *12*(3), 131–139.

Kaplan, D., & Lefton, T. (2005, September 5-11). Molson Coors renewing with NFL. *Street & Smith's Sports Business Journal*, *8*(18), 59.

Kelley, S. W., & Turley, L. W. (2004). The effect of content on perceived affect of Super Bowl commercials. *Journal of Sport Management, 18*(4), 398–420.

Leckenby, J. D., & Stout, P. (1985). Conceptual and methodological issues in persuasion management. In Houston, M. J., & Lutz, R. J. (Eds.), *Marketing communication – Theory and research* (pp. 7–12). Chicago: American Marketing Association.

Lefton, T. (2005, October 3-9). T-Mobile gets $100m NBA connection. *Street & Smith's Sports Business Journal, 8*(22), 36.

Lombardo, J. (2006, April 17-23). Plan for global stores part of Adidas' NBA plans. *Street & Smith's Sports Business Journal, 9*(49), 8.

Madrigal, R. (2000). The influence of social alliances with sports teams on intentions to purchase corporate sponsors' products. *Journal of Advertising, 29*(4), 13–24.

Meenaghan, T. (1991). The role of sponsorship in the marketing communications mix. *International Journal of Advertising, 10*(1), 35–47.

Meenaghan, T. (2001). Understanding sponsorship effects. *Psychology and Marketing, 18*(2), 95–122. doi:10.1002/1520-6793(200102)18:2<95::AID-MAR1001>3.0.CO;2-H

Miyazaki, A. D., & Morgan, A. G. (2001). Assessing market value of event sponsoring: Corporate Olympic sponsorship. *Journal of Advertising Research, 41*(1), 9–15.

Mullin, B. J., Hardy, S., & Sutton, W. A. (2007). *Sport marketing* (3rd ed.). Champaign, IL: Human Kinetics.

O'Guinn, T. O., Allen, C. T., & Semenik, R. J. (2006). *Advertising & integrated brand promotion* (4th ed.). Mason, OH: Thomson.

Ourand, J. (2009, January 5-11). Focused on making the numbers work: ESPN, CBS outline how they expect to justify hefty rights fees for college content. *Street & Smith's Sports Business Journal, 11*(35), 15–19.

Ourand, J., & Lefton, T. (2010, March 15-21). Verizon-NFL deal: Convergence is here. *Street & Smith's Sports Business Journal, 12*(45), 1, 42.

Pedersen, P. M., Miloch, K. S., & Laucella, P. C. (2007). *Strategic sports communication*. Champaign, IL: Human Kinetics.

Pruitt, S. W., Cornwell, T. B., & Clark, J. M. (2004). The NASCAR phenomenon: Auto racing sponsorships and shareholder wealth. *Journal of Advertising Research, 44*(3), 281–296. doi:10.1017/S0021849904040279

Quester, P. G., & Thompson, B. (2001). Advertising and promotion leverage on arts sponsorship effectiveness. *Journal of Advertising Research, 41*(1), 33–47.

Savary, J. (2008). Advocacy marketing: Toyota's secrets for partnering with trendsetters to create passionate brand advocates. *Journal of Sponsorship, 1*(3), 211–224.

Shank, M. (2008). *Sports marketing: A strategic perspective* (4th ed.). Upper Saddle River, NJ: Pearson Prentice Hall.

Shaw, S., & Amis, J. (2001). Image & investment: Sponsorship and women's sport. *Journal of Sport Management, 15*(3), 219–246.

Shrimp, T. A. (2003). *Advertising, promotion. Integrated marketing communications*. Mason, OH: Thompson South-Western.

Sloan, L. R. (1989). The motives of sports fans. In Goldstein, J. H. (Ed.), *Sports, games, and play: Social and psychological viewpoints* (pp. 175–240). Hillsdale, NJ: Lawrence Erlbaum.

Smolianov, P., & Shilbury, D. (2005). Examining integrated advertising and sponsorship in corporate marketing through televised sport. *Sport Marketing Quarterly, 14*(4), 239–250.

Stipp, H., & Schiavone, N. P. (1996). Modeling the impact of Olympic sponsorship on corporate image. *Journal of Advertising Research, 36*(4), 22–28.

Stotlar, D. K. (2001). *Developing successful sport sponsorship plans*. Morgantown, WV: Fitness Information Technology.

Tellis, G. J. (2004). *Effective advertising: Understanding when, how, and why advertising works*. Thousand Oaks, CA: Sage Publications.

Thomaselli, R. (2004, August 9). No fun in games: Steroids, terrorists, election turn Olympics into trial for marketers. *Advertising Age*, 1.

Till, B. D., & Baack, D. W. (2005). Recall and persuasion: Does creative advertising matter? *Journal of Advertising, 34*(3), 47–57.

Till, B. D., & Shimp, T. A. (1998). Endorsers in advertising: The case of negative celebrity information. *Journal of Advertising, 27*(1), 67–82.

Tutko, T. A. (1989). Personality change in the American sport scene. In Goldstein, J. H. (Ed.), *Sports, games, and play: Social and psychological viewpoints* (pp. 111–127). Hillsdale, NJ: Erlbaum.

Ukman, L. (1996). *IEG's complete guide to sponsorship: Everything you need to know about sports, arts, event, entertainment and cause marketing*. Chicago, IL: IEG, Inc.

Underwood, R., Bond, E., & Baer, R. (2001). Building service brands via social identity: Lessons from the sports marketplace. *Journal of Marketing Theory & Practice*, 1-13.

Walliser, B. (2003). An international review of sponsorship research: extension and update. *International Journal of Advertising, 22*(1), 5–40.

Wann, D. L., Royalty, J., & Roberts, A. (2000). The self-presentation of sports fans: Investigating the importance of team identification and self-esteem. *Journal of Sport Behavior, 23*(2), 198–206.

Wenner, L. A. (1989). Media, sports, and society: The research agenda. In Wenner, L. A. (Ed.), *Media, sports, and society* (pp. 13–48). Newbury Park, CA: Sage.

Wenner, L. A., & Gantz, W. (1998). Watching sports on television: Audience experience, gender, fanship, and marriage. In Wenner, L. A. (Ed.), *Mediasport* (pp. 233–251). London: Routledge.

Zillmann, D., Bryant, J., & Sapolsky, B. S. (1989). Enjoyment from sports spectatorship. In Goldstein, J. H. (Ed.), *Sports, games, and play: Social and psychological viewpoints* (pp. 241–278). Hillsdale, NJ: Lawrence Erlbaum.

Chapter 26
Performance-Enhancing Media:
Virtual Advertising in Sports

Jon Mills
University of Alabama, USA

ABSTRACT

With the billions of dollars at stake in sport enterprises, it is not surprising that advertising permeates every facet of athletic competition as companies attempt to increase awareness of their products to the millions of sports fans around the world who continue to make it a multi-billion dollar industry. Today in sports, it seems that everything can be purchased, even "virtual space." For advertisers, however, the proliferation of exposure is not indicative of over-saturation, but rather presents a need for innovative ways to reach their target audiences. Like athletes who use intensive workouts and nutritional supplements, advertisers are looking for performance-enhancing broadcast options. Virtual advertising is a relatively new, performance-enhancing technique that can improve a company's competitive edge. Following an examination of mere exposure theory, this chapter will turn to a discussion of the benefits and opportunities of virtual advertising in sports events, and finally will explore the potential controversies and drawbacks surrounding virtual advertising technology.

INTRODUCTION

In the not too distant past, most fans viewed sports as pure and innocent entertainment. Though it was business, fans only briefly needed to contemplate the enterprising or financial side of sports when controversies arose, such as the Black Sox scandal, Robert Irsay's unexpected move of the Baltimore Colts to Indianapolis, and of course, Pete Rose's alleged sports gambling. Children collected baseball cards and autographs for their own pleasure, Babe Ruth promised to hit a home run for a sick child, and Lou Gehrig was the "luckiest man on earth." But today, sports generate billions of dollars and even the average fan is aware of the ramifications of finance and sports, from contract negotiations for players and coaches, to the cost for Super Bowl ads, and funding for new stadiums and bidding wars over naming rights.

DOI: 10.4018/978-1-60566-792-8.ch026

With the billions of dollars at stake in sport enterprises, it is not surprising that advertising permeates every facet of athletic competition as companies attempt to increase awareness of their products to the millions of sports fans around the world who continue to make it a multi-billion dollar industry. For instance, NBC paid $3.5 billion to hold broadcast rights for the Olympics from years 2000-2008, and paid another $2.2 billion for the broadcast rights from years 2010-2012. Furthermore, scoreboards, ticket stubs, cup holders, and victory parades are also utilized by advertisers to make their company or product name visible. On the field, Reebok paid the NFL millions of dollars for exclusive uniform rights for all NFL teams. High profile athletes, from Derek Jeter, Peyton Manning, and Tiger Woods are paid millions of dollars to wear certain clothing brands, use particular equipment, and be seen drinking specific beverages. In some ways, it appears that anything and everything is for sale. Bryant and Raney (2000) took note of this corporate-first identity that permeates today's sports broadcasts. Though they recognize the history and necessity of commerce in sports, they claim, "of late, however, the commercial skeleton has become the all-too-obtrusive epidermis of sports on the screen" (p. 159). Today in sports, it seems that everything can be purchased, even "virtual space."

For advertisers, however, the proliferation of ads is not indicative of over-saturation, but rather presents a need for innovative ways to reach their target audiences with their products better than their competition in order to break through the clutter. In fact, during the 2003 Marketing Forum, keynote speaker Philip Kotler, a professor of international marketing at Northwestern's Kellogg School of Management, claimed that television advertising no longer works (Abrahams, 2003). His indictment focused on television's antiquated traditional uses. One answer to this and other critiques is virtual advertising. Like athletes who use intensive workouts and nutritional supplements, advertisers are looking for performance-enhancing broadcast options.

Virtual advertising is a relatively new, performance-enhancing technique that can improve a company's competitive edge. Burgi (1997) defines virtual advertising as "real time video insertions into television broadcast" (p. 13). The ads appear to viewers at home as if they are part of the actual, physical event, yet they are only superimposed by computer imaging technology and not visible to event participants, and without disruption of the sports event (Deutsch, 2000). For instance, in Major League Baseball broadcasts, if a camera zooms in on a batter, it may look as if the wall behind him has a sign for a particular phone company on it, when in actuality, it is a blank green screen with digital images visible only to television viewers. The ads truly seem to appear naturally in the setting. When the player moves in front of the sign, the ad never loses its appearance or qualities that would lead the viewer to believe the sign is fabricated. However, a person actually attending the game will see just a blank wall behind home plate. In fact, the technology can be used on blank walls, as well as to cover existing advertisements, create the illusion of freestanding billboards, painted playing surfaces, and even pennants and flags that blow in the wind.

The technology, though now being used by prominent national networks, actually debuted in 1995. During a June 1995 Trenton Thunder minor league baseball game, Comcast Cablevision of New Jersey used the technology to display their logo on the wall behind home plate (Rubel, 1996). During the 1996 and 1997 seasons, both the San Diego Padres and the San Francisco Giants were the first major league teams to incorporate virtual advertising on a regional basis, and ESPN used the technology during its broadcast of their 1997 nationally televised baseball game between the New York Mets and the New York Yankees (Dickson, 1998). Sponsors included well-known companies like MasterCard and Pepsi, as well as an ad for the film *Armageddon*. Following the game and its showcase of this new technology, Bob Jeremiah, ESPN's Vice President of Special

Sales, claimed that sponsors were pleased with the advertisements, and that ESPN would continue to look for ways to use the technology, which they did. By the year 2000, Major League Baseball had committed to using virtual advertisements in at least twenty Sunday night games (Deutsch, 2000). By 2008, nearly all televised MLB games contain virtual advertisements.

These ads are now used in nearly every sport broadcast from baseball and football, to soccer and tennis, and its technology has been widely used during 2008 Summer Olympic Games in Beijing. What becomes part of sport consumers' consciousness as a virtual line in a football broadcast that allowed viewers at home to see the first down marker span the width of the field, has turned into a ubiquitous part of nearly every sports broadcast, from football markers and swimmers' names imposed on their lanes, to sponsored billboards and product placements that change throughout the event. Given the increasing use and acceptance of virtual technology, this chapter will identify key issues that have led to both the need for and adoption of virtual advertising in sports. To do so, Zajonc's (1968; 2001) mere exposure theory will be applied to this context and used to analyze the potential effectiveness of this new advertising technique. Following an examination of mere exposure, this chapter will turn to a discussion of the benefits and opportunities of virtual advertising in sports events, and finally will explore the potential controversies and drawbacks surrounding virtual advertising technology.

MERE EXPOSURE

Building upon a long line of research that demonstrates exposure to a stimulus increases positive feelings toward that stimulus, Zajonc (1968) presented his theory, now known as mere exposure or mere-repeated-exposure (see Bornstein, 1989). Zajonc explains the premise of the mere exposure by claiming that "repeated exposure of the individual to a stimulus is a sufficient condition for the enhancement of his attitude toward it" (p.1). In other words, if the simple and unimposing exposure of a stimulus is repeated, a familiarity is created with the stimulus; that familiarity is transferred to increased positive feelings. Interestingly, Zajonc argues that all that is needed to increase liking is familiarity; there is no need for positive reinforcement or an unconditioned stimulus.

Though the premise is simple, the implications are profound. In contrast to cognitive processing models of persuasion, such as the Elaboration Likelihood Model (Petty & Cacioppo, 1986, 1990), with mere exposure, there is no cognitive "skill" or process undertaken by the subject, nor is there an associated "message" attached to the simple exposure (Bargh, 2001). Further, for mere exposures to affect overall evaluation there is no motivation or purposive effort by the receiver of the repeated message, merely repeated exposure. This almost subliminal form of conditioning is accomplished without the subject's conscious effort of processing, while still generating potentially positive affects. Bornstein (1989) states that there have been numerous studies that show the effects of mere exposure are attained with the subjects being unaware of the stimuli. So, not only does exposure that is unaware to the subjects create the predicted results, more complex and detailed exposures may be less effective. Similarly, the effects from stimuli that are not clearly recognized by the subjects are substantially larger than those that are recognized by the subjects (Bornstein & D'Agostino, 1992; R.B. Zajonc, 2000). When trying to create positive attitudes toward stimuli via mere exposures, the more simple the exposure the more effective.

Bornstein and D'Agostino (1992) illustrated this effect of simple, unnoticed stimuli by examining subliminal stimuli as measured against more blatant stimuli. They showed that the subliminal stimuli fostered higher rankings of "liking" as opposed to the stimuli that was easily recognizable to the subjects. Here, the more obvious the stimulus, the resulting exposure effects were weaker than the less obvious stimulus. Within the relationship between exposure and potential positive attitudes toward the stimuli, mere exposure has a diverse and far reaching application to many contexts, including virtual advertising.

VIRTUAL ADVERTISING AND EXPOSURE

The implications for mere exposure is that advertisers are now choosing to promote their companies and products to the vast audiences attending to sports, who are spending billions of their dollars. When advertisers need to maximize their exposure to their audiences – quantity does matter. As Baker and his colleagues have argued, the amount of attention advertisers' brands get through being shown on television, mentioned as sponsors, advertisers, seen on banners, etc. will affect mere exposure's power through familiarity (Baker, 1999; Baker & Lutz, 1999). Virtual advertising that appears to exist as part of the program itself is one viable option. Applying Zajonc's (1968) work on mere exposure helps explain why this technology might be a powerful new force in advertising. Zajonc demonstrated that the more times a person was exposed to a stimulus, the higher the probability that the person gained a favorable attitude toward the stimulus. As Bornstein (1989) explains, "in short, familiarity leads to liking" (p. 265). Here, this familiarity results from repeated exposure.

Applying the idea of mere exposure within a sports context, one scholar looked at how mere exposure, through sponsorships rather than virtual advertisements, might affect sports fans' perceptions of a company. Bennett (1999) used Zajonc's work on mere exposure as a template to evaluate the effectiveness of particular soccer sponsorships in the U.K. He concluded that the mere exposure of sponsorship not only delivers when it comes to boosting brand awareness, it also gives consumers a sense, true or not, that the sponsor's products/services are used extensively, making them even more desirable. In the case of sponsorships, mere exposure worked. That the same positive relationship should hold true for mere exposure through virtual ads. If consumers consistently see virtual ads, particularly as part of the "scenery" of sports through placements on venue walls and playing surfaces, the exposure is operating to provide a sense of the product as an integral part of the sport itself.

This strategy has high potency potential in light of Bornstein and D'Agostino's (1992) findings discussed above which hold that simple messages can be the most effective means of achieving mere exposure. In virtual ads, the ad itself must stay simple and clean to keep from distracting from the event itself. Thus, the logo or simple visual image can be processed quite subliminally, an important aspect of mere exposure. If done well, then, virtual ads should be frequently shown, and be unobtrusive. In many ways, this defies long-time advertising strategies of becoming the most noticed ad in attempts to break through to the consumer. This technology clearly offers "quantity" as an alternative to "quality" if quality is defined as consciously attended to advertisements.

There is a significant body of evidence that supports the effects of mere exposure, yet for advertisers, the goal is not just to attain familiarity and positive affect, but also to influence buyer behavior. According to Baker (1999) positive affect in absence of buyer behavior is fairly useless in meeting advertisers' goals. Just because a marketing campaign may be memorable or have widespread appeal, if it does not drive sales, it should be rendered useless. Clearly, the goal of companies advertising their products is to obtain a positive change in attitude toward their product or service, ideally with the least amount of effort and financial cost. Baker (1999) asserts that though there are few studies that test mere exposure in advertising research (e.g. Janiszewski, 1993; Obermiller, 1985), that research does support the use of mere exposure in advertising. Importantly, existing studies support mere exposure's central claim that, "unconscious automatic effects of mere exposure are distinct from the deliberate inferences that individuals may make about the conscious familiarity created by advertising exposure" (Baker, 1999).

Extending the discussion of mere exposure in advertising, Baker (1999) posits three ways that mere exposure can affect buyer behavior. The first, brand familiarity, implies that mere exposure can help "relatively unknown brands" compete against one another or well-known brands to compete against one another. Then, if buyers' knowledge or familiarity of brand choices is equivalent, mere exposure can increase familiarity for the well-advertised product and ultimately make them the more familiar, ultimately purchased product.

Quality differentiation and the motivation to deliberate at the purchase point are the other two factors known to affect the effectiveness of mere exposure in advertising contexts (Greenwald & Clark, 1984). Quality differentiation is a factor that operates when competing brands are perceived to be equal in "objective characteristics." In other words, if two toothpastes have equal cavity-fighting protection and whitening ability, the brand the consumer is most familiar with, through mere exposure, will likely be purchased (Baker, 1999). Similarly, if motivation is low to deliberate between brands, familiarity through mere exposure can act as a "tie-breaker" (Baker, 1999; Baker & Lutz, 1999). And, while customers may find traditional advertisements distracting, Bennett and his colleagues (Bennett et al., 2006) found that viewers are not aversive to virtual ads. Specifically, they investigated attitudes toward virtual advertising versus commercial advertising during a sports broadcast. For example, when almost 200 participants watched a segment of a football game, they found that the virtual ads were less irritating and more credible than the traditional commercials. In sum, with all factors being equal, becoming part of the sport landscape through virtual advertising provides the exposure that companies and products need to give them a competitive edge of their own.

BENEFITS AND OPPORTUNITIES OF VIRTUAL ADVERTISING

Non-Broadcast Conducive Sports

First, historically, many sports have conformed to a television-friendly format. As Maidment (2006) notes, Olympic events, Wimbledon tennis championships, and other world class sporting events have tried to adjust their schedules to adapt to American television schedules, despite the difficulties the event timing may present for local audiences. Even baseball's night games have been indicted as pandering to television viewers rather than ticket holders (King, 2008). The adaptations are not actually for American television audiences, but for the advertisers who are targeting those audiences. It only makes sense that a larger audience is available to watch televised sporting events during prime time hours and on weekends, and therefore, those audiences can receive the messages and promotions of the advertisers.

In fact, as several scholars and reporters have noted, sports themselves have adapted rules of play for the benefit of broadcasting (Bennett et al., 2006, Levine, 2008, Maidment, 2006, Zhou, 2004). The National Football League plays four quarters with a halftime, including multiple time-outs allowed for each half. The National Basketball Association follows the same four-quarter, multiple time-out set-up. Many time-outs or time stoppages have even been built into the rules to allow for networks to air television commercials. Yes, television commercials have dictated rule changes for popular sports, which may even alter game strategy. Even the National Collegiate Athletic Association (NCAA) has altered when the clock stops during college football games to allow for maximum commercial opportunities, as requested by the media that air the games. As a result, the NCAA is now battling excessively lengthy games that are difficult for viewers who may not be able to commit three to four hours of viewing time. They are examining ways to shorten the game span. To do so, the number of commercial opportunities will not likely diminish, but new rule changes will limit the number of minutes, and thus plays, during each game. As noted by Levine (2008) "And since the real culprit – television stoppages – is unlike to ever fall in the NCAA's crosshairs, it is once again being suggested that the timing rules be altered." Thus, rather than challenge the authority of broadcasters and advertisers, the NCAA is likely to find other ways, such as rule changes, to shorten games. Television stoppages are not new, and the commercials generate revenue for the networks, and ultimately the universities, conferences, and the NCAA itself. This not only perpetuates colleges' and universities' dependence on this revenue and their desire to be televised, but commercial television's integral role in the success of these relationships.

Given this dependence, some sports have historically been shunned by network broadcasting, thus hurting the potential for those sports gaining exposure to wider audiences, and ultimately popularity. As noted by Bennett, Ferreira, Tsuji, Siders and Cianfrone (2006), without continuous and regimented breaks in action, sports like soccer and hockey have struggled to fit within the modern mold of advertising breaks. Thus, though many televised sports have even changed rules to allow for "television time-outs" that build-in stoppages for commercials, some sports do not allow for such advertising-friendly opportunities. In turn, this lack of coverage weakens advertisers' ability to tap those sports' fan base.

One important benefit of virtual advertising is that it has allowed sports to become more advertising-friendly, which will ultimately allow them to generate more television revenue for sponsors and organizers. With virtual advertising, these sports may get a new lease on life when it comes to the ability to be televised by major networks, and advertisers will have more ways of reaching fans of such sports. Maidment (2006) notes "the money television brings into professional sports transforms them from a one-off spectacle before paying customers at a specific place and time into a global business." Turner and Cusumano (2000) claim that there should be a great deal of interest in a technology that "can enhance the message to consumers, improve the targeting of messages, or slice through the advertising clutter" (p. 51). They assert that virtual technology guides ads to places they weren't before, like potato chip companies being able to advertise on the field during soccer matches, and beef companies can place their logos into bicycle races, like the Tour of Spain on the pavement, on the screens etc.

For instance, the Federation Internationale de Football Association (FIFA), international soccer's chief governing body, calls for two forty-five minute halves to be played during a match, where stoppages and interference are kept to a minimum. Here, virtual billboards can be part of the broadcast, and sponsor's logos can digitally become part of the playing field during the much-uninterrupted broadcast, allowing advertisers to become not merely part of a rare commercial break, but part of the event itself. In fact, according to Turner and Cusumano (2000), one of the advantages of virtual advertising is that advertisers "can have their logo or advertisement 'in camera' at all times, creating what they call "no wastage" (p. 52).

With this application, sports that are not strictly regimented and commercial-friendly become viable and welcomed options for commercial broadcasts. What many see as "niche" sports due to their lack of television success can potentially become as mainstream as professional football and baseball. Chowdhury, Finn, and Olsen (2007) assert that virtual advertising "is also suitable for particular types of programming, such as live sports programs that do not have natural breaks to accommodate advertising inserts" (p. 86). Though one of the United States' most triumphant moments in sports was the 1980 "Miracle on Ice" Olympic hockey team that won the gold medal, professional hockey has not enjoyed the same reverence. There seems to be a "seamless" border between the United States and Canada, where hockey is immensely popular, yet there is an world of difference between the commercial success of the National Hockey League and others major sports leagues. While professional baseball and football, as well as collegiate sports in the U.S. can be seen on every major broadcast network, including many cable networks, professional hockey has a broadcast contract with the Versus cable network, which was previously known as the Outdoor Life Network, with just a fraction of the commercial reach compared with the mammoths carrying the advertising-friendly sports. With virtual advertising, companies can place their ads on the glass, the backboards, the nets, or even on the ice. By doing so, hockey can become a "mainstream sport" for the media, despite the lack of regular commercial stoppages. And, interestingly, the virtual advertising technology itself is well-known to hockey viewers as the "glowing blue puck" that allowed viewers at home to better track the action on the ice (Sweet, 2003).

Unavoidable Advertisements

Second, as consumers are empowered with the ability to control their media consumption, specifically advertising, with the advent of TiVo and similar digital recording devices, advertisers need to examine ways of marketing themselves without being skipped or deleted. Consumers are in more control of their viewing preferences as ever before, with many outlets, including television, Internet and mobile, from which to view content. Many live sporting events are now available online, with limited or no advertisements. Paying for traditional and often expensive commercial spots can be wasteful if those commercials are ignored, deleted or not included in particular outlets. Virtual ads are part of the "actual" event, becoming part of the game, match or field itself.

Obviously the sporting event is the primary reason for the broadcast, where virtual ads are able to tap into the already-present viewers, utilizing a built-in audience. Therefore, while fans may choose to skip or delete ads, viewing the broadcast of the event requires exposure to the virtual advertisements. Chowdhury and colleagues (2007) examined viewers' ability to avoid exposure to advertisements. They claim that as consumer digital recording devices becomes more standard in households, the "technology threatens the business model of current television advertising, which is based on revenue generated from ad placements during breaks in programming " (p. 85). Here, virtual advertising combats any current digital fast-forwarding or deletion. In theory, with the diffusion of home digital recording, commercial breaks might become obsolete. Avoiding advertisements is "a robust behavioral phenomenon demonstrated by television viewers " (p. 85). One of the chief benefits of such devices is that they allow viewers to watch programs on their schedule, putting a premium on maximizing time and schedules. It is apparent that one thing consumers will try to reduce or eliminate during their busy lives is advertisements. With a move toward a more consumer-based interactive type of programming, the future potential of virtual advertising's ability to remain "zap proof" during programming is unrealized.

Market Segmentation Capabilities

Third, given the advances in digital broadcasting, advertisers will not need to advertise to non-relevant groups, as they would by airing advertisements that might not appeal to all of the audience, or by merely purchasing signage at a venue. Segmentation is critical; from national magazines with regional covers, to international video game companies, many marketers are utilizing this potential. Virtual ads can be targeted geographically to particular viewing audiences, using specifically crafted messages, and as the technology improves, the ability to reach more differentiated target audiences will increase (i.e. by race, gender, class, and other demographic variables). Viewers from New York and California watching the Yankees play the Dodgers could see totally different virtual ads, ones that are specific to their local team and location. In fact, during the 2007 World Series, MLB introduced this technology, feeding different virtual ads to Canada, Japan, Latin America and Mexico (PVI, 2007).

This is even more useful when broadcasts span not only different regions, but multiple countries and languages. As many sports continue to span across international borders, so too does its viewing audiences. Major League Baseball and the National Basketball Association have seen a tremendous influx of international players recently, thus creating a borderless audience, yet including many marketing challenges. If the needs and demands of these audiences are realized, the ability for virtual ads to specifically target these groups is extremely valuable. As Moorman et al. state (2007) "planners need additional weapons in the intensifying battle for consumers' attention" (p.132).

According to their website, CKE Restaurants has franchised over 3,000 fast food restaurants in the United States. However, all of their restaurants, though almost identical, do not go under the same name. They operate 1,000 restaurants in the western U.S. called Carl's Jr., and almost 2,000 restaurants in the Midwest and Southeast under the Hardee's name. If CKE had the ability to purchase a single advertisement during a national broadcast, yet with the different brands reaching the different regions simultaneously, virtual advertising's benefits become evident. The ability of organizations with multiple brands and products to reach very specific segments of their consumers would be valuable to many. Similarly, an auto manufacturer such as General Motors, who has many brands and has advertised during many sporting events via traditional means, could also benefit greatly. Convertibles might be more prevalent in warmer regions, where four-wheel drives might be a necessity for consumers in snowy conditions. Through virtual advertising, GM could focus specific products in specific regions during a single broadcast, making a much more efficient use of advertising revenue. The potential for marketers to utilize geographic, demographic and psychographic data when crafting advertising campaigns is immense. With every internet-connected computer containing a unique Internet protocol number, and home digital video recorders also being connected to the web, if the data on each computer or recorder is present, virtual advertising via the Internet and DVR systems could ultimately be customizable on a per-household basis (Deutsch, 2000).

Sony is offering virtual advertisements in its PlayStation 3, which includes sports games. A Sony spokesperson claims that certain games are played by certain types of people, which create opportunities for marketers to target these specific groups with specific messages (AFP, 2008). This supports the opportunities for marketers to reach specific groups with varying messages through virtual advertising. If Sony already knows the characteristics of its various consumers, their ability to craft specific messages allows for a much more efficient marketing strategy.

This ability to reach market segments not only allows marketers to maximize what they can advertise, but also exclude what they can't advertise. Until recently, marketers of liquor products in the U.S. have followed a 50-year self-imposed ban on television advertising of liquor. Cigarette broadcast advertising has been banned in the U.S. since 1971. Similar product advertising is also regulated in Europe. With regulations differing between countries, the ability to *not* include certain brands or products might have legal and regulatory ramifications as well.

Deutsch (2000) indicates that this issue is a universal problem that virtual advertising can help combat. Europe's Formula One auto racing organization has successfully used the technology to display tobacco ads in countries with tobacco-friendly advertising policies, yet omitted those ads from the broadcasts in countries where regulations on tobacco advertising are more stringent.

Dynamic and Interactive Virtual Advertisements

Fourth, virtual advertising benefits not just advertisers, but also media groups and viewers. As revenue for marketing is allocated, advertisers must compete for financial resources. Virtual advertising technology allows broadcast media to provide something other media cannot: animated, changing and dynamic ads. The messages can be changed throughout the coverage, and be adapted to fit the action (Bennett et al., 2006). In other words, virtual ads are not just snapshots, logos, or static pictures; they can be energetic, lively advertisements that move and change. For instance, a shoe company does not just have to put its logo on the electronic billboard, but instead, it can highlight the product spokespeople wearing the product, when those people are central to the game. For instance, when a star soccer player dribbles toward the goal, the shoe company can place his or her image on the field advertisement, and if a goal is scored, the advertisement could change to a celebratory or congratulatory ad. Similarly, a beverage company could show different players drinking their product depending on which team is on offense, or even by the team leading the game hence connecting their product with a winner.

The advertisement can also be instructional or educational, such as the digital caddy sponsored by FedEx in the Professional Golfers' Association (PGA) broadcasts (Thomaselli, 2004). The digital caddy used in PGA broadcasts shows viewers at home recaps of players' performance, including putting success and even provides insider tips on the course positions that would be most helpful for the golfers. According to Liberman (2004), this is not only helpful as a tool to learn the game and evaluate strategy as an armchair golfer, but as networks look for additional sources of advertising revenue without clutter, this provides a seamless and unobtrusive way to sell advertising space.

As the technology continues to develop, Bernstein (2002) states that PVI, an innovator in the virtual technology can "compete with other forms of advertising by making its virtual ads more dynamic, complete with animation, and perhaps some day, interactivity" (p.17) that would lead to viewers' ability to immediately interact with and respond to the ad through obtaining more information about the product, or even ordering the product simply by using the television's remote control. Bernstein calls the potential for interactivity through virtual advertising the industry's "savior in waiting" that will take viewing to the next level. For instance, in the future, if a PGA fan was watching the game, saw the virtual caddy and the ad placed by FedEx, he or she could instantly retrieve FedEx rates via the television screen (linked through the Internet), and even schedule a package pickup. David Stitt of PVI echoed the capabilities behind virtual advertising (Bernstein, 2002). He claimed that the value of the technology is not in the enhancement of a broadcast with features like a virtual first down marker, but in the full dynamic array of benefits to the advertisers. In most cases of advertising, exposure to a brand or product is futile if it does not result in increased revenue. As virtual advertising technology continues to expand, the direct link between advertising exposure and consumer behavior will be easily measurable.

The interactivity of ads can be further heightened by the use of computer and television "cookies" that can determine which ads are most appropriate for the particular viewer (Deutsch, 2000), and ultimately, some scholars predict that the customization of the ads via individual televisions, and demographics preferences is inevitable and beneficial for all parties: viewers see ads for product that interest them, advertisers concentrate their dollars on potential consumers, and media can sell multiple ads for the same virtual space.

Having a more direct relationship with a particular team, event or venue, can enable companies to reap the dynamicand intangible benefits of virtual advertising. With so many consumer products available being marketed through multiple outlets, advertisers need to "connect" with consumers more. In an interview with CNN, Jack Pitney, vice president of marketing for BMW of North America, claims that BMW tends to focus on consumers' psychographic characteristics versus their customary demographic data, like age, gender and location (2008). He claims this marketing strategy looks at a consumer's "mindset" and then BMW can target their different products in a way that resonates with consumers' emotions.

Ultimately, these different emotions and allegiances can be utilized via virtual advertising, tailoring specific products at different times to different groups. This type of targeting is becoming increasingly important for advertisers, as has been seen by the NFL's purchase of consumer viewing habits during the Super Bowl from TiVo. This information allows the NFL to more thoroughly explore its consumers' broadcast behaviors, and utilize that information with potential advertisers in mind (Miller, 2002). Though more primitive than individual targeting, it is clear that the need for segmentation and targeting appropriate audiences is critical, and virtual advertising technology allows marketers to pursue their goals in increasingly sophisticated ways.

CRITICISMS OF VIRTUAL ADVERTISING

In practice, some critics feel that there is no value in virtual advertising and that the entire practice takes away from the coverage of the sports, itself. They argue that sports, in general, are too commercial and this practice continues this problematic trend of consumerism in athletic events (Reich, 1996; Sherman, 2001). Reich asserts that virtual advertising creates negative value for everyone, including the viewers, purists, sponsors, advertisers and broadcasters. He compares virtual ads to the colorization of classic black and white movies, asserting that this technology tampers with "reality." Further, he claims that ultimately overall revenue will decrease as advertisers vie for position within the virtual event, and eschew traditional advertising. Virtual advertising can lead to contentious issues surrounding the authenticity and integrity of a venue or event surrounding a virtually-altered broadcast, or at the very least one seen as intrusive or distracting. Another concern involving the authenticity of an event is the ease at which unofficial sponsors are capable of ambushing corporate sponsorships. Here, the intricate relationships between teams, venues, broadcasters and marketers can be tested. For example, according to Cianfrone, Bennett, Siders, and Tsuji (2006) networks have the ability to replace actual stadium signs with electronic images. Since the networks do not receive revenue from venue signage, this allows them a new revenue stream. As discussed within the legal aspects surrounding sports, Deutsch (2000) indicates that team owners, venue owners, media conglomerates, and advertisers need to wrestle with difficult questions, such as whether virtual ads will supersede stadium signage, or whether advertisements imposed into stadium landscape will result in viewers confusing advertisers with sponsors (which can be significantly more costly), and how the virtual ads will potentially ambush the advertisements that occur in commercial breaks.

Further, addressing virtual advertisings role within media's control of sport reality, Arne Harris, the long-time producer and director of WGN's Chicago Cubs games, fielded complaints from station executives immediately following the introduction of virtual ads into televised Cubs games (Sherman, 2001). Station executives asserted that WGN was compromising the integrity of the broadcast and bringing into question whether the game was televised or "created," by the network. Relating this event to the capabilities of virtual advertising, the authenticity of the broadcast of sporting events can come into question. There is a potential for backlash, either against the event or advertised product if viewers feel they are being misled. Many venues are seen as sacred, and virtual ads have the capacity to "desecrate" the pristine nature and history of these venues.

Virtual advertising literally has the ability to re-write history as it allows for repeated mere exposure, as well as removed exposure. During the 2008 Summer Olympics, Visa, an official Olympic sponsor, ran a campaign titled "Go World." According to Visa's website, the campaign "Celebrated moments that exemplify the Olympic Games spirit." One commercial featured a British sprinter competing in the 400 meters at the 1992 Olympic Games in Barcelona. Derek Redmond injured himself during the race and attempted to limp the final stretch. Redmond's father appeared on the track and, arm in arm, helped his son across the finish line. The original visuals of this poignant moment included Redmond's father being dressed in Nike gear from head to toe. In Visa's updated commercial, Redmond's father appears to be dressed in all white, digitally removing the Nike slogans and logos that were actually there. Visa succeeded in re-writing a historic moment. This can lead to official sponsors of past teams or athletes losing their association in future digital representations and advertisements. There is also the potential to not only removing original products or messages, as Visa did, but to replace them with contemporary, updated images. For example, images of Mary Lou Retton and her 1984 gold medal performance could show her preparation routine to include listening to an iPod, which was not in existence at the time.

Fendrich (2001) not only objects to the change in the event for television viewers, but also claims "Sports events are mere fillers employed as a means to flash sponsors' names on the screen." He claims that all networks are guilty of catering too much to advertisers and that this has too much influence on the actual games being played. Fendrich is not alone in his concerns. Ferguson (2001), claims that media critics oppose the technology, and that the credibility of the broadcast is threatened; he quotes Derrick de Kerckhove, a culture and technology researcher at the University of Toronto, who refers to virtual advertising "electronic littering" (Ferguson, 2001). Even best-selling author Stephen King has weighed in on the ever-increasing advertising in sport, addressing concerns in an article he wrote titled "How TV Ruined Baseball" that appeared in *Entertainment Weekly* (2008). In his essay, he says, "'Sometimes you just want to say to the suits running America's pastime, 'Have you no shame? Is there nothing you won't sell? No disgrace you will not visit on this wonderful game in order to turn a buck?'" (p. 1). Thus, for many pundits and fans, sport has been too long lead by corporate objectives rather than fan appreciation, thus this new turn to virtual advertising represents one more encroachment on many peoples' opportunity for leisure activity and escape.

CONCLUSION

Recently, though not used as a product advertisement, the 2008 Olympics opening ceremony in Beijing came under scrutiny for using digital technology to enhance a fireworks display. The broadcast of the ceremony included what appeared to be 29 synchronized firework "footsteps," representing the previous 29 Olympiads. In actuality, these computer-generated effects were only seen by the television viewing audience. Many major news networks and wire services, including ESPN, MSNBC and the Associated Press, brought attention to the previously recorded digital fireworks that were broadcast as a live event, telling us they were fake and letting us in on the "secret." Yet, these same critics readily offer virtual space to advertisers within sporting events. This technology that allows companies to break through the clutter, create advertising space within the sporting event, and become part of the event itself, can also be used in other applications such as fireworks that are not seen in the sky, but on the monitor. Even today, we could see virtual billboards in a baseball broadcast for products where only sky exists in the actual terrain -- in essence, creating revenue out of thin air.

Virtual advertising is relatively new, but the need for advertisers to get their message into the minds of consumers is not. As we move from phone books to yellowpages.com, encyclopedias to Wikipedia, landlines to cell phones, and VCRs to DVRs, marketers and the media are looking for ways to expose consumers to their product, and to do so repeatedly and with the desired effect. As consumers become more media literate, they recognize that models are airbrushed, that product placement in movies are not accidental, that spokespeople are well-paid, and they are empowered to skip ads through channel surfing and digital editing. Research on mere exposure is clear: familiarity produces results. Thus, while literacy and savvy increases, and ability to elude traditional advertising improves, advertisers must continue to get their companies' messages in front of the consumers. Though critics may not like the practice of using virtual ads in sport events, it clear that the practice will only continue to evolve. Theoretically, better understanding the process and mechanisms of mere exposure, as well as the other relevant variables that teasing out the variables that influence the effects of the ads on consumers, will help advertisers make better choices for positioning their product and allocating their marketing budgets.

REFERENCES

Abrahams, G. (2003, October 16). TV fame loses out to drive for effectiveness. *Marketing Week*, 15.

Agence France-Press. (2008). *Sony says to put virtual ads in PlayStation 3 games*. Retrieved July 22, 2008 http://afp.google.com/article/ALeqM5h-B76UHrOp8aynie9lZxquyizoppg

Baker, W. E. (1999). When can affective conditioning and mere exposure directly influence brand choice? *Journal of Advertising*, *28*, 31–46.

Baker, W. E., & Lutz, J. (1999). The relevance-accessibility model of advertising effectiveness. In Hecker, S. H., & Stewart, D. W. (Eds.), *Nonverbal Communication in Advertising* (pp. 59–84). Lexington, MA: Lexington Books.

Bargh, J. A. (2001). The psychology of the mere. In Bargh, J. A., & Apsley, D. K. (Eds.), *Unraveling the Complexities of Social Life* (pp. 25–37). Washington, DC: American Psychology Association. doi:10.1037/10387-003

Bennett, G., Ferreira, M., Siders, R., Tsuji, Y., & Cianfrone, B. (2006, October). Analysing the effects of advertising type and antecedents on attitude towards advertising in sport. *International Journal of Sports Marketing & Sponsorship*, *8*(1), 62–81.

Bennett, R. (1999). Sports sponsorship, spectator recall and false consensus. *European Journal of Marketing*, *33*, 291–313. doi:10.1108/03090569910253071

Bernstein, A. (2002) Boom! TV advances could disappear –without funding, next wave of innovation might not even make it to screen. *Sports Business Journal*, 17.

Bornstein, R. F. (1989). Exposure and affect: Overview and meta-analysis of research, 1968-1987. *Psychological Bulletin*, *106*, 265–289. doi:10.1037/0033-2909.106.2.265

Bornstein, R. F., & D'Agostino, P. R. (1992). Stimulus recognition and the mere exposure effect. *Journal of Personality and Social Psychology*, *63*, 545. doi:10.1037/0022-3514.63.4.545

Bryant, J., & Raney, A. A. (2000). Sports on the screen. In Zillman, D., & Vorderer, P. (Eds.), *Media Entertainment: The Psychology of Its Appeal* (pp. 153–174). Mahwah, NJ: Lawrence Erlbaum.

Burgi, M. (1997, February 10). TV exec. sees virtual signs. *Mediaweek, 7*(6), 13.

Chowdhury, M. M., Finn, A., & Olsen, G. D. (2007). Investigating the simultaneous presentation of advertising and television programming. *Journal of Advertising, 36*, 85–96. doi:10.2753/JOA0091-3367360306

Cianfrone, B., Bennett, G., Siders, R., & Tsuji, Y. (2006). Virtual advertising and brand awareness. *International Journal of Sport Management and Marketing, 1*(4), 289–310.

Deutsch, A. (2000). Sports broadcasting and virtual adverstisng, Defining the limits of copyright law and the law of unfair competition. *Marquette Sports Law Review, 11*, 41–86.

Dickson, G. (1998). ESPN uses virtual ads for baseball. *Broadcasting & Cable, 128*, 49–50.

Fendrich, H. (2001, April 6). Has sports become filler for the ads? *Associated Press*.

Ferguson, R. (2001, January 10). New TV ads touch down on football field. *Toronto Star*, NEO1.

Greenwald, A. G., & Clark, L. (1984). Audience Involvement in Advertising: Four Levels. *The Journal of Consumer Research, 11*, 581–598. doi:10.1086/208994

Hoyer, W. D., & Brown, S. P. (1990). Effects of brand awareness on choice for a common, repeat purchase product. *The Journal of Consumer Research, 17*, 141–148. doi:10.1086/208544

Janiszewski, C. (1993). Preattentive mere exposure effects. *The Journal of Consumer Research, 20*, 376–392. doi:10.1086/209356

King, S. (2008, August 13). Stephen King: How TV ruined baseball. *Entertainment Weekly*. Retrieved August 13, 2008, from http://www.ew.com/ew/article/0,20218931,00.html

Levine, R. (2008, February 22). *NCAA Finds a Sensible Way To Speed Up Games in College Football.* Retrieved July 15, 2008, from http://www.nysun.com/sports/ncaa-finds-a-sensible-way-to-speed-up-games/71688/

Maidment, P. (2006, December 12). *This Game Is Brought To You By...* Retrieved June 4, 2008, from http://www.forbes.com/2006/12/10/sports-broadcasting-televisions-tech_cx_pm_games06_1212soccer.html

Miller. (2002, April 8). Sports yet to feel full power of new recorders. *Sports Business Journal*, 31.

Moorman, M., Neijens, P. C., & Smit, E. G. (2007). The effects of program involvement on commercial exposure and recall in a naturalistic setting. *Journal of Advertising, 36*, 121–148. doi:10.2753/JOA0091-3367360109

Obermiller, C. (1985). Varieties of mere exposure: The effects of processing style and repetition on affective responses. *The Journal of Consumer Research, 6*, 93–100.

Petty, R. E., & Cacioppo, J. T. (1986). *Communication and persuasion: Central and peripheral routes to attitude change*. New York: Springer-Verlag.

Petty, R. E., & Cacioppo, J. T. (1990). Involvement and persuasion: Tradition versus integration. *Psychological Bulletin, 107*, 367–374. doi:10.1037/0033-2909.107.3.367

Pitney, J. (2008, June 25). *CNN interview*. Retrieved July 15, 2008 from http://www.cnn.com/video/#/video/tech/2008/06/25/am.cho.bmw.ad.cnn?iref=videosearch

PVI launches multiple output system for virtual advertisements during MLB World Series, a technological first. (2007, October 25). *Business Wire*. Retrieved from http://findarticles.com/p/articles/mi_m0EIN/is_2007_Oct_25/ai_n27421866

Reich, R. (1996, November 4). Virtual ads a losing proposition. *Advertising Age*, *67*, 34.

Rubel, C. (1996, May 6). What you see on TV is not what you get at stadium. *Marketing News,* 3012.

Sherman, E. (2001, August 10). Where ads more than meet the eye technology only worsens intrusion. *Chicago Tribune,* 2.

Sweet, D. (2003, January 27). Duo making real progress creating virtual enhancements for sports viewers. *Sports Business Journal*, 22.

Thomaselli, R. (2004, January 12). Adams looks to link sponsors with sorts TV technology. *Advertising Age*, *75*(2), 34.

Turner, P., & Cusumano, S. (2000). Virtual advertising: legal implications for sport. *Sport Management Review*, *3*, 47–70. doi:10.1016/S1441-3523(00)70079-9

Wolinsky, H. (2003, July 15). Sportsvision an All-Star in sports communications. *Chicago Sun-Times,* 45.

Zajonc, R. B. (1968). Attitudinal Effects of Mere Exposure. *Journal of Personality and Social Psychology*, *9*(2), 1–27. doi:10.1037/h0025848

Zajonc, R. B. (2000). Feeling and thinking: Closing the debate over the independence of affect. In Forgas, J. P. (Ed.), *Feeling and thinking: The role of affect in social cognition Studies in emotion and social interaction, second series* (pp. 31–58). Cambridge, UK: Cambridge University Press.

Zajonc, R. B. (2001). Mere exposure: A gateway to the subliminal. *Current Directions in Psychological Science*, *10*, 224–228. doi:10.1111/1467-8721.00154

Zhou, W. (2004). The choice of commercial breaks in television programs: the number, length and timing. *The Journal of Industrial Economics*, *22*(3), 315–326. doi:10.1111/j.0022-1821.2004.00228.x

Chapter 27
Adonis or Atrocious: Spokesavatars and Source Effects in Immersive Digital Environments

Natalie T. Wood
Saint Joseph's University, USA

Michael R. Solomon
Saint Joseph's University, USA

ABSTRACT

A virtual world is an online representation of real world people, products, and brands in a computer-mediated environment (CME). Within the next few years CMEs are likely to emerge as the dominant internet interface. In addition to corporate websites, companies will operate virtual stores where customers can browse and interact with assistants. However, due to the newness of the medium advertisers still struggle to figure out the best way to talk to consumers in these environments–or to decide if they should enter them at all. In this chapter, the authors look at the role of avatars (digital spokes characters) as sources of in-world marketing communications. The authors discuss conceptual issues such as how an avatar's appearance and the ability of the visitor to customize this appearance may influence consumer attitudes and behavior and how conversations with other avatars can serve as a potentially valuable starting point for buzz-building and word of-mouth marketing campaigns. They conclude with some specific suggestions based upon "lessons learned" regarding issues advertisers need to consider when choosing a spokesavatar to communicate with residents of virtual worlds.

WELCOME TO THE METAVERSE

From *Second Life* to *World of Warcraft*, to MTV's *Virtual Pimp My Ride*, millions of consumers live a parallel life in a digital reality. A *virtual world* is an online representation of real world people, products, and brands in a computer-mediated environment (CME). To many mainstream consumers and advertisers, this is largely an unknown or underground phenomenon–but it has real marketing consequences.

DOI: 10.4018/978-1-60566-792-8.ch027

In mid-2007, Charles River Ventures proclaimed that the virtual goods market was worth approximately $1.5 billion and growing rapidly. With more than 150 of these immersive 3D environments now live or currently in development, the number of consumers who come into contact with virtual goods as they navigate these worlds is projected to rise rapidly ("150+ Youth-Oriented" 2008). Indeed, according to one estimate by 2012, 53 percent of kids and 80 percent of active internet users will be members of at least one virtual world ("Kids" 2007, "Virtual Great Enters" 2008).

Clearly virtual environments will be pivotal in fueling new consumer trends over the next decade. McKinsey predicts that "Virtual worlds such as *Second Life* will become an indispensible business tool and vital to the strategy of any company intent on reaching out to the video-game generation" (Richards 2008). *Harvard Business Review* predicts that within the next five years virtual environments are likely to emerge as the dominant internet interface. In addition to corporate websites, companies will operate virtual stores where customers can browse and interact with assistants (Sarvary 2008). To date numerous companies including IBM, GE and Toyota have created CME's for internal and external applications. Eventually, these CME forums may rival traditional, marketer-sponsored e-commerce sites in terms of their influence on consumer decision making and product adoption.

However, due to the newness of the medium advertisers still struggle to figure out the best way to talk to consumers in these environments–or to decide if they should enter them at all. Ironically, this challenge is compounded by the unparalleled latitude both advertisers and consumers possess in these environments to assume virtually (pun intended) any physical form they wish. How will our understanding of *source effects* apply to advertising contexts where a company spokesperson whose *avatar* (or digital representation) is a fiery dragon, a sultry siren, or both at once? How does that company relate to a consumer whose avatar resembles George Bush, a furry creature, or a superhero? Welcome to the wild and wooly world of advertising in virtual worlds.

The influential cyberpunk novel *Snow Crash* by author Neal Stephenson envisioned a virtual world as a successor to the Internet called the *Metaverse*, where everyday people take on glamorous identities in a 3D immersive digital world. The book's main character delivers pizza in RL (real life), but in the Metaverse he is a warrior prince and champion sword fighter (Stephenson 1992). The hugely popular *Matrix* movie trilogy paints a similar (though more sinister) picture of a world that blurs the lines between physical and digital reality.

Today these fictional depictions are coming to life as we witness the tremendous growth of real-time, interactive virtual worlds that allow people to assume **virtual identities** in cyberspace. On these sites, people assume visual identities or avatars ranging from realistic versions of themselves to tricked-out versions with "exaggerated" physical characteristics, or from winged dragons to superheroes. Researchers are just starting to investigate how these online selves will influence consumer behavior and how the identities we choose in CMEs relate to our RL (or "meat world") identities.

Why should advertisers care about a bunch of digital die-hards? Why shouldn't they? After all, they often obsess over the precise appearance of a spokesperson–whether a celebrity, fashion model or "(wo)man-on-the street" because they understand the potency of source effects: Often who says it is just as important as what they say. Indeed a vast corpus of literature dating back at least 50 years attests to the importance of this communications variable (for a detailed review see Joseph 1982).

However, we see little evidence that anything approaching this level of care operates in virtual world environments–even though many advertisers are starting to recognize the potential promotional power of these emerging media formats. So far, anything goes–the virtual platform is so new and the permutations of appearance so vast–that most marketers are still at the early stage of debating just what they should say or do. Worrying about the proper vehicles to deliver this content has yet to appear on the strategic radar. In this chapter, we try to put the question on this radar where it belongs: We look specifically at the role of avatars as sources of in-world marketing communications. We begin with a general discussion of the characteristics of virtual environments and of the avatars that inhabit them. From there we discuss conceptual issues such as how an avatar's appearance and the ability of the visitor to customize this appearance may influence consumer attitudes and behavior and how conversations with other avatars can serve as a potentially valuable starting point for buzz-building and word of-mouth marketing campaigns. We conclude with some specific suggestions based upon "lessons learned" regarding issues advertisers need to consider when they choose a spokesavatar to communicate with residents of virtual worlds.

A New Media Platform

Today's consumers–both young and old–are part and parcel of the new age of advertising that heralds a shift of power from producer to consumer of commercial messages; they are energetic progenitors of consumer-generated content and interact extensively with the brands and organizations that successfully capture their attention. They are equally aloof or even vindictive to those brands that don't. Whereas social networking sites (e.g. MySpace and Facebook) currently receive the majority of attention, some analysts predict that virtual worlds eventually will replace or subsume these platforms (Nowak 2008).

Within the first 6 months of 2008, investors poured $345 million into the virtual worlds space ("$345 Mill" 2008) and within the next 10 years analysts project that 22% of global broadband users will register with at least one virtual world (Gilbert 2008). Eager to join (and market to) the flood of consumers creating virtual lives, many companies have staked their claim in one or more CMEs. A few intrepid advertisers first dipped a toe into this water when they placed their brands in video games and the *advergaming* platform began to form. Game developers driven by a desire to leverage additional revenue joined forces with marketers equally eager to explore new territories in a cluttered media landscape as they incorporated branded products both as props and as part of a game's storyline. The reaction from players has been generally positive; gamers are usually receptive to brand placement because they feel that it adds realism to the game (Nelson 2002). Some mainstream advertisers such as Burger King now take advergaming to the next level as they create *purpose-built advergames*. These use the advertiser's branded mascots, themes, and venues to make the brand a key element of the game (Hyman 2007).

Buoyed by the initial success of advergaming, numerous companies turned their attention to the nascent virtual worlds industry. Unfortunately, many of these efforts failed to live up to expectations and we've been subjected to a slew of negative press. Virtual worlds are a fad, these naysayers claim. Gartner estimates that upwards of 90% of virtual worlds that businesses launch will fail, most within the first 18 months. Yet their analysts also predict that 70 percent of organizations will establish their own private virtual worlds by 2012 (Cavall 2008), which suggests that the *Metaverse* still holds great potential. Despite the number of failures, there are many examples of success including campaigns by Cosmo Girl and Toyota Scion in *There.com* and Nike and Colgate in *Second Life*.

Avatars are Different

The majority of CMEs are 3-D and employ sophisticated computer graphics to produce photorealistic images. Furthermore, unlike many other web environments such as social networking sites individuals enter the world in the form of a a digital persona that they create themselves. These avatars have the ability to walk, fly, teleport, try on clothes, try out products, attend in-world events (educational classes, concerts, political speeches, etc.) and they interact in real time (via textchat, IM and VoIP) with other avatars around the world. This unprecidented level of interactivity facilities consumers' engagement and often creates a *flow state* - a mental state in which the user becomes so immersed and involved in what he is doing that he loses all sense of time and space (Csikszentmihalyi 1991).

Individuals fully immersed in these environments feel a greater sense of social presence than do individuals who visit as casual tourists (Blascovich et al 2002; Schroeder 2002; Slater, Sadagic, Usoh & Schroeder 2000; Short, Williams & Christie 1976). An important part of the in-world experience that facilitates immersion is the avatar the user creates to navigate the space and interact with others. Understanding how to use this space as a marketing and advertising tool first requires an understanding of the role and influence of avatars.

Avatars: Digital Personas

Research on the use of avatars in e-tailing settings tells us that these digital characters vary in function (decorative or proactive), action (animated or motionless), representation (photograph or illustration) and classification (an image of the actual user, a typical person or an idealized image of a model or celebrity) (Wood, Solomon & Englis 2005).

Researchers agree that interacting with avatars may deliver positive benefits to online shoppers (Wood, Solomon & Englis 2005, 2008; Holzwarth, Janiszewski & Neumann 2006; Keeling, Beatty, McGoldrick and Macaulay 2004; Keeling, McGoldrick & Beatty 2006) and that the "right" avatar can help to build trust in the e-tailer (McGoldrick, Keeling & Beatty 2008) and lead to greater levels of satisfaction, confidence and intention to purchase as well as a more positive evaluation of the site's information and entertainment value (Wood et al 2008; Holzwarth et al 2006). Nevertheless, this facilitation is selective; just as is the case with spokespeople in other advertising contexts, an inappropriate avatar can alienate customers (Keeling et al 2004; McBreen et al 2000). This assertion begs the question: Just what makes an avatar effective or appropriate?

Wood, Solomon and Englis (2005) contend that preference for avatar type varies by product category. They found that when respondents shop for appearance-related products (apparel and accessories) they prefer to interact with avatars that depict photographic, idealized images of everyday people and especially celebrities. Malter, Rosa and Garbarino (2008) reported that when users have the ability to try products (e.g. clothing) on an avatar they personally create they express greater confidence in their product evaluations. A user's ability to create an avatar in her own image (whether real or ideal) is one of the unique features of virtual worlds. This feature creates both opportunities and challenges for marketers.

In an effort to understand how avatar appearance influences consumer behavior, Yee (2007) undertook a series of studies in which he manipulated avatar appearance and measured the impact it had on subjects' behavior both in the virtual and the real world. Findings revealed that an individual's virtual appearance (avatar) can have a significant impact in both realms. More specifically, he found that those individuals assigned an attractive avatar are friendlier to virtual strangers than those who were given an unattractive avatar. Individuals assigned taller avatars are more confident and aggressive in virtual world negotiations that those with shorter avatars. Furthermore these changes in behavior are not only observed during the virtual interaction but also outside of the virtual enivonment. In ther words, the physical appearance of the avatar that an individual utilizes to interact with others can impact behavior in the virtual and the real world (Yee 2007). As a result advertisers needs to think carefully about the consumers' avatar with which they interact with in the virtual world as well as the appearance of the avatar/s they employ to communicate with potential customers. The following section addresses these issues.

WHO IS "THERE" IN A VIRTUAL WORLD?

The Avatar as "Self" or "Other"

In the real world, an advertiser can be reasonably sure about just who is the recipient of a persuasive communication[1]. But in virtual worlds individuals are free to experiment with different identities and it is not uncommon for them to have more than one avatar. For example, some people have one avatar that they use for work-related activites and another they use to cruise nightclubs. They can alter their appearance, age, gender or even choose to take on a nonhuman form. They may experiment with personas that are far from their real self, so it can be problematic to infer the true identity of an avatar using traditional visual cues. We may think that we are speaking to a 35-year-old male engineer from Manchester, UK when in reality we are really speaking with a 52-year-old female hair stylist from Manitoba. Advertisers are often left to ponder a Zen-like question: "To whom do we market–the avatar or the "real" person?"

The answer depends largely on the virtual world in question. Reports indicate that in some youth oriented virtual worlds such as *WeeWorld* at least 50 percent of users chat with their real-life friends as their real selves. In contrast, residents in adult-based worlds such as *Second Life* are more likely to use alternative personas (Broitman & Tatar 2008). Whereas for some advertisers this may present a quandary–"how do I determine who is the person behind the persona so I can develop the appropriate messaging?"–some analysts respond that it really does not matter. Regardless of their otherworldly appearance, virtual world residents are often more "virtually" honest than they are in the real world so social desirability biases may in fact diminish (Broitman & Tatar 2008). Residents can express their aspirational selves in a relatively risk-free and anonymous environment, so they may be provide advertisers with a unique insight into their "true" desires.

Spokesavatars

The selection of an appropriate source is central to the marketing communication process, but the choice is a complex one. Advertisers face the challenge to select a source that not only is credible and attractive, but also someone with whom the target audience can identify. *Source credibility*- the extent to which the communicator/source possesses positive characteristics influencing the degree to which the receiver will accept the message, has long been deemed a crucial variable in source selection (Ohanian 1990; Dholakia & Sternthal 1977; Hovland & Weiss 1951).

An abundance of prior research reports that physical attractiveness is a vital cue in this important process of person perception (Kahle & Homer 1985; Baker & Churchill 1977). In traditional advertising, a number of studies conclude that attractive sources are more likely to have a positive impact on the products they advocate and that an increase in the level of perceived attractiveness facilitates positive attitude change (Ohanian 1990; Kahle & Homer 1985; Joseph 1982).

Identification with the source is another mediating variable. The more in common the receiver has with the source the greater the persuasiveness of the message. Identification in this case includes factors such as attitudes, opinions, activities, background, and lifestyle (O'Mahony & Meenaghan 1998). This raises two questions: 1. "Can an avatar be credible, attractive and be represented in a way in which a consumer can identify with it? And, 2. "Can an avatar be persuasive enough to change attitudes and influence decision making?"

As an example, consider the avatars in Figure 1: Are they all equally persuasive? Can a nonhuman or character based avatar be just a persuasive as a realistic human one?\

Figure 1. Sample avatars

Spokescharacters (whether humans, drawings or animations) have been successfully used in advertising since the late 1800's. Traditionally, they were associated with low involvement products such as food items (e.g. Pillsbury Doughboy) and cleaning supplies (e.g. Mr. Clean) but today advertisers employ them to pitch high-involvement purchases such as insurance as well (e.g. The Geico Gecko). The effectiveness of characters is well documented (e.g. Shimp 2003; Fournier 1998) many researchers believe that characters improve brand recognition but also play a significant role to create a strong brand personality (Phillips 1996; Mizerski 1995).

The Disney Corporation in particular exhibits an uncanny knack for creating animated personas that are physical attractive and even (dare we say it?) sexy. Its cast of comely characters includes Jessica Rabbit (Who Framed Roger Rabbit?), Jane (Tarzan), Jasmine (Aladdin), and Ariel (The Little Mermaid). As animation technology has advanced characters have become more human in appearance to the extent that today it is sometimes difficult to determine if the character we are viewing is real or fake. Some of these animated characters are arguably more beautiful than real models. For instance, in 2001 a computer-generated character named Aki Ross from the movie *Final Fantasy* edged out dozens of real life models for the coveted position of cover girl in *Maxim*'s ''Hot 100" supplement. More recently, an art show of portraits of the thirteen most beautiful avatars toured both the real and the virtual world. As our exposure to animated characters in a variety of settings (e.g. entertainment, advertising, product packaging, communications etc) increases so too may our willingness to view them as appropriate sources of information.

As a facilitator of persuasion, avatar attractiveness is what Petty and Cacioppo (1986) classify as a peripheral cue in their Elaboration Likelihood Model (ELM). The ELM contends that those factors that facilitate persuasion vary under different levels of involvement (high versus low). In their research, Petty and Cacioppo (1986) characterize involvement as the extent to which an individual is motivated and able to process all of the details linked with making a decision or gathering information to make decision-making easier. If involvement is high, the consumer will listen carefully to and evaluate the information presented to research a decision (central route). On the other hand, if the involvement is low and he has neither the motivation nor the ability to engage in a detailed evaluation, persuasion emanates from the peripheral route. In this case, non-informational factors such as source attractiveness mediate source persuasion. Prior research provides evidence of spokescharacters' effectiveness when there is a logical fit with the advertised product (cf. Garretson & Burton 2005; Sengupta, Goodstein & Boninger 1997; Miniard et al 1991).

Avatar Match-Up and Brand Personality

Ads transmitted on broadcast media present the same image to an entire audience. In contrast, an advertiser can modify direct or interactive messages for different purchasing contexts or even individual users. Virtual worlds have the potential to take message customization even farther because (at least in theory) they actually allow the recipient to design the source. Wood et al (2005, p.148) pose the question "Is it possible to have a match-up between source and the consumer that will yield similar or even better results than a match-up between the source and the product?" Their research revealed that in online shopping scenarios people do not always respond in a similar fashion to the same avatar. So, what if we instead match the communication source to each user's preferences?

As with other types of consumer-generated media, one of the downsides of handing the asylum over to the inmates (i.e. giving consumers control over a brand's imagery) is that the sources consumers choose may not be consistent with the brand personality a sponsor hopes to communicate. What if the user decides a message source for (say) a financial services ad should take the form of a fire-breathing gremlin wielding a bayonet? What if the female avatar who urges you to try a new fragrance looks like a cross between Carmen Electra and Paris Hilton? How do these images impact consumers' perceptions of the brand's personality that companies have potentially spend millions of dollars to create?

Aaker defines *brand personality* as "…the set of human characteristics associated with a brand" (1997, p.347). In virtual worlds an avatar is the virtual DNA of a brand; "…an icon that can move, morph or otherwise operate freely as the brand's alter ego" (Neumeier 2003). Whereas numerous researchers have examined the dynamics of brand personality in offline communications platforms such as print advertisements (cf. Aitken, Leathar, O'Hagan & Squair 1987; Ang & Lim 2006), virtually no research informs us as to how and if these findings apply in the virtual world. A recent study by Wood and Solomon (2008) extended the match-up hypothesis to the realm of avatar endorsers. This perspective predicts that a source's effectiveness is mediated by the congruence between its' perceived attributes and those of the advertised product (Kamins 1990; Solomon, Ashmore & Longo 1992). This study examined how avatar-based advertising influences consumers' perception, attitude and behavior toward the brand in online promotional contexts. They found scattered support for the match-up hypothesis; this effect appears overall to be more robust for new brands that have yet to establish a firm brand personality as opposed to established brands where the existing image swamps the effect.

Avatar and Group Dynamics

For many virtual world users the primary motivation to spend time in-world is to interact with other people. Many virtual world relationships and interactions mimic those we find in the physical world. Avatars form friendships with other avatars, they discuss real life problems, they argue, they go on virtual dates; some even get married (and divorced), purchase virtual real estate and mourn the death of another without ever meeting in the real world. Therefore it is reasonable to assume that not unlike what we experience in the real world, the dynamics of social influence that are so well-documented in physical contexts–especially those related to conformity and social contagion -- transfer to virtual group relationships as well. Furthermore, just as in the real world the ability to interact with others may lead to an increase in risk-taking behavior in virtual worlds. Individuals may feel more confident to try out new experiences, engage with different products, and experiment more freely when they are in others' company.

These effects may also extend to in-world purchasing. For instance, the retailer Lands' End introduced a "Shop with a Friend" a feature that enables people in different geographic locations to shop together online (Leavitt 2004). This innovative (but woefully understudied) application highlights the potential of immersive technology to impact on both the type and volume of purchases. If individuals have the ability to not only shop together in virtual worlds but also to try items on their avatars to see how they look, there is real potential to spur sales of not only virtual but also real life items such as apparel, fashion accessories, cosmetics, and home furnishings. Today for example, people who play The Sims can import actual pieces of furniture from IKEA into their virtual homes; the use of this sort of platform to accelerate purchases for real homes is unplowed ground.

STRATEGIC ASPECTS OF SPOKESAVATAR SELECTION

In Figure 2, we adapt Wood et al's (2005) typology of avatars for e-tailing to incorporate additional elements applicable to virtual worlds. The model highlights the choices advertisers have available when they select a virtual spokescharacter. The Figure indicates that there are six questions the advertiser should answer during this process:

1. *Function*: Is the avatar going to be merely a prop to display a product such as in traditional advertising or is it going to be proactive and interact with consumers as would a sales or customer service representative?

Figure 2. An avatar typology

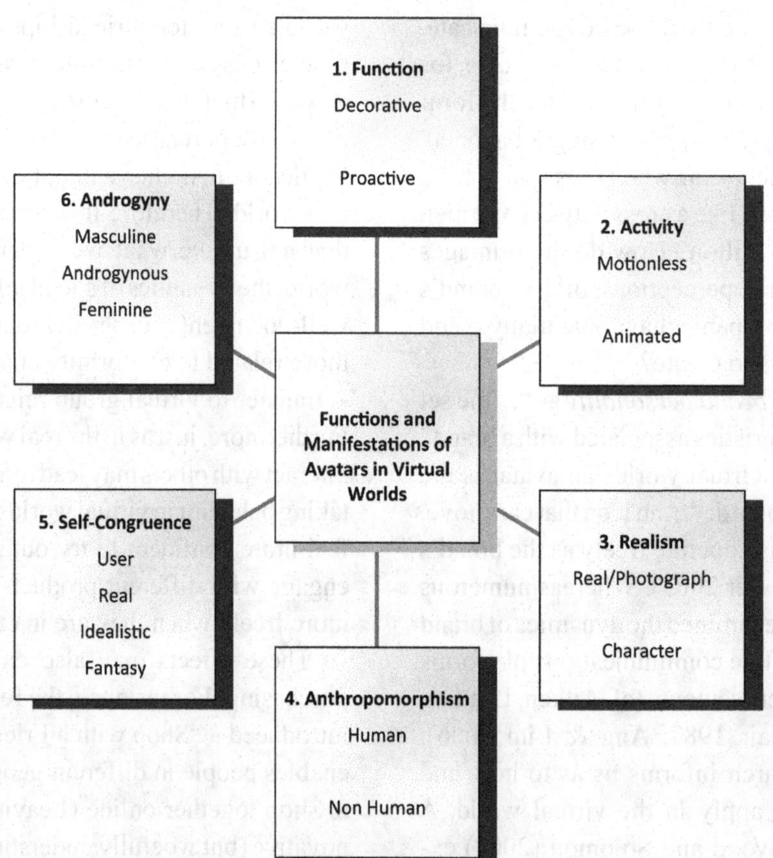

2. *Activity*: How animated does the avatar need to be? While motionless avatars may be acceptable in displays and static advertisements (such as billboards), they may not be as successful in customer interactions. In addition, movement may be desirable to attract attention in a cluttered media environment or perhaps even as a way to demonstrate a product in use.
3. *Realism*: Should the avatar appear realistic (e.g. Aki Ross–*Final Fantasy*) more like a character (e.g. Betty Boop) or somewhere in between (e.g. Princess Fiona–*Shrek*). The choice of avatar may be a function of a number of factors including target market and product category. For instance, younger consumers may respond more favorably to a character whereas adults may be drawn to a more realistic avatar. Realistic avatars may also be more appropriate for apparel and cosmetics whereas characters or hybrid avatars may be more suited for toys and other forms of entertainment.
4. *Anthropomorphism*: Should the avatar resemble a human form or something else? In deciding this, advertisers need to consider the probability that consumers will be able to identify with, and respond favorably to the image presented. Similar to the previous decision the choice here is likely a function of target audience and product category, but also the virtual world in question; non-human avatars are extremely popular and common in worlds such as *Second Life*, but are nonexistent in others (e.g. There.com, *Gaia Online*).
5. *Self-congruence*: Should the avatar mirror the user's own appearance, should it depict another real/typical person, or should it take the form of an idealized image or a fantasy figure? For instance, when shopping for apparel in a virtual environment with the intention of purchasing the item for the real world an avatar created in the user's own image will provide a better indication of product fit and suitability.
6. *Androgyny*: Should the avatar resemble a stereotypical male or female image or be more androgynous? Here consideration needs to be given the brand's image and what avatar will complement it. Is the image more masculine or feminine or perhaps somewhere in between?

In their research on the use of avatar/icon buddies in instant messaging Nowak and Rauh (2008) found people use all information available including characteristics of the avatar and their screen names to reduce uncertainty and make interpersonal judgments. They found that the visual characteristics of the avatar including anthropomorphism, credibility, and androgyny traits influenced perceptions of the individual the figure represented. The authors concluded that the "...wrong avatar can make you, literally, look bad, while using a more credible, more anthropomorphic, less androgynous avatar (whether very masculine or very feminine), will make you appear more credible." (Nowak & Rauh 2008, p. 1490). Dehn & van Mulken (2000) also explored avatar anthropomorphism and caution developers on the desire to create truly anthromorphic characters. They claim that the more "human-like" the avatar characteristics, the greater the risk of failing to match customers' interaction expectations. In terms of gender Guadagno, Blascovich, Bailenson & McCall (2007) found that individuals are more persuaded when the virtual human is the same gender as they are.

Further research suggests that avatar characteristics including anthropomorphism (the degree to which the avatar looks human) and androgyny (the extent to which the avatar possesses both male and female traits) have the ability to influence social liking and perceived credibility–but the directionality of these effects is as yet unclear (Nowak 2004; Nass, Steuer, Tauber, & Reeder 1993). Whereas some researchers have found that more anthropomorphic avatars lead to more positive attributions of credibility than those that are less anthropomorphic (Wexelblat 1998; Koda & Maes 1996), others have found the opposite (Nowak 2004; Nowak & Biocca 2003). Conflicting results can perhaps be explained by the context of the interactions explored and the specific avatars employed (Nowak & Rauh 2008).

In summary, the limited pool of empirical results to date suggests these general guidelines:

1. When selecting avatars as spokescharacters the advertiser should also consider if the brand has a strong personality in the real world. If so the available evidence suggests that the avatar should mimic this personality to the extent possible. For instance, Apple Computers has successfully developed a strong personality for their brand. With actor Justin Long as their spokesperson the brand is presented as innovative, young, and fun. To select a virtual spokescharacter polar opposite to their real world one may result in a rejection of the virtual character as it does not match the personality they associate with the brand.
2. Whereas a more anthropomorphic avatar is recommended, care should be taken not to make it too human in the event that it fails to live up to the expectations of residents. When an avatar appears truly human people expect it to mimic the behaviors and respond as a real person would.
3. Rather than just choosing an androgynous avatar it is preferable to have one that matches the gender of the resident.
4. For customer service interactions it is advisable to let residents choose the avatar with which they want to interact from a preselected group.

THE PATH FORWARD

Analysts' project that by 2015 companies will spend more money on sales and marketing online than offline (Broitman & Tatar 2008). Advertisers today are focused on how to successfully incorporate social networking into their media mix. But given that that virtual worlds are predicted to eventually replace social networking sites it is reasonable to assume that a significant portion of future advertising expenditures will be directed to these environments (Nowak & Rauh 2008) and therefore this is where advertisers should be focusing their attention.

As digital spokeschartacters continue to infiltrate virtual worlds they raise a host of very real questions that need to be answered. For instance, advertisers are often criticized for their use of spokespersons that represent idealized images of beauty. Citrics contend that such images have the potential to negatively impact consumers' self evaluations (cf. Stevens, Hill & Hanson 1994). Will the same results be found in virutal environments? Will interactions with highly attractive spokesavatars in virtual worlds negatively impact a consumer's (real world) self concept and body image? Or perhaps the opposite will be true. In a virtual environment the consumer can choose to create her avatar to reflect her real or her ideal self. In situations where the avatar reflects the ideal self perhaps interactions with highly attractive spokesavatars may have no effect on real world evaluations, or perhaps the effect will be a positive one. Furthermore, technology has evolved to where it is now possible to create virtual clones of real people. Software such as *iClone* uses a simple photograph of a person to create a 3D highly realistic avatar for virtual world use. Will consumers respond to a brand's spokesavatar the same way they respond to him on television or in a magazine? What are the legal implications of cloning a real world famous face? And how do you legally protect virtual world users from cloning your spokesavatar? Finally, in the real world advertisers rely on *Q Scores* to determine the appeal (and potential success) of personalities and characters, but to date no such tool exists for spokesavatars. Do we need a *Q Score* for spokesavatars or will the *Q Score* for a real world celebritity be a valid indicator of their virtual success?

In the 2002 motion picture *Simone,* a disillusioned movie producer digitally creates a synethic actress, who everyone believes to be a real person. What once may have been considered fantasy or science fiction is fast become reality. In the not too distant future the face of your brand may be a virtual one.

REFERENCES

$345 Mill Invested in 39 Virtual Worlds-Related Companies in First 1/2 OF 08. (2008, July 9). Virtual Worlds Management. Retrieved July 15, 2008, from http://www.virtualworldsmanagement.com

Aaker, J. L. (1997). Dimensions of brand personality. *JMR, Journal of Marketing Research, 34*(3), 347–356. doi:10.2307/3151897

Aitken, P. P., Leathar, D. S., O'Hagan, F. J., & Squair, S. I. (1987). Children's awareness of cigarette advertisements and brand imagery. *British Journal of Addiction, 82*, 615–622. doi:10.1111/j.1360-0443.1987.tb01523.x

Ang, S. H., & Lim, E. A. C. (2006). The influence of metaphors and product types on brand personality perceptions and attitudes. *Journal of Advertising, 35*(2), 39–53.

Baker, M. J., & Churchill, G. A. Jr. (1977). The impact of physical attractive models on advertising evaluations. *JMR, Journal of Marketing Research, 14*(4), 538–555. doi:10.2307/3151194

Blascovich, J., & Loomis, J., Beall., Swinth, K., Hoyt, C., & Bailenson, J. N. (2002). Immersive virtual environment technology as a methodological tool for social psychology. *Psychological Inquiry, 1*(3), 103–124. doi:10.1207/S15327965PLI1302_01

Broitman, A., & Tatar, J. (2008, May 30). How to reach real people in a virtual world. *iMedia Connection.* Retrieved July 7, 2008, from http://www.imediaconnection.com/content/19487.asp

Cavall, E. (2008, May 19). 90 Percent of Business-Launched Virtual Worlds Fail. *Wired.* Retrieved May 19, 2008, from http://www.wired.com

Chaney, I. M., Lin, K. H., & Chaney, J. (2004). The effect of billboards within the gaming environment. *Journal of Interactive Advertising, 5*(1).

Csikszentmihalyi, M. (1991). *Flow: The psychology of optimal experience*. New York: Harper & Row.

Dehn, D. M., & van Mulken, S. (2000). The impact of animated interface agents: A review of empirical research. *International Journal of Human-Computer Studies, 52*(1), 1–22. doi:10.1006/ijhc.1999.0325

Dholakia, R., & Sternthal, B. (1977). Highly credible source: Persuasive facilitator or persuasive liability? *The Journal of Consumer Research, 3*(4), 223–232. doi:10.1086/208671

Fournier, S. (1998, March). Consumers and their brands: Developing relationship theory in consumer research. *The Journal of Consumer Research, 24*, 343–373. doi:10.1086/209515

Garretson, J. A., & Burton, S. (2005, October). The role of spokescharacters as advertisement and package cues in integrated marketing communications. *Journal of Marketing, 69*, 118–132. doi:10.1509/jmkg.2005.69.4.118

Gilbert, B. (2008, June 3). Strategy Analytics: Virtual Worlds Projected to Mushroom to Nearly One Billion Users. *Business Wire*. Retrieved June 3, 2008, from http://www.businesswire.com

Greats Enters, V. $1.5 Billion Virtual Goods Market. (2008, June 9). *Business Wire*. Retrieved June 9, 2008, from http://www.businesswire.com

Guadagno, R. E., Blascovich, J., Bailenson, J. N., & Mccall, C. (2007). Virtual humans and persuasion: The effects of agency and behavioral realism. *Media Psychology, 10*(1), 1–22.

Holzwarth, M., Janiszewski, C., & Neumann, M. (2006). The influence of avatars on online consumer shopping behavior. *Journal of Marketing, 70*(4), 19–36. doi:10.1509/jmkg.70.4.19

Hovland, C. I., & Weiss, W. (1951). The Influence of Source Credibility on Communication Effectiveness. *Public Opinion Quarterly, 15*(winter), 635-650.

Hyman, P. (2007, February 7). Burger King Has it Their Way with Advergame Sales. *Hollywood Reporter*.

Joseph, W. B. (1982). The credibility of physically attractive communicators: A review. *Journal of Advertising, 11*(3), 15–24.

Kahle, L. R., & Homer, P. M. (1985). Physical attractiveness of celebrity endorsers: A social, adaptation perspective. *The Journal of Consumer Research, 11*(4), 954–961. doi:10.1086/209029

Kamins, M. A. (1990). An investigation into the 'match-up' hypothesis in celebrity advertising: When beauty may be only skin deep. *Journal of Advertising, 19*(1), 4–13.

Keeling, K., & Beatty, S. McGoldrick, P. J., & Macaulay, L. (2004). Face Value? Customer views of appropriate formats for ECAs in online retailing. In *Hawaii International Conference on System Sciences* (pp. 1-10).

Keeling, K., McGoldrick, P. J., & Beatty, S. (2006). Virtual onscreen Assistants: A viable strategy to support online customer relationship building? In Fitszimons, G. J., & Morwitz, V. G. (Eds.), *Advances in Consumer Research* (*Vol. 34*, pp. 138–144). Duluth, MN: Association for Consumer Research.

Kids, T., & Worlds, V. (2007, September 25). eMarketer. Retrieved October 23, 2007, from http://www.emarketer.com

Koda, T., & Maes, P. (1996). *Agents with Faces: The effects of personification.* Paper presented at the Human-Computer Interaction'96, London.

Leavitt, N. (2004, August 3). Online Clothes Lines. *iMedia Connection*. Retrieved August 14, 2008, from: http://www.imediaconnection.com

Malter, A. J., Rosa, J. A., & Garbarino, E. C. (2008). Using Virtual Models to Evaluate Real Products for Real Bodies. In Lee, A. Y., & Soman, D. (Eds.), *Advances in Consumer Research* (pp. 87–88).

McBreen, H., Shade, P., Jack, M., & Wyard, P. (2000). Experimental assessment of the effectiveness of synthetic personae for multi-modal e-retail applications. In *Proceedings of the Fourth International Conference on Autonomous Agents* (pp. 39-45).

McGoldrick, P. J., Keeling, K. A., & Beatty, S. F. (2008). A typology of roles for avatars in online retailing. *Journal of Marketing Management, 24*(3-4), 433–461. doi:10.1362/026725708X306176

Miniard, P. W., Bhatla, S., Lord, K. R., Dickson, P. R., & Unnava, H. R. (1991, June). Picture-based persuasion processes and the moderating role of involvement. *The Journal of Consumer Research, 18*, 92–107. doi:10.1086/209244

Mizerski, R. (1995, October). The relationship between cartoon trade character recognition and attitude toward product category in young children. *Journal of Marketing, 50*, 58–70. doi:10.2307/1252328

Nass, C., Steuer, J., Tauber, E., & Reeder, H. (1993). *Anthropomorphism, agency, and ethopoea: Computers as social actors*. Paper presented at the Inter Chi'93, Amsterdam, the Netherlands, April 24-29.

Nelson, M. R. (2002). Recall of brand placement in computer/video games. *Journal of Advertising Research, 42*(2), 80–92.

Neumeier, M. (2003). *Brand Innovation: Where the Rubber Meets the Road*. Retrieved from http://www.informit.com

Nowak, A. (2008, April 25). Big Media Muscles in on Virtual Worlds. *Cable360*. Retrieved April 25, 2008, from http://www.cable360.net

Nowak, K. L. (2004). The influence of anthropomorphism and agency on social judgment in virtual environments. *Journal of Computer-Mediated Communication, 9*(2). Retrieved from http://jcmc.indiana.edu/vol9/issue2/nowak.html.

Nowak, K. L., & Biocca, F. (2003). The Effect of the Agency and Anthropomorphism on Users' Sense of Telepresence, Copresence, and Social Presence in Virtual Environments. *Presence: Teleoperators and Virtual Environments, 12*(5), 48 1-494.

Nowak, K. L., & Rauh, C. (2008). Choose your buddy icon carefully: The influence of avatar androgyny, anthropomorphism and credibility in online interactions. *Computers in Human Behavior, 24*, 1473–1493. doi:10.1016/j.chb.2007.05.005

O'Mahony, S., & Meenaghan, T. (1997). The impact of celebrity endorsements on consumers. *Irish Marketing Review, 10*(2), 15–24.

Ohanian, R. (1990). Construction and validation of a scale to measure celebrity endorsers' perceived expertise, trustworthiness, and attractiveness. *Journal of Advertising, 19*(3), 39–52.

peripheral routes to attitude change. New York: Springer/Verlag.

Petty, R. E., & Cacioppo, J. T. (1986). *Communication and persuasion: Central and*

Phillips, B. J. (1996). Defining trade characters and their role in popular culture. *Journal of Popular Culture, 29*(4), 143–158. doi:10.1111/j.0022-3840.1996.1438797.x

Richards, J. (2008, April 23). McKinsey: ignore Second Life at your peril. *Times Online*. Retrieved April 23, 2008, from http://technology.timesonline.co.uk

Sarvary, M. (2008, February). Breakthrough ideas for 2008. *Harvard Business Review*, 17–45.

Schroeder, R. (2002). Social Interaction in Virtual Environments: Key issues, common

Sengupta, J., Goodstein, R. C., & Boninger, D. S. (1997). Cues are not created equal: obtaining attitude persistence under low-involvement conditions. *The Journal of Consumer Research, 23*(March), 351–361. doi:10.1086/209488

Shimp, T. A. (2003). *Advertising, Promotion & Supplemental Aspects of Integrated Marketing Communications*. Cincinnati, OH: South-Western.

Short, J., Williams, E., & Christie, B. (1976). *The Social Psychology of Telecommunications*. London: Wiley.

Slater, M., Sadagic, A., Usoh, M., & Schroeder, R. (2000). Small Group Behavior in

Solomon, M. R., Ashmore, R., & Longo, L. (1992). The beauty match-up hypothesis: congruence between types of beauty and product images in advertising. *Journal of Advertising, 21*(4), 23–34.

Stephens, D. L., Hill, R. P., & Hanson, C. (1994). The beauty myth and female consumers: the controversial role of advertising. *The Journal of Consumer Affairs*, *28*(1), 137–154.

Stephenson, N. (1992). *Snow Crash.* New York: Bantam Books.

themes, and a framework for research. In R. Schroeder (Ed.), *The Social Life of Avatars: Presence and Interaction in Shared Virtual Environments* (pp. 1-18). London: Springer.

aVirtual and Real Environment. (n.d.). A comparative study. *Presence (Cambridge, Mass.)*, *9*(1), 37–51.

Wexelblat, A. (1988). Don't Make That Face: A Report on Anthropomorphizing an Interface. In Coen, M. (Ed.), *Intelligent Environments (AAAI Technical Report)* (pp. 173–179). Menlo Park, CA: AAAI Press.

Wood, N. T., & Solomon, M. R. (2008). Digital Brand Personality: Does the Matchup Hypothesis Extend to Online Environments? In Lee, A. Y., & Soman, D. (Eds.), *Advances in Consumer Research* (pp. 84–85).

Wood, N. T., Solomon, M. R., & Englis, B. G. (2005). Personalisation of online avatars: Is the messenger as important as the message? *International Journal of Internet Marketing and Advertising*, *2*(1/2), 143–161. doi:10.1504/IJIMA.2005.007509

Wood, N. T., Solomon, M. R., & Englis, B. G. (2008). Personalization of the Web interface: The impact of Web avatars on users response to e-commerce sites. *Journal of Website Promotion*, *2*(1/2), 53–69. doi:10.1080/15533610802104133

Yee, N. (2007). The Proteus Effect: Behaviorial Modifications Via Transformations of Digital Self Representation. *The Daedalus Project.* Retrieved August 10, 2008, from http://www.nickyee.com/pubs/Dissertation_Nick_Yee.pdf

150 *Youth-Oriented Virtual Worlds Now Live or Developing.* (2008, August 22). Virtual Worlds Mangement. Retrieved August 24, 2008, from http://www.virtualworldsmanagement.com

ENDNOTE

1 With the caveat that there is always some uncertainty about a receiver's identity, even in direct marketing or online campaigns when we make a leap of faith to assume that the person at the computer is actually the person the advertiser intends to target.

Chapter 28
Sounds of Web Advertising

Iben B. Jessen
Aalborg University, Denmark

Nicolai J. Graakjær
Aalborg University, Denmark

ABSTRACT

Sound seems to be a neglected issue in the study of web ads. Web advertising is predominantly regarded as visual phenomena–commercial messages, as for instance banner ads that we watch, read, and eventually click on–but only rarely as something that we listen to. The present chapter presents an overview of the auditory dimensions in web advertising: Which kinds of sounds do we hear in web ads? What are the conditions and functions of sound in web ads? Moreover, the chapter proposes a theoretical framework in order to analyse the communicative functions of sound in web advertising. The main argument is that an understanding of the auditory dimensions in web advertising must include a reflection on the hypertextual settings of the web ad as well as a perspective on how users engage with web content.

INTRODUCTION

The shouting of the medieval public crier (Dyer 1982, 15) and similar historical instances of commercial announcements (e.g. Bridge 1921) illustrate a long auditory tradition of advertising. In advertising as we know it today, sound seems flourishing and–from a communicative point of view–indispensable in commercial messages in mass communication media such as radio and television (Graakjær & Jantzen 2009a). However, when it comes to web advertising, one is often met with 'sounds of silence' as we will demonstrate empirically below. In a way, research on sounds in web advertising corresponds to this state of affairs, and only a few contributions have dealt considerably with the subject matter (e.g. Jackson & Fulberg 2003, Tsang 2007).

'Silent sounds' have been considered in studies of language in printed advertising (e.g. Myers 1994, Cook 2001) in terms of prosody, rhythm, and rhyme. Likewise, language in web advertising is interestingly demonstrated to have a pronounced spoken characteristic–and thereby

DOI: 10.4018/978-1-60566-792-8.ch028

implies sound. As pointed out by Janoschka (2004), written language in web ads typically plays on face-to-face communication as a means to involve the user: "The use of linguistic features that are typically found in spoken conversations (…) is particularly striking in online advertising interaction. This conceptual orality (…) reflects the affinity between language use and the conception of web ads found in the new communication medium. Characterized by the Web's technical interactivity, the way in which language is utilized in online advertising can create the impression of interpersonal communication and communicative immediacy" (Janoschka 2004, 130). Following Janoschka, the conceptual oral character of the web ad serves as a schema or mental model of how the user is supposed to interact. For instance, a directly addressed question needs an answer; a request must be followed by an act, etc. In this way, the use of language is seen in correspondence to the possibility to interact and thereby 'to answer'.

Thus, sound in web ads is verbally put into play in various ways. First of all, sound appears as implied and invited in the constructed communicative interaction. But sound is also seen as a reference in the communicated address, e.g. imperatives implying sound ('*Turn up the volume*', '*Listen*') and icons indicating sound, e.g. notes, loudspeakers, and play-buttons.

Also visually, web ads sometimes *look* like having sound (see Mass 2002 for a comparable observation regarding printed ads) and 'silent sounds' appear affiliated to visual expressions in various ways. Sound can be implied as a synaesthetic[1] accompaniment–or a kind of 'muted' sound–to the visually highlighted expression of the text (cf. typography and graphics like capitals, bold, italics, underlining, coloured text, etc.), and because such visual means of expressions can be experienced as 'noisy', 'invoking', or 'calling', they are affiliated with auditory conditions. In relation to animated graphics, sound can be experienced in text or visual objects that are looping in sequences. Visiting a website that hosts many animated ads, as for instance an online newspaper, may very well entail a 'noisy' experience, partly due to the abundance of advertising messages featured next to the editorial content, and partly because of the different rhythms of the animated ads which, in an overall view of the website, will probably seem to swing unsystematically. The expression of the specific ad is not necessarily 'noisy', though, and it can appear rather 'rhythmical' and 'musical'. Furthermore, sound associations can arise as 'muted' sound from animated objects that are normally associated with sound as for instance animated cars and moving pictures of people seen talking.

In this regard, web advertising is accompanied by many 'silent sounds'. But what about the real and heard sounds of web advertising? In the following, we will concentrate on the sounds of web ads that we actually hear. These sounds can be grouped in the following four broad categories: speech, music, incidental sounds, and sound effects. The empirical point of departure is a comprehensive material registered in a Danish context in two periods: 2004-2005 and 2008-2009. The material is analysed with the intent to specify the frequency, forms and functions of sound in web ads. In contrast to more limited scopes of previous studies (e.g. Tsang 2007), we will include different types of web ads, and we will not restrict the discussion to specific corporate brands. This allows us to give an empirically substantiated indication of 'normality' when it comes to the (non) presence of sounds in web ads, even though the empirical material can only hardly be considered representative of 'web ads in general' (more to this reservation below). As already hinted at, our findings suggest that sound is not particularly widespread. However, the registered material allows us to make a close examination of the web ads that actually *do* include sound, and the examples lead us to the proposal of an analytical framework. It is the intention that the proposed framework can provide both analysts and designers with useful insights into the (possible) appearances and communicative functions of sound in web ads. In addition, the framework helps to identify relevant future research initiatives.

The chapter is organised in the following manner: Firstly, the chapter provides relevant insights to the conditions of sounds in web ads. Addressing issues of media use and specific characteristics of medium and genre in an intertextual perspective, the first sections will provide a theoretical background for the understanding of sounds in web ads. Secondly, the chapter presents and discusses the empirical material, hereby providing an indication of the frequency and functions of sound in different types of web ads. Thirdly, by way of conclusion, the chapter will present an analytical framework in which to examine the functions of sound in web advertising.

COMMERCIAL SOUNDS AND MEDIA USE

As an introduction to the study of specific sounds in web ads, we will present an overview of some of the differences between sounds in web ads and other instances of commercial sounds from a user's perspective. This introduction will provide the backdrop for the following more specific and detailed presentation of the textual characteristics of web ads that are important to understand sound.

From an overall view, the existence of sound in web ads is accompanied by some ambivalence. Many Internet users seem to experience sound as an intrusive and negative element (Tsang 2007), particularly in relation to web ads surrounded by editorial content as for instance web banners. Accordingly, automatically activated sound is presented on Nielsen's list of *The Most Hated Advertising Techniques*,[2] and, in the creative guidelines from the international association Interactive Advertising Bureau (IAB), it is recommended that audio should be "user initiated, on click",[3] i.e. sound should not turn up as an unwelcome surprise to the users.

Probably, this attitude towards sound in web ads can be explained by the Internet representing a *pull*-media (contrary to *push*-media such as analogue broadcast television), where the user usually expects and experiences a high level of control (cf. one *search* information on the Internet). According to the media typology proposed by Jensen (1999, 163), the web is predominantly a consultative medium. This means that the sudden appearance of sound that the user did not deliberately search for can be experienced as a very intrusive element in the private sphere of the user. Compared to radio and television, sounds of commercials in these media are also often considered uninvited and disturbing (e.g. Schafer 1977, 268ff). However, there are mitigating circumstances: The sound of radio and television plays an important role in establishing both *continuity* (the unbroken and overlapping sequence of events) and *breaks* (the abrupt highlighting of present or upcoming events), useful–if not directly attractive–features of modern radio and television programming matching absent minded listening and viewing. The appearance of sounds on the Internet might perform the same functions for users (one can for instance listen to the radio on the Internet while writing an e-mail), but whereas sounds of radio and television presents (part of) a pre-determined expression which cannot be modified (only avoided), sounds of the Internet are generally to be considered more dependent on the user in the sense that sounds appear as a result of additional choice.

While radio and television arguably present sound *relatively independent* of user activity (cf. the sound on television is mutable, but it usually emerges when the television is switched on), the sound on the Internet is more likely to be *dependent on* (a result of) user activity in various ways. Television is an audio-visual medium presupposing speakers and sound (cf. television sets have always been produced with integrated speakers), whereas the Internet has been conceptualized and used to a greater extent as a visual medium with less focus on sound technology from both producers and users. For instance, it is no rare occurrence for the sound never to appear when opening a computer, in that opening a computer does not necessarily entail switching on speakers. Likewise, when specific web ads come into sight it is not wholly expected for them to carry sound, indicated by the widespread use of imperatives in the ads such as 'turn up the sound' or 'switch me on'.

Specific variants of sounds on web ads warrant a comparison to the commercial sounds (typically in the form of music) in stores. On web banners' linked target ads (e.g. microsites) sounds will sometimes welcome its listeners independently of further user activity than the initial *getting there*. Because the media use and the role of sound do not seem to be quite habituated (as discussed above), it might be argued that for some users these sounds will be met with discomfort and perhaps irritation. An indication of this is the possibility to switch off the music–much unlike a stay in shops, where music is inescapable (only to be avoided through privatised 'cover-music' in for example iPods).

Of course, there are differences between a 'stay-on-a-website' and a 'stay-in-a-store': In stores, the stay is normally sequenced in a relatively well-defined manner (cf. a script for shopping), whereas a stay on a website is usually characterised by a shorter-lasting, not pre-determined exploration or visit, and the stay can be ended any time without important consequence. In other words, the user is *on* the website, whereas the customer is *in* the store, in which the physical setting and spatial experience is co-constructed and modified by music.

In Table 1, the preceding discussion is summed up. In rough outline, the figure indicates essential dissimilarities of sounds in web ads when compared to commercial sounds of stores, radio commercials and television commercials, profiled from a user's perspective.

In the following sections we will focus more specifically on the conditions of sounds in web ads.

THE CONDITIONS OF SOUND IN DIFFERENT TYPES OF WEB ADS

In the present chapter, we use the term 'web ad' as a general term for ad formats on the World Wide Web. In relevant literature, the attempts to specify the different types of ads on the web are numerous (e.g. Rodgers & Thorson 2000, Faber et al. 2004, McMillan 2007). Web ads include a number of graphic formats and technologies, they often integrate multiple modes of expressions, and they can be static, dynamic as well as interactive. Contrary to for instance printed ads and television commercials, which both have

Table 1. Overview of commercial sounds in different media from a user's perspective

	Store	Radio	TV	Internet
Typical degree of receiver attention to commercial sound	Low to medium	Low to high	Low to high	High
Appearance of commercial sound	Ambient	Separate, in ads between editorial content	Separate, in ads between editorial content	Next to editorial content and separate on web pages
Typical degree of user control	Low The listener is exposed to a pre-determined 'auditory architecture'	Medium The listener is exposed to a pre-determined auditory flow	Medium The listener is exposed to a pre-determined audio-visual flow	High The listener is engaged in a user-dependent flow
Musical format and duration	Long, whole pieces of music	Short	Short	Varied

well-defined formats, a web ad is more difficult to define clearly. Obviously, the web ad shares this problem of delimitation with other texts on the Internet, and the challenge is to decide how many links further are related to the context of the ad. When is the ad no longer an ad? Furthermore, it can be difficult to distinguish web advertising from other marketing functions (cf. Faber et al. 2004).

However, in an empirical study of web advertising as the one we refer to here, an operational definition of web advertising is necessary. Unlike a general definition of web advertising that includes all possible types of advertising on the web and that complies with a general definition of advertising (e.g. Dyer 1982, 2), an operational definition is more specific in pointing out what particular kinds of ads that should be included in the study. From an overall perspective, empirical studies on the effectiveness of web ads *either* seem to focus on banner ads (and similar formats),[4] where the advertising message is competing with the surrounding content, *or* employ a broader conception of web advertising *as* commercial websites (see e.g. Hwang & McMillan 2004). It is also a general conception that web ads should be regarded as a hyperlinked connection between an *embedded web ad* on a host website (e.g. a banner ad in an online newspaper) and its *linked target* (for instance a web page about the product, a company website, or a microsite hosting a specific campaign) (e.g. Dahlén 2001, Janoschka 2004). In the present chapter, we stick to the conception of web advertising as a hyperlinked structure starting from the embedded web ad. Thus, we focus on sound in relation to the embedded web ad and its linked target respectively, even if the latter might appear not to comply with a general definition of advertising simply because it does not 'look like advertising' and/or happens to serve other marketing functions.

Therefore, what we claim here about sounds of web advertising must be regarded with the particular operational definition of web ads in mind. However, the proposed analytical framework is intended for a more general use and is believed to be applicable to other types of web ads as well (e.g. commercial websites). It is also necessary to be aware of the different conditions of sound in the embedded web ad and in the linked target ad, respectively. As mentioned, sounds in web ads that are located among other content are in principle *regulated* (cf. the IAB guidelines), whereas structurally independent forms of advertising as for instance the linked targets ads are *less regulated* as regards the use of sound. We will now take a closer look at the media related conditions of sound in web advertising.

THE TEXTUAL CHARACTERISTICS OF THE WEB AD

The web ad is a digital text. This means that it is based on the representational capacities of the computer in which all other media can be simulated by means of the binary alphabet (Finnemann 2001, 23f). In relation to sound, this implies that the use of audio in older media can be simulated and integrated as a component in the digital text, e.g. in the form of a television commercial.

According to Bolter & Grusin (1999), the representation of older media in the digital medium reflects a general logic of *remediation* that appears at the level of the interface in various ways.[5] The remediation of other media can also be considered in a perspective of stages. In his *Media Interaction Cycle,* Leckenby (2005) identifies three phases in the development of a medium: 1) the transference of characteristics from one medium to another ("transference"), 2) the focus on the capabilities specific to the medium ("exclusivity"), and 3) the influence of the new media on older media ("recurrence"). To illustrate the phases Leckenby refers to web ads: "Today's ubiquitous online banner ads are simply a product of taking known methods and ideas and transferring them to the new media from the traditional media, a common occurrence with the advent of a new medium" (Leckenby 2005, 18).[6] Thus, it should be clear that we must understand the web ad text as a result of a complex interplay between existing media forms. We find examples of remediation of 'older' forms of advertising (e.g. billboard ads similar to printed ads, web ads displaying television commercials) as well as examples of new forms of advertising that make use of the unique potentials of the Internet medium (e.g. interactive games, hypertext menus, forms).

However, the web ad's 'borrowing' is not restricted to the level of media, but exists as a common characteristic of advertising as a genre as well. As described by Cook: "Ads draw upon, and thus share features with, many other genres, including political propaganda, conversation, song, film, myth, poetry, fairy tales, soap operas, sitcoms, novels, graffiti, jokes and cartoons (Cook 2001, 12). In an overall perspective it is then appropriate to be aware of the web ad text as a composite form that potentially refers to and borrows from many other modes of expression.

Thus, when analysing sound in web ads, there are a number of other instances of sound in other forms of communications on which it might be necessary to reflect. Figure 1 presents an outline of the related sounds of web advertising. The figure should not be regarded as a complete check list, but as areas that are relevant to consult when dealing with sound in web ads:

To sum up, the figure illustrates that the use of sound in web ads (as well as in other modes of expression) is inspired by different media and genres, and therefore it appears of relevance to consider the occurrence of sound in other advertising media, e.g. sound in radio and television commercials, as well as the use of sound in other genres, e.g. in computer games. However, it is crucial to pay attention to the specific characteristics of the medium in which the sound occurs, including technology as well as media use (cf. Table 1).

Another important characteristic of the web ad text to be mentioned here is its basis in a network of nodes and links (the Internet). From a perspective of communication, Janoschka describes the hyperlinked structure of the web ad as a succession of advertising messages: The web ad consists of an "initial advertising message" (e.g. a banner ad), which links to a "linked advertising message" (the destination of the banner ad, e.g. a web page about the product), and finally an "extended advertising

Figure 1. The related sounds of web advertising

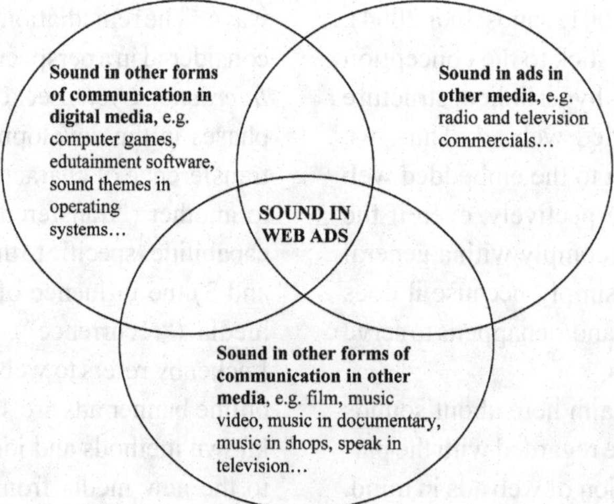

message", which follows from the links on the destination of the banner ad (Janoschka 2004, 49f). In other words, depending on how the limits of the advertising message is decided, the web ad must be regarded as a hypertext or (at least) as a part of a hypertext structure. In this respect, we find it useful to adopt a definition of hypertext as a navigational mechanism in addition to (not opposed to) text: "What hypertext adds to text is primarily that it provides a set of navigational mechanisms which can be used in a variety of ways in our navigation between elements within and between texts" (Finnemann 2001, 42). In our view, the hypertextual feature of the web ad raises an interesting question in relation to sound: What is the function of sound in relation to the hypertextuality of the web ad? We will elaborate on this central question in the remainder of the chapter.

HOW DO WE READ WEB ADS?

The well-known phenomenon of banner blindness (Benway & Lane 1998) indicates that we do not pay much attention to web ads, yet, eyetrack studies have shown that we are not totally blind to commercial messages on the web.[7] Different kinds of empirical studies of what users actually see–and hear–while using the Internet are of course relevant. However, we would like to introduce a general theory of reading hypertexts in order to analyse the specific instances of sound in web ads. The aim is to investigate the functions of sound in relation to the user's potential engagement with the content of the web ad. We regard sound as carrying important communicative functions that shape the user's experience of the web ad, and the challenge is how to analyse sound in relation to the specific medium of the Internet. As mentioned, the purpose is *not* to examine actual users' conceptions of the various auditory phenomena in web ads but from an analytical perspective to be able to describe the functions of sounds in relation to the different types of activities that the user might bring into play when engaging with the ad. Therefore, the first step is to know in which ways the user can orient himself in the web content.

According to Finnemann, digital texts are characterised by *modal shifts* between different modes of reading, representing "a discontinuous process, included as part of the reading process" (Finnemann 2001, 44). Addressing digital texts in general, Finnemann distinguishes between three modes of 'reading': 1) the reading mode, i.e. "reading "as usual" (including skimming etc.)", 2) the link mode, i.e. "navigating and browsing", and 3) the editing mode, i.e. "interactive behaviour changing the future behaviour/content of the system" (Finnemann 2001, 43). In order to understand the role of sound in web ads in relation to how we engage with web content in general, we find it useful to adopt Finnemann's conception of hypertext as facilitating modal switches.

Thus, in the following, we distinguish between three kinds of user activities that can describe the ways in which users read or engage with web ads, namely reading, navigating, editing. In the *mode of reading,* the user for instance listens to and watches a commercial video or simply reads a written text in a banner ad. Unlike the 'simple' reading of the content, the *mode of navigating* obviously involves a more active and tactile contribution by the user, usually by moving or clicking the mouse as a means to browse between parts of the ad's content by the provided links and menus. Finally, in the *mode of editing*, the user contributes with input that has some kind of effect on the content or appearance of the ad. Examples of editing could be the marking of radio buttons and checkboxes as ways of choosing preferences (e.g. the colour of a car, the settings of a game) or the submission of information to the system by filling out forms with numbers and words (e.g. sending orders and contact data).

In the following, we will examine the functions of sound in a comprehensive material of registered web ads in relation to the different modes of user activities. The assumption is that an analytical framework based on the above presented modes of user activity–reading, navigating and editing modes–can be applied on both embedded web ads and linked target ads (as well as other kinds of web ads not discussed in the study), although, obviously, the embedded web ad has more limited conditions as regards sound because of its size and placement. First, the empirical material referred to is presented.

THE EMPIRICAL MATERIAL

The web ads that constitute the empirical material are registered on a Danish sample of websites in 2004-2005 and in 2008-2009.[8] The material from the first period of registration includes 1025 embedded web ads and 613 linked target ads, and the material from the second period of registration includes 221 embedded web ads and 185 linked target ads.[9]

In fact, the absolute majority of the embedded web ads in the material appears without sound, only 1,9% of the registrations from 2004-2005 and 5% of the registrations from 2008-2009 include sound (see Table 2), and when sound actually occurs, it is usually as part of a video, a television commercial or a film trailer, integrated into a banner or a billboard. As regards the linked target ads, sound is neither exactly widespread, even if sound occurs more frequently compared to the embedded web ads: 6,2% of the registered target ads from 2004-2005 and 6,8% of the registered target ads from 2008-2009 include sound (see Table 2).

Even if the share of web ads with sound in the material is rather low, it is notable that the instances of web ads with sound seem to be increasing. However, it should be emphasized that what we report here on sound in web ads must be seen in relation to the specific empirical material,

Table 2. Occurrences of sound in the registered web ads with sound

			Embedded Web Ads		Linked Target Ads	
			2004/2005	**2008/2009**	**2004/2005**	**2008/2009**
Total number of registered web ads			1025	221	613	185
Share of web ads with sound			1,9% (n=19)	5% (n=11)	6,2% (n=38)	8,6% (n=16)
Automatically initiated sound			-	-	**78,9**	**81,3**
		Speech	-	-	15,8	43,8
		Music	-	-	60,5	75,0
		Incidental sounds	-	-	21,1	18,8
		Sound effects	-	-	18,4	-
User-initiated sound			**100**	**100**	**55,3**	**37,5**
	Sound from embedded videos		84,2	45,5	34,2	25,0
		Speech	68,4	36,4	18,4	25,0
		Music	47,4	45,5	21,1	25,0
		Incidental sounds	47,4	18,2	21,1	6,3
		Sound effects	-	-	-	-
	Other instances of sound		15,8	54,5	28,9	12,5
		Speech	10,5	9,1	7,9	-
		Music	-	45,5	5,3	-
		Incidental sounds	5,3	-	2,6	-
		Sound effects	5,3	45,5	21,1	12,5

in particular the applied operational definition and the selection of websites in the sample. It is likely that a focus on other types of websites would have resulted in more ads with sound. Also the Danish context in which the web ads are registered must be acknowledged. The frequency of web ads with sound might vary from country to country, but analysis of cross-cultural differences lies outside the scope of this chapter.

Overall, four categories of sound can be identified in the material:[10]

1) Music, i.e. musicalized sound (typically performed on musical instruments).
2) Speech, i.e. spoken presentations (with direct address in the form of a presenter, a testimonial, or a voice-over, and with indirect address in the form of dialogue).
3) Incidental sounds, i.e. non-spoken and non-musicalized diegetic sounds (supposedly originating from a presented or implied dramatic universe).
4) Sound effects, i.e. non-spoken, non-musicalized, and non-diegetic sounds (typically representing an unrealistic auditory addition to objects showed or implied).

Table 2 presents an overview of the registered sounds in the embedded web ads and in the linked target ads in the empirical material. The figure distinguishes between automatically initiated sound (sounds that 'just turn up') and sound that is initiated by the user.

In all the examples of embedded web ads, sounds are initiated by the user's mouse, i.e. by mouse-over–a more or less deliberate activity–or by clicking on the ad. Such instances are typically formatted as embedded videos of various lengths, and often they bear resemblance to television commercials (thus presenting a case of 'unchanged' representation of the television commercial in another medium, cf. Bolter and Grusin 1999). However, the importance of user activity shows in that the playing of the videos can be modified by the user (which presents a dimension of 'improvement', cf. Bolter and Grusin 1999): If the mouse does not stay on the ad, the video will be interrupted, only to start again when the mouse revisits the ad; a design that makes particular user activities possible (probably not intended by senders), such as *scratching*–the reactivation of a video with very short intervals.

Because it is the user's activity that causes the sound and not the reverse, this 'silent', only potentially auditory ad at first sight presents a peculiar audio-visual advertisement phenomenon. Thus, to *attract attention* is not the primary function of the sound–contrary to the almost archetypal function of sounds in advertising more generally. Rather, the sound emphasizes and sustains attention, so as to prompt the user to leave the mouse where it is (in cases of videos) or to click. It seems that embedded web ads are predominantly visual expressions (pictures, texts–and sometimes animated), attracting attention by various sorts of eye catchers (e.g. colours and movements) or by verbal imperatives. Only in cases when the mouse unintentionally slides across the ad, it makes good sense to consider the sound as attention grabbing; most obvious in cases of highlighted sound in the beginning of the video.

When it comes to the linked target ads, sounds occur more often and more varied compared to sounds in embedded web ads. As mentioned, entering a linked target ad is caused by user activity (click and expectation)–it is an ad that the user deliberately goes for. The advertising message is no longer occurring synchronously with non-commercial, editorial content (contrary to the case of embedded web ads), and the ad text is ready for exploration either right away–following the initial click–or succeeding an introduction in which sounds appear as part of a fixed expression that has to be followed (or skipped).[11]

If we take an overall look at the auditory phenomena that occur in the linked target ads, we can identify automatically initiated sounds in introductions (sometimes including the automatic playing of videos) as well as sound in the 'background' of a web page. We can also identify user initiated sounds comparable to the ones already mentioned in relation to embedded web ads. For instance, sound effects can be heard as a result of mouse-over where the sounds become indexes of the objects seen. Sounds also appear as part of audio-visual expressions such as the 'unchanged' (or perhaps slightly improved) remediation of television commercials or as videos embedded into the design of a microsite, for example as part of a collage, thus presenting a rather sophisticated refashion of television commercials. However, mouse-over initiated videos on linked target ads seem to have somewhat different conditions compared to their status as embedded web ads: Auditory phenomena are not necessarily *up front* (loud and right from the start)–as in many mouse-over initiated embedded ads–because the users' attention can be presupposed, and therefore the need for attention grabbing sounds is less. Furthermore, sounds in linked target ads can be heard in connection with a range of features accessible on the web page, for instance in quizzes, games, immersive scenarios and the like.

We will now take a closer look at the web ads with sound in the registered material in relation to the different modes of user activities, i.e. sound in the mode of reading, in the mode of navigating, and in the mode of editing.

THE FUNCTIONS OF SOUND IN THE MODE OF READING

To a great extent the embedded web ads with sound are videos to be watched and listened to 'as usual', i.e. they are intended to be received in the mode of reading. In the material, the videos in the embedded web ads are most often television commercials or film trailers, but there are also examples of videos related to political campaigns and charity. The use of sound in the videos is evidently very similar to what we hear in audio-visual media in general (cf. Figure 1): We can identify different kinds of speech; the direct address to the user from a presenter, testimonial or voice-over, and the indirect address to the user by means of dialogues between people in a displayed story, and we hear different kinds of music and incidental sounds.

Likewise, in the linked target ads, we find examples of videos 'simply' to be watched and listened to, e.g. presentation videos about the product, television commercials, and film trailers, and often they appear with longer duration compared to the videos of embedded web ads. But, in the linked target ads, we also find instances of sound that appear as part of the web page as such. The sound is automatically initiated when the user enters the web page, and it typically presents itself as part of a short introduction sequence (often in flash design), and/or as sound in the 'background' of the web page as a whole. In the material, we hear different kinds of music, both original and pre-existing, as well as incidental sounds, e.g. sounds from particular settings (for instance a city, a museum, a ski slope, a beach).

Music comes in two forms: Either as predominantly short-lasting, repeated (perhaps slightly varied) musical expressions characterized by groove and sound at the expense of melodic curvature and harmonic progression[12] or as wholly rounded tunes. The latter is comparable to music in stores, where longer-lasting culminating progressions constituted by tuneful, pre-existing pieces of music will typically be heard.[13] However, contrary to the occurrence of pre-existing music in stores–and in radio and television commercials for that matter–the music on a web page can often be identified instantaneously via for instance an icon texted: "You are now hearing…". Pre-existing, often relatively unknown music (to the ordinary user) is sometimes part of the attraction of a linked target ad; the music co-establishes atmosphere and moods (to the possible commercial benefit of the linked target ad and its product), while the pre-existing music is exposed in a rather unobtrusive way. Considered as a kind of co-branding of music and the advertised product, this phenomenon has been prevalent in television commercials for quite some time. However, the linked target ad seems to add new dimensions by providing information on the music (product) instantaneously and simultaneously in an unobtrusive–compared to television commercials–commercial environment.

Considering other types of sounds, speech is occasionally heard as an accompaniment to linked target ads, especially in the short introduction sequences. In videos, speech typically performs the function of more or less explicit commercial presentation (e.g. by way of voice-over, presenter, testimonial, and dialogue). Incidental sounds and sound effects appear during the user's navigation and in different types of games–sometimes supplemented by music–offered on the linked target ad. Occasionally, music from the front page will accompany the sounds of the user's navigation and implies the possibility of overlap between sounds corresponding to different modes of reading; for instance: Music corresponding to the reading mode can perform an auditory background to incidental sounds and sound effects of the modes of navigation and editing mode, respectively (more on this below).

To sum up, three functions of sound can be identified in the reading mode, namely *supportive*, *mood enhancing* and *presenting* functions. Whereas the presenting function of speech (in the form of a presenter, a testimonial, a voice-over, or dialogue) tend to be less dominant, the supportive and mood enhancing functions of sound effects, incidental sounds and music seem to be more widespread. We use the term 'supportive' to refer to a predominantly structuring and underlining function of sound in audio-visual expressions (generally assuming that sound will be subordinate to the visual part to an even greater extent on the Internet compared to television, cf. the discussed media related conditions of sound). We use the term 'mood enhancing' to refer to the usual function of music and incidental sounds in visually uneventful periods, and here sound functions as a rather unspecific moderator of the experience of the web ad (somewhat similar to the experience of being in a store with music). Whereas sounds with a supportive function arguably point *into* the audio-visual expression for instance by emphasizing movements and bridging scenes, sounds of an uneventful visual context are more likely to point *out from* the media text, identifying and positioning the user as for example somebody in need of making a move (see more on this last issue below).

THE FUNCTIONS OF SOUND IN THE MODE OF NAVIGATING

The mode of navigating is constituted by the user's linking or navigating between elements in the ad. In the mode of navigating, sound accentuates or draws attention to the navigational conditions of the web ad text in various ways. In the registered material, we find examples of embedded web ads in which sound is indicating the possibility to link. For instance, the initiation of the sound of a rifle fire by the user's mouse-over in an ad that invites the user to go 'job hunting' (visually illustrated by a savanna with people representing different job positions) can be regarded as a sound that makes the user aware of the existence of a link. At the same time, the thematized sound of the rifle serves as an auditory promise of what the user might expect and thereby motivates the linking.

In the linked target ads, we find similar instances of sound that draw attention to the possibility to link, e.g. in connection with menus (sound effects as well as speech initiated by mouse-over). We find also examples of sounds that stress the navigational movements in relation to a particular object, e.g. sound effects that highlight the zooming in and zooming out of a product. Moreover, in the material, we can identify navigational sounds that, in some respects, overlap with the functions of sound in the reading mode, but that are constituted by the *transition* between different sounds in different parts of the ad. An example is an ad for a car in which the front page displays a new car model on the roof of a skyscraper. The front page is accompanied by incidental sound from the noisy city (with many cars) below, and when the user 'enters' the car for further inspection of its interior details, the user is met with classical music. Obviously, the contrast between the city noise and the classical music is loaded with meaning, but what we would like to point at here is that the contrasting sounds serve as an indicator of where the user is positioned in the structure of the ad. However, transitions between sounds that indicate the position of the user are not necessarily made by contrasts. Other examples in the material show that it is the *difference* (also minor differences) between sounds that positions the user.

Another instance of navigational sound is the use of circular (looped) musical expressions or repeated incidental sounds that alongside the mood enhancing function in the reading mode also seem to function as an incentive to navigate or link. As a result of user expectations of 'pull-ability' (cf. the previous discussion on the Internet as a pull-medium), users might search for a 'link out' (or rather a link 'further into' the universe of the linked target ad) as soon as the sounds stand out as circular, monotonous and stagnant. For example, the repeated playing of 'city noise' on the main navigation page of the above mentioned car ad somehow forces the user to take action, i.e. select which part of the car to be further explored, in order to escape (auditory) boredom.

To sum up, in the mode of navigating, we can point at two dominating functions of sound. Firstly, sounds that function as an *indication of the user's position* for instance by the use of different music in the different levels of the ad's composition. In these cases, the sound emphasizes the location of the user by connecting e.g. specific music or incidental sounds with specific 'spaces' or levels in the ad's structure, and thereby the sound underlines *where* the user is or should be. Secondly, sounds that function as a *marker of link-option*, both directly in the form of sound effects or exclamations and indirectly in the form of circular, repeated sound that urges the user to navigate.

THE FUNCTIONS OF SOUND IN THE MODE OF EDITING

In the mode of editing, the user is actively contributing to the ad. In the registered material, sound in the mode of editing is mainly heard in relation to the user's participation in different kinds of games either in an embedded web ad or in a linked target ad. For instance, the sound of darts hitting a dartboard, the sound of a vase that the user is supposed to smash, or the sound of the user's playing on a piano in a karaoke-like play contest. We also find an example of speak humoristically commenting on the user's performance in a game (e.g. "*What are you doing!*") and a musical fanfare celebrating the user's triumph.

Thus, in the mode of editing, sound functions primarily as a confirmation of the user's input. In contradiction to the mode of navigating where sounds will normally function as motivating activity, the sounds in the mode of editing are rather *confirmatory* in that they function as 'auditory receipts' that are highlighting the *result* of an activity.[14] Most often the sounds are thematized so that they correspond to and emphasize the act that the user is supposed to do (cf. the simulation of a game of darts).

THE COMMUNICATIVE FUNCTIONS OF SOUND IN WEB ADS: AN ANALYTICAL FRAMEWORK

So far, we have examined the sounds of web ads in relation to how we read web texts in general, i.e. as involving modal switches between a reading mode, a navigation mode, and an editing mode. In order to analyse sound, we argue that it is relevant to reflect on the communicative functions of sound in each mode as well as in relation to the switching between modes. Referring to an empirical material, we have outlined what we hear as the typical functions or roles of sound. It is our impression that the presented functions are rather general; however, the findings may not be exhaustive. Figure 2 presents an overview of the functions of sounds in embedded web ads as well as in the linked target ads in relation to the modes of user activities (reading, navigating, editing).

Even though the embedded web ad, because of its limited size, seems less complicated as regards composition and use of sound compared to the linked target ads, the functions of sound presented in Figure 2 both describe the embedded web ad and the linked target ad. In many instances, though, the figure would seem 'too big' since the embedded web ad does not (yet) provide users with the range of options presented in the linked target ads with regard to navigation and use of sound. Moreover, the embedded web ad will not allow the same amount of shifts between different user activities, although they can occur on a reduced scale.

It should be emphasized that the modes of user activities are overlapping and thereby not mutually exclusive. This is why the figure is illustrated as an embedded structure. For instance, music with a predominantly mood enhancing function can form the auditory background of sounds marking options to link or of sounds confirming the user's input. In the registered material, an example of the latter is seen in the game "*Kick out your boy friend*" (addressed at younger women) on a micro-site advertising mineral water. During the game, the playing of *Tu m'as promis* by In-Grid serves as the background for the seemingly 'aggrieved' and 'sweet aggressive' female user's smashing of the boy friend's things.[15] Shifts between levels are also typically marked by different kinds of music or incidental sounds (cf. the contrast between the noise of a city and the playing of classical music inside a car), and depending on shifts in modes of user activity the functions of sound will change and possibly overlap.

As regards the different categories of sound (music, speech, incidental sounds, and sound effects), the presenting function in the reading mode is reserved to speech, the mood enhancing and supportive functions are primarily reserved to music and incidental sounds. All other functions listed in the figure can be constituted by either speech, music, incidental sounds or sound effects, or they can appear as an interplay between all of these. The difference between the categories of sound

Figure 2. Function of sounds in relation to mode of user activity

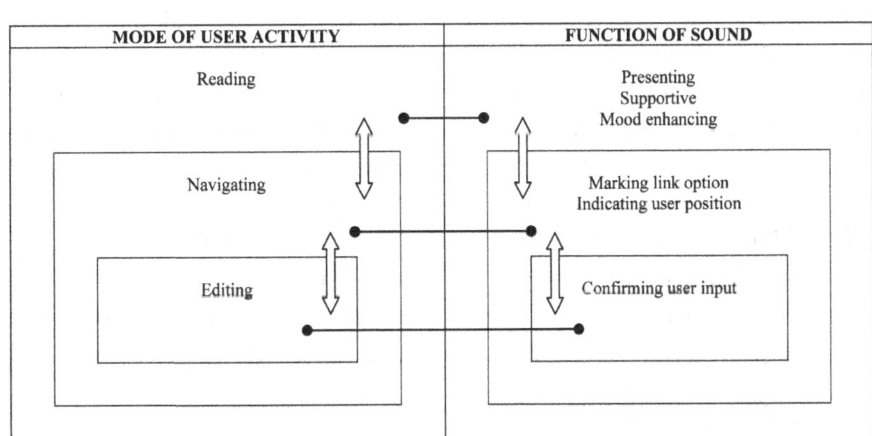

is primarily qualitative, and this is why we find it relevant to distinguish between them as basic variables in the auditory composition of the ad.

Principally, the figure establishes a theoretical framework in which to describe and analyse the communicative functions of sound in web ads. However, the framework might also be useful in a production perspective as a tool to reflect on the different roles of sound and how sound is related to the way we read web texts. As sound in the mode of reading seems quite habituated (cf. the web ads' inspiration from ads in other media illustrated in Figure 1), it thus seems most necessary to concentrate on how sound can accompany the navigating and the editing mode as well as mode switching.

CONCLUSION

The chapter has analysed the appearances, conditions and functions of sounds in web ads. Generally, sounds in web ads can be considered to be a rather rare phenomenon, and this seems in particular to connect to the conditions of sound on the Internet. Thus, technology, design, and media use do not (yet) seem to imply sound in the same (and arguably more consolidated and habituated) way that characterizes the technology, design, and use of e.g. television. However, obviously impressed and optimistic commentators within the advertising business predict that the status of sound will change in the (near) future. For instance animated pictures with sound is considered to represent an effective and impressive means of communication (cf. Gluck & Bruner 2005), and sound is argued to have a great overall potential (Jackson & Fulberg 2003, 7; Tsang 2007). More specifically, the predictions might turn out to hold true, especially of the linked target ads where sounds do not collide with the surrounding context.

However, this study has oriented itself towards present practices and actual instances of sounds. When sound in web ads in fact occurs, a wide variety of functions is involved, and, on a general level, sounds appear user initiated and user dependent compared to commercials in other media. Following this observation, we have argued that sound is a phenomenon to be more or less deliberately 'pulled' from the ads by the users. Actual 'pulling' ranges from the unintended activation of sound in embedded web ads to the intentional exploration of sound on a linked target ad (e.g. pieces of music and games). By combining modes of user activities and functions of sounds, we present Figure 2 as a tool for analysing and designing sounds of web ads. The figure proposes a way to take into account the specific conditions of the digital medium when analysing and designing sound.

Future research could profitably study the responses of actual users to sounds in web ads. It seems that both qualitative media ethnographic approaches and quantitative experimental approaches could be helpful in providing more precise insights into the user's way of handling, understanding and being affected by web ads. Also, further research on the actual prevalence of web ads with sounds needs to be conducted. Obviously, the fact that the empirical material is registered in a Danish context has an influence on the findings. Precisely *what kind of* influence is very hard to pinpoint as there is no available studies to compare with. Future initiatives, in line with the present empirical registrations, would allow for both cross-cultural (synchronic) analysis and mono-cultural (perhaps also cross-cultural) diachronic analysis. Discussions on the functions of sound might also be nuanced or expanded if future research implies 'web ads with sound' as a sample criterion. No doubt that a sample of web ads *all with sounds* would bring further validity to the study of the functions of sound. We hope to have inspired and to have provided the fertile ground for such endeavours.

REFERENCES

Benway, J. P., & Lane, D. M. (1998 December). Banner Blindness: Web Searchers Often Miss Obvious Links. *ITG Newsletter, 1*(3). Retrieved from http://www.internettg.org/newsletter/dec98/banner_blindness.html

Björnberg, A. (2000). Structural relationships of music and images in music videos. In Middleton, R. (Ed.), *Reading Pop - Approaches to textual analysis in popular music* (pp. 347–378). Oxford, UK: Oxford University Press.

Bolter, J. D., & Grusin, R. (1999). *Remediation. Understanding New Media.* Cambridge, MA: The MIT Press.

Bridge, F. (1921). *The old cryes of London.* London: Novello.

Cook, G. (2001). *The Discourse of Advertising* (2nd ed.). London, New York: Routledge.

Cook, N. (1998). *Analysing Musical Multimedia.* Oxford, UK: Oxford University Press.

Dahlén, M. (2001). *Marketing on the Web: Empirical Studies of Advertising and Promotion Effectiveness.* Stockholm, Sweden: EFI, Stockholm School of Economics.

Dyer, G. (1982). *Advertising as Communication.* New York: Routledge. doi:10.4324/9780203328132

Faber, R. J., Lee, M., & Nan, X. (2004). Advertising and the consumer information environment online. *The American Behavioral Scientist, 48*(4), 447–466. doi:10.1177/0002764204270281

Finnemann, N. O. (2001). *The Internet–A New Communicational Infrastructure.* Papers from The Centre for Internet Research, University of Aarhus. Retrieved from http://www.cfi.au.dk/publikationer/cfi/002_finnemann

Gluck, M., & Bruner, R. E. (2005). The Evolution of Rich Media Advertising. Current Market Trends, Success Metrics and Best Practices. *Radar Research & DoubleClick.* Retrieved from http://www.doubleclick.com/

Graakjær, N., & Jantzen, C. (Eds.). (2009a). *Music in advertising–Commercial sounds in media communication and other settings.* Aalborg, Denmark: Aalborg University Press.

Graakjær, N., & Jantzen, C. (2009b). Music for shopping–Supplementary sounds of consumption. In Graakjær, N., & Jantzen, C. (Eds.), *Music in advertising–Commercial sounds in media communication and other settings* (pp. 237–257). Aalborg, Denmark: Aalborg University Press.

Hwang, J.-S., & McMillan, S. J. (2004). How Consumers Think About 'Interactive' Aspects of Web Advertising. In Gao, Y. (Ed.), *Web Systems Design and Online Consumer Behavior* (pp. 69–89). Hershey, PA: Idea Publishing.

Jackson, D. M., & Fulberg, P. (2003). *Sonic branding.* Houndmills, UK: Palgrave. doi:10.1057/9780230503267

Janoschka, A. (2004). *Web Advertising. New forms of communication on the Internet.* Philadelphia, PA: John Benjamins Publishing Company.

Jensen, J. F. (1999). 'Interactivity'–Tracking a New Concept in Media and Communication Studies. In Mayer, P. A. (Ed.), *Computer Media and Communication. A Reader* (pp. 160–187). Oxford, UK: Oxford University Press.

Jessen, I. B. (2010). The Aesthetics of Web Advertising: Methodological Implications for the Study of Genre Development. In Brügger, N. (Ed.), *Web History* (pp. 257–277). New York: Peter Lang.

Leckenby, J. D. (2005). The Interaction of Traditional and New Media. In Stafford, M. R., & Faber, R. J. (Eds.), *Advertising, Promotion, and New Media* (pp. 3–29). Armonk, NY: M. E. Sharpe.

Mass, G. (2002). Musikalische Themen und Motive in Werbeanzeigen–ein Streifzug. In Probst-Effah, G., Schepping, W., & Schneider, R. (Eds.), *Musikalische Volkskunde und Musikpädagogik–Annäherungen und Schnittmengen* (pp. 251–283). Essen, Deutschland: Verlag Die Blauen Eule.

McMillan, S. J. (2007). Internet Advertising: One Face or Many? In Schumann, D. W., & Thorson, E. (Eds.), *Internet Advertising. Theory and Research* (pp. 15–35). Mahwah, NJ: Lawrence Erlbaum Associates.

Myers, G. (1994). *Words in Ads*. London: Edward Arnold.

Rodgers, S., & Thorson, E. (2000). The interactive advertising model: How users perceive and process online ads. *Journal of Interactive Advertising, 1*(1), 26–50. Retrieved from http://jiad.org/vo1/no1/rodgers/.

Schafer, R. M. (1977). *The soundscape. Our sonic environment and the tuning of the world.* Rochester, NY: Destiny Books.

Tsang, L. (2007). Sound and music in website design. In Sexton, J. (Ed.), *Music, sound and multimedia–From the live to the virtual* (pp. 145–171). Edinburgh, UK: Edinburgh University Press.

ENDNOTES

1 In this context synaesthesia refers to the 'weak', socially reproduced form ('quasi-synaesthesia' in Cook's terminology, cf. Cook 1998, 24ff), which finds expression in our everyday experience and vocabulary (e.g. a voice can be clear). It refers to a stimulus in one sense *associating* a stimulus in another sense. In the 'strong' form ('synaesthesia proper' in Cook's terminology), synaesthesia refers to a stimulus of one sense (an E-major chord) *eliciting* a *synchronous experience* in another sense (the colour yellow).

2 Cf. Jakob Nielsen's Alertbox (2004): http://www.useit.com/alertbox/20041206.html

3 Cf. the Rich Media Creative Guidelines from IAB: http://www.iab.net/iab_products_and_industry_services/508676/508767/Rich_Media

4 The term 'banner ad' is often used as a general term for web ad formats located among editorial content. However, these types of ads include many graphic formats and have many names: e.g. banners, rich media banners, skyscrapers, leaderboards, billboards, rectangles, buttons, interstitials, hockey stick, wallpaper, etc.

5 Bolter & Grusin specify "a spectrum of different ways in which digital media remediate their predecessors" and they position digital media products on a scale consisting of 'unchanged' remediation, improvement, refashion and absorption (cf. Bolter & Grusin 1999, 45f).

6 According to Leckenby, the first phase of web advertising is inspired by the outdoor billboard ad in that the static banner ad must also communicate its message in competition with other messages in a very limited space and therefore needs to economise on the amount of information. The second phase is the use of the unique features of the medium, e.g. the dynamic and interactive potential of digital media: "An ad becomes a mini-video game and requires media planners to make connections to new issues in their field such as online order fulfilment operations" (Leckenby 2005, 22). And finally, in the third phase, Leckenby identifies examples of television commercials copying features from the web ad. Leckenby emphasizes that the phases do not necessarily occur in a linear way, but can be present at the same time in the development of a medium. The phases

in the *Media Interaction Cycle* are therefore illustrated as three overlapping circles (cf. Leckenby 2005, 21).

7 Cf. the report from the Poynter Institute: *Eyetrack III. Online Consumer Behavior in the Age of Multimedia* (2004): http://www.poynterextra.org/EYETRACK2004/ (see 'Advertising Results')

8 The sample includes portals, information resources and news media, all selected because of the appeal to a broad target group, a large number of services, many visitors and a broad field of topics. The registrations are made from predefined navigation paths on each website, and the navigation paths cover a wide range of subjects as well, e.g. news, health, sports, culture, business, computer, life style, and communication. For a presentation of the methodological framework of this study, see Jessen (2010).

9 The number of embedded web ads and linked target ads are not identical, mainly because different versions of an embedded web ad within the same campaign can link to the same target ad. Another reason can be that the target ad did not exist.

10 It is important to stress that this categorization is based on a reception perspective (and not for instance on a production perspective).

11 The sounds of the introductions (e.g. to a microsite) typically appear in a pre-arranged flow, not dissimilar to some types of television flow, cf. the gradual absorption of viewers to television programmes such as series and news in which music plays an important role as preparation and characterization (e.g. Tagg and Clarida 2003).

12 In a syntagmatic perspective, and with a geometrical metaphor, the music might be considered to be circular and elliptical rather than linear (inspired by Björnberg 2000).

13 Cf. *stimuli progressions*, a phenomena offered by Muzak for employees (e.g retail managers). Today, the use of original music made by companies like Muzak have decreased in favour of the use of pre-existing music, offered in specific segmented compilations by Muzak and other companies (Graakjær & Jantzen 2009b).

14 An exception is the above mentioned example of the piano game in which the user is supposed to hit the tones of a played melody. Here, interestingly, sound is *both* a result of the user's activity and an input in itself.

15 The aggressive tone of the game is counterbalanced in another more 'loving' game on the same microsite where the user is supposed 'to kiss' (loudly, of course) as many bottles of mineral water as possible.

Chapter 29
Alternative Online Videos in the 2008 U.S. Presidential Election:
Multiple Mix of Media Attributes Approach to Grassroots Mobilization

Gooyong Kim
University of California–Los Angeles, USA

ABSTRACT

This chapter examines a new form of popular political mobilization–online videos. Revising a "mix of attributes approach" to media effects (Eveland, 2003), grassroots participation is included as the Internet's new attribute, which renders a more sociopolitical impact of the medium. Furthermore, to examine its sociopolitical impact, the author suggests a "multiple" mix of attributes approach, which considers extrinsic attributes of audiences' media consumption contexts as well as intrinsic attributes of media configurations. In this regard, the author examines the grassroots participation attribute by interrogating how ordinary people participate in an online public sphere (www.dipdive.com) where they shared and reinforced their support for Obama by producing alternative videos. When it comes to the importance of individuals' critical appropriation of the Internet for political participation, through alternative video production, the potential of transformative human agency by shaping personal narratives toward a better future is realized. In online videos for the Obama campaign, identity politics and the democratization of campaign leadership as extrinsic attributes are enhancing the Internet's network politics for political mobilization. Nevertheless, there is ambivalence of online video's practical impact on society depending on each user's specific motivations and objectives of using it as seen in many cases of destructive, anti-social deployment of the Internet throughout the globe. Therefore, as an educational initiative to implement the multiple mixes of media attributes approach, this chapter concludes by proclaiming that it is a crucial issue for critical pedagogy practitioners to envisage Feenberg's (2002) "radical philosophy of technology" which demands individuals' active intervention in shaping technologies' social applications, as well as its redesign for a more egalitarian purposes. With critical media pedagogy as a premise of the strategic deployment of new media technologies for social change, common people can become leaders of democratic, grassroots political mobilization as well as active, popular pedagogues by producing alternative online videos.

DOI: 10.4018/978-1-60566-792-8.ch029

INTRODUCTION

With cutting-edge online video-sharing technology, everyday authors, camera savvy users, production proficient videographers and lay individuals have much broader space now to engage in sociopolitical matters. By producing more effective audio-visual messages on the Internet, they can participate in the increasingly widening public sphere in which they realize the essence of grassroots democracy and discuss their concerns, interests, and agendas over the nation's political governance. Alternative forms of political mobilization on the Internet are also ever more available for ordinary citizens rather than the conventional political campaign advertisements grasping the public attention nowadays. Especially, with the success of the popular video-sharing website, www.youtube.com, grassroots online videos have become an important player for political campaign during the 2008 U.S. presidential election. During the 2008 campaign, many on-line users vigorously produced alternative campaign videos and distributed them via social network websites such as www.facebook.com and www.myspace.com. Considering Benjamin's (1934) belief that a "reader is at all times ready to become a writer" (p. 225), new digital media technologies can possibly contribute to a revival of the grassroots, egalitarian public sphere, which can lead to a more direct democracy. Yet, we must conceptualize Internet technologies in terms of their "embeddedness in the political economy, social relations, and political environment within which they are produced, circulated, and received" for a more correct understanding and limitations (Kellner, 1995, p. 2). While emergent technologies provide the marginalized with more liberating, counter-hegemonic politics of participation as a means of self-empowerment, they are also imbued with conformist limitations, that is, their embededness in the dominant social and political system that generate social reproduction. In this chapter, I argue that media technologies like YouTube, combined with a transformative pedagogy, can help realize the Internet's potential for democratization.

There have been many efforts to understand how the potential of the Internet can contribute to grassroots based egalitarian democratic governance in society. More specifically, advanced modes of online political communication have been vigorously investigated since the groundbreaking Internet-based strategy of Governor Howard Dean in the 2004 presidential election (Gillmor, 2006; Trippi, 2004). In this regard, Kellner (2005) stresses that the "result of the 2004 election has been the decentering and marginalizing of the importance of the corporate media punditocracy by Internet and blogosphere sources" (p. 306). However, there was not much effort to incorporate voluntary grassroots participations in elections prior to 2008; rather, candidates set up their own campaign Web sites mainly to raise campaign funds, publicize their policies and consolidate more voters online (Sundar, et al., 2003; Williams, et al., 2005; Xenos & Foot, 2005). With the breathtaking speed of the Internet's technological advances and its ubiquity throughout society, the campaign environment for the 2008 presidential election can be characterized as the first major Internet-oriented election.[1] More accurately, the election was a manifestation that substantiates transformative power of the Internet with the critical mass of people trespassing dividing lines between online and offline, pop culture and civic value, and new media and old for a sociopolitical cause.[2] However, there is still a dearth of research on how daily Internet users and a largely wired population make use of a relatively new video-sharing Internet technology in order to recruit, organize and mobilize fellow citizens for major election campaigns.

Among other things in the 2008 election, the sensational popularity of YouTube and the rise of the Democratic Party's nominee, Senator Barack Obama, are major indicators of the complex interconnections between Internet technologies, alternative online videos, grassroots political mobilization, and participatory democracy.[3] To be sure, a main dynamic for Obama to be elected as the Democratic Party's candidate, and the 44th president of the United States, came from a variety of online multi-media materials produced by his technology-savvy supporters. These supporters were largely young, college-educated, and multi-cultural that worked toward boosting the number, and amount, of small donations online as well as offline.

However, we must remember that technologies do not automatically guarantee any sociopolitical utopia; due to ambivalence of technologies' social contribution, such a possibility can only be actualized when the critical mass of individuals endeavors to utilize them for a more just, egalitarian society. Meaning, if provided with proper pedagogic interventions many people become able to employ the unprecedented resources of new media technologies by means of exercising the transformative power of numbers. Consequently, it is both timely and significant to examine how traditionally underrepresented Web-users[4], who did not usually enjoy access to conventional media production and public opinion formation, utilize cutting-edge video-sharing Internet technology to publicize alternative videos as an innovative platform for grassroots political mobilization.

"Multiple" Mix of Attributes Approach to Media Effects

While criticizing a limited view of traditional media effects scholarship that tends to exclusively focus on media content, Eveland (2003) proposes a "mix of attributes approach" that highlights "how media content interacts with other attributes of media, or how the nature of a medium encourages various types of uses" (p. 408). Eveland (2003) indicates a necessity of reassessing media effects by redefining the notion of media that consist of a particular set of attributes which produce certain effects. In other words, "considering specific media as concrete operationalizations" of various attributes, Eveland (2003) believes that a "mix of attributes approach" to media effects can better evaluate each medium's different accommodation of various attributes that produce different effects (p. 397). Accordingly, in order to evaluate media effects correctly, researchers have to identify certain attributes of the media, as well as content, because media effects are a multi-variated mixture of different attributes and content. In essence, the theoretical and practical benefits of applying a "mix of attributes approach" enables researchers to reconsider media effects to be "correlated in terms of their co-occurrence [with different attributes] in various communication technologies" (p. 398). In this respect, Eveland (2003) maintains that researchers should consider various attributes of the Internet, such as interactivity, organization/structure, control, channel, textuality and content.[5]

Although it may be appropriate to examine media effects by identifying a mix of media attributes quantitatively (Eveland, 2003), it may also be dangerous to ignore *qualitative* differences among various media in terms of audiences' context of media consumption and the political economy of the media. Also, he points out that it is important to consider the actual interaction between media's content and the structural arrangements to better assess media effects in reality. In this respect, I believe that Eveland (2003) takes a serious risk of an epistemological confusion, or technological determinism, which conflates a mix of the media's intrinsic attributes with real-world effects that have symbiotic relationships with other external factors, such as cultural, economic, and political contexts of audiences' media consumption. In other words, Eveland's (2003) proposition to measure media effects based on quantitative media attributes sacrifices other important contextual factors regarding an audience's reception of media.

Based on Eveland's mix of media attributes approach, and to better understand the sociopolitical impact of grassroots mobilization in political campaigns via alternative online videos, I propose a "multiple" mix of media attributes model to refine Eveland's conceptualization on media effects. In the model, there are two levels that revise Eveland's earlier attempt. First, I categorize attributes which engender media effects as intrinsic–or extrinsic, which introduces larger contextual elements for individual media experiences. By including participation attributes as new element of the Internet that encourages a broader sociopolitical effect, the multiple mix model endeavors to examine the roles of a medium's infrastructure and application that accommodate active interaction and collaboration between users. Thereby, it can help demonstrate how the Internet's broader space for individuals to organize and mobilize themselves contributes to realizing a more participatory democracy. Considering that different combinations of media attributes produce different effects, identifying and assessing a new attribute will entail an advanced perspective, which explains a more dynamic, "predictive strength" of media effects research by expanding a "repertoire of independent variables" (p. 405). In other words, by indicating the participation attribute of the Internet, it can be argued that researchers will be better able to examine an Internet probability to accommodate grassroots participation in sociopolitical matters. Furthermore, since there should be democratic reconstructions of technologies for us in order to maximize social benefits (Feenberg, 2002), I believe that examining Internet participation attribute can contribute to the progressive re-evaluation of new media technologies by "identifying the combination of factors that would increase the most desirable effects and decrease the most abhorrent media effects" (Eveland, 2003, p. 408). With this perspective, incorporating a participation attribute into Eveland's (2003) "mix of attributes approach" will facilitate a more critical re-appropriation of new media for a sociopolitical goal.

On the other hand, emphasizing the importance of individuals' concrete media experiences, a multiple mix of media attributes model recommends employing a research method designed to investigate intrinsic attributes of media configurations in tandem with holistic interactions and other extrinsic attributes such as culture, society, and politics at large. By extrinsic attributes of media effects, I mean forthcoming results of individuals' attitude toward certain media technologies within larger cultural and political contexts. In other words, it mainly refers to socialized and realized characteristics of certain communication media from users' specific commitment. In considering extrinsic attributes of media effects, researchers will be more able to examine a concrete distinctive sociopolitical impact of new Internet technologies by envisioning the importance of dialectic interactions between the media's technological features and the audiences' subjective appropriation of them. The main theoretical and practical contribution of including the extrinsic attributes of media effects is that it sheds crucial light on the important role of individuals' media consumption and production experiences within larger sociopolitical situations. For example, in the case of the Obama campaign, larger hostile sentiments against the Republican Party played an important role motivating everyday citizens to rely on new Internet technologies as a means of grassroots political mobilization. In this respect, online videos using a multiple mix of attributes approach provided an updated perspective on the relationship between grassroots participation of ordinary people and the communicative effects of online videos in the 2008 presidential campaign.

The Internet and Individuals' Sociopolitical Participation

As Bimber (1999; 2001; 2003) indicates, the Internet as a mode of political communication does not solely entail a "revolution" of political participation. Thus, researchers have to closely investigate other factors that may lead to the political engagements of a number of individuals. In other words, highly developed communication technologies do not automatically guarantee a participatory democratic society. Rather, the Internet is one of conditions that make possible politically motivated people to practice democratic values in society. Just as direct democracy in ancient Greece was possible through direct participation of groups of individuals who were affordable and willing to travel and spend their daytime in the public arenas, the Internet can be a favorable condition that helps reconsider the real value of democratic governance in industrial capitalist societies. In order for democracy to work in society, a more quintessential philosophy must precede, that is an individual's critical sociopolitical consciousness. Without voluntary critical participation of socially conscious people, efficient forms of communication will not revive the essence of democracy as a crucial process of self-governance through collective cooperation. No matter how advanced, secure, or cost-efficient information technologies may be as a kind of intrinsic media attributes,[6] without the practical engagement of civic-minded citizens, and good amounts of socio-politically conscious masses, there ends up being an echo without resonance.[7] Consequently, it is not a "limited effects" media model for grassroots political participation, but the individuals' lack of *interests* and *motivation* that better explains the gap between technological developments of the medium and political engagement.

Bimber (2001) asserts the relationship between information and political engagement is not straight-forward. The traditional instrumental-quantitative approach to the effect of information based on "mechanism links between information availability and levels of engagement" does not successfully explain how Internet's rich and cost-effective provision of political information secures broader political participations (p. 64). Stressing the necessity to examine "how information technology affects attention, salience, affect, schema, and other cognitive phenomena" (p. 64), he believes there are other qualitative factors that induce individuals' political engagement. The instrumental-quantitative model in the political role of information seems equivalent to Eveland's (2003) attempt to evaluate quantitative make-ups of intrinsic media attributes as primers of media effects. Meaning, these elements do not successfully consider the crucial role of human agency in the purposive and practical applications within the real world. Thus, a simple equation between a quantity of information and individuals' political engagement does not hold true. Considering that traditional indicators of political participation such as education, gender, socioeconomic status, age, trust, and political interest exercise direct and strong impacts on individuals' engagement (Bimber, 1999; 2001), my "multiple" mix of attributes approach explains how individuals in different sociopolitical contexts exercise political involvement to accomplish their objectives, according to symbiotic interactions with the media they apply. Having the deliberative importance of political communication in mind, it is more important to remember that the true value of the Internet as a means of political communication is only constructed by how individuals put it into actual deployment with specific civic-minded intentions, with an individual's critical consciousness playing the most important role in shaping the media as a transformative tool. However, it is a difficult pedagogical question to invite people to use online videos for sociopolitical matters, which tend to be used as a medium of entertainment mostly.

Taking into account that all sociopolitical mobilizations are based on the successful utilization of crucial information that marshals the masses, the content/ information of the Internet should equally be stressed with Internet's technological attributes (Bimber, 2000). Content/ information can be classified as both an intrinsic and an extrinsic attribute depending on how one recognizes its function. When one considers media content as a constructive product of social actors, it is an extrinsic attribute that exerts open-ended sociopolitical impacts. However, if media content is classified by how it is created and with what purpose, then it is more of an intrinsic commodity that engenders pre-determined certain effects. The cost-lowering effects of the Internet to circulate content/ information is certainly a groundbreaking contribution. However, the technological innovation of the Internet can only be fulfilled by people's conscious utilization of it with acute purposes in order to realize the wishful thinking of equating the quantity of information and direct participation. To be sure, there is a huge variety of the content/ information available on the Internet from pornography to political manifesto. In this regard, alternative online political videos for the Obama campaign as a strategic innovation of grassroots participation can be considered an extrinsic factor that is imbued with individual contributions.

Compared to text-based and fact-driven information in earlier stages of the Internet, online videos are capable of carrying more contextual, affective, and other cognitive elements. Regarding Internet's communicative structure and multiple sources of information as objective conditions for grassroots political participation, the deployment of online videos in the 2008 election was a subjective factor of a tactical innovation for political mobilization from bottom up. Grasping critical sympathetic attentions and affections from fellow citizens, by sharing vivid testimonies for the necessity of political change based on their everyday experiences, online videos successfully motivate ordinary people to take part in a community of alternative media producers and campaign organizers. Here, rather than technological determinism, which devastates the transformative power of human agency, it is more desirable to understand people's concrete, dialectical appropriation of the Internet for their sociopolitical causes as an extrinsic attribute. While it is certainly true that there is far more access to media production tools than ever before, there is a disparity between the potential and actual utilization of the Internet's productive potential of alternative materials. Also, though some people can create an alternative online video, it is not always the case that they use it with clear sociopolitical intentions.[8] As an indicator of popular YouTube video trends, for example, *Time* magazine's annual report of "Top 10 Viral Videos" reveals that most of the videos in the list are about comedy, parody, spoof, music video, celebrity, or sensational materials, which mostly recirculate the dominant corporate media spectacles just as Juhasz (2009) indicates. From this point of view, there should be much more emphasis on the pedagogical as well as the social implications of alternative content created by socially motivated Internet users as a means of their political participation. Thus, given the importance of the actual nature of alternative grassroot-initiated content, and its correct sociopolitical purposes, it is reasonable to stress pedagogical interventions to motivate, encourage and mobilize common Netizens to do so in their everyday lives.

The Obama Phenomenon and Grassroots Campaign Mobilization

Along with the successful debut of political online videos, the most conspicuous characteristic of the 2008 U.S. Presidential campaign is the rise of a seemingly novice politician, Senator Barack Obama. Among many journalistic accounts for the Obama campaign's success, Collins (2008) maintains that Obama is more than a candidate for the presidential election; rather, he is a major phenomenon in the United States. His first victory in the Democratic Party's primaries and caucuses in Iowa on January 3, 2008 marked an initiation of upward political spirals in popularity that were powered by grassroots participation and mobilization. Under dire cultural/ social/ economic conditions within the Bush Administration, his campaign provided lay people with opportunities to think over problems in their daily lives and get involved in the campaign as a problem-solving process. Others account for the political implication of Obama's Iowa victory as something qualitatively different from the traditional party conventions because of the type of voter, with "57 percent said they were participating for the first time" (Balz et al., 2008, n.p.). It was also reported that for more than 40 percent of the turnout, Obama was the main reason for their participation.[9] The campaign may serve as an exemplar for showing how the transformative power of common people are realized by collective self-organization and mobilization in using technology for democratic governance.

The network nature of Internet communication has been perfectly matched with voluntary and spontaneous participation of grassroots communities of ordinary people (Castells, 2000). By the communicative rationality (Habermas, 1984) with the network politics of the Internet, the conventional notion of formal political participation characterized as one-vote-per-person can be reconditioned to be "direct democracy with grassroots participation" through the unfettered "ideal speech" condition of the Internet public sphere. If this utopian notion of democracy could be realized with individuals' voluntary participations via the Internet, Dewey's (1954) egalitarian notion of democracy as a form of human relationships not as a formal political representation will become more viable. In this respect, individuals' transformative use of the Internet as an extrinsic condition, together with its communicative competence as an intrinsic media factor, proposes a probability to revitalize the democratic self-governance by people (Habermas, 1987).

The changed media landscape for political information production, distribution and consumption encourages individuals to take on a broader space of political participation. During the campaign season, together with large opportunities to produce political information through blog postings and alternative online videos, individuals' major source of campaign-related news marked a shift from conventional mass media such as radio and newspaper to newer media like cable TV or the Internet. For instance, even though television remains as the most dominant news source, "a solid majority of voters now say that they get *any* news about the presidential election from the Internet, with voters between the ages 18 to 29, proclaiming 76%" (Kohut, Doherty, Dimock & Keeter, 2008, pp. 24-5). While the Obama campaign mass-distributed its core message of "change" via TV, on the other hand, it revolutionized social-networking media applications that spread grassroots media content for younger voters. In this regard, Young (2008) summarizes the Obama campaign's effective deployment of Internet media as a "strategy to build his [campaign] brand, and later a more targeted broadcast media schedule that was supported by on-the-ground events and one to one media programs" allowing him to take the Oval Office in the end (n.p.). Nonetheless, more than anything else, it was lay people's civic minded and politically conscious deployment of the Internet technologies that helped implement the transformative politics of technology as a tool of social change.

Thus, the Obama campaign carved out a new rule for the Internet's role in political mobilization and organization. One journalistic account compares Obama campaign's deployment of the Internet to other historic presidential cases: What newspaper was to Jefferson, radio to F.D.R. and television to J.F.K., the Internet was to Obama (Carr, 2008). The most interesting aspect of the Obama campaign's strategic deployment of media for political advertising is that it realized a good mix of new individual media with traditional mass media alike. This combination helped make possible record-breaking online fundraising through grassroots participation. According to TNS Media Intelligence, "Obama campaign spent a record-shattering $ 293 million on TV ads between January 1, 2007 and October 29, 2008 … [while] McCain spent $132 million during the same period" (Delany, 2008, n.p). However, this conventional method of campaigning that consumes large amounts of money was rather auxiliary to the micro level recruiting via a blend of voters' voluntary participation, and new media technologies. Organized by online social-networking applications, e-mail, phone-calls and text-messaging, the campaign not only distributed mass information but also individual supporters efficiently informed, motivated and engaged additional supporters. As one of the most widespread individualized media, e-mail played an important role in persuading individuals to vote. Considering that younger voters usually are defter in utilizing new media applications, one particular advantage of using e-mail is that it reaches an audience with broader age segments though there was socioeconomic gaps in receiving campaign-related issues. For example, "nearly a quarter of voters (24%) say they received email from a campaign or other group urging them to vote in a particular way, up from 14% in the November 2004" (Kohut, Doherty, Dimock & Keeter, 2008, p. 22). Also important to note is the Obama campaign's skillful use of text-messaging contributed toward mobilizing hard-to-engage politically young voters with two-third of voters younger than age 30 voting for Obama,[10] which is at least more than 2.2 million young voter ballots compared to 19.4 million for Kerry in 2004.[11] Considering young adults are actively social-networked in the course of their daily lives, dissemination of grassroots YouTube videos played an important role to catch uncommitted young voters' attention and mobilize them to vote. Pew center supported this claim in its research report that shows 66% of 18-to-29-year-olds who use the Internet has at least one social-networking profile, contrasting to 18% of those age 30 and older (Smith & Rainie, 2008). In sum, it was a good match between the Obama campaign's active strategic deployment of Internet's social-networking capability and young voters' vigorous online engagements. Consequently, the campaign manifested the power of peer-to-peer, bottom-up model of mobilization powered by voluntary participation from millions of "block-walkers, phone-bankers, email-forwarders, Facebook-status-changers, and parent-pesterers, as well as the tens of millions of dollars needed to fund their activities and the online system that organized them" (Delany, 2008, n.p.; Stirland, 2008).

The crux of this political media phenomenon though remains centered on forms of grassroots participation. Major activities for the Obama campaign such as fund-raising, recruiting and organizing campaign volunteers, and developing campaign strategies were largely created by Internet communities.[12] Though supporters' for Republican candidates also utilized Web applications, those for the Democrats surpassed in their aptness of matching Internet's non-hierarchical and synchronized communicative competence with voluntary grassroots participation (Smith, 2009). In other words, the bedrock of the campaign's innovative strategies is a perfect combination of Internet's effective communicative capacity and ordinary people's vigorous grassroots participations (Gibbs, 2008; Keeter, Horowitz & Tyson, 2008; Smith & Rainie, 2008). From this point of view, Maag (2008) considers the race for the Democratic presidential nomination to be a litmus test for a grassroots-centered campaign organization today:

Clinton enjoys endorsements from Ohio's popular governor and many Democratic officeholders. If she retains her (albeit shrinking) lead in the polls, it will mean that a traditional, top-down campaign rooted in the party establishment still can win in the clutch. But if Obama scores an upset, it could prove that a new breed of grassroots campaign—viral, internet-based, built from the ground up by neophytes like Antoinette McCall—is finally ready for prime time. (n.p., emphasis added)

Within the Internet-based political campaign, popular grassroots participants are the essence and motor of a social revolution. Focusing exclusively on major candidates and turning them into mere "horse-race" coverage, traditional journalism privatizes the public good of political campaign events which is a critical process of democratic governance. Simply put, there used to be no place for ordinary people to be major participants in conventional political campaigns as an essential governing process of "democracy." Dissemination applications, such as online videos, afford innovative grassroots political participation thus presenting a paradigm-shift of political mobilization in the age of new media.

Historically, during the 2004 Democratic primary campaign trails, the party's nomination candidate Howard Dean had a weblog, "Blog for America," which was a harbinger that indicated the potential of the Internet in mobilizing a grassroots campaign (Gilmore, 2006; Kahn & Kellner, 2005a; Kerbel & Bloom, 2005; Trippi, 2004). The success of his blog offered some early evidence that the Internet had great potential for promoting grassroots involvement based on voluntary participation. It also provided an increasingly wired population to engage in both their virtual and physical worlds. In other words, individuals not only engaged in political deliberations of the virtual public sphere but also physically entered into the political campaign as a revitalization of grassroots political participation.

The initial stage of grassroots campaign mobilization by Howard Dean in 2004 has been further elaborated in its strategies to use alternative media and extended in its strategy to mobilize undecided voters more recently in the 2008 Presidential election. Grassroots visual materials–as opposed to professionally produced TV commercials–were one of the Obama campaign's fundamental differences from conventional political campaigning (Keeter, Horowitz & Tyson, 2008; Kohut, Keeter, Doherty, & Dimock, 2008; Smith & Rainie, 2008). Here, online videos stand as another method for a qualitative breakthrough of self-organization and communal mobilization. Given the fact that young people's everyday lives are strongly associated with online social networking sites, both the popularity and the spontaneity of grassroots visual material are enormous, especially in comparison with conventional media coverage. It is also remarkable to acknowledge that the conventional broadcasting media outlets have increasingly been incorporating grassroots videos as a way to deliver live reports in their regular programs (e.g., CNN's http://www.ireport.com). Several studies have shown that more than half of social networking websites users are between 35 and 64 years old and comprise a more active voting population than other voting groups (Gueorguieva, 2008). In the 2008 election, Obama received more votes from people active in creating online visual materials and using social networking sites than McCain, constituting 66% votes from the 18-to-29 age group and 52% from the 30-to-44 (Pew Research Center for the People & the Press, 2008).

Thus, the Obama campaign helped to reinvent and reinstate the meaning of democratic politics not as a patronizing model of top-down elitism but as a grassroots model of mutual self-organization and collective governance. More than posting and forwarding political writings and multimedia productions online, Obama supporters devoted themselves to organizing and mobilizing uncommitted fellow Americans to get out and "vote for change" as an extrinsic sociopolitical attribute. In other words, an optimal mix of Internet's intrinsic attribute of participation with extrinsic attributes of American polity came to fruition resulting in the Presidency of Obama. In this regard, Feenberg's (2002) ambiguity of technology was determined upon a dialectical interrelationship between the sociopolitical contexts of the 2008 election and people's practical applications of media technologies. Likewise, from the 2008 election we learned there will be many more social moments when ordinary people are "increasingly bringing Web 2.0 to political activism, developing new watchdog tools" against formal political systems (Caplan, 2008, n.p.). In sum, the most significant outcome of the 2008 election substantiates the heuristic competence of the multiple mix of attributes approach which contemplates Internet's communicative power and people's conscious utilization of it as a means of grassroots mobilization.

"Yes, We Can": A Model of Political Online Videos

Among the enormous volume of alternative media artifacts for the Obama campaign, will.i.am's *"Yes, We Can"* music video is most iconic. It manifests how a powerful online alternative video can be inspirational and persuasive. As a professional musician of the hip-hop group Black Eyed Peas, will.i.am made the *"Yes, We Can"* song and music video after he was inspired and moved by Senator Obama's concession speech at the New Hampshire primary on January 8, 2008. From the inception of this MTV-style music video, it breaks with conventional ways of producing music videos, as will.i.am assembled a variety of artists to participate. He describes:

[I]t was pure inspiration ... so I called my friends ... and they called their friends.... We made the song and video.... Usually this process would take months ... a bunch of record company people figuring out strategies and release dates ... but this time I took it in my own hands ... and we did it together in 48 hours ... and instead of putting it in the hands of profit we put it in the hands of inspiration....[13]

In addition to "*Yes We Can,*" on Dipdive, grassroots-based videos by ordinary people articulated their own agendas and narratives to support Obama.[14] Under the name of "YWC Testimonials," 29 personal videos manifest rationale support for Obama. With a personal narrative form, ordinary supporters in the videos pronounce their own sociopolitical perspectives concerning the importance of their participation as well as the campaign. The main purpose for the videos was to consolidate broader popular support for Obama and to recruit undecided voters sharing the genuine understanding about the election as a means of alternative political mobilization. In this respect, I regard alternative online videos as a unique extrinsic attribute that contributed to motivating, organizing and mobilizing grassroots participants as opposed to an intrinsic media component driven by greed and political agendas. Thus, it is meaningful to examine how online grassroots videos are deployed as an alternative form of political mobilization and its further sociopolitical implications as a part of broader interactions between media's intrinsic technological features and users' extrinsic application. Focusing on personal narratives in the videos, I conducted narrative/ discourse analysis of 29 online videos. By doing it, I explore the sociopolitical resonances of grassroots online videos and analyze how ordinary people make counter-hegemonic use of such media as a tactic to mobilize others online.

Online Videos and Alternative Political Mobilization for the Obama Campaign

Kellner (2008) sketches big moments of the 2008 election campaigns in terms of corporate media spectacles. Throughout the campaign trails, there were so many spectacular moments that were (re) produced by corporate media outlets, such as Palin's lipstick on a fighter dog on the one hand, and created and distributed online by grassroots campaign supporters like "*Yes, We Can*" and "*We are the Ones*" music videos. Though Kellner (2008) is right to point out that there were so many spectacular aspects of the Obama phenomenon and they exercised huge influences on the result of the campaign, in this chapter, I maintain that one needs more detailed analyses on the sociopolitical characteristics of the Obama spectacle based on its producers and contents. In terms of a producer of the Obama spectacle, its success was mainly attributable to grassroots participation in online video production that contained people's vivid narratives of hope for a better future. Considering one major reason why George W. Bush was elected in the 2000 election was that he "successfully pretended" to be a guy in the neighborhood, it was ordinary people who got impressed with Obama's personality, biological hybridity, community service experiences, and potential to serve the common sense of ordinary people who (re) produced, disseminated and ultimately mobilized other people to get him elected as the 44th president of the United States in 2008. Therefore, the 2008 election is a unique case that proved the power of grassroots online video spectacles, which differed decisively from the conventional media spectacles. This is the crux of the Obama spectacle that infiltrated Obama's image as a "new kind of politician representing change and bringing together people of different colors and ethnicities, ages, parts of the nation, and political views" (Kellner, 2008, p. 17).

However, not everyone welcomed alternative online videos that expressed political agendas with visual glitz. Especially, the conventional media outlets criticized that young supporters' activism through online videos is merely a form of consumerism that proliferates the cultish imagery of Obama through glitz media spectacles. For example, Klein (2008) warns that Obama's inspirational and even mesmerizing speech, and young supporters' blind support, could result in a political backlash that reduces its substance to mere rhetoric or spectacle. Because of the visual elements of alternative online videos, Phillips (2008) disparages participants in Obama's grassroots campaign, both online and offline, for replacing "reason, intelligence, stoicism, self-restraint and responsibility [with] credulousness, emotional incontinence, sentimentality, irresponsibility and self-obsession" (n.p.). Further, critics warn that Obama's young supporters seem to be transfixed and "dangerously close to becoming a cult of personality" (Krugman, 2008, n.p.). From this point of view, Klein (2008) argues that will.i.am's *"Yes, We Can"* music video is the center of gravity which draws the attention of young people into the creepy "mass messianism" of Obama.

As Kellner (2008) asserts, media spectacle has become the core ingredient of the presidential election. And it is absolutely true that an "informed and intelligent public thus needs to learn to deconstruct the spectacle to see the real issue behind the election, what interests and ideologies the candidate represent, and what sort of spin, narrative, and media spectacles are being used to sell the candidate" (p. 18). This chapter, however, contends that common Netizens are no longer passive recipients of messages– that is, from the mainstream political elites in the form of MTV-style hip music video, *"Yes, We Can."* The current new media environment offers an entirely different situation that enables individuals to creatively engage in sociopolitical matters. Considering the interlocked relation of knowledge to power (Foucault, 1980) and the relative democratization of access to newer media, the monopoly of knowledge/power becomes fundamentally improbable if not impossible. Unless Althusser (1971)'s concept of the media as an Ideological State Apparatus that interpellates ordinary people as obedient subjects is losing its ground, the strategic deployment of such media technologies enable lay individuals to exercise active sociopolitical agency. In other words, in the age of YouTube, individuals are no longer just consumers of corporate media spectacles; rather, there are a plenty of opportunities to (re) create grassroots media spectacles as a means to fight against the conventional media representations. Considering a diversity of opinions as a fundamental of democracy, grassroots YouTube spectacles for the Obama campaign illustrated a high potential of alternative online video productions as a new form of Gramscian counter-hegemonic cultural politics that is based on individuals' everyday life experiences.

In this regard, with people's grassroots participation, the strategic importance of the conventional media outlets as a means to mobilize campaign supporters is severely challenged. As an alternative means of campaign mobilization, everyday citizens are now able to express their political aspirations effectively via online videos. In this respect, O'Neill (2008) argues that the grassroots campaign is revolutionary because "supporters are not cultish slaves: they are people who have had enough of negative, fear-driven, small-minded politics, of both the Republican and Democratic variety, and now–as they keep telling us–they Want Change" (n.p.). Therefore, it is highly important to reveal how traditionally marginalized, unrepresented people deploy new media technologies to construct and publish their political agendas and mobilize other uncommitted people to participate in the grassroots campaign. With the benefits offered by new media technologies, they can articulate their critical social consciousness and become active leaders toward sociopolitical transformations, thus envisioning the true value of grassroots democracy. Thus, online videos are highly pedagogical as well as political that demand much attention from scholars that deem education to be political endeavors of difference. In terms of the pedagogic implication of videos, this chapter stresses the necessity of critical pedagogic interventions that encourage motivated people to utilize the sociopolitical resources rendered by the Internet technologies as a means of a democratic movement mobilizer in the age of new media.

Critical Media Pedagogy and Situationism

As a new form of critical pedagogy, critical media pedagogy provides individuals with a concrete strategy to exert transformative human agency through producing and distributing alternative media representations in a multi-media society (Kim, forthcoming). When the main purpose of critical pedagogy is to empower students to acquire critical, voluntary human agency that aims for social transformation (McLaren & Farahmandpur, 2005; McLaren & Kincheloe, 2007), critical media pedagogy considers alternative media productions as a form of political engagements to achieve a more egalitarian society. Just as the dominant class deploys mass media as an ideology machine (Sholle & Denski, 1994), it helps individuals to exercise the counter-hegemonic power of alternative media as a means of cultural politics of representation (McLaren, et al., 1995). Considering new media as a means of social transformation, critical media pedagogy prioritizes the ethical goals of progressive education by fostering the sociopolitical impact of grassroots media production, and thus promotes a more egalitarian, direct democracy.[15]

Lay individuals are able to connect their political beliefs by their personal narrative, identity and leadership on the videos with larger collective actions via Internet's communicative infrastructure. In other words, by obtaining the "strategic knowledge" of media's cultural politics that deals with the technical and political operations of the media, they can exercise active human agency to realize participatory democracy "by which less powerful ones struggle for audibility and for access to the technologies of social circulation and by which they fight to promote and defend the interests of their respective social formations" (Foucault, 1980, p. 4). Therefore, a critical analysis of grassroots videos calling for change in the 2008 U.S. Presidential election provides critical media pedagogy with concrete examples of transformative cultural politics that offers both a broad civic impact on sociopolitical arenas and an alternative to the sensationalist "horse-race" campaign coverage of the mainstream U.S. media.

Successful political mobilization requires people to critically scrutinize the objective social conditions and seize new opportunities; out of this dialectical analysis comes strategic knowledge of new media. So, not only should individuals analyze and take over the given situation, they have to carve out an alternative situation for social transformation, for example by producing alternative online videos as a strategic means to mobilize uncommitted supporters. From this point of view, Debord (1967) emphasizes the importance of critical consciousness for reconstructing an alternative social situation in relation to existing social problems mediated by the media. The media system has to be reconstructed because both the media and their spectacle "embody totalitarian varieties of social communication and control" (p. 37) and "[impose] images of the good which is a resume of everything that exists officially ... the guarantor of the systems' totalitarian cohesiveness" (p. 42). Consequently, critical media pedagogy emphasizes the construction of an alternative media situation that disturbs the ordinary and normal in order to jolt people out of their customary, conformative ways of thinking and acting. In this respect, I consider grassroots online videos, such as used during the Obama campaign, a kind of a Situationalist project that aims for a larger societal transformation through individuals' collective engagements in the counter-hegemonic politics of alternative media in their everyday lives.

Extrinsic Attributes: Grassroots Mobilization Perspectives

Regarding the Internet as a resource for social movements, individuals can manage viable alternative strategies for democratic mobilization. Referring to the politics of the media as a "refined instrumentalism" (p. 216), Scott and Street (2000) believe that new media provide the oppressed with unprecedented opportunities for a "new form of political discourse" of liberation (p. 218). In other words, as much as the dominant economic and political powers manipulate the mainstream media to strengthen their ideological hegemony, the marginalized can also deploy counter-hegemony by taking over a new set of sociopolitical opportunities offered by new media. As crucial components for any collective action, organizational as well as communicational conditions created by the Internet are replete with "the creation of networks of networks," a "high degree of co-ordination between movement networks," an "enormous reduction of costs," and a "relative lack of regulation" (p. 230). Likewise, Carroll and Hackett (2006) maintain that "media activism is indeed a diverse field of collective action, bringing us to the related issue of *strategic interaction*" among many sociopolitical constituencies (p. 90, emphasis original). For example, grassroots Obama supporters vigorously utilized social-networking online technologies which they shared crucial campaign information by creating over 2 million personal profiles on MyBrackObama.com, and more than 10 millions on MySpace and Facebook. In this respect, Obama's grassroots campaign politicized the Internet, operating the strategic knowledge of the new media that offers more egalitarian applications of technology for social change. It is this kind of extrinsic attribute of media effects, i.e., the cost-lowering effect for collective action (Polat, 2005), which common Netizens enacting a radical philosophy of technology are drawn toward.

As the most adverse predicament of mobilization, the problem of "free riders" can largely be overcome in the contemporary media situations. Over the course of individuals' decision making processes in stages of any collective action (Olson, 1965), the problem of "free riders" can be considered as a matter of the communicative problem which demands the deliberative consensus from movement constituencies concerning the necessity as well as the possible reward of risky collective action. In order to make any movement successful, unfettered communication is quintessential as Habermas insists. In this vein, Bimber, Flanagin, and Stohl (2005) hold that the high communicative competence and economic benefit of the Internet propose much better conditions for collective action mobilization: "locating and contacting appropriate participants, motivating them make private resources publicly available, persuading them to remain involved despite short-term setbacks and long-term risks, and coordinating their efforts appropriately" (p. 368). While over one million supporters received campaign news by subscribing to Obama's text-message alert system, supporters' communicative and organizational orchestration through the Internet substantiated the importance of simultaneous and free flow of information for campaign mobilization.

To put it differently, online videos for Obama's campaign furthered the possibility to realize McLuhan's proposal of re-tribalization in which the boundaries between the private and the pubic are malleable, as people become encouraged by watching like-minded and, equally important, like-appearing people in the videos. The communality of information and communication is a precursor of any collective action in a new media society so that individuals can share their political agendas and reach consensus. Thus, grassroots online videos have the potential to facilitate "transitions between private and public domains" which make collective action more feasible and successful because "boundary-crossing phenomena lie at the heart of new forms of technology-based action" in which the problem of "traditional free-riding" is ameliorated (Bimber et al., 2005, p. 377).

The transformative power of network politics has given grassroots political participation favorable conditions to operationalize a more egalitarian model of social relationships and voluntary governance. For Salter (2004), "the constitutive structure of the Internet" which is designed to allow "maximum inter-operability" makes possible for civic-minded people to implement the practical "application structure" of the Internet for decentered, interactive, and multi-layered communications (p. 188). During the campaign trails, lay citizens actively participated in organizing supporters by sending e-mails that encouraged others to visit neighborhoods and hold town-hall meetings. Considering the importance of social networks for recruiting possible supporters (Fernandez & McAdam, 1988; Gould, 1991; McAdam, 1986; McAdam & Paulsen, 1993), both Internet's configuration and application attributes fortify the campaign's ability to mobilize supporters with a firm commitment toward a better future. In this respect, seeing that around 200,000 offline gatherings were held by more than 35,000 volunteer groups based on MyBO.com (Vargas, 2008), the network-based grassroots Obama campaign exemplified the fundamental features of autonomous participation.

The network-based politics of the Internet supplies a huge platform for the politics of narrative as a source of political alternatives. Owing to the Internet's multiple, decentered, interactive nodes for grassroots participation, individuals are able to take advantage of new opportunities to publicize the "hidden transcript of subordinate groups" as a form of everyday resistance and alternatives (Scott, 1990, p. 138). Considering narrative as an agency's active involvement in the interpretation of social issues, it plays an important role in promoting the "polyvalence of meaning" as the foundation for alternative perspectives (Polletta, 1998, p. 142). For example, as a protest against Republican efforts to equate Obama with Muslim terrorists, people showed solidarity to him by changing their middle name to "Hussein," which is Obama's political liability on social networking websites such as Facebook.[16] It reveals that people engage language-games[17] in the polyvalence of meaning as an initial stage of their grassroots participation.

In this regard, the politics of narrative can further the diffusion of movements by giving individuals opportunities to construct a "base for mutual identification" and "shared interests" as the bedrock of political mobilization (Nepstad, 2001, p. 22). Considering Obama's popular public support came from his relentless pursue for an egalitarian society, his supporters vigorously reconstructed the narrative of hope in online videos; thereby, they addressed the rationale in their grassroots participation within the dire socioeconomic and political situation such as massive home foreclosures and financial meltdown under the Bush Administration. Moreover, when underrepresented people see a similar person declaring perspectives on politics, they feel entitled to participate in the public discussion because an "effective narrative fosters the audience's identification with the protagonist who embodies the values of the movement" (p. 24). In other words, people multiply their motivation and identity to support by sharing narratives formulated in their everyday lives. Though the degree of agency's narrative is circumscribed by the prescriptive power of discursive hegemony, counter-hegemonic discourse is also possible due to the nature of hegemony and human agency's active engagement in both individual and collective levels through its multi-vocality.[18] Thus, by implementing empowering features of personal narratives as an alternative political perspective, alternative online videos serve to fulfill the potential of supporters' multi-vocality of narrative.

Multi-vocality further illuminates the powerful strategy of identity formation as a subjective condition of mobilization. For instance, a continually repeated slogan for the Obama campaign exclaims "You are the one we've been waiting for." In terms of Bernstein's (1997) category of identity politics, hope/dream for a better future is perpetuated as an "identity for empowerment" (p. 536); unity/prosperity is deployed as an "identity goal" for participation (p. 536); and "change we can believe in" as a catch-phrase serves as an "identity strategy" to recruit the broadest possible supporters (p. 537). Furthermore, identifying the political success of Obama, the grassroots video participants try to project their symbolic desires by conflating Obama's career and their own personal success. In other words, Obama is more than a merely "political" figure who runs for the Oval Office; rather, he is a reincarnation of "forgotten" American dreams for them to pursue. Throughout the videos, people look sanguine and motivated to make a difference by participating in the grassroots political campaign for a better future. For example, Melissa George, who recently obtained American citizenship, believes that "Barack Obama represents and embodies the reasons why I came to this country" in her video on Dipdive.[19] In this respect, moreover, the multi-vocality provides the general Internet audience with broad and sensitive repertoires of their situational identities for support. On the power of identity politics for grassroots political mobilization, Bennett (2003) elaborates:

The ease of creating vast webs of politics enables global activist networks to finesse difficult problems of collective identity that often impede the growth of movements. To a remarkable degree, these networks appear to have undergone scale shifts while containing to accommodate considerable diversity in individual level political identity (p. 164, emphasis added).

This chapter argues that, with the network politics of the Internet for rapid distributions of political agendas, the grassroots online videos furnish enormous resources for everyday citizens to create popular strategies for participatory political mobilization.

With the politics of networks and counter-hegemonic narratives, the grassroots online videos present alternative visions for leadership roles in political mobilization. They suggest a more practical outlook to implement the democratization of leadership roles in campaign mobilization. People in the videos exert visionary leadership roles for political mobilization and carry out the important task of recruiting supporters by proposing both an alternative political prospect and the necessary critical insight to diagnose present conditions. With the non-hierarchical feature of the network, virtually no one can assume a dominant power position in the discursive practices among campaign constituencies, thus realizing the democratization of leadership (Bennett, 2003; Pickard, 2006a; 2006b). In other words, the multi-vocality within online network politics suggests the democratization of leadership roles and the multiple points for recruiting movement supporters because there are complex constraints on dominant leadership roles on the issues of class, gender, race and sexuality. For example, a decreased gap of voter turn-outs between the white population and other racial minorities, as well as the increased turn-out rate of the latter groups, potentially reveals a competence of leadership democratization in campaign mobilization as African-Americans, Asian-Americans and Hispanic-Americans participated in not only producing alternative online videos but also volunteering for the Obama campaign (Lopez & Taylor, 2009). Most of all, the highest increase in African-American females' voter turn-outs from 49.6% in 2004 to 58.2% in 2008 remarked a historic importance of the campaign characterized by grassroots participation and leadership democratization. Thus, considering the importance of the intermediate layer of leadership (Robnett, 1996), the multi-vocality exercised through the network politics of the Internet provides ordinary people to implement the potential of micro-/ meso-leadership and grassroots political mobilization via the Internet.

Online Videos and Politics of Alternative Media

In the grassroots campaign mobilization for Obama, common citizens practiced the theoretical and practical potential of the multiple mixes of attributes approach to the Internet, which provides opportunities to take on the dominant structure of power and knowledge. The uncontested monopoly of knowledge and the control of political news are now challenged by people's critical appropriation of the Internet for more egalitarian social purposes, further validating a participatory model of culture and democracy. With alternative online videos to articulate multiple voices based on the Internet's expanded flow of information, individuals are better able to construct alternative media situations that entail a new field for the conjuncture of media production, civic engagement, political mobilization, and participatory democracy. This new media situation has amplified individuals' capabilities in mutual pedagogy through proliferating new voices and visions, making possible the democratization of knowledge. Meaning, conventional relationships between the producers and the consumers of knowledge have been productively challenged. Thus, grassroots videos on Dipdive exemplify the practical viability of the democratization of knowledge, pedagogy, and political leadership in the age of new media. Within the constraints of the current paper, the widespread use of the Internet to distribute unfounded diatribe and mis-information will not be addressed although the author acknowledges its existence.

Clearly, the main purpose of producing grassroots online videos is to consolidate broader popular support for and to recruit undecided voters for Obama. Along with the politics of identity formation by online videos discussed earlier, people consider Obama's multi-racial and cultural background as an appropriate qualification to unify the country. From minorities' point of view, Obama offers a figurative sense to redeem the long history of racial and ethnic discrimination because he shares their biographical details and experiences. In this regard, Obama's symbolic capital as the first African-American president suggests a new chapter of the U.S. history which seemingly overcomes the multi-layered and chronic shackles of bigotry. Thus, Nia Long, as an African-American woman, affirms the meaning of Obama in the election: "he looks like me and I thought to myself this isn't [only] about him being a black man [but also] it's being a right man."[20] In turn, people expect Obama to help rehabilitate society with justice and harmony by doing "the right things for all people from the poorest to the richest [because] Barack was there for Black, White, Latino, and Asians."[21] In this vein, Christine Kim believes that the campaign is "all about bringing us together as a nation and as a world and healing us as a people."[22] As Freire (1970) asserts the philanthropic, therapeutic power of the pedagogy of the oppressed that gives both oppressors and the oppressed chances to reconcile peacefully, Obama's own stigma based on his skin color brings people united under the common theme of hope and a better future.

In the videos, Obama's community service experience is presented as his qualification to be the U.S. President who can understand the public sentiments and problems of daily lives. Hill Harper, a classmate at Harvard Law School, stresses Obama has committed himself to social justice and equality by turning down all the prestigious positions that naturally come to Harvard Law School graduates which could guarantee his personal prosperity.[23] With a long-term friend's genuine story-telling about Obama's personal history, the video carries an authentic discursive power from his lived experiences. The ontological meaning of Harper's appearance in the video provides supporters with a chance to remind of their "forgotten" ambitions in their school years. Also, as a lifetime community service organizer, Paul Schrade affirms the importance of Obama's local community service experiences to administer policies for broader social equity: "Obama's community organizing experiences really fit into the national office. If one doesn't understand problems of grassroots, being a national officer doesn't help very much."[24] By accentuating the importance of community service experiences, Schrade declares his political belief that the real politician has to take care of not elite lobbyists and multi-billionaires, but ordinary people in the marginalized corners of society. As a grandchild of the revolutionary Cesar Chavez, Christine Chavez praises Obama for inspiring ordinary people to voluntarily participate in the election campaign as something important for themselves as well as the nation. "We don't need a perfect political system, but we need prefect participation. And that's what I'm asking people to do today is to participate to help us change in the word of my grandfather, Cesar Chavez."[25] It reconstitutes the emancipatory value of narratives as construction of identity for the social progressive, forming a community for social change, and creation of voluntary human agency (Mitra, 2002).

As seen above, ordinary people in these grassroots videos are not mindless, brainwashed subjects characterized by the "replacement of reason, intelligence, stoicism, self-restraint and responsibility by credulousness, emotional incontinence, sentimentality, irresponsibility and self-obsession" (Phillips, 2008, n.p.). Even though there are some symptoms of "becoming a cult of [Obama's] personality" in several online sites such as "Obama Girl,"[26] such alternative video participants and producers are well aware of the social, economic, and political importance of the 2008 election and argue that Obama's qualities make him the presidential candidate most likely to work toward a more just society.

Through sharing beliefs, experiences, and political agendas in online videos, political supporters played crucial roles in organizing and mobilizing by providing others with models of political involvement. Not only do grassroots videos supply other uncommitted people with symbolic empowerment while watching, they facilitate others' physical and material participation in the form of small monetary donations or campaign organization volunteers. For example, the Obama campaign collected one hundred and fifty million dollars in one month of September, 2008. Compared to previous records of online fundraising performances which John McCain made six million dollars for his entire campaign in 2000, Howard Dean for twenty-seven million dollars and John Kerry for eighty-four million dollars in 2004, the Obama campaign's small, online donation for September surpassed the previous records all combined (Halperin, 2008). By the end of the election, over "3 million donors made a total of 6.5 million donations online adding up to more than $500 million" (Vargas, 2008, n.p.). Stated differently, videos provide ordinary people with opportunities to construct political participations on the campaign by utilizing new media technologies as a means of political mobilization and the democratization of leadership.

However, there are several limits to production style in the videos. With less than one minute videos, people mostly address their views and agendas in only a few sentences; this limitation led people to state just one main point without providing enough evidence or argument for their support. Considering that a mechanism of reaching consensus is based on uninhibited participation in mutual conversation, the identical format of the videos hinders grassroots video-production participants from exhibiting freer methods of articulating their opinions and agendas. So, even though alternative online videos suggest a possibility to wage a grassroots-initiated counter-hegemonic politics of media representation against corporate media spectacles, it is still confined to limits of mediated communication with time-space distances to engage free, unlimited communicative action.

In this chapter, I examine how common citizens critically appropriated newer Internet media within larger cultural, economic, social and political contexts of the 2008 election, and how it brought about the unprecedented political sensation of grassroots political mobilization. I, however, do not claim their effective deployment of newer media explains exhaustively overall success; rather, as noted earlier, this chapter endeavors to elucidate the new contribution that alternative online video and common Netizens's critical deployment of it rendered the medium's probability to revitalize the essence of democratic governance in the given sociopolitical confinements. In other words, this chapter sheds critical light on the complex relationship between macro extrinsic sociopolitical conditions and micro intrinsic new media factors that made possible via grassroots political organization and mobilization during the campaign trails. Within political communication scholarship that delves into the Internet's roles in political campaign and mobilization, this chapter contributes to understanding the importance of dialectical relationships between individuals, attributes of media technologies and larger sociopolitical contexts. For that matter, it is critical media pedagogy's fundamental task to emphasize that individuals' critical sociopolitical consciousness is a precondition, and capability to employ a newer media technology is necessary for effective political deployment.

Transformative Power of Grassroots and Necessity of Critical Media Pedagogy

The success of the Obama campaign validates the importance of examining how traditionally marginalized people deploy alternative online videos to construct and publish their political agendas and can thus involve themselves in participatory, grassroots democracy by political agenda-setting, mobilization of supporters, and fighting for the transformation of social conditions in their everyday lives. In this regard, grassroots videos and campaign organizations represent highly important political as well as pedagogical implications for the future.

While the concept of pedagogy focuses on the ethical-political dimension of knowledge, critical media pedagogy provides individuals with alternative perspectives on a more strategic deployment of media technologies toward a more just and egalitarian society. Since new opportunities offered by digital media do not automatically secure successful democratic mobilization, this chapter argues for the importance of implementing critical media pedagogy. Considering commodification and individualization as the current trends of the Internet (Brown, 1997; Dawson & Foster, 1996; McChesney, 2002; Wilhelm, 2000), it is a matter of critical pedagogy to motivate people to take advantage of new media for sociopolitical causes. In this respect, by acknowledging the counter-hegemonic power of alternative online videos, critical media pedagogy aims to equip individuals with a "radical philosophy of technology" that cultivates the political operations of the new media technologies to engage the hegemonic power of domination where it is maintained and pursue the counter-hegemonic politics of alternatives (Feenberg, 2002, p. vi). By taking strategic advantage of extrinsic attributes of the Internet, such as cost-lowering conditions to publicize political agenda

(Bennett, 2003; Carroll & Hackett, 2006) and the Internet's boundary-crossing feature as a solution to the problem of "free riding" in collective action (Bimber, et. al., 2005), individuals are positioned to manage unprecedented resources of grassroots political mobilization. More importantly, it revisits the emancipatory power of "praxis" by fusing theory and practices in individuals' everyday lives thanks to Internet's ubiquity for the cultural politics of the media. Thus, Giroux (2001)'s call for "performative pedagogy" becomes ever more possible, which "*translates knowledge back into practice, places theory in the political space of the performative, and invigorates the pedagogical as a practice through which collective struggles can be waged*" by operating the radical philosophy of new media technologies (p. 14, emphasis added).

Keeping in mind the dialectical relationship between sociopolitical conditions of new media technologies and individuals' transformative appropriation of them as discussed in the multiple mixes of media attributes, this chapter sheds critical light on the immense potential of individuals' critical assumption of the Feenberg's (2002) "democratic struggle over technology" for social change (p. 61). Just as Marx (1845) clearly states, there are highly dialectic relationships between human agency and environmental conditions in historical processes, critical media pedagogy provides the marginalized with the practical viability of a counter-hegemonic media culture. In other words, it is necessary to proliferate the transformative power of media production praxis that people can create the "skill of insurgents in devising protest tactics" within "the larger political environment" of new media as seen in the case of online videos for the Obama campaign (McAdam, 1983, p. 737). To this end, people should focus more on the critical use of technology with extrinsic attributes. Thus, it manifests the necessity of pedagogical endeavors that critically incorporate media technologies in the general education settings (Kahn & Kellner, 2005b; Kellner & Share, 2007). Just as ordinary people were able to demonstrate the power of strategic deployment of Internet technologies to realize positive change in the 2008 presidential election, it is recommended that media pedagogy should provide citizens with the up-to-date tools to carry out this analysis and, thus, make it more common to deploy them for social transformation within the cost-lowering structure of the Internet.

REFERENCES

Althusser, L. (1971). *Lenin and Philosophy and Other Essays*. London: New Left Books.

Balz, D., Kornblut, A., & Murray, S. (2008, January 4). Obama Wins Iowa's Democratic Caucuses. *The New York Time*. Retrieved June 7, 2008 from http://www.washingtonpost.com/wp-dyn/content/article/2008/01/03/AR2008010304441_pf.html

Benjamin, W. (1978). *Reflection* (Demetz, P., Ed.). New York: Hartcourt, Brace, Jovanovich.

Bennett, W. L. (2003). Communicating global activism: Strengths and vulnerabilities of networked politics. *Information Communication and Society*, *6*, 143–168. doi:10.1080/1369118032000093860

Bernstein, M. (1997). Celebration and suppression: The strategic uses of identity by the Lesbian and Gay movement. *American Journal of Sociology*, *103*, 531–565. doi:10.1086/231250

Bimber, B. (1999). The internet and citizen communication with government: Does the medium matter? *Political Communication*, *16*(4), 409–428. doi:10.1080/105846099198569

Bimber, B. (2000). The study of information technology and civic engagement. *Political Communication*, *17*(4), 329–333. doi:10.1080/10584600050178924

Bimber, B. (2001). Information and political engagement in America: The search for effects of information technology at the individual level. *Political Research Quarterly*, *54*(1), 53–67.

Bimber, B. (2003). *Information and American Democracy: Technology in the Evolution of Political Power*. Cambridge, UK: Cambridge University Press. doi:10.1017/CBO9780511615573

Bimber, B., Flanagin, A., & Stohl, C. (2005). Reconceptualizing collective action in the contemporary media environment. *Communication Theory*, *15*(4), 365–388. doi:10.1111/j.1468-2885.2005.tb00340.x

Brown, D. (1997). *Cybertrend*. London: Viking.

Caplan, J. (2008, June 30). The Citizen Watchdogs of Web 2.0. *Time*. Retrieved November 18, 2008, from http://www.time.com/time/business/article/0,8599,1819187,00.html

Carr, D. (2008, November 10). How Obama Tapped Into Social Networks' Power. *New York Times*. Retrieved November 11, 2008, from http://www.nytimes.com/2008/11/10/business/media/10carr.html?scp=24&sq=&st=nyt Carroll, W., & Hackett, R. (2006). Democratic Media Activism through the Lens of Social Movement Theory. *Media, Culture & Society, 28*, 83-104.

Castells, M. (2000). *The Rise of the Network Society* (2nd ed.). Malden, MA: Blackwell Publishing.

Collins, S. (2008, January 8). Getting to grips with Obama-mania. *Spiked*. Retrieved June 7, 2008, from http://www.spiked-online.com/index.php?/site/article/4250/

Dawson, M., & Foster, B. J. (1996). Virtual capitalism: The political economy of the information highway. *Monthly Review (New York, N.Y.)*, *48*, 40–59.

Debord, G. (1994). *The Society of the Spectacle*. New York: Zone Books.

Delany, C. (2008, November 5). How the Internet Put Barack Obama in the White House. *TechPresident.com*. Retrieved November 6, 2008, from http://www.techpresident.com/blog/entry/32998/how_the_internet_put_barack_obama_in_the_white_house

Dewey, J. (1954). *Public and its problems*. Denver, CO: Swallow Press Books.

Eveland, W. P. Jr. (2003). A mix of attributes approach to the study of media effects and new communication technologies. *The Journal of Communication*, *53*(3), 395–410. doi:10.1111/j.1460-2466.2003.tb02598.x

Feenberg, A. (2002). *Transforming Technology: A Critical Theory Revisited*. New York: Oxford University Press.

Fernandez, R., & McAdam, D. (1988). Social networks and social movements: multiorganizational fields and recruitment to Mississippi Freedom Summer. *Sociological Forum*, *3*, 357–382. doi:10.1007/BF01116431

Foucault, M. (1980). *Power/knowledge: Selected interviews and other writings* (Gordon, C., Ed.). New York: Pantheon.

Freire, P. (2006). Pedagogy of the Oppressed: 30th Anniversary Ed. New York: Continuum.

Gibbs, N. (2008, November, 05). How Obama Rewrote the Book. *Time*. Retrieved November 18, 2008, from http://www.time.com/time/politics/article/0,8599,1856914,00.html

Gillmor, D. (2006). *We the Media: Grassroots Journalism by the People, for the People*. Sebastopol, CA: O'Reilly Media.

Giroux, H. (2001). Cultural Studies as Performative Politics. *Cultural Studies ↔ Critical Methodologies, 1,* 5-23.

Gould, R. (1991). Multiple networks and mobilization in the Paris Commune, 1871. *American Sociological Review*, *56*, 716–729. doi:10.2307/2096251

Gueorguieva, V. (2008). Voters, MySpace, and YouTube: The impact of alternative communication channels on the 2006 election cycle and beyond. *Social Science Computer Review*, *26*(3), 288–300. doi:10.1177/0894439307305636

Habermas, J. (1984). The Theory of Communicative Action: *Vol. 1. Reason and the Rationalization of Society* (McCarthy, T., Trans.). Boston: Beacon Press.

Habermas, J. (1987). The Theory of Communicative Action: *Vol. 2. Lifeworld and System: A Critique of Functionalist Reason* (McCarthy, T., Trans.). Boston: Beacon Press.

Halperin, M. (2008, November 5). A Campaign of Firsts: Internet Fund-Raising Comes of Age. *Time*. Retrieved November 18, 2008, from http://www.time.com/time/specials/packages/article/0,28804,1856329_1856326_1856295,00.html

Juhasz, A. (2009). Learning the five lessons of YouTube: After trying to teach there, I don't believe the hype. *Cinema Journal*, *48*(2), 145–150. doi:10.1353/cj.0.0098

Kahn, R., & Kellner, D. (2005a). Oppositional politics and the Internet: A critical/ reconstructive approach. *Cultural Politics*, *1*, 75–100. doi:10.2752/174321905778054926

Kahn, R., & Kellner, D. (2005b). Reconstructing technoliteracy: A multiple literacy approach. *E-learning*, *2*(3), 238–251. doi:10.2304/elea.2005.2.3.4

Keeter, S., Horowitz, J., & Tyson, S. (2008, November, 12). *Young Voters in the 2008 Election*. Washington, D.C.: Pew Research Center for the People & the Press. Retrieved November 14, 2008, from http://pewresearch.org/pubs/1031/young-voters-in-the-2008-election

Kellner, D. (1995). *Media culture: Cultural studies, identity and politics between the modern and the postmodern*. New York: Routledge. doi:10.4324/9780203205808

Kellner, D. (2005). The Media and Election 2004. *Cultural Studies ↔ Critical Methodologies, 5*(3), 298-308.

Kellner, D. (2008). Media Spectacle and the 2008 Presidential Election: Some Pre-election Reflections. *Mediascape: UCLA's Journal of Cinema and Media Studies*.

Kellner, D., & Share, J. (2007). Critical media literacy: Crucial policy choices for a twenty-first-century democracy. *Policy Futures in Education*, *5*(1), 59–69. doi:10.2304/pfie.2007.5.1.59

Kerbel, M., & Bloom, J. (2005). Blog for America and Civic Involvement. *Press/ Politics, 10,* 2-27.

Kim, G. (forthcoming). *The Popular as the Political: Critical Media Pedagogy as a Condition for Grassroots Collective Action Mobilization via YouTube Videos*. Ph.D. Dissertation. Los Angeles, CA: University of California.

Klein, J. (2008, February 7). Inspiration vs. Substance. *Time*. Retrieved June 7, 2008, from http://www.time.com/time/nation/article/0,8599,1710721,00.html

Kohut, A., Doherty, C., Dimock, M., & Keeter, S. (2008, November 13). *Republicans Want More Conservative Direction for GOP: High Marks for the Campaign, A High Bar for Obama*. Washington, DC: Pew Research Center for the People & the Press. Retrieved November 14, 2008, from http://people-press.org/report/471/high-bar-for-obama

Kohut, A., Keeter, S., Doherty, C., & Dimock, M. (2008, January, 11). *Social Networking and Online Videos Take Off: Internet's Broader Role in Campaign 2008*. Washington, DC: Pew Research Center for the People & the Press. Retrieved November 14, 2008, from http://www.pewinternet.org/pdfs/Pew_MediaSources_jan08.pdf

Krugman, P. (2008, February 11). Hate Springs Eternal. *The New York Times*. Retrieved June 9, 2008, from http://www.nytimes.com/2008/02/11/opinion/11krugman.html?_r=1&ref=opinion&oref=slogin

Lopez, M. H., & Taylor, P. (2009, April 30). *Dissecting the 2008 Electorate: Most Diverse in U.S. History*. Washington, DC: Pew Research Center. Retrieved May 2, 2009, from http://pewresearch.org/pubs/1209/racial-ethnic-voters-presidential-election

Maag, C. (2008, February 25). Obama's Ohio Grassroots Advantage. *The Time*. Retrieved June 7, 2008, from http://www.time.com/time/politics/article/0,8599,1717150,00.html

Marx, K. (1970). Theses on Feuerbach. In Arthur, C. J. (Ed.), *The German Ideology*. New York: International Publishers.

McAdam, D. (1983). Tactical innovation and the pace of insurgency. *American Sociological Review*, *48*(6), 735–754. doi:10.2307/2095322

McAdam, D. (1986). Recruitment to high-risk activism. *American Journal of Sociology*, *92*, 64–90. doi:10.1086/228463

McAdam, D., & Paulsen, R. (1993). Specifying the relationship between social ties and activism. *American Journal of Sociology*, *99*, 640–667. doi:10.1086/230319

McChesney, R. (2002). The Titanic sails on: Why the Internet won't sink the media giants. In Dines, G., & Humez, J. (Eds.), *Gender, Race and Class in Media*. London: Sage.

McLaren, P., & Farahmandpur, R. (2005). *Teaching Against Global Capitalism and The New Imperialism: A Critical Pedagogy*. Lanham, MD: Rowman & Littlefield.

McLaren, P., Hammer, R., Sholle, D., & Reilly, R. (1995). *Rethinking Media Literacy: A Critical Pedagogy of Representation*. New York: Peter Lang Publishing.

McLaren, P., & Kincheloe, J. (Eds.). (2007). *Critical Pedagogy: Where Are We Now?*New York: Peter Lang Publishing.

Mitra, A. (2002). Theorizing cyberspace: the idea of voice applied to the internet discourse. *New Media & Society*, *4*, 479–498. doi:10.1177/146144402321466778

Nepstad, S. (2001). Creating transnational solidarity: The use of narrative in the U.S.–Central America peace movement. *Mobilization: An International Journal*, *6*, 21–36.

O'Neill. (2008, February 21). Why they're scared of Obamamania. *Spiked*. Retrieved from http://www.spiked-online.com/index.php?/site/article/4556/

Olson, M. (1965). *The Logic ofCollective Action: Public Goods and the Theory of Group*. Cambridge, MA: Harvard University Press.

Pew Research Center for the People & the Press. (2008, November 5). *Inside Obama's Sweeping Victory*. Washington, DC. Retrieved November 14, 2008, from http://pewresearch.org/pubs/1023/exit-poll-analysis-2008 (11/14/08).

Phillips, M. (2008). *Princess Obama*. Retrieved June 9, 2008, from http://www.spectator.co.uk/melaniephillips/503146/

Pickard, V. (2006 a). Assessing the radical democracy of Indymedia: Discursive, technical, and institutional constructions. *Critical Studies in Media Communication*, *23*, 19–38. doi:10.1080/07393180600570691

Pickard, V. (2006 b). United yet autonomous: Indymedia and the struggle to sustain a radical democratic network. *Media Culture & Society*, *28*, 315–336. doi:10.1177/0163443706061685

Polat, R. (2005). The Internet and political participation: Exploring the explanatory links. *European Journal of Communication*, *20*, 435–459. doi:10.1177/0267323105058251

Polletta, F. (1998). It was like a fever… Narrative and identity in social protest. *Social Problems*, *45*, 137–159. doi:10.1525/sp.1998.45.2.03x0163g

Robnett, B. (1996). African-American women in the Civil Rights Movements, 1954-1964: Gender, leadership and micromobilization. *American Journal of Sociology*, *101*, 1661–1693. doi:10.1086/230870

Salter, L. (2004). Structure and forms of use: A contribution to understanding the 'effects' of the internet on deliberative democracy. *Information Communication and Society*, *7*, 185–206. doi:10.1080/1369118042000232648

Scott, A., & Street, J. (2000). From media politics to e-protest: The use of popular culture and new media in parties and social movements. *Information Communication and Society*, *3*(2), 215–240.

Scott, J. (1990). *Domination and the Arts of Resistance: Hidden Transcripts*. New Haven, CT: Yale University Press.

Smith, A. (2009, April 15). *The Internet's Role in Campaign 2008*. Washington, DC: Pew Internet & American Life Project. Retrieved April 15, 2009, from http://pewresearch.org/pubs/1192/internet-politics-campaign-2008

Smith, A., & Rainie, L. (2008, June 15). *The Internet and the Election 2008*. Washington, DC: Pew Internet & American Life Project. Retrieved November 14, 2008, from http://pewresearch.org/pubs/869/politics-goes-viral-online

Stirland, S. L. (2008, November 5). Propelled by Internet, Barack Obama Wins Presidency. *Wired*. Retrieved November 11, 2008, from http://www.wired.com/threatlevel/2008/11/propelled-by-in/

Sundar, S., Kalyanaraman, S., & Brown, J. (2003). Explicating Web site interactivity: impression formation effects in political campaign sites. *Communication Research*, *30*(1), 30–59. doi:10.1177/0093650202239025

Trippi, J. (2004). *The Revolution Will Not Be Televised: Democracy, the Internet, and the Overthrow of Everything*. New York: Regan Books.

Vargas, J. A. (2008, November 20). Obama Raised Half a Billion Online. *The Washington Post*. Retrieved December 12, 2008, from http://voices.washingtonpost.com/44/2008/11/20/obama_raised_half_a_billion_on.html

Wilhelm, A. (2000). *Democracy in the Digital Age: Challenges to Political Life in Cyberspace*. New York: Routledge.

Williams, A., Trammell, K., Postelnicu, M., Landreville, L., & Martin, J. (2005). Blogging and Hyperlinking: use of the Web to enhance viability during the 2004 US campaign. *Journalism Studies*, *6*(2), 177–186. doi:10.1080/14616700500057262

Xenos, M., & Foot, K. (2005). Politics as usual, or politics unusual? Position taking and dialogue on campaign Websites in the 2002 U.S. elections. *The Journal of Communication*, *55*(1), 169–185. doi:10.1111/j.1460-2466.2005.tb02665.x

Young, A. (2008, June 04). Hillary vs. Barack: Who Had the Smartest Media Strategy? *Advertising Age*. Retrieved August 29, 2008, from http://adage.com/campaigntrail/post?article_id=127508

ENDNOTES

1 See Rasiej, A. and Sifry, M.L. (November 12, 2008). The Web: 2008's winning ticket.

Politico. URL: http://www.politico.com/news/stories/1108/15520.html (12/12/08).

2 For example, on relationships between new media and old ones, see Rosenstiel, T, and Kovach, B. (2009). Special Reports: Lessons of the Election. *The State of the News Media: An Annual Report on American Journalism*. Washington, D.C.: The Project for Excellence in Journalism. Available at: http://www.stateofthemedia.org/2009/narrative_special_lessonsoftheelection.php?cat=1&media=12 (3/28/2009)

3 For the social impact of YouTube for the contemporary politics and pedagogy, see Kellner, D. & Kim, G. (2009). YouTube, Politics, and Pedagogy: Some Critical Reflections. In R. Hammer & D. Kellner (eds). *Media/ Cultural Studies: Critical Approaches*. New York: Peter Lang Publishing. Pp. 615 – 636.

4 In this chapter, I use "ordinary people," "lay citizens" and "everyday Netizens" interchangeably to refer to individuals who usually did not have enough access to the media and capability to produce media artifacts as a means of public opinion building, realizing personal interests or sociopolitical participation.

5 For discussions on attributes of the Internet, see Newhagen, J. & Rafaeli, S. (1996). Why Communication Researchers Should Study the Internet. *Journal of Computer-Mediated Communication, 1/4*, and Walther, J. B., Gay, G. & Hancock, J. (2005). How Do Communication and Technology Researchers Study the Internet? *Journal of Communication, 55/3*, 632 – 657.

6 See, For example, Watson, A. and Cordonnier, V. (2002). Voting in the New Millennium: eVoting Holds the Promise to Expand Citizen Choice. Lecture Notes in Computer Science. Springer Berlin / Heidelberg, pp. 234-239; Wolman, D. (2003, October 31). Computer-Enabled Democracy? *Technology Review*. Available at: http://www.technologyreview.com/biomedicine/13344/

7 If one argues the Internet only reflects a herd mentality in society, creating the critical mass of sociopolitical conscious voices online can further an upward spiral of public sentiments/ opinions for grassroots political participation. Even if the Internet only reflects the public mentality of social constituencies, it is important to recognize the public opinion is a concrete outcome of a dialectics of people's interests, deliberation and participation. Therefore, there should be more emphases on the transformative potential of human agency that initiates positive redirection of the public sentiment and pedagogical intervention in lay Netizens's online activities that furthers a political participation.

8 For a reconsideration of users' purposes of deploying YouTube videos, see Kim, G. (2009). The Future of YouTube: Critical Reflections on YouTube Users' Discussion over Its Future. *InterActions: UCLA Journal of Education and Information Studies, 5/2*, Article #4.

9 For the contribution of young adults' voter turn-out, see Pew Research Center for the People & the Press (2008). *Inside Obama's Sweeping Victory*. URL: http://pewresearch.org/pubs/1023/exit-poll-analysis-2008 (11/14/08).

10 See, Pew Research Center for the People & the Press (2008). *Inside Obama's Sweeping Victory*. URL: http://pewresearch.org/pubs/1023/exit-poll-analysis-2008 (11/14/08).

11 See, Falcon, M. (2008, November 5). Youth Turnout Up By 2 Million From 2004. The *New Times*. Available at:http://thecaucus.blogs.nytimes.com/2008/11/05/youth-turn-out-up-by-2-million-from-2004/ (11/5/08)

12 Zephyr Teachout, a former Internet director of the Dean campaign believes that the

Obama campaign's online social networking applications were "in essence, rebuilt and consolidated versions of those created for the Dean campaign" by allowing people to donate money, organize meetings, and distribute media. See, Talbot, D. (2008). How Obama *Really* Did It. *Technology Review, September/October 2008*. Available at: http://www.technologyreview.com/web/21222/?a=f

13 http://yeswecan.dipdive.com/biography/

14 http://yeswecan.dipdive.com/ (YWC Testimonials)

15 For theoretical and practical potential of YouTube from critical media pedagogy's perspective, see Kellner, D. & Kim, G. (2010). YouTube, Critical Pedagogy, and Media Activism. *The Review of Education, Pedagogy and Cultural Studies, 32(1)*, 3 – 36.

16 See Kantor, J. (June 29, 2008). Obama Supporters Take His Name as Their Own. *The New York Times*. http://www.nytimes.com/2008/06/29/us/politics/29hussein.html?ref=politics (7/12/08).

17 For discussions on the relationship between language-games, legitimation, justice and human agency, see Lyotard, J. (1979). *The Postmodern Condition: A Report on Knowledge*. Minneapolis, MN: University of Minnesota Press.

18 See Gramsci, A. (1971). *Selections from the Prison Notebooks*. New York: International Publishers, and Bakhtin, M. (1981). *The Dialogic Imagination: Four Essays*. Austin, TX: University of Texas Press.

19 http://yeswecan.dipdive.com/#/~/videoplayer/0/285/1532/~/

20 http://yeswecan.dipdive.com/#/~/videoplayer/0/285/1591/~/

21 http://yeswecan.dipdive.com/#/~/videoplayer/0/285/1582/~/

22 http://yeswecan.dipdive.com/#/~/videoplayer/0/285/1520/~/

23 http://yeswecan.dipdive.com/#/~/videoplayer/0/285/1524/~/

24 http://yeswecan.dipdive.com/#/~/videoplayer/0/285/1537/~/

25 http://yeswecan.dipdive.com/#/~/videoplayer/0/285/1519/~/

26 http://obamagirl.com/

Chapter 30
What a Difference a Download Makes:
Political Advertising in the Digital Age

Lauren Reichart-Smith
The University of Alabama, USA

Kenny D. Smith
Samford University, USA

ABSTRACT

The Internet has captured the attention of the media, the government and much of the public. It has changed the way Americans receive information and communicate. With a number of political candidates creating MySpace profiles, YouTube videos and Second Life avatars it appears that the Internet and web 2.0 technologies have been leveraged for political advertising and campaigning. In the early literature the Internet and its role in politics had been purely speculative, with research only making vague guesses as to where the Internet would lead politicians in their political ambitions. The following chapter first outlines a historical perspective of political advertising, then examines contemporary forms and avenues of political advertising.

INTRODUCTION

"Thanks for the add!" This statement is not a polite acknowledgment from a constituent to a politician regarding a political advertisement. Rather, in the world of Web 2.0 campaigning, it's a comment from a political candidate's friend on MySpace, thanking the politician for adding that person as a friend. Today, the Internet has captured the attention of the media, the government and much of the public. It has changed the way Americans receive information and communicate. Even the term "Internet" has long since become interchangeable with a variety of expressions, such as new information highway or information superhighway (Pavlik, 1998). A 2006 survey done by Pew/Internet reported that 70% of American adults were Internet users (Lin, 2008).

Beyond going online for information and serving as a way to stay in touch, people are using the Internet to increase their knowledge about politics. During the 2000 election, Web sites became interactive and integrated campaign elements, helping

DOI: 10.4018/978-1-60566-792-8.ch030

to raise money, communicate with supporters, provide positions on issues, organize grassroots supporters, and turn out the vote (Fose, 2002). Fose then went on to say:

The Internet's importance in the political process will increase as more voters learn to use it as an avenue for activism and an opportunity to get information about the candidates. Because of this, candidates will continue to look to the Internet as a way to communicate their message, organize supporters, and raise money (pg. 1).

Of a reported population of 128 million Internet users in 2004, 40% indicated using the Internet for political information during that year's presidential election (Rainie, Horrigan & Cornfield, 2005). Candidate websites flourished in the 2004 election, but as is the ever-changing nature of the Internet, 2008 offered something new–the addition of political candidates–both presidential and local politicians–logging on to social networking sites and developing MySpace and Facebook pages.

In the early literature the Internet and its role in politics had been purely speculative, with research only making vague guesses as to where the Internet would lead politicians in their political ambitions. The future of American politics had been called an "age of Internet democracy" and the residents of the new political system were hypothesized to be known as "netizens." The new medium was predicted as the beginnings of true direct democracy - a vehicle for enabling common citizens, rather than distant elected representatives, to make ongoing policy decisions (Davis, 1999).

A Historical Perspective

Political advertising and campaigning in the United States dates all the way back to the first presidential race. Though there was not a formal discipline of communication studies at that time, the art of rhetoric and persuasion had been in practice since the days of Socrates and Aristotle. A political campaign is an organized effort which seeks to influence the decision making process within a specific group (Shea & Burton, 2001). Communication is the epistemological base by which campaigns begin, proceed, and conclude (Trent & Friedenberg, 2000). Political campaigns are not solely linked to politics; campaigns may include strategies and tactics to move the heads of religious organizations or corporations into and from power, to sell different products, or to encourage people to start or quit a behavior.

At the presidential level George Washington never had this problem. Washington, on the strength of his Revolutionary War heroism, ran unopposed twice. For John Adams the 1796 race changed things forever. It didn't take long for the campaign to turn bitter. Adams' Federalist party intimated that the Democratic-Republicans were involved with revolution in France. Thomas Jefferson and the Democratic-Republicans, in turn, tossed around words like monarchy and aristocracy in taking the Federalists to task for friendly dealings with Britain.

"Other voices in the fall of 1800 were shrill by any period's standard. Murder, robbery, rape, adultery, and incest will all be openly taught and practiced ... The air will be rent with the cries of distress, the soil will be soaked with blood and the nation black with crimes," should Jefferson be elected according to the Connecticut Courant's prediction (Dunn, 2004, p.1).

With the Twelfth Amendment still eight years away, the electoral votes sent John Adams to the presidency and rival Thomas Jefferson into the role of vice president. That was merely the foreshadowing of the next bitter campaign, deemed the Revolution of 1800 by Jefferson who would have his revenge. Both Adams and Jefferson enjoyed long vacations from Washington, but the vice president worked on a campaign biography for a nearby newspaper and also helped influence state elections with correspondence and funding the distribution of campaign pamphlets (Ferling, 2004). The entire affair turned bitter and it would be years before the two Founding Fathers reconciled.

For many years thereafter campaign strategies would adapt to the players, but the techniques were largely the same. Each political hopeful held the approval of supporters who could be found voicing their opinions in speeches, papers, pamphlets and private correspondence. There were, of course, partisan critics with their newspapers and propaganda outlets that would attempt to set the narrative against the opponent.

For decades candidates would put on the appearance of being removed from the campaign. Champion advocates played leading roles as candidates attempt to stay above the vitriol. This move was merely for appearances; the candidates were frequently involved with their supporters and surrogates in crafting the strategy of the election season.

Abraham Lincoln ran under this model. Lincoln's plan was to stay out of view, but oversee the work of his lieutenants to help secure both the nomination and election of 1860. Opposite Lincoln was his famous foil, Stephen Douglas. The Illinois senator was the first presidential candidate to set out on a nationwide speaking campaign (Davis, 2006).

Here we see technological evolutions coming into play. Literature, cartoons images, newspapers, pamphlets, buttons and iconic imagery had long been a conspicuous part of the American campaign season. Now, the candidates could be offered transportation across a rugged frontier that contributed to the changing the face of national electoral politics.

Because of railways and other marginal transportation improvements Senator Douglas' attempt to realign the pre-Civil War South forced other candidates to go out on the road themselves. Needing to reach out to a rapidly growing populace, content needed to reach beyond the borders of their home state. With few exceptions, the front porch campaigns of Warren Harding, William McKinley and James Garfield among the most notable, the game had changed, quickly and forever.

From the long view the evolving modern campaign dovetails nicely with a few concepts: the growth and prosperity of the nation, industrial advances and, often a need to be more innovative than the other candidate. Theodore Roosevelt opened the door to the 20th Century in presidential politics, but those that followed helped usher modernity into campaign politics. Woodrow Wilson was the first president to hold regular news briefings. Calvin Coolidge was the first president to broadcast over radio's airwaves.

It was Franklin Delano Roosevelt who had the benefit of timing to capitalize on emerging media. His famous Fireside Chats reached out to audiences with few other entertainment options at a time when they were willing to hear a calming voice from Washington. It was Roosevelt who boasted of the use of the first presidential plane. What has become known as "Air Force One" has matured into one of the most effective trappings of office for the campaign season; few things are as stirring as seeing that giant plane, with the presidential seal and the commander-in-chief strolling down the steps in your hometown.

Franklin Roosevelt was also the first president to appear on television, speaking to a tiny audience when he helped open the New York World's Fair in 1939. The technology would have to sit out rationing and a World War, but the future was coming into focus. It was one of the heroes of World War II that figured most prominently in the earliest television ads. General Dwight Eisenhower ran primary ads in 1952 and did so again in the general election against Governor Adlai Stephenson. For aspiring politicians, television arrived in full with the Nixon-Kennedy debates in 1960. More than 70 million tuned in to the first of four debates and they learned a lot about the men who would be their president. As Graber (1990) noted "People draw a multitude of inferences from human physical appearance and movements. Many people infer personality characteristics from human physical features" (p. 138).

Kennedy had been campaigning in California prior to the debates and appeared tanned and rested. Nixon, recovering from a bad knee injury, was underweight and refused stage makeup before the debates began. On television the handsome Kennedy ushered in a new image-based political environment opposite the gaunt and perspiring appearance of Nixon. From there campaigns began to understand the practical aspects of how television images affect voter evaluations.

The adaptability of candidates and campaigns to now swiftly-moving technological realities could mean the difference in fund raising or garnering votes. As television entered every home throughout the remainder of the 20th Century the art of appealing to the electorate through the small screen became all the more important. With his style and ease in front of the camera, the former actor turned politician Ronald Regan became known as The Great Communicator.

Thereafter a small industry of political consultants and television pros were pressed into service to get the candidate into every living room. But soon, a curious thing happened: the audience started paying attention to a new small screen in their home.

The Evolution of Political Communication and Political Advertising Theory

Politics, and political thought, may have first found their homes in ancient Greece in the creation of the city-state. Greek thinkers reflected with regard to which form of political organization would be best for the city-state (Sabine, 1961). Some of the most notable creators of political theories include Plato, Aristotle, Cicero, Machiavelli, the Church of England, Thomas Hobbes, John Locke, Kenneth Burke, and Karl Marx. Each sought to define political concepts such as freedom, equality, democracy, and justice. The overarching goal of political theory, then, is to define the meaning of "political" and analyze political systems and political behavior. When talking about political campaigns and advertisements, the focus shifts to political communication theory.

Political decisions and communication theory often work hand in hand, with one frequently influencing the other. Studies of political communication can be broken down into two areas; technique and effects. The technique of political communication focuses on how and why political messages are formed. Effects studies, in large part, are accomplished by examining the impact of the messages delivered.

The earliest records of human communication date back to the 3rd millennium B.C.; rhetoric claims the first citation of formal communication theory (Bryant & Miron, 2006). Definitions of rhetoric are widely varied. Aristotle defined rhetoric as "the faculty wherein one discovers the available means of persuasion in any case whatsoever" (Kennedy, 1991, p.36). "The application of reason to the imagination for the better moving of the will" was how rhetoric was defined by Francis Bacon (Lucaites, Condit, & Caudill, 1999, p. 19). Various other scholars have likened rhetoric to stylistics, or the studies of varieties of language. Merriam-Webster defined rhetoric as "The art of speaking or writing effectively; the study of writing or speaking as a means of communication or persuasion" (Merriam-Webster, 1993). Since rhetoric is a concept that encompasses many different definitions, contemporary rhetoric theory has suggested that the question of what rhetoric is should be discarded and replaced with the question of what rhetoric can be (Lucaites, Condit, & Caudill, 1999). Whatever the definition is the area of rhetoric focuses on the techniques employed in persuasive communication.

The art of speaking effectively centers on a person's oratory skills. The earliest written mention of such skills is found in Homer's *Iliad*, where the main characters were praised for their speaking skills. The success of the speaker was defined by the ability to have such authority over others that the speaker could compel those listening to agree with their position (Bryant & Miron, 2006). Prior to 600 B.C., speaking skill fell largely to the Sophists in Ancient Greece. Theories about rhetoric began in Greece in the 5th century B.C., with Corax and his student Tisias developing an art of rhetoric that was later recognized as having a concept of message organization and the development of arguments from probabilities (Bryant & Miron, 2006; McCroskey & Richmond, 1996).

Socrates, Plato, and Aristotle are names that more readily come to mind when talking about the beginnings of rhetoric. Though Socrates is known for his contributions to philosophy and his development of the Socratic Method of Inquiry, he was ultimately put to death partly because he was suspected of being a sophist - a clever rhetorician who twists words and makes the weaker argument into the stronger (Griswold, 2007). Plato uses his writings *Gorgias* and *Phaedrus* to discount the idea of rhetoric, claiming it can exist separately from the art of speaking. His condemnation in *Gorgias* explains that rhetoric is immoral, dangerous, and unworthy of serious study (Griswold, 2007).

Although Aristotle viewed rhetoric in the same manner as his successors Socrates and Plato, in that rhetoric played on the emotions and failed to use fact for persuasive purposes (Garver, 1994), he is cited as shaping the rhetorical system that would ultimately influence how rhetorical theory was developed through modern times (Bizzell & Herzbeg, 2000). Aristotle's reasoning about rhetoric differs from Plato's in that Aristotle viewed it as a key element of philosophy, along with logic and dialect. *The Republic* opens with the statement "Rhetoric is the counterpoint of Dialectic" (Roberts, 1924/1954). Since debates can take various forms (e.g., philosophical, practical), dialectic and rhetoric can find homes in various forms of debate, and rhetoric was determined to be a part of politics. Aristotle's claim is that dialectic and rhetoric can work in tandem in a system of persuasion that has a basis in knowledge, not in emotion (Corbett, 1984). The debates in ancient Greece took place in public forums, making the person engaged in the debate the orator. The orator's purpose was to persuade, thus came an emphasis on focusing attention on the orator to ensure victory. Successful and influential orators were elevated to special status and power, and it was here that the natural association of oratory and political power began to form (Bryant & Miron, 2006).

Aristotle's greatest contributions fall within the realm of persuasion theory, and the concepts of *ethos* (speaker credibility), *logos* (reasoning that provides truth), and *pathos* (emotions) (Bryant & Miron, 2006). Some of these Greek influences spread beyond Greece as Alexander the Great expanded the empire. As the Roman Empire rose to power, the idea that rhetoric was a part of politics maintained prominence, and the Roman Empire receives credit for spreading this idea across the ancient world (McCroskey & Richmond, 1996). Cicero was one of the strong supporters of this notion, but also established five cannons (invention, arrangement/organization, style, memory, and delivery), proposed three duties/goals (to prove, to delight, and to stir) and theorized on the different styles (plan, middle, and grand) of rhetoric (Bryant & Miron, 2006). It is looking at the concepts created and developed through this point that ties can be made to modern political campaigning and advertising because of the persuasive nature of political messages, and conclusions can be drawn with regards to how deeply the concept of rhetoric–whatever the definition–is tied into political campaigning and advertising.

Political communication finds its roots in the above examples with a heavy emphasis on rhetoric; however modern political communication has become an interdisciplinary field of study. In addition to rhetoric, political communication draws on the fields of communication, political science, journalism, and sociology, as well as several other disciplines (Kaid, 2004). Rhetoric and political communication share the same problem of not having a singular or universally accepted definition, but a simple definition proposed that political communication is the "role of communication in the political process" (Chaffee, 1975, p. 15) may be the best. Modern political communication studies focus on the connections that exist between the politicians, the voters, and the media.

Enter the media. The first forms of mass entertainment began in the first century A.D. within the Roman Empire, as the Roman's enjoyed prosperity with "leisure [becoming] an entitlement across all strata of Roman society" (Zillman, 2000, p. 9). The first mass medium emerged with the invention of the printing press in the 1400s (Bryant & Miron, 2006). At first, the printed book was not meant for mass distribution; rather it was viewed as a place for sacred writings and religious texts to be stored, with access limited to a select few, usually the elite within the society (McQuail, 2000). However, as libraries grew, access to the texts expanded beyond the elite, content began to include secular, practical, and popular texts, and the general public beyond the elites underwent an enlightenment that threatened the control of authorities and promised emancipation and empowerment to the public (Bryant & Miron, 2006). In addition to changes in content, the status of rhetoric underwent a change with the importance of the spoken word decreasing as the importance of the written word increased (Kennedy, 1980).

An example of this is the Lincoln-Douglas debates of 1858. Though only local voters and citizens could attend the debates, newspapers became a powerful instrument in spreading the message. More people were able to receive those messages through the power of the written word than could attend the debates. This was not without problem though. Stenographers from Chicago recorded every word of the debates, which were then reprinted in papers across the United States. However, a bias existed; newspapers with Democratic leanings edited Douglas's speeches, removing any errors and leaving Lincoln's speeches alone. Conversely, newspapers with Republican meanings used the same tactic.

Subsequent communication technologies emerged continuously - the telegraph in the mid-19th century, telephone and film at the end of the 19th century, and radio at the beginning of the 20th century (Fortner, 1994). Print media and film emerged as mass medium, and in the 1920's, electronic media enabled large audiences to become involved in technologically aided communication, giving way to the first true mass communication (Bryant & Miron, 2006). Restricted circulation was lost as commercial and prestige newspapers were established, allowing publications to be distributed to the majority, rather than the minority, of the population (McQuail, 2000). As societies continued to grow, so did the technology, which continuously allowed for more and more 'average' citizens to posses technology that enabled them to receive mass communication, until the norm became the ownership of newspaper subscriptions, then radios, then televisions, then VCR's, and, now, access to computers and the Internet.

Adding media into the relationship between politicians and voters introduces media effect theories. The magic bullet theory/hypodermic needle theory, the two-step flow of communication theory, the limited effects theory, and the theory of the spiral of silence (Noelle-Neumann, 1984) were at one time the four main theories that focused on the media effects with regards to political communication. Agenda setting theory, priming theory, framing theory, diffusion of innovations theory and cultivation theory are also theories that can be studied with regards to political communication.

Arising from thoughts that politicians and governments used the mass media to manipulate messages in order to fuel World War I, the hypodermic needle theory talks about a direct influence on people by mass media (Greenberg & Salwen, 1996). The theory implied mass media had a direct, immediate and powerful effect on its audiences (Katz & Lazarsfeld, 1955). The core suggestion is that the mass media could influence a large group of people directly by 'injecting' them with appropriate messages designed to trigger a desired response (Davis & Baron, 1981). The "panic broadcast" in 1938 became the classic example of how the hypodermic needle theory worked. On October 30, 1938, radio programming was interrupted for the first time with a news bulletin. The news bulletin was actually H.G. Wells' radio edition of *"War of the Worlds"*, and listeners heard Martians had begun an invasion in New Jersey. What resulted was a wave of mass hysteria as people tried to seek shelter, ration their food, raid stores, and flee their homes (Lowrey & DeFleur, 1983).

After World War I, research conducted with regard to consumer behavior found the war propaganda and advertising campaigns were an effective way to manipulate consumer behavior in favor (or support) of the product (Heath & Bryant, 2000). "Messages had only to be loaded, directed to the target, and fired; if they hit their target, then the expected response would be forthcoming" (p. 346). The theory takes on the viewpoints that audience members are simply "passive sheep" (Perloff, 2002, p. 494). In this view, the media becomes a "dangerous drug or a killing force that directly and immediately penetrate a person's system" (Baran, 2001, p. 318). However, this takes the position that the message would affect all people in exactly the same way. This position assumes that, when considering propaganda during a time of war, there is a lack of competing media messages. Also, it assumes that audience will receive the message in exactly the same way (Greenberg & Salwen, 1996). As later shifts in theoretical thinking proved, these assumptions were inaccurate. From opposition from citizens about the United States becoming involved in World War I to war protests today, it is clear that there can be opposing messages, and that people do not receive messages in the exact same manner

The theory was deemed inaccurate after the presidential election of Franklin D. Roosevelt in 1940. Election studies found that the majority of the people were influenced by interpersonal influencers (i.e., 'word-of-mouth' or 'WOM'), and not by mass propaganda (Lazarsfeld, Berelson, & Gaudet, 1968). Heath & Bryant (2000) theorized that the inaccuracy might be due to shortcomings in methodology. Upon the introduction of quantitative and empirically based research after the war, research findings of the hypodermic needle theory were examined and challenged (Greenberg & Salwen, 1996).

The two-step flow of communication theory was formed after the above mentioned election studies were conducted. *The People's Choice* was the study that focused on the process of decision making during a presidential election campaign. As previously mentioned, the results of the study found interpersonal influences had more of an impact than the mass media. These findings gave way to the creation of the two-step flow communication theory, which states that information from the media moves in two distinct stages. Information from the media is first received by individuals who are called opinion leaders (because they normally have some sort of influence over other individuals). The opinion leaders interpret that information, and pass those interpretations down to people within society (Katz, 1987). Individuals are more likely to trust the people they see as opinion leaders than they are to trust the mass media. In other words, an individual is more likely to listen to and be influenced by a family member/friend/leader of a social group they might belong to when trying to make a decision of which politician to vote for because they trust the opinion of that leader.

Limited effects theory (Lang & Lang, 1953) reinforces the idea set forth in the two-step flow theory that media rarely directly influence individuals; rather, individuals are more likely to turn to family, friends, co-workers, or social groups for advice and interpretations. Media only becomes influential when those opinion leaders are influenced. When direct media effects do occur, they only occur in small and isolated incidents. Limited effects theory took the place of the hypodermic needle theory after Klapper (1960) shifted the attention to the role that audiences play in the mass communication process. Selective attention is a pivotal concept within limited effects theory; it explains that people prefer information that fits with their previously held beliefs, and will avoid information that challenges or goes against those beliefs (Graf & Aday, 2008). Lazarsfeld, Berelson & Gaudet (1968) explained selective attention using political messages. People noticed more messages from the candidate they preferred, and often ignored messages from the opponent they disliked. It is then argued that this selectivity went against the notion that was set forth in the hypodermic needle theory that said the mass media directly influenced the audience; instead, thanks to selective attention, it was argued that the mass media only served to reinforce existing beliefs (Klapper, 1949, 1960).

The final media effects theory that looked at voting behavior was the spiral of silence theory. People often end up in a situation where they are afraid to express their views, whether it be a negative opinion about a popular political candidate, or a movie that was widely hated by their peers that they truly enjoyed. Those that do not have an opinion that agrees with the majority often stay silent for fear of ridicule and derision. If they do voice a dissenting opinion, they may end up forced into social isolation, considered to be a pariah that no one will talk to, as if the difference of opinion is a disease that might rub off on them. The above scenarios are the basis for the theory of the spiral of silence.

Noelle-Neumann (1974, 1991) formulated the spiral of silence theory after examining longitudinal survey data concerning the German Election of 1965, of which the two main competing parties were the Christian Democratic Party and the Social Democratic Party. Month after month, the data showed the two parties to be in a dead heat, and predictions about who would win were impossible. In the final time period leading to the election, the survey findings showed a last minute swing in favor of the Christian Democrats. The Christian Democrats won, and Noelle-Neumann systematically examined the relationship between voting intention and expectation of the winner, which gave rise to the theory of the spiral of silence. Several incidents that promoted the Christian Democrats in a positive manner occurred, and Noelle-Neumann hypothesized that the positive images gave supporters a boost that allowed them to speak their opinion, while the positive images made supporters of the Social Democrats feel that they could not share their opinion, and it was the fear of social isolation that caused them to fall silent.

Today the spiral of silence is applied most often to political situations or to people's viewpoints on controversial issues–which often are largely connected to politics. Journal articles that use the spiral of silence boast titles that deal with anti-abortion campaigns, moral reform, community standards for sex and violence, self disclosure on *Donahue*, pluralistic ignorance in prisons and Princess Diana's meanings for women. As mass media continues to have a presence in society, the question of how public opinion is formed will always be present. The other theories mentioned–framing, priming, cultivation theory, diffusion of innovations, and agenda setting–can all work together in multiple combinations to help explain why people think and behave the way that they do.

The difficulty in studying political communication is in the interdisciplinary nature of the field. No one field can lay solid claim to the discipline, and to do so would limit the potential to understand and explore the discipline. When talking about political campaigning and advertising, the areas of communication research that they could best be classified under would be the areas of advertising and propaganda/elections. However, because of the nature of the message in political advertising and campaigning, media effects theories cannot be disregarded. The study of political communication may be interdisciplinary, and similarly the study of political advertising and campaigning is not easily explained within a single discipline.

Advertising research began with print advertising in the 17th century. With the shift in technology at the end of the 19th century/beginning of the 20th century that enabled print media to be mass distributed to the general public, advertising quickly became its own lucrative industry. Delia (1987) points out that national magazines produced after the Civil war were the first place that large-scale advertisements appeared. Advertising agencies began creating ads and campaigns that were run in newspapers and magazines in the beginning of the 20th century. Bryant and Miron (2006) cite this as being the point where the realization for the need for advertising research took place. Though information was still being received by the consumer, exposure and competing messages of advertising meant that persuasion was now the main focus (Curti, 1967; Bryant & Miron, 2006). Similarly, political communication research began to evolve in the same direction, with the focus moving toward persuasion.

Political advertising is regarded as an arm of political communication. It first appeared in campaigns in the 1950s and is now the main avenue for communication between voters and candidates (Kaid, 2004). Kaid's research (1996, 1997, 1999) indicates political advertising research is one of the most significant components within the field of political communication. Political advertising has been defined as "the communication process by which a source (usually a political candidate or party) purchases the opportunity to expose receivers through mass channels to political messages with the intended effect of influencing their political attitudes, beliefs, and/or behaviors" (Kaid, 1981, p. 250). Since the boom and growth of television, the advertisement has become the main form of political oratory, with the political ad being the main way that candidates for the presidency communicate their message to the voting public (Denton, 1988). The design of the political advertisement is twofold: it gives information about the candidate, the candidate's party, or the candidate's agenda that the news media cannot, and it is designed as a persuasive tool (McNair, 2003). The benefit of political advertising is that the candidate has complete control of the message and how it is distributed.

The rules of political televised advertising for candidates are simple: there are no rules. However, broadcast media are regulated by the Federal Communications Commission, and among its many requirements include the provision that access to equal airtime must be given to all legally qualified candidates for federal elective office, and that a disclaimer must be placed on all ads that state the candidate approves the message (Unites States Government Printing Office, 2002).

As a contrast, there is no regulatory body that political advertisers have to answer to, thus there are no rules set forth that apply to the content and form of political advertising (Iyengar & Prior, 1999). Attempts by the news media or Congress to step in and monitor these ads often results in an increase in public cynicism about the two bodies (Iyengar & Prior, 1999; Kaid, 2004). Editorial control of the message is held by the politician, not the journalist; therefore the freedom exists to say what they want, put forth their own agenda, play up their own strengths and attack the weakness of their opponents (McNair, 2003).

Political advertising spending has steadily grown in the past twenty years. The 1988 election found President George H.W. Bush and opponent Michael Dukakis spending a combined $80 million in television ads (Devlin, 1989, McNair, 2003). President George H.W. Bush alone spent over $60 million in 1992 (McNair, 2003) with President Clinton and Ross Perot contributing another $60 million to bring the total up over $120 million (Devlin, 1993). Almost $200 million was spent on advertising time in 1996 (Devlin, 1997), $240 was reportedly spent by the three candidates in 2000 (Devlin, 2001), another $200 million was spent by Bush and Kerry in 2004 (Memmott & Drinkard, 2004)

Current "New" Avenues of Political Advertising

With a number of political candidates creating MySpace profiles, YouTube videos and Second Life avatars it appears the Internet and Web 2.0 technologies have been leveraged for political advertising and campaigning. Political scientist Ithiel de Sola Pool boldly proclaimed electronic communication, of which the Internet is the primary force, the fourth stage in human communications development, following speech, writing, printing, and broadcasting (Davis, 1999).

Since the Internet became a fixture in the majority of U.S. households, it has played a role in political advertising and campaigning. As the Internet becomes less novel and more functional to the everyday user, online campaign tools have become more progressive and interactive. Gary Selnow (1998) noted that 1996 was the first year that political campaigns used the web for mass campaigning; since then its use has increased dramatically in local, state, and federal elections (Benoit & Benoit, 2000; Bimber, 1998; D'Alessio, 1997, 2000; Dulio, Goff, & Thurber 1999; Poupolo, 2001; Schneider & Foot, 2002; Whillock, 1997). For example, by early summer 2003 10 presidential campaigns had already established an active web presence for the 2004 presidential race (Endres & Warnick, 2004). In their 2004 journal article, Endres and Warnick found that campaign Web sites have developed from "a token tool to an absolutely must have tool" (p. 323). Their research discovered that web sites had such an impact on the campaign process that the Institute for Politics, Democracy, and the Internet (IPDI, 2002) published Online Campaigning 2002: A Primer. This was targeted at candidates and campaign managers, and offered instruction on how to strategically use the Internet in campaigns and outlined a set of "best practices" for Internet campaign web sites.

Foot, Xenos, and Schneider (2003) compiled a comprehensive analysis of the U.S. campaign web sites of the 2002 campaign in an attempt to find out if the Internet was changing campaigns and the public sphere. Their study focused on how candidates discussed political issues on campaign web sites to see if universal campaign elements (message construction, issue selection) were adapted or (re)created online. Keeping in mind that the world of the Internet has undergone significant change since their 2003 study, their relevant findings were that candidates tended to provide basic issue stance information online, but avoid direct and indirect forms of issue dialogue. When a campaign was conducted online, the researchers found that intensity in which the campaign was conducted was similar to the intensity found in a traditionally run campaign. Foot et al. indicated that candidates tended to strategically frame their presentation of issue circumstance much in the same way that they would in traditional forms of campaigning. The findings also revealed patterns inconsistent with the 'politics as usual' perspective with regards to past research on politics and the Internet, and yielded two new implications for theorizing about the Internet with regards to online campaigning, pointing out the need for future research in order to obtain a more complete understanding (Endres & Warnick, 2004).

As the Internet continued to grow, users learned how to embrace the concepts of personalization and interactivity. Recognizing individuals' desire for control, companies strived to allow consumers the ability to personalize experience. Internet users saw products and marketing campaigns with the prefix "my" - My AOL, My Yahoo, My Netscape–giving individuals' personalization and adding empowerment to their lives. Personalization is a concept that encompasses many different types of personal control. People began to use the interactivity and flexibility of the Internet to customize their intake of information, their products, and even their social interactions (Shapiro, 1999).

The term *interactivity* refers to a complex and multidimensional concept (Heeter 1989; Newhagen, Cordes and Levy, 1996; Steuer 1992), and there is little agreement on a set of specific conceptual and operational definitions (Kiousis 2002; Lombard and Snyder-Duch 2001; McMillan and Hwang 2002). Interactivity has been defined using various underlying dimensions, but two dimensions appear most frequently in the extant literature: human-message interaction and human-human interaction. These two dimensions hold promise for the examination of interactivity on the Internet because they serve as umbrellas for different definitions and dimensions of previous interactivity studies.

Even though interactivity is not really new to communication fields, computer-mediated communication, especially via the Internet, has added new levels of interactivity beyond what is available in traditional mass communication (Morris and Ogan, 1996; Pavlik, 1998). For example, interactivity on the Internet allows consumers to actively participate in the persuasion process by controlling advertising messages, amount of information, and order of presentation at any time, according to their needs and preferences (Hoffman and Novak 1996). In addition, the commercial value of interactivity has been considerably increased since the advent of the Internet. Advertisers have new tools at their disposal that enable them to send messages to consumers in a more directed, cost efficient manner. With the proper database of information in hand a campaign can drill down to the most precise geographic or demographic cross sections possible.

Geo-Targeting

You're fed up with those gateway surveys on websites. Someone always wants to know your name or your date of birth or hometown. What purpose will these answers ever serve anyway? That information is the foundational basis of an advertising technique known as geo-targeting.

To understand geo-targeting it is important to consider the true meaning of another word. When one broadcasts a signal--in the case of an advertisement or a seed or a live television feed or fertilizer--it is being spread across a chosen dispersal area with hopes of varying degrees of saturation. To mindlessly cover an area with a message a broadcast can be an effective technique. When ad buyers delve further into their formulas, considering the number of eyes that have watched an ad, versus the amount of money spent producing and placing the spot, a general broadcast is often not cost effective.

Consider a mixed urban/rural state with a close race. The urban centers hypothetically vote for one candidate and the rural voters lean the other direction. Historically two southern counties of the state dictate which way the state will go in the next election cycle. A campaign would prefer the ability to advertise to voters in those specific areas directly rather than invest resources in the closest television DMA (designated market area) and hoping for the best. Geo-targeting can allow a message to be dispersed to people on database considerations. If the data has been collected by a local prominent website, or information the campaign or party has gathered, it can be used towards digitally canvassing neighborhoods.

A campaign might wish to shore up its image within the male 24-40 demographic north of downtown. A site that holds this information based on surveys and a web browser's cookies might then be able to share your ad only with men self-described of the certain age from the area of interest. This geo-targeting technique also has uses for smaller races. A potential city councilor needs only to reach the audience in her ward, and not the entire city. If she has the opportunity to do so--and at a smaller cost than a television or radio advertisement--it would be of a larger benefit to her campaign.

There is, of course, a basic televised technique similar to this. As viewers of the 2000 presidential election might recall Vice President Al Gore and Texas Governor George Bush concentrated their television buys on battleground states where the sway of voters was still undetermined. This same theory could be extrapolated into a local dynamic where one media market may generally lean to one candidate, while nearby areas might vote for the opponent. Television has long been a proving ground for advertising based on age groups and a viewer's gender, but this can be a spotty technique owing to programming choices and an audience's drift pattern.

Geo-targeting, however, allows an advertiser to drill down to the core desired audience, to the zip code on a particular website if the hosts have generated the database with such depth. Not every site currently uses or offers this style of advertising, but that might expand as the usefulness of the technique becomes more greatly appreciated.

Websites

The conventional wisdom is that you're campaign isn't much without a website. Like so many other campaign innovations this is a communication method that has trickled down the scale from national to local races. With three-quarters of U.S. adults (Pew, 2008) now accessing the Internet the presence of a website has emerged in a place of prominence that will give a campaign legitimacy, where the absence of such a tool can make a candidate appear out of step.

There are several fundamentally important aspects of campaign websites at this point in the Internet's growth. They can serve as a repository of information on the candidate, his stances and experiences. The website, by the use of blogs can help stir discussion and rally support among a constituency. It can also be an access point for grassroots activity, where proactive supporters can access, download and mass produce campaign literature. Most importantly it can be used as a vehicle to raise money.

Senator Bob Dole actually referred to his web site during his 1996 convention speech (Cornfield, 2005). Neither Governor George Bush nor Vice President Al Gore mentioned a website during their convention speeches in 2000, but that oversight likely won't happen again. The advantages stemming from such a promotion are too important to ignore.

Coming up on the 2004 presidential election, the Internet's influence was beginning its rise to political power. Thorson and Rodgers' (2006) study examined candidate created blogs on campaign Web sites as a form of electronic word of mouth, while Trammell, Tarkowski, Hofmokl and Sapp's (2006) study examined the evolution of online campaigns with specific attention focused on blogs and Web sites. A blog is a form of communication unique to the Internet, noted for their ease of publishing, widespread authorship and varied subject matter from all things popular to arcane. Blogs can be used as educational tools, corporate tools, and are most commonly used as online journals for a wide variety of people. Blogs have proliferated rapidly in recent years, attracting significant attention and generating important legal issues. Software developer Dave Winer one of the first bloggers and a former research fellow at Harvard, defines a blog as "[A] hierarchy of text, images, media objects and data, arranged chronologically, that can be viewed in an HTML browser" (2003, Technically, what is a weblog? ¶ 2). In 2004 Trammell (as cited in Trammell, Williams, Postelnicu & Landreville, 2006) noted that blogs offer greater interactivity, and at higher rates than traditional web pages, owing to the proliferation of links and comment features that allowed readers to leave feedback. Presidential candidates began putting blogs on their sites during the 2004 campaign. The blogs allowed candidates and staff to directly address and interact with website visitors (Thorson & Rodgers, 2006). Blogs, as ostensibly interactive elements designed to enhance the persuasive impact of campaign web sites, provide an opportunity to explore whether (and how) allowing an opportunity for visitors to exchange ideas and opinions has an impact on important attitudinal and behavioral variables (Trammell et al., 2006). While blogs in these two studies were found to have different impacts on voting attitudes and perceptions, such studies have opened up the door for future research.

Max Fose was Sen. John McCain's Internet manager for the 2000 campaign. He pointed to several other advantages of web sites and the Internet in general, among them: unfiltered messages to the electorate, lowering campaign costs, increased message efficacy and the recruitment of campaign volunteers (Powell & Cowart, 2003) Fose's virtual staging ground for grassroots efforts netted the McCain campaign $6.4 million (at the time an online record) and 142,000 volunteers.

How did Fose and the McCain campaign get such results? It worked, Fose said, because the online presence was integrated into the communication platform so completely that the online presence became the platform. Fose found that media drove traffic to the web site to the point that the candidate would mention fund raising success to reporters, who mentioned it in their stories until the coverage just multiplied (Powell & Cowart, 2003).

Money, of course, is the lifeblood of a campaign. Without it, even a natural candidate will struggle for attention. Funding has long captured an important part of the media's attention, often moving in time with the horse race coverage of the polls and the scathing sound bites. McCain, as time would prove, was no one-off in earning money through his online investment.

In the next cycle a little known governor from Vermont would exceed all expectations. Howard Dean raised $15 million in the final months of 2003 and more than $40 million for the year according to fund raising figures reported on by the New York Times. Dean's $40 million lead all Democrats prior to the start of the primary season, including Sen. John Kerry's $29 million (New York Times, 2004). The conventional wisdom was that Dean, a man admittedly behind this particular curve, hired staffers with experience in high level politics and high-technology enterprise to generate the bulk of that money. Thus began a revitalization of interpersonal campaigning. Mass-media was no longer the sole outlet, campaigns could reach out to the public without the media and, even more promising, the electorate was reaching back.

While generating funds online was no secret and everyone was trying it the 2008 election featured two champions of online fund raising. Congressman Ron Paul earned a group of small, but vocal and generous group of supporters in the primary season, breaking several fund raising records including a staggering $4.3 million raised online in a single day (RonPaulGraphs.com, 2008). Patrick Ruffini, a Republican online strategist not affiliated with Paul's campaign, noted "(It) wasn't a huge primary win or a big media hit. His supporters basically willed it into existence. This shows what a healthy, functioning relationship between a campaign and its grassroots actually looks like" (Ruffini, 2007).

It was bottom-up success on an unprecedented scale. Across the aisle candidates were enjoying success as well. The ever-evolving Internet was playing a big role in the success–in money and polling figures--of a young senator from Illinois.

Different from a blog is a social networking site, which focuses on the building and verifying of online social networks for communities of people who share interests and activities, or who are interested in exploring the interests and activities of others. Most social network services are primarily web based and provide a collection of various ways for users to interact, such as chat, messaging, email, video, voice chat, file sharing, blogging, and discussion groups. The main types of social networking services are those which contain directories of some categories (such as former classmates), means to connect with friends (usually with self-description pages), and recommender systems linked to trust. Popular methods now combine many of these, with MySpace and Facebook being the most widely used in 2007 (Nielsen, 2007).

Web sites alone, no matter how dynamic they can become, are no longer enough to keep a candidate in the midst of an ongoing online dialogue. Prior to the 2008 election cycle the Internet blossomed with web 2.0 nomenclature and tools. Web 2.0 came to mean technology and web design to create user-driven content with the ultimate goals of information sharing, collaboration and enhanced creativity.

Suddenly it was even easier for everyday individuals without significant computer coding experience to maintain a presence online. Sites like MySpace and Facebook emerged as some of the most high volume locations on the web. Other technologies emerged to allow users to add their own photos and videos to the web. Phones, too, became an important tool and uploading to the web became push-button easy. More people were able to participate, or host, a part of larger conversations.

It was at this point that social media became valuable tools in a political campaign's arsenal. The electorate not only wanted to hear what the candidate had to say, but now they had the tools and ease to interact with the campaign and occasionally even the candidate as well. When campaigns reached out to the 2.0 audiences they were talking to, and hearing from, a hungry audience. People not content to sit back and wait for the news, sound bites, and answers to come to them were able to easily go online, engage in a conversation and seek out what they were looking for. Progressive strategists realized they now had an opportunity to campaign with greater ease, no filters and no interference to an audience passionate about their cause.

The passion of that audience became a conference campaigns could have with some of their most vocal supporters, using a technology that deals with early adopters. And, for politicians always interesting in courting the youth vote they now had the perfect vehicle. By concentrating online candidates could find motivated individuals, donor success and a younger audience that operated in a world without much consultation of daily newspapers or network news.

Social media, trendy personal hubs like Facebook, photo sharing sites, popular video sites and micro blogging were all part of a larger online construction. In the long 2008 campaign season all the presidential candidates from both major parties had websites. All experimented with many of these other services. And why not? They are free or inexpensive, and most importantly, people were already congregating at these locations for their own online social needs.

In the 2008 race many of the candidates used Facebook, MySpace and Twitter with varying degrees of success (see Reichart, 2008) Name recognition, campaign support, issue identification and fund raising were all important functions of the candidates' online presence. In the aggregate, no one did it better than Sen. Barack Obama.

In addition to dominating the mainstream media with his historic run to become the Democratic nominee, the party's own efforts and his general affability, Obama's campaign nurtured the groundswell of support online. Among the tools at Obama's disposal were: podcasting, Flickr, YouTube, MySpace, Facebook, Twitter and more.

A podcast, for the uninitiated, is something akin to an online radio interview. The strengths of a podcast, from the campaign's perspective are longevity and convenience. While a radio or television interview might be caught by an audience on a single broadcast a podcast can exist online for as long as the host wishes and can be accessed at any time. Even more importantly a podcast can be pulled in by an audience member with one of several automated tools online. Now, as an audience member, you don't even need to seek it out, in can be delivered to your computer for ease of consumption or downloaded to your personal mp3 player, such as an iPod, for you to enjoy on the go.

Flickr is a hosting site that has enjoyed an enormous audience for several years now. It is a simple process to upload your photographs or images to Flickr--free for casual users and at a small price for high-volume uploaders. The site flexes its muscle with a feature called tagging, which is another function of web 2.0. If the campaign uploads a photo and tags it "Obama" it is then grouped with every other Obama photo throughout the Flickr site. At that point anyone on Flickr could search Obama and see your photograph.

On August 29, 2008, the day after Sen. Obama accepted the nomination Flickr returned 163,926 hits for the word "Obama." A search using "Biden" for his running mate Sen. Joe Biden returned 5,431 hits. Obama's Republican opponent Sen. John McCain returned 17,840 hits on Flickr the same day. McCain's running mate, Alaska Governor Sarah Palin returned 2,530 hits. It is worth noting that not all of these numbers represent a photograph; one must consider artistic productions, images from television, commonality of names and so forth, however the usefulness and popularity of Flickr is well illustrated by the statistics.

YouTube grew within the span of a few short years to become the world's dominant video hosting site. Again functionality and ease of use--both to upload a video and to search and play them--are among the primary reasons behind that success. Any campaign with a web site could conceivably host a video on their own domain, but with a few clicks that same video can be uploaded to the third most popular site on the Internet (Alexa.com, 2009b).

Another aspect of YouTube's success has been the simultaneous proliferation of inexpensive and simple video editing software that has become a widespread computing feature. Microsoft and Apple both deliver a basic video editor into their operating system essentially making everyone a potential director. Suddenly anyone with a creative idea is a demonstrable example of two-step flow, passing along their own thoughts and perceptions that could resonate with their audience. Home-based technology is assisting in the creation of new opinion leaders. Parodies, recuts, artistic "mashups" of candidates and music have all become a part of the YouTube dialogue.

Facebook and MySpace are two of the world's primary social networking hubs. According to the Pew Internet & American Life Project's December 2008 tracking survey, 35% of adults have a profile on a social networking site–compared to only 8% in 2005 (Lenhart, 2009). MySpace has fallen to the number two social networking site behind Facebook, with recent statistics claiming over 58 million unique visitors and over 810 million visits per month (CnetNews.com, 2009). In the five years since Facebook originated, it has become the 3rd ranked most visited website behind Google and Yahoo (Alexa.com, 2009a). Facebook ranks 5th worldwide, and in February of 2009 had over 150 million users worldwide, and was still growing (Facebook, 2009). They are sites built with ease of the end user in mind--often to the detriment of the aesthetic, but that would be a different topic altogether. These sites level the playing field. No longer does one need computer coding ability to maintain an online presence, interact with friends, host photos, blog and share their thoughts. They've been so successful as a social gathering place that high end computer users and coders have found that they must also maintain a MySpace and/or Facebook account for networking purposes as a part of their online brand in much the same way as political candidates.

Senator Obama, for example took this one step further by hiring a man named Chris Hughes, who was one of the three co-founders of Facebook. Hughes was put to work running "my.barackobama.com", a site which evolved into something of its own social network for like-minded Obama supporters. Not a software developer himself, Hughes brought an appreciation of how to nurture and manage online communities. Savvy use, and in that particular case a savvy hire, added a great deal to Obama's online impact.

Twitter, one of the latest online success stories, is also a valuable tool for a campaign. It's power in disseminating information about a massive earthquake in China, the 2008 election and the

2009 post-election protests in Iran all helped give Twitter heft as an online tool. Twitter is considered "microblogging" which is to say that you can share anything you'd like that you can fit into 140 characters or less. Twitter users are pooling into nodes and communities as the functionality of the tool is such that you chose who to follow and others chose whether you are interesting enough to follow in their own Twitter feeds.

In some instances this might chip away at the spiral of silence. Twitter audiences are actively cultivated, meaning the user has the ability to seek out voices exclusive to their beliefs and can selectively ignore those that might oppose them or be critical of their voice. There is some degree of reciprocity involved in following Twitter users, so in following a new individual a user will often be given the same courtesy in kind. Over time this could allow a user to build a stream of conversation strictly about issues or stances relative to their own, establishing a network of similar thought while eschewing others.

Twitter is, in fact, new enough that users are still sorting out for themselves the etiquette of the "Twitterverse." The anecdotal stories of the impact and success of Twitter thus far are largely concerned with breaking news, fund raising and other unique grass roots community campaigns, but candidates (national and even some local) are testing the waters. The mobility of Twitter, it can easily be used with any cell phone that supports Short Message Service text messaging, and the immediacy of the tool are tremendous attributes to the Twitter model.

Using these tools effectively benefited Barack Obama greatly on his way to the White House. Joe Rospars, Obama's director of Obama's new-media told *The Washington Post* just after the election that the campaign had more than $500 million in online donations from 3 million donors (Vargas, 2008). Rospars went on to say that the average donation was $80, and the average donor gave more than once. Clearly we've entered into a new age of digital fund raising.

The most challenging aspects for users, candidates and researchers concerning the web's evolution are its innovative character. Rapid development of emerging technologies means things are changing constantly. Today's smash online success, let's say Twitter for one example, might be short-lived, but the next trendy development that bests an existing product as a tool or toy must improve upon the previous item's functionality. Things will only grow faster, more efficient and more innovative. The open-source culture–allowing outside developers to see, use and modify your code to improve or augment an application–existing in much of the online ecosystem contributes to that evolution.

The inevitable question is what's next within the context of a campaign's technological growth? Obama pointed the way there as well: The next revolution will be mobile. He announced Sen. Biden as his running mate by text message. This was shrewd in both the technological and the political campaign sense. It built an instant (and significant) phone bank for the campaign. Nielsen reported that 2.9 million cell phone users signed up to receive such information from the campaign and the novel approach helped further the image of a fresh, young, innovative candidate (CBS News, 2008).

Within an election cycle or two even that experimental text message announcement might seem blasé or antiquated. As technologies evolve and smart phones become smarter and more widespread in the marketplace we'll be getting (and sharing) our news and information in far more innovative, and mobile, ways.

Looking Forward to the Digital Advertising Age

Problems with Digital Advertising and Campaigning

In May of 2008, Lori Drew was indicted by a federal grand jury on one count of conspiracy and three counts of accessing protected computers without authorization to obtain information to inflict emotional distress (CNN, 2008). This woman was accused of creating a fake profile on MySpace and used it to torment Megan Meier, a former friend of Drew's daughter. Ultimately, Meier committed suicide, and her actions were attributed to being the victim of cyber-bullying. Drew was later acquitted (Zavis, 2009). In July of 2008, the Oklahoma Publishing Company and a sportswriter sued a Nebraska football fan who admitted creating a fake news article about two University of Oklahoma quarterbacks, using the publisher's template with which to showcase his satire and posting it on a message board (Ellis, 2008a). The suit was settled later that year (Ellis, 2008b). These are two cases out of numerous incidents that highlight the problem of credibility on the Internet.

Although the digital world gives users access to immediate information at any time, it does not come without its problems. The first, as mentioned, regards the idea of credibility. Credibility research focuses on one of two areas; source and medium. As media have become a primary source for public information, media credibility has received increased scrutiny (Gaziano & McGrath, 1986; Wanta & Hu, 1994; West, 1994). The Internet has been steadily growing in use each year, which tasks researchers to determine how people use it and the effects it has. In the digital age, anyone can be a contributor on the Internet, and the Internet has no government or ethical regulations that control the content that it put forth on it. Hovland & Weiss (1951) were among the first to asses media credibility, and their findings conclude that the messages were more likely to be accepted if the source was deemed trustworthy. As technology continuously advances, it becomes more and more difficult to distinguish a credible source from a less credible source (Andie, 1997).

In the past couple of years, the Internet has taken on a 'viral' aspect; a marketing technique that uses pre-existing social networks (like YouTube or MySpace) to broadcast a message. Viral marketing messages can be spread in several different ways–email forwards, word of mouth, and exposure on social networks. Viral marketing depends on people to pass the message to others on their own volition, and its effect is much like a snowball–the quicker the message is spread, the bigger it becomes.

Senator Hillary Clinton was the subject of a fake ad that was broadcast on YouTube that parodied a 1984 Apple Computer Super Bowl spot that implied Sen. Clinton was the epitome of mind-numbing conformity. Senator Barack Obama was victim to a false email that was spread around the Internet from inbox to inbox for over a year. The anonymous chain e-mail made a claim that Obama is concealing a radical Islamic background, stating that he used the Koran to be sworn in, as well as many other untruthful statements. No prominent political candidate seems immune to such negativity. As stated earlier, the Federal Communications Commission has strict regulations for what can and cannot be broadcast. The Internet does not currently have to adhere to any of these regulations. The viral nature of the Internet allows these fake ads and fake emails unlimited exposure. Essentially, the Internet gives power to anyone willing to make a political commercial. If it is interesting enough, it has the potential to gain wide circulation, influence and audience and perhaps an election. Credibility of these claims is considered by only a few. Credibility on the Internet is left solely to the determination of the individual user.

Easily Accessed Information

Another problem that political campaigns face in the digital age is one of the aspects that the Internet is most appreciated for–the ease in which information can be obtained. Political analyst Dr. Larry Powell agrees that the Internet has definitely played a role in campaigning–a mostly negative role. He has called the Internet a "mistake-based campaign medium" (Kennedy, 2007). Powell further points out that opponents can easily visit a web site to see if there is a mistake made that they can use to their own advantage; additionally, the opponents can take measures that try to inflict harm on the candidate, such as negative messages or inappropriate content.

Though the content can be rapidly changed on any sort of Internet site, if sharp eyes can catch it quickly enough, a mistake can be costly to a political candidate. Unlike the good old days of television advertising, if an ad is run that is more harmful to a candidate than their opponent, there is no more pulling an ad and trying to forget it exists. The nature of the Internet allows bad ads to be played ad nauseum. A bad photograph can be circulated quickly and repeatedly. Digital editing and photoshopping can take a candidate's words and image and put them in a new–and often times negative–context.

Additionally, much like the more traditional media venues of newspaper, radio, and television, there is no way to determine who exactly is privy to your message. There is no membership initiation or proof required to become a part of a political candidate's social networking site, or follow them on Twitter. Supporters and haters alike can be part of these communities. Spies from the opposing camps can monitor discussions and comments on these sites and use them to their own campaign's advantage.

Need for New Theoretical Models

Traditional models of mass communication have taken the form of a linear flow of information, and profess that the audience is a passive receiver of information. In the digital age, both of those statements can prove to be incorrect. The first half of the 20th century saw the domination of linear models that asserted the mass media was responsible for the distribution of messages from centers of information to an audience that was just waiting for the information to be provided to them (Bryant & Miron, 2006). Studies of how the public reacted to such mass persuasion were the foundation for many of the early mass communication theories (Berger & Chaffee, 1987).

It is easy to realize, with the ease of access to the Internet and the popularity of portable media devices that at the very least, the media audience is no longer passive. In today's political climate, voters do not wait for the news at 6 p.m. for campaign trail updates. Rather, they are accessing the latest news from web sites, "friending" candidates on social networking sites, receiving instant updates on their mobile devices, and actively participating in web-based chat and discussion groups. For many years, the point was argued that young people do not pay attention to politics. Today's young adults are proving that they can be well versed in the issues of the day. What they do not do is follow politics in the 'traditional' manner.

McQuail (2000) points out several features that the new electronic mediums of communication present that differ from their predecessors; technology convergence, and unclear lines between content and functions and interpersonal and mass communication. New media allows for increasing levels of activity, user control, user personalization, customization of information, and innovative methods of distribution of messages. When looking at news on the Internet, the idea of convergence has allowed news delivery to grow considerably. Media convergence is more than simply a technological shift, altering the relationship between existing technologies, industries, markets, genres and audiences (Jenkins, 2004). Scholars define convergence as the process of technological integration (Danowski & Choi, 1998; Fidler, 1997; Pavlik, 1998). A mixture of audio, video, graphics, interactivity, and print became a reality with Internet news and has begun to have a lasting impact on news and how news stories are told (Salwen, Garrison & Driscoll, 2004). Most news outlets consider their online sites as supplements to their primary products, but this model has begun to change with the creation of new facilities, and new concepts in new media, multimedia, and media convergence (Salwen, 2004). As media industries are forced to transition from analog to digital, and deregulation begins to occur within the industry, barriers that once existed between different media outlets are becoming weak (Fidler, 1997; Garcia-Murillo & MacInnes, 2001; Waterman, 2000). As more and more new technologies and new media present themselves to the public, the media users will begin the process of determining if the new media is better than the media it is replacing.

The preferred format for online news publishing is a multimedia one. A multimedia environment allows for the presentation of information in text, audio, and video. Written articles are accompanied by voice synthesis, music, color photographs, animated charts, and video footage. Multimedia isn't fixed by ready limits (Elderkin, 1996). The limits are set by the resources news producers commit to news production in this environment rather than by technological capability (Gunter, 2003).

Political advertisements and campaigns have adopted the idea of convergence and have begun to utilize the multimedia platform of delivery. A visitor to a candidate's web site can access as much information as they would like. It becomes the job of the visitor to create their own unique experience with the candidate's site. They can simply look at the front page of the site, and move on. They can choose to watch videos, look at pictures, find out more information on the candidate's background and policies, or to engage in discussion with other visitors to the web site through blog comments or discussion boards.

There has not been a 'new media' model developed to date. Given the variety offered online perhaps one single model will never surface. However, new media certainly challenges much of the theoretical models of media that currently exist. As previously mentioned, many of these models rely on linear communication and a passive audience. Various attempts to create such a model either try to combine structural characteristics of media systems, message exchanges, and user perceptions into a multidimensional construct, or identify one of those facets as the main idea of interactivity (Sundar, 2004). However, the main problem may lie in the fact that there is not one definition that clearly defines exactly what interactivity is. Eveland (2003) criticized traditional media effects studies, suggesting they are too limiting, especially when considering new media technologies, and proposed a mix of attributes approach as a better alternative of study. Bucy & Tao (2007) proposed a mediated model of interactivity that incorporates interactive attitudes, the perceptions of the users of their own self efficacy with the medium, the differences of the individuals using the medium, and various media effects measures. Slater (2007) suggested a reinforcing spirals framework for understanding media selectivity and effects as a dynamic and mutually influencing process. His speculations include the development and maintenance of political subcultures in contemporary societies.

What is most clear amongst the areas of uncertainty is that the traditional models of communication may need a serious overhaul to be considered relevant in the world of digital media. In 'real' life, people often resist expressing their views because they fear some sort of negative consequence. This is the basis for Noelle-Neumann's (1974) theory of the spiral of silence.

However, in the virtual world, there may no longer be a solid grounding for this theory. The Internet potentially removes the concept of social isolation, and without social isolation, the spiral of silence has no grounding in which to exist. Traditionally, social isolation has been represented as a one-dimensional construct organized around the notion of a person's position outside the peer group and refers to isolation from the group as a result of being excluded from the group by peers (Bowker, Bukowski, Zargarpour & Hoza, 1998). From children to adults, literature shows that people understand the concept of isolation and fear the repercussions of being isolated from groups they are a part of. The Internet has the power to free people from the fear of social isolation, and could potentially shut down the spiral of silence. The Internet allows people to intellectually locate within groups of people with like mindsets and similar points of view, but also provides multiple venues in which people can agree or disagree with a wide range of audiences, removing psychological barriers and making possible the large-scale, many-to-many conversations Coleman & Gøtze, (2001) suggested. Unlike traditional mediums that limit participation, the Internet brings the characteristics of empowerment, enormous scales of available information, specific audiences can be targeted effectively and people can be brought together through the medium (O'Hara, 2002).

This is just one example of how new media changes a traditional theory of media. Since the spiral of silence largely deals with political expression, it is easy to see how voters would become more aggressive in voicing their opinions, comfortable in the knowledge that they can find like-minded individuals with relative ease, not to mention silence the voices of opposing and potentially taunting voices with the click of a mouse.

Another example of how a traditional theory might need modification can be viewed with the two-step flow of communication theory. Recall that information in this model passes from the media, down to opinion leaders, then down to the general public. The flow of information moves in a downward pattern. However, politics on the Internet can be viewed in two different lights with this theory. One possible alternative is that information no longer flows in a downward pattern. Political consumers no longer wait for information to come to them; they seek out the information and pass it on. Since the average user now operates as the agent who accesses and distributes information, the information flows laterally. The viral nature of the Internet allows for such a message to be distributed quickly and rapidly. The second potential modification to this theory is that the Internet–specifically sites like YouTube and other social networking sites–perform the opinion leadership function. Social networking sites take over what used to happen in local churches, coffee houses, and water coolers. The same goal–to share information–is able to be done more quickly. This function is no longer in the hands of the mass media. Instead, it goes into the hands of the public who can get online, interact, and email links. Essentially, the two-step downward flow becomes one laterally moving step.

CONCLUSION

The world of political campaigns and advertising has entered a time of great change. As technology moves quickly, political campaign staffs are quick to re-adapt their strategies to fit in with the changing technology. Gone are the days of the passive audience; they have been replaced with a younger generation that often wants the latest technology now, and information and content delivered on their own terms. For all the advantages digital media seems to offer political candidates, it seems there are an equal number of disadvantages, including, perhaps, some that have yet to be discovered. To try to explain the current political playing field using traditional models of mass media and advertising will only serve to limit the overall understanding of the vast potential and capabilities the digital world offers. Taking into consideration how fast technology evolves, it may be more beneficial to better understand the new elements that the new medium brings and create central and lasting definitions that can be applied to various new models. For politicians, they must understand that the days of traditional advertising and campaigning are long gone. Garnering political information and delivering it at the appropriate time and place to the segment needing it for renewed commitment is more than just another step in the game. Rather it holds the potential to be the viral spread of content that becomes a dominant source of belief and support for the tech savvy candidate capable of deploying it.

REFERENCES

Alexa.com. (2009a). *Top sites in the United States* [Electronic Version]. Retrieved March 10, 2009, from http://www.alexa.com/site/ds/top_sites?cc=US&ts_mode=country&lang=none

Alexa.com. (2009b). *Traffic details for YouTube.com*. Retrieved March 3, 2009, from http://www.alexa.com/data/details/traffic_details/youtube.com

Andie, T. (1997). Why web warriors might worry. *Columbia Journalism Review*, *36*(2), 35–39.

Aristotle,. (1991). *On rhetoric: A theory of civil discourse* (Kennedy, G. A., Ed.). New York: Oxford University Press.

Baran, S. J. (2001). *Introduction to mass communication: Media literacy and culture*. Mountain View, CA: Mayfield.

Benoit, W. L., & Benoit, P. J. (2000). The virtual campaign: Presidential primary websites in campaign 2000. *American Journal of Communication*, *3*(3).

Berger, C. R., & Chaffee, S. H. (1987). The study of communication as a science. In Berger, C. R., & Chaffee, S. H. (Eds.), *Handbook of communication science* (pp. 15–19). Newbury Park, CA: Sage.

Bimber, B. (1998). The Internet and political mobilization: Research note on the 1996 election season. *Social Science Computer Review*, *16*(4), 391–401. doi:10.1177/089443939801600404

Bizzell, P., & Herzbeg, B. (2000). *The rhetorical tradition: Readings from the classical times to the present*. Bedford, NY: St. Martin's.

Bowker, A., Bukowski, W., Zargarpour, S., & Hoza, B. (1998). A structural and functional analysis of a two-dimensional model of social isolation. *Merrill-Palmer Quarterly*, *44*(4), 447–463.

Bryant, J. B., & Miron, D. (2006). Historical context and trends in the development of communication theory. In Whaley, B. B., & Samter, W. (Eds.), *Explaining Communication: Contemporary Theories and Exemplars*. Mahwah, NJ: Erlbaum.

Bucy, E. P., & Tao, C. C. (2007). The mediated moderation model of interactivity. *Media Psychology*, *9*, 647–672.

CBSNews. (2008). *Nielsen: 'Obama text' reached 2.9 million* [Electronic Version]. Retrieved August 27, 2008, from http://www.cbsnews.com/stories/2008/08/26/tech/cnettechnews/main4384289.shtml.

Chaffee, S. (1975). *Political communication*. Beverly Hills, CA: Sage Publication.

Cnet.com. (2009). *Whee! New numbers on social network usage* [Electronic Version]. Retrieved March 5, 2009 from http://news.cnet.com/webware/?keyword=statistics.

CNN.com. (2004). *Election Results*. Retrieved June 21, 2008, from http://www.cnn.com/ELECTION/2004/pages/results/states/US/P/00/epolls.0.html

CNN.com. (2008). *Mom indicted in deadly MySpace hoax*. Retrieved July 26, 2008, from http://www.cnn.com/2008/CRIME/05/15/internet.suicide/index.html

Coleman, S., & Gøtze, J. (2001). *Bowling together: Online Public Engagement in Policy Deliberation*. Retrieved March 1, 2009, from http://www.bowlingtogether.net/

Corbett, E. P. J. (1984). *'Introduction' to Aristotle's rhetoric and poetics*. New York: Modern Library.

Cornfield, M. (2005). *The internet and campaign 2004: A look back at the campaigners* [Electronic Version]. Retrieved August 25, 2008, from http://www.pewinternet.org/pdfs/cornfield_commentary.pdf

Curti, M. (1967). The changing concept of human nature in the literature of American advertising. *Business History Review, 41*, 337–345. doi:10.2307/3112645

D'Alessio, D. (1997). Use of the World Wide Web in the 1996 U.S. election. *Electoral Studies, 16*(4), 489–500. doi:10.1016/S0261-3794(97)00044-9

D'Alessio, D. (2000). Adoption of the World Wide Web by American political candidates, 1996-1998. *Journal of Broadcasting & Electronic Media, 44*(4), 556–568. doi:10.1207/s15506878jobem4404_2

Danowski, J. A., & Choi, J. H. (1998). Convergence in the information industries. Telecommunications, broadcasting and data processing 1981-1996. In Sawhney, H., & Barnett, G. A. (Eds.), *Progress in communication sciences* (*Vol. 15*, pp. 125–150). Stamford, CT: Ablex.

Davis, D. B. (2006). *Inhumane bondage: The rise and fall of slavery in the new world*. New York: Oxford University Press.

Davis, D. K., & Baron, S. J. (1981). A history of our understanding of mass communication. In Davis, D. K., & Baron, S. J. (Eds.), *Mass communication and everday life: A perspective on theory and effects*. Belmont, CA: Wadsworth Publishing.

Davis, R. (1999). *The Web of Politics: The Internet's Impact on the American Political System*. New York: Oxford University Press.

Delia, J. G. (1987). Communication study: A history. In Berger, C. R., & Chaffee, S. H. (Eds.), *Handbook of communication science*. Newbury Park, CA: Sage.

Denton, R. E. (1998). *The primetime presidency of Ronald Reagan: The era of the television presidency*. New York: Praeger.

Devlin, L. P. (1989). Contrasts in presidential campaign commercials of 1988. *The American Behavioral Scientist, 32*(4), 389–414. doi:10.1177/0002764289032004006

Devlin, L. P. (1993). Contrasts in presidential campaign commercials of 1992. *The American Behavioral Scientist, 37*(2), 272–290. doi:10.1177/0002764293037002015

Devlin, L. P. (1997). Contrasts in presidential campaign commercials of 1996. *The American Behavioral Scientist, 40*(8), 1058–1084. doi:10.1177/0002764297040008008

Devlin, L. P. (2001). Contrasts in presidential campaign commercials of 2000. *The American Behavioral Scientist, 44*(12), 2338–2369. doi:10.1177/00027640121958366

Dulio, D. A., Goff, D. L., & Thurber, J. A. (1999). Untangled web: Internet use during the 1998 election. *Political Science and Politics, 3*(1), 53–58.

Dunn, S. (2004). *Jefferson's second revolution: The election crisis of 1800 and the triumph of Republicanism*. New York: Houghton Mifflin Company.

Elderkin, K. (1996). *The future of newspaper industry: How electronic newspapers will outrun their competition*. Bloomington, IN: Elderkin Associates.

Ellis, R. (2008a). *Publisher, sportswriter file suit in fake story about Oklahoma quarterbacks*. Retrieved August 3, 2008, from http://newsok.com/article/3270140/

Ellis, R. (2008b). *Settlement reached in Internet hoax about OU QBs*. Retrieved July 3, 2009, from http://newsok.com/settlement-reached-in-internet-hoax-about-ou-qbs/article/3295059

Endres, D., & Warnick, B. (2004). Text-based interactivity in candidate campaign web sites: A case study from the 2002 elections. *Western Journal of Communication, 68*(3), 322–342.

Eveland, W. P. Jr. (2003). A 'mix of attributes' approach to the study of media effects and new communication technology. *The Journal of Communication, 53*, 395–410. doi:10.1111/j.1460-2466.2003.tb02598.x

Facebook.com. (2009). *Press Room* [Electronic Version]. Retrieved March 7, 2009, from http://www.facebook.com/press/info.php?statistics.

Ferling, J. E. (2004). *Adams vs. Jefferson: The election of 1800 and the third American revolution*. New York: Oxford University Press.

Fidler, R. (1997). *Mediamorphosis. Understanding new media*. Thousand Oaks, CA: Pine Forge.

Foot, K. A., Xenos, M., & Schneider, S. M. (2003). *Online Campaigning in the 2002 U.S. Elections: Analyzing House, Senate and Gubernatorial Campaign Web Sites*. Paper presented at the American Political Science Association, Philadelphia.

Fortner, R. S. (1994). Mediated communication theory. In Casmir, F. L. (Ed.), *Building communication theories: A socio/cultural approach*. Hillsdale, NJ: Lawrence Erlbaum Associates.

Fosse, M. (2002, February). The Web goes political: How political candidates and parties are using the Internet to provide information, raise money, mobilize supporters, and get out the vote. *WORLD (Oakland, Calif.), 1*, 17.

Garcia-Murillo, M. A., & MacInnes, I. (2001). FCC organizational structure and regulatory convergence. *Telecommunications Policy, 25*, 431–452. doi:10.1016/S0308-5961(01)00015-5

Garver, E. (1994). *Aristotle's rhetoric: An art of character*. Chicago, IL: University of Chicago Press.

Gaziano, C., & McGrath, K. (1986). Measuring the concept of credibility. *The Journalism Quarterly, 63*, 451–462.

Graber, D. A. (1990). Seeing is remembering. *The Journal of Communication, 40*(3), 134–155. doi:10.1111/j.1460-2466.1990.tb02275.x

Graf, J., & Aday, S. (2008). Selective attention to online political information. *Journal of Broadcasting & Electronic Media, 52*(1), 86–100. doi:10.1080/08838150701820874

Greenberg, B. S., & Salwen, M. B. (1996). Mass communication theory and research: Concepts and models. In Salwen, M. B., & Stacks, D. W. (Eds.), *An Integrated Approach to Communication Theory and Research* (pp. 63–78). Mahwah, NJ: Lawrence Erlbaum Associates.

Griswold, C. (2007). Plato on rhetoric and poetry [Electronic Version]. *The Stanford Encyclopedia of Philosophy* Retrieved June 27, 2008 from http://plato.stanford.edu/archives/sum2007/entries/plato-rhetoric/

Gunter, B. (2003). *News and the Net*. Mahwah, NJ: Lawrence Erlbaum Associates.

Heath, R. L., & Bryant, J. B. (2000). *Human Communication Theory and Research: Concepts, Contexts, and Challenges*. Mahwah, NJ: Lawrence Erlbaum Associates.

Heeter, C. (1989). *Implications of New Interactive Technologies for Conceptualizing Communication in Media Use in the Information Age: Emerging Patterns of Adoption and Consumer Use*. Hillsdale, NJ: Lawrence Erlbaum Associates.

Hoffman, D. L., & Novak, T. P. (1996). Marketing in hypermedia computer-mediated environments: Conceptual foundations. *Journal of Marketing, 60*, 50–68. doi:10.2307/1251841

Hovland, C. I., & Weiss, W. (1951). The influence of source credibility on communication effectiveness. *Public Opinion Quarterly, 15*, 635–650. doi:10.1086/266350

Iyengar, S., & Prior, M. (1999). *Political advertising: What effect on commercial advertisers?* USA: Department of Communication, Stanford University.

Jenkins, H. (2004). The cultural logic of media convergence. *International Journal of Cultural Studies, 7*(1), 33–43. doi:10.1177/1367877904040603

Kaid, L. L. (1981). Political advertising. In Nimmo, D. D., & Sanders, K. R. (Eds.), *Handbook of political communication* (pp. 249–271). Beverly Hills, CA: Sage.

Kaid, L. L. (1996). Political communication. In Salwen, M. B., & Stacks, D. W. (Eds.), *An integrated approach to communication theory and research* (pp. 443–457). Hillsdale, NJ: Lawrence Erlbaum Associates.

Kaid, L. L. (1997). Trends in political communication research. In Trent, J. S. (Ed.), *Communication: View from the helm for the twenty-first century* (pp. 122–126). Needham Heights, MA: Allyn & Bacon.

Kaid, L. L. (1999). Political advertising: A summary of research findings. In Newman, B. (Ed.), *The handbook of political marketing* (pp. 423–438). Thousand Oaks, CA: Sage.

Kaid, L. L. (2004). *The handbook of political communication research.* Mahwah, NJ: Lawrence Erlbaum Associates.

Katz, E. (1987). Communications research since Lazarsfeld. *Public Opinion Quarterly, 51*, S25–S45. doi:10.1086/269068

Katz, E., & Lazarsfeld, P. (1955). *Personal influence*. New York: The Free Press.

Kennedy, G. A. (1980). *Classical rhetoric and its Christian and secular tradition from ancient to modern times.* Chapel Hill, NC: University of North Carolina Press.

Kennedy, G. A. (1991). *Aristotle 'On Rhetoric': A theory of civic discourse.* New York: Oxford University Press.

Kennedy, J. (2007). Cyberspace may not be best place for Birmingham mayoral campaign [Electronic Version]. *The Birmingham News*. Retrieved June 22, 2008, from http://blog.al.com/jkennedy/2007/09/cyberspace_may_not_be_best_pla.html

Kiousis, S. (2002). Interactivity: A concept explication. *New Media & Society, 4*(3), 355–383.

Klapper, J. T. (1949). The effects of mass media. New York: Bureau of Applied Social Research: Columbia University.

Klapper, J. T. (1960). *The effects of mass communication*. Glencoe, IL: The Free Press.

Lang, K., & Lang, G. E. (1953). The unique perspective of television and its effects: A pilot study. *American Sociological Review, 18*, 168–183. doi:10.2307/2087842

Lazarsfeld, P., Berelson, B., & Gaudet, H. (1968). *The people's choice: How the voter makes up his mind in a presidential campaign*. New York: Columbia University Press.

Lazarsfeld, P. F. (1948). Communication research and the social psychologist. In Dennis, W. (Ed.), *Current trends in social psychology*. Pittsburgh, PA: University of Pittsburgh Press.

Lenhart, A. (2009). Social networks grow: Friending mom and dad. *Pew Internet & American Life Project* [Electronic Version]. Retrieved February 25, 2009, from http://www.pewresearch.org/pubs/1079/social-networks-grow

Lin, C. (2008). The effects of the Internet. In Bryant, J., & Oliver, M. B. (Eds.), *Media effects: Advances in theory and research* (3rd ed.). New York: Routledge.

Lombard, M., & Snyder-Duch, J. (2001). Interactive advertising and presence: A framework. *Journal of Interactive Advertising, 1*(2).

Lowrey, S., & DeFleur, M. L. (1983). *Milestones in mass communication research: Media effects*. New York: Longman, Inc.

Lucaites, J. L., Condit, C. M., & Caudill, S. (1999). *Contemporary rhetorical theory*. New York: Guilford Press.

McCroskey, J. C., & Richmond, V. P. (1996). Human communications theory and research: Traditions and models. In Salwen, M. B., & Stacks, D. W. (Eds.), *An integrated approach to communication theory and research*. Mahwah, NJ: Lawrence Erlbaum Associates.

McMillan, S. J., & Hwang, J. (2002). Measures of perceived interactivity: An exploration of the role of direction of communication, user control and time in shaping perceptions of interactivity. *Journal of Advertising, 31*(3), 29–32.

McNair, B. (2003). *An introduction to political communication*. London: Routledge.

McQuail, D. (2000). *McQuail's mass communication theory* (4th ed.). London, England: Sage.

Memmott, M., & Drinkard, J. (2004). Election ad battle smashes record in 2004. *USA Today.* Retrieved July17, 2008, from http://www.usatoday.com/news/washington/2004-11-25-election-ads_x.htm

(2003). *Merriam-Webster's collegiate dictionary* (11th ed.). Springfield, MA: Merriam-Webster.

Morris, M., & Ogan, C. (1996). The Internet as a mass medium. *Journal of Computer-Mediated Communication, 1*(4).

Newhagen, J. E., Cordes, J. W., & Levy, M. R. (1996). Nightly@NBC.com: Audience scope and the perception of interactivity in view mail on the Internet. *The Journal of Communication, 45*(3), 164–175. doi:10.1111/j.1460-2466.1995.tb00748.x

Noelle-Neumann, E. (1974). The spiral of silence: A theory of public opinion. *The Journal of Communication, 24*(2), 43–51. doi:10.1111/j.1460-2466.1974.tb00367.x

Noelle-Neumann, E. (1984). *The spiral of silence: Public opinion–our social skin*. Chicago: University of Chicago Press.

Noelle-Neumann, E. (1991). The theory of public opinion: The concept of the spiral of silence. In Anderson, J. A. (Ed.), *Communication Yearbook* (*Vol. 14*, pp. 339–356). Newbury Park, CA: Sage.

O'Hara, K. (2002). The Internet: A tool for democratic pluralism? *Science as Culture, 11*, 287–298. doi:10.1080/09505430220137298

Online Campaigning 2002: A primer. (2002). Retrieved October 27, 2007, from http://www.ipdi.org/primer2002.html

Pavlik, J. V. (1998). *New Media Technology: Cultural and Commercial Perspectives*. Boston, MA: Allyn and Bacon.

Perloff, R. M. (2002). The third-person effect. In Bryant, J. B., & Zillman, D. (Eds.), *Media Effects: Advances in theory and research* (pp. 489–506). Mahwah, NJ: Lawrence Erlbaum Associates.

Puopolo, S. T. (2001). The Web and U.S. Senate campaigns 2000. *The American Behavioral Scientist, 44*(12), 2030–2047. doi:10.1177/00027640121958474

Powell, L., & Cowart, J. (2003). *Political campaign communication: Inside and out*. Boston: Allyn and Bacon.

Rainie, L., Horrigan, J., & Cornfield, M. (2005). The Internet and campaign 2004. *Pew Internet & American Life Project*. Retrieved July 23, 2008, from http://www.pewinternet.org/Reports/2005/The-Internet-and-Campaign-2004.aspx

Reichart, L. M. (2008). *Will MySpace take me to Washington?* Paper presented at the Popular Culture/American Culture National Conference, San Francisco.

Roberts, W. R. t. (1954). The rhetoric of Aristotle. Oxford, England: Clarendon Press. (Original manuscript published in 1924).

RonPaulGraphs.com. (2008). *The revolution will be digitized* [Electronic Version]. Retrieved August 17, 2008, from http://www.ronpaulgraphs.com./index.html

Ruffini, P. (2007). *What Ron Paul's $4.3M means*. Retrieved August 19, 2008, from http://www.patrickruffini.com/2007/11/06/what-ron-pauls-38m-means/

Sabine, G. H. (1961). *A history of political theory*. New York: Holt, Rinehart and Winston.

Salwen, M. B. (2004). Online news trends. In Salwen, M. B., Garrison, B., & Driscoll, P. (Eds.), *Online news and the public* (pp. 47–80). Mahwah, NJ: Lawrence Erlbaum.

Salwen, M. B., Garrison, B., & Driscoll, P. (2004). *Online news and the public*. Mahwah, NJ: Lawrence Erlbaum.

Schneider, S. M., & Foot, K. (2002). Online structure for political action: Exploring presidential campaign Web sites from the 2000 election. *Javnost The Public*, *9*(2), 43–60.

Selnow, G. W. (1998). *Electronic Whistle-stops: The Impact of the Internet in American Politics*. Westport, CT: Praeger.

Shapiro, A. L. (1999). *The Control Revolution: How the Internet is Putting Individuals in Charge and Changing the World We Know*. New York: Public Affairs.

Shea, D. M., & Burton, M. J. (2001). *Campaign craft: The strategies, tactics, and art of political campaign management*. Westport, CT: Praeger.

Slater, M. D. (2007). Reinforcing spirals: The mutual influence of media selectivity and media effects and their impact on individual behavior and social identity. *Communication Theory*, *17*, 281–303. doi:10.1111/j.1468-2885.2007.00296.x

Steuer, J. (1992). Defining virtual reality: Dimensions determining telepresence. *The Journal of Communication*, *43*(4), 73–93. doi:10.1111/j.1460-2466.1992.tb00812.x

Sundar, S. S. (2004). Theorizing interactivity's effects. *The Information Society*, *20*, 387–391. doi:10.1080/01972240490508072

The 2004 campaign, Dean and Kerry issue fundraising totals. (2004). *The New York Times*.

Thorson, K., & Rodgers, S. (2006). Relationships Between Blogs as eWOM, Interactivity, Perceived Interactivity and Parasocial Interaction. *Journal of Interactive Advertising, special issue on electronic word-of-mouth (eWOM), 6*(2).

Trammell, K. D., Tarkowski, A., Hofmokl, J., & Sapp, A. M. (2006). Rzeczpospolita blogów [Republic of blog]: Examining Polish bloggers through content analysis. *Journal of Computer-Mediated Communication, 11*(3). Retrieved December 13, 2008, from http://jcmc.indiana.edu/vol11/issue3/trammell.html

Trammell, K. D., William, A. P., Postelnicu, M., & Landreville, K. D. (2006). Increasing interactivity in candidate web sites and blogs through text and technical features. *Mass Communication & Society*, *9*(1), 21–44. doi:10.1207/s15327825mcs0901_2

Trent, J. S., & Friedenberg, R. V. (2000). *Political campaign communication: Principles and practices*. Westport, CT: Praeger.

United States Government Printing Office. (2002). *Public law 107-155–Bipartisan campaign reform act of 2002*. [Electronic Version]. Retrieved July 5, 2008 from http://www.gpo.gov/fdsys/pkg/PLAW-107publ155/content-detail.html

Vargas, J. A. (2008). *Obama Raised Half a Billion Online*. Retrieved February 25, 2009 from http://voices.washingtonpost.com/44/2008/11/20/obama_raised_half_a_billion_on.html

Wanta, W., & Hu, Y. (1994). The effects of credibility, reliance, and exposure on media agenda setting: A path analysis model. *The Journalism Quarterly*, *71*(1), 90–98.

Waterman, D. (2000). CBS-Viacom and the effects of media mergers: An economic perspective. *Federal Communications Law Journal*, *52*, 531–550.

West, M. D. (1994). Validating a scale for the measurement of credibility: A covariance structure modeling approach. *The Journalism Quarterly*, *71*(1), 159–168.

Whillock, R. K. (1997). Cyber-politics: The online strategies of 1996. *The American Behavioral Scientist*, *40*(8), 1208–1225. doi:10.1177/0002764297040008018

Winer, D. (2003). What makes a weblog a weblog? Retrieved August 19, 2008, from http://blogs.law.harvard.edu/whatmakesaweblogaweblog.html

Zavis, A. (2009). *MySpace cyber-bullying conviction tentatively dismissed.* Retrieved July 3, 2009 from http://www.latimes.com/news/local/la-me-myspace3-2009jul03,0,6795027.story

Zillman, D. (2000). The coming of media entertainment. In Zillman, D., & Vorderer, P. (Eds.), *Media entertainment: The psychology of its appeal.* Mahwah, NJ: Lawrence Erlbaum Associates.

Chapter 31
Making Personalization Feel More Personal:
A Four-Step Cycle for Advancing the User Experience of Personalized Recommenders and Adaptive Systems

Shailendra Rao
Stanford University, USA

Jeremy N. Bailenson
Stanford University, USA

Clifford Nass
Stanford University, USA

ABSTRACT

The gold standard for customer service is catering to each individual's unique needs. This means providing them undivided attention and helping them find what they want as well as what they will like, based on their prior history. An illustrative metaphor of the ideal interpersonal relationship between retailers and consumers is the "sincere handshake," welcoming a familiar face to a familiar place and saying goodbye until next time, best symbolizes an ideal interpersonal relationship between retailers and consumers. In this chapter the authors offer a four-step cycle of this personalization process, which abstracts the key elements of this handshake in order to make it possible in mass digital consumerism. This model offers an ideal framework for drawing out the key lessons learned from the two previous stages of media evolution, Micro and Mass, as well as from social science and Human Computer Interaction (HCI) to inform the design and further the understanding of the rich capabilities of the current age of Digital Consumerism.

DOI: 10.4018/978-1-60566-792-8.ch031

PERSONALIZATION CYCLE: ABSTRACTING THE KEY ELEMENTS FOR THE HANDSHAKE

The key aspects of the interaction between the customer and retailer that make it feel personalized can be abstracted and broken down into a four-step cycle: 1) Gather user information and needs, 2) Build user model and profile, 3) Match user with appropriate available content, and 4) Present personalized content (see Figure 1).

The first step in the interaction between media, content, product, or service providers and consumers with personalized service is assessing the consumer's demographics and unique preferences. Just as in retail, a key part of this initial assessment is trying to assess their goals- whether they are in search of something specific or browsing a la window-shopping. Once this has been done either through explicit or implicit input, the provider can formulate an internal model of whom the person is and what they might like. Then utilizing this model the provider can determine what available products or services will best suit this particular consumer. Finally, based on the previous three steps, the provider can assess how to best package and frame the recommended content when presenting it to the consumer and follow through accordingly. This personalization process can be conceptualized as a cyclical one as the recommender agent can iterate and continue to refine their understanding and modeling of a user, expand their library of matching content, and improve on how they frame the personalized content when presenting it to each individual consumer. With the cyclical nature and striving for constant improvement the retailer can adhere to the age old adage that the customer is always right.

Together this four step-cycle abstracts the key steps necessary for personalization away from the intricate human production and computing processes necessary for execution. By doing so this model provides a framework for identifying exactly where the insights and future investigations from social science and HCI can help make personalization feel more personal for consumers.

Micro Consumerism: A Friendly Handshake

A frequently visited local video rental store provided an ideal setting for this handshake to take

Figure 1. The personalization process

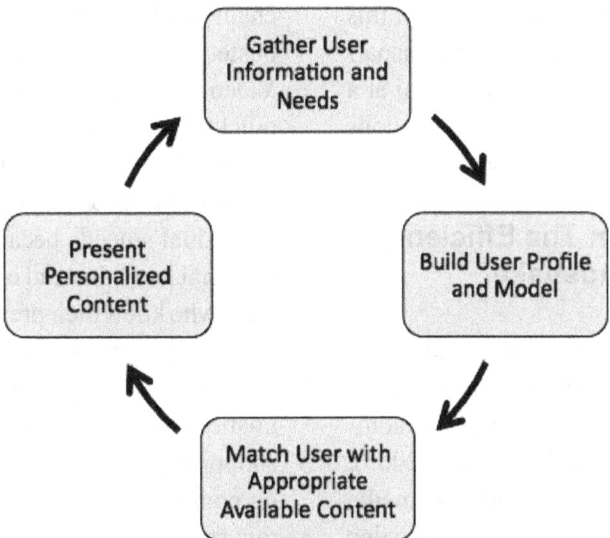

place. At this neighborhood store customers would be welcomed by a friendly greeting from a store clerk or owner, who would ask them how their previous movie recommendations turned out as well as suggest new ones based on the customer's feedback and prior likings. For the customer the purchase process was made infinitely easier and enjoyable because of this personalized service. From the seller's perspective the handshake was a key ingredient in building a better shopping experience and thus a stronger business, by helping project a caring image, increasing sales with targeted recommendations, and cultivating a regular loyal consumer base.

Personalization was a critical factor in making the customer-seller relationship feel truly personalized at this stage of consumerism precisely because of what it did at each aspect of the four-step personalization process. The manner by which the store clerk or owner gathered their customer's needs was important as the right questions were asked in the right manner for each individual. Because the retailer had developed a relationship with the customer and knew how to parse the information they gathered from them, they were able to properly build a profile and model of what each individual would like, which led to a natural matching with appropriate available content (Linden, Smith, & York, 2003). Finally, the store clerk or owner was able to present this personalized content in a targeted and transparent manner, which spoke to each individual at a personal level and made the recommendations and overall service feel more personal.

Mass Consumerism: The Efficient, But Impersonal Handshake

Unfortunately many aspects of this handshake were lost in recent times with the emergence of *mass media* (media designed for a very large audience) (DeFleur & Dennis, 1991; McQuail, 2005), *media consolidation* (the majority of major media outlets owned by a few corporations) (Compaine & Gomery, 2000), and the proliferation of big businesses to the detriment of local mom-and-pop shops such as the neighborhood video rental store, which fostered and were dependent on sincere interpersonal relationships with their clientele. In the name of profit and efficiency truly personalized service and media existed only at the margins of society with special interest venues.

To accrue the benefits of the handshake from Micro Consumerism at each of the four outlined levels of the personalization process which were so critical to the previous model of customer-seller relationship, media conglomerates drew on several strategies to blur the lines between *interpersonal* (Gemeinschaft) and *mass media* (Gesellschaft) (Beniger, 1987). These strategies centered around feigning the sincerity of the handshake commonly found at the previously ubiquitous local video rental store. Strategies for mass media productions to conceal audience size with the aim of generating pseudo-communities include simplicity, personal stories, personal agents, interactivity, emphasis on emotion, and production values. Media providers and retailers used these strategies with varying success however and the handshake frequently found at the neighborhood store was never fully attained in all arenas with the same level of sincerity.

It increasingly became the norm to visit a chain brick and mortar retailer such as Blockbuster (J Nielsen & Mack, 1994) or Hollywood Video (Izard, 1971) as opposed to going to the quickly disappearing neighborhood video rental store. Oftentimes gone with this transition were the familiar faces that were able to attend to each individual's needs because they knew them at a personal level. Instead of being greeted by a store clerk who knew their previous viewing history and could make personalized recommendations based on their prior likings, consumers found themselves unattended and unassisted in a do-it-yourself shopping experience. The burden was primarily on consumers to satisfy their own needs during this stage of media evolution. Critical elements represented in this handshake that made consumerism feel personalized in the previous stage were missing. Consequently the gold standard for customer service normally found in the previous stage of consumerism was lost.

Lost in this transition from Micro Consumerism to Mass Consumerism were the wins at each of the four levels of the personalization process, which were major factors in attaining that friendly handshake between retailers and consumers. Because there was less emphasis on individualized service and fewer opportunities, it was a seemingly impossible challenge to both gather a customer's individual needs and build an accurate profile and model of them fully considering their uniqueness, rather than making gross guesses about them based on their assumed demographic. The consumer also suffered from poorly trained sales people and store representatives who many times lacked a deep understanding of the products and services they were providing (Del Colliano, 2008). Consequently, matching them with appropriate available content and presenting this in a targeted and persuasive way were not strengths of this stage of consumerism.

It would be a mistake to only paint a gloomy picture here however, as this stage in media evolution brought many positives for both providers and consumers. For providers and merchants some of the benefits these changes brought included much more rapid production of higher quality media, larger audiences, and lower costs to production and distribution. Consumers also benefitted with quality standardization, lower prices, and easier access to these media goods.

Digital Consumerism: Reviving the Handshake with the Best of Both Worlds

Over the past decade there has been a seismic shift in these interactions between providers and consumers because of the very recent dramatic technological advances of the digital information age. This has allowed for the possibility of that gold standard of customer service to be reconstructed without losing the efficiency and other tangible benefits of Mass Consumerism. Instead of succumbing to the limitations and impersonal nature of a one-to-many broadcast model, content providers and advertisers can tailor their messages, services, and products to meet the specific needs of a particular individual with a very personalized feel. The symbolic handshake can be resurrected with the technological affordances of the present stage in media evolution.

Innovations in and high adoption rates of cable and digital television, the emergence of the Internet, and the prevalence of mobile phones have created a setting where content providers and advertisers can more effectively feign a personal one-to-one relationship with the members of their target audience through personalized media systems far more intelligently than with the first phase of Mass Consumerism. The technological advances that have set the stage for this shift are numerous and include, but are not limited to, the digitization of content, cheaper and increased storage capacities, advanced machine learning algorithms, faster data transmission speeds, and increasingly ubiquitous cell phone connectivity (Negroponte, 1995). Technology has played a major role in bolstering the efficiency and effectiveness of media suggestions (providers), requests (consumers), transmissions (providers), and reception (consumers).

Personalized recommendation engines best illustrate the extent of the power that this media shift offers. They enable media providers to revive many of those critical elements of the neighborhood corner store, namely being cognizant of each individual consumer's past history and what they might like. By having an understanding of who a consumer is, their tendencies, past attitudes and behaviors, as well as a model of what this means, producers of these recommendation engines can cultivate an intimate relationship with their customers. When done properly and optimally, personalized recommendation systems solve many of the problems that surfaced with the transition to Mass Consumerism. They can revive many of the positives from the more localized and interpersonal consumerism evident in the neighborhood video rental store, and offer new opportunities for advancing consumerism that were not possible in the previous phases.

It has become increasingly common in this present age of media consumerism to use online services to rent or purchase movies in place of the neighborhood video rental store or the massive brick and mortar video chain (Buckley, 2008; eMarketer, 2006, 2007; Reisinger, 2008). Some popular services are Netflix, iTunes Store, and Amazon (Branco, Firth, Encanacao, & Bonato, 2005; Hitwise, 2007; Netflix; *Sharing, Privacy and Trust in Our Networked World*, 2007; Ward, Marsden, Cahill, & Johnson, 2001). All of these services have an underlying recommendation engine, which serves two main functions 1) increase sales by quickly matching consumers with content they will like and 2) make their service feel more personalized for the end consumer by bringing back the aspects of the handshake that were sorely missed with the transition to mass media.

Currently consumers can go to one of these or other e-commerce venues and shop in an online personalized environment for a plethora of products, services, and media content. Across all of these shopping places they can communicate to the retailer what their specific movie interests are either through *explicit* means (self-reports about objective personal characteristics, self-assessments with respect to general dimensions, self-reports on specific evaluations, or responses to test items) or *nonexplicit* ones (naturally occurring actions, previously stored information, low-level indices of psychological states, or signals concerning the current surroundings) (Jameson, 2002). This interactivity between providers and consumers helps foster a relationship that can closely approximate the best aspects of the local neighborhood video rental store shopping experience. Specifically, these online video markets can welcome their customers just like those local shops did, by asking how their previous movie recommendations turned out as well as suggest new ones based on their feedback and past favorites.

Additionally, because of the power afforded by their online recommendation engines these retailers can make new connections with their customers with personalized one-to-one marketing messages via various mediums (email, text messages, other websites) and by allowing them to set up wish lists and notifications. By bringing back the key ingredients that made that handshake possible as well as exploring and experimenting with new opportunities, personalized recommendation systems enable media and content providers to offer customers an easier, more efficient, and more enjoyable purchase process than possible with the previous two stages of consumerism.

But it is important to note that simply having a recommendation engine is not an end all solution to offering a personalized experience, nor a guarantee that the handshake found in the neighborhood store will be revived. Similar to how mass media utilized the techniques outlined by Beniger (Beniger, 1987) to feign sincerity to overcome some of the key problems with Mass Consumerism in terms of providing the handshake, personalized online recommendation systems necessitate a framework based on an empirically grounded understanding of people's interactions to make them feel truly personalized. To take full advantage of the power that digital media affords in this era for empowering consumers with a personalized experience, media theorists, researchers, and producers need to focus on these interactions and experiences from a user centered design perspective.

Personalizing consumer experiences in this current stage of media production and consumption is not only a task for engineers and business experts to tackle and solve. It does not simply consist of issues for computer scientists to work on: improving user modeling, designing better adaptive algorithms to improve accuracy rates, or increasing data transmission speeds. Neither is it just for business strategists to worry about targeting specific markets, expanding inventory, or forming partnerships. A necessary component for the success of online recommendation services and more generally personalized and adaptive systems is a grounding in principles and findings from the interdisciplinary field of HCI and the social sciences.

The four-step personalization process highlights each of the key areas where HCI and social science can advance Digital Consumerism, particularly recommendation systems, to its apex in terms of the relationship between providers and consumers (see Figure 2). Drawing from lessons learned in survey and questionnaire design and privacy can greatly improve how adaptive systems gather user information and needs either explicitly or implicitly. Building user profiles and models by adjusting appropriately for impression management and honesty can make a dramatic impact on the performance of these technologies. Matching users with appropriate available content is a technology problem, but the recommendation mechanisms chosen cannot be done in isolation from user needs. Lastly, understanding the prior work on and future directions for feedback, transparency, timing, and ordering can help ensure that the fruits of the three previous steps are effectively presented to the end consumer.

The cyclical nature of the personalization process afforded by the digital age, parallels repeat visits to the neighborhood corner video store. Much in the same way store clerks at the neighborhood video store cultivated a personal relationship with their loyal costumers, personalized recommendation systems develop this relationship through repeated usage. At its optimized case, the cyclical fashion of this process helps resurrect the handshake, the symbol of the gold standard for customer service.

Chapter Goals

The goals of the remainder of this chapter are two-fold and structured by the framework offered by the four-step cyclical personalization process outlined above: 1) explore and detail how designers of personalized systems can replicate the

Figure 2. Using this model to take digital consumerism to the apex

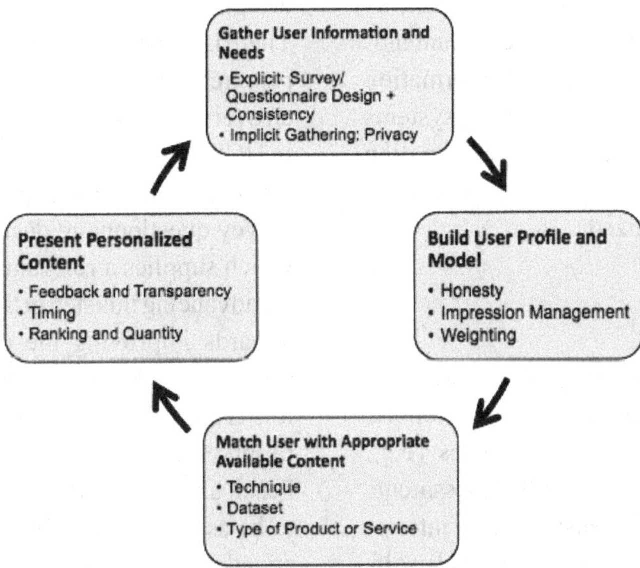

handshake from the local neighborhood corner store, overcome the limitations of the era of Mass Consumerism, and reap the many benefits from the technological advances of the current Digital stage of media evolution and 2) identify open questions and key opportunities in this space for media researchers and theorists to pursue to make personalization feel even more personal.

Gather User Information and Needs

At this stage of the personalization process the chief aim is to collect accurate information about the consumer and identify their individual needs. This phase can be likened to the first encounter between a customer and a store clerk at a video rental store. After the friendly greeting the store clerk's next critical task is to formulate an understanding of whom their customer is and how to best please them. In an ideal case the store clerk puts the customer at ease and encourages them to divulge as much as possible about their background, personality, and interests, which makes it infinitely easier to properly build a mental model of the individual in the next stage of the personalization process. There are two ways for personalization systems to gather information from and the needs of their users: 1) explicitly and 2) implicitly (Jameson, 2002). The following sections outline the respective advantages and disadvantages of both types of information gathering in the context of personalized systems and some specific ways to ensure the information gathering at this stage leads to a user experience that feels more personalized.

Explicit Gathering

Explicit in this case means to gather information about a user including their self-reports about objective personal characteristics (e.g., age, profession, or residence), self-assessments with respect to general dimensions (e.g., interest level, knowledge level, or importance level), self-reports on specific evaluations (e.g., thumbs-up or thumbs-down), and responses to test items (e.g., a standardized battery of questions) (Jameson, 2002). Key benefits to gathering user information explicitly are that it is a quick way to collect user information that is fixed or typically remains static, users know exactly what information about them is being stored and collected which escapes many privacy issues and concerns, and the physical barrier for inputting personal characteristics can be set very low on the web if the inputs are designed with a few radio buttons, check boxes, and drop-down menus. On the other hand, one drawbacks is users have to invest time up front to construct a profile before they can see if the personalization system's recommendations are worth the effort. Moreover, they may not understand the questions and possible answers, they may provide socially desirable answers instead of reflecting their true self, or they may simply look for the answer that requires the least amount of thought to finish the profile building process as fast as possible.

Survey and Questionnaire Design

Explicit information gathering for personalized systems can leverage the rich body of work and lessons learned from survey and questionnaire design to improve upon its validity and reliability. There is a vast array of survey design and research resources readily available. Ozok (2009) provides an overview of survey design and implementation in HCI (Ozok, 2009). Pasek and Krosnick (2010) utilize insights from psychology to optimize survey questionnaire design in political science, which supplies a relevant and applicable review for advancing this step in the personalization cycle towards improving the overall personalization process (Pasek & Krosnick, 2010). At a high level it is critical to be mindful of the three basic rules of survey and questionnaire design enumerated by Pasek and Krosnick. They should 1) be designed to be as easy as possible for the ideal survey respondent, 2) discourage looking for shortcuts and simply looking to satisfy the interviewer, and 3) avoid unnecessary confusion and misunderstandings by adhering to conversational conventions as much as possible. Offering an entire survey and questionnaire design guide for explicit data gathering in the personalization cycle is beyond the scope of this chapter, but there are a few keys to remember which will be outlined here.

Open-Ended Questions vs. Closed Questions

In the context of a personalized recommender it takes a great deal of natural language processing capabilities and places great demands on computing resources to offer open-ended questions and interpret user responses. Consequently, closed questions with a fixed set of answer choices are a natural fit for this context. However, it is important to be cognizant of the drawbacks of closed questions. Unlike open-ended questions, which can require a great deal of thought and effort on the part of the respondent (Oppenheim, 1966), it is easy to quickly flip through closed questions and satisfice. Additionally when numbers are involved in the answer options (e.g. 3 hours, 5 books read, etc.) the midpoint of the offered range implies the norm which sends an implicit message to people and can affect their self-report (Norbert. Schwarz, 1995).

Pasek and Krosnick offer a useful tool when designing closed questions for improving its needs finding ability (Pasek & Krosnick, 2010). Before employing a closed question, it is useful to pretest an open-ended version of it on the population of interest. This helps ensure that the answer choices offered encompass all of the alternatives a user might consider in response to the particular question being asked.

Rating Scales

There are several guidelines about how to make the rating scales for closed ended questions more intuitive for users. These in turn improve the quality of the coding and interpretation done by system designers, researchers, and the corresponding algorithms in play. For *bipolar* dimensions which have a meaningful or interpretable midpoint (e.g. dislike a great deal to like a great deal where the midpoint is neither like nor dislike), 7-point scales have shown to be more reliable (Green & Rao, 1970). Conversely, for *unipolar* dimensions (e.g. not at all important to extremely important where the middle category "somewhat important" does not necessarily imply the absence of importance) ratings have been found to be more reliable when 5-point scales are utilized (Lissitz & Green, 1975).

Despite increasing cognitive costs, adding verbal labels on all rating scales rather than just leaving them only numbered, makes it easier for respondents to interpret the intended meaning behind the answer choices. This increases the reliability and validity of the user's ratings (Jon A. Krosnick & Berent, 1993; Norbert Schwarz, Knauper, Hippler, Noelle-Neumann, & Clark, 1991). These verbal labels should have equally spaced meanings as well (Hofmans, et al., 2007; Norbert Schwarz, Grayson, & Knauper, 1998; Wallsten, Budescu, Rapoport, Zwick, & Forsyth, 1986).

Rating or Ranking

For personalized recommendation systems it is useful to gather user preferences along ordinal dimensions (e.g. 1-Dislike a great deal to 7-Like a great deal) and run corresponding statistical analyses to compare user attitudes across multiple items. In these situations even though they can be more time-consuming for users, ranking questions produce more reliable and valid output than ratings as they are the product of less satisficing (Alwin & Krosnick, 1985; Jon A Krosnick & Alwin, 1987; Miethe, 1985; Reynolds & Jolly, 1980). For example, in the context of a dessert recommendation system attempting to gather a user's fruit delectation, it is more fruitful to ask them to rank their favorites amongst mangoes, strawberries, blueberries, pineapples, etc., rather than inquiring about how much they like each individual fruit and then running the analyses across items.

Ordering Effects

Two ordering effects in particular are important for improving the design of personalized systems at this stage: 1) *response order effects* and 2) *question order effects*. To sidestep both primacy effects, the inclination to select options at the beginning of a list (Belson, 1966), and recency effects, the inclination to select options listed at the end (Kalton, Collins, & Brook, 1978), designers can randomize the order of the answer options presented and utilize *seemingly open-ended questions* (SOEQ) (Pasek & Krosnick, 2010). SOEQ's use a short pause to segment the question from the response choices, which encourages respondents to think through the question as if it were an open-ended one (Holbrook, Krosnick, Moore, & Tourangeau, 2007). For example, in the case of a movie recommendation system trying to gather user likes and dislikes, instead of asking "If you had to pick your favorite gangster movie, would you pick The Godfather I, Goodfellas, Scarface, or Donnie Brasco?" it is better to ask "If you had to pick your favorite gangster movie what would you pick? Would you pick The Godfather I, Goodfellas, Scarface, or Donnie Brasco?", which reduces response order effects.

Four concerns stemming from question order effects are 1) *subtraction*, 2) *perceptual contrast*, 3) *priming*, and 4) *length*. Subtraction results from two nested concepts presented next to each other and it appears the questions although related are intended to be evaluated separately (e.g. a question about Microsoft Internet Explorer followed by one about Microsoft software) (Schuman, Presser, & Ludwig, 1983). Perceptual contrast occurs when two successive questions present a contrast (e.g. attitudes amongst a technophile audience towards Mozilla Firefox may be positively influenced if they are immediately preceded by their assessment of Microsoft Internet Explorer) (Norbert Schwarz & Bless, 1992; Norbert Schwarz & Strack, 1991). Priming happens when earlier questions increase the salience of certain attitudes or beliefs (e.g. preceding questions about Microsoft with those about Windows Vista may increase the chances of a poorer overall evaluation of Microsoft) (Kalton, et al., 1978). In terms of length of survey it is better to ask questions that are of primary importance and utility to the recommendation algorithms in play earlier, rather than later to reduce the chances of satisficing (J. A. Krosnick, 1999). As Pasek and Krosnick note, there is no simple solution for alleviating question order effects other than being cognizant of these aforementioned biases, as oftentimes a particular ordering of a question set is needed for coherence (Pasek & Krosnick, 2010).

Gathering Consistent User Input

Another key consideration when collecting explicitly supplied input is ensuring that the user is providing consistent responses that are not disrupted by system performance or variables in flux such as time of day. Inconsistent user input, particularly those resulting from attempts to game the system, add a tremendous amount of unnecessary confusion for both the underlying recommendation engine's processes as well as for the user. To aid personalized systems in their quest to offer a tailored user experience for each individual it is imperative that the data gathered at this stage in the personalization cycle paints a congruent picture of the user.

The experiment conducted within the context of a fictional and controlled online dating recommender in Rao et. al (2009) (Rao, Hurlbutt, Nass, & JanakiRam, 2009) demonstrated how using a person's own photograph can keep their responses consistent and prevent them from gaming the system when presented with poor quality recommendations. It remains to be seen whether the stabilizing effect of personal photos will wear off over time or whether these results hold in other recommender contexts. However, displaying a person's own photo appears to be one tool designers can add to their arsenal to improve the data gathering stage. In addition to investigating the aforementioned open questions about personal photo, future research can assess whether this is a useful tool for gathering consistent user input through implicit means.

Implicit Gathering

Implicit inputs to formulate user profiles include *naturally occurring actions*, *previously stored information*, *sensing psychological states*, and *deriving information from a user's current surroundings* (Jameson, 2002). Some of the benefits of this style of information gathering about users are that they are not required to invest any cognitive or physical effort and time up front, profiling can be done unobtrusively in the background, and the problems about self-report noted above are avoided. Key concerns about this approach have to do with privacy and transparency. Users may not be comfortable or even realize that personal information and inferences about them are being collected and made. Another limitation is that systems using this method can require users to use the system for quite some time before it is able to collect enough information to make solid and valuable inferences about a person.

Privacy

As it is across the entire personalization process, privacy is a major concern for both users and recommendation system designers. Although this topic applies broadly to the entire personalization process, it is of particular concern for implicit user data gathering and represents the endpoint of the continuum for personalization systems privacy invasiveness (Cranor, 2004). Both Cranor (2004) and Teltzrpw and Kobsa (2004) (Teltzrow & Kobsa, 2004) provide a detailed overview of the many privacy risks, concerns, preferences, laws, and self-regulatory guidelines for personalized systems. The following briefly picks out some key ways to reduce user privacy concerns in this space.

Brodie et. al (2004) found that user willingness to share personal information in an e-commerce setting increased when they were allowed to view, edit, and delete their own data (Brodie, Karat, & Karat, 2004). They also suggested that privacy concerns can be sidestepped for personalized systems if users can specify to the system when it is useful for it to collect their data. Another design guideline offered was to let users manage and select from different identities when interacting with a website as they may be more willing to disclose personal information or be monitored under the guise of a pseudo name. The majority of internet users are concerned about being tracked ("Cyber Dialogue Survey Data Reveals Lost Revenue for Retailers Due to Widespread Consumer Privacy Concerns," 2001) and as Brodie and colleagues posit asking users for explicit consent may be one way to allay their fears. This ties into metaphors about dating and customer service. After the customer has been on a few "dates" with the marketer, it is easier for them to disclose more of their personal information (Godin, 1999).

All of these design guidelines revolve around giving users more control of the data gathering stage which ties into the finding that consumers react more positively to organizations when they have a higher perceived level of control (*A Survey of Consumer Privacy Attitudes and Behaviors*, 2000; Hine & Eve, 1998). Whether information about an individual is being collected through explicit or implicit means, it is critical to be respectful of their concerns and make them feel both in control and cognizant of exactly what is occurring at this stage in the personalization cycle.

Build User Profile and Model

Once the personalized system has gathered an individual user's preference, needs, and goals it is time to the build a model and formulate a profile of the user. This step in the personalization process is about interpreting and assembling all of the user information gathered in the previous phase. The neighborhood video rental store parallel is the clerk taking a few moments and reflecting upon what their customer has intentionally or unintentionally communicated to them as well. This pause helps the store clerk internalize everything they have just learned about their customer through proper listening, deduction, and inference right before seeking appropriate video title recommendations.

Similarly personalized systems at this stage of the personalization process need to correctly assemble the pieces of the puzzle to determine whom exactly the individual user is and what their unique needs are to ensure that it is offering an intelligently personalized experience. To achieve this, the underlying computing algorithms in play here should be driven by an understanding of *impression management*, *correction factors*, and *proper weighting* of the input the consumer has provided explicitly or implicitly in their interactions with the recommendation system.

Impression Management

Understanding people's impression management when interacting with these systems is a key step in ensuring that their entire experience feels personalized. It is critical to always keep in mind that data gathered about the user can be contaminated and corrupted by their own conscious and unconscious efforts to present themselves in a particular light. Failing to do so may lead the personalized system and its underlying algorithms astray and as a consequence, result in sub-optimal recommendations and overall user experience.

This can be likened to the research on *impression management*, *face-work*, and *presentation of self* in human-human interactions (Dillard, Browning, Sitkin, & Sutcliffe, 2000; Goffman, 1956, 1959; Schlenker, 1980; Tedeschi, 1984). The framework which Higgins (1987) uses to categorize the domains of the self is useful for designers of personalized systems to be cognizant of: the *actual self* (who one really is), the *ideal self* (who one would like to be), and the *ought self* (who one feels it is their duty to be) (Higgins, 1987). This trinity of self is applicable in this domain as it outlines the different motivations behind how users represent themselves to an interactive personalized system via explicit and implicit means. For example, a user may misrepresent themselves in a questionnaire that the system needs to learn about their goals and desires by intentionally presenting themselves as how they strive to be, rather than as how they actually are. Likewise when a user is being monitored or under the watch of a personalized system working to profile them, they might change their normal behavior to live up to a version of their self that they think they ought to be (Higgins, 1987). At this stage in the personalization cycle it is imperative to utilize this framework when interpreting the collected user data from the previous step.

It is worth noting that *computer mediated communication* (CMC) between people can have some advantages over human-human interaction with respect to people putting on a different face so to speak. This is illustrated in Bargh et al. (2002) where compared to face-to-face interactions, Internet interactions allowed individuals to better express aspects of their true selves to others (Bargh, McKenna, & Fitzsimons, 2002). In an online setting people felt more comfortable expressing aspects of themselves that they wanted to express in the real world but felt unable to. Furthermore, it may be easier for people to present their various negative aspects given the relative anonymity of online interactions. See Ellison 2006 for a literature review of self-presentation and self-disclosure in online contexts, specifically in CMC (Ellison, 2006). One natural direction for future research in this space is to explore how the various aspects of a user's context, namely time, physical location, and activity, affect their impression management with personalized systems trying to build an accurate and useful profile of them.

Honesty

Hancock et al's (2007) investigation of honesty in the online dating space offers an illustration of why it is critical for designers of interactive systems to not simply take user inputs at face value (Hancock, Toma, & Ellison, 2007). Their study of 40 males and 40 females showed that deception in dating profiles was common: 55.3% of males and 41.5% of females provided deceptive information about their height, 60.5% and 59.0% respectively did so for their weight, and 24.3% and 13.2% misrepresented their age.

More specifically this study offers some specific correction factors for each of these personal attributes. Both men and women overstated their height; on average men did so at .57 inches (SD = .81 inches) and women added on .03 inches (SD = .75 inches). This effect was more pronounced for short men and women. Similarly both men and women underreported their weight, but women did so more than men. On average women said they were 8.48 lbs lighter than they actually were (SD = 8.87 lbs), while men underreported their weight by 1.94 lbs (SD = 10.34). The average age deviation found was .44 years with a range from 3 years younger to 9 years older. No difference in age deception was found between men and women. By applying the results of this study as correction factors system designers in working on online dating matches can appropriately fix the user data that fuels their personalized algorithms, so that it provides a more valid view of the user being profiled.

For the purposes of designing personalized recommendation systems it is not necessarily important why people are misconstruing their actual self to and through digital media; what is important is correcting for it because using raw, uncorrected data to drive the personalization process will result in sub-optimal user experiences. The investigation in Hancock et. al (2007) offers a starting point for research specifically targeted at improving this stage of the personalization process (Hancock, et al., 2007). People's honesty and impression management in other product and service contexts remain unexplored and worthy of much research attention. The specific goal for this work is to determine whether the user data collected actually means what it is supposed to mean and if not, then how to adjust it accordingly. Considerations towards user honesty and their impression management are imperative for driving the personalization algorithms detailed in the next step in the personalization process.

Weighting

Another important consideration at this stage of the personalization process is determining how much value to assign to each of the explicitly and implicitly gathered inputs about an individual user. Rich's work on using stereotypes about a person, particularly their gender and race, to quickly build a small and deep model of them illuminates the potential benefits of properly weighting different traits of a person (Rich, 1979a, 1979b, 1983). This work made use of a system called Grundy, which used a limited set of stereotypes such as feminist, intellectual, sport-person, about a user to generate novel recommendations. Grundy had a much higher success rate of recommending novels that users liked when using these stereotypes about a person than compared to random suggestions. This illustrates how heavily weighting various aspects of an individual user can positively shape the personalized experience being offered.

In short to provide an intelligently personalized experience all of the collected aspects of an individual should not be given the same amount of weight. Research on how much emphasis to place on specific individual user traits during this stage is nowhere near being a closed book. This is not surprising given the diverse array of people and the products and services available for recommendation to them. Consequently concrete guidelines for system designers are not readily available for weighting traits. This leaves ample opportunity for future researchers. It may be the job of computer scientists to devise and adjust these weighting algorithms, but it is the responsibility of social scientists working in this space to explore and determine how much to weight various gathered aspects of an individual user to inform these computing processes.

MATCH USER WITH APPROPRIATE AVAILABLE CONTENT

For personalized recommendation systems this phase in the personalization process is a technology issue, dependent on the recommendation approach and algorithm chosen. On the surface it may seem that social science and HCI methodologies and design principles cannot contribute at this step in the personalization cycle for Digital Consumerism. However, that is not the case as the basis for generating recommendations cannot be disentangled from user perceptions concerning the quality and type of the personalized content, the systems' intelligence level, as well as the system's impact on an individual's cognitive and affective state. With this in mind we provide an overview of the various approaches to recommendation types that exist and are under development.

Techniques Used to Generate Recommendations

Personalized recommendation systems are often grouped into one of five methodologies: 1) *collaborative filtering*, 2) *content-based*, 3) *demographic*, 4) *utility-based* and 5) *knowledge-based* (Burke, 2002; Resnick & Varian, 1997; J. Ben Schafer, Konstan, & Riedl, 1999; Terveen & Hill, 2002). Collaborative filtering is a popular recommendation approach used on the web that filters and evaluates items based on the opinions of other people (J. B. Schafer, Frankowski, Herlocker, & Sen, 2007). Content-based recommendation systems rely on a description of an item and a profile of the user's interests (Michael J. Pazzani & Billsus, 2007). Demographic recommendation systems use personal attributes to categorize its users and make their recommendations according to associated demographic classes (Krulwich, 1997; M. Pazzani & Billsus, 1997; M.J. Pazzani, 1999; Rich, 1979a, 1979b, 1983). Utility-based recommendation systems are centered upon the utility function of each available recommended product or service for a user (Guttman, Moukas, & Maes, 1998). Knowledge-based recommender systems employ their functional knowledge of how an individual user's need is fulfilled by a particular item to provide recommendations (S. Brin & Page, 1998; J. Ben Schafer, et al., 1999; Schmitt & Bergmann, 1999; Towle & Quinn, 2000). Burke (2002) provides a detailed overview and analysis of these five popular recommendation techniques and their associated backgrounds, inputs, and processes (Burke, 2002).

Other adaptive techniques of note are *ability-based, learning personal assistants, critique-based, situational impairment adaption*, and *user interfaces that adapt to the current task* (Gajos & Jameson, 2009). Ability-based user interfaces adapt to the user's individual and actual abilities with respect to dexterity, strength, preferred input/output devices, visual acuity, color perception, etc. and respond accordingly (Gajos, 2007; Gajos & Weld, 2004; Gajos, Wobbrock, & Weld, 2008). Learning personal assistants learn how to help users by observing them perform tasks, and taking over where possible (Faulring, Mohnkern, Steinfeld, & Myers, 2008; Freed, et al., 2008; T. Mitchell, Caruana, Freitag, McDermott, & Zabowski, 1994; Segal & Kephart, 1999; Steinfeld, Bennett, et al., 2007; Steinfeld, Quinones, Zimmerman, Bennett, & Siewiorek, 2007). Critique-based recommendation systems work as a partnership between users and the system where until an acceptable recommendation is offered the user continues to make their preferences and requirements more explicit (Averjanova, Ricci, & Nguyen, 2008; Reilly, Zhang, McGinty, Pu, & Smyth, 2007; Ricci & Nguyen, 2007; Zhang, Jones, & Pu, 2008). Adapting to situational impairments means sensing factors in the user context that may impose adverse or uncommon temporary "disability" (e.g. low lighting, physical activity, or cold fingers) and adapts the user interface to appropriately (Barnard, Yi, Jacko, & Sears, 2007; Kane, Wobbrock, & Smith, 2008; Lin, Goldman, Price, Sears, & Jacko, 2007; MacKay, Dearman, Inkpen, & Watters, 2005; Mizobuchi, Chignell, & Newton, 2005; Mustonen, Olkkonen, & Hakkinen, 2004; Oulasvirta, Tamminen, Roto, & Kuorelahti, 2005; Pascoe, Ryan, & Morse, 2000; A. Sears, Lin, Jacko, & Xiao, 2003; Vadas, Patel, Lyons, Starner, & Jacko, 2006). User interfaces that adapt to the current task modify the presentation and organization of a user interface based on a prediction of the user's next task (Findlater & McGrenere, 2004, 2008; Findlater, Moffatt, McGrenere, & Dawson, 2009; Gajos, Czerwinski, Tan, & Weld, 2006; Gajos, Everitt, Tan, Czerwinski, & Weld, 2008; J. Mitchell & Shneiderman, 1989; Andrew Sears & Shneiderman, 1994).

This categorization offers a useful framework for investigating and understanding the current systems in usage and in development. All of these have associated benefits and tradeoffs and serve different purposes. Across all of these methodologies, including hybrids amongst them, many of the same opportunities to make personalization more personal exist.

Richness of Dataset for Recommendations

Another key factor that has tremendous impact on a personalized recommendation engine's ability to properly match users with appropriate content is the sheer amount of data available for the system to draw upon. Larger datasets improve the quality of the recommendation algorithms' results (Burke, 2002). For example with larger data sets collaborative filtering systems can better match a user with similar users. Similarly with a content-based recommender a larger data set enables the system to better match a user's preferences with the association features of a product. With an existing larger data set in place the system can avoid the cold-start problem, which poses a daunting challenge when new items or new users without any ratings are encountered.

The positives stemming from a larger dataset are obvious, but the interaction between the size of this data and each of the recommendation approaches outlined above is unknown. For example if little background data is available to the recommendation engine about the user and a new piece of recommended content it is not clear whether it would be better to employ a demographic or a content-based recommender in terms of the user's satisfaction with the output and perceptions about the quality of the system. It is unclear if this decision is the same when the dataset powering the recommendation algorithm is sizable. Investigating the role of the amount of data used as the basis of the personalized system's offerings is a future direction for researchers looking to improve personalization at this step in the process.

Type of Product or Service Recommended

Additionally the interaction between the size of the dataset and the type of product or service recommended is an important topic for future research to address. Adding to the previous example, it is unexplored which recommendation approach to select given the limited available dataset for various product types and services. One important distinction to investigate particularly on the web in terms of its impact on the selection of the recommendation algorithm and size of the dataset, is whether the product is a *search product* or an *experience product* (Klein, 1998; Nelson, 1970, 1974, 1976, 1981). Search goods (e.g. cookware, house furnishings, carpets, cameras, garden supplies, and clothing) are products which full information can be assessed prior to purchase. On the other hand, experience goods (e.g. food, drugs, toiletries, books, television, and household appliances) are products which full information cannot be determined prior to purchase without actually using it. Investigating these and other product types are important areas for future research aiming to advance the personalization process and specifically affect the matching user with appropriate content stage.

This section offered an overview of the various recommender system approaches and some key considerations based on the data available for the recommendations and product or type of service being recommended. The next step is for researchers to investigate how the intersections play out in terms of how optimal the resulting recommendations *seem* to users, irrespective of their actual quality. These empirical findings will provide designers with a clear roadmap for deciphering what recommendation approach to select to take advantage of the affordances offered by the digital age and make their personalized offering feel more personal.

PRESENT PERSONALIZED CONTENT

Before reaching this phase in the personalization process cycle the system to some degree has formulated an understanding of the consumer and matched them with appropriate available content. Much like the video rental store clerk or owner, the personalized system knows the customer and has handpicked recommendations just for them. At this stage in the personalization process the recommendation system is ready to present the personalized content to the end user.

Returning back to the local video store analogy, the store clerk or owner does not simply hand off the recommended titles once they have been selected to the customer. They present the personalized content appropriately by framing the recommendation in the context of the individual's past likings and profile. These same principles for presenting personalized content apply for adaptive systems on the web, mobile phones, and desktop computers in Digital Consumerism. Acting like the personalization process is complete once matching content is found by these systems and services would be like a store clerk abruptly handing a regular customer a video and walking away. For personalization to feel truly personal and fully leverage the power of new media technologies, it is critical for these systems to properly situate and position their personalized offerings.

One of the biggest issues with personalization systems is that they operate like a black box; users are unaware of what computer systems think about them and how this information is being used. In general current instantiations of these systems violate one of Nielson's key usability principles concerning system mistakes (Jakob Nielsen & L. Mack, 1994), which prescribes good interface to *help users recognize, diagnose, and recover from errors*. Regardless of how advanced they are, personalized systems in this stage of media evolution and algorithm design will make mistakes some percentage of the time. If systems never reveal their mistake to users at some point during their interaction, users will presumably have a frustrating experience stemming from a difficulty diagnosing and recovering from the system's error.

The consequences of not clearly presenting recommendations can be disastrous. This is evidenced by an anecdote about a TiVo (Li & Kao, 2008) user who is confused about why his TiVo seems fixated on recording programs with homosexual themes, concludes that his TiVo mistakenly thinks he is homosexual, tries to correct this mistake by watching "guy stuff", but ends up overcompensating and getting recommendations all about wars and the military (Zaslow, 2002). There is a wealth of relevant literature from HCI to draw from, namely for framing the recommendation, offering it at the right time, and ranking it appropriately, to improve the personalization process cycle at this step of presenting personalized content to avoid the poor user experiences detailed in this anecdote.

Feedback and Transparency

An underlying HCI principle for good user-centered design is that interfaces must always keep users informed about background system processes. Proper system feedback for users is frequently highlighted as a design necessity (Norman, 1990). Abiding by this principle entails giving user actions an immediate and obvious effect. Applying this design principle to this stage in the personalization process means clearly informing users about why a particular recommendation is tailored to suit their individual needs by clearly explicating the connection to their unique interests and history.

Nielsen's widely used ten usability heuristics for guiding good user interface design also stress the need for appropriate *feedback* (J Nielsen & Mack, 1994). The first of ten design rules of thumb, *visibility of system status*, encourages interface designers to always keep users aware of what the system is doing by providing appropriate feedback in a timely manner. Applying this heuristic to this stage in the personalization process entails these systems keeping consumers aware of its thought processes and how it has arrived at a specific recommendation or tailored effect for each individual.

The broader design principles regarding system feedback encompass the personalization research area of explanations (Tintarev, 2007; Tintarev & Masthoff, 2007a, 2007b). Tintarev and Masthoff's framework for good explanations for personalized recommender systems includes six aims: 1) *transparency*- explaining how the system works, 2) *scrutability*- allowing users to tell the system it is wrong, 3) *effectiveness*- helping users make good decisions, 4) *persuasiveness*- convincing users to try or buy, 5) *efficiency*- helping users make faster decisions, and 6) *satisfaction*- increasing the usability or enjoyment. The transparency, scrutability, effectiveness, efficiency and satisfaction aims are closely tied to Norman design principle of feedback (Norman, 1990) and the relevant aforementioned Nielsen heuristics. These enumerated aspects of good explanations are critical for designers to think through when presenting personalized content. The fourth goal of good explanations persuasiveness taps into the rich domain of persuasive technology (Fogg, 2002). The detailed lessons learned from the broader domain of persuasion and influence (Cialdini, 2008; Petty & Cacioppo, 1996) and benefits for this stage of the personalization process are beyond the scope of this chapter, but important for improving user experiences when presenting personalized content.

According to Herlocker et al. (2000), having an explanation that provides transparency on how the recommendation system works is beneficial for users in several key ways: 1) *Justification*- Explanations provide justification and reasoning for a recommendation, allowing users to decide how much confidence to place in the recommendation. This relates to transparency as detailed by Norman and Tintarev and Masthoff. 2) *User Involvement*- Explanations increase user involvement, allowing users to complete the decision process with their own knowledge. This benefits personalized systems by making them more engaging for users, which is a chief design aim producers in any media space. 3) *Education*- Explanations educate users on the processes used to generate limitations. 4) *Acceptance*- Explanations make the system's strengths and limitations, as well as justifications for suggestions, fully transparent, leading users to greater acceptance of the recommendation system as a decision aid (Herlocker, Konstan, & Riedl, 2000). These two final ways are relevant to the Nielsen heuristic of helping users diagnose and fix errors.

Empirical work in the domain of transparency for improving personalized recommendation systems and more broadly Digital Consumerism, is limited in sheer number of studies and methodology. However, the following work offers a valuable starting point and initial angles for designers to utilize and researchers to pursue.

Herlocker et. al (2000) conducted two studies investigating how best to explain collaborative filtering recommendations for the MovieLens personalized movie recommendation system (Herlocker, et al., 2000). In the first study surveying 78 people they explored how users would respond to various explanations derived from the framework enumerated above. Out of the 21 explanation interfaces tested the best movie recommendation explanations used histograms of the neighbors' ratings, past performance, similarity to other items in the user's profile, and favorite actor or actress. In the second study 210 people were surveyed in this same context to determine whether adding explanation interfaces to a collaborative filtering system would both improve user acceptance of the system and their filtering decisions. According to the exit interviews and qualitative feedback, participants liked it when explanation interfaces were added to MovieLens, but its impact on their filtering decisions was inconclusive from this study.

Cramer et. al (2008) investigated the effects of transparency on trust in and acceptance of personalized recommendations in the context of an user-adaptive art recommender by comparing the impact of three different types of explanations: 1) no transparency, 2) an explanation of why the recommendation had been made, and 3) a rating of how confident the system was that the recommendation would be interesting to the user (Cramer, et al., 2008). The key relevant result of this study indicated that explaining to a user why a recommendation was made increased its acceptance over not having any transparency, but not trust in the system itself. Additionally, showing how certain the recommender was in the recommendation did not influence trust and acceptance.

A user study of 12 people by Sinha and Swearingen (2002) with five music recommender systems making 10 recommendations each suggested that users like and feel more confident in recommendations from transparent systems and they like to know why something was recommended to them by the system even if they already like it (Sinha & Swearingen, 2002). The main design implication from Sinha's user study was that it is not enough for a system to just be accurate; it also needs to reveal its inner logic to its users and let them know why a particular recommendation was thought to be suitable for them.

Taken together this empirical research provides a starting point for work in this area, but it remains mostly an unexplored fertile territory from an empirical standpoint with critical design implications for media theorists and designers left to be discovered. The two studies conducted by Herlocker and colleagues offer support for the importance of transparency in personalized recommendation systems and some possible ways to attain this, but need further investigation in different contexts (Herlocker, et al., 2000). The single variable study design of Cramer et. al does not answer questions about how transparency interacts with key dimensions that frequent the real world, such as fixed and ephemeral aspects of the user and the type of content recommended (Cramer, et al., 2008). The exploration by Sinha is limited by small sample size and it being a user study, rather than a controlled experiment (Sinha & Swearingen, 2002).

Making the inner workings and algorithms of personalized systems transparent to users is a rich topic deserving of much more empirical attention. It remains mostly an unexplored fertile territory with critical design implications for media theorists and designers left to be discovered. A useful framework for continuing the investigation of this topic is revealing a person's states and traits. States include such static aspects of a person such as their age, gender, race and ethnicity, while traits are more ephemeral aspects of a person such as their mood, emotion, and delectation. By utilizing this framework, personalized systems can take advantage of the capabilities of the Digital Consumerism to offer a personalized experience, which acknowledges each individual's unique needs, that was simply not possible in the era of Mass Consumerism. Properly personalized media interfaces particularly in terms of transparency and feedback make every individual feel like the star of the show as the entire media experience is centered on them, regardless of their age, gender, race, religion, socioeconomic status, or even their present affective state.

By profiling, understanding, and appropriately responding to each individual's traits and states, personalized systems create new opportunities. Social groups that have been overlooked and mischaracterized by traditional mass media can now feel as though the permanent and transient aspects of their identity are important, relevant, and considered in their new and more powerful relationships with personalized media. Much like other aspects of the evolution of consumerism within the context of media change, framing and optimizing personalization affords many new advances for consumers to take and feel in control of their increasingly media-centric lives. A full set of design guidelines for personalization based on each of these specific states and traits are currently lacking and offer a new opportunity for researchers interested in advancing this space.

Uncovering transparency guidelines for presenting personalized content has the added benefit of helping users formulate a proper conceptual model (Norman, 1990) of the system. This helps with iteration, improving and refining the recommended output, as the user knows how and what to change about their interactions with the system at the gathering information stage. Additionally this helps the user comprehend how the system uses his or her information at the building and matching stages of the personalization process. The summation of increased user knowledge for these three phases of the personalization cycle helps revive the handshake, the golden standard for customer service.

Timing

In addition to feedback and transparency another way to work towards replicating the symbolic handshake at this stage in the personalization cycle is to present the personalized content at the appropriate time. At the video store the store clerk or owner would wait for the opportune moment to give the customer their personalized recommendation; not interrupting their other activities and using an appropriate transition before making the delivery. It is important for designers of systems for Digital Consumerism to replicate this very same step at this stage in the personalization process.

Panayiotou et. al (2006) detailed the importance of time based personalization, particularly for mobile users equipped with handheld devices (Panayiotou, Andreou, & Samaras, 2006). Mobile user needs are dependent on their context, which is a function of both time and activity. Augmenting user profiles with personalized time metadata enables personalized systems to more appropriately weight user interests with respect to time-zones and ongoing experiences. Panayiotou et al implemented a prototype and their early stage evaluation showed promising results for improving personalization by taking into consideration a user's time based needs.

The importance of proper presentation interval is illustrated in a web experiment conducted by Rao et. al 2009, where altering the presentation intervals of poor dating matches in a personalized online dating recommender affected user frustration levels (Rao, et al., 2009). Specially, participants were more frustrated with the recommendation system when it gave the poor dating matches sequentially, rather than all at the end. In essence seeing no adaptation or improvement repeatedly was frustrating for the participants compared to seeing all the poor results in one final assemblage. The key relevant design implication from this aspect of this study is to avoid continuously showing poor recommendations when possible as opposed to presenting them as a singular collection. This result also illuminates the need for proper transparency and feedback to help people decipher recommendations as well as a mechanism for users to immediately explicitly comment on the results provided.

The various effects of properly timing the presentation of personalized content are an under-researched, yet important area in personalization. Panayitou 2006 and Rao et al 2009 offer a launching pad for investigations in this space (Panayiotou, et al., 2006; Rao, et al., 2009). A future direction for researching timing in recommendation presentation is more rigorous evaluation about how to utilize time-based knowledge about an individual user appropriately within the context of their daily lives. Another direction is looking at the effects of varying presentation intervals for both good recommendations and other domains beyond dating matches. It is also potentially important to give consumers the opportunity to access the recommendations when they feel so inclined (e.g., the value of periodicity in library rental and renewal schemes).

Ranking and Quantity

Transparency and feedback guide *how* to present, timing deals with *when* to present, and ranking in the case of multiple recommendations concerns *what order* to present. Revisiting the video store analogy when the store clerk is ready to present the recommendations if there are multiple items, to offer a truly personalized experience, they order them in a sensible manner with respect to both ranking and quantity.

With the advent of the web and the ubiquity of the digitized content it became critical to associate a rank with each chunk of information and present them accordingly. Google's web search and associated Page Rank exemplify this concept; web pages across the entire World Wide Web are indexed, ranked, and presented in an intelligent order with respect to a user's search query (Sergey Brin, 1998; Sergey Brin, Motwani, Page, & Winograd, 1998; S. Brin & Page, 1998). Ranking is a major advancement of the digital era as it enables personalized ordering and packaging of content. For example, one basketball fan may prefer to see all NBA video clips first and then NCAA clips, while another may prefer the opposite. Such tailoring for each individual consumer at the level of ranking and ordering content was simply not possible in the era of Macro Consumerism where mass production and delivery was such a critical component for success, because of the major resulting time inefficiency. In the age of Digital Consumerism however it is attainable.

The Gricean conversational maxim of *quantity* stresses making the contribution as informative as required and not excessive (Grice, 1975). Much in the same way it is important for recommendation systems to not overwhelm their users with content during the presentation stage. At the video store the store clerk might have hundreds of movies that they think a customer might like, but they only present them with a few carefully selected titles at once. Similarly on a web search engine like Google even though there are often hundreds, if not thousands of search results for popular queries, by default only the top ten results are displayed (Weld, et al., 2003). It is important for designers of personalized recommendation systems to resist the temptation to offer too many recommendations given the oftentimes plethora of available content and the ease with which to suggest it in the digital age.

Personalized ranking of content has been an area of much interest for researchers and is evident in the ongoing work on personalized web search (Ark, Dryer, & Lu, 1999; de Vrieze, van Bommel, & van der Weide, 2004; Picard). In the coming years research in this space should only expand. Another key future direction for research in this space is investigating the intersections between the number of recommendations to present for various domains and each user's corresponding state and traits. A person's static mental capacity as well as their context can heavily impact how many recommendations they can handle before running into the problem of cognitive overload (Kirsh, 2000). It is critical for interfaces in this Digital age of consumerism to continue to investigate ways to intelligently account for these individual factors in this stage of the personalization process.

CONCLUSION

By building upon the lessons learned from Micro and Mass Consumerism, HCI, and social science with respect to the four-step personalization process outlined and explored in this chapter- 1) Gather user information and needs, 2) Build user model and profile, 3) Match user with appropriate available content, and 4) Present personalized content)- Digital Consumerism particularly in the domain of personalized recommendation systems can radically advance the user experience. For designers working within this space, utilizing the design guidelines at each of these four phases will aid in the production of interactions that more closely approximate the handshake, which symbolizes the gold standard for customer service. For researchers and media theorists the abstracted key aspects of personalization illuminate future directions for inquiry and how to contextualize this work within the larger master goal of improving the interpersonal relationship between retailers and consumers. This framework offers a common ground for all of the diverse communities working within the fields of consumerism and personalized systems to work together towards the continued progression of reviving the friendly handshake of Micro Consumerism without losing the benefits of Macro Consumerism in this technologically rich stage of media evolution.

REFERENCES

(2000). *A Survey of Consumer Privacy Attitudes and Behaviors*. Rochester, NY: Harris Interactive.

Alwin, D. F., & Krosnick, J. A. (1985). The measurement of values in surveys: A comparison of ratings and rankings. *Public Opinion Quarterly*, *49*(4), 535–552. doi:10.1086/268949

Ark, W. S., Dryer, D. C., & Lu, D. J. (1999). The Emotion Mouse. In *Proceedings of HCI International (the 8th International Conference on Human-Computer Interaction) on Human-Computer Interaction: Ergonomics and User Interfaces* (Vol. 1, pp. 818 - 823). Hillsdale, NJ: L. Erlbaum Associates Inc.

Averjanova, O., Ricci, F., & Nguyen, Q. N. (2008). *Map-Based Interaction with a Conversational Mobile Recommender System*. Paper presented at the Proceedings of the 2008 The Second International Conference on Mobile Ubiquitous Computing, Systems, Services and Technologies.

Bargh, J. A., McKenna, K. Y., & Fitzsimons, G. M. (2002). Can you see the real me? Activation and expression of the "true self" on the Internet. *The Journal of Social Issues*, *58*(1), 33–48. doi:10.1111/1540-4560.00247

Barnard, L., Yi, J. S., Jacko, J. A., & Sears, A. (2007). Capturing the effects of context on human performance in mobile computing systems. *Personal and Ubiquitous Computing*, *11*(2), 81–96. doi:10.1007/s00779-006-0063-x

Belson, W. A. (1966). The effects of reversing the presentation order of verbal rating scales. *Journal of Advertising Research*, *6*, 30–37.

Beniger, J. (1987). Personalization of mass media and the growth of pseudo-community. *Communication Research*, *14*(3), 352. doi:10.1177/009365087014003005

Branco, P., Firth, P., Encanacao, L. M., & Bonato, P. (2005). *Faces of Emotion in Human-Computer Interaction.* Paper presented at the CHI 2005, Portland, Oregon, USA.

Brin, S. (1998). Extracting Patterns and Relations from the World Wide Web. *WebDB*, 172-183.

Brin, S., Motwani, R., Page, L., & Winograd, T. (1998). What can you do with a Web in your pocket? *IEEE Data Eng. Bull.*, *21*, 37–47.

Brin, S., & Page, L. (1998). The Anatomy of a Large-Scale Hypertextual Web Search Engine. *Computer Networks and ISDN Systems, 30*(1-7), 107-117.

Brodie, C., Karat, C., & Karat, J. (2004). Creating an E-Commerce Environment where Consumers are Willing to Share Personal Information. In Karat, C., Blom, J. O., & Karat, J. (Eds.), *Designing Personalized User Experiences in eCommerce*. Dordrecht, The Netherlands: Kluwer Academic Publishers. doi:10.1007/1-4020-2148-8_11

Buckley, S. (2008). *The Internet killed the video store: New options emerge to obtain video content.* Retrieved from http://www.telecommagazine.com/article.asp?HH_ID=AR_3884

Burke, R. (2002). Hybrid recommender systems: Survey and experiments. *User Modeling and User-Adapted Interaction, 12*(4), 331–370. doi:10.1023/A:1021240730564

Cialdini, R. B. (2008). *Influence: Science and Practice*. Needham Heights, MA: Allyn & Bacon.

Compaine, B. M., & Gomery, D. (2000). *Who Owns the Media?: Competition and Concentration in the Mass Media Industry* (3rd ed.). Mahwah, NJ: Lawrence Erlbaum Associates.

Cramer, H., Evers, V., van Someren, M., Ramlal, S., Rutledge, L., & Stash, N. (2008). The effects of transparency on trust and acceptance in interaction with a content-based art recommender. *User Modeling and User-Adapted Interaction*, 5.

Cranor, L. F. (2004). 'I Didn't Buy It for Myself' Privacy and Ecommerce Personalization. In Karat, C., Blom, J. O., & Karat, J. (Eds.), *Designing Personalized User Experiences in eCommerce.* Dordrecht, The Netherlands: Kluwer Academic Publishers.

Cyber Dialogue Survey Data Reveals Lost Revenue for Retailers Due to Widespread Consumer Privacy Concerns. (2001). *Cyber Dialogue.* Retrieved from http://www.cyberdialogue.com/news/releases/2001/11-07-uco-retail.html de Vrieze, P., van Bommel, P., & van der Weide, T. (2004). A Generic Adaptivity Model in Adaptive Hypermedia. *Adaptive Hypermedia And Adaptive Web-Based Systems.*

DeFleur, M. L., & Dennis, E. E. (1991). *Understanding Mass Communication.* Retrieved from http://regents.state.oh.us.

Del Colliano, J. (2008). *Circuit City Files For Chapter 11 Bankruptcy After Years of Bad Decisions and Aggressive Tactics.* Retrieved from http://hometheaterreview.com/circuit-city-files-for-chapter-11-bankruptcy-after-years-of-bad-decisions-and-aggressive-tactics/

Dillard, C., Browning, L. D., Sitkin, S. B., & Sutcliffe, K. M. (2000). Impression Management and the use of procedures at the Ritz-Carlton: Moral standards and dramaturgical discipline. *Comunication Studies, 51.*

Ellison, N. (2006). Managing impressions online: Self-presentation processes in the online dating environment. *Journal of Computer-Mediated Communication, 11*, 415–441. doi:10.1111/j.1083-6101.2006.00020.x

eMarketer. (2006). *Online Video Becomes a Real Business: Welcome to the MoneyTube.*

eMarketer. (2007). *Retail Adapts to Digital Movie Rentals: Going to rent a movie? Don't forget your iPod.*

Faulring, A., Mohnkern, K., Steinfeld, A., & Myers, B. (2008). *Successful User Interfaces for RADAR.* Paper presented at the CHI 2008 Workshop on Usable Artificial Intelligence.

Findlater, L., & McGrenere, J. (2004). *A comparison of static, adaptive, and adaptable menus.* Paper presented at the Proceedings of the SIGCHI conference on Human factors in computing systems.

Findlater, L., & McGrenere, J. (2008). *Impact of screen size on performance, awareness, and user satisfaction with adaptive graphical user interfaces.* Paper presented at the Proceeding of the twenty-sixth annual SIGCHI conference on Human factors in computing systems.

Findlater, L., Moffatt, K., McGrenere, J., & Dawson, J. (2009). *Ephemeral adaptation: the use of gradual onset to improve menu selection performance.* Paper presented at the Proceedings of the 27th international conference on Human factors in computing systems.

Fogg, B. J. (2002). *Persuasive Technology: Using Computers to Change What We Think and Do.* San Francisco, CA: Morgan Kaufmann.

Freed, M., Carbonell, J., Gordon, G., Hayes, J., Myers, B., Siewiorek, D., et al. (2008). *RADAR: A Personal Assistant that Learns to Reduce Email Overload.* Paper presented at the Twenty-Third Conference on Artificial Intelligence.

Gajos, K. Z. (2007). *Automatically generating user interfaces adapted to users' motor and vision capabilities.* Paper presented at the UIST '07, New York, NY.

Gajos, K. Z., Czerwinski, M., Tan, D. S., & Weld, D. S. (2006). *Exploring the design space for adaptive graphical user interfaces.* Paper presented at the Proceedings of the working conference on Advanced visual interfaces.

Gajos, K. Z., Everitt, K., Tan, D. S., Czerwinski, M., & Weld, D. S. (2008). *Predictability and accuracy in adaptive user interfaces.* Paper presented at the Proceeding of the twenty-sixth annual SIGCHI conference on Human factors in computing systems.

Gajos, K. Z., & Jameson, A. (2009). *Course Notes: New Paradigms for Adaptive Interaction.* Paper presented at the Conference on Human Factors in Computing Systems, Boston, MA.

Gajos, K. Z., & Weld, D. S. (2004). *Supple: automatically generating uuser interfaces.* Paper presented at the IUI '04, New York, NY.

Gajos, K. Z., Wobbrock, J. O., & Weld, D. S. (2008). *Improving the performance of motor-impaired users with automatically-generated, ability-based interfaces.* Paper presented at the Conference on Human Factors in Computing Systems, Florence, Italy.

Godin, S. (1999). *Permission Marketing: Turning Strangers into Friends, and Friends into Customers.* New York, NY: Simon & Schuster Adult Publishing Group.

Goffman, E. (1956). Embarrassment and social interaction. *American Journal of Sociology, 62*(3), 264–271. doi:10.1086/222003

Goffman, E. (1959). *The Presentation of Self in Everyday Life.* New York: Doubleday.

Green, P. E., & Rao, V. R. (1970). Rating scales and information recovery. How many scales and response categories to use? *Journal of Marketing, 34*(3), 33–39. doi:10.2307/1249817

Grice, H. P. (1975). Logic and Conversation. In P. Cole & J. L. Morgan (Eds.), Syntax and Semantics, Vol. 3, Speech Acts. New York: Academic Press.

Guttman, R. H., Moukas, A. G., & Maes, P. (1998). Agent-mediated electronic commerce: A survey. *The Knowledge Engineering Review, 13*(2), 147–159. doi:10.1017/S0269888998002082

Hancock, J. T., Toma, C., & Ellison, N. (2007). *The truth about lying in online dating profiles.* Paper presented at the Conference on Human Factors in Computing Systems, San Jose, California.

Herlocker, J., Konstan, J., & Riedl, J. (2000, December 2-6, 2000). *Explaining Collaborative Filtering Recommendations.* Paper presented at the ACM 2000 Conference on Computer Supported Cooperative Work.

Higgins, E. T. (1987). Self-discrepancy: A theory relating self and affect. *Psychological Review, 94*(3), 319–340. doi:10.1037/0033-295X.94.3.319

Hine, C., & Eve, J. (1998). Privacy in the Marketplace. *The Information Society, 14*(4), 253–262. doi:10.1080/019722498128700

Hitwise. (2007). *Hitwise Industry Report for Shopping and Classifieds.*

Hofmans, J., Theuns, P., Baekelandt, S., Mairesse, O., Schillewaert, N., & Cools, W. (2007). Bias and changes in perceived intensity of verbal qualifiers effected by scale orientation. *Survey Research Methods, 1*(2), 97–108.

Holbrook, A. L., Krosnick, J. A., Moore, D., & Tourangeau, R. (2007). Response order effects in dichotomous categorical questions presented orally: The impact of question and respondent attributes. *Public Opinion Quarterly, 71*(3), 325–348. doi:10.1093/poq/nfm024

Izard, C. (1971). *The face of emotion.* New York: Appleton-Century-Cofts.

Jameson, A. (2002). Adaptive interfaces and agents. In Jacko, J., & Sears, A. (Eds.), *Handbook of human-computer interaction* (pp. 305–330). New York: Lawrence Erlbaum Associates.

Kalton, G., Collins, M., & Brook, L. (1978). Experiments in wording opinion questions. *Applied Statistics, 27*(2), 149–161. doi:10.2307/2346942

Kane, S. K., Wobbrock, J. O., & Smith, I. E. (2008). *Getting off the treadmill: evaluating walking user interfaces for mobile devices in public spaces.* Paper presented at the Proceedings of the 10th international conference on Human computer interaction with mobile devices and services.

Kirsh, D. (2000). A few thoughts on cognitive overload. *Intellectica,* 19–51.

Klein, L. R. (1998). Evaluating the potential of interactive media through a new lens: search versus experience goods. *Journal of Business Research, 41*(3), 195–203. doi:10.1016/S0148-2963(97)00062-3

Krosnick, J. A. (1999). Survey research. *Annual Review of Psychology, 50,* 537–567. doi:10.1146/annurev.psych.50.1.537

Krosnick, J. A., & Alwin, D. F. (1987). An evaluation of a cognitive theory of response-order effects in survey measurement. *Public Opinion Quarterly, 51*(2), 201–219. doi:10.1086/269029

Krosnick, J. A., & Berent, M. K. (1993). Comparisons of party identification and policy preferences: The impact of survey question format. *American Journal of Political Science, 37*(3), 941–964. doi:10.2307/2111580

Krulwich, B. (1997). Lifestyle finder: Intelligent user profiling using large-scale demographic data. *AI Magazine, 18,* 37–45.

Li, Y. M., & Kao, C. P. (2008). *TREPPS: A Trust-based Recommender System for Peer Production Services.* Expert Systems With Applications.

Lin, M., Goldman, R., Price, K. J., Sears, A., & Jacko, J. (2007). How do people tap when walking? An empirical investigation of nomadic data entry. *International Journal of Human-Computer Studies, 65*(9), 759–769. doi:10.1016/j.ijhcs.2007.04.001

Linden, G., Smith, B., & York, J. (2003). *Amazon.com Recommendations: Item-to-item collaborative filtering.*

Lissitz, R. W., & Green, S. B. (1975). Effect of the number of scale points on reliability: A Monte Carlo approach. *The Journal of Applied Psychology, 60*(1), 10–13. doi:10.1037/h0076268

MacKay, B., Dearman, D., Inkpen, K., & Watters, C. (2005). *Walk 'n scroll: a comparison of software-based navigation techniques for different levels of mobility.* Paper presented at the Proceedings of the 7th international conference on Human computer interaction with mobile devices \&, services.

McQuail, D. (2005). *McQuail's Mass Communication Theory.* Retrieved from http://books.google.com

Miethe, T. D. (1985). Validity and reliability of value measurements. *The Journal of Psychology, 119*(5), 441–453.

Mitchell, J., & Shneiderman, B. (1989). Dynamic versus static menus: an exploratory comparison. *SIGCHI Bull., 20*(4), 33–37. doi:10.1145/67243.67247

Mitchell, T., Caruana, R., Freitag, D., McDermott, J., & Zabowski, D. (1994). Experience with a learning personal assistant. *Communications of the ACM, 37*(7), 81–91. doi:10.1145/176789.176798

Mizobuchi, S., Chignell, M., & Newton, D. (2005). *Mobile text entry: relationship between walking speed and text input task difficulty.* Paper presented at the Proceedings of the 7th international conference on Human computer interaction with mobile devices \&, services.

Mustonen, T., Olkkonen, M., & Hakkinen, J. (2004). *Examining mobile phone text legibility while walking.* Paper presented at the CHI '04 extended abstracts on Human factors in computing systems.

Negroponte, N. (1995). *Being Digital.* New York: Vintage Publishing.

Nelson, P. J. (1970). Information and consumer behavior. *The Journal of Political Economy, 78*(2), 311–329. doi:10.1086/259630

Nelson, P. J. (1974). Advertising as information. *The Journal of Political Economy, 82*(4), 729–754. doi:10.1086/260231

Nelson, P. J. (1976). Economic value of advertising. In Brozen, Y. (Ed.), *Advertising and Society* (pp. 109–141). New York: New York University Press.

Nelson, P. J. (1981). Consumer information and advertising. In Galatin, M., & Leiter, R. D. (Eds.), *Economics of Information* (pp. 42–77). Boston: N. Nijhoff Publishers.

Netflix. (n.d.). Retrieved from http://www.netflix.com/

Nielsen, J., & Mack, R. L. (1994). *Usability Inspection Methods.* New York: John Wiley & Sons.

Nielsen, J., & Mack, R. L. (Eds.). (1994). *Heuristic Evaluation.* New York: John Wily & Sons.

Norman, D. (1990). *The design of everyday things.*

Oppenheim, A. N. (1966). *Questionnaire Design and Attitude Measurement.* New York: Basic Books.

Oulasvirta, A., Tamminen, S., Roto, V., & Kuorelahti, J. (2005). *Interaction in 4-second bursts: the fragmented nature of attentional resources in mobile HCI.* Paper presented at the Proceedings of the SIGCHI conference on Human factors in computing systems.

Ozok, A. A. (2009). Survey Design and Implementation in Human Computer Interaction. In Jacko, J., & Sears, A. (Eds.), *Human-Computer Interaction: Development Process* (pp. 253–271). Mahwah, NJ: Lawrence Erlbaum Associates.

Panayiotou, C., Andreou, M., & Samaras, G. (2006). Using time and activity in personalization for the mobile user. In *MobiDE '06: Proceedings of the 5th ACM international workshop on Data engineering for wireless and mobile access*.

Pascoe, J., Ryan, N., & Morse, D. (2000). Using while moving: HCI issues in fieldwork environments. *ACM Transactions on Computer-Human Interaction*, 7(3), 417–437. doi:10.1145/355324.355329

Pasek, J., & Krosnick, J. A. (2010). Optimizing Survey Questionnaire Design in Political Science: Insights From Psychology. In Leighley, J. (Ed.), *Oxford Handbook of American Elections and Political Behavior*. Oxford, UK: Oxford University Press.

Pazzani, M., & Billsus, D. (1997). Learning and revising user profiles: The identification of interesting web sites. *Machine Learning*, *27*(3), 313–331. doi:10.1023/A:1007369909943

Pazzani, M. J. (1999). A framework for collaborative, content-based and demographic filtering. *Artificial Intelligence Review*, *13*, 393–408. doi:10.1023/A:1006544522159

Pazzani, M. J., & Billsus, D. (2007). Content-Based Recommendation Systems. In Brusilovsky, P., Kobsa, A., & Nejdl, W. (Eds.), *The Adaptive Web* (*Vol. 4321*, pp. 325–341). Berlin, Germany: Springer-Verlag. doi:10.1007/978-3-540-72079-9_10

Petty, R. E., & Cacioppo, J. T. (1996). *Attitudes And Persuasion: Classic And Contemporary Approaches*. Boulder, CO: Westview Press.

Picard, R. W. (n.d.). *Toward computers that recognize and respond to user emotion-References*. Retrieved from http://research.ibm.com

Rao, S. R., Hurlbutt, T., Nass, C., & JanakiRam, N. (2009). *My Dating Site Thinks I'm a Loser: effects of personal photos and presentation intervals on perceptions of recommender systems.* Paper presented at the Conference on Human Factors in Computing Systems, Boston, MA.

Reilly, J., Zhang, J., McGinty, L., Pu, P., & Smyth, B. (2007). *Evaluating compound critiquing recommenders: A real-user study.* Paper presented at the Eighth Annual Conference on Electronic Commerce.

Reisinger, D. (2008, February 8). *Why Blockbuster brick-and-mortars will be gone in five years*. Retrieved from http://news.cnet.com/8301-13506_3-9867493-17.html

Resnick, P., & Varian, H. R. (1997). Recommender systems. *Communications of the ACM*, *40*(3), 56–58. doi:10.1145/245108.245121

Reynolds, T. J., & Jolly, J. P. (1980). Measuring personal values: An evaluation of alternative methods. *JMR, Journal of Marketing Research*, *17*(4), 531–536. doi:10.2307/3150506

Ricci, F., & Nguyen, Q. N. (2007). Acquiring and revising preferences in a critique-based mobile recommender system. *IEEE Intelligent Systems*, *22*(3), 22–29. doi:10.1109/MIS.2007.43

Rich, E. (1979a). *Building and exploiting user models* [Ph. D. Thesis]. Retrieved from http://csa.com

Rich, E. (1979b). *User modeling via stereotypes*. Cognitive Science.

Rich, E. (1983). Users are Individuals: Individualizing User Models. *International Journal of Man-Machine Studies*.

Schafer, J. B., Frankowski, D., Herlocker, J., & Sen, S. (2007). Collaborative Filtering Recommender Systems. In Brusilovsky, P., Kobsa, A., & Nejdl, W. (Eds.), *The Adaptive Web* (*Vol. 4321*). Berlin, Germany: Springer-Verlag. doi:10.1007/978-3-540-72079-9_9

Schafer, J. B., Konstan, J., & Riedl, J. (1999). *Recommender Systems in E-Commerce*. Paper presented at the Proceedings of the 1st ACM conference on Electronic commerce.

Schlenker, B. R. (1980). *Impression Management: The Self-Concept, Social Identity, and Interpersonal Relations*. Monterey, CA: Brooks/Cole.

Schmitt, S., & Bergmann, R. (1999 June). *Applying case-based reasoning technology for product selection and customization in electronic commerce environments.* Paper presented at the 12th Bled Electronic Commerce Conference, Bled, Slovenia.

Schuman, H., Presser, S., & Ludwig, J. (1983). The norm of even-handedness in surveys as in life. *American Sociological Review*, *48*(1), 112–120. doi:10.2307/2095149

Schwarz, N. (1995). What respondents learn from questionnaires: The survey interview and the logic of conversation. *International Statistical Review*, *63*(2), 153–168. doi:10.2307/1403610

Schwarz, N., & Bless, H. (1992). Scandals and the public's trust in politicians: Assimilation and contrast effects. *Personality and Social Psychology Bulletin*, *18*(5), 574–579. doi:10.1177/0146167292185007

Schwarz, N., Grayson, C. E., & Knauper, B. (1998). Formal features of rating scales and the interpretation of question meaning. *International Journal of Public Opinion Research*, *10*(2), 177–183.

Schwarz, N., Knauper, B., Hippler, H.-J., Noelle-Neumann, E., & Clark, L. (1991). Rating scales: Numeric values may change the meaning of scale labels. *Public Opinion Quarterly*, *55*(4), 570–582. doi:10.1086/269282

Schwarz, N., & Strack, F. (1991). Context effects in attitude surveys: Applying cognitive theory to social research. *European Review of Social Psychology*, *2*, 31–50. doi:10.1080/14792779143000015

Sears, A., Lin, M., Jacko, J., & Xiao, Y. (2003). When Computers Fade. Pervasive Computing and Situationally-Induced Impairments and Disabilities. In Stephanidis, C., & Jacko, J. (Eds.), *Human-Computer Interaction: Theory and Practice (Part II)* (pp. 1298–1302). Hillsdale, NJ: Lawrence Erlbaum Associates.

Sears, A., & Shneiderman, B. (1994). Split menus: effectively using selection frequency to organize menus. *ACM Transactions on Computer-Human Interaction*, *1*(1), 27–51. doi:10.1145/174630.174632

Segal, R. B., & Kephart, J. O. (1999). *MailCat: An Intelligent Assistant for Organizing E-Mail.* Paper presented at the Third International Conference on Autonomous Agents.

Sharing, Privacy and Trust in Our Networked World. (2007). OCLC: Online Computer Library Center- Harris Interactive.

Sinha, R., & Swearingen, K. (2002). The role of transparency in recommender systems. *Conference on Human Factors in Computing Systems.*

Steinfeld, A., Bennett, R. S., Cunningham, K., Lahut, M., Quinones, P. A., Wexler, D., et al. (2007). *Evaluation of an Integrated Multi-Task Machine Learning System with Humans in the Loop.*

Steinfeld, A., Quinones, P. A., Zimmerman, J., Bennett, R. S., & Siewiorek, D. (2007). *Survey Measures for Evaluation of Cognitive Assistants.* Paper presented at the NIST Performance Metrics for Intelligent Systems Workshop.

Tedeschi, J. T. (Ed.). (1984). *Impression Management Theory and Social Psychological Research.* New York: Academic Press.

Teltzrow, M., & Kobsa, A. (2004). Impacts of User Privacy Preferences on Personalized Systems: A comparative study. In Karat, C., Blom, J. O., & Karat, J. (Eds.), *Designing Personalized User Experiences in eCommerce*. Dordrecht, The Netherlands: Kluwer Academic Publishers. doi:10.1007/1-4020-2148-8_17

Terveen, L., & Hill, W. (2002). Human-Computer Collaboration in Recommender Systems. In Caroll, J. M. (Ed.), *Human-Computer Interaction in the New Millennium*. Addison-Wesley.

Tintarev, N. (2007, Jan 1). *Explaining Recommendations.* Paper presented at the Doctoral Consortium ACM Recommender Systems '07, Minneapolis, MN.

Tintarev, N., & Masthoff, J. (2007a, Jan 1). *A Survey of Explanations in Recommender Systems.* Paper presented at the Workshop on Recommender Systems and Intelligent User Interfaces associated with ICDE'07, Istanbul, Turkey.

Tintarev, N., & Masthoff, J. (2007b). *Effective Explanations of Recommendations: User-Centered Design.* Paper presented at the ACM Recommender Systems '07, Minneapolis, MN.

Towle, B., & Quinn, C. (2000). Knowledge Based Recommender Systems Using Explicit User Models, Menlo Park, CA.

Vadas, K., Patel, N., Lyons, K., Starner, T., & Jacko, J. (2006). *Reading on-the-go: a comparison of audio and hand-held displays*. Paper presented at the Proceedings of the 8th conference on Human-computer interaction with mobile devices and services.

Wallsten, T. S., Budescu, D. V., Rapoport, A., Zwick, R., & Forsyth, B. (1986). Measuring the vague meanings of probability terms. *Journal of Experimental Psychology. General*, *115*(4), 348–365. doi:10.1037/0096-3445.115.4.348

Ward, R. D., Marsden, P. H., Cahill, B., & Johnson, C. (2001). *Using skin conductivity to detect emotionally significant events in human-computer interaction.* Paper presented at the IHM-HCI.

Weld, D., Anderson, C., Domingos, P., Etzioni, O., Gajos, K., Lau, T., et al. (2003). Automatically personalizing user interfaces. In IJCAI03, Acapulco, Mexico, August.

Zaslow, J. (2002, November 26, 2002). If TiVo Thinks You Are Gay, Here's How To Set It Straight - Amazon.com Knows You, Too, Based on What You Buy, Why All the Cartoons? *The Wall Street Journal,* 1.

Zhang, J., Jones, N., & Pu, P. (2008). *A visual interface for critiquing-based recommender systems*. Paper presented at the Proceedings of the 9th ACM conference on Electronic commerce.

Chapter 32
From Consumers to Producers:
Engagement through User-Generated Advertising Contests

Kelli S. Burns
University of South Florida, USA

ABSTRACT

If reality television is any indication, people have an interest in being known. For some, creating and possibly starring in some form of user-generated content can be a route to being a reality star. The Internet provides a way for consumers to share their documentaries, antics, music videos, and even commercials with other users. Several marketers have capitalized on this trend by combining the desire of users to create their own content with the time-honored concept of a sweepstakes. The purpose of this chapter is to present a model of consumer engagement that encompasses user-generated advertising content. The model will then be placed into context by discussing specific examples from 15 user-generated advertising contests and making theoretical connections for each of the key contest elements.

INTRODUCTION

The declining effectiveness of television advertising has been attributed to viewers who use their DVRs to zip through commercials, shrinking television audiences, and the increase of advertising messages, trends that are expected to continue, according to a 2006 McKinsey & Co. report (Klaassen, 2006). Viewers are also turning to the Internet to watch their favorite programs, in some cases, free of commercial interruptions (Hansell, 2005). Faced with these challenges, advertisers are employing new strategies and looking to the Web for a way to engage consumers in a brand conversation. While consumers have always had some degree of control over the brand, they now have more methods to communicate about their brand experience. Web users have already demonstrated they are eager to share their documentaries, antics, music videos, and even commercials with other users through sites such as YouTube. In response to these challenges and opportunities, advertisers are learning how to harness the energy of consumers willing to create brand content, potentially

DOI: 10.4018/978-1-60566-792-8.ch032

creating a higher level of engagement between consumers and brands.

This chapter examines user-generated advertising contests, which are used as a way to motivate consumers to produce advertising content, often a 30-second commercial. Precursors to user-generated advertising include jingle contests and customer testimonials (Klein, 2008). Although much has been written about user-generated advertising contests in trade journals and the mainstream media, no previous study has aggregated these contests to deepen understanding of this trend and its theoretical implications.

The use of the term user-generated advertising can encompass 30-second spots, but also images or films. Advertisers have also solicited other types of user-generated content from consumers such as stories, videos, and photos that are personal expressions of an individual's relationship with a brand. Some user-generated advertising is inspired solely by the producer and is generally created for a product either loved or despised. The foremost example of this type of content is George Masters' homemade iPod commercial, which was posted to his Web site in 2004 and then circulated to 37,000 viewers through blogs and e-mail (Kahney, 2004). This ad is widely regarded as the first consumer-generated commercial that was a "pure ad" and not parody or political commentary (Kahney, 2004).

User-generated content is not a panacea for the advertiser. The risks involve the creation and distribution of subversive messages and the inability of the producer to truly understand the brand and product positioning as well as the audience (Mills, 2006). Consumers can also be critical of this marketing tactic. Heinz's "Top This TV" contest generated online comments that Heinz is lazy and looking for cheap labor (Story, 2007). In addition, although creative costs are lower because the advertiser often relies on the creator to produce the actual spot, the advertiser still has costs associated with promoting and administering the contest as well as promoting the final spot and paying for media space (Story, 2007). User-generated advertising, however, is a novel concept that has created another way for advertisers to engage with consumers and tap their creativity.

Agency executives have speculated whether user-generated advertising will replace agency-generated advertising (Morrissey, 2006). This trend may create a new role for agencies as they are needed to promote contests that solicit user-generated advertising, drive consumers to the contest Web site, and promote the winning spot, as Frito-Lay's agency Goodby, Silverstein & Partners in San Francisco did for the Doritos contest. Another perspective is that the proliferation of low quality user-generated content may actually create a backlash against its use and be a vindication for advertisers (Snoddy, 2007).

This chapter examines user-generated advertising contests and places them into the context of an engagement model of advertising. This research will examine the various elements of this model—the advertisers, producers, and consumers—in addition to content and media by describing how the contests addressed each element, discussing the theoretical considerations, and offering suggestions for future research. The analysis of user-generated contests also provides insight for practitioners into the variety of ways these contests are administered.

ADVERTISING ENGAGEMENT MODEL

The traditional model of communication is a model of information transmission whereby the source sends a message to a receiver. Lasswell (1948) characterized this process as "who says what to whom in what channel with what effect." Even prior to widespread use of the Internet, Stern (1994) described the shortcomings of the model:

Despite the postulation of noise and feedback, the traditional model fails to capture the interactivity of communicative intercourse between advertisers and consumers in several ways: it presumes that the source and recipient are singular constructs; it does not account for message content that can be activated in a variety of forms; and it assumes a passive message recipient as the object of information transmitted by the source (p. 5).

Other scholars have noted that the rise of digital media requires a rethinking of traditional models of communication (Perry, 2002).

Rappaport (2007) presented three new advertising models, with the one called the engagement model being the most applicable to user-generated advertising. This model applies when brands are both highly relevant and emotionally connected to consumers and changes the notion of advertising effectiveness measures. As Rappaport (2007) stated:

Standard learning and persuasion measures ... are ceding ground to interest in understanding what we can think of as brands' social aspects—they are the ability to involve, inform, and entertain, and longer term, to co-evolve with consumers through the creation and ongoing development of brand meaning (p. 138).

These new outcomes will present a challenge to the advertising industry as it moves to create and adopt new measures of effectiveness.

The engagement model of advertising consists of three groups involved in creating brand meaning—advertisers, consumers, and producers (see Figure 1). The intersection of advertisers and producers captures the willingness of people to create and share brand messages with advertisers, whether initiated by the advertiser or the producer. These producers can also share brand content with consumers, and consumers can provide feedback, a process facilitated by the Internet. The intersection between advertisers and consumers occurs when consumers have an opportunity to engage with the brand, possibly on a Web site or a social networking profile. Finally, the center of the diagram is where these three groups converge and advertisers solicit content from producers for the purpose of sharing it with consumers. The overlapping areas in this model also acknowledge that from the ranks of consumers come producers; these producers act as advertisers by communicating a brand message; and advertisers are active consumers of the information they receive from producers.

USER-GENERATED AD CONTESTS

The engagement model of advertising will be discussed in this section by describing the role of advertisers, the motivations of producers, and the involvement of consumers, as well as the nature of the content created and the use of media.

To be considered user-generated advertising content, the producer must actually generate something original, whether text, images, or a commercial, that will be used as an advertisement or has a brand message. In addition, for the purpose of this study of advertising contests, the user-generated content needs to be judged in some manner resulting in the acknowledgement of a winner or winners. Fifteen contests running at any time between January 2006 and June 2007 are used to explore this model and are presented in Table 1.

Advertiser/Sponsor

The advertiser is often the impetus for the creation of user-generated advertising content and exerts a great deal of control over the creative execution of the ad. Advertisers set the tone for the content by providing a creative assignment to insure that the commercial has the appropriate brand message. In the Doritos contest, entrants were told to demonstrate how Doritos are "big, bold and packed with more flavor-power than a seven-course meal" by showing "all-out, passion-soaked, Doritos-loving, competitive action." Moe's

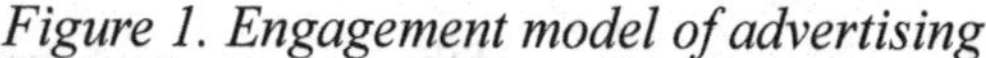
Figure 1. Engagement model of advertising

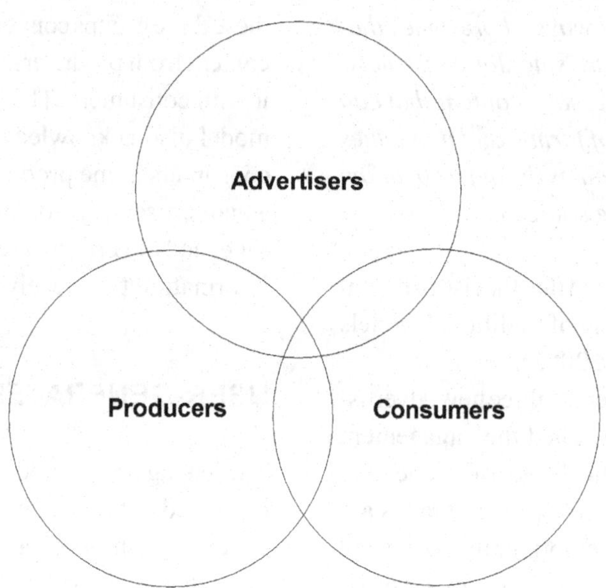

Table 1. User-generated advertising contest summary

Brand	Campaign	Web site	Dates
Chevrolet	Chevy Super Bowl College Ad Challenge	www.cbs.com/chevy intranet.edventurepartners.com/samprograms/Chevrolet_sb/default.asp	9/29/2006-2/4/2007
Chipotle	30 Seconds of Fame	www.chipotle.com/30secondsoffame (no longer maintained)	10/2006-11/2006
Converse	Chuck Taylor All Star Shoe	http://www.converse.com/index.asp?bhcp=1# (no longer maintained)	8/2004-2006
Doritos	Crash the Super Bowl	promotions.yahoo.com/doritos	10/10/2006-2/4/2007
Dove	Dove Cream Oil	www.dovecreamoil.com/	12/14/2006-2/25/2007
Heinz	Top this TV	www.topthistv.com	4/16/2007-9/10/2007
MasterCard	Priceless	www.priceless.com (no longer maintained)	3/2006
Moe's Southwest	Burrito in Every Hand	moes.sharkle.com	7/10/2006-2/2007
Mozilla	Firefox Flicks	www.firefoxflicks.com	12/21/2005-4/14/2006
NFL	Pitch Us Your Idea for the Best NFL Super Bowl Commercial Ever. Seriously.	www.nfl.com/superad	10/31/2006-2/1/2007
National Sunflower Association	Grab 'em by the Sack	www.grabembythesack.com	3/2007-6/17/2007
Sony	Sony HD (Current TV)	www.currenttv.com/make/vc2/sonyhd	Spring 2007
Southwest Airlines	Wanna Get Away	www.wannagetaway.com	12/12/2006-2/20/2007
Tahoe	Apprentice Challenge	www.chevyapprentice.com (no longer maintained)	3/13/2006-4/10/2006
Vegas.com	Direct the Next Vegas.Commercial	www.cinevegas.com/vegascom/	5/4/2007-6/14/2007

Southwest Grill sought ads that supported the mission of a burrito in every hand. Dove wanted ads that communicated the features and benefits of Dove Cream Oil, emphasized real beauty, were simple and uncluttered, and showed natural and self-assured women. Some creative assignments were less specific, such as Chipotle's that asked entrants to represent Chipotle and its personality, or National Sunflower Association's contest that wanted entrants to address why someone should grab a sack of sunflower seeds. In summary, most contests provided entrants with some sort of creative brief to guide the creation of the content.

Many of the advertisers in this study also had requirements for the use of the logo, product, tagline, and/or URL in the user-generated ad. While some contests did not express any requirements, Converse specifically made it optional and Southwest requested no brand mention. In these two cases, the sponsor added an end tag to each submission.

Content is also controlled by the way advertisers construct the judging process. In every contest examined except National Sunflower Association and Sony, representatives from the agency or sponsor had some level of involvement in choosing either the finalists or the grand prize winner. The outcome of some contests, including Chevrolet and Vegas.com, was completely controlled by the advertiser or sponsor. Another popular method is to have a panel choose finalists and then allow viewers to choose the winner. For example, five finalists were selected by a panel of judges in the Doritos "Crash the Super Bowl" contest and viewers voted on the winner. A panel chose 15 semi-finalists in the Heinz "Top This TV" contest, from which consumers chose the winners. The reverse method where the panel selects the winners from the top vote-getters was used by Moe's Southwest Grill. Two of the contests awarded separate prizes for the judges' selection and the popular vote. Southwest used a panel for the grand prize winner and awarded first, second, and third places based on consumer votes. Chipotle had a creative winner judged by a panel and a most-viewed winner. In a novel approach, NFL used a panel to narrow the pool to 12 semi-finalists, then the viewers, the director, and a panel of agency and sponsor executives voted, with each of their votes counting one-third toward the entry's final score. Finally, as mentioned above, Sony and National Sunflower Association winners were selected by the viewers.

The advertiser also often outlines the criteria for the selection of finalists or winners and assigns a point value for each. For Doritos and Dove, finalists were chosen based on originality and creativity; adherence to assignment and regulations; and overall appeal. Of the 10 contests specifically stating their selection criteria, creativity and originality were the most popular criteria, followed by overall/audience appeal or marketability, appropriateness to theme, adherence to assignment or regulations, connection to brand, quality of production, quality of acting or writing, and concept or content. Other criteria mentioned included likelihood to motivate the audience to use the product; proper format for entry; use of logo, name, and tagline; and creativity of jingle or soundtrack.

Another important role of the advertiser is to publicize the contest. Web sites, Internet advertising, and television advertising are three commonly used methods. Advertisers who sponsored contests directed toward a student population, such as Chevrolet, created profiles in MySpace and Facebook. Mozilla used a grassroots campaign to publicize its contest. Heinz advertised its "Top This TV" contest on ketchup bottles and on television.

Producer

At the very heart of user-generated contests are the creators or producers of the content, which sponsors will control by determining who can enter the contest. While some contests are promoted to the general public, sponsors may also solicit entries from professionals. Some contests are closed to all but a specified group, with Chevrolet and Moe's targeting college students and Dove targeting women. Many contests, however, were open to the general public, including Doritos, Mozilla, Southwest, Converse, Vegas.com, NFL, and the National Sunflower Association. Of this group, Converse and Doritos also pitched the contest to film students, Mozilla pitched to film/ad/TV/multimedia students and aspiring professionals, and Vegas.com pitched to film students and professionals. Opening the contest to the general public and pitching it to people in the field practically insures that the contest will generate a large pool of entries and that at least some of the entries will be of professional quality.

While many people are acquiring the basic skills necessary to shoot, edit, and upload a video to the Web, several winners of user-generated advertising contests have had professional experience. The grand-prize winner of the Doritos "Crash the Super Bowl" contest was a five-person team from Five Point Productions, a North Carolina firm that specializes in creative video production. In fact, the five Doritos finalists were either aspiring or experienced filmmakers (Tanaka, 2007). Gino Bona, winner of the NFL contest, is the director of business development for a Portland, Maine, marketing firm (Anfuso, 2007). Mozilla's winner was Pete Macomber, who creates video, commercials, and screenplays, and a runner-up was Jeff Gill, a junior studying animation at Savannah College of Art and Design (Walker, 2006). Brian Lazzaro, who won the Vegas.com commercial, is a graduate of NYU film school and a professional videographer (Jaffee, 2007). Heinz's winner, Andrew Dobson of Wheelersburg, Ohio, runs a one-man production shop (O'Malley, 2007). Lindsay Miller, Dove's grand prize winner, was a station manager for VTV, the student-run television station of Vanderbilt University. Miller currently works as an assistant production coordinator at a television production company in Santa Monica, Calif. (Malinee, 2007). Brian Cates, one of the producers of the winning Southwest ad, works in video production at Newchurch in Oklahoma City. In fact, in every contest where a single winner could be identified except National Sunflower Association, the winner was somehow affiliated with a creative industry.

The number of entries for each contest ranged 38 to 100,000 (see Table 2). The Converse Gallery, for example, elicited over 2,000 entries (Rose, 2006), while Doritos received more than 1,000 submissions (Mills, 2007). The Heinz competition generated about 8,000 entries, but only 4,000 were approved for posting (Heinz Company Release, 2007). Mozilla's contest received 280 entries (Walker, 2006). The contests with the highest number of entries were also the easiest to enter and required very little technical expertise. In MasterCard's contest, producers added the classic "Priceless" text to a video. In Tahoe's contest, producers were supplied video and developed a mash-up commercial using their own text.

The chance to win a prize and possibly receive national exposure may motivate some producers. A popular prize for the winning commercial is an airing of the spot before a national television audience. More publicity can be garnered for the winner if the airing occurs during a highly-rated program such as the Super Bowl XLI, as in the case of Doritos, NFL, and Chevrolet, or the 79th Annual Academy Awards,® as in the case of Dove. Southwest's winning ad ran during the NBA playoffs on TNT. In a majority of contests, the winning ad was aired on television. The remaining contests all used a variety of approaches for making the winning ad accessible to consumers. In the Chipotle contest, the winning ad was featured on the Web site with the possibility, but no guarantee, that the ad would be shown on television. The ads for National Sunflower Association and Moe's are only available on the Web site. Mozilla's winning ad was one of 11 that viewers then voted on to determine which four ads would be shown on television. While the winning ad was not guaranteed a television spot, the voting resulted in it earning a spot. Finally, the prize for

Table 2. Total entries per contest

Brand	Contest	No. of Entries
Chevrolet	Chevy Super Bowl College Ad Challenge	820
Chipotle	30 Seconds of Fame	70
Converse	Chuck Taylor All Star Shoe	2,000 (76 for current topic)
Doritos	Crash the Super Bowl	Over 1,000
Dove	Dove Cream Oil	1,200
Heinz	Top this TV	8,000 (4,000 approved)
MasterCard	Priceless	100,000
Moe's Southwest	Burrito in Every Hand	38 (on Web site)
Mozilla	Firefox Flicks	280
NFL	Pitch Us Your Idea for the Best NFL Super Bowl Commercial Ever. Seriously.	1,700
National Sunflower Association	Grab 'em by the Sack	55
Sony	Sony HD (Current TV)	81
Southwest Airlines	Wanna Get Away	149
Tahoe	Apprentice Challenge	30,000
Vegas.com	Direct the Next Vegas.Commercial	Unknown

Vegas.com was to direct an ad for Vegas.com, but the rules did not indicate that this ad would follow the same concept as the winning ad.

In a majority of contests, the winner received a cash prize (or gift certificate) ranging from $1,000 to $57,000. Six contests did not involve a financial reward. In some contests, including Converse, Dove, Doritos, and Heinz, finalists also received a cash prize ranging from $1,000 to $10,000. A trip is another common element of the prize either at the finalist stage or as a grand prize. In some cases, finalists traveled to a location where the winner would be announced. Dove finalists traveled to Los Angeles, Doritos finalists to Miami, Chevrolet finalists to Michigan, and Vegas.com finalists to Las Vegas. The NFL winner won a trip to the Super Bowl as well as a trip to Los Angeles to watch the production of the commercial. Some contests involve product prizes for grand prize winners or finalists, such as vacations or airline tickets for Southwest's grand prize winner and the first three places determined by popular voting, T-shirts for weekly National Sunflower Association winners/finalists, hardware for Mozilla's second and third place winners, and an NFL gift pack worth $500 for the NFL contest finalists. Moe's grand prize winner received burritos for life.

Some contests allow the producer's personality or background to be exposed. Visitors to the Converse site can read the director's commentary and biography and get contact information for the filmmaker. The Chevrolet site hosts an episodic documentary that followed the student teams throughout the selection process. The Sony ads hosted on Current TV's Web site offer the producer a MySpace-like profile page with links to Web sites or e-mails. Through Jumpcut, Doritos entrants also had a profile page.

Advertisers should question whether entrants are motivated at all by their relationship with the brand. Some entrants might be trying to break into the advertising or film industries and view entering contests as a way to do this. Walker (2006) described contest entries not as examples of "co-creation," but as "co-promotion," as winners attempt to use the contest to promote themselves.

Mozilla contest runner-up Jeff Gill described himself as "a huge contest guy" (Walker, 2006). Craig Kuehne, who also entered Mozilla's contest, features his Doritos entry on his blog (homepage.mac.com/craigkuehne/index.html). Dan Cunliffe II, who won the National Sunflower Association contest, also won $500 from a toy company for a 30-second video and $5,000 for an American Idol video contest (Tice, 2007). Tyson Ibele, who submitted a Sony ad he created while an animator at MAKE, was also entering the Mozilla contest (Petrecca, 2006). Heinz contest winner Andrew Dobson includes a bottle of ketchup in new business proposals as a way to remind people of his winning work (O'Malley, 2007). For contests that solicit entries from film or advertising students, are the advertisers looking for talent? For contests that solicit entries from the general public, are the advertisers seeking to further engage the consumer in a brand conversation?

Contest entries may gain additional exposure through the process of viral advertising. When a company creates a viral message, the intent is for it to be distributed by consumers among their networks of friends and family (Porter & Golan, 2006). Contest entrants have employed viral advertising tactics to further promote themselves and the contest through blogs, Web sites, or social media profiles. The winner of the Doritos contest, Five Point Productions, hosted a blog at www.5pointproductions.com/doritos.html that included a link to the Doritos contest voting page. Dan Cunliff II, the winner of the National Sunflower Association contest, used the URL voteforminot.com to promote his entry, driving traffic to the site through fliers sent home with schoolchildren and through the encouragement of community leaders (Tice, 2007). A search of Facebook and MySpace reveals student-created sites on both asking friends to vote for Chipotle entries. Doritos' contest entrants also used MySpace pages (Tanaka, 2007).

Consumers

The Internet offers the ability to measure exposure to user-generated content. In the case of the Doritos contest, winning commercial "Live the Flavor" was viewed by 667,711 people and finalist "Check-Out Girl" was viewed by 638,032. The other three finalists were all watched more than 200,000 times. The gallery of entries had 600 million views during Super Bowl week (Mills, 2007). Chipotle's most-viewed ad was seen over 8 million times with the second most-viewed ad seen almost 7.8 million times. Heinz's entries had 2.3 million views, representing 80,000 hours of viewing (Heinz Company Release, 2007). Mozilla's second place ad had 29,000 votes and an additional 23,000 views on YouTube (Walker, 2006). Over 200,000 people voted for the NFL pitches (Anfuso, 2007). Even the National Sunflower Association had 115,000 views during grand prize voting and 257,000 views during the contest. The winning Chevrolet ad has been viewed 63,445 times on YouTube and Dove's winning ad had over 40,000 views on AOL Video. The winning Southwest ad had over 20,000 views and Moe's most-watched ad was seen almost 14,000 times on Sharkle. Top rated ads Sony ads on Current TV had thousands of views.

The entries and the sponsor can get additional exposure if the technology allows the consumer to blog or send the video to a friend, both also being ways to enhance interactivity. For the Sony ads on Current TV, users can post comments, as well as post the video to a blog, e-mail it, "Digg" it, or tag it as a delicious link. Mozilla's system allowed users to get a link to embed in a blog or Web site, e-mail the video, or download the video. Converse, Southwest, and Moe's allowed the user to e-mail the video. The Doritos entries could be posted to a Web site or e-mailed; Dove offered the same capabilities as well as sending the video via instant messaging. Heinz used IM and e-mail as well.

Consumers also interact with user-generated ads by casting votes. In many of the contests examined, consumers have a vote that counts toward selecting a winner, most often the grand prize winner but sometimes an alternative winner. For example, Dove used a panel of judges to select ten semi-finalists and then used another panel to narrow the field to three finalists. Consumers then selected a winner from the top three. Similarly, after Doritos selected five finalists in its "Crash the Super Bowl" contest, Web site visitors voted for the winning commercial, which was shown during the Super Bowl XLI broadcast. As mentioned earlier, sometimes consumers have no involvement in voting for the grand prize winner. Southwest used a panel of judges to name a grand prize winner, although it did utilize consumers to select first, second, and third place winners who received prizes ranging from a three-day vacation for four to a Southwest destination to two Southwest tickets. Chipotle awarded $20,000 to a creative winner judged solely by the panel and $10,000 to a most-viewed winner. In the Chevrolet college student contest, viewers were able to vote for the team they thought would win, but the votes did not count toward the selection of a winner. Consumers like to be able to have some impact on the final outcome and have expressed frustration when their comments or votes do not count.

The anonymity of the Web has created situations whereby consumers are vindictive toward the advertising producers. In the case of Mozilla, comments turned cruel and insulting, rather than constructive, and several entrants asked for their videos to be removed from the site (Firefox Flicks Backstage, 2006). The contest administrators disabled the comment function until they could develop a solution.

Content

The content of a user-generated ad is most influenced by the amount or type of content provided by the sponsor as a starting point. In some contests, the advertiser provides the video and the producer then adds the text, as in the case of MasterCard's "Priceless" campaign. In Tahoe's contest, producers developed a mash-up video consisting solely of footage provided by the advertiser. In other cases, such as in the contests for Dove and Doritos, producers have a much higher degree of creative control and are asked to create an original video, pitch, script, or storyboard. In addition, some contests provided graphics or video of the logo and/or product lineup, music, or sound effects to assist in the creative process.

One way to analyze content is to classify its format. For the contests included in this study, the content requirements are specific. The content might look like a commercial for the brand, as in the case of Doritos, Heinz, and Dove. In another variation, producers were asked to make a vignette without a brand message that would be incorporated into a commercial. Southwest used this strategy for their "Wanna Get Away" contest by asking producers to show uncomfortable or embarrassing scenes from which a person might want to "get away." Southwest then added its own logo to the producer's 20-second video. Converse solicits 24-second films from consumers. Not intended as advertisements for the brand, the films are inspired by the values of Converse. Two contests, Chevrolet and NFL, sought ideas from entrants, with Chevrolet requiring a script and storyboard and NFL allowing entrants to make a 90-second pitch with no video or audio materials. In MasterCard's Priceless contest, producers were provided with the video and asked to fill in the missing phrases. Only the Vegas.com contest allowed entrants to submit 60 seconds of either a pitch, an "acting-out" of the idea, or a rough-cut version of the commercial. Despite the range in the format, according to a press release from Vegas.com, the contest generated many professional-quality entries (Vegas.com, 2007).

Another way to classify the content is to examine whether the final version of the advertisement was created by the producer or whether the idea was generated by the producer then professionally produced by the advertising agency. Most contests used the version submitted by the producer while some were shot or re-shot by the advertising agency. However, some ads did not run on television so it was not critical for these to be of professional quality. In the case of Doritos, Dove, Southwest, and others, the producer created the commercial that ran on television. In Chevrolet's contest for college students, agency Campwell-Ewald invited the top five teams to its office in Warren, Mich., chose the best concept, and then professionally shot the commercial based on the winning idea. The NFL also professionally produced a commercial based on the winning idea. Working in collaboration with the CineVegas Film Festival, Vegas.com awarded on opportunity for the winner to be able to direct the next Vegas.com commercial.

User-generated advertising contests have been known to produce subversive advertising messages, as in the case of Chevrolet's user-generated advertising contest launched in March 2006 to promote the Tahoe SUV. The company provided images and music for producers to develop their own 30-second spots. This campaign generated approximately 30,000 commercials (Rose, 2006), but backfired when subversive themes emerged, such as GM's contribution to global warming, social irresponsibility, or the poor quality of the cars, as well as profane and sexually explicit messages. While company officials stated that they expected some negative ads to be submitted, they were satisfied that more than 80% of the entries had positive themes (Sandoval, 2006). In MasterCard's "Priceless" campaign, 200 of the 10,000 entries were considered inappropriate (Petrecca, 2007). Interestingly, these two contests provided consumers with the highest degree of content. Although the content allowed these companies to control the creative execution of the commercials, it perhaps encouraged consumers to consider subversive messages.

Medium

Contest entries are made available for viewing through the contest Web site, on video sites such as YouTube or Yahoo! Video, on television, or in print. For most contests, the grand prize was an airing of the winning commercial (or a commercial directed by the winner) on television. Sony and Converse both ran the commercials of several contests winners. Chipotle and Mozilla noted that the airing of the winning commercial was a possibility, but not a guarantee. For the winners of the Tahoe, Moe's, and National Sunflower Association contests, their commercial was not intended for television. Several contests, such as Doritos, not only aired the winner, but another top entry. Heinz aired five finalists to generate publicity for voting. Mozilla aired the four most popular commercials in two markets. The winning MasterCard commercial ran as a television spot in 2006 (Tanaka, 2007).

Some contest sponsors partner with video sites to utilize their technological capabilities. For example, Doritos' entries were created in and uploaded to Jumpcut and powered by Yahoo! video, Dove's entries were hosted by AOL Video, and the entries for Southwest, Heinz, and Chipotle entries were hosted by YouTube. Moe's used Sharkle, Vegas.com used a service called VideoEgg, and Mozilla powered its videos with Revver. In addition, video sites, such as YouTube, offer a wealth of inventory of all kinds of user-generated content and many of the contest entries find their way here.

After the contests ended, some contest sites maintained all entries, while highlighting the winner and finalists. The contest Web sites for Doritos, Converse, and Southwest, for example, hosted all or almost all entries. Some contest sites hosted just the winning ad. Two sites, Dove and Vegas.com, maintained only the grand prize winner and the finalists.

THEORETICAL FRAMEWORK AND FUTURE RESEARCH

This section will explore each of the key elements of user-generated advertising contests from a theoretical perspective and suggest topics for future research.

Advertisers

The use of user-generated advertising contests by advertisers raises the issue of whether this strategy affects consumer attitudes toward the advertiser. A report released by the AMA who partnered with Opinion Research Corp. for the study indicated that adults perceive user-generated content to be more customer-friendly, more creative, and more innovative than agency-generated advertising (Wood, 2006). Younger adults (between the ages of 18 and 24), however, are more skeptical of user-generated advertising than older adults (between the ages of 25-64). Younger consumers are more likely to say that advertisers who use user-generated advertising are less trustworthy, less socially responsible, and less customer-friendly (Wood, 2006). These findings should be somewhat troubling for advertisers who are using user-generated advertising contests to target a younger demographic.

Defined as "a learned predisposition to respond in a consistently favorable or unfavorable manner to the sponsoring organization" (Lutz, 1985, p. 53), attitude toward the advertiser represents an affective response to an advertisement. In the attitude toward the ad model, perceptions of the advertiser, including advertiser credibility, are expected to influence attitude toward the advertiser (MacKenzie & Lutz, 1989). Perceptions emanate from consumers' past experiences and information about the company. Advertiser attitude was found to have a strong positive correlation with attitude toward the ad under ad pretest conditions (MacKenzie & Lutz, 1989). The relationship between attitude toward the advertiser and attitude toward the ad should be explored in future studies of user-generated content to determine under what circumstances the two concepts are correlated.

Research has demonstrated that credibility of the source is an important factor in the effectiveness of persuasive messages (Austin & Pinkleton, 2006). Consumers may perceive the *source* of the message to be the producer of the ad, the person appearing in the ad, the advertiser, or possibly all three. Credibility is defined as the extent to which the source is perceived to have relevant expertise, can be trusted as having an objective opinion, and exhibits attractiveness (Ohanian, 1990). The source considered in Ohanian's (1990) research is the spokesperson appearing in the advertisement.

A distinct concept from spokesperson credibility is corporate credibility, which impacts the company's image or reputation (Newell & Goldsmith, 2001). This construct can be measured using Newell and Goldsmith's (2001) Corporate Credibility Scale which includes eight items, with four items measuring corporate trustworthiness and four measuring corporate expertise. Lafferty, Goldsmith, and Newell (2002) tested the Dual Credibility Model, which integrates corporate and spokesperson credibility, and found that consumers can differentiate between the presenter and the corporate sponsor of the ad. Furthermore, while endorser credibility was found to have a more profound direct effect on attitude toward the ad than corporate credibility, corporate credibility was directly related to all three advertising-related variables (i.e., attitude toward the ad, attitude toward the brand, and purchase intention) (Lafferty, Goldsmith, & Newell, 2002). User-generated ads may exhibit a higher level of source credibility because consumers are likely to trust the opinion of a peer who created the ad or a lower lever because the message is not emanating directly from the advertiser. A better understanding of perceived source may help to advance knowledge of the appropriate application of user-generated advertising.

Producers

The producer can be studied by examining the motivations for creating the content. Daugherty, Eastin, and Bright (2008) examined the functional sources of motivation to create user-generated content and the impact of motivations on attitude toward creating user-generated content. Based on the postulation that attitudes serve personality functions, Katz (1960) developed a typology of four personality functions—utilitarian, knowledge, ego-defensive, and value expressive. Adding the social function of Clary et al. (1998) to Katz's (1960) typology and applying the concepts to user-generated content, Daugherty, Eastin, and Bright (2008) found that the ego-defensive and social functions have a positive and significant relationship with attitudes toward creating user-generated content, while the value-expressive function had a negative relationship. Therefore, those producers who exhibit the ego-defensive motivation, which helps to minimize self-doubt and experience a sense of community, and the social motivation, which allows them to associate with others and participate in activities considered favorable to others, will have more favorable attitudes toward creating user-generated content (Daugherty, Eastin, & Bright, 2008). Exploring this social function as well as other motivations may provide additional insight as to how to mobilize contest entrants, which has both theoretical and practical applications for advertisers.

Advertising contests also have implications for brand-building. Branding has long been used to create social networks among consumers in an effort to generate enthusiasm for a brand and encourage consumers to remain loyal (Schultz, 2007). A recent study by Dou and Krishnamurthy (2007) examined how product and service providers are using the Web to build brands, focusing on the specific elements of a brand's Web site. Consumer involvement in advertising contests might even be considered a form of "branding Reformation," whereby "marketing professionals used to be the high-priest gatekeepers, but now we can all have a direct relationship with the Almighty Brand" (Walker, 2006, p. 20 paraphrasing Grant McCracken). For this reason, sponsors should examine their objectives to ensure they are in line with the entrants to get the most out of their efforts. Future research in this area of user-generated content could focus on the relationship between the producer and the brand and consider the branding benefits of contest entrants and other content creation promotions.

The creation of user-generated advertising might evoke a high involvement situation for producers, whereby they persuade themselves of the benefits of a product through the intense process of creating an ad. Petty and Cacioppo (1986) incorporate the concept of involvement in their Elaboration Likelihood Model (ELM), which directs those who are motivated and able to process a message to a central route to persuasion involving elaborated arguments. In contrast, elaborated arguments are not effective for those unmotivated and unable to cognitively process a message, requiring communicators to rely on peripheral cues in the peripheral route to persuasion (Petty & Cacioppo, 1986). The study of user-generated advertising provides for a unique application of ELM whereby the ad creator might be hastening the process of persuasion through intimate interactions with the brand.

Consumers

While Web site statistics are available and useful for advertisers, the literature does not reveal an understanding of the motivations of consumers. Uses and gratifications theory helps explain why people use certain media by classifying how people make decisions about media use and the needs fulfilled by those choices (Katz, Blumler, & Gurevitch, 1973). Uses and gratifications makes three assumptions: the audience actively uses media to provide gratifications, audience members will identify a need prior to making a media choice, and media outlets compete with other methods for satisfying needs (Katz et al., 1973). Future research in the area of user-generated advertising should examine the uses and gratifications of consumers who watch and comment on the entries.

In an application of uses and gratifications to Web site usage, Ko, Cho, and Roberts (2005) found high information, convenience, and social interaction to account for length of time spent on a Web site, and consumers with high information needs were more likely to engage in human-message interaction. Consumers with high convenience and social interaction needs will engage in human-human interaction, which was found to have more impact on attitude toward the site than human-message interaction (Ko, Cho, & Roberts, 2005). Those who engage more in human-message and human-human interactions evaluate Web sites more positively, leading to favorable attitudes toward brands and higher purchase intentions (Ko, Cho, & Roberts, 2005).

User-generated advertising often provides opportunities for consumers to interact with the producers of the ad or the ad itself. Cho and Leckenby (1997) classified existing definitions of interactivity in terms of user-machine interactions, user-user interactions, and user-message interactions. Applying these definitions to the Internet, user-machine interactivity allows the user to change the look of the Web site or navigate the site through links; user-user interactivity refers to communication between two people mediated by the Internet; and user-message interactivity allows for control of advertising messages on the Internet. Interactivity is important for its documented link to positive user attitudes (Cho & Leckenby, 1999).

Liu and Shrum (2002) used a definition of interactivity that combined Cho and Leckenby's (1997) perspective: "We define interactivity as follows: The degree to which two or more communication parties can act on each other, on the communication, and on the messages and the degree to which such influences are synchronized." Of Liu and Shrum's (2002) three dimensions of interactivity—active control, two-way communication, and synchronicity—the dimension that most applies to user-generated advertising contests is two-way communication. Two-way communication is predicted to be positively related to cognitive involvement and user satisfaction (Liu & Shrum, 2002).

McQuail's (1987) typology of motivations of mass media use offers additional insight for user-generated content and its consumers. While the information, entertainment, and personal identity reasons may apply, it is the personal relationships and social interaction reason that is particularly useful for understanding consumption of user-generated advertising. When user-generated content is available on the Web, it often allows consumers to connect with others. Some of the advertising contests reviewed, for example, make it possible for consumers to comment on the entries. Furthermore, two-way communication is possible when consumers are able to comment on the entries and contest entrants respond.

The ELM (Petty & Cacioppo, 1986) also applies to the study of user-generated advertising consumers. Research should explore whether consumers have higher levels of involvement when viewing consumer-generated advertisements as opposed to agency advertisements. The added features of comment functions, voting, and pass-along power may further enhance involvement levels.

Research could also explore how a consumer becomes a producer of user-generated content. Daugherty, Eastin, and Bright (2008) found that people are more likely to create blogs or Web sites and post in discussion forums than read blogs, Web sites, or other forum posts. In contrast, people are more likely to consume videos, photos, audio, and wiki sites than create them. These differences are surmised to be attributed to the desire of people to use more text-based online communication for self-expression and their limited skills to create and post video and audio (Daugherty, Eastin, & Bright, 2008).

Content

Further research could examine whether user-generated advertising content confuses consumers. Producers have been known to make their entries available to others on sites such as YouTube. These entries may communicate a subversive brand message or at the very least, a message that is not consistent with that of the company. Research could also examine whether the availability of critical messages creates a distrust of ad messages in general.

Content can also be studied by classifying the creative strategy of the user-generated advertising content. Creative strategy has been described as a combination of message content and creative execution (Laskey, Day, & Crask, 1989; Ray, 1982; Shimp & Delozier, 1986). Laskey, Day, and Crask (1989), for example, described creative strategy as "what is being said in an advertisement as well as how it is said." While some scholars limit the definition of creative strategy to message content, creative strategy can encompass both message content and creative execution. Advertisers are encouraged to use the same strategy for all marketing communications (Kim, McMillan, & Hwang, 2005).

Message content often falls into one of two general categories with one focusing on product attributes and benefits and the other emphasizing brand image (Laskey, Fox, & Crask, 1995). Puto and Wells (1984) described this distinction as informational or transformational. Previous typologies of message strategies that are more detailed than the simple informational/transformational dichotomy include Laskey, Day, and Crask's (1989) typology of nine message strategies divided into the informational and transformational approaches.

The five creative strategies of the informational approach include Comparative, Unique Selling Proposition (USP), Preemptive, Hyperbole, and Generic Information. The four creative strategies of the transformational approach include User Image, Brand Image, Use Occasion, and Generic Transformation. Using Laskey, Day, and Crask's (1989) typology, user-generated advertising content can be examined to see if it is consistent with other advertisements produced by the agency for the brand and to also examine the difference between winning ads and other entries.

Creative execution refers to the way a message is presented and the context of that presentation. The Marketing Science Institute's typology (cited in Schmalensee, 1983) examines the format, product, presenter, visuals, music, and sexual content. Added to this typology by Koudelova and Whitelock (2001) is the category of humor as examined by Weinberger and Spotts (1989). The creative execution of user-generated advertising can be examined to determine if it is consistent with other agency-produced advertisements for the brand or if there is a difference between winning ads and other entries.

Other areas of research to explore would be attitudes toward user-generated ads and attitudes toward the brand. Attitude toward the ad has been found to be a mediator of brand attitude, brand choice, and purchase intentions (MacKenzie & Lutz, 1989; MacKenzie, Lutz, & Belch, 1986; Mitchell & Olson, 1981). A meta-analysis by Brown and Stayman (1992) confirmed a significant relationship between attitude toward the ad and brand attitudes, brand-related cognitions, and purchase intention. The significance of brand attitude is its documented link to purchase intentions (Brown & Stayman, 1992). Additional research could explore whether attitude toward the ad is as strongly correlated with advertising-related variables for user-generated advertising as it is for agency-generated advertising or whether consumers disassociate user-generated advertising from the brand itself, reducing the impact of attitude toward the ad.

Media

The concept of synergy has relevance in a user-generated campaign because consumer ads often air on television and are hosted on the Web. Synergy first requires that multiple communication tools or vehicles are applied within a campaign (Chang & Thorson, 2004). Achieving synergy then occurs in one of four ways: having a unified image, speaking in a consistent voice, being a good listener, or being a world-class citizen (Duncan, 1993). In testing the effectiveness of television-Web synergy compared to repetition of either television or Web, Chang and Thorson (2004) found that synergy led to higher attention, higher perceived message credibility, and more total and positive thoughts. Chang and Thorson (2004) concluded that multiple sources not only elicited more thoughts, but also led to more central processing than repetition, which relied more on peripheral cues.

Attitudes toward online advertising have been explored in number of studies, but many of these focus on Web formats, such as banner ads or pop-ups (Burns & Lutz, 2006, 2008; Cho, 2003; Wolin & Korgaonkar, 2003; Yang, 2003). Research could explore attitudes toward online video advertisements. Another area for future research would be the role of involvement in watching user-generated ads on the Web versus television commercials. It is assumed that involvement levels will be higher, thereby enhancing cognitive processing.

DISCUSSION

The engagement model of advertising is more complex than traditional models and it is hoped that the complexity has been thoroughly explicated here in the context of user-generated advertising contests. The advertiser, once the sender of the message, invites participation from a targeted group, sets up the boundaries for the creation of the content, and serves as a gatekeeper for appropriate content. The producer, once a passive receiver of the message, has an invitation to communicate about the brand, which may or may not have occurred without the inspiration of a contest. Consumers may engage in a dialogue with the producer of the ad, further defining the brand. Engaging with producers and consumers involves using new and social media, where more interactivity can occur. The engagement model presented serves as a method to analyze the various components of user-generated advertising contests and also define areas for future research. The model provides additional insight into the phenomenon of user-generated content and will hopefully motivate scholars to develop theory and address issues in this area.

That said, the trend of user-generated content raises additional concerns for the industry. Advertisers need to consider whether seeking and sharing user-generated advertising is the best way to engage consumers. An initial concern would be whether subversive messages are possible, as in the case of the Chevy Tahoe. Another question would be whether the brand engenders devotion, as in the case of the National Football League (Fine, 2007). As Fine (2007) described, "Many big advertisers sell commodities—soap powder, paper goods—that lack logos people tattoo on their torsos or paint on their faces" (p. 24). Thus, if people do not feel a brand connection, they may not be able to be motivated to create advertisements for it.

Another issue for the industry is whether user-generated advertising is more effective than traditional advertising and if so, locating the source or sources of this impact. Producers of the ad may experience increases in advertising effects through their intense involvement with the brand while creating the ad. Consumers may experience greater advertising effects watching ads created by their peers. The effects may occur as producers and consumers engage in dialogue. The use of the Web as a vehicle for showcasing these ads may have greater impact on viewers than television commercials. Measuring all these components will help bridge understanding for this new advertising strategy.

REFERENCES

Anfuso, D. (2007, January 10). NFL selects user-gen Super Bowl ad. *iMedia Connection*. Retrieved June 26, 2007, from http://www.imediaconnection.com/news/13175.asp

Austin, E. W., & Pinkleton, B. E. (2006). *Strategic public relations management* (2nd ed.). Mahwah, NJ: Lawrence Erlbaum Associates.

Brown, S. P., & Stayman, D. M. (1992). Antecedents and consequences of attitude toward the ad: A meta-analysis. *The Journal of Consumer Research, 19*(1), 34–51. doi:10.1086/209284

Burns, K. S., & Lutz, R. J. (2006). The function of format: Consumer responses to six online advertising formats. *Journal of Advertising, 35*(1), 53–63. doi:10.2753/JOA0091-3367350104

Burns, K. S., & Lutz, R. J. (2008). Web users' perceptions of and attitudes toward online advertising formats. *International Journal of Internet Marketing and Advertising, 4*(4), 281–301. doi:10.1504/IJIMA.2008.019150

Chang, Y., & Thorson, E. (2004). Television and Web advertising synergies. *Journal of Advertising, 33*(2), 75–84.

Cho, C.-H. (2003). The effectiveness of banner advertisements: involvement and click-through. *Journalism & Mass Communication Quarterly, 80*(3), 623–645.

Cho, C.-H., & Leckenby, J. D. (1997). Internet-related programming technology and advertising. In M. C. Macklin (Ed.), *Proceedings of the 1997 Conference of the American Academy of Advertising* (pp. 69). Cincinnati, OH: American Academy of Advertising.

Cho, C.-H., & Leckenby, J. D. (1999). Interactivity as a measure of advertising effectiveness: Antecedents and consequences of interactivity in Web advertising. In M. S. Roberts (Ed.), *Proceedings of the 1999 Conference of the American Academy of Advertising* (pp. 162-179). Gainesville, FL: American Academy of Advertising.

Clary, E. G., Snyder, M., Ridge, R., Copeland, J., Stukas, A., Haugen, J., & Miene, P. (1998). Understanding and assessing the motivations of volunteers: A functional approach. *Journal of Personality and Social Psychology, 74*(6), 1516–1530. doi:10.1037/0022-3514.74.6.1516

Daugherty, T., Eastin, M. S., & Bright, L. (2008). Exploring consumer motivations for creating user-generated content. *Journal of Interactive Advertising, 8*(2). Retrieved August 8, 2008, from http://jiad.org/article101

Dou, W., & Krishnamurthy, S. (2007). Using brand Websites to build brands online: A product versus service brand comparison. *Journal of Advertising Research, 47*(2), 193–206. doi:10.2501/S0021849907070225

Duncan, T. (1993). Integrated marketing? It's synergy. *Advertising Age, 64*(10), 22.

Fine, J. (2007, February 19). What makes citizen ads' work. *BusinessWeek*, (4022), 24.

Firefox Flicks Backstage. (2006, May 1). *Flicks comments and ratings*. Retrieved June 26, 2007, from http://www.firefoxflicks.com/backstage/page/6.

Hansell, S. (2005, August 1). More people turn to the Web to watch TV. *New York Times*. Retrieved June 26, 2007, from http://www.nytimes.com/2005/08/01/technology/01video.html?pagewanted=1&ei=5070&en=738e29c3e0711720&ex=1184558400.

Heinz. (2007, August 11). *Heinz 'Top This!' campaign tops list of consumer-generated efforts* [Company Release]. Retrieved March 19, 2009, from http://www.prweb.com/releases/2007/08/prweb545964.htm

Jaffee, L. (2007, June 20). California man wins Vegas.com ad contest. *Promo Xtra.* Retrieved June 26, 2007, from http://promomagazine.com/contests/news/california_man_wins_vegas_ad_contest_062007/index.html

Kahney, L. (2004, December 13). Home-brew iPod ad opens eyes. *Wired.* Retrieved June 25, 2007, from http://www.wired.com/gadgets/mods/commentary/cultofmac/2004/12/66001

Katz, D. (1960). The functional approach to the study of attitudes. *Public Opinion Quarterly, 24,* 27–46. doi:10.1086/266945

Katz, D., Blumler, J. G., & Gurevitch, M. (1973). Uses and gratifications research. *Public Opinion Quarterly, 37,* 509–523. doi:10.1086/268109

Kim, J., McMillan, S. J., & Hwang, J.-S. (2005). Strategies for Super Bowl advertising: An analysis of how the Web is integrated into campaigns. *Journal of Interactive Advertising, 6*(1). Retrieved June 15, 2007, from http://jiad.org/vol6/no1/kim

Klaassen, A. (2006, August 7). Major turnoff: McKinsey slams TV's selling power. *Advertising Age, 77*(32), 1–2.

Klein, K. E. (2008, January 3). Should your customers make your ads? *BusinessWeek Online.*

Ko, H., Cho, C.-H., & Roberts, M. S. (2005). Internet uses and gratifications: A structural equation model of interactive advertising. *Journal of Advertising, 34*(2), 57–70.

Koudelova, R., & Whitelock, J. (2001). A cross-cultural analysis of television advertising in the UK and Czech Republic. *International Marketing Review, 18*(3), 286–300. doi:10.1108/02651330110695611

Lafferty, B., Goldsmith, R. E., & Newell, S. J. (2002). The dual credibility model: The influence of corporate and endorser credibility. *Journal of Marketing Theory and Practice, 10*(3), 1–12.

Laskey, H. A., Day, E., & Crask, M. R. (1989). Typology of main message strategies for television commercials. *Journal of Advertising, 18*(1), 36–41.

Laskey, H. A., Fox, R. J., & Crask, M. R. (1995). The relationship between advertising message strategy and television commercial effectiveness. *Journal of Advertising Research, 35*(2), 31–39.

Lasswell, H. D. (1948). The structure and function of communication in society. In Schramm, W., & Roberts, D. F. (Eds.), *The process and effects of mass communication* (pp. 84–99). Urbana, IL: University of Illinois Press.

Liu, Y., & Shrum, L. J. (2002). What is interactivity and is it always such a good thing? Implications of definition, person, and situation for the influence of interactivity on advertising effectiveness. *Journal of Advertising, 31*(4), 53–64.

Lutz, R. J. (1985). Affective and cognitive antecedents of attitude toward the ad: A conceptual framework. In Alwitt, L. F., & Mitchell, A. A. (Eds.), *Psychological processes and advertising effects: Theory, research, and applications* (pp. 45–63). Hillsdale, NJ: Lawrence Erlbaum Associates, Inc., Publishers.

MacKenzie, S. B., & Lutz, R. J. (1989). An empirical examination of the structural antecedents of attitude toward the ad in an advertising pretesting context. *Journal of Marketing, 53*(2), 48–65. doi:10.2307/1251413

MacKenzie, S. B., Lutz, R. J., & Belch, G. E. (1986). The role of attitude toward the ad as a mediator of advertising effectiveness: A test of competing explanations. *JMR, Journal of Marketing Research, 23*(2), 130–143. doi:10.2307/3151660

Malinee, A. (2007, March 1). Alumna bathes in media spotlight after winning Dove competition. *Inside Vandy*. Retrieved June 29, 2007, from http://www.insidevandy.com/drupal/node/3473

McQuail, D. (1987). *Mass communication theory: An introduction* (2nd ed.). Newbury Park, CA: Sage.

Mills, E. (2006, April 4). Advertisers look to grassroots marketing. *CNETNews.com*. Retrieved June 26, 2007, from http://news.com.com/2102-1024_3-6057300.html.

Mills, E. (2007, March 20). Frito-Lay turns to netizens for ad creation. *CNET News.com*. Retrieved June 9 2007, from http://news.com.com/2100-1024_3-6168881.html

Mitchell, A. A., & Olson, J. C. (1981). Are product attributes beliefs the only mediator of advertising effects on brand attitude? *JMR, Journal of Marketing Research, 18*(3), 318–332. doi:10.2307/3150973

Morrissey, B. (2006, September 15). For Super Bowl ad, Doritos turns to users. *Adweek*. Retrieved June 9, 2007, from http://www.adweek.com/aw/iq_interactive/article_display.jsp?vnu_content_id=1003122828

Newell, S. J., & Goldsmith, R. E. (2001). The development of a scale to measure perceived corporate credibility. *Journal of Business Research, 52*(3), 235. doi:10.1016/S0148-2963(99)00104-6

O'Malley, G. (2007, September 18). Heinz anticipates another success with consumer ads. *MediaPost*.

Ohanian, R. (1990). Construction and validation of a scale to measure celebrity endorsers' perceived expertise, trustworthiness, and attractiveness. *Journal of Advertising, 19*(3), 39–52.

Perry, D. K. (2002). *Theory and research in mass communication: Context and consequences* (2nd ed.). Mahwah, NJ: Lawrence Erlbaum Associates.

Petrecca, L. (2006, March 27). Amateur advertisers get a chance. *USA Today*. Retrieved June 26, 2007, from http://www.usatoday.com/money/advertising/2006-03-27-amateur-advertisers_x.htm

Petrecca, L. (2007, June 21). Madison Avenue wants you! (or at least your videos). *USA Today*. Retrieved June 26, 2007, from http://www.usatoday.com/printEd./money/20070621/cannes_cover.art.htm

Petty, R. E., & Cacioppo, J. T. (1986). *Communication and persuasion: Central and peripheral routes to attitude change*. New York: Springer-Verlag.

Porter, L., & Golan, G. (2006). From subservient chickens to brawny men: A comparison of viral advertising to television advertising. *Journal of Interactive Advertising, 6*(2). Retrieved March 19, 2009, from http://www.jiad.org/vol6/no2/

Puto, C. P., & Wells, W. D. (1984). Informational and transformational advertising: The differential effects of time. In Kinnear, T. C. (Ed.), *Advances in Consumer Research, XI* (pp. 638–643). Provo, UT: Association for Consumer Research.

Rappaport, S. D. (2007). Lessons from online practice: New advertising models. *Journal of Advertising Research, 47*(2), 135–141. doi:10.2501/S0021849907070158

Ray, M. (1982). *Advertising and communication management*. Englewood Cliffs, NJ: Prentice Hall.

Rose, F. (2006). Commercial break. *Wired, 14*(12). Retrieved June 26, 2007, from http://www.wired.com/wired/archive/14.12/tahoe.html

Sandoval, G. (2006, April 3). GM slow to react to nasty ads. *CNET News*. Retrieved June 26, 2007, from http://news.com.com/GM+slow+to+react+to+nasty+ads/2100-1024_3-6057143.html

Schmalensee, D. H. (1983). Today's top priority advertising research questions. *Journal of Advertising Research, 23*(2), 49–60.

Schultz, D. E. (2007). Social call. *Marketing Management, 16*(4), 10–11.

Shimp, T. A., & Delozier, W. (1986). *Promotion management and marketing communication*. New York: CBS College Publishing.

Snoddy, R. (2007, January 17). User content won't kill off old media. *Marketing*, 18.

Stern, B. B. (1994). A revised communications model for advertising: Multiple dimensions of the source, the message, and the recipient. *Journal of Advertising, 23*(2), 5–15.

Story, L. (2007, May 26). The high price of creating free ads. *New York Times*. Retrieved June 26, 2007, from http://www.nytimes.com/2007/05/26/business/26content.html?pagewanted=1&ei=5088&en=f5244987dc59d9d0&ex=1337832000

Tanaka, W. (2007, January 29). D.I.Y. ads. *Red Herring*. Retrieved June 26, 2007, from http://www.redherring.com/Article.aspx?a=20955&hed=D.I.Y.+Ads.

Tice, L. (2007, June 24). Video contest goes to seed. *SunJournal.com*. Retrieved July 11, 2007, from http://www.sunjournal.com/story/218125-3/LewistonAuburn/Video_contest_goes_to_seed/

Vegas.com. (2007, June 18). *Winner chosen for Direct the Next Vegas.commercial contest* [Company Release]. Retrieved July 11, 2007, from http://www.vegas.com/about/releases/vegascommercialwinner061807.html

Walker, R. (2006, May 28). Free advertising. *New York Times Magazine*, 20.

Weinberger, M. G., & Spotts, H. E. (1989). Humour in U.S. versus U.K. TV commercials: A comparison. *Journal of Advertising, 18*(2), 39–44.

Wolin, L. D., & Korgaonkar, P. (2003). Web advertising: Gender difference in beliefs, attitudes, and behavior. *Internet Research, 13*(5), 375–385. doi:10.1108/10662240310501658

Wood, C. (2006, December 5). User-generated content is building brand affinity: AMA. *DMNews*. Retrieved June 26, 2007, from http://www.dmnews.com/cms/dm-news/research-studies/39243.html.

Yang, C. C. (2003). Internet users' attitude toward and beliefs about Internet advertising: exploratory research from Taiwan. *Journal of International Consumer Marketing, 15*(4), 43–65. doi:10.1300/J046v15n04_03

Compilation of References

Aaker, D. A. (1996). *Building Strong Brands*. New York: The Free Press.

Aaker, J. L. (1997, August). Dimensions of brand personality. *JMR, Journal of Marketing Research*, 347–356. doi:10.2307/3151897

Aaker, J., Brumbaugh, A., & Grier, S. (2000). Non-target market effects and viewer distinctiveness: The impact of target marketing on attitudes. *Journal of Consumer Psychology*, *9*(3), 127–140. doi:10.1207/S15327663JCP0903_1

Aaker, J. L., Benet-Martinez, V., & Garolera, J. (2001). Consumption symbols as carriers of culture: A study of Japanese and Spanish brand personality constructs. *Journal of Personality and Social Psychology*, *81*(3), 492–508. doi:10.1037/0022-3514.81.3.492

Aaker, J. L. (1997). Dimensions of brand personality. *JMR, Journal of Marketing Research*, *34*(3), 347–356. doi:10.2307/3151897

Aarsand, P. A. (2007). Children's consumption of computer games. In Katz, J. E. (Ed.), *Handbook of Mobile Communication Studies* (pp. 47–62). Cambridge, MA: MIT Press.

Abdullatif, H. I., & Hamadah, L. N. (2005). The factorial structure of the desirability of control scale among kuwaiti subjects. *Social Behavior and Personality*, *33*(3), 307–312. doi:10.2224/sbp.2005.33.3.307

Abell, S. C., Harkheimer, R., & Nguyen, S. E. (1998). Intellectual evaluations of adolescents via human figure drawings: An empirical comparison of two methods. *Journal of Clinical Psychology*, *54*, 811–815. doi:10.1002/(SICI)1097-4679(199810)54:6<811::AID-JCLP8>3.0.CO;2-J

Abell, S. C., Heiberger, A. M., & Johnson, J. E. (1994). Cognitive evaluations of young adults by means of human figure drawings: An empirical investigation of two methods. *Journal of Clinical Psychology*, *50*, 900–904. doi:10.1002/1097-4679(199411)50:6<900::AID-JCLP2270500614>3.0.CO;2-3

Abell, S. C., Von Briesen, P. D., & Watz, L. S. (1996). Intellectual evaluations of children using human figure drawings: An empirical investigation of two methods. *Journal of Clinical Psychology*, *52*, 67–74. doi:10.1002/(SICI)1097-4679(199601)52:1<67::AID-JCLP9>3.0.CO;2-T

Abelson, R. P., & Prentice, D. A. (1989). Beliefs as possessions: A functional perspective. In A. R. Pratkanis, S. J. Breckler, & Ag. G. Greenwald (Eds.), *Attitude Structure and Function* (pp. 361-381). Hillsdale, NJ: Erlbaum.

Abiona, T. C., Onayade, A. A., Ijadunola, K. T., Obiajunwa, P. O., Aina, O. I., & Thairu, L. N. (2006). Acceptability, feasibility and affordability of infant feeding options for HIV-infected women: A qualitative study in south-west Nigeria. *Maternal and Child Nutrition*, *2*, 134–144. doi:10.1111/j.1740-8709.2006.00050.x

Aboud, F. E., & Mendelson, M. J. (1998). Determinants of friendship selection and quality: developmental perspective. In W. M. Bukowski, A. F. Newcomb & W. W. Hartup (Eds.), *The company they keep: Friendship in Childhood and adolescence* (pp. 87-112). NY: New York: Cambridge University Press.

Abraham, L., & Kumar, A. (1999). Sexual experiences and their correlates among college students in Mumbai City in India. *International Family Planning Perspectives*, *25*(3), 139–146. doi:10.2307/2991963

Abrahams, G. (2003, October 16). TV fame loses out to drive for effectiveness. *Marketing Week*, 15.

Absolut Top Bartender on Facebook. (n.d.). Retrieved from http://www.facebook.com/AbsolutTopBartender?ref=search

Acar, A. (2007). Testing the effects of incidental advertising exposure in online gaming environment. *Journal of Interactive Advertising*, *8*(1), 1–36.

DOI: 10.4018/978-1-60566-792-8.chcrf

AccuStream iMedia Research. (2008, January). *Professional and UGV Market Size 2005 - 2008: Views, Category and Brand Share Analysis.*

Achbar, M., Abbot, J., & Bakan, J. (Directors). (2005). *The Corporation* [Motion Picture]. USA: Zeitgeist Films.

Activision. (2004). *Activision and Nielsen Entertainment team to provide standardized measurement metrics for video game audiences.* Press release. Retrieved October 1, 2008 from http://investor.activision.com/ReleaseDetail.cfm?releaseid=149231

Adamic, L. A., & Glance, N. (2005). The Political Blogosphere and the 2004 US Election: Divided They Blog. In *Proceedings of the 3rd international Workshop on Link Discovery* (pp. 36-43).

Adcentricity. (n.d.). Retrieved from http://www.adcentricity.com

Adkinson, W. F., Eisenach, J. A., & Lenard, T. M. (2002). *Privacy Online: A Report on the Information Practices and Policies of Commercial Web Sites.* Washington, DC: Progress & Freedom Foundation. Retrieved July 15, 2008, from http://www.pff.org/publications/privacyonlinefinalael.pdf

Adler, P. T. (1970). Evaluation of the figure drawing technique: Reliability, factorial structure, and diagnostic usefulness. *Journal of Consulting and Clinical Psychology, 35,* 52–57. doi:10.1037/h0029645

Adler, P. T. (1971). Ethnic and socio-economic status differences in human figure drawings. *Journal of Consulting and Clinical Psychology, 36,* 344–354. doi:10.1037/h0031125

Admin. (2008). *Product Placement on Youtube: A New Advertising Approach?* Retrieved from http://payperclickoffer.com/product-placement-on-youtube-a-new-advertising-approach/

Adorno, T. (1941). *On Popular Music.*

Adorno, T. (n.d.). *Culture Industry Reconsidered.* Retrieved February 26, 2009, from http://libcom.org/library/culture-industry-reconsidered-theodor-adorno

Adrian, A. (2007). I™: Avatars as trade marks. *Computer Law & Security Report, 23*(5), 436–448. doi:10.1016/j.clsr.2007.07.002

Advertising Age. (2007). *Digital Marketing and Media Fast Pack.*

Agence France-Press. (2008). *Sony says to put virtual ads in PlayStation 3 games.* Retrieved July 22, 2008 http://afp.google.com/article/ALeqM5hB76UHrOp8aynie9lZxquyizoppg

Agoramoorthy, G., & Minna, J. H. (2007). India's homosexual discrimination and health consequences. *Revista de Saude Publica, 41*(4), 657–660. doi:10.1590/S0034-89102006005000036

Ahlkvist, J. (2006). *Sociology of Mass Media.* USA: Unpublished Lecture, University of Denver.

Ahn, S. J., Bailenson, J., Fox, J., & Jabon, M. (in press). Using automated facial expression analysis for emotion and behavior prediction. In Doeveling, K., von Scheve, C., & Konijn, E. A. (Eds.), *Handbook of Emotions and Mass Media.* New York: Routledge.

Ahrens, F. (2006). The nearly personal touch: Marketers use Avatars to put an animated face with the name. *The Washington Post.* Retrieved December 7, 2007, from http://www.washingtonpost.com/wp-dyn/content/article/2006/07/14/AR2006071401587.html

Aikman, K. G., Belter, R. W., & Finch, A. J. Jr. (1992). Human figure drawings: Validity in assessing intellectual level and academic achievement. *Journal of Clinical Psychology, 48,* 114–119. doi:10.1002/1097-4679(199201)48:1<114::AID-JCLP2270480116>3.0.CO;2-Y

Aitken, P. P., Leathar, D. S., O'Hagan, F. J., & Squair, S. I. (1987). Children's awareness of cigarette advertisements and brand imagery. *British Journal of Addiction, 82,* 615–622. doi:10.1111/j.1360-0443.1987.tb01523.x

Ajzen, I. (1988). *Attitudes, personality, and behavior.* Chicago: Open University Press.

Ajzen, I., & Fishbein, M. (1980). *Understanding Attitudes and Predicting Social Behavior.* Englewood Cliffs, NJ: Prentice-Hall.

Akerlof, G. (1970). The market for 'Lemons': Quality uncertainty and the market mechanism. *The Quarterly Journal of Economics, 84,* 488–500. doi:10.2307/1879431

Alexa.com. (2009a). *Top sites in the United States* [Electronic Version]. Retrieved March 10, 2009, from http://www.alexa.com/site/ds/top_sites?cc=US&ts_mode=country&lang=none

Alexa.com. (2009b). *Traffic details for YouTube.com.* Retrieved March 3, 2009, from http://www.alexa.com/data/details/traffic_details/youtube.com

Alexander, A., Owers, J., Carveth, R., Hollifielf, C. A., & Greco, A. N. (Eds.). (2004). *Media Economics, Theory and Practice.* Hillsdale, NJ: Lawrence Erlbaum Associates Inc.

Allan, K., & Burridge, K. (2006). *Forbidden Words: Taboo and the censoring of language.* Cambridge, UK: Cambridge University Press. doi:10.1017/CBO9780511617881

Allport, G. W. (1961). *Pattern and Growth in Personality.* New York: Holt, Rinehart and Winston.

Allport, G. W. (1935). Attitudes. In Murchison, C. (Ed.), *Handbook of social psychology* (pp. 798–844). Worcester, MA: Clark University Press.

Allsop, D., Bassett, B., & Hoskins, J. (2007). Word-of-Mouth research: Principles and applications. *Journal of Advertising Research, 47*(4), 398–411. doi:10.2501/S0021849907070419

Alpert, S. R., Karat, J., Karat, C.-M., Brodie, C., & Vergo, J. G. (2003). User attitudes regarding a user-adaptive ecommerce web site. *User Modeling and User-Adapted Interaction, 13*, 373–396. doi:10.1023/A:1026201108015

Althaus, S. L., & Tewksbury, D. (2000). Patterns of internet and traditional news media use in a networked community. *Political Communication, 17*, 21–45. doi:10.1080/105846000198495

Altheide, D. (1996). The news media, the problem frame, and the production of fear. *The Sociological Quarterly, 38*(4), 647–668. doi:10.1111/j.1533-8525.1997.tb00758.x

Altheide, D. L., & Grimes, J. N. (2005, September). War programming: The propaganda project and the Iraq War. *The Sociological Quarterly, 46*(4), 617–643. doi:10.1111/j.1533-8525.2005.00029.x

Althusser, L. (1971). *Lenin and Philosophy and Other Essays*. London: New Left Books.

Alwin, D. F., & Krosnick, J. A. (1985). The measurement of values in surveys: A comparison of ratings and rankings. *Public Opinion Quarterly, 49*(4), 535–552. doi:10.1086/268949

Amato, C. H., Peters, C. L. O., & Shao, A. T. (2005). An exploratory investigation into NASCAR fan culture. *Sport Marketing Quarterly, 14*(2), 71–83.

Ambati, B. K., Ambati, J., & Rao, A. M. (1997). Dynamics of knowledge and attitudes about AIDS among the educated in southern India. *AIDS Care, 9*(3), 319–330. doi:10.1080/09540129750125118

America's Army. (2008). In *Wikipedia, The free encyclopedia.* Retrieved August 24, 2008 from http://en.wikipedia.org/wiki/America's_Army#cite_note-Turse-33

American Marketing Association Conference Proceedings:2006AMA Winter Educators' Conference (Vol. 17, pp. 226-231).

Anckar, B., Walden, P., & Jelassi, T. (2002). Creating customer value in online grocery shopping. *International Journal of Retail & Distribution Management, 30*(4), 211–220. doi:10.1108/09590550210423681

Andersen, L. P., Tufte, B., Rasmussen, J., & Chan, K. (2007). Tweens and new media in Denmark and Hong Kong. *Journal of Consumer Marketing, 24*(6), 340–350. doi:10.1108/07363760710822927

Anderson, C. A., & Bushman, B. J. (2001). Effects of violent games on aggressive behavior, aggressive cognition, aggressive affect, physiological arousal and prosocial behavior: a meta-analytic review of the scientific literature. *Psychological Science, 12*(5), 353–359. doi:10.1111/1467-9280.00366

Anderson, C. (2006). *The Long Tail: Why the Future of Business is Selling Less*. New York: Hyperion Press.

Anderson, J. R. (1974). Retrieval of propositional information from long-term memory. *Cognitive Psychology, 6*, 451–474. doi:10.1016/0010-0285(74)90021-8

Anderson, J. R., & Reder, L. M. (1999). The fan effect: New results and new theories. *Journal of Experimental Psychology. General, 128*(2), 186–197. doi:10.1037/0096-3445.128.2.186

Anderson, N. (2006). Most gamers do not agree that advertising makes games more realistic. *Ars Technica.* Retrieved October 5, 2008 from http://arstechnica.com/news.ars/post/20061002-7879.htm

Andie, T. (1997). Why web warriors might worry. *Columbia Journalism Review, 36*(2), 35–39.

Anfuso, D. (2007, January 10). NFL selects user-gen Super Bowl ad. *iMedia Connection.* Retrieved June 26, 2007, from http://www.imediaconnection.com/news/13175.asp

Ang, S. H., & Lim, E. A. C. (2006). The influence of metaphors and product types on brand personality perceptions and attitudes. *Journal of Advertising, 35*(2), 39–53.

Aoki, K., & Downes, E. J. (2003). An analysis of young people's use of and attitudes toward cell phones. *Telematics and Informatics, 20*(4), 349–364. doi:10.1016/S0736-5853(03)00018-2

Appelbaum, A. (2001, June). The Constant Customer. *Gallup Management Journal.*

Appiah, O. (2001). The effects of ethnic identification on Black and White adolescents' evaluation of ads. *Journal of Advertising Research, 41*(5), 7–22.

Appiah, O. (2002). Black and White viewers' perception and recall of occupational characters on television. *The Journal of Communication, 52*(4), 776–793. doi:10.1111/j.1460-2466.2002.tb02573.x

Appiah, O. (2003). Americans online: Differences in surfing and evaluating race-targeted web sites by Black and White users.

Journal of Broadcasting & Electronic Media, *47*(4), 534–552. doi:10.1207/s15506878jobem4704_4

Appiah, O. (2006). Rich media, poor media: The impact of audio/video vs. text/picture testimonial ads on browsers' evaluations of commercial web sites and online products. *Journal of Current Issues and Research in Advertising*, *28*(1), 73–86.

Appiah, O. (2007). The effectiveness of typical-user testimonial ads on Black and White browsers' evaluations of products on commercial web sites: Do they really work? *Journal of Advertising Research*, *47*(1), 14–27. doi:10.2501/S0021849907070031

Appiah, O. (2004). Effects of ethnic identification on web browsers attitudes toward, and navigational patterns on, race-targeted sites. *Communication Research*, *31*(3), 312–337. doi:10.1177/0093650203261515

Applegate, E. C. (1998). *Personalities and Products: A Historical Perspective on Advertising in America*. London: Praeger.

Araujo, P. D. (2008). *Is India's population at risk of contracting HIV?* Retrieved January 20, 2009, from http://www.voxeu.org/index.php?q=node/1651

Ariely, D. (2000). Controlling the information flow: Effects on consumers' decision making and preferences. *The Journal of Consumer Research*, *27*(2), 233–248. doi:10.1086/314322

Aristotle,. (1991). *On rhetoric: A theory of civil discourse* (Kennedy, G. A., Ed.). New York: Oxford University Press.

Ark, W. S., Dryer, D. C., & Lu, D. J. (1999). The Emotion Mouse. In *Proceedings of HCI International (the 8th International Conference on Human-Computer Interaction) on Human-Computer Interaction: Ergonomics and User Interfaces* (Vol. 1, pp. 818 - 823). Hillsdale, NJ: L. Erlbaum Associates Inc.

Arlidge, J. (2004, January 4). The new melting pot: Forget Black, forget White. The future is generation EA. *The Observer,* 19.

Armel, K. C. (2008). *Changes in energy usage as indicators of audience engagement in sustainability messaging*. Retrieved from http://www.archive.org/details/ChangesInEnergyUsageAsIndicatorsOfAudienceEngagement.

Arnould, E. J., & Thompson, C. J. (2005). Consumer culture theory (CCT): Twenty years of research. *The Journal of Consumer Research*, *31*(4), 868–883. doi:10.1086/426626

Ashworth, L., & Free, C. (2006). Marketing dataveillance and digital privacy: Using theories of justice to understand consumers' online privacy concerns. *Journal of Business Ethics*, *67*, 107–123. doi:10.1007/s10551-006-9007-7

Aspan, M. (2008, February 11). How Sticky Is Membership on Facebook? Just Try Breaking Free. *The New York Times*. Retrieved from http://www.nytimes.com/2008/02/11/technology/11facebook.html?_r=2&ref=business&oref=slogin.

Au, W. J. (2001). Playing God. *Lingua Franca: The Review of Academic Life*, *11*(7), 12–13.

Au, T. K., & Romo, L. F. (1996). Building a coherent conception of HIV transmission: A new approach to AIDS education. In Medin, D. (Ed.), *The Psychology of Learning and Motivation* (pp. 193–237).

Au, T. K., Roma, L. F., & DeWitt, J. E. (1999). Considering children's folk biology in health education. In Siegal, M., & Peterson, C. (Eds.), *Children's Understanding of Biology and Health* (pp. 209–234). Cambridge, UK: Cambridge Studies in Cognitive and Perceptual Development.

Au, W. J. (2008). *Second Life marketing: Still strong*. Retrieved on 05/07/08 from http://www.businessweek.com/technology/content/may2008/tc2008054_665274.htm

Austin, E. W., & Pinkleton, B. E. (2006). *Strategic public relations management* (2nd ed.). Mahwah, NJ: Lawrence Erlbaum Associates.

Auter, P. J., & Lane, R. Jr. (1999). Locus of control, parasocial interaction and usage of TV ministry programs. *Journal of Communication and Religion*, *22*(1), 93–120.

Auty, S., & Lewis, C. (2004, September). Exploring children's choice: The reminder effect of product placement. *Psychology and Marketing*, *21*, 697–713. doi:10.1002/mar.20025

Averjanova, O., Ricci, F., & Nguyen, Q. N. (2008). *Map-Based Interaction with a Conversational Mobile Recommender System*. Paper presented at the Proceedings of the 2008 The Second International Conference on Mobile Ubiquitous Computing, Systems, Services and Technologies.

Avert. (n.d.). *Abstinence*. Retrieved January 26, 2009, from http://www.avert.org/abstinence.htm

Avert. (n.d.). *Overview of HIV and AIDS in India*. Retrieved January 26, 2009, from http://www.avert.org/aidsindia.htm

Ayto, J., & Simpson, J. (Eds.). (2005). *The Oxford Dictionary of Modern Slang*. Oxford, UK: Oxford University Press.

Babin, L. A., & Carder, S. T. (1996). Viewers' recognition of brands placed within a film. *International Journal of Advertising*, *15*(2), 140–151.

Babrow, A. S., & Swanson, D. L. (1988). Disentangling antecedents of audience exposure levels: Extending expectancy-value analyses of gratifications sought from television news. *Communication Monographs*, *55*, 1–21. doi:10.1080/03637758809376155

Bagdikian, B. H. (2000). *The Media Monopoly*. Boston: Beacon Press.

Bagwell, C. L. Schmidt, Michelle. E., Newcomb, A. F. &., & Bukowski, W. M. (2001). Friendship and peer rejection as predictors of adult adjustment, In. In W. Damon, (series Ed.) and D. W. Nangle & C. A. Erdley (vol.Eds.)., *New directions for child and adolescent development: no.91. The role of friendship in psychology adjustment* (pp. 25-49). SF: San Francisco: Jossey-Bass.

Bailenson, J. N., Beall, A. C., Loomis, J., Blascovich, J., & Turk, M. (2005). Transformed social interaction, augmented gaze, and social influence in immersive virtual environments. *Human Communication Research*, *31*, 511–537. doi:10.1111/j.1468-2958.2005.tb00881.x

Baker, C. E. (2007). *Media Concentration and Democracy: Why Ownership Matters*. Cambridge, MA: Cambridge University Press.

Baker, W. E. (1999). When can affective conditioning and mere exposure directly influence brand choice? *Journal of Advertising*, *28*, 31–46.

Baker, M. J., & Churchill, G. A. Jr. (1977). The impact of physical attractive models on advertising evaluations. *JMR, Journal of Marketing Research*, *14*(4), 538–555. doi:10.2307/3151194

Baker, W. E., & Lutz, J. (1999). The relevance-accessibility model of advertising effectiveness. In Hecker, S. H., & Stewart, D. W. (Eds.), *Nonverbal Communication in Advertising* (pp. 59–84). Lexington, MA: Lexington Books.

Baker, C. (2006). What's all the Blog about? *The Washington Times*. Retrieved May 6, 2008, from http://www.washingtontimes.com/specialreports/20040814-114043-3023r.htm

Baker, S., & Heather, G. (2005, May 2). Blogs will Change Your Business. *Business Week*, 57-67.

Bakir, A., Blodgett, J. G., & Rose, G. M. (2008, June). Children's responses to gender-role stereotyped advertisements. *Journal of Advertising Research*, (June): 255–266. doi:10.2501/S002184990808029X

Bakos, Y. (1997). Reducing buyer search costs: Implications for electronic marketplaces. *Management Science*, *43*(12), 1676–1692. doi:10.1287/mnsc.43.12.1676

Bakos, Y., & Brynjolfsson, E. (1999, December). Bundling information goods: Pricing, profits, and efficiency. *Management Science*, *45*, 1613–1630. doi:10.1287/mnsc.45.12.1613

Balasubramanian, S. K., Karrh, J. A., & Patwardhan, H. (2006). Audience response to product placements: An integrative framework and future research agenda. *Journal of Advertising*, *35*(3), 115–141. doi:10.2753/JOA0091-3367350308

Bales, R. F. (1950). *Interaction process analysis. MA*. Reading, MA: Addison-Wesley.

Balkin, J. M., & Noveck, B. S. (Eds.). (2006). *The state of play: Law, games, and virtual worlds*. New York: New York University Press.

Ballard, M. E., & Lineberger, R. (1999). Video games and confederate gender: Effects on reward and punishment given by college males. *Sex Roles*, *41*, 541–558. doi:10.1023/A:1018843304606

Ballentyne, D., & Varey, R. J. (2006). Creating value-in-use through marketing interaction: The exchange logic of relating, communicating, and knowing. *Marketing Theory*, *6*(3), 335–348. doi:10.1177/1470593106066795

Balz, D., Kornblut, A., & Murray, S. (2008, January 4). Obama Wins Iowa's Democratic Caucuses. *The New York Time*. Retrieved June 7, 2008 from http://www.washingtonpost.com/wp-dyn/content/article/2008/01/03/AR2008010304441_pf.html

Bandura, A. (1986). *Social Foundations of Thought and Action: A Social Cognitive Theory*. Englewood Cliffs, NJ: Prentice Hall.

Bandura, A. (2001). Social cognitive theory of mass communication. *Media Psychology*, *3*, 265–299. doi:10.1207/S1532785XMEP0303_03

Bandura, A. (1997). *Self-efficacy: The Exercise of Control*. New York: W.H. Freeman.

Bang, H., & Reece, B. B. (2003). Minorities in children's television commercials: New improved, and stereotyped. *The Journal of Consumer Affairs*, *37*(1), 42–67.

Bangeman, E. (2008, January 24). Growth in gaming in 2007 far outpaces movies, music. *ARS Technica*. Retrieved May 30, 2008, from http://arstechnica.com/news.ars/post/20080124-growth-of-gaming-in-2007-far-outpaces-movies-music.html

Bao, Y., & Shao, A. T. (2002, June). Nonconformity advertising to teens. *Journal of Advertising Research*, (June): 56–65.

Baran, S. J. (2001). *Introduction to mass communication: Media literacy and culture*. Mountain View, CA: Mayfield.

Barbaro, M., & Zeller, T. (2006, August 9). A Face is Exposed for AOL Searcher No. 4417749. *The New York Times*. Retrieved June 15, 2009, from http://www.nytimes.com/2006/08/09/technology/09aol.html?ex=1312776000

Bargh, J. A., McKenna, K. Y., & Fitzsimons, G. M. (2002). Can you see the real me? Activation and expression of the "true self" on the Internet. *The Journal of Social Issues, 58*(1), 33–48. doi:10.1111/1540-4560.00247

Bargh, J. A. (2001). The psychology of the mere. In Bargh, J. A., & Apsley, D. K. (Eds.), *Unraveling the Complexities of Social Life* (pp. 25–37). Washington, DC: American Psychology Association. doi:10.1037/10387-003

Barlow, A. K. J., Siddiqui, N. Q., & Mannion, M. (2004). Developments in information and communication technologies for retail marketing channels. *International Journal of Retail & Distribution Management, 32*(2/3), 157–163. doi:10.1108/09590550410524948

Barnard, L., Yi, J. S., Jacko, J. A., & Sears, A. (2007). Capturing the effects of context on human performance in mobile computing systems. *Personal and Ubiquitous Computing, 11*(2), 81–96. doi:10.1007/s00779-006-0063-x

Barnes, S. (2007). Virtual worlds as a medium for advertising. *The Data Base for Advances in Information Systems, 38*(4), 45–55.

Barry, T. E. (2002). In defense of the hierarchy of effects: A rejoinder to weilbacher. *Journal of Advertising Research, 42*(3), 44–47.

Barry, T. E., & Howard, D. (1990). A review and critique of the hierarchy of effects in advertising. *International Journal of Advertising, 9*(2), 121–135.

Barry, T. (1987). The Development of the Hierarchy of Effects, An Historical Perspective. In Leigh, J. H., & Martin, C. R. (Eds.), *Current Issues and Research in Advertising* (pp. 251–295). Ann Arbor, MI: University of Michigan.

Bartle, R. (1990). *Early MUD history.* Retrieved from http://www.mud.co.uk/richard/mudhist.htm

Bartle, R. A. (2006). Why governments aren't gods and gods aren't governments. *First Monday.* Retrieved March 1. 2008. from http://firstmonday.org/issues/special11_9/bartle/

Bass, F. M. (1969). A new product growth model for consumer durables. *Management Science, 15*(January), 215–227. doi:10.1287/mnsc.15.5.215

Bauman, Z. (1995). *Life in fragments: essays in postmodern morality.* Oxford, UK: Basil Blackwell.

Baylor, A. L., & Kim, Y. (2003). *The role of gender and ethnicity in pedagogical agent perception.* Paper presented at the E-Learn (World Conference on E-Learning in Corporate, Government, Healthcare, & Higher Education), Phoenix, AZ. Retrieved July 8, 2004 from http://pals.fsu.edu/publications.html.

Baylor, A. L., Shen, E., & Huang, X. (2003). *Which pedagogical agent do learners choose? The effects of gender and ethnicity.* Paper presented at the E-Learn (World Conference on E-Learning in Corporate, Government, Healthcare, & Higher Education), Phoenix, AZ.

Baym, N. K., Zhang, Y. B., & Lin, M. C. (2004). Social interactions across media. *New Media & Society, 6*(3), 299–318. doi:10.1177/1461444804041438

Baym, N. (1998). The emergency of online community. In Jobes, S. G. (Ed.), *Cybersociety 2.0.* Thousand Oaks, CA: Sage.

BBC. (2004). *'Blog' Picked as Word of the Year.* Retrieved September 18, 2007, from http://news.bbc.co.uk/1/hi/technology/4059291.stm

BBC. (2005). *News Corporation in $580m Internet Buy.* Retrieved on September 1, 2008, from http://news.bbc.co.uk/1/hi/business/4695495.stm.

Beal, B. (2004). Are RSS Feeds the Next Great Marketing Tool? *SearchCRM.com.* Retrieved May 14, 2008, from http://searchcrm.techtarget/com/originalcontent/0,289142.sid//gci1017317,00.html

Beane, T. P., & Ennis, D. M. (1987). Market segmentation: A review. *European Journal of Marketing, 21*(5), 20–43. doi:10.1108/EUM0000000004695

Beattie, A. E., & Mitchell, A. A. (1985). The relationship between advertising recall and persuasion: An experimental investigation. In Alwitt, L. F., & Mitchell, A. A. (Eds.), *Psychological processes and advertising effects* (pp. 129–155). Hillsdale, NJ: Erlbaum.

Beckman, R. (2008, September 3). Facebook Ads Target You Where it Hurts. *Washington Post,* C01. Retrieved from http://www.washingtonpost.com/wp-dyn/content/article/2008/09/02/AR2008090202956.html

Bee-Gates, D. (2006). *"I want it": navigating childhood in a materialistic world.* London: Palgrave-MacMillan.

Beer, D. (2008). Social Network(ing) sites…revisiting the story so far: a response to danah boyd & Nicole Ellison. *Journal of Computer-Mediated Communication, 13,* 252–275. doi:10.1111/j.1083-6101.2008.00408.x

Belch, G. E., & Belch, M. A. (2001). *Advertising and promotion: An integrated marketing communications perspective* (5th ed.). New York: McGraw-Hill Irwin.

Belch, G. E., Ceresino, G., & Belch, M. A. (1985). Parental and teenage child influences in family decision making. *Journal of Business Research, 13,* 163–176. doi:10.1016/0148-2963(85)90038-4

Belk, R. W. (1988, September). Possessions and extended self. *The Journal of Consumer Research, 15*(September), 139–168. doi:10.1086/209154

Bell, G. D. (1967). Self-confidence and persuasion in car buying. *JMR, Journal of Marketing Research, 4*(1), 46–52. doi:10.2307/3150163

Bellamy, R. V. Jr, & Traudt, P. J. (2000). Television branding as promotion. In Eastman, S. T. (Ed.), *Research in media promotion* (pp. 127–159). Mahwah, NJ: Lawrence Erlbaum Publishing.

Bellamy, R. V. Jr. (1998). The evolving television sports marketplace. In Wenner, L. A. (Ed.), *Mediasport* (pp. 73–87). London: Routledge.

Belsky, J., Steinberg, L., & Draper, P. (1991). Childhood experience, interpersonal development, and reproductive strategy: an evolutionary theory of socialization. *Child Development, 62*, 647–670. doi:10.2307/1131166

Belson, W. A. (1966). The effects of reversing the presentation order of verbal rating scales. *Journal of Advertising Research, 6*, 30–37.

Bendapudi, N., & Leone, R. P. (2003). Psychological implications of customer participation in co-production. *Journal of Marketing, 67*(1), 14–28. doi:10.1509/jmkg.67.1.14.18592

Benedicktus, R. L., & Andrews, M. L. (2006). Building trust with consensus information: The effects of valence and sequence direction. *Journal of Interactive Advertising, 6*(2), 17–29.

Beniger, J. (1987). Personalization of mass media and the growth of pseudo-community. *Communication Research, 14*(3), 352. doi:10.1177/009365087014003005

Benjamin, W. (1978). *Reflection* (Demetz, P., Ed.). New York: Hartcourt, Brace, Jovanovich.

Benkler, Y. (2006). *The wealth of networks: How social production transforms markets and freedom*. New Haven, CT: Yale University Press.

Bennett, L. R. (2000). Sex talk, Indonesian youth and HIV/AIDS. *Development Bulletin Australian Development Studies Network, 52*, 54–57.

Bennett, G., Ferreira, M., Siders, R., Tsuji, Y., & Cianfrone, B. (2006, October). Analysing the effects of advertising type and antecedents on attitude towards advertising in sport. *International Journal of Sports Marketing & Sponsorship, 8*(1), 62–81.

Bennett, R. (1999). Sports sponsorship, spectator recall and false consensus. *European Journal of Marketing, 33*, 291–313. doi:10.1108/03090569910253071

Bennett, W. L. (2003). Communicating global activism: Strengths and vulnerabilities of networked politics. *Information Communication and Society, 6*, 143–168. doi:10.1080/1369118032000093860

Benoit, W. L., & Benoit, P. J. (2000). The virtual campaign: Presidential primary websites in campaign 2000. *American Journal of Communication, 3*(3).

Benton, J. E., & Daniel, P. L. (1996). Learning to talk about taboo topics: A first step in examining cultural diversity with preservice teachers. *Equity & Excellence in Education, 29*(3), 8–17. doi:10.1080/1066568960290303

Benway, J. P., & Lane, D. M. (1998 December). Banner Blindness: Web Searchers Often Miss Obvious Links. *ITG Newsletter, 1*(3). Retrieved from http://www.internettg.org/newsletter/dec98/banner_blindness.html

Berg A. (1997, January 17). op. cit., NPR, Talk of the Nation Science Friday, Transcript # 97011702-211, available on Lexis/Nexis computerized database service.

Berger, C. R., & Chaffee, S. H. (1987). The study of communication as a science. In Berger, C. R., & Chaffee, S. H. (Eds.), *Handbook of communication science* (pp. 15–19). Newbury Park, CA: Sage.

Berger, K. S. (2006). *The developing person: through childhood and adolescence* (7th ed.). N.Y.: New York: Worth Publishers., 7th ed.

Berkowitz, D. (2008, July 17). The Chutzpah of Facebook's 'Jewdar. www.mediapost.com. Retrieved June 15, 2009, from http://www.mediapost.com/publications/?fa=Articles.showArticle&art_aid=86800

Berndt, T. J., & Murphy, L. M. (2002). Influences of friends and friendships: myths, truths, and research recommendations. In R. V. Kail (Ed.), *Advances in child development and behavior*, (vVol. 30, (pp. pp. 275-310). San Diego, CA: Academic Press.

Bernieri, F., Davis, J., Rosenthal, R., & Knee, C. (1994). Interactional synchrony and rapport: Measuring synchrony in displays devoid of sound and facial affect. *Personality and Social Psychology Bulletin, 20*, 303–311. doi:10.1177/0146167294203008

Bernstein, M. (1997). Celebration and suppression: The strategic uses of identity by the Lesbian and Gay movement. *American Journal of Sociology, 103*, 531–565. doi:10.1086/231250

Bernstein, A. (2002) Boom! TV advances could disappear–without funding, next wave of innovation might not even make it to screen. *Sports Business Journal*, 17.

Best, N. (2010, February 9). Super Bowl new king of TV. *New York Newsday*, A5.

Better Breastfeeding, Healthier Lives: Women with HIV Face Crucial Breastfeeding Decisions. (n.d.). Population Reports. Retrieved February 18, 2009, from http://www.infoforhealth.org/pr/l14/7.shtml

Bhatnaghar, N., & Wan, F. (2009). *Dual Impacts of Self-Character Similarity: The Moderating Role of Narrative Immersion on Product Placement Effects.* Working paper, Asper School of Business, University of Manitoba.

Bianco, A. (2004, July 12). The vanishing mass market: New technology. Product proliferation. Fragmented media. Get ready: It's a whole new world. *Business Week*, 61-68.

Bickart, B., & Schindler, R. M. (2001). Internet forums as influential sources of consumer information. *Journal of Interactive Marketing, 15*(3), 31–40. doi:10.1002/dir.1014

Bierma, N. (2002). Our Online Diarist Finds it Easy to Get Lost in the Blog. *Chicago Tribune.* Retrieved May 2, 2008, from http://www.chicagotribune.com/search/dispatcher.front?Query=weblogs&target=article

Bimber, B. (1999). The internet and citizen communication with government: Does the medium matter? *Political Communication, 16*(4), 409–428. doi:10.1080/105846099198569

Bimber, B. (2000). The study of information technology and civic engagement. *Political Communication, 17*(4), 329–333. doi:10.1080/10584600050178924

Bimber, B. (2001). Information and political engagement in America: The search for effects of information technology at the individual level. *Political Research Quarterly, 54*(1), 53–67.

Bimber, B. (2003). *Information and American Democracy: Technology in the Evolution of Political Power.* Cambridge, UK: Cambridge University Press. doi:10.1017/CBO9780511615573

Bimber, B., Flanagin, A., & Stohl, C. (2005). Reconceptualizing collective action in the contemporary media environment. *Communication Theory, 15*(4), 365–388. doi:10.1111/j.1468-2885.2005.tb00340.x

Bimber, B. (1998). The Internet and political mobilization: Research note on the 1996 election season. *Social Science Computer Review, 16*(4), 391–401. doi:10.1177/089443939801600404

Biocca, F., Harms, C., & Burgoon, J. K. (2003). Toward a more robust theory and measure of social presence: Review and suggested criteria. *Presence (Cambridge, Mass.), 12*(5), 456–480. doi:10.1162/105474603322761270

Bio-Medicine. (2005). *Youth becoming sexually active at a younger age.* Retrieved January 20, 2009, from http://www.bio-medicine.org/medicine-news/Youth-Becoming-Sexually-Active-At-A-Younger-Age-5886-1/

Biswas, R. (2003). India's youth programs to combat AIDS must be diverse and widespread. *Population Reference Bureau.* Retrieved January 20, 2009, from http://www.prb.org/Articles/2003/IndiasYouthProgramstoCombat AIDSMustBeDiverseandWidespread.aspx

Bizzell, P., & Herzbeg, B. (2000). *The rhetorical tradition: Readings from the classical times to the present.* Bedford, NY: St. Martin's.

Björnberg, A. (2000). Structural relationships of music and images in music videos. In Middleton, R. (Ed.), *Reading Pop - Approaches to textual analysis in popular music* (pp. 347–378). Oxford, UK: Oxford University Press.

Blackmon, W. D. (1994). Dungeons and dragons: The use of a fantasy game in the psychotherapeutic treatment of a young adult. *American Journal of Psychotherapy, 48*, 624–632.

Blackshaw, P. (2005, June 25). The Pocket Guide to Consumer-Generated Media. *The ClickZ network.* Retrieved June 20, 2008, from http://www.clickz.com/showPage.html?page=3515576

Blackwell, R. D., Miniard, P. W., & Engel, J. F. (2001). *Consumer Behavior.* Ft. Worth, TX: Harcourt College Publishers.

Blascovich, J., Loomis, J., Beall, A., Swinth, K., Hoyt, C., & Bailenson, J. (2002). Immersive virtual environment technology as a research tool for social psychology. *Psychological Inquiry, 13*, 103–125. doi:10.1207/S15327965PLI1302_01

Blizzard.com. (2008). *World of Warcraft reaches new milestone: 10 million subscribers.* Retrieved January 22, 2008, from http://eu.blizzard.com/en/press/080122.html

Blumler, J. G., & Katz, E. (1974). *The uses of mass communications: Current perspectives on gratifications research.* Beverly Hills, CA: Sage.

Bogost, I. (2007). *Persuasive games: The expressive power of videogames.* Cambridge, MA: The MIT Press.

Bogost, I. (2005, June 11). Beer, nudity, and Pac-Man. *Water Cooler Games.* Retrieved August 20, 2008 from http://www.watercoolergames.org/archives/000416.shtml

Bolter, J. D., & Grusin, R. (1999). *Remediation. Understanding New Media.* Cambridge, MA: The MIT Press.

Boneva, B., Quinn, A., Kraut, R., Kiesler, S., & Shklovski, I. (2006). Teenage communication in instant messaging era, In. In

R. Kraut, M. Brynin and & S. Kiesler (Eds.). *Computers, Phones and the Internet: domesticating information Technology* (pp. 201-218). NY: New York: Oxford University Press.

Boorstin, D. J. (1974). *The Americans: The Democratic Experience*. New York: Vintage.

Bornstein, R. F. (1989). Exposure and affect: Overview and meta-analysis of research, 1968-1987. *Psychological Bulletin, 106*, 265–289. doi:10.1037/0033-2909.106.2.265

Bornstein, R. F., & D'Agostino, P. R. (1992). Stimulus recognition and the mere exposure effect. *Journal of Personality and Social Psychology, 63*, 545. doi:10.1037/0022-3514.63.4.545

Botermans, J., Burrett, T., Van Delft, P., & Van Splunteren, C. (1989). *The World of Games: Their Origins and History, How to Play Them and How to Make Them*. New York: Facts on File, Inc.

Boulos, K. M. N., Lee, H., & Wheeler, S. (2007). Second Life: An overview of the potential of 3-D virtual worlds in medical and health education. *Health Information and Libraries Journal, 24*, 233–245. doi:10.1111/j.1471-1842.2007.00733.x

Bowker, A., Bukowski, W., Zargarpour, S., & Hoza, B. (1998). A structural and functional analysis of a two-dimensional model of social isolation. *Merrill-Palmer Quarterly, 44*(4), 447–463.

Bowlby, J. (1969). *Attachment and loss: Attachment. (vVol. 1)*. Harmondsworth, UK: Penguin.

Bowman, L. L., Levine, L. E., Waite, B. M., & Gendron, M. (2010). Can students really multitask? An experimental study of instant messaging while reading. *Computers & Education, 54*, 927–931. doi:10.1016/j.compedu.2009.09.024

Boyd, D. M., & Ellison, N. B. (2007). Social network sites: Definition, history and scholarship. *Journal of Computer-Mediated Communication, 12*(1). Retrieved from http://jcmc.indiana.edu/vol13/issue1/boyd.ellison.html.

Bracken, C. C. (2007). *That was a great ad: The impact of high definition television commercials on audiences' attitudes toward brands*. Presented to the second annual Persuasive Conference, Stanford, CA.

Bradlow, E. T., & Schmittlein, D. C. (2000). The little engines that could: Modeling the performance of World Wide Web search engines. *Marketing Science, 19*(1), 43–62. doi:10.1287/mksc.19.1.43.15180

Branco, P., Firth, P., Encanacao, L. M., & Bonato, P. (2005). *Faces of Emotion in Human-Computer Interaction.* Paper presented at the CHI 2005, Portland, Oregon, USA.

Brandt, M., & Johnson, G. (1997). *Power Branding: Building Technology Brands for Competitive Advantage*. Newtonville, MA: International Data Group.

Bransford, J., Brown, A. L., & Cocking, R. R. (Eds.). (1999). *How people learn: Brain, mind, experience, and school*. Washington, DC: National Academy Press.

Breakwell, G. M. (1986). *Coping with threatened identities*. London: Methuen.

Brewer, M. B. (1991). The social self: On being the same and different at the same time. *Personality and Social Psychology Bulletin, 17*, 475–482. doi:10.1177/0146167291175001

Bridge, F. (1921). *The old cryes of London*. London: Novello.

Briggs, R., & Hollis, N. (1997). Advertising on the Web: Is there response before click-through? *Journal of Advertising Research, 3*(2), 33–45.

Brin, S., Motwani, R., Page, L., & Winograd, T. (1998). What can you do with a Web in your pocket? *IEEE Data Eng. Bull., 21*, 37–47.

Brin, S. (1998). Extracting Patterns and Relations from the World Wide Web. *WebDB*, 172-183.

Brin, S., & Page, L. (1998). The Anatomy of a Large-Scale Hypertextual Web Search Engine. *Computer Networks and ISDN Systems, 30*(1-7), 107-117.

Brint, S. (2001). Gemeinshaft revisited: A critique and reconstruction of the community concept. *Sociological Theory, 12*(1).

British Library. (n.d.). Retrieved from http://www.bl.uk/reshelp/findhelprestype/news/index.html

Brito, P. Q. (2008). *Conceptualizing and illustrating the digital lifestyle of youth*. Working Paper no. 300. Faculdade de Economia - Universidade do Porto. Portugal.

Brodie, C., Karat, C., & Karat, J. (2004). Creating an E-Commerce Environment where Consumers are Willing to Share Personal Information. In Karat, C., Blom, J. O., & Karat, J. (Eds.), *Designing Personalized User Experiences in eCommerce*. Dordrecht, The Netherlands: Kluwer Academic Publishers. doi:10.1007/1-4020-2148-8_11

Broitman, A., & Tatar, J. (2008, May 30). How to reach real people in a virtual world. *iMedia Connection*. Retrieved July 7, 2008, from http://www.imediaconnection.com/content/19487.asp

Bronack, S., Riedl, R., Tashner, J., & Greene, M. (2006). Learning in the zone: A social constructivist framework for distance education in a 3D virtual world. In. *Proceedings of Society for*

Information Technology and Teacher Education International Conference, 2006, 268–275.

Brown, D. R. (2000). Editor's note. *GAIN: AIGA Journal of Design for the Network Economy, 1*(1), 2–3.

Brown, S. L., Tilton, A., & Woodside, D. M. (2002). The case for online communities. *The McKinsey Quarterly, 1*, 11.

Brown, J. J., & Reingen, P. H. (1987). Social ties and word-of-mouth referral behavior. *The Journal of Consumer Research, 14*(November), 350–362. doi:10.1086/209118

Brown, D. (1997). *Cybertrend*. London: Viking.

Brown, S. P., & Stayman, D. M. (1992). Antecedents and consequences of attitude toward the ad: A meta-analysis. *The Journal of Consumer Research, 19*(1), 34–51. doi:10.1086/209284

Brown, E. (2006). *Product Placement on the Rise in Video Games: Marketers Desperate to Engage well-to-do market of 132 Million Gamers.* Retrieved from http://www.msnbc.msn.com/id/13960083/

Bruner, G. C., & Kumar, A. (2000). Web commercials and advertising hierarchy-of-effects. *Journal of Advertising Research, 40*(1/2), 35–42.

Bryant, J. A., Jackson, A. S., & Smallwood, A. M. K. (2006). IMing, text messaging, and adolescent social networks. *Journal of Computer-Mediated Communication, 11*, 577–592. doi:10.1111/j.1083-6101.2006.00028.x

Bryant, J. B., & Miron, D. (2006). Historical context and trends in the development of communication theory. In Whaley, B. B., & Samter, W. (Eds.), *Explaining Communication: Contemporary Theories and Exemplars*. Mahwah, NJ: Erlbaum.

Bryant, J., & Raney, A. A. (2000). Sports on the screen. In Zillman, D., & Vorderer, P. (Eds.), *Media Entertainment: The Psychology of Its Appeal* (pp. 153–174). Mahwah, NJ: Lawrence Erlbaum.

Buckingham, D. (2007). That's edutainment. New media, marketing and education in the home, In. In K. M. Ekström and & B. Tufte. (Eds.), *Children, media and consumption* (pp. 33-46). Gothenburg, Sweden: Nordicom.

Buckler, G. (2009). Businesses tap new markets with social media: Twitter, blogs and Facebook are becoming enterprise tools in their own right. *Special small business, business, Technology.* Retrieved from http://www6.lexisnexis.com/publisher/EndUser?Action=UserDisplayFullDocument&orgId=101735&topicId=101800040&docId=l:952641936&start=5

Buckley, S. (2008). *The Internet killed the video store: New options emerge to obtain video content.* Retrieved from http://www.telecommagazine.com/article.asp?HH_ID=AR_3884

Bucy, E. P., & Tao, C. C. (2007). The mediated moderation model of interactivity. *Media Psychology, 9*, 647–672.

Buijzen, M., & Mens, C. (2007). Adult mediation of television advertising effects: a comparison of factual, evaluative, and combined strategies. *Journal of Children and Media, 1*(2), 177–191. doi:10.1080/17482790701339233

Bulik, B. (2008, May 5). Is your consumer using social media? [from Communication & Mass Media Complete database.]. *Advertising Age, 79*(18), 12–13. Retrieved September 4, 2008.

Burger, J. M., & Cooper, H. M. (1979). The desirability of control. *Motivation and Emotion, 3*(4), 381–393. doi:10.1007/BF00994052

Burger, J. M. (1984). Desirability of control, locus of control and proneness to depression. *Journal of Personality, 52*, 71–89. doi:10.1111/j.1467-6494.1984.tb00551.x

Burger, J. M. (1985). Desirability of control and achievement-related behaviors. *Journal of Personality and Social Psychology, 48*(6), 1520–1533. doi:10.1037/0022-3514.48.6.1520

Burger, J. M. (1992). Desirability of control and academic performance. *Canadian Journal of Behavioural Science, 24*(2), 147–155. doi:10.1037/h0078716

Burger, J. M., & Cooper, H. M. (1979). The desirability of control. *Motivation and Emotion, 3*(4), 381–393. doi:10.1007/BF00994052

Burgi, M. (1997, February 10). TV exec. sees virtual signs. *Mediaweek, 7*(6), 13.

Burke, R. (2002). Hybrid recommender systems: Survey and experiments. *User Modeling and User-Adapted Interaction, 12*(4), 331–370. doi:10.1023/A:1021240730564

Burke, K. (2008, May 1). E-commerce link: Humanizing the Web. *Target Marketing*. Retrieved August 6, 2008, from http://www.targetmarketingmag.com/story/reprints.bsp?sid=95879&var=story

Burnett, K. F., Magel, P. E., Harrington, S., & Taylor, C. B. (1989). Computerized assisted behavioral health counseling for high school students. *Journal of Counseling Psychology, 36*(1), 63–67. doi:10.1037/0022-0167.36.1.63

Burns, R. B. (1979). *The Self-Concept: Theory, Measurement, Development, and Behavior*. New York: Longman.

Burns, K. S., & Lutz, R. J. (2006). The function of format: Consumer responses to six online advertising formats. *Journal of Advertising, 35*(1), 53–63. doi:10.2753/JOA0091-3367350104

Burns, K. S., & Lutz, R. J. (2008). Web users' perceptions of and attitudes toward online advertising formats. *International Journal of Internet Marketing and Advertising, 4*(4), 281–301. doi:10.1504/IJIMA.2008.019150

Burns, E. (2005). Nike iD steps into NBA 2K6. *The ClickZ Network.* Retrieved August 12, 2008 from http://www.clickz.com/showPage.html?page=3552726.

Burns, N. (2008). *Barfly Channels: Media engagement and measurement at the point of consumption.* Retrieved from http://www.archive.org/details/Media_Engagement_And_Measurement

Burns, N. M. (2008). *Establishing cost and effectiveness rationale for digital out of home media* (White Paper). Barfly Networks.

Burns, N. M. (2009, April). *In-store Persuasive Technologies.* Presented at Persuasive Technology 2009 Meeting, Claremont College, USA.

Buroker, J. (2009, April 1). Use online social networks to market your company. *Wisconsin State Journal, 22.*

Burton Snowboards. (n.d.). Retrieved from http://www.burton.com

Business Week. (2006). The Future of the Blog. *Business Week Online.* Retrieved February 18, 2008, from http://www.businessweek.com/print/innovte/content/feb2006/id20060224_155318.html

BuyMMOAccounts.com. (n.d.) Retrieved February 10, 2009, from http://www.buymmoaccounts.com

Byrn, E. (1999). *Altavista History.* Retrieved from March 13, 2008, http://www.clubi.ie/webserch/engines/altavist/history.htm

Cacioppo, J. T., & Petty, R. E. (1982). The need for cognition. *Journal of Personality and Social Psychology, 42*(1), 116–131. doi:10.1037/0022-3514.42.1.116

Campbell, M. C., & Kirmani, A. (2000, June). Consumers' use of persuasion knowledge: The effects of accessibility and cognitive capacity on perceptions of an influence agent. *The Journal of Consumer Research, 27,* 69–83. doi:10.1086/314309

Campbell, R. (2006). Teenage girls and cellular phones: discourse of independence, safety and 'rebellion.'. *Journal of Youth Studies, 9*(2), 195–212. doi:10.1080/13676260600635649

Campbell, S. (2008). Mobile technology and the body: apparatgeist, fashion, and function. In Katz, J. E. (Ed.), *Handbook of Mobile Communication Studies* (pp. 153–164). Cambridge, MA: MIT Press.

Caplan, J. (2008, June 30). The Citizen Watchdogs of Web 2.0. *Time.* Retrieved November 18, 2008, from http://www.time.com/time/business/article/0,8599,1819187,00.html

Captivate. (n.d.). Retrieved from http://www.captivate.com

Carlin, D. (2006, November 14). Can Daily Motion Challenge YouTube? *BusinessWeek.com.* Retrieved April 1, 2008, from http://www.businessweek.com/globalbiz/content/nov2006/gb20061114_086712.htm?chan=search

Carlson, E. A., Sroufe, L. A., & Byron, E. (2004). The construction of experience: a longitudinal study of representation and behavior. *Child Development, 75,* 66–83. doi:10.1111/j.1467-8624.2004.00654.x

Carlton, D. W., & Perloff, J. M. (2005). *Modern Industrial Organization* (4th ed.). New York: Addison-Wesley.

Carr, D. (2008, November 10). How Obama Tapped Into Social Networks' Power. *New York Times.* Retrieved November 11, 2008, from http://www.nytimes.com/2008/11/10/business/media/10carr.html?scp=24&sq=&st=nyt Carroll, W., & Hackett, R. (2006). Democratic Media Activism through the Lens of Social Movement Theory. *Media, Culture & Society, 28,* 83-104.

Carter, S. (Ed.). (2006). In *Historical statistics of the United States* (Millennial Ed.). Cambridge, UK: Cambridge University Press.

Cassell, J., & Bickmore, T. (2000). External manifestations of trustworthiness in the interface. *Communications of the ACM, 43*(12), 50–56. doi:10.1145/355112.355123

Cassidy, J. (2006). Me media: How hanging out on the Internet became big business. *New Yorker (New York, N.Y.), 82*(13), 50.

Cassidy, W. (2002, December 17). Top 10 gaming grails. *GameSpy.* Retrieved August 18, 2008, from http://archive.gamespy.com/top10/december02/grails/

Castells, M. (2000). *The Rise of the Network Society* (2nd ed.). Malden, MA: Blackwell Publishing.

Castronova, E. (2002). On virtual economies. *CESifo Working Paper No. 752. Category 9: Industrial Organization (July),* 1-39. Retrieved from http://ssrn.com/abstract_id=338500

Caudill, E. M., & Murphy, P. E. (2000). Consumer online privacy: Legal and ethical issues. *Journal of Public Policy & Marketing, 19*(1), 7–19. doi:10.1509/jppm.19.1.7.16951

Cavall, E. (2008, May 19). 90 Percent of Business-Launched Virtual Worlds Fail. *Wired*. Retrieved May 19, 2008, from http://www.wired.com

CBSNews. (2008). *Nielsen: 'Obama text' reached 2.9 million* [Electronic Version]. Retrieved August 27, 2008, from http://www.cbsnews.com/stories/2008/08/26/tech/cnettechnews/main4384289.shtml.

Celsi, R. L., & Olson, J. C. (1988). The role of involvement in attention and comprehension processes. *The Journal of Consumer Research, 15*(2), 210–224. doi:10.1086/209158

Census of India. Census Data. (2001). *Literacy Rate: India–Part 3.* Retrieved from http://www.censusindia.net/ results/provindia3.html

Chadha, M. (2007 April). Indian state bans sex education. *BBC News*. Retrieved January 20, 2009, from http://news.bbc.co.uk/2/hi/south_asia/6523371.stm

Chaffee, S. H., & Metzger, M. J. (2001). The end of mass communication? *Mass Communication & Society, 4*(4), 365–379. doi:10.1207/S15327825MCS0404_3

Chaffee, S. (1975). *Political communication.* Beverly Hills, CA: Sage Publication.

Chakrabarti, D., Agarwal, D., & Josifovski, V. (2008). Contextual Advertising by Combining Relevance with Click Feedback. In *Search: Ranking & Retrieval Enhancement, International World Wide Web Conference Committee (IW3C2)*, April 21–25, 2008, Beijing, China.

Chan, E., & Vorderer, P. (2006). Massively multiplayer online games. In Vorderer, P., & Bryant, J. (Eds.), *Playing video games: Motives, responses, and consequences* (pp. 181–194). Mahwah, NJ: Lawrence Erlbaum Associates, Inc.

Chandler, M. J., Lalonde, C. E., Sokol, B. W., Bryan, W. & ., & Hallet, D. (2003). Personal persistence, identity development and suicide: a study of native and non-native North American adolescents. Monographs of the Society for research. *Child Development, 68*(2), serial n°273.

Chandon, J. L., Chtourou, M. S., & Fortin, D. R. (2003, June). Effects of configuration and exposure levels on responses to Web advertisements. *Journal of Advertising Research*, 217–222.

Chandran, S., & Morwitz, V. G. (2005, September). Effects of participative pricing on consumers' cognitions and actions: A goal theoretic perspective. *The Journal of Consumer Research, 32*, 249–259. doi:10.1086/432234

Chaney, I. M., Lin, K.-H., & Chaney, J. (2004). The effect of billboards within the gaming environment. *Journal of Interactive Media, 5*(1), 54–69.

Chang, H. H., & Wang, I. C. (2008). An investigation of user communication behavior in computer mediated environments. *Computers in Human Behavior, 24*(5), 2336–2356. doi:10.1016/j.chb.2008.01.001

Chang, Y., & Thorson, E. (2004). Television and Web advertising synergies. *Journal of Advertising, 33*(2), 75–84.

Changchien, W. S., Lee, C.-F., & Hsu, Y.-J. (2004, July). Online personalized sales promotion in electronic commerce. *Expert Systems with Applications, 27*(1), 35–52. doi:10.1016/j.eswa.2003.12.017

Charles, G. (2006, September 27). Audi Hunts Music Ties for Podcasts to Support TT. *Marketing*, 5.

Charlton, T., Panting, C., & Hannan, A. (2002). Mobile telephone ownership and usage among 10- and 11 year-olds: participation and exclusion. *Emotional & Behavioural Difficulties, 7*(3), 152–163.

Chatterjee, P., Hoffman, D. L., & Novak, T. P. (2003). Modeling the clickstream: Implications for web-based advertising efforts. *Marketing Science, 22*(4), 520–541. doi:10.1287/mksc.22.4.520.24906

Chatterjee, P. (2001). Online reviews: Do consumers use them? *Advances in Consumer Research. Association for Consumer Research (U. S.), 28*, 129–133.

Chatterjee, P., Hoffman, D. L., & Novak, T. P. (2003, October). Modeling the clickstream: implications for Web-based advertising efforts. *Marketing Science, 22*(4), 520–541. doi:10.1287/mksc.22.4.520.24906

Chen, J., Shohamy, D., Ross, V., Reeves, B., & Wagner, A. D. (in press). The impact of social belief on the neurophysiology of learning and memory. *Journal of the Society for Neuroscience.*

Cheng, L., Farnham, S., & Stone, L. (2002). Lessons learned: Building and deploying shared virtual environments. In Schroeder, R. (Ed.), *The social life of avatars: Presence and interaction in shared virtual environments* (pp. 90–111). London: Springer Verlag.

Cheong, H. J., & Morrison, M. A. (2008). Consumers' reliance on product information and recommendations found in UGC. *Journal of Interactive Advertising, 8*(2). Retrieved July 30, 2008, from http://www.jiad.org/article103

Chiou, J., & Cheng, C. (2003). Should a company have message boards on its websites? *Journal of Interactive Marketing, 17*(3), 50–61. doi:10.1002/dir.10059

Chiu, H., Hsieh, Y., Kao, Y., & Lee, M. (2007). The determinants of e-mail receivers' disseminating behaviors on the Internet. *Journal of Advertising Research, 47*(4), 524–534. doi:10.2501/S0021849907070547

Cho, C. (2003). Factors influencing the clicking of banner ads on the WWW. *Cyberpsychology & Behavior, 6*(2), 201–215. doi:10.1089/109493103321640400

Cho, C.-H., & Cheon, H. J. (2004). Why do people avoid advertising on the Internet? *Journal of Advertising, 33*(4), 89–97.

Cho, C.-H. (2003). The effectiveness of banner advertisements: involvement and click-through. *Journalism & Mass Communication Quarterly, 80*(3), 623–645.

Cho, C.-H., & Leckenby, J. D. (1997). Internet-related programming technology and advertising. In M. C. Macklin (Ed.), *Proceedings of the 1997 Conference of the American Academy of Advertising* (pp. 69). Cincinnati, OH: American Academy of Advertising.

Cho, C.-H., & Leckenby, J. D. (1999). Interactivity as a measure of advertising effectiveness: Antecedents and consequences of interactivity in Web advertising. In M. S. Roberts (Ed.), *Proceedings of the 1999 Conference of the American Academy of Advertising* (pp. 162-179). Gainesville, FL: American Academy of Advertising.

Cho, Y. S., Yong-Sauk, H., & Jae-Chase, P. (2002). The DN Grid Model for E-Positioning in E-Business Environment. In *International Academy of E-Business Conference Proceedings*, Las Vegas, NE (pp. 46-49).

Choi, D., & Kim, J. (2004). Why people continue to play online games: In search of critical design factors to increase customer loyalty to online contents. *Cyberpsychology & Behavior, 7*, 11–24. doi:10.1089/109493104322820066

Chowdhury, M. M., Finn, A., & Olsen, G. D. (2007). Investigating the simultaneous presentation of advertising and television programming. *Journal of Advertising, 36*, 85–96. doi:10.2753/JOA0091-3367360306

Christ, P. E., & Peele, C. A. (2008). Virtual worlds: Personal jurisdiction and click-wrap licenses. *Intellectual Property & Technology Law Journal, 20*(1), 1–6.

Christopher, L. (2008, March 20). Advertisers Go Net Native. *Seybold Report: Analyzing Publishing Technologies, 8*(6), 5-14. Retrieved September 4, 2008, from Academic Search Premier database. comScore. (2006). *Social networking sites continue to attract record numbers as Myspace.com surpasses 50 Million U.S. visitors in May*. Retrieved March 13, 2008 from http://www.comscore.com/press/release.asp?press=906

Chung, D. (2005). Something for nothing: Understanding purchasing behaviors in virtual environments. *Cyberpsychology & Behavior, 8*, 538–554. doi:10.1089/cpb.2005.8.538

Cialdini, R. B. (2008). *Influence: Science and Practice*. Needham Heights, MA: Allyn & Bacon.

Cianfrone, B., Bennett, G., Siders, R., & Tsuji, Y. (2006). Virtual advertising and brand awareness. *International Journal of Sport Management and Marketing, 1*(4), 289–310.

Cichocki, M. (2007). HIV Around the World–India. *About.com*. Retrieved March 14, 2009, from http://aids.about.com/od/clinicaltrials/a/india.htm

Claeson, M., & Alexander, A. (2008, July). Tackling HIV In India: Evidence-based priority setting and programming. *Health Affairs, 27*(4), 1091–1102. doi:10.1377/hlthaff.27.4.1091

Clary, E. G., Snyder, M., Ridge, R., Copeland, J., Stukas, A., Haugen, J., & Miene, P. (1998). Understanding and assessing the motivations of volunteers: A functional approach. *Journal of Personality and Social Psychology, 74*(6), 1516–1530. doi:10.1037/0022-3514.74.6.1516

Clemmons, L., & Coulibaly, Y. (2000). Turning the ordinary into the extraordinary: The green pendelu and maternal health in Mali. *Dioro Approach Project Report*. Retrieved January 20, 2009, from http://www.comminit.com/ drum_beat_55.html

Clifford, S., & Helft, M. (2008, May 19). Online Search Ads Faring Better than Expensive Displays. *The New York Times*. Retrieved from http://www.nytimes.com/2008/05/19/technology/19online.html

CmdrTaco. (1999, September 9). *Slashdot Moderation*. Retrieved April 17, 2003, from http://slashdot.org/moderation.shtml

Cnet.com. (2009). *Whee! New numbers on social network usage* [Electronic Version]. Retrieved March 5, 2009 from http://news.cnet.com/webware/?keyword=statistics.

CNN. (2005). The Rise and Rise of Corporate Blogs. *CNN.com*. Retrieved June 22, 2008, from http://www.cnn.com/2005/BUSINESS/12/20/company.blogs/index.html

CNN.com. (2004). *Election Results*. Retrieved June 21, 2008, from http://www.cnn.com/ELECTION/2004/pages/results/states/US/P/00/epolls.0.html

CNN.com. (2008). *Mom indicted in deadly MySpace hoax.* Retrieved July 26, 2008, from http://www.cnn.com/2008/CRIME/05/15/internet.suicide/index.html

Coates, K., & Sauter, W. (2007). Communication: Telecoms, Media and Internet. In Faull, J., & Nikpay, A. (Eds.), *The EC Law of Competition* (2nd ed.). Oxford, UK: Oxford University Press.

Cole, H., & Griffiths, M. D. (2007). Social interactions in massively multiplayer online role-playing gamers. *Cyberpsychology & Behavior, 10*(4), 575–583. doi:10.1089/cpb.2007.9988

Coleman, S., & Gøtze, J. (2001). *Bowling together: Online Public Engagement in Policy Deliberation.* Retrieved March 1, 2009, from http://www.bowlingtogether.net/

Colley, R. (1961). *Defining Advertising Goals for Measured Advertising Results.* New York: Association of National Advertisers.

Collins, S. (2008, January 8). Getting to grips with Obama-mania. *Spiked.* Retrieved June 7, 2008, from http://www.spiked-online.com/index.php?/site/article/4250/

Common Cause Education Fund. (2005). *The fallout from the Telecommunications Act of 1996: Unintended Consequences and Lessons Learnt, Common Cause, Holding Power Accountable.* Washington, DC: Common Cause Education Fund.

Compaine, B. M., & Gomery, D. (2000). *Who Owns the Media?: Competition and Concentration in the Mass Media Industry* (3rd ed.). Mahwah, NJ: Lawrence Erlbaum Associates.

Compared to Last Year, Advertisers Rely Less on Print Ads and More on Internet and Digital. (2009, July). Harris Interactive.

comScore. (2008). *Social Networking Explodes Worldwide as Sites Increase as Sits Increase their Focus on Cultural Relevance.* Retrieved June 26, 2009, from http://www.comscore.com/index.php/Press_Events/Press_Releases/2008/08/Social_Networking_World_Wide/(language)/eng-US

ComScore. (2008, February 12). *New Study Shows that Heavy Clickers Distort Reality of Display Advertising Click-Through Metrics.* Retrieved from http://www.comscore.com/press/release.asp?press=2060

Conti, G., & Sobieski, E. (2007). An Honest Man Has Nothing to Fear: User Perceptions on Web-based Information Disclosure. In *Symposium On Usable Privacy and Security (SOUPS) 2007*, July 18-20, Pittsburgh, PA, USA.

Converse. (n.d.). Retrieved March 8, 2009, from http://www.converse.com/index.aspx?mode=c1&bhcp=1#CATEGORYC1

Cook, G. (2001). *The Discourse of Advertising* (2nd ed.). London, New York: Routledge.

Cook, N. (1998). *Analysing Musical Multimedia.* Oxford, UK: Oxford University Press.

Cook, W. (2007, February 20). *First opinion. An ARF research review for integration marketing and communication limited's market contact audit ™ methodology.*

Cooley, C. H., & Schubert, H. J. (1998). *On self and the social organization.* Chicago: University of Chicago Press.

Copps, M. (2003, January 16). Crunch Time at the FCC. *The Nation.* Retrieved on September 18, 2008, from http://www.thenation.com/doc/20030203/copps

Corbett, E. P. J. (1984). *'Introduction' to Aristotle's rhetoric and poetics.* New York: Modern Library.

Cornfield, M. (2005). *The internet and campaign 2004: A look back at the campaigners* [Electronic Version]. Retrieved August 25, 2008, from http://www.pewinternet.org/pdfs/cornfield_commentary.pdf

Corn-Revere, R., & Carveth, R. (2004). Economics and Media Regulation. In Alexander, A. (Eds.), *Media Economics: Theory and Practice.* Hillsdale, NJ: Lawrence Erlbaum Associates Inc.

Cornwell, T. B., & Maignan, I. (1998). An international review of sponsorship research. *Journal of Advertising, 27*(1), 1–21.

Cornwell, T. B., Roy, D. P., & Steinard, E. A. (2001). Exploring manager's perceptions of the impact of sponsorship on brand equity. *Journal of Advertising, 30*(2), 41–51.

Correa, M., & Gisselquist, D. (2006). Routes of HIV transmission in India: assessing the reliability of information from AIDS case surveillance. *International Journal of STD & AIDS, 17*, 731–735. doi:10.1258/095646206778691194

Cottrell, J. (2007). *Social Networks in youth and Adolescence* (2nd ed.). London: Routledge.

Coulter, R. A., Zaltman, G., & Coulter, K. S. (2001). Interpreting consumer perceptions of advertising: An application of the Zaltman metaphor elicitation technique. *Journal of Advertising, 30*(4), 1–21.

Court issues warrants against Shilpa Shetty, Richard Gere. (2007, April 26). *Hindustan Times.* Retrieved January 13, 2007, from http://www.hindustantimes.com/StoryPage/StoryPage.aspx?id=b307da1b-cec7-419f-9e65-6108d797dbb3&ParentID=eda501ca-affe-4d4d-a93f-05a591421050&,amp,amp,amp,amp,amp,amp, amp,amp,amp,amp,amp,&Headline=Court+issues+warrants+against+Shilpa%2C+Gere

Cova, B., & Cova, V. (2002). Tribal marketing: The tribalisation of society and its impact on the conduct of marketing. *European Journal of Marketing, 36*(5), 595–620. doi:10.1108/03090560210423023

Cover, R. (2006). Audience inter/active: Interactive media, narrative control and reconceiving audience history. *New Media & Society, 18*(1), 139–158. doi:10.1177/1461444806059922

Cowley, E., & Barron, C. (2008). When product placement goes wrong: The effects of program liking and placement prominence. *Journal of Advertising, 37*(1), 89–98. doi:10.2753/JOA0091-3367370107

Cox, T. (2008). *Convergence of digital media and convenience retailing.* Retrieved from http://www.archive.org/details/ConvergenceOfDigitalMediaAndConvenienceRetailing.

Coyle, J. R., & Thorson, E. (2001). The effects of progressive levels of interactivity and vividness in web marketing sites. *Journal of Advertising, 30*(3).

Cramer, K. M., & Perreault, L. A. (2006). Effect of predictability, actual controllability, and awareness of choice on perceptions of control. *Current Research in Social Psychology, 11*(8), 111–126.

Cramer, H., Evers, V., van Someren, M., Ramlal, S., Rutledge, L., & Stash, N. (2008). The effects of transparency on trust and acceptance in interaction with a content-based art recommender. *User Modeling and User-Adapted Interaction*, 5.

Crane, R., & Sornette, D. (2008). Robust dynamic classes revealed by measuring the response function of a social system. *Proceedings of the National Academy of Sciences of the United States of America, 105*(41), 15649–15653. doi:10.1073/pnas.0803685105

Cranor, L. F. (2004). 'I Didn't Buy It for Myself' Privacy and Ecommerce Personalization. In Karat, C., Blom, J. O., & Karat, J. (Eds.), *Designing Personalized User Experiences in eCommerce*. Dordrecht, The Netherlands: Kluwer Academic Publishers.

Creamer, M. (2007, July 23). At last, the reviews are In Wal-Mart wakes up to the power of the people. *Advertising Age*.

Critcher, C. (2006). *Critical readings: moral panics and the media*. London: Open University Press.

Croft, M. (2006, April 20). Sports sponsorship; Biggest is not always the best. *Marketing Week*, 45.

Cross, J. (2005). HD Era coming to gaming. ExtremeTech. Retrieved January 15, 2006 from http://www.extremetech.com/article2/0,1558,1774523,00.asp?kc=ETRSS02129TX1K0 00532

Croteau, D., & Hoynes, W. (2003). *Media Society* (3rd ed.). Thousand Oaks, CA: Pine Forge Press. Davis, M. (2006). *Current Radio Topics*. Unpublished Lecture, University of Denver, USA.

Csikszentmihalyi, M. (1997). *Finding flow: the psychology of engagement with everyday life*. New York: Basic Books.

Csikszentmihalyi, M. (1990). *Flow: The psychology of optimal experience*. New York: Harper and Row.

Csikszentmihalyi, M., & Halton, E. (1981). *The Meaning of Things: Domestic Symbols and the Self.* Cambridge, UK: Cambridge University Press.

Culnan, M. J., & Milberg, S. J. (1998). *The Second Exchange: Managing Customer Information in Marketing Relationships*. Unpublished Working Paper, Georgetown University.

Curti, M. (1967). The changing concept of human nature in the literature of American advertising. *Business History Review, 41*, 337–345. doi:10.2307/3112645

Curwen, P. (2005). Consolidation in the USA: Does Bigger Mean Better. *Rearview, 7*(5). Retrieved from http://www.emeraldinsight.com/Insight/ViewContentServlet?Filename=Published/NonArticle/Articles/27207eab.001.html

Cyber Dialogue Survey Data Reveals Lost Revenue for Retailers Due to Widespread Consumer Privacy Concerns. (2001). *Cyber Dialogue*. Retrieved from http://www.cyberdialogue.com/news/releases/2001/11-07-uco-retail.html de Vrieze, P., van Bommel, P., & van der Weide, T. (2004). A Generic Adaptivity Model in Adaptive Hypermedia. *Adaptive Hypermedia And Adaptive Web-Based Systems*.

Dahl, R. E. (2004). Adolescent brain development: a period of vulnerabilities and opportunities, Keynote address. *Annals of the New York Academy of Sciences, 1021*, 1–22. doi:10.1196/annals.1308.001

Dahlén, M. (2001). *Marketing on the Web: Empirical Studies of Advertising and Promotion Effectiveness*. Stockholm, Sweden: EFI, Stockholm School of Economics.

D'Alessio, D. (1997). Use of the World Wide Web in the 1996 U.S. election. *Electoral Studies, 16*(4), 489–500. doi:10.1016/S0261-3794(97)00044-9

D'Alessio, D. (2000). Adoption of the World Wide Web by American political candidates, 1996-1998. *Journal of Broadcasting & Electronic Media, 44*(4), 556–568. doi:10.1207/s15506878jobem4404_2

Dalrymple, J. (2008). *Facebook Continues to Dominate Social Networking Sites*. Retrieved on August 21, 2008, from http://

www.networkworld.com/news/2008/081208-facebook-continues-to-dominate-social.html?fsrc=rss-webservices.

Damasio, A. R. (2004). *Looking for Spinoza*. London: Random House.

Danowski, J. A., & Choi, J. H. (1998). Convergence in the information industries. Telecommunications, broadcasting and data processing 1981-1996. In Sawhney, H., & Barnett, G. A. (Eds.), *Progress in communication sciences* (*Vol. 15*, pp. 125–150). Stamford, CT: Ablex.

Darian, J. C. (1998). Parent-child decision making in children's clothing stores. *International Journal of Retail and Distribution Management*, *26*(11), 421–428. doi:10.1108/09590559810246377

Daugherty, T., Eastin, M. S., & Bright, L. (2008). Exploring consumer motivations for creating user-generated content. *Journal of Interactive Advertising*, *8*(2). Retrieved from http://www.jiad.org/.

Daugherty, T., Gangadharbatla, H., & Bright, L. (in press). Presence and persuasion. In Bracken, C. C., & Skalski, P. (Eds.), *Immersed in media: Telepresence in everyday life*. New York: Routledge.

Daugherty, T., Eastin, M., & Gangadharbatla, H. (2005). e-CRM: Understanding Internet Confidence and Implications for Customer Relationship Management. In I. Clarke III & T. B. Flaherty (Eds.), *Advances in Electronic Marketing*. Hershey, PA: Idea Group Publishing, Inc.

Davenport, T. H., & Beck, J. C. (2001). *The attention economy: understanding the new currency of business*. Harvard Business School Press.

Davidson, S. (2007). From Spam to Stern, Advertising law and the Internet. In Schumann, D. W., & Thorson, E. (Eds.), *Internet Advertising, Theory and Research* (pp. 427–471). Mahwah, NJ: Lawrence Erlbaum Associates.

Davis, F. D., Bagozzi, R. P., & Warshaw, P. R. (1989). User acceptance of computer technology: A comparison of two theoretical models. *Management Science*, *35*(8), 982–1003. doi:10.1287/mnsc.35.8.982

Davis, D. B. (2006). *Inhumane bondage: The rise and fall of slavery in the new world*. New York: Oxford University Press.

Davis, R. (1999). *The Web of Politics: The Internet's Impact on the American Political System*. New York: Oxford University Press.

Davis, D. K., & Baron, S. J. (1981). A history of our understanding of mass communication. In Davis, D. K., & Baron, S. J. (Eds.), *Mass communication and everday life: A perspective on theory and effects*. Belmont, CA: Wadsworth Publishing.

Davis, W. (2008, March 10). Company accused of posting self-serving reviews. *Media Post Publications*. Retrieved August 6, 2008, from http://www.mediapost.com/publications/index.cfm?fuseaction=Articles.showArticleHomePage&art_aid=78101

Davis, W. (2009a, May 1). Free Speech Trumps Privacy Online. *Daily Online Examiner*. Retrieved June 15, 2009, from http://www.mediapost.com/publications/?fa=Articles.showArticle&art_aid=105258

Davis, W. (2009b, May 12). FTC's Leibowitz Opts for BT Opt-In. *Daily Online Examiner*. Retrieved June 15, 2009, from http://www.mediapost.com/publications/?fa=Articles.showArticle&art_aid=105954

Dawson, M., & Foster, B. J. (1996). Virtual capitalism: The political economy of the information highway. *Monthly Review (New York, N.Y.)*, *48*, 40–59.

De Bruyn, A., & Lilien, G. L. (2008). A multi-stage model of word of mouth through electronic referrals. *International Journal of Research in Marketing*, *25*, 151–163. doi:10.1016/j.ijresmar.2008.03.004

de Nood, D., & Attema, J. (2006). *Second Life: The Second Life of virtual reality*. EPN Report.

Dean, D. H. (2002). Associating the corporation with a charitable event through sponsorship: Measuring the effects on corporate community relations. *Journal of Advertising*, *31*(4), 77–88.

Debord, G. (1994). *The Society of the Spectacle*. New York: Zone Books.

DeCharms, R. (1968). *Personal Causation*. New York: Academic Press.

deChernatony, L. (2001, February). Succeeding with brands on the Internet. *Brand Management*, *8*(3), 186–193. doi:10.1057/palgrave.bm.2540019

Declerck, C. H., Boone, C., & De Brabander, B. (2006). On feeling in control: A biological theory for individual differences in control perception. *Brain and Cognition*, *62*, 143–176. doi:10.1016/j.bandc.2006.04.004

DeFleur, M., & Dennis, E. E. (2002). *Understanding mass communication* (7th ed.). Boston, MA: Houghton Mifflin.

Dehn, D. M., & van Mulken, S. (2000). The impact of animated interface agents: A review of empirical research. *International*

Journal of Human-Computer Studies, *52*(1), 1–22. doi:10.1006/ijhc.1999.0325

Deighton, J. A., & Kornfeld, L. (2007). Digital Interactivity: Unanticipated Consequences for Markets, Marketing and Consumers [Electronic Version]. *HBS Working Papers*. Retrieved from http://www.hbs.edu/research/pdf/08-017.pdf

Del Colliano, J. (2008). *Circuit City Files For Chapter 11 Bankruptcy After Years of Bad Decisions and Aggressive Tactics*. Retrieved from http://hometheaterreview.com/circuit-city-files-for-chapter-11-bankruptcy-after-years-of-bad-decisions-and-aggressive-tactics/

Delany, C. (2008, November 5). How the Internet Put Barack Obama in the White House. *TechPresident.com*. Retrieved November 6, 2008, from http://www.techpresident.com/blog/entry/32998/how_the_internet_put_barack_obama_in_the_white_house

Delia, J. G. (1987). Communication study: A history. In Berger, C. R., & Chaffee, S. H. (Eds.), *Handbook of communication science*. Newbury Park, CA: Sage.

Deliso, M. (2006, August 28). RSS, Podcasts are Worthwhile Investments. *Advertising Age*, *77*(35), 4.

Dellarocas, C., Zhang, X., & Awad, N. F. (2007). Exploring the value of online product reviews in forecasting sales: The case of motion pictures. *Journal of Interactive Marketing*, *21*(4), 23–45. doi:10.1002/dir.20087

Dellarocas, C. (2003). The digitization of word of mouth: Promise and challenges of online feedback mechanisms. *Management Science*, *49*(10), 1407–1424. doi:10.1287/mnsc.49.10.1407.17308

Dellarocas, C., Award, N., & Zhang, X. (2004). *Exploring the Value of Online Reviews to Organization: Implications for Revenue Forecasting and Planning.*

Demaria, R., & Wilson, J. L. (2004). *High Score! The Illustrated History of Electronic Games*. Emeryville, CA: McGraw-Hill/Osborne.

Demetriou, A., Christou, C., Spanoudis, G. & ., & Platsidou, M. (2002). The development of mental processing: efficiency, working memory, and thinking. *Monographs of the Society for research in Child Development, 67*(1), serial n°268.

Denton, R. E. (1998). *The primetime presidency of Ronald Reagan: The era of the television presidency*. New York: Praeger.

Derlega, V., & Barbee, A. P. (Eds.). (1998). *HIV and social interaction*. Thousand Oaks, CA: Sage Publications.

Desphande, R., & Stayman, D. (1994). A tale of two cities: Distinctiveness theory and advertising effectiveness. *JMR, Journal of Marketing Research*, *31*, 57–64. doi:10.2307/3151946

Deutsch, A. (2000). Sports broadcasting and virtual adverstisng, Defining the limits of copyright law and the law of unfair competition. *Marquette Sports Law Review*, *11*, 41–86.

Devlin, L. P. (1989). Contrasts in presidential campaign commercials of 1988. *The American Behavioral Scientist*, *32*(4), 389–414. doi:10.1177/0002764289032004006

Devlin, L. P. (1993). Contrasts in presidential campaign commercials of 1992. *The American Behavioral Scientist*, *37*(2), 272–290. doi:10.1177/0002764293037002015

Devlin, L. P. (1997). Contrasts in presidential campaign commercials of 1996. *The American Behavioral Scientist*, *40*(8), 1058–1084. doi:10.1177/0002764297040008008

Devlin, L. P. (2001). Contrasts in presidential campaign commercials of 2000. *The American Behavioral Scientist*, *44*(12), 2338–2369. doi:10.1177/00027640121958366

Dewey, J. (1954). *Public and its problems*. Denver, CO: Swallow Press Books.

Dhillon, A. (2006). The land of Kama Sutra chokes on a kiss. *The Age*. Retrieved January 20, 2009, from http://www.theage.com.au/news/entertainment/the-land-of-kama-sutra-chokes-on-a-kiss/2006/12/15/1166162320089.html

Dholakia, R., & Sternthal, B. (1977). Highly credible source: Persuasive facilitator or persuasive liability? *The Journal of Consumer Research*, *3*(4), 223–232. doi:10.1086/208671

Diaz, S. (2007, August 31). On the Internet, A Tangled Web Of Classified Ads With So Many Sites, Sifting Is Difficult. *Washington Post*, D01. Retrieved July 30, 2008, fromhttp://www.washingtonpost.com/wp-dyn/content/article/2007/08/30/AR2007083002046_pf.html

Dickens, C. (1837). *The Posthumous Papers of the Pickwick Club*. Oxford, UK: Chapman and Hall.

Dickey, I. J., Lewis, W. F., & Siemens, J. C. (2007). The evolution of Internet weblogs: History, current trends, and projections of usage in marketing strategy. *Journal of Business and Behavioral Sciences*, *19*(1), 91–102.

Dickey, M. J. (2005). Three-dimensional virtual worlds and distance learning: Two case studies of active worlds as a medium for distance education. *British Journal of Educational Technology*, *36*(3), 439–451. doi:10.1111/j.1467-8535.2005.00477.x

Dickson, G. (1998). ESPN uses virtual ads for baseball. *Broadcasting & Cable*, *128*, 49–50.

Dietmar, C. (2005). Mobile communication in couple relationship. In Nyiri, K. (Ed.), *A sense of place: the global and local in mobile communication* (pp. 201–208). Vienna, Austria: Passagen Verlag.

Digital Life America. (2009, May). Solution Research Group Program. Retrieved from http://www.srgnet.com/us/programs.html

Dillard, J. P., & Nabi, R. L. (2006). The persuasive influence of emotion in cancer prevention and detection message. *The Journal of Communication*, *56*(S1), S123–S139. doi:10.1111/j.1460-2466.2006.00286.x

Dillard, C., Browning, L. D., Sitkin, S. B., & Sutcliffe, K. M. (2000). Impression Management and the use of procedures at the Ritz-Carlton: Moral standards and dramaturgical discipline. *Comunication Studies, 51*.

DiPaola, S., Dorosh, D., & Brandt, G. (n. d.). *Ratava's line: Emergent learning and design using collaborative virtual worlds*. Retrieved March 1, 2008, from http://ivizlab.sfu.ca/research/colabdesign/dipaolaF1.pdf

Direct Marketing Association. Email Delivery Best Practices for Marketers and List Owners, http://www.the-dma.org/antispam/EmailBPFINAL.pdf October 2005, pp.2-10. Retrieved March 1, 2009]

Direct2Dell. (n.d.). Retrieved from http://en.community.dell.com/blogs/direct2dell/

Dishion, T. J., & Owen, L. D. (2002). A longitudinal analysis of friendship and substance use: bidirectional influence from adolescence to adulthood. *Developmental Psychology*, *38*, 480–491. doi:10.1037/0012-1649.38.4.480

DMD. (2007). Diversified media design, combined storey, and market truths limited. In *The virtual brand footprint: The marketing opportunity in Second Life.*

Dolnicar, S., & Jordaan, Y. (2007). A market-oriented approach to responsibly managing information privacy concerns in direct marketing. *Journal of Advertising*, *36*(2), 123–149. doi:10.2753/JOA0091-3367360209

Dominick, J. R. (1999). Who do you think you are? Personal home pages and self-presentation on the World Wide Web. *Journalism & Mass Communication Quarterly*, *76*(4), 646–658.

Donada, C. (2002). E-Business and the Automotive Industry: What Stakes for the European Dealers? *International Academy of E-Business Conference Proceedings*, International Academy of E-Business, Las Vegas, NE, 76-79.

Donahue, M. (2007). Setting up shop on Second Life. *Pharmaceutical Executive*, *27*(11), 8–10.

Donohew, L., Palmgreen, P., & Rayburn, J. D. II. (1987). Social and psychological origins of media use: A lifestyle analysis. *Journal of Broadcasting & Electronic Media*, *31*(3), 255–278.

Dooling, D. J., & Lachman, R. (1971). Effects of comprehension on retention of prose. *Journal of Experimental Psychology*, *88*(2), 216–222. doi:10.1037/h0030904

Dou, W., & Krishnamurthy, S. (2007). Using brand Websites to build brands online: A product versus service brand comparison. *Journal of Advertising Research*, *47*(2), 193–206. doi:10.2501/S0021849907070225

Douglas, M. (2002). *Purity and Danger*. London: Routledge & Kegan Paul.

Douglas, M., & Isherwood, B. (1979). *The World of Goods*. New York: Basic.

Downie, L., & Kaiser, R. G. (2002). *The News About the News: American Journalism in Peril*. New York: Random House.

Doyle, P. (1994). *Marketing Management & Strategy*. Upper Saddle River, NJ: Prentice-Hall.

Drèze, X., & Husshern, F.-X. (2003). Internet advertising: Is anybody watching? *Journal of Interactive Marketing*, *17*(4), 8–23. doi:10.1002/dir.10063

Driver, E., Jackson, P., Moore, C., & Schooley, C. (2008, January 7). Getting Real Work Done In Virtual Worlds. *Forrester Research*. Retrieved April 30, 2008, from http://www.forrester.com/Research/Document/Excerpt/0,7211,43450,00.html

Drotner, K. (2005). Mediatized childhoods: discourses, dilemmas and directions. In Qvortrup, J. (Ed.), *Studies in Modern Childhood* (pp. 39–58). London: Palgrave-MacMillan.

Du Plessis, E. (2005). *The Advertised Mind*. London: Kogan Page.

Ducheneaut, N., Moore, R. J., & Nickell, E. (2007). Virtual third places: A case study of sociability in massively multiplayer games. *Computer Supported Cooperative Work*, *16*, 129–166. doi:10.1007/s10606-007-9041-8

Dulio, D. A., Goff, D. L., & Thurber, J. A. (1999). Untangled web: Internet use during the 1998 election. *Political Science and Politics*, *3*(1), 53–58.

Duncan, D. J. (1978). Leisure types: Factor analyses of leisure profiles. *Journal of Leisure Research*, *10*, 113–125.

Duncan, T. (1993). Integrated marketing? It's synergy. *Advertising Age*, *64*(10), 22.

Dunn, S. (2004). *Jefferson's second revolution: The election crisis of 1800 and the triumph of Republicanism*. New York: Houghton Mifflin Company.

Durlach, N., & Slater, M. (2000). Presence in shared virtual environments and virtual togetherness. *Presence (Cambridge, Mass.)*, *9*(2), 214–217. doi:10.1162/105474600566736

Dyer, G. (1982). *Advertising as Communication*. New York: Routledge. doi:10.4324/9780203328132

Eagly, A. H., & Chaiken, S. (1993). *The Psychology of Attitudes*. Fort Worth, TX: Harcourt Brace Janovich College Publishers.

Eastin, M. S. (2005). Teen internet use: Relating social perceptions and cognitive models to behavior. *Cyberpsychology & Behavior*, *8*(1), 62–71. doi:10.1089/cpb.2005.8.62

Eastin, M. S., & LaRose, R. L. (2000). Internet self-efficacy and the psychology of the digital divide. *Journal of Computer-Mediated Communication*, *6*. Retrieved from http://www.ascusc.org/jcmc/vol6/issue1/eastin.html.

Eastin, M. S. (2002). Diffusion of e-commerce: An analysis of the adoption of four e-commerce activities. *Telematics and Informatics*, *19*(3), 251–267. doi:10.1016/S0736-5853(01)00005-3

Eastin, M. S., Yang, M.-S., & Nathanson, A. I. (2006, June). Children of the net: An empirical exploration into the evaluation of internet content. *Journal of Broadcasting & Electronic Media*, *50*(2), 211–230. doi:10.1207/s15506878jobem5002_3

Eastin, M., Appiah, O., & Cicchirllo, V. (2009). Identification and the influence of cultural stereotyping on postvidogame play hostility. *Human Communication Research*, *35*, 337–356. doi:10.1111/j.1468-2958.2009.01354.x

Eastin, M. S., & Daugherty, T. (2005). Past, Current, and Future Trends in Mass Communication. In Kimmel, A. (Ed.), *Marketing Communication: Emerging Trends and Developments*. Oxford, UK: Oxford University Press.

Eastin, M., & LaRose, R. (2003). *A social cognitive explanation of Internet uses and gratifications: Toward a new theory of media attendance.* Paper presented at the annual meeting of the International Communication Association, Marriott Hotel, San Diego, CA.

Ebersole, S. (1997). A brief history of virtual reality and its social applications. *Encyclopedia of interactive media*. Retrieved February 3, 2009 from http://faculty.colostate- pueblo.edu/samuel.ebersole/336/eim/papers/vrhist.html

Economist. (2006). *It's the Links, Stupid*. Retrieved September 26, 2007, from http://www.economist.com/surveys/displaystory.cfm?story_id=6794172

Edery, D. (2006). Reverse product placement in virtual worlds. *Harvard Business Review*, *84*(12), 24–24.

Edwards, C. (2006). Another world. *Engineering and Technology*, *1*(9), 28–32. doi:10.1049/et:20060904

Edwards, J. (2009, July 29). *BNET's Ad Agency Layoff Counter: 34,828 Jobs Lost.* Retrieved from http://industry.bnet.com/advertising/1000433/bnets-ad-agency-layoff-counter/

Eighmey, J. (1997, May). Profiling user responses to commercial websites. *Journal of Advertising Research*, 59–67.

Ekind, D. (1979). *The child and society: essays in applied child development. NY*. New York: Oxford University Press.

Ekström, K. M. (2007, July). Parental consumer learning or 'keeping up with the children.'. *Journal of Consumer Behaviour*, *6*(July-August), 203–217. doi:10.1002/cb.215

Elderkin, K. (1996). *The future of newspaper industry: How electronic newspapers will outrun their competition*. Bloomington, IN: Elderkin Associates.

Elias, T. (2008). *A tale of two social contexts: Race-specific testimonials on commercial web sites and their effects on numeric majority and numeric minority consumer attitudes*. Paper presented at the Advertising Division of the Annual Convention of the Association for Education and Journalism and Mass Communication, Chicago, IL., August 2008.

Elliot, M. T., & Speck, P. S. (1998, January). Consumer perceptions of advertising clutter and its impact across various media. *Journal of Advertising Research*, 29–41.

Ellis, R. (2008a). *Publisher, sportswriter file suit in fake story about Oklahoma quarterbacks*. Retrieved August 3, 2008, from http://newsok.com/article/3270140/

Ellis, R. (2008b). *Settlement reached in Internet hoax about OU QBs*. Retrieved July 3, 2009, from http://newsok.com/settlement-reached-in-internet-hoax-about-ou-qbs/article/3295059

Ellison, N., Steinfield, C., & Lampe, C. (2007). The Benefits of Facebook "Friends:" Social Capital and College Students' Use of Online Social Network Sites. *Journal of Computer-Mediated Communication*, *12*, 1143–1168. doi:10.1111/j.1083-6101.2007.00367.x

Ellison, N. (2006). Managing impressions online: Self-presentation processes in the online dating environment. *Journal of Computer-Mediated Communication*, *11*, 415–441. doi:10.1111/j.1083-6101.2006.00020.x

eMarketer. (2006). *Online Video Becomes a Real Business: Welcome to the MoneyTube.*

eMarketer. (2006a). *Brands to Spend $1.8 Billion on Social Networking Sites by 2010*. Retrieved August 29, 2007 from http://www.emarketer.com/Article.aspx?id=1004085

eMarketer. (2006b). *Social networking online boosts bottom line*. Retrieved August 29, 2007, from http://www.emarketer.com/Article.aspx?id=1004313

eMarketer. (2007). *Retail Adapts to Digital Movie Rentals: Going to rent a movie? Don't forget your iPod.*

eMarketer. (2008). *Social Networking Marketing: Where Too Next*. Retrieved on August 19, 2008, from http://www.emarketer.com/Report.aspx?code=emarketer_2000433

Endres, D., & Warnick, B. (2004). Text-based interactivity in candidate campaign web sites: A case study from the 2002 elections. *Western Journal of Communication*, *68*(3), 322–342.

Entertainment Software Association. (2007). *Computer and video game industry reaches $18.85 billion in 2007*. Retrieved on April 29, 2008, from http://www.theesa.com/archives/2008/01/computer_and_vi_1.php

Entertainment Software Association. (2008). *Essential facts about the computer and video game industry*. Retrieved on April 29, 2008, from http://www.theesa.com/facts/pdfs/ESA_EF_2008.pdf

Entman, R. M., & Rojecki, A. (2000). Advertising Whiteness. In Entman, R. M., & Rojecki, A. (Eds.), *The Black Image in the White Mind*. Chicago: University of Chicago Press.

Erickson, J. (1996, June 30). Are Those Who Go Online To Send Junk Mail Out of Line? Growth of Unsolicited Direct Mail on Internet Raises Questions of Privacy. *Star Tribune*, 3D.

Erikson, E. H. (1968). *Identity: youth and crisis. NY*. New York: Norton.

Ernst & Young. (1999). *The Second Annual Ernst & Young Internet Shopping Study: The Digital Channel Continues to Gather Steam*. Ernst & Young Publication, Ernst & Young LLP.

Erwin, P. (1998). *Friendship in childhood and adolescence*. London: Routledge.

Escalas, J. E. (2004). Imagine yourself in the product: Mental simulation, narrative transportation, and persuasion. *Journal of Advertising*, *33*(2), 37–48.

Escalas, J. E. (2007, March). Self-referencing and persuasion: Narrative transportation versus analytical elaboration. *The Journal of Consumer Research*, *33*, 421–429. doi:10.1086/510216

Espinoza, J., & Garza, R. (1985). Social group salience and inter-ethnic cooperation. *Journal of Experimental Social Psychology*, *21*, 380–392. doi:10.1016/0022-1031(85)90037-X

Evaluation of Abstinence Education Programs Funded Under Title V. Section 510. (n.d.). *Mathematica Policy Research, Inc.* Retrieved January 26, 2009, from http://www.mathematica-mpr.com/welfare/abstinence.asp#reports

Evans, M., Wedande, G., Ralston, L., & Hul, S. (2001). Consumer interaction in the virtual era: Some qualitative insights. *Qualitative Market Research: An International Journal*, *4*(3), 150–159. doi:10.1108/13522750110393053

Eveland, W. P. Jr. (2003). A mix of attributes approach to the study of media effects and new communication technologies. *The Journal of Communication*, *53*(3), 395–410. doi:10.1111/j.1460-2466.2003.tb02598.x

Ewen, S. (1976). *Captains of Consciousness*. New York: McGraw-Hill.

Faber, R. J., Lee, M., & Nan, X. (2004). Advertising and the consumer information environment online. *The American Behavioral Scientist*, *48*(4), 447–466. doi:10.1177/0002764204270281

Facebook.com. (2009). *Press Room* [Electronic Version]. Retrieved March 7, 2009, from http://www.facebook.com/press/info.php?statistics.

Fang, M. C., McCarthy, E. P., & Singer, D. E. (2004). Are patients more likely to see physicians of the same sex? Recent national trends in primary care medicine. *American Journal of Public Health*, *117*(8), 575–581.

Faranda, W. T. (2001). A scale to measure the cognitive control form of perceived control: Construction and preliminary assessment. *Psychology and Marketing*, *18*(12), 1259–1281. doi:10.1002/mar.1052

Farber, C. (2007, November 29). Facebook Beacon Update: No Activities Published Without Users Proactively Consenting. *ZDnet.com*. Retrieved June 1, 2009, from http://blogs.zdnet.com/BTL/?p=7188

Farkas, M. G. (2007). *Social software in libraries: Building collaboration, communication, and community online*. Medford, NJ: Information Today.

Farmer, M. A., & Sandoval, G. (2001, July 9). Webvan Delivers its Last Word: Bankruptcy. *CNET News*. Retrieved March 12, 2009, from http://news.cnet.com/2100-1017-269594.html

Farrelly, G. (1999). *Search Engines: Evolution and Revolution*. Retrieved May 18, 2008, from http://webhome.idirect.com/~glenjenn/search/history1.htm

Faulring, A., Mohnkern, K., Steinfeld, A., & Myers, B. (2008). *Successful User Interfaces for RADAR.* Paper presented at the CHI 2008 Workshop on Usable Artificial Intelligence.

Fawkes, P. (2008 February). *Initial thoughts on mind-control gaming, electronics & gadgets, gaming & virtual worlds.* Retrieved May 29, 2008, from *http://www.psfk.com/category/gaming-virtual-worlds/page/2*

Faylor, C. (2008). PlayStation 3 getting true 3D visual support in 2009, claims developer. *Shacknews*. Retrieved February 3, 2009 from http://www.shacknews.com/onearticle.x/56514

Fazio, R. H., & Olson, M. A. (2003). Implicit measures in social cognition research: Their meaning and use. *Annual Review of Psychology, 54*, 297–327. doi:10.1146/annurev.psych.54.101601.145225

Fazio, R. H., & Towles-Schwen, T. (1999). The MODE Model of Attitude-Behavior Processes. In Chaiken, S., & Trope, Y. (Eds.), *Dual Process Theories in Social Psychology* (pp. 97–116). New York: Guilford.

Fazio, R. H. (1986). How Do Attitudes Guide Behavior? In Sorrentino, R. M., & Higgins, E. T. (Eds.), *Handbook of Motivation and Cognition* (pp. 204–243). New York: Guilford.

FCC. (2008). *The FCC and its Regulatory Authority*. Retrieved on August 23, 2008, from http://www.fcc.gov/aboutus.html

Feenberg, A. (2002). *Transforming Technology: A Critical Theory Revisited.* New York: Oxford University Press.

Feldman, L. P., & Hornik, J. (1981, March). The use of time: An integrated conceptual model. *The Journal of Consumer Research, 7*, 407–419. doi:10.1086/208831

Fendrich, H. (2001, April 6). Has sports become filler for the ads? *Associated Press.*

Fennell, R. (1993). Using humor to teach responsible sexual health decision making and condom comfort. *Journal of American College Health, 42*(1), 37–39.

Ferguson, D. A., & Perse, E. M. (2000). The World Wide Web as a functional alternative to television. *Journal of Broadcasting & Electronic Media, 44*, 155–194. doi:10.1207/s15506878jobem4402_1

Ferguson, R. (2001, January 10). New TV ads touch down on football field. *Toronto Star*, NEO1.

Ferling, J. E. (2004). *Adams vs. Jefferson: The election of 1800 and the third American revolution.* New York: Oxford University Press.

Fernandez, R., & McAdam, D. (1988). Social networks and social movements: multiorganizational fields and recruitment to Mississippi Freedom Summer. *Sociological Forum, 3*, 357–382. doi:10.1007/BF01116431

Fetscherin, M., & Lattemkmann, C. (2007). *User Acceptance of Virtual Worlds: An Explorative Study about Second Life*. Winter Park, FL: Rollins College.

Fidler, R. (1997). *Mediamorphosis. Understanding new media.* Thousand Oaks, CA: Pine Forge.

Findlater, L., & McGrenere, J. (2004). *A comparison of static, adaptive, and adaptable menus*. Paper presented at the Proceedings of the SIGCHI conference on Human factors in computing systems.

Findlater, L., & McGrenere, J. (2008). *Impact of screen size on performance, awareness, and user satisfaction with adaptive graphical user interfaces*. Paper presented at the Proceeding of the twenty-sixth annual SIGCHI conference on Human factors in computing systems.

Findlater, L., Moffatt, K., McGrenere, J., & Dawson, J. (2009). *Ephemeral adaptation: the use of gradual onset to improve menu selection performance*. Paper presented at the Proceedings of the 27th international conference on Human factors in computing systems.

Fine, J. (2007, February 19). What makes citizen ads' work. *BusinessWeek*, (4022), 24.

Finnemann, N. O. (2001). *The Internet–A New Communicational Infrastructure*. Papers from The Centre for Internet Research, University of Aarhus. Retrieved from http://www.cfi.au.dk/publikationer/cfi/002_finnemann

Firefox Flicks Backstage. (2006, May 1). *Flicks comments and ratings*. Retrieved June 26, 2007, from http://www.firefoxflicks.com/backstage/page/6.

Fischer, E., Bristor, J., & Gainer, B. (1996). Creating or escaping community? An exploratory study of Internet consumers' behaviours. *Advances in Consumer Research. Association for Consumer Research (U. S.), 23*, 178–182.

Flanagin, A., J., & Metzger, M., J. (2000). Perceptions of Internet information credibility. *Journalism & Mass Communication Quarterly, 77*(3), 515–540.

Fleming, T. (1976). *How it was in advertising: 1776-1976.* Mandan, ND: Crain Books.

Flichy, P. (1999). The construction of new digital media. *New Media & Society, 1*(1), 33–38. doi:10.1177/1461444899001001006

Foehr, U. G. *Media Multitasking among American Youth: Prevalence, Predictors, and Pairings.* Menlo Park, CA: The Henry J. Kaiser Foundation.

Fogel, J., Albert, S. M., Schnabel, F., Ditkoff, B. A., & Neugut, A. I. (2002). Internet use and social support in women with breast cancer. *Health Psychology, 21*(4), 398–404. doi:10.1037/0278-6133.21.4.398

Fogg, B. J. (2002). *Persuasive Technology: Using Computers to Change What We Think and Do*. San Francisco, CA: Morgan Kaufmann.

Fogg, B. J., & Tseng, H. (1999). The Elements of Computer Credibility. In *Proceedings of the SIGCHI Conference on Human Factors in Computing Systems: The CHI is the Limit* (pp. 80-87).

Fong, J., & Burton, S. (2006). Electronic word-of-mouth: A comparison of stated and revealed Behavior on electronic discussion boards. *Journal of Interactive Advertising, 6*(2), 61–70.

Foot, K. A., Xenos, M., & Schneider, S. M. (2003). *Online Campaigning in the 2002 U.S. Elections: Analyzing House, Senate and Gubernatorial Campaign Web Sites.* Paper presented at the American Political Science Association, Philadelphia.

Forrester. (2006). *Profiling Europe's Bloggers: What Marketers Need to Know before Entering the Blogosphere*. Retrieved July 15, 2008, from http://www.forrester.com/ER/Press/Release/0,1769,1112,00.html

Fortner, R. S. (1994). Mediated communication theory. In Casmir, F. L. (Ed.), *Building communication theories: A socio/cultural approach*. Hillsdale, NJ: Lawrence Erlbaum Associates.

Fortunato, J. A. (2001). *The ultimate assist: The relationship and broadcast strategies of the NBA and television networks*. Cresskill, NJ: Hampton Press.

Fortunato, J. A. (2008). Using message content to communicate a brand association: Olympic television advertising. *Journal of Sponsorship, 1*(3), 248–257.

Fortunato, J. A., & Richards, J. (2007). Reconciling sports sponsorship exclusivity with antitrust law. *Texas Review of Entertainment & Sports Law, 8*, 33–48.

Fortunato, J. A., & Dunnam, A. E. (2004). The negotiation philosophy for corporate sponsorship of sports properties. In Pitts, B. G. (Ed.), *Sharing best practices in sports marketing* (pp. 99–111). Morgantown, WV: Fitness Information Technology, Inc.

Fosse, M. (2002, February). The Web goes political: How political candidates and parties are using the Internet to provide information, raise money, mobilize supporters, and get out the vote. *WORLD (Oakland, Calif.), 1*, 17.

Foucault, M. (1980). *Power/knowledge: Selected interviews and other writings* (Gordon, C., Ed.). New York: Pantheon.

Fournier, S. (1998). Consumers and their brands: Developing relationship theory in consumer research. *The Journal of Consumer Research, 24*(4), 343–353. doi:10.1086/209515

Fox, M. (2006). *The video games guide*. London: Boxtree Ltd.

Frankl, V. (1959). *Man's Search for Meaning*. New York: Simon & Schuster.

Franz, R., & Wolkinger, T. (2003). Customer Integration with Virtual Communities. Case Study: The online community of the largest regional newspaper in Austria. In *Proceedings of the Hawaii International Conference on System Sciences*, January 6-9, 2003, Big Island, Hawaii.

Freed, L. (2007, March 1). Customer product reviews: Key to driving satisfaction, loyalty and conversion. *Foresee Results*. Retrieved on August 1, 2008, from http://www.ForeSeeResults.com

Freed, M., Carbonell, J., Gordon, G., Hayes, J., Myers, B., Siewiorek, D., et al. (2008). *RADAR: A Personal Assistant that Learns to Reduce Email Overload.* Paper presented at the Twenty-Third Conference on Artificial Intelligence.

Freeman, J., Steed, A., & Zhou, B. (2005). Rapid scene modelling, registration, and specification for mixed reality systems. In *Proceedings of ACM virtual reality software and technology* (pp. 147-150), Monterey, CA.

Freire, P. (2006). *Pedagogy of the Oppressed: 30th Anniversary Ed.* New York: Continuum.

Freud, S. (1962, original 1923). *The ego and Id.*, London: Hogarth Press. (Original manuscript published in 1923).

Frey, B. S., & Jegen, R. (2001). Motivation crowding theory. *Journal of Economic Surveys, 15*(5), 589. doi:10.1111/1467-6419.00150

Friestad, M., & Wright, P. (1994). The persuasion knowledge model: How people cope with persuasion attempts. *The Journal of Consumer Research, 21*(1), 1–31. doi:10.1086/209380

Friestad, M., & Wright, P. (1995). Persuasion knowledge: Lay people's and researchers' beliefs about the psychology of persuasion. *The Journal of Consumer Research, 22*(1), 62–74. doi:10.1086/209435

Friestad, M., & Wright, P. (1999). Everyday persuasion knowledge. *Psychology and Marketing, 16*(2), 185–194. doi:10.1002/(SICI)1520-6793(199903)16:2<185::AID-MAR7>3.0.CO;2-N

Fry, J. (2006). Blog Epitaphs? Get Me Rewright! *The Wall Street Journal Online*. Retrieved February 27, 2008, from http://online.wsj.com/article_print/SB114072068850081570.html

Fu, F. L., Su, R. C., & Yu, S. C. (2010). EGameFlow: A scale to measure learners' enjoyment of e-learning games. *Computers & Education, 52*, 101–112. doi:10.1016/j.compedu.2008.07.004

Fujioka, Y. (2005). Emotional TV viewing and minority audience: How Mexican Americans process and evaluate TV news about in-group members. *Communication Research, 32*(5), 566–593. doi:10.1177/0093650205279210

Fulcher, J., & Scott, J. (2007). *Sociology*, (3rd ed.), NY: New York: Oxford University Press.

Funk, D., & James, J. (2001). The psychological continuum model: A conceptual framework for understanding an individual's psychological connection to sport. *Sport Management Review, 4*(2), 119–150. doi:10.1016/S1441-3523(01)70072-1

Furse, D. H., Punj, G., & Stewart, D. W. (1984). A typology of individual search strategies among purchasers of new automobiles. *The Journal of Consumer Research, 10*(4), 417–431. doi:10.1086/208980

Gaggioli, A., Mantovani, F., Castelnuovo, G., Wieberhold, B., & Riva, G. (2003). Avatars in clinical psychology: A framework for the clinical use of virtual humans. *Cyberpsychology & Behavior, 6*, 117–125. doi:10.1089/109493103321640301

Gajos, K. Z. (2007). *Automatically generating user interfaces adapted to users' motor and vision capabilities.* Paper presented at the UIST '07, New York, NY.

Gajos, K. Z., & Jameson, A. (2009). *Course Notes: New Paradigms for Adaptive Interaction.* Paper presented at the Conference on Human Factors in Computing Systems, Boston, MA.

Gajos, K. Z., & Weld, D. S. (2004). *Supple: automatically generating uuser interfaces.* Paper presented at the IUI '04, New York, NY.

Gajos, K. Z., Czerwinski, M., Tan, D. S., & Weld, D. S. (2006). *Exploring the design space for adaptive graphical user interfaces.* Paper presented at the Proceedings of the working conference on Advanced visual interfaces.

Gajos, K. Z., Everitt, K., Tan, D. S., Czerwinski, M., & Weld, D. S. (2008). *Predictability and accuracy in adaptive user interfaces.* Paper presented at the Proceeding of the twenty-sixth annual SIGCHI conference on Human factors in computing systems.

Gajos, K. Z., Wobbrock, J. O., & Weld, D. S. (2008). *Improving the performance of motor-impaired users with automatically-generated, ability-based interfaces.* Paper presented at the Conference on Human Factors in Computing Systems, Florence, Italy.

Gangadharbatla, H. (2008). Facebook Me: Collective self-esteem, need to belong, and Internet self-efficacy as predictors of the iGeneration's attitudes toward social networking sites. *Journal of Interactive Advertising, 8*(2). Retrieved September 4, 2008, from http://www.jiad.org/article100

Garau, C. (2008). The influence of advergames on players' behaviour: An experimental study. *Electronic Markets, 18*(2), 106–116. doi:10.1080/10196780802044859

Garcia, D., & Valdes, R. (2004). Blogs Present Unique Challenges and Opportunities for Advertisers. *Gartner Report.*

Garcia-Murillo, M. A., & MacInnes, I. (2001). FCC organizational structure and regulatory convergence. *Telecommunications Policy, 25*, 431–452. doi:10.1016/S0308-5961(01)00015-5

Gardner, B., & Levy, S. J. (1955, March). The product and the brand. *Harvard Business Review*, 33–39.

Gardner, P. (2001, June 1). Games with a day job: Putting the power of games to work. *Gamasutra.* Retrieved August 18, 2008 from http://www.gamasutra.com/features/20010601/gardner_01.htm

Garfield, B. (2009). *The Chaos Scenario.* Stielstra Publishing.

Garretson, J. A., & Burton, S. (2005, October). The role of spokescharacters as advertisement and package cues in integrated marketing communications. *Journal of Marketing, 69*, 118–132. doi:10.1509/jmkg.2005.69.4.118

Garris, R., Ahlers, R., & Driskell, J. E. (2002). Games, motivation, and learning: A research and practice model. *Simulation & Gaming, 33*, 441–467. doi:10.1177/1046878102238607

Gartner, Inc. (2007, April 24). *Gartner says 80 percent of active Internet users will have a second life in the virtual world by the end of 2011.* Retrieved May 29, 2008, from http://gartner.com/it/page.jsp?id=503861

Garver, E. (1994). *Aristotle's rhetoric: An art of character.* Chicago, IL: University of Chicago Press.

Gaudiosi, J. (2006). Product placement to die for. *Wired.* Retrieved April 25, 2008 from http://www.wired.com/wired/archive/14.04/gads.html.

Gaziano, C., & McGrath, K. (1986). Measuring the concept of credibility. *The Journalism Quarterly, 63*, 451–462.

Gebhardt, W. A., & Brosschot, J. F. (2002). Desirability of control: Psychometric properties and relationships with locus of control, personality, coping, and mental and somatic complaints in three Dutch samples. *European Journal of Personality, 16*, 423–438. doi:10.1002/per.463

Gee, J. P. (2003). *What video games have to teach us about learning and literacy. NY*. New York: Palgrave MacMillan.

Geertz, C. (1974). Myth, symbol and culture. *Proceedings of the American Academy of Arts and Sciences, 101*, 1.

Gentile, D. A., & Gentile, J. R. (2008). Violent video games as exemplary teachers: a conceptual analysis. *Journal of Youth and Adolescence, 37*, 127–141. doi:10.1007/s10964-007-9206-2

Gentleman, A. (2007, May). Sex education curriculum angers Indian conservatives. *International Herald Tribune| ASIA-Pacific*. Retrieved January 20, 2009, from http://www.iht.com/articles/2007/05/24/africa/letter.php

Gerba, B. (2008, January 1). Media Metrics: Finding the Darjeeling Limit. *MediaPost Magazines*.

Gerbner, G. (1969). *Towards 'Cultural Indicators': The Analysis of Mass Mediated Public Message Systems*.

Gerdes, J. Jr, Stringam, B. B., & Brookshire, R. G. (2008). An integrative approach to assess qualitative and quantitative consumer feedback. *Electronic Commerce Research, 8*(4), 217–234. doi:10.1007/s10660-008-9022-0

Gere, C. (2002). *Digital Culture*. London: Reaktion Books.

Gere faces Indian arrest warrant. (2007, April 27). *BBC News*. Retrieved January 13, 2009, from http://news.bbc.co.uk/2/hi/entertainment/6596163.stm

Gere kiss sparks India protests. (2007, April 16). *BBC News*. Retrieved January 13, 2009, from http://news.bbc.co.uk/2/hi/entertainment/6560371.stm

Ghani, J. A., & Deshpande, S. P. (1994). Task characteristics and the experience of optimal flow in human-computer interaction. *The Journal of Psychology, 128*(4), 381–391.

Ghose, A., & Yang, S. (2008). Analyzing Search Engine Advertising: Firm Behavior and Cross-Selling in Electronic Markets. In *Internet Monetization–Sponsored Search, International World Wide Web Conference Committee (IW3C2)*, April 21–25, 2008, Beijing, China.

Gibbs, N. (2008, November, 05). How Obama Rewrote the Book. *Time*. Retrieved November 18, 2008, from http://www.time.com/time/politics/article/0,8599,1856914,00.html

Giddens, A. (1976). *New rules of the sociological methods*. London: Hutchinson.

Gilbert, B. (2008, June 3). Strategy Analytics: Virtual Worlds Projected to Mushroom to Nearly One Billion Users. *Business Wire*. Retrieved June 3, 2008, from http://www.businesswire.com

Giles, M. (2008). *Customer centricity: monetizing authentic customer connections across the consumer journey*. Retrieved from http://www.archive.org/details/CustomerCentricity

Gillmor, D. (2006). *We the Media: Grassroots Journalism by the People, for the People*. Sebastopol, CA: O'Reilly Media.

Giroux, H. (2001). Cultural Studies as Performative Politics. *Cultural Studies ↔Critical Methodologies, 1*, 5-23.

Gladwell, M. (2002). *The tipping point: how little things can make a big difference*. New York: Little, Brown & Company.

Glass, Z. (2007). The effectiveness of product placement in video games. *Journal of Interactive Advertising, 8*(1). Retrieved from http://www.jiad.org/article96.

Gleick, J. (1987). *CHAOS: Making a New Science*. New York: Penguin Books.

Gluck, M., & Bruner, R. E. (2005). The Evolution of Rich Media Advertising. Current Market Trends, Success Metrics and Best Practices. *Radar Research & DoubleClick*. Retrieved from http://www.doubleclick.com/

Godek, J., & Yates, J. F. (2005). Marketing to Individual Consumers Online: The Influence of Perceived Control. *Online Consumer Psychology*, 225-244.

Godes, D., & Mayzlin, D. (2004). Using online conversations to study word-of-mouth communication. *Marketing Science, 23*(4), 545–560. doi:10.1287/mksc.1040.0071

Godin, S. (1999). *Permission Marketing: Turning Strangers into Friends, and Friends into Customers*. New York, NY: Simon & Schuster Adult Publishing Group.

Goel, L., & Mousavidin, E. (2007). vCRM: Virtual customer relationship management. *The Data Base for Advances in Information Systems, 38*(4), 56 60.

Goffman, E. (1959). *The presentation of self in everyday life*. Harmondsworth, UK: Penguin.

Goffman, E. (1963). *Stigma: Notes on the management of spoiled identity*. Englewood Cliffs, NJ: Prentice Hall.

Goffman, E. (1956). Embarrassment and social interaction. *American Journal of Sociology, 62*(3), 264–271. doi:10.1086/222003

Golan, G. J., & Zaidner, L. (2008). Creative strategies in viral advertising: An application of Taylor's six-segment message strategy wheel. *Journal of Computer-Mediated Communication*, *13*(4), 959–972. doi:10.1111/j.1083-6101.2008.00426.x

Goldsmith, R. E., & Horowitz, D. (2006). Measuring motivations for online opinion speaking. *Journal of Interactive Advertising*, *6*(2), 1–16.

Gong, L., & Nass, C. (2007). When a talking-face computer agent is half-human and half-humanoid: Human identity and consistency preference. *Human Communication Research*, *33*, 163–193. doi:10.1111/j.1468-2958.2007.00295.x

Gong, L., Appiah, O., & Elias, T. (2007). *See minorities through the lens of ethnic identity: Reflected onto racial representations of real humans and virtual humans*. Paper presented at the annual convention of the National Communication Association.

Good, N., Dhamija, R., Grossklags, J., Thaw, D., Aronowitz, S., Mulligan, D., & Konstan, J. (2005). Stopping Spyware at the Gate: A User Study of Privacy, Notice and Spyware. In *Symposium on Usable Privacy and Security (SOUPS)*, July 6-8, 2005, Pittsburgh, PA.

Goodman, D., Bradley, N. L., Paras, B., Williamson, I. J., & Bizzochi, J. (2006). Video gaming promotes concussion knowledge acquisition in youth hockey players. *Journal of Adolescence*, *29*, 351–360. doi:10.1016/j.adolescence.2005.07.004

Goodstein, A. (2007). *Totally wired: what teen and tweens are really doing online. NY*. New York: St.Martin's Press.

Goodwin, C. (1991). Privacy: Recognition of a consumer right. *Journal of Public Policy & Marketing*, *19*(Spring), 149–166.

Google Zeitgiest Archive. (2002). Retrieved April 22, 2008, from http://www.google.com/press/zeitgeist/archive.html

Gould, R. (1991). Multiple networks and mobilization in the Paris Commune, 1871. *American Sociological Review*, *56*, 716–729. doi:10.2307/2096251

Graakjær, N., & Jantzen, C. (Eds.). (2009a). *Music in advertising–Commercial sounds in media communication and other settings*. Aalborg, Denmark: Aalborg University Press.

Graakjær, N., & Jantzen, C. (2009b). Music for shopping–Supplementary sounds of consumption. In Graakjær, N., & Jantzen, C. (Eds.), *Music in advertising–Commercial sounds in media communication and other settings* (pp. 237–257). Aalborg, Denmark: Aalborg University Press.

Graber, D. A. (1990). Seeing is remembering. *The Journal of Communication*, *40*(3), 134–155. doi:10.1111/j.1460-2466.1990.tb02275.x

Grabowski, A., & Kruszewska, N. (2007). Experimental study of the structure of a social network and human dynamics in a virtual society. *International Journal of Modern Physics*, *18*(10), 1527–1535. doi:10.1142/S0129183107011480

Graf, J., & Aday, S. (2008). Selective attention to online political information. *Journal of Broadcasting & Electronic Media*, *52*(1), 86–100. doi:10.1080/08838150701820874

Graham, J., & Havlena, W. (2007). Finding the missing link: Advertising's impact on word of mouth, Web searches, and site visits. *Journal of Advertising Research*, *47*(4), 427–435. doi:10.2501/S0021849907070444

Graham, F. K. (1997). Afterward: Pre-attentive processing and passive and active attention. In Lang, P. J., Simons, R. F., & Balaban, M. (Eds.), *Attention and Orienting: Sensory and Motivational Processes* (pp. 417–452). Hillsdale, NJ: Erlbaum.

Graham, J. (2008, May 21). Online reviews can help grow a business: More consumer prowl Web looking for recommendations. *USA Today*.

Granbois, D. H. (1968, October). Improving the study of customer in-store behavior. *Journal of Marketing*, *32*, 28–32. doi:10.2307/1249334

Grannis, K., & Davis, E. (2008 April 8). Online Sales to Climb Despite Struggling Economy. *Forrester Research.* Retrieved January 13, 2009, from http://forrester.com

Graves, L. (2008). A second life for higher Ed. *U.S. News & World Report*, *144*(2), 49–50.

Greats Enters, V. $1.5 Billion Virtual Goods Market. (2008, June 9). *Business Wire*. Retrieved June 9, 2008, from http://www.businesswire.com

Green, M. C., & Brock, T. C. (2000). The role of transportation in the persuasiveness of public narratives. *Journal of Personality and Social Psychology*, *79*(5), 701–721. doi:10.1037/0022-3514.79.5.701

Green, P. E., & Rao, V. R. (1970). Rating scales and information recovery. How many scales and response categories to use? *Journal of Marketing*, *34*(3), 33–39. doi:10.2307/1249817

Green, A. (2007 March). Are viewers engaged with advertising? Does it matter? *WARC Media FAQ*. Retrieved October 25, 2008, from http://www.warc.com/LandingPages/Generic/Results.asp?Ref=76

Greenberg, B. S., & Brand, J. E. (n.d.). Commercials in the classroom: The impact of channel one advertising. *Journal of Advertising Research*, *34*(1), 18–27.

Greenberg, B. S., & Salwen, M. B. (1996). Mass communication theory and research: Concepts and models. In Salwen, M. B., & Stacks, D. W. (Eds.), *An Integrated Approach to Communication Theory and Research* (pp. 63–78). Mahwah, NJ: Lawrence Erlbaum Associates.

Greenwald, A. G., & Clark, L. (1984). Audience Involvement in Advertising: Four Levels. *The Journal of Consumer Research, 11*, 581–598. doi:10.1086/208994

Greenwald, A. G. (1968). Cognitive learning, cognitive response to persuasion, and attitude change. In Greenwald, T. B., & Ostrom, T. (Eds.), *Psychological Foundations of Attitudes* (pp. 147–170). New York: Academic Press.

Grice, H. P. (1975). Logic and Conversation. In P. Cole & J. L. Morgan (Eds.), *Syntax and Semantics, Vol. 3, Speech Acts*. New York: Academic Press.

Griffiths, M. D., Davies, M. N. O., & Chappell, D. (2003). Breaking the stereotype: The case of online gaming. *Cyberpsychology & Behavior, 6*, 81–91. doi:10.1089/109493103321167992

Griffiths, M. D., Davies, M. N. O., & Chappell, D. (2004a). Online computer gaming: A comparison of adolescent and adult gamers. *Journal of Adolescence, 27*, 87–96. doi:10.1016/j.adolescence.2003.10.007

Griffiths, M. D., Davies, M. N. O., & Chappell, D. (2004b). Demographic factors and playing variables in online computer gaming. *Cyberpsychology & Behavior, 7*, 479–487. doi:10.1089/cpb.2004.7.479

Grigorovici, D. M., & Constantin, C. D. (2004). Experiencing interactive advertising beyond rich media: Impacts of ad type and presence on brand effectiveness in 3D gaming immersive virtual environments. *Journal of Interactive Media, 5*(1), 31–53.

Grise, M., & Gallupe, B. (2000). Information overload: Addressing the productivity paradox in face-to-face electronic meeting. *Journal of Management Information Systems, 16*(3), 157–185.

Griswold, C. (2007). Plato on rhetoric and poetry [Electronic Version]. *The Stanford Encyclopedia of Philosophy* Retrieved June 27, 2008 from http://plato.stanford.edu/archives/sum2007/entries/plato-rhetoric/

Grohs, R., & Reisinger, H. (2005). Image transfer in sports sponsorships: An assessment of moderating effects. *International Journal of Sports Marketing & Sponsorship, 1*, 42–48.

Gronau, R. (1977, December). Leisure, home production, and work: The theory of the allocation of time revisited. *The Journal of Political Economy, 85*, 1099–1123. doi:10.1086/260629

Gross, R., Acquisti, A., & Heinz, A. (2005). Information Revelation and Privacy in Online Social Networks. In *Proceedings of the 2005 ACM workshop on Privacy in electronic society* (pp. 71-80).

Grossman, L. (2006, December 13). Time's person of the year: you. *TIME*. Retrieved July18, 2008, from http://www.time.com/time/magazine/article/0,9171,1569514,00. html? cnn=yes

Gruen, T. W., Osmonbekov, T., & Czaplewski, A. J. (2006). eWOM: The impact of customer-to-customer online know-how exchange on customer value and loyalty. *Journal of Business Research, 59*(4), 449–456. doi:10.1016/j.jbusres.2005.10.004

Grunfeld, V. (1975). *Games of the World: How to Make Them How to Play Them, How They Came to Be*. New York: Holt, Rinehart and Winston.

Grüter, B., Mielke, A., & Oks, M. (. (2005). Mobile gaming–experience design. In *Proceedings from pervasive: The 3rd International Conference on Pervasive Computing*, Munich.

Guadagno, R., Blascovish, J., Bilenson, J., & Mccall, C. (2007). Virtual humans and persuasion: The effects of agency and behavioral realism. *Media Psychology, 10*, 1–22.

Gueorguieva, V. (2008). Voters, MySpace, and YouTube: The impact of alternative communication channels on the 2006 election cycle and beyond. *Social Science Computer Review, 26*(3), 288–300. doi:10.1177/0894439307305636

Gunter, B., Furnham, A., & Frost, C. (1994). Recall by young people of television advertisements as a function of programme type and audience evaluation. *Psychological Reports, 75*, 1107–1120.

Gunter, B. (2003). *News and the Net*. Mahwah, NJ: Lawrence Erlbaum Associates.

Gupta, P. B., & Lord, K. R. (1998). Product placement in movies: The effect of prominence and mode on audience recall. *Journal of Current Issues in Research and Advertising, 20*(1), 47–59.

Gustafson, D. H., Hawkins, R., Pingree, S., McTavish, F., Arora, N. K., & Mendenhall, J. (2001). Effect of computer support on younger women with breast cancer. *Journal of General Internal Medicine, 16*(7), 435–445. doi:10.1046/j.1525-1497.2001.016007435.x

Guttman, R. H., Moukas, A. G., & Maes, P. (1998). Agent-mediated electronic commerce: A survey. *The Knowledge Engineering Review, 13*(2), 147–159. doi:10.1017/S0269888998002082

Gwinner, K. P. (1997). A model of image creation and image transfer in event sponsorship. *International Marketing Review, 14*(3), 145–158. doi:10.1108/02651339710170221

Gwinner, K. P., & Eaton, J. (1999). Building brand image through event sponsorship: The role of image transfer. *Journal of Advertising, 28*(4), 47–58.

Habermas, J. (1984). The Theory of Communicative Action: *Vol. 1. Reason and the Rationalization of Society* (McCarthy, T., Trans.). Boston: Beacon Press.

Habermas, J. (1987). The Theory of Communicative Action: *Vol. 2. Lifeworld and System: A Critique of Functionalist Reason* (McCarthy, T., Trans.). Boston: Beacon Press.

Hagel, J., & Armstrong, A. G. (1997). *Net gain: Expanding markets through virtual communities*. Boston: Harvard Business School Press.

Haidt, J., & Rodin, J. (1999). Control and efficacy as interdisciplinary bridges. *Review of General Psychology, 3*(4), 317–337. doi:10.1037/1089-2680.3.4.317

Hair, J. F., Anderson, R. E., Tatham, R. L., & Black, W. C. (1998). *Multivariate Data Analysis* (5th ed.). Upper Saddle River, NJ: Prentice Hall.

Halperin, M. (2008, November 5). A Campaign of Firsts: Internet Fund-Raising Comes of Age. *Time*. Retrieved November 18, 2008, from http://www.time.com/time/specials/packages/article/0,28804,1856329_1856326_1856295,00.html

Hancock, J. T., Toma, C., & Ellison, N. (2007). *The truth about lying in online dating profiles*. Paper presented at the Conference on Human Factors in Computing Systems, San Jose, California.

Handshake Marketing and Business Development. (n.d.) Retrieved from http://www.handshakemarketing.com

Hans, H. B., Neumann, M. M., Haber, T. E., & Mader, F. (2006). Virtual sales agents. In

Hansell, S. (2005, August 1). More people turn to the Web to watch TV. *New York Times*. Retrieved June 26, 2007, from http://www.nytimes.com/2005/08/01/technology/01video.html?pagewanted=1&ei=5070&en=738e29c3e0711720&ex=1184558400.

Hansell, S. (2008). *A second leader for Second Life*. Retrieved on 05/07/08 from http://bits.blogs.nytimes.com/2008/05/05/a-second-leader-for-second-life/

Hansell, S. (2009, March 19). An Icon That Says They're Watching You. *Bits Blog - The New York Times*. Retrieved June 15, 2009, from http://bits.blogs.nytimes.com/2009/03/19/an-icon-that-says-theyre-watching-you/

Harai, T. T., Lampert, S. I., & Wilzig, S. L. (2007). Information processing of advertising among young people: The elaboration likelihood model as applied to youth. *Journal of Advertising Research, 47*(3), 326–340. doi:10.2501/S0021849907070341

Hardey, M. (2001). 'E-health': The Internet and the transformation of patients into consumers and producers of health knowledge. *Information Communication and Society, 4*(3), 388–405.

Hardin, R. (2002). *Trust and Trustworthiness*. New York: Russell Sage Foundation.

Hargittai, E. (2008). Whose space? Differences among users and non-users of social network sites. *Journal of Computer-Mediated Communication, 13*, 276–297. doi:10.1111/j.1083-6101.2007.00396.x

Harmon, R., & Coney, H. (1982). The persuasive effects of source credibility in buy and lease situations. *JMR, Journal of Marketing Research, 19*(May), 255–260. doi:10.2307/3151625

Harper, N. (1979). *Human Communication Theory: The History of a Paradigm*. Rochelle Park, NJ: Hayden Book Company, Inc.

Harris, R. J. (2004). *A cognitive psychology of mass communication* (4th ed.). Mahwah, NJ: Lawrence Erlbaum Associates.

Harris, P. (2007). Inside out: The realities of virtual business. *J@pan Inc., 74*(Nov/Dec).

Hart, C., & Blackshaw, P. (2006 January). Internet Inferno. *Marketing Management,* 19-25.

Hartman, C. L., & Kiecker, P. L. (1991). Marketplace influencers at the point of purchase: The role of purchase pals in consumer decision making. In *1991 AMA summer educators' conference proceedings* (pp. 461–469). Chicago: American Marketing Association.

Harvey, B. (2001). Measuring the effects of sponsorship. *Journal of Advertising Research, 41*(1), 59–65.

Haselager, G. J. T., Cillessen, A. H. N., Van Lieshout, C. F. M., Riksen-Walraven, J. M. A., & Hartup, W. W. (2002). Heterogeneity among peer-rejected boys across middle childhood: developmental pathways of social behaviour. *Developmental Psychology, 38*, 446–456. doi:10.1037/0012-1649.38.3.446

Haubl, G., & Trifts, V. (2000). Consumer decision making in online shopping environments: The effects of interactive decision aids. *Marketing Science, 19*(1), 4–21. doi:10.1287/mksc.19.1.4.15178

Hauseman, A. V., & Siekpe, J. S. (2008). The effect of web interface features on consumer online purchase intentions. *Journal of Business Research, 62*, 5–13. doi:10.1016/j.jbusres.2008.01.018

Haven, B. (2007, August). *Marketing's New Key Metric: Engagement*. Forrester Research Report.

Hayden, T. (2008). *Successfully executing integrated experiences in today's alternative reality*. Retrieved from http://www.archive.org/details/SuccessfullyExecutingIntegratedExperiencesInTodaysAlternativeReality

Hayles, N. K. (1999). *How we became posthuman: virtual bodies in cybernetics, literature, and informatics*. Chicago: University of Chicago Press.

Haythornthwaite, C. (2000). Online personal networks. *New Media & Society*, *2*(2), 195–226. doi:10.1177/14614440022225779

Heath, R. G. (2000). Low involvement processing–a new model of brands and advertising. *International Journal of Advertising*, *19*(3), 287–298.

Heath, R. L., & Bryant, J. B. (2000). *Human Communication Theory and Research: Concepts, Contexts, and Challenges*. Mahwah, NJ: Lawrence Erlbaum Associates.

Heath, R. (2007). *Emotional persuasion in advertising: a hierarchy-of-processing model*. Working Paper 2007.07, School of Management, University of Bath.

Heatherton, T. F., & Polivy, J. (1991). Development and validation of a scale for measuring state self-esteem. *Journal of Personality and Social Psychology*, *60*, 895–910. doi:10.1037/0022-3514.60.6.895

Heaton, T. (2009, July 20). *CPM rates are falling (Thank God)*. Message posted to http://www.thepomoblog.com/

Hebdige, D. (1979). *Subculture: The Meaning Of Style*. London: Routledge. doi:10.4324/9780203139943

Heeter, C. (1992). Being there: the subjective experience of presence. *Presence (Cambridge, Mass.)*, *1*(2), 262–271.

Heeter, C. (1989). *Implications of New Interactive Technologies for Conceptualizing Communication in Media Use in the Information Age: Emerging Patterns of Adoption and Consumer Use*. Hillsdale, NJ: Lawrence Erlbaum Associates.

Hein, K. (2007, August 6). Teen talk is, like, totally branded. *Brandweek*. Retrieved August, 1, 2008, from http://www.kellerfay.com/?page_id=123

Heinz. (2007, August 11). *Heinz 'Top This!' campaign tops list of consumer-generated efforts* [Company Release]. Retrieved March 19, 2009, from http://www.prweb.com/releases/2007/08/prweb545964.htm

Helm, B. (2009, April 7). Will Targeted TV Ads Justify Higher Fees? *Business Week*. Retrieved June 15, 2009, from http://www.businessweek.com/magazine/content/09_16/b4127000389178.htm

Hemp, P. (2006). Avatar-based marketing. *Harvard Business Review*, *84*(6), 48–56.

Hendaoui, A., Limayem, A., & Thompson, C. W. (2008, January). 3D social virtual world: Research issues and challenges. *IEEE Internet Computing*, 88–92. doi:10.1109/MIC.2008.1

Hendriks-Vettehen, P. G., Schaap, G., & Schlosser, S. (2004). What men and women think while watching the news: An exploration. *Communications: The European Journal of Communication Research*, *29*, 235–251.

Hennig-Thurau, T., Gwinner, K. P., Walsh, G., & Gremler, D. D. (2004). Electronic word-of-mouth via consumer-opinion platforms: What motivates consumers to articulate themselves on the Internet? *Journal of Interactive Marketing*, *18*(1), 38–52. doi:10.1002/dir.10073

Herek, G. M. (1987). Can functions be measured? A new perspective on the functional approach to attitudes. *Social Psychology Quarterly*, *50*(4), 285–303. doi:10.2307/2786814

Herek, G. M., & Glunt, E. K. (1988). An epidemic of stigma: Public reactions to AIDS. *The American Psychologist*, *43*(11), 886–891. doi:10.1037/0003-066X.43.11.886

Herlocker, J., Konstan, J., & Riedl, J. (2000, December 2-6, 2000). *Explaining Collaborative Filtering Recommendations*. Paper presented at the ACM 2000 Conference on Computer Supported Cooperative Work.

Herman, A., Coombe, R. J., & Kaye, L. (2006). Your Second Life? Goodwill and the performativity of intellectual property in online digital gaming. *Cultural Studies*, *20*(2/3), 184–210. doi:10.1080/09502380500495684

Herman, L., Horwitz, J., Kent, S., & Miller, S. (2008). The history of video games. *Gamespot*. Retrieved February 10, 2008, from http://www.gamespot.com/gamespot/features/video/hov/

Herr, P. M. (1986). Consequences of priming: Judgment and behavior. *Journal of Personality and Social Psychology*, *51*(6), 1106–1115. doi:10.1037/0022-3514.51.6.1106

Herring, S. C., Kouper, I., Scheidt, L. A., & Wright, E. L. (2004). Women and Children Last: The Discursive Construction of Weblogs. *Into the Blogosphere: Rhetoric, Community, and Culture of Weblogs*. Retrieved August, 23, 2008, from http://blog.lib.umn.edu/blogosphere/women_and_children.html

Hersh, A. (2006). *I know how you feel: A person-centered approach to supportive messages in online breast cancer groups.* Paper presented at the annual International Communication Association, New York, NY.

Hessel, E. (2009, May 28). Gray Lady Juicing up Digital Ads. *Forbes.com*. Retrieved June 15, 2009, from http://www.forbes.com/2009/05/28/new-york-times-business-media-advertising.html

Hewitt, D. (2009, January 28). Computer and video game industry tops $22 billion in 2008 (press release). *Entertainment Software Association*. Retrieved September 27, 2009, from http://www.theesa.com/newsroom/release_detail.asp?releaseID=44

Higgins, E. T. (1987). Self-discrepancy: A theory relating self and affect. *Psychological Review, 94*(3), 319–340. doi:10.1037/0033-295X.94.3.319

Higgins, E. T., & King, G. A. (1981). Accessibility of Social Constructs: Information Processing Consequences of Individual and Contextual Variability. In Cantor, N., & Kihlstrom, J. F. (Eds.), *Personality, Cognition and Social Interaction*. Hillsdale, NJ: Erlbaum.

Hinduja, S., & Patchin, J. W. (2008). Personal information of adolescents on Internet: a quantitative content analysis of MySpace. *Journal of Adolescence, 31*, 125–146. doi:10.1016/j.adolescence.2007.05.004

Hine, C., & Eve, J. (1998). Privacy in the Marketplace. *The Information Society, 14*(4), 253–262. doi:10.1080/019722498128700

Hinton, A. (2006). We live here: Games, third places and the information architecture of the future. *Bulletin of the American Society for Information Science and Technology, 32*(6), 17–21. Retrieved May 30, 2009, from http://www.asis.org/Bulletin/Aug-06/hinton.html

Hitwise. (2007). *Hitwise Industry Report for Shopping and Classifieds*.

Hlem, B., & Kiley, D. (2009, January 12). Edgy advertising in a tenuous time. *Business Week*, 48.

Ho, J., & Tang, K. (2001). Towards an Optimal Resolution to Information Overload: An Infomediary Approach. In *Proceedings of the 2001 International ACM SIGGROUP Conference Supporting Group Work* (pp. 91-96). Boulder, CO: ACM Press.

Hodder, C. (2002). *God and Gap: What has Asda got to do with Jerusalem? Branding and being a Christian in the 21st century—some Reflections*. Retrieved January 21, 2008, from http://wwwinstitutefor brand leadership.org/Chris_Hodder-Brands_and_Theology.htm

Hof, R. (2006 October). *Unrepentant PayPerPost Gets Funding*. Retrieved September 26, 2007, from http://www.businessweek.com/the_thread/techbeat/archives/2006/10/unrepentant_pay.html

Hof, R. (2007, April 16). The Coming Virtual Web. *Business Week*. Retrieved June 15, 2007, from http://www.businessweek.com/technology/content/apr2007/tc20070416_780263.htm

Hoffer, E. (1951). *The True Believer*. New York: Harper & Row Publishers, Inc.

Hoffman, D. L., & Novak, T. P. (1996). Marketing in hypermedia computer-mediated environments: Conceptual foundations. *Journal of Marketing, 60*(July), 50–68. doi:10.2307/1251841

Hoffman, D. L., & Novak, T. P. (1996, January). A new marketing paradigm for electronic commerce. *The Information Society, 13*, 43–54.

Hoffman, D. L., & Patrali, C. (1995). Commercial Scenarios for the Web: Opportunities and Challenges. *Journal of Computer-Mediated Communication, 1*(3). Retrieved May 6, 2008, from http://www3.interscience.wiley.com/journal/120837666/abstract?CRETRY=1&SRETRY=0

Hoffman, D. L., Novak, T. P., & Chatterjee, P. (1995). *Commercial Scenarios for the Web: Opportunities and Challenges*. Retrieved May 24, 2008, from http//slum.huji.ac.il/Vol1/issue3/hoffman.html

Hofmans, J., Theuns, P., Baekelandt, S., Mairesse, O., Schillewaert, N., & Cools, W. (2007). Bias and changes in perceived intensity of verbal qualifiers effected by scale orientation. *Survey Research Methods, 1*(2), 97–108.

Hogg, M., Terry, D., & White, K. (1995). A tale of two theories: A critical comparison of identity theory with social identity theory. *Social Psychology Quarterly, 58*, 255–269. doi:10.2307/2787127

Hogg, M. A., Hardie, E. A., & Reynolds, K. J. (1995). Prototypical similarity, self-categorization, and depersonalized attraction: A perspective on group cohesiveness. *European Journal of Social Psychology, 25*(2), 159–177. doi:10.1002/ejsp.2420250204

Hogg, M. A. (2004). Social categorization, depersonalization, and group behavior. In Brewer, M. B., & Hewstone, M. (Eds.), *Self and social identity*. London: Blackwell Publishing.

Holbrook, M. B., & Hirschman, E. C. (1982). The experiential aspects of consumption: consumer fantasies, feelings, and fun. *The Journal of Consumer Research, 9*(2), 132–140. doi:10.1086/208906

Holbrook, A. L., Krosnick, J. A., Moore, D., & Tourangeau, R. (2007). Response order effects in dichotomous categorical questions presented orally: The impact of question and respondent attributes. *Public Opinion Quarterly*, *71*(3), 325–348. doi:10.1093/poq/nfm024

Hollis, N. (2005, June). Ten years of learning on how online advertising builds brands. *Journal of Advertising Research*, (June): 255–268. doi:10.1017/S0021849905050270

Holloway, S. L., & Valentine, G. (2003). *Cyberkids: children in the information age*. London: Routledge.

Holt, D. B. (1995). How consumers consume: A typology of consumption practices. *The Journal of Consumer Research*, *22*(1), 1–25. doi:10.1086/209431

Holzwarth, M., Janiszewski, C., & Neumann, M. M. (2006). The influence of avatars on online consumer shopping behavior. *Journal of Marketing*, *70*(4), 19–36. doi:10.1509/jmkg.70.4.19

Horovitz, B. (2010, March 5). Oscar advertisers hope to build buzz on Twitter, Facebook. *USA Today*. Retrieved March 5, 2010, from http://www.usatoday.com/money/media/2010-03-05-oscarsocial05_ST_N.htm

Horwitz, R. B. (2005). On media concentration and the diversity question. *The Information Society*, *21*(3), 181–204. doi:10.1080/01972240490951908

Horwitz, J. (2004, September 23). Advertising and cross-promotion. *Jupiter Research*. Retrieved August 19, 2008 from http://www.jupiterresearch.com/bin/item.pl/research:concept/111/id=95647/

Hou, J., & Rego, C. (2002). *Internet Marketing: an Overview*. University of Mississippi Working Paper. Retrieved June 15, 2007 from http://faculty.bus.olemiss.edu/crego/papers/hces0802.pdf

Hovland, C., Janis, I., & Kelley, H. (1953). *Communication and Persuasion*. New Haven, CT: Yale University Press.

Hovland, C. I., & Weiss, W. (1951). The influence of source credibility on communication effectiveness. *Public Opinion Quarterly*, *15*, 635–650. doi:10.1086/266350

Howell, M. (2007). The history of federal abstinence-only funding.*Advocates for Youth*. Retrieved March 15, 2009, from http://www.advocatesforyouth.org/publications/factsheet/fshistoryabonly.pdf

Hoyer, W. D., & Brown, S. P. (1990). Effects of brand awareness on choice for a common, repeat purchase product. *The Journal of Consumer Research*, *17*, 141–148. doi:10.1086/208544

Hrastnik, R. (2005). The Full Circle of RSS Marketing Power. *RSS-Specifications.com*. Retrieved November 16, 2007, from http://www.rss-specifications.com/full-circle-rss.htm

Hsu, S. H., Lee, F., & Wu, M. (2005). Designing action games for appealing to buyers. *Cyberpsychology & Behavior*, *8*, 585–591. doi:10.1089/cpb.2005.8.585

Hu, N., Pavlou, P. A., & Zhang, J. (2006). Can Online Reviews Reveal a Product's True Quality? Empirical Findings and Analytical Modeling of Online Word-of-Mouth Communication. In *Proceedings of the 7th ACM Conference on Electronic Commerce* (pp. 324-330).

Huang, C., Shen, Y., Lin, H., & Chang, S. (2007). Bloggers' motivations and behaviors: A model. *Journal of Advertising Research*, *47*(4), 472–484. doi:10.2501/S0021849907070493

Huang, M.-H. (2003). Designing Website Attributes to Induce Experiential Encounters. In *Computers in Human Behavior* (Vol. 19, pp. 425-442). Retrieved April 25, 2003, from http://www.elsevier.com/locate/comphumbeh/

Hugues, J. (2007). From virtual sex to no sex*? Ethical Technology*. Retrieved March 1, 2008, from http://ieet.org/index.php/IEET/more/hughes20070228/

Huhtamo, E. (1999). From cybernation to interaction: a contribution to an archeology of interactivity. In Lunenfeld, I. P. (Ed.), *The Digital Dialectic: New Essays on New Media* (pp. 96–110). Cambridge, MassMA: The MIT Press.

Hulu. (n.d.). Retrieved from http://www.hulu.com

Human Factors Engineering. (n.d.). Retrieved March 8, 2009, from http://reliability.sandia.gov/Human_Factor_Engineering/human_factor_engineering.html

Hung, K. H., & Li, S. Y. (2007). The influence of eWOM on virtual consumer communities: Social capital, consumer learning, and behavioral outcomes. *Journal of Advertising Research*, *47*(4), 485–495. doi:10.2501/S002184990707050X

Hunt, S. D. (1991). *Modern marketing theory: Critical issues in the philosophy of marketing science*. Cincinnati, OH: South-Western Publishing Co.

Hussain, Z., & Griffiths, M. D. (2008). Gender swapping and socializing in cyberspace: an exploratory study. *Cyberpsychology & Behavior*, *11*(1), 47–53. doi:10.1089/cpb.2007.0020

Hwang, J.-S., & McMillan, S. J. (2004). How Consumers Think About 'Interactive' Aspects of Web Advertising. In Gao, Y. (Ed.), *Web Systems Design and Online Consumer Behavior* (pp. 69–89). Hershey, PA: Idea Publishing.

Hyman, P. (2007, February 7). Burger King Has it Their Way with Advergame Sales. *Hollywood Reporter*.

IAB. (2006). Interactive advertising revenues grow 30% to a record $12.5 billion in '05. *Interactive Advertising Bureau.* Retrieved April 12, 2006, from http://iab.printthis.clickability.com/pt/cpt?action=cpt&title=IAB+Press+Release&expire=&urlID=17977334&fb=Y&url=http://www.iab.net/news/pr_2006_04_20.asp&partnerID=297

IDC. (2008May). U.S. Internet Advertising 2008–2012 Forecast and Analysis: Defying Economic Crisis.

IDC. (2008, May 30). *IDC Finds Internet Advertising Keeps Growing Fast Despite Economic Difficulties.* IDC Press release. Retrieved from http://www.idc.com/getdoc.jsp?containerId=prUS21260308

India Together. (2008 September). *Their secret status and a riskyschooling.* Retrieved January 20, 2009, from http://www.indiatogether.org/2007/sep/chi-aidskids.htm

India's Shyness towards Sexual Education Fuelling AIDS. (2002, November 1). *The HIV Update International, 2*(37).

In-game advertising. (2008). In *Wikipedia, the Free Encyclopedia.* Retrieved April 25, 2008 from http://en.wikipedia.org/wiki/In-game_advertising#cite_note-adweek-0

In-Store Marketing Institute. (n.d.). Retrieved from http://www.instoremarketer.org

Internet World Statistics. (2008). *Internet Usage Statistics, the Big Picture*. Retrieved August 19, 2008, from http://www.internetworldstats.com/stats.htm

Iosifidis, P. (2005). The Application of EC Competition Policy to the Media Industry, *International Journal on Media Management, 7*(3\4), 103-111.

Irwin, R. L., Lachowetz, T., Cornwell, T. B., & Clark, J. S. (2003). Cause-related sport sponsorship: An assessment of spectator beliefs, attitudes, and behavioral intentions. *Sport Marketing Quarterly, 12*(3), 131–139.

Ishii, K. (2006). Implications of mobility: the uses of personal communication media in everyday life. *The Journal of Communication, 56*, 346–365. doi:10.1111/j.1460-2466.2006.00023.x

Ito, M., & Daisuke, O. (2009). Technosocial Situations: Emergent Structurings of Mobile Email Use. In Ito, M., Matsuda, M., & Okabe, D. (Eds.), *Personal, Portable, Intimate: Mobile Phones in Japanese Life*. Cambridge, MA: MIT Press.

Ito, M., & Okabe, D. (2005). Intimate connections: contextualizing Japanese youth and mobile messaging. In R. Harper, L. Palen and & A. Taylor (Eds.). *The inside text: social, cultural and design perspectives of SMS* (pp. 127-146). Dordrecht, The Netherlands: Springer.

Iyengar, S., & Kinder, D. M. (1987). *News that Matters*. Chicago, IL: University of Chicago Press.

Iyengar, S., & Prior, M. (1999). *Political advertising: What effect on commercial advertisers?* USA: Department of Communication, Stanford University.

Izard, C. (1971). *The face of emotion*. New York: Appleton-Century-Cofts.

Jackson, D. M., & Fulberg, P. (2003). *Sonic branding*. Houndmills, UK: Palgrave. doi:10.1057/9780230503267

Jaffe, J. (2004, February 18). Case study: See what happens. *iMedia Connection.* Retrieved July 17, 2008, from http://www.imediaconnection.com/printpage/printpage.aspx?id=2821

Jaffee, L. (2007, June 20). California man wins Vegas.com ad contest. *Promo Xtra*. Retrieved June 26, 2007, from http://promomagazine.com/contests/news/california_man_wins_vegas_ad_contest_062007/index.html

James, M., Hoff, T., Davis, J., & Graham, R. (2005). Leveraging the powerof the media to combat HIV/AIDS. *Health Affairs, 24*(3), 854–857. doi:10.1377/hlthaff.24.3.854

Jameson, A. (2002). Adaptive interfaces and agents. In Jacko, J., & Sears, A. (Eds.), *Handbook of human-computer interaction* (pp. 305–330). New York: Lawrence Erlbaum Associates.

Jan, T. (2006). *Parents rip school over gay storybook*. The Boston Globe. Retrieved March 16, 2009, from http://www.boston.com/news/local/articles/2006/04/20/parents_rip_school_over_gay_storybook/

Jana, R. (2006). Is that a video game—or an ad? *Business Week.* Retrieved October 1, 2008 from http://www.businessweek.com/innovate/content/jan2006/id20060124_792815.htm

Janiszewski, C. (1993). Preattentive mere exposure effects. *The Journal of Consumer Research, 20*, 376–392. doi:10.1086/209356

Janoschka, A. (2004). *Web Advertising. New forms of communication on the Internet*. Philadelphia, PA: John Benjamins Publishing Company.

Jansen, B. J., & Resnick, M. (2006). An examination of searchers' perceptions of non-sponsored and sponsored links during ecommerce Web searching. *Journal of the American Society for Information Science and Technology, 57*, 1949–1961. doi:10.1002/asi.20425

Jansz, J., & Martens, L. (2005). Gaming at a LAN event: the social context of playing video games. *New Media & Society, 7*(3), 333–355. doi:10.1177/1461444805052280

Jee, J., & Lee, W. N. (2002). Antecedents and consequences of perceived interactivity: An exploratory study. *Journal of Interactive Advertising*, *3*(1), 1–26.

Jehmlich, D. (2007). Gamevertising: An interactive advertising experience. *Trendburo*. Retrieved February 11, 2009 from http://www.trendbuero.de/index.php?f_articleId=1880&f_categoryId=155

Jenkins, H. (2004). The cultural logic of media convergence. *International Journal of Cultural Studies*, *7*(1), 33–43. doi:10.1177/1367877904040603

Jensen, J. F. (1999). 'Interactivity'–Tracking a New Concept in Media and Communication Studies. In Mayer, P. A. (Ed.), *Computer Media and Communication. A Reader* (pp. 160–187). Oxford, UK: Oxford University Press.

Jensen, C., Farnham, S. D., Drucker, S. M., & Kollock, P. (2000 April). *The effect of communication modality on cooperation in online environment.* Paper presented at the CHI, Hague, Netherlands.

Jesdanun, A. (2008). Cell Phones Represent a New Media for Companies. *Single Touch*. Retrieved March 1, 2009, from http://www2.singletouch.net/content/view/86/109/

Jessen, I. B. (2010). The Aesthetics of Web Advertising: Methodological Implications for the Study of Genre Development. In Brügger, N. (Ed.), *Web History* (pp. 257–277). New York: Peter Lang.

Jhally, S. (n.d.). *Advertising and the End of the World*. Lecture. Retrieved February 26, 2009, from http://www.sutjhally.com/audiovideo

Jiang, Z., & Benbasat, I. (2002). *Virtual Product Experience: Effects of Visual & Functionality Control of Products on Perceived Diagnosticity in Electronic Shopping*. University of British Columbia.

Jin, S. A., & Bolebruch, J. (2008). *Effects of Apple's spokes-avatar on iPhone advertising in Second Life*. Working paper presented at the 27th annual Advertising and Consumer Psychology Conference of the Society for Consumer Psychology, Philadelphia, 2008.

Jin, S. A., & Sung, Y. (2008). *Effects of brand personality on advertising in Second Life*. Working paper presented at the 27th annual Advertising and Consumer Psychology Conference of the Society for Consumer Psychology, Philadelphia, 2008.

John, D. R. (1999, December). Consumer socialization of children: a retrospective looks at twenty-five years of research. *Journal of Advertising Research*, (December): 183–213.

John, F. Kennedy School of Government, Harvard University. (2007). *A National Study in Confidence in Leadership, National Leadership Index 2007*. Retrieved from http://www.hks.harvard.edu/leadership/images/CPLpdf/cpl_index%202007%20(3).pdf.

John, F. Kennedy School of Government, Harvard University. (2008). *A National Study in Confidence in Leadership, National Leadership Index 2008 Draft*. Retrieved from http://content.ksg.harvard.edu/leadership/images/CPLpdf/nli%20report.pdf

Johnson, D. R., & Post, D. (1996). Law and Borders: The Rise of Law in Cyberspace. *Stanford Law Review*, *48*(1), 13–67.

Johnson, T. J., & Kaye, B. K. (2002). Webelievability: A path model examining how convenience and reliance predict online credibility. *Journalism & Mass Communication Quarterly*, *79*(3), 619–642.

Johnson, T. J., & Kaye, B. K. (2004). Wag the blog: How reliance on traditional media and the Internet influence credibility perceptions of weblogs among blog users. *Journalism & Mass Communication Quarterly*, *81*(3), 622–642.

Johnson, T. J., Kaye, B. K., Bichard, S. L., & Wong, W. J. (2007). Every blog has its day: Politically-interested Internet users' perceptions of blog credibility. *Journal of Computer-Mediated Communication*, *13*(1), 100–122. doi:10.1111/j.1083-6101.2007.00388.x

Johnson, H. M. (1961). *Sociology: a systematic introduction*. London: Routledge & Keegan Paul.

Johnson, J. E., & Christie, J. F. (2009). Play and digital media. *Computers in the Schools*, *26*, 284–289. doi:10.1080/07380560903360202

Joinson, A. N. (2001). Self-disclosure in computer-mediated communication: the role of self-awareness and visual anonymity. *European Journal of Social Psychology*, *31*, 177–192. doi:10.1002/ejsp.36

Jones, K. O., Denham, B. E., & Springston, J. K. (2006). Effects of mass and interpersonal communication on breast cancer screening: Advancing agenda-setting theory in health contexts. *Journal of Applied Communication Research*, *34*(1), 94–113. doi:10.1080/00909880500420242

Jones, C., Ramanau, R., Cross, S., & Healing, G. (2010). Net generation or digital natives: Is there a distinct new generation entering university? *Computers & Education*, *54*, 722–732. doi:10.1016/j.compedu.2009.09.022

Jones, H., & Soltren, J. H. (2005). *Facebook: Threats to Privacy.* Cambridge, MA: Massachusetts Institute of Technology.

Retrieved on April 30, 2008 from http://www.swiss.ai.mit.edu/6095/student-papers/fall05-papers/facebook.pdf

Jones, T. L. (n.d.). The O.J. Simpson Murder Trial: Prologue. *True TV*. Retrieved on February 25, 2009, from http://www.trutv.com/library/crime/notorious_murders/famous/simpson/index_1.html

Jordan, N. (1968). *Themes in Speculative Psychology*. London: Tavistock Publications.

Joseph, W. B. (1982). The credibility of physically attractive communicators: A review. *Journal of Advertising, 11*(3), 15–24.

Journal of Virtual Worlds. (2008). *Consumer Behavior in Virtual Worlds*. Special Issue, 1(November). (http://www.jvwr.com).

Juhasz, A. (2009). Learning the five lessons of YouTube: After trying to teach there, I don't believe the hype. *Cinema Journal, 48*(2), 145–150. doi:10.1353/cj.0.0098

Just, N., & Latzer, M. (2000). EC competition policy and market power control in the Mediamatics Era. *Telecommunications Policy, 24*, 395–411. doi:10.1016/S0308-5961(00)00035-5

Kadavasal, M. D., Dhara, K. K., Wu, X., & Krishnaswamy, V. (2007). Mixed reality for enhancing business communications using virtual worlds. In *Proceedings of the 2007 ACM symposium on Virtual reality software and technology* (pp. 233-234).

Kaferer, J. N. (1992). *Strategic Brand Management: New Approaches to Creating and Evaluating Brand Equity*. London: Logan Page.

Kahle, L. R., & Homer, P. M. (1985). Physical attractiveness of celebrity endorsers: A social, adaptation perspective. *The Journal of Consumer Research, 11*(4), 954–961. doi:10.1086/209029

Kahn, R., & Kellner, D. (2005a). Oppositional politics and the Internet: A critical/ reconstructive approach. *Cultural Politics, 1*, 75–100. doi:10.2752/174321905778054926

Kahn, R., & Kellner, D. (2005b). Reconstructing technoliteracy: A multiple literacy approach. *E-learning, 2*(3), 238–251. doi:10.2304/elea.2005.2.3.4

Kahney, L. (2000). The web the way it was. *Wired News*. Retrieved June 23, 2008, from http://www.wired.com/news/culture/0,1284,34006-2,00.html?tw=wn_story_page_next1

Kahney, L. (2004, December 13). Home-brew iPod ad opens eyes. *Wired*. Retrieved June 25, 2007, from http://www.wired.com/gadgets/mods/commentary/cultofmac/2004/12/66001

Kaid, L. L. (2004). *The handbook of political communication research*. Mahwah, NJ: Lawrence Erlbaum Associates.

Kaid, L. L. (1999). Political advertising: A summary of research findings. In Newman, B. (Ed.), *The handbook of political marketing* (pp. 423–438). Thousand Oaks, CA: Sage.

Kaid, L. L. (1981). Political advertising. In Nimmo, D. D., & Sanders, K. R. (Eds.), *Handbook of political communication* (pp. 249–271). Beverly Hills, CA: Sage.

Kaid, L. L. (1996). Political communication. In Salwen, M. B., & Stacks, D. W. (Eds.), *An integrated approach to communication theory and research* (pp. 443–457). Hillsdale, NJ: Lawrence Erlbaum Associates.

Kaid, L. L. (1997). Trends in political communication research. In Trent, J. S. (Ed.), *Communication: View from the helm for the twenty-first century* (pp. 122–126). Needham Heights, MA: Allyn & Bacon.

Kail, R. (2000). Speed of information processing: development change and links to intelligence. *Journal of School Psychology, 38*, 51–61. doi:10.1016/S0022-4405(99)00036-9

Kakihara, M., & Sørensen, C. (2002). Mobility: An Extended Perspective, *IEEE. Published iIn the Proceedings of the Hawai'i International Conference on System Sciences*, January 7-10, Big Island, Hawaii.

Kalaignanam, K., Kushwaha, T., & Varadarajan, P. (2008). Marketing operations efficiency and the Internet: An organizing framework. *Journal of Business Research, 61*(4), 300–308. doi:10.1016/j.jbusres.2007.06.019

Kalakota, R., & Robinson, M. (2001). *E-Business 2.0: Roadmap for Success*. Reading, MA: Addison-Wesley.

Kalehoff, M. (2009, April 3). A Note About Tracking Cookies, MediaPost Publications, Onelinespin@mediapost.com. Retrieved from http://www.mediapost.com/publications/?fa=Articles.showArticle&art_aid=103459.

Kalton, G., Collins, M., & Brook, L. (1978). Experiments in wording opinion questions. *Applied Statistics, 27*(2), 149–161. doi:10.2307/2346942

Kalyanam, K., & McIntyre, S. (2002). The e-marketing mix: A contribution of the e-tailing wars. *Journal of the Academy of Marketing Science, 30*(4), 487–499. doi:10.1177/009207002236924

Kamins, M. A. (1990). An investigation into the 'match-up' hypothesis in celebrity advertising: When beauty may be only skin deep. *Journal of Advertising, 19*(1), 4–13.

Kane, S. K., Wobbrock, J. O., & Smith, I. E. (2008). *Getting off the treadmill: evaluating walking user interfaces for mobile devices in public spaces*. Paper presented at the Proceedings of the 10th international conference on Human computer interaction with mobile devices and services.

Kang, H. S., & Yang, H. D. (2006). The visual characteristics of avatars in computer-mediated communication: Comparison of internet relay chat and instant messenger as of 2003. *International Journal of Human-Computer Studies, 64*, 1173–1183. doi:10.1016/j.ijhcs.2006.07.003

Kaplan, D., & Lefton, T. (2005, September 5-11). Molson Coors renewing with NFL. *Street & Smith's Sports Business Journal, 8*(18), 59.

Kaptein, M. C., Markopoulos, P., de Ruyter, B., & Aarts, E. (2009). Persuasion in ambient intelligence. *Journal of Ambient Intelligence and Humanized Computing, 1*(1), 43–56. doi:10.1007/s12652-009-0005-3

Kardes, F. R. (2002). *Consumer Behavior and Managerial Decision Making* (2nd ed.). Upper Saddle River, NJ: Pearson Education, Inc.

Karrh, J. A. (1998). Brand placement: A review. *Journal of Current Issues and Research in Advertising, 20*(2), 31–49.

Katz, D. (1960). The functional approach to the study of attitudes. *Public Opinion Quarterly, 24*, 27–46. doi:10.1086/266945

Katz, E. (1959). Mass communication research and the study of popular culture: An editorial note on a possible future for this journal. *Studies in Public Communications, 2*, 1–6.

Katz, E., Blumler, J. G., & Gurevitch, M. (1973). Uses and gratification research. *Public Opinion Quarterly, 37*(4), 509–523. doi:10.1086/268109

Katz, J. E., & Aakhus, M. A. (Eds.). (2002). *Perpetual contact: Mobile communication, private talk, public performance*. Cambridge, UK: Cambridge University Press. doi:10.1017/CBO9780511489471

Katz, E. (1987). Communications research since Lazarsfeld. *Public Opinion Quarterly, 51*, S25–S45. doi:10.1086/269068

Katz, E., & Lazarsfeld, P. (1955). *Personal influence*. New York: The Free Press.

Katz, E., Blumer, J. G., & Gurevitch, M. (1974). Utilization of mass communication by the individual. In Blumer, J. G., & Katz, E. (Eds.), *The uses of mass communications: Current perspectives on gratification research* (pp. 19–32). Beverly Hills, CA: Sage.

Katz, J. E., & Acord, S. K. (2008). Mobile games and entertainment. In Katz, J. (Ed.), *Handbook of Mobile Communication Studies* (pp. 153–164). Cambridge, MA: MIT Press.

Katz, J. E., Lever, K. M., & Chen, Y. F. (2008). Mobile music as environmental control and prosocial entertainment. In Katz, J. E. (Ed.), *Handbook of Mobile Communication Studies* (pp. 367–376). Cambridge, MA: MIT Press.

Katz, J. E., & Sugiyama, S. (2005). Mobile phones as fashion statements: the co-creation of mobile communication's public meaning. In R. Ling and & P. Pedersen (Eds,), *Mobile communications: re-negotiation of the social sphere* (pp. 81-63), London: Springer.

Kaye, B., & Johnson, T. (2002, March). Online and in the know: Uses and gratifications of the Web for political information. [from Communication & Mass Media Complete database.]. *Journal of Broadcasting & Electronic Media, 46*(1), 54. Retrieved September 4, 2008. doi:10.1207/s15506878jobem4601_4

Kaynar, O., & Amichai-Hamburger, Y. (2008). The effects of need for cognition on internet use revisited. *Computers in Human Behavior, 24*(2), 361–371. doi:10.1016/j.chb.2007.01.033

Keating, D. P. (. (2004). Cognitive and brain development. In R. M. Lerner and& L. D. Steinberg (Eds.), *Handbook of Adolescent Psychology* (2nd ed., pp. 45-84) 2nd ed., NJ: Hoboken, NJ: Wiley.

Keeling, K., McGoldrick, P. J., & Beatty, S. (2006). Virtual on-screen Assistants: A viable strategy to support online customer relationship building? In Fitszimons, G. J., & Morwitz, V. G. (Eds.), *Advances in Consumer Research* (*Vol. 34*, pp. 138–144). Duluth, MN: Association for Consumer Research.

Keeling, K., & Beatty, S. McGoldrick, P. J., & Macaulay, L. (2004). Face Value? Customer views of appropriate formats for ECAs in online retailing. In *Hawaii International Conference on System Sciences* (pp. 1-10).

Keeter, S., Horowitz, J., & Tyson, S. (2008, November, 12). *Young Voters in the 2008 Election*. Washington, D.C.: Pew Research Center for the People & the Press. Retrieved November 14, 2008, from http://pewresearch.org/pubs/1031/young-voters-in-the-2008-election

Keiningham, T. L. (2007). A longitudinal examination of net promoter and firm revenue growth. *Journal of Marketing, 71*(3). doi:10.1509/jmkg.71.3.39

Kelleher, T. a. M., B. M. (2006). Organizational blogs and the human voice: relational strategies and relational outcomes. *Journal of Computer-Mediated Communication, 11*(2), 395–414. doi:10.1111/j.1083-6101.2006.00019.x

Kelley, S. W., & Turley, L. W. (2004). The effect of content on perceived affect of Super Bowl commercials. *Journal of Sport Management, 18*(4), 398–420.

Kellner, D. (1995). *Media culture: Cultural studies, identity and politics between the modern and the postmodern*. New York: Routledge. doi:10.4324/9780203205808

Kellner, D., & Share, J. (2007). Critical media literacy: Crucial policy choices for a twenty-first-century democracy. *Policy Futures in Education*, *5*(1), 59–69. doi:10.2304/pfie.2007.5.1.59

Kellner, D. (2005). The Media and Election 2004. *Cultural Studies ↔ Critical Methodologies, 5*(3), 298-308.

Kellner, D. (2008). Media Spectacle and the 2008 Presidential Election: Some Pre-election Reflections. *Mediascape: UCLA's Journal of Cinema and Media Studies*.

Kelly, K. (1994 January). Will Wright: The mayor of SimCity. *Wired*.

Kelly, K. (2007). Predicting the Next 5,000 Days of the Web. *TED: Ideas Worth Spreading*. Retrieved October 1, 2008, from http://www.ted.com/index.php/talks/kevin_kelly_on_the_next_5_000_days_of_the_web.html.

Kelman, H. C. (1958). Compliance, identification, and internalization: Three processes of attitude change. *The Journal of Conflict Resolution*, *2*, 51–60. doi:10.1177/002200275800200106

Kennedy, G. A. (1980). *Classical rhetoric and its Christian and secular tradition from ancient to modern times*. Chapel Hill, NC: University of North Carolina Press.

Kennedy, G. A. (1991). *Aristotle 'On Rhetoric': A theory of civic discourse*. New York: Oxford University Press.

Kennedy, J. (2007). Cyberspace may not be best place for Birmingham mayoral campaign [Electronic Version]. *The Birmingham News*. Retrieved June 22, 2008, from http://blog.al.com/jkennedy/2007/09/cyberspace_may_not_be_best_pla.html

Kennish, F. (2003, March 3). In-Game advertising do's and don'ts. *iMedia Conncection*. Retrieved on September 30, 2008 from http://www.imediaconnection.com/content/8489.asp

Kent, S. L. (2001). *The ultimate history of video games*. New York: Three Rivers Press.

Kent, S. L. (2003). *Alternate reality: The history of massively multiplayer online games*. Retrieved July 20, 2008, from http://archive.gamespy.com/amdmmog/week1/

Kerbel, M., & Bloom, J. (2005). Blog for America and Civic Involvement. *Press/ Politics, 10,* 2-27.

Kerlinger, F. H. (1986). *Foundations of Behavioral Research* (3rd ed.). New York: Holt, Reinhart & Winston.

Kern, D., Harding, M., Storz, O., Davis, N., & Schmidt, A. (2008). Shaping How Advertisers See Me: User Views on Implicit and Explicit Profile Capture. In *CHI 2008*, April 5-10, 2008, Florence, Italy, ACM.

Kerr, A. (2006). *The business and culture of digital games: Gamework/Gameplay*. Thousand Oaks, CA: Sage.

Kids, T., & Worlds, V. (2007, September 25). eMarketer. Retrieved October 23, 2007, from http://www.emarketer.com

Kiecker, P., & Hartman, C. L. (1994). Predicting buyers' selection of interpersonal sources: The role of strong and weak ties. In Allen, C. T., & John, D. R. (Eds.), *Advances in consumer research* (*Vol. 21*, pp. 464–469). Provo, UT: Association for Consumer Research.

Kiehne, T. P. (2004). *Social Networking Systems: History, Critique, and Knowledge Management Potentials. Mimeo*. School of Information, The University of Texas at Austin.

Kim, J., Kardes, F. R., & Herr, P. H. (1989). Consumer expertise and the vividness effect: Implications for judgment and inference. *Advances in Consumer Research. Association for Consumer Research (U. S.)*, *18*, 90–93.

Kim, H., Kim, G. J., Park, H. W., & Rice, R. E. (2007). Configurations of relationships in different media: FtF, email, instant messenger, mobile phone, and SMS. *Journal of Computer-Mediated Communication*, *12*, 1183–1207. doi:10.1111/j.1083-6101.2007.00369.x

Kim, M. (2008). The creative commons and copyright protection in the Digital Era: uses of creative commons licenses. *Journal of Computer-Mediated Communication*, *13*, 187–209. doi:10.1111/j.1083-6101.2007.00392.x

Kim, A. (1994). Pulp Nonfiction. *Entertainment Weekly*. Retrieved on February 25, 2009, from http://www.ew.com/ew/article/0,302832,00.html

Kim, G. (forthcoming). *The Popular as the Political: Critical Media Pedagogy as a Condition for Grassroots Collective Action Mobilization via YouTube Videos*. Ph.D. Dissertation. Los Angeles, CA: University of California.

Kim, H., Lyons, K., & Cunningham, M. A. (2008, January). Towards a Theoretically-Grounded Framework for Evaluating Immersive Business Models and Applications. In *Proceedings of the 41st Annual Hawaii International Conference on System Sciences*.

Kim, J., McMillan, S. J., & Hwang, J.-S. (2005). Strategies for Super Bowl advertising: An analysis of how the Web is integrated into campaigns. *Journal of Interactive Advertising, 6*(1). Retrieved June 15, 2007, from http://jiad.org/vol6/no1/kim

Kim, P., Sorcar, P., Um, Sujung, Chung, H., & Lee, Y. (2008). Effects of episodic variations in web-based avian influenza education: influence of fear and humor on perception, comprehension, retention and behavior. *Health Education Research.* Retrieved from doi:10.1093/her/cyn031

King, S. (2008, August 13). Stephen King: How TV ruined baseball. *Entertainment Weekly*. Retrieved August 13, 2008, from http://www.ew.com/ew/article/0,20218931,00.html

Kiousis, S. (2002). Interactivity: A concept explication. *New Media & Society, 4*(3), 355–383.

Kirby, D. (2002). The impact of schools and school programs upon adolescent sexual behavior. *Journal of Sex Research, 39*(1), 27–33. doi:10.1080/00224490209552116

Kirby, D. (2002). Effective approaches to reducing adolescent unprotected sex, pregnancy, and childbearing. *Journal of Sex Research, 39*(1), 51–57. doi:10.1080/00224490209552120

Kirby, D., Laris, B. A., & Rolleri, L. A. (2007). Sex and HIV education programs: Their impact on sexual behaviors of young people throughout the world. *The Journal of Adolescent Health, 40*(3), 206–217. doi:10.1016/j.jadohealth.2006.11.143

Kirby, D., Obasi, A., & Laris, B. A. (2006). The effectiveness of sex education and HIV education interventions in schools in developing countries. *World Health Organization Technical Report Series, 938*, 103–150.

Kirby, D., Short, L., Collins, J., Rugg, D., Kolbe, L., & Howard, M. (1994). School-based programs to reduce sexual risk behaviors: A review of effectiveness. *Public Health Reports (Washington, D.C.), 109*(3), 339–360.

Kirkpatrick, D., & Roth, D. (2005). Why there's no escaping the blog. *Fortune, 151*(1), 32–37.

Kirkpatrick, M. (2006, June 30). PayPerPost.com Offers to Sell Your Soul. *TechCrunch.com*. Retrieved September 24, 2007, from http://www.techcrunch.com/2006/06/30/payperpostcom-offers-to-buy-your-soul/.

Kirsh, D. (2000). A few thoughts on cognitive overload. *Intellectica*, 19–51.

Klaassen, A. (2008, April 7). Actions louder than words on social nets. [from Communication & Mass Media Complete database.]. *Advertising Age, 79*(14), 3–33. Retrieved September 4, 2008.

Klaassen, A. (2006, August 7). Major turnoff: McKinsey slams TV's selling power. *Advertising Age, 77*(32), 1–2.

Klaassen, A. (2007). Real Revolution isn't Facebook's Ad Plan: Zuckerberg makes Big Claims, but Future Lies in Power of Peer-to-Peer. *Adage.com*. Retrieved November 19, 2007, from http://adage.com/digital/article?article_id=121929

Klaassen, A. (2007, November 26). Facebook's Bid Ad Plan: If Users Like You, They'll be Your Campaign. *Advertising Age*. Retrieved February 1, 2008, from http://adage.com/digital/article?article_id=121806&search_phrase=%22social+ads%22

Klaassen, A. (2009, April 27). Speaking of Augmented Reality, Here's a 3-D Sasquatch: Latest Ad From Jerky Maker Jack Link's Uses Webcam to Create Image. *AdAge.Com*. Retrieved June 15, 2009, from http://adage.com/digitalnext/article?article_id=136287

Klaassen, A. (2009, January 29). Online CPM Prices Take Tumble. *Advertising Age*.

Klapper, J. T. (1960). *The effects of mass communication.* Glencoe, IL: The Free Press.

Klapper, J. T. (1949). *The effects of mass media.* New York: Bureau of Applied Social Research: Columbia University.

Klein, C. T. F., & Helweg-Larsen, M. (2002). Perceived control and the optimistic bias: A meta-analytic review. *Psychology & Health, 17*(4), 437–446. doi:10.1080/0887044022000004920

Klein, L. R. (2003). Creating virtual product experiences: the role of telepresence. *Journal of Interactive Marketing, 17*(1), 42–55. doi:10.1002/dir.10046

Klein, L. R. (1998). Evaluating the potential of interactive media through a new lens: search versus experience goods. *Journal of Business Research, 41*(3), 195–203. doi:10.1016/S0148-2963(97)00062-3

Klein, J. (2008, February 7). Inspiration vs. Substance. *Time*. Retrieved June 7, 2008, from http://www.time.com/time/nation/article/0,8599,1710721,00.html

Klein, K. (2008, August 7). Are Social Networking Sites Useful for Business? *Business Week Online*. Retrieved September 3, 2008, from Academic Search Premier database.

Klein, K. E. (2008, January 3). Should your customers make your ads? *BusinessWeek Online.*

Klues, J. (2008, April 11). *Media Today.* Presentation to University of Illinois at Urbana-Champaign Department of Advertising Faculty, Illini Center, Chicago.

Klug, G. C., & Schell, J. (2006). Why people play games: An industry perspective. In Vorderer, P., & Bryant, J. (Eds.), *Play-*

ing video games: Motives, responses, and consequences (pp. 91–100). Mahwah, NJ: Lawrence Erlbaum.

Knobloch-Westerwick, S., Appiah, O., & Alter, S. (2008). News selection patterns as a function of race: The discerning minority and the indiscriminating majority. *Media Psychology, 11*(3), 400–417. doi:10.1080/15213260802178542

Ko, H., Cho, C. H., & Roberts, M. S. (2005). Internet uses and gratifications: A structural equation model of interactive advertising. *Journal of Advertising, 34*(2), 57–70.

Koda, T., & Maes, P. (1996). *Agents with Faces: The effects of personification.* Paper presented at the Human-Computer Interaction'96, London.

Koeppel, P. (2007). Use today's web technologies to connect with your customers. *Agency Sales, 37*(9), 28–29.

Kohut, A., Doherty, C., Dimock, M., & Keeter, S. (2008, November 13). *Republicans Want More Conservative Direction for GOP: High Marks for the Campaign, A High Bar for Obama.* Washington, DC: Pew Research Center for the People & the Press. Retrieved November 14, 2008, from http://people-press.org/report/471/high-bar-for-obama

Kohut, A., Keeter, S., Doherty, C., & Dimock, M. (2008, January, 11). *Social Networking and Online Videos Take Off: Internet's Broader Role in Campaign 2008.* Washington, DC: Pew Research Center for the People & the Press. Retrieved November 14, 2008, from http://www.pewinternet.org/pdfs/Pew_MediaSources_jan08.pdf

Kollock, P. (1999). The production of trust in online markets. In Lawler, E. J., Macy, M., Thyne, S., & Walker, H. A. (Eds.), *Advances in Group Processes (Vol. 16)*. Greenwich, CT: JAI Press.

Konar, E. (2008). *Integrating engagement across the customer context.* Retrieved from http://www.archive.org/details/IntegratingEngagementAcrossTheCustomerContext

Kopelman, L. M. (2002). If HIV/AIDS is punishment, who is bad? *The Journal of Medicine and Philosophy, 27*(2), 231–243. doi:10.1076/jmep.27.2.231.2987

Korgaonkar, P., & Wolin, L. (1999). A multivariate analysis of web usage. *Journal of Advertising Research, 39*(2), 53–68.

Koskinen, I. (2008). Mobile multimedia: uses and social consequences. In Katz, J. E. (Ed.), *Handbook of Mobile Communication Studies* (pp. 241–257). Cambridge, MA: MIT Press.

Kottke, J. (2003). *It's Weblog Not Web Log.* Retrieved September 30, 2007, from http://www.kottke.org/03/08/its-weblog-not-web-log

Koudelova, R., & Whitelock, J. (2001). A cross-cultural analysis of television advertising in the UK and Czech Republic. *International Marketing Review, 18*(3), 286–300. doi:10.1108/02651330110695611

Kover, A. J., Stephen, M. G., & James, W. L. (1995). Creativity vs. effectiveness? An integrating classification for advertising. *Journal of Advertising Research, 6*, 29–38.

Kozinets, R. V. (2002). The field behind the screen: Using netnography for marketing research in online communities. *JMR, Journal of Marketing Research, 39*(1), 61–72. doi:10.1509/jmkr.39.1.61.18935

Kozinets, R. V. (1999). E-tribalized marketing?: The strategy implications of virtual communities of consumption. *European Management Journal, 17*(3), 252–264. doi:10.1016/S0263-2373(99)00004-3

Krishnamurthy, S. (2003). *E-Commerce Management.* Mason, OH: South-Western.

Krosnick, J. A. (1999). Survey research. *Annual Review of Psychology, 50*, 537–567. doi:10.1146/annurev.psych.50.1.537

Krosnick, J. A., & Alwin, D. F. (1987). An evaluation of a cognitive theory of response-order effects in survey measurement. *Public Opinion Quarterly, 51*(2), 201–219. doi:10.1086/269029

Krosnick, J. A., & Berent, M. K. (1993). Comparisons of party identification and policy preferences: The impact of survey question format. *American Journal of Political Science, 37*(3), 941–964. doi:10.2307/2111580

Krugman, H. E. (1962). An application of learning theory to TV copy testing. *Public Opinion Quarterly, 26*, 626–634. doi:10.1086/267132

Krugman, P. (2008, February 11). Hate Springs Eternal. *The New York Times.* Retrieved June 9, 2008, from http://www.nytimes.com/2008/02/11/opinion/11krugman.html?_r=1&ref=opinion&oref=slogin

Krulwich, B. (1997). Lifestyle finder: Intelligent user profiling using large-scale demographic data. *AI Magazine, 18*, 37–45.

Kuchinskas, S. (2004). *Marqui Product Placement in Blogs.* Retrieved from http://www.internetnews.com/ec-news/article.php/3440401

Kurien, M., Thomas, K., Ahuja, R. C., Patel, A., Shyla, P. R., Wig, N., & Mangalani, M., Sathyanathan, Kasthuri, A., Vyas, B., Brogen, A., Sudarsanam, T. D., Chaturvedi, A., Abraham, O. C., Tharyan, P., Selvaraj, K. G., Mathew, J., & India CLEN HIV Screening Study Group. (2007). Screening for HIV infection by health professionals in India. *The National Medical Journal of India*, *20*(2), 59–66.

Kurtenbach, E. (2005 June). 'Freedom,' 'democracy' taboo words on Chinese Internet. *The Associated Press*. Retrieved January 20, 2009, from http://www.usatoday.com/tech/news/2005-06-14-chineseInternet_x.htm

Kzero. (2008). *The virtual worlds universe*. Retrieved August 30, 2008, from http://www.kzero.co.uk/blog/?page_id=2092

La Ferla, R. (2003, December 28). *Generation E. A.: Ethnically Ambiguous*. Retrieved December 28, 2003, from http://www.nytimes.com/2003/12/28/fashion/28ETHN.html

Labaton, S. (2000, June 6). AT&T's Acquisition of MediaOne Wins Approval by FCC. *The New York Times*.

Labaton, S. (2004, June 23). Senate Votes to Restore Media Limits. *The New York Times*.

Lafferty, B., Goldsmith, R. E., & Newell, S. J. (2002). The dual credibility model: The influence of corporate and endorser credibility. *Journal of Marketing Theory and Practice*, *10*(3), 1–12.

Lahelma, E. (2002). School is for friends: secondary school as lived and remembered. *British Journal of Sociology of Education*, *23*(3), 367–381. doi:10.1080/0142569022000015418

Lal, R., & Sarvary, M. (1999). When and how is the Internet likely to decrease price competition? *Marketing Science*, *18*(4), 485–503. doi:10.1287/mksc.18.4.485

Lang, A. (2000). The limited capacity model of mediated message processing. *The Journal of Communication*, 46–70. doi:10.1111/j.1460-2466.2000.tb02833.x

Lang, A. (2006). Using the limited capacity model of motivated mediated message processing to design effective cancer communication messages. *The Journal of Communication*, *56*(S1), S57–S80. doi:10.1111/j.1460-2466.2006.00283.x

Lang, K., & Lang, G. E. (1953). The unique perspective of television and its effects: A pilot study. *American Sociological Review*, *18*, 168–183. doi:10.2307/2087842

Laroche, M., Yang, Z., McDougall, G. H. G., & Bergeron, J. (2005). Internet versus bricks-and-mortar retailers: An investigation into intangibility and its consequences. *Journal of Retailing*, *81*(4), 251–267. doi:10.1016/j.jretai.2004.11.002

LaRose, R., & Eastin, M. S. (2004). A social cognitive explanation of Internet. Uses and gratifications: Toward a new model of media attendance. *Journal of Broadcasting & Electronic Media*, *48*(3), 358–377. doi:10.1207/s15506878jobem4803_2

LaRose, R., Mastro, D., & Eastin, M. S. (2001). Understanding internet usage: A social-cognitive approach to uses and gratifications. *Social Science Computer Review*, *19*(4), 395–413. doi:10.1177/089443930101900401

LaRose, R., & Eastin, M. S. (2002). Is online buying out of control? Electronic commerce and consumer self-regulation. *Journal of Broadcasting & Electronic Media*, *46*(4), 549–564. doi:10.1207/s15506878jobem4604_4

Larson, R., & Wilson, S. (2004). Adolescence across Place and Time: Globalization and the Changing Pathways to Adulthood. In Lerner, R., & Steinberg, L. (Eds.), *Handbook of adolescent psychology* (pp. 299–330). New York: Wiley.

Laskey, H. A., Day, E., & Crask, M. R. (1989). Typology of main message strategies for television commercials. *Journal of Advertising*, *18*(1), 36–41.

Laskey, H. A., Fox, R. J., & Crask, M. R. (1995). The relationship between advertising message strategy and television commercial effectiveness. *Journal of Advertising Research*, *35*(2), 31–39.

Lasswell, H. D. (1948). The structure and function of communication in society. In Schramm, W., & Roberts, D. F. (Eds.), *The process and effects of mass communication* (pp. 84–99). Urbana, IL: University of Illinois Press.

Lastowka, F. G., & Hunter, D. (2006). Virtual worlds: A primer. In Balkin, J. M. (Ed.), *The state of play: Law, games, and virtual worlds*. New York: New York University Press.

Lavidge, R. J., & Steiner, G. A. (1961). A model for predictive measurements of advertising effectiveness. *Journal of Marketing*, *25*(4), 59–62. doi:10.2307/1248516

Law, S., & Braun, K. A. (2000). I'll have what she's having: Gauging the impact of product placements on viewers. *Psychology and Marketing*, *17*(12), 1059–1075. doi:10.1002/1520-6793(200012)17:12<1059::AID-MAR3>3.0.CO;2-V

Lawor, M. A. (2008), What do children do with advertising?–a uses and gratifications' perspective, In *Child and Teen Consumption 2008 Conference*, Trondheim, Norway.

Lawrie, M. (2002). *Parallels in MUD and IRC history*. Retrieved from http://www.ircnet.org/History/jarkko-mjl.html

Lazarsfeld, P., Berelson, B., & Gaudet, H. (1968). *The people's choice: How the voter makes up his mind in a presidential campaign*. New York: Columbia University Press.

Lazarsfeld, P. F. (1948). Communication research and the social psychologist. In Dennis, W. (Ed.), *Current trends in social psychology*. Pittsburgh, PA: University of Pittsburgh Press.

Leary, M. R., & Schreindorfer, L. S. (1998). The stigmatization of HIV and AIDS: rubbing salt in the wound. In Derlega, V. J., & Barbee, A. P. (Eds.), *HIV and Social Interaction* (pp. 12–29). Thousand Oaks, CA: Sage Publications.

Leavitt, N. (2004, August 3). Online Clothes Lines. *iMedia Connection*. Retrieved August 14, 2008, from: http://www.imediaconnection.com

Leblebici, H., Salancik, G. R., Copay, A., & King, T. (1991). Institutional change and the transformation of interorganizational fields: An organizational history of the U.S. radio broadcasting industry. *Administrative Science Quarterly, 35*, 333–363. doi:10.2307/2393200

Leckenby, J. D., & Stout, P. (1985). Conceptual and methodological issues in persuasion management. In Houston, M. J., & Lutz, R. J. (Eds.), *Marketing communication – Theory and research* (pp. 7–12). Chicago: American Marketing Association.

Leckenby, J. D. (2005). The Interaction of Traditional and New Media. In Stafford, M. R., & Faber, R. J. (Eds.), *Advertising, Promotion, and New Media* (pp. 3–29). Armonk, NY: M. E. Sharpe.

Lederman, L. (2007). Stranger than fiction: Taxing virtual worlds. *New York University Law Review, 82*(6), 1620–1672.

Lee, M., & Faber, R. J. (2007). Effects of product placement in on-line games on brand memory: A perspective of the limited-capacity model of attention. *Journal of Advertising, 36*(4), 75–90. doi:10.2753/JOA0091-3367360406

Lee, E.-J., & Nass, C. (2002). Experimental tests of normative group influence and representation effects in computer-mediated communication: When interacting via computers differs from interacting with computers. *Human Communication Research, 28*, 349–381. doi:10.1093/hcr/28.3.349

Lee, S., Hwang, T., & Lee, H. H. (2006). Corporate blogging strategies of the Fortune 500 companies. *Management Decision, 44*(3), 316–334. doi:10.1108/00251740610656232

Lee, D. H., & Park, C. W. (2007, September). Conceptualization and measurement of multidimensionality of integrated marketing communications. *Journal of Advertising Research*, (September): 222–236. doi:10.2501/S0021849907070274

Lee, M., & Ferguson, M. (2002). Effects of anti-tobacco advertisements based on risk-taking tendencies: Realistic fear vs. vulgar humor. *Journalism & Mass Communication Quarterly, 79*(4), 945–963.

Lee, M., & Faber, R. J. (2007). Effects of product placement in on-line games on brand memory: A perspective of the limited-capacity model of attention. *Journal of Advertising, 36*, 75–90. doi:10.2753/JOA0091-3367360406

Lefton, T. (2005, October 3-9). T-Mobile gets $100m NBA connection. *Street & Smith's Sports Business Journal, 8*(22), 36.

Lenhart, A. (2009). Social networks grow: Friending mom and dad. *Pew Internet & American Life Project* [Electronic Version]. Retrieved February 25, 2009, from http://www.pewresearch.org/pubs/1079/social-networks-grow

Lenhart, A. (2009, January 14). Adult and Social Networking Websites. *Pew Internet & American Life Project, 2009*. Retrieved June 27, 2009, from http://www.pewinternet.org/~/media//Files/Reports/2009/PIP_Adult_social_networking_data_memo_FINAL.pdf.pdf

Lenhart, A., & Madden, M. (2005). Teen content creators and consumers. *Pew Internet and Life Project*. Retrieved June 25, 2006 from http://www.pewinternet.org/pdfs/PIP_Teens_ Content_Creation.pdf

Lenhart, A., & Madden, M. (2007, January 7). Social Networking Websites and Teens: An Overview. *Pew Internet & American Life Project, 2007*. Retrieved August 25, 2007, from http://www.pewinternet.org/PPF/r/198/report_display.asp

Lenhart, A., Madded, M., & Smith, A. (2007). Teens and Social Media: The Use of Social Media Gains a Greater Foothold in Teen Life as they Embrace the Conversational Nature of Interactive Online Media. *The Pew Internet & American Life Project*. Retrieved May 12, 2008 from http://www.pewInternet.org/PPF/r/230/report_display.asp

Lenhart, A., Madden, M., & Hitlin, P. (2005). *Teens and Technology: youth are leading the transition to a fully wired and mobile nation*. Retrieved from http://www.pewinternet.org/

Lenhart, A., Rainie, L., & Lewis, O. (2001). *Teenage life online: the rise of the instant-message generation and the internet's impact on friendship and family relationship*. Retrieved from http://www.pewinternet.org/

Leung, L., & Wei, R. (2000). More than just talk on the move: uses and gratifications of cellular phones. *Journalism & Mass Communication Quarterly, 77*(2), 308–320.

Levine, R. (2008, February 22). *NCAA Finds a Sensible Way To Speed Up Games in College Football*. Retrieved July 15, 2008, from http://www.nysun.com/sports/ncaa-finds-a-sensible-way-to-speed-up-games/71688/

Levy, N. (2005). Mario Monti's legacy in EC merger control. *Competition Policy International, 1*(1), 99–132.

Levy, S. J. (1959, July). Symbols for sale. *Harvard Business Review*, *37*, 117–124.

Lewis, J. (2007). *Social Networking: Examining User Behavior*. Retrieved August 29, 2007, from http://www.webpronews.com/topnews/2007/04/10/social-networking-examining-user-behavior

Li, H., Edwards, S., & Lee, J. (2002). Measuring the intrusiveness of advertisements: Scale development and validation. *Journal of Advertising*, *31*(2), 37–47.

Li, H., Daugherty, T., & Biocca, F. (2001). Characteristics of virtual experience in electronic commerce: A protocol analysis. *Journal of Interactive Marketing*, *15*(3), 13–30. doi:10.1002/dir.1013

Li, H., Daugherty, T., & Biocca, F. (2002). Impact of 3-D advertising on product knowledge, brand attitude, and purchase intention: The mediating role of presence. *Journal of Advertising*, *31*(3), 43–58.

Li, H., Daugherty, T., & Biocca, F. (2003). The role of virtual experience in consumer learning. *Journal of Consumer Psychology*, *13*(4), 395–407. doi:10.1207/S15327663JCP1304_07

Li, X., & Hitt, L. M. (in press). Self selection and information role of online product reviews. *Information Systems Research*.

Li, H., & Bukovac, J. I. (1999). Cognitive impact of banner ad characteristics: An experimental study. *Journalism and Mass Communication*, *76*(2), 341–354.

Li, Y. M., & Kao, C. P. (2008). *TREPPS: A Trust-based Recommender System for Peer Production Services*. Expert Systems With Applications.

Li, H., & Leckenby, J. D. (2007). Examining the Effectiveness of Internet Advertising Formats. In Schumann, D. W., & Thorson, E. (Eds.), *Internet Advertising, Theory and Research* (pp. 203–224). Mahwah, NJ: Lawrence Erlbaum Associates.

Li, C., Bernoff, J., Fiorentino, R., & Glass, S. (2007, April 19). Social technographics: Mapping participation in activities forms the foundation of a social strategy. *Forrester Research*. Retrieved June 11, 2008, from http://www.forrester.com/Research/Document/Excerpt/0,7211,42057,00.html

Liang, T.-P., Lai, H.-J., & Ku, Y.-C. (2006). Personalized content recommendation and user satisfaction: Theoretical synthesis and empirical findings. *Journal of Management Information Systems*, *23*(3), 45–70. doi:10.2753/MIS0742-1222230303

Licope, C., & Smoreda, Z. (2005). Are social networks technologically embedded? How networks are changing today with changes in communication technology. *Social Networks*, *27*, 317–335. doi:10.1016/j.socnet.2004.11.001

Licoppe, C. (2008). The mobile phone's ring. In Katz, J. E. (Ed.), *Handbook of Mobile Communication Studies, (pp* (pp. 139–152). Cambridge, MA: MIT Press.

Lieberman, M. S., & Goldstein, B. A. (2005). Self-help on-line: An outcome evaluation of breast cancer bulletin boards. *Journal of Health Psychology*, *10*(6), 855–862. doi:10.1177/1359105305057319

Lightfoot, M., Comulada, W., & Stover, G. (2007). Computerized HIV preventive intervention for adolescents: Indications of efficacy. *American Journal of Public Health*, *97*(6), 1027–1030. doi:10.2105/AJPH.2005.072652

Lin, C. A. (1999). Online service adoption likelihood. *Journal of Advertising Research*, *39*(2), 79–89.

Lin, M., Goldman, R., Price, K. J., Sears, A., & Jacko, J. (2007). How do people tap when walking? An empirical investigation of nomadic data entry. *International Journal of Human-Computer Studies*, *65*(9), 759–769. doi:10.1016/j.ijhcs.2007.04.001

Lin, C. (2008). The effects of the Internet. In Bryant, J., & Oliver, M. B. (Eds.), *Media effects: Advances in theory and research* (3rd ed.). New York: Routledge.

Linden Lab. (2007). *Economics*. Retrieved May 2008, from http://lindenlab.com/pressroom/general/factsheets/economics

Linden, G., Smith, B., & York, J. (2003). *Amazon.com Recommendations: Item-to-item collaborative filtering*.

Lindgaard, G., Fernandes, G., Dukek, C., & Brown, J. (2006). Attention web designers: you have 50 miliseconds to make a good first impression! *Behaviour & Information Technology*, *25*(2), 115–126. doi:10.1080/01449290500330448

Lindstrøm, M. & ., & Seybold, P. B. (2004). *Brand Child: remarkable insights into the minds of today's global kids and their relationship with brands*. USA. New York: Kogan Page.

Lindstrom, M. (2002, July 23). Brand games: your move. *The Clickz Network*. Retrieved August 18, 2008, from http://www.clickz.com/showPage.html?page=1430331

Ling, R. (2000). "We will be reached": the use of mobile phone telephony among Norwegian youth. *Information Technology & People*, *13*, 102–120. doi:10.1108/09593840010339844

Ling, R. (2007). Children, youth, and mobile communication. *Journal of Children and Media*, *1*(1), 60–67. doi:10.1080/17482790601005173

LinkedIn. (2008). *About LinkedIn*. Retrieved on August 19, 2008, from http://www.linkedin.com

Lissitz, R. W., & Green, S. B. (1975). Effect of the number of scale points on reliability: A Monte Carlo approach. *The Journal of Applied Psychology, 60*(1), 10–13. doi:10.1037/h0076268

Lister, M., Dovey, J., Giddings, S., Grant, I., & Kelly, K. (2003). *New Media: a critical introduction*. London: Routledge.

Little, J. D. C. (1979). Decision support systems for marketing managers. *Journal of Marketing, 43*, 11. doi:10.2307/1250143

Litvin, S. W., Goldsmith, R. E., & Pan, B. (2008). Electronic word-of-mouth in hospitality and tourism management. *Tourism Management, 29*(3), 458–468. doi:10.1016/j.tourman.2007.05.011

Liu, Y., & Shrum, L. J. (2002). What is interactivity and is it always such a good thing? Implications of definition, person, and situation for the influence of interactivity on advertising effectiveness. *Journal of Advertising, 31*(4), 53–64.

Liu, Y. (2006). Word-of-mouth for movies: Its dynamics and impact on box office receipts. *Journal of Marketing, 70*, 74–89. doi:10.1509/jmkg.70.3.74

Liu, Y. (2003). Developing a scale to measure the interactivity of websites. *Journal of Advertising Research, 43*(2), 207–216.

Liu, H. (2008). Social network profiles as taste performances. *Journal of Computer-Mediated Communication, 13*, 252–275. doi:10.1111/j.1083-6101.2007.00395.x

Lives in Focus. (2008). *Living with HIV/AIDS in India*. Retrieved January 20, 2009, from http://www.livesinfocus.org/aids/2006/

Livingstone, S. (1999). New media, new audiences? *New Media & Society, 1*(1), 59–66. doi:10.1177/1461444899001001010

Locander, W. B., & Spivey, W. A. (1978). A functional approach to attitude measurement. *JMR, Journal of Marketing Research, 15*(4), 576–587. doi:10.2307/3150627

Lohr, S. (2007, October 10). Free the Avatars. *The New York Times*. Retrieved May 29, 2008, from http://bits.blogs.nytimes.com/2007/10/10/free-the-avatars/

Lohtia, R., Donthu, N., & Hershberger, E. K. (2003). The impact of content and design elements on banner advertising click-through rates. *Journal of Advertising Research, 43*, 410–418.

Lombard, M., & Snyder-Duch, J. (2001). Interactive advertising and presence: A framework. *Journal of Interactive Advertising, 1*(2).

Lombard, M., & Ditton, T. (1997). At the heart of it all: The concept of presence. *Journal of Computer Mediated Communication, 3*(2). Retrieved April 20, 2005 from http://jcmc.indiana.edu/vol3/issue2/lombard.htm

Lombardo, J. (2006, April 17-23). Plan for global stores part of Adidas' NBA plans. *Street & Smith's Sports Business Journal, 9*(49), 8.

Loos, P. (2003). *Avatar, in lexicon electronic business* (Schildhauer, T., Ed.). Munich, Germany: Oldenbourg.

Lopez, M. H., & Taylor, P. (2009, April 30). *Dissecting the 2008 Electorate: Most Diverse in U.S. History*. Washington, DC: Pew Research Center. Retrieved May 2, 2009, from http://pewresearch.org/pubs/1209/racial-ethnic-voters-presidential-election

Lorayne, H., & Lucas, J. (1974). *The memory book*. New York: Ballantine.

Lovison, B. (2009). A tale of two avatars. *Gaming Insider.* Retrieved February 10, 2009 from http://www.mediapost.com/publications/?fa=Articles.showArticle&art_aid=99894

Lowood, H. (2006). A brief biography of computer games. In Vorderer, P., & Bryant, J. (Eds.), *Playing Video Games: Motives, Responses and Consequences* (pp. 25–42). Mahwah, NJ: Lawrence Erlbaum Associates.

Lowrey, S., & DeFleur, M. L. (1983). *Milestones in mass communication research: Media effects*. New York: Longman, Inc.

Lucaites, J. L., Condit, C. M., & Caudill, S. (1999). *Contemporary rhetorical theory*. New York: Guilford Press.

Lucas, K., & Sherry, J. L. (2004). Sex differences in video game play: A communication-based explanation. *Communication Research, 31*, 499–523. doi:10.1177/0093650204267930

Lunar Lander. (2008, April 4). In *Arcade-History.* Retrieved August 18, 2008 from http://www.arcade-history.com/index.php?page=detail&id=1417

Luria, A. R. (1968). *The mind of the mnemonist*. New York: Avon.

Lusch, R. F., Vargo, S. L., & O'Brien, M. (2007). Competing through service: insights from service-dominant logic. *Journal of Retailing, 83*(1), 5–18. doi:10.1016/j.jretai.2006.10.002

Lutz, R. J. (1985). Affective and cognitive antecedents of attitude toward the ad: A conceptual framework. In Alwitt, L. F., & Mitchell, A. A. (Eds.), *Psychological processes and advertising effects: Theory, research, and applications* (pp. 45–63). Hillsdale, NJ: Lawrence Erlbaum Associates, Inc., Publishers.

Lwin, M., Wirtz, J., & Williams, J. D. (2007). Consumer online privacy concerns and responses: A power-responsibility equilibrium perspective. *Journal of the Academy of Marketing Science*, *35*, 572–585. doi:10.1007/s11747-006-0003-3

Lynch, D., Vernon, R. F., & Smith, M. L. (2001). Critical thinking and the web. *Journal of Social Work Education*, *37*(2), 381–386.

Lyotard, J.-F. (1979). *The Postmodern Condition.*

Maag, C. (2008, February 25). Obama's Ohio Grassroots Advantage. *The Time*. Retrieved June 7, 2008, from http://www.time.com/time/politics/article/0,8599,1717150,00.html

Macgill, A. R. (n.d.). Parent and Teen Internet use. *Pew Internet & American Life Report*. Retrieved May 16, 2008 from http://www.pewInternet.org/PPF/r/225/report_display.asp

Machover, K. (1953). *Personality Projection in the Drawing of the Human Figure*. Springfield, IL: Charles C. Thomas.

MacInnes, I. (2006). Property rights, legal issues, and business models in virtual world communities. *Electronic Commerce Research*, *6*(1), 39–56. doi:10.1007/s10660-006-5987-8

MacInnis, D. J., & Jawroski, B. J. (1989). Information processing from advertisements: toward an integrative framework. *Journal of Marketing*, *53*(4), 1–23. doi:10.2307/1251376

MacKay, B., Dearman, D., Inkpen, K., & Watters, C. (2005). *Walk 'n scroll: a comparison of software-based navigation techniques for different levels of mobility*. Paper presented at the Proceedings of the 7th international conference on Human computer interaction with mobile devices \&, services.

MacKenzie, S. B., & Lutz, R. J. (1989). An empirical examination of the structural antecedents of attitude toward the ad in an advertising pretesting context. *Journal of Marketing*, *53*(2), 48–65. doi:10.2307/1251413

MacKenzie, S. B., Lutz, R. J., & Belch, G. E. (1986). The role of attitude toward the ad as a mediator of advertising effectiveness: A test of competing explanations. *JMR, Journal of Marketing Research*, *23*(2), 130–143. doi:10.2307/3151660

MacKeogh, K. (2001). National Strategies for the Promotion of On-Line Learning in Higher Education. *European Journal of Education*, *36*(2), 223–236. doi:10.1111/1467-3435.00061

MacMillan, D. (2009, January 12). Online Video Ads: A Bag of Tricks, the five most common types of ads you'll see in videos on the Web, and how they're used. *Businessweek*. Retrieved March 13, 2009, from http://www.businessweek.com/technology/content/jan2009/tc20090126_305941.htm

Macsai, D. (2008, August 22). Marketing to millennials. *Business Week*, August 22.

Madell, D. E., & Muncer, S. J. (2007). Control over social interactions: an approach for young people's use of the Internet and mobile communications? *Cyberpsychology & Behavior*, *10*(1), 137–140. doi:10.1089/cpb.2006.9980

Madhok, A. (2008). *The invited conversation: personalized and integrated communication platform*. Retrieved from http://www.archive.org/details/TheInvitedConversationPersonalizedAndIntegratedCommunicationPlatform

Madrigal, R. (2000). The influence of social alliances with sports teams on intentions to purchase corporate sponsors' products. *Journal of Advertising*, *29*(4), 13–24.

Madsen, H. (1996 December). Reclaim the Deadzone. The Beleaguered Web Banner can be Zapped into an Effective and Eye-Popping Advertising Shingle, but Radical Surgery Awaits. *Wired*, *4*(12). Retrieved June 24, 2008, from http://www.wired.com/wired/archive/4.12/esmadsen.htm

Maffesoli, M. (1996). *The Time of the Tribes: The Decline of Individualism in Mass Society*. London: Sage.

Magarian, G. P. (2008). Substantive Media Regulation in Three Dimensions. *Villanova Public Law and Legal Theory Working Paper Series*. Working Paper No 2008-05.

Magill, K. (2006, March 1). Petco tests product reviews. *Direct*. Retrieved July 24, 2008, from http://directmag.com/disciplines/email/marketing_petco_tests_product/

Mahatanankoon, P., & O'Sullivan, P. (2008). Attitude toward mobile text messaging: an expectancy-based perspective. *Journal of Computer-Mediated Communication*, *13*, 973–992. doi:10.1111/j.1083-6101.2008.00427.x

Maher, L., Liew, M., Gu, P., & Lan, N. D. (2005). An agent approach to supporting collaborative design in 3D virtual worlds. *Automation in Construction*, *14*(2), 189–195. doi:10.1016/j.autcon.2004.07.008

Maidment, P. (2006, December 12). *This Game Is Brought To You By...* Retrieved June 4, 2008, from http://www.forbes.com/2006/12/10/sports-broadcasting-televisions-tech_cx_pm_games06_1212soccer.html

Maine, H. (2004). *Ancient Law*. New Brunswick, NJ: Transaction Publishers.

Malavade, J. A., Shah, S. R., Shah, J. J., & Shah, R. M. (2002). *Ethical and legal issues in HIV/AIDS counseling and testing, 2002 International Conference on AIDS* (Abstract No. ThPeE7902). Retrieved on January 28, 2009, from http://gateway.nlm.nih.gov/MeetingAbstracts/ma?f=102250984.html

Malhotra, N. K. (1981). A scale to measure self-concept, person concepts, and product concepts. *JMR, Journal of Marketing Research, 18*, 456–464. doi:10.2307/3151339

Malinee, A. (2007, March 1). Alumna bathes in media spotlight after winning Dove competition. *InsideVandy*. Retrieved June 29, 2007, from http://www.insidevandy.com/drupal/node/3473

Malter, A. J., Rosa, J. A., & Garbarino, E. C. (2008). Using Virtual Models to Evaluate Real Products for Real Bodies. In Lee, A. Y., & Soman, D. (Eds.), *Advances in Consumer Research* (pp. 87–88).

Mangleburg, T. F., Doney, P. M., & Bristol, T. (2004). Shopping with friends and teens' susceptibility to peer influence. *Journal of Retailing, 80*(2), 101–116. doi:10.1016/j.jretai.2004.04.005

Mangleburg, T. F., & Bristol, T. (1998). Socializations of adolescents' skepticism toward advertising. *Journal of Advertising, 28*(3), 11–20.

Manovich, L. (2002). *The Language of New Media*. Cambridge, MA: MIT Press.

Maragos, N. (2005, March 7) Serious games summit: Advergaming for private and public interests. *Gamasutra*. Retrieved August 18, 2008, from http://www.gamasutra.com/view/feature/2209/postcard_from_gdc_2005_serious_.php

Margolin, V., Brichta, I., & Brichta, V. (1979). *The promise and the product: 200 Years of American advertising posters*. New York: Macmillan.

Marken, G. A. (2005). To blog or not to blog, that is the question. *Public Relations Quarterly, 50*(3), 31–33.

Markillie, P. (2004, May 15). A perfect market. *Economist, 371*(8375), 3.

Markus, H., & Nurius, P. (1986). Possible selves. *The American Psychologist, 41*, 954–969. doi:10.1037/0003-066X.41.9.954

Martensen, A. (2007). Mobile phones and tweens' needs, motivations and values. Segmentation based on means-end chains. In Ekström, K. M., & Tufte, B. (Eds.), *Children, media and consumption* (pp. 107–126). Gothenburg, Sweden: Nordicom.

Marx, K. (1970). Theses on Feuerbach. In Arthur, C. J. (Ed.), *The German Ideology*. New York: International Publishers.

Marx, K. (1975). *The German Ideology*. London: Lawrence & Wishart. (Original manuscript published in 1845).

Mason, P., & Davis, B. (2007). More than the words: Using stance-shift analysis to identify crucial opinions and attitudes in online focus groups. *Journal of Advertising Research, 47*(4), 496–506. doi:10.2501/S0021849907070511

Mason, R. (1994). *Using communications media in open and flexible learning*. London: Kogan Page.

Mass, G. (2002). Musikalische Themen und Motive in Werbeanzeigen–ein Streifzug. In Probst-Effah, G., Schepping, W., & Schneider, R. (Eds.), *Musikalische Volkskunde und Musikpädagogik–Annäherungen und Schnittmengen* (pp. 251–283). Essen, Deutschland: Verlag Die Blauen Eule.

Massive Incorporated. (n.d.) Retrieved February 10, 2009, from http://www.massiveincorporated.com

Masters, T. N., Beadnell, B. A., Morrison, D. M., Marilyn, J. H., & Gillmore, M. R. (2008). The Opposite of sex? Adolescents' thoughts about abstinence and sex, and their sexual behavior. *Perspectives on Sexual and Reproductive Health, 40*(2), 87–93. doi:10.1363/4008708

Mastro, D. (2003). Social identity approach to understanding the impact of television messages. *Communication Monographs, 70*(2), 98–113. doi:10.1080/0363775032000133764

Matthes, J., Schemer, C., & Wirth, W. (2007). More than meets the eye: Investigating the hidden impact of brand placements in television magazines. *International Journal of Advertising, 26*(4), 477–503.

Max, K. (2008, June). *Media engagement - developing consistent measures across multiple media channels*. Budapest, Hungary: ESOMAR Worldwide Multi Media Measurement (WM3).

Mayer-Schonberger, J., & Crowley, J. (2006). Napster's second life?: The regulatory challengers of virtual worlds. *Northwestern University Law Review, 100*(4), 1775–1826.

McAdam, D. (1983). Tactical innovation and the pace of insurgency. *American Sociological Review, 48*(6), 735–754. doi:10.2307/2095322

McAdam, D. (1986). Recruitment to high-risk activism. *American Journal of Sociology, 92*, 64–90. doi:10.1086/228463

McAdam, D., & Paulsen, R. (1993). Specifying the relationship between social ties and activism. *American Journal of Sociology, 99*, 640–667. doi:10.1086/230319

McBreen, H., Shade, P., Jack, M., & Wyard, P. (2000). Experimental assessment of the effectiveness of synthetic personae for multi-modal e-retail applications. In *Proceedings of the Fourth International Conference on Autonomous Agents* (pp. 39-45).

McCarty, J. A. (2004). Product placements: The nature of the practice and potential avenues of inquiry. In Shrum, L. J.

(Ed.), *The Psychology Of Entertainment Media: Blurring the Lines Between Entertainment and Persuasion*. Mahwah, NJ: Lawrence Erlbaum.

McChesney, R. W. (1999). *Rich Media Poor Democracy: Communication Politics in Dubious Times*. Champaign, IL: University of Illinois Press.

McChesney, R. (2002). The Titanic sails on: Why the Internet won't sink the media giants. In Dines, G., & Humez, J. (Eds.), *Gender, Race and Class in Media*. London: Sage.

McClure, R. F., & Mears, F. G. (1984). Video game players: Personality characteristics and demographic variables. *Psychological Reports*, *55*, 271–276.

McConnell, C. (1996, February 12). Mega-Merger gets FCC Nod. *Broadcasting and Cable*.

McCroskey, J. C., & Richmond, V. P. (1996). Human communications theory and research: Traditions and models. In Salwen, M. B., & Stacks, D. W. (Eds.), *An integrated approach to communication theory and research*. Mahwah, NJ: Lawrence Erlbaum Associates.

McEnallhy, M. R., & deChernatony, L. (1999). The evolving nature of branding: Consumer and managerial considerations. *Academy of Marketing Science Review*, *2*, 1–26.

McGill, A. L., & Anand, P. (1989). The effect of vivid attributes on the evaluation of alternatives: The role of differential attention and cognitive elaboration. *The Journal of Consumer Research*, *16*, 188–196. doi:10.1086/209207

McGoldrick, P. J., Keeling, K. A., & Beatty, S. F. (2008). A typology of roles for avatars in online retailing. *Journal of Marketing Management*, *24*(3-4), 433–461. doi:10.1362/026725708X306176

McGuire, W., McGuire, V., Child, P., & Fujioka, T. (1978). Salience of ethnicity in the spontaneous self-concept as a function of one's ethnic distinctiveness in the social environment. *Journal of Personality and Social Psychology*, *36*(5), 511–520. doi:10.1037/0022-3514.36.5.511

McGuire, W. J. (1969). The nature of attitudes and attitude change. In Lindzey, G., & Aronson, E. (Eds.), *Handbook of Social Psychology* (*Vol. 3*, pp. 136–314). Reading, MA: Addison-Wesley.

McIntyre, T. (2008). *MSNBC joins MySpace to combat the Facebook-ABC alliance*. Retrieved September 3, 2008, from http://tech.blorge.com/Structure:%20/2008/04/24/msnbc-joins-myspace-to-combat-the-facebook-abc-alliance-2/

McKeanna, K. Y. A., Green, A. S., & Gleason, M. E. J. (2002). Relationship formation on the Internet: what's the big attraction? *The Journal of Social Studies*, *58*(1), 9–31.

McKechnie, G. E. (1974). The psychological structure of leisure: Past behavior. *Journal of Leisure Research*, *6*, 27–35.

McKenna, R. (1991). *Relationship Marketing: Successful Strategies for the Age of the Customers*. Reading, MA: Addison-Wesley Publishing Company.

McKnight, D. H., & Kacmar, C. J. (2007). Factors and Effects of Information Credibility. In *Proceedings of the Ninth International Conference on Electronic Commerce* (pp. 423-432).

McLaren, P., & Farahmandpur, R. (2005). *Teaching Against Global Capitalism and The New Imperialism: A Critical Pedagogy*. Lanham, MD: Rowman & Littlefield.

McLaren, P., Hammer, R., Sholle, D., & Reilly, R. (1995). *Rethinking Media Literacy: A Critical Pedagogy of Representation*. New York: Peter Lang Publishing.

McLaren, P., & Kincheloe, J. (Eds.). (2007). *Critical Pedagogy: Where Are We Now?* New York: Peter Lang Publishing.

McLeod, J., & Lin, L. (2010). A child's power in game-play. *Computers & Education*, *54*, 517–527. doi:10.1016/j.compedu.2009.09.003

McLuhan, M., Hutchon, K., & McLuhan, E. (1978). Multimedia: The laws of the media. *English Journal*, *67*(8). doi:10.2307/815039

McLuhan, M. (1969). *Connterblast*. London: Rapp & Whiting.

McLuhan, M. (2001,original 1964). *Understanding Media*. London: Routledge.

McMillan, S. J., & Hwang, J. S. (2002). Measures of perceived interactivity: An exploration of the role of direction of communication, user control, and time in shaping perceptions of interactivity. *Journal of Advertising*, *31*(3), 29–42.

McMillan, S. J. (2007). Internet Advertising: One Face or Many? In Schumann, D. W., & Thorson, E. (Eds.), *Internet Advertising. Theory and Research* (pp. 15–35). Mahwah, NJ: Lawrence Erlbaum Associates.

McMillan, D. (2009). What Works in Online Video Advertising. *Business Week*. Retrieved March 8, 2009, from http://www.businessweek.com/technology/content/jan2009/tc20090126_341533.htm

McNair, B. (2003). *An introduction to political communication*. London: Routledge.

McQuail, D., & Windahl, S. (1993). *Communication models for the study of mass communication* (2nd ed.). London: Longman.

McQuail, D. (2000). *McQuail's mass communication theory* (4th ed.). London, England: Sage.

McQuail, D. (1987). *Mass communication theory: An introduction* (2nd ed.). Newbury Park, CA: Sage.

McQuail, D., Blumler, J., & Brown, R. (1972). The television audience: a revised perspective. In McQuail, D. (Ed.), *Sociology of Mass Communication*. London: Longman.

McQuail, D. (2005). *McQuail's Mass Communication Theory.* Retrieved from http://books.google.com

McTaggart, J. (2004). Fresh direct. *Progressive Grocer, 83*(4), 58–60.

Mead, G. (1934, original 1927). *Mind, self and society*. Chicago: University of Chicago Press. (Original manuscript published in 1927).

Media, P. Q. (2005). *Product Placement Spending in Media 2005*. Retrieved from http://www.pqmedia.com/product-placement-spending-in-media.html

Medical News Today. (2007 May). *Sex education bans hinder India's efforts to curb spread Of HIV, NACO official says*. Retrieved January 20, 2009, from http://www.medicalnewstoday.com/articles/71487.php

Medical News Today. (2007 November). *MAC AIDS Fund survey of people in nine countries finds misconceptions, stigma*. Retrieved September 2, 2008, from http://www.medicalnewstoday.com/articles/89000.php

Meenaghan, T. (1991). The role of sponsorship in the marketing communications mix. *International Journal of Advertising, 10*(1), 35–47.

Meenaghan, T. (2001). Understanding sponsorship effects. *Psychology and Marketing, 18*(2), 95–122. doi:10.1002/1520-6793(200102)18:2<95::AID-MAR1001>3.0.CO;2-H

Melby, T. (2008). How Second Life seeps into real life. *Contemporary Sexuality, 42*(1), 1–6.

Memmott, M., & Drinkard, J. (2004). Election ad battle smashes record in 2004. *USA Today.* Retrieved July 17, 2008, from http://www.usatoday.com/news/washington/2004-11-25-election-ads_x.htm

Mennecke, B. E., Terando, W. D., Janvrin, D. J., & Dilla, W. N. (2007). It's just a game, or is it? Real money, real income, and real taxes in virtual worlds. *Communications of the Association for Information Systems, 20*, 134–141.

Menon, S., & Soman, D. (2002). Managing the power of curiosity for effective web advertising strategies. *Journal of Advertising, 31*(3), 1–14.

Messinger, P. R. (1995). *The marketing paradigm: A guide for general managers*. Cincinnati, OH: Southwestern College Publishing.

Messinger, P. R., Stroulia, E., Lyons, K., Bone, M., Niu, A., Smirnov, K., & Perelgut, S. (2009b, June). Virtual worlds—past, present, and future: New directions in social computing. *Decision Support Systems, 47*(3), 204–228. doi:10.1016/j.dss.2009.02.014

Messinger, P. R., & Ge, X. (2009). The Future of the Market Research Profession. In Smith, C., Kisiel, K., & Morrison, J. (Eds.), *Working through Synthetic Worlds* (pp. 15–44). Burlington, VT, USA: Ashgate Publishing Company.

Messinger, P. R., Li, J., Stroulia, E., Galletta, D., Ge, X., & Choi, S. (2009a). Seven challenges to combining human and automated service. *Canadian Journal of Administrative Sciences*.

Messinger, P. R., Stroulia, E., & Lyons, K. (2008). A typology of virtual worlds: A historical overview and future directions. *Journal of Virtual Worlds Research, 1*(1). Retrieved May 30, 2009, from http://journals.tdl.org/jvwr/article/view/291/222

Metcalfe's Law. (n.d.). searchnetworking.com. Retrieved March 8, 2000, from http://searchnetworking.techtarget.com/sDefinition/0,sid7_gci214115,00.html

Methenitis, M. (2007). A tale of two worlds: New U.S. gambling laws and the MMORPG. *Gaming Law Review, 11*(4), 436–439. doi:10.1089/glr.2007.11404

Metheringham, R. (1964, December). Measuring the net cumulative coverage of a print campaign. *Journal of Advertising Research*.

Metzger, M. J., Flanagin, A. J., Eyal, K., Lemus, D. R., & McCann, R. M. (2003). Credibility for the 21st century: Integrating perspectives on source, message, and media credibility in the contemporary media environment. *Communication Yearbook, 27*, 293–335. doi:10.1207/s15567419cy2701_10

Meyers Levy, J., & Malaviya, P. (1999). Consumers' processing of persuasive advertisements: An integrative framework of persuasion theories. *Journal of Marketing, 63*, 45–60. doi:10.2307/1252100

Microsoft. (2006, November 29). *Women Rule in Malaysian Blogosphere*. Retrieved from http://www.microsoft.com/malaysia/press/archive2006/linkpage4337.mspx

Midgley, D. F. (1983). Patterns of interpersonal information seeking for the purchase of a symbolic product. *JMR, Journal of Marketing Research, 20*(1), 74–83. doi:10.2307/3151414

Miethe, T. D. (1985). Validity and reliability of value measurements. *The Journal of Psychology, 119*(5), 441–453.

Milgrom, P., & Roberts, J. (1992). *Economics, Organization and Management*. Englewood Cliffs, NJ: Prentice Hall.

Miller, R. K. (2007). *The 2007 entertainment, Media & advertising market research handbook (RKM1471789)*. Loganville, GA: Richard K. Miller & Associates.

Miller, R. (2008, October 30). Obama billed 44.5K for in-game advertising. *JoyStiq*. Retrieved January 14, 2009, from http://www.joystiq.com/2008/10/30/obama-billed-44-5k-for-in-game-advertising/

Miller. (2002, April 8). Sports yet to feel full power of new recorders. *Sports Business Journal*, 31.

Mills, E. (2006, April 4). Advertisers look to grassroots marketing. *CNET News.com*. Retrieved June 26, 2007, from http://news.com.com/2102-1024_3-6057300.html.

Mills, E. (2007, March 20). Frito-Lay turns to netizens for ad creation. *CNET News.com*. Retrieved June 9 2007, from http://news.com.com/2100-1024_3-6168881.html

Milne, G. R. (2000). Privacy and ethical issues in database/interactive marketing and public policy: A research framework and overview of the special issue. *Journal of Public Policy & Marketing, 19*(1), 1–6. doi:10.1509/jppm.19.1.1.16934

Milne, G. R., Bahl, S., & Rohm, A. (2008). Toward a framework for assessing covert marketing practices. *Journal of Public Policy & Marketing, 27*(Spring), 57–62. doi:10.1509/jppm.27.1.57

Milne, G. R., & Culnan, M. J. (2004). Strategies for reducing online privacy risks: Why consumers read (or don't read) online privacy notices. *Journal of Interactive Marketing, 18*(Summer), 15–29. doi:10.1002/dir.20009

Milne, G. R., Rohm, A. J., & Bahl, S. (2004). Consumers' protection of online privacy and identity. *The Journal of Consumer Affairs, 38*(2), 217–232.

Miniard, P. W., Bhatla, S., Lord, K. R., Dickson, P. R., & Unnava, H. R. (1991, June). Picture-based persuasion processes and the moderating role of involvement. *The Journal of Consumer Research, 18*, 92–107. doi:10.1086/209244

Ministry of Home Affairs, Government of India. (1860). *The Indian Penal Code, Section 377*. Retrieved January 20, 2009, from http://www.mha.nic.in/

Mishra, A. (2007 March). India: 70% rural women in Bihar not aware of HIV/AIDS: survey. *Hindustan Times*. Retrieved February 14, 2009, from http://www.hindustantimes.com/news/181_1926931,000900030002.htm

Mitchell, J., & Shneiderman, B. (1989). Dynamic versus static menus: an exploratory comparison. *SIGCHI Bull., 20*(4), 33–37. doi:10.1145/67243.67247

Mitchell, T., Caruana, R., Freitag, D., McDermott, J., & Zabowski, D. (1994). Experience with a learning personal assistant. *Communications of the ACM, 37*(7), 81–91. doi:10.1145/176789.176798

Mitchell, A. A., & Olson, J. C. (1981). Are product attributes beliefs the only mediator of advertising effects on brand attitude? *JMR, Journal of Marketing Research, 18*(3), 318–332. doi:10.2307/3150973

Mitchell, C., & Reid-Walsh, J. (Eds.). (2005). *Seven going on seventeen–tween studies in the culture of girlhood*. N.Y.: New York: Peter Lang Publ. Inc.

Mitchell, J. J. (1973). Networks, norms and institutions. In J. Boissevain & J. J. Mitchell (Eds)(Eds.), *Network analysis: studies in human interaction* (pp. 15-35). The Hague, Netherlands: Mouton.

Mitra, S. (2001). The death of media regulation in the age of the Internet. *Legislation and Public Policy, 4*, 415–438.

Mitra, A. (2002). Theorizing cyberspace: the idea of voice applied to the internet discourse. *New Media & Society, 4*, 479–498. doi:10.1177/146144402321466778

Mittal, B. (1994). Public assessment of TV advertising: faint and harsh criticism. *Journal of Advertising Research, 34*(1), 35–53.

Miyata, K., Boase, J., & Wellman, B. (2008). The Social Effects of Keitai and Personal Computer Email in Japan. In Katz, J. E. (Ed.), *Handbook of Mobile Communication Studies* (pp. 209–222). Cambridge, MA: MIT Press.

Miyazaki, A. D. (2008). Online privacy and the disclosure of cookie use: Effects on consumer trust and anticipated patronage. *Journal of Public Policy & Marketing, 27*(1), 19–33. doi:10.1509/jppm.27.1.19

Miyazaki, A. D., & Morgan, A. G. (2001). Assessing market value of event sponsoring: Corporate Olympic sponsorship. *Journal of Advertising Research, 41*(1), 9–15.

Mizerski, R. (1995, October). The relationship between cartoon trade character recognition and attitude toward product category in young children. *Journal of Marketing, 50*, 58–70. doi:10.2307/1252328

Mizobuchi, S., Chignell, M., & Newton, D. (2005). *Mobile text entry: relationship between walking speed and text input task difficulty*. Paper presented at the Proceedings of the 7th international conference on Human computer interaction with mobile devices \&, services.

Mohr, M. S. (1997). *The New Games Treasury*. New York: Houghton Mifflin Company.

Moore, R. E. (2003). From genericide to viral marketing: on brand. *Language & Communication, 23*, 331–357. doi:10.1016/S0271-5309(03)00017-X

Moore, R. S., Stammerjohan, C. A., & Coulter, R. A. (2005). Banner advertiser-web site context congruity and color effects on attention and attitudes. *Journal of Advertising, 34*(2), 71–84.

Moore, E. S., & Lutz, J. R. (2000, June). Children, advertising and product experiences: a multimethod inquiry. *Journal of Advertising Research*, (June): 31–48.

Moorman, M., Neijens, P. C., & Smit, E. G. (2007). The effects of program involvement on commercial exposure and recall in a naturalistic setting. *Journal of Advertising, 36*, 121–148. doi:10.2753/JOA0091-3367360109

Morris, C. W. (1938). *Foundations of the Theory of Signs*. Chicago: University of Chicago Press.

Morris, M., & Ogan, C. (1996). The Internet as a mass medium. *Journal of Computer-Mediated Communication, 1*(4).

Morrissey, B. (2005). *Advertisers Try to Reach Users With Different Buying Behavior*. Dateline New York.

Morrissey, B. (2006, September 15). For Super Bowl ad, Doritos turns to users. *Adweek*. Retrieved June 9, 2007, from http://www.adweek.com/aw/iq_interactive/article_display.jsp?vnu_content_id=1003122828

Morrissey, B. (2009, May 25). Real Time: The Web's New Prime Time. *Adweek.com*. Retrieved from http://www.adweek.com/aw/content_display/news/digital/e3i15f4e2b3b4a487b-3b5cd5347ebd07cbf

Mort, G. S., & Rose, T. (2004). The effect of product type on value linkages in the means-end chain: Implications for theory and method. *Journal of Consumer Behaviour, 3*, 221–234. doi:10.1002/cb.136

Moses, L. J., & Baldwin, D. A. (2005). What can the study of cognitive development reveal about children's ability to appreciate and cope with advertising? *Journal of Public Policy & Marketing, 24*(2), 186–201. doi:10.1509/jppm.2005.24.2.186

Moshman, D. (1999). *Adolescent psychological development: rationality, morality and identity*. Mahwah, NJ: Eribaum.

Moulds, J. (2007, September 14). *Blogs: The Latest Tool in Decision-Making*. Retrieved September 24, 2007, from http://www.telegraph.co.uk/money/main.jhtml?xml=/money/2007/09/14/bcnblogs114.xml

Mukherjee, K. (2005 June). Indian, Pakistani prostitutes discuss AIDS lessons. *Reuters NewMedia*. Retrieved January 20, 2009, from http://www.aegis.com/news/re/2005/RE050641.html

Mukherjee, K. (2007 July). Sex education creates storm in AIDS-stricken India. *Washingtonpost.com*. Retrieved on January 20, 2009, from http://www.washingtonpost.com/wp-dyn/content/article/2007/07/14/AR2007071401390.html

Mullin, B. J., Hardy, S., & Sutton, W. A. (2007). *Sport marketing* (3rd ed.). Champaign, IL: Human Kinetics.

Mulpuru, S. (2008, May 7). The State of Online Retailing 2008: Marketing Report. *Forrester Research, Inc.* Retrieved January 9, 2009, from http://www.forrester.com

Muniz, A., & O'Guinn, T. (2001). Brand communities. *The Journal of Consumer Research, 27*(4), 412–432. doi:10.1086/319618

Muniz, A., & O'Guinn, T. (1996). Brand community and the sociology of brands. In Corfman, K. P., & Lynch, J. G. (Eds.), *Advances in Consumer Research*. Provo, UT: Association For Consumer Research.

Murchu, I. O., Breslin, J., & Decker, S. (2004). *Online Social and Business Networking Communities*. DERI Technical Report, August 2004.

Murray, S. (2005). High art/low life: The art of playing Grand Theft Auto. *PAJ a Journal of Performance and Art, 27*(80), 91–98. doi:10.1162/1520281053850866

Mustonen, T., Olkkonen, M., & Hakkinen, J. (2004). *Examining mobile phone text legibility while walking*. Paper presented at the CHI '04 extended abstracts on Human factors in computing systems.

Myers, D. G. (1998). *Social Psychology* (9th ed.). New York: McGraw-Hill.

Myers, G. (1994). *Words in Ads*. London: Edward Arnold.

Myths and Facts about HIV/AIDS. (n.d.). *Global strategies for HIV prevention, rural education and development*. Sahaya International, International Training and Education Center on HIV. Retrieved on January 20, 2009, from http://go2itech.org/pdf/p06-db/db-50922-02.pdf

Nabi, R. L., & Kremar, M. (2004). Conceptualizing media enjoyment as attitude: implications for mass media effects research. *Communication Theory, 14*(4), 288–310. doi:10.1111/j.1468-2885.2004.tb00316.x

Nail, J. (2007). Visibility versus surprise: Which drives the greatest discussion of Super Bowl advertisements? *Journal of Advertising Research, 47*(4), 412–419. doi:10.2501/S0021849907070420

Nardi, B. A., Schiano, D. J., & Gumbrecht, M. (2004). Blogging as Social Activity, or, Would You Let 900 Million People Read Your Diary? In *Proceedings of the 2004 ACM Conference on Computer Supported Cooperative Work* (pp. 222-231).

Nass, C., & Moon, Y. (2000). Machines and mindlessness: Social responses to computers. *The Journal of Social Issues, 56*(1), 81–103. doi:10.1111/0022-4537.00153

Nass, C., & Brave, S. (2005). *Wired for speech: How voice activates and advances the human-computer relationship*. Cambridge, MA: MIT Press.

Nass, C. (2008). *Understanding and leveraging emotional engagement*. Retrieved from http://www.archive.org/details/UnderstandingAndLeveragingEmotionalEngagement

Nass, C., Steuer, J., Tauber, E., & Reeder, H. (1993). *Anthropomorphism, agency, and ethopoea: Computers as social actors*. Paper presented at the Inter Chi'93, Amsterdam, the Netherlands, April 24-29.

National AIDS Control Organization. (2007). *HIV Sentinel Surveillance and HIV Estimation 2007: A Technical Brief*. Retrieved on March 16, 2009, from http://www.nacoonline.org/upload/Publication/M&E%20 Surveillance.% 20Research/HIV%20 Sentinel%20Surveillance%20and%20HIV%20Estimation%20 2007_A%20Technical%20Brief.pdf

National AIDS Control Organization. (n.d.). *About NACO*. Retrieved September 2008, from http://www.nacoonline.org/About_NACO/

National AIDS Control Organization. (n.d.). *Funding of the National AIDS Control Programme Phase-II*. Retrieved January 25, 2009, from http://www.nacoonline.org/About_NACO/Funds_and_Expenditures/

National AIDS Control Organization. (n.d.). *Health Minister Launches Third Phase of NACP*. Retrieved January 25, 2009, from http://www.nacoonline.org/NACO_Action/Media__Press_Release/

National AIDS Control Organization. (n.d.). *Monthly updates on AIDS*. Retrieved August 2006, from http://www.nacoonline.org/NACO

National AIDS Control Organization. (n.d.). *Organisational Structure*. Retrieved September 2008, from http://www.nacoonline.org/About_NACO/Organisanal_Structure/

Natkin, S. (2006). *Video games & interactive media: A glimpse at new digital entertainment*. Wellesley, MA: A. K. Peters, Ltd.

Naughton, J. (2006). *Our Changing Media Ecosystem in Communications: The Next Decade, a collection of essays prepared for the UK Office of Communications* (Richards, E., Foster, R., & Kiedrowski, T., Eds.). London: Ofcom.

Nayak, J., & Bose, R. (1997). Making sense, talking sexuality: India reaches out to its youth. *SIECUS Report, 25*(2), 19–21.

Nebolsky, C., Yee, N. K., Petrushin, V. A., & Gershman, A. V. (2003). Using virtual worlds for corporate training. In *Proceedings of the 3rd IEEE International Conference on Advanced Learning Technologies (ICALT'03)*.

Neer, K. (2003). *How Product Placement Works*. Retrieved from http://money.howstuffworks.com/product-placement.htm

Negroponte, N. (1995). *Being digital*. New York: Vintage.

Nelsen, M. R. (2002). Recall of brand placements in computer/video games. *Journal of Advertising Research, 42*, 80–92.

Nelson, M. R., & Otnes, C. C. (2005). Exploring cross-cultural ambivalence: A netnography of intercultural wedding message boards. *Journal of Business Research, 58*(1), 89–95. doi:10.1016/S0148-2963(02)00477-0

Nelson, M. R., Yaros, R. A., & Keum, H. (2006). Examining the influence of telepresence on spectator and player processing of real and fictitious brands in a computer game. *Journal of Advertising, 35*(4), 87–99. doi:10.2753/JOA0091-3367350406

Nelson, P. J. (1970). Information and consumer behavior. *The Journal of Political Economy, 78*(2), 311–329. doi:10.1086/259630

Nelson, P. J. (1974). Advertising as information. *The Journal of Political Economy, 82*(4), 729 751. doi:10.1086/260231

Nelson, P. J. (1976). Economic value of advertising. In Brozen, Y. (Ed.), *Advertising and Society* (pp. 109–141). New York: New York University Press.

Nelson, P. J. (1981). Consumer information and advertising. In Galatin, M., & Leiter, R. D. (Eds.), *Economics of Information* (pp. 42–77). Boston: N. Nijhoff Publishers.

Nepstad, S. (2001). Creating transnational solidarity: The use of narrative in the U.S.–Central America peace movement. *Mobilization: An International Journal, 6*, 21–36.

Netflix. (n.d.). Retrieved from http://www.netflix.com/

Netpop/U.S. (2006). *Study of purchase influencers*.

Neumeier, M. (2003). *Brand Innovation: Where the Rubber Meets the Road*. Retrieved from http://www.informit.com

Newell, J., Salmon, C. T., & Chang, S. (2006). The hidden history of product placement. *Journal of Broadcasting & Electronic Media, 50*(4), 575–594. doi:10.1207/s15506878jobem5004_1

Newell, S. J., & Goldsmith, R. E. (2001). The development of a scale to measure perceived corporate credibility. *Journal of Business Research, 52*(3), 235. doi:10.1016/S0148-2963(99)00104-6

Newhagen, J. E., Cordes, J. W., & Levy, M. R. (1996). Nightly@NBC.com: Audience scope and the perception of interactivity in view mail on the Internet. *The Journal of Communication, 45*(3), 164–175. doi:10.1111/j.1460-2466.1995.tb00748.x

Newsom, G. (2008). Prop 8 battle rages over whether gay marriage would be taught in schools. *Los Angeles Times*. Retrieved March 16, 2009, from http://articles.latimes.com/2008/oct/19/local/me-gayschools19

Nguyen, H. Q., Carrieri-Kohlman, V., Rankin, S. H., Slaughter, R., & Stulbarg, M. S. (2004). Internet-based patient education and support interventions: A review of evaluation studies and directions for future research. *Computers in Biology and Medicine, 34*(2), 95–112. doi:10.1016/S0010-4825(03)00046-5

Nguyen, H. Q., Cuenco, D., Wolpin, S., Benditt, J., & Carrieri-Kohlman, V. (2007). Methodological considerations in evaluating eHealth interventions. *Canadian Journal of Nursing Research, 39*(1), 116–134.

Nichovich, S. G. (2005). The effect of involvement on ad judgment in a video game environment: The mediating role of presence. *Journal of Interactive Advertising, 6*(1). Retrieved from http://www.jiad.org/article67.

Niederhoffer, K., Mooth, R., Wiesenfeld, D., & Gordon, J. (2007). The origin and impact of CPG new-product buzz: Emerging trends and implications. *Journal of Advertising Research, 47*(4), 420–426. doi:10.2501/S0021849907070432

Niederhoffer, K. (2008). *Measuring engagement in social media and new online media: new perspectives on measuring involvement*. Retrieved from http://www.archive.org/details/MeasuringEngagementInSocialMediaAndNewOnlineMedia

Nielsen, J., & Mack, R. L. (1994). *Usability Inspection Methods*. New York: John Wiley & Sons.

Nielsen, J., & Mack, R. L. (Eds.). (1994). *Heuristic Evaluation*. New York: John Wily & Sons.

Nielsen Shutters, P. R. I. S. M. *Initiative*. (2009, January 26). The Market Research Industry Online. Retrieved from http://www.mrweb.com/drno/news9467.htm

Nikerson, A. B., & Nagle, R. J. (2005). Parent and peer attachment in late childhood and early adolescence. *The Journal of Early Adolescence, 25*, 223–249. doi:10.1177/0272431604274174

Nikken, P., & Jansz, J. (2007). Playing restricted videogames: relations with game ratings and parental mediation. *Journal of Children and Media, 1*(3), 227–243. doi:10.1080/17482790701531862

Nisbet, R. A. (1970). *The social bond.*, N.Y.New York: Knopf.

Noam, E. M. (2006, June). Deregulation and market concentration: An analysis of post-1996 consolidations. *Federal Communications Law Journal, 58*, 539–549.

Nobel, N. (2006). *Aesthetics and gratification: Sexual practices in virtual environments*. Working Paper. Trinity University, San Antonio, TX

Noble, R. (2007). *Worldwide HIV & AIDS statistics commentary*. Retrieved March 15, 2009, from http://www.avert.org/worlstatinfo.htm

Noelle-Neumann, E. (1974). The spiral of silence: A theory of public opinion. *The Journal of Communication, 24*(2), 43–51. doi:10.1111/j.1460-2466.1974.tb00367.x

Noelle-Neumann, E. (1984). *The spiral of silence: Public opinion–our social skin*. Chicago: University of Chicago Press.

Noelle-Neumann, E. (1991). The theory of public opinion: The concept of the spiral of silence. In Anderson, J. A. (Ed.), *Communication Yearbook* (*Vol. 14*, pp. 339–356). Newbury Park, CA: Sage.

Norman, D. (1990). *The design of everyday things*.

Nowak, K. L., & Biocca, F. (2003). The effect of the agency and anthropomorphism on users' sense of telepresence, copresence, and social presence in virtual environments. *Presence (Cambridge, Mass.), 12*(5), 481–494. doi:10.1162/105474603322761289

Nowak, K. L., & Rauh, C. (2006). The influence of the avatar on online perceptions of anthropomorphism, androgyny, credibility, homophily, and attraction. *Journal of Computer-Mediated Communication, 11*, 153–178. doi:10.1111/j.1083-6101.2006.tb00308.x

Nowak, K. L. (2004). The influence of anthropomorphism and agency on social judgment in virtual environments. *Journal of Computer-Mediated Communication, 9*(2). Retrieved from http://jcmc.indiana.edu/vol9/issue2/nowak.html.

Nowak, K. L., & Rauh, C. (2008). Choose your buddy icon carefully: The influence of avatar androgyny, anthropomorphism and credibility in online interactions. *Computers in Human Behavior*, *24*, 1473–1493. doi:10.1016/j.chb.2007.05.005

Nowak, A. (2008, April 25). Big Media Muscles in on Virtual Worlds. *Cable360*. Retrieved April 25, 2008, from http://www.cable360.net

Nowson, S., & Oberlander, J. (2006). *The Identity of Bloggers: Openness and Gender in Personal Weblogs*. Paper Presented at the AAAI Spring Symposium - Technical Report.

Nussenbaum, E. (2004, August 22). Video game makers go Hollywood. Uh-oh. *New York Times*, 5.

Nuttall, C. (2007, January 30). Burger King's whopping games sales. *Financial Times*. Retrieved August 18, 2008 from http://blogs.ft.com/techblog/2007/01/burger-kings-whhtml/

Nuyens, G. (2008) *Engaging avatars and their operators*. Retrieved from http://www.archive.org/details/EngagingAvatarsAndTheirOperators

O'Guinn, T. O., Allen, C. T., & Semenik, R. J. (2006). *Advertising & integrated brand promotion* (4th ed.). Mason, OH: Thomson.

O'Keefe, D. J. (2002). *Persuasion: Theory & Research* (2nd ed.). Thousand Oaks, CA: Sage Publications, Inc.

O'Mahony, S., & Meenaghan, T. (1997). The impact of celebrity endorsements on consumers. *Irish Marketing Review*, *10*(2), 15–24.

O'Malley, G. (2007, September 18). Heinz anticipates another success with consumer ads. *MediaPost*.

O'Neill. (2008, February 21). Why they're scared of Obamamania. *Spiked*. Retrieved from http://www.spiked-online.com/index.php?/site/article/4556/

Oakes, P. J., Haslam, S. A., & Turner, J. C. (1994). *Stereotyping and social reality*. Oxford, UK: Blackwell.

Oakley, A., Fullerton, D., Holland, J., Arnold, S., France-Dawson, M., Kelley, P., & McGrellis, S. (1995). Sexual health education interventions for young people: A methodological review. *British Medical Journal*, *310*, 158–162.

Oates, C. J., Blades, M., & Gunter, B. (2002). Children and television advertising. *Journal of Consumer Behaviour*, *1*(3), 238–245. doi:10.1002/cb.69

Obermiller, C. (1985). Varieties of mere exposure: The effects of processing style and repetition on affective responses. *The Journal of Consumer Research*, *6*, 93–100.

Odden, L. (2009, April 1). Comprehensive guide to social media marketing from marketingsherpa. *Wisconsin State Journal*, 22.

OECD. (2008). *OECD Statistics*. Retrieved from http://www.oecd.org/

Ohanian, R. (1990). Construction and validation of a scale to measure celebrity endorsers' perceived expertise, trustworthiness, and attractiveness. *Journal of Advertising*, *19*(3), 39–52.

O'Hara, K. (2002). The Internet: A tool for democratic pluralism? *Science as Culture*, *11*, 287–298. doi:10.1080/09505430220137298

Ohman, A. (1997). As fast as the blink of an eye: Evolution preparedness for preattentive processing of threat. In Lang, P. J., Simons, R. F., & Balaban, M. (Eds.), *Attention and Orienting: Sensory and Motivational Processes* (pp. 165–184). Hillsdale, NJ: Erlbaum.

Okazaki, S. (2008). Determinant factors of mobile-based word-of-mouth campaign referral among Japanese adolescents. *Psychology and Marketing*, *25*(8), 714–731. doi:10.1002/mar.20235

Okazaki, S., Skapa, R., & Grande, R., I. (2008). Capturing global youth: mobile gaming in the U.S., Spain, and the Czech Republic. *Journal of Computer-Mediated Communication*, *13*, 827–855. doi:10.1111/j.1083-6101.2008.00421.x

Olga, K. (2007, May 22). Virtual World Gold Rush. *BusinessWeek.com*. Retrieved June 15, 2007, from http://www.businessweek.com/technology/content/may2007/tc20070522_380944.htm

Oliver, M. B. (2002). Individual differences in media effects. In Bryant, J., & Zillmann, D. (Eds.), *Media effects: Advances in theory and research* (pp. 507–524). Hillsdale, NJ: Lawrence Erlbaum Associates, Inc.

Olson, M. (1965). *The Logic of Collective Action: Public Goods and the Theory of Group*. Cambridge, MA: Harvard University Press.

Ondrejka, C. (2006). Escaping the gilded cage: User-created content and building the metaverse. In Balkin, J. M. (Ed.), *The state of play: Law, games, and virtual worlds*. New York: New York University Press.

Online Campaigning 2002: A primer. (2002). Retrieved October 27, 2007, from http://www.ipdi.org/primer2002.html

Online Classified Use Soaring in US. *Pew Survey*. (2009, May 22). Retrieved from http://www.pewinternet.org/Media-Mentions/2009/Online-classified-use-soaring-in-US-Pew-survey.aspx

Ophir, E., Nass, C. I., & Wagner, A. D. (2009). Cognitive control in media multitaskers. *Proceedings of the National Academy of*

Sciences of the United States of America, *106*(37), 15583–15587. doi:10.1073/pnas.0903620106

Oppenheim, A. N. (1966). *Questionnaire Design and Attitude Measurement*. New York: Basic Books.

Ordover, J., Saloner, G., & Salop, S. (1990, March). Equilibrium vertical foreclosure. *The American Economic Review*, *80*, 127–142.

Oregon Bar Press Broadcasters Council. (2000). *Media Handbook on Oregon Law and Court System*. Retrieved on September 25, 2008, from http://www.open-oregon.com/New_Pages/media_handbook/toc.html

Orlandi, M. A., Dozier, C. E., & Marta, M. A. (1990). Computer-assisted strategies for substance abuse prevention: Opportunities and barriers. *Journal of Consulting and Clinical Psychology*, *558*(4), 425–431. doi:10.1037/0022-006X.58.4.425

Oser, K. (2005, August 8). Marketers wrestle with hard–to-control content. *Advertising Age*, 20.

Osgood, C. E., Succi, J. G., & Tannenbaum, T. H. (1957). *The Measurement of Meaning*. Chicago: University of Illinois Press.

Oskman, V., & Turtiainen, J. (2004). Mobile communication as a social stage. *New Media & Society*, *6*(3), 319–339. doi:10.1177/1461444804042518

Ostrow, A. (2009). *Social Networking Sites More Popular than Email*. Retrieved June 27, 2009, from http://mashable.com/2009/03/09/social-networking-more-popular-than-email/

Oulasvirta, A., Tamminen, S., Roto, V., & Kuorelahti, J. (2005). *Interaction in 4-second bursts: the fragmented nature of attentional resources in mobile HCI*. Paper presented at the Proceedings of the SIGCHI conference on Human factors in computing systems.

Ourand, J. (2009, January 5-11). Focused on making the numbers work: ESPN, CBS outline how they expect to justify hefty rights fees for college content. *Street & Smith's Sports Business Journal*, *11*(35), 15–19.

Ourand, J., & Lefton, T. (2010, March 15-21). Verizon-NFL deal: Convergence is here. *Street & Smith's Sports Business Journal*, *12*(45), 1, 42.

Owen, B. M. (2008). The temptation of media regulation. *Regulation*, 8–12.

Owen, D. (2000). Using Search Engines and Portals. In G. J. Swinfen (Ed.), *E-Media* (pp. 89-96). Henley-on-Thames, UK: Admap Publications.

Oxford Dictionaries. (2008). *Concise Oxford English Dictionary (11th Ed. Revised)*. Oxford, UK: Oxford University Press.

Ozok, A. A. (2009). Survey Design and Implementation in Human Computer Interaction. In Jacko, J., & Sears, A. (Eds.), *Human-Computer Interaction: Development Process* (pp. 253–271). Mahwah, NJ: Lawrence Erlbaum Associates.

Padma, T. V. (2005 May). *Experts dispute Indian claims of huge drop in HIV cases*. Retrieved March 15, 2009, from http://www.scidev.net/en/news/experts-dispute-indian-claims-of-huge-drop-in-hiv.html

Page, R. (2006, November 11). General Session Summary: Andrew Heyward on the Power of the Remote and the Rise of New Media. *Public Relations Society of America*.

Pahl, R. (2000). *On friendship. Cambridge*. Cambridge, MA: Polity Press.

Paivio, A. (1986). *Mental Representativeness: A Dual Coding Approach*. New York: Oxford University Press.

Palda, K. S. (1966). *The measurement of cumulative advertising effects*. Englewood Cliffs, NJ: Prentice-Hall.

Palmgreen, P., & Rayburn, J. D. II. (1985). A comparison of gratification models of media satisfaction. *Communication Monographs*, *52*, 334–346. doi:10.1080/03637758509376116

Palmgreen, P., Wenner, L. A., & Rayburn, J. D. II. (1980). Relations between gratifications sought and obtained: A study of television news. *Communication Research*, *7*, 161–192. doi:10.1177/009365028000700202

Palser, B. (2005). News a la carte. *American Journalism Review*, *27*(1). Retrieved June 4, 2008, from http://www.questia.com/googleScholar.qst,jsessionid=LlbL4QxyLTqRhFdrwJ9hTpHQcnnG3yd2kpvtWpzyJSnffhL1CycG!-553604554?docId=5008837690

Panayiotou, C., Andreou, M., & Samaras, G. (2006). Using time and activity in personalization for the mobile user. In *MobiDE '06: Proceedings of the 5th ACM international workshop on Data engineering for wireless and mobile access*.

Papacharissi, Z., & Rubin, A. M. (2000). Predictors of Internet use. *Journal of Broadcasting & Electronic Media*, *44*(2), 175–196. doi:10.1207/s15506878jobem4402_2

Papacharissi, Z., & Rubin, A. M. (2000). Predictors of internet use. *Journal of Broadcasting & Electronic Media*, *44*(2), 175–196. doi:10.1207/s15506878jobem4402_2

Papadopoulou, P. (2007). Applying virtual reality for trust-building e-commerce environments. *Virtual Reality (Waltham Cross)*, *11*(2), 107–127. doi:10.1007/s10055-006-0059-x

Parasraman, A., & Zinkhan, G. M. (2002). Marketing to and serving customers through the internet: An overview and research agenda. *Journal of the Academy of Marketing Science*, *30*(4), 286–295. doi:10.1177/009207002236906

Park, D., Lee, J., & Han, I. (2007). The effect of on-line consumer reviews on consumer purchasing intention: The moderating role of involvement. *International Journal of Electronic Commerce*, *11*(4), 125–148. doi:10.2753/JEC1086-4415110405

Park, S., & Ha, L. (2005). Interactivity in consumer commenting functions: A comparison of Korean and U.S. leading retail websites. In *Proceedings of the American Academy of Advertising Asia-Pacific Conference*, Hong Kong.

Parks, L. (2008 April). Peer reviews drive online buyers: Bath & Body Works kicks up conversion rate using customer comments. *Stores*. Retrieved August 4, 2008, from http://www.stores.org/Current_Issue/2008/04/edit8/index.asp

Parlato, M., & Seidel, R. (Eds.). (1998). *Large Scale Application of Nutrition Behavior Change Approaches: Lessons from West Africa*. Arlington, VA: Basic Support for Institutionalizing Child Survival (BASICS) Project. Retrieved February 10, 2009, from http://www.pronutrition.org/files/Large%20Scale%20BCC%20 Approaches.PDF

Parsons, T. (1951). *The social system. NY*. New York: Free press.

Pascoe, J., Ryan, N., & Morse, D. (2000). Using while moving: HCI issues in fieldwork environments. *ACM Transactions on Computer-Human Interaction*, *7*(3), 417–437. doi:10.1145/355324.355329

Pasek, J., & Krosnick, J. A. (2010). Optimizing Survey Questionnaire Design in Political Science: Insights From Psychology. In Leighley, J. (Ed.), *Oxford Handbook of American Elections and Political Behavior*. Oxford, UK: Oxford University Press.

Passikoff, R., Keys, B., & Schultz, D. E. (2007, October). Cross-media Engagement Evaluations. *Admap Magazine*.

Pavlik, J. V. (1998). *New Media Technology: Cultural and Commercial Perspectives*. Boston, MA: Allyn and Bacon.

Pazzani, M., & Billsus, D. (1997). Learning and revising user profiles: The identification of interesting web sites. *Machine Learning*, *27*(3), 313–331. doi:10.1023/A:1007369909943

Pazzani, M. J. (1999). A framework for collaborative, content-based and demographic filtering. *Artificial Intelligence Review*, *13*, 393–408. doi:10.1023/A:1006544522159

Pazzani, M. J., & Billsus, D. (2007). Content-Based Recommendation Systems. In Brusilovsky, P., Kobsa, A., & Nejdl, W. (Eds.), *The Adaptive Web* (*Vol. 4321*, pp. 325–341). Berlin, Germany: Springer-Verlag. doi:10.1007/978-3-540-72079-9_10

Pechmann, C., & Stewart, D. W. (1990). The effects of comparative advertising on attention, memory, and purchase intentions. *The Journal of Consumer Research*, *17*(September), 180–191. doi:10.1086/208548

Pedersen, P. M., Miloch, K. S., & Laucella, P. C. (2007). *Strategic sports communication*. Champaign, IL: Human Kinetics.

Pennebaker, J. W., Mehl, M. R., & Niederhoffer, K. (2003). Psychological aspects of natural language use: Our words, our selves. *Annual Review of Psychology*, *54*, 547–577. doi:10.1146/annurev.psych.54.101601.145041

Pennebaker, J. W., Booth, R. J., & Francis, M. E. (2007). *Linguistic Inquiry and Word Count (LIWC2007), a text analysis program*. Austin, TX: LIWC.net.

Perez, M. (2008, June). Mobile gaming revenue to hit $4.5 billion. *Information Week*. Retrieved

Perloff, R. M. (2007). *The dynamics of persuasion*. New York: Lawrence Erlbaum Associates.

Perloff, R. M. (2002). The third-person effect. In Bryant, J. B., & Zillman, D. (Eds.), *Media Effects: Advances in theory and research* (pp. 489–506). Mahwah, NJ: Lawrence Erlbaum Associates.

Perry, D. (2002). Theories of Media Audiences. In *Theory and Research in Mass Communication* (2nd ed., pp. 70–92). Mahwah, NJ: Lawrence Erlbaum Associates.

Perry, D. K. (2002). *Theory and Research in Mass Communication: Contexts and Consequences* (2nd ed.). Mahwah, NJ: Lawrence Erlbaum Associates.

Perry, A. (2005). When silence kills. *TIME ASIA*. Retrieved January 15, 2009, from http://www.time.com/time/asia/ covers/501050606/story.html

Perse, E., & Greenberg Dunn, D. (1998). The utility of home computers and media use: Implications of multimedia and connectivity. *Journal of Broadcasting & Electronic Media*, *42*, 435–456.

Peters, E., Lipkus, I., & Diefenbach, M. A. (2006). The functions of affect in health communications and in the construction of health preferences. *The Journal of Communication*, *56*(S1), S140–S162. doi:10.1111/j.1460-2466.2006.00287.x

Petrecca, L. (2006, March 27). Amateur advertisers get a chance. *USA Today*. Retrieved June 26, 2007, from http://www.usatoday.com/money/advertising/2006-03-27-amateur-advertisers_x.htm

Petrecca, L. (2007, June 21). Madison Avenue wants you! (or at least your videos). *USA Today*. Retrieved June 26, 2007, from http://www.usatoday.com/printEd./money/20070621/cannes_cover.art.htm

Petty, R. E., & Cacioppo, J. T. (1986). *Communication and Persuasion: Central and Peripheral Routes to Attitude Change*. New York: Springer Verlag.

Petty, E. P., & Brinol, P. (2008). From single to multiple to metacognitive processes. *Perspectives on Psychological Science, 3*(2), 137–147. doi:10.1111/j.1745-6916.2008.00071.x

Petty, R. E., Fazio, R. H., & Briñol, P. (Eds.). (2009). *Attitudes: Insights From the New Implicit Measures*. New York: Psychology Press.

Petty, R. E., & Cacioppo, J. T. (1990). Involvement and persuasion: Tradition versus integration. *Psychological Bulletin, 107*, 367–374. doi:10.1037/0033-2909.107.3.367

Petty, R. E., & Cacioppo, J. T. (1996). *Attitudes And Persuasion: Classic And Contemporary Approaches*. Boulder, CO: Westview Press.

Pew Research Center for the People & the Press. (2008, November 5). *Inside Obama's Sweeping Victory*. Washington, DC. Retrieved November 14, 2008, from http://pewresearch.org/pubs/1023/exit-poll-analysis-2008 (11/14/08).

Phillips, B. J. (1996). Defining trade characters and their role in popular culture. *Journal of Popular Culture, 29*(4), 143–158. doi:10.1111/j.0022-3840.1996.1438797.x

Phillips, J. (2008, July 2). Performance, Performance, Performance. *Metrics Insider*. Retrieved June 15, 2009, from http://www.mediapost.com/publications/index.cfm?fa=Articles.showArticle&art_aid=85886

Phillips, M. (2008). *Princess Obama*. Retrieved June 9, 2008, from http://www.spectator.co.uk/melaniephillips/503146/

Phinney, J. S. (1990). Ethnic identity in adolescents and adults: Review of research. *Psychological Bulletin, 108*, 499–514. doi:10.1037/0033-2909.108.3.499

Phinney, J. S. (1992). The multigroup ethnic identity measure: A new scale for use with diverse groups. *Journal of Adolescent Research, 7*(2), 156–176. doi:10.1177/074355489272003

Piaget, J. (1952, original 1936). *The origins of intelligence in children*. Oxford, UK: International University Press. (Original manuscript published in 1936).

Picard, R. W. (n.d.). *Toward computers that recognize and respond to user emotion-References*. Retrieved from http://research.ibm.com

Pickard, V. (2006 a). Assessing the radical democracy of Indymedia: Discursive, technical, and institutional constructions. *Critical Studies in Media Communication, 23*, 19–38. doi:10.1080/07393180600570691

Pickard, V. (2006 b). United yet autonomous: Indymedia and the struggle to sustain a radical democratic network. *Media Culture & Society, 28*, 315–336. doi:10.1177/0163443706061685

Pigna, K. (2008). Presidential candidate ads appear in Burnout Paradise. *1Up.com*. Retrieved October 14, 2008 from http://www.1up.com/do/newsStory?cId=3170635

Pilieci, V. (2008, February 18). *Video game is free -- just watch onscreen ads*. Winnipeg Free Press. Retrieved March 1, 2008, from http://www.winnipegfreepress.com/canada/story/4127803p-4721275c.html

Pilotta, J. J., Schultz, D. E., & Drenik, G. (2004). Simultaneous media usage: a critical consumer orientation to media planning. *Journal of Consumer Behaviour, 30*(3).

Pinsky, L. E., & Wipf, J. E. (2001). Innovations in education and clinical practice. *Journal of General Internal Medicine, 15*, 805–810. doi:10.1046/j.1525-1497.2000.05129.x

Piotrow, P., Kincaid, D. L., Rimon, J. G., & Rinehart, W. (1997). *Health Communication: Lessons from family planning and reproductive health*. Westport, CT: Praeger.

Pitney, J. (2008, June 25). *CNN interview*. Retrieved July 15, 2008 from http://www.cnn.com/video/#/video/tech/2008/06/25/am.cho.bmw.ad.cnn?iref=videosearch

Pitta, D. A., & Fowler, D. (2005). Online consumer communities and their value to new product developers. *Journal of Product and Brand Management, 14*(5), 283–291. doi:10.1108/10610420510616313

Plummer, J., Rappaport, S., Hall, T., & Barocci, R. (2007). *The online advertising playbook: proven strategies and tested tactics from the advertising research foundation*. Hoboken, NJ: John Wiley & Sons, Inc.

Plummer, J., Cook, B., Diforio, D., Schachter, B., Sokolyanskaya, I., Korde, T., & Heath, R. (2007). *Measures of engagement: Volume II*. Advertising Research Foundation, White Paper (March).

Pogue, D. (2009, January 19). Belkin employee paid users for good reviews. *New York Times*. Retrieved February 16, 2009, from http://pogue.blogs.nytimes.com/2009/01/19/belkin-employee-paid-users-for-good-reviews/?scp=1&sq=belkin%20 employee%20&st=Search

Point of Purchase Advertising International (POPAI). (2003, January). *In-store advertising becomes a measured medium*. Convenience Channel Study.

Polat, R. (2005). The Internet and political participation: Exploring the explanatory links. *European Journal of Communication*, *20*, 435–459. doi:10.1177/0267323105058251

Polletta, F. (1998). It was like a fever… Narrative and identity in social protest. *Social Problems*, *45*, 137–159. doi:10.1525/sp.1998.45.2.03x0163g

Pollock, M. (2005). *Colormute: Race talk dilemmas in an American school*. Princeton, NJ: Princeton University Press.

Pompper, D., Kinnally, W., & McClung, S. (2005, May 26). *Appealing to Abandoning Adolescents: Radio Use Motivation Factors and Time Spent Listening*. Conference Papers -- International Communication Association. Retrieved September 4, 2008, from Communication & Mass Media Complete database.

Pong. (2008). Retrieved May 30, 2008, from http://en.wikipedia.org/wiki/Pong

Population Services International (PSI). (2003). *Balbir Pasha: HIV/AIDS Campaign is the talk of Mumbai*. Retrieved January 20, 2009, from www.psi.org/resources/pubs/balbir-pasha.pdf

Porter, C. E. (2004). A typology of virtual communities: A multi-disciplinary foundation for future research. *Journal of Computer-Mediated Communication*, *10*(1).

Porter, S. B. (1993). Public knowledge and attitudes about AIDS among adults in Calcutta, India. *AIDS Care*, *5*(2), 169–176. doi:10.1080/09540129308258597

Porter, L., & Golan, G. (2006). From subservient chickens to brawny men: A comparison of viral advertising to television advertising. *Journal of Interactive Advertising*, *6*(2). Retrieved March 19, 2009, from http://www.jiad.org/vol6/no2/

Posner, E. A. (2002). *Law and Social Norms*. Cambridge, MA: Harvard University Press.

Poupolo, S. T. (2001). The Web and U.S. Senate campaigns 2000. *The American Behavioral Scientist*, *44*(12), 2030–2047. doi:10.1177/00027640121958474

Powell, L., & Cowart, J. (2003). *Political campaign communication: Inside and out*. Boston: Allyn and Bacon.

PR Newswire US. (2006, September 21). *Free Podcast Tours Give Visitors an Insider's Look at Philadelphia, New Downloadable Audio Tours Offer Yet Another Way for Visitors to Explore the City*. Retrieved May 18, 2008, from http://www.gophila.com/Go/PressRoom/pressreleases/Free_Podcast_Tours_Give_Visitors_an_Insiders_Look.aspx

Pradhan, B. K., Sundar, R., & Singh, S. K. (2006). Socio-Economic Impact of HIV and AIDS in India. *United Nations Development Programme*. New Delhi, India: New Concept Information Systems Pvt. Ltd. Retrieved January 28, 2009, from http://data.undp.org.in/hivreport/India_Report.pdf

Prahalad, C. K., & Ramaswamy, V. (2004). *The Future Of Competition: Co-Creating Unique Value With Customers*. Cambridge, MA: HBS Press.

Pramanik, S., Chartier, M., & Koopman, C. (2006). HIV/AIDS stigma and knowledge among predominantly middle-class high school students in New Delhi, India. *The Journal of Communicable Diseases*, *38*(1), 57–69.

Pravettoni, G., Leotta, S. N., & Lucchiari, C. (2008). The eye caught in the Net: A study on attention and motivation in virtual environment exploration. *The European Journal of Cognitive Psychology*, *20*, 955–966. doi:10.1080/09541440701804564

Preece, J., Nonnecke, B., & Andrews, D. (2004). The top five reasons for lurking: improving community experiences for everyone. *Computers in Human Behavior*, *2*(1).

Prensky, M. (2001). Digital natives, digital immigrants. *On the Horizon. NCB University Press*, *9*(5), 1–9.

Prensky, M. (2004). *The emerging online life of the digital native: what they do differently because of technology, and how they do it*. Retrieved from http://www.marcprensky.com.

Presbrey, F. (1929). *The History and Development of Advertising*. New York: Doubleday.

PricewaterhouseCoopers. (2008). *Interactive Advertising Bureau Internet Advertising Revenue Report*.

ProvenModels. (n. d.). *AIDA sales funnel*. Retrieved May 30, 2009, from http://www.provenmodels.com/547/aida-sales-funnel/lewis

Pruitt, S. W., Cornwell, T. B., & Clark, J. M. (2004). The NASCAR phenomenon: Auto racing sponsorships and shareholder wealth. *Journal of Advertising Research*, *44*(3), 281–296. doi:10.1017/S0021849904040279

Puto, C. P., & Wells, W. D. (1984). Informational and transformational advertising: The differential effects of time. In Kinnear,

T. C. (Ed.), *Advances in Consumer Research, XI* (pp. 638–643). Provo, UT: Association for Consumer Research.

PVI launches multiple output system for virtual advertisements during MLB World Series, a technological first. (2007, October 25). *Business Wire*. Retrieved from http://findarticles.com/p/articles/mi_m0EIN/is_2007_Oct_25/ai_n27421866

Qiu, L., & Benbasat, I. (2005). Online consumer trust and live help interfaces: The effects of text-to-speech voice and three-dimensional avatars. *International Journal of Human-Computer Interaction, 19*, 75–94. doi:10.1207/s15327590ijhc1901_6

Quester, P. G., Karunaratna, A., & Goh, L. K. (2000). Self-Congruity and product evaluation. *Journal of Consumer Marketing, 17*, 525–537. doi:10.1108/07363760010349939

Quester, P. G., & Thompson, B. (2001). Advertising and promotion leverage on arts sponsorship effectiveness. *Journal of Advertising Research, 41*(1), 33–47.

Raacke, J., & Bonds-Raacke, J. (2008). MySpace and Facebook: Applying the uses and gratifications theory to exploring friend-networking sites. *Cyberpsychology & Behavior, 11*(2), 169–174. doi:10.1089/cpb.2007.0056

Ragusa, J. M., & Bochenek, G. M. (2001). Collaborative virtual design environments. *Communications of the ACM, 44*(12), 40–43. doi:10.1145/501317.501339

Rainie, L., Horrigan, J., & Cornfield, M. (2005). The Internet and campaign 2004. *Pew Internet & American Life Project*. Retrieved July 23, 2008, from http://www.pewinternet.org/Reports/2005/The-Internet-and-Campaign-2004.aspx

Rao, S. R., Hurlbutt, T., Nass, C., & JanakiRam, N. (2009). *My Dating Site Thinks I'm a Loser: effects of personal photos and presentation intervals on perceptions of recommender systems.* Paper presented at the Conference on Human Factors in Computing Systems, Boston, MA.

Rappaport, S. (2007). Why we talk: The truth behind word-of-mouth: Seven reasons your customers will or will not talk about your brand. *Journal of Advertising Research, 47*(4), 535–536. doi:10.2501/S0021849907070560

Rappaport, S. D. (2007). Lessons from online practice: new advertising models. *Journal of Advertising Research, 47*(2), 135–141. doi:10.2501/S0021849907070158

Ray, M. (1982). *Advertising and communication management.* Englewood Cliffs, NJ: Prentice Hall.

Ray, M. (1973). Marketing Communication and the Hierarchy of Effects. In Clarke, P. (Ed.), *New Models for Communication Research* (*Vol. 2*, pp. 146–175). Beverley Hills, CA: Sage.

Rayburn, J. D. (1996). Uses and gratifications. In Salwen, M. B., & Stacks, D. W. (Eds.), *An integrated approach to communications theory and research* (pp. 97–119). Mahwah, NJ: Lawrence Erlbaum Associates, Inc.

Redjimi, G., & Lert, F. (1993). Images of AIDS among teenagers and young adults. *AIDS Care, 5*(4), 449–465. doi:10.1080/09540129308258014

Reeves, B., & Read, J. L. (2009). *Total Engagement: Using Games and Virtual World in Change the Way We Work and Play.* Cambridge, MA: Harvard Business Press.

Reeves, R. (1961). *Reality in Advertising.* New York: Alfred A. Knopf.

Reeves, B., & Nass, C. (1996). *The media equation: How people treat computers, television, and new media like real people and places.* New York: Cambridge University Press.

Reich, R. (1996, November 4). Virtual ads a losing proposition. *Advertising Age, 67*, 34.

Reichart, L. M. (2008). *Will MySpace take me to Washington?* Paper presented at the Popular Culture/American Culture National Conference, San Francisco.

Reilly, J., Zhang, J., McGinty, L., Pu, P., & Smyth, B. (2007). *Evaluating compound critiquing recommenders: A real-user study.* Paper presented at the Eighth Annual Conference on Electronic Commerce.

Reisinger, D. (2008, February 8). *Why Blockbuster brick-and-mortars will be gone in five years.* Retrieved from http://news.cnet.com/8301-13506_3-9867493-17.html

Report Card HIV Prevention for Girls and Young Women. (n.d.). *United Nations Population Fund.* Retrieved January 28, 2009, from www.unfpa.org/hiv/docs/report-cards/india.pdf

Report of the Commission for Africa. (n.d.). *Commission for Africa.* Retrieved January 29, 2009, from http://www.commissionforafrica.org/english/report/thereport/english/11-03-05_cr_report.pdf

Report, M. A. (2008). *Limbo-GfK, produced in conjunction with GFK/NOP research. Q2 2008.* Retrieved March 1, 2009, from http://mmaglobal.com/uploads/Limbo_MAR_Report_Q2_2008.pdf

Resnick, P., & Varian, H. R. (1997). Recommender systems. *Communications of the ACM, 40*(3), 56–58. doi:10.1145/245108.245121

Reuters. (2006 March). *Asia-Pacific countries must end cultural taboos about sex, discrimination, to curb HIV/AIDS epidemic, advocate says*. Retrieved January 20, 2009, from http://www.kaisernetwork.org/daily_reports/ print_report.cfm?DR_ID=36203&dr_cat=4

Reynolds, K. E., & Beatty, S. E. (1999). Customer benefits and company consequences of customer–salesperson relationships in retailing. *Journal of Retailing, 75*(1), 11–32. doi:10.1016/S0022-4359(99)80002-5

Reynolds, T. (2007). Friendship networks, social capital and ethnic identity: researching the perspectives of Caribbean young people in Britain. *Journal of Youth Studies, 10*(4), 383–398. doi:10.1080/13676260701381192

Reynolds, T. J., & Jolly, J. P. (1980). Measuring personal values: An evaluation of alternative methods. *JMR, Journal of Marketing Research, 17*(4), 531–536. doi:10.2307/3150506

Rheingold, H. (1993). *The Virtual Community: Homesteading on the Electronic Frontier*. New York: Addison Wesley.

Ricci, F., & Nguyen, Q. N. (2007). Acquiring and revising preferences in a critique-based mobile recommender system. *IEEE Intelligent Systems, 22*(3), 22–29. doi:10.1109/MIS.2007.43

Rich, E. (1979b). *User modeling via stereotypes*. Cognitive Science.

Rich, E. (1979a). *Building and exploiting user models* [Ph. D. Thesis]. Retrieved from http://csa.com

Rich, E. (1983). Users are Individuals: Individualizing User Models. *International Journal of Man-Machine Studies*.

Rich, M. (2008). In Book for Young, Two Views on Product Placement. *New York Times*. Retrieved from http://www.nytimes.com/2008/02/19/books/19cathy.html?_r=1&oref=slogin

Richard Gere cleared of obscenity. (2008, March 14). *BBC News*. Retrieved January 13, 2009, from http://news.bbc.co.uk/2/hi/south_asia/7295797.stm

Richards, J. (2008, April 23). McKinsey: ignore Second Life at your peril. *Times Online*. Retrieved April 23, 2008, from http://technology.timesonline.co.uk

Ridings, C., & Gefen, D. (2004). Virtual Community Attraction: Why People Hang Out Online. *Journal of Computer-Mediated Communication, 10*(1). Retrieved August 29, 2007, from http://jcmc.indiana.edu/vol10/issue1/ridings_gefen.html

Riegner, J. C. (2007). Word of mouth on the Web: The impact of Web 2.0 on consumer purchase decisions. *Journal of Advertising Research, 47*(4), 436–447. doi:10.2501/S0021849907070456

Rifon, N. J., LaRose, R., & Choi, S. M. (2005). Your privacy is sealed: Effects of Web privacy seals on trust and personal disclosures. *The Journal of Consumer Affairs, 39*(2), 339–362. doi:10.1111/j.1745-6606.2005.00018.x

Ritson, M., & Elliott, R. (1999). The social uses of advertising: an ethnographic study of adolescent advertising audiences. *The Journal of Consumer Research, 26*(3), 260–277. doi:10.1086/209562

Roberts, M. L., Wortzel, L. H., & Berkeley, R. L. (1981). Mother's attitudes and perceptions of children's influence and their effect on family consumption. *Advances in Consumer Research. Association for Consumer Research (U. S.), 8*, 730–735.

Roberts, W. R. t. (1954). *The rhetoric of Aristotle*. Oxford, England: Clarendon Press. (Original manuscript published in 1924).

Robertson, T. S. (1971). *Innovation and the Consumer*. New York: Holt, Rinehart & Winston.

Robinson, J. (1977). *How American Use Time: A Social-Psychological Analysis of Everyday Behavior*. New York: Praeger.

Robinson, F., Sandoval, N., Baldwin, J., & Sanderson, P. R. (2005). Breast cancer education for Native American women: Creating culturally relevant communications. *Clinical Journal of Oncology Nursing, 9*(6), 689–692. doi:10.1188/05.CJON.689-692

Robinson, H., Wysocka, A., & Hand, C. (2007). Internet advertising effectiveness: The effect of design on click-through rates for banner ads. *International Journal of Advertising, 26*(4), 527–541.

Robnett, B. (1996). African-American women in the Civil Rights Movements, 1954-1964: Gender, leadership and micromobilization. *American Journal of Sociology, 101*, 1661–1693. doi:10.1086/230870

Rodgers, S., Wang, Y., Rettie, R., & Alpert, F. (2007). The Web motivation inventory: replication, extension, and application to Internet advertising. *International Journal of Advertising, 26*(4), 447–476.

Rodgers, S., & Thorson, E. (2000). The interactive advertising model: How users perceive and process online ads. *Journal of Interactive Advertising, 1*(1), 26–50. Retrieved from http://jiad.org/vo1/no1/rodgers/.

Rodgers, S., Cannon, H. M., & Moore, J. (2007). Segmenting Internet Markets. In Schumann, D. W., & Thorson, E. (Eds.), *Internet Advertising, Theory and Research* (pp. 149–183). Mahwah, NJ: Lawrence Erlbaum Associates, Publishers.

Rogers, E. M. (1995). *The Diffusion of Innovations* (4th ed.). New York: Free Press.

Rokeach, S. J. B., & DeFleur, M. L. (1976). A dependency model of mass-media effects. *Communication Research*, *3*(1), 3–21. doi:10.1177/009365027600300101

Ron, D., & Tasra, D. (2007). Effective marketing with blogs. *EventDV*, *20*(10), 26.

RonPaulGraphs.com. (2008). *The revolution will be digitized* [Electronic Version]. Retrieved August 17, 2008, from http://www.ronpaulgraphs.com./index.html

Rose, F. (2006). Commercial break. *Wired*, *14*(12). Retrieved June 26, 2007, from http://www.wired.com/wired/archive/14.12/tahoe.html

Rosen, E. (2000). *The anatomy of buzz: How to create word-of-mouth marketing*. New York: Doubleday.

Rosen, L. D. (2007). *Me, MySpace, and I: parenting the net generation. NY*. New York: Palgrave-MacMillan.

Rosen, L. D., Cheever, N. A., Cummings, C., & Felt, J. (2008). The impact of emotionality and self-disclosure on online dating versus traditional dating. *Computers in Human Behavior*, *24*, 2124–2157. doi:10.1016/j.chb.2007.10.003

Rosenkrans, G. (2009). The creativeness and effectiveness of online interactive rich media advertising. *Journal of Interactive Advertising*, *9*(2). Retrieved from http://www.jiad.org/article114.

Rosenman, M. A., Smith, G., Maher, M. L., Ding, L., & Marchant, D. (2007). Multidisciplinary collaborative design in virtual environments. *Automation in Construction*, *16*(1), 37–44. doi:10.1016/j.autcon.2005.10.007

Rosenwald, M. (2010, March 29). Reputations at stake, companies try to alter word of mouth online. *Washington Post*. Retrieved March 31, 2010, from http://www.washingtonpost.com/wp-dyn/content/article/2010/03/28/AR2010032802905.html?hpid=sec-tech

Rothman, A. J., Bartels, R. D., Wlaschin, J., & Salovey, P. (2006). The strategic use of gain and loss framed messages to promote healthy behavior: How theory can inform practice. *The Journal of Communication*, *56*, S202–S220. doi:10.1111/j.1460-2466.2006.00290.x

Rotter, J. B. (1966). Generalized expectancies for internal versus external control of reinforcement. *Psychological Monographs*, *80*, 9–28.

Roush, W. (2005). August) Social machines. *Technology Review*.

Rovee-Collier, C., Hayne, H., & Colombo, M. (2001). *The development of implicit and explicit memory*. Amsterdam: John Benjamins.

Roy, U., & Kodkani, S. S. (1999). Product modeling within the framework of the World Wide Web. *IIE Transactions*, *31*(7), 667–678. doi:10.1080/07408179908969867

Royse, P., Lee, J., Undrahbuyan, B., Hopson, M., & Consalvo, M. (2007). Women and games: technologies of the gendered self. *New Media & Society*, *9*, 555–576. doi:10.1177/1461444807080322

Rozendaal, E., Buijzen, M., & Valkenburg, P. (2008). Comparing children's and adults' cognitive defenses to television advertising. In *Child and Teen Consumption 2008 Conference*, Trondheim, Norway.

Rubel, C. (1996, May 6). What you see on TV is not what you get at stadium. *Marketing News*, 3012.

Rubenstein, H., & Griffiths, C. (2001). Branding matters more on the Internet. *Brand Management*, *8*(6), 394–404. doi:10.1057/palgrave.bm.2540039

Rubin, A. M. (1993). The effect of locus of control on communication motivation, anxiety, and satisfaction. *Communication Quarterly*, *41*(Spring), 161–171.

Rubin, A. M. (1983). Television uses and gratifications: The interaction of viewing patterns and motivations. *Journal of Broadcasting*, *27*, 37–52.

Rubin, A. M. (2002). The uses-and-gratifications perspective of media effects. In Bryant, J., & Zillmann, D. (Eds.), *Media Effects: Advances in theory and research* (2nd ed., pp. 525–548). Mahwah, NJ: Lawrence Erlbaum.

Rubin, A. M. (2002). The uses-and-gratifications perspective of media effects. In Bryant, J., & Zillmann, D. (Eds.), *Media effects: Advances in theory and research* (2nd ed., pp. 525–548). Mahwah, NJ: Lawrence Erlbaum.

Ruffini, P. (2007). *What Ron Paul's $4.3M means*. Retrieved August 19, 2008, from http://www.patrickruffini.com/2007/11/06/what-ron-pauls-38m-means/

Ruggerio, T. E. (2000, February). Uses and gratifications theory in the 21st century. *Mass Communication & Society*, *3*(1), 3–37. doi:10.1207/S15327825MCS0301_02

Russell, C. A. (2002, December). Investigating the effectiveness of product placements in television shows: The role of modality and plot connection congruence on brand memory and attitude. *The Journal of Consumer Research*, *29*, 306–318. doi:10.1086/344432

Russell, M. G. (2009). Narrowcast pricebook-driven persuasion: Engagement at point of influence, purchase and consumption in distributed retail environments. *Journal of Software*, *4*(4). doi:10.4304/jsw.4.4.365-373

Russell, M. G. (2009). The call for creativity in new metrics for liquid media. *Journal of Interactive Advertising, 9*(2).

Russell, M. G. (2008c). Benevolence and effectiveness: persuasive technology's spillover effects in retail settings. In Oinas-Kukkonen, H. (Eds.), *Persuasive 2008* (pp. 94–103). Berlin: Springer-Verlag. doi:10.1007/978-3-540-68504-3_9

Russell, M. G. (2008a). Engagement Pinball. In *3rd Annual Customer Engagement Survey, Report 2009, cScape | eConsultancy 2008*. Retrieved March 1, 2009, from http://www.cscape.com/features/Pages/customer-engagement-register.aspx

Russell, M. G. (2008b). *Wait marketing in fast-paced retail settings*. Retrieved from http://www.archive.org/details/WaitMarketingInFast-pacedRetailSettings

Ryan, C. (2001). Virtual reality in marketing. *Direct Marketing, 63*(12), 57–62.

Sabha, R. (2007). Sex Education in Curriculum. *National AIDS Control Organization.* Retrieved January 25, 2009, from http://www.nacoonline.org/NACO_Action/Media__Press_Release/

Sabine, G. H. (1961). *A history of political theory*. New York: Holt, Rinehart and Winston.

Sachdev, P. (1998). Sex on campus: A preliminary study of knowledge, attitudes and behaviour of university students in Delhi, India. *Journal of Biosocial Science, 30*(1), 95–105. doi:10.1017/S0021932098000959

Saiva Siddhanta Church. (2006). *Saiva Siddhanta Church*. Retrieved June 1, 2006, from http://www.himalayanacademy.com/

Salen, K., & Zimmerman, E. (2005). Game design and meaningful play. In Rasessens, J., & Goldstein, J. (Eds.), *Handbook of computer game studies* (pp. 59–80). Cambridge, MA: MIT Press.

Salisch, M. V., Oppl, C., & Kristen, A. (2006). What attracts children? In Vorderer, P., & Bryant, J. (Eds.), *Playing video games: Motives, responses, and consequences* (pp. 147–163). Mahwah, NJ: Lawrence Erlbaum.

Salter, L. (2004). Structure and forms of use: A contribution to understanding the 'effects' of the internet on deliberative democracy. *Information Communication and Society, 7*, 185–206. doi:10.1080/1369118042000232648

Salwen, M. B., Garrison, B., & Driscoll, P. (2004). *Online news and the public*. Mahwah, NJ: Lawrence Erlbaum.

Salwen, M. B. (2004). Online news trends. In Salwen, M. B., Garrison, B., & Driscoll, P. (Eds.), *Online news and the public* (pp. 47–80). Mahwah, NJ: Lawrence Erlbaum.

Sampson, J. P., & Kruboltz, J. D. (1991). Computer assisted instruction: A missing link in counseling. *Journal of Counseling and Development, 69*(5), 395–397.

Samuel, G. S. (2005, November 10). *Australian Communications and Media Authority, 1st Annual Conference*.

Sandburg, A. (2008). 82% positive to in-game ads, someone call Ripley's! *That video game Blog*. Retrieved September 30, 2008 from http://www.thatvideogameblog.com/2008/06/18/82-react-positively-to-in-game-advertisement/

Sandhana, L. (2005). Pacman comes to life virtually. *BBC News*. Retrieved February 3, 2009, from http://news.bbc.co.uk/2/hi/technology/4607449.stm

Sandoval, G. (2006, April 3). GM slow to react to nasty ads. *CNETNews*. Retrieved June 26, 2007, from http://news.com.com/GM+slow+to+react+to+nasty+ads/2100-1024_3-6057143.html

Santelli, J., Ott, M. A., Lyon, M., Rogers, J., Summers, D., & Schleifer, R. (2006). Abstinence and abstinence-only education: A review of U.S. policies and programs. *The Journal of Adolescent Health, 38*, 72–81. doi:10.1016/j.jadohealth.2005.10.006

Sappenfield, M. (2007). In India, A Public Kiss is Not Just a Kiss. *The Christian Science Monitor*. Retrieved September 17, 2008, from http://www.csmonitor.com/2007/0430/p01s03-wosc.html

Sarvary, M. (2008, February). Breakthrough ideas for 2008. *Harvard Business Review*, 17–45.

Sass, E. (2007, August 13). Overview: Cross-Media Measurement Takes Off. *Media Daily News*. Retrieved from http://www.mediapost.com/publications/index.cfm?fa=Articles.showArticle&art_aid=65499

Savary, J. (2008). Advocacy marketing: Toyota's secrets for partnering with trendsetters to create passionate brand advocates. *Journal of Sponsorship, 1*(3), 211–224.

Sayre, S. (2001). *Qualitative Methods for Marketplace Research*. Thousand Oaks, CA: Sage.

Schafer, R. M. (1977). *The soundscape. Our sonic environment and the tuning of the world*. Rochester, NY: Destiny Books.

Schafer, J. B., Frankowski, D., Herlocker, J., & Sen, S. (2007). Collaborative Filtering Recommender Systems. In Brusilovsky, P., Kobsa, A., & Nejdl, W. (Eds.), *The Adaptive Web* (*Vol. 4321*). Berlin, Germany: Springer-Verlag. doi:10.1007/978-3-540-72079-9_9

Schafer, J. B., Konstan, J., & Riedl, J. (1999). *Recommender Systems in E-Commerce*. Paper presented at the Proceedings of the 1st ACM conference on Electronic commerce.

Schau, H. J., & Gilly, M. C. (2003). We are what we post? Self-presentation in personal web space. *The Journal of Consumer Research*, *30*(3), 385–404. doi:10.1086/378616

Schilling, M. A. (2006). Game not over: Competitive dynamics in the video game industry. In Lampel, J., Shamsie, J., & Lant, T. K. (Eds.), *The Business of Culture: Strategic Perspectives on Entertainment Media* (pp. 75–104). Mahwah, NJ: Lawrence Erlbaum Associates.

Schindler, R. M., & Bickart, B. (2005). Published word of mouth: Referable, consumer-generated information on the Internet. In Haugtvedt, C. P., Machleit, K. A., & Yalch, R. (Eds.), *Online consumer psychology: Understanding and influencing consumer behavior in the virtual world* (pp. 35–61). Mahwah, NJ: LEA.

Schlenker, B. R. (1980). *Impression Management: The Self-Concept, Social Identity, and Interpersonal Relations*. Monterey, CA: Brooks/Cole.

Schmalensee, D. H. (1983). Today's top priority advertising research questions. *Journal of Advertising Research*, *23*(2), 49–60.

Schmitt, S., & Bergmann, R. (1999 June). *Applying case-based reasoning technology for product selection and customization in electronic commerce environments.* Paper presented at the 12th Bled Electronic Commerce Conference, Bled, Slovenia.

Schneider, L. P., & Cornwell, T. B. (2005). Cashing in on crashes via brand placement in computer games: The effects of experience and flow on memory. *International Journal of Advertising*, *24*(3), 321–343.

Schneider, E. F., Lang, A., Shin, M., & Bradley, S. D. (2004). Death with a story: How story impacts emotional, motivational, and physiological responses to first-person shooter video games. *Human Communication Research*, *30*, 361–375. doi:10.1093/hcr/30.3.361

Schneider, S. M., & Foot, K. (2002). Online structure for political action: Exploring presidential campaign Web sites from the 2000 election. *Javnost The Public*, *9*(2), 43–60.

Schouten, J., & McAlexander, J. (1995). Subcultures of consumption: An ethnography of the new bikers. *The Journal of Consumer Research*, *22*(1), 43. doi:10.1086/209434

Schramm, W., & Roberts, D. F. (1961). *The Process and Effects of Mass Communication*. Urbana, IL: University of Illinois Press.

Schroeder, R. (2002). Social Interaction in Virtual Environments: Key issues, common

Schultz, D. E. (2007). Social call. *Marketing Management*, *16*(4), 10–11.

Schuman, H., Presser, S., & Ludwig, J. (1983). The norm of even-handedness in surveys as in life. *American Sociological Review*, *48*(1), 112–120. doi:10.2307/2095149

Schumann, D. W., & Thorson, E. (2007). *Internet Advertising: Theory and Research*. San Francisco: Lawrence Erlbaum Associates.

Schutz, W. C. (1966). *The Interpersonal Underworld*. Palo Alto, CA: Science and Behavior Books.

Schwarz, N. (1995). What respondents learn from questionnaires: The survey interview and the logic of conversation. *International Statistical Review*, *63*(2), 153–168. doi:10.2307/1403610

Schwarz, N., & Bless, H. (1992). Scandals and the public's trust in politicians: Assimilation and contrast effects. *Personality and Social Psychology Bulletin*, *18*(5), 574–579. doi:10.1177/0146167292185007

Schwarz, N., Grayson, C. E., & Knauper, B. (1998). Formal features of rating scales and the interpretation of question meaning. *International Journal of Public Opinion Research*, *10*(2), 177–183.

Schwarz, N., Knauper, B., Hippler, H.-J., Noelle-Neumann, E., & Clark, L. (1991). Rating scales: Numeric values may change the meaning of scale labels. *Public Opinion Quarterly*, *55*(4), 570–582. doi:10.1086/269282

Schwarz, N., & Strack, F. (1991). Context effects in attitude surveys: Applying cognitive theory to social research. *European Review of Social Psychology*, *2*, 31–50. doi:10.1080/14792779143000015

Scott, W. A. (1955). Reliability of content analysis: The case of nominal scale coding. *Public Opinion Quarterly*, *17*, 321–325. doi:10.1086/266577

Scott, A., & Street, J. (2000). From media politics to e-protest: The use of popular culture and new media in parties and social movements. *Information Communication and Society*, *3*(2), 215–240.

Scott, J. (1990). *Domination and the Arts of Resistance: Hidden Transcripts*. New Haven, CT: Yale University Press.

Sears, A., & Shneiderman, B. (1994). Split menus: effectively using selection frequency to organize menus. *ACM Transactions on Computer-Human Interaction*, *1*(1), 27–51. doi:10.1145/174630.174632

Sears, A., Lin, M., Jacko, J., & Xiao, Y. (2003). When Computers Fade. Pervasive Computing and Situationally-Induced Impairments and Disabilities. In Stephanidis, C., & Jacko, J. (Eds.),

Human-Computer Interaction: Theory and Practice (Part II) (pp. 1298–1302). Hillsdale, NJ: Lawrence Erlbaum Associates.

Second Life. (2007). Economy Statistics. *Second Life*. Retrieved June 15, 2007, from http://blog.secondlife.com/2006/12/12/growth-of-second-life-community-and-economy/

Second Life. (2010), Monthly customer spending distribution. Retrieved May 4, 2010, from http://secondlife.com/statistics/economy-data.php

Secondlife. (2008). *Programs*. Retrieved on August 8, 2009, from http://secondlifegrid.net/programs/education

SeeSaw Network. (n.d.). Retrieved from http://www.seesawnetworks.com

Segal, R. B., & Kephart, J. O. (1999). *MailCat: An Intelligent Assistant for Organizing E-Mail.* Paper presented at the Third International Conference on Autonomous Agents.

Self, C. S. (1996). *Credibility. An Integrated Approach to Communication Theory and Research*. Mahwah, NJ: Erlbaum.

Selnow, G. W. (1998). *Electronic Whistle-stops: The Impact of the Internet in American Politics*. Westport, CT: Praeger.

Sen, S., & Lerman, D. (2007). Why are you telling me this? An examination into negative consumer reviews on the Web. *Journal of Interactive Marketing, 21*(4), 76–94. doi:10.1002/dir.20090

Senecal, S., & Nantel, J. (2004). The influence of online product recommendations on consumers' online choices. *Journal of Retailing, 80*(2), 159–169. doi:10.1016/j.jretai.2004.04.001

Senecal, S., & Nantel, J. (2004). The influence of online product recommendations on consumers' online choices. *Journal of Retailing, 80*, 159–169. doi:10.1016/j.jretai.2004.04.001

Sengupta, S. (2002). In the eyes of the beholder: The relevance of skin tone and facial features of African American Female models to advertising effectiveness. *Communication Reports, 16*(2), 210–220.

Sengupta, J., Goodstein, R. C., & Boninger, D. S. (1997). Cues are not created equal: obtaining attitude persistence under low-involvement conditions. *The Journal of Consumer Research, 23*(March), 351–361. doi:10.1086/209488

Senser, R. (2008). *New media engagement as a virtuous process*. Retrieved from http://www.archive.org/details/NewMediaEngagementAsAVirtuousProcess.

Severin, W. J., & Tankard, J. W. Jr. (1992). *Communication Theories: Origins, Methods, and Uses in the Mass Media* (3rd ed.). White Plains, NY: Longman Publishing Group.

Severin, W. J., & Tankard, J. W. Jr. (1997). *Communications theories: origins, methods, and uses in the mass media* (4th ed.). White Plains, NY: Langman.

Sex education runs into trouble. (2007, August). *BBC News*. Retrieved January 20, 2009, from http://news.bbc.co.uk/1/hi/world/south_asia/6949714.stm

Shah, S. P. (2006). Visibility in Mumbai producing the spectacle of Kamathipura: The politics of red light. *Cultural Dynamics, 18*(3), 269–292. doi:10.1177/0921374006071615

Shamdasani, P. H., Stanaland, A. J. S., & Tan, J. (2001, July). Location, location, location: Insights for advertising placement on the web. *Journal of Advertising Research*, 7–21.

Shank, M. (2008). *Sports marketing: A strategic perspective* (4th ed.). Upper Saddle River, NJ: Pearson Prentice Hall.

Shapiro, A. L. (1999). *The Control Revolution: How the Internet is Putting Individuals in Charge and Changing the World We Know*. New York: Public Affairs.

Sharing, Privacy and Trust in Our Networked World. (2007). OCLC: Online Computer Library Center- Harris Interactive.

Sharma, R. (2001). More than a quarter of India's youngsters have premarital sex. *British Medical Journal, 322*(7286), 575. doi:10.1136/bmj.322.7286.575

Sharma, B. (2008 September). Making inroads. *Tehelka*. Retrieved January 20, 2009, from http://www.tehelka.com/story_main40.asp?filename=Ws130908makinginroads.asp

Sharma, P. (2005 December). Sex education still off the charts. *India Together*. Retrieved January 20, 2009, from http://www.indiatogether.org/2005/dec/edu-notaboo.htm#src

Shaw, S., & Amis, J. (2001). Image & investment: Sponsorship and women's sport. *Journal of Sport Management, 15*(3), 219–246.

Shea, D. M., & Burton, M. J. (2001). *Campaign craft: The strategies, tactics, and art of political campaign management*. Westport, CT: Praeger.

Sheehan, K. B. (2002). Toward a typology of Internet users and online privacy concerns. *The Information Society, 18*(1), 21–32. doi:10.1080/01972240252818207

Sheehan, K. B. (1999). An investigation of gender differences in online privacy concerns and resultant behaviors. *Journal of Interactive Marketing, 13*, 24–38. doi:10.1002/(SICI)1520-6653(199923)13:4<24::AID-DIR3>3.0.CO;2-O

Sheehan, K. B., & Hoy, M. G. (1999). Flaming, complaining, abstaining: How online users respond to privacy concerns. *Journal of Advertising, 28*(3), 37–51.

Shelanski, H. A. (2006). Antitrust law as mass media regulation: Can merger standards protect the public interest? *California Law Review, 94*, 370–421. doi:10.2307/20439038

Shepard, J. M. (2007). *Sociology*. New York: Thomson Wadsworth.

Sherman, E. (2001, August 10). Where ads more than meet the eye technology only worsens intrusion. *Chicago Tribune,* 2.

Sherry, J. L. (2004). Flow and media enjoyment. *Communication Theory, 14*(4), 328–347. doi:10.1111/j.1468-2885.2004.tb00318.x

Sherry, J. L. (2001). The effects of violent video games on aggression: a meta-analysis. *Human Communication Research, 27*(3), 409–432.

Sherry, J. F. Jr. (1983). Gift giving in anthropological perspective. *The Journal of Consumer Research, 10*(2), 157. doi:10.1086/208956

Sherry, J. L. (2004). Flow and media enjoyment. *Communication Theory, 14*(4), 328–347. doi:10.1111/j.1468-2885.2004.tb00318.x

Sherry, J. L., Lucas, K., Greenberg, B. S., & Lachlan, K. (2006). Video game uses and gratifications as predicators of use and game preference. In Vorderer, P., & Bryant, J. (Eds.), *Playing video games: Motives, responses, and consequences* (pp. 213–224). Mahwah, NJ: Lawrence Erlbaum Associates, Inc.

Shetty defends Richard Gere kiss. (2007, April 17). *BBC News.* Retrieved January 13, 2009, from http://news.bbc.co.uk/1/hi/entertainment/6563425.stm

Shields, M. (2006, April 17). Gaming's growth spurt. *MediaWeek, 16*, 7.

Shields, M. (2006). In-game ads could reach $2 billion. *Adweek.* Retrieved April 25, 2008, from http://www.adweek.com/aw/national/article_display.jsp?vnu_content_id=1002343563

Shields, M. (2008). *SplashCast Launches Product Placement Platform: The Startup Produces Mini, Multimedia Applications That Users Can Add to Their MySpace and Facebook Pages.* Retrieved from http://www.mediaweek.com/mw/content_display/esearch/e3i90cbbc45ee5b571635f598a25fc68192.

Shimp, T., Wood, S., & Smarandescu, L. (2007). Self-generated advertisements: Testimonials and the perils of consumer exaggeration. *Journal of Advertising Research, 47*(4), 453–461. doi:10.2501/S002184990707047X

Shimp, T. A. (2003). *Advertising, Promotion & Supplemental Aspects of Integrated Marketing Communications*. Cincinnati, OH: South-Western.

Shimp, T. A., & Delozier, W. (1986). *Promotion management and marketing communication*. New York: CBS College Publishing.

Shin, D., & Kim, W. (2007). *Uses and Gratifications of Digital Multimedia Broadcasting: What People Do with Digital Multimedia Broadcasting?* Conference Papers -- International Communication Association, Retrieved September 4, 2008, from Communication & Mass Media Complete database.

Shiv, B., & Fedhorikhin, A. (1999). Heart & mind in conflict: the interplay of affect and cognition in consumer decision making. *The Journal of Consumer Research, 26*(3), 278–292. doi:10.1086/209563

Shocker, A. D., Srivastava, R. K., & Ruekert, R. W. (1994, May). Challenges and opportunities facing brand management. *JMR, Journal of Marketing Research*, 149–158. doi:10.2307/3152190

Short, J., Williams, E., & Christie, B. (1976). *The social psychology of telecommunications*. London: John Wiley and Sons.

Shull, E. (2006, October 26). *Welcome to Blogitive*. Retrieved September 29, 2007, from http://www.blogitive.com/2006/10/26/welcome-to-blogitivewelcome-to-blogitive/#more-3

Shutz, T. (2000). Mass media and concept of interactivity: an exploratory study of online forums and reader email. *Media Culture & Society, 22*(2), 205–221. doi:10.1177/016344300022002005

Sicilia, M., & Ruiz, S. (2007). The role of flow in website effectiveness. *Journal of Interactive Advertising, 8*(1). Retrieved on February 29, 2008 from http://www.jiad.org/vol8/no1/ruiz/index.htm

SIECUS. (1996). Issues and answers. Fact sheet on sexuality education. *Sexuality Information and Education Council of the United States Report, 24*(6), 1–4.

Siegal, C. (2004). *Internet Marketing. Foundations and Applications*. Boston, MA: Houghton Mifflin Company.

Siegel, D. L., Coffey, T. J. & ., & Livingstone, G. (2001). *The great tween buying machine–marketing to today's tweens*. N.Y.: New York: Paramount M.P. Inc.

Sifry, D. (2007). *The State of the Live Web*. Retrieved September 11, 2008, from http://technorati.com/weblog/2007/04/328.html

Sify News. (2007 March). *No sex education in Madhya Pradesh schools*. Retrieved January 20, 2009, from http://sify.com/news/fullstory.php?id=14412544

Siklos, R. (2006, October 19). A virtual world but real money. *The New York Times*. Retrieved August 18, 2008 from http://www.nytimes.com/2006/10/19/technology/19virtual.html?_r=1&oref=slogin

Simon, M. (2008). Dupre's MySpace page evolves with scandal. *CNN online*. Retrieved March 14, 2008 from http://www.cnn.com/2008/US/03/13/ashley.myspace/index.html

Sinclair, B. (2008, October 14). Obama campaigns in Burnout, 17 other games. *GameSpot*. Retrieved January 14 from http://www.gamespot.com/news/6199379.html

Singh, B. P. (2007). Rajasthan court issues warrant against Gere. *Hindustan Times*. Retrieved January 13, 2009, from http://www.hindustantimes.com/storypage/storypage.aspx?id=3307c846-cfce-489d-b220-1b399b9759ee&ParentID=eda501ca-affe-4d4d-a93f-05a591421050&&Headline=Rajasthan+court+issues+warrant+against+Gere

Singhal, A., & Rogers, E. M. (1999). *Entertainment-education: A communication strategy for social change*. Mahwah, NJ: Lawrence Erlbaum Associates.

Singhal, A., & Rogers, E. M. (2003). *Combating AIDS communication strategies in action*. New Delhi, India: Sage Publications.

Sinha, R., & Swearingen, K. (2002). The role of transparency in recommender systems. *Conference on Human Factors in Computing Systems*.

SinoCast. (2006). *China's Blog User Base Expected to Approach 100mn Next Year*. Retrieved July 18, 2008, from http://findarticles.com/p/articles/mi_hb5562/is_200607/ai_n22733639?tag=artBody,col1

Sipress, A. (2006, December 26). Where real money meets virtual reality, the jury is still out. *Washington Post*. Retrieved March 1, 2008, from http://www.washingtonpost.com/wp-dyn/content/article/2006/12/25/AR2006122500635.html

Sirgy, M. J. (1982). Self-Concept in consumer behavior: A critical review. *The Journal of Consumer Research, 9*, 287–295. doi:10.1086/208924

Sirgy, M. J. (1985). Using self-congruity and ideal congruity to predict purchase motivation. *Journal of Business Research, 13*, 195–206. doi:10.1016/0148-2963(85)90026-8

Sirgy, M. J. (1986). *Self-Congruity: Toward a Theory of Personality and Cybernetics*. New York: Praeger.

Sivaramakrishnan, S., Wan, F., & Tang, Z. (2007). Giving an e-human touch to e-tailing: The moderating roles of static information quantity and consumption motive in the effectiveness of an anthropomorphic information agent. *Journal of Interactive Marketing, 21*(1), 60–75. doi:10.1002/dir.20075

Skalski, P., & Tamborini, R. (2007). The role of social presence in interactive agent-based persuasion. *Media Psychology, 10*, 385–413.

Skalski, P. (2007). *Game modding. Presentation delivered to Visualization and Digital Imaging Lab*. University of Minnesota Duluth.

Skalski, P., Tamborini, R., Glazer, E., & Smith, S. (2009). Effects of humor on presence and recall of persuasive messages. *Communication Quarterly, 57*(2), 136–153. doi:10.1080/01463370902881619

Slater, M. D. (2007). Reinforcing spirals: The mutual influence of media selectivity and media effects and their impact on individual behavior and social identity. *Communication Theory, 17*, 281–303. doi:10.1111/j.1468-2885.2007.00296.x

Slater, M., Sadagic, A., Usoh, M., & Schroeder, R. (2000). Small Group Behavior in

Sloan, L. R. (1989). The motives of sports fans. In Goldstein, J. H. (Ed.), *Sports, games, and play: Social and psychological viewpoints* (pp. 175–240). Hillsdale, NJ: Lawrence Erlbaum.

Slocombe, M. (2005). Men spend more money on video games than music: Nielsen report. *Digital-Lifestyles*. Retrieved November 1, 2006 from http://digital-lifestyles.info/display_page.asp?section=cm&id=2091

Smith, R. A., Wallston, B. S., Wallston, K. A., Forsberg, P. R., & King, J. E. (1984). Measuring desirability of control of health care processes. *Journal of Personality and Social Psychology, 47*, 415–426. doi:10.1037/0022-3514.47.2.415

Smith, E. J. (1999). *Radiant Mind* (1st ed.). New York: Riverhead Books.

Smith, D., Menon, S., & Sivakumar, K. (2005). Online peer and editorial recommendations, trust, and choice in virtual markets. *Journal of Interactive Marketing, 19*(3), 15–37. doi:10.1002/dir.20041

Smith, T., Coyle, J., Lightfoot, E., & Scott, A. (2007). Reconsidering models of influence: The relationship between consumer social networks and word-of-mouth effectiveness. *Journal of Advertising Research, 47*(4), 387–397. doi:10.2501/S0021849907070407

Smith, H. J., Milberg, S. J., & Burke, S. J. (1996). Information privacy: Measuring individuals' concerns about organizational practices. *Management Information Systems Quarterly, 20*(2), 167–196. doi:10.2307/249477

Smith, E. R., Murphy, J., & Coats, S. (1999). Attachment to groups: theory and management. *Journal of Personality and Social Psychology, 77*, 94–110. doi:10.1037/0022-3514.77.1.94

Smith, G., Kippax, S., Aggleton, P., & Tyrer, P. (2003). HIV/AIDS school based education in selected Asia-Pacific countries. *Sex Education, 3*(1), 3–21. doi:10.1080/1468181032000052126

Smith, M. B. (1973). Political attitudes. In Knutson, J. (Ed.), *Handbook of political psychology* (pp. 57–82). San Francisco: Jossey-Bass.

Smith, A. (2008). New Numbers for Blogging and Blog Readership. Retrieved March 16, 2009, from http://www.pewinternet.org/Commentary/2008/July/New-numbers-for-blogging-and-blog-readership.aspx/.

Smith, A. (2009, April 15). *The Internet's Role in Campaign 2008*. Washington, DC: Pew Internet & American Life Project. Retrieved April 15, 2009, from http://pewresearch.org/pubs/1192/internet-politics-campaign-2008

Smith, A., & Rainie, L. (2008, June 15). *The Internet and the Election 2008*. Washington, DC: Pew Internet & American Life Project. Retrieved November 14, 2008, from http://pewresearch.org/pubs/869/politics-goes-viral-online

Smith, A., & Wood, P. (2005, July 1). *Online advertising for the gamer generation.* Retrieved

Smith, J. W. (2006 January). A Marketplace of Social Engagement. *Marketing Management*, 52.

Smolianov, P., & Shilbury, D. (2005). Examining integrated advertising and sponsorship in corporate marketing through televised sport. *Sport Marketing Quarterly, 14*(4), 239–250.

Smythe, J. M. (2007). Beyond self-selection in video game play: An experimental examination of the consequences of massively multiplayer online role-playing game play. *Cyberpsychology & Behavior, 10*(5), 717–721. doi:10.1089/cpb.2007.9963

Snider, M. (2006, July 11). WWII shows no battle fatigue. *USA Today.*

Snoddy, R. (2007, January 17). User content won't kill off old media. *Marketing*, 18.

Snyder, C. R., & Fromkin, H. L. (1980). *Uniqueness: The human pursuit of difference*. New York: Plenum.

Snyder, P. (2004, June 28). Wanted: Standards for viral marketing. *Brandweek, 45*(26), 21.

Socialtext.net. (2008). *Fortune 500 Business Blogging Wiki.* Retrieved August 19, 2008, from http://www.asia.socialtext.net/bizblogs/index.cgi

Society for Adolescent Medicine. (2006). Abstinence-only education policies and programs: A position paper of the Society for Adolescent Medicine. *The Journal of Adolescent Health, 38*(1), 83–87. doi:10.1016/j.jadohealth.2005.06.002

Sohn, D., & Lee, B. (2005). Dimensions of Interactivity: Differential Effects of Social and Psychological Factors. *Journal of Computer-Mediated Communication*, 10(3), article 6. Retrieved July 18, 2008 from http://jcmc.indiana.edu/vol10/issue3/sohn.html

Solomon, S., & Chakraborty, A. (2004). A review of the HIV epidemic in India. *AIDS Education and Prevention, 12*(3A), 155–169. doi:10.1521/aeap.16.3.5.155.35534

Solomon, S., Kumarasamy, N., Ganesh, A. K., & Amalraj, R. E. (1998). Prevalence and risk factors of HIV-1 and HIV-2 infection in urban and rural areas in Tamil Nadu, India. *International Journal of STD & AIDS, 9*, 98–103. doi:10.1258/0956462981921756

Solomon, M. R., Ashmore, R., & Longo, L. (1992). The beauty match-up hypothesis: congruence between types of beauty and product images in advertising. *Journal of Advertising, 21*(4), 23–34.

Sommer, R., Wynes, M., & Brinkley, G. (1992). Social facilitation effects in shopping behavior. *Environment and Behavior, 24*(3), 285–297. doi:10.1177/0013916592243001

Song, S., & Lee, J. (2007). Key factors of heuristic evaluation for game design: towards massively multi-player online role-playing game. *International Journal of Human-Computer Studies, 65*(8), 709–723. doi:10.1016/j.ijhcs.2007.01.001

Song, I., Larose, R., Eastin, S. M., & Lin, C. A. (2004). Internet gratifications and Internet addiction: on the uses and abuses of new media. *Cyberpsychology & Behavior*, *7*(4), 384–394. doi:10.1089/cpb.2004.7.384

Sonnenreich, W. (1997). A History of Search Engines. Retrieved July 12, 2008, from http://www.wiley.com/legacy/compbooks/sonnenreich/history.html

Sorcar, P. (2009). *Teaching Taboo Topics Without Talking About Them: An Epistemic Study of a New Approach to HIV/AIDS Prevention Education in India.* Published Doctoral Dissertation, Stanford University.

Spoehr, K. T. (1994). Enhancing the acquisition of conceptual structures through hypermedia. In Kate, M. (Ed.), *Classroom lessons: Integrating cognitive theory and classroom practice* (pp. 75–101). Cambridge, MA: MIT Press.

Srinivasan, S. S., Anderson, R., & Ponnavolu, K. (2002). Customer loyalty in e-commerce: An exploration of its antecedents and consequences. *Journal of Retailing, 78*(1), 41–50. doi:10.1016/S0022-4359(01)00065-3

Srull, T. K., & Wyer, R. S. (1978). Category accessibility and social perception: some implications for the study of person memory and interpersonal judgments. *Journal of Personality and Social Psychology, 37*, 841–856.

Staff, I. G. N. (2003, January 10). Dante, meet Diesel. *IGN.* Retrieved February 11, 2008 from http://ps2.ign.com/articles/382/382175p1.html

Stafford, T. F., Stafford, M. R., & Schkade, L. L. (2004). Determining uses and gratifications for the Internet. *Decision Sciences, 35*(2), 259–285. doi:10.1111/j.00117315.2004.02524.x

Stanage, N. (2007). *From Second Life to second-degree murder.* Retrieved on 04/18/08 www.guardian.co.uk/commentisfree/2007/jan/16/fromsecondlifetoseconddegr

Stauss, B. (1997). Global word of mouth, service bashing on the Internet is thorny issue. *Marketing Management, 6*(3), 28–30.

Steel, E. (2009, May 6). Sprucing up Online Display Ads. *Wall Street Journal.com.* Retrieved from http://online.wsj.com/article/SB124156876159389809.html

Steinberg, L. (2004). Risk taking in adolescence: what changes, and why? *Annals of the New York Academy of Sciences, 1021*, 51–58. doi:10.1196/annals.1308.005

Steinfeld, A., Bennett, R. S., Cunningham, K., Lahut, M., Quinones, P. A., Wexler, D., et al. (2007). *Evaluation of an Integrated Multi-Task Machine Learning System with Humans in the Loop.*

Steinfeld, A., Quinones, P. A., Zimmerman, J., Bennett, R. S., & Siewiorek, D. (2007). *Survey Measures for Evaluation of Cognitive Assistants.* Paper presented at the NIST Performance Metrics for Intelligent Systems Workshop.

Steinkuehler, C. A. (2006). Why game (culture) studies now? *Games and Culture, 1*(1), 97–102. doi:10.1177/1555412005281911

Steinkuehler, C. A., & Williams, D. (2006). Where everybody knows your (screen) name: online games as "third places". *Journal of Computer-Mediated Communication, 11*, 885–909. doi:10.1111/j.1083-6101.2006.00300.x

Stephens, D. L., Hill, R. P., & Hanson, C. (1994). The beauty myth and female consumers: the controversial role of advertising. *The Journal of Consumer Affairs, 28*(1), 137–154.

Stephenson, N. (1992). *Snow Crash.* New York: Bantam Books.

Stern, B. B. (1994). A revised communications model for advertising: Multiple dimensions of the source, the message, and the recipient. *Journal of Advertising, 23*(2), 5–15.

Steuer, J. (1992). Defining virtual reality: Dimensions determining telepresence. *The Journal of Communication, 43*(4), 73–93. doi:10.1111/j.1460-2466.1992.tb00812.x

Steuer, J. (1995). Defining virtual reality: Dimensions determining telepresence. In Biocca, F., & Levy, M. R. (Eds.), *Communication in the age of virtual reality* (pp. 33–56). Hillsdale, NJ: LEA.

Stevenson, V. S. (2007). *VSS Communications Industry Forecast 2007-2011.*

Stewart, B. (1996). *Summary MUD history.* Retrieved from http://www.livinginternet.com/d/di_major.htm

Steyer, A., Garcia-Bardidia, R., & Quester, P. (2006). Online discussion groups as social networks: An empirical investigation of word-of-mouth on the Internet. *Journal of Interactive Advertising, 6*(2), 51–60.

Stinson, T. (2008). *Consumer understanding as a foundation for creating audience engagement.* Retrieved from http://www.archive.org/details/ConsumerUnderstandingAsAFoundation-ForCreatingAudienceEngagement

Stipp, H., & Schiavone, N. P. (1996). Modeling the impact of Olympic sponsorship on corporate image. *Journal of Advertising Research, 36*(4), 22–28.

Stirland, S. L. (2008, November 5). Propelled by Internet, Barack Obama Wins Presidency. *Wired.* Retrieved November 11, 2008, from http://www.wired.com/threatlevel/2008/11/propelled-by-in/

Storedotburton on Twitter. (n.d.). Retrieved from http://twitter.com/storedotburton

Story, L. (2007, August 6). It's An Ad, Ad, Ad, Ad World. *The New York Times.* Retrieved July 15, 2008, from http://www.nytimes.com/2007/08/06/business/media/06digitas.html

Story, L. (2007, May 26). The high price of creating free ads. *New York Times.* Retrieved June 26, 2007, from http://www.nytimes.com/2007/05/26/business/26content.html?pagewanted=1&ei=5088&en=f5244987dc59d9d0&ex=1337832000

Stotlar, D. K. (2001). *Developing successful sport sponsorship plans*. Morgantown, WV: Fitness Information Technology.

Stromer-Galley, J. (2000). On-line interaction and why candidates avoid it. *The Journal of Communication*, (Autumn): 111–132. doi:10.1111/j.1460-2466.2000.tb02865.x

Strong, E. K. (1925). Theories of selling. *The Journal of Applied Psychology*, *9*, 75–86. doi:10.1037/h0070123

Subrahmanyam, K., Greenfield, P. M., & Tynes, B. (2004). Constructing sexuality and identity in an online teen chat room. *Journal of Applied Developmental Psychology*, *25*(6), 651–666. doi:10.1016/j.appdev.2004.09.007

Subramani, M. R., & Rajagopalan, B. (2003). Knowledge-sharing and influence in online social networks via viral marketing. *Communications of the ACM*, *46*(12), 300–307. doi:10.1145/953460.953514

Sudha, R. T., Vijay, D. T., & Lakshmi, V. (2005). Awareness, attitudes, and beliefs of the general public towards HIV/AIDS in Hyderabad, A capital city from South India. *Indian Journal of Medical Sciences*, *59*(7), 307–316. doi:10.4103/0019-5359.16506

Sujan, M., Bettman, J. R., & Baumgartner, H. (1993). Influencing consumer judgments using autobiographical memories: A self-referencing perspective. *JMR, Journal of Marketing Research*, *30*(4), 422–436. doi:10.2307/3172688

Suler, J. (2004). The online disinhibition effect. *Cyberpsychology & Behavior*, *7*(3), 321–326. doi:10.1089/1094931041291295

Sullivan, E. A. (2008, February 15). Consider your source: As e-commerce sites add consumer-generated review systems, marketers and consumers hope truth trumps disingenuousness. *Marketing News*, 16-18.

Sullivan, H. S. (1947, original 1939). *Conception of modern psychiatry*, NY: New York: W.W. Norton. (Original manuscript published in 1939).

Sun, T., Youn, S., Wu, G., & Kuntaraporn, M. (2006). Online word-of-mouth (or mouse), An exploration of its antecedents and consequences. *Journal of Computer-Mediated Communication*, *11*(4), 1104–1127. doi:10.1111/j.1083-6101.2006.00310.x

Sundar, S., Kalyanaraman, S., & Brown, J. (2003). Explicating Web site interactivity: impression formation effects in political campaign sites. *Communication Research*, *30*(1), 30–59. doi:10.1177/0093650202239025

Sundar, S. S. (2004). Theorizing interactivity's effects. *The Information Society*, *20*, 387–391. doi:10.1080/01972240490508072

Sundaram, V. (2007 December). Let's NOT talk about sex, baby. *New America Media*. Retrieved September 1, 2008, from http://news.newamericamedia.org/news/view_article.html?article_id=e5589d57e3d6e65b0e17efb1fd28bba4

Surowiecki, J. (2006). *The Wisdom of Crowds*. New York: Anchor.

Svensson, P. (2005, February 24). Sony builds pizza-order function into 'Everquest II'. *USA Today.* Retrieved August 19, 2008 from http://www.usatoday.com/tech/products/services/2005-02-24-sony-pizza_x.htm

Swanson, K. (2007). Second Life: A science library presence in virtual reality. *Science & Technology Libraries*, *27*(3), 79–86. doi:10.1300/J122v27n03_06

Sweet, D. (2003, January 27). Duo making real progress creating virtual enhancements for sports viewers. *Sports Business Journal*, 22.

Sweetser, P., & Wyeth, P. (2005). GameFlow: A model for evaluating player enjoyment in games. *ACM computers in Entertainment*, *3*(3), 1-23.

Swensen, C. H. (1968). Empirical evaluations of human figure drawings: 1057-1966. *Psychological Bulletin*, *70*, 20–44. doi:10.1037/h0026011

Swenson, C. H. (1957). Empirical evaluations of human figure drawings. *Psychological Bulletin*, *54*, 431–463. doi:10.1037/h0041404

Tajfel, H. (1974). Social identity and intergroup behaviour. *Social Sciences Information. Information Sur les Sciences Sociales*, *13*(2), 65–93. doi:10.1177/053901847401300204

Tajfel, H., & Wilkes, A. (1963). Classification and quantitative judgments. *The British Journal of Psychology*, *54*, 101–114.

Tajfel, H., & Turner, J. C. (1986). The social identity theory of intergroup behavior. In Worchel, S., & Austin, W. G. (Eds.), *Psychology of intergroup relations* (pp. 7–24). Chicago, IL: Nelson-Hall.

Tamborini, R., Eastin, M., Skalski, P., Lachlan, K., Fediuk, T., & Brady, R. (2004). Violent virtual video games. *Journal of Broadcasting & Electronic Media*, *48*(3), 335–357.

Tamborini, R., & Skalski, P. (2006). The role of presence in the experience of electronic games. In Vorderer, P., & Bryant, J. (Eds.), *Playing video games: Motives, responses, and consequences*. Mahwah, NJ: Lawrence Erlbaum Associates.

Tambyah, S. K. (1996). Life on the net: The reconstruction of self and community. In Corfman, K. P., & Lynch, J. G. (Eds.),

Advances in Consumer Research. Provo, UT: Association for Consumer Research.

Tanaka, W. (2007, January 29). D.I.Y. ads. *Red Herring*. Retrieved June 26, 2007, from http://www.redherring.com/Article.aspx?a=20955&hed=D.I.Y.+Ads.

Taplin, J. (2006). The IP TV Revolution. In Castells, M., & Gustavo, C. (Eds.), *The Network Society: From Knowledge to Policy*. Washington, DC: Johns Hopkins Center for Transatlantic Relations.

Tapscott, D. (1998). *Growing-up digital: the rise of the net generation., NY*. New York: McGraw-Hill.

Target Rating Point. (n.d.). Wikipedia. Retrieved from http://en.wikipedia.org/wiki/Target_Rating_Point

Tarrant, M., MacKenzie, L., & Hewitt, L. A. (2006). Friendship group identification, multidimensional self-concept, and experience of developmental tasks in adolescence. *Journal of Adolescence, 29*, 627–640. doi:10.1016/j.adolescence.2005.08.012

Tauder, A. R. (2006). Getting ready for the next generation of marketing communications. *Journal of Advertising Research*, 1–4.

Taylor, C. R. (2003). Consumer privacy and the market for customer information. *The Rand Journal of Economics, 35*(4), 631–650. doi:10.2307/1593765

Taylor, S. E. (1981). The Interface of Cognitive and Social Psychology. In Harvey, J. (Ed.), *Cognition, Social Behavior, and the Environmen* (pp. 189–211). Hillsdale, NJ: Erlbaum.

Tedeschi, J. T. (Ed.). (1984). *Impression Management Theory and Social Psychological Research*. New York: Academic Press.

Tellis, G. J. (2004). *Effective advertising: Understanding when, how, and why advertising works*. Thousand Oaks, CA: Sage Publications.

Teltzrow, M., & Kobsa, A. (2004). Impacts of User Privacy Preferences on Personalized Systems: A comparative study. In Karat, C., Blom, J. O., & Karat, J. (Eds.), *Designing Personalized User Experiences in eCommerce*. Dordrecht, The Netherlands: Kluwer Academic Publishers. doi:10.1007/1-4020-2148-8_17

Terveen, L., & Hill, W. (2002). Human-Computer Collaboration in Recommender Systems. In Caroll, J. M. (Ed.), *Human-Computer Interaction in the New Millennium*. Addison-Wesley.

Terveen, L., & Hill, W. (2001). Beyond recommender systems: helping people help each other. In Carroll, J. (Ed.), *HCI In The New Millennium*. Reading, MA: Addison-Wesley.

Tharp, M. C. (2001). *Marketing and consumer identity in multicultural America*. Thousand Oaks, CA: Sage Publication.

The 2004 campaign, Dean and Kerry issue fund-raising totals. (2004). *The New York Times*.

The Center for Media Research. (2008, August 1). *Online Advertising Shows Significant Impact on Brand Awareness*. Research Brief. Retrieved from http://www.mediapost.com/publications/?fa=Articles.showArticle&art_aid=87420

The Center for Media Research. (2008, July 15). *Internet Ad Growth Percentage High, But Traditional Ad Dollars Higher*. Research Brief. Retrieved from http://www.mediapost.com/publications/index.cfm?fa=Articles.showArticle&art_aid=86497

The Radicati Group, Inc. (2007). *Addressing information overload in corporate email: the economics of user attention*. Whitepaper by The Radiciati Group, Inc. Palo Alto, CA. Retrieved from http://www.seriosity.com/downloads/Seriosity%20White%20Paper%20-%20Information%20Overload.pdf

Thody, P. (1997). *Don't Do IT! A dictionary of the forbidden*. New York: St. Martin's Press.

Thomaselli, R. (2004, August 9). No fun in games: Steroids, terrorists, election turn Olympics into trial for marketers. *Advertising Age*, 1.

Thomaselli, R. (2004, January 12). Adams looks to link sponsors with sorts TV technology. *Advertising Age, 75*(2), 34.

Thompson, S. C., Thomas, C., & Armstrong, W. (1998). Illusion of control, underestimations, and accuracy: A control heuristic explanation. *Psychological Bulletin, 123*(2), 143–161. doi:10.1037/0033-2909.123.2.143

Thompson, R. A. (2005). Multiple relationships multiply considered. *Human Development, 48*, 102–107. doi:10.1159/000083221

Thompson, C. (2006 April). Google's China problem (and China's Google Problem). *The New York Times*. Retrieved January 20, 2009, from http://www.nytimes.com/2006/04/23/magazine/23google.html?_r=1&pagewanted=print

Thompson, J. B. (1995, original 1971). *The media and Modernity: social theory of media*. Cambridge: Polity Press. (Original manuscript published in 1971).

Thorson, K. S., & Rodgers, S. (2006). Relationships between blogs as eWOM and interactivity, perceived interactivity, and parasocial interaction. *Journal of Interactive Advertising, 6*(2), 39–50.

Thurman, N. (2008). Forums for citizen journalists? Adoption of user generated content initiatives by online news media. *New Media & Society, 10*(1), 139–157. doi:10.1177/1461444807085325

Tice, L. (2007, June 24). Video contest goes to seed. *SunJournal.com*. Retrieved July 11, 2007, from http://www.sunjournal.com/story/218125-3/LewistonAuburn/Video_contest_goes_to_seed/

Till, B. D., & Baack, D. W. (2005). Recall and persuasion: Does creative advertising matter? *Journal of Advertising, 34*(3), 47–57.

Till, B. D., & Shimp, T. A. (1998). Endorsers in advertising: The case of negative celebrity information. *Journal of Advertising, 27*(1), 67–82.

Tingstad, V. (2003). *Children's chat on the net: a study of social encounters in two Norwegian chat rooms*. Trondheim, Norway: NOSEB/NTNU.

Tintarev, N. (2007, Jan 1). *Explaining Recommendations.* Paper presented at the Doctoral Consortium ACM Recommender Systems '07, Minneapolis, MN.

Tintarev, N., & Masthoff, J. (2007a, Jan 1). *A Survey of Explanations in Recommender Systems.* Paper presented at the Workshop on Recommender Systems and Intelligent User Interfaces associated with ICDE'07, Istanbul, Turkey.

Tintarev, N., & Masthoff, J. (2007b). *Effective Explanations of Recommendations: User-Centered Design.* Paper presented at the ACM Recommender Systems '07, Minneapolis, MN.

Toffler, A. (1980). *The third wave*. New York: Bantam.

Tong, S. T., Heide, B. V. D., & Lanwell, L. (2008). Too much of a good thing? The relationship between number of friends and interpersonal impressions on Facebook. *Journal of Computer-Mediated Communication, 13*, 531–549. doi:10.1111/j.1083-6101.2008.00409.x

Touchtunes. (n.d.). Retrieved from http://www.touchtunes.com/barfly.html

Towle, B., & Quinn, C. (2000). *Knowledge Based Recommender Systems Using Explicit User Models*, Menlo Park, CA.

Townsend, J. (2007). Second Life is just the first step for brands in virtual worlds. *Marketing Week, 30*(26), 28.

Trammell, K. D., William, A. P., Postelnicu, M., & Landreville, K. D. (2006). Increasing interactivity in candidate web sites and blogs through text and technical features. *Mass Communication & Society, 9*(1), 21–44. doi:10.1207/s15327825mcs0901_2

Trammell, K. D., Tarkowski, A., Hofmokl, J., & Sapp, A. M. (2006). Rzeczpospolita blogów [Republic of blog]: Examining Polish bloggers through content analysis. *Journal of Computer-Mediated Communication, 11*(3). Retrieved December 13, 2008, from http://jcmc.indiana.edu/vol11/issue3/trammell.html

Travis, D. (2001). Branding in the digital age. *The Journal of Business Strategy, 22*(3), 14–18. doi:10.1108/eb040166

Trent, J. S., & Friedenberg, R. V. (2000). *Political campaign communication: Principles and practices*. Westport, CT: Praeger.

Trippi, J. (2004). *The Revolution Will Not Be Televised: Democracy, the Internet, and the Overthrow of Everything.* New York: Regan Books.

Trudell, G., & Kolkin, E. (1999, September 27). Traditional Values in a High-Tech World. *InformationWeek*, 233-238.

Tsai, C. (2006). What is the Internet? Taiwanese high school students' perceptions. *Cyberpsychology & Behavior, 9*(6), 767–771. doi:10.1089/cpb.2006.9.767

Tsang, L. (2007). Sound and music in website design. In Sexton, J. (Ed.), *Music, sound and multimedia–From the live to the virtual* (pp. 145–171). Edinburgh, UK: Edinburgh University Press.

Turcotte, S. (1995). *Gimme a Bud! The feature film product placement industry*. Unpublished Master's thesis, Austin, Texas, University of Texas.

Turkle, S. (1995). *Life on the screen: identity in the age of the Internet. NY*. New York: Simon and Schuster.

Turkle, S. (2008). Always-on/always-on-you: the tethered self. In Katz, I. J. (Ed.), *Handbook of Mobile Communication Studies* (pp. 121–137). Cambridge, MA: MIT Press.

Turkle, S. (2004). Whither psychoanalysis in computer culture? *Psychoanalytic Psychology: Journal of the Division of Psychoanalysis, vol.21*(-no.1), pp. 16-30.

Turner, J. H. (2002). *Face-to-face: toward a sociological theory of interpersonal behavior*. Stanford, CA: Stanford University Press.

Turner, P., & Cusumano, S. (2000). Virtual advertising: legal implications for sport. *Sport Management Review, 3*, 47–70. doi:10.1016/S1441-3523(00)70079-9

Turner, R. (1962). Role-taking. Process versus conformity. In Rose, A. (Ed.), *Human behaviour and social process*. London: Routledge & Kegan Paul.

Turow, J., Hennessy, M., & Bleakley, A. (2008). Consumers' understanding of privacy rules in the marketplace. *The Journal of Consumer Affairs, 42*(3), 411–424. doi:10.1111/j.1745-6606.2008.00116.x

Turow, J. (2003). *Online Privacy: The System is Broken*. Report from the Annenberg Public Policy Center of the University of Pennsylvania. Retrieved from http://www.asc.upenn.edu/usr/jturow/internet-privacy-report/36-page-turow-version-9.pdf

Tutko, T. A. (1989). Personality change in the American sport scene. In Goldstein, J. H. (Ed.), *Sports, games, and play: Social and psychological viewpoints* (pp. 111–127). Hillsdale, NJ: Erlbaum.

TV Viewing and Internet Use are Complementary. (2008, October). New York: Nielsen Reports.

Ukman, L. (1996). *IEG's complete guide to sponsorship: Everything you need to know about sports, arts, event, entertainment and cause marketing*. Chicago, IL: IEG, Inc.

UNAIDS. (2004). *Action Against AIDS Must Address Epidemic's Increasing Impact on Women, Says UN Report*. Retrieved January 20, 2009, from http://www.unifem.org/news_events/story_detail.php?StoryID=130

UNAIDS. (2007). *2.5 million people living with HIV in India*. Retrieved March 28, 2008, from http://www.unaids.org/en/KnowledgeCentre/Resources/FeatureStories/archive/2007/20070704_India_new_data.asp

UNAIDS. (2007). *AIDS epidemic update*. Press Release. Retrieved January 20, 2009, from http://www.unaids.org/en/HIV_data/2007EpiUpdate/default.asp

UNAIDS. (2007). *Annex 1: HIV and AIDS estimates and data, 2007 and 2001*. Retrieved January 21, 2009, from http://data.unaids.org/pub/GlobalReport/2008/jc1510_2008_global_report_pp211_234_en.pdf

Underwood, R., Bond, E., & Baer, R. (2001). Building service brands via social identity: Lessons from the sports marketplace. *Journal of Marketing Theory & Practice*, 1-13.

UNFPA. (2004). Working with Communities and Faith-based Organizations. *Culture Matters*. Retrieved January 29, 2009, from http://www.unfpa.org/upload/lib pub file/426 filename CultureMatters_2004.pdf

United States Government Printing Office. (2002). *Public law 107-155–Bipartisan campaign reform act of 2002*. [Electronic Version]. Retrieved July 5, 2008 from http://www.gpo.gov/fdsys/pkg/PLAW-107publ155/content-detail.html

Universal-McCann. (2009).Wave 4. Retrieved March 2010, from http://universalmccann.bitecp.com/wave4/Wave4.pdf/.

University of Chicago. (n.d.). *The Society for Social Research*. Retrieved February 26, 2009, from http://ssr1.uchicago.edu/PRELIMS/Theory/durkheim.html

Urban, G. L., Sultan, F., & Qualls, W. (2000). Making trust the center of your Internet strategy. *Sloan Management Review*, *1*, 39–48.

Urban, G. L. (2004). *Digital Marketing Strategy*. Upper Saddle River, NJ: Prentice-Hall.

Vadas, K., Patel, N., Lyons, K., Starner, T., & Jacko, J. (2006). *Reading on-the-go: a comparison of audio and hand-held displays*. Paper presented at the Proceedings of the 8th conference on Human-computer interaction with mobile devices and services.

Valdiserri, R. (2002). HIV/AIDS stigma: An impediment to public health. *American Journal of Public Health*, *92*(3), 341–342. doi:10.2105/AJPH.92.3.341

Valkenburg, P. M., & Peter, J. (2007). Preadolescents' and adolescents' online communication and their closeness to friends. *Developmental Psychology*, *43*(2), 267–277. doi:10.1037/0012-1649.43.2.267

Valkenburg, P. M., & Peter, J. (2007). Online Communication and Adolescent Well-Being: Testing the Stimulation Versus the Displacement Hypothesis. *Journal of Computer-Mediated Communication*, *13*, 1169–1182. doi:10.1111/j.1083-6101.2007.00368.x

Valkenburg, P. M., Peter, J., & Schouten, P. (2006). Friend networking sites and their relationship to adolescents' well-being and social self-esteem. *Cyberpsychology & Behavior*, *9*(5), 584–590. doi:10.1089/cpb.2006.9.584

van Dolen, W. M., Dabholkar, P. A., & de Ruyter, K. (2007). Satisfaction with online commercial group chat: The influence of perceived technology attributes, chat group characteristics, and advisor communication style. *Journal of Retailing*, *83*(3), 339–358. doi:10.1016/j.jretai.2007.03.004

van Lent, M. (2008, February). The business of fun. *Computer*, *41*, 101–103. doi:10.1109/MC.2008.64

van Reijmersdal, E. A., Neijens, P. C., & Smit, E. G. (2007). Effects of television brand placement on brand image. *Psychology and Marketing*, *24*(5), 403–420. doi:10.1002/mar.20166

Varadarajan, Y. (2002). Marketing strategy and the internet: An organizing framework. *Journal of the Academy of Marketing Science*, *30*(4), 296–312. doi:10.1177/009207002236907

Vargas, J. A. (2008, November 20). Obama Raised Half a Billion Online. *The Washington Post*. Retrieved December 12, 2008, from http://voices.washingtonpost.com/44/2008/11/20/obama_raised_half_a_billion_on.html

Vargo, S. L., & Lusch, R. F. (2004). Evolving to a new dominant logic for marketing. *Journal of Marketing*, *68*(1), 1–7. doi:10.1509/jmkg.68.1.1.24036

Vargo, S. L., & Lusch, R. F. (2006). Service-dominant logic: Reactions, reflections, and refinements. *Marketing Theory*, *6*(3), 281–288. doi:10.1177/1470593106066781

Vasalou, A., Joinson, A., Banziger, T., Goldie, P., & Pitt, J. (2008). Avatars in social media: balancing accuracy, playfulness and embodied messages. *International Journal of Human-Computer Studies*, *66*, 801–811. doi:10.1016/j.ijhcs.2008.08.002

Vasalou, M., Joinson, A. N., & Pitt, J. (2007). Constructing my online self: avatars that increase self-focused attention. In *Proceedings of the SIGCHI conference on Human factors in computing systems* (pp. 445-448). New York: ACM Press.

Veda, Q. (2008). *Engaging Enterprise Audiences In New Media*. Retrieved from http://www.archive.org/details/EngagingEnterpriseAudiencesInNewMedia

Vedrashko, I. (2006). *Advertising in computer games*. Unpublished master's thesis, Massachusetts Institute of Technology, Cambridge.

Vegas.com. (2007, June 18). *Winner chosen for Direct the Next Vegas.commercial contest* [Company Release]. Retrieved July 11, 2007, from http://www.vegas.com/about/releases/vegascommercialwinner061807.html

Verma, R. K., Sureender, S., & Guruswamy, M. (1997). What do school children and teachers in rural Maharashtra think of AIDS and sex? *Health transition review: The cultural, social, and behavioural determinants of health*, S7, 481-486.

Verna, P. (2007 June). User-Generated Content: Will Web 2.0 Pay Its Way? *eMarketer*, 1-31.

Verna, P. (2008 February). Video game advertising. *eMarketer*. Retrieved September 27, 2009, from http://www.emarketer.com/Reports/All/Emarketer_2000485.aspx

Verna, P. (2009 June). Digital entertainment meets social media. *eMarketer*. Retrieved September 27, 2009, from http://www.emarketer.com/Reports/All/Emarketer_2000580.aspx

Vickers, A. (2007). Smart Growth in an Era of Digital Disruption. *Avenue A | Razorfish Insight*, Retrieved July 1, 2007, from http://www.avenuea-razorfish.com

Vignoles, V., Chryssochoou, X., & Breakwell, G. M. (2000). The distinctiveness principle: Identity, meaning, and bounds of cultural relativity. *Personality and Social Psychology Review*, *4*(4), 337–354. doi:10.1207/S15327957PSPR0404_4

Vijian, P. (2009). India Targets 3.5 Billion Free Condoms To Curb HIV/Aids. *Bernama.Com Malaysian National News Agency*. Retrieved February 18, 2009, from http://www.bernama.com.my/bernama/v3/news.php?id=389722

Vikas, A., Manz, C. C., & Glick, W. H. (1998). An organizational memory approach to information management. *Academy of Management Review*, *23*(4), 796–809. doi:10.2307/259063

Vilpponen, A., Winter, S., & Sundqvist, S. (2006). Electronic word-of-mouth in online environments: Exploring referral network structure and adoption behavior. *Journal of Interactive Advertising*, *6*(2), 63–77.

Viscusi, K., Harrington, J., & Vernon, J. (2005). *Economics of Regulation and Antitrust*. Cambridge, MA: MIT Press.

vJive. (n.d.). Retrieved from www.vjivenetworks.com

Vlahov, D., & Junge, B. (1998). The role of needle exchange programs in HIV prevention. *Public Health Reports (Washington, D.C.)*, *1*(113Supplement), 75–80.

Vollmers, S., & Mizerski, R. (1994). A Review and Investigation into the Effectiveness of Product Placements in Films. In K. Whitehill King (Eds.), *Conference Proceedings of the 1994 Conference of the American Academy of Advertising* (pp. 97-102). Athens, GA: American Academy of Advertising.

Von Hoffman, C. (2007). *Are marketers dying on Second Life?* Retrieved on 05/07/08 www.brandweek.com/bw/news/recent_display.jsp?vnu_content_id=1003563242&imw=Y

Vorderer, P., Klimmt, C., & Ritterfled, U. (2004). Enjoyment: At the heart of media entertainment. *Communication Theory*, *14*, 388–408. doi:10.1111/j.1468-2885.2004.tb00321.x

Vorderer, P. (2000). Interactive Entertainment and Beyond. In Zillmann, D., & Vorderer, P. (Eds.), *Media Entertainment: The Psychology of Its Appeal* (pp. 21–36). Mahwah, NJ: Lawrence Erlbaum.

Vorderer, P., Hartmann, T., & Klimmt, C. (2003). *Explaining the enjoyment of playing video games: The role competition*. Paper presented to the ACM International Conference Proceeding of the second international conference on entertainment computing.

Vorro, A. (2009). Building the network: Recognizing the potential for relationship building, a number of insurers turn to social media. *Insurance Networking News: Executive Strategies for Technology Management*, *4*(12), 1542–4901.

Vygotsky, L. S. (1978, original 1935). *Mind in society: the development of higher psychological processes*. Cambridge, MA: Harvard University Press. (Original manuscript published in 1935).

Walker, R. (2008). *Buying In the secret dialogue between what we buy and who we are*. New York: Random House.

Walker, R. (2006, May 28). Free advertising. *New York Times Magazine*, 20.

Walkerdine, V. (2007). *Children, gender and video games. NY.* New York: Palgrave-MacMillan.

Wallechinsky, D., & Wallace, I. (1975-1981). *History of Advertising: Ancient History, Middle Ages and the Early Days.* Retrieved from Trivia Library website: http://www.trivia-library.com/a/history-of-advertising-ancient-history-middle-ages-and-the-early-days.htm

Wallendorf, M., & Arnould, E. J. (1988). My favorite things: A cross-cultural inquiry into object attachment, possessiveness, and social linkage. *The Journal of Consumer Research, 14*(4), 531–547. doi:10.1086/209134

Wallenius, M., Punamäaki, R. L., & Rimpelåa, A. (2007). Digital game playing and direct and indirect aggression in early adolescence: the roles of age, social intelligence, and parent-child communication. *Journal of Youth and Adolescence, 36*, 325–336. doi:10.1007/s10964-006-9151-5

Walliser, B. (2003). An international review of sponsorship research: extension and update. *International Journal of Advertising, 22*(1), 5–40.

Wallsten, T. S., Budescu, D. V., Rapoport, A., Zwick, R., & Forsyth, B. (1986). Measuring the vague meanings of probability terms. *Journal of Experimental Psychology. General, 115*(4), 348–365. doi:10.1037/0096-3445.115.4.348

Walsh, K. R., & Pawlowski, S. D. (2002). Virtual reality: a technology in need of IS research. *Communications of the Association for Information Systems, 8*, 297–313.

Walters, C. (2009, February 15). Facebook's New Terms Of Service: 'We Can Do Anything We Want With Your Content. Forever.' *The Consumerist.* Retrieved from http://consumerist.com/5150175/facebooks-new-terms-of-service-we-can-do-anything-we-want-with-your-content-forever

Walther, J. B., Wang, Z., & Loh, T. (2004). The effect of top-level domains and advertisements on health web site credibility. *Journal of Medical Internet Research, 6*(3), e24. doi:10.2196/jmir.6.3.e24

Walther, J. B. (2007). Selective self-presentation in computer-mediated communication: Hyperpersonal dimensions of technology, language, and cognition. *Computers in Human Behavior, 23*, 2538–2557. doi:10.1016/j.chb.2006.05.002

WAN. (2008). World Press Trends: Newspapers are a Growth Business. *World Association of Newspapers.* Retrieved August 23, 2008, from http://www.wan-press.org/print.php3?id_article=17377

Wang, A. (2006). Advertising engagement: A driver of message involvement on message Effects. *Journal of Advertising Research, 46*(4), 355–368. doi:10.2501/S0021849906060429

Wang, H., Lee, M., & Wang, C. (1998). Consumer privacy concerns About internet marketing. *Communications of the ACM, 41*(3), 63–70. doi:10.1145/272287.272299

Wann, D. L., Royalty, J., & Roberts, A. (2000). The self-presentation of sports fans: Investigating the importance of team identification and self-esteem. *Journal of Sport Behavior, 23*(2), 198–206.

Wanta, W., & Hu, Y. (1994). The effects of credibility, reliance, and exposure on media agenda setting: A path analysis model. *The Journalism Quarterly, 71*(1), 90–98.

Ward, R. D., Marsden, P. H., Cahill, B., & Johnson, C. (2001). *Using skin conductivity to detect emotionally significant events in human-computer interaction.* Paper presented at the IHM-HCI.

Warf, B. (2003). Mergers and acquisitions in the telecommunications industry, growth and change. *Journal of Urban and Regional Policy, 34*(3), 321–344.

Waterman, D. (2000). CBS-Viacom and the effects of media mergers: An economic perspective. *Federal Communications Law Journal, 52*, 531–550.

Watson, R. T., Leyl, F., Pitt, P. B., & Zinkhan, G. M. (2002). U-commerce: Expanding the universe of marketing. *Journal of the Academy of Marketing Science, 30*(4), 332–347. doi:10.1177/009207002236909

Watson, G., & Johnson, D. (1972). *Social psychology: Issues and insights.* Philadelphia: J.B. Lippincott.

Watson, J. (2008). *Media Communication: an introduction to theory and process* (3rd ed.). London: Palgrave-MacMillan.

Watts, D. J., Dodds, P., & Newman, M. (2002). Identity and search in social networks. *Science, 296*(5571), 1302–1306. doi:10.1126/science.1070120

Watzlawick, P., Bavelas, J. B., & Jackson, D. D. (1967). *Pragmatics of Human Communication.* New York: Norton & Co.

Weaver, D. T., & Oliver, M. B. (2000 June). *Television Programs and Advertising: Measuring the Effectiveness of Product Placement within Seinfeld.* Paper presented to the Mass Communication Division at the 50th annual conference of the International Communication Association (ICA), Acapulco, Mexico.

Weber, M. (1978). *Economy and Society, Vol. 1*. Berkeley, CA: University of California Press.

Webster, J., Trevino, L. K., & Ryan, L. (1993). The dimensionality and correlates of flow in human-computer interactions. *Computers in Human Behavior*, *9*(4), 411–426. doi:10.1016/0747-5632(93)90032-N

Webster, J. G., Phalen, P. F., & Lichty, L. W. (2006). *Ratings Analysis: Theory and Practice of Audience Research* (3rd ed.). Mahwah, NJ: LEA Lawrence Erlbaum Associates.

Wei, M.-L., Fischer, E., & Main, K. J. (2008). An examination of the effects of activating persuasion knowledge on consumer response to brands engaging in covert marketing. *Journal of Public Policy & Marketing*, *27*(1), 34–44. doi:10.1509/jppm.27.1.34

Wei, R. (2007). Effects of playing violent videogames on Chinese adolescents' pro-violence attitudes, attitudes toward others, and aggressive behavior. *Cyberpsychology & Behavior*, *10*(3), 371–372. doi:10.1089/cpb.2006.9942

Weibel, D., Wissmath, B., Habegger, S., Yves, S., & Rudolf, G. (2008). Playing online games against computer- vs. human-controlled opponents: Effects on presence, flow, and enjoyment. *Computers in Human Behavior*, *24*, 2274–2291. doi:10.1016/j.chb.2007.11.002

Weilbacher, W. M. (2001). Point of view: Does advertising cause a hierarchy of effects? *Journal of Advertising Research*, *41*(6), 19–26.

Weinberger, M. G., & Spotts, H. E. (1989). Humour in U.S. versus U.K. TV commercials: A comparison. *Journal of Advertising*, *18*(2), 39–44.

Weinberger, M. C., & Dillon, W. R. (1980). The effects of unfavorable product information. In Olson, J. C. (Ed.), *Advances in Consumer Research* (*Vol. 7*, pp. 528–532). Ann Arbor, MI: Association for Consumer Research.

Weiser, E. (2000). Gender differences in Internet use patterns and Internet application preferences: a two-sample comparison. *Cyberpsychology & Behavior*, *4*, 167–178. doi:10.1089/109493100316012

Weld, D., Anderson, C., Domingos, P., Etzioni, O., Gajos, K., Lau, T., et al. (2003). Automatically personalizing user interfaces. In *IJCAI03*, Acapulco, Mexico, August.

Wenger, E., McDermott, R., & Snyder, W. (2002). *Cultivating communities of practice: a guide to managing knowledge*. Harvard Business School Press.

Wenger, E., & Snyder, W. (2000). Communities of practice: the organizational frontier. *Harvard Business Review*, (January-February): 139–145.

Wenger, E. (2004). Knowledge management is a donut: shaping your knowledge strategy with communities of practice. *Ivey Business Journal* (January).

Wenner, L. A. (1989). Media, sports, and society: The research agenda. In Wenner, L. A. (Ed.), *Media, sports, and society* (pp. 13–48). Newbury Park, CA: Sage.

Wenner, L. A., & Gantz, W. (1998). Watching sports on television: Audience experience, gender, fanship, and marriage. In Wenner, L. A. (Ed.), *Mediasport* (pp. 233–251). London: Routledge.

West, M. D. (1994). Validating a scale for the measurement of credibility: A covariance structure modeling approach. *The Journalism Quarterly*, *71*(1), 159–168.

West, D. (2005). Editorial. *Journal of Advertising Research, 24*(3), 267-268. Retrieved May 16, 2008, from http://www.businessweek.com/magazine/content/07_40/b4052072.htm?campaign_id=nws_insdr_sep21&link_position=link3

Wexelblat, A. (1988). Don't Make That Face: A Report on Anthropomorphizing an Interface. In Coen, M. (Ed.), *Intelligent Environments (AAAI Technical Report)* (pp. 173–179). Menlo Park, CA: AAAI Press.

Whang, L. S., & Chang, G. (2004). Lifestyles of virtual world residents: Living in the on-line game Lineage. *Cyberpsychology & Behavior*, *7*(5), 592–600.

What's culture got to do with HIV and AIDS? Why the global strategy for HIV and AIDS needs to adopt a cultural approach. (2007). *HealthLink Worldwide*. Retrieved January 29, 2009, from http://www.healthlink.org.uk/PDFs/findings7_hiv_culture.pdf

Wheaton, B. (2003). A subculture of commitment. In Rinehart, R. E., & Sydnor, S. (Eds.), *To The Extreme: Alternative Sports, Inside And Out*. Albany, NY: State University of New York.

Whillock, R. K. (1997). Cyber-politics: The online strategies of 1996. *The American Behavioral Scientist*, *40*(8), 1208–1225. doi:10.1177/0002764297040008018

White, R. (2007, October). Engagement, involvement and attention. *Admap*, *487*, 23–24.

White, T. B., Zahay, D. L., Thorbjornsen, H., & Shavitt, S. (2008). Getting too personal: Reactance to highly personalized email solicitations. *Marketing Letters*, *19*, 39–50. doi:10.1007/s11002-007-9027-9

Whittler, T. E. (1989). Viewers' processing of actor's race and message claims in advertising stimuli. *Psychology and Marketing, 6*, 287–309. doi:10.1002/mar.4220060405

Whittler, T. E. (1991). The effects of actors' race in commercial advertising: Review and extension. *Journal of Advertising, 20*(1), 54–60.

Wierville, C. (2008) *Customer engagement and product/service innovation*. Retrieved from http://www.archive.org/details/CustomerEngagementAndProductServiceInnovation.

Wikipedia. (n.d.). *Blogosphere*. Retrieved June 15, 2008, from http://en.wikipedia.org/wiki/Blogosphere

Wildstrom, S. (1996, November 11). They're Watching You Online. *Business Week*. Retrieved from http://www.businessweek.com/1996/46/b350141.htm

Wilhelm, A. (2000). *Democracy in the Digital Age: Challenges to Political Life in Cyberspace*. New York: Routledge.

Wilkes, R. E., & Valencia, H. (1989). Hispanics and Blacks in television commercials. *Journal of Advertising, 18*(1), 19–25.

Willadsen-Jensen, E. C., & Ito, T. A. (2006). Ambiguity and the timecourse of racial perception. *Social Cognition, 24*(5), 580–606. doi:10.1521/soco.2006.24.5.580

Williams, D., Yee, N., & Caplan, S. E. (2008). Who plays, how much, and why? Debunking the stereotypical gamer profile. *Journal of Computer-Mediated Communication, 13*, 993–1018. doi:10.1111/j.1083-6101.2008.00428.x

Williams, R. (1961). *Long revolutions*. London: Penguin.

Williams, R. (1976). *Keywords: a vocabulary of culture and society*. Glasgow, UK: Fontana.

Williams, D. (2006). Virtual cultivation: Online worlds, offline perceptions. *The Journal of Communication, 56*, 69–87. doi:10.1111/j.1460-2466.2006.00004.x

Williams, A., Trammell, K., Postelnicu, M., Landreville, L., & Martin, J. (2005). Blogging and Hyperlinking: use of the Web to enhance viability during the 2004 US campaign. *Journalism Studies, 6*(2), 177–186. doi:10.1080/14616700500057262

Wilska, T. A. (2003). Mobile phone use as part of young people's consumption styles. *Journal of Consumer Policy, 26*, 441–463. doi:10.1023/A:1026331016172

Winer, D. (1999). *The History of Weblogs*. Retrieved May 17, 2008, from http://newhome.weblogs.com/history of Weblogs The Wall Street Journal. (2006, August 2). *McDonald's Seeks Young Adults in Their Realm – Podcasts, Bars*. Retrieved May 2, 2008, from http://www.cattlenetwork.com/content.asp?contentid=56797

Winer, D. (2003). What makes a weblog a weblog? Retrieved August 19, 2008, from http://blogs.law.harvard.edu/whatmakesaweblogaweblog.html

Winkler, T., & Buckner, K. (2006). Receptiveness of gamers to embedded brand messages in advergames: Attitudes towards product placement. *Journal of Interactive Advertising, 7*(1), 37–46.

Winn, P. (2009). State of the Blogosphere 2008. Retrieved March 16, 2010, from http://technorati.com/blogging/article/state-of-the-blogosphere-introduction/.

Winter, D. (2008). *Arcade Pong*. Retrieved February 10, 2008, from http://www.pong-story.com/arcade.htm

Wirth, W., Hartmann, T., Bocking, S., Vorderer, P., Klimmt, C., & Schramm, H. (2007). A process model of the formation of spatial presence experiences. *Media Psychology, 9*, 493–525.

Wise, K., Bolls, P. D., Kim, H., Venkataraman, A., & Meyer, R. (2008). Enjoyment of advergames and brand attitudes: The impact of thematic relevance. *Journal of Interactive Advertising, 9*(1). Retrieved from http://www.jiad.org.

Wober, M., & Gunter, B. (1982). Television and personal threat: Fact or artifact? A British survey. *The British Journal of Social Psychology, 21*, 239–247.

Wodak, A., & Cooney, A. (2006). Do needle syringe programs reduce HIV infection among injecting drug users: a comprehensive review of the international evidence. *Substance Use & Misuse, 41*(6-7), 777–813. doi:10.1080/10826080600669579

Wolak, J., Mitchell, K. J., & Finkelhor, D. (2003). Escaping or connecting? Characteristics of youth who form close online relationships. *Journal of Adolescence, 26*, 105–119. doi:10.1016/S0140-1971(02)00114-8

Wolfgang, A. K., Zenker, S. I., & Viscusi, T. (1984). Control Motivation and the Illusion of Control in Betting on Dice. *The Journal of Psychology, 116*, 67–72.

Wolin, L. D., & Korgaonkar, P. (2003). Web advertising: Gender difference in beliefs, attitudes, and behavior. *Internet Research, 13*(5), 375–385. doi:10.1108/10662240310501658

Wolinsky, H. (2003, July 15). Sportsvision an All-Star in sports communications. *Chicago Sun-Times,* 45.

Wong, W. C., Lee, A., & Tsang, K. K. (2004). Correlates of sexual behaviors with health status and health perception in Chinese adolescents: A cross-sectional survey in schools. *AIDS Patient Care and STDs*, *18*(8), 470–480. doi:10.1089/1087291041703656

Wong, M. (2004, October 18). Advertisments inserted into video games. *redOrbit.* Retrieved August 19, 2008 from http://www.redorbit.com/news/technology/94730/advertisements_inserted_into_video_ga mes/#

Wood, R. T. A., Griffiths, M. D., Chappell, D., & Davies, M. N. O. (2004). The structural characteristics of video games: a psycho-structural analysis. *Cyberpsychology & Behavior*, *7*(1), 1–10. doi:10.1089/109493104322820057

Wood, N. T., Solomon, M. R., & Englis, B. G. (2005). Personalisation of online avatars: Is the messenger as important as the message? *International Journal of Internet Marketing and Advertising*, *2*(1/2), 143–161. doi:10.1504/IJIMA.2005.007509

Wood, N. T., Solomon, M. R., & Englis, B. G. (2008). Personalization of the Web interface: The impact of Web avatars on users response to e-commerce sites. *Journal of Website Promotion*, *2*(1/2), 53–69. doi:10.1080/15533610802104133

Wood, N. T., & Solomon, M. R. (2008). Digital Brand Personality: Does the Matchup Hypothesis Extend to Online Environments? In Lee, A. Y., & Soman, D. (Eds.), *Advances in Consumer Research* (pp. 84–85).

Wood, C. (2006, December 5). User-generated content is building brand affinity: AMA. *DMNews*. Retrieved June 26, 2007, from http://www.dmnews.com/cms/dm-news/research-studies/39243.html.

Woodcock, B. S. (2006). *MMOG chart*. Retrieved July 20, 2009, from http://www.mmogchart.com

Woods, B. S., & Murphy, P. K. (2002). Separated at birth: the shared lineage of research on conceptual change and persuasion. *International Journal of Educational Research*, *35*(7-8), 633–649. doi:10.1016/S0883-0355(02)00007-1

Woodside, A. G., & Sims, J. T. (1976). Retail sales transactions and customer 'purchase pal' effects on buying behavior. *Journal of Retailing*, *52*(3), 57–64.

World of WarCraft. *Character* (n.d.). Retrieved on August 5, 2009, from http://www.worldofwarcraft.com/wrath/features/gameplay/achievements.xml

World of WarCraft. *Player vs. player* (n.d.). Retrieved on August 4, 2009, from http://www.worldofwarcraft.com/info/basics/duels.html

Wright, P. (1974, October). The harassed decision maker: Time pressures, distractions, and the use of evidence. *The Journal of Applied Psychology*, *59*, 555–561. doi:10.1037/h0037186

Wright, P. (2002, March). Marketplace metacognition and social intelligence. *The Journal of Consumer Research*, *28*, 677–682. doi:10.1086/338210

Wright, K. (2000). Perceptions of on-line support providers: an examination of perceived homophily, source credibility, communication and social support within on-line support groups. *Communication Quarterly*, *48*(1), 44–59.

Wright, J. (2006). *Blog Marketing: The Revolutionary New Way to Increase Sales, Build Your Brand, and Get Exceptional Results*. New York: McGraw-Hill.

Wright, P., Friestad, M., & Boush, D. M. (2005). The development of marketplace persuasion knowledge in children, adolescents, and young adults. *Journal of Public Policy & Marketing*, *24*(2), 222–233. doi:10.1509/jppm.2005.24.2.222

Wrong, D. (1961). The oversocialized concept of main in modern sociology. *American Sociological Review*, 26.

Wu, G. (2006). Conceptualization and measuring the perceived interactivity of websites. *Journal of Current Issues and Research in Advertising*, *28*(Spring), 87–104.

Wu, G. (2006). Conceptualizing and measuring the perceived interactivity of websites. *Journal of Current Issues and Research in Advertising*, *28*(1), 87–104.

Wu, G. (1999). Perceived interactivity and attitude toward web sites. In Marilyn, S. Roberts, E. (Eds.) Proceedings of the American Academy of Advertising Conference, 254-262.

Xenos, M., & Foot, K. (2005). Politics as usual, or politics unusual? Position taking and dialogue on campaign Websites in the 2002 U.S. elections. *The Journal of Communication*, *55*(1), 169–185. doi:10.1111/j.1460-2466.2005.tb02665.x

Yahoo. Games. (2007). *Grand theft auto IV: Five reasons you want it.* Retrieved April 29, 2009, from http://videogames.yahoo.com/events/grand-theft-auto-iv/grand-theft-auto-iv-five-reasons-you-want-it/1199905

Yang, M., & Roskos-Ewoldsen, D. R. (2007). The effectiveness of brand placements in the movies: Levels of placements, explicit and implicit memory, and brand-choice behavior. *The Journal of Communication*, *57*, 469–489. doi:10.1111/j.1460-2466.2007.00353.x

Yang, M., Roskos-Ewoldsen, D. R., Dinu, L., & Arpan, L. M. (2006). The effectiveness of 'in-game' advertising: Comparing college students' explicit and implicit memory for brand names. *Journal of Advertising*, *35*(4), 143–152. doi:10.2753/JOA0091-3367350410

Yang, K. C. C. (2007). Factors influencing internet users' perceived credibility of news-related blogs in Taiwan. *Telematics and Informatics*, *24*(2), 69–85. doi:10.1016/j.tele.2006.04.001

Yang, C. C. (2003). Internet users' attitude toward and beliefs about Internet advertising: exploratory research from Taiwan. *Journal of International Consumer Marketing*, *15*(4), 43–65. doi:10.1300/J046v15n04_03

Yang, M., Roskos-Ewoldsen, B., & Roskos-Ewoldsen, D. R. (2004). Mental models of for brand placement. In Shrum, L. J. (Ed.), *The psychology of entertainment media: Blurring the lines between entertainment and persuasion*. Mahwah, NJ: Lawrence Erlbaum Associates.

Yang, S. (2003 June). Researchers warn that AIDS in India could become as dire as in Africa. *UC Berkeley News*. Retrieved January 20, 2009, from http://www.berkeley.edu/news/media/releases/2003/06/19_india.shtml

Yang, Y. (2004). *New Data Mining and Marketing Approaches for Customer Segmentation and Promotion Planning on the Internet*. Retrieved July 10, 2008, from http://en.scientificcommons.org/7595063

Yaveroglu, I., & Donthu, N. (2008). Advertising repetition and placement issues in on-line environments. *Journal of Advertising*, *37*, 31–43. doi:10.2753/JOA0091-3367370203

Yee, N. (2006). The demographics, motivations, and derived experiences of users of massively multi-user online graphical environments. *Presence (Cambridge, Mass.)*, *15*(3), 309–329. doi:10.1162/pres.15.3.309

Yee, N., & Bailenson, J. (2007). The Proteus Effect: The effect of transformed self-representation on behavior. *Human Communication Research*, *33*(3), 271–290. doi:10.1111/j.1468-2958.2007.00299.x

Yee, N., Bailenson, J., Urbanek, M., Chang, F., & Merget, D. (2007). The unbearable likeness of being digital: The persistence of nonverbal social norms in online virtual environments. *Cyberpsychology & Behavior*, *10*(1), 115–121. doi:10.1089/cpb.2006.9984

Yee, N. (2007). Motivations to play online. *Cyberpsychology & Behavior*, *9*(6), 772–775. doi:10.1089/cpb.2006.9.772

Yee, N. (2005). The Psychology of Massively Multi-User Online Role-Playing Games: Motivations, Emotional Investment, Relationships and Problematic Usage. In Schroder, R., & Alexson, A. (Eds.), *Avatars at Work and Play: Collaboration and interaction in shared virtual environments*.

Yee, N. (2007). *The daedalus project*. Retrieved on August 5, 2009, from http://www.nickyee.com/daedalus/

Yee, N. (2007). The Proteus Effect: Behaviorial Modifications Via Transformations of Digital Self Representation. *The Daedalus Project*. Retrieved August 10, 2008, from http://www.nickyee.com/pubs/Dissertation_Nick_Yee.pdf

Yo! Noid Shrine. (n.d.). Retrieved September 12, 2008 from http://www.nesplayer.com/yonoid/noids.htm

Yoo, C. Y. (2008). Unconscious processing of Web advertising: Effects on implicit memory, attitude toward the brand, and consideration set. *Journal of Interactive Marketing*, *22*(2), 2–18. doi:10.1002/dir.20110

Yoo, C. S. (2002). Vertical Integration and Media Regulation in the New Economy. *Vanderbilt Public Law and Legal Theory*. Working Paper 2002-01.

Youn, S. (2008). Family communication influences on teens' online consumer socialization. In, *Child and Teen Consumption 2008 Conference*, Trondheim, Norway.

Young, K. S. (2001). *Caught in the net: how to recognize the signs of Internet addiction and winning a strategy recover., NY*. New York: Wiley.

Young, A. (2008, June 04). Hillary vs. Barack: Who Had the Smartest Media Strategy? *Advertising Age*. Retrieved August 29, 2008, from http://adage.com/campaigntrail/post?article_id=127508

Youth-Oriented Virtual Worlds Now Live or Developing. (2008, August 22). Virtual Worlds Mangement. Retrieved August 24, 2008, from http://www.virtualworldsmanagement.com

Yun, G. W., Park, S., & Ha, L. (2008). Influence of cultural dimensions on online interactive review feature implementations: A comparison of Korean and U.S. retail websites. *Journal of Interactive Marketing*, *22*(3), 40–50. doi:10.1002/dir.20116

Zaheer, K. (2007 May). Get real and save Indian youth from AIDS–official. *Reuters UK*. Retrieved January 20, 2009, from http://uk.reuters.com/article/healthNews/idUKDEL6968520070517?feedType

Zaichkowsky, J. L. (1985). Measuring the involvement construct in marketing. *The Journal of Consumer Research*, *12*(3), 341–352. doi:10.1086/208520

Zajonc, R. B., & Marcus, H. (1982). Affective and cognitive factors in preferences. *The Journal of Consumer Research*, *9*(2), 123–131. doi:10.1086/208905

Zajonc, R. B. (1968). Attitudinal Effects of Mere Exposure. *Journal of Personality and Social Psychology*, *9*(2), 1–27. doi:10.1037/h0025848

Zajonc, R. B. (2001). Mere exposure: A gateway to the subliminal. *Current Directions in Psychological Science*, *10*, 224–228. doi:10.1111/1467-8721.00154

Zajonc, R. B. (2000). Feeling and thinking: Closing the debate over the independence of affect. In Forgas, J. P. (Ed.), *Feeling and thinking: The role of affect in social cognition Studies in emotion and social interaction, second series* (pp. 31–58). Cambridge, UK: Cambridge University Press.

Zaslow, J. (2002, November 26, 2002). If TiVo Thinks You Are Gay, Here's How To Set It Straight - Amazon.com Knows You, Too, Based on What You Buy, Why All the Cartoons? *The Wall Street Journal,* 1.

Zavis, A. (2009). *MySpace cyber-bullying conviction tentatively dismissed.* Retrieved July 3, 2009 from http://www.latimes.com/news/local/la-me-myspace3-2009jul03,0,6795027.story

Zhang, J., Jones, N., & Pu, P. (2008). *A visual interface for critiquing-based recommender systems*. Paper presented at the Proceedings of the 9th ACM conference on Electronic commerce.

Zhao, S., Grasmuck, S., & Martin, J. (2008). Identity construction on Facebook - Digital empowerment in anchored relationships. *Computers in Human Behavior*, *24*, 1816–1836. doi:10.1016/j.chb.2008.02.012

Zhou, W. (2004). The choice of commercial breaks in television programs: the number, length and timing. *The Journal of Industrial Economics*, *22*(3), 315–326. doi:10.1111/j.0022-1821.2004.00228.x

Zillman, D. (2000). The coming of media entertainment. In Zillman, D., & Vorderer, P. (Eds.), *Media entertainment: The psychology of its appeal.* Mahwah, NJ: Lawrence Erlbaum Associates.

Zillmann, D., Bryant, J., & Sapolsky, B. S. (1989). Enjoyment from sports spectatorship. In Goldstein, J. H. (Ed.), *Sports, games, and play: Social and psychological viewpoints* (pp. 241–278). Hillsdale, NJ: Lawrence Erlbaum.

Zinkhan, G. M., Qualls, W. J., & Biswas, A. (1990). The use of Blacks in magazine and television advertising: 1946 to 1986. *The Journalism Quarterly*, *67*(3), 547–553.

Zool. (2008, October 10). In *Wikipedia, the Free Encyclopedia.* Retrieved October 12, 2008, from http://en.wikipedia.org/wiki/Zool

Zuckerberg, M. (2007, December 5). *Thoughts on Beacon.* Message posted to http://blog.facebook.com/blog.php?post=7584397130

About the Contributors

Matthew S. Eastin, (Ph.D., Michigan State University) is an Associate Professor in the Department of Advertising, College of Communication, at The University of Texas at Austin. He is also the Director of the Texas Media Research Lab and Faculty Associate of the Energy Institute at The University of Texas at Austin. Matthew S. Eastin's research focuses on new media behavior. From this perspective, he has investigated information processing as well as the social and psychological factors associated with game play involvement, new media adoption, e-commerce, e-health, and organizational use. Generally, his research utilizes information processing as a central mechanism to new media experiences (i.e., affect, identification, perceptions, etc.) and knowledge acquisition. Dr. Eastin's research can be found in the *Journal of Communication, Communication Research, Human Communication Research, Journal of Broadcasting & Electronic Media, CyberPsychology & Behavior, Journal of Computer-Mediated Communication, and Computers in Human Behavior*, to name a few. Currently, Dr. Eastin serves on the Editorial Boards for the *Journal of Broadcasting & Electronic Media and I/S: A Journal of Law and Policy for the Information Society.*

Terry Daugherty (Ph.D., Michigan State University) is a Research Fellow for the Suarez Applied Marketing Research Laboratory and Taylor Institute for Direct Marketing, as well as an Assistant Professor in the Department of Marketing, at The University of Akron. His research focuses on exploring strategic, social, and technological issues within consumer psychology involving the mass media. Terry's research has appeared in the *Journal of Consumer Psychology, Journal of Advertising, Psychology & Marketing, Journal of Interactive Marketing, Journal of Computer-Mediated Communication, International Journal of Electronic Marketing & Retailing, International Journal of Internet Marketing & Advertising, Journal of Interactive Advertising*, and *American Journal of Business*, among numerous others. Prior to joining UA, Terry worked in the media industry as well as conducted research at the M.I.N.D. Lab at Michigan State University, eLab in the Owen Graduate School of Management at Vanderbilt University, and was the Director of the Media Research Lab in the Department of Advertising at The University of Texas.

Neal Burns (Ph.D., McGill University) is a Professor in the Department of Advertising, College of Communication, at The University of Texas at Austin. He also has been appointed as an Adjunct Professor at the University of California San Francisco (UCSF) Center for AIDS Prevention Studies (CAPS). He was senior partner and director of research and account planning at Carmichael Lynch Advertising from 1985 – when Carmichael Lynch and The Burns Group combined their resources to become one of the strongest and highly respected agencies in the country – until 1997 when The InterPublic Group acquired the Agency and he joined the faculty at The University of Texas at Austin. Neal was also an adjunct faculty member at the University of Minnesota teaching classes in consumer behavior and advertising, high technology marketing and ethics. Earlier in his career Burns served as associate executive director for the Higher Education Coordinating Board in Minnesota; director of marketing for the Systems & Research Division of Honeywell Inc.; and head of the Environmental Stress Branch of the US Navy's Air Crew Equipment Laboratory working with the Project Mercury Team. Burns has published more than75 articles and papers and his work had been honored with dozens of advertising awards. At the University of Texas at Austin, Dr. Burns is the founder and director of the Advertising Department's account planning program. He has served as director of the Center for Brand Research since 2002. He is also a member of the Faculty Council and the Latino Media Studies Committee.

***

Tamara L. Ansons is a Doctoral Candidate in the Brain and Cognitive Sciences area of the Department of Psychology at the University of Manitoba.

Osei Appiah, (Ph.D., Associate Professor, The Ohio State University) has a deep-seated interest in how ethnic minority consumers use and are affected by both media and media messages. His research is driven by a desire to discover more effective ways to reach ethnic minorities with messages they can identify with and trust. This is particularly important given ethnic minorities are difficult to reach with media messages because many believe media messages are directed at the general market and doubt messages from mainstream sources. Dr. Appiah's research attempts to uncover the most effective ways to get ethnic minorities to attend to and act upon messages from traditional and new media.

Jeremy Bailenson is founding director of Stanford University's Virtual Human Interaction Lab and an associate professor in the Department of Communication at Stanford. He earned a B.A. cum laude from the University of Michigan in 1994 and a Ph.D. in cognitive psychology from Northwestern University in 1999. After receiving his doctorate, he spent four years at the Research Center for Virtual Environments and Behavior at the University of California, Santa Barbara as a Post-Doctoral Fellow and then an Assistant Research Professor. Bailenson's main area of interest is the phenomenon of digital human representation, especially in the context of immersive virtual reality. He explores the manner in which people are able to represent themselves when the physical constraints of body and veridically-rendered behaviors are removed. Furthermore, he designs and studies collaborative virtual reality systems that allow physically remote individuals to meet in virtual space, and explores the manner in which these systems change the nature of verbal and nonverbal interaction.

Lisa M. Bennett completed her undergraduate studies at the University of California at Irvine, where she received her B.A. in Psychology. She pursued a career in marketing while in the private sector and obtained her M.B.A. from San Francisco State University. Her career exposed her to the challenges businesses face when trying to reach the right audience with the right message at the right time in the digital world. She is passionate about utilizing targeted virtual consumer behavior to understand how businesses can improve their online marketing efforts. She spends her time offline with photography, the great outdoors, and her family in Apple Valley, CA.

Laura F. Bright, (Ph.D., University of Texas at Austin) is an Assistant Professor of Strategic Communication at Texas Christian University. Her research focuses on understanding marketing and consumer behavior within interactive environments as well as how those types of media are created and consumed. Laura can be reached at http://www.brightwoman.com.

Pedro Quelhas Brito, Assistant Professor at School of Economics - University of Porto. Ph.D. at UMIST, United Kingdom, M.A., University of Porto. His research focus on consumer psychology applied to tourism, retailing and new media. Dr. Brito has investigated the pre-adolescents integration of digital instruments in the context of their social network management. He is author, co-author and editor of several books and chapters as well as articles published in journals devoted to marketing, consumer ethics and communication. He is director of several executive Master and post-graduation programs in business and tourism management.

Mike Buncher (B.A., University of Minnesota Duluth) is a graduate student in the Department of Communication at Michigan State University. His research interests include video games, music, and mood management through media.

Kelli S. Burns, Ph.D. is an assistant professor in the School of Mass Communications at the University of South Florida . Her research interests include social media use in public relations; the intersection of social media and popular culture; and online and user-generated advertising. She is the author of the 2009 book *Celeb 2.0: How Social Media Foster Our Fascination with Popular Culture*. Her research has been published in the *Journal of Advertising*, *Journal of New Communications Research*, *Newspaper Research Journal*, and the *International Journal of Interactive Marketing and Advertising*. Burns received a doctorate in mass communication from the University of Florida where she was a presidential fellow, a master's degree in mass communication from Middle Tennessee State University , and a bachelor's degree in mathematics and business administration from Vanderbilt University . Her work experience includes positions in marketing communications and market research.

Cheryl Campanella Bracken (Ph.D., Temple University) is an associate professor in the School of Communication at Cleveland State University. Her research interests include psychological processing of media. She is intrigued by the role of various screens in the lives of media users and focuses on telepresence. Her research has been published in *Media Psychology*, *Journal of Communication*, and *Journal of Broadcasting & Electronic Media*. She has co-edited three special issues of *Presence: Teleoperators and Virtual Environments* and is on the Board of Directors of the International Society for Presence Research.

Sejung Marina Choi is Associate Professor of Advertising at the University of Texas at Austin. She received her Ph.D. in Mass Media and M.A. in Advertising from Michigan State University. Dr. Choi's research interests are in the areas of source credibility, consumer-brand relationships, new media and cross-cultural consumer behavior. Her current projects investigate how source credibility perceptions are formed and subsequently influence the message effectiveness in the context of celebrity endorsements in advertising and mediated communications on the Internet. Dr. Choi's work has been published in various conference proceedings, several book chapter and the *Journal of Advertising, Psychology & Marketing, Journal of Consumer Affairs, Journal of Popular Culture, Journal of Current Issues and Research in Advertising, Journal of Marketing Communications, Journal of Computer Mediated Communication, International Journal of Advertising*, among others. Prior to her graduate degrees, Dr. Choi worked in the advertising agency business, particularly in account management. Her past clients include various multinational advertisers and local advertisers.

Shu-Chuan Chu (PhD University of Texas at Austin) is an Assistant Professor in the College of Communication at DePaul University. Her main research areas are social media, cross-cultural consumer behavior, electronic word-of-mouth, and brand personality. Her work has been published or forthcoming in the *Journal of Interactive Advertising, Journal of International Consumer Marketing, Journal of Marketing Communications*, among others.

Vincent Cicchirillo's research focuses upon the study of new media technologies. Primarily, upon the influence of video game play features and contexts on post-game play outcomes. Of particular interest is the examination of character representations within video games (i.e., race & gender) and how that influences outcomes related to identification, positive & negative valence, as well as aggression. This research also examines the effect of stereotypical representations within violent video games. Furthermore, this work examines player motivations for online gaming and how that impacts information-processing of in-game content. Other research interests include cyber-bullying and teasing behaviors among college students. His research has appeared in the *Journal of Broadcasting and Electronic Media, Human Communication Research, Journal of Social Psychology*, and *Communication Research Reports*. Also, he has a single author book chapter in the *Handbook of Research on Digital Media and Advertising* and a co-authored book chapter in the *Handbook of Research on Computer Mediated Communication.*

Irene Dickey is a Lecturer at the University of Dayton's School of Business Administration. She teaches a broad scope of marketing courses at the undergraduate and graduate levels, and in numerous executive development and leadership programs. Ms. Dickey has published in such journals as the Journal of Business and Behavioral Sciences, and the Journal of E-Business, and has presented at many academic and practitioner conferences and meetings. Much of her research focuses on digital marketing. Ms. Dickey serves as the Director of the P&G Marketing Competition, and serves on several boards and committees. She has won four teaching awards. She received her undergraduate degree in Management and Marketing from The University of Dayton. After graduation, she received her MBA in Finance from Wright State University.

Troy Elias (Ph.D., The Ohio State University) is an Assistant Professor in the Department of Advertising in the College of Journalism and Communications at the University of Florida. His research interest is in social influence, with an emphasis on race and ethnicity, information and communication technology, and Internet advertising. His research explores the impact of social identity and psychological distinctiveness on consumer attitudes in new media environments. He has taught courses in *Social Influence in New Media Environments, Advertising Design and Graphics, Communication Technology, Visual Communication*, and *Persuasion*. He has published in the *Journal of Advertising Research*, and in 2008, he was awarded the Barrow Minority Doctoral Student scholarship.

John A. Fortunato, Ph. D., is an associate professor at Fordham University in the School of Business, Area of Communication and Media Management. He has published articles in *Public Relations Review, Journal of Interactive Advertising, Journal of Sports Media*, and the *Journal of Sponsorship*. He is also the author of *Making Media Content* and *Commissioner: The Legacy of Pete Rozelle*. Dr. Fortunato previously taught at the University of Texas at Austin in the Department of Advertising and Public Relations and he received his Ph. D. from Rutgers University in the School of Communication, Information, and Library Science.

Harsha Gangadharbatla (Ph.D., University of Texas) is an assistant professor in the school of journalism and communication at University of Oregon. His research focuses on new and emerging media, social and economic effects of advertising, and environmental communication. His publications have appeared (or are forthcoming) in the *Journal of Current Issues and Research in Advertising, International Journal of Advertising , Journal of Interactive Advertising, Journal of Computer-Mediated Communication* and various other conferences.

Xin Ge is an assistant professor at the University of Northern British Columbia, Canada. She received her Ph.D. in Marketing from the School of Business at the University of Alberta, Canada. Her research interests include constructive consumer preferences, strategic presentation of product information, market signals, and consumer behavior in virtual worlds. She has recently published in *Journal of Retailing, Journal of Virtual Worlds Research,* and *Canadian Journal of Administrative Science.*

Nicolai Jørgensgaard Graakjær, Ph.D., is an Associate Professor at the Department of Communication & Psychology, Aalborg University, Denmark. Nicolai Graakjær's research interests include Musicology, Media Studies and Social Psychology, and he has published contributions within these fields. Among contributions are the Ph.D. thesis *Music in Television Commercials* (2008) and the edited volume *Music in Advertising – Commercial Sounds in Media Communication and Other Settings* (eds. Graakjær & Jantzen, Aalborg University Press, 2009).

Iben Bredahl Jessen, MA, is working on a Ph.D. dissertation on web advertising as part of the research project *Market Communication and Aesthetics* at the Department of Communication & Psychology, Aalborg University, Denmark. Her research includes an empirical study of web ads in a Danish context. In her dissertation she examines web advertising from a media aesthetic perspective with focus on multisemiotic analysis and genre development. Among contributions are "The Aesthetics of Web Advertising: Methodological Implications for the Study of Genre Development" in the edited volume *Web History* (ed. N. Brügger, Peter Lang, 2010).

Helen Katz is a Senior Vice President, Director of Research at Starcom Mediavest Group, where she focuses on advanced video research, and research contract negotiations. She joined SMG in May 2001 as a Strategic Research Director at GM Planworks, working for General Motors. Prior to that, Helen had her own media research consultancy where she worked with agencies and research suppliers across the advertising and marketing industry. Before that, Helen spent 18 months at Zenith Media in New York as the VP, Director of Strategic Research, working with clients such as Toyota, Bell Atlantic (Verizon), HSBC, M&M Mars, and General Mills. Helen's media research career began in 1989 at DDB Needham Chicago, where she worked for 10 years for clients such as McDonald's, Anheuser-Busch, General Mills, State Farm Insurance, Dial, Clorox, Helene Curtis/Unilever, and Discover Card. In 2008, Helen was the recipient of an Advertising Research Foundation "Great Minds" award for research innovation.

Gooyong Kim is a Ph.D. candidate at the Graduate School of Education & Information Studies, UCLA. He has completed his dissertation about people?s grassroots collective action mobilization for sociopolitical matters utilizing new media technologies. Specifically, YouTube videos for mass movements such as the Obama campaign in the 2008 U.S. presidential election and Korea?s Candlelight protests are the subjects of the dissertation research. His previous works have investigated the transformative potential of YouTube as a pedagogic tool and a new model of the Brechtian politics of aesthetics in the age of Web 2.0. Generally, he is interested in theorizing the intersectionality between agency, structure, media technology, aesthetics, critical pedagogy, and social transformation.

Jason P. Leboe is the Associate Head (Undergraduate Studies) and an Associate Professor in the Brain and Cognitive Sciences area of the Department of Psychology at the University of Manitoba.

William F. Lewis is an Associate Professor of Marketing in the School of Business Administration at the University of Dayton. He earned his Ph.D. from the University of Cincinnati, and his M.B.A. from Michigan State University. He has published in the *Journal of the Academy of Marketing Science, European Journal of Marketing, Journal of Business and Behavioral Sciences, Journal of Financial Education, Issues in Accounting Education, Journal of Business Ethics,* and the *Journal of E-Business.* Dr. Lewis is the winner of a "Best Paper" award at an annual conference of the Academy of Marketing Science. He has won six teaching awards and a life-time service award at the University of Dayton. While serving with Chrysler Corporation he had responsibilities in the areas of Budget and Accounting Control, Investment Analysis, Profit Analysis, Corporate Income Tax Division, Accounting Department of the Chrysler

Chemical Division, and Corporate Treasury where he had responsibility for $10,500,000 in Accounts Receivable from 750 customers of the Marine and Industrial Division in the United States and Canada.

Paul R. Messinger is Associate Professor of Marketing at the University of Alberta School of Business and IBM Faculty Fellow in the Centre for Advanced Studies program at the IBM Toronto Laboratory. He recently served as Principle Investigator of the Research Alliance "Harnessing the Web-Interaction Cycle for Canadian Competitiveness" for the Social Science and Humanities Research Council of Canada and as Founding Director of the University of Albert School of Retailing. Paul currently serves on the Editorial Board of the journal *Marketing Science* and as guest editor for two special issues on eService of the *Canadian Journal of Administrative Sciences.* Paul's research focuses on e-commerce, 3D mediated virtual worlds, service science, emerging retail formats, dynamic pricing, and recommendation systems; his publication outlets include *Marketing Science, Journal of Retailing, Journal of Economic Dynamics and Control, Decision Support Systems, Canadian Journal of Administrative Sciences, Journal of Virtual Worlds Research, Journal of Business Research,* and *Journal of Retailing and Consumer Services.* For more details, see http://www.business.ualberta.ca/pmessinger/

Jon Michael Mills is ABD at the University of Alabama in Mass Communication, with a focus on Sports Communication. His research interests include non-traditional marketing in sports, media in sports, and campaigns, with corporate naming rights of sports venues being a major component. He previously worked in consumer and sports marketing for an international firm in Chicago, with clients that included Kellogg, Harley Davidson and Hasbro. This experience includes Olympic sponsorships, special events at Major League Baseball games, and crisis communications. Jon currently resides in Tuscaloosa, Alabama, with his wife and three children.

Jang Ho Moon is a Ph.D. student in Advertising at the University of Texas at Austin. He received his M.A. in Strategic Public Relations from University of Southern California. His areas of research interest are the effect of marketing communication activities through new media, with a focus on virtual environments, social networking website, and high-definition television broadcasting. His work has been published in various conference proceedings.

Dilip Mutum is a doctoral researcher at the Warwick Business School, University of Warwick in the UK. He has worked with various organisations in different capacities, including a stint as a sub-editor in a magazine company and as a web developer. Prior to starting his PhD studies, Dilip was a lecturer at Universiti (spelling in Malay) Utara Malaysia, Malaysia. His research interests include issues related to emerging web technologies, social media and online consumer behaviour. He is an active blogger and is posting constant updates on Twitter.

Clifford Nass (Ph.D., Princeton U., Sociology) is the Thomas M. Storke Professor at Stanford University, with appointments in communication, computer science, education, and sociology. He is also Director of the Communication between Humans and Interactive Media (CHIMe) Lab, co-Director of the Kozmetsky Global Collaboratory, and co-Director of the Center for Automotive Research at Stanford (CARS). He is author of three books—The Media Equation, Wired for Speech, and The Man Who Lied to His Laptop (forthcoming in 2010)--and over 125 papers on social-psychological aspects of human-technology interaction and non-parametric statistics. He is the founder of the Computers Are Social Actors paradigm. His current research foci are the psychology and design of automotive interfaces, mobile interfaces, and human-robot interaction and the cognitive and social consequences of chronic multitasking.

Michelle R. Nelson is Associate Professor in the Department of Advertising at the University of Illinois at Urbana-Champaign. Nelson's research, professional marketing communication experience and teaching focus on intra-cultural and international advertising and consumer behavior and digital media. She has researched and worked in Denmark and England before assuming academic responsibilities in the United States. Nelson has published more than 35 book chapters and articles in journals such as *Journalism and Mass Communication Quarterly, Journal of Advertising, Journal of Advertising Research, Journal of Consumer Psychology, Journal of Cross-Cultural Psychology* and *Journal of Public Relations Research.* In addition to 12 years of teaching, Nelson also has professional experience in nonprofit, trade and high-tech organizations.

Gregory O'Toole works in media theory, research and development as a self-termed technomadologist. Technomadology is the study of the contemporary technology-dependent nomadic human culture, information theory, intermedia, and the creative process of generating experimental research, methods, art, and literature as critical discourse toward a greater understanding of the prevailing social, economic, and political condition(s). In brief, Greg is interested in understanding the mediated system in hopes of educating and advancing a comprehensive civil literacy. Currently, Greg is writing a theoretical analysis of mass media and cultural effect as his doctoral dissertation. He is also the principal media theorist and test coordinator for a new body of scientific research exploring neurological effects of media through Electroencephalographic examinations. For his work Greg has received grant funds and recognition awards from the National Endowment for the Arts, Montana Arts Council, International Memefest, Colorado Book Award, and the Valparaiso University Poetry Review among many others. His exploratory academic, literary and visual art work has been published and exhibited around the world in venues such as the New York Times, Denver Post, Chicago Sun-Times, Rhonda Schaller Gallery New York, Kotka Finland Photographic Center, British Journal of Educational Technology, International Journal of the Arts in Society, and the Rocky Mountain Communication Review. Greg currently works as a multimedia specialist and web developer at The Pennsylvania State University and is on the faculty of The Art Institute of Pittsburgh Online Division in Web Design and Interactive Media.

Sung-Yeon Park (Ph.D., University of Wisconsin-Madison, 2004) is an assistant professor at Bowling Green State University. She studies advertising and marketing messages and their effects from multiple perspectives, including the psychological mechanisms of the effect, the impact on individuals, and the implications for the society and culture. In the new media context, she has been focusing on the messages, perceptions, and the influence of user-generated online information. She published many articles in leading communication journals and the highest concentration of her publications to date can be found on the effects of media on women's perceptions of their bodies. She was a visiting professor at Leo Burnett Worldwide in the summer of 2008 and is currently serving as the editorial review board member of *Communication Research.*

Melvin Prince holds a Ph.D. degree from Columbia University. He is a professor of marketing at Southern Connecticut State University. He teaches graduate courses in marketing research, consumer behavior and advertising. Past academic appointments include teaching and research positions at Brandeis University, Fordham University, Pace, Iona College and Quinnipiac University. Dr. Prince is also President of Prince Associates and provides analytic counsel to research companies and their clients. He spearheaded the research and development of the instant coupon machine, a breakthrough in-store promotional device. His previous industry experience includes marketing research directorships at advertising agencies, manufacturing companies and the media. He worked in this capacity for BBDO and Marsteller agencies, National Brand Scanning, J. B. Williams and Scholastic Magazines. He is a member of the American Marketing Association, American Statistical Association, Association for Consumer Research, and the Society for Consumer Psychology, a division of the American Psychological Association.

Shailendra Rao is a PhD candidate at Stanford University focusing on Human Computer Interaction in the Department of Communication. His research primarily focuses on advancing the user experience of personalized recommendations systems on the web. He is a member of the Communication between Humans and Interactive Media (CHIMe) Lab and a former member of the Interactive Cognition Lab (ICL) at the University of California, San Diego (UCSD). He earned a B.S. with distinction in Cognitive Science specializing in Human Computer Interaction at UCSD as well as a M.A. in Media Studies from Stanford University.

Shelly Rodgers is an associate professor of strategic communication at the University of Missouri, School of Journalism. Research areas include Internet advertising, user-generated content, social media, and health communication. Rodgers is nationally ranked as one of the most productive and most cited researchers in her field. Her research, funded by more than $8 million in federal and state grants, has been published in leading academic advertising and communication journals including the *Journal of Advertising, Journal of Advertising Research, Journal of Interactive Advertising, Journal of Current Issues in Research and Advertising, International Journal of Advertising, Social Marketing Research, Journal of Communication,* and *Journal of Health Communication.*

Martha G. Russell is Associate Director of Media X at Stanford University, Senior Research Scholar at the Human Sciences and Technology Advanced Research (H*STAR) Institute at Stanford University and a Fellow at the Institute for Innovation, Creativity and Capital (IC2) at The University of Texas at Austin. Dr. Russell studies the persuasive impact of interactive and place-based media and is developing new metrics for new media, including social media and the emerging integrated, device-centered media in personal area networks. She also studies innovation ecosystems using data-driven visualization methods for systems analysis. Dr. Russell serves on the advisory boards of the *Journal of Interactive Advertising* and the *Journal of Electronics.*

Geraldine Ryan is a lecturer in Economics at University College Cork, Ireland. Geraldine was awarded a Joint Honours BA Degree (Economics and Geography) and an MA in Economics from University College Cork and she holds a PhD in Economics from Warwick University. Her principal research interest is in the area of stock price predictability. She has published in this area in *Applied Financial Economics.* In addition, she has also published a number of pieces on information and incentive problems in economics and knowledge management. She is the joint holder of IRCHSS and Invest NI funding (with Dr. Bernadette Power) investigating SME Succession Issues in Ireland.

Heather M. Schulz is a Ph.D. student, University of Texas at Austin (Advertising); M.S., University of Illinois at Urbana-Champaign (Advertising); B.J. University of Nebraska - Lincoln (Advertising). Heather's primary research interests center on conspicuous consumption and the identities consumers create and communicate through the use of mass-mediated brands. Research on this topic will illuminate how brands function in the creation of individual identity as well as social culture. This lens of analysis focuses on post-purchase consumer behavior in addition to advertising's role in interpersonal relationships. Her work has been presented at the American Academy of Advertising (AAA) conference, the Transformative Consumer Research conference (TCR), the Society for Consumer Psychology conference, and the Center for Health Promotion Research (CHPR) conference.

Brian Sheehan is an Associate Professor at the S.I. Newhouse School of Public Communications at Syracuse University. He teaches courses in advertising, advertising management and practice, and interactive advertising/e-branding. Prior to his switch to academia in 2008, Brian spent 25 years with Saatchi & Saatchi Advertising. After 5 years in Saatchi's New York office, he spent the next 11 years overseas, working in Hong Kong, Tokyo, and Sydney. Most recently, Brian was chairman and CEO of Team One advertising (a division of Saatchi & Saatchi). During his career, Brian has worked on many top national and international brands, including Toyota, General Mills, Procter & Gamble, Hilton, British Airways, IKEA, TIME, News Corporation, Bayer, DuPont, Sara Lee, Kodak, Ritz-Carlton, Castrol and Hewlett-Packard. Brian continues his relationship with Saatchi & Saatchi as a consultant, and he has consulted recently for Petrobras, Brazil's national energy company. He is also an advisory board member of Fuhu, a China-US based internet-software company, and Mission/Metrix, a digital applications company.

Edward Shinnick is a Senior lecturer in Economics at University College Cork. He received his BA degree (Economics and Mathematics) and Master's degree (Economics) from University College Cork. He received his Ph.D. from the University of Strathclyde in 1999. His research areas include competition in markets & industries, privatisation, competition policy, regulation and business strategy, where he has published a number of papers in a range of national and international journals, book chapters and edited book volumes. Most recent publications cover the area of, economic incentives and the knowledge economy, regulatory reform in Irish legal services, corruption and governance issues and competition in Bus transport. Dr Shinnick has undertaken economic consultancy work for industry, serves on the Board of a State Agency, is an International Reviewer for the *Czech Science Foundation,* and serves on the editorial boards of the *International Journal of Public Policy* and the *International Economics and Economic Policy.*

Paul Skalski (Ph.D., Michigan State University) is an assistant professor in the School of Communication at Cleveland State University. His scholarship focuses primarily on interactive entertainment and persuasion. His work has appeared in journals such as *Media Psychology, Journal of Broadcasting and Electronic Media,* and *Communication Research.* He teaches courses on video games, mass communication, new media, persuasion, and research methods and is currently serving as Graduate Program Director in the School of Communication at Cleveland State University.

Lauren Reichart Smith will serve as an Assistant Professor of Public Relations at Auburn University beginning in the Fall of 2010. She earned her Ph.D. in Communication and Information Sciences from the University of Alabama in 2010. A former television producer, Lauren's main research interests lie in media portrayals, media effects, and new media theories. She earned her B.A. from Fairfield University and her M.A. from University of Alabama-Birmingham.

Kenny D. Smith is the student media adviser and director of the digital video center at Samford University where he works with students developing cross-platform journalism skills. Kenny is also pursuing a doctorate in communication and information sciences from the University of Alabama. A veteran journalist with experience in all mass media formats, his research centers on social media, convergence journalism and mobile media news. He holds a bachelor's degree from Auburn University and a master's degree from the University of Alabama at Birmingham.

Michael R. Solomon, Ph.D. is Professor of Marketing and Director of the Center for Consumer Research in the Haub School of Business at Saint Joseph's University in Philadelphia. Prof. Solomon's primary research interests include consumer behavior and lifestyle issues, branding strategy, the symbolic aspects of products, the psychology of fashion, marketing applications of virtual worlds and the development of visually-oriented online research methodologies. His textbook, *Consumer Behavior: Buying, Having, and Being*, published by Prentice Hall is widely used in universities throughout North America, Europe, and Australasia and is now in its ninth edition. He is the first author of *LAUNCH! Advertising and Promotion in Real Time* (Flat World Knowledge), which is the first open platform commercial textbook. His most recent trade book, *The Truth about What Customers Want*, was published in October 2008 by FT (*Financial Times*) Press.

Piya Sorcar is the CEO and Founder of TeachAIDS, where she leads a team of interdisciplinary experts to develop pedagogically-grounded and evidence-based HIV/AIDS prevention materials. The interactive animated materials are used around the world, including South Africa, India, China, Botswana, United States, and Canada. Piya was previously a Program Advisor for Stanford's Learning, Design & Technology Master's Program and a founding board member of XRI Inc., a California-based nonprofit which specializes in the development and evaluation of rich media Internet-based medical and literacy applications. Piya holds a Ph.D. in Learning Sciences & Technology Design and International Comparative Education and an M.A. in Education from Stanford. She graduated summa cum laude from the University of Colorado at Boulder with a B.A. in Economics, B.S. in Journalism, and B.S. in Information Systems. She has been an invited speaker at numerous universities including Caltech, Columbia, Tsinghua, Utrecht, and Yale.

Yongjun Sung is Assistant Professor of Advertising at the University of Texas at Austin. He received his Ph.D. in Mass Communication and M.A. in Advertising from University of Georgia. Dr. Sung's research focuses on brand personality, brand commitment, consumer-brand relationships, brand placement, and cross-cultural consumer psychology. He has published or has work forthcoming in *Journal of Consumer Psychology, Psychology & Marketing, Journal of Advertising, Journal of Public Policy and Marketing, Journal of Marketing Communications, International Journal of Advertising, Journal of Brand Management, Journal of Consumer Behaviour, Journal of International Consumer Marketing, Journalism & Mass Communication Quarterly, and Journal of Health Communication*, among others.

Gülnur Tumbat is an Assistant Professor of Marketing at San Francisco State University. She got her PhD from University of Utah with emphasis on interpretive consumer behavior research. Her research interests lie at the intersections of consumer experiences, technology, and marketplaces; built, digital, or otherwise. She can be reached at http://www.gulnurtumbat.com

Fang Wan is an Associate Professor of Marketing and Ross Johnson Research Fellow in the I. H. Asper School of Business at the University of Manitoba.

Qing Wang is Professor of Marketing and Innovation at the Warwick Business School, University of Warwick in the UK. Prior to joining Warwick in 2000, she was a faculty member at SPRU, Sussex University. She has held visiting professor positions at several universities including Duke University, Insead, and Tsinghua University. Professor Qing Wang is a Fellow of the Royal Society of Medicine in the UK, Academic Member of the Marketing Science Institute in the U.S., and External Expert in China's National Research Centre for Technological Innovation. Her research is concerned with consumer adoption intention for really new products and services, the co-evolution of consumer learning and firm strategies and capabilities, and the branding strategies of Chinese technology-based companies. She has published in leading refereed journals including *Journal of Marketing Research, Journal of Product Innovation Management*, and *Research Policy* among others. She is the winner of the 2009 Robert D. Buzzell Marketing Science Institute (MSI) Best Paper Award for making the most significant contribution to marketing practice and thought. She is the principal investigator for a number of research projects including AXA Grant and MSI grant and was also involved in a number of ESRC programmes including the ESRC Centre for Complex Product Systems (CoPs).

Ye Wang is a doctoral student of strategic communication at the University of Missouri, School of Journalism, where she received her MA degree in strategic communication in 2008. Her research interests include interactive advertising and its application to health communication and international advertising. She has published in *International Journal of Advertising*, and has presented conference papers at the American Academy of Advertising's annual conference.

Natalie T. Wood (Ph.D., Auburn University) is Assistant Professor of Marketing, Erivan K. Haub School of Business, Saint Joseph's University. Prof. Wood has published in journals such as *The Journal of Consumer Behaviour, Marketing Education Review, The International Journal of Internet Marketing and Advertising* and *The Journal of Website Promotion.* She is the co-editor of *Virtual Social Identity and Consumer Behavior* published by M.E. Sharpe and is the author of the *Marketing in Virtual Worlds* published by Prentice Hall. She is also an Advisory Editor for the *Journal of Virtual Worlds Research.*

Antony Young is CEO of based in New York and is CEO of Optimedia International US Inc., a Publicis Groupe owned media strategy and buying agency. He has spent twenty plus years in the business, holding CEO roles in Asia/Pacific, the UK and the US. Mr. Young has been responsible for developing strategy and executing media campaigns for some of the most influential global brands, which include Sony, Coca-Cola, T-Mobile, L'Oréal, McDonald's, Nokia, Procter & Gamble and Toyota. He co-authored "*Profitable Marketing Communications*", a business marketing book that details his insights into how world class companies have been able to deliver marketing return on investment. He launched one of the first media agencies in China, which became the largest agency in that market in 2000. He was also a founding partner and CEO of an independent digital marketing company AdXplorer, which was later sold to Morningstar a digital media investment group. Antony writes a monthly column on brand media strategy for Advertising Age.

Gi Woong Yun (Ph. D. University of Wisconsin-Madison) is an assistant professor at Bowling Green State University. His research interests are mostly about Internet as media. He works on social psychological theories of communication, online interactive forums, Internet research methodology, and more. He has published articles in various journals including *Journal of Computer Mediated Communication, Communication Research, Journalism & Mass Communication Quarterly, Media Psychology*, and other communication related journals. His current research projects are selective posting online, newspaper online business model, online media framing, and others.

Index

A

B

C

D

E

F

G

R

S

T

U

Y